GW00694289

Main Cities
of Europe
2009

Commitments

"This volume was created at the turn of the century and will last at least as long".

This foreword to the very first edition of the MICHELIN Guide, written in 1900, has become famous over the years and the Guide has lived up to the prediction. It is read across the world and the key to its popularity is the consistency of its commitment to its readers, which is based on the following promises.

THE MICHELIN GUIDE'S COMMITMENTS

Anonymous inspections: our inspectors make regular and anonymous visits to hotels and restaurants to gauge the quality of products and services offered to an ordinary customer. They settle their own bill and may then introduce themselves and ask for more information about the establishment. Our readers' comments are also a valuable source of information, which we can then follow up with another visit of our own.

Independence: Our choice of establishments is a completely independent one, made for the benefit of our readers alone. The decisions to be taken are discussed around the table by the inspectors and the editor. The most important awards are decided at a European level. Inclusion in the Guide is completely free of charge.

Selection and choice: The Guide offers a selection of the best hotels and restaurants in every category of comfort and price. This is only possible because all the inspectors rigorously apply the same methods.

Annual updates: All the practical information, the classifications and awards are revised and updated every single year to give the most reliable information possible.

Consistency: The criteria for the classifications are the same in every country covered by the MICHELIN Guide.

... and our aim: to do everything possible to make travel, holidays and eating out a pleasure, as part of Michelin's ongoing commitment to improving travel and mobility.

Dear Reader

Welcome to the 28th edition of the 'Main Cities of Europe' guide. This guide is aimed primarily at the international business traveller who regularly journeys throughout Europe but it is equally ideal for those wishing to discover the delights of some of Europe's most romantic and culturally stimulating cities for a weekend break or special occasion.

Entry in the MICHELIN Guide is completely free of charge and it continues to be compiled by our professionaly trained teams of full-time inspectors from across Europe who make their assessments anonymously in order to ensure complete impartiality and independence. Their mission is to check the quality and consistency of the amenities and services provided by the hotels and restaurants throughout the year and our listings are updated annually in order to ensure the most up-to-date information.

Most of the establishments featured have been hand-picked from our other national guides and therefore our European selection is, effectively, a best-of-the-best listing.

In addition to the user-friendly layout the guide contains key thematic words which succinctly convey the style of the establishment; practical and cultural information on each country and each city; suggestions on when to go, what to see and what to eat.

This year we have expanded the guide to include Florence and Turin in Italy.

Thank you for your support and please continue to send us your comments. We hope you will enjoy travelling with the 'Main Cities of Europe' guide 2009.

Consult the MICHELIN Guide at
www.ViaMichelin.com
and write to us at:
themichelinguide-europe@uk.michelin.com

Contents

Contents

COUNTRIES

Classification & Awards

The MICHELIN Guide selection lists the best hotels and restaurants in each category of comfort and price. The establishments we choose are classified according to their levels of comfort and, within each category, are listed in order of preference.

🏨	XXXXX	Luxury in the traditional style
🏨	XXXX	Top class comfort
🏨	XXX	Very comfortable
🏨	XX	Comfortable
🏠	X	Quite comfortable
	🍺	Pubs serving good food
	♈/	Tapas bars
↑		Other recommended accommodation
without rest.		This hotel has no restaurant
with rm		This restaurant also offers accommodation

THE AWARDS

To help you make the best choice, some exceptional establishments have been given an award in this year's Guide. They are marked ✿ or 🍃 and **Rest**.

THE BEST CUISINE

Michelin stars are awarded to establishments serving cuisine, of whatever style, which is of the highest quality. The cuisine is judged on the quality of ingredients, the skill in their preparation, the combination of flavours, the levels of creativity, the value for money and the consistency of culinary standards.

✿✿✿	**Exceptional cuisine, worth a special journey** One always eats extremely well here, sometimes superbly.
✿✿	**Excellent cooking, worth a detour**
✿	**A very good restaurant in its category**

RISING STARS

These establishments, listed in red, are the best in their present category. They have the potential to rise further, and already have an element of superior quality; as soon as they produce this quality consistently, and in all aspects of their cuisine, they will be hot tips for a higher award. We've highlighted these promising restaurants so you can try them for yourselves; we think they offer a foretaste of the gastronomy of the future.

GOOD FOOD AT MODERATE PRICES

⊛ **Bib Gourmand**

Establishments offering good quality cuisine at reasonable prices (the actual price limit varies from country to country according to the relative costs).

PLEASANT HOTELS AND RESTAURANTS

Symbols shown in red indicate particularly pleasant or restful establishments: the character of the building, its décor, the setting, the welcome and services offered may all contribute to this special appeal.

🏠 to 🏠🏠🏠🏠 **Pleasant hotels**

✕ to ✕✕✕✕✕ **Pleasant restaurants**

OTHER SPECIAL FEATURES

As well as the categories and awards given to the establishment, Michelin inspectors also make special note of other criteria which can be important when choosing an establishment.

LOCATION

If you are looking for a particularly restful establishment, or one with a special view, look out for the following symbols:

🐾 **Quiet hotel**

🐾 **Very quiet hotel**

≼ **Interesting view**

≼ **Exceptional view**

WINE LIST

If you are looking for an establishment with a particularly interesting wine list, look out for the following symbol:

🍇 **Particularly interesting wine list**

This symbol might cover the list presented by a sommelier in a luxury restaurant or that of a simple restaurant where the owner has a passion for wine. The two lists will offer something exceptional but very different, so beware of comparing them by each other's standards.

Facilities & Services

30 rm	Number of rooms
AC	Air conditioning (in all or part of the establishment)
⚥	Establishment with areas reserved for non-smokers.
♿	Establishment at least partly accessible to those of restricted mobility
🍽	Meals served in garden or on terrace
SAT	Satellite TV
☎	Fast internet access in bedrooms
(¡)	Wireless Internet access
Spa	Wellness centre: an extensive facility for relaxation and well-being
))) *ʃ*	Sauna – Exercise room
⇘ ⊡	Swimming pool: outdoor or indoor
⌗	Garden
✗	Tennis court
⚑	Equipped conference room
⇔	Private dining rooms
⇨ ⇖ P P	Valet parking – Garage – Car park, enclosed parking
May-October	Dates when open, as indicated by the hotelier
M	Nearest metro station

Prices

These prices are given in the currency of the country in question. Valid for 2009 the rates shown should only vary if the cost of living changes to any great extent.

SERVICE AND TAXES

Except in Greece, Hungary, Poland and Spain, prices shown are inclusive, that is to say service and V.A.T. included. In the U.K. and Ireland, s = service included. In Italy, when not included, a percentage for service is shown after the meal prices, eg. (16 %).

MEALS

Meals 40/56	Set meal prices
Carte	'à la carte' meal prices

HOTEL

86 rm ♥ 650/750	Lowest and highest price for a comfortable single
♥♥ 750/890	and a best double room
⌧ 60/120	Prices include breakfast

BREAKFAST

⌧ 20	Price of breakfast (where not included in rate)

CREDIT CARDS

Credit cards accepted by the establishment:

AE ⓓ ⓜⓒ *VISA* American Express – Diners Club – MasterCard – Visa

How to use this guide

PRACTICAL & TOURIST INFORMATION

Pages with practical information on every country and city: public transport, tourist information offices, main sites and attractions (museums, monuments, theatres, etc), with a directory of shop addresses and examples of loal specialities to take home.

RESTAURANTS

XXXXX à X

The most pleasant : in red.

STARS

❀❀❀ Worth a special journey.

❀❀ Worth a detour.

❀ A very good restaurant.

BIB GOURMAND ⊛

Good food at moderate prices.

RESTAURANTS & HOTELS

The country is indicated by the coloured strip down the side of the page: dark for restaurants, light for hotels.

HOTELS

🏠🏠🏠 à 🏠

The most pleasant : in red.

10

LIVING THE CITY

Paris wouldn't be Paris *sans* its Left and Right Banks. The **Left Bank** takes in the city south of the Seine; the **Right Bank** comprises the north and west. There are twenty **arrondissements** (quarters) set within the **Boulevard Périphérique**. The **Ile de la Cité** is the nucleus around which the city grew and the oldest quarters around this site are the 1ˢᵗ, 2ⁿᵈ, 3ʳᵈ, 4ᵗʰ arrondissements on the Right Bank and 5ᵗʰ and 6ᵗʰ on the Left Bank. The remaining arrondissements fan out in a clockwise direction from here. Landmarks are universally known: the **Eiffel Tower** and the **Arc de Triomphe** are to the west of the centre (though on different sides of the river), the **Sacré-Coeur** is to the north, **Montparnasse Tower** to the south, and, of course, **Notre-Dame Cathedral** slap bang in the middle (of the Seine).

PRACTICAL INFORMATION

ARRIVAL-DEPARTURE

Roissy-Charles-de-Gaulle Airport is 23km northeast of Paris and b- will cost around €45. A- to Montparnasse every 15m-

day pass-

CHAMPS-ÉLYSÉES, ÉTOILE, PALAIS DES C

Le Petit Four (Martin)

2 rue François 1ᵉʳ (1st) Ⓜ Palais-Royal – 𝒞 01 12 96 45 27 – petit.four@wanadoo.fr – Fax 01 12 96 46 28

Rest (closed in august) 75 €, 185/240 € and a la carte 150/2

Spec. Foie gras chaud au vinaigre de cidre. Saint-Pierre p Colvert rôti au miel.

◆ Luxury ◆ Inventive ◆

In the gardens of the Palais-Royal, sumptuous Empire rated with splendid "pictures under glass". The insp- worthy of this historic monument.

Au Pied de Porc

15 bd Voltaire (11th) Ⓜ République – 𝒞 01 40 13 7 – Pieddeporc@gmw.net – Fax 01 42 13 77 09 – cl

Rest – 29 €, 32/72 € and a la carte 37/61 €

◆ Classic ◆ Trendly ◆

Pigs trotters are the speciality of this renow late into the night since opened in 1946. C fruits designs.

ÉTOILE – CHAMPS-ÉLYSÉES

Rond-point des Champs-Él

Palazzo Amédée Ⓜ Marceau

25 av. Rabelais (8th) – reservation@

– 𝒞 01 45 12 24 24 – 500 €, s

– Fax 01 45 12 23 23

145 rm 🛏 – 🍴 350 € below

Rest – See **Le jardin** below

Rest **La Cour** – a la carte 50/

Spec. Tartare de bar et saun

chocolats grands crus.

◆ Palace ◆ Stylich ◆

Classic style in the luxuric gallery, stunning design ming, green-filled terra when the weather tur

Le Faubourg St-

15 r. des Ecuries (7th

– reservations@fa

174 rm 🛏 – 🍴 2

Rest **Café du F**

carte 60/90 €

◆ Busines

This "Faubo tech room decor, rest

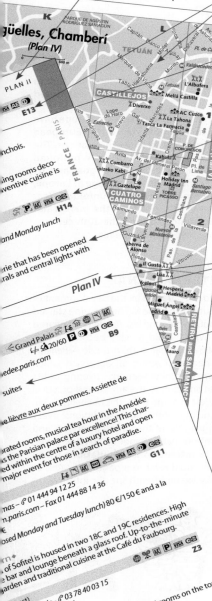

LOCATION

The country, the town, the district and the map.

LOCATING THE ESTABLISHMENT

Location and coordinates on the town plan, with principal sights.

ADDRESS

All the information you need to make a reservation and find the establishment.

FACILITIES & SERVICES

See also page 8.

DESCRIPTION OF THE ESTABLISHMENT

Atmosphere, style and character.

CLASSIFICATION BY DISTRICT

With the corresponding plan number.

PRICES

See also page 9.

KEY WORDS

If you are looking for a specific type of establishment, these key words will help you make your choice more quickly.

→ **For hotels,** the first word explains the **establishment type** (chain hotel, business, luxury, etc); the second one describes the **décor** (modern, stylish, design, etc) and sometimes a third will be used to complete the picture.

→ **For restaurants,** the first word relates to the **type of cuisine** and the second the **atmosphere**.

---

güelles, Chamberí
(Plan IV)

PLAN II

VISA AE ①
E13

nchois.

ing rooms deco-
ventive cuisine is

P AC VISA ⑮
H14

and Monday lunch

rie that has been opened
rals and central lights with

Plan IV

Grand Palais
♿ ⏰20/60 P ① VISA
B9

edee.paris.com

suites

le lièvre aux deux pommes. Assiette de

rated rooms, musical tea hour in the Amédée
s the Parisian palace par excellence! This char-
ed within the centre of a luxury hotel and open
major event for those in search of paradise.
G11

nas – ℰ 01 444 94 12 25
n.paris.com – Fax 01 444 88 14 36

osed Monday and Tuesday lunch) 80 €/150 € and a la

of Sofitel is housed in two 18C and 19C residences. High
bar and lounge beneath a glass roof. Up-to-the-minute
arden and traditional cuisine at the Café du Faubourg.
Z3

Concorde – ℰ 03 78 40 03 15
78 73 76

out rest)

cheerful rooms on the top

11

The Michelin Guide and Europe

Whether it be for business or pleasure, travellers throughout Europe know that they can rely on the Michelin Guide. For over a century, it has been their companion, first in France and then beyond the dotted borderlines printed on the Michelin maps.

Over the last hundred years, the boundaries of Europe have been extended and the circle of gold stars on the European flag has had to adjust in order to welcome other nations. The Michelin Guide has always kept abreast of these profound changes on the ground, in keeping with its goal and its motto: *serving the traveller*. Indeed, in its coverage of Europe, it has witnessed the history of the continent as it unfolded. Year after year, the guide's publication or absence from the market has reflected the great upheavals experienced during the 20th century, with its vicissitudes, crises, eras of prosperity and peace.

THE MICHELIN GUIDE: MULTILINGUAL AND INTERNATIONAL

Inspired by its success in France and encouraged by the development of the automobile industry throughout Europe, the Michelin Guide started to spread the concept to neighbouring countries: *Belgique* appeared in 1904 – the second volume in what would quickly become a true European-wide collection. The following year, a third guide – *Benelux* – was published. The collection began to adopt an approach which would include **tourist information**, with new sections covering sights and excursions not to be missed, in addition to the advice and practical information already in the guides. At the same time, the Michelin Guide collection started to espouse Michelin's international ambitions: every new title was published in the language(s) of the country, services and main facilities were indicated by **symbols** that everyone could understand, and several pages were devoted to **international regulations** useful for travellers. Consequently readers could refer to a page dedicated to «General European Traffic Rules», for example, with specific information

regarding which side of the road to drive on in every European country. It is interesting to note that, at the time, the Michelin Guide included Turkey as part of Europe, with information about traffic in that country.

MICHELIN TRAVELS ABROAD

The Michelin Guide began to expand throughout Europe and use other languages. In 1908 *The Michelin Guide to France* was published, an **adaptation in English** of the original French guide, and two years later two new titles were published: *Deutschland* und *Schweiz* and *España y Portugal*. The following year (1911) three more guides

were published, expanding the collection still further: *British Isles, Alpes et Rhin*, and the exotic *Les pays du Soleil*, covering not only the Côte d'Azur, Corsica and Italy, but also North Africa and Egypt! And that same year, all of these guides were translated into English.

This unprecedented expansion marked the start of the company's desire to spread throughout Europe and North Africa. Proof of the successful formula of the Michelin Guides was summed up in an advertising poster of the era showing Bibendum – the Michelin Man – proudly demonstrating that the total number of copies of the Michelin guide collection, if piled up, would be equivalent to 60 times the height of St Paul's Cathedral in London!

Success was then interrupted in 1939, with the start of the **Second World War**. From 1940 to 1944, the absence of the guide revealed the torment which Europe was going through. When the guide finally reappeared, it was «*for official use only*», printed in Washington to accompany the officers of the Allied forces during the Normandy Landings.

FROM A
EUROPEAN COLLECTION...

The 1950s brought new growth, with Michelin maps now covering all of Western Europe. But it was in the 1960s that the Michelin Guide collection really started to take on a **European dimension**, taking a step by step approach to expansion. In 1964, after a half century's absence, *Deutschland* reappeared (without the GDR and East Berlin), followed ten years later by *Great Britain & Ireland*. Meanwhile, the shorter *Paris* and *London* guides appeared on the shelves, based on information taken from the national guides, and revealing an interest in large **European capital cities**. In order to remain the indispensable companion for travellers throughout Europe, the guides would from then on follow the model of *France*: enhanced with more information, including a **rigorous selection of fine restaurants**.

...TO A GUIDE FOR EUROPE

Means of transport were becoming more and more diversified and journey times were shortening considerably, encouraging faster travel and trips made more often and over longer distances than ever before. Michelin needed to bring tourists and business travellers alike a guide which covered the relevant areas, and at the same time cross the borders of the new Europe to the north and to the east.

1982 saw the chance to do this. The first guide devoted to Europe was born of a **partnership** with *Times-Life Magazine* and appeared under the title *20 Cities/ Villes EUROPE*. The guide was written in English and twenty thousands copies were published. The selection of establishments adopted for the guide took the best hotel and restaurant addresses in each category from the «country» guides, following the criteria guaranteeing **a constant level of quality**, above and beyond specific national considerations.

The huge success of this first edition led the company to repeat the experience. The following year, Copenhagen and Vienna were included in the guide: until then, no guide existed which covered these cities, and the more global title *Main Cities of Europe* was adopted in 1984 with more than 50 towns and cities – some of them capitals, but also the other large influential cities in **20 countries**.

Who does not recognise the famous red cover of the Michelin Guide today? Since the beginning of the 20th century, the Guide has established itself throughout Europe thanks to quality, service and up-to-date selection. From Oslo to Athens, Lisbon to Budapest, the 23 titles in the collection (including the latest city guides to Hong Kong and Tokyo) recommend over 25000 hotels and 16000 restaurants, including over 1800 starred restaurants, and 1200 town plans. With new introductions and practical information on every country and every town and city selected, the 2009 vintage of *Main Cities of EUROPE* offers you the very best. Happy reading and bon voyage with Michelin!

AUSTRIA
ÖSTERREICH

PROFILE

→ **AREA:**
83 853 km²
(32 376 sq mi).

→ **POPULATION:**
8 150 000 inhabitants
(est. 2005), density =
97 per km².

→ **CAPITAL:**
Vienna (conurbation
1 892 000
inhabitants).

→ **CURRENCY:**
Euro (€); rate of
exchange: € 1 = US$
1.32 (Jan 2009).

→ **GOVERNMENT:**
Parliamentary
republic and federal
state (since 1955).
Member of European
Union since 1995.

→ **LANGUAGE:**
German.

→ **SPECIFIC PUBLIC
HOLIDAYS:**
Epiphany
(6 January); Corpus
Christi
(late May/June);
National Day
(26 October);
Immaculate

Conception
(8 December);
St. Stephen's Day
(26 December).

→ **LOCAL TIME:**
GMT + 1 hour in
winter and GMT
+ 2 hours in summer.

→ **CLIMATE:**
Temperate
continental with cold
winters – high snow
levels – and warm
summers (Vienna:
January: 0°C, July:
20°C).

→ **INTERNATIONAL
DIALLING CODE:**
00 43 followed
by area code
without initial 0 and
then the local
number.

→ **EMERGENCY:**
Police: ☏ **133**;
Medical Assistance:
☏ **144**;
Fire Brigade: ☏ **122.**

→ **ELECTRICITY:**
220 volts AC, 50Hz;
2-pin round-shaped
continental plugs

VIENNA

→ **FORMALITIES**
Travellers from
the European
Union (EU),
Switzerland, Iceland
and the main
countries of North
and South America
need a national
identity card or
passport (America:
passport required)
to visit Austria for
less than three
months (tourism or
business purpose).
For visitors from
other countries
a visa may be
required, in addition
to a passport,
especially for those
wishing to stay for
longer than three
months. We advise
you to check with
your embassy before
travelling.

VIENNA
WIEN

Population: 1 573 000 (conurbation 1 892 000) – Altitude: 156m.

R. Mauritius/PHOTONONSTOP

Beethoven, Brahms, Mozart, Haydn, Strauss...not a bad list of former residents, by any stretch of the imagination. One and all, they succumbed to the opulent aura of Vienna, a city where an appreciation of the arts is as conspicuous as its famed big cream cakes. Sumptuous architecture and a refined air reflect the city's historical position as the seat of the powerful Habsburg dynasty and former epicentre of the Austro-Hungarian Empire. This is a city where the words rococo and baroque could have been invented.

Despite its grand image, Vienna is propelling itself into the twenty-first century with a handful of seriously innovative hotspots, most notably the MuseumsQuartier cultural complex, a stone's throw from the mighty Hofburg Imperial Palace. This is not a big city, although its vivid image gives that impression. The compact centre teems with elegant shops, fashionable coffee-houses and grand avenues, and the empire's awesome nineteenth-century remnants keep visitors' eyes fixed forever upwards.

LIVING THE CITY

Many towns and cities are defined by their ring roads, but Vienna can boast a truly upmarket version: the **Ringstrasse**, a showpiece boulevard that cradles the inner city and the riches that lie therein. Just outside here – to the southwest - are the districts of **Neubau** and **Spittelberg**, both of which have taken on a quirky, modernistic feel, exemplified by the outstanding **MuseumsQuartier**, and a buzzing coterie of hip galleries and bars. To the east of town in the Leopoldstadt quarter lies **Prater,** the green lung of Vienna, and home to some of the world's oldest merry-go-rounds. Further out, southwest of the city, lies the suburban area utterly enhanced by the grandeur of the Schönbrunn palace. Where in all this is the blue Danube? Surprisingly enough, the great river of waltzing legend plays less of a role than many other city waterways as it flows some way out to the northeast of the city. Of more 'strategic' relevance to visitors is the Danube Canal, which divides the centre from the northern and eastern suburbs.

PRACTICAL INFORMATION

ARRIVAL-DEPARTURE

Wien-Schwechat Airport is 19km from the city centre. The City Airport Express train to Wien Mitte takes 16min and leaves every 30min. A taxi will cost around €30 and take 30min.

TRANSPORT

The Vienna Card, which allows unlimited travel on the whole of the city's public transport network for 72hr and offers a discount to sights, cafes, restaurants and shops, can be bought from the Tourist Office, at your hotel or from ticket offices of the Vienna Transport Authority. You can also purchase Rover tickets for 24hr or 72hr. The city's buses, trams and metro are renowned for their excellent efficiency.

There are around eighty bus routes around the city. Night buses run every half-hour throughout the small hours. The trams run every five to ten minutes, and there are timetables at every stop. You can bet your Sachertorte on them arriving exactly on time!

This is not a drivers' city. With its profusion of one-way streets, tramways and difficult-to-find parking spots, Vienna is most definitely somewhere to discover by foot or by public transport.

EXPLORING VIENNA

Take a ruling dynasty, give it six hundred years of power and influence, and what have you got? Answer: a city bursting with imperial pomp and palaces, a high-brow concoction set fair to impose and overawe. You've got Vienna. This is Europe's *grand dame*, where former royal palaces burst with treasure troves of art, white stallions trot daintily amongst visitors and classical concerts are performed in streets crammed with regal delights. The era of the Habsburgs came crashing to an uncomfortable end at the climax of World War I, but you only have to stroll around the old town, embraced by the Ringstrasse, to come face-to-face with its former glories. One location sums it all up: the **Hofburg**, or Imperial Palace. It dominates this famous area, and is a small town in itself, an immense palace complex with extensions and add-ons depending on the whim of successive Habsburg rulers. Two of the city's most famous institutions are based here: the **Vienna Boys' Choir** and the **Spanish Riding School**. You could spend all your time at the Hofburg, wandering around the Imperial Apartments, decked out with Biedermeier portraits and Bohemian crystal chandeliers, or following the melodramatic events of Empress Elisabeth's life in the Sisi Museum.

→ TOWERING GLORY

In time, though, you'll more than likely want to stroll the quarter-mile north to Vienna's second great visitor magnet, **St Stephen's Cathedral**, towering over Stephansplatz Square. Its chevron style mosaic roof and skeletal spires are iconic landmarks, and its near-450ft. tower (completed in 1433) means it can be seen from all over the city. Climb its 343 steps and you can return the favour. Your bird's eye view will take in a whole holiday's worth of museums and galleries, so cherry-pick the best, and your footsteps will invariably lead you to the **Art History Museum** on Maria-Theresien Platz. It's stacked with centuries of Habsburg-acquired artistic gems: the Picture Gallery is hung with 16C and 17C masters such as Titian, Caravaggio and Rubens, and there are other superb collections, including those of Roman and Egyptian antiquity.

→ QUIRKY QUARTIER

Anyone who knew Vienna before 2001 will wonder what's happened to the imperial stables, just over the road from the Art History Museum. These days, you won't see any horses, but you will find the impressively trendy **MuseumsQuartier.**

This is now one of the biggest cultural complexes in the world, and its irresistible quirkiness draws visitors twenty-four hours a day (the courtyards and alleyways here never close; its cafés and bars think along much the same lines). The MQ is home to an awesome array of artists and art spaces, galleries and museums. Its defining attraction is a massive white cube – the Leopold Museum – which has five floors of 19C and 20C art, the highlights being Austria's 'dynamic duo' Klimt and Schiele: the latter's world-famous Reclining Woman is here.

Find your way out of the MQ, head east along the Ringstrasse, and before you can say Don Giovanni you're at the **Staatsoper**, or State Opera House. This is possibly the most cherished building of them all to locals, and has had a special place in Viennese hearts since it opened to the strains of Mozart in 1869. Designed in grandiose Italian Renaissance style, there's an invariable throng of people getting in line for their cheap standing-room tickets. If you can't make it to a concert here, then try the Musikverein further east. Also built in the 1860s, it matches the Opera House in terms of popularity, not least because its acoustics are second-to-none, its décor is sumptuous, and it's home to the globally renowned Vienna Philharmonic. When the play's the thing, the Viennese head back west along the Ringstrasse to the Burgtheater. You can't miss it: it's right opposite the grand neo-Gothic City Hall. Some go to the Burgtheater just to clap eyes on the sumptuously decorated staircases that define the place. Others go for the city's finest drama productions.

→ BEL-EPOQUE

Just when you think this box of treasures has given up all its golden contents, along comes a palace that even outdoes the Hofburg. The **Belvedere** is southeast of the centre, and its two superb Baroque mansions, atop a sweeping garden, offer wonderful vistas of central Vienna. One of these imposing buildings (the grander of the two, the Upper Belvedere,) houses the wondrous Austrian Art Gallery, which boasts an impressive collection of works by Klimt, plus a notable selection by Schiele. Great paintings by Van Gogh and Monet are here, too. Not to be totally outdone, the Lower Belvedere showcases treasures with a medieval, baroque and Golden Age hue.

→ THE AVANT GARDE

To be honest, the area of Leopoldstadt, to the east of the city, isn't going to win any tourism awards. On the whole, it's pretty suburban, and pretty uninteresting, save for two shining lights. The Hundertwasserhaus, by the Danube Canal, is a fifty-apartment housing complex. In 1983, avant-garde architect Friedensreich Hundertwasser took it by the scruff of the neck and converted it into an eyeball-popping explosion of colour and wavy lines, a higgledy-piggledy jumble of textures that draws tourists united by one common denominator – the dropped jaw. Meanwhile, across the canal, the more conservative Prater is a traditional magnet for suburban dwellers and visiting hordes alike;

this vast park has been welcoming all comers for nearly two hundred and fifty years. It's a vast place, with a funfair, tracts of woodland, a miniature railway and a planetarium. Its giant Ferris wheel lifts you above the skyline in rickety red gondolas, and on high you can see right across to St Stephen's Cathedral. If you love the aroma of candyfloss and the twinkling tinkle of the merry-go-round, then you might want to forget the more *fin-de-siècle* attractions of Vienna, and hang round the Prater instead.

One little quarter even the most devout Prater lover would not wish to miss out on lies just beyond the Museums-Quartier. It's called Spittelberg, and it comprises half a dozen parallel, narrow cobbled streets that have retained their eighteenth-century appeal, a taste of Old Vienna beyond the Ringstrasse. There's a modern twist here: this charming district now has a new lease of life, enhanced by a string of bars, cafés and stylish art galleries, smartly entwined with the Baroque and Biedermeier houses that have been carefully restored to their former glory.

CALENDAR HIGHLIGHTS

Vienna's cultural highlights, not to anyone's great surprise, have a predominantly musical flavour, kicking off in January with the world-famous New Year's Day Concert at the Musikverein; almost as fancy are the balls which waltz through the city in deepest winter. Two of the more glitzy are the Practitioners' Ball (January) and the Opera Ball (February), when pink carnations and *The Blue Danube* are obligatory. Springtime is heralded by April's City Festival, and free musical concerts are the backbone here. A couple of cultural biggies hit town in June. The Vienna Festival is a huge event with music and theatrical highlights

VIENNA IN...

→ ONE DAY
A tram ride round the Ringstrasse (two and a half miles), St Stephen's Cathedral, a section of the Hofburg Palace, cream cakes at a smart café

→ TWO DAYS
MuseumsQuartier, Spittelberg, Hundertwasserhaus, Prater

→ THREE DAYS
A day at the Belvedere, a night at the opera

being shared out, while the Danube Island Festival is a three-day extravaganza of free concerts by bands from far and wide with the added allure of it all happening on the river's dinky islands. Later in the month and into July the vibe changes with the Vienna Jazz Festival, which spreads itself to hip venues across the city, while later in the summer the mood changes once again with KlangBogen, a chance to catch top opera and classical performers in a widely-renowned series of concerts. November brings the twenty-year-old festival Wien Modern, which succeeds in adding a cutting edge to contemporary classical music. It's not all batons, bass and big beats in this city – September's Literature Festival lasts for twenty four hours and features Austria's leading authors reading from their works non-stop around the clock – an "adventure in the head" - while the Viennale in October is Austria's biggest festival of film.

EATING OUT

Vienna is the spiritual home of the café ; the landing stage of Europe's first coffee bean (or so legend has it). Austrians drink nearly twice as much coffee as beer, astonishingly over a pint a day per head of population. A sweet tooth characterises the city: chunky mounds of glistening cream cakes enhance the window displays of most eateries. Is there a visitor to Vienna who hasn't succumbed to the sponge of the Sachertorte? Reflecting its empire days, the city's restaurants are many-pronged, so if you wish to eat your way around the globe, you shouldn't have a problem here. Viennese food is essentially the food of Bohemia, which means that meat has a strong presence on the plate. Beef, veal, pork, alongside potatoes, dumplings or cabbage, gives you pretty much the picture - be sure to try traditional boiled beef or the ubiquitous Wiener Schnitzel, deep-fried breaded veal. Also worth experiencing are the Heurigen, the traditional Austrian wine taverns which are found in Grinzing, Heiligenstadt, Neustift and Nussdorf. Elsewhere, there are snug cafés and sushi bars, tasty trattorias and tapas bars. MuseumsQuartier and Spittelberg are great places to head for to get good food and avoid the tourist centre scrum. If you want to eat on the hoof, the place to go is Naschmarkt, Vienna's best market, where the ethnic range of stalls spills over into the vibrant little restaurants dishing up everything from a plateful of noodles to a steaming, spicy curry. When it comes to tipping, if you're in the more relaxed, local pubs and wine taverns, just round up the bill, otherwise add on ten per cent.

→ UNDERGROUND SPY NETWORK

Much of cinema's iconic The Third Man was filmed in Vienna – and in particular, the sewers. Harry Lime spent an unforgettable period scurrying round beneath strasse level. He had a lot of sewer to choose from: there are about three thousand miles' worth in the city. About half can be walked, and you can sample them for yourself on various tours.

→ HOLIDAYING HAPSBURGS

Where did the Hapsburgs go for summer retreat? Answer: the grandiose **Schönbrunn Palace** three miles southwest of the centre. It's Austria's answer to Versailles, boasting a seventy foot high Palm House and a Hall of Mirrors where Mozart played. The whole complex is a symmetrical masterwork of 1500 rooms that in its day would have housed more than a thousand servants. Nowadays it welcomes over six and a half million visitors a year.

Palais Coburg 🚗 🏡 🛖 🖻 ❖ ↩ rm 📶 🎵 🚵 🚐 VISA ⮾ AE ①
Coburgbastei 4 ✉ *1010* – Ⓜ *Stubentor* – 𝒞 *(01) 51 81 80* – *hotel.residenz@palais-coburg.com* – *Fax (01) 51 81 81 00* – *www.palais-coburg.com*
35 suites ⚏ – †490/2140 € ††490/2140 € **E2**
Rest *WeinBistro* – 𝒞 *(01) 51 81 88 70* – Menu 29/44 € – Carte 21/41 € 🍴
◆ Grand Luxury ◆ Historic ◆ Modern ◆
This impressive, carefully restored palace from 1840 is an extremely elegant address that offers pleasant, modern luxury. Some of the individual suites are spread over two floors. The pleasantly bright garden pavilion and wine bar constitute the WeinBistro.

Imperial 🕰 🛖 🗚 ↩ rm 📶 🎵 🚵 VISA ⮾ AE ①
Kärntner Ring 16 ✉ *1015* – Ⓜ *Karlsplatz* – 𝒞 *(01) 50 11 00* – *hotel.imperial@luxurycollection.com* – *Fax (01) 50 11 04 10*
– *www.luxurycollection.com/imperial* **E3**
138 rm – †369/900 € ††369/900 €, ⚏ 39 € – 31 suites
Rest *Imperial* – 𝒞 *(01) 50 11 03 56 (closed July) (dinner only) (booking advisable)* Carte 54/79 €
Rest *Café Imperial* – 𝒞 *(01) 50 11 03 89* – Carte 33/58 €
◆ Palace ◆ Grand Luxury ◆ Historic ◆
The Grand Hotel, dated from 1873, is a magnificent building that has kept a touch of the past. The ambience is refined and elegant, from the wonderful stylish lobby through to the rooms and suites. A restaurant offering a refined and exclusive ambience. The Café Imperial offers all the flair of a Viennese coffee house.

Grand Hotel 🕰 🕰 ❖ 🗚 ↩ rm 📶 🎵 🚵 🚐 VISA ⮾ AE ①
Kärntner Ring 9 ✉ *1010* – Ⓜ *Karlsplatz* – 𝒞 *(01) 51 58 00* – *sales@grandhotelwien.com* – *Fax (01) 5 15 13 12* – *www.grandhotelwien.com*
205 rm – †340/440 € ††390/490 €, ⚏ 30 € – 11 suites **E3**
Rest *Le Ciel* – 𝒞 *(01) 5 15 80 91 00 (closed Sunday)* Carte 48/72 €
Rest *Unkai* – 𝒞 *(01) 5 15 80 91 10 (closed Monday lunch)* Menu 38/99 €
– Carte 24/60 €
Rest *Grand Café* – 𝒞 *(01) 5 15 80 91 20* – Carte 28/48 €
◆ Grand Luxury ◆ Classic ◆
The Grand Hotel offers classical and elegant rooms luxuriously decorated with a historical flair. There is a sushi bar inside the hotel. Le Ciel is an elegant restaurant on the 7th floor with a beautiful terrace. The Unkai features Japanese cuisine.

Sacher 🕰 ⮾ 🛖 ❖ 🗚 ↩ rm 📶 🎵 🚵 🚐 VISA ⮾ AE ①
Philharmonikerstr. 4 ✉ *1010* – Ⓜ *Karlsplatz* – 𝒞 *(01) 51 45 60* – *wien@sacher.com* – *Fax (01) 51 45 68 10* – *www.sacher.com* **D3**
152 rm – †355/460 € ††355/460 €, ⚏ 31 € – 7 suites
Rest *Anna Sacher* – 𝒞 *(01) 51 45 68 40 (closed July - August and Monday)* Menu 62/94 € – Carte 39/77 €
Rest *Rote Bar* – 𝒞 *(01) 51 45 68 41* – Carte 31/72 €
◆ Luxury ◆ Traditional ◆ Classic ◆
This Viennese institution, established in 1876, has style and elegance with first-class service and a beautiful recreational area. Suites with terrace and view of Vienna. Anna Sacher provides classical elegance. The Rote Bar is sumptuously bedecked in red velvet and serves delicious traditional cuisine.

Bristol 🕰 ❖ rest 🗚 ↩ rm 📶 🎵 🚵 🚐 VISA ⮾ AE ①
Kärntner Ring 1 ✉ *1015* – Ⓜ *Karlsplatz* – 𝒞 *(01) 51 51 60* – *hotel.bristol@luxurycollection.com* – *Fax (01) 51 51 65 50* – *www.luxurycollection.com/bristol*
140 rm – †245/750 € ††245/750 €, ⚏ 35 € – 10 suites **D3**
Rest *Korso* – see below
Rest *Sirk* – *(from 30 June - 27 August only lunch)* Menu 26/39 €
– Carte 37/64 €
◆ Luxury ◆ Traditional ◆ Classic ◆
A stylish hotel with professional service. The Prince of Wales suite is sumptuous and luxurious and features its own fitness and sauna rooms. Enjoy beautiful views over the State Opera House through the large windows of the Sirk restaurant.

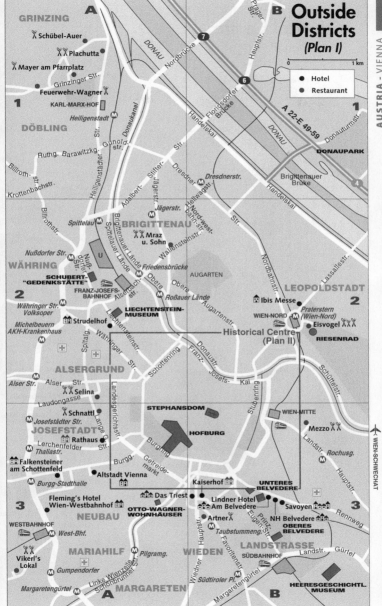

Outside Districts
(Plan I)

0   1 km

● Hotel
● Restaurant

GRINZING

Ẋ Schübel-Auer

ẊẊ Plachutta

Ẋ Mayer am Pfarrplatz

Feuerwehr-Wagner Ẋ

KARL-MARX-HOF

Heiligenstadt

DÖBLING

Ruthg. Barawitzkg.

Billroth-str.

Krottenbachstr.

Spittelau

Nußdorfer Str.

WÄHRING

SCHUBERT-"GEDENKSTÄTTE"

FRANZ-JOSEFS-BAHNHOF

Währinger Str. Volksoper

Michelbeuern AKH-Krankenhaus

Strudelhof

LIECHTENSTEIN-MUSEUM

BRIGITTENAU

ẊẊ Mraz u. Sohn

Friedensbrücke

Roßauer Lände

AUGARTEN

ALSERGRUND

Alser Str.   Alser   Str.

ẊẊ Selina

Laudongasse

Ẋ Schnattl

Josefstädter Str.

JOSEFSTADT

Rathaus

Lerchenfelder Str. Thaliastr.

Falksteiner am Schottenfeld

Burgg-Stadthalle

Fleming's Hotel Wien-Westbahnhof

NEUBAU

WESTBAHNHOF

West-Bhf.

Ẋ Vikerl's Lokal

MARIAHILF

Pilgramg.

Gumpendorfer

Margaretengürtel

MARGARETEN

Linke Wienzeile Schönbrunner Str.

OTTO-WAGNER-WOHNHÄUSER

STEPHANSDOM

HOFBURG

Altstadt Vienna

Das Triest

Artner Ẋ

Taubstummeng.

WIEDEN

Wiedner Haupt.

SÜDBAHNHOF

Südtiroler Pl.

Favoritenstr.

DONAU

Nordbrücke

Prager Str.

Hauptstr.

Floridsdorfer Brücke

A 22-E 49-59

DONAU

Handelskai

Donauturmstr.

DONAUPARK

Brigittenauer Brüke

Dresdnerstr.

Hellwagstr.

Jägerstr.

Nord-west. bahnstr.

Wallensteinstr.

Obere

Obere

Augartenstr.

Nordbahnstr.

Lassallestr.

LEOPOLDSTADT

Ibis Messe

WIEN-NORD (Wien-Nord)

Praterstern

Eisvogel ẊẊẊ

RIESENRAD

→ Historical Centre (Plan II)

Donaustr.

Franz-Josefs-

Schottenring

Kai

Stubenring

WIEN-MITTE

Mezzo ẊẊ

Landstr. Rochusg.

Burgring

Getreide-markt

Kaiserhof

Lindner Hotel Am Belvedere

UNTERES BELVEDERE

Savoyen

NH Belvedere

OBERES BELVEDERE

Prinz-Eugen-Str.

Rennweg

LANDSTRASSE

Landstr. Gürtel

Margaretengürtel

HEERESGESCHICHTL. MUSEUM

→ WIEN-SCHWECHAT

25

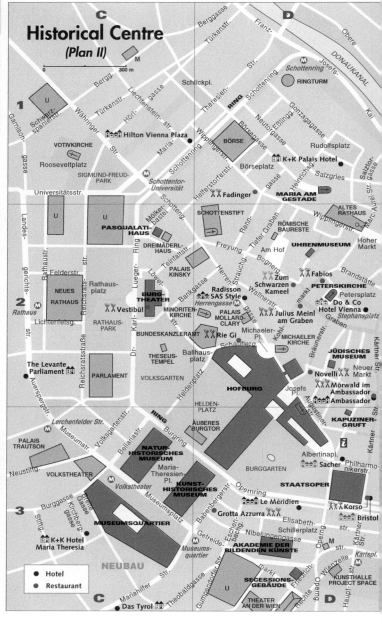

Historical Centre
(Plan II)

AUSTRIA - VIENNA

0 — 300 m

● Hotel
● Restaurant

26

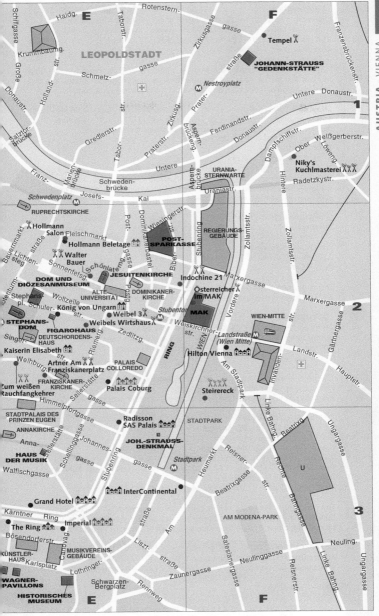

Rotenstern-gasse

Haidg.

Schilligasse

Große

Donaustr.

Salztor-brücke

Krummbaumg.

LEOPOLDSTADT

Taborstr.

Schmelz-

Holland-

Gredlerstr.

Tabor-

Marien-brücke

Franz-

Josefs-

Schweden-brücke

Kai

gasse

Zirkusgasse

Nestroyplatz

Prater-

Aspern-brücke

Ferdinandstr.

Untere

Untere Donaustr.

Donaustr.

Aspern-brücke

Uranistr.

Tempel

JOHANN-STRAUSS "GEDENKSTÄTTE"

Dampfschiffstr.

Ober-Weißgerberstr.

Löweng.

Hintere

Niky's Kuchlmasterei

Radetzkystr.

URANIA-STERNWARTE

REGIERUNGS-GEBÄUDE

Zollamtstr.

Zollamtsstr.

Marxergasse

Marxergasse

Schwedenplatz

RUPRECHTSKIRCHE

Bauermarkt

Hollmann Salon

Fleischmarkt

Hollmann Beletage

Walter Bauer

Lichten-steig

Sonnenfelsg.

straße

DOM UND DIÖZESANMUSEUM

Stephans-pl.

Schuler-str.

Wollzeile

ALTE UNIVERSITÄT

JESUITENKIRCHE

Bäcker-

Schönlate

DOMINIKANER-KIRCHE

Weibel 3

Weibels Wirtshaus

Wiesingerstr.

Dominikanerbastei

Biber-

Stubenring

Indochine 21

POST-SPARKASSE

Österreicher im MAK

Stubentor

MAK

Vordere

WIEN-MITTE

STEPHANS-DOM

FIGAROHAUS

DEUTSCHORDENS-HAUS

Singer-

Kaiserin Elisabeth

Weihburg-

König von Ungarn

Zedlitzg.

Riemer-

Weiskirchner-str.

Landstraße (Wien Mitte)

Hilton Vienna

Gärtnergasse

Landstr.

Hauptstr.

Artner Am Franziskanerplatz

FRANZISKANER-KIRCHE

Zum weißen Rauchfangkehrer

Himmelpfortgasse

Seilerstätte

Palais Coburg

PALAIS COLLOREDO

RING

Am Stadtpark

Steirereck

Linke Bahng.

Beatrix

Ungargasse

STADTPALAIS DES PRINZEN EUGEN

ANNAKIRCHE

Anna-

HAUS DER MUSIK

Walfischgasse

Seilerstätte

Schellinggasse

Johannes-

Radisson SAS Palais

Stubenring

gasse

JOH.-STRAUSS-DENKMAL

Stadtpark

STADTPARK

Heumarkt

Reisner-

Beatrixgasse

str.

Fechte

Bahrng.

U

Kärntner Ring

Grand Hotel

The Ring

Bösendorferstr.

KÜNSTLER-HAUS

Karlsplatz

Imperial

InterContinental

Canovag.

straße

Am

MUSIKVEREINS-GEBÄUDE

Lothringer-

Liszt-

straße

Zaunergasse

AM MODENA-PARK

Salesianergasse

Neulinggasse

Reisnerstr.

Linke Bahng.

Neuling-

Ungargasse

WAGNER-PAVILLONS

HISTORISCHES MUSEUM

Schwarzen-Bergplatz

Rennweg

E

F

27

Le Méridien

*Opernring 13 ⊠ 1010 – Ⓜ Karlsplatz – ℰ (01) 58 89 00 – info.vienna@
lemeridien.com – Fax (01) 5 88 90 90 90 – www.lemeridien.com/vienna*
294 rm – ♦179/579 €, ♦♦179/579 €, ⊆ 28 € – 17 suites   **D3**
Rest *Shambala* – Carte 38/58 €
◆ Chain hotel ◆ Business ◆ Modern ◆
Behind its classical façade, this hotel is surprising with its tasteful, thoroughly
modern design. The rooms are equipped with the latest high-tech fittings. The distinctive design of the hotel is also present in the Shambala restaurant.

InterContinental

*Johannesgasse 28 ⊠ 1037 – Ⓜ Stadtpark – ℰ (01) 71 12 20 – vienna@
ihg.com – Fax (01) 7 13 44 89 – www.intercontinental.com/vienna*
453 rm – ♦289/349 € ♦♦289/349 €, ⊆ 27 € – 32 suites   **E3**
Rest – Carte 31/58 €
◆ Chain hotel ◆ Luxury ◆ Classic ◆
This business hotel is situated by the city park. It boasts a lavish interior with a
sophisticated, elegant hall and contemporary rooms with high-tech fittings. There
is a lovely view from the top floor. A touch of the Mediterranean in this restaurant
with open kitchen and winter garden.

Hilton Vienna Plaza

Schottenring 11 ⊠ 1010 – Ⓜ Schottentor-Universität
*– ℰ (01) 31 39 00 – info.viennaplaza@hilton.com – Fax (01) 31 39 02 20 09
– www.hilton.at/wienplaza*   **C1**
218 rm – ♦139/400 € ♦♦139/400 €, ⊆ 27 € – 13 suites
Rest – Carte 30/47 €
◆ Chain hotel ◆ Functional ◆
This city-centre hotel features spacious and technologically functional rooms as
well as luxurious designer suites. Restaurant with a modern atmosphere.

Savoyen

*Rennweg 16 ⊠ 1030 – Ⓜ Karlsplatz – ℰ (01) 20 63 30 – savoyen@
austria-trend.at – Fax (01) 2 06 33 92 10 – www.austria-trend.at/sav*
309 rm – ♦150/300 € ♦♦150/350 €, ⊆ 19 € – 43 suites   *Plan I* **B3**
Rest – Carte 29/41 €
◆ Luxury ◆ Contemporary ◆
The hotel is located inside the imposing building of the former State Printing
Office. The spacious modern, elegant rooms are reached via an impressive atrium
extending six floors upwards. A light, modern restaurant in orange shades.

Radisson SAS Palais

Parkring 16 ⊠ 1010 – Ⓜ Stadtpark – ℰ (01) 51 51 70
*– sales.vienna@radissonsas.com – Fax (01) 5 12 22 16
– www.palais.vienna.radissonsas.com*   **E3**
247 rm – ♦169/299 € ♦♦169/299 €, ⊆ 25 € – 9 suites
Rest *Le siècle* – ℰ (01) 5 15 17 34 40 (closed 14 July - 31 August, Sunday and
bank holidays) Menu 57/85 € – Carte 53/107 €
Rest *Palais Café* – ℰ (01) 5 15 17 34 70 – Carte 28/54 €
◆ Chain hotel ◆ Luxury ◆ Classic ◆
This hotel across from the City Park consists of two connected 19th-century palace
buildings. Stylish appointments fit the historical setting. Le siècle : a classical restaurant with a beautiful view over the park. Palais Café in the winter garden.

Hilton Vienna

Am Stadtpark 3 ⊠ 1030 – Ⓜ Landstraße – ℰ (01) 71 70 00
– reservations.vienna@hilton.com – Fax (01) 7 13 06 91 – www.hilton.at
579 rm – ♦139/399 € ♦♦139/399 €, ⊆ 27 € – 41 suites   **F2**
Rest – Carte 28/54 €
◆ Chain hotel ◆ Luxury ◆ Modern ◆
A large conference hotel in a central location with an atrium hall and modern
guestrooms. The executive level on the 15th floor has a beautiful roof terrace
with wonderful views. Restaurant features a contemporary style.

AUSTRIA - VIENNA

Ambassador

AC 🛜 🖻 📶 🖾 VISA ☯ AE ①

Kärntner Str. 22 ⊠ 1010 – 🖾 *Stephansdom –* 𝒞 *(01) 96 16 10 – office@ambassador.at – Fax (01) 5 13 29 99 – www.ambassador.at* **D2**
86 rm – ♦267/452 € ♦♦333/567 €, � 25 €
Rest *Mörwald im Ambassador* – see below
♦ Business ♦ Modern ♦
A successful combination of traditional and modern characterises the stylish, technically well-equipped rooms. The themed rooms are named after famous people.

Do & Co Hotel Vienna

≤ 🚗 🛜 ₺ AC 🛜 rm 🖾 📶 🛜 VISA

Stephansplatz 12 (6 th floor) ⊠ 1010 – 🖾 *Stephansplatz –* 𝒞 *(01) 2 41 88 – hotel@doco.com – Fax (01) 24 18 84 44 – www.doco.com* **D2**
43 rm – ♦245/410 € ♦♦245/410 €, � 29 € **Rest –** Carte 31/56 €
♦ Business ♦ Design ♦
This attractive hotel, which is characterised by its high quality facilities and modern design, is in a privileged location, facing the Stephansdom. European and Asian dishes are served from the visible kitchen on the seventh floor. Pleasant views can be enjoyed from the restaurant and terrace.

The Ring

🔏 🛜 ₺ AC 🛜 🖾 📶 🛜 VISA ☯ AE ①

Kärntner Ring 8 ⊠ 1010 – 🖾 *Karlsplatz –* 𝒞 *(01) 22 12 20 – reservation@theringhotel.com – Fax (01) 22 12 29 00 – www.theringhotel.com*
68 rm – ♦290/700 € ♦♦340/750 €, � 23 € **E3**
Rest – Menu 39/55 € – Carte 34/53 € 🍴
♦ Townhouse ♦ Modern ♦
This beautiful historical townhouse in the city centre is home to a hotel maintained in a tasteful, modern style. The heritage protected lift is not to be missed. An international range of dishes is available in the restaurant.

Radisson SAS Style

🔏 🛜 ₺ 🛜 rm 🖾 📶 🛜 VISA ☯ AE ①

Herrengasse 12 ⊠ 1010 – 🖾 *Herrengasse –* 𝒞 *(01) 22 78 00 – info.style@radissonsas.com – Fax (01) 2 27 80 77 – www.style.vienna.radissonsas.com*
78 rm – ♦260/315 € ♦♦260/330 €, � 28 € – 6 suites **D2**
Rest *Sapori* – *(closed 2 weeks August, Sunday and bank holidays)*
Carte 39/53 €
♦ Health hotel ♦ Design ♦
This former bank building is impressive with its classical façade and elegant, modern interior. A sauna has been built in the former vault. The Sapori restaurant offers an international range of dishes.

Das Triest

🛜 🛜 AC 🛜 rm 🖾 📶 🔏 VISA ☯ AE ①

Wiedner Hauptstr. 12 ⊠ 1040 – 🖾 *Karlsplatz –* 𝒞 *(01) 58 91 80 – office@dastriest.at – Fax (01) 5 89 18 18 – www.dastriest.at* *Plan I* **B3**
72 rm � – ♦220/240 € ♦♦280/290 € – 3 suites
Rest – *(closed Saturday lunch, Sunday)* Menu 46 € – Carte 31/52 €
♦ Business ♦ Design ♦
Located close to the centre, the functional, well-designed guestrooms of this hotel bear the hallmark of Sir Terence Conran. The modern restaurant serves Italian cuisine. The attractive inner courtyard is very pleasant.

Lindner Hotel Am Belvedere

🔏 🛜 ₺ AC 🛜 🔏 🛜

Rennweg 12 ⊠ 1030 – 🖾 *Karlsplatz –* 𝒞 *(01) 79 47 70* VISA ☯ AE ①
– info.wien@lindnerhotels.at – Fax (01) 79 47 79 29 – www.lindner.de
219 rm – ♦150/399 € ♦♦150/399 €, � 19 € *Plan I* **B3**
Rest – Carte 30/48 €
♦ Business ♦ Modern ♦
This modern city hotel has well-equipped, high-tech rooms with clean lines. They have a lovely view over the Belvedere castle and the Botanical Gardens. European and Asian cuisine can be enjoyed in the 'Taste it!' restaurant, while the wine tavern offers regional dishes.

AUSTRIA - VIENNA

NH Belvedere without rest   🐾 🕸 & 🆔 ⇔ 🖼 🕪 🏖 VISA ⑩ AE ①
Rennweg 12a ⊠ 1030 – ⓜ Karlsplatz – ℰ (01) 2 06 11 – nhbelvedere@
nh-hotels.com – Fax (01) 2 06 11 15 – www.nh-hotels.com   *Plan I* **B3**
114 rm – †104/205 € **††**104/205 €, ⥶ 16 €
♦ Chain hotel ♦ Modern ♦
This hotel in the classicist building of the former State Printing Office offers
modern rooms, some with views over the Botanical Gardens. Bistro with snacks.

The Levante Parliament   🛋 🆔 ⇔ rm 🖼 🕪 🏖 VISA ⑩ AE ①
Auerspergstr. 9 ⊠ 1080 – ⓜ Rathaus – ℰ (01) 22 82 80 – parliament@
thelevante.com – Fax (01) 2 28 28 28 – www.thelevante.com   **C2**
70 rm ⥶ – **†**220 € **††**286 €   **Rest** – *(closed Sunday)* Carte 24/44 €
♦ Townhouse ♦ Design ♦
The hotel with its bright stone façade stands out with its modern, purist design
and state-of-the-art technology. It is decorated with glassworks lent by Nemtoi
and photographs by Curt Themessl. The restaurant offers international cuisine.

Kaiserhof without rest   🐾 🕸 🆔 ⇔ 🖼 🕪 🏖 VISA ⑩ AE ①
Frankenberggasse 10 ⊠ 1040 – ⓜ Karlsplatz – ℰ (01) 5 05 17 01 – wien@
hotel-kaiserhof.at – Fax (01) 5 05 88 75 88 – www.hotel-kaiserhof.at
74 rm ⥶ – **†**130/180 € **††**165/280 € – 3 suites   *Plan I* **B3**
♦ Traditional ♦ Art Deco ♦
Guests receive friendly and attentive service in this beautifully furnished hotel built
in 1896 – two floors are especially modern. Snack menu in the bar.

Fleming's Hotel Wien-Westbahnhof   🐾 🕸 & 🆔 ⇔ 🖼 🕪
Neubaugürtel 26 ⊠ 1070 – ⓜ West-Bahnhof   🏖 VISA ⑩ AE ①
– ℰ (01) 22 73 70 – wien@flemings-hotels.com – Fax (01) 2 27 37 99 99
– www.flemings-hotels.com   *Plan I* **A3**
146 rm ⥶ – **†**89/315 € **††**125/351 € – 4 suites   **Rest** – Carte 20/35 €
♦ Business ♦ Modern ♦
The business hotel close to the west railway station has been maintained in a thoroughly modern style. All the rooms possess glassed-in bathrooms. Restaurant
with a brasserie-style atmosphere.

Hollmann Beletage   🕸 🆔 ⇔ 🖼 🕪 VISA ⑩ AE ①
Köllnerhofgasse 6 ⊠ 1010 – ⓜ Stephansplatz – ℰ (01) 9 61 19 60 – hotel@
hollmann-beletage.at – Fax (01) 9 61 19 60 33 – www.hollmann-beletage.at
25 rm ⥶ – **†**150/200 € **††**150/200 €   **E2**
Rest *Hollmann Salon* – see below
♦ Townhouse ♦ Design ♦
A personal, individual address in an ideal location. This small hotel successfully
combines the classical framework of the old townhouse with a trendy design.
Films about Vienna and Austria are shown in the hotel's small cinema.

K+K Hotel Maria Theresia without rest   🕸 🆔 ⇔ 🖼 🕪 🏖 🏖
Kirchberggasse 6 ⊠ 1070 – ⓜ Volkstheater – ℰ (01)   VISA ⑩ AE ①
5 21 23 – kk.maria.theresia@kuk.at – Fax (01) 5 21 23 70 – www.kkhotels.com
123 rm ⥶ – **†**190/215 € **††**260/285 €   **C3**
♦ Business ♦ Modern ♦
Located in the artists' quarter of Spittelberg, this hotel has especially nicely fitted
rooms with views over Vienna. The bar in the spacious lobby offers a small menu.

Rathaus without rest   ⇔ 🖼 🕪 🏖 VISA ⑩ AE ①
Lange Gasse 13 ⊠ 1080 – ⓜ Rathaus – ℰ (01) 4 00 11 22 – office@
hotel-rathaus-wien.at – Fax (01) 4 00 11 22 88 – www.hotel-rathaus-wien.at
40 rm – †118/138 € **††**148/198 €, ⥶ 15 €   *Plan I* **A3**
♦ Townhouse ♦ Historic ♦ Design ♦
This smart, historical townhouse combines an old building and a clearly modern
style with the motto 'Wein-Design'. Here you can stay in spacious, airy 'Winzer'
rooms and enjoy an excellent buffet breakfast in the morning.

AUSTRIA - VIENNA

Altstadt Vienna without rest   🔲 ↳ 📺 ⁿ⁰ 🆚 ⊕ 🅰🄴 ⓪
Kirchengasse 41 ⊠ 1070 – Ⓜ Volkstheater – 𝒞 (01) 5 26 33 99 – hotel@
altstadt.at – Fax (01) 5 23 49 01 – www.altstadt.at   *Plan I* **A3**
42 rm ⊏ – †119/169 € ††139/209 € – 8 suites
♦ Traditional ♦ Design ♦
This patrician house is an individual, homely location with a historical charm. It is dotted with select objets d'art, and the rooms designed by Matteo Thun are exquisitely decorated.

Falkensteiner Am Schottenfeld without rest   🏠 🔲 ↳ 📺 ⁿ⁰
Schottenfeldgasse 74 ⊠ 1070   🖧 🕾 🆚 ⊕ 🅰🄴 ⓪
– Ⓜ Burggasse Stadthalle – 𝒞 (01) 5 26 51 81 – schottenfeld@falkensteiner.com
– Fax (01) 52 65 18 11 60 – www.falkensteiner.com/schottenfeld   *Plan I* **A3**
95 rm – †157/169 € ††199/219 €, ⊏ 19 €
♦ Business ♦ Contemporary ♦
This hotel, which is perfect for seminars, has a very large reception area. It offers modern, functional guestrooms decorated in light tones.

Kaiserin Elisabeth without rest   🔲 📺 ⁿ⁰ 🖧 🆚 ⊕ 🅰🄴 ⓪
Weihburggasse 3 ⊠ 1010 – Ⓜ Stephansplatz – 𝒞 (01) 51 52 60 – info@
kaiserinelisabeth.at – Fax (01) 51 52 67 – www.kaiserinelisabeth.at
63 rm ⊏ – †126/180 € ††216/245 €   **E2**
♦ Traditional ♦ Classic ♦
This beautiful townhouse near the Stephansdom has been in operation since 1809. An elegant hotel with a pretty roofed inner courtyard.

König von Ungarn   🔲 rm 📺 🕾 🖧 🆚 ⊕ 🅰🄴 ⓪
Schulerstr. 10 ⊠ 1010 – Ⓜ Stephansplatz – 𝒞 (01) 51 58 40 – hotel@kvu.at
– Fax (01) 51 58 48 – www.kvu.at   **E2**
33 rm ⊏ – †150/170 € ††215 €   **Rest** – *(dinner only)* Carte 24/36 €
♦ Traditional ♦ Classic ♦
Located behind the Stephansdom is this classically decorated 16C building, with lots of style and warm colours. Don't miss the attractive courtyard. The restaurant is located in a house that Mozart once lived in.

Das Tyrol without rest   🏠 🔲 ↳ 📺 ⁿ⁰ 🕾 🆚 ⊕ 🅰🄴 ⓪
Mariahilfer Str. 15 ⊠ 1060 – Ⓜ Museumsquartier – 𝒞 (01) 5 87 54 15
– reception@das-tyrol.at – Fax (01) 58 75 41 59 – www.das-tyrol.at
30 rm ⊏ – †109/209 € ††149/259 €   **C3**
♦ Family ♦ Modern ♦
This lovingly restored corner building is home to tastefully decorated rooms with modern furnishings. Paintings by Viennese artists adorn the walls.

K+K Palais Hotel without rest   🔲 ↳ 📺 🕾 🆚 ⊕ 🅰🄴 ⓪
Rudolfsplatz 11 ⊠ 1010 – Ⓜ Schwedenplatz – 𝒞 (01) 5 33 13 53
– kk.palais.hotel@kuk.at – Fax (01) 5 33 13 53 70 – www.kkhotels.com
66 rm ⊏ – †190 € ††260 €   **D1**
♦ Traditional ♦ Contemporary ♦
Guests are offered functional rooms. The warm colours of which create a cosy atmosphere in this historical Stadtpalais close to the centre.

Strudlhof without rest   🏠 ♿ 🔲 ↳ 📺 🕾 🖧 🅿 🕾 🆚 ⊕ 🅰🄴 ⓪
Pasteurgasse 1 ⊠ 1090 – Ⓜ Währinger Str.-Volksoper – 𝒞 (01) 3 19 25 22
– hotel@strudlhof.at – Fax (01) 31 92 52 28 00 – www.strudlhof.at
84 rm ⊏ – †142/152 € ††189/212 €   *Plan I* **A2**
♦ Business ♦ Functional ♦
This hotel offers technologically well equipped guest rooms. A stylish setting for your business function in this former palace.

Ibis Messe   ♿ 🔲 ↳ rm 📺 ⁿ⁰ 🖧 🕾 🆚 ⊕ 🅰🄴 ⓪
Lassallestr. 7a ⊠ 1020 – Ⓜ Praterstern – 𝒞 (01) 21 77 00 – h2736@accor.com
– Fax (01) 21 77 05 55 – www.ibishotels.com   *Plan I* **B2**
166 rm – †69/89 € ††87/107 €, ⊏ 10 €   **Rest** – Carte 17/26 €
♦ Chain hotel ♦ Functional ♦
This hotel, ideally suited to business guests, is located in the vicinity of the Prater and offers modern, functional rooms.

XXXX ✿✿

Steirereck (Heinz Reitbauer Jun.)

Am Heumarkt 2a (at Stadtpark) ✉ 1030 – Ⓜ Stadtpark – ☎ (01) 7 13 31 68 – wien@steirereck.at – Fax (01) 71 33 16 82 – www.steirereck.at – closed Saturday - Sunday and bank holidays **F2**

Rest – *(booking advisable)* Menu 49 € (lunch)/105 € – Carte 55/91 €

Rest *Meierei* – *(closed Saturday dinner, Sunday dinner and bank holidays)* Menu 36 € (dinner) – Carte 28/40 €

Spec. Lauwarmer Artischockensalat mit Kräutern. Lamm aus eigener Landwirtschaft. Reh mit Wald- und Wiesenaromaten.

◆ Inventive ◆ Luxury ◆

Creative, contemporary dishes are prepared here with utmost care from excellent local products. From the terrace there is a very pleasant view over the Stadtpark. Meierei is a cheese and milk bar occupying part of the restaurant. Its regional menu includes cakes and tarts.

XXX

Korso – Hotel Bristol

Kärntner Ring 1 ✉ 1015 – Ⓜ Karlsplatz – ☎ (01) 51 51 65 46 – palm@restaurantkorso.at – Fax (01) 51 51 65 75 – www.luxurycollection.com/bristol – closed 3 - 30 August and Saturday lunch **D3**

Rest – Menu 48 € (lunch)/86 € – Carte 56/88 €

◆ Classic ◆ Elegant ◆

This restaurant with its classical, stylish atmosphere recalls the noble ambience of the traditional Grand Hotel. A highlight is the illuminated onyx wall.

XXX

Eisvogel

Riesenradplatz 5 (Prater) ✉ 1022 – Ⓜ Praterstern – ☎ (01) 9 08 11 16 31 00 – eisvogel@riesenradplatz.at – Fax (01) 9 08 11 16 31 01 – www.riesenradplatz.at *Plan I* **B2**

Rest – Menu 26/35 € – Carte 30/35 €

◆ Viennese cuisine ◆ Elegant ◆

An elegant restaurant offering regional cuisine in what was formerly a 19C city inn. In summer, the lively atmosphere of the Prater can be enjoyed from the terrace located in front of the ferris wheel.

XXX

Niky's Kuchlmasterei with rm

Obere Weissgerberstr. 6 ✉ 1030 – ☎ (01) 7 12 90 00 – office@kuchlmasterei.at – Fax (01) 7 12 90 00 16 – www.kuchlmasterei.at – closed Sunday and bank holidays, except in December

7 suites – †250 € ††250 €, ☕ 13 € **F1**

Rest – Menu 19 € (lunch)/52 € – Carte 35/58 €

◆ International ◆ Cosy ◆

Rich decor and original artwork set the tone in this unique restaurant. Beautiful terrace and large wine cellar. Individual, exclusive suites.

XXX

Julius Meinl am Graben

Graben 19 (1st floor) ✉ 1010 – Ⓜ Stephansplatz – ☎ (01) 5 32 33 34 60 00 – restaurant@meinlamgraben.at – Fax (01) 5 32 33 34 12 90 – www.meinlamgraben.at – closed Sunday and bank holidays **D2**

Rest – *(booking essential)* Menu 35 € (lunch)/92 € (dinner) – Carte 46/70 €

◆ Classic ◆ Elegant ◆

In a gourmet shop rich in tradition you will find this popular restaurant with classical cuisine. The window seats provide a lovely view over the Graben and Pestsäule.

XXX

Grotta Azzurra

Babenbergerstr. 5 ✉ 1010 – Ⓜ Museumsquartier – ☎ (01) 5 86 10 44 – office@grotta-azzurra.at – Fax (01) 5 86 10 44 15 – www.grotta-azzura.at – closed Monday **D3**

Rest – Menu 38/58 € – Carte 32/53 €

◆ Italian ◆ Friendly ◆

Austria's oldest Italian restaurant exists since the beginning of the '50s. Details such as high ceilings, beautiful candlesticks and artwork create a special atmosphere.

XXX **Mörwald im Ambassador**   AK VISA ◐◑ AE ①

Kärntner Str. 22 (1st floor) ✉ *1010* – Ⓜ *Stephansplatz* – ℰ *(01) 96 16 11 61*
– *ambassador@moerwald.at* – *Fax (01) 96 16 11 60* – *www.moerwald.at*
Rest – *(booking advisable)* Menu 29 € (lunch)/110 €   **D2**
– Carte 28/74 € ✿
 ♦ French ♦ Fashionable ♦
The classical restaurant with French-style cuisine is connected to the impressive
Atrium Bar. The conservatory, with its open glass front in the summer, offers
views over the new market.

XX **Mraz & Sohn**   ☷ P VISA ◐◑
✿

Wallensteinstr. 59 ✉ *1200* – Ⓜ *Friedensbrücke* – ℰ *(01) 3 30 45 94* – *Fax (01)*
3 50 15 36 – *www.mraz-sohn.at*
– *closed 24 December - 7 January, 6 - 14 April, 10 - 30 August, Saturday*
- Sunday and bank holidays   **Plan I A2**
Rest – *(booking advisable)* Menu 39/89 € – Carte 47/65 € ✿
Spec. Kaisergranat mit dekonstruiertem Kochsalat. Illusion von der gegrillten
Taube mit geräuchertem Spitzkohl und Apfelstampf. Kirschkollektion.
 ♦ Inventive ♦ Individual ♦
This individual restaurant has an impressive wine cellar and is a real family busi-
ness. The cuisine is modern and creative and is prepared by the third generation
of the Mraz family.

XX **Selina**   VISA ◐◑ AE ①

Laudongasse 13 ✉ *1080* – Ⓜ *Rathaus* – ℰ *(01) 4 05 64 04* – *Fax (01)*
4 08 04 59 – *www.selina.at*   **Plan I A2**
Rest – Menu 49/72 € – Carte 21/40 €
 ♦ International ♦ Friendly ♦
In a modern, elegant setting with a southern touch, refined international and
Mediterranean/Middle Eastern cuisine is served.

XX **Novelli**   ☷ VISA ◐◑ AE ①

Bräunerstr. 11 ✉ *1010* – Ⓜ *Herrengasse* – ℰ *(01) 5 13 42 00* – *novelli@*
haslauer.at – *Fax (01) 5 12 37 52 50* – *www.novelli.at*
– *closed Sunday*   **D2**
Rest – *(booking advisable)* Carte 39/58 €
 ♦ Mediterranean ♦ Trendy ♦
Italian cuisine is coupled with friendly service. Robust, warm colours lend a Mediterranean atmosphere to this modern restaurant.

XX **Vestibül**   � ⇥ VISA ◐◑ AE ①
☺

Dr. Karl-Lueger-Ring 2 (at Burgtheater) ✉ *1010* – Ⓜ *Herrengasse* – ℰ *(01)*
5 32 49 99 – *restaurant@vestibuel.at* – *Fax (01) 5 32 49 99 10* – *www.vestibuel.at*
– *closed Sunday and bank holidays, July - August also Saturday*   **C2**
Rest – Menu 22 € (lunch)/47 € – Carte 30/55 € ✿
 ♦ International ♦ Classic ♦
This restaurant recalls the historical, stylish atmosphere of the Burgtheater with its
extensive stucco work and beautiful marble. Delicious regional and Mediterranean
cuisine.

XX **Walter Bauer**   AK VISA ◐◑ AE ①
✿

Sonnenfelsgasse 17 ✉ *1010* – Ⓜ *Stubentor* – ℰ *(01) 5 12 98 71*
– *restaurant.walter.bauer@aon.at* – *Fax (01) 5 12 98 71*
– *closed 24 December - 4 January, 13 - 19 April, 20 July - 16 August*
and Saturday - Monday lunch   **E2**
Rest – *(booking advisable)* Menu 69 € – Carte 45/65 € ✿
Spec. Gänseleberterrine mit Brioche. Steinbutt an der Gräte gebraten.
Geschmortes Ochsenbackerl.
 ♦ Inventive ♦ Cosy ♦
Somewhat hidden in the old town in a pretty square, this restaurant with cross
vaulting has a sophisticated atmosphere. The menu combines modern and tradi-
tional dishes in which top quality products are used.

XX **Zum weißen Rauchfangkehrer**   AK ⇔ VISA ⬤⬤

Weihburggasse 4 ⊠ 1010 – Ⓜ Stephansplatz – ℰ (01) 5 12 34 71
– rauchfangkehrer@utanet.at – Fax (01) 5 12 34 71 28
– www.weisser-rauchfangkehrer.at
– closed 13 July - 16 August and Sunday - Monday   **E2**
Rest *– (dinner only) (booking advisable)* Carte 49/89 € 🏛

♦ Viennese cuisine ♦ Traditional ♦

Established in 1848, this traditional inn offers comfortable lounges with fresh Viennese cuisine. Excellent selection of Austrian wines.

XX **Artner am Franziskanerplatz**   ⇔ VISA ⬤⬤ ⑩

Franziskanerplatz 5 – Ⓜ Stephansplatz – ℰ (01) 5 03 50 34
– franziskanerplatz@artner.co.at – Fax (01) 5 03 50 34 15 – www.artner.co.at
Rest *–* Menu 23 € (lunch)/75 € – Carte 34/44 €   **E2**

♦ Contemporary ♦ Trendy ♦

This modern restaurant with its contemporary cuisine is located near the Stephansdom, in the small square in front of the Franciscan Church. There is a pleasant room in the vaulted cellar.

XX **Fabios**   🍴 AK VISA ⬤⬤ AE ⑩

Tuchlauben 6 ⊠ 1010 – Ⓜ Stephansplatz – ℰ (01) 5 32 22 22 – fabios@
fabios.at – Fax (01) 5 32 22 25 – www.fabios.at
– closed Sunday   **D2**
Rest *– (booking essential)* Carte 51/72 €

♦ Mediterranean ♦ Trendy ♦

The atmosphere in this modern restaurant is lively and cosmopolitan. The restaurant is located at the end of the pedestrian zone and serves creative Mediterranean cuisine.

XX **Indochine 21**   🍴 AK VISA ⬤⬤ AE ⑩

Stubenring 18 ⊠ 1010 – Ⓜ Stubentor – ℰ (01) 5 13 76 60 – restaurant@
indochine.at – Fax (01) 5 13 76 60 16 – www.indochine.at   **E2**
Rest *–* Menu 35/88 € – Carte 41/70 €

♦ Fusion ♦ Exotic ♦

This Asian-inspired restaurant in a classical townhouse offers high-class fusion cooking with a hint of Indo-China. There is an attractive little terrace in front of the building.

XX **Zum Schwarzen Kameel**   🍴 AK ⇔ VISA ⬤⬤ AE ⑩

Bognergasse 5 ⊠ 1010 – Ⓜ Herrengasse – ℰ (01) 5 33 81 25 – info@kameel.at
– Fax (01) 5 33 81 25 23 – www.kameel.at
– closed Sunday and bank holidays   **D2**
Rest *– (booking essential)* Menu 30 € (lunch)/76 € – Carte 35/73 €

♦ Austrian ♦ Traditional ♦

This traditional building has kept the same name since it opened in 1618. The former spice shop developed into a beautiful Art Nouveau restaurant with a pleasant coffee house flair. It serves regional and high quality international dishes, and has a delicatessen.

XX **RieGi**   🍴 VISA ⬤⬤ AE ⑩
£3

Schauflergasse 6 ⊠ 1010 – Ⓜ Herrengasse – ℰ (01) 5 32 91 26 – world@
barbaro.at – Fax (01) 5 32 91 26 20 – www.riegi.at
– closed 1 week early January, end July - mid August and Sunday - Monday
Rest *–* Menu 45/78 € – Carte 46/62 €   **D2**
Spec. Cannelloni mit Kalbsbries, Morcheln und grünem Spargel. Gänseleberterrine auf Rosinenbrioche mit Pinienkernen und Beerenauslesegelee. Kabeljau mit Zitronen-Olivenöl-Emulsion.

♦ International ♦ Friendly ♦

Located close to the Hofburg, this friendly and modern restaurant has an eye-catching ceiling with blue lights. International cuisine with a Mediterranean influence is served under this original 'sky'. Food is also served on the small terrace behind the building.

AUSTRIA - VIENNA

Mezzo
Esteplatz 6 ⊠ *1030* – Ⓜ *Landstraße* – ℰ *(01) 7 15 51 48* – *mezzo@mezzo.cc*
– *Fax (01) 7 15 51 48* – *www.mezzo.cc*
– *closed 25 December - 7 January, Saturday - Sunday and bank holidays*
Rest – Menu 28/65 € – Carte 28/42 € *Plan I* **B3**
◆ International ◆ Fashionable ◆
Located close to the centre, this restaurant serves international cuisine with Mediterranean and regional influences, in a simple, modern decor. Dining is also on the attractive terrace in front of the building.

Fadinger
Wipplingerstr. 29 ⊠ *1010* – Ⓜ *Schottentor-Universität* – ℰ *(01) 5 33 43 41*
– *restaurant@fadinger.at* – *Fax (01) 5 32 44 51* – *www.fadinger.at*
– *closed 10 - 16 August, Saturday lunch, Sunday and bank holidays*
Rest – *(booking advisable)* Menu 22 € (lunch)/55 €
– Carte 24/57 € 🍴 **D1**
◆ International ◆ Friendly ◆
An attractive location near the stock exchange with an extremely lively atmosphere. The tasty menu is both international and regional with a good selection of wines.

Österreicher im MAK
Stubenring 5 (at Museum MAK) ⊠ *1010* – Ⓜ *Stubentor* – ℰ *(01) 7 14 01 21*
– *office@oesterreicherimmak.at* – *Fax (01) 7 10 10 21*
– *www.oesterreicherimmak.at* **F2**
Rest – Carte 24/42 €
◆ Austrian ◆ Minimalist ◆
In the historical building of the Museum for Applied Arts, in a modern atmosphere with clean lines, regional dishes are served. Outdoor dining area.

Schnattl
Lange Gasse 40 ⊠ *1080* – Ⓜ *Rathaus* – ℰ *(01) 4 05 34 00* – *schnattl@aon.at*
– *Fax (01) 4 05 34 00* – *www.schnattl.com*
– *closed 2 weeks after Easter, 2 weeks end August, Saturday - Sunday and bank holidays* *Plan I* **A3**
Rest – *(dinner only)* Menu 38/55 € – Carte 34/45 €
◆ Regional ◆ Cosy ◆
This well-run restaurant with its regional cuisine is located on the edge of the inner city. In the summer an inviting terrace in the inner courtyard complements the comfortable rooms.

Weibels Wirtshaus
Kumpfgasse 2 ⊠ *1010* – Ⓜ *Stubentor* – ℰ *(01) 5 12 39 86* – *Fax (01) 5 12 39 86*
– *www.weibel.at* **E2**
Rest – *(booking advisable)* Menu 38 € – Carte 24/41 €
◆ Viennese cuisine ◆ Cosy ◆
This cosy, traditional restaurant is located in the city center. Friendly service and Viennese cuisine are served in the restaurant as well as on the outdoor terrace.

Weibel 3
Riemergasse 1 ⊠ *1010* – Ⓜ *Stubentor* – ℰ *(01) 5 13 31 10* – *Fax (01)*
5 13 31 10 – *www.weibel.at*
– *closed Monday, Sunday and bank holidays* **E2**
Rest – *(dinner only) (booking advisable)* Menu 36 € – Carte 28/52 €
◆ Spanish ◆ Intimate ◆
This pretty little restaurant serves Mediterranean cuisine. The tables are very close together, creating a cosy atmosphere.

Artner
Floragasse 6 ⊠ *1040* – Ⓜ *Taubstummengasse* – ℰ *(01) 5 03 50 33* – *wieden@*
artner.co.at – *Fax (01) 5 03 50 34* – *www.artner.co.at*
– *closed Saturday lunch, Sunday and bank holidays lunch* *Plan I* **B3**
Rest – Menu 35/50 € – Carte 25/50 €
◆ Regional ◆ Fashionable ◆
A simple, modern restaurant where guests can enjoy contemporary regional dishes with international influences. Good value lunch menu.

AUSTRIA - VIENNA

X
☺
Tempel   ↳ 🚾 ⑩ 🅰🅴 ⓞ
Praterstr. 56 ☒ 1020 – Ⓜ Nestroyplatz – ℰ (01) 2 14 01 79
– restaurant.tempel@utanet.at – Fax (01) 2 14 01 79
– closed 21 December - 6 January, Saturday lunch, Sunday - Monday
Rest – Menu 16 € (lunch)/41 € – Carte 26/39 €   **F1**
♦ Regional ♦ Bistro ♦
This cosy, bistro-style restaurant in a courtyard offers regional cuisine with international influence and reasonably priced lunchtime menu that changes daily. Beautiful terrace.

X
Hollmann Salon – Hotel Hollmann Beletage   🚾 ⑩ 🅰🅴 ⓞ
Grashofgasse 3 (at Heiligenkreuzerhof) ☒ 1010 – Ⓜ Stephansplatz – ℰ (01)
9 61 19 60 40 – essen@hollmann-salon.at – Fax (01) 9 61 19 60 44
– www.hollmann-salon.at
– closed Sunday and bank holidays   **E2**
Rest – Menu 34/49 € – Carte 25/44 €
♦ Regional ♦ Rustic ♦
The restaurant is located approximately 100m from the hotel of the same name in the Heiligenkreuzerhof, a beautiful Baroque inner courtyard in the old town. The restaurant offers regional dishes.

OUTER DISTRICTS   *Plan I*

🏠
Landhaus Fuhrgassl-Huber without rest   🚗 🎐 ↳ 🖭 🚗
Rathstr. 24 (by Krottenbachstraße A1) ☒ 1190   🚾 ⑩ 🅰🅴 ⓞ
– ℰ (01) 4 40 30 33 – landhaus@fuhrgassl-huber.at – Fax (01) 4 40 27 14
– www.fuhrgassl-huber.at
38 rm ☂ – †85/95 € ††135/145 €
♦ Family ♦ Country house ♦ Cosy ♦
This family-run establishment offers homey, attractively furnished rooms in a country-house atmosphere. In the summer, enjoy breakfast in the lovely inner courtyard. Extensive buffet.

XX
☺
Vikerl's Lokal   ↳ ⓞ
Würffelgasse 4 ☒ 1150 – Ⓜ Westbahnhof – ℰ (01) 8 94 34 30 – office@
vikerls.at – Fax (01) 8 94 34 30 – www.vikerls.at
– closed 1 week early January, 2 weeks end July - early August and Saturday
lunch, Sunday dinner - Monday also July - August Saturday lunch, Sunday
- Monday   **A3**
Rest – (booking advisable) Carte 20/46 €
♦ Regional ♦ Traditional ♦
On the edge of the city centre is this restaurant made up of attractive rustic dining rooms. Regional cuisine is served with friendly service directed by the patron.

XX
Plachutta   🎐 🚾 ⑩ 🅰🅴 ⓞ
Heiligenstädter Str. 179 ☒ 1190 – ℰ (01) 3 70 41 25 – nussdorf@plachutta.at
– Fax (01) 3 70 41 25 20 – www.plachutta.at
– closed 2 weeks end July - early August   **A1**
Rest – Carte 24/44 €
♦ Austrian ♦ Cosy ♦
This friendly establishment serves a variety of delicious beef dishes: hearty soups served in copper pots feature various gourmet cuts of meat.

XX
Eckel   🎐 ✤ 🚾 ⑩ 🅰🅴 ⓞ
Sieveringer Str. 46 (by Billrothstraße A1) ☒ 1190 – ℰ (01) 3 20 32 18
– restaurant.eckel@aon.at – Fax (01) 3 20 66 60 – www.restauranteckel.at
– closed 24 December - 12 January, 9 - 24 August and Sunday - Monday
Rest – Carte 23/48 €
♦ Regional ♦ Family ♦
This country house features beautiful rooms, some with wood paneling. Traditional cuisine served. Beautiful terrace.

AUSTRIA - VIENNA

✗ **Schübel-Auer**   🛖 *VISA* 🅾🅾 🅰🅴 🅾

Kahlenberger Str. 22 (Döbling) ✉ *1190 – ☎ (01) 3 70 22 22 – daniela.somloi@
schuebel-auer.at – Fax (01) 3 70 22 22 – www.schuebel-auer.at
– closed 4 - 14 April, 22 December - February and Sunday - Monday*
Rest – *(open from 4pm)* Menu 18/38 € (buffet)   **A1**
  ◆ Buffet ◆ Wine bar ◆

Built in 1642 as a wine-grower's house with mill, this traditional building was carefully renovated in 1972 and then lovingly furnished. Courtyard terrace.

✗ **Feuerwehr-Wagner**   🛖 *VISA* 🅾🅾 🅰🅴 🅾

Grinzingerstr. 53 (Heiligenstadt) ✉ *1190 – ☎ (01) 3 20 24 42 – heuriger@
feuerwehrwagner.at – Fax (01) 3 20 91 41 – www.feuerwehrwagner.at*
Rest – *(open from 4pm)* Menu 10/24 € (buffet)   **A1**
  ◆ Buffet ◆ Wine bar ◆

This typical, traditional Austrian wine tavern is greatly appreciated by regulars. Find
a cosy, rustic decor with dark wood and simple tables. The terraced garden is particularly nice.

✗ **Mayer am Pfarrplatz**   🛖 *VISA* 🅾🅾 🅰🅴 🅾

Pfarrplatz 2 (Heiligenstadt) ✉ *1190 – ☎ (01) 3 70 12 87 – mayer@pfarrplatz.at
– Fax (01) 3 70 47 14 – www.pfarrplatz.at
– closed 22 December - mid January*
Rest – *(open Monday – Saturday from 4pm)* Carte 11/26 € (buffet)   **A1**
  ◆ Buffet ◆ Wine bar ◆

A textbook traditional Austrian wine tavern: rustic furnishings, traditional Viennese
folk music, and an attractive courtyard terrace. Of note: Beethoven lived here in
1817.

AT THE AIRPORT

 NH Vienna Airport   🍴 🅺 ⇄ rm 📺 "📶" 🛋 🅿 *VISA* 🅾🅾 🅰🅴 🅾

Einfahrtstr. ✉ *1300 – ☎ (01) 70 15 10 – nhviennaairport@nh-hotels.com
– Fax (01) 7 01 51 95 71 – www.nh-hotels.com*
500 rm – 🛏90/320 € 🛏🛏90/320 €, �🍽 19 €
Rest – Menu 59 € – Carte 38/66 €
  ◆ Business ◆ Modern ◆

In the hotel across from the arrival hall, guests are welcomed by a spacious, simple
and elegant lobby and rooms decorated in a tasteful modern or classical style. The
restaurant is characterised by clean lines and an open floor plan.

BELGIUM
BELGIQUE - BELGIË

PROFILE

→ **AREA:**
30 513 km²
(11 781 sq mi)

→ **POPULATION:**
10 710 000
inhabitants (est.
2005), nearly 55%
Flemish, 33%
Walloons and about
10% foreigners.
Density = 351 per
km².

→ **CAPITAL:**
Brussels (1 018 804
inhabitants).

→ **CURRENCY:**
Euro (€); rate of
exchange: € 1 = US$
1.32 (Jan 2009).

→ **GOVERNMENT:**
Constitutional
parliamentary
monarchy
(since 1830) and a
federal state (since
1994). Member of
European Union
since 1957 (one
of the 6 founding
countries).

→ **LANGUAGES:**
French (Wallonia),
Flemish (Flanders),
German (Eastern
cantons); most
Belgians also speak
English.

→ **SPECIFIC PUBLIC
HOLIDAYS:**
National
Day (21 July),
Armistice Day 1918
(11 November).

→ **LOCAL TIME:**
GMT + 1 hour in
winter and GMT
+ 2 hours in summer.

→ **CLIMATE:**
Temperate maritime
with cool winters
and mild summers
(Brussels: January:
2°C, July: 18°C);
more continental
towards the
Ardennes. Rainfall
evenly distributed
throughout the year.

→ **INTERNATIONAL
DIALLING CODE:**
00 32 followed
by local number
without the initial **0**.
Electronic
directories: www.
skynet.be,
www.belgacom.be

→ **EMERGENCY:**
Police: ☎ **101**;
Medical Assistance
and Fire Brigade:
☎ **100**; Police or
Medical Assistance
from cellular phones :
☎ **112**.

→ **ELECTRICITY:**
220 volts AC, 50Hz;
2-pin round-shaped
continental plugs.

→ **FORMALITIES**
Travellers from the
European Union
(EU), Switzerland,
Iceland and the main
countries of North
and South America
need a national
identity card or
passport (America:
passport required)
to visit Belgium
for less than three
months (tourism or
business purpose).
For visitors from
other countries
a visa may
be required, in
addition to a
passport, especially
for those wishing to
stay for longer than
three months. We
advise you to check
with your embassy
before travelling.

BRUSSELS
BRUXELLES/BRUSSEL

Population: 1 031 215 – Altitude: approx 100m

Tips/PHOTONONSTOP

It's not every city where you can employ a 16C century map and accurately navigate your way around. Or where there are enough restaurants to dine somewhere new every day for five years. Or where you'll find a museum dedicated to the comic strip. But then every city is not Brussels. Unfortunately tagged a 'grey' capital because of its associations with the suited hordes of the European Union, those who've actually visited the place know it to be, by contrast, a buzzing town, the home of art nouveau, with a wonderful maze of medieval alleys and great places to eat.

It's warm and friendly, with a cosmopolitan outgoing feel, due in no small part to its turbulent history, which has seen it under frequent occupation. The idea of multiculturalism has long been part and parcel of life for the Bruxellois, who believe, generally speaking, that you shouldn't take things too seriously. They have a soft spot for street music and puppets, Tintin and majorettes. They do their laundry in communal places like the Wash Club, and have restaurants with names such as 'L'Idiot du Village' and 'Morte Subite' (Sudden Death). Not so grey, after all…

LIVING THE CITY

The area where all visitors wend is the area that historically belonged to the poorer elements of Brussels, the Lower Town, and in particular the **Grand Place**. Its northwest and southern quarters (Ste-Catherine and The Marolles) are of particular interest. To the east, higher up an escarpment, lies the Upper Town, which, literally and symbolically, has always had a penchant for looking down at its westerly neighbour. This is the traditional home of the aristocracy, and it encircles the landmark Parc de Bruxelles. Further east in the Upper Town is the **European Parliament** area, which is saved from itself by two rather lovely parks. Two suburbs of interest are St.Gilles, to the southwest, and Ixelles, to the southeast, where trendy bars and Art Nouveau are the order of the day.

PRACTICAL INFORMATION

ARRIVAL-DEPARTURE

Brussels-National Airport is 14km northeast of the city centre. Take the Airport City Express train which runs every 20min and takes 25min. A taxi will cost approximately €30. Eurostar trains run from Brussels-Midi, which is a 20min walk from the city centre or else take the Metro, Lines 4, 55 or 56.

TRANSPORT

Buses, trams and metro all run efficiently in Brussels. You can buy a single short distance ticket, or if you're in the city for a while, 5-10 journey cards and one-day travelcards. These are available from metro stations, travel authority (STIB/MIVB) offices, tourist information centres and newsagents.

Remember to stamp your ticket before each journey. Machines are on every metro station concourse and every tram or bus. The ticket is valid for an hour, and you can hop on and off all forms of public transport as often as you like. Roving inspectors impose heavy on-the-spot fines for anyone caught without a valid ticket.

EXPLORING BRUSSELS

Brussels is a rollicking city, living up to its Brueghelesque depictions, albeit

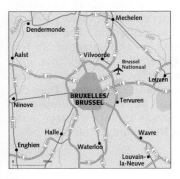

without the medieval accoutrements. It's somewhere that's fun just to wander around, buoyed up by frites and chocolate, two 'delicacies' which announce themselves practically every step of the way. There's no better place to get a feel for Brussels than at its Lower Town heart, the Grand Place, whose Baroque magnificence makes it the world's most uniformly satisfying square. The awesomely Gothic, 15C **Town Hall** engenders enough import to take up a whole side; powerful trade guilds took up the cudgels in the late 17C and created superbly harmonious buildings in Flemish Renaissance style to complete the magical whole. No wonder Victor Hugo famously described it as "La plus belle place du monde". Around and about the Grand Place is a mix of ancient cobbled lanes; most of the thoroughfares tumbling into the main hub have a time scale that ranges from the Middle Ages up to the 18C.

The **Lower Town** is at its most magical going northwest from the Grand Place. This is a cobweb of spidery lanes topped off by dinky squares. The one that draws most visitors is Place Ste Catherine: some come for its eponymous church with curvaceous Baroque belfry, but most are seduced by its fashionable aura, inspired by a plethora of great seafood restaurants. Around here are to be found an intriguing assemblage of late 19C bourgeois houses: they're a mix of the elegant and the run-down, giving the quarter its slightly battered charm. Just up the way from here is one of the city's finest churches, St-Jean-Baptiste-au-Beguinage, decked out in fanciful Flemish Baroque detail.

→ SOUTHERN COMFORT

If you're after a feel of old working class life, then head to the **Marolles** quarter at the southern extremity of the Lower Town. The former stronghold of Flemish weavers and craftsmen, it possesses its own (dying out) fruity dialect, the city's best daily flea market, and a neat collection of antique and suitably 21C interior design shops. Step a little way east from here, and you're on the ridge of the Upper Town, the posh side of the city with its pre-planned wide boulevards and squares. Those very same workmen from the Marolles would have crossed this 'border' to beaver away and create the elegant town houses which give the Place du Grand Sablon its abidingly popular air. Riding up the slope of the escarpment that slices Brussels in two, this is a wealthy and smart area where Art Nouveau meets grand Neoclassical. The trendy bars here act as a magnet for al fresco people-watchers in the summer months.

→ ART ATTACK

In spite of a history spanning over a thousand years, it's fair to say Brussels doesn't boast the best museum scene in Europe. There are certainly a good number of them, but only a few seem to have any great confidence in themselves; others lean towards the mundane. So make sure you choose a good one, and chief amongst these is the **Museum of Ancient Art**, allied to the Museum of Modern Art, near the Place Royale in the Upper Town. Together they make up the Musées Royaux des Beaux Arts. Pay your money, take your choice: will you settle for the finest collection of Flemish art in the world, with many Old Masters such as Rubens, Brueghel the Elder and van Dyck (Ancient), or will you shell out your euros on a comprehensive eight floors of 20C art featuring Magritte, Monet and Gauguin (Modern)? Either way you can't lose, but don't try to do justice to both in one day: you'll never manage it.

→ MUSIC TO YOUR EYES

The two-buses-together scenario applies to Brussels' museums. You've only just recovered from the glories of the Beaux Arts, when along comes another spellbinder, just across Place Royale. The Musical Instrument Museum is housed in a wonderful Art Nouveau building of glass and wrought-iron that was once home to the Old England company (whose name still adorns the eye-catching black façade). Inside, over three floors, the collection of instruments is breathtaking, having grown steadily from its humble nineteenth century origins. If it emits a sound, then it's probably here, from a medieval Cornemuse to a Tibetan temple trumpet, via every kind of international and European music making vessel imaginable. What's more, there's a top-floor restaurant which rewards you with superb views.

You don't have to travel much further to find somewhere to actually go and hear some music: the **Palais des Beaux-Arts** is Brussels' top cultural venue, with the city's largest classical music auditorium, home to the Belgian National Orchestra. If your taste is more operatic, then across in the Lower Town is the nineteenth century **La Monnaie**, one of the best opera venues in Europe. It has a rousing claim to fame: in 1830, a nationalist aria sung here provoked the audience to take to the streets and rebel against their Dutch rulers, setting Belgium on its path to independence. Most productions here are sold out months in advance. Concertgoers remain as rapt as ever by the music, though these days they have a tendency to remain in their seats till the end.

→ PARKING FINE

It would appear that the life of the Bruxellois was so bound up in medieval urban intrigue and revelry that they forgot about the addition of parkland. Not quite true: there is the **Parc de Bruxelles** in the heart of the Upper Town, but it's often seen as little more than a quick shortcut to the metro rather than a green oasis to stop and linger. The best park in the city is way over to the east in Euroland: the **Parc du Cinquantenaire** has a grand arch based on the Arc de Triomphe, a fine collection of old cars housed in a palace, a renowned museum for decorative arts and ancient civilisations, and wonderful walks watched over by old elms and plane trees. Close by is another park worth a meander: Parc Leopold, which has a lake to sit by, and a lot of politicians to bypass.

Many people come to Brussels for a close encounter with **Art Nouveau**. This is the city where architecturally it all started, led by local architect Victor Horta in the late nineteenth century. In the 1890s, over two thousand new houses were built in the style. The bad news is that many have been demolished, or are in use as private houses or offices. The good news is that just about every Brussels street retains details of Art Nouveau, and Horta's house, down south on the borderline between Ixelles and St Gilles, is an absorbing museum containing many artefacts from his time spent there. Stick around these two southern suburbs for the best array of Art Nouveau buildings. Both are pretty hot, too, for their café and street life scenes. Ixelles, in particular, boasts an arty, bohemian feel – certainly enough for the likes of Marx, Dumas and Rodin, who all lived here awhile.

BRUSSELS IN...

→ ONE DAY
Grand Place, Place Ste Catherine, Musees Royaux des Beaux Arts, fish restaurant at Ste-Catherine

→ TWO DAYS
Marolles, Place du Grand Sablon, Musical Instrument Museum, concert at
Palais des Beaux-Arts or La Monnaie

→ THREE DAYS
Parc du Cinquantenaire, Horta's house, a tour of St Gilles and Ixelles

CALENDAR HIGHLIGHTS

Important festivals kick off early in the New Year in Brussels. Pleasingly, with the iffy weather outside, they take place indoors. January sees Europe's first big film festival of the year, the Brussels festival, and a month later the imposing Palais des Beaux-Arts hosts the engrossing Antiques Fair. At the same time, the city's comic strip heritage comes to the fore at the International Comic Strip and Cartoon Festival. And staying with the world of publishing, the Brussels Book Fair engrosses hundreds of visitors, also in February. March and April boasts a real highlight with Ars Musica, a well-renowned celebration of contemporary music. May's Kunsten Festival des Arts is a showcase for exciting new names in dance and theatre, while classical lovers feed their fixation at the Queen Elisabeth Music Contest,

also in May, during which Europe's top student musicians gather to play. If you want to know what people got up to in Renaissance times, go to July's famed Ommegang, in which two thousand participants take to the Grand Place dressed as nobles, soldiers and jesters (book well in advance for this one). Don't book, but drive up to the Drive-In Movies, every July to September at Esplanade du Cinquantenaire: blockbusters are shown on weekend evenings. Back on the musical front, there are classical shows all over the city in the Brussels Summer Festival (July and August) and gyrating hips aplenty on the Place du Chatelain for the Fiesta Latina, also in August. September's Lucky Town Festival is a very cool event indeed, with trendy cafes hosting a range of concerts.

EATING OUT

As long as your appetite hasn't been sated at the chocolatiers, or you haven't had your hand in a cone full of frites from a street stall, then you'll relish the dining experience in Brussels: this is a city where it's almost impossible to eat badly. In fact, food is one of the best reasons for visiting. Some say that the EU decamped here en masse because of the wealth of fine restaurants. As long as you stay off the main tourist drag (ie, Rue des Bouchers) then you're guaranteed somewhere good to eat within a short strolling distance and that doesn't just mean Moules Frites, which is so popular that some restaurants serve it all year but it really should be enjoyed from August until March. There are lots of places to enjoy Belgian dishes such as lobster from Ostend, eels served with green herbs, and waterzooi (chicken or fish stew simmered in water and ser-

ved with vegetables). Wherever you're eating, at whatever price range, food is invariably well cooked, often bursting with innovative touches, and served with pride, albeit mixed with a slice of self-deprecating Belgian humour. As a rule of thumb, the Lower Town has the best places to eat, with the Ste-Catherine quarter's fish and seafood establishments the pick of the bunch. You'll also find a mini Chinatown here. Because of the city's cosmopolitan character, there are dozens of international restaurants, ranging from the expected cluster of French and Italian dining spots, to the more unusual Moroccan, Tunisian and Congolese destinations. Belgium beers are famous the world over and come served in special glasses but it is not just found in the taverns; you can also discover a few dishes involving the use of beer.

45

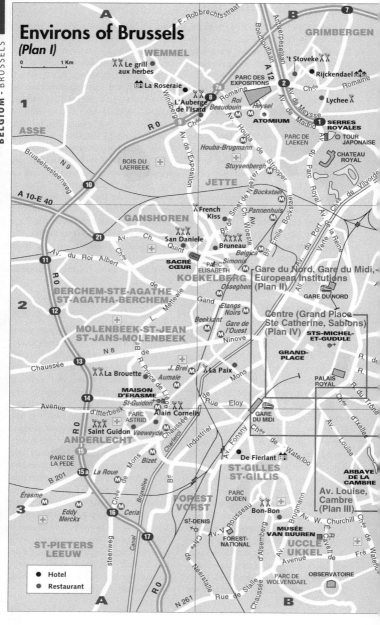

Environs of Brussels
(Plan I)

0 ___ 1 Km

A

F. Robbrechtsstraat

WEMMEL

Le grill
aux herbes

La Roseraie

L'Auberge
de l'Isard

PARC DES
EXPOSITIONS

Romaine

Roi
Beaudouin

Heysel

ATOMIUM

ASSE

Brusselsesteenweg

N 9

A 10-E 40

BOIS DU
LAERBEEK

Av. de l'Exposition

JETTE

Houba-Brugmann

Stuyvenbergh

GANSHOREN

French
Kiss

San Daniele
Quint

Bruneau

SACRÉ
CŒUR

Belgica

Simonis

PARC
ELISABETH

KOEKELBERG

Ossegem

BERCHEM-STE-AGATHE
ST-AGATHA-BERCHEM

Gand

Etangs
Noirs

Beekkant

Gare de
l'Ouest

MOLENBEEK-ST-JEAN
ST-JANS-MOLENBEEK

N 8

Ninove

Chaussée

La Brouette

Aumale

J. Brel

La Paix

Mons

MAISON
D'ERASME

St-Guidon

Alain Cornelis

Avenue

d'Itterbeek

PARC
ASTRID

Saint Guidon

Veeweyde

ANDERLECHT

Chaussée

Charleroi

Industriel

Rue Eloy

PARC DE
LA PEDE

Bizet

B 201

La Roue

Érasme

Eddy
Merckx

Ceria

ST-PIETERS
LEEUW

steenweg

Canal

FOREST
VORST

ST-DENIS

PARC
DUDEN

Rousseau

Bon-Bon

FOREST-
NATIONAL

d'Alsemberg

de Naeststalle

Rue de Stalle

Chaussée

N 261

R 0

B

GRIMBERGEN

't Stoveke

Rijckendael

Chée

Romaine

Lychee

Av. de Meysse

Av. de Madrid

Houba

de

SERRES
ROYALES

TOUR
JAPONAISE

PARC DE
LAEKEN

CHATEAU
ROYAL

Parc Royal

Chée de Vilvorde

Bockstael

Pannenhuis

Emile Bockstael

Verte la Reine

Gare du Nord, Gare du Midi,
European Institutions
(Plan II)

GARE DU NORD

Centre (Grand Place
Ste Catherine, Sablons)
(Plan IV)

STS-MICHEL-
ET-GUDULE

GRAND-
PLACE

PALAIS
ROYAL

R. du Trône

Av. d'Ixelles

GARE
DU MIDI

Chée

de Waterloo

Av. Fonsny

De Fierlant

ST-GILLES
ST-GILLIS

Louise

ABBAYE
DE LA
CAMBRE

Av. Louise,
Cambre
(Plan III)

Av. W. Churchill

MUSÉE
VAN BUUREN

UCCLE
UKKEL

PARC DE
WOLVENDAEL

OBSERVATOIRE

Chée de Waterloo

- ● Hotel
- ● Restaurant

A

B

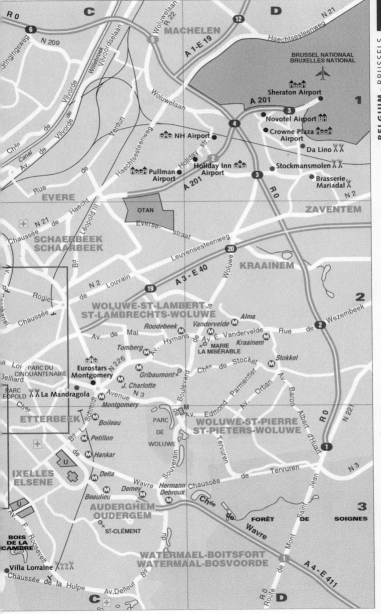

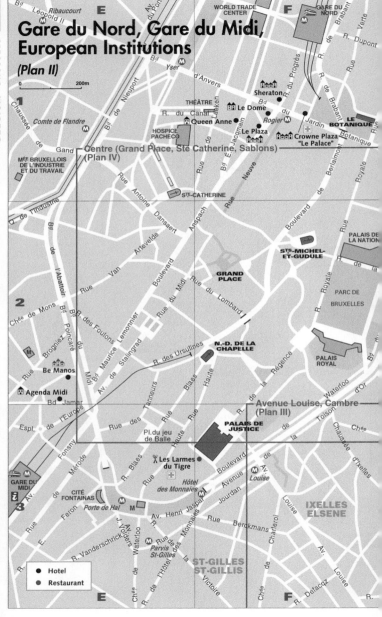

Gare du Nord, Gare du Midi, European Institutions

(Plan II)

0 ___ 200m

E · **F**

WORLD TRADE CENTER

GARE DU NORD

Bd Léopold II · Ribaucourt · Av. du Port

R. Verte · R. Dupont

Bd d'Yser

Bd de Nieuport

Chaussée de Gand · Comte de Flandre

Av. d'Anvers

R. de Brabant

THÉÂTRE

Le Dome

R. du Canal

Queen Anne

Sheraton

Le Plaza

Rogier

LE BOTANIQUE

HOSPICE PACHECO

Crowne Plaza "Le Palace"

Jardin Botanique

Centre (Grand Place, Ste Catherine, Sablons) (Plan IV)

MÉE BRUXELLOIS DE L'INDUSTRIE ET DU TRAVAIL

Rue Neuve

Royale

Rue Antoine Dansaert

STE-CATHERINE

Anspach

Boulevard de Berlaimont

Q. de l'Industrie

Rue Van Artevelde

STS-MICHEL-ET-GUDULE

PALAIS DE LA NATION

Rue de la

Boulevard

GRAND PLACE

Rue du Midi

Rue du Lombard

R. de la Régence

Royale

PARC DE BRUXELLES

Chée de Mons · Bd de l'Abattoir

Bd des Foulons

Bd Poincaré

Rue du Midi

Rue Maurice Lemonnier

N.-D. DE LA CHAPELLE

PALAIS ROYAL

Bé Manos

Av. de Stalingrad

R. des Ursulines

Rue Blaes

Rue Haute

Waterloo

Agenda Midi

Bd Jamar

Avenue Louise, Cambre (Plan III)

Espl. de l'Europe

Rue des Tanneurs

Pl. du jeu de Balle

PALAIS DE JUSTICE

Bd de la Toison d'Or

Chaussée d'Ixelles

Fonsny

Métrode

Rue Blaes

Rue Haute

Les Larmes du Tigre

Boulevard

Av. Louise

GARE DU MIDI

CITÉ FONTAINAS

Hôtel des Monnaies

Avenue

Rue Jourdan

IXELLES ELSENE

Av. Feron · Porte de Hal

Av. Henri Jaspar

Rue des Monnaies

Rue Berckmans

Louise

R. Vanderschrick

Parvis St-Gilles

ST-GILLES ST-GILLIS

Chée de Charleroi

Av. Louise

Chée de Waterloo

Victoire

R. Defacqz

E · **F**

● Hotel
● Restaurant

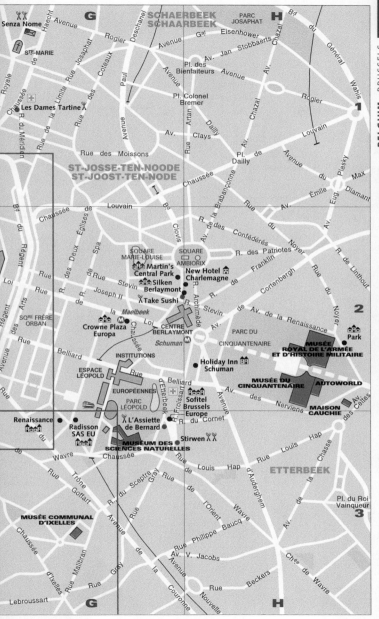

Senza Nome

STE-MARIE

Les Dames Tartine

SCHAERBEEK
SCHAARBEEK

PARC JOSAPHAT

Eisenhower

Av. Jan Stobbaerts

Pl. des Bienfaiteurs

Pl. Colonel Bremer

Pl. de Dailly

ST-JOSSE-TEN-NOODE
ST-JOOST-TEN-NODE

Louvain

SQUARE MARIE-LOUISE

Martin's Central Park

Silken Berlaymont

Take Sushi

SQUARE AMBIORIX

New Hotel Charlemagne

Maelbeek

Crowne Plaza Europa

CENTRE BERLAYMONT

Schuman

INSTITUTIONS

ESPACE LÉOPOLD

EUROPÉENNES

PARC LÉOPOLD

Renaissance

Radisson SAS EU

L'Assiette de Bernard

MUSÉUM DES SCIENCES NATURELLES

Stirwen

SQRE FRÈRE ORBAN

PARC DU CINQUANTENAIRE

Holiday Inn Schuman

MUSÉE ROYAL DE L'ARMÉE ET D'HISTOIRE MILITAIRE

Park

MUSÉE DU CINQUANTENAIRE

AUTOWORLD

MAISON CAUCHIE

Sofitel Brussels

Europe

ETTERBEEK

Pl. du Roi Vainqueur

MUSÉE COMMUNAL D'IXELLES

Lebroussart

49

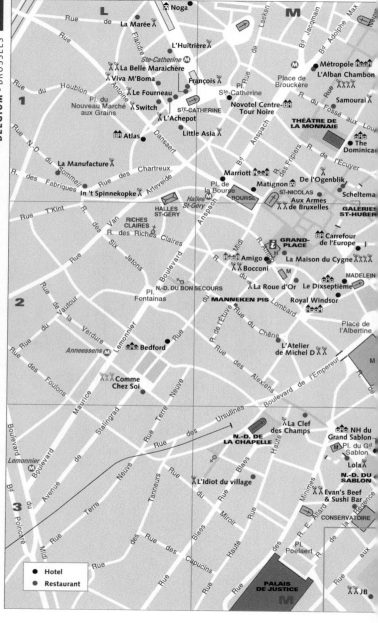

Hotel
Restaurant

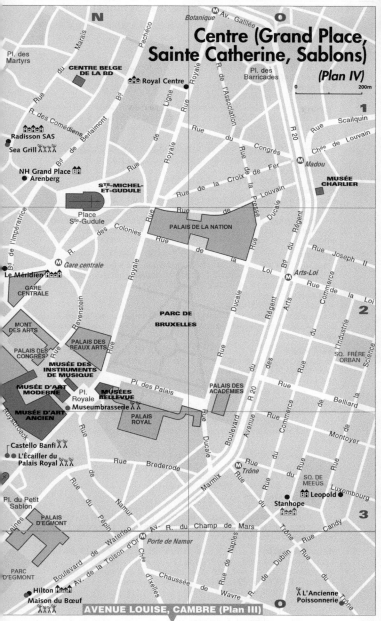

Centre (Grand Place, Sainte Catherine, Sablons)
(Plan IV)

0 — 200m

Pl. des Martyrs

CENTRE BELGE DE LA BD

Royal Centre

Radisson SAS
Sea Grill

NH Grand Place
Arenberg

STS-MICHEL-ET-GUDULE

Place Ste-Gudule

Le Méridien
GARE CENTRALE

MONT DES ARTS
PALAIS DES CONGRÈS

PALAIS DES BEAUX ARTS

MUSÉE DES INSTRUMENTS DE MUSIQUE

MUSÉE D'ART MODERNE

MUSÉE D'ART ANCIEN

Pl. Royale
Museumbrasserie

MUSÉES BELLEVUE

PALAIS ROYAL

Castello Banfi
L'Écailler du Palais Royal

Pl. du Petit Sablon

PALAIS D'EGMONT

PARC D'EGMONT

Hilton
Maison du Bœuf

Botanique
Av. Galilée

Pl. des Barricades

Scailquin

Chée de Louvain

Madou

MUSÉE CHARLIER

PALAIS DE LA NATION

Gare centrale

PARC DE BRUXELLES

Arts-Loi

Rue Joseph II

SQ. FRÈRE ORBAN

PALAIS DES ACADÉMIES

Belliard

Montoyer

Rue Tróne

SQ. DE MEEUS

Leopold

Stanhope

Porte de Namur

L'Ancienne Poissonnerie

AVENUE LOUISE, CAMBRE (Plan III)

BELGIUM - BRUSSELS

Radisson SAS Royal
r. Fossé-aux-Loups 47 ⊠ 1000 – ℰ 0 2 219 28 28
– info.brussels@radissonsas.com – Fax 0 2 219 62 62
– www.royal.brussels.radissonsas.com   **N1**
271 rm – ♦139/349 € ♦♦139/349 €, ⊊ 28 € – 10 suites
Rest *Sea Grill* – see below
Rest *Atrium* – ℰ 0 2 227 31 70 – Menu 35/50 € bi – Carte 29/60 €
◆ Palace ◆ Personalised ◆
Impressive modern glass atrium, remains of the city's fortifications, and extremely comfortable suites and guestrooms. Bar with comic book decor. Breakfast room adorned with wooden railway sleepers. A contemporary style brasserie illuminated by natural light through the glass roof.

Hilton
bd de Waterloo 38 ⊠ 1000 – ℰ 0 2 504 11 11 – Fax 0 2 504 21 11
– www.hilton.com   **N3**
428 rm – ♦109/505 € ♦♦109/505 €, ⊊ 33 € – 4 suites
Rest *Maison du Bœuf* – see below
Rest *Café d'Egmont* – ℰ 0 2 504 13 33 – Menu 40 € – Carte 38/69 €
◆ Chain hotel ◆ Grand Luxury ◆ Functional ◆
This imposing high-rise chain hotel, located between the upper and lower sections of the city, is a popular choice for international business travellers. Cuisine from around the world is on offer beneath the Café d'Egmont's Art Deco glass roof.

Amigo
r. Amigo 1 ⊠ 1000 – ℰ 0 2 547 47 47 – reservations.amigo@
roccofortecollection.com – Fax 0 2 513 52 77 – www.roccofortehotels.com
154 rm – ♦640/780 € ♦♦660/800 €, ⊊ 30 € – 19 suites   **M2**
Rest *Bocconi* – see below
◆ Palace ◆ Personalised ◆
Once a prison, this attractive building has retained a touch of the Spanish Renaissance. A collection of artwork, chic modern rooms and impeccable service for its upmarket clientele.

Le Plaza
bd A. Max 118 ⊠ 1000 – ℰ 0 2 278 01 00 – reservations@leplaza.be
– Fax 0 2 278 01 01 – www.leplaza.be   *Plan II* **F1**
184 rm – ♦120/1100 € ♦♦140/1100 €, ⊊ 29 € – 6 suites
Rest – *(closed Saturday lunch and Sunday)* Menu 55 € – Carte 60/72 €
◆ Palace ◆ Personalised ◆
A 1930s building imitating the George V hotel in Paris. Classic public areas, large cosy guestrooms and a superb Baroque theatre used for receptions and events. An elegant bar and restaurant beneath an attractive dome painted with a trompe l'œil sky.

Métropole
pl. de Brouckère 31 ⊠ 1000 – ℰ 0 2 217 23 00 – info@metropolehotel.be
– Fax 0 2 218 02 20 – www.metropolehotel.com   **M1**
290 rm ⊊ – ♦130/389 € ♦♦140/419 € – 8 suites
Rest *L'Alban Chambon* – see below
◆ Palace ◆ Luxury ◆ Historic ◆
Late-19C palace overlooking Place de Brouckère. Period lobby and lounges, retro-style lounge bar with columns, a piano and Chesterfield furniture. Luxurious bedrooms and suites. Breakfast to a backdrop of Indian decor.

Royal Windsor
r. Duquesnoy 5 ⊠ 1000 – ℰ 0 2 505 55 55 – resa.royalwindsor@
warwickhotels.com – Fax 0 2 505 55 00 – www.royalwindsorbrussels.com
260 rm – ♦120/645 € ♦♦120/645 €, ⊊ 29 € – 6 suites   **M2**
Rest – Menu 19/28 € – Carte 27/57 €
◆ Personalised ◆
Luxury, comfort and refinement are the hallmarks of this hotel, which has undergone recent refurbishment. Superb service. A varied choice of traditional dishes, bistro cuisine and Belgian specialities.

Marriott

r. A. Orts 7 (opposite stock exchange) ✉ *1000 –* ✆ *0 2 516 90 90 – mhrs.brussels@marriotthotels.com – Fax 0 2 516 90 00 – www.marriottbrussels.com* **M1**

214 rm – 524 € 524 €, ☕ 25 € – 4 suites **Rest** – Carte 33/66 €

◆ Luxury ◆ Personalised ◆

A famous piece of local folklore (The Marriage of Mademoiselle Beulemans) was conceived behind the 1900 façade adjoining the Stock Exchange. Chic public areas. Bedrooms with every creature comfort. A brasserie with an open kitchen serving grilled dishes and American-style cuisine. Lunch buffet.

Le Méridien

Carrefour de l'Europe 3 ✉ *1000 –* ✆ *0 2 548 42 11 – info.brussels@lemeridien.com – Fax 0 2 548 40 80 – www.lemeridien.com/brussels*

224 rm – 149/525 € 149/525 €, ☕ 29 € **N2**

Rest *L'Épicerie* – *(closed 21 July – 25 August, Saturday lunch and Sunday dinner)* Menu 48/70 € – Carte 52/100 €

◆ Luxury ◆ Personalised ◆

Built in the 1990s opposite the central station, the Méridien's curved façade is palatial in style. Elegant lobby, varying categories of guestroom, and excellent seminar facilities. A traditional dining room in which the cuisine follows a similar theme.

The Dominican

r. Léopold 9 ✉ *1000 –* ✆ *0 2 203 08 08 – info@thedominican.carlton.be – Fax 0 2 203 08 07 – www.thedominican.be* **M1**

147 rm – 475/525 € 475/525 €, ☕ 27 € – 3 suites

Rest – *(open until 11pm)* Carte 30/66 €

◆ Luxury ◆ Business ◆ Personalised ◆

The artist Jacques-Louis David lived in this former Dominican cloister from 1816 to 1825. Nowadays it is a smart hotel with a subtle combination of the old and new. A fashionable lounge-restaurant open continuously from morning to late in the evening. Contemporary cuisine.

Le Dixseptième without rest

r. Madeleine 25 ✉ *1000 –* ✆ *0 2 517 17 17 – info@ledixseptieme.be – Fax 0 2 502 64 24 – www.ledixseptieme.be* **M2**

19 rm ☕ – 140/400 € 140/430 € – 5 suites

◆ Luxury ◆

This townhouse dating from the 17C was once the official residence of the Spanish ambassador in the city. Elegant lounges, attractive inner courtyard, and guestrooms embellished with furniture of varying styles.

Bedford

r. Midi 135 ✉ *1000 –* ✆ *0 2 507 00 00 – info@hotelbedford.be – Fax 0 2 507 00 10 – www.hotelbedford.be* **L2**

326 rm ☕ – 260/340 € 300/380 €

Rest – *(closed 15 July – 15 August)* Carte approx. 50 €

◆ Personalised ◆

For many years the same family has run this hotel near the Manneken Pis and Grand Place. Spacious guestrooms and numerous meeting rooms, including a former textile workshop. French and Belgian cuisine to a backdrop of distinctly British decor.

NH du Grand Sablon

r. Bodenbroek 2 ✉ *1000 –* ✆ *0 2 518 11 00 – nhdugrandsablon@nh-hotels.com – Fax 0 2 512 67 66 – www.nh-hotels.com*

190 rm – 89/290 € 89/305 €, ☕ 25 € – 6 suites **M3**

Rest – *(closed 15 July – 15 August, Sunday and bank holidays)* Menu 44 € bi/58 € bi – Carte 24/42 €

◆ Business ◆ Personalised ◆

A hotel steeped in tradition and a stone's throw from the city's prestigious royal museums. Spacious public areas, well-appointed guestrooms, and fully equipped meeting rooms. An Italian restaurant specialising in daily specials and buffets. Live music on Sundays.

Royal Centre without rest

r. Royale 160 ⊠ 1000 – ℰ 0 2 219 00 65 – hotel@royalcentre.be
– Fax 0 2 218 09 10 – www.royalcentre.be **N1**
73 rm ⊂⊃ – ∮150/750 € ∮∮170/850 €
♦ Business ♦ Functional ♦

This hotel is at the heart of the European institutions district. The modern guest-rooms are of varying sizes and spread across eight floors. Marble lobby-entrance hall and comfortable lounge.

Carrefour de l'Europe without rest

r. Marché-aux-Herbes 110 ⊠ 1000 – ℰ 0 2 504 94 00 – info@carrefourhotel.be
– Fax 0 2 504 95 00 – www.carrefourhotel.be **M2**
59 rm ⊂⊃ – ∮99/310 € ∮∮99/330 € – 6 suites
♦ Functional ♦

Despite having been built just a decade or so ago, this hotel between the Grand Place and the central train station blends in perfectly with the architecture of the Ilot Sacré. Reasonably sized, functional guestrooms.

NH Grand Place Arenberg

r. Assaut 15 ⊠ 1000 – ℰ 0 2 501 16 16 – nhgrandplace@nh-hotels.com
– Fax 0 2 501 18 18 – www.nh-hotels.com **N1**
155 rm – ∮75/315 € ∮∮75/315 €, ⊂⊃ 19 €
Rest – (closed Saturday and Sunday) Menu 27 € – Carte 28/38 €
♦ Business ♦ Personalised ♦

This chain hotel is an ideal base from which to explore the Ilot Sacré district. Rest-rained but warm decor in the contemporary guestrooms. Special features aimed at female guests. A modern restaurant serving international cuisine.

Novotel Centre - Tour Noire

r. Vierge Noire 32 ⊠ 1000 – ℰ 0 2 505 50 50 – H2122@
accor.com – Fax 0 2 505 50 00 – www.novotel.com **M1**
217 rm – ∮100/300 € ∮∮100/300 €, ⊂⊃ 18 €
Rest – Menu 30 € bi – Carte 33/44 €
♦ Business ♦ Functional ♦

A modern chain hotel incorporating remains of the city's first wall, including a res-tored tower. Large bedrooms, meeting rooms, aqua-centre, fitness room and sauna. A contemporary, brasserie-style restaurant.

Atlas without rest ⚭

r. Vieux Marché-aux-Grains 30 ⊠ 1000 – ℰ 0 2 502 60 06 – info@atlas.be
– Fax 0 2 502 69 35 – www.atlas.be **L1**
88 rm ⊂⊃ – ∮75/225 € ∮∮85/250 €
♦ Functional ♦

This extensively modernised 18C townhouse is situated in a lively part of the city renowned for its Belgian fashion boutiques. The majority of the hotel's rooms over-look the courtyard.

Noga without rest

r. Béguinage 38 ⊠ 1000 – ℰ 0 2 218 67 63 – info@nogahotel.com
– Fax 0 2 218 16 03 – www.nogahotel.com **L1**
19 rm ⊂⊃ – ∮75/95 € ∮∮85/110 €
♦ Classical ♦

A welcoming mansion in a quiet part of the city. Pleasant lounge, nautically the-med bar, attractive guestrooms, and a stairwell displaying photos of the Belgian royal family.

Queen Anne without rest

bd E. Jacqmain 110 ⊠ 1000 – ℰ 0 2 217 16 00 – info@queen-anne.be
– Fax 0 2 217 18 38 – www.queen-anne.be *Plan II* **F1**
60 rm ⊂⊃ – ∮65/160 € ∮∮75/180 €
♦ Modern ♦

This glass-fronted building fronts one of the city's major streets. Compact, soberly decorated guestrooms with discreet designer touches. Those that have been newly renovated are preferable.

BELGIUM - BRUSSELS

Matignon without rest   🔲 🎥 💻 ᵗᵗ *VISA* ⓘ AE

r. Bourse 10 ⌂ 1000 – 𝒞 0 2 511 08 88 – hotelmatignon@skynet.be
– Fax 0 2 513 69 27 – www.hotelmatignon.be   **M1**
37 rm ⌁ – ♯90/105 € ♯♯105/120 €
♦ Functional ♦
This hotel close to the city's stock exchange has been run by the same family for
two decades. Well-maintained guestrooms, including a dozen junior suites.

Agenda Midi without rest   🖩 🔲 🎥 ᵗᵗ *VISA* ⓘ AE ①

bd Jamar 11 ⌂ 1060 – 𝒞 0 2 520 00 10 – midi@hotel-agenda.com
– Fax 0 2 520 00 20 – www.hotel-agenda.com   *Plan II* **E2**
35 rm ⌁ – ♯85/115 € ♯♯85/130 €
♦ Functional ♦
Located a stone's throw from the Midi TGV station. The Agenda Midi offers its
guests well-maintained, regularly renovated bedrooms; those to the rear are
recommended. Business corner. Buffet breakfast.

🏵🏵🏵🏵
🕸🕸 **Sea Grill** – H. Radisson SAS Royal   🕭 🖩 💠 ⊐ᵗ *VISA* ⓘ AE ①

r. Fossé-aux-Loups 47 ⌂ 1000 – 𝒞 0 2 217 92 25 – marc.meremans@
radissonsas.com – Fax 0 2 227 31 27 – www.seagrill.be
– closed 1ˢᵗ - 4 January, 21 February - 1ˢᵗ March, 11 - 19 April, 18 July -
16 August, 31 October - 8 November, Saturday, Sunday and bank holidays
Rest – Menu 120/245 € bi – Carte 108/145 € 🕸   **N1**
Spec. Crabe royal de Norvège au gros sel d'algues et d'épices, beurre
blanc ou huile d'olive. Ris de veau et homard, béarnaise au jus de presse.
Turbot rôti à l'arête, sauce choron ou béarnaise d'huîtres, pommes pont-
neuf.
♦ Seafood ♦
Scandinavian style decor in salmon tones provides the backdrop for an ambitious
fish and seafood inspired menu created by a leading Belgian celebrity chef. Exten-
sive wine list. Smoking lounge.

🏵🏵🏵🏵 **La Maison du Cygne**   🖩 💠 ⊐ᵗ Ｐ *VISA* ⓘ AE ①

r. Charles Buls 2 ⌂ 1000 – 𝒞 0 2 511 82 44 – info@lamaisonducygne.be
– Fax 0 2 514 31 48 – www.lamaisonducygne.be
– closed 3 weeks in August, end December, Saturday lunch, Sunday and bank
holidays   **M2**
Rest – Menu 76 € bi/116 € bi – Carte 65/108 €
♦ Traditional ♦
This prestigious 17C building on the Grand Place was once home to the city's but-
chers' guild. Varied traditional cuisine and opulent decor. International clientele.

🏵🏵🏵🏵 **Maison du Bœuf** – H. Hilton, 1st floor   ⪕ 🕭 🖩 💠 ⊐ᵗ

bd de Waterloo 38 ⌂ 1000 – 𝒞 0 2 504 11 11
– maisonduboeuf.brussels@hilton.com – Fax 0 2 504 21 11 – www.hilton.com
– closed 2 - 18 January, 1ˢᵗ - 16 August, Saturday lunch and Sunday
Rest – Menu 65/115 € bi – Carte 78/130 €   **N3**
♦ Traditional ♦
A chic, traditional setting provides the backdrop for an appetising menu, which
includes a choice of beef dishes, such as the famous rib of beef, which is carved
at your table. The tables facing the park are preferable.

🏵🏵🏵🏵
🕸🕸 **Bruneau** (Jean-Pierre Bruneau)   🏠 🖩 💠 ⊐ᵗ (dinner) *VISA* ⓘ AE ①

av. Broustin 75 ⌂ 1083 – 𝒞 0 2 421 70 70 – restaurant_bruneau@skynet.be
– Fax 0 2 428 97 26 – www.bruneau.be
– closed 1ˢᵗ - 10 February, August, holiday Thursdays, Tuesday and Wednesday
Rest – Menu 95/195 € – Carte 81/194 € 🕸   *Plan I* **B2**
Spec. Jalousie de ris de veau croustillant. Ravioles de céleri aux truffes.
Galette de pigeon de Vendée.
♦ Contemporary ♦
A renowned restaurant offering a perfect balance between the traditional and the
innovative, while at the same time showcasing regional cuisine. Impressive wine
list. Outdoor terrace for summer dining.

BELGIUM - BRUSSELS

XXXX **L'Alban Chambon** – H. Métropole   〔AC〕 ⇌ 〔⌂〕 〔VISA〕 〔◉◎〕 〔AE〕 〔①〕
pl. de Brouckère 31 ⊠ 1000 – ℰ 02 217 23 00 – info@metropolehotel.be
– Fax 02 218 02 20 – www.metropolehotel.com
– closed 13 July - 16 August, Saturday lunch, Sunday, Monday and bank
holidays   M1
Rest – Menu 45/120 € bi – Carte 78/94 €
♦ A la mode ♦ Formal ♦
The name of the Métropole's restaurant pays homage to its architect. Classic cuisine in an old ballroom embellished with period furniture.

XXX **Comme Chez Soi**   〔AC〕 ⇌ 〔⌂〕 〔VISA〕 〔◉◎〕 〔AE〕 〔①〕
❀❀ *pl. Rouppe 23 ⊠ 1000 – ℰ 02 512 29 21 – info@commechezsoi.be*
– Fax 02 511 80 52 – www.commechezsoi.be
– closed 24 February, 14 April, 1st May, 12 July - 10 August, 3 November,
Wednesday lunch, Sunday and Monday   L2
Rest – *(pre-book)* Menu 76/190 € – Carte 98/199 €
Spec. Émincés de Saint-Jacques juste saisies au naturel, fine gelée à la truffe
du Vaucluse. Moelleux de plates de Florenville au crabe, crevettes grises,
caviar nelge et beurre blanc d'huîtres à la ciboulette. Sablé breton, marmelade de citrons confits, sorbet au citron vert et basilic.
♦ Inovative ♦ Formal ♦
A Brussels institution founded in 1926. Bistro-style comfort in the Horta inspired
main dining room. Homemade classics alongside more imaginative dishes. Numerous dishes for two people. The tables closer to the kitchens are perhaps preferable.

XXX **L'Écailler du Palais Royal** (Richard Hahn)   〔AC〕 〔VISA〕 〔AE〕 〔①〕
❀ *r. Bodenbroek 18 ⊠ 1000 – ℰ 02 512 87 51 – lecaillerdupalaisroyal@skynet.be*
– Fax 02 511 99 50 – www.lecaillerdupalaisroyal.be
– closed August, Christmas – New Year and Sunday   N3
Rest – Carte 60/114 €
Spec. Demi homard rôti, confit d'aubergine et mangue, émulsion à l'absinthe. Ravioli de homard au curry léger. Blancs de saint-pierre grillés et tempura de fleur de courgette safranée.
♦ Seafood ♦ Cosy ♦
Elegant and cosy oyster bar frequented by a mix of diplomats, politicians and top
executives for the past 40-years. A choice of benches or chairs, with additional seating at the bar and round tables upstairs. Refined fish and seafood to the fore, with
the occasional modern touch.

XXX **San Daniele** (Franco Spinelli)   〔AC〕 ⇌ 〔VISA〕 〔◉◎〕 〔AE〕 〔①〕
❀ *av. Charles-Quint 6 ⊠ 1083 – ℰ 02 426 79 23 – Fax 02 426 92 14*
– www.san-daniele.be
– closed 2 weeks at Easter, mid-July - 15 August, 1 week at Christmas, Sunday,
Monday and bank holidays   *Plan I* **A2**
Rest – Menu 75 € – Carte 48/92 € 🕸
Spec. Ravioli de homard et courgettes, jus de crustacés. Aiguillette de thon
rouge grillée, émulsion à la menthe. Panna cotta à la fève tonka, glace au
lait confit, délice "exotic".
♦ Italian ♦ Elegant ♦
An attractive dining room serving typical Italian cuisine accompanied by an enticing Italian wine list. Friendly, attentive service from the Spinelli family.

XX **Aux Armes de Bruxelles**   〔🛋〕 〔AC〕 ⇌ 〔VISA〕 〔◉◎〕 〔AE〕 〔①〕
r. Bouchers 13 ⊠ 1000 – ℰ 02 511 55 98 – dingeveld@groupeflo.fr
– Fax 02 514 33 81 – www.auxarmesdebruxelles.be   M1
Rest – *(open until 11pm)* Menu 35/47 € – Carte 29/78 €
♦ Traditional ♦ Brasserie ♦
A veritable Brussels institution in the Ilot Sacré district, which has been honouring
Belgian culinary traditions since 1921. Contrasting dining rooms, a lively atmosphere and a new chef at the helm.

BELGIUM - BRUSSELS

XX Museumbrasserie
pl. Royale 3 ⊠ 1000 – ℰ 0 2 508 35 80 – info@museumfood.be
– Fax 0 2 508 34 85 – www.museumfood.be
– closed 1 week in January, 20 July – 10 August, Monday and official museum
closing days   **N2**
Rest – Menu 36 € – Carte 38/65 €
• Brasserie • Design •
A trendy brasserie inside the Musées Royaux des Beaux-Arts. Cuisine reflecting the
patriotic tastes of chef and culinary adviser Peter Goossens of Hof van Cleve fame.
Decor designed by Antoine Pinto.

XX Bocconi – H. Amigo
r. Amigo 1 ⊠ 1000 – ℰ 0 2 547 47 15 – bocconirestaurant@
roccofortecollection.com – Fax 0 2 513 52 77 – www.ristorantebocconi.com
Rest – *(open until 11pm)* Menu 45/89 € bi – Carte 48/93 €   **M2**
• Italian • Fashionable •
This renowned Italian restaurant occupies a luxury hotel near the Grand Place.
Modern brasserie-style decor provides the backdrop for enticing Italian cuisine.

XX La Belle Maraîchère
pl. Ste-Catherine 11 ⊠ 1000 – ℰ 0 2 512 97 59 – Fax 0 2 513 76 91
– www.labellemaraichere.com
– closed 2 weeks during carnival, late July – early August, Wednesday and
Thursday   **L1**
Rest – Menu 35/54 € – Carte 36/94 €
• Seafood •
This welcoming, family-run restaurant is a popular choice for locals with charmingly nostalgic decor in the dining room. Enticing traditional cuisine, including
fish, seafood and game depending on the season, as well as high quality sauces.
Attractive set menus.

XX Castello Banfi
r. Bodenbroek 12 ⊠ 1000 – ℰ 0 2 512 87 94 – castellobanfi@hotmail.com
– Fax 0 2 512 87 94 – www.castellobanfi.be
– closed 9 - 31 August, Sunday and Monday   **N3**
Rest – Menu 55 € – Carte 38/102 €
• Italian • Formal •
Behind the 1729 façade is this restaurant whose name has been taken from a large
wine estate in Tuscany. Cuisine and wines from both France and Italy.

XX JB
r. Grand Cerf 24 ⊠ 1000 – ℰ 0 2 512 04 84 – restaurantjb@tele2.be
– Fax 0 2 511 79 30 – www.restaurantjb.be
– closed Saturday lunch and Sunday   **M3**
Rest – Menu 25/45 € bi – Carte 51/69 €
• Traditional • Family •
A well-respected, family-run restaurant established in 1979. For 30-years, the
owner-chef has been preparing delicious and affordable menus combining traditional and contemporary influences with a focus on wonderful sauces. Lloyd
Loom chairs, Italian crystal, and a predominantly yellow colour scheme. Small terrace with wood decking.

XX Evan's Beef & Sushi Bar
r. Régence 25 ⊠ 1000 – ℰ 0 2 503 13 78 – Fax 0 2 503 12 79
– closed Monday   **M3**
Rest – Carte 29/49 €
• Japanese • Fashionable •
A new, trendy Japanese restaurant opened in 2008 on a busy street between Sablon and the Palais de Justice. Two concepts: a sushi bar on the ground floor and
teppanyaki grill on the floor above.

BELGIUM - BRUSSELS

XX **L'Atelier de Michel D**   🛋 VISA ⬥ AE ①

pl. de la Vieille Halle aux Blés 31 ⊠ 1000 – ℰ 0 2 512 57 00
– ateliermicheld@live.be – Fax 0 2 512 57 00
– www.ateliermicheld.be
– closed Wednesday dinner, Saturday lunch and Sunday   **M2**
Rest – Menu 30/65 € bi – Carte 42/58 €
♦ A la mode ♦ Formal ♦
Michel Doukissis is at his best in this contemporary restaurant. Find a black and white decor, open kitchen serving seasonally inspired cuisine, popular 'menu du marché' and friendly, attentive service.

X **La Manufacture**   🛋 ⬥ 🛏️ VISA ⬥ AE ①
☺
r. Notre-Dame du Sommeil 12 ⊠ 1000 – ℰ 0 2 502 25 25 – info@
manufacture.be – Fax 0 2 502 27 15 – www.manufacture.be
– closed Saturday lunch, Sunday and bank holidays   **L1**
Rest – (open until 11pm) Menu 35/70 € bi – Carte 33/49 €
♦ Brasserie ♦
Metals, wood, leather and granite provide the decor in this lively, trendy brasserie in the former workshop of a famous Belgian luggage maker. Contemporary cuisine.

X **Lola**   🄰🄲 VISA ⬥ AE
pl. du Grand Sablon 33 ⊠ 1000 – ℰ 0 2 514 24 60
– restaurant.lola@skynet.be – Fax 0 2 514 26 53
– www.restolola.be   **M3**
Rest – (open until 11.30pm) Carte 38/58 €
♦ Brasserie ♦
Friendly brasserie with a contemporary decor serving Italian dishes based on the freshest ingredients. Choice of chairs or benches, or opt to dine at the bar.

X **L'Huîtrière**   🛋 ⬥ VISA ⬥ AE ①
quai aux Briques 20 ⊠ 1000 – ℰ 0 2 512 08 66 – huitriere@skynet.be
– Fax 0 2 512 12 81 – www.huitriere.eu   **L1**
Rest – Menu 25/47 € – Carte 42/71 €
♦ Seafood ♦ Bistro ♦
Traditionally prepared fish and seafood served to a backdrop of old Brussels, including wood panelling and Bruegel-inspired murals. The house speciality here is lobster with sea urchin butter.

X **De l'Ogenblik**   🛋 ⬥ VISA ⬥ AE ①
Galerie des Princes 1 ⊠ 1000 – ℰ 0 2 511 61 51 – ogenblik@scarlet.be
– Fax 0 2 513 41 58 – www.ogenblik.be
– closed Sunday and bank holidays lunch   **M1**
Rest – (open until midnight) Menu 51/71 € bi – Carte 48/70 €
♦ Bistro ♦
This restaurant popular with the city's business crowd has the appearance of an old café. Traditional cuisine including typical bistro dishes. The same chef has been working here since 1975.

X **Samourai**   🄰🄲 ⬥ VISA ⬥ AE ①
r. Fossé-aux-Loups 28 ⊠ 1000 – ℰ 0 2 217 56 39 – Fax 0 2 771 97 61
– www.samourai-restaurant.be
– closed 1ˢᵗ - 21 August, 24 December - 6 January, Sunday lunch and Tuesday
Rest – Menu 65/90 € – Carte 47/110 €   **M1**
♦ Japanese ♦ Minimalist ♦
A Japanese restaurant that opened in 1975 near the Théâtre de la Monnaie. Dining rooms on three floors with a Japanese decorative theme. Authentic dishes based around quality products and adapted slightly to Western tastes.

La Roue d'Or   VISA ⓒⓞ AE Ⓞ

r. Chapeliers 26 ⊠ 1000 – ℰ 02 514 25 54 – roue.dor@hotmail.com
– Fax 02 512 30 81 – closed 12 July - 12 August   **M2**
Rest – *(open until midnight)* Carte 31/58 €
♦ Bistro ♦ Brasserie ♦

A typical old Brussels café with a friendly atmosphere. Traditional brasserie-style
dishes in addition to a few Belgian specialities. Decor includes Magritte-style
murals and a superb clock.

Scheltema   🕼 AC ⇄ VISA ⓒⓞ AE Ⓞ

r. Dominicains 7 ⊠ 1000 – ℰ 02 512 20 84 – scheltema@skynet.be
– Fax 02 512 44 82 – www.scheltema.be
– closed 24 and 25 December and Sunday   **M1**
Rest – *(open until 11.30pm)* Menu 37/90 € bi – Carte 40/74 €
♦ Seafood ♦ Brasserie ♦

An attractive old brasserie located in the city's Ilot Sacré district. Traditional dishes
and daily specials with fish and seafood specialities. A lively atmosphere and a
pleasant retro-style wooden decor.

La Marée   🕼 AC ⇄ VISA ⓒⓞ AE Ⓞ

r. Flandre 99 ⊠ 1000 – ℰ 02 511 00 40 – Fax 02 511 86 19
– www.lamaree-sa.com
– Closed 20 June - 15 July, Christmas, New Year, Sunday and Monday
Rest – Carte 25/64 €   **L1**
♦ Seafood ♦

A convivial restaurant with a focus on simple decor and uncomplicated cuisine,
with an emphasis on fish and seafood. Kitchen in full view of customers. Portuguese dishes on request.

Switch   🕼 AC VISA ⓒⓞ AE

r. Flandre 6 ⊠ 1000 – ℰ 02 503 14 80 – info@switchrestofood.be
– Fax 02 502 58 75 – www.switchrestofood.be
– closed 22 July - 13 August, Monday lunch and Sunday   **L1**
Rest – Menu 30/34 € – Carte 33/45 €
♦ Bistro ♦

Friendly staff, a contemporary bistro-style feel, and high quality dishes, including a
reasonably priced lunch and a flexible 'switch' menu. Innovative, traditional cuisine.

Le Fourneau   AC VISA ⓒⓞ AE

pl. Ste-Catherine 8 ⊠ 1000 – ℰ 02 513 10 02 – evant@skynet.be
Fax 02 513 10 07 – closed 5-12 January, 13 July-3 August, Sunday and Monday
Rest – Carte approx. 40 €   **L1**
♦ Design ♦

Enticing southern French cuisine best enjoyed at the bar, from where you can
watch the chef at work in the high-tech kitchen in front of you. Plenty of flexibility,
with a choice of mini portions as a starter and main dishes priced according to
weight. No reservation required.

Little Asia   AC ⇄ VISA ⓒⓞ AE

r. Ste-Catherine 8 ⊠ 1000 – ℰ 02 502 88 36 – littleasia@skynet.be
– Fax 02 511 96 06 – www.littleasia.be – closed Sunday and bank holidays
Rest – *(open until 11pm)* Menu 35/75 € bi – Carte 24/63 €   **L1**
♦ Vietnamese ♦

A restaurant known for its well-prepared Vietnamese specialities, modern decor
and smiling waitresses, overseen by a charming female owner.

Viva M'Boma   🕼 AC VISA ⓒⓞ

r. Flandre 17 ⊠ 1000 – ℰ 02 512 15 93 – Fax 02 469 42 84
– closed 3 - 17 August, 30 December - 4 January, Monday dinner,
Tuesday dinner, Wednesday and Sunday   **L1**
Rest – Carte 23/32 €
♦ Bistro ♦ Family ♦

A popular canteen style restaurant in an old butcher's with closely packed tables
and white tiles on the walls. Specialities from Brussels and around Belgium, including limitless offal dishes. Small terrace.

La Clef des Champs 🦿 AC VISA ⓴ AE ①

r. Rollebeek 23 ⊠ 1000 – ℰ 0 2 512 11 93 – info@clefdeschamps.be
– Fax 0 2 502 42 32 – www.clefdeschamps.be
– closed Sunday dinner and Monday **M3**
Rest – Menu 34/60 € bi – Carte 42/50 €
♦ Traditional ♦ Family ♦

This family-run restaurant established in 1984 is known for its unpretentious, generous cuisine focusing on the best of French regional cooking. An elegant decor of large mirrors, crystal chandeliers, ceruse panelling and open-backed chairs.

L'Idiot du village VISA ⓴ AE

r. Notre Seigneur 19 ⊠ 1000 – ℰ 0 2 502 55 82
– closed 15 July – 15 August, 23 December - 3 January, Saturday and Sunday
Rest – *(open until 11pm)* Carte 36/63 € **M3**
♦ Bistro ♦

A restaurant with a friendly welcome. Charmingly kitsch decor, intimate ambience, and bistro-style cuisine with a contemporary flourish.

Les Larmes du Tigre 🦿 ⟷ VISA ⓴ AE ①

r. Wynants 21 ⊠ 1000 – ℰ 0 2 512 18 77 – larmesdutigre@skynet.be
– Fax 0 2 502 10 03 – www.leslarmesdutigre.be – closed Saturday lunch
Rest – Menu 35 € – Carte 28/41 € *Plan II* **F3**
♦ Thai ♦ Exotic ♦

This restaurant behind the Palais de Justice has been serving exotic and delicate Thai cuisine since 1985. Dine beneath the umbrella adorned ceiling or outdoors in fine weather. Sunday lunch and dinner buffet.

In 't Spinnekopke 🦿 AC ⟷ VISA ⓴ AE ①

pl. du Jardin aux Fleurs 1 ⊠ 1000 – ℰ 0 2 511 86 95 – info@spinnekopke.be
– Fax 0 2 513 24 97 – www.spinnekopke.be
– closed Saturday lunch and Sunday **L1**
Rest – *(open until 11pm)* Menu 42 € bi/55 € bi – Carte 31/60 €
♦ Bistro ♦

A charming inn so typical of Brussels, with a bistro-style ambience and a menu that pays homage to the traditions of Belgian brasseries. Terrace on the square.

L'Achepot 🦿 ⟷ VISA ⓴ AE

pl. Ste-Catherine 1 ⊠ 1000 – ℰ 0 2 511 62 21 – Fax 0 2 511 62 21
– www.achepot.be – closed second fortnight July, Sunday and bank holidays
Rest – Menu 40 € – Carte 31/51 € **L1**
♦ Bistro ♦

A well-established, friendly bistro with a menu board offering a mix of local and southern French dishes. Several dining rooms, plus a lively pavement terrace.

François 🦿 AC ⟷ ⌂ VISA ⓴ AE ①

quai aux Briques 2 ⊠ 1000 – ℰ 0 2 511 60 89 – Fax 0 2 502 61 80
– www.restaurantfrancois.be – closed August, Sunday and Monday
Rest – Menu 39/44 € – Carte 40/105 € **L1**
♦ Seafood ♦ Brasserie ♦

A traditional restaurant next door to a fishmonger's and run by the same family since the 1930s. An understandable emphasis on fish and seafood served to a maritime inspired decorative backdrop.

QUARTIER LOUISE-CAMBRE *Plan III*

Conrad 🦿 🛁 ⊛ 🕸 🖿 ᵫ AC ⁒ 🖂 🏋 ⌂ 🏧 VISA ⓴ AE

av. Louise 71 ⊠ 1050 – ℰ 0 2 542 42 42 – brusselsinfo@conradhotels.com
– Fax 0 2 542 42 00 – www.conradhotels.com **J1**
254 rm – ♦649/749 € ♦♦679/779 €, � 38 € – 15 suites
Rest *Café Wiltcher's* – ℰ 0 2 542 48 50 – Carte 59/84 €
♦ Personalised ♦

The Conrad offers modern luxury within the walls of an historic building dating from 1918. Attractive and stylish guestrooms, excellent leisure and spa options, as well as extensive conference facilities. A café with a popular lunch buffet.

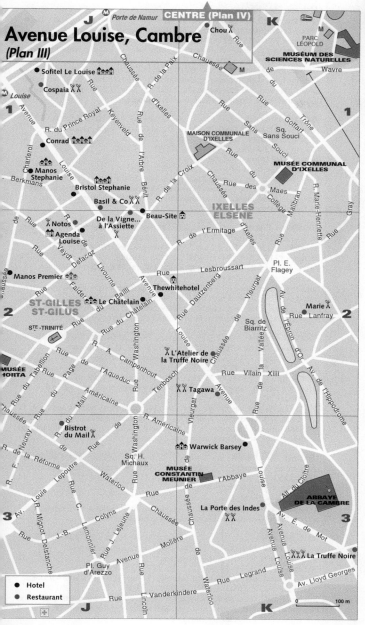

Avenue Louise, Cambre
(Plan III)

CENTRE (Plan IV)

Porte de Namur

Chou

PARC LÉOPOLD

MUSÉUM DES SCIENCES NATURELLES

Wavre

Sofitel Le Louise

Cospaia

Louise

Avenue

Charleroi

R. du Prince Royal

Keyenveld

Chaussée

Rue de la Paix

d'Ixelles

Conrad

Rue de l'Arbre Bénit

Chaussée

Rue du Trône

Goffart

Sq. Sans Souci

MAISON COMMUNALE D'IXELLES

MUSÉE COMMUNAL D'IXELLES

Manos Stephanie

Louise

Berkmans

Bristol Stephanie

Basil & Co

De la Vigne... à l'Assiette

Beau-Site

IXELLES ELSENE

Rue de la Croix

Chaussée

Rue des

Maes

Rue du Collège

R. Marie-Henriette

Rue Gray

Notos

Agenda Louise

Veydt

Défacqz

Livourne

R. de l'Ermitage

Rue d'Ixelles

Rue Malibran

Rue

Faider

Rue

Manos Premier

Avenue

Rue

Lesbroussart

Pl. E. Flagey

Thewhitehotel

ST-GILLES ST-GILUS

du

Bailli

Le Châtelain

Rue Dauzenberg

Vleurgat

Av. de l'Étron d'Or

Marie

Rue Lanfray

STE-TRINITÉ

Rue du Châtelain

Louise

Sq. de Biarritz

Av. de la Vallée

MUSÉE HORTA

Rue du Tabellion

Rue de la Page

R. A. Campenhout

Chaussée

de

L'Atelier de la Truffe Noire

Rue Vilain XIIII

Av. de l'Hippodrome

Rue de l'Aqueduc

Américaine

Tenbosch

Avenue

Tagawa

Chaussée

Rue

Bistrot du Mail

R. Américaine

Rue de Neuray

Rue du Mail

Washington

Sq. H. Michaux

Warwick Barsey

Vleurgat

R. de la Réforme

Lepoutre

Waterloo

Rue

MUSÉE CONSTANTIN MEUNIER

de l'Abbaye

Louise

All. du Cloître

ABBAYE DE LA CAMBRE

Av. Louis Mignot

J.-B. Lemonnier

Colyns

Rue J. Lejeune

Chaussée

de

La Porte des Indes

Av. E. de Mot

Rue Delstanche

Pl. Guy d'Arezzo

Avenue

Molière

Waterloo

Rue Legrand

Avenue Louise

La Truffe Noire

Av. Lloyd Georges

Rue

Rue Vanderkindere

Lincoln

●	Hotel
●	Restaurant

0   100 m

BELGIUM - BRUSSELS

Bristol Stephanie

av. Louise 91 ✉ *1050 – ✆ 0 2 543 33 11 – hotel_bristol@bristol.be – Fax 0 2 538 03 07 – www.bristol.be* **J1**

139 rm – 380/415 € 380/415 €, ☕ 27 € – 3 suites

Rest – *(closed 27 June - 30 August, 19 December - 3 January, Saturday and Sunday)* Menu 44 € – Carte 54/67 €

◆ Luxury ◆ Business ◆ Personalised ◆

A luxury hotel with attractive guestrooms (49 of which have been renovated) spread between two interconnecting buildings. Superb, Norwegian-style suites. Classic, traditional cuisine in a Scandinavian setting.

Sofitel Le Louise

av. de la Toison d'Or 40 ✉ *1050 – ✆ 0 2 514 22 00 – H1071@accor.com – Fax 0 2 514 57 44 – www.sofitel.com* **J1**

169 rm – 130/495 € 130/495 €, ☕ 30 € – 1 suite

Rest *Crystal Lounge* – Carte 43/73 €

◆ Chain hotel ◆ Business ◆ Modern ◆

An escalator skirting an unusual lace mural leads to the lobby of this hotel. It was refurbished in 2008 by the interior designer Antoine Pinto and has attractive guestrooms. Attractive menu, sophisticated decor, plus a cocktail bar with a display of Val Saint-Lambert crystal carafes.

Warwick Barsey

av. Louise 381 ✉ *1050 – ✆ 0 2 649 98 00 – res.warwickbarsey@warwickhotels.com – Fax 0 2 640 17 64 – www.warwickbarsey.com*

98 rm – 115/430 € 115/430 €, ☕ 27 € – 1 suite **FV**

Rest – *(closed Saturday lunch and Sunday)* Menu 28 € – Carte 35/72 €

◆ Luxury ◆ Business ◆

Attractively refurbished in neo-Classical and Napoleon III style, this hotel teeming with character is located near the Bois de la Cambre. Elegant lounge and public areas, and cosy guestrooms featuring every creature comfort. Personalised service. A lounge and restaurant with refined modern-classic décor by Jacques Garcia.

Manos Premier

chaussée de Charleroi 102 ✉ *1060 – ✆ 0 2 537 96 82 – manos@manoshotel.com – Fax 0 2 539 36 55 – www.manoshotel.com* **J2**

45 rm ☕ – 315 € 350 € – 5 suites

Rest *Kolya* – *✆ 0 2 533 18 30 (closed 25 December - 1st January, Saturday lunch and Sunday) (open until 11pm)* Menu 45/70 € bi – Carte 39/54 €

◆ Luxury ◆ Business ◆

The Manos Premier has the grace of a late-19C townhouse with its rich Louis XV and Louis XVI furnishings. If possible, book a room overlooking the garden. Authentic oriental hammam in the basement. Stylish restaurant, veranda and lounge bar. Chic and elegant decor, plus a charming patio.

Manos Stéphanie without rest

chaussée de Charleroi 28 ✉ *1060 – ✆ 0 2 539 02 50 – manos@manoshotel.com – Fax 0 2 537 57 29 – www.manoshotel.com* **J1**

50 rm ☕ – 295 € 325 € – 5 suites

◆ Luxury ◆ Stylish ◆

A townhouse with warm, classically styled guestrooms with a contemporary feel and light wood furnishings. Cupola above the breakfast room.

Le Châtelain

r. Châtelain 17 ✉ *1000 – ✆ 0 2 646 00 55 – info@le-chatelain.net – Fax 0 2 646 00 88 – www.le-chatelain.net* **J2**

107 rm – 125/375 € 155/475 €, ☕ 25 € – 2 suites

Rest – *(closed Sunday lunch and Saturday)* Menu 79/89 € – Carte 40/51 €

◆ Luxury ◆ Business ◆ Personalised ◆

This new hotel offers a choice of large, contemporary guestrooms with a full range of creature comforts. Plush lobby area, well-equipped fitness room, plus a small town garden. This restaurant has a continental menu that also features Asian dishes.

Agenda Louise without rest

r. Florence 6 ✉ 1000 – ✆ 0 2 539 00 31 – louise@hotel-agenda.com – Fax 0 2 539 00 63 – www.hotel-agenda.com **J2**

37 rm ☕ – †135/150 € ††150 €

◆ Business ◆ Functional ◆

Spacious modern guestrooms and friendly, attentive staff are the main selling points of this hotel near the Avenue Louise. Buffet breakfast. Small garden.

Thewhitehotel without rest

av. Louise 212 ✉ 1050 – ✆ 0 2 644 29 29 – info@thewhitehotel.be – Fax 0 2 644 18 78 – www.thewhitehotel.be **J2**

53 rm ☕ – †95/165 € ††95/165 €

◆ Family ◆ Business ◆ Design ◆

A designer hotel with a name that says it all! In addition to the white decor throughout, the hotel displays works by Belgian artists and designers. Obliging staff and large, immaculate guestrooms.

Beau-Site without rest

r. Longue Haie 76 ✉ 1050 – ✆ 0 2 640 88 89 – info@beausitebrussels.com – Fax 0 2 640 16 11 – www.beausitebrussels.com **J1-2**

38 rm ☕ – †75/169 € ††75/179 €

◆ Classical ◆

A sober, functional, but friendly family-run hotel occupying a small corner building just 100m from one of Brussels' most select streets. Reasonably spacious bedrooms.

Villa Lorraine

av. du Vivier d'Oie 75 ✉ 1000 – ✆ 0 2 374 31 63 – info@villalorraine.be – Fax 0 2 372 01 95 – www.villalorraine.be – closed 6 - 27 July and Sunday

Rest – Menu 130 € bi/150 € bi – Carte 78/165 € *Plan I* **C3**

◆ Traditional ◆ Formal ◆

An attractive restaurant opened in 1953 on the edge of the Bois de la Cambre. Superb setting, a delightful chestnut shaded terrace, plus an outstanding wine cellar.

La Truffe Noire

bd de la Cambre 12 ✉ 1000 – ✆ 0 2 640 44 22 – luigi.ciciriello@truffenoire.com – Fax 0 2 647 97 04 – www.truffenoire.com – closed first week January, first week Easter, first fortnight August, Sunday and Monday **K3**

Rest – Menu 50/174 € bi – Carte 80/195 €

◆ Italian ◆ Formal ◆

Run by its charismatic owner, 'The Black Truffle' certainly lives up to its name with the famous Tuber Melanosporum featuring heavily on the menu. Elegant decor, plus an impressive, artistically illustrated wine list. Patio-terrace.

Basil & Co

av. Louise 156 ✉ 1050 – ✆ 0 2 642 22 22 – louise@basil-co.be – Fax 0 2 642 22 25 – www.basil-co.be – closed 1 week after Easter, 3 weeks in August, late December, Saturday and Sunday **J1**

Rest – Menu 35/115 € – Carte 35/64 €

◆ Fashionable ◆

An attractive private townhouse with high ceilings and a trendy decor. Cuisine from around the world, including tapas, set menus and wines by the glass.

Cospaia

r. Capitaine Crespel 1 ✉ 1050 – ✆ 0 2 513 03 03 – info@cospaia.be – Fax 0 2 513 45 72 – www.cospaia.com – closed Saturday lunch and Sunday

Rest – Carte 38/73 € **J1**

◆ Contemporary ◆

A trendy restaurant on the corner of an upmarket shopping centre. Refined cuisine and elegant contemporary decor designed by Marcel Wolterinck.

BELGIUM - BRUSSELS

Tagawa
XX   AC ⇔ P VISA ⑩ AE ①

av. Louise 279 ⊠ 1050 – ℰ 02 640 50 95 – o.tagawa@scarlet.be
– Fax 02 648 41 36 – closed 10 - 15 August, late December, third Monday of
every month and Sunday   **K2**
Rest – Menu 35/65 € – Carte 21/110 €
♦ Japanese ♦ Exotic ♦

An unassuming Japanese restaurant hidden away at the end of a shopping gallery.
Typical ambience in the dining room, kimono clad waitresses, and a private lounge
with tatami mats on the floor.

La Porte des Indes
XX   AC ⇔ VISA ⑩ AE ①

av. Louise 455 ⊠ 1050 – ℰ 02 647 86 51 – brussels@laportedesindes.com
– Fax 02 640 30 59 – www.laportedesindes.com
– closed 1st January and Sunday lunch   **K3**
Rest – Menu 43/78 € bi – Carte 33/71 €
♦ Indian ♦ Exotic ♦

Enjoy authentically flavoured, colourful cuisine at La Porte des Indes (The Gateway
to the Indies). Antique furnishings from the subcontinent provide the decor.

L'Atelier de la Truffe Noire
X   ⌂ AC VISA ⑩ AE ①

av. Louise 300 ⊠ 1050 – ℰ 02 640 54 55 – gil@atelier.truffenoire.com
– Fax 02 648 11 44 – www.atelier.truffenoire.com
– closed Monday dinner and Sunday   **K2**
Rest – Menu 35/49 € – Carte 42/86 €
♦ Bistro ♦

A modern bistro whose originality and success are down to its efficient service and
varied Italian cuisine that includes the celebrated truffle. Small terrace.

Notos
X   ⌂ VISA ⑩ AE
☺

r. Livourne 154 ⊠ 1000 – ℰ 02 513 29 59 – info@notos.be – www.notos.be
– closed 3 weeks in August, 1 week late December, Sunday and Monday
Rest – (open until 11pm) Menu 35/60 € – Carte 40/60 €   **J2**
♦ Greek ♦ Brasserie ♦

A 'new generation' Greek restaurant located in what used to be a garage. Restrained contemporary setting, authentic Greek dishes with a modern touch, and a
good selection of Hellenic wines.

Marie
X   AC VISA ⑩ AE
❀

r. Alphonse De Witte 40 ⊠ 1050 – ℰ 02 644 30 31 – Fax 02 644 27 37
– closed 19 July - 18 August, 21 December - 6 January, Saturday lunch, Sunday
and Monday   **K2**
Rest – Menu 60 € – Carte 48/64 € ⌂
Spec. Brandade de morue à l'huile d'olive et concassée de tomates au pistou.
Homard "demoiselle" au four, brunoise de légumes à l'estragon, pomme et curry
doux. Côte de veau "sous la mère" rôtie au jus, risotto aux légumes et parmesan.
♦ Bistro ♦ Traditional ♦

A very pleasant bistro serving high quality traditional cuisine. Interesting decor and
an extensive choice of wines (particularly by the glass) presented by the attentive
sommelier.

Bistrot du Mail
X   ⌂ AC ⌂P VISA ⑩ AE
❀

r. Mail 81 ⊠ 1050 – ℰ 02 539 06 97 – contact@bistrotdumail.be
– www.bistrotdumail.be
– closed 7 - 14 April, 15 July - 15 August, 24 - 31 December, Saturday lunch,
Sunday and Monday   **J3**
Rest – Menu 60 € – Carte 60/74 €
Spec. Langoustines rôties au gingembre, voile de passion et pastèque, écume
de shizo. Pigeonneau de Warêt en pot-au-feu de morilles aux xérès, pommes
grenailles. Crème caramélisée au thé vert, pêches et pistaches croquantes.
♦ Contemporary ♦ Fashionable ♦

A bistro serving personalised cuisine amid elegant decor. Wood floors, large bay
windows, grey and aubergine coloured walls and modern canvases. Friendly,
attentive service. Valet parking.

De la Vigne... à l'Assiette   AC VISA ●● AE

r. Longue Haie 51 ⊠ *1000 – ℰ 02 647 68 03 – Fax 02 647 68 03*
– closed Christmas – New Year, Saturday lunch, Sunday and Monday
Rest – Menu 21/35 € – Carte 37/51 €   **J2**
♦ Bistro ♦

This 'gastro bistro' serves unusual, hearty cuisine washed down with a choice of
reasonably priced world wines. Professional and knowledgeable staff.

EUROPEAN INSTITUTIONS   *Plan II*

Stanhope   🛎 ⅃♨ 🕙 ᴠ AC ↩ 🔲 🖐 ⇨ 🚗 VISA ●● AE ⓪

r. Commerce 9 ⊠ *1000 – ℰ 02 506 91 11 – info@stanhope.be*
– Fax 02 512 17 08 – www.stanhope.be
– closed Christmas – New Year   **KZ**
99 rm – †165/525 € ††185/545 €, � 25 € – 9 suites
Rest Brighton – *(lunch only during Easter holidays and mid July-mid August)*
Menu 55/69 € – Carte 72/96 €
♦ Luxury ♦ Stylish ♦

The splendours of the Victorian era are brought to life in this British-style townhouse. It offers varying categories of rooms, including superb suites and duplexes.
An elegant restaurant serving contemporary cuisine.

Renaissance   ⅃♨ 🕙 🔲 ᴠ AC ↩ 🔲 🖐 ⇨ 🚗 VISA ●● AE ⓪

r. Parnasse 19 ⊠ *1050 – ℰ 02 505 29 29 – renaissance.brussels@*
renaissancehotels.com – Fax 02 505 22 76 – www.renaissancebrussels.com
256 rm – †79/499 € ††79/499 €, � 25 € – 6 suites   **G3**
Rest – ℰ 02 505 25 81 *(closed lunch Saturday, Sunday and bank holidays)*
Menu 29 € – Carte 34/59 €
♦ Business ♦ Modern ♦

A modern chain hotel adjoining the European institutions district. Well-appointed
bedrooms, studios in the annexe, conference rooms, business facilities, and a
'health academy'.

Radisson SAS EU   ᴠ rm AC ↩ 🔲 🖐 🚗 VISA ●● AE ⓪

r. Idalie 35 ⊠ *1050 – ℰ 02 626 81 11 – info.brusseleu@radissonsas.com*
– Fax 02 626 81 12 – www.brussels.eu.radissonsas.com   **G3**
145 rm – †89/800 € ††89/800 €, � 27 € – 4 suites
Rest *(closed Saturday lunch and Sunday lunch)* Menu 30 € – Carte approx. 35 €
♦ Business ♦ Modern ♦

New, ultra contemporary-style hotel offering three types of rooms: Fresh, Chic and
Fashion. Favoured by a business clientele and European civil servants. Classic, modern
cuisine served at your table or at the large, designer bar. Trendy, contemporary decor.

Sofitel Brussels Europe *without rest*   ⅃ᴠ AC ↩ 🔲 🖐 🚗

pl. Jourdan 1 ⊠ *1040 – ℰ 02 235 51 00 – H5282@*   VISA ●● AE ⓪
accor.com – Fax 02 235 51 01 – www.sofitel-brussels-europe.com
137 rm – †450 € ††450 €, � 25 € – 12 suites   **G3**
♦ Palace ♦ Business ♦ Design ♦

A modern luxury hotel overlooking a busy square at the heart of the European
institutions district. Glass hall-atrium, leisure facilities, and fully equipped rooms,
junior suites and suites.

Eurostars Montgomery   ⅃♨ 🕙 AC ↩ 🔲 🖐 🚗 VISA ●● AE ⓪

av. de Tervuren 134 ⊠ *1150 – ℰ 02 741 85 11 – reservations@*
eurostarsmontgomery.com – Fax 02 741 85 00 – www.eurostarshotels.com
61 rm – †120/360 € ††120/380 €, � 20 € – 2 suites   *Plan I* **C2**
Rest – *(closed Saturday and Sunday)* Carte 37/61 €
♦ Business ♦ Modern ♦

An elegant and intimate business hotel facing the Square Montgomery. Early-20C
façade, guestrooms of varying styles, penthouses, lounge-library, English bar, fitness room and sauna. A cosy restaurant serving international cuisine to an upmarket clientele.

Crowne Plaza Europa

r. Loi 107 ⊠ *1040 – 𝒞 0 2 230 13 33 – info@europahotelbrussels.com*
– Fax 0 2 230 03 26 – www.europahotelbrussels.com   **G2**
236 rm – ♦260 € ♦♦290 €, ⊆ 25 € – 2 suites
Rest *The Gallery – 𝒞 0 2 400 48 48 (closed August, last week December,*
Saturday lunch and Sunday lunch) Carte 33/61 €
◆ Business ◆ Functional ◆

This 16-storey chain hotel is at the heart of the European institutions district. Comfortable guestrooms, modern lobby, fitness room, conference facilities and business centre. The Gallery is known for its fashionable decor, global menu and lunch and dinner buffets.

Silken Berlaymont

bd Charlemagne 11 ⊠ *1000 – 𝒞 0 2 231 09 09 – hotel.berlaymont@*
hoteles-silken.com – Fax 0 2 230 33 71 – www.hotelsilkenberlaymont.com
214 rm – ♦89/355 € ♦♦89/355 €, ⊆ 25 € – 2 suites   **G2**
Rest *L'Objectif – (closed Saturday lunch and Sunday lunch)* Menu 38 €
– Carte 37/55 €
◆ Business ◆ Modern ◆

A hotel with bright, updated guestrooms split between two interlinked modern buildings. Interior decor based on the theme of contemporary photography. Contemporary dining room serving varied and inventively presented cuisine.

Martin's Central Park

bd Charlemagne 80 ⊠ *1000 – 𝒞 0 2 230 85 55*
– mcp@martinshotels.com – Fax 0 2 230 56 35 – www.martinshotels.com
97 rm – ♦210/360 € ♦♦240/360 €, ⊆ 20 € – 3 suites   **G2**
Rest *– (closed 17 July - 23 August, 18 December - 12 January, Saturday lunch,*
Sunday lunch and bank holidays) Menu 29 € – Carte 37/52 €
◆ Chain hotel ◆ Traditional ◆ Modern ◆

A modern hotel near the Berlaymont building with three categories of guestrooms and excellent business and seminar facilities. Designer public areas adorned with snapshots of Hollywood stars. Trendy brasserie with a decor and special effects inspired by the world of film. Lounge bar.

Park *without rest*

av. de l'Yser 21 ⊠ *1040 – 𝒞 0 2 735 74 00 – info@parkhotelbrussels.be*
– Fax 0 2 735 19 67 – www.parkhotelbrussels.be   **H2**
53 rm ⊆ – ♦115/398 € ♦♦135/424 € – 1 suite
◆ Classical ◆

This intimate hotel comprising of two impressive mansions dating from 1903 that face the Parc du Cinquantenaire. Traditional breakfast room overlooking an attractive town garden.

Leopold

r. Luxembourg 35 ⊠ *1050 – 𝒞 0 2 511 18 28 – reservations@hotel-leopold.be*
– Fax 0 2 514 19 39 – www.hotel-leopold.be   *Plan IV* **O3**
111 rm ⊆ – ♦150/260 € ♦♦170/280 €
Rest *Salon Les Anges – (closed Saturday lunch and Sunday) (lunch only*
except Friday and Saturday) Menu 35 € – Carte 43/63 €
◆ Business ◆ Functional ◆

The Leopold continues to expand and improve at the same time. Smart public areas, welcoming guestrooms, and a large winter garden used as a breakfast room. Classic cuisine served in a romantic and refined atmosphere. Relaxed brasserie serving a range of dishes.

Holiday Inn Schuman *without rest*

r. Breydel 20 ⊠ *1040 – 𝒞 0 2 280 40 00 – hotel@*
holiday-inn-brussels-schuman.com – Fax 0 2 282 10 70
– www.holiday-inn.com/brusselschuman   **H2**
59 rm – ♦69/450 € ♦♦69/465 €, ⊆ 22 € – 2 suites
◆ Business ◆ Functional ◆ Chain hotel ◆

Robert Schuman, the creator of the EEC, would probably have enjoyed staying in this hotel: the rooms offer all the facilities required by visiting European politicians and civil servants.

New Hotel Charlemagne without rest

bd Charlemagne 25 ✉ *1000 –* ℰ *02 230 21 35*
– brusselscharlemagne@new-hotel.be – Fax 0 2 230 25 10 – www.new-hotel.com
68 rm – ♦99/425 €, ♦♦99/425 €, �^ 22 €
H2
♦ Business ♦ Family ♦ Functional ♦
Located between the Square Ambiorix and the Berlaymont complex, this small,
functional hotel is popular with European civil servants and diplomats. The renovated guestrooms are perhaps preferable.

Stirwen

chaussée St-Pierre 15 ✉ *1040 –* ℰ *02 640 85 41 – alaintroubat@hotmail.com*
– Fax 0 2 648 43 08 – www.stirwen.resto.be – closed Saturday and Sunday
Rest – Menu 45/65 € bi – Carte 44/60 €
G3
♦ Formal ♦
A restaurant with a plush, elegant feel enhanced by attractive Belle Époque-style
wood decor. Traditional cuisine, include specialities from around France. Popular
with diplomats.

La Mandragola

av. de Tervuren 59 ✉ *1040 –* ℰ *02 736 17 01 – info@lamandragola.be*
Fax 0 2 736 67 85 – www.lamandragola.be – closed Saturday lunch and Sunday
Rest – Menu 45/60 € bi – Carte 48/61 €
Plan I **C2**
♦ Italian ♦
La Mandragola occupies a mansion along a busy road. Authentic Italian-
Mediterranean cuisine served to a backdrop of contemporary decor or on the
front terrace.

L'Ancienne Poissonnerie

r. Trône 65 ✉ *1050 –* ℰ *02 502 75 05 – info@anciennepoissonnerie.be*
– Fax 0 2 219 12 39 – www.anciennepoissonnerie.be
– closed first 2 weeks August, Saturday lunch and Sunday
Plan IV **O3**
Rest – *(open until 11pm)* Carte 31/50 €
♦ Italian ♦ Minimalist ♦
A designer influenced, family-run Italian restaurant in a former Art Nouveau fish-
monger's. Open kitchen, and period decor including the façade and painted wall
tiles. No menu.

Take Sushi

bd Charlemagne 21 ✉ *1000 –* ℰ *02 230 56 27 – Fax 0 2 231 10 44*
– closed Sunday lunch and Saturday
G2
Rest – Menu 27/49 € bi – Carte 36/57 €
♦ Japanese ♦ Minimalist ♦
Established in 1985, this Japanese restaurant in the heart of the European district
has a sushi bar and courtyard terrace. Typical bento (box) set menus. Particularly
popular weekday lunchtimes.

L'Assiette de Bernard

pl. Jourdan 48 ✉ *1040 –* ℰ *02 230 89 35 – reservation@assiettedebernard.be*
– Fax 0 2 231 10 73 – www.assiettedebernard.be
– closed 23 December - 3 January, Saturday lunch and Sunday
G3
Rest – Menu 27/35 € – Carte 45/56 €
♦ Brasserie ♦
This restaurant resembling a high quality brasserie is a popular haunt for locals.
Traditional menu choices with a greater focus on fish and seafood than meat
dishes. Lobster a speciality.

Chou

pl. de Londres 4 ✉ *1050 –* ℰ *02 511 92 38 – info@restaurantchou.eu*
– www.restaurantchou.eu
– closed 21 July - 10 August, Saturday and Sunday
Plan III **K1**
Rest – Menu 40 € – Carte 49/61 €
♦ Contemporary ♦
A decor featuring soft lighting, casting moulds for tables, a sloping dresser and a
red plexiglass floor above the wine cellar. The name refers to the French owner,
who plays the piano in the restaurant.

BELGIUM - BRUSSELS

Crowne Plaza "Le Palace"
r. Gineste 3 ⊠ 1210 – ℰ 02 203 62 00 – info@cpbxl.be
– Fax 02 203 55 55 – www.crowneplazabrussels.com   **F1**
346 rm – †99/350 € ††99/350 €, � 10 € – 8 suites
Rest – *(closed Saturday lunch and Sunday lunch)* Menu 35 € – Carte approx.
40 €
♦ Business ♦ Classical ♦
This Belle Époque palace has rediscovered its splendour and celebrated its centenary in 2008. Impressively elegant public areas, a brand new bar, neo-retro style guestrooms and new suites. Cosmopolitan cuisine to a backdrop of chic and trendy decor.

Sheraton
pl. Rogier 3 ⊠ 1210 – ℰ 02 224 31 11
– reservations.brussels@sheraton.com – Fax 02 224 34 56
– www.sheraton.com/brussels   **F1**
486 rm – †375/430 € ††375/455 €, ⊃ 27 € – 22 suites
Rest – Menu 32/48 € – Carte 41/59 €
♦ Business ♦ Modern ♦
Imposing tower hotel with superb facilities for a mainly international business and conference clientele. Spacious standard and club rooms, as well as numerous suites. Attractive contemporary bar. Traditional cuisine in this hotel restaurant facing Place Rogier. Lunch buffet.

Le Dome
bd du Jardin Botanique 12 ⊠ 1000 – ℰ 02 218 06 80
– dome@skypro.be – Fax 02 218 41 12 – www.hotel-le-dome.be   **F1**
125 rm ⊃ – †90/218 € ††100/253 €
Rest – Carte approx. 35 €
♦ Chain hotel ♦ Business ♦ Functional ♦
A building with a façade dating from 1900 and a dome that stands proudly over Place Rogier. Art Nouveau decor in the hotel's guestrooms and public areas. A modern brasserie with a mezzanine. The menu focuses on traditional Belgian fare, in addition to a choice of salads and snacks.

Senza Nome (Giovani Bruno)
r. Royale Ste-Marie 22 ⊠ 1030 – ℰ 02 223 16 17 – senzanome@skynet.be
– Fax 02 223 16 17 – www.senzanome.be
– closed mid-July – mid-August, late December, Saturday lunch and Sunday
Rest – *(pre-book)* Menu 60 € – Carte 52/64 €   **G1**
Spec. Sardines farcies, chapelure aux herbes, pecorino et pignons de pin.
Osso buco sans os, jus de cuisson, purée de pommes de terre et légumes
de saison. Parfait givré à la grappa et au miel.
♦ Italian ♦
The best of Italian cuisine and wine are on offer in this restaurant near the Halles de Schaerbeek. Welcoming decor and popular with politicians and celebrities. Bookings essential for lunch and dinner.

Les Dames Tartine
chaussée de Haecht 58 ⊠ 1210 – ℰ 02 218 45 49
– Fax 02 218 45 49
– closed first 3 weeks August, Christmas – New Year, Saturday lunch, Sunday
and Monday   **G1**
Rest – Menu 34/45 € – Carte 40/53 €
♦ Traditional ♦ Rustic ♦
Two women run this small, traditional and old-style restaurant. It has an intimate atmosphere with old family photos on the walls. Excellent menu based around fresh produce and a well-stocked wine cellar.

Be Manos
⊕ 🕉 AC 🔲 ¶¹ ☈ 🚗 VISA ⊕ AE ⊕

Square de l'Aviation 23 ⊠ *1070 –* ℰ *0 2 520 65 65 – stay@bemanos.com*
– Fax 0 2 520 67 67 – www.bemanos.com – closed Christmas – New Year
59 rm ⊑ – ♦345 € ♦♦480 € – 1 suite *Plan II* **E2**
Rest *Be Lella – (closed Saturday lunch and Sunday)* Menu 45/70 €
– Carte 35/59 €
♦ Luxury ♦ Design ♦

This boutique hotel was opened in 2007 in a trendy district of Anderlecht. Ultra-fashionable public areas and guestrooms created by a team of designers. Spa and terraces. This very trendy restaurant serves both Belgian and Brussels specialities.

De Fierlant *without rest*
↳ 🔲 ¶¹ ☈ VISA ⊕ AE

r. De Fierlant 67 ⊠ *1190 –* ℰ *0 2 538 60 70 – info@hoteldefierlant.be*
– Fax 0 2 538 91 99 – www.hoteldefierlant.be **B3**
40 rm ⊑ – ♦60/150 € ♦♦65/160 €
♦ Functional ♦

The De Fierlant is located between the Midi TGV train station and the Forest-National concert hall. Well-maintained guestrooms, modern (buffet) breakfast area, lounge and bar.

XXX Saint Guidon
AC ⇔ P VISA ⊕ AE

av. Théo Verbeeck 2 ⊠ *1070 –* ℰ *0 2 520 55 36 – saint-guidon@skynet.be*
– Fax 0 2 523 38 27 – www.saint-guidon.be – closed 20 June - 22 July,
21 December - 2 January, Saturday, Sunday and days of club home games
Rest *– (lunch only)* Menu 45 € – Carte 59/100 € **A3**
♦ Traditional ♦

This popular restaurant is located inside the RSC Anderlecht football stadium with views of the pitch. Refined, traditional cuisine served by an attentive and professional staff.

XX Bon-Bon (Christophe Hardiquest)
🌟 AC ⇔ VISA ⊕ AE ⊕

r. Carmélites 93 ⊠ *1180 –* ℰ *0 2 346 66 15 – christophe.hardiquest@*
belgacom.net – Fax 0 2 538 79 82 – www.bon-bon.be
– closed first week January, 1 week during Easter holidays, 21 July - 15 August,
Saturday lunch, Sunday, Monday and bank holidays **B3**
Rest *– (pre-book)* Menu 67/105 € – Carte 68/104 €
Spec. Homard au sauternes et gingembre fumé. Raviole de jaune d'œuf à la truffe. Lard confit 36 heures, sauce charcutière.
♦ Contemporary ♦

Wood panelling, parquet floors, mirrors and grey velvet provide the decor in this restaurant. It serves modern dishes created using certified, and often unusual, products.

XX Alain Cornelis
🌁 VISA ⊕ AE ⊕

av. Paul Janson 82 ⊠ *1070 –* ℰ *0 2 523 20 83 – alaincornelis@skynet.be*
– Fax 0 2 523 20 83 – www.alaincornelis.be
– closed first week Easter holidays, first 2 weeks August, Christmas – New Year,
Wednesday dinner, Saturday lunch and Sunday **A3**
Rest – Menu 32/65 € bi – Carte 32/45 €
♦ Traditional ♦ Elegant ♦

A restaurant with a somewhat grand, traditional ambience, with cuisine and service in the same vein. Garden terrace close to an ornamental pool. Set menu and à la carte choices.

XX La Brouette
🌁 AC VISA ⊕ AE ⊕

bd Prince de Liège 61 ⊠ *1070 –* ℰ *0 2 522 51 69 – info@labrouette.be*
– Fax 0 2 522 51 69 – www.labrouette.be – closed 2-4 January, carnival time,
1 week at Easter, 21 July-15 August, Saturday lunch, Sunday dinner and Monday
Rest – Menu 35/55 € 🌿 **A2**
♦ A la mode ♦ Friendly ♦

Restaurant with an interior renovated in grey and claret tones, and adorned with artistic photos taken by the owner-cum-sommelier, who is a permanent presence in the dining room. The 'Brouette' menu is particularly recommended.

La Paix (David Martin) ⟷ 🆅🅸🆂🅰 ⬤⬤ 🅰🅴

r. Ropsy-Chaudron 49 (opposite the slaughterhouse) (opposite abattoirs)
⊠ 1070 – 𝓒 02 523 09 58 – restaurantlapaix@skynet.be – Fax 02 520 10 39
– www.lapaix1892.com – closed July, Christmas – New Year, Saturday and
Sunday   **B2**
Rest – (lunch only except Friday) Carte 42/65 €
Spec. Lard et poitrine de porc pie noir fondant, laquage à la japonaise. Côte
de bœuf Simmental élevé en Bavière, os à moelle poché, sauce au choix.
Pain perdu croustillant, glace vanille bourbon, compote de pommes.
♦ Bistro ♦ Brasserie ♦
A traditional brasserie in which the French chef explores and reinvents bistro cui-
sine in an ambience that is reminiscent of the Belgian capital. Kitchen in view of
diners, wood floors and high ceilings. An excellent address that has retained its
culinary soul!

ATOMIUM QUARTER   *Plan I*

Rijckendael ◈ 🎣 🏛 🖼 rm 🌿 📶 🔾 🅿 🚗 🆅🅸🆂🅰 ⬤⬤ 🅰🅴 ⓞ

Luitberg 1 ⊠ 1853 Strombeek-Bever – 𝓒 02 267 41 24 – restaurant.rijckendael@
vhv-hotels.be – Fax 02 267 94 01 – www.rijckendael.be   **B1**
49 rm ⌧ – ♦60/195 € ♦♦80/215 €
Rest – (closed last 3 weeks July – first week August and Sunday dinner)
Menu 42/70 € bi – Carte 38/68 €
♦ Business ♦ Classical ♦
This modern-style hotel is located in a residential district with easy access to the
Atomium and Heysel stadium. Functional guestrooms. Private car park. Restaurant
with rustic charm in an old farmhouse dating from 1857. Classic, traditional cuisine.

La Roseraie 🏛 🖼 🌿 📶 🅿 🆅🅸🆂🅰 ⬤⬤ 🅰🅴 ⓞ

De Limburg Stirumlaan 213 ⊠ 1780 Wemmel – 𝓒 02 456 99 10
– hotel@laroseraie.be – Fax 02 460 83 20 – www.laroseraie.be   **A1**
8 rm ⌧ – ♦107/250 € ♦♦130/300 €
Rest – (closed 20 - 30 July, 24 - 30 December, Saturday lunch, Sunday dinner
and Monday) Menu 32/66 € bi – Carte 43/67 €
♦ Classical ♦
La Roseraie is a friendly, family-run hotel occupying a 1930s building. Meticulous
guestrooms decorated according to different themes, such as African, Japanese,
Roman, etc. A classic style restaurant where a piano acts as the lobster tank!

't Stoveke (Daniel Antuna) 🖼 ⟷ 🆅🅸🆂🅰 ⬤⬤ 🅰🅴

Jetsestraat 52 ⊠ 1853 Strombeek-Bever – 𝓒 02 267 67 25 – info@tstoveke.be
– www.tstoveke.be – closed August, 26 December – first week January,
Saturday lunch, Sunday dinner, Tuesday and Wednesday   **B1**
Rest – (number of covers limited, pre-book) Menu 45/70 € bi – Carte approx. 50 €
Spec. Carpaccio de bœuf au foie d'oie et à la truffe d'hiver. Pigeon d'Anjou
rôti, clamart de petit-pois et oignons, belles de Fontenay. Parfait à l'orange
et caramel d'amandes, espuma de framboises, soupçon de menthe.
♦ Traditional ♦ Family ♦
Occupying a modernised house (both inside and out) in a residential district near
the Heysel stadium. Enticing à la carte and set menu choices encompassing the
traditional and contemporary. Kitchens visible from the dining room, plus an
attractive hidden terrace.

Le gril aux herbes 🖼 🌿 🅿 🆅🅸🆂🅰 ⬤⬤ 🅰🅴

Brusselsesteenweg 21 ⊠ 1780 Wemmel – 𝓒 02 460 52 39 – evant@skynet.be
– Fax 02 461 19 12
– closed 24 December - 1st January, Saturday lunch and Sunday
Rest – Menu 60/90 € bi – Carte 55/129 €   **A1**
Rest La table d'Evan – Carte approx. 40 €
♦ A la mode ♦
Two dining concepts, the Gril aux Herbes and the newly created La table d'Evan.
A fusion of traditional/contemporary gastronomy to a backdrop of chic, neo-
Baroque decor.

L'Auberge de l'Isard

Romeinsesteenweg 964 ✉ 1780 Wemmel – ✆ 0 2 479 85 64 – info-reservation@isard.be – Fax 0 2 479 16 49 – www.isard.be – closed 1 week during Easter holidays, 2 weeks in August, Thursday dinner, Sunday dinner and Monday

Rest – Menu 38/77 € bi – Carte 47/75 € **B1**

◆ Contemporary ◆

Located between the ring road and Heysel stadium. Modern dining room with round tables and comfortable armchairs. Pergolas on the terrace. Extensive, contemporary à la carte, lunch and set menus, including one devoted to lobster.

French Kiss

r. Léopold Ier 470 ✉ 1090 – ✆ 0 2 425 22 93 – www.restaurantfrenchkiss.be – closed 1st January, 27 July - 17 August and Monday **B2**

Rest – Menu 32 € – Carte 30/46 €

◆ Traditional ◆ Friendly ◆

A pleasant restaurant renowned for its excellent grilled dishes and impressive wine list. Dining area with a low ceiling and bright paintings adding colour to the brick walls.

Lychee

r. De Wand 118 ✉ 1020 – ✆ 0 2 268 19 14 – Fax 0 2 268 19 14 – closed Monday except bank holidays **B1**

Rest – *(open until 11pm)* Menu 17/48 € – Carte 18/68 €

◆ Chinese ◆ Family ◆

An Asian restaurant founded in 1981 between the Chinese pavilion and the Chaussée Romaine. Chinese-Japanese cuisine (including a teppanyaki option), numerous menus, plus very affordable lunch specials.

AIRPORT & NATO

Plan I

Sheraton Airport

Brussels National airport ✉ 1930 Zaventem – ✆ 0 2 710 80 00 – reservations.brussels@sheraton.com – Fax 0 2 710 80 80 – www.sheraton.com/brusselsairport **D1**

292 rm – †395/495 € ††395/520 €, ☕ 25 € – 2 suites **Rest** Menu 48/62 €

◆ Business ◆ Modern ◆

This comfortable chain hotel is part of the airport terminal. Redesigned lounges and public areas, and bright, contemporary bedrooms. Popular with business travellers. A full range of guest services.

Crowne Plaza Airport

Da Vincilaan 4 ✉ 1831 Diegem – ✆ 0 2 416 33 33 – cpbrusselsairport@whgeu.com – Fax 0 2 416 33 44 – www.crowneplaza.com/cpbrusselsarpt **D1**

312 rm – †445 € ††445 €, ☕ 21 € – 3 suites

Rest – *(open until 11pm)* Menu 30/46 € bi – Carte 35/58 €

◆ Business ◆ Luxury ◆ Modern ◆

This upmarket chain hotel is located in a business district close to the airport. Central atrium, well-appointed guestrooms, a full range of conference facilities, fitness room and sauna. Club floor with a private lounge. A restaurant with an adjoining lounge bar. Buffet lunch midweek. Terrace overlooking a public park.

Pullman Airport

Bessenveldstraat 15 ✉ 1831 Diegem – ✆ 0 2 713 66 66 – H0548@accor.com – Fax 0 2 721 43 45 – www.pullmanhotels.com **C1**

125 rm – †85/360 € ††85/360 €, ☕ 23 €

Rest ***La Pléiade*** – ✆ *0 2 713 66 48 (closed July – August, Sunday lunch, Friday dinner and Saturday)* Carte 40/55 €

◆ Business ◆ Functional ◆

Quiet, cosy guestrooms, seven meeting rooms and a variety of leisure facilities are on offer in this hotel along the motorway, just 4km from Zaventem airport. A friendly bar and restaurant with the feel of an upmarket brasserie.

NH Airport

*De Kleetlaan 14 ⊠ 1831 Diegem – ℰ 0 2 203 92 52 – nhbrusselsairport@
nh-hotels.com – Fax 0 2 203 92 53 – www.nh-hotels.com* **D1**
234 rm – †90/320 € ††90/320 €, ⌑ 20 €
Rest – *(closed Friday dinner, Saturday and Sunday)* Menu 34 € – Carte 35/60 €
♦ Business ♦ Modern ♦

Business hotel with a resolutely modern feel in a business district near the airport.
Well-soundproofed rooms to counteract the noise from passing trains nearby.
Modern lounge bar and restaurant with an international menu and buffet options.

Holiday Inn Airport

*Holidaystraat 7 ⊠ 1831 Diegem – ℰ 0 2 720 58 65 – info@
hibrusselsairport.com – Fax 0 2 720 41 45 – www.holiday-inn.com/bru-airport*
310 rm – †95/375 € ††95/450 €, ⌑ 22 € **D1**
Rest – *(closed Friday and Saturday) (dinner only)* Menu 46 € bi/68 € bi
– Carte 39/54 €
♦ Business ♦ Classical ♦

A 1970s hotel near the airport that has just embarked on an extensive programme
of modernisation. Extensive leisure and business facilities. Contemporary in style,
with traditional à la carte choices and buffet menus.

Novotel Airport

*Leonardo Da Vincilaan 25 ⊠ 1831 Diegem – ℰ 0 2 725 30 50 – H0467@
accor.com – Fax 0 2 721 39 58 – www.novotel.com* **D1**
209 rm – †100/260 € ††110/270 €, ⌑ 18 €
Rest – *(open until midnight)* Menu 31 € – Carte 29/42 €
♦ Business ♦ Functional ♦

Convenient for stopover or business travellers, this Novotel is being gradually
upgraded in line with the rest of the chain. Outdoor pool, fitness centre and meeting rooms. Modern brasserie with buffet menus (except weekends).

Stockmansmolen

*H. Henneaulaan 164 ⊠ 1930 Zaventem – ℰ 0 2 725 34 34 – info@
stockmansmolen.be – Fax 0 2 725 75 05 – www.stockmansmolen.be
– closed last 2 weeks July – first week August, Christmas – New Year, Saturday
and Sunday* **D1**
Rest – Menu 56/98 € bi – Carte 65/94 €
♦ Brasserie ♦

This 13C water mill has a brasserie downstairs and a restaurant upstairs with the
decor combining old and modern. The best option is the traditionally inspired set
menu.

Da Lino

*Vilvoordelaan 9 ⊠ 1930 Zaventem – ℰ 0 2 720 01 08 – info@dalino.be
– Fax 0 2 725 42 66 – www.dalino.be
– closed Saturday lunch and Monday* **D1**
Rest – Carte 34/52 €
♦ Italian ♦

A family-run Italian restaurant renowned for its authentic menu. Charming dining
area with a wall painting of the owner's native Sicilian village. Vine covered arbour
on the terrace.

Brasserie Mariadal

*Kouterweg 2 ⊠ 1930 Zaventem – ℰ 0 2 720 59 30 – info@brasseriemariadal.be
– Fax 0 2 720 59 29 – www.brasseriemariadal.be
– closed 24 and 31 December* **D1**
Rest – Menu 33/49 € bi – Carte 23/54 €
♦ Brasserie ♦

A modern brasserie recently established in an attractive manor house overlooking
a public park and lake. Retro-style orangerie, courtyard terrace and play area. Traditional à la carte menu.

ANTWERP
ANVERS – ANTWERPEN

Population: 466 203 – Altitude: sea level

A. Kouprianoff/www.tourismebelgique.com

Antwerp calls itself the pocketsize metropolis, and with good reason. Although it's Belgium's second-largest port with a population of half a million, it still retains a compact intimacy, defined by bustling squares and narrow streets. It's a place with many facets, not least its marked link to Rubens and the diamond trade; in recent years it's become a fashion hotspot due to the success of the renowned design collective The Antwerp Six in the 1990s.

The city's centre teems with ornate gabled guildhouses. In summer, open-air cafés line the area beneath the towering cathedral, giving the place a festive, almost bohemian air. It's a fantastic place to shop; besides the clothing boutiques, there are antiques emporiums and diamond stores that can't help but entice the eye. That's to say nothing of the chocolate shops, whose window displays are a visitor attraction in themselves. Bold regeneration projects have transformed the skyline over the last decade, and the waterfront has undergone a big change with its decrepit warehouses starting a new life as ritzy storerooms of twenty-first century commerce. Nightlife here is the best in Belgium, while the beer is savoured with a cellar bar reverence, a satisfied sniff and a glorious gargle, the way others in Europe might treat a vintage wine.

LIVING THE CITY

Antwerp lies on the east bank of the **River Scheldt**. The **Old Town** is defined by **Grote Markt** and **Groenplaats**, and slightly further east, The **Meir** shopping street. These are a kind of dividing line between Antwerp's north and south. The city can be defined as an island, cut off from the suburbs by a ring road. North of the centre is **Het Eilandje**, the hip former warehouse area. To the east is the **Diamond District** and the main **railway station**. Antique and bric-a-brac shops are in abundance in the 'designer heart' **Het Zuid** south of the centre. This is also where you'll find the best museums and art galleries. The smart suburb of **Zurenborg** is to the southeast.

PRACTICAL INFORMATION

ARRIVAL-DEPARTURE

If arriving at Brussels (Zaventem) Airport take the SN Brussels Airlines shuttle bus to Central Station which runs on the hour and takes 45min. Antwerpen-Deurne Airport is 7km from the city - take bus number 16 to Pelikaanstraat. International and inter-city trains both stop at Antwerpen-Central and Antwerpen-Berchem stations.

TRANSPORT

Antwerp has an efficient network of trams, buses and premetro, which is a tram that runs underground at some stage of the journey. Invest in a Dagpas Stad – a city day pass – which gives unlimited travel on the whole of the city's public transport system; it's obtainable on board buses and trams and from De Lijn kiosks.

On many occasions you'll find it quicker to walk around, for this is a compact city made for pedestrians. Or if you want to get about by bike, head into the Tourism Antwerp in Grote Markt for more information.

EXPLORING ANTWERP

Antwerp is a feast for the eyes. It can give you medieval character, Gothic splendour and scintillating fashion creations in a single three-hundred-and-sixty degree visual sweep. Although steeped in modern folklore due to the exploits of its now legendary designers-with-attitude, Antwerp is essentially a fine old Flanders town, living easily with its old age. Stroll just off the central Grote Markt to get a feel for its ancient bones. Off the adjacent **Oude Koornmarkt** you'll find **Vlaeykensgang**, a baffling maze of alleys that date back to the 16C. There's a little square here that allows you to wallow in the atmosphere of bygone times. Take a deep breath and head back out into the full glare of tourist heaven – Grote Markt is the heart of the Old Centre, and the home of Antwerp's finest sixteenth century architecture, including the awesome town hall and a selection of wonderfully impressive guildhouses. Gaze at the iconic **Brabo Fountain** in the middle of the square and you gaze at the very epicentre of the city.

MAKING ITS MARKT

Grote Markt's great Gothic cathedral, **Onze Lieve Vrouwekathedraal** (Our Lady's Cathedral) holds two titles of distinction: it's the largest Gothic church in the Low Countries, and the most popular visitor attraction in Flanders. Nearly five hundred years old, its intricate spire dominates the skyline, but its greatest treasures await within. Despite the beautiful nooks, crannies, altars and aisles, all eyes inevitably fall on four paintings by Rubens, including two spectacular triptychs. There's another fine church nearby: **Carolus Borromeuskerk** took six years to build in the early 17C and the result is a fabulously ornate baroque confection: it would have been even more spectacular if thirty nine ceiling paintings by Rubens hadn't been destroyed in a fire in 1718. Confound your disappointment by heading into the church's beautiful square. It's called **Hendrik Conscienceplein**, and rivals Grote Markt for the old town's top plaudits. Stop here for a drink at one of its smart cafés.

RUBENS QUEUE

No apologies for bringing up the name of Antwerp's most famous son again. **Rubens' House** is situated just off the Meir shopping street. It's easy to find, just attach yourself to the queues of tourists waiting at the front door. This is where almost all of his great works were produced; its collections are on an intimate scale, with only ten paintings by Rubens to see, but the house gives you a vivid picture of his personality and his daily life. He would have approved of the **Royal Museum of Fine Arts** (way down south of the centre), not least because it devotes two of its large rooms to his paintings. There are over seven thousand works here, making it one of the most important collections in Europe. You'll also find Van Eyck, Magritte, Breughel the Younger and Memling in an eclectic array of highlights. Unlike Rubens' House, the light and airy rooms allow you some welcome space to manoeuvre. What if your tastes are more up-to-date? Well, for a modern hit, head west a little way to the river where you'll find the **Museum of Contemporary Art**, an old grain silo converted into a happening space of post-1970 artworks, grungy and cutting-edge pieces with a decent place to squat. This is a modernist's heaven but, for the most dynamic gallery in Antwerp, you have to retrace your steps and head back towards the centre. Only five years old, **MoMu** chronicles the history of fashion in what is now one of Europe's leading design cities. Its permanent collection is fascinating, but what really draw the crowds are the hip and happening temporary exhibits, a fitting tribute to the Antwerp 6, whose exploits took the fashion world by storm twenty years ago. To enhance the modish experience, you can dine in a seriously snazzy brasserie and flick through the coolest pages in the zeitgeist in the glossily smart bookshop.

SMART STRAAT-EGY

MoMu is flush in the heart of Het Zuid, the neighbourhood just south of the old centre. Twenty years ago, this was a rundown quarter with art nouveau buildings that had pretty much gone to seed. Largely as a result of the fashion industry waving its magic wand over the area, it's now the most glamorous address in town; smart boutiques and chic dressers meet at every turn. Two of the city's best shopping streets run parallel here. **Nationalestraat** is a wide nineteenth-century boulevard of designer stores (a more discerning address than the nearby mainstream Meir), while a short stroll to its west is **Kloosterstraat**, the antiques street of Antwerp. Rummage through the bizarre artefacts tumbling onto the pavement, and you'll sooner or later find something truly out of this world. That's the theory, and often enough it bears fruit (or something a little more exotic).

To get a feel for the city's nicely weighted schizophrenia (the old town balanced by the new 'hipdom'), take a hike to two of its suburbs. Zurenborg is a village-like quarter in the 'far' southeast of Antwerp, by the railway line leading up towards the station. The wealthy merchant classes built it up, and today it's where the city's moneyed bohemians and artists live. There are sumptuous belle-epoque buildings here; the most interesting walk is up and down the seven avenues that fan out from **Draakplaats Tramplein**, where you can take in the fine – not to say eccentic – art nouveau buildings. Right up the other end of town is Het Eilandje, a one-time collection of mangy warehouses and storage facilities that the world steered clear of. Nowadays it's alive with quirky shops, cafes and offices; notable names have moved in, including Antwerp 6 fashion guru Dries Van Noten, whose workshop and office is based in a local warehouse.

ROCK SOLID

Another aspect of the city is the area around the mighty Centraal station, a terminus that ranks as one of Europe's finest, with its sweeping staircases and vaulted dome. It's relevant that the station displays a wealth of gold gilt, because this is also the **Diamond District**, a grungy kind of area after dark, but during the day the centre of the city's historic diamond industry, where many billions of euros' worth of shiny things are handled each year. If the sight of all those sparklers proves too much, take a pew at the nearby triangular shaped **Stadspark**, Antwerp's largest green space, where you can watch the cosmopolitan mix that for many decades has defined the area. Take a deep breath, then head back to that diamond shop to double-check the price of that rock…

CALENDAR HIGHLIGHTS

Laundry Day only comes once a year in Antwerp, but the hip Het Eilandje area cleans up when it happens early every September. This is the coolest event of the year, bringing in forty thousand revellers who dance to the various DJs at outdoor stages in the area. Why Laundry Day? Well, the first one in the mid-1990s was held at a weekend, when Belgians traditionally hang their washing out to dry…Later in the month, it's the turn of architecture addicts to hit the streets for Open Monument Day, when various historic buildings, usually closed to the public, open their doors for a day. The city is well known for its antiques, and in March this reputation comes to the fore when twenty thousand visitors head to the Bouwcentrum for the Eurantica Antwerp Antiques Festival, a grand fair with paintings,

ANTWERP IN...

→ **ONE DAY**
Grote Kerk, Our Lady's Cathedral, MoMu, Het Zuid

→ **TWO DAYS**
Rubens' House, Royal Museum of Fine Arts, a stroll across to the Left Bank via the Sint-Anna tunnel

→ **THREE DAYS**
Het Eilandje, a river trip, Kloosterstraat, Nationalestraat

jewellery, furniture and objets d'art up for grabs. May brings out revellers for five weeks of ghost trains and roller-coasters at the Sinksefoor funfair, which takes over a capacious square in southern Antwerp. The free carillon concerts on Monday nights between May and September have become hugely popular.The Groenplaats is heaving in June with ale quaffers for Beer Passion Weekend, with over 150 tipples on offer. You can lie on Antwerp Beach through the summer – a long stretch of sand in the dock area south of the centre boasting terraces with comfy sun-loungers - or, in July, you might prefer classical music at the Festival of Flanders (at venues across the city), or the International Summer Festival, which has street theatre, open-air cinema and jazz concerts happening on various city squares. Antwerp wouldn't be Antwerp without Rubens, and the Rubens Market in August sees Grote Markt's traders donning their best sixteenth century garb in honour of the great man.

EATING OUT

With Antwerp being Europe's second-largest commercial port, it's no surprise that fish and seafood play a big part in the local diet. The menus of Flanders are heavily influenced by proximity to the North Sea, lush meadows and canals swarming with eels. But the eating culture in Antwerp offers a lot more than crustacean flavours. With its centuries old connection to more exotic climes, there's no shortage of fragrant spices such as cinnamon finding their way regularly into local dishes: check out the rich stews so beloved by the locals. Having such a high ratio of trend-setting types flitting around, there's always a good chance of finding a restaurant devoted to the latest in food fads. If you want to eat with the chic, hang around the Het Eilandje dockside or the rejuvenated ancient warehouses south of Grote Markt. For early risers, grand cafés are a popular port of call here. They're open nice and early in the morning, and are ideal for a slow coffee and trawl through the papers. Overall, though, the city boasts the same tempting Belgian gastronomic specialities as Brussels (eg, stewed eel in chervil sauce, mussels in various sauces, dishes with rabbit, beef stew and chicory), the focus in Antwerp is more on contemporary cuisine, matched with up-to-date décor. Don't miss out on the local chocolate, shaped like a hand in keeping with the local legend which tells of a Roman soldier who cut off the hand of a giant and threw it in the river, and in the process gave the city its name: Hand werpen, meaning 'to throw a hand'. And make sure you try your hand at the local beer: Antwerp's Konings brewery serves the popular keuninkske, served in a glass shaped like an open bowl.

→ SCHELDT SHOCKED

The best view of Antwerp's dramatic skyline is from the west bank of the Scheldt. Firstly, stroll through the listed Sint-Anna tunnel with its lovely art deco interior, and, at the other side, go 'wow' as you take in the superb panoramic view of the city from the Left Bank.

The river has always been Antwerp's lifeline, and you can make the most of it on fifty-minute river cruises, which depart from Steenplein on a regular basis in the afternoons. The trip offers up a taste of the city's maritime history; you'll also get a good look at modern riverside landmarks such as the unmistakable Palace of Justice, an iconic twenty-first century building that resembles a white-sailed ship – fittingly, in a city whose port has been its fortune.

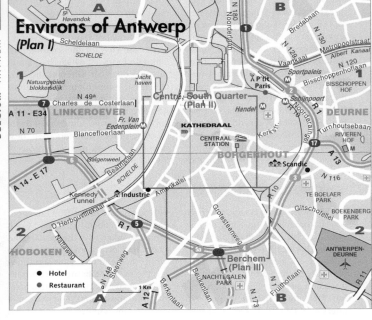

Environs of Antwerp
(Plan I)

- ● Hotel
- ● Restaurant

1 Km

CENTRE (Old Town and Main Station)   *Plan II*

Hilton

Groenplaats 32 – ☎ 03 204 12 12 – anrhitwsal@hilton.com – Fax 03 204 12 13
– www.antwerp.hilton.com   **D2**
199 rm – ♦149/369 € ♦♦149/369 €, ☞ 25 € – 12 suites
Rest *Brasserie Terrace Café* – Menu 39 € – Carte 39/59 €

♦ Luxury ♦

A luxury hotel established in 1994 within the walls of the superb, early-20C Grand
Bazar building. Sumptuous Belle Époque ballroom. Suites facing the city, standard
guestrooms overlooking the courtyard. Views of the cathedral and busy Groenplaats from the Terrace Café's veranda.

Park Plaza Astrid

Koningin Astridplein 7 ✉ 2018 – ☎ 03 203 12 34 – ppaares@pphe.com
– Fax 03 203 12 51 – www.parkplazaantwerp.com   **F2**
244 rm – ♦129/304 € ♦♦129/304 €, ☞ 20 € – 3 suites
Rest – (closed Sunday lunch) Carte 36/51 €

♦ Luxury ♦

This luxurious modern hotel, characterised by its original architecture, stands on
the edge of a busy square near the main train station. Renovated public areas
and large attractive bedrooms that have been refurbished. Modern dishes served
in a bright and trendy canteen-style dining room with a wood floor and views of
the city.

BELGIUM - ANTWERP

Radisson SAS Park Lane

Van Eycklei 34 ⊠ 2018 – ℰ 03 285 85 85
— *guest.antwerp@radissonsas.com – Fax 03 285 85 86 – www.radissonsas.com* **VISA ◑ AE ⓘ**
160 rm – †115/199 € ††115/199 €, � 27 € – 14 suites **E3**
Rest – Carte approx. 45 €
♦ Business ♦

This luxury hotel popular with business travellers is located along a main road, opposite a public park. Two types of comfortable rooms and several suites. Excellent conference facilities. A restaurant with a glass ceiling, giving it the feel of a winter garden. Bar to one side.

De Witte Lelie without rest ⌂

Keizerstraat 16 – ℰ 03 226 19 66 – hotel@dewittelelie.be – Fax 03 234 00 19
— *www.dewittelelie.be* **D1**
7 rm – †295 € ††295 €, ⊆ 20 € – 3 suites
♦ Luxury ♦

This small and tranquil luxury hotel occupies a series of 17C houses. Considerable charm and cosy bedrooms with refined decoration. Relaxing patio.

't Sandt without rest

Het Zand 17 – ℰ 03 232 93 90 – reservations@hotel-sandt.be
— *Fax 03 232 56 13 – www.hotel-sandt.be* **C2**
28 rm ⊆ – †155/285 € ††175/305 € – 1 suite
♦ Luxury ♦

An old building with a neo-Rococo façade close to the banks of the Escaut river. Personalised rooms, a delighted rooftop terrace, and highly attentive service.

Theater

Arenbergstraat 30 – ℰ 03 203 54 10 – info@theater-hotel.be – Fax 03 233 88 58
— *www.vhv-hotels.be* **E2**
122 rm – †110/220 € ††130/240 €, ⊆ 20 € – 5 suites
Rest – *(closed 17 July - 16 August, 21 December - 3 January, Saturday and Sunday)* Carte 33/45 €
♦ Business ♦ Classical ♦

A comfortable, modern hotel ideally situated close to the Bourla Theatre and Rubens' House. Two types of spacious accommodation – the contemporary guestrooms or those that are more British in style. Welcoming lounge. A formal restaurant serving a mix of fusion and traditional cuisine.

Rubens without rest ⌂

Oude Beurs 29 – ℰ 03 222 48 48 – hotel.rubens@glo.be – Fax 03 225 19 40
— *www.hotelrubensantwerp.be* **D1**
35 rm ⊆ – †145/170 € ††150/230 € – 1 suite
♦ Classical ♦

A quiet and welcoming renovated house close to the Grand Place and cathedral. The best rooms open out onto a courtyard that is decked out in flowers in summer.

Hyllit without rest

De Keyserlei 28 (access via Appelmansstraat) ⊠ 2018 – ℰ 03 202 68 00
— *info@hyllithotel.be – Fax 03 202 68 90 – www.hyllithotel.be* **E2**
123 rm – †110/190 € ††130/215 €, ⊆ 20 € – 4 suites
♦ Business ♦

A modern hotel with a cosy lounge bar, large bedrooms and contemporary suites. There is an attractive swimming pool with Roman decor, as well as views of the city's rooftops at breakfast.

De Keyser without rest

De Keyserlei 66 ⊠ 2018 – ℰ 03 206 74 60 – info@dekeyserhotel.be
— *Fax 03 232 39 70 – www.vhv-hotels.be* **F2**
120 rm – †110/165 € ††130/165 €, ⊆ 20 € – 3 suites
♦ Business ♦ Classical ♦

A great location with easy access to the train station and tramway. Modern lobby, plus two generations and three categories of guestrooms (standard, junior suites and suites).

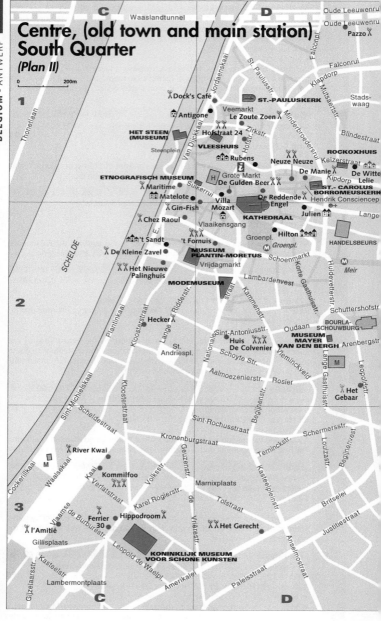

Centre, (old town and main station) South Quarter
(Plan II)

0   200m

Waaslandtunnel

Oude Leeuwenru.
Oude Leeuwenru.
Pazzo ✗

Falconpl.
Falconrui
Klapdorp

St. Pauluestr.
Stads-
waag

✗ Dock's Café
Veemarkt
ST.-PAULUSKERK
Le Zoute Zoen ✗✗
Hofstraat 24
Zirkstr.

Antigone
Minderbroedersrui
Blindestraat

HET STEEN
(MUSEUM)
Steenplein

VLEESHUIS
Hofstr.

ROCKOXHUIS
Keizerstraat
Neuze Neuze
Rubens
De Manie ✗
Kipdorp
De Witte
Lelie

Grote Markt
De Gulden Beer ✗✗
ST.- CAROLUS
BORROMEUSKERK
Hendrik Consciencepl.

ETNOGRAFISCH MUSEUM
✗ Maritime
Suikerrui
De Reddende
Engel
Lange

Matelote
Villa
Mozart
KATHEDRAAL
Julien

Gin-Fish
Vlaaikensgang
Hilton

✗ Chez Raoul
Groenpl.
HANDELSBEURS

't Sandt
't Fornuis
Groenpl.

✗ De Kleine Zavel
MUSEUM
PLANTIN-MORETUS
Schoenmarkt
Meir

✗✗ Het Nieuwe
Palinghuis
Vrijdagmarkt
Korte Gasthuisstr.

MODEMUSEUM
Lambardenvest

Schuttershofstr.

Hecker ✗
Lange Ridderstr.
Kammenstr.

BOURLA-
SCHOUWBURG

Sint-Antoniusstr.
Huis ✗✗✗
De Colvenier
Oudaan
MUSEUM
MAYER
VAN DEN BERGH
Arenbergstr.

St.
Andriespl.
Nationale
Schoyte Str.
Vleminckveld
Lange Gasthuisstr.
Leopoldstr.

Aalmoezenierstr.
Rosier
✗ Het
Gebaar

Sint-Rochusstraat
Begijnenstr.
Schermersstr.

Kronenburgstraat
Teninckstr.
Louizastr.

Begijnenvest

✗ River Kwai
Geuzenstr.
Kasteelpleinstr.
Britselei

Kaai
Kommilfoo
✗✗✗
Volksstr.
Marnixplaats
Justitiestr.

Verlatstraat
Karel Rogierstr.
Tolstraat
Anselmostraat

Ferrier
30
Hippodroom ✗
de Vriesstr.
✗✗ Het Gerecht

✗ l'Amitié
Gillisplaats

KONINKLIJK MUSEUM
VOOR SCHONE KUNSTEN

Lambermontplaats
Leopold de Waelpl.
Amerikalei
Palesstraat

Thonetlaan

SCHELDE

Plankinkaai
Kloosterstraat
Sint-Michielskaai
Kloosterstraat
Scheldestraat

Cockerillkaai
Waalsekaai
Vlaamse de Burburstr.
Kasteelstr.
Glijzelaarsstr.

C   D

1

2

3

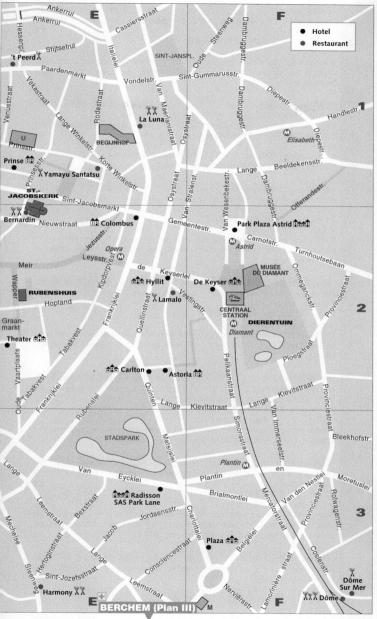

BELGIUM - ANTWERP

Plaza without rest 🔲 🕭 🏶 🛆 🚗 💳 ⓓ 🄰🄴 ①
Charlottalei 49 ⊠ 2018 – ⸿ 0 3 287 28 70 – book@plaza.be – Fax 0 3 287 28 71
– www.plaza.be **F3**
81 rm � – †118/225 € ††118/240 €
♦ Business ♦
A welcoming hotel with an English feel, including wood panelling and Chesterfield chairs in the lounge. Victorian bar, large bedrooms, cosy suites and a pleasant breakfast area.

Carlton without rest 🔲 🕭 🖭 🏶 🛆 🚗 💳 ⓓ 🄰🄴 ①
Quinten Matsijslei 25 ⊠ 2018 – ⸿ 0 3 231 15 15 – info@
carltonhotel-antwerp.com – Fax 0 3 225 30 90 – www.carltonhotel-antwerp.com
138 rm – †80/189 € ††80/189 €, ⊆ 15 € – 1 suite **E2**
♦ Business ♦ Classical ♦
A comfortable, 1980s style hotel near the diamond district and a local park. Several types of bedroom, as well as studios for longer stays.

Julien without rest 🔲 🕭 🖭 🏶 💳 ⓓ 🄰🄴
Korte Nieuwstraat 24 – ⸿ 0 3 229 06 00 – info@hotel-julien.com
– Fax 0 3 233 35 70 – www.hotel-julien.com **D2**
11 rm ⊆ – †170/280 € ††170/280 €
♦ Luxury ♦
The carriage entrance of this intimate hotel opens out onto a street with a tramway. Cosy interior combining classic, rustic and designer features. Attractive modern rooms.

Matelote without rest 🔲 🕭 🏶 💳 ⓓ 🄰🄴
Haarstraat 11a – ⸿ 0 3 201 88 00 – info@matelote.be – Fax 0 3 201 88 08
– www.matelote.be **C1-2**
9 rm – †120/240 € ††120/240 €, ⊆ 10 €
♦ Luxury ♦ Modern ♦
The Matelote's main selling points are the friendly service and the chic designer feel, which is in stark contrast to the 16C walls. Breakfast in the neighbouring restaurant.

Astoria without rest 🛋 🔲 🕭 🖭 🏶 🚗 💳 ⓓ 🄰🄴 ①
Korte Herentalsestraat 5 ⊠ 2018 – ⸿ 0 3 227 31 30 – res@astoria-antwerp.com
– Fax 0 3 227 31 34 – www.astoria-antwerp.com **E2**
66 rm ⊆ – †100/140 € ††115/165 €
♦ Business ♦ Functional ♦
A hotel dating from the 1990s overlooking a quiet residential street close to the diamond district. Functional, identically furnished guestrooms.

Colombus without rest 🛋 🖵 🕭 🏶 🚗 💳 ⓓ 🄰🄴 ①
Frankrijklei 4 – ⸿ 0 3 233 03 90 – colombushotel@skynet.be – Fax 0 3 226 09 46
– www.colombushotel.com **E2**
32 rm ⊆ – †97 € ††117 €
♦ Classical ♦
This central family-run hotel near the Meir shopping street is recognisable by its attractive neo-Classical façade. Art Nouveau lounge and breakfast room, pleasant guestrooms and an attractive small swimming pool.

Prinse without rest ⸱ 🏶 🛆 🚗 💳 ⓓ 🄰🄴 ①
Keizerstraat 63 – ⸿ 0 3 226 40 50 – hotel-prinse@skynet.be – Fax 0 3 225 11 48
– www.hotelprinse.be
– closed 24 - 26 December **E1**
34 rm ⊆ – †105/120 € ††125/135 €
♦ Classical ♦
A quiet 16C private mansion offering spacious, contemporary comfort. Courtyards embellished with box plants. Modern breakfast room, plus a designer lounge.

Villa Mozart without rest ⟨ 🕙 ⅍ ℱ VISA ☺ AE ①
Handschoenmarkt 3 – ℰ *0 3 231 30 31 – info@villamozart.be*
– Fax 0 3 231 56 85 – www.villa-mozart.be   **D1**
25 rm ⊿ – ✦114 € ✦✦130 €
◆ Functional ◆
A good location in the bustling city centre between the Grand Place and the cathedral. The latter is visible from three-quarters of the classically furnished guestrooms.

Antigone without rest 🕮 ⅍ ℱ **P** VISA ☺ AE ①
Jordaenskaai 11 – ℰ *0 3 231 66 77 – info@antigonehotel.be – Fax 0 3 231 37 74*
– www.antigonehotel.be   **D1**
20 rm ⊿ – ✦75/95 € ✦✦80/95 €
◆ Functional ◆
An old corner house on the banks of the Escaut near the Steen Museum. Smart, renovated façade embellished with blue window awnings. Reasonably priced, functional and modern guestrooms.

't Fornuis (Johan Segers) ⟷ VISA ☺ AE ①
Reyndersstraat 24 – ℰ *0 3 233 62 70 – fornuis@skynet.be – Fax 0 3 233 99 03*
– closed 20 July – 16 August, Christmas – New Year, Saturday, Sunday and
bank holidays   **D2**
Rest *– (pre-book)* Menu 90/140 € bi – Carte 59/118 € ⅜
Spec. Salade de crabe frais. Langue d'agneau, gros haricots blancs et sauce au madère. Barbue pochée et caviar.
◆ Traditional ◆ Rustic ◆
Fine classic cuisine and a good wine list are on offer in this old Antwerp house. Display of miniature stoves on the ground floor, rustic dining rooms upstairs. No menus, just a choice of daily specials outlined by the chef at your table.

Huis De Colvenier 🕮 ⟷ **P** VISA ☺ AE ①
Sint-Antoniusstraat 8 – ℰ *0 3 226 65 73 – info@colvenier.be – Fax 0 3 227 13 14*
– www.colvenier.be
– closed carnival week, Easter week, August, Saturday lunch, Sunday and Monday
Rest *– (set menu only)* Menu 70/125 € bi ⅜   **D2**
◆ Traditional ◆ Retro ◆
A restaurant occupying a townhouse dating from 1879. Dine to a backdrop of chic, classic decor or beneath the glass roof. Elaborate menu that is announced at your table by the chef. Impressive wine list.

Dôme (Julien Burlat) 🕮 VISA ☺ AE ①
Grote Hondstraat 2 ⊠ *2018 –* ℰ *0 3 239 90 03 – info@domeweb.be*
– Fax 0 3 239 93 90 – www.domeweb.be
– closed 2 weeks in August, 24 December – 7 January, Saturday lunch, Sunday
and Monday   **F3**
Rest *–* Menu 69/93 € bi – Carte 63/84 € ⅜
Spec. Cuisses de grenouilles, réglisse, salade Cecina de Buey. Féra du Léman pochée au beurre salé, girolles, vandouvan. Pigeon de Vendée, pommes de terre de Noirmoutier, ragoût de morilles et asperges sauvages (en saison).
◆ Contemporary ◆
Savour delicate and inventive modern cuisine in the circular dining room beneath a 19C neo-Baroque stucco dome. Very popular 'carte blanche' menu, and a studiously compiled wine list presented by the qualified young sommelier. Highly professional service.

Neuze Neuze ⟷ VISA ☺ AE ①
Wijngaardstraat 19 – ℰ *0 3 232 27 97 – neuzeneuze@telenet.be*
– Fax 0 3 225 27 38 – www.neuzeneuze.be
– closed 21-29 February, 9-23 August, Wednesday lunch, Saturday lunch and Sunday
Rest *–* Menu 53/88 € bi – Carte 48/80 €   **D1**
◆ Retro ◆
A restaurant comprising of five small 16C houses. The perfect setting for a business meal or romantic dinner for two. Classic cuisine with a modern twist. Intimate atmosphere and attentive service.

La Luna
🗛 ⊯ 🆅🅸🆂🅰 🌐 🅰🅴 ⓘ

*Italiëlei 177 – ℰ 0 3 232 23 44 – info@laluna.be – Fax 0 3 232 24 41
– www.laluna.be
– closed Easter, 1st - 15 August, Christmas – New Year, Saturday lunch, Sunday
and Monday*   **E1**
Rest – Menu 65 € – Carte 50/81 € ⅏
◆ Design ◆

A refined restaurant with lunar designer decor by Jean De Meulder (1996). Tasty
cuisine featuring a variety of cosmopolitan influences (France, Italy and Japan),
and a comprehensive wine list.

De Gulden Beer
≤ 🈲 🗛 ⇲ 🆅🅸🆂🅰 🌐 🅰🅴 ⓘ

*Grote Markt 14 – ℰ 0 3 226 08 41 – Fax 0 3 232 52 09
– closed Wednesday*   **D1**
Rest – Menu 37/75 € – Carte 38/66 €
◆ Italian ◆

This old house with a fine stepped gable is located on the Grand Place. There are
attractive views from the bay windows on the first floor, and from the terrace.
Authentic Italian cuisine.

Harmony
🈲 🗛 ⇲ ⊯ 🆅🅸🆂🅰 🌐 🅰🅴

*Mechelsesteenweg 169 ✉ 2018 – ℰ 0 3 239 70 05 – info@
diningroomharmony.com – Fax 0 2 343 48 61 – www.diningroomharmony.com
– closed 25 July - 12 August, 22 December - 6 January, Saturday lunch and
Wednesday*   **E3**
Rest – Menu 30/75 € bi – Carte 44/61 €
◆ Retro ◆

A restaurant with a modern culinary focus amid a retro decor of parquet flooring,
fluted Art Deco pilasters, Lloyd Loom chairs and refined contemporary lighting.
Valet parking.

Het Nieuwe Palinghuis
🗛 🆅🅸🆂🅰 🌐 🅰🅴

*Sint-Jansvliet 14 – ℰ 0 3 231 74 45 – hetnieuwepalinghuis@skynet.be
– Fax 0 3 231 50 53 – www.hetnieuwepalinghuis.be
– closed 12 January - 1st February, June, 1st - 10 September, Monday and
Tuesday*   **C2**
Rest – Menu 39/110 € bi – Carte 48/94 €
◆ Seafood ◆

Located close to the pedestrian tunnel beneath the Escaut, this restaurant specialises in fish and seafood. Nostalgic maritime photos on the walls of the dining room.
Front terrace.

Hofstraat 24
⇲ 🆅🅸🆂🅰 🌐 🅰🅴

*Hofstraat 24 – ℰ 0 3 225 05 45 – hofstraat24@skynet.be – Fax 0 3 225 05 45
– www.hofstraat24.be
– closed 2 weeks at Easter, first 2 weeks August, 2 weeks at Christmas,
Wednesday and Sunday*   **D1**
Rest – (dinner only) Carte 48/68 €
◆ Cosy ◆

Behind the imposing white façade are three dining rooms: one crowned by a glass
roof, and two decorated in a modern rustic style, one of which contains a library.

Bernardin
🈲 ⊯ 🆅🅸🆂🅰 🌐

*Sint-Jacobsstraat 17 – ℰ 0 3 213 07 00 – info@restaurantbernardin.be
– Fax 0 3 232 49 96 – www.restaurantbernardin.be
– closed 1 week at Easter, last 2 weeks August, late December, Saturday lunch,
Sunday and Monday*   **E2**
Rest – Menu 33/44 € bi – Carte 46/68 €
◆ Contemporary ◆

A 17C house that has been renovated both inside and out. Plain, modern dining
room decorated in white, light grey and black. Attractive patio terrace in the shadow of St Jacob's church.

BELGIUM - ANTWERP

De Manie
🛋 ⇄ VISA ◐◉ AE ⓪

H. Conscienceplein 3 – ℰ 03 232 64 38 – demanie@euphonynet.be
– Fax 03 232 64 38
– closed 28 February - 4 March, 12 August - 2 September, Sunday except lunch
outside of school holidays, and Wednesday **D1**
Rest – Menu 29/60 € bi – Carte 50/66 €
♦ Classic ♦
A quiet restaurant with a summer terrace fronting a pretty square in front of the
Baroque style St Charles Borromeo church. A few tables on the mezzanine.

Dock's Café
🛋 AC ⇄ 🛏 VISA ◐◉ AE

Jordaenskaai 7 – ℰ 03 226 63 30 – info@docks.be – Fax 03 226 65 72
– www.docks.be
– closed Sunday **D1**
Rest – (open until 11pm) Menu 24/40 € – Carte 33/77 €
♦ Brasserie ♦
A brasserie and oyster bar with a futuristic, ocean liner inspired decor. Dining room
with a mezzanine and neo-Baroque staircase. Advance booking recommended.

De Kleine Zavel
VISA ◐◉ AE

Stoofstraat 2 – ℰ 03 231 96 91 – info@dekleinezavel.be – Fax 03 231 79 01
– www.dekleinezavel.be
– closed Saturday lunch and Monday **C2**
Rest – Menu 60 € – Carte 44/67 €
♦ Bistro ♦
This restaurant offers classic and bistro dishes, along with daily specials and a good
value lunch. The decor comprises of wood floors, bare tables, an old bar and a
relaxed atmosphere.

De Reddende Engel
🛋 ⇄ VISA ◐◉ AE ⓪

Torfbrug 3 – ℰ 03 233 66 30 – de.reddende.engel@telenet.be
– Fax 03 233 73 79 – www.de-reddende-engel.be
– closed mid-August - mid-September, Saturday lunch, Tuesday and Wednesday
Rest – Menu 27/35 € – Carte 31/53 € **D1**
♦ Traditional ♦ Rustic ♦
This restaurant occupies a rustic style 17C house near the cathedral. Gastronomic à
la carte menu focusing on southern France, including dishes such as bouillabaisse
and cassoulet.

Le Zoute Zoen
⇄ VISA ◐◉ AE

Zirkstraat 17 – ℰ 03 226 92 20 – lezoutezoen@telenet.be – Fax 03 231 01 30
– closed Saturday lunch and Monday **D1**
Rest – Menu 27/65 € bi – Carte 29/50 €
♦ Retro ♦
This intimate and cosy bistro offers some of the best value gastronomic fare in the
city with its hearty, contemporary cuisine. Relaxed service with a smile.

Gin-Fish (Didier Garnich)
AC ⇄ VISA ◐◉ AE ⓪

Haarstraat 9 – ℰ 03 231 32 07 – Fax 03 231 08 13
– closed 1st - 15 January, 15 June – 6 July, Sunday and Monday
Rest – (dinner only) (number of covers limited, pre-book) (set **D1-2**
menu only) Menu 65/80 € bi
Spec. Préparations où entre la pêche du jour. Glace tournée minute.
♦ Seafood ♦
Good fish and seafood prepared and served at the counter with just a single menu
on offer. Friendly staff.

Het Gebaar
🛋 VISA ◐◉

Leopoldstraat 24 – ℰ 03 232 37 10 – hetgebaar@pandora.be
– Fax 03 293 72 32 – www.hetgebaar.be
– closed Sunday and Monday **D2**
Rest – (lunch only) Carte approx. 50 €
♦ Innovative ♦ Cosy ♦
A welcoming restaurant in an old cottage style house on the edge of a botanical
garden. Inventive molecular style cuisine and delicate desserts.

Maritime

🖼 AC VISA ⊙ AE ⓪

Suikerrui 4 – 𝒞 0 3 233 07 58 – restaurant.maritime@pandora.be
– Fax 0 3 233 07 58 – www.maritime.be
– closed Wednesday and Thursday   **C1**
Rest – Carte 40/63 € 🕸

♦ Seafood ♦ Family ♦

A seafood restaurant with bright red tablecloths serving plentiful mussels and eel dishes in season. Excellent choice of Burgundies. Attentive service courtesy of the owner.

Hecker

🖼 ⇔ VISA ⊙ AE ⓪

Kloosterstraat 13 – 𝒞 0 3 234 38 34 – info@hecker.be – Fax 0 2 343 48 61
– www.hecker.be
– closed 25 July - 12 August, 22 December - 6 January, Monday lunch and
Wednesday   **C2**
Rest – Menu 48 € – Carte 39/53 €

♦ Wine bar ♦

A trendy bistro with a wine bar feel located next door to an antique shop, the main business activity in this district. Small, original menu accompanied by a good choice of wines from around the world.

Pazzo

AC ⇔ VISA ⊙ AE ⓪

Oude Leeuwenrui 12 – 𝒞 0 3 232 86 82 – pazzo@skynet.be – Fax 0 3 232 79 34
– www.pazzo.be
– closed 20 July – 17 August, Saturday, Sunday and bank holidays
Rest – (open until 11pm) Carte 40/68 € 🕸   **D1**

♦ Contemporary ♦

Located near the docks, this former warehouse has been converted into a contemporary brasserie with a lively atmosphere. Mediterranean and Asian inspired cuisine with excellent wine recommendations from the owner-cum-sommelier.

Dôme Sur Mer

🖼 VISA ⊙

Arendstraat 1 ⊠ 2018 – 𝒞 0 3 281 74 33 – info@domeweb.be
– Fax 0 3 239 93 90 – www.domeweb.be
– closed 2 weeks in September, 24 December – 12 January, Saturday lunch,
Sunday and Monday   **F3**
Rest – (open until 11.30pm) Carte 38/97 €

♦ Seafood ♦

This manor house has been transformed into a trendy seafood brasserie. It has a whitewashed decor punctuated by several bluish coloured aquariums full of goldfish.

't Peerd

🖼 AC ⇔ VISA ⊙ AE ⓪

Paardenmarkt 53 – 𝒞 0 3 231 98 25 – resto_t_peerd@yahoo.com
– Fax 0 3 231 59 40 – www.tpeerd.be
– closed Tuesday and Wednesday   **E1**
Rest – Menu 30/62 € bi – Carte 45/74 €

♦ Traditional ♦ Rustic ♦

A pleasant small restaurant with rustic decor and an equestrian theme. Typical ambience, where the owner has been at the helm since 1970. Traditional menu, including a number of horse meat specialities.

Yamayu Santatsu

AC ⇔ VISA ⊙ AE

Ossenmarkt 19 – 𝒞 0 3 234 09 49 – Fax 0 3 234 09 49
– closed Sunday lunch and Monday   **E1**
Rest – Menu 40/65 € bi – Carte 31/57 €

♦ Japanese ♦ Exotic ♦

A lively and authentic Japanese restaurant that only uses the best hand picked ingredients, and prepares sushi in full view of diners. Assorted à la carte options with four different menus for two people.

Chez Raoul ⌂ VISA ⓪

Vlasmarkt 21 – ℰ 03 213 09 77 – Fax 0 32 13 16 50 – www.chezraoul.be
– closed 14 July – early August, Sunday lunch, Wednesday and Thursday
Rest – Carte 47/60 €   **C2**
◆ Traditional ◆
Refined cuisine amid a warm, bistro decor of red brick, red benches, tables packed close together, wood floors and bar. Attractive display of wine bottles plus a daily specials board.

Lamalo AC ⇔ VISA ⓪

Appelmansstraat 21 ⊠ 2018 – ℰ 03 213 22 00 – ikaz@telenet.be
– Fax 0 3 234 22 26 – www.lamalo.com
– closed 1st - 23 August, Friday and Saturday   **E2**
Rest – Menu 42/68 € bi – Carte 35/63 €
◆ Cosy ◆
This restaurant in Antwerp's diamond district is popular with the city's Jewish community. An interesting menu of Mediterranean inspired kosher cuisine.

P'tit Paris ⌂ VISA ⓪ AE

Lange Lobroekstraat 41 ⊠ 2060 – ℰ 03 272 52 72 – reservatie@petitparis.be
– Fax 0 3 236 22 56 – www.petitparis.be
– closed first 2 weeks August, Saturday lunch and Sunday   *Plan I* **B1**
Rest – Carte 38/62 €
◆ Seafood ◆
This former butcher's workshop near the abattoirs has been transformed into a restaurant specialising in fish and seafood, with white tiling and an open kitchen. The blackboard menus conveyed along the rails in the ceiling once used to transport carcasses.

SOUTH QUARTER AND BERCHEM   *Plan III*

Crowne Plaza ⌂ 㐂 🔐 🔲 ☕ rest AC ⇎ 🖥 ☎ 🏋 P 🚗

G. Legrellelaan 10 ⊠ 2020 – ℰ 03 259 75 00 – info@   VISA ⓪ AE ⓪
cpantwerp.com – Fax 0 3 238 64 31 – www.crowneplaza.com   **BS**
262 rm – †185/230 € ††185/230 €, ⊡ 21 € – 2 suites
Rest – Menu 55/140 € – Carte 38/101 €
◆ Business ◆ Functional ◆
A hotel and conference centre near the ring road and a main road heading into the centre of the city. The modernised guestrooms are the best option here. Fitness centre, sauna and indoor swimming pool. A new restaurant menu is currently being studied.

Firean 🎍 AC ☎ 🚗 VISA ⓪ AE ⓪

Karel Oomsstraat 6 ⊠ 2018 – ℰ 03 237 02 60 – info@hotelfirean.com
– Fax 0 3 238 11 68 – www.hotelfirean.com
– closed 1st - 24 August and 19 December – 4 January   **G1**
12 rm ⊡ – †149/175 € ††174/185 €   **Rest Minerva** – see below
◆ Luxury ◆
A hotel full of character occupying an attractive Art Deco house dating from 1929. Courtyard terrace, public areas in period style, and personalised guestrooms with antique furniture. Superb staff and impeccable service.

Industrie without rest ☎ 🚗 VISA ⓪ AE ⓪

Emiel Banningstraat 52 – ℰ 03 238 66 00 – info@hotelindustrie.be
– Fax 0 3 238 86 88 – www.hotelindustrie.be   *Plan I* **A2**
13 rm ⊡ – †57/69 € ††69/77 €
◆ Classical ◆
This small hotel occupies two townhouses with meticulously furnished rooms. It is located close to two interesting museums and the city's new and unique law courts.

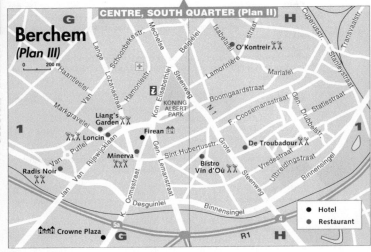

XXX **Minerva** – H. Firean   A/C VISA ⚫⚫ AE ①
Karel Oomsstraat 36 ⊠ 2018 – ℰ 0 3 216 00 55 – info@restaurantminerva.be
– Fax 0 3 216 00 55 – www.hotelfirean.com
– closed first week January, last week July – first 2 weeks August, last week
December, Sunday and Monday   **G1**
Rest – Carte 50/91 €
  ♦ Traditional ♦ Formal ♦
A chic restaurant named after a pre-war make of Belgian car. The Minerva occupies
a former garage, where the old inspection pit (now covered by glass) has been
retained. Classic cuisine.

XXX **Kommilfoo**   A/C VISA ⚫⚫ AE ①
Vlaamse Kaai 17 ⊠ 2000 – ℰ 0 3 237 30 00 – kommilfoo@resto.be
– Fax 0 3 237 30 00
– closed 15 - 31 July, Saturday lunch, Sunday and Monday   *Plan II* **C3**
Rest – Menu 50/60 € – Carte 48/79 €
  ♦ Cosy ♦
Restaurant occupying an old warehouse with contemporary decor including Lloyd
Loom chairs. Inventive cuisine.

XXX **Loncin**   🍴 A/C ⇔ **P** VISA ⚫⚫ AE
Markgravelei 127 ⊠ 2018 – ℰ 0 3 248 29 89 – info@loncinrestaurant.be
– Fax 0 3 248 38 66 – www.loncinrestaurant.be
– closed Saturday lunch and Sunday   **G1**
Rest – Menu 85/108 € bi – Carte 45/112 € 🍷
  ♦ Traditional ♦ Formal ♦
An early-20C house with elegant decor and an owner who is a keen hunter. A
menu geared towards traditional dishes with plentiful game in season. A solid
wine list with a good choice of half-bottles.

BELGIUM - ANTWERP

XX **Liang's Garden** 🄰🄲 ⇔ 🆅🅸🆂🅰 ⬤ 🄰🄴 ①

Markgravelei 141 ✉ 2018 – ℰ 0 3 237 22 22 – liangsgarden@skynet.be
– Fax 0 3 248 38 34 – www.liangsgarden.be
– closed 6 July - 2 August and Sundays   **G1**
Rest – Menu 45/90 € bi – Carte 31/78 €
♦ Chinese ♦ Exotic ♦
A stalwart of Chinese cuisine in the city! A spacious and elegant restaurant where the authentic menu covers specialities from Canton (dim sum), Peking (duck) and Szechuan (fondue).

XX **Radis Noir** 🄰🄲 ⇔ 🆅🅸🆂🅰 ⬤ 🄰🄴 ①

Desguinlei 186 ✉ 2018 – ℰ 0 3 238 37 70 – radisnoir@skynet.be
– Fax 0 3 238 39 07 – www.radisnoir.be
– closed 8 - 15 April, 19 July - 12 August, 24 December - 4 January, Wednesday dinner, Saturday lunch and Sunday   **G1**
Rest – Menu 52/88 € bi – Carte 53/97 €
♦ Minimalist ♦
Behind the Black Radish's old red brick façade, modernised with frosted plate glass, is an attractive dining room in minimalist, contemporary style. Concise, yet frequently updated menu choices.

XX **De Troubadour** 🄰🄲 ⇔ 🄿 🆅🅸🆂🅰 ⬤ 🄰🄴 ①
☺

Driekoningenstraat 72 – ℰ 0 3 239 39 16 – info@detroubadour.be
– Fax 0 3 230 82 71 – www.detroubadour.be
– closed first 3 weeks August, Sunday and Monday   **H1**
Rest – Menu 33 € – Carte 35/59 €
♦ Contemporary ♦
A modern, cosy dining room where the gregarious owner fosters a warm and friendly atmosphere. Classic, creative à la carte options, as well as appetising menus and daily specials announced at your table. Parking available (prior booking required).

XX **Bistro Vin d'Où** 🍴 🄰🄲 ⇔ 🆅🅸🆂🅰 ⬤ 🄰🄴 ①

Terlinckstraat 2 – ℰ 0 3 230 55 99 – tomfluit@skynet.be – Fax 0 3 230 40 71
– www.vindou.be
– closed Easter, first 2 weeks September, Christmas holidays, Saturday lunch and Sunday   **H1**
Rest – Menu 31/65 € – Carte 36/65 €
♦ Brasserie ♦
This old house in a residential area has been refurbished in the style of an elegant bistro. Courtyard terrace with teak furnishings and boxwood hedging. A new chef at the helm in 2008.

XX **O'Kontreir** 🄰🄲 ⇔ 🆅🅸🆂🅰 ⬤ 🄰🄴

Isabellalei 145 ✉ 2018 – ℰ 0 3 281 39 76 – info@okontreir.com
– Fax 0 3 237 92 06 – www.okontreir.com
– closed 20 July - 4 August, 24 December - 5 January, Saturday lunch, Sunday lunch, Monday and Tuesday   **H1**
Rest – Menu 30/70 € bi – Carte 38/62 €
♦ Contemporary ♦
This restaurant located in the Jewish quarter serves modern, creative cuisine. Its setting is a contemporary lounge-style with a contrasting black and white decor. Dining room with mezzanine.

XX **Het Gerecht** 🍴 ⇔ 🆅🅸🆂🅰 ⬤

Amerikalei 20 – ℰ 0 3 248 79 28 – restaurant@hetgerecht.be – Fax 0 3 248 79 28
– www.hetgerecht.be
– closed last 2 weeks July – first week August, Saturday lunch, Sunday and Monday   *Plan II* **D3**
Rest – Menu 29/87 € bi – Carte 50/62 €
♦ Contemporary ♦
Contemporary cuisine prepared by the male chef, with the female half of the partnership running the front of house. Cosy, modern and elegant decor, plus a decked courtyard terrace enclosed by brick walls.

Hippodroom

Leopold de Waelplaats 10 – ☎ 0 3 248 52 52 – resto@hippodroom.be – Fax 0 3 238 71 67 – www.hippodroom.be – closed 1st January, Saturday lunch and Sunday Plan II **C3**

Rest – *(open until 11pm)* Carte 38/63 €

◆ Brasserie ◆

A modern brasserie in a mansion adjoining the Fine Arts Museum. A globetrotting menu popular with clientele from the artistic world. Terraces to the front and rear.

River Kwai

Vlaamse Kaai 14 – ☎ 0 3 237 46 51 – info@riverkwai.be – www.riverkwai.be – closed 1st - 15 June, Christmas – New Year and Wednesday Plan II **C3**

Rest – *(dinner only except Thursday and Friday)* Menu 32/45 € bi – Carte 30/49 €

◆ Thai ◆ Exotic ◆

This Thai restaurant, with its authentic neo-colonial decor, occupies a building constructed in 1906. Dining rooms on the ground floor and above, as well as a small, enclosed wood terrace.

l'Amitié

Vlaamse Kaai 43 – ☎ 0 3 257 50 05 – info@lamitie.net – Fax 0 3 257 59 05 – www.lamitie.net – closed 6 - 29 June, 29 August - 6 September, late December, Saturday lunch, Sunday and Monday Plan II **C3**

Rest – Menu 50/80 € bi – Carte 54/71 €

◆ Contemporary ◆ Bistro ◆

This newcomer is full of culinary promise, with its bistro style menu focusing on French and Mediterranean dishes. Contemporary dining room and a small wood-decked terrace.

Ferrier 30

Leopold de Waelplaats 30 – ☎ 0 3 216 50 62 – Fax 0 3 216 99 94 – www.ferrier.be – closed Wednesday Plan II **C3**

Rest – *(open until 11pm)* Carte 33/53 €

◆ Italian ◆

Generous Italian cuisine, fashionable black and white decor, attentive service, plus a terrace overlooking the Fine Arts Museum. The more intimate basement dining room is used at busy times.

AT THE AIRPORT *Plan I*

Scandic

rm

Luitenant Lippenslaan 66 ✉ 2140 Borgerhout – ☎ 0 3 235 91 91 – info-antwerp@scandic-hotels.com – Fax 0 3 235 08 96 – www.scandichotels.com/antwerpen **B2**

201 rm – †110/190 € ††128/208 € – 3 suites

Rest – *(closed Saturday lunch and Sunday lunch)* Carte 32/46 €

◆ Functional ◆ Chain hotel ◆

This chain hotel is located near the ring road, a railway station, the Zilvercentrum (museum) and a golf course. Well-appointed guestrooms, as well as meeting rooms, swimming pool and fitness centre. A rather formal brasserie with a large teak terrace.

CZECH REPUBLIC
ČESKÁ REPUBLIKA

PROFILE

→ **AREA:**
78 864 km² (30 449 sq mi).

→ **POPULATION:**
10 241 000 inhabitants (est. 2005), density = 130 per km².

→ **CAPITAL:**
Prague (population 1 141 000 inhabitants).

→ **CURRENCY:**
Czech crown (Kč); rate of exchange: CZK 100 = € 3.89 = US$ 4.92 (Dec 2008).

→ **GOVERNMENT:**
Parliamentary republic (since 1993). Member of European Union since 2004.

→ **LANGUAGE:**
Czech; also German and English.

→ **SPECIFIC PUBLIC HOLIDAYS:**
Liberation Day (8 May); St. Cyril and St. Methodius Day (5 July); Martyrdom of Jean Hus (6 July); Czech Statehood Day (28 September); Independence Day (28 October); Freedom and Democracy Day (17 November); Boxing Day (26 December).

→ **LOCAL TIME:**
GMT + 1 hour in winter and GMT + 2 hours in summer.

→ **CLIMATE:**
Temperate continental with cold winters and warm summers (Prague: January: 0°C, July: 20°C).

→ **INTERNATIONAL DIALLING CODE:**
00 420 followed by area code (Prague: 2), and then the local number.

→ **EMERGENCY:**
Police: ☎ 158; Ambulance: ☎ 155; Fire Brigade: ☎ 150.

→ **ELECTRICITY:**
220 volts AC, 50Hz; 2-pin round-shaped continental plugs.

PRAGUE

→ **FORMALITIES**
Travellers from the European Union (EU), Switzerland, Iceland and the main countries of North and South America need a national identity card or passport (America: passport required) to visit Czech Republic for less than three months (tourism or business purpose). For visitors from other countries a visa may be required, in addition to a passport, especially for those wishing to stay for longer than three months. We advise you to check with your embassy before travelling.

PRAGUE
PRAHA

Population: 1 141 000 – Altitude: 250m

Siméone/PHOTONONSTOP

The most important thing to remember about Prague is that its history stretches back to the Dark Ages. In the ninth century a princely seat comprising a simple walled-in compound was built where today stands the castle. In the tenth century the first bridge over the Vltava arrived. By the thirteenth century the enchanting cobbled alleyways below the castle were complete. Wherever you tread here, the musty scent of the past travels with you. But Prague has come of age and in many ways it's had to. It now receives ten times as many visitors as it did 20 years ago, and that figure could jump to double again (15 million) by 2010. Europe's most perfectly preserved capital now proffers consumer choice as well as medieval marvels. Its state-of-the-art shopping malls and pulsing nightlife bear testament to its popularity with tourists, the iron glove of communism long since having given way to the silk purse of western consumerism. These days there are practically two versions of Prague - the lively, youthful version which has spawned the unfortunate, headline grabbing epithet of 'stag party central', and the sedate, enchanting version most people have succumbed to, the 'city of a hundred spires', where cathedrals, churches, chapels and monasteries – exuberant and extraordinary - prod the skyline. And this is the city, prosperous, cosmopolitan and orderly, where music of all shades seeps into your senses.

LIVING THE CITY

The four main zones of Prague were originally independent towns in their own right. The river Vltava winds its way through their heart, and they're linked by the iconic Charles Bridge, possibly the most charismatic of Europe's spans. On the west side lie Hradèany, the castle quarter, built on a rock spur commanding the river bend, and Malá Strana, Prague's most perfectly preserved district at the bottom of the castle hill. Over the river are Staré Město, the old town with its vibrant medieval square and outer boulevards, and Nové Město, the new town, which is the city's commercial heart extending south and east of the old town. It's where you find Wenceslas Square and it's where Prague's suited and booted new execs hang out and the young things go to party.

PRACTICAL INFORMATION

ARRIVAL-DEPARTURE

Ruzyně (Prague Airport) is 20km west of the city. Take a taxi displaying 'Airport Cars' sign ; this should cost around CZK650. The shuttle bus leaves every 30min. International trains stops at Hlavni nádraží.

TRANSPORT

Trams and buses are frequent in Prague and run from early morning to past midnight. There's also a 49-station Metro comprising three lines and covering much of the city. All three are invariably cheap.

Be wary of taxis. Although regulations specify rates, it's not uncommon to be grossly overcharged. Always use a designated rank, and avoid flagging down a cab anywhere.

If you think you'll be public transport hopping on a pretty regular basis, then buy a short-term season pass that allows unlimited travel on bus, tram, metro and Petrin funicular.

EXPLORING PRAGUE

No other capital in Europe can match Prague's enviable mix of Medieval, Gothic, Baroque and art nouveau. It creates a heady fairytale patchwork set off by glinting spring sunshine

or a pure blanket of winter snow. The city's laid-back citizens sit in their gloomily atmospheric pubs and relax with a beer, leaving the hard work to the tourists. Outside, many of those are trying to decide just how to fit the jigsaw pieces together…museums, art galleries, churches, synagogues, a chamber concert in an ornate chapel. Or perhaps they're trying to find their way around the labyrinthine web of lanes and passageways that may link those very tourist landmarks.

→ YOU'LL BE A-MAZED

If you're all set to 'do' Staré Město or Malá Strana, be prepared to lose yourself in a maze of crooked streets and narrow alleyways; don't be afraid to peek down passageways and slip into secret courtyards hemmed in by old-style dwellings. The real itch of Prague is feeling you haven't discovered it until it's concocted a way of getting you lost. As confused as you may be, you can take heart in the knowledge that before too long you'll end up by the Vltava or catch sight of a recognizable landmark. If it all gets a little bit too claustrophobic, you can take refuge in the Nové Město. Here the medieval town planner has taken pity on the confused visitor and the streets and squares are logically laid out, as typified by the broad boulevard of **Wenceslas Square**.

To get a real perspective on the city, everyone – and we mean everyone – takes a stroll over the **Charles Bridge** (completed in 1402) with its various bronze saints staring down implacably on the never-ending shuffle of passers-by. At each end is a tower, open to visitors, both offering superb views from their roofs. This merely whets the appetite for the climb up to **Prague Castle**, with its commanding cliff-top outlook. Its scale is breathtaking; quite simply, it's the biggest ancient castle in the world. So big that within its third courtyard stands the immense Gothic structure that is **St Vitus Cathedral,** complete with massive main tower, scintillating rose window, spectacular stained-glass windows, and a chapel to St Wenceslas that glitters with gold, silver and semi-precious stones. There are other jewels in the Castle's crown, such as the Royal Garden, the Old Royal Palace and the Summer Palace, while close by are the smart boutiques of the tiny, magical Golden Lane, where Franz Kafka, at number 22, wrote much of his work. There's so much to take in around here that it might be worth doing it in more than one visit.

→ **THROUGH TICK AND TYN**

If you just love the warm glow of big crowds, then cross the river for another fix. This time the masses gather every hour in Staré Město's Old Town Square beneath the Orloj, or **Astronomical Clock,** which has three hands to show the position of the sun, moon and stars. On the hour, with the crowds in tow, carved figures do a turn, death wags his hourglass, and a cockerel crows to bring the drama to its conclusion. There are other great charms to the historical square (aside from the ubiquitous restaurants and bars to rest weary feet); every hue and nuance of architectural style vies for attention in the shape of the rococo Kinsky Palace, the Gothic/Baroque House of the Stone Bell, the Renaissance façade of Storch House, and the dramatic twin spires signalling the great Gothic landmark of the Church of Our Lady Before Tyn. Here, inside the richly adorned interior, search out the tomb of Tycho Brahe, Renaissance astronomer, who lost the tip of his nose in a duel, had it replaced in gold and silver, and died when his bladder burst after an excess of beer and wine. He might have appreciated the Municipal House, an art nouveau masterpiece close to Old Town Square where you can wine and dine in luxuriously refined surroundings. It's a great place for concerts, too.

To the north of Staré Město is Josefov, the Jewish quarter, where the Old Jewish Cemetery is a fascinating place to visit. Hemmed in by buildings and high walls, there was only so much space for the 12,000 tombstones, and these topple across each other in chaotic disarray. The synagogues of the area remain, some used as museums outlining the long history of Jews in Prague, others as places of worship. The Old-New Synagogue, near the cemetery, is one of Europe's oldest functioning synagogues, and boasts an eye-catching high brick gable and an atmospheric feel. Josefov is a rather small area that does get packed, so a good time to go along is early in the day.

→ GRAND NATIONAL

At the other end of town, at the southern end of Wenceslas Square, looms the brooding bulk of another great Prague institution, **the National Museum.** With its vast natural history and archaeology collections, it's a city institution, but some may find the most intriguing aspect of the place its cavernous atrium and grand staircases (incidentally, there are many quirky museums in Prague, devoted to the likes of spiders and scorpions, medieval torture and Barbie). The National Museum is a towering experience under a big roof, and you can get a similar kind of awesome hit at **the National Theatre**, south of Charles Bridge by the river, an opulent home of opera, ballet and theatre, full of lavish decorations from the country's top nineteenth century artistic talents.

To appreciate a complete contrast, head back over the river to **Petrin Hill,** which towers gloriously over Malá Strana's dappled squares and aristocratic palaces. It offers great vistas over the city, and features lots of leafy trails that criss-cross the surface. Sitting atop of it all is Prague's mini Eiffel Tower, the Petrin Tower, gifting you more stunning views. Heading back down to river level, you might be surprised to find the John Lennon Wall, painted after his murder in 1980, covered in graffiti, slightly tatty and peeling, but preserved as a totem to free expression.

However hard-wired to the newly opened-up, globalized world Prague aspires to be, it'll surely never lose its magical medieval appeal. It's at its best in the winter with damp mists swirling off the river, and the crowds mysteriously evaporated. In November or February, you can walk unsullied across Charles Bridge and appreciate this stunning city at its best.

CALENDAR HIGHLIGHTS

There's an English language paper in the city, **The Prague Post**, which is particularly good for listing details of what's on where. And there are so many people handing out leaflets announcing recitals and concerts that your hand will soon start to feel like a mini JCB. Many of these events are worth looking into, so don't just stuff that bit of paper away in your pocket. The Prague Spring Festival, which takes place in May and offers a scintillating variety of classical concerts at many venues, is internationally lauded, but there's also an Autumn Festival in September, and a Winter

PRAGUE IN...

→ ONE DAY
Old Town Square, the astronomical clock, Charles Bridge, Prague Castle, take it all in on Petrin Hill

→ TWO DAYS
Josefov, the National Theatre, Golden Lane

→ THREE DAYS
Wenceslas Square and the National Museum, across the bridge for a detailed look round Malá Strana

Festival in January, so…if you miss one, remember there'll be another along soon. Fans of gipsy roots music have a treat every May, with the World Roma Festival, which, as well as gipsy music, features films and theatre shows in various locations. Dance Prague, every June, is another highlight of the cultural year, while, without employing a trace of the city's trademark irony,

June the third is devoted to the death of Kafka, with admirers flocking to his burial place. December is a good time to be in Old Town Square, with its huge Christmas tree and surrounding markets selling all manner of things you might not really want. On New Year's Eve, the square is a manic place to be, and the fireworks over the castle are something else.

EATING OUT

Prague was and still is to an extent famous for its infinite variety of dumplings. These were the glutinous staple that saw locals through the long years of stark Communist rule. It's still as easy as bumping into another tourist on Charles Bridge to get the favoured local nosh: pork, pickled cabbage and dumplings. You can also mix the likes of schnitzel, beer and ginger cake for a ridiculously cheap outlay. But since '89's Velvet Revolution, Prague has undergone a bit of a foodie revolution, and the heavy traditional cuisine is now served, in the better establishments, with a creative flair and international approach. Global menus are now common currency here. Less palatably, the city has earned a reputation for rather straight-faced and indifferent service: lots of restaurants include a tip in your final bill, so check closely to make sure you don't tip twice. It's worth remembering that lunch is the main meal of the Czech day, and many restaurants have shut up shop well before midnight.

Czechs consume more beer than anyone else in the world, and there are some excellent microbrewery tipples to be had. In Staré Město there's a very popular establishment, with an amazing selection of beers, conveniently called Alcohol Bar. Harder to find in the city, but well worth the effort, are the brilliant flea markets, which set up their stalls depending on the time of year. A good place to check out details is the Globe English language bookstore by the Vltava near the National Theatre. Everyone knows everything there, and the coffee's good too!

→ RISING DAMP

The floods of 2002 were a wake-up call to locals that the Vltava is no respecter of the tourist trade. The costs reached some 70 billion crowns in structural damage and loss of visitors. Although buildings were smartly renovated in good time, the city has learnt its lesson and the authorities have built a new flood wall and early warning system in case the river decides to put them to the test again.

Environs of Prague
(Plan I)

0   1 km

RUZYNĚ

A

B

1

2

3

Podbabská

DEJVICE

BUBENEČ

U

Horoměřická

Evropská

Korunovační

Horákové

Milady

nábřeží Edvarda

VOKOVICE

Evropská

7

PRAŽSKÝ
HRAD

Křížovnická

STŘEŠOVICE

Karmelit-
ská

KARLŮV
MOST

BŘEVNOV

BŘEVNOVSKÝ
KLÁŠTER

Patočkova

Masarykovo
nábřeží

Bělohorská

Pod stadiony

Rašínovo
nábřeží

przijp

Prague Centre
(Plan II)

Kukulova

MOTOL

SMÍCHOV

KOŠÍŘE

Smíchovské
nádraží

Radlická

Radlická

5

Bucharova

Jinonice

RADLICE

STODŮLKY

JINONICE

Nové Butovice

Radlická

Hůrka

Jeremiášova

| Hotel |
| Restaurant |

HLUBOČEPY

A

B

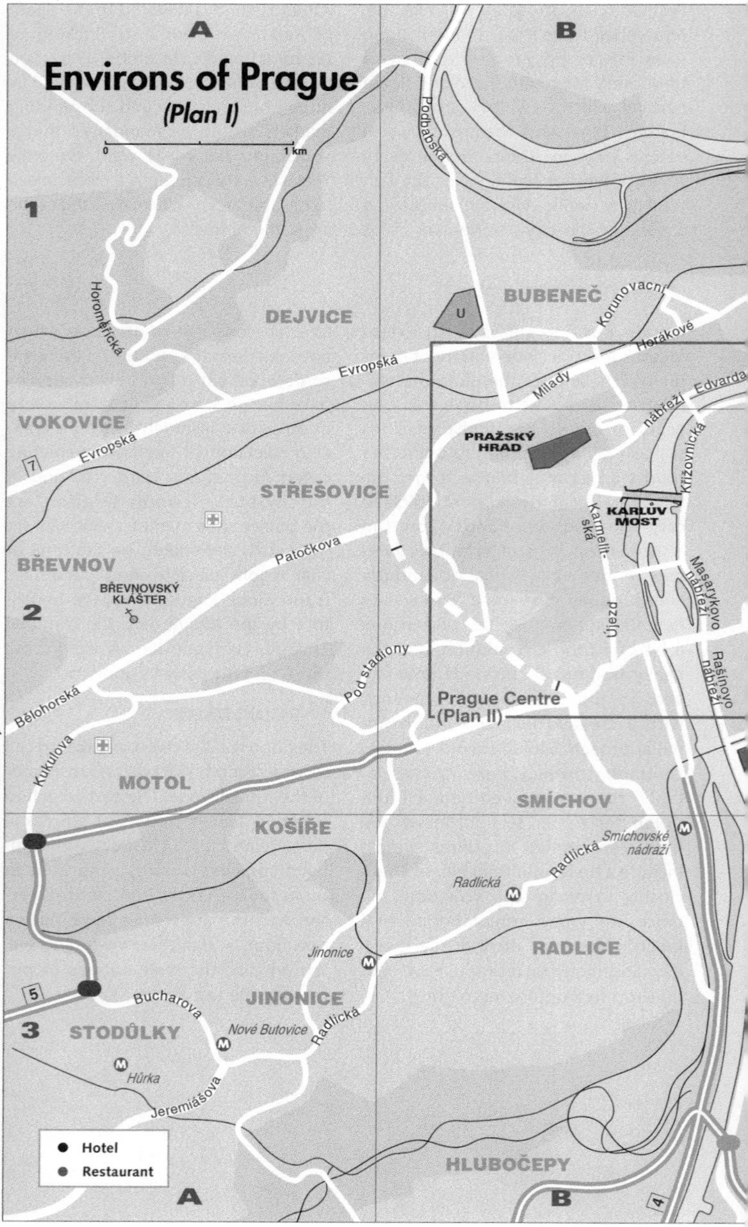

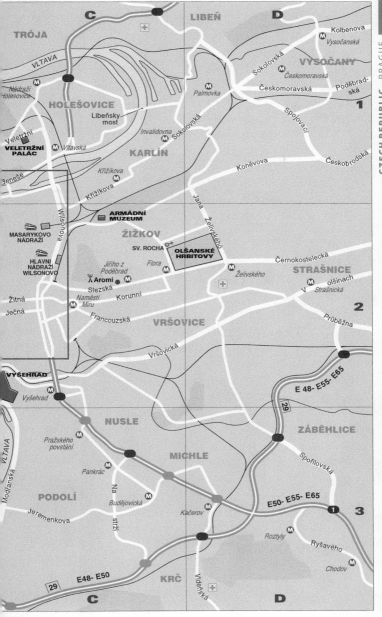

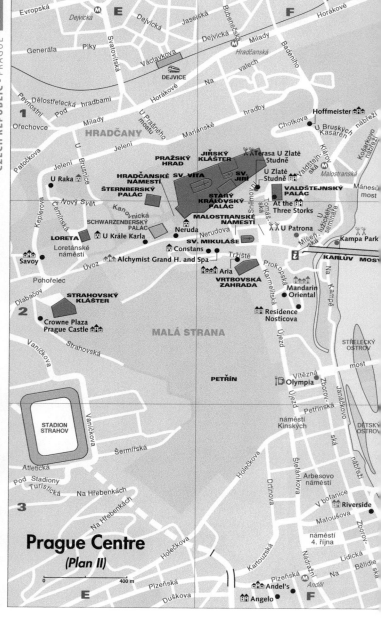

Prague Centre
(Plan II)

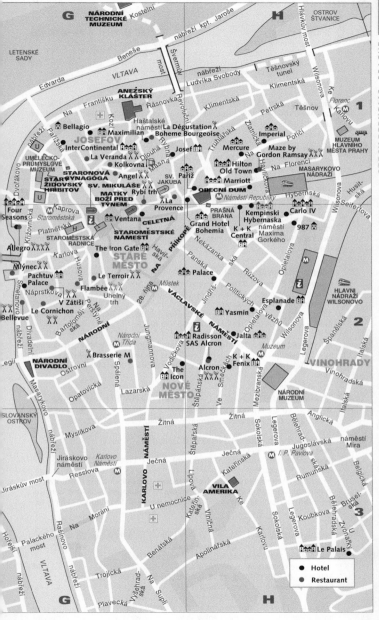

CZECH REPUBLIC - PRAGUE

Four Seasons   𝟱 ⌂ & 𝔸𝔺 ⇜ 🖵 ¶ 𝔸 𝒱𝑰𝑺𝑨 ⑳ 𝔸𝔼 ⓞ
2A Veleslavínova 1098/2a ✉ 110 00 – ⓜ Staroměstská – ✆ 221 427 000
– reservations.prg@fourseasons.com – Fax 221 426 0 00
– www.fourseasons.com/prague   G2
141 rm – ♦9190 CZK ♦♦9700 CZK, ⌾ 970 CZK – 20 suites
Rest Allegro – see below
♦ Grand Luxury ♦ Modern ♦

Imposing riverside hotel composed of three 3 buildings - the Classical, the Renaissance and the Baroque - and united by modern main building. High standard of service. Luxuriously appointed rooms.

Carlo IV   𝟱 ⑳ ⌂ 🖵 & 𝔸𝔺 ⇜ rm 🖵 ☎ 𝔸 ⌾ 𝒱𝑰𝑺𝑨 ⑳ 𝔸𝔼 ⓞ
Senovážné Nám. 13 ✉ 110 00 – ⓜ Náměsti Republiky – ✆ 224 593 111
– reservation@carloiv.boscolo.com – Fax 224 593 0 00
– www.boscolohotels.com   H2
150 rm – ♦4600/12770 CZK ♦♦4600/12770 CZK, ⌾ 640 CZK – 2 suites
Rest Box Block – Menu 1447 CZK (dinner) – Carte 913/1573 CZK
♦ Grand Luxury ♦ Stylish ♦

Unabashed luxury personified: very impressive former bank with stunning marble lobby, ornate ceiling and pillars. Bedrooms in the original building the most spacious and luxurious. A stylish restaurant serving modern Italian and international dishes.

Kempinski Hybernská   ⌖ 𝟱 𝔸𝔺 🖵 ¶ 𝔸 𝒱𝑰𝑺𝑨 ⑳ 𝔸𝔼 ⓞ
Hybernská 12 ✉ 110 00 – ⓜ Namesti Republiky – ✆ 226 226 111
– concierge.prague@kempinski.com – Fax 226 226 1 23
– www.kempinski-prague.com   H2
13 rm – ♦9746 CZK ♦♦9746 CZK – **62 suites** – ♦16672/128250 CZK, ⌾ 769 CZK
Rest – Menu 800 CZK (lunch) – Carte 880/1690 CZK
♦ Historic ♦ Stylish ♦

200 year old listed building, now host to a smart hotel with delightful glass-topped atrium. Walls adorned with international art lead to luxurious bedrooms displaying thoughtful extras. Cosy bar; spacious modern dining room with wide-ranging menu.

Radisson SAS Alcron   ⌖ 𝟱 ⌂ & 𝔸𝔺 ⇜ rm 🖵 ¶ 𝔸 ⌾
Štěpánská 40 ✉ 110 00 – ⓜ Muzeum   𝒱𝑰𝑺𝑨 ⑳ 𝔸𝔼 ⓞ
– ✆ 222 820 000 – sales.prague@radissonsas.com – Fax 222 820 1 00
– www.alcron.cz   H2
200 rm – ♦5700/7500 CZK ♦♦8200 CZK, ⌾ 610 CZK – 6 suites
Rest Alcron – see below
Rest La Rotonde – Menu 850 CZK (lunch) – Carte 1100/1250 CZK
♦ Luxury ♦ Business ♦ Modern ♦

1930s building refurbished to a high standard. Original art deco theme carried through to include the spacious, comfortable, well-equipped bedrooms. Immaculately laid out restaurant with a stylish art deco theme and an outdoor summer terrace.

Inter-Continental   ≤ 𝟱 ⑳ ⌂ 🖵 & 𝔸𝔺 ⇜ rm 🖵 ☎ 𝔸 ⌾
Pařížská 30 ✉ 110 00 – ⓜ Staroměstská   𝒱𝑰𝑺𝑨 ⑳ 𝔸𝔼 ⓞ
– ✆ 296 631 111 – prague@ihg.com – Fax 226 631 2 16
– www.intercontinental.com/prague   G1
349 rm – ♦5810/7590 CZK ♦♦5810/7590 CZK, ⌾ 711 CZK – 23 suites
Rest Zlata Praha – Carte 1175/2240 CZK
♦ Grand Luxury ♦ Modern ♦

Prague's first luxury hotel provides all of the facilities expected of an international hotel. Elegant bedrooms, most enjoy views of the river or the old part of the city. Contemporary cooking with fine wines and stunning views of the city skyline

Le Palais 🀫 *ᵭᴕ* 🕮 ᷝ 뎠 ᷝ ᷝ 뎠 ᷝ 🕮 ᷝ 뎠 ᷝ 🖅 **VISA** 🕮 **AE** 🕕

U Zvonařky 1 ✉ *120 00* – **Ⓜ** *I. P. Pavlova* – ✆ *234 634 111* – *info@
palaishotel.cz* – *Fax 234 634 6 35* – *www.palaishotel.cz*   **H3**
60 rm ⌑ – 💲8880 CZK 💲💲9390 CZK – 12 suites
Rest – Menu 564/1115 CZK – Carte 1064/1343 CZK
◆ Luxury ◆ Classic ◆

Elevated, affluent and quiet location overlooking city for Belle Epoque style converted late 19C mansion. Luxurious bedrooms with traditional comforts and equipment; corner rooms more spacious. Contemporary, seasonal cooking and attentive
service in Le Papillon; delightful outlook from terrace.

Marriott *ᵭᴕ* 🕮 ᷝ 뎠 ᷝ 🕮 ᷝ rm 🖅 ᷝ 뎠 ᷝ **VISA** 🕮 **AE** 🕕

V Celnici 8 ✉ *110 00* – **Ⓜ** *Náměsti Republiky* – ✆ *222 888 888*
– *prague.marriott@marriotthotels.com* – *Fax 222 888 8 89*
– *www.marriottprague.com*   **H1**
258 rm – 💲6100/7800 CZK 💲💲6100/7800 CZK, ⌑ 670 CZK – 35 suites
Rest – Carte 730/1205 CZK
◆ Business ◆ Classic ◆

International hotel boasting first-class conference and leisure facilities. Committed
service and modern, smart bedrooms with all the latest mod cons. Brasserie offers
a wide selection of cuisine from American, French to traditional Czech.

Hilton Old Town *ᵭᴕ* 🕮 ᷝ 뎠 ᷝ 🕮 ᷝ 🖅 ᷝ 뎠 ᷝ **VISA** 🕮 **AE** 🕕

V Celnici 7 ✉ *111 20* – **Ⓜ** *Náměsti Republiky*
– ✆ *221 822 100* – *reservations.prague@hilton.com* – *Fax 221 822 2 00*
– *www.hilton.com*   **H1**
302 rm – 💲4375/8150 CZK 💲💲4375/8150 CZK, ⌑ 575 CZK – 3 suites
Rest *Maze by Gordon Ramsay* – see below
◆ Business ◆ Modern ◆

Located in the heart of the city, this hotel has recently been fully refurbished
and boasts an art deco style lobby with white marble and gold décor. Modern,
functional bedrooms.

Palace 🕮 ᷝ 🕮 ᷝ 뎠 ᷝ rm 🖅 ᷝ 뎠 ᷝ 🖅 ᷝ **VISA** 🕮 **AE** 🕕

Panská 12 ✉ *111 21* – **Ⓜ** *Můstek* – ✆ *224 093 111* – *info@palacehotel.cz*
– *Fax 224 221 2 40* – *www.palacehotel.cz*   **H2**
122 rm ⌑ – 💲5500/8250 CZK 💲💲6250/8750 CZK – 2 suites
Rest *Gourmet Club* – Menu 350/1190 CZK – Carte 1160/1765 CZK
◆ Traditional ◆ Classic ◆

Original Viennese art nouveau style façade dating back to 1909. Elegant interior;
bedrooms combine period furniture with modern facilities and services. Classic
club ambience and fine dining off broad global menu.

Paříž *ᵭᴕ* 🕮 ᷝ 뎠 ᷝ rm 🖅 ᷝ 뎠 ᷝ **VISA** 🕮 **AE** 🕕

U obecniho domu 1 ✉ *110 00* – **Ⓜ** *Náměsti Republiky* – ✆ *222 195 195*
– *booking@hotel-pariz.cz* – *Fax 224 225 4 75* – *www.hotel-pariz.cz*
83 rm – 💲10500 CZK 💲💲10500 CZK, ⌑ 650 CZK – 3 suites   **H1**
Rest *Sarah Bernhardt* – Menu 550 CZK (lunch) – Carte 920/1300 CZK
◆ Traditional ◆ Classic ◆

Culturally and historically, a landmark famed for its neo-gothic, art nouveau architecture. Original staircase with preserved window panels. Sound-proofed rooms;
corner rooms are larger. Fine example of art nouveau in Sarah Bernhardt restaurant.

Grand Hotel Bohemia ᷝ 🕮 ᷝ rm 🖅 ᷝ 뎠 ᷝ 🖅 ᷝ **VISA** 🕮 **AE** 🕕

Králodvorská 4 ✉ *110 00* – **Ⓜ** *Náměsti Republiky* – ✆ *234 608 111* – *office@
grandhotelbohemia.cz* – *Fax 222 329 5 45* – *www.grandhotelbohemia.cz*
78 rm ⌑ – 💲5870/7400 CZK 💲💲5870/7400 CZK   **H1**
Rest – Menu 600/1090 CZK – Carte 950/1630 CZK
◆ Traditional ◆ Classic ◆

Classic 1920s hotel, in an ideal location for tourists, with a splendid neo-Baroque
ballroom. Comfortable bedrooms are generously proportioned and service professional. Large, classic restaurant with a menu of Czech/international dishes.

CZECH REPUBLIC - PRAGUE

CZECH REPUBLIC - PRAGUE

Jalta 🏠🏠🏠 🛋 ⅚ 📠 ⅙ rm 📺 ⁽ᵞ⁾ 🏊 VISA ⓪ 🅰 ⓪

Václavské Nám. 45 ⊠ *110 00 –* ⓜ *Muzeum –* ℰ *222 822 111 – booking@*
hoteljalta.com – Fax 222 822 8 33 – www.hoteljalta.com   **H2**
89 rm ⌑ – ♦4500/6000 CZK ♦♦4500/6000 CZK – 5 suites
Rest *Hot* – Carte 555/995 CZK
 ◆ Traditional ◆ Stylish ◆

Hotel with classic 1950s façade overlooking Wenceslas Square, celebrating its 50th
anniversary this year. Spacious, modern, well equipped bedrooms with art deco
styling and furniture. Stylish modern restaurant offering steaks and pasta.

Mercure 🏠🏠🏠 🛋 ⅚ 📠 ⅙ rm 📺 ⁽ᵞ⁾ VISA ⓪ 🅰 ⓪

Na Poříčí 7 ⊠ *110 00 –* ⓜ *Náměstí Republiky –* ℰ *221 800 800 – h3440@*
accor.com – Fax 221 800 8 01 – www.accor.com   **H1**
173 rm – ♦4000/5000 CZK ♦♦4000/5000 CZK, ⌑ 415 CZK – 1 suite
Rest *Felice* – *(Closed Saturday and Sunday lunch)* Menu 375 CZK – Carte
approx. 500 CZK
 ◆ Business ◆ Functional ◆

Modern hotel behind ornate 19C façade: many original features remain. Kafka worked here for seven years when it was insurance offices. Ask for a more spacious
deluxe room. Restaurant named after one of Kafka's lovers: modern Parisian brasserie; pleasant terrace.

Imperial 🏠🏠🏠 ⅙₅ 🏊 ⅚ 📠 ⅙ 📺 ⁽ᵞ⁾ 🏊 ⟨⟩ VISA ⓪ 🅰 ⓪

Na Poříčí 15 ⊠ *110 00 –* ⓜ *Náměsti Republiky –* ℰ *246 011 600 – info@*
hotel-imperial.cz – Fax 246 011 6 70 – www.hotel-imperial.cz
– Closed 20-26 September   **H1**
126 rm – ♦7800/9100 CZK ♦♦8060/9360 CZK, ⌑ 520 CZK
Rest – Carte 530/890 CZK
 ◆ Business ◆ Retro ◆

Newly restored hotel, originally built in 1914, featuring fine ceramic mosaics in an
art deco style. Dark wood bedrooms combine retro styling with modern comforts.
Popular, open plan restaurant serving seasonal menu, with a remarkable backdrop
of colourfully tiled pillars and walls.

Pachtuv Palace without rest ⅏ ⟨ ⟩ ⅙₅ 📺 ⁽ᵞ⁾ VISA ⓪ 🅰 ⓪

Karolíny Světlé 34 ⊠ *110 00 –* ⓜ *Staroměstská –* ℰ *234 705 111 – reception@*
pachtuvpalace.com – Fax 234 705 1 12 – www.pachtuvpalace.com
20 rm – ♦7585/9870 CZK ♦♦8480/11565 CZK – **30 suites**   **G2**
– ♦♦15830/79666 CZK, ⌑ 643 CZK
 ◆ Traditional ◆ Cosy ◆

17C residence with commanding views over the city. Large and luxurious
bedrooms and suites blend antique furniture with modern accessories. Relaxing
courtyard terrace.

Josef without rest ⅏ ⅚ 📠 ⅙ 🏊 ⟨⟩ VISA ⓪ 🅰 ⓪

Rybná 20 ⊠ *110 00 –* ⓜ *Náměsti Republiky –* ℰ *221 700 111 – reservation@*
hoteljosef.com – Fax 221 700 9 99 – www.hoteljosef.com   **G1**
109 rm ⌑ – ♦3295/5030 CZK ♦♦3550/5030 CZK
 ◆ Townhouse ◆ Design ◆

Stylish boutique hotel with light glass lobby, bar and breakfast room. Design-led
bedrooms; deluxe rooms have ultra modern glass bathrooms.

Yasmin 🛋 ⅙₅ ⅏ ⅚ 📠 ⅙ 📺 ⁽ᵞ⁾ 🏊 ⟨⟩ VISA ⓪ 🅰 ⓪

Politických vězňu 12/913 ⊠ *110 00 –* ⓜ *Muzeum –* ℰ *234 100 111 – info@*
hotel-yasmin.cz – Fax 234 110 1 01 – www.hotel-yasmin.cz   **F2**
198 rm ⌑ – ♦5563/6693 CZK ♦♦5563/6693 CZK
Rest – ℰ 234 100 100 Menu 510 CZK – Carte 824/900 CZK
 ◆ Business ◆ Modern ◆

Modern and design-led centrally located hotel. Stylish lobby leads into winter garden and cool lounge. Modular bedrooms in soft shades of sage with black-tiled
bathrooms. Colourful and casual dining room with vast Asian menu specialising
in noodles.

CZECH REPUBLIC - PRAGUE

Maximilian without rest   🕭 🔟 🚿 🖼 ⁽¹⁾ 🕍 🚖 🚾 🚳 🔚 ①

Haštalská 14 ⊠ 110 00 – ⓜ Náměsti Republiky – ✆ 225 303 111
– reservations@maximilianhotel.com – Fax 225 303 1 10
– www.maximilianhotel.com **G1**
70 rm ⌧ – †2782/4440 CZK ††3040/4830 CZK – 1 suite
◆ Business ◆ Modern ◆

Converted apartment block in quiet area near St Agnes Convent. Designer boutique style prevails. Glass and steel breakfast room. Basement Thai massage spa. Contemporary rooms.

Ventana without rest   🔟 🖼 ⁽¹⁾ 🚾 🚳 🔚 ①

Celetná 7 ⊠ 110 00 – ⓜ Náměsti Republiky – info@
ventana-hotel.cz – Fax 221 776 6 03 – www.ventana-hotel.cz **G2**
24 rm ⌧ – †4340/6000 CZK ††5362/7532 CZK – 5 suites
◆ Traditional ◆ Classic ◆

Tranquil hotel near the Old Town market, featuring art deco style lobby. Spacious, well-equipped bedrooms in modern, muted hues; loft rooms on top floor have separate lounge.

K + K Central   🖐 🕉 🕭 🔟 🚿 rm 🖼 ⁽¹⁾ 🕍 🚖 🚾 🚳 🔚 ①

Hybernská 10 ⊠ 110 00 – ⓜ Náměsti Republiky – ✆ 225 022 000
– hotel.central@kkhotels.cz – Fax 225 022 1 41 – www.kkhotels.com/central
126 rm ⌧ – †7200 CZK ††7720 CZK – 1 suite **H2**
Rest – (in bar) Carte approx. 694 CZK
◆ Business ◆ Modern ◆

Beautifully restored hotel with elegant art nouveau façade; interior is blend of ultra modern and period décor. Glass and steel breakfast gallery in old theatre. Modish rooms. Light dishes in bar/restaurant.

The Icon   🔟 ⁽¹⁾ 🚾 🚳 🔚 ①

Vljame 6 ⊠ 110 00 – ⓜ Muzeum – ✆ 724 723 138 – info@iconhotel.eu
– Fax 221 634 1 05 – www.iconhotel.eu **G2**
29 rm ⌧ – †6150/6662 CZK ††6662 CZK – 2 suites   **Rest** – Carte 390/730 CZK
◆ Business ◆ Modern ◆

Centrally located hotel that's done away with convention: a colourful interior displays regularly changing artwork, staff choose their outfits and the bright, modern bedrooms have a hip feel. Formal bar area serves a large à la carte with daily specials.

The Iron Gate   🍴 🔟 🖼 ⁽¹⁾ 🚾 🚳 🔚 ①

Michalská 19 ⊠ 110 00 – ⓜ Staroměstská – ✆ 225 777 777 – hotel@
irongate.cz – Fax 225 777 7 78 – www.irongate.cz **G2**
13 rm – †6522 CZK ††6522 CZK – **30 suites** ⌧ – †10515/23958 CZK
Rest Železná vrata – Carte 605/1120 CZK
◆ Traditional ◆ Classic ◆

Hidden away in Old Town's cobbled street maze. 14C origins; attractive central courtyard. Large rooms with antique furniture or painted beams; some duplex suites. Khajuraho in basement for Indian cuisine.

Esplanade   🚿 🖼 🕍 🚾 🚳 🔚 ①

Washingtonova 1600-19 ⊠ 110 00 – ⓜ Muzeum – ✆ 224 501 111
– esplanade@esplanade.cz – Fax 224 229 3 06 – www.esplanade.cz
74 rm ⌧ – †3572/5890 CZK ††4060/5890 CZK **H2**
Rest – Menu 643 CZK – Carte 667/1132 CZK
◆ Traditional ◆ Classic ◆

Charming and atmospheric; this art nouveau building is something of an architectural gem. Original features abound; bedrooms enjoy style and a timeless elegance. International menu offered in friendly surroundings.

K + K Fenix

Ve Smečkách 30 ✉ *110 00* – Ⓜ *Muzeum* – ✆ *225 012 000* – *hotel.fenix@ kkhotels.cz* – *Fax 222 012 9 99* – *www.kkhotels.com* **H2**
128 rm ⌷ – 🛏6946 CZK 🛏🛏7405 CZK **Rest** – *(in bar)* Menu 643 CZK
♦ Business ♦ Modern ♦
Located off Wenceslas Square; up to date interior behind a classic façade. Bedrooms vary in size and shape but all are smart, clean and comfortable. Simple bathrooms. Light dishes in lounge bar.

Bellagio

U Milosrdných 2 ✉ *110 00* – Ⓜ *Staroměstská* – ✆ *221 778 999* – *info@ bellagiohotel.cz* – *Fax 221 778 9 00* – *www.bellagiohotel.cz* **G1**
46 rm – 🛏4607/6409 CZK 🛏🛏5121/6821 CZK, ⌷ 360 CZK – 1 suite
Rest *Isabella* – Carte 675/1225 CZK
♦ Business ♦ Stylish ♦
Quiet, converted apartment block near the river. Basement vaulted bar/breakfast room. Airy, attractive bedrooms, well equipped in warm colours. Impressive bathrooms. Restaurant is Mediterranean style.

987 without rest

Senovážné 15 ✉ *110 00* – Ⓜ *Náměsti Republiky* – ✆ *255 737 200*
– *reservations@987praguehotel.com* – *Fax 222 210 3 69*
– *www.987praguehotel.com* **H2**
80 rm – 🛏3090/6200 CZK 🛏🛏3090/6200 CZK – 3 suites
♦ Traditional ♦ Modern ♦
Well located, value-for-money hotel with cosy atmosphere and well-equipped, comfortable bedrooms, featuring modern design and furnishings. Colourful ground floor breakfast room.

Allegro – at Four Seasons Hotel

Veleslavínova 1098/2a ✉ *110 00* – Ⓜ *Staroměstská* – ✆ *221 426 880*
– *Fax 221 426 0 00* – *www.fourseasons.com/prague* **G2**
Rest – Menu 1380 CZK (lunch) – Carte 2090/3220 CZK
Spec. Scallops and langoustines with apple tapioca and oyster soup. Duo of venison with quince and smoked chestnut purée. Autumn fruits in pomegranate syrup with torrone parfait.
♦ Italian ♦ Formal ♦
Elegant, luxurious restaurant overlooking river. Talented Italian chef creates innovative, harmoniously-balanced Italian dishes using prime quality ingredients; popular set menus include selected wines by the glass.

Alcron – at Radisson SAS Alcron Hotel

Štěpánská 40 ✉ *110 00* – Ⓜ *Muzeum* – ✆ *222 820 038* – *sales.prague@ radissonsas.com* – *Fax 222 820 1 00* – *www.prague.radissonsas.com*
– *Closed Sunday* **H2**
Rest – *(booking essential) (dinner only)* Carte 700/800 CZK
♦ Seafood ♦ Design ♦
An Art Deco mural after de Lempicka dominates this intimate, semi-circular restaurant. Creative and classic seafood served by friendly, professional staff.

Flambée

Husova 5 ✉ *110 00* – Ⓜ *Můstek* – ✆ *224 248 512* – *flambee@flambee.cz*
– *Fax 224 248 5 13* – *www.flambee.cz* **G2**
Rest – Carte 1100/1760 CZK
Rest *Cafe Bistro 'F'* – ✆ *224 401 236* – Menu 255/615 CZK – Carte 225/475 CZK
♦ Traditional ♦ Formal ♦
Elegant fine dining in established cellar restaurant dating from 11C. Well-judged classics prepared using quality produce; flambéed food a speciality. Formal yet friendly service. Cafe Bistro 'F' - above the restaurant - is a little modern eatery serving simpler international dishes.

XXX
ε3 **Maze by Gordon Ramsay** – at Hilton Old Town   AC 4/ ✧

V Celnici 7 ✉ *111 21* – Ⓜ *Náměsti Republiky*   VISA ⓒ AE ①
– ℰ 221 822 303 – mazeprague@gordonramsay.com – Fax 221 325 6 46
– www.gordonramsay.com   **H1**
Rest – Menu 650 CZK (lunch) – Carte 1250/1500 CZK
Spec. Beetroot with Sairass cheese, pine nuts and Cabernet Sauvignon dressing. Halibut with lobster risotto, mussels and parsley butter. Chocolate and orange fondant with beurre noisette ice cream.
◆ French ◆ Brasserie ◆
Set rather unusually in the rear of a hotel and modelled on Gordon Ramsay's London outlet, this elegant restaurant boasts art deco styling and precise, confident, classical cooking.

XX **Bellevue**   ≤ ☆ AC VISA ⓒ AE

Smetanovo Nábřeží 18 ✉ *110 00* – Ⓜ *Staroměstská* – ℰ *222 221 443*
– bellevue@zatisigroup.cz – Fax 222 220 4 53 – www.zatisigroup.cz
– Closed 24 December   **G2**
Rest – Carte 1180/1570 CZK
◆ Traditional ◆ Formal ◆
Refurbished restaurant in elegant 19C building, affording views of river and royal palace. Contemporary styling in pastel shades; dine on international cuisine as the nightly piano plays.

XX **La Degustation Bohême Bourgeoise**   ☆ AC 4/ VISA ⓒ AE ①

Haštalská 18 ✉ *110 00* – Ⓜ *Náměsti Republiky* – ℰ *222 311 234 – boheme@ambi.cz – Fax 222 311 2 35 – www.ladegustation.cz*
– Closed 24 December, Sunday, Monday and Friday-Saturday lunch
Rest – Menu 690/2650 CZK ⅜   **G1**
◆ Modern ◆ Intimate ◆
Modern L-shaped restaurant with dark wood interior and intimate atmosphere. Talented kitchen produces innovative, flavourful cooking; regularly changing menus include 3 tasting menus which reflect the best produce available.

XX **Le Terroir**   ☆ AC VISA ⓒ AE ①
☺
Vejvodova 1 ✉ *110 00* – Ⓜ *Můstek* – ℰ *222 220 260 – rezervace@leterroir.cz*
– Fax 222 220 2 60 – www.leterroir.cz
– Closed Sunday and Monday   **G2**
Rest – Menu 490/1090 CZK – Carte 1110/1340 CZK ⅜
◆ Innovative ◆ Rustic ◆
Cobbled courtyard and steps descending past wine store to atmospheric vaulted 10C cellar. Personally run; superb wine list. Good value, accomplished, Pan-European cooking.

XX **La Veranda**   AC VISA ⓒ AE ①

Elišky Krásnohorské 2 ✉ *110 00* – Ⓜ *Staroměstská* – ℰ *224 814 733 – office@laveranda.cz – Fax 224 814 5 96 – www.laveranda.cz*   **G1**
Rest – Carte 785/1010 CZK
◆ Innovative ◆ Design ◆
Charming restaurant in the old Jewish district; with stylish, contemporary décor in the sunny colours of the Mediterranean. Well-prepared, flavoursome modern cooking.

XX **Le Cornichon**   VISA ⓒ
☺
Betlemska 9 ✉ *110 00* – Ⓜ *Mustek* – ℰ *222 211 766 – info@cornichon.cz*
– www.cornichon.cz   **G2**
Rest – *(closed Sunday and Monday) (booking advisable) (dinner only)*
Carte 592/863 CZK
◆ French ◆ Friendly ◆
Charming, personally run city centre restaurant with modern bistro-style décor. As the name implies, it has a French owner, French chef and specialises in well-judged, classical French cooking.

CZECH REPUBLIC - PRAGUE

XX **V Zátiši**   [AC] [↤] [VISA] [●●] [AE] [●]

Liliová 1, Betlémské Nám. ⊠ *110 00 –* ⓜ *Můstek –* ℰ *222 221 155 – vzatisi@
zatisigroup.cz – Fax 222 220 6 29 – www.zatisigroup.cz
– Closed 24 December*   **G2**
Rest *– (booking essential at dinner)* Menu 850/990 CZK – Carte 985/1335 CZK
♦ Modern ♦ Cosy ♦

Well run, slick and dependable restaurant offering modern, well-priced cuisine within a range of four rooms which are intimate in places, and more stylish in others. Traditional Czech dishes; Asian influences.

XX **Mlýnec**   [↜] [🏠] [VISA] [●●] [AE] [●]

Novotného Lávka 9 ⊠ *110 00 –* ⓜ *Staroměstská –* ℰ *221 082 208 – mlynec@
zatisigroup.cz – Fax 221 082 3 91 – www.zatisigroup.cz
– Closed 24 December*   **G2**
Rest – Menu 790/990 CZK – Carte 920/1420 CZK
♦ Contemporary ♦ Retro ♦

Spacious and contemporary; popular with tourists because of setting. Modern dishes combined with Czech classics. Terrace views of Charles Bridge on fine summer evenings.

XX **Rybí trh**   [🏠] [AC] [VISA] [●●] [AE] [●]

Týnský dvůr 5 ⊠ *110 00 –* ⓜ *Námĕsti Republiky –* ℰ *224 895 447 – info@
rybitrh.cz – Fax 224 895 4 49 – www.rybitrh.cz*   **G1**
Rest – Menu 690/1890 CZK – Carte 720/2060 CZK
♦ Seafood ♦ Friendly ♦

Modern restaurant which lives up to its name - Fish Market - with fresh seafood on crushed ice before open-plan kitchen; fish tanks and adjacent wine shop. Creative, contemporary cooking.

XX **Angel**   [AC] [VISA] [●●] [AE] [●]

V Kolkovne 7 ⊠ *110 00 –* ⓜ *Starometsska –* ℰ *773 222 422 – info@
angelrestaurant.cz – www.angelrestaurant.cz
– closed Christmas and Sunday dinner*   **G1**
Rest – Menu 450 CZK (lunch) – Carte 670/970 CZK
♦ Asian ♦ Design ♦

Spacious restaurant close to the smart shopping streets, with smart gold décor, coral-like lighting and an understated Asian feel. Precise cooking uses simple techniques to create clean flavours.

X **Aromi**   [🏠] [↤] [VISA] [●●] [AE] [●]
☺

Mánesova 78/1442 ⊠ *120 00 –* ⓜ *Jiřiho z Poděbrad –* ℰ *222 713 222 – info@
aromi.cz – Fax 222 713 4 44 – www.aromi.cz
– Closed Christmas*   **C2**
Rest *– (booking essential at dinner)* Menu 145 CZK (lunch) – Carte 575/
1075 CZK 🍷
♦ Italian ♦ Rustic ♦

Buzzy neighbourhood restaurant boasts spacious, rustic interior with big, chunky wood tables and open kitchen. Great value, authentic Italian dishes and quality wine list.

X **Brasserie M**   [🏠] [AC] [VISA] [●●] [AE] [●]

Vladislavova 17 ⊠ *110 00 –* ⓜ *Národni Třída –* ℰ *224 054 070 – info@
brasseriem.cz – Fax 224 054 4 40 – www.brasseriem.cz
– Closed Christmas and Sunday*   **G2**
Rest – Menu 195 CZK (lunch) – Carte 445/1185 CZK 🍷
♦ French ♦ Bistro ♦

Central but away from touristy main streets. Big, high-ceilinged room with dominant open-plan kitchen and French accent to décor. Well-priced Gallic favourites on menu too.

La Provence   [AC] ⅓ [VISA] ⁐ [AE] ①

Štupartská 9 ⊠ *110 00 Praha –* ❻ *Náměsti Republiky –* ☏ *296 826 155*
– kontakt@laprovence.cz – Fax 224 819 5 70 – www.kampagroup.com
Rest – Carte 735/1325 CZK   **G1**
◆ French ◆ Brasserie ◆

Ground floor is in classic French brasserie style with etched mirrors, tile mosaics and Gallic scenes. More intimate basement room with Mediterranean feel and menu to match.

Kolkovna   ⌂ [AC] ⅓ [VISA] ⁐ [AE] ①

V Kolkovně 8 ⊠ *110 00 –* ❻ *Staroměstská –* ☏ *224 819 701 – info@kolkovna.cz – Fax 224 819 7 00 – www.kolkovna.cz*   **G1**
Rest – Menu 250/400 CZK – Carte 279/655 CZK
◆ Traditional ◆ Inn ◆

Atmospheric Czech Pilsner Urquell bar/restaurant: old pictures, tools and advertisements line green walls under vaulted ceilings. Huge traditional dishes and excellent beers.

ON THE LEFT BANK   *Plan II*

Mandarin Oriental   ▮ゟ ❀ 氐 [AC] ⅓ rm ▥ ☏ ⅗ ⇌ [VISA] ⁐ [AE] ①

Nebovidská 459/1 ⊠ *118 00 –* ❻ *Malostranská –* ☏ *233 088 888*
– moprg-reservations@mohg.com – Fax 233 088 6 68
– www.mandarinoriental.com   **F2**
77 rm – ♛6400/9732 CZK ♛♛6907/10245 CZK, ⌑ 515 CZK – 22 suites
Rest *Essensia* – Menu 745 CZK (lunch) – Carte 1053/1593 CZK
◆ Luxury ◆ Stylish ◆

Housed within a 14C monastery, the hotel opened in 2006 and is more boutique in style than most in this group. Spa within the former chapel. Luxurious and sleek bedrooms. Vaulted, chic dining room with contemporary lighting; menu a blend of European and Asian.

Aria   ⌂ ▮ゟ 氐 [AC] ⅓ rm ▥ ♚ ⅗ [P] ⇌ [VISA] ⁐ [AE] ①

Tržiště 9 ⊠ *118 00 –* ❻ *Malostranská –* ☏ *225 334 111 – stay@aria.cz*
– Fax 225 334 6 66 – www.aria.cz   **F2**
43 rm ⌑ – ♛5612/7915 CZK ♛♛5612/7915 CZK – 9 suites
Rest *Coda* – Menu 590 CZK (lunch) – Carte 1100/1640 CZK
◆ Luxury ◆ Design ◆

Stylishly overlooking lovely castle gardens; boasts strong music orientation, including library and rooms themed individually to different music genres. Personable service. Choose from the international menu in intimate Coda or eat on the stunning summer rooftop terrace.

Alchymist Grand H. and Spa   ⌂ ▮ゟ ❀ ⫸ [AC] ⅓ rm ♚ ⅗

Tržíště 19 ⊠ *118 00 –* ❻ *Malostranská*
– ☏ 257 286 011 – info@alchymisthotel.com – Fax 257 286 0 17   [VISA] ⁐ [AE] ①
– www.alchymisthotel.com   **F2**
37 rm ⌑ – ♛7717/8575 CZK ♛♛7717/8575 CZK – 9 suites
Rest *Aquarius* – Menu 1000 CZK – Carte 1000/2000 CZK
◆ Luxury ◆ Classic ◆

Four 15C Renaissance and Baroque houses on UNESCO street, sympathetically restored and offering sumptuous style. Beautiful spa; enchanting rooms with 16C-19C artefacts. Formal restaurant and café opening onto a courtyard; contemporary cuisine.

Savoy   ▮ゟ ⫸ 氐 [AC] ⅓ rm ▥ ☏ ⅗ ⇌ [VISA] ⁐ [AE] ①

Keplerova 11 ⊠ *118 00 –* ☏ *224 302 430 – info@savoyhotel.cz*
– Fax 224 302 1 28 – www.savoyhotel.cz   **E2**
55 rm ⌑ – ♛8678 CZK ♛♛8678 CZK – 6 suites
Rest *Hradčany* – Menu 663 CZK (lunch) – Carte 929/1623 CZK
◆ Luxury ◆ Classic ◆

Timeless charm; popular with statesmen. Strength lies in its classically styled bedrooms, which are spacious, tasteful, well equipped and benefit from high levels of service. Bright formal dining room with glass ceiling and distant city view.

CZECH REPUBLIC - PRAGUE

Crowne Plaza Prague Castle
ᕫ 🅰🅲 ↳ rest 🆂🅰 🅿 ♨

Strahovská 128 ⊠ *118 00* – ✆ *226 080 000*   🆅🅸🆂🅰 ◑ 🅰🅴 ◍
– *reservations@cpcastle.com* – *Fax 226 080 2 00* – *www.cpcastle.com*
135 rm – 🛏4700/5500 CZK 🛏🛏4700/5500 CZK, ⬭ 520 CZK – 3 sui-   **E2**
tes
Rest – Carte 805/1240 CZK
♦ Business ♦ Historic ♦

Comfortable hotel in unique location next to the castle, within the site of the Stra-
hov Monastery. Bedrooms in the old building, which dates from the 16C, are the
more spacious. International dishes served in restaurant.

Andel's
🛗 🕉 ᕫ 🅰🅲 ↳ rm 🆂🅰 🅿 ♨ 🌁 🆅🅸🆂🅰 ◑ 🅰🅴 ◍

Stroupeznického 21 ⊠ *150 00* – Ⓜ *Anděl* – ✆ *296 889 688* – *info@*
andelshotel.com – *Fax 296 889 9 99* – *www.andelshotel.com*   **F3**
257 rm ⬭ – 🛏6256/7575 CZK 🛏🛏6813 CZK – 33 suites
Rest *Oscar's* – Carte 591/951 CZK
Rest *Nagoya* – ✆ *251 511 724 (closed Christmas-New Year and Sunday)*
Menu 500 CZK – Carte 500/1500 CZK
♦ Business ♦ Modern ♦

Stylish modern hotel with distinctively minimalist appeal; luxurious apartments in
adjacent block. Conference and fitness centres. Well-equipped rooms with all mod
cons. Informal dining in Oscar's brasserie; simple international menu. Nagoya offers
traditional Japanese dishes.

Hoffmeister
🌁 ᕫ 🅰🅲 ↳ rm 🆂🅰 🅿 ♨ 🌁 🆅🅸🆂🅰 ◑ 🅰🅴 ◍

Pod Bruskou 7 ⊠ *118 00* – Ⓜ *Malostranská* – ✆ *251 017 111* – *hotel@*
hoffmeister.cz – *Fax 251 017 1 20* – *www.hoffmeister.cz*   **F1**
43 rm – 🛏5407/6179 CZK 🛏🛏6437/7467 CZK, ⬭ 386 CZK – 5 suites
Rest *Ada* – Carte 977/1363 CZK
♦ Traditional ♦ Classic ♦

Unprepossessing façade but inside full of artworks by Adolf Hoffmeister; son owns
hotel. Eclectic range of classically decorated bedrooms plus 15C steam room. Elegant restaurant with original Adolf Hoffmeister cartoons. Attentive service; classical
French cooking.

Riverside *without rest*
← 🅰🅲 ↳ 🆂🅰 🅿 🆅🅸🆂🅰 ◑ 🅰🅴 ◍

Janáčkovo Nábřeži 15 ⊠ *150 00* – Ⓜ *Anděl* – ✆ *225 994 611* – *info@*
riversideprague.com – *Fax 225 994 6 12* – *www.riversideprague.com*
42 rm – 🛏7532 CZK 🛏🛏7532 CZK, ⬭ 383 CZK – 3 suites   **F3**
♦ Business ♦ Modern ♦

An early 20C riverside façade conceals relaxing modern hotel with castle view. Efficient service. Very well-appointed bedrooms with luxurious bathrooms; many with
views.

U Zlaté Studně 🕉
← 🅰🅲 🆂🅰 🅿 🆅🅸🆂🅰 ◑ 🅰🅴 ◍

U Zlaté Studně 166/4 ⊠ *118 00* – Ⓜ *Malostranská* – ✆ *257 011 213* – *hotel@*
goldenwell.cz – *Fax 257 533 3 20* – *www.goldenwell.cz*   **F1**
17 rm – 🛏5790 CZK 🛏🛏7695 CZK – 2 suites
Rest Terasa U Zlaté Studně – *see below*
♦ Historic ♦ Classic ♦

16C Renaissance building in quiet spot between the castle and Ladeburg Gardens.
Inviting bedrooms - most boasting city views - are richly furnished but uncluttered.

At The Three Storks
🅰🅲 ↳ 🆂🅰 🅿 ♨ 🆅🅸🆂🅰 ◑ 🅰🅴 ◍

Tomášská 20 ⊠ *118 00* – Ⓜ *Malostranská* – ✆ *257 210 779* – *utricapu@ok.cz*
– *Fax 257 212 9 67* – *www.utricapu.cz*   **F1**
20 rm ⬭ – 🛏3577/6406 CZK 🛏🛏3831/8336 CZK
Rest – Menu 300/500 CZK – Carte 530/700 CZK
♦ Townhouse ♦ Modern ♦

Renovated 17C house with white 19C façade. Modern lobby bar and panoramic
lift. Choice between superior and deluxe bedrooms; the latter are more spacious;
all have luxury bathrooms. Modern restaurant with clean, bright interior, serving
international and Czech dishes.

CZECH REPUBLIC - PRAGUE

Residence Nosticova 🛁   🎦 🛜 **P** VISA ⓒ AE ①

Nosticova 1, Malá Strana ⊠ 118 00 – Ⓜ Malostranská – ℰ 257 312 513
– info@nosticova.com – Fax 257 312 5 17 – www.nosticova.com **F2**
7 rm ☲ – †4470/4980 CZK ††5230/7020 CZK – 4 suites
Rest *Alchymist* – ℰ 257 312 518 (closed Monday) Carte 945/1250 CZK
♦ Townhouse ♦ Classic ♦

Tastefully refurbished 17C town house in a quiet, cobbled side street near the river. Stylish suites - all with their own kitchen - combine modern and antique furnishings and works of art. French cuisine served in flamboyantly-styled restaurant.

Angelo without rest   ঌ 🗚 ⅃⁄ 🎦 ⁽ᵎ⁾ 🖫 🛌 VISA ⓒ AE ①

Radlicka 1g ⊠ 150 00 – Ⓜ Anděl – ℰ 234 801 111 – info@angelohotel.com
– Fax 234 809 9 99 – www.angelohotel.com **F3**
168 rm ☲ – †6294 CZK ††6809 CZK
♦ Business ♦ Modern ♦

Behind its sister hotel, Andel's, this is a colourfully decorated and relaxed hotel. Spacious bedrooms, with showers and large beds; Executive rooms on the top two floors.

U Raka without rest 🛁   🚘 🗚 🎦 ⁽ᵎ⁾ **P** VISA ⓒ AE

Černínská 10 ⊠ 118 00 – ℰ 220 511 100 – info@romantikhotel-uraka.cz
– Fax 233 358 0 41 – www.romantikhotel-uraka.cz **E1**
6 rm ☲ – †2250/2625 CZK ††3625/6000 CZK
♦ Family ♦ Cosy ♦

Tucked away, two timbered cottages in a rustic Czech style creating a charming little hotel. Cosy, comfy and inviting. Clean-lined rooms in warm brick and wood. Friendly welcome.

U Krále Karla without rest   🎦 ⁽ᵎ⁾ VISA ⓒ AE ①

Úvoz 4 ⊠ 118 00 – ℰ 257 531 211 – ukrale@iol.cz – Fax 257 533 5 91
– www.romantichotels.cz **E2**
19 rm ☲ – †2500/3500 CZK ††3000/4000 CZK
♦ Historic ♦ Classic ♦

Below the castle: rebuilt in 1639 into a Baroque house; the style of furniture endures. Bags of character: every bedroom features stained glass and a stencilled wood ceiling.

Neruda   🚘 🗚 ⅃⁄ 🎦 ⁽ᵎ⁾ 🛌 VISA ⓒ AE ①

Nerudova 44 ⊠ 118 00 – ℰ 257 535 557 – info@hotelneruda.cz
– Fax 257 531 4 92 – www.hotelneruda.eu **E2**
42 rm ☲ – †2170/3192 CZK ††2298/3574 CZK   **Rest** – Carte 613/766 CZK
♦ Townhouse ♦ Modern ♦

Castle dominates views from rooftop terrace. Modern style complements 14C ceiling and architecture; poet Neruda's quotes decorate walls. Spacious, well soundproofed rooms. Simple but attractive café/restaurant offering popular dishes.

Constans without rest   🗚 ⅃⁄ 🎦 🛌 🛌 VISA ⓒ AE ①

Břetislavova 309 ⊠ 110 00 – Ⓜ Malostranská – ℰ 234 091 818 – hotel@
hotelconstans.cz – Fax 234 091 8 60 – www.hotelconstans.cz **F2**
31 rm – †3062/6125 CZK ††3318/6125 CZK, ☲ 275 CZK
♦ Townhouse ♦ Classic ♦

Three converted townhouses transformed by recent renovation, situated in quiet street. Very spacious bedrooms with period furniture and well equipped, marble bathrooms.

Kampa Park   ≤ 🛌 VISA ⓒ AE ①

Na Kampě 8b, Malá Strana ⊠ 118 00 – Ⓜ Malostranská – ℰ 296 826 102
– kontakt@kampapark.com – Fax 257 533 2 23 – www.kampagroup.com
Rest – (booking essential at dinner) Carte 1185/1755 CZK **F2**
♦ Modern ♦ Fashionable ♦

Celebrity heavy; stunningly located at water's edge by Charles Bridge. Capacious, contemporary interior; heated terraces: good view likely. Modern global menus.

CZECH REPUBLIC - PRAGUE

XX **Terasa U Zlaté Studně** – at U Zlaté Studně Hotel ≤ 😤 AC

U Zlaté Studně 4 ⊠ 118 00 – **Ⓜ** *Malostranská* VISA ⓪③ AE ⑩
– ℰ 257 533 322 – restaurant@goldenwell.cz – Fax 257 535 0 40
– www.terasauzlatestudne.cz **F1**
Rest – Carte 1405/2350 CZK
♦ Modern ♦ Design ♦

Beautiful skyline views from a clean-lined top-floor restaurant and terrace, reached
by its own lift. Affable staff; full-flavoured modern dishes.

XX **U Patrona** � VISA ⓪③ AE ⑩

Dražického Nám. 4 ⊠ 118 00 – **Ⓜ** *Malostranská – ℰ 257 530 725*
– upatrona@upatrona.cz – Fax 257 530 7 23 – www.upatrona.cz **F2**
Rest – Carte 800/950 CZK
♦ Traditional ♦ Cosy ♦

Charming period house near Charles Bridge. Elegant ground floor restaurant or larger upstairs room with window into kitchen. French-influenced classics and Czech
specialities.

🛏 **Olympia** AC VISA ⓪③ AE ⑩

Vítězná 7 ⊠ 110 00 – **Ⓜ** *Národni Třída – ℰ 251 511 080 – info@*
olympia-restaurant.cz – Fax 251 511 0 79 – www.olympia-restaurant.cz
Rest – Carte 350/605 CZK **F2**
♦ Traditional ♦ Inn ♦

The menu of Czech specialities is a carnivore's delight, with generous portions and
assured flavours. A relaxed and easy-going pub atmosphere pervades this converted bank.

DENMARK
DANMARK

PROFILE

→ **Area:**
43 069 km² (16 629 sq mi) excluding the Faroe Islands and Greenland.

→ **Population:**
5 432 000 inhabitants (est. 2005), density = 126 per km².

→ **Capital:**
Copenhagen (conurbation 1 426 000 inhabitants).

→ **Currency:**
Danish Krone (DKK) divided into 100 øre; rate of exchange: DKK 1 = € 0.13 = US$ 0.17 (Dec. 2008).

→ **Government:**
Constitutional parliamentary (single chamber) monarchy (since 1849). Member of European Union since 1973.

→ **Languages:**
Danish; many Danes also understand and speak English.

→ **Specific public holidays:**
Maundy Thursday (the day before Good Friday); Good Friday (Friday before Easter); Prayer Day (4th Friday after Easter); Constitution Day (5 June); Boxing Day (26 December).

→ **Local time:**
GMT + 1 hour in winter and GMT + 2 hours in summer.

→ **Climate:**
Temperate northern maritime with cold winters and mild summers Copenhagen: January: 1°C, July: 18°C).

→ **International dialling code:**
00 45 followed by full local number. Directory Enquiries: ☏ 118; International Directory Enquiries: ☏ 113.

→ **Emergency:**
Dial ☏ 112 for Police, Ambulance and Fire Brigade.

→ **Electricity:**
220 volts AC, 50Hz; 2-pin round-shaped continental plugs.

→ **Formalities**
Travellers from the European Union (EU), Switzerland, Norway, Iceland and

the main countries of North and South America need a national identity card or passport (America: passport required) to visit Denmark for less than three months (tourism or business purpose). For visitors from other countries a visa may be required, in addition to a passport, especially for those wishing to stay for longer than three months. If you plan to visit Greenland or Faroe Islands while in Denmark, you must purchase a visa in advance in your own country. We advise you to check with your embassy before travelling.

COPENHAGEN
KØBENHAVN

Population: 514 000 (conurbation 1 426 000) Altitude: approx 13m above sea level

Mauritius/PHOTONONSTOP

You have to go right over to the far eastern coast of Denmark to find Copenhagen. It stares straight across the Öresund Straight at Sweden, as though anxious to leave its own shores. They've even built a bridge connecting it to Malmö on the other side. But once you've idled away some time in the Danish capital, you'll wonder why anyone might ever want to leave. This bright, sleek city has a nicely digestible, compact feel and is an easy place to discover on foot. It's a laid-back, hassle-free city generally free from threatening behaviour, and there are lots of elegant, smartly designed buildings to look at. The people fall pretty much into that category, too.

Though Denmark is one of the richest countries in the world, the citizens of Copenhagen are not given to brashness; if anything, they get embarrassed by what they call their provincialism, at being way out on the margins of Europe. But at the same time, they have an infectious enthusiasm for the arts and a world-renowned appreciation of design. Ingest this alongside a good cup of coffee, an open fire and sleek, cosy surroundings, and you'll be partaking of Danish hygge, a word much prized by locals loosely translated as 'warm conviviality'. To the list can now be added good food: fresh regional ingredients have revolutionized the menus of Copenhagen's hip restaurants.

LIVING THE CITY

Some cities overwhelm you, and give the impression that there's too much of them to take in. Not Copenhagen. Most of its key sights are neatly compressed within its central **Slotsholmen** 'island', an area that enjoyed its first golden age in the early seventeenth century in the reign of Christian IV, when it became a harbour of great consequence. It has canals on three sides and opposite the harbour is the area of **Christianshavn**, home of the legendary freewheeling 'free-town' community of Christiania. Further up from the centre are **Nyhavn**, the much-photographed canalside with brightly coloured buildings where the sightseeing cruises leave from, and the elegant **Frederiksstaden**, whose wide streets contain palaces and museums. West of centre is where Copenhageners love to hang out: the **Tivoli Gardens**, a kind of magical fairyland. Slightly more down-to-earth are the western suburbs of Vesterbro and Nørrebro, which were run-down areas given a street credible spit and polish for the 21st century.

PRACTICAL INFORMATION

ARRIVAL-DEPARTURE

Copenhagen Airport is located in Kastrup, 9km southeast of the city. The new extension to the metro allows you to now travel to the centre in 15min. A taxi, meanwhile, will cost about Kr200 and take 25min.

TRANSPORT

If you wish to dart about the city by rail, the metro – opened only in 2002 – is a triumph of sleek, smooth, beautifully detailed efficiency.

Want to see as much of Copenhagen as possible without continually digging into your pocket for cash? Get a Copenhagen Card, which gives free entry to all museums and galleries, as well as free bus, train and metro travel. Get one from the main tourist office just across the road from the central railway station.

It's not every day you're offered a free city bike ride but brightly painted bicycles, lined up in racks, are available for the deposit of a Dkr20 coin. The coin releases a cycle from a stand for an unlimited period and is retrieved when the cycle is returned to any of the 150 stands in the city. It takes about two hours to circumnavigate the major attractions.

It's possible to see the city...by kayak. Kajak Ole (that's Ole's Kayaks) can get you paddling round the central harbour area for a very different perspective. No previous experience is necessary, and it beats taking a crowded bus.

The medieval centre of Copenhagen is a walker's paradise, compounded by the fact that the longest shopping street in Europe, **Strøget**, is these days pedestrianised. (It's actually a collective name for five streets running from east to west, in case you're looking for Strøget on a map). Some of the world's top retail names are squashed into its eastern end, while for half a mile further west run fountains, churches, squares and cafés (and a wealth of shops, of course). The cluster of grand brand names gives a clue to Copenhagen's love affair with design and style. Turn any corner in the central area and you'll find an elegant 17C building rubbing shoulders with a sleek example from the modern age.

The city's royal history stretches back for a millennium, and the rich architectural legacy is seen in its castles, museums and palaces. These merge so well with the new buildings around them that you might well think they were made for each other. The city presents a user-friendly modern ambience with its extensive waterfronts, quirky little shops and hundreds of cafés, but it also boasts world class art collections, museums, and impressive parks, gardens and lakes, all of which bear the mark of an earlier time. A design footprint of impeccable taste remains a pedestrian's constant companion. Even the airport has smart wooden floors and a clean, fresh charm about it.

➜ DESIGNED TO PLEASE

The place to go to find out what's causing the latest aesthetic stir is the **Danish Design Centre** just south of Tivoli on the splendidly named Hans Christian Andersens Boulevard. It's a beautiful, five-storey, smoked-glass building opened in 2000 that houses temporary exhibitions and interactive installations. And it's right opposite one of Copenhagen's crown jewels, the nineteenth century **Ny Carlsberg**

Glyptotek, which contains a superb art collection including world-renowned French Impressionist paintings housed in a graceful modern extension. To complete a stylish trio, all within the space of half a mile, head to the waterfront to take in the **Black Diamond**, a dramatic name for a radical building. Not yet a decade old, it's the extension to the old Royal Library, and the clash of styles is breathtaking. So is the Black Diamond's reflective surface (made up of glass, silk concrete, sandstone, maple and granite) which changes colour moment by moment as it ripples against the water and sky.

The most recent of the modernist eye-catchers to turn heads is over the canal on Dock Island: the colossal **Opera House** was opened in 2005 and its knife-edge roof abuts the water, leaning across towards the rococo royal palaces on the other side (a fact that horrified some locals at the time). It's nine floors high, on a scale with the Met in New York, and is seen as a kind of gargantuan twin of The Black Diamond. Until recently, Copenhagen was an almost exclusively low-rise city, but these two big, bold intruders have certainly stirred up the cool, calm Danish waters.

➜ TIVOLI OR NOT TIVOLI...

For a more traditional experience, it's hard to beat the **National Gallery** (in a lovely park setting in the northern area of Rosenborg), with its superb collection of Matisse paintings, or the National Museum in the heart of town. This imposing centerpiece is housed in a gorgeous one-time royal palace, and boasts some of the finest rooms in the city. It also lays claim to the most extensive collection of Danish artefacts in the world. Star turn must be the 3,500 year-old Sun Chariot unearthed by a Sjaelland farmer in 1902; it's exquisite to look at, still bearing some of its gold leaf. Walk a few blocks down from here and you come to that city icon so traditional that it would make even the Sun Chariot feel like a new cart on the block: the **Tivoli Gardens** seem to have been around forever (they actually opened in 1843) and, judging by admission figures, it seems the whole of Scandinavia has been taken for a ride here. There are roller-coasters, open air shows, troubadours, jugglers, orchestras, parades, ice-cream and beer stands. At night Tivoli turns into a fairyland with over 100,000 lights illuminating the sky as the Demon rollercoaster whirls through the air and fireworks crackle heavenwards. The whole smorgasbord of innocent delights might not be to everyone's taste, considering the refined air of the rest of Copenhagen, but in the end even the biggest cynic is usually won over by the relentlessly magical atmosphere. And if you really can't stand all the showground stuff, you can at least admire the lovely lake, gushing fountains and eye-catching flowerbeds.

→ THE ROYAL FAMILIARITY

It might seem strange to visitors that egalitarian Denmark stands fast behind a monarchy, but the Danes love their populist, chain-smoking Queen Margrethe II, and tourists love to visit where she lives, **Amalienborg Palace,** in the posh Frederiksstaden part of town. Its four palaces stand around a rather grand cobbled square, and when Margrethe is in, a flag flies from the roof. There's a rumour that if they

sing loud enough from the new Opera House opposite, the production can be enjoyed from the royal apartments. At the diametrically opposite end of the tourist radar scan, but no less a tourist attraction, is the free state of **Christiania**, an eastern section of Christianshavn that until 1971 was a military camp. When it was abandoned, hundreds of hippies moved in and attracted hundreds more from around Denmark. Their concepts of recycling, solar and wind power have over time become mainstream, and the government has allowed the 'free state' to continue as a social experiment. With three quarters of a million tourists coming to visit a year, an odd 'human zoo' ambience can prevail.

These days, the edgier parts of town are to the west – **Vesterbro** and **Nørrebro.** They offer a couple of interesting alternatives to the city centre for those wanting a taste of how Copenhageners live. Vesterbro was a rough quarter sprawling from the Central station, but regeneration has given it a creative boost, with a younger, racially mixed population running bohemian cafés, trendy clothes emporiums and independent design shops. Nørrebro's deep, dark working-class streets were fashioned in the mid-19th century, and the 1970s and 80s saw a wave of Muslim immigrants come into the area. These days it's home to vinyl stores, junk shops, coffee dens and middle-class teenagers drawn by its ethnic appeal.

COPENHAGEN IN...

→ ONE DAY
Walk along Strøget, visit The National Museum, Ny Carlsberg Glyptotek, Black Diamond on waterfront; sit at Nyhavn and watch the boats go by.

→ TWO DAYS
Spend most of the day in Tivoli Gardens; head on across to the trendy Vesterbro; take in the Opera House and Christiania

→ THREE DAYS
The royal palaces at Frederiksstaden; a train ride along the Danish coastline

CALENDAR HIGHLIGHTS

Spring and summer are the times to visit Copenhagen for its festivals (deepest winter is a time of hibernation in Denmark). You can get your bearings at the May Day Festival when brass bands and marchers descend on Faelled Park (in the shadow of the national stadium in Osterbro) for much food, drink and music. There's more beer to be consumed at the Copenhagen Beer Festival, also in May: you don't just have to put up with Carlsberg here but can enjoy the offerings from microbreweries too. Dance it all off at the Latin American Festival, in venues around the city centre in May, when rhythms from Cuba and Brazil typically include salsa, samba and tango. June kicks off with the Whitsun Carnival in Faelled Park, while lagers are to the fore again at the St Hans Eve Festival, in the same park and along the northern beaches near the city, as locals celebrate the longest day of the year. Northern Europe's largest music festival, a four-day rock jaunt at Roskilde, is a 25-minute train journey away from the capital in June, while jazz lovers can gorge themselves with 600 concerts as the Jazz Festival takes over the city in July. The more sophisticated Ballet Festival, featuring the Royal Danish Ballet, is in August, and pre-1971 Bentleys, Bugattis and Alfa Romeos make their own kind of music at the Copenhagen Historic Grand Prix in the same month. Finally, if you go to see the Little Mermaid while you're in the city, try the 23 August – that was the date in 1913 she was placed in her location at the harbour, so they call it her birthday.

EATING OUT

Copenhagen's reputation for its food just keeps getting bigger and bigger. The city's dining establishments manage to marry Danish dining traditions such as herring or frikkadeller meatballs with global influences to impressive effect. So impressive that in recent times the city has earned itself more Michelin stars, for its crisp and precise cooking, than any other in Scandinavia. Top- and bottom-end restaurants and cafés – those most expensive and those most cheap - are pretty well catered for but the trick is to find one that fits the mid-range, so be warned: you could use up much energy trying to locate a smart restaurant with reasonable prices. Many good restaurants blend French methods and dishes with fresh regional ingredients and innovative touches and there is a trend towards fixed price, no choice menus involving several courses. Danes love their coffee and drink more of it per capita than anywhere else; you're guaranteed a good, strong cup all around the city. There's no need to tip, as it should be included in the cost of the meal. Danes, though, have a very good reputation as cheerful, helpful waiting staff, so you might feel like adding a bit extra.

➜ ROUND AND ROUND WE GO

You don't have to go to the top of Black Diamond or the Opera House to get a view over the city. The **Rundetårn** (Round Tower), just off Strøget, is Europe's oldest working observatory, and from the top of its long spiral staircase you get a fine vista of Copenhagen's low-rise symmetry.

➜ FALLEN LADY

She may be a tourist attraction, but locals aren't that keen on The **Little Mermaid**. In her near century long residence along the Langelinie docks she's been painted red, had her head hacked off and arm lopped off – and then, in 2003, she was actually bombed into the water! Are residents trying to tell us something?

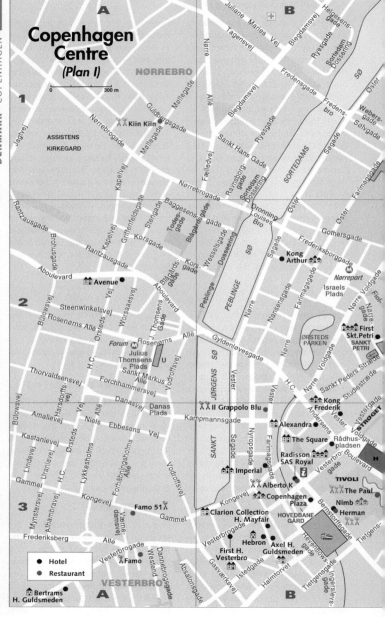

Copenhagen Centre
(Plan I)

NØRREBRO

ASSISTENS
KIRKEGARD

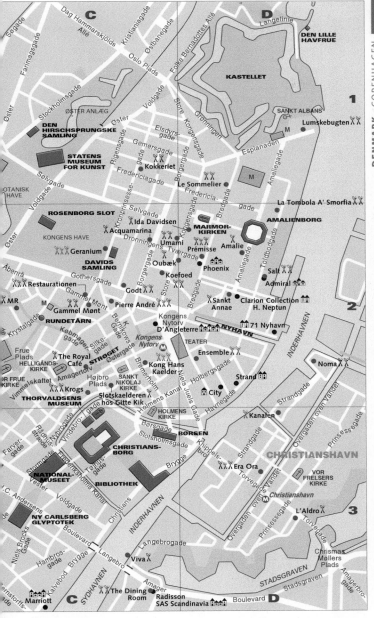

DEN LILLE HAVFRUE

KASTELLET

Langelinie

Dag Hammarskjölds Allé

Kristianiagade

Østbanegade

Oslo Plads

Folke Bernadottes Allé

Søgade

Farimagsgade

Stockholmsgade

ØSTER ANLÆG

Stockholmsgade

Øster

Øster Voldgade

DEN HIRSCHSPRUNGSKE SAMLING

STATENS MUSEUM FOR KUNST

Sølvgade

OTANISK HAVE

Voldgade

Elsdyrsgade

Store Kongensgade

Gemersgade

Rigensgade

Fredericiagade

Kokkeriet ⋔⋔

SANKT ALBANS

Lumskebugten ⋔⋔

M

Esplanaden

Amaliegade

Le Sommelier ●

⋔⋔

Fredericia- gade

M

La Tombola A' Smorfia ⋔⋔

ROSENBORG SLOT

Sølvgade

⋔ Ida Davidsen

⋔ Acquamarina

KONGENS HAVE

Dronningens

MARMOR- KIRKEN

⋔⋔⋔ Geranium

DAVIDS SAMLING

Umami ⋔⋔⋔

Tværgade

AMALIENBORG

Borgergade

Prémisse ⋔⋔⋔

Amalie ⋔

Gothersgade

Store Kongensgade

Oubæk ●

Phoenix 🏛🏛

Salt ⋔⋔

⋔⋔⋔ Restaurationen

● Koefoed

Bredgade

Amaliegade

Toldbodgade

Abenrå

Godt ⋔⋔

Admiral 🏛🏛

Gammel Mønt

⋔ MR

M

Pierre André ⋔⋔⋔

⋔ Sankt Annae

Clarion Collection H. Neptun 🏛🏛

Gammel Mønt

Bredgade

RUNDETÅRN

Krystalgade

Købmager gade

Silke gade

Bernikows

K.

Kongens Nytorv

D'Angleterre 🏛🏛

⋔⋔ **NYHAVN**

🏛🏛 71 Nyhavn

INDERHAVNEN

Frue Plads

Østergade

Kongens Nytorv M

TEATER

Ensemble ⋔⋔

HELLIGÅNDS- KIRKE

⋔ The Royal Café

STRØGET

Noma ⋔⋔

R FRUE KIRKE

Vimmelskaftet

Amagertorv

SANKT NIKOLAJ KIRKE

Kong Hans Kaelder ⋔

Holbergsgade

Strand 🏛🏛

Niels Juels Gade

THORVALDSENS MUSEUM

⋔⋔ Krogs

Højbro Plads

Slotskaelderen hos Gitte Kik

Bremerholm

🏛 **City**

Havnegade

Holmens Kanal

HOLMENS KIRKE

⋔ Kanalen

Rådhus-

Nybro- gade

Vindebro- gade

Børsen

⋔⋔⋔ Era Ora

Slotsholmsgade

BØRSEN

Knippels- bro

Strandgade

CHRISTIANSHAVN

Farver- gade

Stormgade

Hestemølle-

Tøms gade

CHRISTIANS- BORG

Brygge

Overgaden oven Vandet

VOR FRELSERS KIRKE

NATIONAL- MUSEET

Christians Kanal

BIBLIOTEK

Torvegade

Christianshavn

J.C. Andersens

Vester

Voldgade

L'Aldro ⋔

Prinsessegade

Torvegade

NY CARLSBERG GLYPTOTEK

Niels Brocks Gade

Boulevard

Christmas Møllers Plads

Amagerbro gade

Hambros- gade

Kalvebod Brygge

Langebro

Viva ⋔

Langebrogade

Amager

STADSGRAVEN

Stadsgraven

amsforts-

🏛🏛🏛 Marriott

C

SYDHAVNEN

⋔⋔ The Dining Room

Radisson SAS Scandinavia 🏛🏛🏛

Boulevard D

121

D'Angleterre

🖾 *Ló ₥ ⊠ AC ↔ ☞ ¶* 🏖 VISA ☎ AE ⓪

Kongens Nytorv 34 ✉ *1022 K –* Ⓜ *Kongens Nytorv – 🕾 33 12 00 95*
– dangleterre@dangleterre.dk – Fax 33 12 11 18 – www.dangleterre.dk
117 rm – 🛉2680 DKK 🛉🛉2680/3060 DKK, ☲ 175 DKK – 6 suites **C2**
Rest – Menu 285 DKK (lunch) – Carte 385/700 DKK
♦ Grand Luxury ♦ Traditional ♦ Classic ♦
Elegant 18C hotel in the heart of Copenhagen, overlooking New Royal Square.
Luxurious lobby, grand ballroom and popular afternoon teas set the tone. Stylish
suites boast classical décor and antique furniture. Restaurant offers French and
Danish dishes.

Copenhagen Marriott

≤ 🖾 *Ló ₥ Ġ AC ↔ ☞* 🕾 🏖 **P**

Kalvebod Brygge 5 ✉ *1560 V – 🕾 88 33 99 00* VISA ☎ AE ⓪
– mhrs.cphdk.reservations@marriotthotels.com – Fax 88 33 13 99
– www.marriott.com/cphdk **C3**
392 rm – 🛉1899/4999 DKK 🛉🛉1899/4999 DKK, ☲ 195 DKK – 9 suites
Rest *Terraneo* – Carte 275/495 DKK
♦ Luxury ♦ Business ♦ Modern ♦
Striking glass-fronted hotel with amazing views over the water, Tivoli and the city.
Bedrooms are handsomely appointed; top-floor executive rooms share a stylish
private lounge. Buffet lunch is followed by Mediterranean dishes at dinner.

First Hotel Skt.Petri

🖾 *Ġ AC ↔ ☞ ¶* 🏖 🕭 VISA ☎ AE ⓪

Krystalgade 22 ✉ *1172 K –* Ⓜ *Nørreport – 🕾 33 45 91 00*
– reservation@hotelsktpetri.com – Fax 33 45 91 10
– www.hotelsktpetri.com **B2**
257 rm – 🛉1495/2495 DKK 🛉🛉1695/2695 DKK, ☲ 195 DKK – 11 suites
Rest *Bleu* – Menu 290 DKK (lunch) – Carte 380/495 DKK
♦ Luxury ♦ Business ♦ Design ♦
Former department store set in central Copenhagen, close to old St Peter's Church.
Spacious open-plan atrium leads to bright, stylish bedrooms, boasting contemporary design features by Per Arnoldi. Modern restaurant offers a mix of European
and Asian dishes.

Radisson SAS Scandinavia

≤ *Ló ₥ ⊠ ↔ Ġ ↔ ☞ ¶* 🏖 **P**

Amager Boulevard 70 ✉ *2300 S – 🕾 38 15 65 00* VISA ☎ AE ⓪
– copenhagen@radissonsas.com – Fax 38 15 65 01
– www.scandinavia.copenhagen.radissonsas.com **C3**
538 rm – 🛉900/2395 DKK 🛉🛉1000/2395 DKK, ☲ 185 DKK – 4 suites
Rest *The Dining Room* – see below
Rest *Blue Elephant –* 🕾 *33 96 59 70 (dinner only)* Menu 405 DKK – Carte 340/
585 DKK
Rest *Kyoto –* 🕾 *33 32 16 74 (dinner only)* Menu 310 DKK – Carte 200/700 DKK
♦ Business ♦ Classic ♦
Modern tower block hotel boasting spectacular views and a busy lobby playing
host to a bar, casino and even shops. Bright, original bedrooms are themed in ten
different styles. Blue Elephant serves authentic Thai cuisine; Kyoto offers Japanese
fare.

Radisson SAS Royal

≤ *Ló ₥ Ġ AC ↔ ☞ ¶* 🏖 **P** 🕭

Hammerichsgade 1 ✉ *1611 V – 🕾 33 42 60 00* VISA ☎ AE ⓪
– copenhagen@radissonsas.com – Fax 33 42 61 00 – www.radissonsas.com
– Closed Christmas and 1 week January **B3**
258 rm – 🛉1495/2295 DKK 🛉🛉1895/2495 DKK, ☲ 195 DKK – 2 suites
Rest *Alberto K* – see below
Rest *Café Royal* – Menu 345 DKK (dinner)
♦ Luxury ♦ Business ♦ Modern ♦
Huge hotel block which dominates the skyline to the west of Tivoli: the first Radis-
son SAS to be built in the world. Offering superb views, all bedrooms are designed
by Arne Jacobsen. Ground floor brasserie-style café.

Imperial   🔍 AC ↔ 📺 📞 🛅 ⇔ VISA ⚫ AE ①

Vester Farimagsgade 9 ⊠ 1606 V – ℰ 33 12 80 00 – imperial@imperialhotel.dk
– Fax 33 12 80 03 – www.imperialhotel.dk   **B3**
239 rm – †1115/2040 DKK ††1315/2215 DKK, � 150 DKK – 1 suite
Rest *The Grill Room* – *(Closed 22 June-24 August, Sunday, Monday and Bank Holidays) (dinner only)* Menu 445 DKK – Carte 475/575 DKK
Rest *Imperial Brasserie* – ℰ 33 43 20 83 *(closed 24-31 December)*
Menu 320 DKK – Carte 325/525 DKK
♦ Business ♦ Modern ♦
Spacious mid 20C hotel set on a wide city thoroughfare. Comfortable, well-serviced bedrooms range in size and are elegantly decorated with stylish modern furnishings. Resident pianist in The Grill Room, less formal dining in Imperial Brasserie.

Copenhagen Plaza   AC ↔ 📺 📞 🛅 ⇔ VISA ⚫ AE ①

Bernstorffsgade 4 ⊠ 1577 V – ℰ 33 14 92 62 – copenhagenplaza@ profilhotels.dk – Fax 33 93 93 62 – www.profilhotels.dk   **B3**
89 rm – †2150/2350 DKK ††2350 DKK, ⊆ 145 DKK – 2 suites
Rest – *(closed Sunday)* Menu 380 DKK (dinner) – Carte 243/438 DKK
♦ Traditional ♦ Cosy ♦
Commissioned in the early 20C by King Frederik VIII, a venerable hotel overlooking Tivoli gardens. Cosy, classically styled bedrooms and atmospheric library bar. Modern, welcoming brasserie serves internationally influenced dishes.

Kong Arthur without rest   🏠 ⚫ 🌿 ↔ 📺 📞 🛅 P VISA ⚫ AE ①

Nørre Søgade 11 ⊠ 1370 K – ⓜ Nørreport – ℰ 33 11 12 12 – hotel@ kongarthur.dk – Fax 33 32 61 30 – www.kongarthur.dk   **B2**
155 rm – †1640/1840 DKK ††2040 DKK, ⊆ 135 DKK
♦ Traditional ♦ Business ♦ Classic ♦
Pleasant hotel with nice spa, set on an elegant 19C residential avenue close to Peblinge Lake. Tastefully decorated bedrooms are divided between four buildings. Good buffet breakfast.

Nimb   🏠 ↔ 📺 📞 🛅 VISA ⚫ AE ①

Bernstorffsgade 5 ⊠ 1577 V – ℰ 88 70 00 00 – info@nimb.dk – Fax 88 70 00 99 – www.nimb.dk   **B3**
13 rm – †2900/4900 DKK ††5900/8500 DKK, ⊆ 275 DKK
Rest *Herman* – *see below*
Rest *Brasserie* – Menu 395 DKK
♦ Luxury ♦ Design ♦
Luxury hotel situated beside Tivoli Gardens and boasting an elegant ballroom, delicatessen, dairy and chocolaterie. 12 of the beautifully appointed bedrooms have garden views. Informal Brasserie also has a great outlook.

Admiral   ≤ 🌿 ↔ 📺 📞 🛅 P VISA ⚫ AE ①

Toldbodgade 24-28 ⊠ 1253 K – ⓜ Kongens Nytorv – ℰ 33 74 14 14 – admiral@admiralhotel.dk – Fax 33 74 14 16 – www.admiralhotel.dk
366 rm – †1475/1810 DKK ††1855/2890 DKK, ⊆ 130 DKK   **D2**
Rest *Salt* – see below
♦ Business ♦ Modern ♦
Converted 1780s grain-drying warehouse set on the harbour front. A maritime theme runs throughout the hotel, with the compact bedrooms complementing its rustic charm.

Island   ≤ 🏠 ♨ 🌿 AC ↔ 📺 📞 🛅 P VISA ⚫ AE ①

Kalvebod Brygge 53 (via Kalvebod Brygge C 3) ⊠ 1560 V – ℰ 33 38 96 00 – copenhagenisland@arp-hansen.dk – Fax 33 38 96 01 – www.copenhagenisland.dk
325 rm – †900/2025 DKK ††1575/3860 DKK, ⊆ 150 DKK
Rest *The Harbour* – Menu 358 DKK (dinner) – Carte 344/494 DKK
♦ Business ♦ Design ♦
Gleaming glass and steel structure on a man-made island in the harbour. Bedrooms – some with balconies – are well-equipped and boast city or water views; allergy friendly rooms available. Stylish multi-levelled lounge bar and restaurant with harbour views; menu to suit all tastes.

DENMARK - COPENHAGEN

Phoenix
⇪ ⛶ 📶 ♨ VISA ⓸ 🅰🅴 ⓸

Bredgade 37 ⊠ 1260 K – Ⓜ *Kongens Nytorv –* ℰ *33 95 95 00*
– phoenixcopenhagen@arp-hansen.dk – Fax 33 33 98 33
– www.phoenixcopenhagen.dk **D2**
210 rm – ♥1865/2095 DKK ♥♥2905 DKK, ⊂⊃ 150 DKK – 3 suites
Rest Von Plessen *– (Closed Sunday and Monday)* Menu 295/368 DKK – Carte 415/555 DKK
♦ Traditional ♦ Classic ♦

Set in the lively modern art and antiques district, an elegant 17C hotel boasting a grand marble lobby. Bedrooms come in various shapes, with décor in a style inspired by Louis XVI. Smart basement dining room serves French inspired cuisine.

Kong Frederik
⇪ ⛶ 📶 ♨ VISA ⓸ 🅰🅴 ⓸

Vester Voldgade 25 ⊠ 1552 V – ℰ *33 12 59 02 – kongfrederik@hotelkf.dk*
– Fax 33 93 59 01 – www.hotelkf.dk
– Closed Christmas and New Year **B3**
108 rm – ♥1300/1540 DKK ♥♥1780 DKK, ⊂⊃ 135 DKK – 2 suites
Rest Le Coq Rouge *–* ℰ *33 42 48 48 (Closed Sunday)* Menu 350 DKK (dinner)
– Carte 202/459 DKK
♦ Traditional ♦ Classic ♦

Elegant building set in a good location. Traditionally styled décor and dark wood panelling feature throughout, with period furniture continuing the theme in the comfy bedrooms. Atmospheric restaurant offers French brasserie-style dishes.

The Square *without rest*
🅰🅒 ⇪ ⛶ ♨ ☏ ♨ VISA ⓸ 🅰🅴 ⓸

Rådhuspladsen 14 ⊠ 1550 V – ℰ *33 38 12 00 – thesquare@arp-hansen.dk*
– Fax 33 38 12 01 – www.thesquare.dk **B3**
267 rm – ♥1825 DKK ♥♥2085 DKK, ⊂⊃ 110 DKK
♦ Business ♦ Modern ♦

Contemporary hotel ideally located in Town Hall Square. Good sized bedrooms display a 'square' theme in their décor, fabrics and furnishings. 6th floor breakfast room boasts city rooftop views.

Clarion Collection H. Mayfair *without rest*
🅰🅒 ⇪ ⛶ 📶 ♨ VISA ⓸ 🅰🅴 ⓸

Helgolandsgade 3 ⊠ 1653 V – ℰ *70 12 17 00*
– cc.mayfair@choice.dk – Fax 33 23 96 86 – www.choicehotels.dk
– Closed Christmas-New Year **B3**
102 rm ⊂⊃ *–* ♥895/2195 DKK ♥♥995/2395 DKK – 4 suites
♦ Business ♦ Modern ♦

Fully renovated in 2008, this well-run hotel displays classical English furniture, a relaxing bar and fresh, modern bedrooms created by leading Scandinavian designers. Good buffet breakfast.

Strand *without rest*
⇪ ⛶ 📶 ♨ VISA ⓸ 🅰🅴 ⓸

Havnegade 37 ⊠ 1058 K – Ⓜ *Kongens Nytorv –* ℰ *33 48 99 00*
– copenhagenstrand@arp-hansen.dk – Fax 33 48 99 01
– www.copenhagenstrand.dk **D2**
172 rm – ♥1655/1995 DKK ♥♥1995 DKK, ⊂⊃ 110 DKK – 2 suites
♦ Business ♦ Modern ♦

Set in a useful central location in an 1869 harbourside warehouse; formerly a paper factory. Comfy bedrooms – some with harbour views – boast bright colours and polished wood furniture.

Avenue *without rest*
⇪ ⛶ 📶 ♨ 🅿 VISA ⓸ 🅰🅴 ⓸

Åboulevard 29, Frederiksberg C ⊠ 1960 – Ⓜ *Forum –* ℰ *35 37 31 11 – info@ avenuehotel.dk – Fax 35 37 31 33 – www.avenuehotel.dk*
– Closed Christmas-New Year **A2**
68 rm ⊂⊃ *–* ♥995/1250 DKK ♥♥1195/1550 DKK
♦ Business ♦ Design ♦

Housed within a building dating back to 1899, this hotel boasts a nice lounge, relaxing bar and courtyard patio. Comfortable bedrooms are smart, well-equipped and have a bright, crisp style.

DENMARK - COPENHAGEN

71 Nyhavn ⪅ ⭭⭥ 🖃 ☎ 💳 ⦿ 🄰🄴 ⓞ

Nyhavn 71 ⊠ 1051 K – Ⓜ Kongens Nytorv – ℰ 33 43 62 00 – 71nyhavnhotel@ arp-hansen.dk – Fax 33 43 62 01 – www.71nyhavnhotel.dk **D2**
144 rm – ♱1135/1830 DKK ♱♱1335/2030 DKK, ⫘ – 6 suites
Rest *Parkhus Kaelder* – *(Closed Sunday and Bank Holidays)* Menu 410 DKK
♦ Business ♦ Stylish ♦

Converted spice warehouse set by the canal, where charming wooden beams and low ceilings are offset by smart, modern furnishings and water views; comfortable bedrooms. Cellar restaurant offers seasonally inspired French cuisine.

First Hotel Vesterbro 🄰🄲 ⭭⭥ 🖃 🕪 🕍 🚕 💳 ⦿ 🄰🄴 ⓞ

Vesterbrogade 23-29 ⊠ 1620 V – ℰ 33 78 80 00 – reception.copenhagen@ firsthotels.dk – Fax 33 78 80 80 – www.firsthotels.com **B3**
400 rm – ♱1745 DKK ♱♱1945 DKK, ⫘ 155 DKK
Rest – *(Closed Sunday and Bank Holidays)* Carte 250/325 DKK
♦ Business ♦ Functional ♦

Large, modern hotel with glass and metal façade, set on a busy avenue. Furnished in a contemporary style with dark wood floors, bedrooms are bright, airy and well-appointed. Informal restaurant offers international dishes.

Axel H. Guldsmeden 🕪 ⭭⭥ 🖃 ☎ 🕍 💳 ⦿ 🄰🄴 ⓞ

Helgolandsgade 11 ⊠ 1653 K – ℰ 33313266 – booking@hotelguldsmeden.dk – Fax 33 31 69 70 – www.hotelguldsmeden.dk **B3**
129 rm – ♱1495/1995 DKK ♱♱1995 DKK, ⫘ 125 DKK
Rest – *(residents only)* Menu 295 DKK (dinner)
♦ Business ♦ Design ♦

Stylish hotel close to the station, with open-plan lounge and bar. Modern, comfortable bedrooms are decorated in a Balinese style; most boast four-posters beds and some have balconies. Restaurant serves buffet only.

Alexandra 🚕 ⭭⭥ rm 🖃 🕪 🅿 💳 ⦿ 🄰🄴 ⓞ

H.C. Andersens Boulevard 8 ⊠ 1553 V – ℰ 33 74 44 44 – reservations@ hotel-alexandra.dk – Fax 33 74 44 88 – www.hotel-alexandra.dk – Closed 24-27 December **B3**
61 rm ⫘ – ♱1295/1695 DKK ♱♱1495/1695 DKK
Rest *Bistro Copenhagen* – ℰ 33 74 44 66 (Closed Sunday) (dinner only) Menu 398 DKK – Carte 364/423 DKK
♦ Traditional ♦ Design ♦

Classical hotel close to the city centre. Bedrooms are uniquely styled and there's an entire allergy friendly floor; 13 'design rooms' boast smart Danish furniture and original paintings. Restaurant has a Mediterranean tone.

Clarion Collection H. Neptun *without rest* ⭭⭥ 🖃 🕪 🕍

Sankt Annae Plads 18-20 ⊠ 1250 K 💳 ⦿ 🄰🄴 ⓞ
– Ⓜ Kongens Nytorv – ℰ 33 96 20 00 – cc.neptun@choice.dk – Fax 33 96 20 66 – www.choicehotels.dk
– Closed 22 December-3 January **D2**
133 rm ⫘ – ♱995/1395 DKK ♱♱1195/1795 DKK
♦ Business ♦ Functional ♦

Converted from two characterful houses in a residential area of the popular Nyhavn district. Bedrooms, decorated with light wood furniture, have a good range of facilities. Courtyard breakfast room.

City *without rest* ⭭⭥ 🖃 🕪 🕍 💳 ⦿ 🄰🄴 ⓞ

Peder Skrams Gade 24 ⊠ 1054 K – Ⓜ Kongens Nytorv – ℰ 33 13 06 66 – hotelcity@hotelcity.dk – Fax 33 13 06 67 – www.hotelcity.dk **D2**
81 rm ⫘ – ♱1200/1450 DKK ♱♱1500/1750 DKK
♦ Business ♦ Functional ♦

Modern hotel set between the city and the docks. Refurbished bedrooms boast designer Danish furniture, flat screen TVs and monochrome jazz photos – some are yet to be completed.

Bertrams H. Guldsmeden

Vesterbrogade 107 ⊠ *1620 V* – ℰ *33 25 04 05*
– bertrams@hotelguldsmeden.dk – Fax 33 25 04 02
– www.hotelguldsmeden.dk   **A3**
47 rm – †1210/1495 DKK ††1455/1795 DKK, ⊡ 100 DKK
Rest – *(Closed Sunday) (dinner only)* Menu 150 DKK
♦ Townhouse ♦ Personalised ♦
Younger sister to Axel H. Guldsmeden, this hotel shares the same bright décor.
Bedrooms look out onto a courtyard – some have four-poster beds or balconies.
Good organic breakfasts. Warm, café-style restaurant offers a set menu.

Hebron without rest

Helgolandsgade 4 ⊠ *1653 V* – ℰ *33 31 69 06* – *info@hebron.dk*
– Fax 33 31 90 67 – www.hebron.dk
– Closed Christmas   **B3**
93 rm ⊡ – †1000 DKK ††1350 DKK – 6 suites
♦ Traditional ♦ Functional ♦
When it opened in 1900 this was one of the biggest hotels in the city – and some
of its original features still remain. Close to the gardens and shopping centre, it
boasts smart, simple bedrooms.

Kong Hans Kaelder

Vingårdsstraede 6 ⊠ *1070 K* – ❶ *Kongens Nytorv* – ℰ *33 11 68 68*
– kontakt@konghans.dk – Fax 33 32 67 68 – www.konghans.dk
– Closed 3 weeks July-August, 1 week Christmas and Sunday   **C2**
Rest – *(booking essential) (dinner only)* Carte 810/920 DKK
Spec. Langoustines with chicory and vanilla. Monkfish with polenta, articho-
kes and olives. Valrhona chocolate 'in the jar' with raspberries.
♦ Classic ♦ Formal ♦
Discreetly located down a side street in a vaulted Gothic cellar, in one of the oldest
buildings in town. A friendly, dedicated team offer fine dining and innovative
menus.

Geranium (Soren Ledet/Rasmus Kofoed)

Kronprinsessegade 13 ⊠ *1306* – ℰ *33 11 13 04* – *info@restaurantgeranium.dk*
– www.restaurantgeranium.dk
– Closed 3 weeks Christmas-New Year, Saturday lunch, Sunday and
Monday   **C2**
Rest – *(booking essential) (set menu only)* Menu 465/698 DKK
Spec. King crab with salad cress, cucumber and dill. Roe deer with beet-
root, mushrooms and herbs. Elderberry jelly with white chocolate and
elderflower.
♦ Innovative ♦ Friendly ♦
Delightfully located in an 18C tea pavilion in the King's Garden. Passionate kitchen
uses organic, biodynamic ingredients to create original, flavoursome dishes. 100%
organic wine list.

Herman – at Nimb Hotel

Bernstorffsgade 5 ⊠ *1577 V* – ℰ *88 70 00 00* – *info@nimb.dk – Fax 88 70 00 99*
– www.nimb.dk
– Closed Saturday lunch and Sunday   **B3**
Rest – *(booking advisable)* Menu 475/850 DKK
Spec. Foie gras with cherry and beetroot. Pigeon with mushrooms and
wood sorrel. Sønderjysk cake table.
♦ Contemporary ♦ Formal ♦
Split-level restaurant with terrace and lovely views over Tivoli gardens. Upper level
tables are backed by a glass wall looking into the kitchen. 6 course menu offers
modern Danish cooking, matched with wine.

XXX
ξ3
Formel B (Rune Jochumsen/Kristian Møller)   🔳 ↳ ⇔ 𝖵𝖨𝖲𝖠 ⓌⓈ 𝖠𝖤 ⓪
Vesterbrogade 182-184, Frederiksberg (via Vesterbrogade C 3)
✉ *1800 C* – ℰ *33 25 10 66* – *info@formel-b.dk* – *www.formel-b.dk*
– *Closed 13 July - 4 August, Christmas and Sunday*
Rest – *(booking essential) (dinner only)* Menu 800/850 DKK 🏵
Spec. Langoustine with baby vegetables and pickled green tomatoes. Pigeon with
apples, celeriac and truffle sauce. Passion fruit 'en surprise' with liquorice ice cream.
   ◆ Innovative ◆ Design ◆
Sleek, intimate restaurant with dynamic serving team and well-chosen wine list.
Seasonal Danish ingredients are used to create precisely-crafted modern French
dishes, served on beautiful china.

XXX
Mielcke & Hurtigkarl   🍷 ↳ 𝖵𝖨𝖲𝖠 ⓌⓈ 𝖠𝖤 ⓪
Runddel 1 (via Frederiksberg Allé C 3) ✉ *2000 Frederiksberg* – ℰ *38 34 84 36*
– *Fax 38 76 13 93* – *www.mielcke-hurtigkarl.dk*
– *Open April-21 December. Closed Monday and Tuesday and from October -
21 December for lunch and Sunday and Wednesday.*
Rest – *(booking essential)* Menu 425/750 DKK
   ◆ Innovative ◆ Formal ◆
Elegant restaurant set in the beautiful Fredriksberg Gardens. Set menu offers
modern dishes crafted from quality ingredients. Owners use their time off to travel
the world in search of inspiration.

XXX
Restaurationen   ↳ 𝖵𝖨𝖲𝖠 ⓌⓈ 𝖠𝖤 ⓪
Møntergade 19 ✉ *1116 K* – Ⓜ *Kongens Nytorv* – ℰ *33 14 94 95*
– *Fax 33 14 85 30* – *www.restaurationen.com*
– *Closed July-August, Christmas-New Year, Easter, Sunday and Monday*   **C2**
Rest – *(booking essential) (dinner only) (set menu only)* Menu 765 DKK 🏵
   ◆ Classic ◆ Friendly ◆
Well-established, personally run restaurant with formal service and comprehensive
wine list. Set menu offers accomplished, classically based Danish cooking, using
well sourced ingredients.

XXX
ξ3
Era Ora   🍷 ↳ 𝖵𝖨𝖲𝖠 ⓌⓈ 𝖠𝖤 ⓪
Overgaden neden Vandet 33B ✉ *1414 K* – Ⓜ *Christianshavn*
– ℰ *32 54 06 93* – *era-ora@era-ora.dk* – *Fax 32 96 02 09* – *www.era-ora.dk*
– *Closed Christmas,1 January, Easter and Sunday*   **D3**
Rest – *(booking essential at dinner) (set menu only)* Menu 350/850 DKK 🏵
Spec. Marinated halibut with egg plant and olive oil. Guinea fowl with
polenta and rosemary. Panna cotta and rhubarb sorbet.
   ◆ Italian ◆ Formal ◆
Discreet canalside restaurant with elegant Mediterranean styling, pleasant terrace
and formal service. Expertly chosen wines complement well-conceived, precisely
executed Italian dishes.

XXX
Prémisse   ↳ ⇔ 𝖵𝖨𝖲𝖠 ⓌⓈ 𝖠𝖤 ⓪
Dronningens Tvaergade 2 ✉ *1302 K* – Ⓜ *Kongens Nytorv*
– ℰ *33 11 11 45* – *mail@premisse.dk* – *Fax 33 11 11 68* – *www.premisse.dk*
– *Closed 13 July-10 August, 23-30 December, lunch November-April, Sunday,
Monday and Bank Holidays*   **D2**
Rest – Menu 400/750 DKK
   ◆ French ◆ Formal ◆
17C vaulted cellar restaurant with modern stylish décor and wine cellar on view.
Open-plan kitchen serves a classically based French menu, which includes some
original flavours.

XXX
Pierre André   ↳ 𝖵𝖨𝖲𝖠 ⓌⓈ 𝖠𝖤 ⓪
Ny Østergade 21 ✉ *1101 K* – Ⓜ *Kongens Nytorv* – ℰ *33 16 17 19* – *info@
pierreandre.dk* – *Fax 33 16 17 72* – *www.pierreandre.dk* – *Closed 4 weeks July-
August, Christmas-New Year, Easter, Sunday, Monday and Bank Holidays*
Rest – *(booking essential) (dinner only)* Menu 450 DKK – Carte   **C2**
635/775 DKK
   ◆ French ◆ Formal ◆
Elegant dining room with comfortable seating and stylish décor, set in an attrac-
tive old building. Cooking has a classical French base. Efficient, attentive service.

DENMARK - COPENHAGEN

XXX Krogs　　　　　　　　　　　　AC 🌿 VISA ⚫⚫ AE ①

Gammel Strand 38 ⊠ 1201 K – 𝒞 33 15 89 15 – krogs@krogs.dk
– Fax 33 15 83 19 – www.krogs.dk – Closed Sunday　　　　**C2**
Rest *– (booking essential) (dinner only)* Menu 575 DKK – Carte 735/1030 DKK
◆ Seafood ◆ Formal ◆

Characterful 18C house pleasantly located next to the canal. High ceilinged classical dining room with large end window. Attractively presented seafood dishes. Formal service.

XX Ensemble (Morten Schou)　　　　　🌿 VISA ⚫⚫ AE ①

Tordenskjoldsgade 11 ⊠ 1055 K – ⓜ Kongens Nytorv – 𝒞 33 11 33 52
– kontakt@restaurantensemble.dk – Fax 33 11 33 92 – www.restaurantensemble.dk
– Closed July, 2 weeks Christmas, Easter, Sunday and Monday
Rest *– (set menu only) (booking advisable) (dinner only)* Menu 450/800 DKK 🍸
Spec. Langoustine with celeriac, sorrel and consommé. Pigeon with wild mushrooms and thyme. Blueberries in birch syrup with vanilla ice cream.
◆ Modern ◆ Formal ◆

Whites, greys and bright lighting contribute to a fresh, clean feel. Keen team serve modern 6 course set menu of original, well-crafted dishes, making good use of quality ingredients.

XX Noma (Rene Redzepi)　　　　　🌿 ⟷ VISA ⚫⚫ AE ①

Strandgade 93 ⊠ 1401 K – ⓜ Christianshavn – 𝒞 32 96 32 97 – booking@
noma.dk – www.noma.dk – Closed last 3 weeks July, between Christmas and
New Year, Monday lunch and Sunday　　　　**D2**
Rest *– (booking essential)* Menu 725/1100 DKK – Carte 675/950 DKK
Spec. Langoustine, seaweed and oyster emulsion. Musk ox with milk skin and truffle purée. Sheep's milk mousse with sorrel granité.
◆ Innovative ◆ Design ◆

Stylish restaurant displaying a charming, rustic simplicity. Quality Nordic ingredients contribute to stimulating, innovative dishes that test the usual culinary boundaries. Smooth service.

XX MR (Mads Refslund)　　　　AC 🌿 ⟷ VISA ⚫⚫ AE ①

Kultorvet 5 ⊠ 1175 K – 𝒞 33 91 09 49 – mr@mr-restaurant.dk – www.mr-restaurant.dk
– Closed 13 July-3 August, Christmas-New Year and Sunday　　　　**C2**
Rest *(booking essential) (dinner only)* Menu 596/1006 DKK – Carte approx. 700 DKK
Spec. Mackerel with walnuts, lemon and cep dust. Chicken with cockscomb, kidney and salad roots. 'Aroma of the trees in the forest'.
◆ Modern ◆ Fashionable ◆

18C townhouse set on a paved square, with stylish lounge and private 2nd floor dining room. 1st floor restaurant serves creative dishes with Danish influences. Knowledgeable service.

XX Kiin Kiin (Lertchai Treetawatchaiwong)　　AC 🌿 ⟷ VISA ⚫⚫ AE ①

Guldbergsgade 21 ⊠ 2200 – 𝒞 35 35 75 55 – kiin@kiin.dk
– Fax 35 35 75 59 – www.kiin.dk – Closed Christmas and Sunday　　　　**A1**
Rest *– (booking essential) (dinner only) (set menu only)* Menu 750 DKK
Spec. Frozen red curry with lobster. Quail in coconut milk with galangal and wild mushrooms. Passion fruit with baby oranges and cashews.
◆ Thai ◆ Exotic ◆

Spacious 1st floor restaurant offering precise, authentic cooking – a modern interpretation of classical Thai – with balanced, delicate flavours. Comfy sitting room boasts Thai furnishings.

XX Kokkeriet (Lasse Askov)　　　　🌿 ⟷ VISA ⚫⚫ AE ①

Kronprinsessegade 64 ⊠ 1306 K – 𝒞 33 15 27 77 – info@kokkeriet.dk
– Fax 33 15 27 75 – www.kokkeriet.dk – Closed July, Christmas, Sunday and Monday
Rest *– (dinner only)* Menu 650 DKK　　　　**C1**
Spec. Veal tartare with smoked eel, roe and poached egg yolk. Braised lamb with mushrooms, watercress pesto and lamb jus. Pear, chestnuts and browned butter cream.
◆ Modern ◆ Friendly ◆

Smart, intimate restaurant with stylish furnishings and a bright, friendly neighbourhood feel. Inventive 6 course modern menu and matching wines are served by an enthusiastic team.

DENMARK - COPENHAGEN

XX **Umami**   AC ⑤ VISA ◯◯ AE ①
Store Kongensgade 59 ⊠ 1264 – ⓜ Kongens Nytorv – ℰ 33 38 75 00
– mail@restaurantumami.dk – Fax 33 38 75 15 – www.restaurantumami.dk
– Closed 22-30 December   **C-D2**
Rest – *(dinner only)* Carte 380/800 DKK
  ♦ Japanese ♦ Fashionable ♦
Elegant contemporary restaurant with stylish tables and a choice of eating areas,
including a sushi bar. Modern Japanese cuisine displays some French influences.
Popular cocktail bar.

XX **Godt**   VISA ◯◯ ①
Gothersgade 38 ⊠ 1123 K – ⓜ Kongens Nytorv
– ℰ 33 15 21 22 – restaurant.godt@get2net.dk
– www.restaurant-godt.dk
– Closed early July-early August, 13-17 October, Christmas-New Year, Easter,
Sunday, Monday and Bank Holidays   **C2**
Rest – *(dinner only, set menu only)* Menu 500/660 DKK
  ♦ Classic ♦ Friendly ♦
Small but stylish modern restaurant with old WWII shells acting as candle holders.
Classic European and French cuisine is served in 3, 4 or 5 courses. Friendly service
from the owner.

XX **Il Grappolo Blu**   ⑤ VISA ◯◯ AE ①
Vester Farimagsgade 35 ⊠ 1606 V – ℰ 33 11 57 20
– ilgrappoloblu@ilgrappoloblu.com – Fax 33 12 57 20 – www.ilgrappoloblu.com
– Closed July, Easter, Christmas, Saturday lunch and Sunday   **B3**
Rest – *(set menu only)* Menu 545/750 DKK
  ♦ Italian ♦ Friendly ♦
Hidden behind an unpromising façade, this small, personally run restaurant boasts
wood panelling, ornate carving and a cosy, intimate atmosphere. Authentic Italian
cuisine.

XX **Salt** – at Admiral Hotel   ⩽ 🕭 P VISA ◯◯ AE ①
Toldbodgade 24-28 ⊠ 1253 K – ⓜ Kongens Nytorv – ℰ 33 74 14 44 – info@
saltrestaurant.dk – Fax 33 74 14 16 – www.saltrestaurant.dk   **D2**
Rest – Menu 375 DKK – Carte 375/510 DKK
  ♦ Modern ♦ Design ♦
Modern version of a Parisian brasserie, set in an 18C warehouse with huge expo-
sed beams. Danish buffet and à la carte at lunch, more extensive modern menu at
dinner.

XX **Frederiks Have**   🕭 ⑤ VISA ◯◯ AE ①
Smallegade 41/Virgina Vej ⊠ 2000 Frederiksberg – ⓜ Frederiksberg
– ℰ 38 88 33 35 – info@frederikshave.dk – Fax 38 88 33 37
– www.frederikshave.dk – Closed Christmas, Easter and Sunday
Rest – Menu 235/358 DKK – Carte 340/495 DKK
  ♦ Modern ♦ Neighbourhood ♦
Well-established restaurant in leafy residential area, with homely ambience and
delightful terrace. Monthly menus offer a fairly-priced choice of modern and tradi-
tional Danish cooking.

XX **Gammel Mønt**   ⑤ VISA ◯◯ AE ①
Gammel Mønt 41 ⊠ 1117 K – ⓜ Kongens Nytorv – ℰ 33 15 10 60 – info@
gammel-moent.dk – Fax 33 15 10 60 – www.gammel-moent.dk
– closed July and Bank Holidays   **C2**
Rest – *(lunch only)* Menu 395 DKK – Carte 315/660 DKK
  ♦ Traditional ♦ Cosy ♦
Half-timbered 18C house with striking red façade and monthly-changing modern
art on the walls; set in a smart commercial district. Traditional, seasonal cooking
offers an interesting range of herring dishes.

DENMARK - COPENHAGEN

XX   **Le Sommelier**   ↳ *VISA* **◉◉** **AE** **①**

Bredgade 63-65 ⊠ 1260 K – ℰ 33 11 45 15 – mail@lesommelier.dk
– Fax 33 11 59 79 – www.lesommelier.dk – Closed Christmas-New Year
Rest – Menu 395 DKK – Carte 365/465 DKK ✿   **D1**
♦ French ♦ Brasserie ♦

Popular brasserie serving classic French dishes, set in the heart of the old town. The owners' passion for wine shows through their display of posters, memorabilia and good 'by the glass' list.

XX   **LaTombola A'Smorfia**   ↳ *VISA* **◉◉** **AE** **①**

Toldbodgade 55 ⊠ 1253 – ℰ 33 14 57 20 – info@latombola.dk
– Fax 33 12 57 20 – www.latombola.dk – Closed Christmas-New Year, Easter,
Sunday and lunch mid September-mid April   **D2**
Rest – Menu 248/373 DKK – Carte approx. 433 DKK
♦ Italian ♦ Brasserie ♦

Spacious, airy Italian brasserie decorated with tombola-themed numbers and offering the chance to win your meal for free. Daily changing dishes visit all corners of Italy.

XX   **Lumskebugten**   🏠 ↳ *VISA* **◉◉** **AE** **①**

Esplanaden 21 ⊠ 1263 K – ℰ 33 15 60 29 – mail@lumskebugten.dk
– Fax 33 32 87 18 – www.lumskebugten.dk
– Closed 22 December-2 January, Sunday and Saturday lunch   **D1**
Rest – Menu 405/425 DKK – Carte 395/615 DKK
♦ Traditional ♦ Cosy ♦

Mid 19C pavilion by the quayside, decorated with interesting maritime memorabilia and old paintings on the walls. The queen of Denmark has her birthday lunch here. Traditional Danish cuisine.

XX   **The Dining Room** – at Radisson SAS Scandinavia Hotel   ⇐ ↳ **P**

25th Floor, Amager Boulevard 70 ⊠ 2300 S   *VISA* **◉◉** **AE** **①**
– ℰ 33 96 58 58 – info@thediningroom.dk – Fax 33 96 55 00
– www.thediningroom.dk – Closed July, Sunday, Monday and Bank Holidays
Rest – *(dinner only)* Menu 415 DKK – Carte approx. 584 DKK   **C3**
♦ Modern ♦ Friendly ♦

Situated on the 25th floor of the Radisson SAS Scandinavia, this independently run restaurant offers a modern à la carte menu and wonderful panoramic views of the city.

XX   **Alberto K** – at Radisson SAS Royal Hotel   ⇐ **AC** **P** *VISA* **◉◉** **AE** **①**

Hammerichsgade 1 ⊠ 1611 V – ℰ 33 42 61 61 – copenhagen@radissonsas.com
Fax 33 42 61 00 – www.radissonsas.com– Closed Christmas and 1 week January
Rest – *(closed Sunday) (dinner only)* Menu 600/750 DKK   **B3**
♦ Italian influences ♦ Design ♦

Set on the 29th floor of the Radisson SAS Royal, this contemporary restaurant offers fabulous city views. A friendly team serve Italian influenced cuisine from a modern, open-kitchen.

XX   **Koefoed**   *VISA* **◉◉** **AE** **①**

Landgreven 3 (basement) ⊠ 1301 – Ⓜ Kongens Nytorv – ℰ (56) 48 22 24
– koefoed@mtz.dk – www.restaurant-koefoed.dk
– Closed 20 December-5 January and Sunday in winter   **C2**
Rest – Menu 225/425 DKK
♦ Traditional ♦ Intimate ♦

Intimate restaurant, divided into several small rooms. Celebrates the island of Bornholm, from where everything comes from the ingredients to the glassware. Dinner a more formal affair.

X   **Kanalen**   ⇐ 🏠 ↳ **P** *VISA* **◉◉** **AE** **①**

Christianshavn-Wilders Plads 1-3 ⊠ 1403 K – Ⓜ Christianshavn
– ℰ 32 95 13 30 – info@restaurant-kanalen.dk – Fax 32 95 13 38
– www.restaurant-kanalen.dk – Closed Christmas, Sunday and Bank Holidays
Rest – *(booking essential)* Menu 290/360 DKK – Carte 360/538 DKK   **D3**
♦ Danish ♦ Friendly ♦

Former Harbour Police office, delightfully located on the canalside with a romantic terrace. Simple, elegant décor and informal atmosphere. Well balanced menu of modern Danish cooking.

X **Famo 51** ⇔ VISA ⚫⚫

Gammel Kongevej 51 ⊠ 1610 – ℰ 33 22 22 50 – famo@mail.tele.dk
– Fax 33 22 19 93 – www.osteriafamo.dk
– Closed 3 weeks July, 2 weeks Christmas, 1 week Easter and Sunday
Rest *– (booking essential) (dinner only)* Menu 400/500 DKK   **A3**
♦ Italian ♦ Friendly ♦
Relaxed restaurant with informal atmosphere and intimate two-tabled cellar. Surprise 10 course menu changes daily, offering rustic Italian cooking and fresh, unfussy flavours.

X **Acquamarina** AC ⇔ VISA ⚫⚫ AE ⓪

Borgergade 17 a ⊠ 1300 – Ⓜ Kongens Nytorv – ℰ 33 11 17 21 – mail@
acquamarina.dk – Fax 33 12 17 21 – www.acquamarina.dk
– closed Christmas, 1 January, Easter Monday and Sunday
Rest *– (set menu only)* Menu 325/450 DKK   **C2**
♦ Seafood ♦ Minimalist ♦
This is the third restaurant in the stable of Era Ora. Bright yet understated in design, with a fashionable reputation. Specialises in seasonal seafood, prepared with an Italian accent.

X **M/S Amerika** ⇔ VISA ⚫⚫ AE ⓪

Dampfaergevej 8 (Pakhus 12, Amerikakaj) (via Folke Bernadottes Allée C 1)
⊠ 2100 K – ℰ 35 26 90 30 – info@msamerika.dk – Fax 35 26 91 30
– www.msamerika.dk
– Closed 21 December-2 January, Sunday and Bank Holidays
Rest *–* Menu 285/325 DKK *–* Carte 355/455 DKK
♦ Modern ♦ Brasserie ♦
Characterful restaurant with open-kitchen and popular summer terrace, set in an attractive quayside location. Simple, traditional lunch menu; more contemporary offerings at dinner.

X **Famo** ⇔ VISA ⚫⚫
☺

Saxogade 3 ⊠ 1662 – ℰ 33 23 22 50 – famo@mail.tele.dk – Fax 33 22 19 93
– www.osteriafamo.dk
– Closed 3 weeks August, 2 weeks Christmas, 1 week Easter and Monday
Rest *– (booking essential) (dinner only)(set menu only)*   **A3**
Menu 350 DKK
♦ Italian ♦ Bistro ♦
Popular, personally run Italian eatery with relaxed, informal atmosphere. No written menus – good value, authentic regional dishes are described by the owners. Chatty, attentive service.

X **Fiasco** ⇔ VISA ⚫⚫ AE ⓪

Gammel Kongevej 176, Frederiksberg (via Gammel Kongevej A 3) ⊠ 1850 C
– ℰ 33 31 74 87 – fiasco@tiscali.dk – Fax 33 31 74 87 – www.fiasco.dk
– Closed July, Christmas-New Year, Sunday and Monday
Rest *– (dinner only and set menu only)* Menu 275/335 DKK
♦ Italian ♦ Friendly ♦
Modern Italian restaurant located to the west of the city centre. Bright dining room boasts large picture windows and has a fresh, airy feel. Carefully prepared authentic Italian dishes.

X **L'Altro** AC ⇔ VISA ⚫⚫ AE ⓪
☺

Torvegade 62 ⊠ 1400 K – Ⓜ Christianshavn – ℰ 32 54 54 06 – laltro@laltro.dk
– Fax 32 54 54 06 – www.laltro.dk
– Closed Christmas, 1 January, Easter and Sunday
Rest *– (booking essential) (dinner only) (set menu only)* Menu 340 DKK   **D3**
♦ Italian ♦ Intimate ♦
Pleasant Italian restaurant divided between the ground floor and a characterful wine cellar basement. 'Mama's Kitchen' serves well-priced Tuscan and Umbrian home cooking.

X

☺

Oubaek   ⅙ VISA ⦿ AE ⦿

Store Kongensgade 52 ⊠ *1264 –* Ⓜ *Kongens Nytorv –* ℰ *33 32 32 09*
– rasmus-oubaek@mail.dk – www.rasmusoubaek.dk
– Closed last week July-first week August, Christmas, New Year, Easter,
Saturday and Sunday   **C-D2**
Rest *– (booking essential at dinner)* Carte approx. 435 DKK
♦ Classic ♦ Bistro ♦

Unassuming Danish restaurant with tables on a mezzanine level above the kitchen.
Carefully prepared, classical bistro-style dishes are competitively priced. Friendly,
informal service.

X

Viva   ≤ 淦 ⅙ VISA ⦿ AE ⦿

Langebrogade Kaj 570 ⊠ *1411 K –* Ⓜ *Christianshavn –* ℰ *27 25 05 05 – viva@*
restaurantviva.dk – www.restaurantviva.dk
– Closed Christmas-New Year   **C3**
Rest *–* Menu 285/345 DKK *–* Carte 295/480 DKK
♦ Modern ♦ Minimalist ♦

A converted German tug boat moored on the river, with a stylish minimalist interior and pleasant top deck terrace. The eclectic menu displays a modern international style.

IN TIVOLI

XXX

🕄

The Paul *(Paul Cunningham)*   淦 AK ⅙ ⇔ VISA ⦿ AE ⦿

Vesterbrogade 3 ⊠ *1630 K –* ℰ *33 75 07 75 – info@thepaul.dk*
– Fax 33 75 07 76 – www.thepaul.dk
– Closed late September-mid November, Christmas Eve-Easter and Sunday
Rest *– (set menu only)* Menu 450/850 DKK 瀿   **B3**
Spec. Oysters, cockles and mussels with shell water gel. Pigeon with morels,
white asparagus and woodruff. Candied beetroot with ewe's milk sorbet.
♦ Innovative ♦ Elegant ♦

Elegant 20C glass-domed building set by the lake in Tivoli gardens. Open-plan kitchen boasts chef's table. Modern, innovative menus make excellent use of Danish
produce. Attentive service.

SMØRREBRØD *The following list of simpler restaurants and cafés/*
bars specialise in Danish open sandwiches and are generally open
from 10.00am to 4.00pm.

X

Sankt Annae   ⅙ VISA ⦿ AE ⦿

Sankt Annae Plads 12 ⊠ *1250 K –* Ⓜ *Kongens Nytorv –* ℰ *33 12 54 97*
– Fax 33 15 16 61 – www.restaurantsanktannae.dk   **D2**
Rest *– (booking essential) (lunch only)* Carte 150/250 DKK
♦ Traditional ♦ Cosy ♦

Pretty terraced building in a popular part of town, with pleasant décor and cosy,
rustic feel. Typical menu of smørrebrød taken at the counter next to the kitchen.
Prompt, efficient service.

X

Amalie   ⅙ VISA ⦿ AE ⦿

Amaliegade 11 ⊠ *1256 K –* Ⓜ *Kongens Nytorv –* ℰ *33 12 88 10*
– jjmaltesen@mail.dk – Fax 33 12 88 10 – www.restaurantamalie.dk
– Closed July, Easter, Christmas-New Year, Sunday and Bank Holidays
Rest *– (booking essential) (lunch only)* Menu 208 DKK *–* Carte 202/292 DKK
♦ Traditional ♦ Friendly ♦   **D2**
Pleasant family run restaurant with a clean style and helpful service, situated in a
pretty 18C townhouse. Menu offers a good choice of fish and herring; ideal for a
traditional Danish lunch.

The Royal Cafe
☆ 戸 AC VISA ⬤ AE ⬤

Amagertorv 6 ✉ 1160 K – ✆ 38 14 95 27 – lo@hellohello.dk
– www.theroyalcafe.dk   **C2**
Rest – *(lunch only)* Menu 125 DKK
◆ Modern ◆ Fashionable ◆
Part of the Royal Copenhagen china shop, this narrow, quirkily designed 'café' is
the place to be. Crossing smørrebrød with sushi to create intricate 'smushies', it
brings smørrebrød into the 21C.

Ida Davidsen
☆ ⬤ VISA ⬤ AE ⬤

Store Kongensgade 70 ✉ 1264 K – Ⓜ Kongens Nytorv – ✆ 33 91 36 55
– reservation@idadavidsen.dk – Fax 33 11 36 55 – www.idadavidsen.dk
– Closed early July-early August, Easter, Christmas-mid January, Saturday,
Sunday and Bank Holidays   **D2**
Rest – *(lunch only)* Carte 195/300 DKK
◆ Smørrebrød ◆ Family ◆
Set on a busy city centre street, this open sandwich bar offers a full range of typical
smørrebrød. Run by the same family for five generations it's becoming a local
household name.

Slotskælderen hos Gitte Kik
☆ ⬤ VISA ⬤ AE ⬤

Fortunstræ 4 ✉ 1065 K – ✆ 33 11 15 37
– Closed July, Sunday, Monday and Bank Holidays   **C2**
Rest – *(booking essential) (lunch only)* Carte 46/85 DKK
◆ Smørrebrød ◆ Family ◆
Adorned with portraits and city scenes, this established restaurant is the bench-
mark for this style of cuisine. Choose around three dishes of authentic homemade
smørrebrød from the counter.

ENVIRONS OF COPENHAGEN

at Nordhavn North : 3 km by Østbanegade and Road 2

Bo Bech at Paustian
☆ 戸 AC ⬤ P. VISA ⬤ AE ⬤
✿

Kalkbraenderiløbskaj 2 ✉ 2100 – ✆ 39 18 55 01 – mail@bobech.net
– Fax 39 18 55 01 – www.bobech.net
– closed 3 weeks July and Sunday
Rest – *(booking essential)* Menu 350/750 DKK – Carte 565/860 DKK
Spec. Avocado wafers with caviar and almond. Hare in blood sauce with
lemon and Brussels sprouts. Smoked chocolate with porous pors bubbles.
◆ Innovative ◆ Design ◆
Stylish restaurant set on a redeveloped marina. The appealing set menus include
classical 'Jean-Anthelme Brillant-Savarin', original, innovative 'Alchemist' and vege-
tarian 'Chlorophyll'.

at Hellerup North : 7.5 km by Østbanegade and Road 2 - ✉ 2900 Hellerup

Hellerup Parkhotel
⬤ ⬤ rm ⬤ ⬤ P. VISA ⬤ AE ⬤

Strandvejen 203 ✉ 2900 – ✆ 39 62 40 44 – info@hellerupparkhotel.dk
– Fax 39 45 15 90 – www.hellerupparkhotel.dk
– Closed 22 December-2 January
71 rm – ✝999/1950 DKK ✝✝1295/2240 DKK, ⬳ 155 DKK
Rest *Saison* – see below
Rest *La Rocca* – ✆ 39 95 66 55 *(closed 2 weeks July, Christmas and Bank Holi-*
days) (dinner only) Menu 325 DKK
◆ Business ◆ Classic ◆
Attractive, classical hotel located in an affluent suburb north of the city. Bedrooms
vary in size and colour but are equal in their level of comfort and provision of faci-
lities. Popular with locals, La Rocca, to the side of the hotel, offers Italian cuisine and
a pleasant terrace.

XX **Saison** – at Hellerup Parkhotel   🗚 **P** 𝘝𝘐𝘚𝘈 ⊕⊕ 🅰🅴 ⓘ
Strandvejen 203 ✉ *2900 –* 𝒞 *39 95 66 55 – info@hellerupparkhotel.dk*
– Fax 39 45 15 90 – www.saison.dk
– closed 22 December- 2 January, Sunday and Bank Holidays
Rest – Carte 350/645 DKK
♦ Seasonal cuisine ♦ Friendly ♦
Bright, airy restaurant located in a hotel, boasting high ceilings and large windows.
Carefully prepared dishes are crafted from quality ingredients. Cellar plays host to a
cookery school.

at Skovshoved North : 10 km by Østbanegade and Road 2

🏠 **Skovshoved**   😤 ⅙ rest 🆎 📶 🈯 **P** 𝘝𝘐𝘚𝘈 ⊕⊕ 🅰🅴 ⓘ
Strandvejen 267 ✉ *2920 Charlottenlund –* 𝒞 *39 64 00 28 – reception@*
skovshovedhotel.com – Fax 39 64 06 72 – www.skovshovedhotel.com
– Closed 24-26 December and 1 January
20 rm – 🛏1100/1500 DKK 🛏🛏1475/1700 DKK, � 135 DKK – 2 suites
Rest – Menu 285/495 DKK – Carte 475/565 DKK
♦ Inn ♦ Cosy ♦
Set in a charming village, this welcoming inn dates back to the 1660s. Fully refur-
bished in 2003 it offers cosy bedrooms, most with balconies looking out to sea.
Warm, inviting restaurant with pleasant terrace offers both modern and classical
cuisine.

at Søllerød North : 20 km by Tagensvej (take the train to Holte then taxi) - ✉ 2840 Holte

XXX **Søllerød Kro**   😤 ⅙ ✿ **P** 𝘝𝘐𝘚𝘈 ⊕⊕ 🅰🅴 ⓘ
❀ *Søllerødvej 35* ✉ *2840 K –* 𝒞 *45 80 25 05 – mail@soelleroed-kro.dk*
– Fax 45 80 22 70 – www.soelleroed-kro.dk
– Closed 3 weeks July, 1 week February, Easter, 24 December, Monday and
Tuesday
Rest – Menu 375/695 DKK – Carte 630/1160 DKK 🏮
Spec. Baeri caviar 'en surprise'. Lobster with morels and white asparagus.
Seasonal Danish berries with vanilla.
♦ Classic ♦ Inn ♦
Characterful 17C thatched inn with stylish Danish rustic-bourgeois décor and a
delightful courtyard terrace. Classical French cooking displays subtle Danish influ-
ences; luxury ingredients abound.

at Kastrup Airport Southeast : 10 km by Amager Boulevard

🏨 **Hilton Copenhagen Airport**   ← ₤ᴚ 🎋 🖹 ᴋ 🆎 ⅙ 🆑 📶 🈯 🚗
Ellehammersvej 20, Kastrup ✉ *2770 –* 𝒞 *32 50 15 01*   𝘝𝘐𝘚𝘈 ⊕⊕ 🅰🅴 ⓘ
– res.copenhagen-airport@hilton.com – Fax 32 44 55 58 – www.hilton.com
375 rm – 🛏1075/2595 DKK 🛏🛏1075/3695 DKK, ⊂ 190 DKK – 1 suite
Rest *Hamlet* – – Carte 378/525 DKK
Rest *Horizon* – – Carte 378/525 DKK
♦ Business ♦ Modern ♦
This smart business hotel can be accessed directly from airport arrivals via a glass
walkway. Its bright, contemporary bedrooms boast Scandinavian furnishings and
modern facilities. Formal open-plan restaurant offers Nordic specialities, while
beneath the vast atrium, Horizon's open kitchen provides a buffet menu.

FINLAND
SUOMI

PROFILE

→ **AREA:**
338 145 km²
(130 558 sq mi).

→ **POPULATION:**
5 225 000 inhabitants
(est. 2005), density =
15 per km².

→ **CAPITAL:**
Helsinki (conurbation
1 151 000
inhabitants).

→ **CURRENCY:**
Euro (€); rate of
exchange: € 1 = US$
1.32 (Jan 2009).

→ **GOVERNMENT:**
Parliamentary
republic (since 1917).
Member of European
Union since 1995.

→ **LANGUAGES:**
Finnish (a Finno-
Ugric language
related to Estonian)
spoken by 92% of
Finns, Swedish (6%)
and Sami (some 7 000
native speakers).
English is widely
spoken.

→ **SPECIFIC PUBLIC
HOLIDAYS:**
Epiphany (6 January);
Good Friday (Friday
before Easter);
Midsummer's
Eve Day (mid June);
Independence Day
(6 December); Boxing
Day (26 December).

→ **LOCAL TIME:**
GMT + 2 hours in
winter and GMT +
3 hours in summer.

→ **CLIMATE:**
Temperate
continental with very
cold winters and mild
summers (Helsinki:
January: -7°C, July:
17°C). Midnight sun:
the sun never sets for
several weeks around
Midsummer in the
north. Snow settles
in early December to
April in the south and
centre of the country.
Northern Lights
(*Aurora Borealis*)
visible in the north
on clear, dark nights;
highest frequency
in Feb-Mar and Sep-
Oct.

→ **INTERNATIONAL
DIALLING CODE:**
00 358 followed by
area code (Helsinki: 9)
and then the local
number.

→ **EMERGENCY:**
Fire Brigade,
Ambulance, Police:
✆ **112**.

→ **ELECTRICITY:**
220 volts AC,
50Hz; 2-pin round-
shaped continental
plugs.

HELSINKI

→ **FORMALITIES**
Travellers from the
European Union
(EU), Switzerland,
Iceland and the main
countries of North
and South America
need a national
identity card or
passport (America:
passport required) to
visit Finland for less
than three months
(tourism or business
purpose). For visitors
from other countries
a visa may be
required, in addition
to a passport,
especially for those
wishing to stay for
longer than three
months. If you plan
to visit Russia while
in Finland, you
must purchase an
appropriate visa in
advance in your own
country. We advise
you to check with
your embassy before
travelling.

HELSINKI
HELSINGFORS

Population; 583 000 (conurbation 1 151 000) – Altitude: sea level

www.visitfinland.com

Cool, clean and chic, the 'Daughter of the Baltic' sits prettily on a peninsula, jutting out between the landmasses of its historical overlords, Sweden and Russia. Surrounded on three sides by water, Helsinki is a busy port, but that only tells a small part of the story: forests grow in abundance around here and trees reach down to the lapping shores. This is a striking city to look at: it was rebuilt in the nineteenth century after fire, and many of the buildings have a handsome neoclassical or art nouveau façade. Shoppers can browse the picturesque outdoor food and tourist markets stretching along the main harbour, where island-hopping ferries ply their trade.

Wherever you are here, you get the feeling of man and nature thinking pretty much along the same lines. In a country with over 200,000 lakes it would be pretty hard to escape a green sensibility, and the Finnish capital has made sure that concrete and stone have never taken priority over its distinctive features of trees, water and open space. There are bridges at every turn connecting the city's varied array of small islands, and a ten kilometre strip of parkland acts as a spine running vertically up from the centre. Renowned as a city of cool, it's somewhere that also revels in a hot nightlife and even hotter saunas – this is where they were invented. And if your blast of dry heat has left you wanting a refreshing dip, there's always a freezing lake close at hand.

137

LIVING THE CITY

The harbour is the hub of Helsinki. Arrive by boat and **Senate Square,** identified by the proud lines of its Lutheran cathedral, beckons in the background. To your east juts the headland of **Katajanokka,** while moving away from the harbour the city centre continues to the northwest, pierced by the elongated **Mannerheimintie** shopping street. To the east as you proceed along this thoroughfare is **Töölönlahti Bay**, the southern-most tip of **Central Park's** gloriously green spine. To the west is **Sibelius Park**, named after Finland's greatest composer. Helsinki sits in an archipelago and islands around it include **Suomenlinna** to the south, which houses an eighteenth century sea fortress, now a UNESCO World Heritage site.

PRACTICAL INFORMATION

ARRIVAL-DEPARTURE

Helsinki-Vantaa Airport is 19km north of the city. By taxi it'll cost around €30 and take 20-30min. There are also buses to Central Bus Station which will take 40min.

TRANSPORT

Getting across Helsinki is fast and easy: trams and buses whizz you round efficiently. A single ticket is cheap and good for any transfers you make within an hour: buy them from the driver, ticket machines, kiosks, metro stations or ferry terminal.

If you expect to use public transport often, it might be worth buying a tourist ticket, valid for one, three or five days and available from railway station, ticket machines or tourist office.

The Helsinki Card is another good option: it's valid for one, two or three days with a sliding scale of prices, and allows you unlimited transport plus free admission to museums and attractions.

There are regular ferries from the harbour to Suomenlinna; they sail a little less frequently to the other main islands.

EXPLORING HELSINKI

There's something about a harbour. See one and it becomes the pivotal part of a town or city. In Helsinki

that feeling is accentuated by the grand hubbub of the daily market that takes place there. It's a colourful gathering of farmers and fishermen, traders and crafts people, and the buzzy atmosphere is enhanced by the aromas from impromptu cafés selling fresh and smoked fish grilled on planks of cedar. For the surrounding elegant neoclassical look, we can thank the German architect Carl Engel, who engraved on a clean slate nearly 200 years ago. This chunk of the city is an ideal place just to stroll round for an hour or two, enjoying the juxtaposition of fine architecture and waterfront life.

When it comes to cathedrals, you'll encounter double vision as you step off your boat onto the waterside. The vivid green dome of the **Lutheran Cathedral** has been a focal point for visitors for over 150 years, standing majestically up the hill from the harbour in **Senate Square**. The buildings that surround it create a fine symmetry; this is recognized as one of Europe's most aesthetically satisfying squares. Dominating the far side of the harbour, meanwhile, is **Uspensky Cathedral,** western Europe's largest Orthodox church, a confident testimony to Russia's past influence in Finland. It has thirteen gold cupolas, and an equally elaborate interior redolent of black marble and glinting gold. Helsinki spreads westwards along the boutique-edged avenues of **Esplanadi,** a strip of parkland that comes alive on summer evenings as everyone promenades during the long hours of light.

This is a city that takes its culture seriously. There are a host of good museums within a small area up from Senate Square and Esplanadi. The **Ateneum** (National Gallery) is a suitably grand building to house the best of Finnish art, given international enhancement by a splattering of works by Gauguin, Cézanne, Degas, Modogliani and Van Gogh. Half a mile up the road stands the eye-catching, decade old **Kiasma,** a picture itself with its curvy zinc roof and vertical aluminium elevations. This is the home of Finnish modern art, complete with theatre for experimental drama, dance and music. Carry on a little further up Mannerheimintie and you reach the **National Museum**, another show-stopping building, chock full with Finnish artefacts from prehistoric times to the present day. The sense of classy cool so permeates these places that it's no surprise to find a museum itself dedicated to style: The **DesignMuseo** (go back south past Esplanadi) pits all the famous design styles side-by-side in a kaleidoscope of good taste, with a main emphasis on Finnish masters of the art.

→ NOUVEAU RICH

If you get a slight feeling of déjà vu when your eyes alight on the DesignMuseo's art nouveau exhibits, there's a good chance you've already spent some time in Katajanokka, the art nouveau quarter of the city jutting out like a wiggly foot as you approach the harbour by boat. art nouveau took off in Helsinki as the Arts and Crafts Movement of the early twentieth century happily coincided with a flowering of inspired Finnish architects, and dozens of their landmark buildings are found in eye-catching clusters, chief of which is Katajanokka, the first neighbourhood of this type in Europe, and still the continent's best preserved. As you walk along its streets, you'll notice fine stone ornamentation, dreamy towers and fanciful details of all kinds. Two other examples of jaw-dropping art nouveau are the **Helsinki Railway Station** with its sumptuous interior and iconic lamp-holding figures to welcome you in (if somewhat menacingly), and the **Pohjola** insurance building, near Esplanadi, which mixes stone with local wood to dramatic effect. Head to the west of the city, though, for one of Finland's top visitor attractions. **Temppeliaukio**, or the Church in the Rock, is exactly that. It was hollowed out from living bedrock in 1969, and to visit is like staring at an altar in a quarry. The copper roof offsets the deadening effect of the granite walls, and the acoustics are stunning: it's a top-notch venue for concerts.

→ SOUR NOTE

The world of Finnish music is dominated by one man…**Jean Sibelius**. In Helsinki they think so much of him they not only gave him a monument, they gave him a park to go with it. It's in the west of the city and the monument certainly caused a stir when it was unveiled back in 1967. Made up of a collection of different sized metallic pipes that make their own kind of music when the wind blows, it was subject to a torrent of abuse at the time because people couldn't see the connection with Sibelius. So they added a statue of his head (some way from the pipes) and things quietened down. Judge for yourself. Whatever you may think, the park is a lovely, peaceful place to take a stroll, and it's very close to the water's edge. The best place to hear the music of Sibelius is the impressive **Finlandia Hall**, opposite the National Museum and overlooking Toolo Bay. It's a stunning building of white marble and black granite to remind you of a piano keyboard, and its acoustics do wonders for the likes of the Helsinki Philharmonic who regularly hold court there.

→ GOING UNDERGROUND

This is an excellent city for shopping. Just looking in the windows is like a lesson in artistic design. Actually, just looking in the windows may be your wisest move, especially if you're on a tight budget, as prices tend to shoot in a distinctly northerly direction. The smartest shops are around Esplanadi and Mannerheimintie, where fashion, furniture, jewellery and homeware stores jostle for attention. Go to Senate Square and its surrounds for handicrafts and art shops. If the weather's bad, you can hide from it beneath the central streets in a maze of connected underground passages replete with shops, cafés, restaurants and food markets. You could spend a day browsing down there without ever emerging into daylight!

A short ferry trip to the island of Suomenlinna is a good idea in the summer. Certainly UNESCO thinks so: it made the sea fortress on the island's headland a World Heritage Site in 1991. The fortress, built by the Swedes in the mid-eighteenth century, was used as a defence against Russia, and some of the island's 900-strong population now lives in its converted naval buildings. There are several museums and exhibition halls, balanced by delightful walks, bays and coves, making it a good location for a whole day's excursion. The calm of the island is a kind of microcosm of Helsinki: a restful place that seems to run quietly, smoothly and apparently without much effort.

HELSINKI IN...

→ ONE DAY

Harbour market place, Uspensky Cathedral, Lutheran Cathedral, Katajanokka, a slow stroll up Mannerheimintie taking in the cultural sights

→ TWO DAYS

A ferry to Suomenlinna and most of the day at the sea fortress, Church in the Rock, the lively nightlife of Fredrikinkatu area (west of city)

→ THREE DAYS

A trip through Central Park, the Sibelius monument, the design area round Esplanadi

CALENDAR HIGHLIGHTS

Helsinki has been around since 1550, and Helsinki Day, its birthday, is celebrated on 12 June. There are plenty of festivities and events around the city – Esplanadi and Senate Square are filled with music and the performing arts, while sailing boats in the harbour let you on-board (for a fee). Also in June, Juhannus (midsummer) is celebrated with bonfires and gusto. Football fans can get a summer fix at the International Youth Tournament when hundreds of young players from around the world gather to compete for the Helsinki Cup. August's Helsinki Festival includes a Night of Arts with street shows till dawn, as well as classical music, dance, theatre and visual arts. Herring lovers should make for the Market Square in October – the Baltic Herring Festival has been held here for over 200 years. Traditional Christmas markets light up the harbour in December, when there's also the dramatic Lucia Parade to the Lutheran Cathedral.

EATING OUT

Jacques Chirac may not have been very complimentary about the Finnish diet but he had clearly never visited any of the superbly stylish restaurants in Helsinki regularly serving imaginative cuisine where local – and we mean local – ingredients are very much to the fore. Produce is sourced from the country's abundant lakes, forests and seas, so that your menu will assuredly be laden with the likes of reindeer, smoked reindeer, reindeer's tongue, elk in aspic, lampreys, Arctic char, Baltic herring, snow grouse and cloudberries. Generally speaking, complicated, fussy preparations are overlooked for those that let the natural flavours shine through. In the autumn, markets are piled high with woodland mushrooms, often from Lapland, and chefs make the most of this bounty. Local alcoholic drinks include schnapps, vodka and liqueurs made from local berries, while *lakka* (made from cloudberries) and *mesimarja* (brambleberries) are definitely worth discovering – you may not find them in any other European city. You'd find coffee anywhere in Europe, but not to the same extent as here: Finns are among the world's biggest coffee drinkers. In the gastronomic restaurants, lunch is a simpler affair with limited choice. Many serve customers until 11pm, and most of the time service charges are included in restaurant bills.

➜ WILD CITY

If you go for a walk in Central Park, you'll be surrounded by animal life. These include weasel, raccoon dog, muskrat, elk, arctic and brown hare. Birds are everywhere in the spring; in particular keep an eye open for Eurasian jay, dunnock, red-breasted flycatcher and garden and wood warblers.

➜ OLYMPIAN HEIGHTS

Although Helsinki is a pretty low-lying city, you can reach the heights at the 240ft Olympic Stadium tower, built in 1938. The view takes in the whole of the city and the outlying Gulf of Finland.

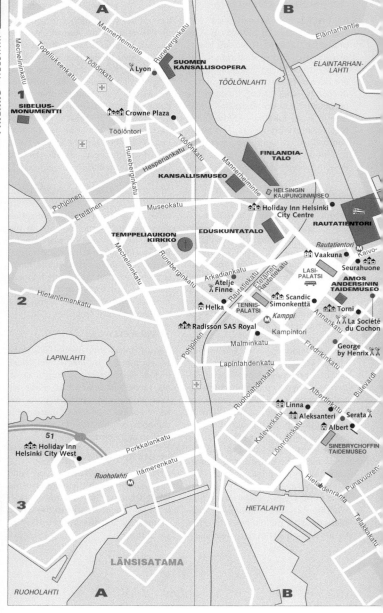

Mannerheimintie
Topeliuksenkatu
Mechelininkatu
Töölönkatu
Runeberginkatu
Eläintarhantie

A

B

Lyon

SUOMEN KANSALLISOOPERA

ELÄINTARHAN-LAHTI

TÖÖLÖNLAHTI

1

SIBELIUS-MONUMENTTI

Crowne Plaza

Töölöntori

FINLANDIA-TALO

Hesperiankatu
Töölönkatu
Runeberginkatu
Mannerheimintie

KANSALLISMUSEO

HELSINGIN KAUPUNGINMUSEO

Pohjoinen
Eteläinen

Museokatu

Holiday Inn Helsinki City Centre

RAUTATIENTORI

TEMPPELIAUKION KIRKKO

EDUSKUNTATALO

Rautatientori

Vaakuna
Kaivo-

Mechelininkatu
Runeberginkatu

Arkadiankatu

Seurahuone

Atelje Finne

Rautatiekatu
Eteläinen Rautatiekatu

LASI-PALATSI

AMOS ANDERSININ TAIDEMUSEO

2

Hietaniemenkatu

Helka

TENNIS-PALATSI

Scandic Simonkenttä

Torni

Radisson SAS Royal

Kamppi

La Société du Cochon

Annankatu

Pohjoinen

Kampintori

Malminkatu

Fredrikinkatu

George by Henrix

LAPINLAHTI

Lapinlahdenkatu

Ruoholahdenkatu

Albertinkatu
Bulevardi

Kalevankatu

Linna

Aleksanteri

Serata

Lönnrotinkatu

Albert

SINEBRYCHOFFIN TAIDEMUSEO

51

Holiday Inn Helsinki City West

Porkkalankatu

Itämerenranta

Hietalahdenranta
Punavuoren

Ruoholahti

3

HIETALAHTI

Telakkakatu

LÄNSISATAMA

A

B

RUOHOLAHTI

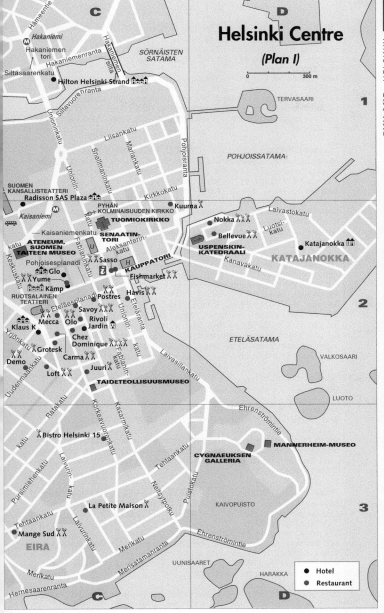

Helsinki Centre
(Plan I)

0   300 m

Hämeentie

Hakaniemi
Hakaniemen tori
Hakaniemenranta
Siltasaarenkatu
Hakaniemen silta

SÖRNÄISTEN SATAMA

Hilton Helsinki Strand

TERVASAARI

Siltavuorenranta
Unioninkatu
Liisankatu

Maariankatu

Pohjoisranta

POHJOISSATAMA

Snellmaninkatu

SUOMEN KANSALLISTEATTERI
Radisson SAS Plaza

Kirkkokatu

PYHÄN KOLMINAISUUDEN KIRKKO
Kuurna

Nokka

Laivastokatu

Kaisaniemi

TUOMIOKIRKKO

Bellevue

Luotsikatu

Kaisaniemenkatu

SENAATIN-TORI

Katajanokka

ATENEUM, SUOMEN TAITEEN MUSEO

Aleksanterin-katu

USPENSKIN-KATEDRAALI

KATAJANOKKA

Keskuskatu

Fabianin-

Kanavakatu

Pohjoisesplanadi
Sasso
KAUPPATORI

Glo
Yume
Kämp
Fishmarket

RUOTSALAINEN TEATTERI

Postres
Havis

Eteläesplanadi

Unioninkatu

Eteläranta

Savoy
Mecca   Olo
Rivoli
Jardin

ETELÄSATAMA

VALKOSAARI

Klaus K
Chez Dominique

Yrjönkatu

Grotesk

Carma

Uudenmaankatu

Demo

Fabianin-katu

Juuri

Loft

Laivasillankatu

LUOTO

TAIDETEOLLISUUSMUSEO

Ratakatu

Korkeavuorenkatu

Kasarminkatu

Ehrenströmintie

Bistro Helsinki 15

Lapurin-katu

Pursimiehenkatu

MANNERHEIM-MUSEO

Tehtaankatu

CYGNAEUKSEN GALLERIA

Neitsytpolku

Puistokatu

KAIVOPUISTO

La Petite Maison

Tehtaankatu

Laivurinkatu

Merikatu

Mange Sud

EIRA

Merikatu

Merisatamanranta

Ehrenströmintie

UUNISAARET

HARAKKA

Hernesaarenranta

● Hotel
● Restaurant

143

FINLAND - HELSINKI

Kämp 🛱 ₤₅ 🕙 🕸 🕭 座 喠 ⩽ 嗯 ⑪° 🖓 🛆 VISA ✪ 亞 ①
Pohjoisesplanadi 29 ⌧ *00100* – ⓜ *Kaisaniemi* – 𝒸 *(09) 576 111* – *hotelkamp@*
hotelkamp.fi – *Fax (09) 576 11 22* – *www.hotelkamp.fi* **C2**
174 rm – 🛉169/455 € 🛉🛉184/455 €, � 29 € – 5 suites
Rest Yume – see below
Rest *Kämp Café* – Menu 31 € (lunch) – Carte 39/63 €
 ♦ Grand Luxury ♦ Business ♦ Stylish ♦
Luxurious 19C hotel with superb spa and fitness suite. Well-equipped, elegant
bedrooms boast spacious marble bathrooms. Nightclub offers good champagne
selection; tempting cocktail list in the bar. Brasserie-style Kämp Café serves international dishes.

Crowne Plaza ⩽ ₤₅ 🕙 🕸 ◻ 座 喠 ⩽ rm 嗯 ⑪° 🖓 🖘
Mannerheimintie 50 ⌧ *00260* – 𝒸 *(09) 2521 0000* VISA ✪ 亞 ①
– *helsinki.cph@restel.fi* – *Fax (09) 2521 39 99* – *www.crowneplaza-helsinki.fi*
345 rm – 🛉115/339 € 🛉🛉136/360 €, ⊃ 25 € – 4 suites **A1**
Rest *Macu* – Menu 25/43 € – Carte dinner 31/48 €
 ♦ Business ♦ Modern ♦
Spacious hotel specialising in conferences. Comfortable, contemporary bedrooms
boast good facilities (the higher the better) and city or lake views. Fitness room,
pool and day spa cost extra. Warm, welcoming restaurant offers Mediterranean
cuisine.

Hilton Helsinki Strand ⩽ ₤₅ 🕸 ◻ 座 喠 ⩽ 嗯 ⑪° 🖓 🖘
John Stenbergin Ranta 4 ⌧ *00530* – ⓜ *Hakaniemi* VISA ✪ 亞 ①
– 𝒸 *(09) 393 51* – *helsinkistrand@hilton.com* – *Fax (09) 3935 32 55*
– *www.hilton.com* **C1**
185 rm – 🛉122/370 € 🛉🛉122/370 €, ⊃ 25 € – 7 suites
Rest *Bridges* – *(Sunday brunch only)* Menu 32/40 € – Carte 36/61 €
 ♦ Luxury ♦ Business ♦ Modern ♦
Spacious waterfront hotel with classical '80s design, an impressive atrium and a
smart relaxation/fitness centre. Bedrooms boast marble bathrooms; some have
water views. Restaurant offers a mix of classics and local cuisine.

Glo ₤₅ 🕙 🕸 座 喠 ⩽ 嗯 ⑪° 🖓 VISA ✪ 亞 ①
Kluuvikatu 4 ⌧ *00100* – ⓜ *Kaisaniemi* – 𝒸 *(010) 3444 400* – *glo@*
palacekamp.fi – *Fax (010) 3444 4 01* – *www.palacekamp.fi* **C2**
140 rm ⊃ – 🛉139/330 € 🛉🛉139/330 € – 4 suites
Rest *Cocina* – *(Closed Sunday)* Menu 28/54 € – Carte 30/57 €
 ♦ Luxury ♦ Modern ♦
Stylish, centrally located hotel with good spa/fitness facilities and complimentary
bicycles. Spacious bedrooms boast contemporary furniture and high-tech equip-
ment. Bar has lively atmosphere at weekends. Smart Spanish restaurant offers
Catalan inspired cuisine.

Klaus K ₤₅ 🕙 🕸 喠 ⩽ 嗯 ⑪° 🖓 VISA ✪ 亞 ①
Bulevardi 2 ⌧ *00120* – ⓜ *Rautatientori* – 𝒸 *(20) 770 4700* – *rooms@*
klauskhotel.com – *Fax (20) 770 47 30* – *www.klauskhotel.com*
– *Closed 22-25 December* **C2**
135 rm – 🛉194/374 € 🛉🛉229/399 €, ⊃ 22 € – 2 suites
Rest *Ilmatar* – 𝒸 *(20) 770 4714 (Closed Monday dinner, Saturday dinner and
Sunday)* Menu 50 € (dinner) – Carte 43/52 €
Rest *Toscanini* – 𝒸 *(20) 770 4713 (Closed lunch Sunday and Bank Holidays)*
Menu 23/44 € – Carte dinner 30/52 €
 ♦ Business ♦ Design ♦
Late 19C landmark building with great façade; stylish interior is design to reflect
The Kalevala's 'emotion contrasts'. Four styles of bedroom; bar and disco on
ground floor. Modern Finnish cuisine in contemporary Ilmatar and modern Tuscan
cuisine in lively Toscanini.

Radisson SAS Royal   🕉 ⅙ AC ⅙ rm SAT 🛰 🕯 🖧 ⤏ VISA 🚗 AE ⑩

Runeberginkatu 2 ⊠ 00100 – Ⓜ Kamppi – ℰ (20) 1234 701
– reservations.finland@radissonsas.com – Fax (20) 1234 7 02
– www.radissonsas.com
– Closed 5 days Christmas   **B2**
255 rm � – ♦175/215 € ♦♦175/215 € – 7 suites
Rest *Grill it!* – Carte 27/64 €
♦ Business ♦ Modern ♦

Two-winged hotel with pleasant bar, set close to the metro station. Spacious bedrooms boast grey marble bathrooms; 'Business class' rooms offer increased level of facilities and inclusive breakfast. Restaurant serves typical grill menu.

Radisson SAS Plaza   ⅙ 🕉 ⅙ AC ⅙ rm SAT 🕯 🖧 ⤏

Mikonkatu 23 ⊠ 00100 – Ⓜ Kaisaniemi   VISA 🚗 AE ⑩
– ℰ (20) 1234 703 – reservations.finland@radissonsas.com – Fax (20) 1234 7 04
– www.plaza.helsinki.radissonsas.com   **C1-2**
291 rm ⊑ – ♦100/190 € ♦♦120/220 € – 1 suite
Rest *Pääkonttori* – *(Closed lunch Saturday, Sunday and in summer)*
Carte 33/47 €
♦ Business ♦ Historic ♦

Early 20C building set close to the station – formerly a company HQ – and recently completed by a modern wing. Choice of 'Italian', 'Nordic' or 'Classic' bedrooms. Elegant Italian restaurant boasts impressive columns and stained glass windows.

Torni   🕉 AC ⅙ rm SAT 🕯 🖧 VISA 🚗 AE ⑩

Yrjönkatu 26 ⊠ 00100 – Ⓜ Rautatientori – ℰ (20) 1234 604 – torni.helsinki@
sokoshotels.fi – Fax (09) 4336 71 00 – www.sokoshotels.fi
– Closed Christmas   **B2**
146 rm – ♦99/215 € ♦♦99/235 €, ⊑ 22 € – 6 suites
Rest – *(Closed Sunday and Bank Holidays)* Menu 39/47 € – Carte 37/59 €
♦ Business ♦ Stylish ♦

Charming early 20C city centre hotel with 11 floor tower and a real sense of history. Warm, elegant décor with choice of 'art deco', 'functionalism' or 'art nouveau' bedrooms. Three bars, and pleasant art deco restaurant offering various types of cooking.

Holiday Inn Helsinki   ⅙ 🕉 ⅙ AC ⅙ rm SAT 🕯 🖧 P̃ ⤏

Messuaukio 1 (near Pasila Railway Station)   VISA 🚗 AE ⑩
(North : 5 km by Mannerheimintie, Nordenskiöldink, Savonkatu off Ratapihantie)
⊠ 00520 – ℰ (09) 150 900 – helsinki.holidayinn@restel.fi – Fax (09) 150 9 01
– www.restel.fi/holidayinn
239 rm ⊑ – ♦120/285 € ♦♦150/285 € – 5 suites
Rest *Terra Nova* – Carte 33/46 €
♦ Business ♦ Modern ♦

Set just outside the city – but close to a station – in the Masscentrum Fair Centre, this chain hotel is popular for conferences. Bright, warm bedrooms offer increasing levels of facilities. Welcoming Terra Nova serves international cuisine.

Holiday Inn Helsinki City West   ⅙ 🕉 ⅙ AC ⅙ SAT 🕯

Sulhasenkuja 3 ⊠ 00180 – Ⓜ Ruoholahti   VISA 🚗 AE ⑩
– ℰ (09) 4152 1000 – helsinki.hihcw@restel.fi – Fax (09) 4152 12 99
– www.hi-helsinkiwest.fi   **A3**
256 rm – ♦99/235 € ♦♦147/283 €, ⊑ 18 €
Rest *Fokka* – *(Closed lunch Saturday and Sunday)* Menu 35 € (lunch) – Carte
dinner 24/58 €
♦ Business ♦ Modern ♦

Set in a business park well away from the city centre but close to a station. Modern bedrooms display touches of colour, pleasant furniture and excellent soundproofing; compact bathrooms. Contemporary restaurant serves international cuisine.

Scandic Simonkenttä

Simonkatu 9 ⊠ 00100 – Ⓜ Kamppi – ℰ (09) 68 380 – simonkentta@
scandichotels.com – Fax (09) 68 3 81 11 – www.scandichotels.com
– Closed 23-27 December   **B2**
357 rm ☲ – ♦98/267 € ♦♦118/287 € – 3 suites
Rest Simonkatu – *(Closed Sunday)* Menu 24/38 € – Carte 28/45 €
♦ Business ♦ Modern ♦
Contemporary hotel in the heart of the city with attractive glazed façade. Bright
bedrooms display lots of wood and have some good views; superior rooms feature
private saunas. Restaurant offers a good choice of local and international cuisine.

Holiday Inn Helsinki City Centre

Elielinaukio 5 ⊠ 00100 – Ⓜ Rautatientori
– ℰ (09) 5425 5000 – helsinki.hihcc@restel.fi – Fax (09) 5425 52 99
– www.holiday-inn.com/hihelsinkicc   **B2**
174 rm – ♦155/283 € ♦♦295/313 €, ☲ 18 €
Rest Verde – *(Closed Sunday and lunch Saturday and Bank Holidays)* (buffet
lunch) Menu 9 € (lunch) – Carte 27/55 €
♦ Business ♦ Functional ♦
Contemporary city centre hotel, located close to the post office, station and main
shopping areas. Most of the modern bedrooms boast good city views; compact bathrooms. Restaurant serves international and Finnish recipes crafted from local produce.

Seurahuone

Kaivokatu 12 ⊠ 00100 – Ⓜ Rautatientori – ℰ (09) 69 141
– helsinki.seurahuone@restel.fi – Fax (09) 691 40 10 – www.hotelliseurahuone.fi
118 rm – ♦135/199 € ♦♦155/210 €, ☲ 19 €   **B2**
Rest – *(Closed Sunday)* Menu 40/46 € – Carte 43/58 €
♦ Historic ♦ Classic ♦
Early 20C hotel set by the station, where a sympathetic renovation has managed to
retain an period feel. Varying sized bedrooms display dark wood furniture and
Gustave Klimt prints. Traditional bar and an elegant restaurant with decorated ceiling and chandeliers.

Katajanokka

Vyökatu 1 ⊠ 00160 – ℰ (09) 686 450 – sales@bwkatajanokka.fi
– Fax (09) 670 2 90 – www.bwkatajanokka.fi   **D2**
106 rm ☲ – ♦107/259 € ♦♦154/295 €
Rest Jailbird – *(dinner only)* Carte 30/58 €
♦ Historic ♦ Modern ♦
Pleasantly restored late 19C former prison with high ceilinged corridors and original staircases still in situ. Old cells are now modern, comfortable, well-equipped
bedrooms. Large basement restaurant serves international cuisine and features a
preserved prison cell.

Vaakuna

Asema-aukio 2 ⊠ 00100 – Ⓜ Rautatientori – ℰ (20) 1234 610
– vaakuna.helsinki@sokoshotels.fi – Fax (09) 4337 71 00 – www.sokoshotels.fi
– Closed 9-13 April, 18-21 June and 23-27 December   **B2**
258 rm ☲ – ♦105/210 € ♦♦115/245 € – 12 suites
Rest – *(Closed Sunday)* Menu 25/72 € – Carte 31/52 €
♦ Business ♦ Historic ♦
Central hotel built for the 1952 Olympics, displaying a mix of original features and
contemporary styling. Spacious corner suites boast private saunas; some rooms
have balconies with views. 10th floor restaurant displays beautiful décor and offers
great city views; international dishes.

Aleksanteri

Albertinkatu 34 ⊠ 00180 – Ⓜ Kamppi – ℰ (20) 1234 643
– aleksanteri.helsinki@sokoshotels.fi – Fax (20) 1234 6 44 – www.sokoshotels.fi
– Closed 1 week Christmas   **B3**
151 rm ☲ – ♦88/228 € ♦♦98/238 €   **Rest Fransmanni** – Carte 25/49 €
♦ Business ♦ Modern ♦
Two renovated buildings set by the Alexander Theatre. The 1920s building offers
modern, comfortable well-equipped bedrooms, while the 1880s building boasts
larger rooms and more characterful features. Restaurant serves French cuisine.

FINLAND - HELSINKI

Linna 🐾   ⟨icons⟩

Lönnrotinkatu 29 ⊠ 00180 – ⓜ Kamppi – ℰ (010) 344 4100
– linna@palacekamp.fi – Fax (010) 344 41 01
– www.palacekamp.fi   **B3**
47 rm ☷ – †240/260 € ††260 € – 1 suite
Rest – *(Closed Sunday and Monday) (dinner only)* Menu 42 € – Carte 43/54 €
♦ Business ♦ Modern ♦
Early 20C landmark building with striking art nouveau styling, contemporary interior and stylish meeting rooms. Bedrooms, located in a more recent extension, boast good soundproofing. Cosy dining room offers classical French cooking.

Pasila   ⟨icons⟩

Maistraatinportti 3 (North : 5 km by Mannerheimintie, Nordenskiöldink off Vetuvitie) ⊠ 00240 – ℰ (20) 1234 613 – pasila.helsinki@sokoshotels.fi
– Fax (09) 143 7 71 – www.sokoshotels.fi
– Closed 18-31 December
178 rm ☷ – †71/165 € ††80/250 €
Rest *Sevilla* – *(closed July)* Carte 18/25 €
♦ Business ♦ Modern ♦
Spacious hotel set in a peaceful area close to the Hartwall Arena and Congress Centre; popular with business users during the week. Modern bedrooms display local decoration and furnishings. Informal Spanish-influenced restaurant; popular menu with grills.

Helka   ⟨icons⟩

Pohjoinen Rautatiekatu 23 ⊠ 00100 – ⓜ Kamppi – ℰ (09) 613 580
– reservations@helka.fi – Fax (09) 441 0 87 – www.helka.fi
– Closed 23-27 December   **B2**
146 rm ☷ – †94/177 € ††117/177 € – 3 suites
Rest *Helkan keittiö* – *(Buffet lunch)* Menu 35 € (dinner) – Carte dinner 32/44 €
♦ Business ♦ Functional ♦
Early 20C building re-designed around the concept of 'nature'. Well-kept, contemporary bedrooms display huge photos of flora and fauna on white walls. In the restaurant, classic Finnish cuisine can be enjoyed amongst real tree trunks and large forest photos.

Albert   ⟨icons⟩

Albertinkatu 30 ⊠ 00120 – ⓜ Kamppi – ℰ (20) 1234 638
– albert.helsinki@sokoshotel.fi – Fax (20) 1234 6 39
– www.sokoshotels.fi
– Closed 2 weeks Christmas   **B3**
95 rm ☷ – †78/218 € ††88/228 €
Rest *Trenta* – *(Closed Saturday lunch and Sunday)* Menu 35/57 €
– Carte 32/42 €
♦ Business ♦ Modern ♦
Late 19C building with welcoming lounge bar set opposite reception. Standard bedrooms are compact but well-equipped, especially for business users; superior are slightly larger. Contemporary Trenta offers an Italian menu.

Rivoli Jardin without rest   ⟨icons⟩

Kasarmikatu 40 ⊠ 00130 – ⓜ Kaisaniemi – ℰ (09) 681 500 – rivoli.jardin@ rivoli.fi – Fax (09) 656 9 88 – www.rivoli.fi
– Closed 23-26 December   **C2**
55 rm ☷ – †125/215 € ††145/245 €
♦ Business ♦ Classic ♦
Small city centre hotel with 1980s styling, pleasant breakfast room and comfortable, functional bedrooms; top floor rooms boast terraces. Now fully air conditioned throughout.

FINLAND - HELSINKI

Chez Dominique (Hans Valimaki/Matti Wikberg)

Rikhardinkatu 4 ⊠ *00130* – 🚇 *Rautatientori*
– ℰ *(09) 612 7393* – *info@chezdominique.fi* – *Fax (09) 612 4 42 20*
– *www.chezdominique.fi*
– *Closed 23-26 December,Sunday and Bank Holidays* **C2**
Rest – *(booking essential)* Menu 36 € (lunch), 99/139 € – Carte 93/107 €
Spec. Lobster poached in vanilla butter with avocado lasagna. Anjou pigeon "pastille cacao" and pigeon consommé. "Exotic fruit salad" eucalyptus and pineapple jus.
♦ Inventive ♦ Elegant ♦
Sleek, elegant restaurant that's just celebrated its 10th year. Highly accomplished, original dishes display top ingredients, bold flavours and delicate touches. Surprise dinner menus Mon and Sat.

Savoy

Eteläesplanadi 14 (8th floor) ⊠ *00130* – 🚇 *Kaisaniemi* – ℰ *(09) 6128 5330*
– *kai.kallio@royalravintolat.com* – *Fax (09) 628 7 15*
– *www.royalravintolat.com*
– *Closed Easter, Midsummer, 23 December-6 January, Saturday and Sunday*
Rest – Menu 58 € (lunch)/125 € – Carte 79/92 € **C2**
♦ Finnish ♦ Formal ♦
Elegant 8th floor restaurant dating back to 1937, boasting excellent panoramic views from its terrace. Carefully sourced organic ingredients create largely classical, Finnish dishes.

Nokka

Kanavaranta 7F ⊠ *00160* – ℰ *(09) 6128 5600* – *Fax (09) 260 00 59*
– *www.royalravintolat.com*
– *Closed Easter, Midsummer, 20 December-5 January, lunch Saturday and Sunday* **D2**
Rest – *(booking essential)* Menu 40 € (lunch), 59/69 € – Carte dinner 42/64 €
♦ Modern Finnish ♦ Elegant ♦
Converted harbourside warehouse with three striking rooms: an elegant bar, red-brick dining room and glazed wine cellar. Modern Finnish cuisine relies on small farm producers.

Postres (Vesa Parviainen/Samuli Wirgentius)

Eteläesplanadi 8 ⊠ *00130* – 🚇 *Kaisaniemi* – ℰ *(09) 663 300* – *info@postres.fi*
– *Fax 663 3 01* – *www.postres.fi*
– *Closed 10-13 April, 23 December-7 January, 4 weeks July, Saturday lunch, Sunday and Monday* **C2**
Rest – Menu 29 € (lunch), 53/69 € – Carte dinner 62/73 €
Spec. Lobster bolognese, caviar and parmesan. Lamb with salad jardinière. Chocolate and almond praline with chocolate sorbet.
♦ Modern ♦ Design ♦
19C building with modern styling and elegant hues, set on a famous esplanade. Contemporary Scandinavian dishes display French techniques and innovative touches. Knowledgeable sommelier.

Havis

Eteläranta 16 ⊠ *00130* – ℰ *(09) 6128 5800* – *myyntipalvelu@royalravintolat.com* – *Fax (09) 6869 56 56* – *www.royalravintolat.com/havis*
– *Closed Easter, 23-27 December, Sunday October-April and lunch Saturday and Sunday* **C2**
Rest – Menu 43 € (lunch), 50/70 € – Carte 45/72 €
♦ Seafood ♦ Elegant ♦
19C harbourside restaurant serving carefully crafted seafood dishes. Two rooms – one with elegant vaulted ceiling and maritime knick-knacks, the other with contemporary open kitchen and terrace.

XX **Olo**   🗚 ⇔ ⇔ 💳 ⓪ AE ⓪

Kasarmikatu 44 ✉ *00130 –* Ⓜ *Kaisaniemi –* ℰ *(09) 665 565 – info@ olo-ravintola.fi – Fax (09) 665 5 75 – www.olo-ravintola.fi*
– Closed Easter, 3 weeks July, Christmas, Saturday lunch, Monday dinner and Sunday   **C2**
Rest – Menu 33 € (lunch), 47/84 € – Carte dinner 54/71 €
♦ Contemporary ♦ Elegant ♦
Well run, modern city centre restaurant with elegant wine cellar and kitchen studio for private dining. Contemporary Finnish dishes use quality ingredients; more elaborate menus at dinner.

XX **Sasso**   🗚 ⇔ 💳 ⓪ AE ⓪

Pohjoisesplanadi 17 ✉ *00170 Helsinki –* Ⓜ *Kaisaniemi –* ℰ *(09) 1345 6240 – tables@palacekamp.fi – Fax (09) 1345 62 42 – www.palacekamp.fi*
– Closed Christmas, Easter, Midsummer and Sunday   **C2**
Rest – Menu 59 € (dinner) – Carte 36/50 €
♦ Italian ♦ Fashionable ♦
Spacious harbourside restaurant decorated in contemporary brown hues, with stylish bar and lounge. Modern north Italian dishes are crafted from top Scandinavian ingredients.

XX **Demo** (Tommi Tuominen/Teemu Aura)   ⇔ 💳 ⓪ AE ⓪
ॐ

Uudenmaankatu 11 ✉ *00120 Helsinki –* Ⓜ *Rautatientori –* ℰ *(09) 228 90 840 – demo@restaurantdemo.fi – Fax (09) 228 90 8 41 – www.restaurantdemo.fi*
– Closed 2 weeks Christmas and New Year, July, Sunday, Monday and Bank Holidays   **C2**
Rest – (booking essential) (dinner only) Menu 58 € – Carte 59/73 €
Spec. Slow-cooked duck with pear purée and almond milk. Pigeon stuffed with herbs and a port wine sauce. Hazelnut soufflé with almond ice cream.
♦ Modern Finnish ♦ Trendy ♦
Cosy restaurant with informal, candle-lit atmosphere. Mix of modern French and Finnish dishes, with a popular 'menu of the day'. Assured, highly confident cooking uses quality local produce.

XX **FishMarket**   🗚 ⇔ 💳 ⓪ AE ⓪

Pohjoisesplanadi 17 ✉ *00170 Helsinki –* Ⓜ *Kaisaniemi –* ℰ *(09) 1345 6220 – sales@palacekamp.fi – Fax (09) 1345 62 22 – www.palacekamp.fi*
– Closed Christmas, Easter, Midsummer, Sunday, and Monday in July
Rest – (dinner only) Carte 43/68 €   **C2**
♦ Seafood ♦ Elegant ♦
Several different dining areas set within the basement of a former pharmacy, with elegant décor and contemporary Scandinavian furnishings. Seasonal seafood menus use good ingredients.

XX **Yume** – at Kämp Hotel   🍴 🗚 ⇔ 💳 ⓪ AE ⓪

Kluuvikatu 2 ✉ *00100 –* Ⓜ *Kaisaniemi –* ℰ *(09) 5840 9356 – sales@ palacekamp.fi – Fax (09) 5761 15 15 – www.palacekamp.fi*
– Closed Christmas, Easter, Midsummer, Sunday, Bank Holidays and Saturday lunch   **C2**
Rest – Menu 57 € (dinner) – Carte 28/58 €
♦ Japanese ♦ Fashionable ♦
Contemporary restaurant set in the Kämp Hotel, with pleasant, seasonal décor. Menus present a wide selection of Japanese cuisine, with some dishes adapted to suit European tastes.

XX **Mecca**   🗚 ⇔ 💳 ⓪ AE ⓪
☺

Korkeavuorenkatu 34 ✉ *00130 –* Ⓜ *Kaisaniemi –* ℰ *(09) 1345 6200 – tables@ palacekamp.fi – Fax (09) 1345 62 19 – www.palacekamp.fi*
– Closed Christmas, Midsummer, Sunday and Bank Holidays   **C2**
Rest – (dinner only) Menu 38/64 €
♦ Innovative ♦ Fashionable ♦
Contemporary restaurant with lively atmosphere; the chef's abstract art adorns the walls. Creative cuisine displays strong techniques and top ingredients. Menus include 'Street Food' and a seven course 'Mystery Trip'.

FINLAND - HELSINKI

XX Carma (Markus Aremo)   AC ↳ VISA ⦾ AE ⦿
Ludviginkatu 3-5 ⊠ 00100 – Ⓜ Rautatientori – ℰ (09) 673 236 – carma@
carma.fi – www.carma.fi
– Closed Easter, July, 22-28 December, Saturday lunch and Sunday   C2
Rest – (booking essential) Menu 36 € (lunch), 49/69 € – Carte dinner 60/67 €
Spec. Tuna with scallop cream and red onion vinaigrette. Pigeon with
almond purée and raspberry sauce. Pear with tonka bean and milk choco-
late mousse.
♦ Modern ♦ Design ♦
Small, intimate dining room decorated in grey, with purple designer chairs. Cooking mixes modern and traditional, French and Scandinavian. The chef is a master
chocolatier.

XX Loft   ⛱ AC ↳ ⇄ VISA ⦾ AE ⦿
Yrjönkatu 18 ⊠ 00120 – Ⓜ Rautateintori – ℰ (09) 4281 2500 – loft@
ravintolaloft.fi – www.ravintolaloft.fi
– Closed Easter, July, Monday dinner and Sunday   C2
Rest – Menu 45 € (lunch), 51/65 € – Carte 39/52 €
♦ Scandinavian ♦ Design ♦
Modern restaurant – formerly a girls' school – with spacious rooms, high ceilings
and contemporary furniture. Seasonal Scandinavian dishes source quality produce
from small Finnish producers.

XX George by Henri'x   AC ↳ ⇄ VISA ⦾ AE ⦿
Kalevankatu 17 ⊠ 00100 – Ⓜ Kamppi – ℰ (010) 270 1702 – george@henrix.fi
– Fax (010) 672 7 89 – www.henrix.fi
– Closed Christmas, lunch in July, Saturday lunch and Sunday   B2
Rest – Menu 31 € (lunch), 64/70 € – Carte dinner 56/65 €
♦ Modern ♦ Intimate ♦
Smart 19C townhouse with warm, welcoming atmosphere and cosy feel. Cooking
combines good Finnish ingredients and traditional bases with modern influences
and imaginative Asian hints.

XX Mange Sud   AC ↳ VISA ⦾ AE ⦿
Tehtaankatu 34 D2 ⊠ 00150 – ℰ (020) 711 8350 – mail@mangesud.fi
– Fax (020) 711 83 59 – www.mangesud.fi
– Closed 21 December-6 January, Midsummer, Sunday and Monday
Rest – (dinner only) Menu 48/62 € – Carte 50/60 €   C3
♦ Mediterranean ♦ Minimalist ♦
Contemporary restaurant in the south of the city. Two dining rooms boast original
period tiling and modern furnishings. Ambitious chef creates new versions of old
Mediterranean recipes.

XX La Société du Cochon   AC ↳ VISA ⦾ AE ⦿
Mannerheimintie 14, (1st floor) ⊠ 00100 – Ⓜ Rautatientori – ℰ (020)
761 9888 – info@cochon.fi – Fax (020) 761 98 89 – www.cochon.fi
– Closed 24-26 December, 1 January, Good Friday, Midsummer and Bank
Holidays   B2
Rest – (Sundays brunch only) Menu 27 € (lunch)/39 € – Carte 50/61 €
♦ Brasserie ♦ Brasserie ♦
Bright, spacious restaurant with striking modern décor and pleasant feel. French
brasserie-style recipes use seasonal, organic ingredients and display contemporary
touches.

XX Bellevue   AC ↳ VISA ⦾ AE ⦿
Rahapajankatu 3 ⊠ 00160 – Ⓜ Kaisaniemi – ℰ (09) 179 560 – info@
restaurantbellevue.com – Fax (09) 636 9 85 – www.restaurantbellevue.com
– Closed Christmas, Midsummer, lunch in July and Sunday   D2
Rest – Menu 30 € (lunch) – Carte 44/66 €
♦ Russian ♦ Cosy ♦
Opened in 1917, a trendy townhouse restaurant boasting several dining rooms
adorned with old paintings and Russian knick-knacks. Authentic Russian cuisine
proudly maintains tradition.

Grotesk
🛱 AC ⇕ ⇆ VISA ◑ AE ⓞ

Ludviginkatu 10 ✉ *00130 –* **Ⓜ** *Rautatientori – ℰ ((10)) 470 2100 – grotesk@*
grotesk.fi – Fax ((10)) 470 21 01 – www.grotesk.fi
– Closed Christmas, Saturday lunch and Sunday **C2**
Rest – Menu 24 € (lunch) – Carte dinner 38/49 €
♦ Modern Finnish ♦ Fashionable ♦

Trendy restaurant with stylish black and red décor, canopy-covered patio terrace
and buzzy atmosphere. Modern Finnish cooking is heart-warming and flavoursome. Lounge bar open in the evening.

Bistro Helsinki 15
AC ⇕ VISA ◑ AE ⓞ

Korkeavuorenkatu 4B – ℰ (09) 4242 7650 – bistro@bistrohelsinki.fi – Fax (09)
679 4 72 – www.bistrohelsinki.fi
– Closed Christmas-New Year, Easter, Sunday and Monday **C3**
Rest – *(dinner only)* Carte dinner 36/46 €
♦ Italian ♦ Bistro ♦

Elegant neighbourhood restaurant, re-named to reflect the change in ownership.
Inspired Italian cooking has a modern edge and also incorporates some Finnish
touches.

Solna
AC ⇕ ⇆ VISA ◑ AE ⓞ

Solnantie 26 (North West : 5 km by Mannerheimintie, Tukholmankatu,
Paciusgatan and Munkkiniemen puistotie) ✉ *00330 – ℰ (09) 477 8400*
– tarjous@solna.fi – Fax (09) 241 44 22 – www.solna.fi
– Closed Christmas, Easter, July, Saturday lunch and Sunday dinner
Rest – Menu 40 € (lunch), 42/51 € – Carte dinner 41/45 €
♦ Scandinavian ♦ Bistro ♦

Contemporary neighbourhood restaurant with bistro-style dining rooms, set in a
residential area 20mins away from the city centre. Good value Scandinavian cooking with some French twists.

Lyon
AC VISA ◑ AE ⓞ

Mannerheimintie 56 ✉ *00260 – ℰ (09) 408 131 – ravintola.lyon@kolumbus.fi*
– Fax (09) 422 0 74 – www.ravintolalyon.fi
– Restricted opening in summer. Closed Easter, July, Christmas, Sunday,
Monday and Saturday lunch and Bank Holidays **A1**
Rest – Menu 30 € (lunch), 42/68 € – Carte 47/56 €
♦ French ♦ Bistro ♦

Well-established restaurant with traditional French bistro feel, set close to the
Opera. Wide-ranging menus offer seasonal French and vegetarian dishes crafted
from good Finnish ingredients.

La Petite Maison
⇕ VISA ◑ AE ⓞ

Huvilakatu 28A ✉ *00150 – ℰ (010) 270 1704 – sales@henrix.fi – Fax (09)*
6842 56 66 – www.henrix.fi
– Closed Christmas, July, Sunday and Monday **C3**
Rest – *(booking essential) (dinner only)* Menu 69/79 €
♦ French ♦ Cosy ♦

The name says it all: a small French restaurant. Two one-choice set menus available: one 'Classical', the other 'Regional', featuring regularly-changing dishes from
different areas of France.

Serata
⇕ VISA ◑ AE ⓞ

Bulevardi 32 ✉ *00120 –* **Ⓜ** *Kamppi – ℰ (09) 680 1365 – serata@serata.net*
– www.serata.net
– Closed 20 December-7 January, Easter, Sunday, Monday dinner, Saturday
lunch and Bank Holidays **B3**
Rest – *(booking essential at dinner)* Menu 20 € (lunch), 46/59 €
♦ Italian ♦ Friendly ♦

Laid-back Italian restaurant with convivial atmosphere and comprehensive wine
list. Authentic cooking offers a one-choice set menu 'of the day'; more elaborate
dishes at dinner.

X **Ateljé Finne**   Ⓐ🅒 ↵ VISA ⓄⓈ AE ⓄⒾ
Arkadiankatu 14 ⊠ 00100 – Ⓜ Kamppi – ℰ ((09)) 493 110 – info@ateljefinne.fi
– Fax ((040)) 411 53 16 – www.ateljefinne.fi
– Closed Christmas, Sunday and Monday, lunch in July   **B2**
Rest – Menu 39 € (dinner) – Carte lunch 23/36 €
♦ Modern Finnish ♦ Bistro ♦
Formerly the studio of famous Finnish sculptor Gunnar Finne, now three small
bistro-style dining rooms decorated with local art. Local dishes are given contem-
porary and international twists.

X **Juuri**   Ⓐ🅒 ↵ ⇔ VISA ⓄⓈ AE ⓄⒾ
Korkeavuorenkatu 27 ⊠ 00130 – ℰ (09) 635 732 – ravintola@juuri.fi – Fax (09)
635 7 32 – www.juuri.fi
– Closed 6 December, Christmas and Midsummer   **C2**
Rest – *(booking advisable)* Carte 39/54 €
♦ Finnish ♦ Bistro ♦
Small bistro set close to the Design Museum, serving traditional Finnish cuisine
with some innovative touches (including tapas-style starters). More concise lunch
menu.

X **Kuurna**   ↵ VISA ⓄⓈ AE ⓄⒾ
Meritullinkatu 6 ⊠ 00170 – Ⓜ Kaisaniemi – ℰ (09) 670 849 – info@kuurna.fi
– www.kuurna.fi
– Closed 2 weeks Christmas, 22 June-31 July, Sunday and Monday
Rest – *(booking essential) (dinner only)* Menu 35 €   **C2**
♦ Finnish ♦ Friendly ♦
Small restaurant with vaulted ceiling – seats just twenty. Set menu offers three
choices and blackboard supplements; seasonal Finnish cooking with an occasional
contemporary touch.

at Helsinki-Vantaa Airport North : 19 km by A 137

 Hilton Helsinki Vantaa   ⅃₆ 🐾 ⅏ Ⓐ🅒 ↵ rm 🄲 🛜 ⅃⅄ 🄿
Lentäjänkuja 1 ⊠ 01530 – ℰ (09) 732 20   VISA ⓄⓈ AE ⓄⒾ
– helsinkivantaa.airport@hilton – Fax (09) 732 2 22 11
– www.helsinki-vantaa-airport.hilton.com
241 rm – ♥125/335 € ♥♥125/370 €, � 25 € – 5 suites
Rest Gui – Menu 32 € (lunch) – Carte 44/64 €
♦ Business ♦ Modern ♦
Spacious glass hotel with relaxed ambience, 3mins from the international terminal.
Soundproofed bedrooms boast locally designed furniture, good facilities and large
bathrooms; some have saunas. Contemporary restaurant serves Finnish and international dishes.

FRANCE

PROFILE

→ **AREA:**
551 500 km²
(212 934 sq mi).

→ **POPULATION:**
63 800 000
inhabitants (est.
2008), density
= 110 per km².

→ **CAPITAL:**
Paris (conurbation
11 577 000
inhabitants).

→ **CURRENCY:**
Euro (€); rate
of exchange:
€ 1 = US$ 1.32 (Jan
2009).

→ **GOVERNMENT:**
Parliamentary
republic (since
1946). Member of
European Union since
1957 (one of the 6
founding countries).

→ **LANGUAGE:**
French.

→ **SPECIFIC PUBLIC
HOLIDAYS:**
Victory Day 1945
(8 May), Bastille
Day-National Day
(14 July), Armistice
Day 1918
(11 November).

→ **LOCAL TIME:**
GMT + 1 hour
in winter and GMT
+ 2 hours in
summer.

→ **CLIMATE:**
Temperate with cool
winters and warm
summers (Paris:
January: 3°C, July:
20°C). Mediterranean
climate in the south
(mild winters, hot
and sunny summers,
occasional strong
wind called the
mistral).

→ **INTERNATIONAL DIALLING
CODE:**
00 33 followed
by regional code
without the initial 0
and then the local
number.

→ **EMERGENCY:**
Police: ☏ 17;
Ambulance: ☏ 15;
Fire Brigade: ☏ 18.

→ **ELECTRICITY:**
220 volts AC,
50Hz. 2-pin round-
shaped continental
plugs.

→ **FORMALITIES**
Travellers from the
European Union
(EU), Switzerland,
Iceland and the main
countries of North
and South America
need a national
identity card or
passport (America:
passport required)
to visit France for less
than three months
(tourism or business
purpose). For visitors
from other countries
a visa may be
required, in addition
to a passport,
especially for those
wishing to stay for
longer than three
months. We advise
you to check with
your embassy before
travelling.

Population (est.2008): 2 166 000 (conurbation 11 577 000) – Altitude: 60m

R. Visage/SUNSET

It may be the city of a hundred and one clichés, but Paris never fails to come up with the goods. The French capital is one of the truly great cities of the world, a metropolis that eternally satisfies the desires of its beguiled visitors. With its harmonious layout, typified by the grand geometric boulevards radiating from the Arc de Triomphe like the spokes of a wheel, Paris is designed to enrapture.

Despite its ever-widening tentacles, most of the things worth seeing are contained within the city's ring road, the Boulevard Périphérique. The very heart of Paris is an island, the Ile de la Cité, where over two thousand years ago Celtic tribes first eked out a living. Later the Romans took control, attracted by the strategic possibilities of this settlement in the middle of the Seine. In time, a series of French kings achieved the centralisation of France, with Paris its cultural, political and economic nerve centre. Romance still pervades the streets of the twenty-first century city – a stroll along the Left Bank conjures images of Doisneau's magical monochrome photographs, while the narrow, cobbled streets of Montmartre vividly call up the colourful cool of Toulouse-Lautrec. But Paris is not resting on its laurels. New buildings and new cultural sensations are never far away: most recent has been the headline-grabbing Musée du Quai Branly. Les Grands Travaux are forever in the wings, waiting to inspire.

LIVING THE CITY

Paris wouldn't be Paris *sans* its Left and Right Banks. The **Left Bank** takes in the city south of the Seine; the **Right Bank** comprises the north and west. There are twenty **arrondissements** (quarters) set within the **Boulevard Périphérique**. The **Ile de la Cité** is the nucleus around which the city grew and the oldest quarters around this site are the 1st, 2nd, 3rd, 4th arrondissements on the Right Bank and 5th and 6th on the Left Bank. The remaining arrondisements fan out in a clockwise direction from here. Landmarks are universally known: the **Eiffel Tower** and the **Arc de Triomphe** are to the west of the centre (though on different sides of the river), the **Sacré-Coeur** is to the north, **Montparnasse Tower** to the south, and, of course, **Notre-Dame Cathedral** slap bang in the middle (of the Seine).

PRACTICAL INFORMATION

ARRIVAL-DEPARTURE

Roissy-Charles-de-Gaulle Airport is 23km northeast of Paris and by taxi will cost around €45. Air France Bus to Montparnasse or Porte Maillot runs every 15min. Orly Airport is 14km south and a taxi will be approximately €35. The Air France Bus runs to Invalides or Montparnasse. The Eurostar runs from the Gare du Nord, on the Rue de Dunkerque in the 10th arrondissement.

TRANSPORT

Paris has an excellent public transport system, and it's inexpensive too. Choose between the bus or the metro. A single ticket has a flat fare however far you travel; a carnet (book of ten tickets) works out at very good value for money.

There are three different travel cards you can also buy. Paris Visite is a one-day pass for three zones, or five-day pass for five zones; Mobilis is a one-day pass giving unlimited travel in either zones 1-2, or zones 1-8; Carte Orange is a weekly or monthly pass valid from Monday-Sunday or from the first of the month, offering an advantageous rate (you'll need a photograph for this one).

In 2007 Paris introduced the Velib. It's a self-service bicycle system – you pick up one of the twenty thousand bikes stationed at any of 750 points across the city, and leave it at another one. Subscription is a euro a day - the first half-hour of the journey is free, then after that you pay another euro if you require another half hour. Swiping a normal travel card will free up your bike – then it's just you versus the Parisian traffic…

EXPLORING PARIS

There are so many ways to enjoy the aura of Paris that even those who have never set foot in the city will recognise the familiar poetic selling points. A boat trip along the **Seine**; a café pose in **Boulevard St Germain**; the majestic glories of Notre-Dame cathedral; the utterly emblematic **Eiffel Tower**; a casual meander through the arty alleyways of **Montmartre** (enjoying the fabulous view, of course); the importance of the **Louvre's** mighty collection; getting to grips with the

Centre Pompidou (still futuristic after thirty years). However often you're reminded of them, these are images that never lose their power to seduce.

More than any other European city, Paris is defined by its river. The Seine slices its way through the centre, dividing the capital into two distinct areas. The Left Bank has, for centuries, been the home of poets, writers and artists. Inspired by the proximity of **the Sorbonne**, France's first university, radicals and intellectuals have throughout the ages flourished their quills and philosophised upon the world; many of their tracts can be found languishing in *les bouquinistes*, the Seine-side bookstalls it's impossible not to stop and browse over. Latin speaking students of the Sorbonne gave this area its name; today the **Latin Quarter** is filled with art galleries, cafés and bookshops. It's still the done thing to linger in the legendary cafés and brasseries of Boulevard St-Germain and reflect on more than the price of handbags in the smart boutiques lining the street. The classic trio – **Café de Flore, Les Deux Magots** and **Brasserie Lipp** – sit within a beguiling proximity to each other: a triangle of culinary and intellectual temptation.

→ THE SEINE CHOICE

Many of the major sights of Paris are famously strung out along the river, like an imposing architectural necklace. Two, of more recent vintage, have created quite a stir on the waterfront. If you're in Paris in the summer time, go down to the river at the eastern end of the Louvre, in the shadow of the **Pont des Arts**, and there you'll find sandy beaches, palm trees, ice-cream stalls, water sprinklers and deckchairs, not to mention fitness classes, too. This is **Paris Plage**, which, over the last five years, has become a bit of an institution. Further west, in the long shadow of the Eiffel Tower, a new museum (opened in 2006) has been pulling in visitors by the thousand. The **Musée du Quai Branly** squats low like a barge and invites you in along a sensuously swooping white ramp, while inside, mud-coloured walls form the dimly lit backdrop to powerful displays of tribal and folk art from France's colonial past. This was President Chirac's pet project, and it's shaping up to become as popular as those of his predecessors Pompidou and Mitterrand.

→ CREATING AN IMPRESSION

Mind you, it'll have to go some to catch the city's other artistic institutions. Further east along the riverfront, for example, the magical **Musée d'Orsay** continues to inspire. Everything about it is striking, from its Industrial Age railway station shell to its fabulous collections of nineteenth century art, which read like the greatest hits of Impressionist painting; realists and symbolists are there too, and substantial arrays of Van Gogh, Gauguin and Cézanne. Across the Seine, The Louvre – the museum to end all museums – is where to go for a daunting array of antiquities and French neo-classical grandeur, while the Centre Pompidou brings you bang up to date with a peerless collection of works by the likes of Picasso, Kandinsky, Matisse and Miro, right up to the latest trends.

→ EAST SIDE STORY

Taking a trip on the water doesn't have to mean taking a trip on the Seine. There's a hauntingly evocative sojourn you can take to a forgotten Paris – a liquid journey that takes you right under the **Bastille**. The **Canal Saint-Martin** winds its way up the eastern side of the city from the **Porte de l'Arsenal**, just below the Bastille, to **Parc de la Villette**, some four kilometres away. Alleys of chestnut trees cloak the peaceful, still waters of the two hundred year old canal, at one point just a stone's throw from the roaring **Place de la République**. The journey includes idyllic stretches with arching iron footbridges and boatman's pathways. It has ghoulish landmarks, too: the elegant **Maison des Morts** is where they used to pay rewards for bodies fished from the canal, and immediately below the Bastille, in a deep, dark netherworld, the boat slows to reveal a crypt, wherein lie the remains of the victims of the revolutions of 1830 and 1848. Open-topped tourist boats cover the fascinating two-and-a-half hour trip a few times a day.

→ THREE CEMETERIES

A cemetery may not be on every city's visitor hit-list, but every city isn't Paris, which has three great *cimetières*, full of history's rich and famous, and **Père-Lachaise** is the greatest of them all. Visit this massive sea of sepulchres, where the only movement appears to be the flapping of crows' wings above the deadly calm, and you'll pick out a long list of the great and the good who happen to have brea-

thed their last in the city. Then you'll understand the wisdom of the saying: "You haven't lived until you've died in Paris". The twelfth century lovers Abelard and Heloise were the first to be reburied here, and in the last two hundred years, they've been followed by a veritable A-list Who's Who. The range is phenomenal, from Chopin to Jim Morrison, Balzac to Piaf, Rossini to Oscar Wilde and Molière to Isadora Duncan. Despite the great clamour they may have made in their lives, they now rest in a stunningly tranquil oasis of peace, the largest green space in Paris.

For contrast, what better than the life-affirming paintings of the twentieth century's most acclaimed artist. The **Picasso Museum** is hidden in a fine seventeenth century mansion in **Rue de Thorigny**, a back street in the fascinating **Marais Quarter**. It holds nearly four thousand of his works, from childhood sketches to important late works.

CALENDAR HIGHLIGHTS

Whatever your fancy, Paris can satisfy it. March is a good time for book lovers to indulge a wordy fix: the Salon du Livre Paris at the Parc des Expositions Paris-Nord Villepinte is a five day orgy *des mots* with a shelf-full of performances, while Poets' Springtime has over five thousand well versed events in streets, cafés, markets, museums,

schools and stations. Later in the year, October's Reading Festival boasts hundreds of written word events. The music world takes to the City of Light with an eclectic flourish. The Open-Air Classical Music Festival on weekends in August and September brings world-class performers to Parc Floral, and in the same month Jazz à la Villette,

PARIS IN...

→ ONE DAY
Eiffel Tower and a boat trip on the Seine, Musée d'Orsay, people watching in a St-Germain brasserie

→ TWO DAYS
Musée du Quai Branly (or The Louvre), Montmartre, Picasso Museum and the Marais

→ THREE DAYS
Père-Lachaise, Canal Saint-Martin, Centre Pompidou

in Parc de la Villette, grows annually in stature as a home for innovative, experimental jazz. Dramatic Spanish rhythms cut through the springtime air in March's International Flamenco Festival at Le Grand Rex. Meantime, in north-east Paris, Seine St-Denis chills to the Banlieues Bleues, also in March. If your springtime fancy turns to art, then head to Art Paris, at Grand Palais, for a high quality small collection of paintings, sculptures and photos. You can stay up late either at La Nuit des Musées (May) when museums keep their doors open until 1am, or at Nuit Blanche (October) when it seems every public space in the city lets you in for a nocturnal cultural nose around. Catch a diverse programme of movies at springtime's Paris Film Festival, at the Cinéma Gaumont Marignan on the Champs-Élysées, or indulge your taste for wine at October's Montmartre Grape Harvest Festival (la Butte has its own vineyard). Hang around for a month and you can carouse on the Carrousel du Louvre at November's Great Wines Fair. If your taste is for beer and chips, a world away from the cultural clichés of Paris, then lose yourself amongst five million others at Europe's largest funfair, the Foire du Trône, at Pelouse de Reuilly, in the spring.

EATING OUT

Three hundred years ago, the social philosopher Montesquieu famously said, "Lunch kills half of Paris, supper the other half." Food plays such an important role in Gallic life that eating well is deemed a citizen's birthright. Stroll around any part of the capital and lavish looking shops offer perfectly presented treats: the Place de la Madeleine, for instance, has a lip-smacking range of treats. Parisians are intensely knowledgeable about their food and wine to the extent that restaurant, bistro and brasserie offerings here are of a higher quality than just about any other European city. Mind you, the French capital has had a lot on its plate in recent years with the rest of Europe seemingly playing catch up, by way of strong gastronomic performances coming from the likes of Barcelona, London and Copenhagen. As though Paris would rest on its laurels! Young chefs have taken up the cudgels and are opening their own crowd-pulling bistros and inventing their own styles; they've broken away from more formulaic regimes to achieve their own goals. They can call on the strongest backup team around: specialist produce shops line every Parisian thoroughfare, and there are not far short of a hundred city-wide markets teeming with fresh produce. Remember, when eating in Paris, to enjoy your meal at a leisurely pace – this is the city, after all, that practically shuts up shop at 12.30pm for lunch. People think nothing of spending up to three hours at the table, so if you're pressed for time, go to a brasserie or café. A service charge of fifteen per cent is normally included in the price of the meal, but locals leave an additional five per cent in smaller restaurants, and five to ten per cent in the grander establishments, which pride themselves on their service. (If you think the service has been a bit brusque or haughty, just remember that a Parisian waiter walks on average between six and twelve miles a day attending to customers' whims).

OPEN SATURDAY AND SUNDAY

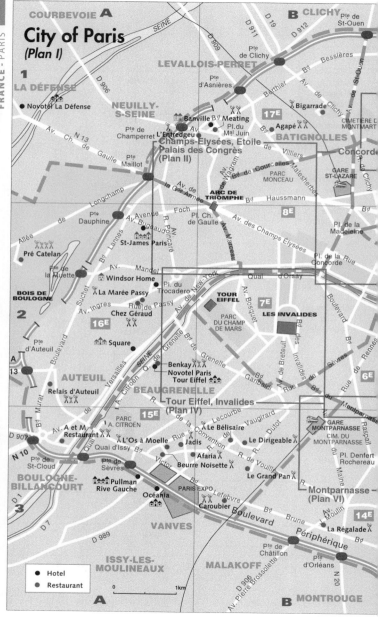

City of Paris
(Plan I)

COURBEVOIE **A**

B CLICHY

Pte de St-Ouen

SEINE

1

LA DÉFENSE

LEVALLOIS-PERRET

Pte de Clichy

● Novotel La Défense

NEUILLY-S-SEINE

Pte d'Asnières

Bigarrade ✗

CIMETIÈRE DE MONTMARTRE

Banville ✗ Meating

Pl. du M^{al} Juin

Agapé ✗ ✗

BATIGNOLLES

Pte de Champerret

L'Entredgeu

Champs-Elysées, Etoile Palais des Congrès (Plan II)

Concorde

Pte Maillot

PARC MONCEAU

GARE ST-LAZARE

ARC DE TRIOMPHE

Haussmann

Pl. de la Madeleine

Pte Dauphine

Avenue

Pl. Ch. de Gaulle

Av. des Champs Elysées

St-James Paris

Pl. de la Rue Concorde

8^E

Pré Catelan ✗✗✗✗

BOIS DE BOULOGNE

Pte de la Muette

Windsor Home

Pl. du Trocadéro

Quai d'Orsay

✗ La Marée Passy

TOUR EIFFEL

7^E

LES INVALIDES

Chez Géraud ✗✗

PARC DU CHAMP DE MARS

16^E

Pte d'Auteuil

Square

6^E

A

13

AUTEUIL

Benkay ✗✗✗

Novotel Paris Tour Eiffel

Relais d'Auteuil ✗✗✗

BEAUGRENELLE

Tour Eiffel, Invalides (Plan IV)

GARE MONTPARNASSE

CIM. DU MONTPARNASSE

15^E

✗ Le Bélisaire

A et M Restaurant ✗✗

PARC A. CITROËN

Le Dirigeable ✗

✗ L'Os à Moelle

Jadis ✗

Quai d'Issy

Afaria ✗

Pl. Denfert Rochereau

Pte de St-Cloud

Beurre Noisette ✗

Le Grand Pan ✗

BOULOGNE-BILLANCOURT

Pte de Sèvres

Pullman Rive Gauche

PARIS EXPO

Montparnasse (Plan VI)

Océania

Caroubier ✗✗

14^E

VANVES

La Régalade ✗

3

Périphérique

Pte de Châtillon

Pte d'Orléans

ISSY-LES-MOULINEAUX

MALAKOFF

| ● | Hotel |
| ● | Restaurant |

0   1km

A

B MONTROUGE

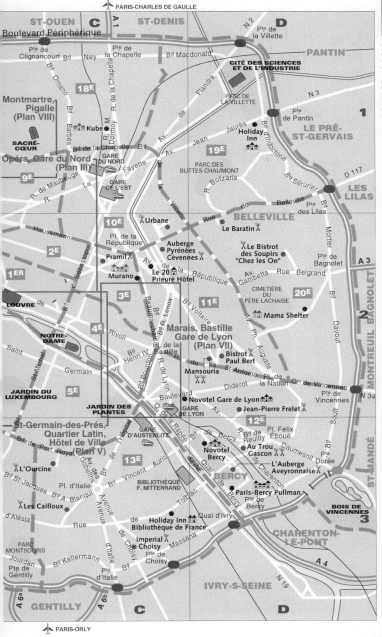

PARIS-CHARLES DE GAULLE

A1

ST-OUEN
Boulevard Périphérique

ST-DENIS

N 2

Pte de
la Villette

C

D

Pte de
Clignancourt

Bd Ney

Pte de
la Chapelle

Bd Macdonald

PANTIN

CITÉ DES SCIENCES
ET DE L'INDUSTRIE

N 3

Montmartre,
Pigalle
(Plan VIII)

18E

PARC DE
LA VILLETTE

Pte
de Pantin

LE PRÉ-
ST-GERVAIS

SACRÉ-
CŒUR

Kube

Bd de la Chapelle

GARE
DU NORD

Jaurès

Bd d'Indochine

Holiday
Inn

Opéra, Gare du Nord
(Plan III)

9E

GARE
DE L'EST

19E

PARC DES
BUTTES CHAUMONT

Bd Sérurier

D 117

LES
LILAS

R. de Maubeuge

Villette

R. Botzaris

de

Belleville

Pte
des Lilas

Haussmann

10E

Urbane

Rue

BELLEVILLE

Le Baratin

Mortier

Pl. de la
République

Auberge
Pyrénées
Cévennes

Le Bistrot
des Soupirs
"Chez les On"

Pte de
Bagnolet

A 3

2E

Pramil

Av.
de
la

Bd de Sébastopol

1ER

Murano

Le 20
Prieuré Hôtel

République

Av. Gambetta Rue Belgrand

MONTREUIL BAGNOLET

LOUVRE

de

3E

Bd Beaumarchais

Bd R. Lenoir

CIMETIÈRE
DU
PÈRE LACHAISE

20E

Davout

2

NOTRE-
DAME

4E

Rivoli

11E

Bd Voltaire

Mama Shelter

Saint

Bd Henri IV

Pl. de la
Bastille

Marais, Bastille
Gare de Lyon
(Plan VII)

Germain

St-Michel

Bd de Lyon

du
Mansouria

Bistrot
Paul Bert

St-Antoine

Auguste

JARDIN DU
LUXEMBOURG

5E

JARDIN DES
PLANTES

Boulevard

Diderot

Pl. de
la Nation

Crs de Vincennes

N 34

Pte de
Vincennes

ST-MANDÉ

GARE
DE LYON

Novotel Gare de Lyon

St-Germain-des-Prés,
Quartier Latin,
Hôtel de Ville
(Plan V)

GARE
D'AUSTERLITZ

de la Rapée

Av.

Jean-Pierre Frelet

12E

L'Ourcine

Bd de Port-Royal

13E

Bd St-Jacques

Bd A. Blanqui

Les Cailloux

d'Alésia

Bd des Gobelins

Pl. d'Italie

Avenue

Vincent Auriol

Quai

d'Austerlitz

SEINE

Quai de Bercy

BIBLIOTHÈQUE
F. MITTERRAND

Tolbiac

de Bercy

Bd de Bercy

Novotel
Bercy

Au Trou
Gascon

Bd de
Reuilly

Pl. Félix
Eboué

Daumesnil

L'Auberge
Aveyronnaise

Pte
Dorée

BOIS DE
VINCENNES

3

PARC
MONTSOURIS

Jourdan
Pte de
Gentilly

Bd Kellermann

Holiday Inn
Bibliothèque de France

Imperial
Choisy

Rue

de

Quai d'Ivry

Masséna

Paris-Bercy Pullman

Pte de
Bercy

CHARENTON-
LE-PONT

A 4

A 6a

A 6b

GENTILLY

Avenue d'Italie

Pte de
Choisy

Pte
d'Italie

IVRY-S-SEINE

N 19

C

D

PARIS-ORLY

167

Champs-Élysées, Étoile, Palais des Congrès
(Plan II)

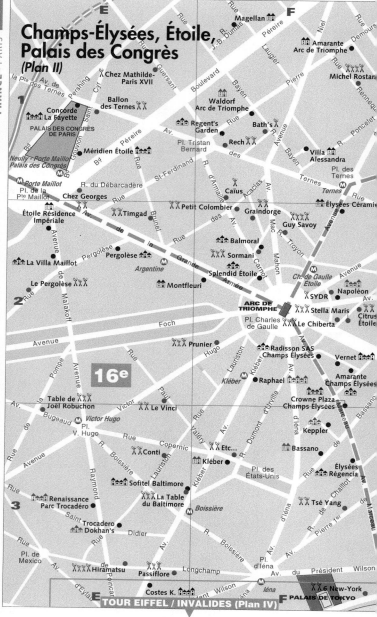

Magellan

Amarante Arc de Triomphe

Michel Rostan

Chez Mathilde-Paris XVII

Ballon des Ternes

Waldorf Arc de Triomphe

Concorde La Fayette

PALAIS DES CONGRÈS DE PARIS

Regent's Garden

Bath's

Méridien Étoile

Pl. Tristan Bernard

Rech

Villa Alessandra

Neuilly - Porte Maillot Palais des Congrès

Pl. des Ternes

Porte Maillot

R. du Débarcadère

Chez Georges

Caïus

Élysées Céram

Étoile Résidence Impériale

Timgad

Petit Colombier

Graindorge

Guy Savoy

Balmoral

La Villa Maillot

Pergolèse

Sormani

Le Pergolèse

Argentine

Splendid Étoile

Montfleuri

Ch. de Gaulle Étoile

Napoléon

SYDR

ARC DE TRIOMPHE

Stella Maris

Citrus Étoile

Pl. Charles de Gaulle

Le Chiberta

Foch

Prunier

Radisson SAS Champs Élysées

Vernet

16e

Kléber

Raphael

Amarante Champs Élysées

Crowne Plaza Champs Élysées

Table de Joël Robuchon

Victor Hugo

Le Vinci

Keppler

Pl. V. Hugo

Copernic

Conti

Bassano

Kléber

Pl. des États-Unis

Élysées Régencia

Sofitel Baltimore

La Table du Baltimore

Boissière

Tsé Yang

Renaissance Parc Trocadéro

Trocadéro

Dokhan's

Didier

Pl. de Mexico

Hiramatsu

Passiflore

Longchamp

Pl. d'Iéna

Av. du Président Wilson

Iéna

Costes K.

6 New-York

TOUR EIFFEL / INVALIDES (Plan IV)

PALAIS DE TOKYO

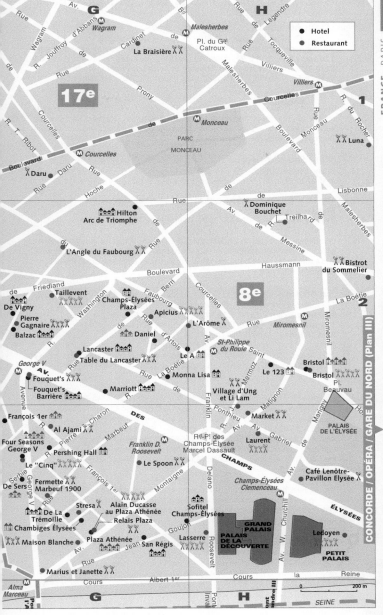

Hotel
Restaurant

Av. d'Abbans
G
Rue
Wagram
Rue Jouffroy
Av. de Wagram
Cardinet
de
Bd Malesherbes
Rue de Légendre
H
Rue de Tocqueville
Villiers
Villiers
Courcelles
R. du Rocher
1

La Braisière

Pl. du Gal Catroux

17e

Prony

de

Courcelles

Monceau

PARC MONCEAU

Boulevard de Courcelles

Monceau

Luna

Courcelles

Boulevard

Daru

Hoche

Rue

Lisbonne

Rue

Dominique Bouchet

Treilhard

Messine

Malesherbes

Hilton
Arc de Triomphe

de

Rue

L'Angle du Faubourg

Boulevard

Friedland

Berri

Faubourg

Courcelles

Haussmann

8e

La Boétie

Bistrot du Sommelier

2

De Vigny

Taillevent

Washington

Champs-Élysées Plaza

Apicius

L'Arôme

Miromesnil

Miromesnil

Pierre Gagnaire

Balzac

Daniel

Rue d'Artois

St-Philippe du Roule

Saint

Lancaster
Table du Lancaster

Le A

Bristol

George V

Rue

La Boétie

Monna Lisa

Le 123

Bristol

Fouquet's

Av.

Rue

Mermoz

Pl. Beauvau

Fouquet's Barrière

Marriott

de

Village d'Ung et Li Lam

Matignon

PALAIS DE L'ÉLYSÉE

François 1er

Avenue

Charon

Marbeuf

Ponthieu

Market

Ho

Al Ajami

Pierre

Franklin D. Roosevelt

Rd-Pt des Champs-Élysée Marcel Dassault

Av.

Gabriel

Marigny

Four Seasons George V

Pershing Hall

Laurent

Le "Cinq"

François 1er

Le Spoon

CHAMPS

Av.

Café Lenôtre-Pavillon Elysée

Fermette Marbeuf 1900

Montaigne

Champs-Élysées Clemenceau

Delano

ÉLYSÉES

De Sers

Stresa

Alain Ducasse au Plaza Athénée

De La Trémoille

Relais Plaza

Sofitel Champs-Élysées

GRAND PALAIS

Churchill

Chambiges Élysées

Maison Blanche

Plaza Athénée

Goujon

Lasserre

San Régis

PALAIS DE LA DÉCOUVERTE

Ledoyen

PETIT PALAIS

Marius et Janette

Rue

Jean Goujon

Roosevelt

Cours Albert 1er

Cours

la Reine

Alma Marceau

G

Pont Alexandre III

H

SEINE

0   200 m

169

Plaza Athénée

(8th) – **Ⓜ** *Alma Marceau* – *𝒞 01 53 67 66 65 – reservations@
plaza-athenee-paris.com – Fax 01 53 67 66 66 – www.plaza-athenee-paris.com*
146 rm – †595/650 € ††740/790 €, �2 50 € – 45 suites   **G3**
Rest *Alain Ducasse au Plaza Athénée* et *Le Relais Plaza* – see below
Rest *La Cour Jardin* – *𝒞 01 53 67 66 02 (open mid May-mid September)*
Carte 82/118 €

♦ Palace ♦ Grand Luxury ♦ Classical ♦

The luxury Parisian hotel par excellence: sumptuous Classic or Art Deco style
rooms, afternoon teas with music in the Gobelins gallery, stunning designer bar,
and luxurious Dior beauty salon. The charming, greenery-filled terrace of La Cour
Jardin opens when the weather turns nice.

Four Seasons George V

31 av. George-V (8th) – **Ⓜ** *George V*
– *𝒞 01 49 52 70 00 – reservation.paris@fourseasons.com – Fax 01 49 52 70 10
– www.fourseasons.com/paris*   **G3**
197 rm – †770/1520 € ††770/1520 €, ⊏⊐ 49 € – 48 suites
Rest *Le Cinq* – see below
Rest *La Galerie* – *𝒞 01 49 52 30 01* – Carte 95/157 €

♦ Palace ♦ Grand Luxury ♦ Personalised ♦

Completely renovated in an 18C style, the George V has luxurious bedrooms,
which are extremely spacious by Paris standards. Beautiful collections of art work
and a superb spa. In summer, the tables in this restaurant are set out in the delightful interior courtyard.

Le Bristol

112 r. Fg St-Honoré (8th) – **Ⓜ** *Miromesnil* – *𝒞 01 53 43 43 00 – resa@
lebristolparis.com – Fax 01 53 43 43 01 – www.lebristolparis.com*   **H2**
123 rm – †650 € ††710/1200 €, ⊏⊐ 55 € – 38 suites
Rest *Le Bristol* – see below

♦ Palace ♦ Grand Luxury ♦ Stylish ♦

1925 luxury hotel set around a magnificent garden. Sumptuous rooms, mainly
Louis XV or Louis XVI-style with an exceptional "boat" swimming pool on the top
floor.

Raphael

17 av. Kléber (16th) ⊠ 75116 – **Ⓜ** *Kléber* – *𝒞 01 53 64 32 00 – reservation@
raphael-hotel.com – Fax 01 53 64 32 01 – www.raphael-hotel.com*
45 rm – †345/505 € ††345/605 €, ⊏⊐ 39 € – 37 suites   **F2**
Rest *Les Jardins Plein Ciel* – *𝒞 01 53 64 32 30 (open from May to September
and closed Saturday lunch and Sunday)* Menu 75 € (weekdays)
Rest *La Salle à Manger* – *(closed August, Saturday and Sunday)*
Carte 50/200 €

♦ Grand Luxury ♦ Palace ♦ Stylish ♦

The Raphael, built in 1925, offers a superb wood-panelled gallery, refined rooms, a
rooftop terrace with a panoramic view and a trendy English bar. A lovely view of
Paris and traditional cuisine in the Jardins Plein Ciel (seventh floor). Superb dining
room in Grand Hotel style.

Renaissance Parc-Trocadéro without rest ⌂

55 av. R. Poincaré (16th) ⊠ 75116
– **Ⓜ** *Victor Hugo* – *𝒞 01 44 05 66 66 – restaurant.lerelais@
renaissancehotels.com – Fax 01 44 05 66 00 – www.marriott.com*
116 rm – †229/690 € ††249/750 €, ⊏⊐ 27 € – 4 suites   **E3**

♦ Grand Luxury ♦ Modern ♦

The rooms are elegant and pleasingly British in atmosphere. All are well equipped
(with Wifi) and distributed around a garden terrace. Part of the bar decor is by
Arman.

FRANCE - PARIS

Fouquet's Barrière
46 av. George-V (8th) – Ⓜ *George V* – ℰ *01 40 69 60 00*   VISA ⓄⓄ ΛΞ Ⓞ
– hotelfouquets@lucienbarriere.com – Fax 01 40 69 60 35
– www.fouquets-barriere.com   **G2**
86 rm – ♦710/1190 € ♦♦710/1190 €, ☲ 46 € – 21 suites
Rest *Fouquet's* – see below
Rest *Le Diane* – (closed 19 July-10 August, 3-11 January, Sunday and Monday)
Menu 68 € (weekday lunch), 90/135 € – Carte 109/155 €
♦ Grand Luxury ♦ Modern ♦
The latest hotel of the Barrière group offers 16,000m² of luxury: décor bearing the Garcia stamp, modern comfort, high technology, spa and garden. A hushed ambience at Le Diane with its brightly-lit niches adorned with flowers. Contemporary cuisine.

Hilton Arc de Triomphe
51 r. de Courcelles (8th) – Ⓜ *Courcelles* – ℰ *01 58 36 67 00*   VISA ⓄⓄ ΛΞ
– reservations.adt@hilton.com – Fax 01 58 36 67 84 – www.hilton.fr
463 rm – ♦295/650 € ♦♦295/650 €, ☲ 30 € – 50 suites   **G2**
Rest *Safran* – ℰ *01 58 36 67 96* – Menu 40 € (lunch) – Carte 50/75 €
♦ Luxury ♦ Chain hotel ♦ Personalised ♦
This new hotel, inspired by the liners of the 1930s, has successfully created their luxurious and refined atmosphere. Elegant Art Deco rooms designed by Jacques Garcia, patio with a fountain, fitness centre etc. At Safran, contemporary cuisine influenced by the flavours and scents of Asia.

Crowne Plaza Champs Elysées
64 av. Marceau (8th) – Ⓜ *George V* – ℰ *01 44 43 36 36*   VISA ⓄⓄ ΛΞ Ⓞ
– reservations@crowneplazaparischampselysees.com – Fax 0142 84 10 30
– www.crowneplazaparischampselysees.com   **F2**
56 rm – ♦450/1500 € ♦♦450/1500 €, ☲ 30 €
Rest – (opening planned in spring)
♦ Luxury ♦ Business ♦ Modern ♦
This new hotel in the Golden Triangle is a stone's throw from Place de l'Étoile, the ideal location for business meetings. Behind its Haussmann façade and fine red lacquer carriage door lies an interior decor by Bruno Borréone, an associate of Philippe Starck. A gourmet restaurant is scheduled to open in spring 2009.

Lancaster
7 r. Berri (8th) – Ⓜ *George V* – ℰ *01 40 76 40 76* – *restaurant@hotel-lancaster.fr*
– Fax 01 40 76 40 00 – www.hotel-lancaster.fr   **G2**
46 rm – ♦270/320 € ♦♦425/520 €, ☲ 37 € – 11 suites
Rest *La Table du Lancaster* – see below
♦ Luxury ♦ Classical ♦
Boris Pastoukhoff paid for his lodging in this hotel with paintings, thus adding richly to this former mansion's stylish décor. Its discreet luxury was also beloved by Marlene Dietrich.

Sofitel Baltimore
88 bis av. Kléber (16th) ✉ *75116* – Ⓜ *Boissière* – ℰ *01 44 34 54 54* – *h2789@*
accor.com – Fax 01 44 34 54 44 – www.baltimore-sofitel.com
103 rm – ♦470/890 € ♦♦470/890 €, ☲ 26 € – 1 suite   **E3**
Rest *Table du Baltimore* – see below
♦ Luxury ♦ Modern ♦
Simple furniture, trendy fabrics, old photos of the city of Baltimore: the contemporary decor of the rooms contrasts with the architecture of this 19C building.

Vernet
25 r. Vernet (8th) – Ⓜ *Charles de Gaulle-Etoile* – ℰ *01 44 31 98 00*
– reservations@hotelvernet.com – Fax 01 44 31 85 69 – www.hotelvernet.com
50 rm – ♦290/340 € ♦♦290/340 €, ☲ 30 € – 9 suites   **F2**
Rest *Les Élysées* – ℰ *01 44 31 98 98* – Menu 45 € (lunch) – Carte 51/73 €
♦ Luxury ♦ Classical ♦
A fine building dating from the 1920s, with a dressed-stone façade and wrought-iron balconies. Empire- or Louis XVI-style rooms. Fashionable bar and grill. Both the chic, bistro-style traditional cuisine and the glass-roofed dining room and bar have a modern feel.

Champs-Élysées Plaza without rest
35 r. de Berri (8th) – Ⓜ *George V* – ℰ *01 53 53 20 20*
– *info@champselyseesplaza.com* – *Fax 01 53 53 20 21*
– *www.champselyseesplaza.com*   **G2**
35 rm – ♦490/690 € ♦♦490/690 €, ⌷ 24 € – 10 suites
♦ Luxury ♦ Personalised ♦
The spacious and elegant rooms of this refurbished hotel sport a happy marriage of period and more contemporary furniture. Lovely sitting room with fireplace. Fitness facilities.

Napoléon
40 av. Friedland (8th) – Ⓜ *Charles de Gaulle-Etoile* – ℰ *01 56 68 43 21*
– *napoleon@hotelnapoleon.com* – *Fax 01 47 66 82 33*
– *www.hotelnapoleonparis.com*   **F2**
101 rm – ♦540/640 € ♦♦540/640 €, ⌷ 26 € – 30 suites
Rest – *(closed dinner, Saturday and Sunday)* Carte 55/80 €
♦ Luxury ♦ Personalised ♦
A stone's throw from Place de l'Étoile, this hotel-museum honours the emperor's memory via autographs, figurines and paintings from the period. Plush Directoire- or Empire-style rooms. A traditional menu served in the restrained, cosy, wainscoted restaurant.

Balzac without rest
6 r. Balzac (8th) – Ⓜ *George V* – ℰ *01 44 35 18 00* – *reservation-balzac@*
jjwhotels.com – *Fax 01 44 35 18 05* – *www.hotelbalzac.com*   **G2**
57 rm – ♦420/500 € ♦♦470/550 €, ⌷ 38 € – 13 suites
♦ Luxury ♦ Classical ♦
Hotel completely refurbished in luxury style, with neo-Classical décor, a vibrant colour scheme and references to the writer Balzac. Period furniture and high-tech facilities in the guestrooms.

Costes K. without rest
81 av. Kléber (16th) ⊠ *75116* – Ⓜ *Trocadéro* – ℰ *01 44 05 75 75* – *reception@*
hotelcostesk.com – *Fax 01 44 05 74 74* – *www.hotelcostesk.com*   **E3**
83 rm – ♦300/350 € ♦♦350/400 €, ⌷ 20 €
♦ Luxury ♦ Minimalist ♦
This hotel by Ricardo Bofill is ultra-modern. It invites you to enjoy the discreet calm of its vast rooms with their pure lines, laid out around a Japanese-style patio.

San Régis
12 r. J. Goujon (8th) – Ⓜ *Champs-Elysées Clemenceau* – ℰ *01 44 95 16 16*
– *message@hotel-sanregis.fr* – *Fax 01 45 61 05 48* – *www.hotel-sanregis.fr*
41 rm – ♦350/745 € ♦♦465/745 €, ⌷ 36 € – 3 suites   **G3**
Rest – *(closed August and Sunday)* Menu 40 € *(weekdays lunch)*
– Carte 49/63 €
♦ Luxury ♦ Personalised ♦
This 1857 townhouse has been remodelled with taste. A fine staircase adorned with stained glass and statues leads to delightful guestrooms furnished with a diverse range of furniture. The hotel's exquisitely appointed restaurant occupies a subdued but luxurious and exclusive lounge-library.

Le Méridien Étoile
81 bd Gouvion St-Cyr (17th) – Ⓜ *Neuilly-Porte Maillot* – ℰ *01 40 68 34 34*
– *guest.etoile@lemeridien.com* – *Fax 01 40 68 31 31* – *www.lemeridien.com/etoile*
1025 rm – ♦175/475 € ♦♦175/475 €, ⌷ 25 € – 21 suites   **E1**
Rest L'Oneroc – ℰ *01 40 68 30 40 (closed from end July to end August, 20-28 December, Saturday and Sunday)* Menu 44 € *(weekdays)*/75 € – Carte 52/90 €
Rest La Terrasse du Jazz – ℰ *01 40 68 30 42* – Carte 25/49 €
♦ Business ♦ Modern ♦
Facilities at this huge hotel include a jazz club, bar, boutiques and an impressive conference centre. Black granite and shades of beige predominate in the contemporary-style guestrooms. The Orenoc reflects current tastes in food, and has warm, colonial-style decor. An updated menu and live music with the Sunday brunch at the Jazz Club Lounge.

FRANCE - PARIS

Concorde Lafayette ≤ 🕭 🖭 ↳ rm 🖭 ⁽¹⁾ 🖧 VISA ⓞ AE ⓞ

3 pl. Gén. Koenig (17th) – **Ⓜ** *Porte Maillot* – *𝒞 01 40 68 50 68* – *booking@ concorde-hotels.com* – *Fax 01 40 68 50 43* – *www.concorde-lafayette.com*
931 rm – ♦150/600 € ♦♦150/600 €, ☲ 28 € – 21 suites   **E1**
Rest *La Fayette* – *𝒞 01 40 68 51 19* – Menu 45 € (lunch) – Carte 46/69 €
♦ Business ♦ Modern ♦

This 33-floor tower, part of the city's convention centre, offers wonderful views of Paris from most of its spacious and comfortable rooms, as well as from the panoramic bar. Eat as much as you like at the buffet of the La Fayette restaurant.

De Vigny 🖭 rm ↳ rm 🖭 ⁽¹⁾ 🖘 VISA ⓞ AE ⓞ

9 r. Balzac (8th) – **Ⓜ** *George V* – *𝒞 01 42 99 80 80* – *reservation@ hoteldevigny.com* – *Fax 01 42 99 80 40* – *www.hoteldevigny.com*   **G2**
26 rm – ♦290/395 € ♦♦290/440 €, ☲ 39 € – 11 suites
Rest *Baretto* – *(closed 15-24 August)* Menu 60 € bi/95 € bi – Carte 54/84 €
♦ Luxury ♦ Personalised ♦

A discreet stylish hotel close to the Champs-Elysées. The snug rooms are graced with personalised touches including a few four-poster beds. Cosy fireside lounge. The Baretto serves traditional cuisine in a stylish, low-key atmosphere and Art Deco setting.

Marriott 🖙 🖪 🕭 🖦 rm 🖭 ↳ 🖭 ⁽¹⁾ 🖧 🖘 VISA ⓞ AE ⓞ

70 av. des Champs-Élysées (8th) – **Ⓜ** *Franklin D. Roosevelt* – *𝒞 01 53 93 55 00* – *mhrs.pardt.ays@marriotthotels.com* – *Fax 01 53 93 55 01*
– *www.marriott.com/pardt*   **G2**
174 rm – ♦355/775 € ♦♦355/775 €, ☲ 29 € – 18 suites
Rest *Sur les Champs* – *𝒞 01 53 93 55 44 (closed Saturday lunch and Sunday lunch)* Menu 45 € – Carte 65/90 €
♦ Luxury ♦ Chain hotel ♦ Classical ♦

Enjoy American efficiency combined with lavish comfort in this smart hotel. Most of the guestrooms overlook the Champs-Élysées. Traditional dishes and grills are served in the contemporary decor of the restaurant (red and chocolate tones) and on the terrace.

La Trémoille 🖪 🕭 rm 🖭 ↳ rm 🖭 ⁽¹⁾ 🖧 VISA ⓞ AE ⓞ

14 r. Trémoille (8th) – **Ⓜ** *Alma Marceau* – *𝒞 01 56 52 14 00* – *reservation@ hotel-tremoille.com* – *Fax 01 40 70 01 08* – *www.hotel-tremoille.com*
90 rm – ♦315/485 € ♦♦370/570 €, ☲ 37 € – 3 suites   **G3**
Rest *Louis2* – *(closed Saturday lunch, Sunday and holidays)* Menu 48/68 €
– Carte 49/70 €
♦ Luxury ♦ Modern ♦

The hotel has been successfully refurbished with contemporary decor combining the old and the ultra-modern, the latest high-tech equipment, and marble bathrooms with Portuguese tiles. Refurbished, comfortable and lit up by a skylight, the Louis 2 serves modern cuisine.

Keppler without rest 🖪 🖟 🕭 🖭 ↳ 🖭 ⁽¹⁾ 🖧 VISA ⓞ AE ⓞ

10 r. Keppler (16th) ✉ *75116* – **Ⓜ** *George V* – *𝒞 01 47 20 65 05* – *hotel@ keppler.fr* – *Fax 01 47 23 02 29* – *www.keppler.fr*   **F3**
34 rm – ♦325/350 € ♦♦350/390 €, ☲ 22 € – 5 suites
♦ Luxury ♦ Personalised ♦

This luxurious, sophisticated establishment is the work of designer Pierre-Yves Rochon. A magical blend of styles, materials and light sets the tone in the lobby and rooms.

Trocadero Dokhan's without rest 🖭 ↳ 🖭 ⁽¹⁾ VISA ⓞ AE ⓞ

117 r. Lauriston (16th) ✉ *75116* – **Ⓜ** *Trocadéro* – *𝒞 01 53 65 66 99*
– *reservation@dokhans.com* – *Fax 01 53 65 66 88*
– *www.dokhans-sofitel-paris.com*   **E3**
45 rm – ♦450/500 € ♦♦450/500 €, ☲ 27 € – 4 suites
♦ Townhouse ♦ Personalised ♦

Attractive town house (1910) with Palladian architecture and neo-Classical interior decor. 18C celadon wood panelling in the cosy lounges and intimate champagne bar.

FRANCE - PARIS

De Sers

41 av. Pierre 1er de Serbie (8th) – Ⓜ George V – ℰ 01 53 23 75 75 – contact@
hoteldesers.com – Fax 01 53 23 75 76 – www.hoteldesers.com   **G3**
49 rm ⌷ – ♦299/550 € ♦♦299/550 € – 3 suites
Rest – (closed August) Carte 50/85 €
♦ Luxury ♦ Modern ♦

Successfully refurbished late-19C townhouse. While the hall has kept its original
character, the rooms are thoroughly modern. The food reflects current tastes and
is served in a designer dining room or, in summer, on the pleasant terrace.

François 1er without rest

7 r. Magellan (8th) – Ⓜ George V – ℰ 01 47 23 44 04 – hotel@
hotel-francois1er.fr – Fax 01 47 23 93 43 – www.the-paris-hotel.com
40 rm – ♦300/390 € ♦♦325/490 €, ⌷ 22 € – 2 suites   **G3**
♦ Luxury ♦ Personalised ♦

Carrara marble, mouldings, curios, antique furniture and a plethora of paintings set
the lavish decor created by French architect Pierre Yves Rochon. Substantial buffet
breakfasts.

La Villa Maillot without rest

143 av. Malakoff (16th) ✉ 75116 – Ⓜ Porte Maillot – ℰ 01 53 64 52 52
– resa@lavillamaillot.fr – Fax 01 45 00 60 61 – www.lavillamaillot.fr
39 rm – ♦230/415 € ♦♦230/415 €, ⌷ 28 € – 3 suites   **E2**
♦ Luxury ♦ Classical ♦

A step away from Porte Maillot. Soft colours, a high level of comfort and good
soundproofing in the rooms. Glassed-in space for breakfasts, opening onto the
greenery.

Daniel

8 r. Frédéric Bastiat (8th) – Ⓜ St-Philippe du Roule – ℰ 01 42 56 17 00
– danielparis@relaischateaux.com – Fax 01 42 56 17 01
– www.hoteldanielparis.com   **G2**
25 rm – ♦350/500 € ♦♦420/500 €, ⌷ 27 € – 1 suite
Rest – Menu 80 € – Carte 45/67 €
♦ Luxury ♦ Personalised ♦

This hotel likes travel! Furniture and objects brought back from all over the world
combined with a variety of patterned fabrics create a refined and welcoming
decor for Parisian globetrotters.

Sofitel Champs-Élysées

8 r. J. Goujon (8th) – Ⓜ Champs-Elysées Clemenceau
– ℰ 01 40 74 64 64 – h1184-re@accor.com – Fax 01 40 74 79 66
– www.sofitel-champselysees-paris.com   **G-H3**
40 rm – ♦410/500 € ♦♦410/510 €, ⌷ 27 €
Rest Les Signatures – ℰ 01 40 74 64 94 (closed 1-23 August, 25 December-
3 January, Saturday, Sunday and Bank Holidays) (lunch only) Menu 41/49 €
– Carte 52/61 €
♦ Chain hotel ♦ Luxury ♦ Personalised ♦

A Second Empire building shared with the Press Club of France. The rooms have a
contemporary new look and are equipped with state-of-the-art facilities. Business
centre. Minimalist decor and a lovely terrace. A restaurant popular with journalists.

Splendid Étoile

1bis av. Carnot (17th) – Ⓜ Charles de Gaulle-Etoile – ℰ 01 45 72 72 00 – sales@
groupefrontenac.com – Fax 01 45 72 72 01 – www.hsplendid.com
54 rm – ♦310/400 € ♦♦310/400 €, ⌷ 25 € – 3 suites   **F2**
Rest Le Pré Carré – Menu 34 € (dinner) – Carte 34/69 €
♦ Traditional ♦ Classical ♦

Beautiful classical façade with wrought-iron balconies. Spacious rooms full of character, embellished with Louis XV furnishings; some look out onto the Arc de
Triomphe.

Pergolèse without rest   ⟨icons⟩

3 r. Pergolèse (16th) ✉ 75116 – **Ⓜ** Argentine – ✆ 01 53 64 04 04
– hotel@pergolese.com – Fax 01 53 64 04 40 – www.hotelpergolese.com
40 rm – †230 € ††260/390 €, ⊑ 18 €

◆ Business ◆ Design ◆

E2

Restrained 16th arrondissement chic on the outside hides a successful designer interior combining mahogany, glass bricks, chrome and bright colours. Breakfast facing a pleasant patio.

Radisson SAS Champs-Élysées   ⟨icons⟩

78 av. Marceau (8th) – **Ⓜ** Charles de Gaulle-Etoile
– ✆ 01 53 23 43 43 – reservations.paris@radissonsas.com – Fax 01 53 23 43 44
– www.champselysees.paris.radissonsas.com   F2
46 rm – †300/600 € ††300/700 €, ⊑ 29 €
Rest *La Place* – (closed 1-23 August, 25 December-3 January, Saturday and Sunday) Menu 50/80 € – Carte 65/84 €

◆ Chain hotel ◆ Luxury ◆ Modern ◆

A new hotel occupying the former headquarters of Louis Vuitton. Restful, contemporary rooms, high-tech equipment (plasma TVs) and excellent soundproofing. Updated menu and small courtyard terrace at La Place restaurant.

Élysées Régencia without rest   ⟨icons⟩

41 av. Marceau (16th) ✉ 75116 – **Ⓜ** George V – ✆ 01 47 20 42 65 – info@regencia.com – Fax 01 49 52 03 42 – www.regencia.com   F3
43 rm – †195/275 € ††215/295 €, ⊑ 19 €

◆ Family ◆ Design ◆

Tastefully renovated in a designer style, this hotel offers modern, stylish rooms (blue, fuchsia or aniseed), an elegant sitting room, and a bar/library (red and chocolate coloured wainscoting).

Regent's Garden without rest   ⟨icons⟩

6 r. P. Demours (17th) – **Ⓜ** Ternes – ✆ 01 45 74 07 30 – hotel.regents.garden @wanadoo.fr – Fax 01 40 55 01 42 – www.bestwestern-regents.com
39 rm – †290/440 € ††290/440 €, ⊑ 19 €   F1

◆ Traditional ◆ Design ◆

Townhouse commissioned by Napoleon III for his doctor, now fully refurbished in a boutique hotel style. Fashionable bedrooms, Japanese garden, and Ecolabel certified.

Balmoral without rest   ⟨icons⟩

6 r. Gén. Lanrezac (17th) – **Ⓜ** Charles de Gaulle-Etoile – ✆ 01 43 80 30 50
– hotel@hotelbalmoral.fr – Fax 01 43 80 51 56 – www.hotel-balmoral.com
57 rm – †135/145 € ††150/185 €, ⊑ 10 €   F2

◆ Traditional ◆ Personalised ◆

A personalised welcome and calm atmosphere characterise this old hotel (1911) a stone's throw from the Étoile. Brightly coloured bedrooms, and elegant wood panelling in the lounge.

Pershing Hall   ⟨icons⟩

49 r. Pierre Charron (8th) – **Ⓜ** George V – ✆ 01 58 36 58 00
– info@pershinghall.com – Fax 01 58 36 58 01
– www.pershinghall.com   G3
20 rm – †329/470 € ††329/470 €, ⊑ 26 € – 6 suites
Rest – Menu 59 € – Carte 60/90 €

◆ Luxury ◆ Modern ◆

Once the home of General Pershing, then a veterans club and finally a charming hotel designed by Andrée Putman. Chic interior, original and enchanting hanging garden. Behind the curtain of glass beads, the decor is trendy and the cuisine fashionable. Lounge evenings.

Chambiges Élysées without rest   ⚠ 🅰️ ↩ 📶 📺 🛜 VISA 🌐 AE ①

8 r. Chambiges (8th) – Ⓜ Alma Marceau – ℰ 01 44 31 83 83 – reservation@
hotelchambiges.com – Fax 01 40 70 95 51 – www.hotelchambiges.com
32 rm ⊑ – ♦280/320 € ♦♦280/320 € – 2 suites   **G3**
♦ Luxury ♦ Personalised ♦

Wood panelling, lovely hangings and fabrics and period furniture depict the cosy
romantic allure of this fully renovated hotel. Snug rooms and a pretty interior
garden.

Le A without rest   ⚠ 🅰️ ↩ 📺 📶 VISA 🌐 AE ①

4 r. d' Artois (8th) – Ⓜ St-Philippe du Roule – ℰ 01 42 56 99 99 – hotel-le-a@
wanadoo.fr – Fax 01 42 56 99 90 – www.hotel-le-a-paris.com   **G-H2**
25 rm – ♦365/660 € ♦♦365/660 €, ⊑ 23 € – 1 suite
♦ Luxury ♦ Modern ♦

F. Hybert, a visual artist, and F. Méchiche, an interior designer, masterminded this
trendy hotel (or museum, perhaps?) in black and white. Relaxing lounge-library
and bar-lounge.

Kléber without rest   🅰️ ↩ 📺 📶 🧖 VISA 🌐 AE ①

7 r. Belloy (16th) ⊠ 75116 – Ⓜ Boissière – ℰ 01 47 23 80 22 – kleberhotel@
wanadoo.fr – Fax 01 49 52 07 20 – www.kleberhotel.com   **F3**
23 rm – ♦99/299 € ♦♦99/299 €, ⊑ 14 € – 1 suite
♦ Traditional ♦ Classical ♦

The sitting rooms of this 1853 hotel have Louis XV style furniture, original frescoes
and old paintings. Exposed stonework and parquet floors in the rooms.

Bassano without rest   🅰️ ↩ 📺 📶 VISA 🌐 AE ①

15 r. Bassano (16th) ⊠ 75116 – Ⓜ George V – ℰ 01 47 23 78 23 – info@
hotel-bassano.com – Fax 01 47 20 41 22 – www.hotel-bassano.com
33 rm – ♦195/275 € ♦♦215/295 €, ⊑ 19 € – 1 suite   **F3**
♦ Family ♦ Personalised ♦

Cosy atmosphere, wrought-iron furniture, sunny fabrics (it feels like being at a
friend's home in Provence, but is only a few hundred metres from the Champs-Elysées.

Montfleuri without rest   🛁 ⚠ 🅰️ ↩ 📺 📶 VISA 🌐 AE ①

21 av. Grande Armée (16th) ⊠ 75116 – Ⓜ Charles de Gaulle-Etoile
– ℰ 01 45 00 33 65 – montfleuri@wanadoo – Fax 01 45 00 06 36
– www.montfleuri.fr   **E-F2**
42 rm – ♦230/250 € ♦♦270/290 €, ⊑ 14 € – 3 suites
♦ Modern ♦

Two steps from the Arc de Triomphe, this hotel has been entirely redecorated in a
modern style. Peaceful, refined rooms in muted tones, elegantly furnished and
adorned with fine fabrics.

Monna Lisa   🅰️ 📺 📶 VISA 🌐 AE ①

97 r. La Boétie (8th) – Ⓜ St-Philippe du Roule – ℰ 01 56 43 38 38 – contact@
hotelmonnalisa.com – Fax 01 45 62 39 90 – www.hotelmonnalisa.com
22 rm – ♦250/280 € ♦♦250/280 €, ⊑ 22 €   **G-H2**
Rest *Caffe Ristretto* – (closed 3-24 August, 20-28 December, Saturday and
Sunday) Carte 48/66 €
♦ Luxury ♦ Minimalist ♦

This fine hotel built in 1860 is a showpiece for audacious Italian design. Larger
rooms on the street side. The Caffe Ristretto offers a delicious journey through
the specialities of the Italian peninsula in a wonderfully modern setting.

Le 123 without rest   🅰️ ↩ 📺 📶 VISA 🌐 AE ①

123 r. du Fg St Honoré (8th) – Ⓜ St-Philippe du Roule – ℰ 01 53 89 01 23
– hotel.le123@astotel.com – Fax 01 45 61 09 07 – www.astotel.com
41 rm – ♦269/420 € ♦♦309/450 €, ⊑ 24 €   **H2**
♦ Luxury ♦ Personalised ♦

Contemporary decor and a mixture of styles, materials and colours. The personalised rooms, which are decorated with fashion sketches, are as appealing as they
are unusual.

FRANCE - PARIS

Waldorf Arc de Triomphe without rest
36 r. Pierre Demours (17th) – **Ⓜ** *Ternes*
– *𝒞 01 47 64 67 67 – arc@hotelswaldorfparis.com – Fax 01 40 53 91 34*
– *www.hotelswaldorfparis.com*   **F1**
44 rm – ♦320/460 € ♦♦340/460 €, ⊆ 20 €
◆ Business ◆ Design ◆

Attractively refurbished, elegant contemporary rooms. Good fitness centre, a small pool, sauna and steam bath: ideal after a hard day's work or sightseeing!

Amarante Arc de Triomphe without rest
25 r. Th.-de-Banville (17th) – **Ⓜ** *Pereire*
– *𝒞 01 47 63 76 69 – amarante-arcdetriomphe@jjwhotels.com*
– *Fax 01 43 80 63 96 – www.jjwhotels.com*   **F1**
50 rm – ♦140/250 € ♦♦140/250 €, ⊆ 22 €
◆ Chain hotel ◆

This hotel has Directoire-style rooms which are popular with its business clientele. Attic-type rooms on the top floor, with some rooms opening onto the patio.

Étoile Résidence Impériale without rest
155 av. de Malakoff (16th) ⊠ *75116* – **Ⓜ** *Porte Maillot*
– *𝒞 01 45 00 23 45 – reservation@residenceimperiale.com – Fax 01 45 01 88 82*
– *www.residenceimperiale.com*   **E2**
37 rm – ♦100/260 € ♦♦100/260 €, ⊆ 14 €
◆ Traditional ◆ Personalised ◆

Well-soundproofed hotel, with theme rooms (Africa, Asia, etc.). Some have retained their exposed beams, while others open onto the patio.

Villa Alessandra without rest ⑤
9 pl. Boulnois (17th) – **Ⓜ** *Ternes* – *𝒞 01 56 33 24 24 – alessandra@*
leshotelsdeparis.com – Fax 01 56 33 24 30 – www.villa-alessandra.com
49 rm – ♦310 € ♦♦320 €, ⊆ 18 €   **F1**
◆ Business ◆ Functional ◆

This Ternes quarter hotel is on a delightful quiet little square and is appreciated for its calm. Colours of southern France in the rooms, with wrought-iron beds and painted wood furniture.

Élysées Céramic without rest
34 av. Wagram (8th) – **Ⓜ** *Ternes* – *𝒞 01 42 27 20 30 – info@*
elysees-ceramic.com – Fax 01 46 22 95 83 – www.elysees-ceramic.com
57 rm – ♦195/205 € ♦♦220/230 €, ⊆ 12 €   **F2**
◆ Family ◆ Retro ◆

The Art Nouveau glazed stoneware façade (1904) is an architectural gem. The interior lives up to the same standard with furniture and decor in the same spirit. Several balconies.

Magellan without rest ⑤
17 r. J.-B. Dumas (17th) – **Ⓜ** *Porte de Champerret* – *𝒞 01 45 72 44 51 – paris@*
hotelmagellan.com – Fax 01 40 68 90 36 – www.hotelmagellan.com
72 rm – ♦103/137 € ♦♦152 €, ⊆ 14 €   **F1**
◆ Business ◆ Design ◆

Large, functional rooms in a handsome edifice dating from 1900. Breakfast is served in the small pavilion at the end of the garden in summer. Art Deco-style lounge.

Le "Cinq" – Hôtel Four Seasons George V
31 av. George V (8th) – **Ⓜ** *George V* – *𝒞 01 49 52 71 54 – lecinq.par@*
fourseasons.com – Fax 01 49 52 71 81 – www.fourseasons.com   **G3**
Rest – Menu 85 € (lunch), 155/220 € – Carte 225/340 € 綫
Spec. Tartine de pied et oreille de porc. Pithiviers de gibier (season). Macaron au caramel.
◆ Innovative ◆ Luxury ◆

The superb dining room, a majestic evocation of the Grand Trianon, opens onto a delightful interior garden. A refined atmosphere, good wine list and classic cuisine.

FRANCE - PARIS

XXXXX · සිසිසි **Alain Ducasse au Plaza Athénée** – Hôtel Plaza Athénée 　　🏧

25 av. Montaigne (8th) – Ⓜ Alma Marceau 　　　　🚾 ⓒⓔ 🅰🇪 ⓞ
– ☏ 01 53 67 65 00 – adpa@alain-ducasse.com – Fax 01 53 67 65 12
– www.alain-ducasse.com
– Closed 17 July-25 August, 18-30 December, Monday lunch, Tuesday lunch,
Wednesday lunch, Saturday and Sunday 　　　　　　　　　　**G3**
Rest – Menu 260/360 € – Carte 215/395 € 🕸
Spec. Caviar osciètre d'Iran, langoustines rafraîchies. Volaille de Bresse, sauce
Albufera (15 oct.-31 déc;). Fraises des bois en coupe rafraîchie.
　◆ Innovative ◆ Luxury ◆
The sumptuous regency décor has been redone with a mind to design and
organza. Inventive dishes from a talented team coached by Ducasse and 1001
selected wines: the palatial life!

XXXXX · සිසිසි **Le Bristol** – Hôtel Bristol 　　　🕱 🏧 ⅃⅄ 📶 🚾 ⓒⓔ 🅰🇪 ⓞ

112 r. Fg St-Honoré (8th) – Ⓜ Miromesnil – ☏ 01 53 43 43 00 – resa@
lebristolparis.com – Fax 01 53 43 43 01 – www.lebristolparis.com 　**H2**
Rest – Menu 95 € (lunch)/220 € – Carte 124/230 € 🕸
Spec. Macaronis farcis, truffe noire, artichaut et foie gras de canard. Poularde
de Bresse cuite en vessie aux écrevisses. Précieux chocolat nyangbo, cacao
liquide et fine tuile croustillante.
　◆ Innovative ◆ Luxury ◆
With its splendid wood panelling, the winter dining room resembles a small
theatre. The summer dining room overlooks the hotel's charming garden.

XXXXX · සිසිසි **Ledoyen** 　　　🏧 ⇄ 📶 🅿 🚾 ⓒⓔ 🅰🇪 ⓞ

8 av. Dutuit (carré Champs-Élysées) (8th) – Ⓜ Champs Elysées Clemenceau
– ☏ 01 53 05 10 01 – simiand@ledoyen.com – Fax 01 47 42 55 01
– www.ledoyen.com
– Closed 3-25 August, Monday lunch, Saturday and Sunday 　　**H3**
Rest – Menu 88 € (lunch), 199/299 € – Carte 160/285 € 🕸
Spec. Grosses langoustines bretonnes, émulsion d'agrumes. Blanc de turbot
de ligne juste braisé, pommes rattes truffées. Croquant de pamplemousse
cuit et cru au citron vert.
　◆ Innovative ◆ Luxury ◆
This neo-classical lodge built on the Champs Élysées in 1792 offers delicious surf n'
turf cuisine, magnificent Napoleon III décor and a view of the gardens designed by
Hittorff.

XXXXX · සිසි **Taillevent** 　　　　🏧 ⇄ 🚾 ⓒⓔ 🅰🇪 ⓞ

15 r. Lamennais (8th) – Ⓜ Charles de Gaulle-Etoile – ☏ 01 44 95 15 01 – mail@
taillevent.com – Fax 01 42 25 95 18 – www.taillevent.com
– Closed 25 July-24 August, Saturday, Sunday and Bank Holidays
Rest – (number of covers limited, pre-book) Menu 80 € (lunch)/ 　　**G2**
190 € – Carte 128/219 € 🕸
Spec. Epeautre du pays de Sault en risotto, cuisses de grenouilles dorées.
Langoustines royales croustillantes, marmelade d'agrumes et thé vert. Tarte
renversée au chocolat et au café grillé.
　◆ Classic ◆ Luxury ◆
Wainscoting and works of art adorn this former private residence dating from the
19C. It was once home to the Duke of Morny, and is now a guardian of French
haute cuisine. Exquisite cuisine and magnificent wine list.

XXXXX · සිසි **Apicius** (Jean-Pierre Vigato) 　　　🍽 🏧 ⇄ 📶 🅿 🚾 ⓒⓔ 🅰🇪 ⓞ

20 r. d'Artois (8th) – Ⓜ St-Philippe du Roule – ☏ 01 43 80 19 66
– restaurant-apicius@wanadoo.fr – Fax 01 44 40 09 57
– www.restaurant-apicius.com
– Closed August, Saturday, Sunday and holidays 　　　　　　**G2**
Rest – Menu 160 € – Carte 130/190 € 🕸
Spec. Déclinaison sur le thème des langoustines. Tourte de canard façon
grande cuisine bourgeoise. Grand dessert au caramel.
　◆ Innovative ◆ Elegant ◆
This elegant restaurant, in a townhouse, is adorned with 19C Flemish paintings
and 17C Indian sculptures. Up-to-date cuisine and superb wine list.

Lasserre

XXXXX
ҔуӠ

🛦🄲 ⇄ ⌂ 🆅🅸🆂🅰 🆅 🄰🄴 ⓞ

17 av. F.-D.-Roosevelt (8th) – Ⓜ *Franklin D. Roosevelt –* 🕾 *01 43 59 53 43*
– lasserre@lasserre.fr – Fax 01 45 63 72 23 – www.restaurant-lasserre.com
*– Closed August, Saturday lunch, Monday lunch, Tuesday lunch, Wednesday
lunch and Sunday* **H3**
Rest – Menu 75 € (lunch)/185 € – Carte 130/180 € 🕸

Spec. Macaroni à la truffe et au foie gras. Pigeon André Malraux. Timbale
Elysée Lasserre.
    ◆ Traditional ◆
Considered an institution by Parisian gourmets, the neo-Classical dining room fea-
tures objets d'art and an amazing retractable roof. Classic menu; superb wine list.

Guy Savoy

XXXX
ҔуӠҔуӠ

🛦🄲 ⇄ ⌂ 🆅🅸🆂🅰 🆅 🄰🄴 ⓞ

18 r. Troyon (17th) – Ⓜ *Charles de Gaulle-Etoile –* 🕾 *01 43 80 40 61 – reserv@*
guysavoy.com – Fax 01 46 22 43 09 – www.guysavoy.com
– Closed August, 24 December-2 January, Saturday lunch, Sunday and Monday
Rest – Menu 275/345 € – Carte 140/270 € 🕸 **F2**
Spec. Huîtres en nage glacée. Bar en écailles grillées aux épices douces. Noir
(dessert).
    ◆ Innovative ◆ Trendy ◆
Glasswork, leather and Wenge, works by great names in contemporary art, African
sculptures and refined, inventive cuisine make this the inn for the 21C par excellence.

Michel Rostang

XXXX
ҔуӠ

🛦🄲 ⇄ ⌂ 🆅🅸🆂🅰 🆅 🄰🄴 ⓞ

20 r. Rennequin (17th) – Ⓜ *Ternes –* 🕾 *01 47 63 40 77 – rostang@*
relaischateaux.com – Fax 01 47 63 82 75 – www.michelrostang.com
– Closed 3-25 August, Monday lunch, Saturday lunch and Sunday
Rest – Menu 78 € (lunch), 165/285 € – Carte 133/222 € 🕸 **F1**
Spec. Carte des truffes et "sandwichs" à la truffe (15 Dec. to mid March). Grosse
sole de ligne meunière, marinière de coquillages au curry mauri. Tarte chaude
au chocolat amer.
    ◆ Classic ◆ Elegant ◆
Wainscoting, Robj statuettes, works by Lalique, and Art Deco stained glass make
this both a luxurious and unusual setting. Exquisite cuisine and outstanding wine
list.

Pierre Gagnaire

XXXX
ҔуӠҔуӠ

🛦 🄲 ⌂ 🆅🅸🆂🅰 🆅 🄰🄴 ⓞ

6 r. Balzac (8th) – Ⓜ *George V –* 🕾 *01 58 36 12 50 – p.gagnaire@wanadoo.fr*
– Fax 01 58 36 12 51 – www.pierre-gagnaire.com
– Closed Sunday lunch and Saturday **G2**
Rest – Menu 105/255 € – Carte 230/449 €
Spec. Gelée de poivron doux au citron, thon rouge confit et foie gras de
canard. Galinette de Palamos braisée et poêlée de blettes aux petits pois.
Le dessert "Rouge".
    ◆ Innovative ◆ Trendy ◆
The low key, chic, contemporary décor (light wood panelling, modern art) pales
before the unrestrained score played by a spellbinding chef/jazz player. Music
maestro please!

Hiramatsu

XXXX
ҔуӠ

🛦🄲 ⇄ ⌂ (dinner) 🆅🅸🆂🅰 🆅 🄰🄴 ⓞ

52 r. Longchamp (16th) ✉ *75116 –* Ⓜ *Trocadéro –* 🕾 *01 56 81 08 80 – paris@*
hiramatsu.co.jp – Fax 01 56 81 08 81 – www.hiramatsu.co.jp
– Closed 1-30 August, 1-8 January, Saturday and Sunday **E3**
Rest – *(number of covers limited, pre-book)* Menu 48 € (lunch), 95/130 €
– Carte 104/125 € 🕸
Spec. Gourmandise de homard et pigeon fumé. Fines lamelles d'agneau,
compotée d'oignons blancs et jus de truffe au thym. Gâteau au chocolat "Hiramatsu".
    ◆ Innovative ◆ Elegant ◆
Beneath his Japanese sign, Hiramatsu honours French cuisine with inventiveness
and talent. High-class gastronomy in an extremely elegant setting decorated with
flowers. Magnificent wine list.

Laurent

41 av. Gabriel (8th) – 🚇 *Champs Elysées Clemenceau* – 𝄐 *01 42 25 00 39*
– *info@le-laurent.com* – *Fax 01 45 62 45 21* – *www.le-laurent.com*
– *Closed 23 December-5 January, Saturday lunch, Sunday and Bank Holidays*
Rest – Menu 80/160 € – Carte 136/225 €   **H3**
Spec. Araignée de mer dans ses sucs en gelée, crème de fenouil. Flanchet de veau de lait braisé, blettes à la moelle et au jus (April-October). Glace vanille minute en corolle.
◆ Classic ◆ Luxury ◆
A stone's throw from the Champs Élysées, this former hunting lodge belonging to Louis XIV with its elegant shaded terraces has a loyal following. Traditional cuisine and a good wine list.

Prunier

16 av. Victor-Hugo (16th) – 🚇 *Charles de Gaulle-Etoile* – 𝄐 *01 44 17 35 85*
– *maison-prunier3@wanadoo.fr* – *Fax 01 44 17 90 10*
– *www.caviarhouse-prunier.com*
– *Closed August, Sunday and Bank Holidays*   **F2**
Rest – Menu 59 € (lunch)/175 € – Carte 69/159 €
◆ Seafood ◆ Retro ◆
Superb listed Art Deco interior (black marble, mosaics, stained glass) at this institution, created in 1925 by the architect Boileau. Excellent fish and seafood (caviar, salmon etc).

La Table du Lancaster – Hôtel Lancaster

7 r. Berri (8th) – 🚇 *George V* – 𝄐 *01 40 76 40 18*
– *restaurant@hotel-lancaster.fr* – *Fax 01 40 76 40 00* – *www.hotel-lancaster.fr*
Rest – Menu 95 € (lunch)/150 € – Carte 92/143 €   **G2**
Spec. Cuisses de grenouilles au tamarin, chou-fleur en copeaux. Pièce de thon au ponzu, sur un riz "koshi hikari". Soufflé au citron et sirop au miel d'acacia.
◆ Innovative ◆ Friendly ◆
Inventive food supervised by Michel Troisgros, and a pleasant, contemporary setting (Chinese prints) opening onto the garden. A fitting restaurant for the Lancaster.

La Table de Joël Robuchon

16 av. Bugeaud (16th) ✉ *75116* – 🚇 *Victor Hugo* – 𝄐 *01 56 28 16 16*
– *latabledejoelrobuchon@wanadoo.fr* – *Fax 01 56 28 16 78*   **E3**
Rest – Menu 55 € bi (lunch)/150 € – Carte 60/155 €
Spec. Langoustine en papillotes croustillantes au basilic. Caille au foie gras et caramélisée avec une pomme purée truffée. Chocolat tendance crème onctueuse au chocolat Araguani, glace chocolat au biscuit "oréo".
◆ A la mode ◆ Fashionable ◆
In this elegant setting you are sure to enjoy your meal here: sample tapas style snacks and classic dishes subtly updated by Joël Robuchon.

Maison Blanche

15 av. Montaigne (8th) – 🚇 *Alma Marceau* – 𝄐 *01 47 23 55 99* – *reservations@maison-blanche.fr* – *Fax 01 47 20 09 56* – *www.maison-blanche.fr*
– *Closed Saturday lunch and Sunday lunch*   **G3**
Rest – Menu 55 € (weekday lunch) – Carte 95/185 €
◆ A la mode ◆ Elegant ◆
On top of the Théâtre des Champs Élysées, whose loft-duplex design features a huge glass roof facing the golden dome of Les Invalides. Languedoc-inspired cuisine.

Fouquet's

99 av. Champs Élysées (8th) – 🚇 *George V* – 𝄐 *01 40 69 60 50* – *fouquets@lucienbarriere.com* – *Fax 01 40 69 60 35* – *www.lucienbarriere.com*
Rest – Menu 78 € – Carte 76/188 €   **G2**
◆ Traditional ◆
A listed dining room, updated by J. Garcia, a terrace that is popular come summer or winter and brasserie cuisine: Fouquet's has been catering to the jet set since 1889.

THE ARTISTRY OF CHAMPAGNE

BRUT PREMIER

LOUIS ROEDERER
CHAMPAGNE

BRUT   REIMS

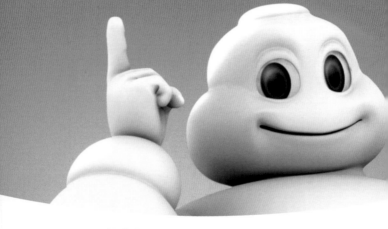

XXX ❀
La Table du Baltimore – Hôtel Sofitel Baltimore ᴀᴄ 🍴
1 r. Léo Delibes (16th) ✉ *75016 –* Ⓜ *Boissière* ᴠɪꜱᴀ ⓒⓞ ᴀᴇ ⓞ
– ☎ 01 44 34 54 34 – h2789-fb@accor.com – Fax 01 44 34 54 44
– www.hotel-baltimore-paris.com
– Closed August, Saturday and Sunday
Rest – Menu 48 € bi (lunch)/75 € – Carte 62/85 €   **E3**
Spec. Le tourteau. La volaille. Le chocolat.
♦ A la mode ♦ Friendly ♦
Period wood panelling, modern furnishings, warm colours and a collection of
drawings characterise this restaurant. Gourmet up-to-date cuisine.

XXX ❀
Le Chiberta ᴀᴄ ⟺ ᴠɪꜱᴀ ⓒⓞ ᴀᴇ ⓞ
3 r. Arsène-Houssaye (8th) – Ⓜ *Charles de Gaulle-Etoile – ☎ 01 53 53 42 00*
– chiberta@guysavoy.com – Fax 01 45 62 85 08 – www.lechiberta.com
– Closed 1-23 August, Christmas holidays, Saturday lunch and Sunday
Rest – Menu 60/155 € bi – Carte 86/124 €   **F2**
Spec. Crème de carotte "citronnelle-gingembre" et gambas éclatées aux épices.
Lièvre à la royale et gratin de macaroni aux champignons sauvages (October-
December). Soufflé vanille et glace caramel.
♦ Innovative ♦ Design ♦
A serene atmosphere, soft lighting and simple décor designed by J.M. Wilmotte
(dark colours and unusual wine bottle walls) provide the setting for inventive cui-
sine supervised by Guy Savoy.

XXX
Sormani ᴀᴄ ⟺ 🍴 ᴠɪꜱᴀ ⓒⓞ ᴀᴇ
4 r. Gén. Lanrezac (17th) – Ⓜ *Charles de Gaulle-Etoile – ☎ 01 43 80 13 91*
– sasormani@wanadoo.fr – Fax 01 40 55 07 37
– Closed 1ˢᵗ-25 August, Saturday, Sunday and holidays
Rest – Carte 60/200 € 🍷   **F2**
♦ Italian ♦ Formal ♦
Latin charm predominates in this restaurant near the Place de l'Etoile, with its new
decor (red tones and Murano-glass chandeliers), dolce vita atmosphere and Italian
cuisine.

XXX ❀
Le Pergolèse (Stéphane Gaborieau) ᴀᴄ 🍴 ᴠɪꜱᴀ ⓒⓞ ᴀᴇ
40 r. Pergolèse (16th) ✉ *75116 –* Ⓜ *Porte Maillot – ☎ 01 45 00 21 40*
– le-pergolese@wanadoo.fr – Fax 01 45 00 81 31 – www.lepergolese.com
– Closed 3 weeks in August, Saturday and Sunday   **E2**
Rest – Menu 42 € bi/95 € – Carte 75/110 €
Spec. Ravioli de langoustines, duxelles de champignons, émulsion de crusta-
cés au foie gras. Aiguillette de Saint-Pierre meunière, cannelloni farcis aux
multi saveurs. Feuilles d'ananas en raviole, fruits exotiques et sorbet fromage
blanc.
♦ Classic ♦ Fashionable ♦
Yellow wall hangings, pale wood wainscoting and surprising sculptures reflect in
the mirrors, forming an elegant decor a step away from select Avenue Foch.
Impeccable classic cuisine.

XXX ❀
Passiflore (Roland Durand) ᴀᴄ 🍴 ᴠɪꜱᴀ ⓒⓞ ᴀᴇ ⓞ
33 r. Longchamp (16th) ✉ *75116 –* Ⓜ *Trocadéro – ☎ 01 47 04 96 81*
– passiflore@club-internet.fr – Fax 01 47 04 32 27
– www.restaurantpassiflore.com
– Closed 20 July-20 August, Monday lunch, Saturday lunch and Sunday
Rest – Menu 42 €, 49/65 € – Carte 50/60 €   **E3**
Spec. Gratin de macaroni au foie gras. Tournedos de pied de cochon. Fraî-
cheur d'aloe vera à l'orange.
♦ A la mode ♦ Fashionable ♦
An unassumingly elegant decor of ethnic inspiration (yellow tones and wood
panelling) and a classic, personalised cuisine combine to rejoice the taste buds of
Parisian society.

XXX
ध

Stella Maris (Tateru Yoshino)   AC ⌐🍴 VISA ⦿ AE ①

4 r. Arsène Houssaye (8th) – Ⓜ *Charles de Gaulle-Etoile* – ✆ *01 42 89 16 22*
– stella.maris.paris@wanadoo.fr – Fax 01 42 89 16 01 – www.tateruyoshino.com
– Closed 10-22 August, Saturday lunch, Sunday and Bank Holidays
Rest – Menu 49 € (weekday lunch), 99/130 € – Carte 119/163 €   **F2**
Spec. Millefeuille de thon rouge mariné, aubergine, tapenade et caviar Fran-
çais. Tête de veau en cocotte, crête de coq et œuf frit. Kouing-aman façon
Penthièvre.
♦ A la mode ♦ Design ♦

A pleasant restaurant with a refined decor and warm welcome near the Arc de
Triomphe. Classic French cuisine with a modern touch added by a skilful Japanese chef.

XX
Tsé Yang   AC ⇔ VISA ⦿ AE

25 av. Pierre 1er de Serbie (16th) ✉ *75116* – Ⓜ *léna* – ✆ *01 47 20 70 22*
– Fax 01 47 20 75 34 – www.tseyang.fr   **F3**
Rest – Menu 49/59 € – Carte 45/90 €
♦ Chinese ♦ Luxury ♦

Two interior designers have revamped this chic temple of traditional Chinese cuisine. Black dominates the decor with gold coffered ceiling, attractive settings, etc.

XX
Le Relais Plaza – Hôtel Plaza Athénée   AC VISA ⦿ AE ①

25 av. Montaigne (8th) – Ⓜ *Alma Marceau* – ✆ *01 53 67 64 00 – reservation@*
plaza-athenee-paris.com – Fax 01 53 67 66 66 – www.plaza-athenee-paris.com
– Closed August   **G3**
Rest – Menu 50 € – Carte 68/148 €
♦ Classic ♦ Brasserie ♦

The chic, intimate 'local' for the nearby fashion houses. Timeless atmosphere and
beautiful 1930s decor inspired by the Normandie cruise ship. Classic, refined cuisine.

XX
Spoon   AC ⌐🍴 VISA ⦿ AE ①

12 r. Marignan (8th) – Ⓜ *Franklin D. Roosevelt* – ✆ *01 40 76 34 44*
– spoon-paris@hotelmarignan.fr – Fax 01 40 76 34 37 – www.spoon.tm.fr
– Closed August, 25 December-3 January, Saturday and Sunday   **G3**
Rest – Menu 36 €, 80/120 € bi – Carte approx. 69 € ℬ
♦ Innovative ♦ Design ♦

A smart designer decor and an open kitchen set the fun scene by Alain Ducasse,
whose fusion menu mingles with more traditional dishes. Exceptional wines from
around the globe.

XX
Conti   AC VISA ⦿ AE ①

72 r. Lauriston (16th) ✉ *75116* – Ⓜ *Boissière* – ✆ *01 47 27 74 67*
– Fax 01 47 27 37 66 – Closed 3-23 August, 25 December-1 January, Saturday,
Sunday and Bank Holidays   **E3**
Rest – Menu 34 € – Carte 47/75 € ℬ
♦ Italian ♦ Intimate ♦

Red and black predominate in this restaurant's decor, where mirrors and crystal
chandeliers glitter. Italian cuisine; wonderful wine list.

XX
Fermette Marbeuf 1900   AC VISA ⦿ AE ①

5 r. Marbeuf (8th) – Ⓜ *Alma Marceau* – ✆ *01 53 23 08 00 – fermettemarbeuf@*
blanc.net – Fax 01 53 23 08 09 – www.fermettemarbeuf.com   **G3**
Rest – Menu 32 € – Carte 36/78 €
♦ Traditional ♦ Retro ♦

One must reserve a table to enjoy the Art Nouveau decor of this glass dining hall dating
back to 1898 and discovered by chance in the course of renovation. Classic cuisine.

XX
Marius et Janette   🍴 AC ⌐🍴 VISA ⦿ AE ①

4 av. George V (8th) – Ⓜ *Alma Marceau* – ✆ *01 47 23 41 88*
– Fax 01 47 23 07 19 – www.mariusjanette@yahoo.fr   **G3**
Rest – Menu 48 € – Carte 90/140 €
♦ Seafood ♦ Bistro ♦

The name of this restaurant recalls Robert Guédiguian's films and Marseille's Esta-
que quarter. Elegant nautical decor, a pleasant street terrace and seafood fare.

FRANCE - PARIS

XX Timgad
21 r. Brunel (17th) – Ⓜ *Argentine* – ℰ *01 45 74 23 70* – *contact@timgad.fr*
– *Fax 01 40 68 76 46* – *www.timgad.fr*   **E2**
Rest – Menu 69 € bi/113 € bi – Carte 40/85 €
◆ Moroccan ◆ Friendly ◆

Delve into the past splendour of the city of Timgad: the elegant Moorish decor of the rooms was carried out by Moroccan stucco-workers. Fragrant North African cuisine.

XX Citrus Étoile
6 r. Arsène-Houssaye (8th) – Ⓜ *Charles de Gaulle-Étoile* – ℰ *01 42 89 15 51*
– *info@citrusetoile.fr* – *Fax 01 42 89 28 67* – *www.citrusetoile.fr*
– *Closed 8-19 August, 21 December-3 January, Saturday, Sunday and holidays*
Rest – Menu 49/120 € – Carte 88/118 €   **F2**
◆ A la mode ◆

Chef Gilles Épié invites you to sample rich cuisine that is full of new flavours inspired by his travels in California and Japan. Elegant, simple décor and a delicious welcome.

XX L'Angle du Faubourg
195 r. Fg St-Honoré (8th) – Ⓜ *Ternes* – ℰ *01 40 74 20 20*
– *resa@angledufaubourg.com* – *Fax 01 40 74 20 21* – *www.taillevent.com*
– *Closed August, Saturday, Sunday and Bank Holidays*   **G2**
Rest – Menu 38/75 € – Carte 63/93 € 🏵
Spec. Sablé de thon aux épices. Saint-Jacques rôties à la vanille bourbon. Macaron moelleux à la banane et passion.
◆ A la mode ◆ Friendly ◆

On the corner of Rue du Faubourg-St-Honoré and Rue Balzac. This modern bistrot serves skilfully updated classic cuisine to suit current tastes. Simple decor.

XX etc...
2 r. La Pérouse (16th) ✉ *75016* – Ⓜ *Kléber* – ℰ *01 49 52 10 10*
– *etc@groupeepicure.com* – *Fax 01 49 52 10 11*
– *Closed Saturday lunch and Sunday*   **F3**
Rest – Menu 68 € bi (lunch) – Carte approx. 85 €
Spec. Fraîcheur de tourteau. Noix d'entrecôte de boeuf Hereford, laquée de soja-ciboulette. Caramel au goût de carambar glacé.
◆ A la mode ◆ Trendy ◆

An unassumingly elegant decor of ethnic inspiration (yellow tones and wood panelling) and a classic, personalised cuisine combine to rejoice tthe taste buds of Parisian society.

XX Rech
62 av. des Ternes (17th) – Ⓜ *Ternes* – ℰ *01 45 72 29 47*
– *restaurant.rech@free.fr* – *Fax 01 45 72 41 60* – *www.esprit-bistrot.com*
– *Closed 26 July-24 August, 24 December-1 January, Sunday and Monday*
Rest – Menu 34 € (lunch)/55 € – Carte 50/85 €   **F1**
◆ Seafood ◆ Retro ◆

Recently renovated, Art Deco-inspired dining rooms (mirrors, stained glass) at this venerable restaurant. Principally fine fish and seafood specialities, but the odd meat dish too.

XX Agapé
51 r. Jouffroy-d'Abbans (17th) – Ⓜ *Wagram* – ℰ *01 42 27 20 18*
– *www.agape-paris.fr* – *Fax 01 43 80 68 09* – *www.agape-paris.fr*
Rest – *(closed August, Saturday and Sunday)* Menu 39 €   *Plan I* **B1**
(weekday lunch), 77/110 € – Carte 57/79 €
Spec. Veau cru-fumé de Corrèze, citron vert-vanille et fines herbes. Pigeonneau de Sologne, endive carmine et abricot. Chocolat-café Panama.
◆ A la mode ◆ Minimalist ◆

This new restaurant, whose name means love in Greek, will appeal to gourmets. It has a chic, minimalist decor and a concise enticing menu.

Graindorge   XX 🍴   VISA ◎ AE

15 r. Arc de Triomphe (17th) – **M** *Charles de Gaulle-Étoile –* ✆ *01 47 54 00 28*
– le.graindorge@wanadoo.fr
– Closed 1ˢᵗ-15 August, Saturday lunch and Sunday   **F2**
Rest – Menu 28 € (weekdays), 34/50 € – Carte 44/50 €
• Flemish cuisine • Retro •

Here you can choose between beer and wine, generous Flemish cuisine and appealing market dishes in an attractive Art Deco setting.

Bistrot du Sommelier   XX   AC ⇔ VISA ◎ AE

97 bd Haussmann (8th) – **M** *St-Augustin –* ✆ *01 42 65 24 85*
– bistrot-du-sommelier@noos.fr – Fax 01 53 75 23 23
– www.bistrotdusommelier.com
– Closed 1-30 August, 24 December-4 January, Saturday and Sunday
Rest – Menu 39 € (lunch), 65 € bi/110 € bi – Carte 52/62 € 🎐   **H2**
• A la mode • Bistro •

This bistro of free-flowing Bacchanalian pleasure belongs to Philippe Faure-Brac, elected World's Best Sommelier in 1992.

La Braisière (Jacques Faussat)   XX ✿   AC VISA ◎ AE ①

54 r. Cardinet (17th) – **M** *Malesherbes –* ✆ *01 47 63 40 37 – labraisiere@free.fr*
– Fax 01 47 63 04 76
– Closed 26 July-23 August, 1-10 January, Saturday lunch and Sunday
Rest – Menu 38 € (lunch)/110 € – Carte 53/65 € 🎐   **G1**
Spec. Gâteau de pomme de terre au foie gras et aux girolles (season). Saint-Jacques poêlées (autumn-winter). Figues rôties aux fruits d'automne, crème de marrron et épices de la joie (autumn).
• South-western France •

Comfortable, modern restaurant decorated in a tasteful restrained style. The menu is influenced by the cuisine of southwest France, changes with the seasons and the chef's whims.

Market   XX   AC ⇔ VISA ◎ AE

15 av. Matignon (8th) – **M** *Franklin D. Roosevelt –* ✆ *01 56 43 40 90*
– prmarketsa@aol.com – Fax 01 43 59 10 87 – www.jean-georges.com
Rest – Carte 53/80 €   **H3**
• Fusion • Design •

A trendy establishment with a prestigious location. Wood and marble decor, including African masks in niches. Mixed cuisine (French, Italian and Asian).

6 New-York   XX   AC VISA ◎ AE ①

6 av. New-York (16th) ✉ *75016 –* **M** *Alma Marceau –* ✆ *01 40 70 03 30*
– 6newyork@wanadoo.fr – Fax 01 40 70 04 77 – www.6newyork.fr
– Closed August, Saturday lunch and Sunday   **F3**
Rest – Menu 30 € (lunch) – Carte 42/64 €
• A la mode • Design •

The sign gives you a clue to the address but does not tell you that this stylish bistro prepares dishes perfectly suited to its modern and refined setting.

Le Vinci   XX   AC ⇔ (dinner) VISA ◎ AE

23 r. P. Valéry (16th) ✉ *75116 –* **M** *Victor Hugo –* ✆ *01 45 01 68 18 – levinci@wanadoo.fr – Fax 01 45 01 60 37*
– Closed 2-24 August, Saturday and Sunday   **E2-3**
Rest – Carte 45/75 €
• Italian • Formal •

Tasty Italian cuisine, pleasant colourful interior and friendly service (a highly-prized establishment a step away from the chic shopping in Avenue Victor-Hugo.

Le Ballon des Ternes   XX   ⇔ VISA ◎ AE

103 av. Ternes (17th) – **M** *Porte Maillot –* ✆ *01 45 74 17 98*
– leballondesternes@fr.oleane.com – Fax 01 45 72 18 84   **E1**
Rest – Carte 40/65 €
• Brasserie • Brasserie •

No, you have not had a glass of wine too many! The table set upside down on the ceiling is part of the 1900 decor of this brasserie next to the Palais des Congrès.

XX **Al Ajami**   AC VISA 🌐 ⓪

58 r. François 1ᵉʳ (8th) – Ⓜ *George V* – 𝒞 *01 42 25 38 44* – *ajami@free.fr*
– Fax 01 42 25 38 39 – www.ajami.com   **G3**
Rest – Menu 28 € (weekdays)/48 € – Carte 35/60 €
 ♦ Lebanese ♦ Elegant ♦

This temple of traditional Lebanese cuisine is the Parisian branch of a Beirut establishment in operation since 1920. Near East decor, family ambiance and many
regulars.

XX **Village d'Ung et Li Lam**   AC VISA 🌐 AE ⓪

10 r. J. Mermoz (8th) – Ⓜ *Franklin D. Roosevelt* – 𝒞 *01 42 25 99 79*
– menez.lam@orange.fr – Fax 01 42 25 12 06
– Closed Saturday lunch and Sunday lunch   **H2**
Rest – Menu 19/35 € – Carte 25/35 €
 ♦ Thai ♦ Exotic ♦

Ung and Li welcome you into a very original Asian setting: suspended aquariums
and a flooring of glass and sand tiles. Chinese-Thai cuisine.

XX **Chez Georges**   🏠 ⇔ ⌂🍴 VISA 🌐 AE

273 bd Péreire (17th) – Ⓜ *Porte Maillot* – 𝒞 *01 45 74 31 00* – *chez-georges@*
hotmail.fr – Fax 01 45 72 18 84 – www.chez-georges.com   **E1**
Rest – Carte 42/75 €
 ♦ Brasserie ♦ Bistro ♦

An institution in Paris since 1926, the ambience and decor of this brasserie are perfectly in keeping with its appetising bistro cuisine. Menu and daily suggestions.

X **Dominique Bouchet**   AC ⇔ ⌂🍴 VISA 🌐 AE
ⓔ
11 r. Treilhard (8th) – Ⓜ *Miromesnil* – 𝒞 *01 45 61 09 46* – *dominiquebouchet@*
yahoo.fr – Fax 01 42 89 11 14 – www.dominique-bouchet.com
– Closed in August, Saturday, Sunday and Bank Holidays   **H2**
Rest – (pre-book) Carte 57/97 € ❀
Spec. Croustillant de tête de veau aux poireaux et oeufs mimosa. Macaronis
de homard sur purée de champignons et coulis de carapaces. Pêche glacée
et crème brûlée a la vanille Bourbon (June-September).
 ♦ A la mode ♦

Tasteful contemporary decor, a friendly atmosphere and delicious, traditionally-
based cuisine using market produce are the hallmarks of this small, successful
and trendy bistro.

X **L'Arôme**   AC VISA 🌐 AE
ⓔ
3 r. St-Philippe-du-Roule (8th) – Ⓜ *St-Philippe-du-Roule* – 𝒞 *01 42 25 55 98*
– contact@larome.fr – Fax 01 42 25 55 97 – www.larome.fr
– Closed 2-23 August, 19-28 December, Saturday and Sunday   **H2**
Rest – Menu 36 € (lunch), 70/114 € bi – Carte 55/75 €
Spec. Cannelloni de tourteau décortiqué et daïkon au pamplemousse. Foie
gras de canard poêlé au cacao amer. Tarte aux pommes façon tatin.
 ♦ A la mode ♦

A chic 'neo-bistro' run by Eric Martins (in the dining room) and Thomas Boullault
(in the kitchen). Simple decor in shades of coral pink and taupe. Open kitchen.
Modern cuisine.

X **Café Lenôtre - Pavillon Elysée**   🏠 ♿ AC ⇔ ⌂🍴 🅿

10 av. Champs-Elysées (8th)   VISA 🌐 AE ⓪
– Ⓜ *Champs Elysées Clemenceau* – 𝒞 *01 42 65 85 10* – *webmaster@lenotre.fr*
– Fax 01 42 65 76 23 – www.lenotre.fr
– Closed 3 weeks in August, 1 week in February, Monday dinner and Sunday
dinner from November to February   **H3**
Rest – Carte 45/65 €
 ♦ A la mode ♦ Trendy ♦

This elegant pavilion built for the 1900 World Fair has been treated to a make over.
It houses a boutique, a catering school and a distinctly modern restaurant.

FRANCE - PARIS

Le Stresa
⬛ VISA ⬤⬤ AE ⓘ

7 r. Chambiges (8th) – ⓜ Alma Marceau – 🕿 01 47 23 51 62
– Closed August, 20 December-3 January, Saturday and Sunday **G3**
Rest – *(pre-book)* Carte 70/120 €
♦ Italian ♦ Family ♦

Golden Triangle trattoria frequented by a very jet-set clientele. Paintings by Buffet and compressed sculptural art by César – artists also appreciate the Italian cuisine here.

Caïus
⬛ VISA ⬤⬤ AE

6 r. d'Armaillé (17th) – ⓜ Charles de Gaulle-Etoile – 🕿 01 42 27 19 20
– Fax 01 40 55 00 93 – Closed Saturday and Sunday **F1**
Rest – Menu 39 €
♦ Innovative ♦ Trendy ♦

Every day, the chef of this smart bistro chalks up his new personalised recipes made with spices and 'forgotten' produce. Minimalist modern decor.

Bath's
⬛ VISA ⬤⬤ AE
☙

25 r. Bayen (17th) – ⓜ Ternes – 🕿 01 45 74 74 74 – contact@baths.fr
– Fax 01 45 74 71 15 – www.baths.fr
– Closed August, Sunday and Bank Holidays **E7**
Rest – Menu 42 € (weekdays) – Carte 50/70 €
Spec. Cassolette d'oeufs brouillés. Filet de boeuf de Salers aux épices douces. Riz au lait, compotée d'ananas.
♦ A la mode ♦ Design ♦

Contemporary artwork, and sculpture by the owner grace the modern decor of this restaurant, enhanced by an orange and black colour scheme. Tasty market-fresh cuisine.

SYDR
& ⬛ VISA ⬤⬤ AE

6 r. de Tilsitt (8th) – ⓜ Charles de Gaulle-Etoile – 🕿 01 45 72 41 32 – sydrerie@ orange.fr – Fax 01 45 72 41 79
– Closed 3 weeks in August, Saturday lunch, Monday dinner and Sunday
Rest – Menu 28/48 € – Carte 36/48 € **F2**
♦ A la mode ♦ Minimalist ♦

This post-modern cider bar created by Alain Dutournier and Philippe Sella is extremely minimalist in style. Regional cuisine with a modern twist, plus a bar offering tapas and cider tastings.

Daru
⬛ 🍴 (dinner) VISA ⬤⬤ AE

19 r. Daru (8th) – ⓜ Courcelles – 🕿 01 42 27 23 60 – restaurant.daru@ wanadoo.fr – Fax 01 47 54 08 14 – www.daru.fr – Closed August and Sunday
Rest – Menu 28 € (weekdays lunch)/34 € – Carte 60/90 € **G1**
♦ Russian ♦ Formal ♦

Founded in 1918, Daru was the first Russian grocery store in Paris. Today it still offers customers a choice of zakouskis, blinis and caviar in its red and black interior.

Chez Mathilde-Paris XVII
VISA ⬤⬤
☺

41 r. Guersant (17th) – ⓜ Porte Maillot – 🕿 01 45 74 75 27 – contact@ chezmathilde.fr – www.chezmathilde.fr
– Closed 26 July-26 August, 24 December-1st January, Saturday **E1**
Rest – Carte approx. 25 €
♦ Bistro ♦

The chef's bistro-style market based cuisine is listed on a blackboard. A modest family-run restaurant far from the Parisian trendy set.

L'Entredgeu
VISA ⬤⬤
☺

83 r. Laugier (17th) – ⓜ Porte de Champerret – 🕿 01 40 54 97 24
– Fax 01 40 54 96 62
– Closed 25 April-7 May, 5-25 August, 22-29 December, Sunday and Monday
Rest – Menu 32 € *Plan I* **AB1**
♦ Bistro ♦

Friendly welcome, decor with touches of south western France, lively atmosphere, menu chalked up on a blackboard, market fresh cuisine and a tongue-twisting name to boot.

Le Meurice   🏨 *L₅* 🕃 ⚅ rm 🄰🄲 ⟷ rm 🄲🄰🄳 ⸙ 🔏 VISA ⓿ 🄰🄴 ⓿

228 r. Rivoli (1st) – Ⓜ Tuileries – ℰ 01 44 58 10 10
– reservations@lemeurice.com – Fax 01 44 58 10 15
– www.lemeurice.com   **J3**
137 rm – ♦565/665 € ♦♦625/805 €, ⌂ 36 € – 23 suites
Rest le Meurice – see below
Rest Le Dali – ℰ 01 44 58 10 44 – Carte 60/95 €
♦ Palace ♦ Grand Luxury ♦ Historic ♦

One of the first luxury hotels, built in 1817, converted into a "palace" in 1907.
Sumptuous rooms and a superb top floor suite with a breathtaking view of Paris.
Philippe Starck has added a touch of modernity in the lobby area. An impressive
canvas by Ara Starck adorns the ceiling of the Dali.

Ritz   🏠 *L₅* ⚅ 🄲 🄰🄲 ⟷ rm 🄲🄰🄳 ⸙ VISA ⓿ 🄰🄴 ⓿

15 pl. Vendôme (1st) – Ⓜ Opéra – ℰ 01 43 16 30 30 – resa@ritzparis.com
– Fax 01 43 16 33 75 – www.ritzparis.com   **K3**
123 rm – ♦770 € ♦♦770 €, ⌂ 67 € – 36 suites
Rest L'Espadon – see below
Rest Bar Vendôme – ℰ 01 43 16 33 63 – Carte 92/131 €
♦ Grand Luxury ♦ Palace ♦ Stylish ♦

In 1898, César Ritz opened the 'perfect hotel' of his dreams, boasting Valentino,
Proust, Hemingway and Coco Chanel among its guests. Exquisitely sophisticated.
Superb pool. A chic interior and superb terrace can be found at the Bar Vendôme,
which turns into a tearoom in the afternoon.

Crillon   *L₅* 🄰🄲 ⟷ rm 🄲🄰🄳 ⸙ 🔏 VISA ⓿ 🄰🄴 ⓿

10 pl. de la Concorde (8th) – Ⓜ Concorde – ℰ 01 44 71 15 00
– crillon@crillon.com – Fax 01 44 71 15 02
– www.crillon.com   **J3**
119 rm – ♦770 € ♦♦770/1220 €, ⌂ 49 € – 28 suites
Rest Les Ambassadeurs – see below
Rest L'Obélisque – ℰ 01 44 71 15 15 – Menu 54 € – Carte 54/110 €
♦ Palace ♦ Grand Luxury ♦ Stylish ♦

This 18C townhouse has kept its sumptuous, decorative features. The bedrooms,
decorated with wood-furnishings, are magnificent. A French style luxury hotel
through-and-through.

Park Hyatt   🏠 *L₅* ⚅ 🕃 🄰🄲 ⟷ rm 🄲🄰🄳 ⸙ 🔏 🚗 VISA ⓿ 🄰🄴 ⓿

5 r. de la Paix (2nd) – Ⓜ Opéra – ℰ 01 58 71 12 34
– paris.vendome@hyatt.com – Fax 01 58 71 12 35
– www.paris.vendome.hyatt.fr   **K3**
168 rm – ♦800 € ♦♦800 €, ⌂ 48 € – 22 suites
Rest Le Pur' Grill – see below
Rest Les Orchidées – ℰ 01 58 71 10 61 (lunch only) Carte 61/123 €
♦ Luxury ♦ Personalised ♦

This group of five Haussmannian buildings has been converted into an ultra-
modern luxury hotel with contemporary decor by Ed Tuttle. Collection of modern
art, a spa and high-tech equipment throughout. Cuisine in keeping with current
tastes, served to diners beneath a glass roof.

Intercontinental Le Grand   *L₅* ⚅ 🕃 🄰🄲 ⟷ 🄲🄰🄳 ⸙ 🔏 🄿 🚗

2 r. Scribe (9th) – Ⓜ Opéra – ℰ 01 40 07 32 32
VISA ⓿ 🄰🄴 ⓿
– legrand@ihg.com – Fax 01 42 66 12 51 – www.ichotelsgroupe.com
442 rm – ♦360/750 € ♦♦360/750 €, ⌂ 38 € – 28 suites   **K2**
Rest Café de la Paix – see below
♦ Palace ♦ Stylish ♦

This illustrious luxury hotel, opened in 1862, was refurbished in 2003. An admirable
mix of Second Empire style and modern comforts.

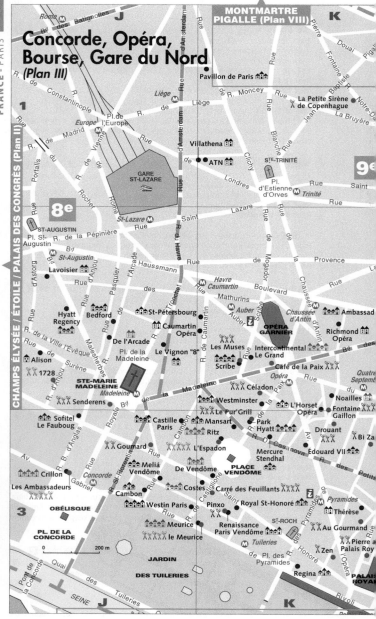

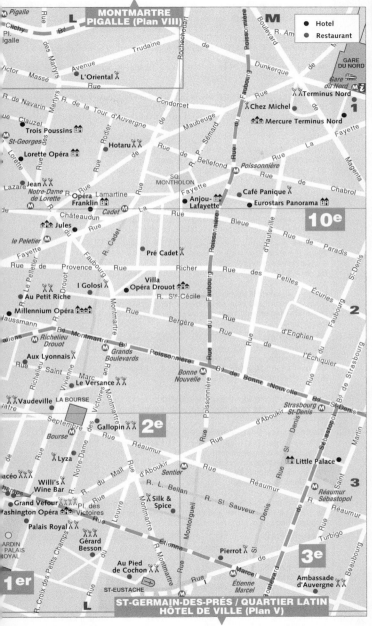

MONTMARTRE
PIGALLE (Plan VIII)

● Hotel
● Restaurant

M Pigalle

Clichy
Pl.
igalle

L'Oriental

/ictor Massé

R. de Navarin

ue Clauzel
St-Georges

Trois Poussins

Lorette Opéra

Hotaru

Jean
Notre-Dame
de Lorette

Opéra
Franklin

Châteaudun

Jules

le Peletier

Fayette

Rue de Provence

I Golosi

Au Petit Riche

Millennium Opéra

Richelieu
Drouot

Aux Lyonnais

Le Versance

Vaudeville LA BOURSE

Septembre

Bourse

Lyza

acéo

Willi's
Wine Bar

Grand Vefour
ashington Opéra

Palais Royal

JARDIN
PALAIS
ROYAL

Gérard
Besson

Au Pied
de Cochon

ST-EUSTACHE

GARE
DU NORD

Terminus Nord

Chez Michel

Mercure Terminus Nord

Poissonnière

Café Panique

Anjou-
Lafayette

Eurostars Panorama

10e

Pré Cadet

Villa
Opéra Drouot

Grands
Boulevards

Bonne
Nouvelle

2e

Gallopin

Silk &
Spice

Little Palace

Réaumur
Sébastopol

Pierrot

3e

Ambassade
d'Auvergne

Strasbourg
St-Denis

1er

L

ST-GERMAIN-DES-PRÉS / QUARTIER LATIN
HÔTEL DE VILLE (Plan V)

The Westin Paris

3 r. Castiglione (1st) – **M** Tuileries – ℰ 01 44 77 11 11 – reservation.01729@
starwoodhotels.com – Fax 01 44 77 14 60 – www.westin.com/paris
440 rm – ✝390/750 € ✝✝390/750 €, ⇆ 37 € – 29 suites **J3**
Rest Le First – ℰ 01 44 77 10 40 (Closed August) Menu 32 € (weekdays lunch)/
75 € – Carte 80/95 €
Rest La Terrasse – ℰ 01 44 77 10 40 (Open 15 April-30 September) Menu 32 €
(weekday lunch)/75 € – Carte 80/95 €
♦ Luxury ♦ Traditional ♦ Stylish ♦
A splendid hotel built in 1878, whose rooms (some with views of the Tuileries) are
decorated in the style of the 19C. Sumptuous Napoleon III sitting rooms. Smart and
refined modern boudoir atmosphere at Le First. The courtyard is secluded from the
Paris hurly-burly.

Scribe

1 r. Scribe (9th) – **M** Opéra – ℰ 01 44 71 24 24 – h0663@accor.com
– Fax 01 42 65 39 97 – www.hotel-scribe-paris.com **K2**
204 rm – ✝570/1150 € ✝✝570/1150 €, ⇆ 35 € – 9 suites
Rest Café Lumière – Carte 63/152 €
♦ Grand Luxury ♦ Palace ♦ Personalised ♦
Housed in a grand Haussmann style building, this hotel has been completely reno-
vated and is much appreciated for its discreet luxury. The world première of the
Lumière brothers' first film screening was held here in 1895. Spa. Cosy, slightly Bri-
tish ambiance at the Café Lumière, brightened by a glass roof. Modern menu.

Costes

239 r. St-Honoré (1st) – **M** Concorde – ℰ 01 42 44 50 00 – Fax 01 42 44 50 01
– www.hotelcostes.com **J-K3**
82 rm – ✝400 € ✝✝550 €, ⇆ 32 € – 3 suites **Rest** – Carte 80/140 €
♦ Luxury ♦ Personalised ♦
Updated Napoleon III style in the hotel's purple and gold guestrooms. Splendid Italianate courtyard and impressive fitness centre. An extravagant luxury hotel popular with the hip crowd. The restaurant of the Hôtel Costes is a shrine to the latest
lounge trend.

De Vendôme

1 pl. Vendôme (1st) – **M** Opéra – ℰ 01 55 04 55 00 – reservations@
hoteldevendome.com – Fax 01 49 27 97 89 – www.hoteldevendome.com
19 rm – ✝450/550 € ✝✝535/630 €, ⇆ 32 € – 10 suites **K3**
Rest – Menu 40 € – Carte 61/83 €
♦ Grand Luxury ♦ Palace ♦ Stylish ♦
Place Vendôme provides the splendid backdrop for this fine 18C townhouse converted into a luxury hotel. Bedrooms with antique furniture, marble fittings and
high tech equipment.

Renaissance Paris Vendôme

4 r. Mont-Thabor (1st) – **M** Tuileries – ℰ 01 40 20 20 00
– francereservations@marriotthotels.com – Fax 01 40 20 20 01
– www.renaissanceparisvendome.com **K3**
97 rm – ✝330/620 € ✝✝330/620 €, ⇆ 29 € – 12 suites
Rest Pinxo – see below
♦ Business ♦ Traditional ♦ Cosy ♦
A 19C building converted into a contemporary hotel with interesting decor from
the 1930s to 1950s. Honey and chocolate tones and wood predominate in the
high-tech bedrooms. Attractive Chinese bar.

Castille Paris

33 r. Cambon (1st) – **M** Madeleine – ℰ 01 44 58 44 58 – reservations@
castille.com – Fax 01 44 58 44 00 – www.castille.com **J3**
91 rm – ✝260/820 € ✝✝260/820 €, ⇆ 28 € – 17 suites
Rest Il Cortile – 37 r. Cambon, ℰ 01 44 58 45 67 (closed August, 24-30
December, Saturday and Sunday) Menu 48/95 € – Carte 53/80 €
♦ Luxury ♦ Traditional ♦ Personalised ♦
Delightful Venetian-inspired decor in the Opéra wing, with black and white chic in
the Rivoli wing (in reverence to nearby fashion house Chanel). Il Cortile serves
Italian cuisine in a Villa d'Este-style dining room. Attractive patio-terrace.

Westminster   🛏 AC � rm 📺 📞 ⅏ 🚗 VISA ⦿ AE ⓞ

13 r. de la Paix (2nd) – Ⓜ Opéra – ℰ 01 42 61 57 46
– resa.westminster@warwickhotels.com – Fax 01 42 60 30 66
– www.hotelwestminster.com   **K2**
102 rm – †280/630 € ††280/630 €, ☕ 28 € – 22 suites
Rest *Le Céladon* – see below
Rest *Le Petit Céladon* – ℰ 01 47 03 40 42 (closed August, Monday, Tuesday, Wednesday, Thursday and Friday) Menu 55 €
◆ Luxury ◆ Cosy ◆

In was in 1846 that this elegant hotel took the name of its most loyal guest, the Duke of Westminster. Sumptuous rooms, luxurious apartments. The hall is redecorated every season. The Céladon becomes the Petit Céladon at the weekend, with a simplified menu and more relaxed service.

Hyatt Regency   🛏 ♿ rm AC ⅏ rm 📺 🍴 ⅏ 🚗 VISA ⦿ AE ⓞ

24 bd Malhesherbes (8th) – Ⓜ Madeleine – ℰ 01 55 27 12 34
– paris.madeleine@hyatt.com – Fax 01 55 27 12 35
– www.paris.madeleine.hyatt.com   **J2**
86 rm – †295/515 € ††330/545 €, ☕ 42 €
Rest *Café M* – (closed Sunday dinner) Menu 47 € (weekdays)/54 €
◆ Luxury ◆ Chain hotel ◆ Modern ◆

A distinctly contemporary interior that is both restrained and warm depicts this hotel: lobby-sitting rooms by Eiffel, spacious personalised rooms and a sauna and hammam. The delicious modern cuisine served at the Café M make it very popular. Champagne bar in the evening.

Millennium Opéra   🍴 ♿ rm AC ⅏ rm 📺 📞 ⅏ VISA ⦿ AE ⓞ

12 bd Haussmann (9th) – Ⓜ Richelieu Drouot – ℰ 01 49 49 16 00 – opera@
millenniumhotels.fr – Fax 01 49 49 17 00 – www.millenniumhotels.com
157 rm – †180/500 € ††200/550 €, ☕ 25 € – 6 suites   **L2**
Rest *Brasserie Haussmann* – ℰ 01 49 49 16 64 – Carte 29/55 €
◆ Luxury ◆ Business ◆ Modern ◆

This 1927 hotel has lost none of its period lustre. Tastefully appointed rooms with Art Deco furniture. Modern facilities. Carefully renovated with modern decor, and typical brasserie fare at the Brasserie Haussman.

Ambassador   🍴 🛏 AC ⅏ rm 📺 ⅏ ⊑ VISA ⦿ AE ⓞ

16 bd Haussmann (9th) – Ⓜ Richelieu Drouot – ℰ 01 44 83 40 40
– ambass@concorde-hotels.com – Fax 01 44 83 40 57
– www.hotelambassador-paris.com   **K2**
294 rm – †200/500 € ††200/500 €, ☕ 28 € – 8 suites
Rest *16 Haussmann* – ℰ 01 48 00 06 38 – Menu 44/52 € – Carte 48/59 €
◆ Luxury ◆ Business ◆ Classical ◆

Painted panels, crystal chandeliers and antiques adorn this elegant hotel dating from the 1920s. The renovated rooms are decorated in simple, contemporary style; the others somewhat more traditional. At 16 Haussmann, the royal blue and gold colour scheme is enhanced by light-coloured wood, red Starck chairs and views of the lively boulevard through the large windows.

Bedford   ♿ rm AC 📺 🍴 ⅏ VISA ⦿ AE

17 r. de l'Arcade (8th) – Ⓜ Madeleine – ℰ 01 44 94 77 77 – reservation@
hotel-bedford.com – Fax 01 44 94 77 97 – www.hotel-bedford.com
135 rm – †172 € ††228 €, ☕ 19 € – 10 suites   **J2**
Rest – (Closed August, Saturday, Sunday and Bank Holidays) (lunch only)
Menu 42 € – Carte 63/75 €
◆ Luxury ◆ Personalised ◆

This hotel, built in 1860 in the well-heeled Madeleine district, offers guests tastefully decorated rooms of varying size. 1900s-style decor with an abundance of decorative, stucco motifs and a lovely cupola. The restaurant room is the Bedford's real jewel.

FRANCE - PARIS

Regina 🍴 & rm 🆎 🖥 rm 🖥 📶 🛎 🅥🅘🅢🅐 🆒 🆎 📀

2 pl. des Pyramides (1st) – 🅜 *Tuileries –* 📞 *01 42 60 31 10 – reservation@
regina-hotel.com – Fax 01 40 15 95 16 – www.regina-hotel.com* **K3**
120 rm – 🛏375 € 🛏🛏375 €, ⌷ 32 € – 10 suites **Rest** – Carte 35/55 €
◆ Traditional ◆ Business ◆ Personalised ◆

The Art Nouveau decor of this 1900 hotel has been preserved. Superb lobby and
the rooms, rich in antique furniture, are quieter on the patio side; some offer views
of the Eiffel Tower. Dining room with a pretty Majorelle fireplace and popular courtyard-terrace.

Cambon without rest 🆎 🖥 📶 🅥🅘🅢🅐 🆒 🆎 📀

3 r. Cambon (1st) – 🅜 *Concorde –* 📞 *01 44 58 93 93 – info@hotelcambon.com
– Fax 01 42 60 30 59 – www.hotelcambon.com* **J3**
40 rm – 🛏230/290 € 🛏🛏330/370 €, ⌷ 19 € – 2 suites
◆ Traditional ◆ Functional ◆

Between the gardens of the Tuileries and Rue St-Honoré, pleasant rooms combining contemporary furniture, attractive engravings and old paintings. Regular
clientele.

Royal St-Honoré without rest 🆎 🔌 🖥 📶 🅥🅘🅢🅐 🆒 🆎 📀

221 r. St-Honoré (1st) – 🅜 *Tuileries –* 📞 *01 42 60 32 79 – rsh@hroy.com
– Fax 01 42 60 47 44 – www.hotel-royal-st-honore.com* **K3**
72 rm – 🛏340/390 € 🛏🛏390/440 €, ⌷ 22 €
◆ Business ◆ Traditional ◆ Classical ◆

An opulent-looking 19C building on the site of the former Hôtel de Noailles. Elegant and refined guestrooms, with Louis XVI decor in the breakfast room. Cosy bar.

Villa Opéra Drouot without rest & 🆎 🔌 🖥 📶 🅥🅘🅢🅐 🆒 🆎 📀

2 r. Geoffroy Marie (9th) – 🅜 *Grands Boulevards –* 📞 *01 48 00 08 08 – drouot@
leshotelsdeparis.com – Fax 01 48 00 80 60* **L2**
29 rm – 🛏129/310 € 🛏🛏139/320 €, ⌷ 20 €
◆ Business ◆ Stylish ◆

A surprising and subtle blend of Baroque decor and the latest in elegant comfort in
these rooms embellished with wall hangings, velvets, silks and wood panelling.

Meliá Vendôme without rest 🆎 🔌 🖥 📶 🛎 🅥🅘🅢🅐 🆒 🆎

8 r. Cambon (1st) – 🅜 *Concorde –* 📞 *01 44 77 54 00 – melia.vendome@
solmelia.com – Fax 01 44 77 54 01 – www.solmelia.com* **J3**
83 rm – 🛏379 € 🛏🛏399 €, ⌷ 28 € – 4 suites
◆ Business ◆ Traditional ◆ Functional ◆

Smart, restrained decor in tones of red and gold. Bedrooms with period furniture,
elegant lounge with a Belle Époque glass roof, chic bar and attractive breakfast
area.

Édouard VII 🆎 🔌 🖥 📶 🅥🅘🅢🅐 🆒 🆎 📀

39 av. Opéra (2nd) – 🅜 *Opéra –* 📞 *01 42 61 56 90 – info@edouard7hotel.com
– Fax 01 42 61 47 73 – www.edouard7hotel.com* **K3**
71 rm – 🛏220/360 € 🛏🛏250/500 €, ⌷ 25 € – 7 suites
Rest *Angl' Opéra –* 📞 *01 42 61 86 25 –* Menu 29 € (lunch) – Carte 48/58 €
◆ Luxury ◆ Modern ◆

Edward VII, Prince of Wales liked to stay here on his trips through Paris. Spacious,
luxurious rooms. Dark wood panelling and stained glass decorate the bar. The
warm contemporary decor of the Angl' Opéra is as pleasant as its unusual fusion
food.

Mercure Terminus Nord without rest & 🆎 🔌 🖥 📶 🛎

12 bd Denain (10th) – 🅜 *Gare du Nord*
– 📞 *01 42 80 20 00 – h2761@accor.com – Fax 01 42 80 63 89* 🅥🅘🅢🅐 🆒 🆎 📀
– www.mercure.com **M1**
236 rm – 🛏148/298 € 🛏🛏178/348 €, ⌷ 16 €
◆ Chain hotel ◆ Business ◆ Cosy ◆

A sympathetic renovation has restored this 19C hotel to its former glory. Art Nouveau stained glass, "British" decor and a cosy atmosphere give it the air of an elegant Victorian mansion.

FRANCE - PARIS

Pavillon de Paris without rest
   ⚿ 🗚 ↩ 📠 🛜 P VISA ◉◉ AE ①

7 r. Parme (9th) – ⓜ Liège – ℰ 01 55 31 60 00 – mail@pavillondeparis.com
– Fax 01 55 31 60 01 – www.pavillondeparis.com   **K1**

30 rm – 🛏215/240 € 🛏🛏270/296 €, � 21 €

◆ Luxury ◆ Design ◆

Contemporary-style hotel in a quiet street. The rooms are on the small side, but have a sober, luxurious decor and a pleasant intimate atmosphere. Japanese garden in the mini-courtyard.

Washington Opéra without rest
   ⚿ 🗚 ↩ 📠 🛜 VISA ◉◉ AE ①

50 r. Richelieu (1st) – ⓜ Palais Royal – ℰ 01 42 96 68 06 – hotel@
washingtonopera.com – Fax 01 40 15 01 12 – www.washingtonopera.com
36 rm – 🛏190/275 € 🛏🛏245/335 €, ⊒ 13 €   **L3**

◆ Traditional ◆ Luxury ◆ Classical ◆

Former townhouse of the Marquise de Pompadour. Directoire or 'Gustavian'-style rooms. The 6th floor terrace offers beautiful views over the gardens of the Palais-Royal.

Mercure Stendhal without rest
   🗚 ↩ 📠 🛜 VISA ◉◉ AE ①

22 r. D. Casanova (2nd) – ⓜ Opéra – ℰ 01 44 58 52 52 – h1610@accor.com
– Fax 01 44 58 52 00 – www.mercure.com   **K3**

20 rm – 🛏270/410 € 🛏🛏290/420 €, ⊒ 17 €

◆ Luxury ◆ Modern ◆

On the trail of the famous writer, stay in the "Red and Black" suite of this stylish residence. Smart, personalised rooms and snug lounge-bar with fireplace.

Mansart without rest
   🗚 📠 🛜 VISA ◉◉ AE ①

5 r. des Capucines (1st) – ⓜ Opéra – ℰ 01 42 61 50 28 – mansart@
espritfrance.com – Fax 01 49 27 97 44 – www.esprit-de-france.com
57 rm – 🛏160 € 🛏🛏170/345 €, ⊒ 13 €   **K3**

◆ Business ◆ Traditional ◆ Functional ◆

Close to Place Vendôme, this hotel pays homage to Mansart, architect to Louis XIV. Classic rooms furnished in Empire or Directoire style. A more modern lobby-lounge.

L'Horset Opéra without rest
   🗚 ↩ 📠 🛜 VISA ◉◉ AE ①

18 r. d'Antin (2nd) – ⓜ Opéra – ℰ 01 44 71 87 00 – reservation@
hotelhorsetopera.com – Fax 01 42 66 55 54 – www.hotelhorsetopera.com
54 rm ⊒ – 🛏180/265 € 🛏🛏195/295 €   **K2**

◆ Luxury ◆ Cosy ◆

Colourful wall hangings, warm wood panelling and fine furnishings add style to the rooms of this traditional hotel a short distance from the Garnier Opera House. Cosy lounge.

Jules without rest
   🖼 ⚿ 🗚 ↩ 📠 🛜 VISA ◉◉ AE ①

49 r. La Fayette (9th) – ⓜ Le Peletier – ℰ 01 42 85 05 44 – info@hoteljules.com
– Fax 01 49 95 06 60 – www.hoteljules.com   **L2**

101 rm – 🛏285/500 € 🛏🛏285/500 €, ⊒ 20 €

◆ Traditional ◆ Business ◆ Cosy ◆

This hotel has embraced contemporary design without sacrificing any of its inherent elegance. Bright and lively breakfast room (orange decor with floral motif). Gym.

St-Pétersbourg without rest
   🗚 📠 🛜 ⚿ VISA ◉◉ AE ①

33 r. Caumartin (9th) – ⓜ Havre Caumartin – ℰ 01 42 66 60 38 – info@
hotelpeters.com – Fax 01 42 66 53 54 – www.hotelsaintpetersbourg.com
100 rm ⊒ – 🛏141/210 € 🛏🛏181/267 €   **J2**

◆ Traditional ◆ Classical ◆

A large, traditional, family-run hotel. Elegant entrance with chandeliers and a marble floor, numerous lounges and meeting rooms. Spacious guestrooms.

Sofitel le Faubourg

15 r. Boissy d'Anglas (8th) – **Ⓜ** *Concorde*
– ☎ *01 44 94 14 14* – *h1295-gr@accor.com* – *Fax 01 44 94 14 28*
– *www.sofitel.com* **J3**
163 rm – †450/550 € ††550/850 €, ⌖ 32 € – 10 suites
Rest *Café Faubourg* – *(closed August, Saturday lunch and Sunday lunch)*
Menu 37 € – Carte 58/70 €
◆ Chain hotel ◆ Luxury ◆ Modern ◆

This Sofitel is housed in two buildings, one 18C, the other 19C. Rooms with high-tech facilities; a 1930s bar; plus a lounge with a glass roof. Trendy decor, relaxing interior garden and modern cuisine at the Café Faubourg.

Richmond Opéra *without rest*

11 r. Helder (9th) – **Ⓜ** *Chaussée d'Antin* – ☎ *01 47 70 53 20*
– *paris@richmond-hotel.com* – *Fax 01 48 00 02 10* **K2**
59 rm – †136/151 € ††156/171 €, ⌖ 10 €
◆ Traditional ◆ Classical ◆

The spacious, elegant rooms almost all give onto the courtyard. The lounge is rather grandly decorated in the Empire style.

Noailles *without rest*

9 r. de la Michodière (2nd) – **Ⓜ** *Quatre Septembre* – ☎ *01 47 42 92 90*
– *goldentulip.denoailles@wanadoo.fr* – *Fax 01 49 24 92 71*
– *www.hoteldenoailles.com* **K2**
58 rm – †205/265 € ††215/280 €, ⌖ 15 € – 4 suites
◆ Traditional ◆ Modern ◆

Bold contemporary elegance behind a pretty old façade. Minimalist decor in the rooms, most of which open onto a patio-terrace. Fashionable lounges.

De l'Arcade *without rest*

9 r. Arcade (8th) – **Ⓜ** *Madeleine* – ☎ *01 53 30 60 00*
– *reservation@hotel-arcade.com* – *Fax 01 40 07 03 07* – *www.hotel-arcade.com*
48 rm – †168/190 € ††203/420 €, ⌖ 13 € **J2**
◆ Luxury ◆ Family ◆ Personalised ◆

The marble and wood panels in the hall and lounges, and the soft colours and carefully-chosen furniture in the rooms, all contribute to the charm of this elegant and discreet hotel near the Madeleine.

ATN *without rest*

21 r. d'Athènes (9th) – **Ⓜ** *St-Lazare* – ☎ *01 48 74 00 55* – *atn@atnhotel.fr*
– *Fax 01 42 81 04 75* – *www.atnhotel.fr* **K1**
36 rm – †139/350 € ††149/360 €, ⌖ 11 €
◆ Design ◆

Situated a stone's throw from St-Lazare station, completely refurbished hotel in a trendy, contemporary style. Quality materials and attention to detail add to the appeal.

Lorette Opéra *without rest*

36 r. Notre-Dame de Lorette (9th) – **Ⓜ** *St-Georges* – ☎ *01 42 85 18 81*
– *hotel.lorette@astotel.com* – *Fax 01 42 81 32 19* – *www.astotel.com*
84 rm – †136/240 € ††136/240 €, ⌖ 14 € **L1**
◆ Business ◆ Modern ◆

The decor in this completely renovated hotel is a harmonious mix of bare stone and designer style. Pleasant, contemporary rooms; breakfast is served in the cellar with its vaulted ceiling.

Eurostars Panorama *without rest*

9 r. des Messageries (10th) – **Ⓜ** *Poissonnière* – ☎ *01 47 70 44 02* – *info@
eurostarspanorama.com* – *Fax 01 40 22 91 09* – *www.eurostarshotels.com*
43 rm – †100/540 € ††100/540 €, ⌖ 10 € **M1**
◆ Business ◆ Personalised ◆

Brand new hotel in ultra-contemporary style. Designer decor with references to French culture.

FRANCE - PARIS

Villathéna without rest   🚫 🅰️ ↫ 🖥️ ☎ 🆅🆂🆁 ⊕ 🅰🅴

23 r. d'Athènes (9th) – Ⓜ St-Lazare – ℰ 01 44 63 07 07 – reservation@
villathena.com – Fax 01 44 63 07 60 – www.villathena.com   **K1**
43 rm – ♦119/385 € ♦♦119/385 €, ☲ 17 €
♦ Modern ♦

Housed in the former Social Security offices, this brand-new hotel has a resolutely
contemporary feel. Lobby decorated in red, white and black; well-appointed guestrooms with light wood furniture.

Le Lavoisier without rest   🚫 🅰️ ↫ 🖥️ ☎ 🆅🆂🆁 ⊕ 🅰🅴 ⓘ

21 r. Lavoisier (8th) – Ⓜ St-Augustin – ℰ 01 53 30 06 06 – info@
hotellavoisier.com – Fax 01 53 30 23 00 – www.hotellavoisier.com
27 rm – ♦179/300 € ♦♦179/300 €, ☲ 14 € – 3 suites   **J2**
♦ Luxury ♦ Modern ♦

Contemporary rooms, cosy little library-cum-lounge also serving as a bar, and a
vaulted breakfast room are the hallmarks of this hotel in the St-Augustin district.

Little Palace   ⓖ rm 🅰️ ↫ rm 🖥️ ☎ 🆅🆂🆁 ⊕ 🅰🅴 ⓘ

4 r. Salomon de Caus (3rd) – Ⓜ Réaumur Sébastopol – ℰ 01 42 72 08 15
– info@littlepalacehotel.com – Fax 01 42 72 45 81 – www.littlepalacehotel.com
53 rm – ♦170/230 € ♦♦190/265 €, ☲ 15 € – 4 suites   **M3**
Rest – (closed 2 August-1st September, Friday dinner, Saturday and Sunday)
♦ Traditional ♦ Personalised ♦

A charming address with decor combining Belle Époque and contemporary styles.
Attractive guestrooms; those on the fifth and sixth floors have a balcony with
views of Paris. Lovely brown, sculpted wood panelling, light tones and minimalist
furniture can be found in the restaurant.

Le Vignon without rest   🅰️ ↫ 🖥️ ☎ 🆅🆂🆁 ⊕ 🅰🅴 ⓘ

23 r. Vignon (8th) – Ⓜ Madeleine – ℰ 01 47 42 93 00 – reservation@
hotelvignon.com – Fax 01 47 42 04 60 – www.levignon.com   **J2**
28 rm – ♦190/330 € ♦♦195/360 €, ☲ 20 €
♦ Business ♦ Personalised ♦

A friendly, discreet hotel just a few steps from Place de la Madeleine. Cosy rooms
– those on the top floor have been refurbished in a distinctly contemporary style.

Thérèse without rest   🅰️ ↫ 🖥️ ☎ 🆅🆂🆁 ⊕ 🅰🅴 ⓘ

5 r. Thérèse (1st) – Ⓜ Pyramides – ℰ 01 42 96 10 01 – info@hoteltherese.com
– Fax 01 42 96 15 22 – www.hoteltherese.com   **K3**
43 rm – ♦155/320 € ♦♦155/320 €, ☲ 13 €
♦ Traditional ♦ Business ♦ Personalised ♦

The charm of this hotel lies in its refined contemporary decor of paintings, attractive fabrics and pastel shades. Vaulted breakfast room occupying the former cellars.

Opéra Franklin without rest   🅰️ ↫ 🖥️ ☎ 🆅🆂🆁 ⊕ 🅰🅴 ⓘ

19 r. Buffault (9th) – Ⓜ Cadet – ℰ 01 42 80 27 27 – info@operafranklin.com
– Fax 01 48 78 13 04 – www.operafranklin.com   **L1**
67 rm – ♦146/203 € ♦♦189/247 €, ☲ 13 €
♦ Business ♦ Classical ♦

Located in a quiet street, this business hotel is built around a central courtyard.
Large lobby with a glass roof and bar. Functional, simply decorated rooms.

Caumartin Opéra without rest   ↫ 🖥️ ☎ 🆅🆂🆁 ⊕ 🅰🅴 ⓘ

27 r. Caumartin (9th) – Ⓜ Havre Caumartin – ℰ 01 47 42 95 95
– hotel.caumartin@astotel.com – Fax 01 47 42 88 19 – www.astotel.com
40 rm – ♦155/240 € ♦♦165/240 €, ☲ 14 €   **J2**
♦ Minimalist ♦

This small hotel in the Grand Magasins district has had a complete face-lift. Contemporary-style guestrooms with immaculate white bathrooms.

Anjou Lafayette without rest   🔲 ↯ 📺 📶 💳 ⓞⓞ 🄰🄴 ⓞ

4 r. Riboutté (9th) – ⓜ Cadet – 𝒞 01 42 46 83 44 – hotel.anjou.lafayette
@wanadoo.fr – Fax 01 48 00 08 97 – www.hotelanjoulafayette.com
39 rm – †98/170 € ††118/190 €, ⌷ 12 €   **M1**
◆ Traditional ◆ Modern ◆

Near the leafy Square Montholon, with its Second Empire wrought-iron gates, this
hotel offers guests comfortable, soundproofed rooms decorated in warm tones.

Les Trois Poussins without rest   & 🔲 ↯ 📺 📶 💳 ⓞⓞ 🄰🄴 ⓞ

15 r. Clauzel (9th) – ⓜ St-Georges – 𝒞 01 53 32 81 81 – h3p@les3poussins.com
– Fax 01 53 32 81 82 – www.les3poussins.com   **L1**
40 rm – †106/156 € ††109/171 €, ⌷ 10 €
◆ Traditional ◆ Classical ◆

Elegant rooms offering several levels of comfort. View of Paris from the top floors.
Prettily vaulted breakfast room. Small courtyard-terrace.

Alison without rest   ↯ 📺 📶 💳 ⓞⓞ 🄰🄴 ⓞ

21 r. de Surène (8th) – ⓜ Madeleine – 𝒞 01 42 65 54 00 – hotel.alison@
orange.fr – Fax 01 42 65 08 17 – www.hotelalison.com   **J2**
34 rm – †96/172 € ††118/192 €, ⌷ 10 €
◆ Family ◆ Functional ◆

A family hotel in a quiet street near the Théâtre de la Madeleine with an entrance
hall decorated with modern paintings. Neat and tidy, functional bedrooms, with
attic-style rooms on the 6th floor.

le Meurice – Hôtel Le Meurice   🔲 ⇔ 🍽 💳 ⓞⓞ 🄰🄴 ⓞ

228 r. Rivoli (1st) – ⓜ Tuileries – 𝒞 01 44 58 10 55 – restaurant@lemeurice.com
– Fax 01 44 58 10 76 – www.lemeurice.com
– Closed 1-30 August, 20 February-7 March, Saturday and Sunday
Rest – Menu 90 € (lunch)/220 € – Carte 205/290 € ℬ   **J-K3**
Spec. Poulet à la bouteille "Aniel Zélie" généreusement truffé, salade de jeu-
nes pousses (winter). Dos de saumon de l'Adour confit, chou aux écorces
d'orange et fumet au genièvre. Fuseaux croustillants au chocolat lacté, truffe
blanche à la fleur de sel.
◆ Innovative ◆ Luxury ◆

Dining room in the style of the age of Louis XIV, inspired by the State Apartments
of Versailles, and talented modern cuisine by Yannick Alleno: a palace for gourmets!

Les Ambassadeurs – Hôtel Crillon   🔲 ⇔ 🍽 💳 ⓞⓞ 🄰🄴 ⓞ

10 pl. Concorde (8th) – ⓜ Concorde – 𝒞 01 44 71 16 16 – ambassadeurs@
crillon.com – Fax 01 44 71 15 02 – www.crillon.com
– Closed August, Sunday and Monday   **J3**
Rest – Menu 92 € (weekdays lunch)/220 € – Carte 168/273 € ℬ
Spec. Blanc à manger d'œuf et truffe noire (January-March). Pigeonneau
désossé, foie gras de canard et jus à l'olive. Comme un vacherin aux fruits
de saison.
◆ Innovative ◆ Luxury ◆

This splendid dining room was once the ballroom of an 18C mansion. Sophisticated, inventive cuisine and a superb wine list.

L'Espadon – Hôtel Ritz   🏠 🔲 ⇔ 🍽 💳 ⓞⓞ 🄰🄴 ⓞ

15 pl. Vendôme (1st) – ⓜ Opéra – 𝒞 01 43 16 30 80 – espadon@ritzparis.com
– Fax 01 43 16 33 75 – www.ritzparis.com   **K3**
Rest – Menu 80 € (lunch), 105/340 € bi – Carte 170/266 € ℬ
Spec. Emietté de tourteau, jaune d'oeuf fumé et caviar impérial. Sole aux
coquillages, confit de pommes de terre au beurre demi-sel. Millefeuille "Tra-
dition Ritz", crème glacée caramel.
◆ Classic ◆ Elegant ◆

The restaurant is weighed down with gold and drapery. In this magical setting,
Michel Roth's faultlessly classic cuisine finds its true expression. Impeccable service.

XXXX ξξ ξξ **Le Grand Véfour**   🅰🅒 ⇨ ➡️ 💳 ⬥ 🅰🅔 ⬥

17 r. Beaujolais (1st) – Ⓜ *Palais Royal* – ☏ *01 42 96 56 27* – *grand.vefour@wanadoo.fr* – *www.grand-vefour.com*
– *Closed 20-24 April, 2-31 August, 24 December-1 January, Friday dinner, Saturday and Sunday*   **L3**
Rest – Menu 88 € (weekdays lunch)/268 € – Carte 210/230 € 🕮
Spec. Ravioles de foie gras, crème foisonnée truffée. Parmentier de queue de bœuf aux truffes. Palet noisette et chocolat au lait, glace au caramel brun et prise de sel de Guérande.
  ♦ *Innovative* ♦ *Romantic* ♦
Many famous personalities have dined in the elegant Directoire-style *salons* of this luxurious restaurant, located in the gardens of the Palais-Royal. Innovative cuisine created by an inspired chef.

XXXX ξξ ξξ **Carré des Feuillants** (Alain Dutournier)   🅰🅒 ⇨ ➡️ 💳 ⬥ 🅰🅔 ⬥

14 r. Castiglione (1st) – Ⓜ *Tuileries* – ☏ *01 42 86 82 82* – *carredesfeuillants@orange.fr* – *Fax 01 42 86 07 71* – *www.carredesfeuillants.fr*
– *Closed August, Saturday and Sunday*   **K3**
Rest – Menu 58 € (weekdays lunch)/175 € – Carte 137/176 € 🕮
Spec. Huîtres de Marennes, caviar d'Aquitaine et algues marines (except summer). Turbot sauvage rôti, riz noir et asperges vertes (spring-summer). Cerises burlat en jubilé façon "forêt verte" (summer).
  ♦ *A la mode* ♦ *Luxury* ♦
A modern restaurant on the site of the former Feuillants convent enhanced by contemporary works of art. The modern menu shows distinct Gascon influences and there is a superb choice of wines and armagnacs.

XXX ξξ ξξ **Senderens**   🅰🅒 ⇨ ➡️ 💳 ⬥ 🅰🅔 ⬥

9 pl. de la Madeleine (8th) – Ⓜ *Madeleine* – ☏ *01 42 65 22 90* – *restaurant@senderens.fr* – *Fax 01 42 65 06 23* – *www.senderens.fr*
– *Closed 2-24 August*   **J2**
Rest – Menu 110/150 € bi – Carte 89/120 € 🕮
Spec. Langoustines croustillantes, coriandre et livèche. Morue des îles Féroé en brandade et pousses de salade. Fine dacquoise au poivre de Séchouan, marmelade de citron confit, glace au gingembre.
  ♦ *Innovative* ♦ *Design* ♦
This luxurious establishment, which is always extremely lively, boasts a successful marriage of designer furniture and Art Nouveau wood panelling by Majorelle. Creative cuisine and a fine choice of accompanying wines.

XXX ξξ **Le Céladon** – Hôtel Westminster   🅰🅒 ⇨ ➡️ 💳 ⬥ 🅰🅔 ⬥

15 r. Daunou (2nd) – Ⓜ *Opéra* – ☏ *01 47 03 40 42* – *cmoisand@leceladon.com* – *Fax 01 42 61 33 78* – *www.leceladon.com*
– *Closed August, Saturday and Sunday*   **K2**
Rest – Menu 55 € (weekdays lunch), 82/110 € – Carte 90/120 €
Spec. Thon rouge et sardine bretonne marinés et rôtis à la chermoula. Turbot côtier rôti au beurre salé, salade de charlotte grillée. Chocolat, sablé à la fleur de sel et sabayon.
  ♦ *A la mode* ♦ *Romantic* ♦
Sophisticated decor that combines Regency-style furniture, green walls and a collection of Chinese porcelain. Cuisine suited to current tastes.

XXX ξξ **Gérard Besson**   🅰🅒 ➡️ 💳 ⬥ 🅰🅔 ⬥

5 r. Coq Héron (1st) – Ⓜ *Louvre Rivoli* – ☏ *01 42 33 14 74* – *gerard.besson4@libertysurf.fr* – *Fax 01 42 33 85 71* – *www.gerardbesson.com*
– *Closed 25 July-24 August, Monday lunch, Saturday lunch and Sunday*
Rest – Menu 130 € – Carte 125/160 € 🕮   **L3**
Spec. Fricassée de homard "Georges Garin". Gibier (October-mid December.). Fenouil confit aux épices, glace vanille de Tahiti.
  ♦ *Traditional* ♦ *Formal* ♦
Elegant restaurant near Les Halles decorated in beige tones with still life paintings and Jouy wall hangings. Reinterpreted classic cuisine, game specialities and a good wine list.

XXX **Café de la Paix** – Intercontinental Le Grand   🔥 AC ⇔ ➡️🍴

12 bd Capucines (9th) – **Ⓜ** *Opéra* – 𝒞 *01 40 07 36 36*   VISA ⓦ AE Ⓞ

– *info@cafedelapaix.fr* – *Fax 01 40 07 36 13* – *www.cafedelapaix.fr*

Rest – Menu 47 € (lunch)/85 € – Carte 62/100 €   **K2**

♦ A la mode ♦ Brasserie ♦

Fine murals, gold wainscoting and French Second Empire-inspired furniture: this famous luxury brasserie, open from 7am to midnight is still the place to meet in Paris.

XXX **Le Pur' Grill** – Hôtel Park Hyatt   ➡️🍴 VISA ⓦ AE Ⓞ

ⓈⒺⒺ

5 r. de la Paix (2nd) – **Ⓜ** *Opéra* – 𝒞 *01 58 71 10 60* – *paris.vendome@ hyatt.com* – *www.paris.vendome.hyatt.fr*

– *closed August*   **K3**

Rest – *(dinner only)* Menu 135/300 € bi – Carte 97/185 €

Spec. Sashimi de langoustines sur l'idée d'une pinacolada. Bar de ligne confit à l'huile d'olive, supions, sauce tonato (september). Sablé breton au beurre demi-sel, marmelade figues et cassis, crème glacée au shizo.

♦ A la mode ♦

Simplicity and refinement best describe the modern dinner menu served in the chic and contemporary rotunda-shaped dining room (kitchen in full view). Attractive summer terrace.

XXX **Drouant**   🍴 AC 🥢 ⇔ ➡️🍴 VISA ⓦ AE

16 pl. Gaillon (2nd) – **Ⓜ** *Quatre Septembre* – 𝒞 *01 42 65 15 16*

– *a.westermann@orange.fr* – *Fax 01 49 24 02 15* – *www.drouant.com*

Rest – Menu 43 € (lunch)/54 € – Carte 56/86 € 🍷   **K3**

♦ A la mode ♦ Elegant ♦

Under the auspices of Antoine Westermann, the legendary Goncourt restaurant is enjoying a new lease of life: elegant, opulent, yet uncluttered decor, dotted with antiques and a modern menu.

XXX **La Fontaine Gaillon**   🍴 AC ⇔ ➡️🍴 VISA ⓦ AE Ⓞ

pl. Gaillon (2nd) – **Ⓜ** *Quatre Septembre* – 𝒞 *01 47 42 63 22*

– *lafontainegaillon@cegetel.net* – *Fax 01 47 42 82 84*

– *www.la-fontaine-gaillon.com*

– *Closed 1-23 August, Saturday and Sunday*   **K2-3**

Rest – Menu 43 € (weekdays lunch), 49/58 € – Carte 60/70 €

♦ Seafood ♦ Cosy ♦

Seafood dishes and wine selection supervised by the actor Gérard Depardieu in a graceful, 17C townhouse. Stylish decor and terrace with central fountain.

XXX **Macéo**   ⇔ VISA ⓦ

15 r. Petits-Champs (1st) – **Ⓜ** *Bourse* – 𝒞 *01 42 97 53 85* – *info@ maceorestaurant.com* – *Fax 01 47 03 36 93* – *www.maceorestaurant.com*

– *Closed 1-17 August, Saturday lunch, Sunday and Bank Holidays*

Rest – Menu 32 € (weekdays)/60 € – Carte 50/62 € 🍷   **L3**

♦ Innovative ♦ Friendly ♦

Lively French Second Empire setting: period mirrors combine with modern furnishings. Updated cuisine, a vegetarian menu and international wine list. Friendly lounge-bar.

XX **1728**   AC 🥢 ⇔ VISA ⓦ AE

8 r. d'Anjou (8th) – **Ⓜ** *Madeleine* – 𝒞 *01 40 17 04 77* – *restaurant1728@ wanadoo.fr* – *Fax 01 42 65 53 87* – *www.restaurant-1728.com*

– *Closed 5-25 August and Sunday*   **J2**

Rest – Carte 55/121 € 🍷

♦ A la mode ♦ Romantic ♦

An 18C town house where La Fayette lived from 1827 until his death. Modern cuisine with an international accent served in stylish rooms adorned with wainscoting and period furniture.

XX **Goumard**   AC ⟷ ⟶ VISA ●● AE ①

9 r. Duphot (1st) – Ⓜ Madeleine – ℰ 01 42 60 36 07 – goumard.philippe@
wanadoo.fr – Fax 01 42 60 04 54 – www.goumard.com   **J3**
Rest – Menu 39/49 € bi – Carte 49/70 €
♦ Seafood ♦
Esteemed 100-year-old Parisian restaurant where major artists including Majorelle,
Lalique and Labouret have enhanced the Art Deco setting. Fine seafood menu.

XX **Pierre au Palais Royal**   AC VISA ●● AE

10 r. Richelieu (1st) – Ⓜ Palais Royal – ℰ 01 42 96 09 17 – pierreaupalaisroyal@
wanadoo.fr – Fax 01 42 96 26 40 – www.pierreaupalaisroyal.com
– closed August, Saturday lunch and Sunday   **K3**
Rest – Menu 39/54 €
♦ A la mode ♦ Neighbourhood ♦
Change of course for this establishment: a dining room redecorated in black and
white, in a simple, chic effect, and dishes inspired by the southwest, a region that
the owner promotes with passion.

XX **Palais Royal**   ⛱ AC VISA ●● AE ①

110 Galerie de Valois - Jardin du Palais Royal (1st) – Ⓜ Bourse
– ℰ 01 40 20 00 27 – palaisrest@aol.com – Fax 01 40 20 00 82
– www.restaurantdupalaisroyal.com
– closed 21 December-10 January and Sunday   **L3**
Rest – Carte 50/75 €
♦ Traditional ♦ Retro ♦
Beneath the windows of Colette's apartment, an Art Deco-style restaurant with an
idyllic terrace, opening onto the Palais-Royal garden.

XX **Jean**   AC ¼↗ ⟷ VISA ●● AE ①
£3

8 r. St-Lazare (9th) – Ⓜ Notre-Dame-de-Lorette – ℰ 01 48 78 62 73
– chezjean@wanadoo.fr – Fax 01 48 78 66 04 – www.restaurantjean.fr
– Closed 27 July-17 August, 23-27 February, Saturday and Sunday
Rest – Menu 46 € (lunch), 65/85 € – Carte 70/77 €   **L1**
Spec. Foie gras, risotto et figues au vinaigre de Xérès (season). Pigeon et
ravioles de foie de volaille au jus chocolaté (season). Pêche de vigne pochée
au vin blanc (season).
♦ Innovative ♦ Friendly ♦
Tempting modern cuisine served in this redecorated restaurant. The bistro spirit
has made way for a cosy atmosphere (striped fabrics, flowery motifs, mosaic
floor). Lounge on the first floor.

XX **Au Petit Riche**   AC ⟷ VISA ●● AE ①

25 r. Le Peletier (9th) – Ⓜ Richelieu Drouot – ℰ 01 47 70 68 68 – aupetitriche@
wanadoo.fr – Fax 01 48 24 10 79 – www.aupetitriche.com
– Closed Saturday from 14 July to 20 August and Sunday   **L2**
Rest – Menu 31/37 € bi – Carte 32/64 € ⛯
♦ Traditional ♦ Brasserie ♦
Bench seats in red velvet, etched mirrors, and elegant tables: the charm of the sit-
ting room that was the height of fashion in the 19C remains intact here. Cuisine
inspired by the Tours region and a good choice of wines from the Loire valley.

XX **Gallopin**   AC ⟷ VISA ●● AE ①

40 r. N.-D.-des-Victoires (2nd) – Ⓜ Bourse – ℰ 01 42 36 45 38
– administration@brasseriegallopin.com – Fax 01 42 36 10 32
– www.brasseriegallopin.com   **L3**
Rest – Menu 30/36 € bi – Carte 30/50 €
♦ Brasserie ♦ Retro ♦
Named after its former owners, this brasserie opposite the Palais Brongniart, sports
a plush, Victorian (1876) decor. Speedy service and excellent choice of bistro-style
dishes.

XX **La Luna**   AC VISA ◯◯ AE

69 r. Rocher (8th) – Ⓜ Villiers – ℰ 01 42 93 77 61 – laluna75008@yahoo.fr
– Fax 01 40 08 02 44 – www.restaurant-laluna.fr
– Closed 1-24 August and Sunday   *Plan II* **H1**
Rest – Carte 87/110 €
♦ Fish ♦ Friendly ♦

An Art Deco setting, peaceful ambience and fine cuisine based on fish and seafood delivered fresh from the Atlantic.

XX **Au Pied de Cochon**   ⌂ AC �>♀ VISA ◯◯ AE ◯

6 r. Coquillière (1st) – Ⓜ Châtelet-Les Halles – ℰ 01 40 13 77 00
– pieddecochon@blanc.net – Fax 01 40 13 77 09 – www.pieddecochon.com
Rest – Menu 26 € – Carte 35/66 €   **L3**
♦ Brasserie ♦ Brasserie ♦

Famous Parisian brasserie well known among night owls since it opened in 1947. Long, traditional menu (pauper's platter, seafood).

XX **Ambassade d'Auvergne**   AC ⟷ VISA ◯◯ AE
ⓐ
22 r. Grenier St-Lazare (3rd) – Ⓜ Rambuteau – ℰ 01 42 72 31 22 – info@
ambassade-auvergne.com – Fax 01 42 78 85 47
– www.ambassade-auvergne.com   **M3**
Rest – Menu 30 € – Carte 31/47 €
♦ De Terroir ♦ Friendly ♦

True ambassadors of a province rich in flavours and traditions: Auvergne style furniture and décor, products, recipes and local wines.

XX **Terminus Nord**   AC ⟷ VISA ◯◯ AE

23 r. Dunkerque (10th) – Ⓜ Gare du Nord – ℰ 01 42 85 05 15
– Fax 01 40 16 13 98 – www.terminusnord.com   **M1**
Rest – Menu 32 € – Carte 35/45 €
♦ Brasserie ♦ Brasserie ♦

High ceilings, frescoes, posters and sculptures are reflected in the mirrors of this brasserie that successfully mixes Art Deco and Art Nouveau. Cosmopolitan clientele.

XX **Au Gourmand**   AC VISA ◯◯
ⓐ
17 r. Molière (1st) – Ⓜ Pyramides – ℰ 01 42 96 22 19 – Fax 01 42 96 05 72
– www.augourmand.fr
– Closed 21-25 May, 10-17 August, 24-28 December, Saturday lunch, Sunday
and Bank Holidays   **K3**
Rest – Menu 30/105 € – Carte 65/80 € ⅄
♦ Traditional ♦ Neighbourhood ♦

Traditional cuisine with a contemporary twist (including a menu based on Joël Thiébault's famous vegetables) prepared by a self-taught chef. Knowledgeable sommelier and friendly, welcoming ambience.

XX **Pinxo** – Hôtel Renaissance Paris Vendôme   AC ⌁♀ VISA ◯◯ AE ◯

9 r. d'Alger (1st) – Ⓜ Tuileries – ℰ 01 40 20 72 00 – Fax 01 40 20 72 02
– www.pinxo.fr
– Closed 3 weeks in August   **K3**
Rest – Carte 48/70 €
♦ Innovative ♦ Fashionable ♦

A restaurant with minimalist furniture, black and white shades, an open kitchen and understated but stylish decoration, serving simple, tasty dishes à la Dutournier.

XX **Vaudeville**   VISA ◯◯ ◯

29 r. Vivienne (2nd) – Ⓜ Bourse – ℰ 01 40 20 04 62 – Fax 01 40 20 14 35
– www.vaudevilleparis.com   **L2**
Rest – Menu 24/32 € – Carte 35/60 €
♦ Brasserie ♦ Brasserie ♦

This large brasserie with its sparkling Art Deco details in pure Parisian style has become the 'canteen' of numerous journalists. It is also especially lively after theatre performances. Classical menu.

XX **Le Versance** `AK` `≠` `VISA` `OO` `AE`

16 r. Feydeau (2nd) – Ⓜ *Bourse –* ℰ *01 45 08 00 08 – contact@leversance.fr*
– Fax 01 45 08 47 99 – www.leversance.fr
– Closed August, 24 December-5 January, Saturday lunch, Sunday and Monday
Rest – Menu 38 € bi (weekdays lunch) – Carte 54/71 €   **L2**
♦ A la mode ♦ Fashionable ♦
A tasteful combination of elegant modern (white/grey tones, designer furniture)
and period decor (exposed beams, stained glass). Contemporary cuisine from a
globetrotting chef.

XX **Hotaru** `VISA` `OO`

18 r. Rodier (9th) – Ⓜ *Notre-Dame-de-Lorette –* ℰ *01 48 78 33 74*
– www.hotaru.fr
– Closed Sunday and Monday   **L1**
Rest – Menu 35/60 € – Carte 33/60 €
♦ Japanese ♦
No-frills decor at this new Japanese restaurant installed in a former inn. Traditional,
fish-based cuisine.

X **Aux Lyonnais** `AK` `⟷` `VISA` `OO` `AE`
😊
32 r. St-Marc (2nd) – Ⓜ *Richelieu Drouot –* ℰ *01 42 96 65 04 – auxlyonnais@*
online.fr – Fax 01 42 97 42 95 – www.esprit-bistrot.com
– Closed 26 July-24 August, 24 December-2 January, Saturday lunch, Sunday
and Monday   **L2**
Rest – *(pre-book)* Menu 32 € – Carte 40/49 €
♦ Lyons cuisine ♦ Bistro ♦
This bistro founded in 1890 offers delicious, intelligently updated Lyonnais recipes.
A delightfully retro setting: bar counter, bench seating, bevelled mirrors and moul-
dings.

X **Café Panique** `VISA` `OO` `AE`
😊
12 r. des Messageries (10th) – Ⓜ *Poissonnière –* ℰ *01 47 70 06 84*
– www.cafepanique.com   **M1**
Rest – Menu 20 € (lunch)/33 € – Carte approx. 44 €
♦ A la mode ♦ Intimate ♦
Former textile workshop converted into a loft-style restaurant: skylight, mezzanine,
temporary exhibitions and modern dishes from an open-plan kitchen.

X **La Petite Sirène de Copenhague** `VISA` `OO` `AE`
😊
47 r. N.-D. de Lorette (9th) – Ⓜ *St-Georges –* ℰ *01 45 26 66 66*
– Closed 1-31 August, 23 December-2 January, Saturday lunch, Sunday and
Monday   **K1**
Rest – *(pre-book)* Menu 29 € (lunch)/34 € – Carte 43/71 €
♦ Danish ♦ Cosy ♦
A tasteful dining room, colour washed walls and soft Danish lighting set the scene
for original recipes from Andersen's homeland. Attentive service.

X **Zen** `🍴` `AK` `VISA` `OO` `AE`
😊
8 r. de L'Echelle (1st) – Ⓜ *Palais Royal –* ℰ *01 42 61 93 99 – mondial.paris@*
wanadoo.fr – Fax 01 40 20 92 91 – www.restaurant-zen.fr.cc
– Closed 10-20 August   **K3**
Rest – Menu 18 € (lunch), 30/60 € – Carte 20/30 €
♦ Japanese ♦
Japanese restaurant with typically extensive menu, yet refreshingly untraditional in
its decor: clean curving lines, white and acid green colour scheme.

X **Willi's Wine Bar** `VISA` `OO`
😊
13 r. Petits-Champs (1st) – Ⓜ *Bourse –* ℰ *01 42 61 05 09 – info@*
williswinebar.com – Fax 01 47 03 36 93 – www.williswinebar.com
– Closed 9-24 August, Sunday and Bank Holidays   **L3**
Rest – Menu 27 € (lunch)/35 € `🍷`
♦ Bistro ♦ Wine bar ♦
A collection of posters created for the establishment by modern artists decorates
this very friendly wine bar. Bistro cuisine and carefully selected vintage wines.

FRANCE - PARIS

I Golosi
[AC] [VISA] [CO]

6 r. Grange Batelière (9th) – Ⓜ *Richelieu Drouot –* ℰ *01 48 24 18 63 – i.golosi@wanadoo.fr – Fax 01 45 23 18 96 – Closed 8-20 August, Saturday dinner and Sunday*
Rest – Carte 25/45 € ⅜
L2

◆ Italian ◆ Minimalist ◆

On the 1st floor, Italian designer decor with a minimalism made up for by the joviality of the service. Café, shop and little spot for tasting things on the ground floor. Italian cuisine.

Liza
[AC] [VISA] [CO] [AE]

14 r. de la Banque (2nd) – Ⓜ *Bourse –* ℰ *01 55 35 00 66 – info@restaurant-liza.com – Fax 01 40 15 04 60 – www.restaurant-liza.com*
Rest – Menu 18 € (weekdays lunch), 23/50 € – Carte 35/70 €
L3

◆ Lebanese ◆

Stylish Lebanese address (oriental designer decor with a "lounge" feel) offering a refined interpretation of traditional dishes.

Silk & Spice
[AC] ⇔ [VISA] [CO] [AE] ①

6 r. Mandar (2nd) – Ⓜ *Sentier –* ℰ *01 44 88 21 91 – paris@groupsilkandspice.com – Fax 01 42 21 36 25 – www.groupsilkandspice.com*
Rest – Menu 21 € (lunch), 32/60 € – Carte 48/61 €
L3

◆ Thai ◆ Exotic ◆

Elegant and intimate setting at this Thai restaurant with orchids, tropical wood and low-key lighting.

Le Pré Cadet
[AC] [VISA] [CO] [AE]

10 r. Saulnier (9th) – Ⓜ *Cadet –* ℰ *01 48 24 99 64 – Fax 01 73 77 39 49 – Closed 1st-8 May, 3-21 August, 24 December-1st January, Saturday lunch and Sunday*
Rest – *(number of covers limited, pre-book)* Menu 30 € – Carte 50/70 €
L2

◆ Traditional ◆ Friendly ◆

This friendly, convivial restaurant in the vicinity of the 'Folies' is renowned for rough and ready dishes, such as veal brawn - its pride and joy. Very good coffee list.

Pierrot
⌂ [AC] [VISA] [CO] [AE]

18 r. Étienne Marcel (2nd) – Ⓜ *Etienne Marcel –* ℰ *01 45 08 00 10 – Fax 01 42 77 35 92 – Closed 9-28 August and Sunday*
Rest – Menu 50 € bi/70 € bi
M3

◆ Traditional ◆ Bistro ◆

Bistro in the Sentier district offering a discovery tour of the flavours of the Aveyron. Free-range meat from the Aubrac, duck confit, foie gras, etc. Pavement terrace.

Chez Michel
[VISA] [CO]

10 r. Belzunce (10th) – Ⓜ *Gare du Nord –* ℰ *01 44 53 06 20 – Fax 01 44 53 61 31 – Closed 2 weeks in August, Monday lunch, Saturday and Sunday*
Rest – Menu 32/55 €
M1

◆ Traditional ◆ Bistro ◆

Unpretentious and popular retro-style bistro proposing delicious traditional dishes, with a slight Breton slant (the chef's origins and name!) Excellent game in season.

Bi Zan
⇔ [VISA] [CO] [AE]

56 r. Ste-Anne (2nd) – Ⓜ *Quatre Septembre –* ℰ *01 42 96 67 76*
Rest – Menu 60/150 € – Carte 60/250 €
K3

◆ Japanese ◆ Minimalist ◆

Popular address (the name refers to a mountainous region of Japan) in minimalist style. Sushi counter, intimate upstairs dining room and interesting saké list.

TOUR EIFFEL, INVALIDES
Plan IV

Sezz without rest
& [AC] ↳ [GAT] ⁉ ⌂ [VISA] [CO] [AE] ①

6 av. Frémiet (16th) – ⊠ *75016 –* Ⓜ *Passy –* ℰ *01 56 75 26 26 – mail@hotelsezz.com – Fax 01 56 75 26 16 – www.hotelsezz.com*
22 rm – ♦285/340 € ♦♦335/470 €, � 25 € – 5 suites
N2

◆ Luxury ◆ Design ◆

Revamped hotel in a modern style: spacious, minimalist interior (shades of grey, giant vases), hi-tech gadgets and attentive staff. Steam bath and Jacuzzi.

FRANCE - PARIS

Mercure Suffren Tour Eiffel 🛜 🕭 🕭 rm 📶 🖑 rm 🖼️ 🏊 🅿️
20 r. Jean Rey (15th) – Ⓜ Bir-Hakeim   VISA ⓪ AE ①
– ✆ 01 45 78 50 00 – h2175@accor.com – Fax 01 45 78 91 42
– www.mercure.com   **N2**
405 rm – ♦175/310 € ♦♦190/310 €, � 20 €   **Rest** – Carte 30/45 €
♦ Chain hotel ♦ Business ♦ Functional ♦
This modern building in the heart of the capital stands out with its verdant reception and environs. Rooms are perfectly soundproofed and some have views of the Eiffel Tower. The dining room opens onto a pleasant terrace surrounded by trees and greenery.

Bourgogne et Montana without rest   📶 🖼️ 🕸️ VISA ⓪ AE ①
3 r. de Bourgogne (7th) – Ⓜ Assemblée Nationale – ✆ 01 45 51 20 22
– bmontana@bourgogne-montana.com – Fax 01 45 56 11 98 – bourgogne-
montana.com   **Q1**
28 rm ⊑ – ♦180/200 € ♦♦200/290 € – 4 suites
♦ Traditional ♦ Personalised ♦
Elegance and beauty fill every room of this discreet 18C hotel. The top floor rooms offer superb views over the "Palais-Bourbon" (French Parliament buildings).

Le Walt without rest   🕭 📶 🖑 🖼️ 🕸️ VISA ⓪ AE ①
37 av. de La Motte Picquet (7th) – Ⓜ Ecole Militaire – ✆ 01 45 51 55 83
– lewalt@inwoodhotel.com – Fax 01 47 05 77 59 – www.lewaltparis.com
25 rm – ♦275/325 € ♦♦295/345 €, ⊑ 19 €   **P2**
♦ Personalised ♦
The imposing reproductions of classical masterpieces and "panther" or "zebra" bedspreads add originality to the comfortable, contemporary rooms.

Muguet without rest   📶 🖑 🖼️ 🕸️ VISA ⓪ AE
11 r. Chevert (7th) – Ⓜ Ecole Militaire – ✆ 01 47 05 05 93 – muguet@
wanadoo.fr – Fax 01 45 50 25 37 – www.hotelmuguet.com   **P2**
43 rm – ♦106 € ♦♦140 €, ⊑ 10 €
♦ Business ♦ Family ♦ Functional ♦
Hotel spruced up in a classic spirit. Sitting room furnished in Louis Philippe style, well-appointed rooms (seven overlook the Eiffel Tower or the Invalides), veranda and small garden.

Eiffel Park Hôtel without rest   📶 🖑 🖼️ 🕸️ VISA ⓪ AE ①
17bis r. Amélie (7th) – Ⓜ La Tour Maubourg – ✆ 01 45 55 10 01 – reservation@
eiffelpark.com – Fax 01 47 05 28 68 – www.eiffelpark.com   **P1**
36 rm – ♦135/260 € ♦♦135/260 €, ⊑ 12 €
♦ Personalised ♦
From the Indian and Chinese artefacts to the ethnic fabrics, exoticism reigns throughout this elegant hotel. Even more unusual, it boasts a rooftop summer terrace complete with beehives.

Relais Bosquet without rest   📶 🖼️ 🕸️ VISA ⓪ AE ①
19 r. Champ-de-Mars (7th) – Ⓜ Ecole Militaire – ✆ 01 47 05 25 45 – hotel@
relaisbosquet.com – Fax 01 45 55 08 24 – www.hotelrelaisbosquet.com
40 rm – ♦135/185 € ♦♦155/210 €, ⊑ 15 €   **P2**
♦ Traditional ♦ Business ♦ Classical ♦
This discreet hotel has a prettily furnished Directoire style interior. The classic style rooms feature the same attention to detail with thoughtful little touches.

Londres Eiffel without rest   📶 🖼️ 🕸️ VISA ⓪ AE ①
1 r. Augereau (7th) – Ⓜ Ecole Militaire – ✆ 01 45 51 63 02 – info@
londres-eiffel.com – Fax 01 47 05 28 96 – www.londres-eiffel.com   **O2**
30 rm – ♦165 € ♦♦185 €, ⊑ 14 €
♦ Family ♦ Personalised ♦
Cosy hotel done up in warm colours near the leafy paths of the Champ-de-Mars. The second building, reached through a small courtyard, has quieter rooms.

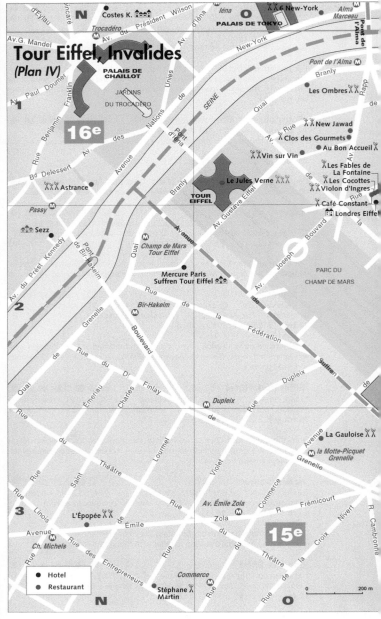

Tour Eiffel, Invalides
(Plan IV)

16e

15e

Costes K.

Av.G. Mandel

Av. du Président Wilson

Trocadéro

Iéna

PALAIS DE TOKYO

6 New-York

Alma Marceau

Pont de l'Alma

Av. d'Eylau

Raymond Poincaré

N

New-York

Pont de l'Alma

PALAIS DE CHAILLOT

JARDINS DU TROCADÉRO

Av. Paul Doumer

Rue Franklin

Rue Benjamin

Bd Delessert

Astrance

Passy

Sezz

Av. du Prést Kennedy

Pont de Bir-Hakeim

Quai

SEINE

Pont d'Iéna

Avenue des Nations Unies

Av. de New-York

Quai Branly

Branly

Les Ombres

Rue

New Jawad

Clos des Gourmets

Au Bon Accueil

Vin sur Vin

Le Jules Verne

TOUR EIFFEL

Av. Gustave Eiffel

Les Fables de La Fontaine

Les Cocottes

Violon d'Ingres

Café Constant

Londres Eiffel

Avenue

Champ de Mars Tour Eiffel

Mercure Paris Suffren Tour Eiffel

Quai

Bir-Hakeim

Rue de

Av. de la Bourdonnais

Av. Joseph Bouvard

PARC DU CHAMP DE MARS

Av. de la Fédération

Av. de Suffren

Boulevard de Grenelle

Rue du Dr Finlay

Charles

Rue Émeriau

Dupleix

Rue Dupleix

La Gauloise

la Motte-Picquet Grenelle

Quai

Théâtre

Rue Saint

Rue Lourmel

Rue Violet

Av. Émile Zola

Rue du Commerce

Frémicourt

L'Épopée

Rue Émile

Zola

R. Théâtre

Croix

Nivert

R. Cambronne

Avenue Ch. Michels

Rue Linois

Rue des Entrepreneurs

Commerce

Stéphane Martin

Rue du Commerce

Rue

Rue de la

Rue

N

O

0   200 m

● Hotel
● Restaurant

FRANCE PARIS

SEINE

Q

Pont de la Concorde

Pont Alexandre III

Quai

d'Orsay

Quai d'Orsay

Thiou

Fabert

Galliéni

AEROGARE DES INVALIDES

ASSEMBLÉE NATIONALE

Pétrossian

Mal Maubourg

Le Divellec

l'Université

Invalides

1

l'Université

L'Affriolé

Le Petit Bordelais

Il Vino d'Enrico Bernardo

Rue

ESPLANADE

R. de Constantine

Bourgogne et Montana

Chez l'Ami Jean

Av. Bosquet

Saint

Dominique

Tour

Rue

DES INVALIDES

Saint

Dominique

Bourgogne

Eiffel Park Hôtel

Chez les Anges

la Tour Maubourg

Auguste

P'tit Troquet

153 Grenelle

Grenelle

la Tour Maubourg

Rue

de

G

Rue

Du Cadran

Relais Bosquet

Rue

Bosquet

Picquet

De Varenne

Invalides

Varenne

Rue

ST-GERMAIN-DES-PRÉS / QUARTIER LATIN HÔTEL DE VILLE (Plan V)

Champ-de-Mars

LES INVALIDES

Vaneau

Arpège

Muguet

Rue

de

Varenne

Bourdonnais

Bd

Motte

Walt

École Militaire

Avenue

de

Tourville

Av.

des

7e

3

ÉCOLE MILITAIRE

la

Av.

D'Chez Eux

Lowendal

Duquesne

Ségur

Breteuil

Av.

de Villars

Boulevard

Rue

de

Babyl

de

Rue

d'Estrées

Duquesne

St-François Xavier

Vaneau

Avenue

Rue

Oudinot

Aida

Avenue

de

de

R. Eblé

des

Invalides

Vaneau

Cambronne

Rue

Sèvres

Boulevard

Ségur

Suffren

Garibaldi

Sèvres Lecourbe

Avenue

Saxe

Rue

de

Duroc

Bd du Montparnasse

Rue

Miollis

R. F.

Bonvin

Le Troquet

Lecourbe

Falguière

Vaugirard

P

MONTPARNASSE (Plan VI)

Du Cadran without rest   🏧 ⇆ 📺 ⁽ᵗ⁾ 𝚟𝚒𝚜𝚊 ⓿ 🄰🄴 ⓪

10 r. du Champ-de-Mars (7th) – Ⓜ Ecole Militaire – ✆ 01 40 62 67 00 – info@
cadranhotel.com – Fax 01 40 62 67 13 – www.hotelducadran.com
41 rm – ♦150/230 € ♦♦150/230 €, ⌑ 13 €   **P2**
♦ Traditional ♦ Business ♦ Modern ♦
This hotel near the lively Rue Cler market is in store for a total makeover. Contemporary style in all the rooms, 17C fireplace in the sitting room, and vaulted dining room.

De Varenne without rest ⌖   🏧 📺 ⁽ᵗ⁾ 𝚟𝚒𝚜𝚊 ⓿ 🄰🄴

44 r. Bourgogne (7th) – Ⓜ Varenne – ✆ 01 45 51 45 55 – info@
hoteldevarenne.com – Fax 01 45 51 86 63 – www.hoteldevarenne.com
25 rm – ♦125/177 € ♦♦135/197 €, ⌑ 10 €   **Q2**
♦ Family ♦
A quietly located hotel adorned with French Empire and Louis XVI style furniture.
In summer, breakfast is served in a small, leafy courtyard.

Champ-de-Mars without rest   📺 ⁽ᵗ⁾ 𝚟𝚒𝚜𝚊 ⓿

7 r. du Champ-de-Mars (7th) – Ⓜ Ecole Militaire – ✆ 01 45 51 52 30
– reservation@hotelduchampdemars.com – Fax 01 45 51 64 36
– www.hotelduchampdemars.com   **P2**
25 rm – ♦89 € ♦♦95 €, ⌑ 8 €
♦ Cosy ♦
Small hotel with an English atmosphere, between the Champ-de-Mars and the Invalides. Dark green façade, cosy rooms (soon to be renovated) and neat "Liberty" style decor.

Arpège (Alain Passard)   🏧 ⇿ 𝚟𝚒𝚜𝚊 ⓿ 🄰🄴 ⓪
❀❀❀ 84 r. de Varenne (7th) – Ⓜ Varenne – ✆ 01 45 51 47 33 – arpege.passard@
wanadoo.fr – Fax 01 44 18 98 39 – www.alain-passard.com
– Closed Saturday and Sunday   **Q2**
Rest – Menu 135 € (lunch)/360 € – Carte 190/285 €
Spec. Couleur, saveur, parfum et dessin du jardin, cueillette éphémère.
Volaille de pays "Grande Tradition". Tarte aux pommes bouquet de rose.
♦ Innovative ♦ Formal ♦
Choose the elegant modern dining room, with rare wood and glass decorations by Lalique, rather than the basement. Savour dazzling vegetable garden-based cuisine by a master chef and poet of the land.

Le Jules Verne   ⩽ 🏧 ⌔ 𝚟𝚒𝚜𝚊 ⓿ 🄰🄴 ⓪
❀ 2nd floor Eiffel Tower, private lift, South pillar (7th) – Ⓜ Bir-Hakeim
– ✆ 01 45 55 61 44 – Fax 01 47 05 29 41 – www.lejulesverne-paris.com
Rest – Menu 85 € (weekdays lunch), 165/200 €   **O1**
– Carte 190/242 €
Spec. Pressé de volaille et foie gras. Pavé de turbot aux girolles. Ecrou au chocolat et praliné croustillant.
♦ A la mode ♦
Although the views of Paris remain the same, the décor in this famous restaurant in the Eiffel Tower has been modernised. For a truly memorable experience, book a window table.

Astrance (Pascal Barbot)   🏧 ⇆ 𝚟𝚒𝚜𝚊 ⓿ 🄰🄴 ⓪
❀❀❀ 4 r. Beethoven (16th) ✉ 75016 – Ⓜ Passy – ✆ 01 40 50 84 40
– Closed 1-3 March, 1-5 May, 30 May-3 June, 11-15 July, August, 1-8 November, Christmas holidays, Saturday, Sunday and Monday   **N1**
Rest – (number of covers limited, pre-book) Menu 70 € (lunch), 120/290 € bi ⌖
Spec. Agrumes, herbes sauvages, fleurs et coquillages. Langoustines, girolles, concombre et pistache. Chocolat blanc et framboise.
♦ Innovative ♦ Minimalist ♦
In an intimate decor, sample the inventive cuisine of a chef at the height of his art in the 'surprise menu'. Equally outstanding wine and service. An unforgettable culinary experience.

FRANCE - PARIS

Le Divellec (Jacques Le Divellec)

107 r. Université (7th) – **Ⓜ** Invalides – ℰ 01 45 51 91 96 – ledivellec@noos.fr
– Fax 01 45 51 31 75
– Closed 25 July-25 August, 25 December-2 January and Sunday
Rest – Menu 55 € – Carte 110/205 €   **P-Q1**
Spec. Emincé de langoustines aux truffes. Gros turbot de ligne rôti. Harmonie des compotes.
◆ Seafood ◆ Formal ◆
This restaurant, devoted to outstanding seafood, is just a stone's throw from Les Invalides and offers customers a feeling of the ocean in the centre of Paris. The prosperous clientele relish this establishment in the administration district. The décor is a bit out-dated.

Pétrossian

144 r. de l'Université (7th) – **Ⓜ** Invalides – ℰ 01 44 11 32 32 – Fax 01 44 11 32 35
– Closed August, Sunday and Monday   **P1**
Rest – Menu 35 € (lunch)/90 € – Carte 65/110 €
◆ Seafood ◆ Formal ◆
The Petrossians have treated Parisians to caviar from the Caspian sea since 1920. Above the boutique, inventive cuisine is served in a comfortable, elegant dining room.

Le Violon d'Ingres (Christian Constant et Stéphane Schmidt)

135 r. St-Dominique (7th) – **Ⓜ** Ecole Militaire
– ℰ 01 45 55 15 05 – violondingres@wanadoo.fr – Fax 01 45 55 48 42
– www.leviolondingres.com
– Closed in August, Sunday and Monday
Rest – Menu 49 € (weekdays)/65 € – Carte 49/60 €   **O1**
Spec. Foie gras d'oie brioché, gelée au pinot noir. Suprême de bar croustillant aux amandes, ravigote aux câpres de Sicile. Feuillantine au chocolat guanaja
◆ Classic ◆ Fashionable ◆
This elegant dining room in the style of a contemporary bistro is a meeting point for gourmets, attracted by quality cuisine that enhances the produce and seasons without braking with tradition.

Il Vino d'Enrico Bernardo

13 bd La Tour-Maubourg (7th) – **Ⓜ** Invalides – ℰ 01 44 11 72 00 – info@ilvinobyenricobernardo.com – Fax 01 44 11 72 01
– www.ilvinobyenricobernardo.com   **P1**
Rest – Menu 50 € bi (lunch), 95 € bi/1000 € bi – Carte 90/140 €
Spec. Calamars poêlés, caviar d'aubergine et poivrons confits (summer). Duo d'agneau, ballotines et côtelettes rôties, purée de petits pois et légumes croquants (autumn). Melon et abricots en salade, coulis de fruits exotiques, glace au fromage blanc et miel (summer).
◆ A la mode ◆ Elegant ◆
Choose the wine and let the meal take care of itself! In his chic designer restaurant, the Best Sommelier 2004 reverses the trend by linking the food to the wine.

Les Ombres

27 quai Branly (7th) – **Ⓜ** Alma Marceau – ℰ 01 47 53 68 00
– ombres.restaurant@elior.com – Fax 01 47 53 68 18 – www.lesombres.fr
Rest – Menu 38 € (lunch)/95 € – Carte 38/95 €   **O1**
◆ A la mode ◆ Trendy ◆
This restaurant enjoys fine views of the Eiffel Tower and its nocturnal illuminations from the roof-terrace of the Musée du Quai Branly. Contemporary dining.

Vin sur Vin

20 r. de Monttessuy (7th) – **Ⓜ** Pont de l'Alma – ℰ 01 47 05 14 20
– Closed 1-11 May, August, 24 December-6 January, Monday except dinner from September to March, Saturday lunch and Sunday   **O1**
Rest – (number of covers limited, pre-book) Carte 88/138 €
Spec. Galette de pied de cochon. Ris de veau de lait français. Soufflé chaud.
◆ Classic ◆ Cosy ◆
Warm welcome, elegant decor, delicious traditional dishes and extensive wine list (600 vintages) – full marks for this restaurant close to the Eiffel Tower!

153 Grenelle

153 r. de Grenelle (7th) – **Ⓜ** La Tour Maubourg – ℰ 01 45 51 54 12
– jjjouteux@gmail.com **P1-2**
Rest – Menu 35 € (weekdays)/59 € – Carte approx. 60 €
♦ Traditional ♦ Cosy ♦

Taken over by a new chef, this restaurant has been treated to a soothing, elegant, classical interior (grey colour scheme, fresh flowers, artwork). Traditional fare.

Chez les Anges

54 bd de la Tour Maubourg (7th) – **Ⓜ** La Tour Maubourg – ℰ 01 47 05 89 86
– mail@chezlesanges.com – Fax 01 47 05 45 56 – www.chezlesanges.com
– Closed Saturday and Sunday **P1**
Rest – Menu 34/40 € – Carte 44/73 € ⅋⅋
♦ Traditional ♦

A trendy atmosphere, minimalist contemporary decor and long counter where you can take a seat to sample the tasty cuisine, half-traditional, half-modern.

New Jawad

12 av. Rapp (7th) – **Ⓜ** Ecole Militaire – ℰ 01 47 05 91 37 – Fax 01 45 50 31 27
Rest – Menu 16/42 € – Carte 21/42 € **O1**
♦ Indian-Pakistani ♦ Friendly ♦

Pakistani and Indian specialities, attentive service and a plush, cosy setting characterise this restaurant in the vicinity of the Pont de l'Alma.

Thiou

49 quai d'Orsay (7th) – **Ⓜ** Invalides – ℰ 01 40 62 96 50 – Fax 01 40 62 97 30
– closed August, Saturday lunch and Sunday **P1**
Rest – Carte 45/90 €
♦ Thai ♦

Thiou is the nickname of the lady chef of this restaurant, often mentioned in the press, whose regular customers include celebrities. Thai dishes served in a discreetly exotic, comfortable dining room.

Auguste (Gaël Orieux)

54 r. Bourgogne (7th) – **Ⓜ** Varenne – ℰ 01 45 51 61 09 – orieux.gael@
wanadoo.fr – Fax 01 45 51 27 34 – www.restaurantauguste.fr
– Closed 3-24 August, Saturday and Sunday **Q1**
Rest – Menu 35 € (lunch) – Carte 62/94 €
Spec. Huitres creuses en gelée à la diable. Rouget de roche au confit de poivrons doux. Soufflé au chocolat pur Caraïbe
♦ A la mode ♦ Design ♦

The pleasant colourful decor of this up-to-date establishment is the setting for a cuisine that is as flavourful as it is inventive. A fine tribute to Auguste Escoffier.

Le Petit Bordelais

22 r. Surcouf (7th) – **Ⓜ** Invalides – ℰ 01 45 51 46 93 – contact@
le-petit-bordelais.fr – Fax 01 45 50 30 11 – www.lepetit-bordelais.com
– Closed 26 July-18 August, Sunday and Monday **P1**
Rest – Menu 19 € (lunch), 33/45 € – Carte 48/66 €
♦ A la mode ♦ Fashionable ♦

New address offering a good choice of wines by the glass, particulary Bordeaux. Intimite decor in red and moka tones, velvet banquettes.

D'Chez Eux

2 av. Lowendal (7th) – **Ⓜ** Ecole Militaire – ℰ 01 47 05 52 55 – contact@
chezeux.com – Fax 01 45 55 60 74 – www.chezeux.com
– closed 1st-18 August and Sunday **P2**
Rest – Menu 42 € (lunch) – Carte 55/75 €
♦ De Terroir ♦ Rustic ♦

For 40 years customers have been seduced by this restaurant where hearty dishes from Auvergne and southwest France are served by waiters in smocks in a "provincial inn" atmosphere.

FRANCE - PARIS

XX **La Gauloise** 🏠 ⇔ VISA ◎ AE
59 av. La Motte-Picquet (15th) – ⓜ *La Motte Picquet Grenelle*
– ℰ 01 47 34 11 64 – Fax 01 40 61 09 70   **O3**
Rest – Carte 33/45 €
♦ Traditional ♦ Neighbourhood ♦
This 1900 brasserie must have seen many celebrities pass through, judging from
the signed photos on the walls. A pleasant, kerbside terrace.

XX **L'Épopée** AK VISA ◎ AE
89 av. Émile-Zola (15th) – ⓜ *Charles Michels* – ℰ *01 45 77 71 37* – *lepopee@*
hotmail.fr – *Fax 01 45 77 71 37* – *www.lepopee.fr*
– Closed 9-17 August, 24 December-5 January and Sunday   **N3**
Rest – Menu 35 €
♦ Traditional ♦ Family ♦
Despite the grandeur of its name (The Epic), this is a small, convivial restaurant.
Regulars keep coming back for its excellent wine list and traditional cuisine.

X **Au Bon Accueil** AK VISA ◎ AE
☺ *14 r. Monttessuy (7th)* – ⓜ *Pont de l'Alma* – ℰ *01 47 05 46 11*
– mail@chezlesanges.com – *Fax 01 45 56 15 80*
– www.aubonaccueilparis.com
– Closed 7-20 August, Saturday and Sunday   **O1**
Rest – Menu 27/31 € – Carte 54/75 €
♦ A la mode ♦
Beneath the shadow of the Eiffel Tower, this modern restaurant and small adjacent room offer delicious up-to-date dishes pleasantly reflecting the changing
seasons.

X **Les Fables de La Fontaine** (Sébastien Gravé) 🏠 AK VISA ◎ AE
🌸 *131 r. Saint-Dominique (7th)* – ⓜ *Ecole Militaire* – ℰ *01 44 18 37 55*
– violondingres@wanadoo.fr – *Fax 01 44 18 37 57*
– www.lesrestaurantsdeconstant.com   **O1**
Rest – Menu 80 € – Carte 56/78 €
Spec. Fine tarte de rouget façon pissaladière. Saint-Jacques à la plancha à
l'écrasé de topinambour et châtaigne. Gâteau basque.
♦ Seafood ♦ Fashionable ♦
Bistro dedicated to seafood set in a small dining room (brown tones, bench seats,
tiles and blackboards) and on a summer terrace. Short, well thought-out menu and
good wines available by the glass.

X **Stéphane Martin** AK VISA ◎
☺ *67 r. des Entrepreneurs (15th)* – ⓜ *Charles Michels* – ℰ *01 45 79 03 31*
– resto.stephanemartin@free.fr – *Fax 01 45 79 44 69*
– www.stephanemartin.com
– Closed 19-27 April, 1-24 August, 20 December-4 January, Sunday and
Monday   **N3**
Rest – Menu 22 € (weekday lunch)/35 € – Carte 50/64 €
♦ A la mode ♦
This inviting restaurant with a library theme (mural of bookshelves), serves up-to-
date market fresh cuisine.

X **Le Clos des Gourmets** VISA ◎
☺ *16 av. Rapp (7th)* – ⓜ *Alma Marceau* – ℰ *01 45 51 75 61*
– closdesgourmets@wanadoo.fr – *Fax 01 47 05 74 20*
– www.closdesgourmets.com
– Closed 1-25 August, Sunday and Monday   **O1**
Rest – Menu 29 € (lunch)/35 €
♦ A la mode ♦
Many regulars love this discreet restaurant decorated in warm colours. The tempting menu varies according to the availability of market produce.

Aida (Koji Aida) ⚔ ⚙ 🔄 *VISA* ◑◎ *AE*
1 r. Pierre Leroux (7th) – Ⓜ *Vaneau –* ℰ *01 43 06 14 18 – Fax 01 43 06 14 18*
– www.aidaparis.com
– Closed 3 weeks in August, February holiday and Monday **Q3**
Rest *– (dinner only) (number of covers limited, pre-book)* Menu 140/160 € ⚜
Spec. Foie gras chaud et radis blanc cuits vapeur et miso de Kyoto. Chateaubriand cuit au teppanyaki. Wagashi.
◆ Japanese ◆ Minimalist ◆
A Zen feel to this discreet Japanese restaurant with a bar counter and private dining room. Japanese cuisine and teppanyaki menus, and a rich list of Burgundy wines chosen by the passionate chef.

P'tit Troquet *VISA* ◑◎
28 r. de l'Exposition (7th) – Ⓜ *Ecole Militaire –* ℰ *01 47 05 80 39*
– Fax 01 47 05 80 39
– Closed August, Saturday lunch, Monday lunch and Sunday **P2**
Rest *– (number of covers limited, pre-book)* Menu 32 € – Carte approx. 42 €
◆ Traditional ◆ Retro ◆
This bistro is certainly as small as its name suggests! But it has so much going for it: a nostalgic charm (old advertisements, soda siphons and period bar counter), friendly atmosphere and tasty market fresh cuisine.

L'Affriolé ⚔ *VISA* ◑◎
17 r. Malar (7th) – Ⓜ *Invalides –* ℰ *01 44 18 31 33*
– closed 3 weeks in August, Sunday and Monday **P1**
Rest – Menu 19 € bi (lunch), 23/34 €
◆ A la mode ◆ Bistro ◆
This bistro's chef prepares seasonal dishes with fresh market produce, which are announced as daily specials on the blackboard or in a set menu that changes every month.

Chez l'Ami Jean ⚔ *VISA* ◑◎
27 r. Malar (7th) – Ⓜ *La Tour Maubourg –* ℰ *01 47 05 86 89 – Fax 01 45 55 41 82*
– Closed August, 23 December-2 January, Sunday and Monday **P1**
Rest – Menu 34 €
◆ De Terroir ◆ Rustic ◆
Chez l'Ami Jean offers tasty, copious dishes, with market produce, and from Southwest France (game specialities in season) in a warm, Basque Country setting.

Le Troquet *VISA* ◑◎
21 r. François Bonvin (15th) – Ⓜ *Cambronne –* ℰ *01 45 66 89 00*
– Fax 01 45 66 89 83
– Closed 1 week in May, 1-24 August, 24 December-1 January, Sunday and Monday
Rest – Menu 30 € (lunch), 32/42 € **P3**
◆ De Terroir ◆ Neighbourhood ◆
An authentic Parisian bar: single set menu shown on a slate, retro-style dining room and tasty market based cuisine. For locals... and others!

Café Constant *VISA* ◑◎
139 r. Saint-Dominique (7th) – Ⓜ *Ecole Militaire –* ℰ *01 47 53 73 34*
– violondingres@wanadoo.fr – Fax 01 45 55 48 42
– www.lesrestaurantsdeconstant.com
– Closed Sunday and Monday **O1**
Rest – Carte 30/40 €
◆ Traditional ◆ Bistro ◆
This annexe designed by Christian Constant and housed in an old café displays convivial simplicity. You can enjoy good value gourmet bistro cuisine.

Les Cocottes *VISA* ◑◎
135 r. St Dominique (7th) – Ⓜ *Ecole Militaire – violondingres@wanadoo.fr*
– www.lesrestaurantsdeconstant.com – Closed Sunday **O1**
Rest – Carte 24/45 €
◆ A la mode ◆ Fashionable ◆
The concept of this friendly establishment, more bar (high counter) than restaurant, lies in its reinvented bistro cuisine, served in cast-iron casserole dishes. No booking.

Lutetia Ⅰ₆ AC ⅍ rm 🖳 🎤 ⅏ VISA ⓒⓞ AE ①

45 bd Raspail (6th) – Ⓜ Sèvres Babylone – 𝒞 01 49 54 46 46
– lutetia-paris@lutetia-paris.com – Fax 01 49 54 46 00
– www.lutetia-paris.com **R2**
231 rm – ♦450/600 € ♦♦460/610 €, ☲ 28 € – 11 suites
Rest *Paris* – see below
Rest *Brasserie Lutetia* – 𝒞 01 49 54 46 76 – Menu 43 € – Carte 60/73 €
◆ Luxury ◆ Art Deco ◆

Built in 1910, this luxury hotel on the Left Bank has lost none of its sparkle. It happily blends Art Deco fixtures with contemporary details (sculptures by César, Arman, etc). Refurbished rooms. Popular with well-heeled Parisians, the Brasserie Lutetia is renowned for its seafood.

Victoria Palace *without rest* Ⅵ AC ⅍ 🖳 🎤 ⅏ 🚗 VISA ⓒⓞ AE ①

6 r. Blaise-Desgoffe (6th) – Ⓜ St-Placide – 𝒞 01 45 49 70 00
– info@victoriapalace.com – Fax 01 45 49 23 75
– www.victoriapalace.com **R3**
62 rm – ♦273/620 € ♦♦273/620 €, ☲ 18 €
◆ Traditional ◆ Stylish ◆

Small luxury hotel with undeniable charm: toiles de Jouy, Louis XVI-style furniture and marble bathrooms in the rooms. Paintings, red velvet and porcelain in the lounges.

Pont Royal Ⅰ₆ ⅓ AC ⅍ 🖳 📞 ⅏ VISA ⓒⓞ AE ①

7 r. Montalembert (7th) – Ⓜ Rue du Bac – 𝒞 01 42 84 70 00 – hpr@
hotel-pont-royal.com – Fax 01 42 84 71 00 – www.hotel-pont-royal.com
65 rm – ♦410 € ♦♦550 €, ☲ 27 € – 10 suites **R1**
Rest *L'Atelier de Joël Robuchon* – see below
◆ Luxury ◆ Stylish ◆

Bold colours and mahogany walls adorn the bedrooms; the romance of the salad days of St-Germain-des-Prés with all the comfort of an elegant "literary hotel"!

Duc de St-Simon *without rest* ⅌ 🖳 🎤 VISA ⓒⓞ AE ①

14 r. St-Simon (7th) – Ⓜ Rue du Bac – 𝒞 01 44 39 20 20
– duc.de.saint.simon@wanadoo.fr – Fax 01 45 48 68 25
– www.hotelducdesaintsimon.com **R1**
34 rm – ♦225/290 € ♦♦250/290 €, ☲ 15 €
◆ Luxury ◆ Business ◆ Stylish ◆

Cheerful colours, wood panelling, antique furniture and objects. The atmosphere here is that of a beautiful house of olden times, with the additional appeal of a friendly welcome and peaceful surroundings.

D'Aubusson *without rest* ⅓ AC ⅍ 🖳 🎤 ⅏ 🅿 🚗 VISA ⓒⓞ AE ①

33 r. Dauphine (6th) – Ⓜ Odéon – 𝒞 01 43 29 43 43 – reservations@
hoteldaubusson.com – Fax 01 43 29 12 62 – www.hoteldaubusson.com
49 rm – ♦275/305 € ♦♦275/305 €, ☲ 25 € **T2**
◆ Luxury ◆ Cosy ◆

A 17C townhouse with character, offering elegant, renovated rooms with Versailles parquet and Aubusson tapestries. There are jazz evenings at the Café Laurent at the weekend.

Relais Christine *without rest* ⅌ Ⅰ₆ AC 🖳 🎤 ⅏ 🚗 VISA ⓒⓞ AE ①

3 r. Christine (6th) – Ⓜ St-Michel – 𝒞 01 40 51 60 80 – contact@
relais-christine.com – Fax 01 40 51 60 81 – www.relais-christine.com
51 rm – ♦380/780 € ♦♦380/780 €, ☲ 30 € **T2**
◆ Traditional ◆ Historic ◆ Personalised ◆

Breakfast is served in a 13C vaulted room of this mansion, built on a medieval site. Handsome cobbled courtyard, fitness facilities, and rooms with a personal touch.

1er

7e

2

6e

3

Quai

Passerelle Léopold Sédar Senghor

Quai Anatole France

SEINE

des Tuileries

Paris Royal
Musée du Louvre

Rue

MUSÉE
DU LOUVRE

Assemblée
Nationale

D'Orsay

MUSÉE
D'ORSAY

Rue de France

Quai Voltaire

Quai

Pont du Carrousel

François Mitterrand

Boulevard Saint

Le Bellechasse

Rue de Bac

Pont Royal

Rue de Solférino

Bersoly's

Lille

Q. Malaquais

Quai

Pont des Arts

35° Ouest

Verneuil

Verneuil

Pont
Royal

l'Université

Lenox
St-Germain

Rue Bonaparte

Rue Mazarine

Gaya Rive Gauche
par Pierre Gagnaire

Montalembert

L'Atelier de
Joël Robuchon

Saint
Vincent

L'Hôtel

Le Restaurant

Rue du Bac

Duc de Saint-Simon

K+K Hôtel Cayré

Germain

Bel Ami
St-Germain-des-Prés

Millésime Hôtel

Alcazar

St-Germain

Boulevard de Grenelle

St-Germain-des-Prés
Au Manoir
St-Germain-des-Prés

ST-GERMAIN
DES PRÉS

Jacob

Buci

Rue de Buci

Rue de

Varenne

Pas de Calais

Madison

Mabillon

Artus

Saint

Left Bank
St-Germain

Germain

Rue de Babylone

Cigale Récamier

St-Sulpice

Rennes

Rue de Colombier

Bonaparte

Esprit
Saint-Germain

Saint

Sulpice

Relais
St-Germain

Rue de l'Odéon

Rue de Sèvres

Sèvres Babylone

Paris

Raspail

Lutétia

Rue du Cherche

Rue du Midi

ST-SULPICE

Relais
St-Sulpice

Odéon Hôtel

L'Épi Dupin

Hélène Darroze-
La Salle à Manger

Rue d'Assas

L'Abbaye

Relais Médicis

Rue de

PALAIS DU
LUXEMBOURG

Boulevard Raspail

Rue de Rennes

St-Placide

Vaugirard

La Maison du Jardin

Guynemer

JARDIN

DU LUXEMBOURG

Rue d'Assas

St-Grégoire

Victoria
Palace

Rue de Rennes

Littré

Rue du Départ

Pl.
du 18 Juin
1940

Rue du Montparnasse

Notre-Dame
des Champs

Ste-Beuve

Notre-Dame

Rue

Auguste Comte

R. Saint

Boulevard

Montparnasse
Bienvenüe

TOUR

Montparnasse

Sensing

Des Académies
et des Arts

Villa des

Rue des

Raspail

d'Assas

Cerisaie

La Coupole

212

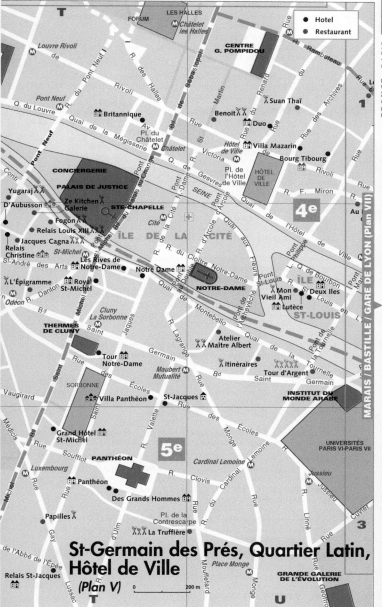

Hotel
Restaurant

LES HALLES
FORUM
Châtelet
les Halles

CENTRE
G. POMPIDOU

Louvre Rivoli

Rue de Rambuteau

Rue du Renard

Rue des Archives

Pont Neuf

Q. du Louvre

Britannique

Benoit

Suan Thaï

Duo

Hôtel
de Ville

Villa Mazarin

Bourg Tibourg

CONCIERGERIE

PALAIS DE JUSTICE

Yugaraj

D'Aubusson

Ze Kitchen
Galerie

STE-CHAPELLE

Fogon

Relais Louis XIII

Jacques Cagna

Relais
Christine

St-Michel

Les Rives de
Notre-Dame

Notre Dame

L'Épigramme

Royal
St-Michel

Cluny
La Sorbonne

THERMES
DE CLUNY

Tour
Notre-Dame

Maubert
Mutualité

Atelier
Maître Albert

Itinéraires

Tour d'Argent

SORBONNE

Villa Panthéon

St-Jacques

Grand Hôtel
St-Michel

PANTHÉON

Luxembourg

Panthéon

Des Grands Hommes

Papilles

Pl. de la
Contrescarpe

La Truffière

Relais St-Jacques

St-Germain des Prés, Quartier Latin, Hôtel de Ville
(Plan V)

0   200 m

213

Relais St-Germain   🔲 ↳ rm 🔲 🕽 *VISA* 🔲 AE ⑪

9 carrefour de l'Odéon (6th) – **Ⓜ** *Odéon* – ℰ *01 44 27 07 97 – hotelrsg@*
wanadoo.fr – Fax 01 46 33 45 30 – www.hotelrsg.com   **S2**
22 rm ⊑ – ♦180/220 € ♦♦230/285 €
Rest *Le Comptoir* – *(number of covers limited, pre-book)* Menu 50 € (weekdays dinner) A la carte 35/80 € (lunch)
  ♦ Luxury ♦ Traditional ♦ Historic ♦
Elegant hotel comprising three 17C buildings. Polished beams, shimmering fabrics
and antique furniture. Elegant hotel comprising three 17C buildings. Polished
beams, shimmering fabrics and antique furniture.

Bel Ami St-Germain des Prés *without rest*   🔲 ⑪ 🔲 AE ⑪

7 r. St-Benoit (6th) – **Ⓜ** *St-Germain des Prés*   ⑪ 🔲 *VISA* 🔲 AE ⑪
– ℰ 01 42 61 53 53 – contact@hotel-bel-ami.com – Fax 01 49 27 09 33
– www.hotel-bel-ami.com   **S2**
112 rm – ♦245/620 € ♦♦245/620 €, ⊑ 25 €
  ♦ Traditional ♦ Minimalist ♦
This attractive building may well be 19C in origin but the era of Maupassant is long
gone! Resolutely modern interior where minimalist luxury rubs shoulders with hi-
tech gadgets and a relaxed ambience.

Buci *without rest*   ♿ 🔲 🔲 ⑪ 🔲 *VISA* 🔲 AE ⑪

22 r. Buci (6th) – **Ⓜ** *Mabillon* – ℰ *01 55 42 74 74 – reservations@buci-hotel.com*
– Fax 01 55 42 74 44 – www.buci-hotel.com   **S2**
24 rm – ♦190/220 € ♦♦220/335 €, ⊑ 18 € – 5 suites
  ♦ Traditional ♦ Personalised ♦
An elegant midnight blue façade gives an idea of the tone of this boutique hotel.
The stylish guestrooms have canopies on the beds and English period furniture,
while others sport a more contemporary look.

L'Abbaye *without rest* ⌂   🔲 🔲 ⑪ *VISA* 🔲 AE

10 r. Cassette (6th) – **Ⓜ** *St-Sulpice* – ℰ *01 45 44 38 11 – hotel.abbaye@*
wanadoo.fr – Fax 01 45 48 07 86 – www.hotel-abbaye.com   **S2**
40 rm ⊑ – ♦232/261 € ♦♦427/472 € – 4 suites
  ♦ Luxury ♦ Traditional ♦ Stylish ♦
Hotel in a former 18C convent combining old-world charm with modern comfort.
Pleasant veranda, duplex apartment with a terrace, and stylish rooms. Some overlook a delightful patio.

Littré *without rest*   🔲 ↳ 🔲 ⑪ 🔲 🚗 *VISA* 🔲 AE

9 r. Littré (6th) – **Ⓜ** *Montparnasse Bienvenüe* – ℰ *01 53 63 07 07 – hotellittre@*
hotellittreparis.com – Fax 01 45 44 88 13 – www.hotellittreparis.com
88 rm – ♦315 € ♦♦315/550 €, ⊑ 20 € – 2 suites   **R3**
  ♦ Traditional ♦ Personalised ♦
Classic building, halfway between Saint Germain des Prés and Montparnasse. The
stylish rooms are all very comfortable. Magnificent view from the top floor.

L'Hôtel   🔲 🔲 ↳ 🔲 ⑪ *VISA* 🔲 AE ⑪

13 r. des Beaux-Arts (6th) – **Ⓜ** *St-Germain-des-Prés* – ℰ *01 44 41 99 00 – stay@*
l-hotel.com – Fax 01 43 25 64 81 – www.l-hotel.com   **S1**
20 rm – ♦280/370 € ♦♦345/740 €, ⊑ 18 € – 4 suites
Rest Le Restaurant – see below
  ♦ Luxury ♦ Historic ♦ Personalised ♦
This hotel is where Oscar Wilde passed away, leaving an unpaid bill behind him. It
sports a vertiginous well of light and an extravagant decor by Garcia (Baroque,
French Empire and Oriental).

Esprit Saint-Germain *without rest*   🔲 ♿ 🔲 ↳ 🔲 🕽

22 r. Saint-Sulpice (6th) – **Ⓜ** *Mabillon*   *VISA* 🔲 AE ⑪
– ℰ 01 53 10 55 55 – contact@espritsaintgermain.com – Fax 01 53 10 55 56
– www.espritsaintgermain.com   **S2**
28 rm – ♦320/790 € ♦♦320/790 €, ⊑ 26 €
  ♦ Luxury ♦ Design ♦
Elegant and contemporary rooms pleasantly combining red, chocolate and beige
colours with modern paintings and furniture; bathrooms with slate walls.

Montalembert 🛜 AC ⇌ rm ⁽¹⁾ 🏊 🛋 VISA ⚫ AE ⓪

*3 r. Montalembert (7th) – Ⓜ Rue du Bac – ℰ 01 45 49 68 68 – welcome@
montalembert.com – Fax 01 45 49 69 49 – www.montalembert.com*
56 rm – †340/520 € ††340/520 €, ⌑ 24 € – 7 suites   **R1**
Rest – Carte 56/87 €

◆ Luxury ◆ Modern ◆

Dark wood, leather, glass and steel, with tobacco, plum and lilac-coloured decor.
The rooms combine all the components of contemporary style. Designer dining
room, terrace protected by a boxwood partition, and cuisine for appetites large
and small!

Pas de Calais without rest AC 📺 ⓦ VISA ⚫ AE ⓪

*59 r. des Saints-Pères (6th) – Ⓜ St-Germain-des-Prés – ℰ 01 45 48 78 74
– infos@hotelpasdecalais.com – Fax 01 45 44 94 57
– www.hotelpasdecalais.com*   **R2**
38 rm – †145/160 € ††155/180 €, ⌑ 15 €

◆ Traditional ◆ Family ◆ Functional ◆

The hotel lobby is lit by a glass ceiling and has a beautiful vertical garden made up
of orchids. Lovely rooms with individual touches; exposed beams on the top floor.

K+K Hotel Cayré without rest 🛏 ⅙ AC ⇌ 📺 ⓦ VISA ⚫ AE ⓪

*4 bd Raspail (7th) – Ⓜ Rue du Bac – ℰ 01 45 44 38 88 – reservations@
kkhotels.fr – Fax 01 45 44 98 13 – www.kkhotels.com/cayre*   **R1-2**
125 rm – †248/406 € ††280/448 €, ⌑ 26 €

◆ Luxury ◆ Business ◆ Modern ◆

The discreet Haussmann façade contrasts with the elegant designer rooms within.
Fitness centre (with sauna), elegant lounge and bar serving simple bistro-style
dishes.

Madison without rest ≤ AC 📺 ⁽¹⁾ VISA ⚫ AE ⓪

*143 bd St-Germain (6th) – Ⓜ St-Germain des Prés – ℰ 01 40 51 60 00 – resa@
hotel-madison.com – Fax 01 40 51 60 01 – www.hotel-madison.com*
52 rm ⌑ – †175/195 € ††235/255 €   **S2**

◆ Traditional ◆ Personalised ◆

Camus loved to stay at this hotel with its elegant rooms. Choose one on the top
floors, refurbished in a chic, cosy, modern style. Some rooms have views of the
church.

Villa Panthéon without rest ⅙ AC ⇌ 📺 ⁽¹⁾ VISA ⚫ AE ⓪

*41 r. des Écoles (5th) – Ⓜ Maubert Mutualité – ℰ 01 53 10 95 95 – pantheon@
leshotelsdeparis.com – Fax 01 53 10 95 96 – www.leshotelsdeparis.com*
59 rm – †160/380 € ††195/450 €, ⌑ €   **T2**

◆ Traditional ◆ Stylish ◆

The reception, guestrooms and bar (fine selection of whiskies) have a British feel
created by parquet floors, colourful hangings, exotic wooden furniture and Liberty
style light fixtures.

Left Bank St-Germain without rest ⅙ AC ⇌ 📺 ⁽¹⁾ VISA ⚫ AE ⓪

*9 r. de l'Ancienne Comédie (6th) – Ⓜ Odéon – ℰ 01 43 54 01 70 – reservation@
hotelleftbank.com – Fax 01 43 26 17 14 – www.paris-hotels-charm.com*
31 rm ⌑ – †160/260 € ††170/280 €   **S2**

◆ Traditional ◆ Family ◆ Classical ◆

Wainscoting, damask, Jouy drapes, Louis XIII style furniture and half-timbered walls
set the scene. Some rooms command views of Notre Dame.

Millésime without rest ⤷ AC 📺 ⁽¹⁾ VISA ⚫ AE ⓪

*15 r. Jacob (6th) – Ⓜ St-Germain des Prés – ℰ 01 44 07 97 97 – reservation@
millesimehotel.com – Fax 01 46 34 55 97 – www.millesimehotel.com*
21 rm – †190 € ††220 €, ⌑ 16 €   **S2**

◆ Traditional ◆ Family ◆ Cosy ◆

Colours of the south and select furniture and fabrics create a warm atmosphere in
the splendid rooms at this hotel. Superb 17C staircase, patio and fine vaulted
dining room.

FRANCE - PARIS

Bourg Tibourg without rest   AC ⁽ᵗ⁾ VISA ◍ AE ◑

19 r. Bourg Tibourg (4th) – Ⓜ Hôtel de Ville – ✆ 01 42 78 47 39 – hotel@
bourgtibourg.com – Fax 01 40 29 07 00 – www.hotelbourgtibourg.com
30 rm – ♦180 € ♦♦230/360 €, � 16 €   **U1**
♦ Luxury ♦ Personalised ♦
The lovely personalised guestrooms in this boutique hotel are decorated in a
variety of styles (neo-Gothic, Baroque or Oriental). A little gem in the heart of the
Marais quarter.

Saint Vincent without rest   & AC ⇪ ⁽ᵗ⁾ VISA ◍ AE ◑

5 r. Pré aux Clercs (7th) – Ⓜ Rue du Bac – ✆ 01 42 61 01 51 – reservation@
hotel-st-vincent.com – Fax 01 42 61 01 54 – www.hotel-st-vincent.com
22 rm – ♦210/240 € ♦♦210/240 €, ⊆ 13 € – 2 suites   **R-S1**
♦ Luxury ♦ Personalised ♦
A delightful luxury hotel in the heart of the Left Bank. This 18C private mansion is
home to warm, spacious rooms appointed in a Napoleon III spirit.

Le Bellechasse without rest   AC ⇪ ⁽ᵗ⁾ VISA ◍ AE ◑

8 r. de Bellechasse (7th) – Ⓜ Musée d'Orsay – ✆ 01 45 50 22 31 – info@
lebellechasse.com – Fax 01 45 51 52 36 – www.lebellechasse.com   **R1**
34 rm – ♦290/390 € ♦♦340/390 €, ⊆ 21 €
♦ Luxury ♦ Personalised ♦
Top couturier Christian Lacroix designed the rooms of this hotel. He has joyfully
mixed colour with antique and modern details to create an almost dreamlike but
distinctly fashionable setting.

Les Rives de Notre-Dame without rest   ≤ AC 🖻 ⁽ᵗ⁾

15 quai St-Michel (5th) – Ⓜ St-Michel   VISA ◍ AE ◑
– ✆ 01 43 54 81 16 – hotel@rivesdenotredame.com – Fax 01 43 26 27 09
– www.rivesdenotredame.com   **T2**
10 rm – ♦170/550 € ♦♦170/550 €, ⊆ 14 €
♦ Traditional ♦ Family ♦ Classical ♦
Splendidly preserved 16C edifice whose spacious Provençal-style rooms all overlook the Seine and Notre Dame. Top floor penthouse.

Royal St-Michel without rest   AC ⇪ 🖻 ℰ ⁽ᵗ⁾ VISA ◍ AE ◑

3 bd St-Michel (5th) – Ⓜ St-Michel – ✆ 01 44 07 06 06
– hotelroyalsaintmichel@wanadoo.fr – Fax 01 44 07 36 25
– www.hotelroyalsaintmichel.com   **T2**
39 rm – ♦169/260 € ♦♦179/290 €, ⊆ 15 €
♦ Family ♦ Traditional ♦ Modern ♦
On the Boulevard St Michel, opposite the fountain of the same name, this hotel
enjoys an excellent location in the heart of the lively Latin Quarter. Attractive,
modern rooms.

Deux Iles without rest   AC 🖻 ⁽ᵗ⁾ VISA ◍ AE

59 r. St-Louis-en-l'Ile (4th) – Ⓜ Pont Marie – ✆ 01 43 26 13 35 – info@
hoteldesdeuxiles.com – Fax 01 43 29 60 25 – www.hoteldesdeuxiles.com
17 rm – ♦155/165 € ♦♦195 €, ⊆ 12 €   **U2**
♦ Modern ♦
A few yards from the capital's most popular ice-cream parlour, this establishment
has comfortable, cane furnished, peaceful rooms and cosy lounges (one of which
is vaulted and one with a fireplace).

Relais Médicis without rest   AC 🖻 ⁽ᵗ⁾ VISA ◍ AE ◑

23 r. Racine (6th) – Ⓜ Odéon – ✆ 01 43 26 00 60 – reservation@
relaismedicis.com – Fax 01 40 46 83 39 – www.relaismedicis.com   **S2**
16 rm ⊆ – ♦142/172 € ♦♦172/258 €
♦ Traditional ♦ Personalised ♦
A hint of Provence enhances the rooms of this hotel near the Odeon theatre; those
overlooking the patio are quieter. Interesting antique furniture.

FRANCE - PARIS

Au Manoir St-Germain-des-Prés without rest
153 bd St-Germain (6th) – **M** St-Germain des Prés
– 𝒞 01 42 22 21 65 – reservation@hotelaumanoir.com – Fax 01 45 48 22 25
– www.paris-hotels-charm.com   **S2**
28 rm ⌑ – †200 € ††300 €
◆ Traditional ◆ Stylish ◆
This elegant hotel facing the Flore and Deux Magots (famous St Germain des Prés cafés) has been fully renovated. It retains its bourgeois charm with murals, wood panelling and antiques.

St-Grégoire without rest
43 r. Abbé-Grégoire (6th) – **M** St-Placide – 𝒞 01 45 48 23 23 – hotel@
saintgregoire.com – Fax 01 45 48 33 95 – www.hotelsaintgregoire.com
20 rm – †195/250 € ††250/300 €, ⌑ 14 €   **R3**
◆ Traditional ◆ Cosy ◆
Elegant and welcoming decor at this establishment. Two of the rooms have small leafy terraces. Attractive vaulted breakfast room.

Panthéon without rest
19 pl. Panthéon (5th) – **M** Luxembourg – 𝒞 01 43 54 32 95 – reservation@
hoteldupantheon.com – Fax 01 43 26 64 65 – www.hoteldupantheon.com
36 rm – †89/300 € ††99/310 €, ⌑ 13 €   **T3**
◆ Traditional ◆ Cosy ◆
The cosy or Louis XVI-style rooms command a view of the dome of the Pantheon. Attractive lounge and vaulted breakfast room.

Des Grands Hommes without rest
17 pl. Panthéon (5th) – **M** Luxembourg – 𝒞 01 46 34 19 60 – reservation@
hoteldesgrandshommes.com – Fax 01 43 26 67 32
– www.hoteldesgrandshommes.com   **T3**
31 rm – †80/310 € ††90/310 €, ⌑ 13 €
◆ Traditional ◆ Historic ◆
Facing the Panthéon, pleasant hotel decorated in Directoire style (antique furnishings). Over half the rooms overlook the final resting place of some of France's most eminent citizens.

Villa Mazarin without rest
6 r. des Archives (4th) – **M** Hôtel de Ville – 𝒞 01 53 01 90 90 – paris@
villamazarin.com – Fax 01 53 01 90 91 – www.villamazarin.com   **U1**
29 rm – †140/380 € ††140/380 €, ⌑ 12 €
◆ Modern ◆
With its high tech equipment (wifi, flat screen TVs) and mix of modern and period furniture, this comfortable hotel near the Hôtel de Ville combines tradition and modernity.

Tour Notre-Dame without rest
20 r. Sommerard (5th) – **M** Cluny la Sorbonne – 𝒞 01 43 54 47 60
– reservation@la-tour-notre-dame.com – Fax 01 43 26 42 34
– www.tour-notre-dame.com   **T2**
48 rm – †110/190 € ††120/250 €, ⌑ 13 €
◆ Traditional ◆ Family ◆ Stylish ◆
This hotel is very well situated, almost adjoining the Cluny museum. Comfortable, recently-renovated rooms. Those at the back are quieter.

Relais St-Sulpice without rest
3 r. Garancière (6th) – **M** St-Sulpice – 𝒞 01 46 33 99 00 – relaisstsulpice@
wanadoo.fr – Fax 01 46 33 00 10 – www.relais-saint-sulpice.com   **S2**
26 rm – †178/217 € ††178/217 €, ⌑ 12 €
◆ Traditional ◆ Personalised ◆
Appealing hotel not far from the Sénat and the Luxembourg gardens housing spacious, well-decorated rooms. Those at the back are very quiet.

Grand Hôtel St-Michel without rest   🅰 🆔 🅰 🆔 🆅🆂🅰 🆗 🅰🅴 🅾

19 r. Cujas (5th) – Ⓜ Luxembourg – 𝒞 01 46 33 33 02 – grand.hotel.st.michel @wanadoo.fr – Fax 01 40 46 96 33 – www.grand-hotel-st-michel.com
47 rm – 🛏170/290 € 🛏🛏170/350 €, ⌕ 17 € – 1 suite   **T3**
  ✦ Family ✦ Traditional ✦ Classical ✦

Hotel in a Haussmannian building offering comfortable rooms adorned with painted furniture. Napoleon III-style lounge. Breakfast served beneath a vaulted ceiling.

Notre Dame without rest   ◁ 🆔 ⇙ 🅰 🆔 🆅🆂🅰 🆗 🅰🅴 🅾

1 quai St-Michel (5th) – Ⓜ St-Michel – 𝒞 01 43 54 20 43 – hotel.denotredame@ libertysurf.fr – Fax 01 43 26 61 75 – http://www.hotel-paris-notredame.com/
26 rm – 🛏159/199 € 🛏🛏159/199 €, ⌕ 7 €   **T2**
  ✦ Traditional ✦ Family ✦ Cosy ✦

The cosy little rooms in this hotel have all been refurbished and are air-conditioned and well appointed. Most rooms have a view over Notre-Dame cathedral.

Relais St-Jacques without rest   🅰 🆔 🆔 ⚄ 🆅🆂🅰 🆗 🅰🅴 🅾

3 r. Abbé de l'Épée (5th) – Ⓜ Luxembourg – 𝒞 01 53 73 26 00 – info@ relais-saint-jacques.com – Fax 01 43 26 17 81 – www.relais-saint-jacques.com
22 rm – 🛏189/370 € 🛏🛏189/370 €, ⌕ 17 €   **T3**
  ✦ Traditional ✦ Family ✦ Stylish ✦

Rooms of various styles (Directoire, Louis Philippe, etc.), a glass-roofed breakfast room, Louis XV lounge and 1920s bar, make this a stylish hotchpotch hotel!

Artus without rest   🆔 🆔 🆅🆂🅰 🆗 🅰🅴 🅾

34 r. de Buci (6th) – Ⓜ Mabillon – 𝒞 01 43 29 07 20 – info@artushotel.com – Fax 01 43 29 67 44 – www.artushotel.com   **S2**
27 rm ⌕ – 🛏195/305 € 🛏🛏195/305 €
  ✦ Traditional ✦ Design ✦

Contemporary yet intimate, with modern bedrooms ornamented with antiques, an attractive vaulted cellar, designer bar, and paintings from nearby galleries on display.

Odéon without rest   🆔 🆔 🆔 🆅🆂🅰 🆗 🅰🅴 🅾

3 r. Odéon (6th) – Ⓜ Odéon – 𝒞 01 43 25 90 67 – odeon@odeonhotel.fr – Fax 01 43 25 55 98 – www.odeonhotel.fr   **S2**
33 rm – 🛏130 € 🛏🛏190/270 €, ⌕ 12 €
  ✦ Family ✦ Classical ✦

The façade, stone walls and exposed beams bear witness to the age of this building (17C). Personalised guestrooms, some with views of the Eiffel Tower.

Verneuil without rest   🆔 🆔 🆅🆂🅰 🆗 🅰🅴 🅾

8 r. Verneuil (7th) – Ⓜ Rue du Bac – 𝒞 01 42 60 82 14 – info@hotelverneuil.com – Fax 01 42 61 40 38 – www.hotelverneuil.com   **S1**
26 rm ⌕ – 🛏157 € 🛏🛏200/260 €
  ✦ Cosy ✦

This old building on the Left Bank is decorated in the style of a private house. Elegant rooms adorned with 18C prints. Serge Gainsbourg lived opposite.

Lenox St-Germain without rest   🆔 🆔 🆔 🆅🆂🅰 🆗 🅰🅴 🅾

9 r. de l'Université (7th) – Ⓜ St-Germain des Prés – 𝒞 01 42 96 10 95 – hotel@ lenoxsaintgermain.com – Fax 01 42 61 52 83 – www.lenoxsaintgermain.com
32 rm – 🛏135/180 € 🛏🛏160/295 €, ⌕ 14 € – 2 suites   **R-S1**
  ✦ Art Deco ✦

A discreetly luxurious Art Deco style depicts this hotel. Rooms are a little on the small side but attractively decorated. "Egyptian" frescoes adorn the breakfast room. Pleasant bar.

D'Orsay without rest   🅰 🆔 🆔 ⚄ 🆅🆂🅰 🆗 🅰🅴 🅾

93 r. Lille (7th) – Ⓜ Solférino – 𝒞 01 47 05 85 54 – orsay@espritfrance.com – Fax 01 45 55 51 16 – www.esprit-de-france.com   **R1**
41 rm – 🛏155/210 € 🛏🛏177/370 €, ⌕ 13 €
  ✦ Traditional ✦ Classical ✦

The hotel occupies two handsome, late-18C buildings. Attractive classical style rooms and welcoming lounge overlooking a small leafy patio.

St-Germain without rest   AK SAT ((°)) VISA OO AE

88 r. du Bac (7th) – **Ⓜ** Rue du Bac – *𝒞* 01 49 54 70 00 – info@
hotel-saint-germain.fr – Fax 01 45 48 26 89 – www.hotel-saint-germain.fr
29 rm – ⵧ150/240 € ⵧⵧ150/240 €, ⌷ 12 €   **R2**
♦ Family ♦ Personalised ♦
Empire, Louis-Philippe, high-tech design, antique objects, contemporary paintings
- the charm of variety. Comfortable library, patio pleasant in summer.

Duo without rest   ⅃ゟ ゟ AK SAT ((°)) VISA OO AE ①

11 r. Temple (4th) – **Ⓜ** Hôtel de Ville – *𝒞* 01 42 72 72 22 – contact@
duoparis.com – Fax 01 42 72 03 53 – www.duoparis.com   **U1**
56 rm – ⵧ130/240 € ⵧⵧ200/480 €, ⌷ 15 € – 2 suites
♦ Modern ♦
The trendily refurbished second wing with its warm vivid tones has given new life
to this hotel that is full of character. The same family has run it for three generations. Fitness facilities.

Lutèce without rest   AK SAT ((°)) VISA OO AE

65 r. St-Louis-en-l'Ile (4th) – **Ⓜ** Pont Marie – *𝒞* 01 43 26 23 52 – info@
hoteldelutece.com – Fax 01 43 29 60 25 – www.hoteldelutece.com
23 rm – ⵧ155 € ⵧⵧ195 €, ⌷ 12 €   **U2**
♦ Functional ♦
The rustic charm of this mansion on the Ile St-Louis is particularly popular with
American visitors. Modernised guestrooms with a country feel, plus attractive old
woodwork in the lounge.

Britannique without rest   AK SAT ((°)) VISA OO AE ①

20 av. Victoria (1st) – **Ⓜ** Châtelet – *𝒞* 01 42 33 74 59 – mailbox@
hotel-britannique.fr – Fax 01 42 33 82 65 – www.hotel-britannique.fr
39 rm – ⵧ128/160 € ⵧⵧ152/279 €, ⌷ 13 €   **T1**
♦ Traditional ♦ Family ♦ Cosy ♦
Founded by an English family during the reign of Queen Victoria, this hotel has
retained its elegantly British Imperial charm and refined exotic feel. Charming
lounge.

Bersoly's without rest   AK SAT ((°)) VISA OO AE

28 r. de Lille (7th) – **Ⓜ** Musée d'Orsay – *𝒞* 01 42 60 73 79 – hotelbersolys@
wanadoo.fr – Fax 01 49 27 05 55 – www.bersolyshotel.com
– Closed 10-21 August   **R-S1**
16 rm – ⵧ130/140 € ⵧⵧ150/170 €, ⌷ 10 €
♦ Traditional ♦ Business ♦ Personalised ♦
Impressionist nights in this 17C building in which each room honours an artist
whose works are displayed in the nearby Musée d'Orsay (Renoir, Gauguin, etc.).

St-Jacques without rest   ((°)) VISA OO AE ①

35 r. des Écoles (5th) – **Ⓜ** Maubert Mutualité – *𝒞* 01 44 07 45 45
– hotelsaintjacques@wanadoo.fr – Fax 01 43 25 65 50
– www.paris-hotel-stjacques.com   **T2**
36 rm – ⵧ97 € ⵧⵧ105/189 €, ⌷ 10 €
♦ Traditional ♦ Family ♦ Stylish ♦
Modern comfort allies with old-style charm in the rooms of this hotel. Library with
18C and 19C works. Breakfast room with Roaring Twenties cabaret-style decor.

La Tour d'Argent   ⪡ AK ⇕ ⌂ゃ VISA OO AE ①

15 quai Tournelle (5th) – **Ⓜ** Maubert Mutualité – *𝒞* 01 43 54 23 31 – resa@
latourdargent.com – Fax 01 44 07 12 04 – www.latourdargent.com
– Closed August and Monday   **U2**
Rest – Menu 75 € (lunch) – Carte 250/300 € ⅏
Spec. Quenelles de brochet "André Terrail". Caneton "Tour d'Argent". Crêpes
"Belle Epoque".
♦ Traditional ♦ Luxury ♦
The 'skyline' dining room offers a magnificent view of Notre Dame Cathedral.
Exceptional wine list, famous Challans duck and a celebrity clientele since the
16C. An institution!

219

FRANCE - PARIS

XXX ✿
Paris – Hôtel Lutetia   🕭 🗚 ⇔ ☞ 📶 **VISA** ⦾ **AE** ⓪
45 bd Raspail (6th) – Ⓜ Sèvres Babylone – ℰ 01 49 54 46 90
– lutetia-paris@lutetia-paris.com – Fax 01 49 54 46 00
– www.lutetia-paris.com
– Closed August, 24-30 December, Saturday, Sunday and Bank Holidays
Rest – Menu 60 € bi (weekdays lunch), 80/130 €   **R2**
– Carte 65/145 €
Spec. Homard breton au tartare de betterave, tétragone à l'huile de noisette. Langoustine dorées, fleurs de courgettes aux girolles et aux amandes fraîches. Fruits rouges et noirs, palet de noix de coco, coque de sucre filé, jus chaud à la fraise.
♦ A la mode ♦ Cosy ♦
In keeping with the style of the hotel, the Sonia Rykiel Art Deco dining room reproduces one of the lounges from the Normandie ocean liner. Inspired updated cuisine.

XXX ✿
Jacques Cagna   🗚 ☞ (dinner) **VISA** ⦾ **AE** ⓪
14 r. Grands Augustins (6th) – Ⓜ St-Michel – ℰ 01 43 26 49 39
– restaurant@jacques-cagna.com – Fax 01 43 54 54 48
– www.jacques-cagna.com
– Closed 1-26 August, Monday lunch, Saturday lunch and Sunday
Rest – Menu 45 € (lunch)/100 € – Carte 104/170 €   **T2**
Spec. Langoustines de l'atlantique en croustillant. Gibier (season). Paris-Brest au praliné à l'ancienne.
♦ Traditional ♦ Rustic ♦
Located in one of the oldest homes in old Paris, the comfortable dining hall is embellished by massive rafters, 16C woodwork and Flemish paintings. Refined cuisine.

XXX ✿✿
Relais Louis XIII (Manuel Martinez)   🗚 ⇔ ☞ **VISA** ⦾ **AE** ⓪
8 r. Grands Augustins (6th) – Ⓜ Odéon – ℰ 01 43 26 75 96 – contact@
relaislouis13.com – Fax 01 44 07 07 80 – www.relaislouis13.com
– Closed August, 22 December-3 January, Sunday and Monday   **T2**
Rest – Menu 80 € (weekday dinner), 110/170 € bi – Carte 141/166 € 🍴
Spec. Ravioli de homard breton, foie gras et crème de cèpes. Caneton challandais rôti entier aux épices douces et fortes. Millefeuille à la vanille bourbon.
♦ Classic ♦ Cosy ♦
The building dates from the 16C and there are three Louis XIII-style dining rooms with balustrades, tapestries and open stonework. The cuisine is subtle and up-to-date.

XXX ✿✿
Hélène Darroze-La Salle à Manger   🗚 ½ ☞ **VISA** ⦾ **AE** ⓪
4 r. d'Assas (6th) – Ⓜ Sèvres Babylone – ℰ 01 42 22 00 11 – reservation@
helenedarroze.com – Fax 01 42 22 25 40   **R2**
Rest – (1st floor) (Closed lunch from 20 July to 30 August, Sunday and Monday) Menu 72 €, 175/280 € – Carte 111/189 € 🍴
Rest *Le Salon* – (closed 27 July-30 August, Sunday and Monday)
Menu 88/180 € – Carte 45/110 € 🍴
Spec. Riz carnaroli acquarello noir et crémeux, chipirons au chorizo et tomates confites, jus au persil, émulsion de parmesan. Grosses langoustines bretonnes rôties aux épices tandoori, mousseline de carottes aux agrumes. Pigeonneau fermier de Racan flambé au capucin et foie gras de canard des Landes grillé au feu de bois.
♦ South-western France ♦ Cosy ♦
Modern, low-key and soft décor in tones of aubergine and orange, where you can enjoy delicious cuisine and wines from the southwest. On the ground floor, Hélène Darroze presides over the Salon, serving tapas and snacks with a rustic Landes accent.

XXX **La Truffière**   AC VISA OO AE O

4 r. Blainville (5th) – **M** *Place Monge – ℰ 01 46 33 29 82*
– restaurant.latruffiere@wanadoo.fr – Fax 01 46 33 64 74 – www.latruffiere.com
– Closed 20-26 December, Sunday and Monday   **T3**
Rest – Menu 28 € (weekdays lunch), 50/125 € – Carte 99/110 € ஃ
 ♦ Traditional ♦ Cosy ♦

A 17C house home to three dining rooms. One is rustic with bare beams and the other two are vaulted. Traditional cuisine from southwest France and a fine wine list.

XX **Cigale Récamier**   🍴 AC VISA OO

4 r. Récamier (7th) – **M** *Sèvres Babylone – ℰ 01 45 48 86 58*
– Closed Sunday   **R2**
Rest – Carte 55/65 €
 ♦ Traditional ♦ Friendly ♦

A welcoming establishment with a clientele of writers and editors. Classic cuisine and sweet and savoury soufflé specialities, renewed every month. Peaceful terrace.

XX **Benoit**   AC ⇄ VISA OO AE

ஃ *20 r. St-Martin (4th) –* **M** *Châtelet-Les Halles – ℰ 01 42 72 25 76*
– restaurant.benoit@wanadoo.fr – Fax 01 42 72 45 68 – www.esprit-bistrot.com
– Closed 26 July-25 August and 25 February-2 March   **U1**
Rest – Menu 38 € (lunch) – Carte 55/84 €
Spec. Escargots en coquille, beurre d'ail et fines herbes. Filet de sole nantua, épinards à peine crémés. Tête de veau traditionnelle sauce ravigote.
 ♦ Classic ♦ Bistro ♦

Alain Ducasse runs this chic and lively bistro, one of the oldest in Paris. Traditional cuisine, respecting the soul of this authentic and delightful establishment.

XX **Yugaraj**   AC VISA OO AE O

14 r. Dauphine (6th) – **M** *Odéon – ℰ 01 43 26 44 91 – contact@yugaraj.com*
– Fax 01 46 33 50 77
– Closed August, Monday lunch and Thursday lunch   **T1**
Rest – Menu 28/66 € – Carte 36/48 €
 ♦ Indian ♦ Exotic ♦

New look but the same refinement at this highly acclaimed Indian restaurant with its museum-like decor (wood panelling, silks and antiques). Comprehensive menu.

XX **Le Restaurant** – Hôtel L'Hôtel   AC VISA OO AE O

ஃ *13 r. des Beaux-Arts (6th) –* **M** *St-Germain-des-Prés – ℰ 01 44 41 99 01 – eat@l-hotel.com – Fax 01 43 25 64 81 – www.lerestaurantparis.com*
– Closed 4-29 August, 21-29 December, Sunday and Monday   **S1**
Rest – Menu 95/155 € bi – Carte 95/130 €
Spec. Cèpe en ravioles et grillé, truffe marinée et jus corsé de champignons (autumn). Bar de ligne, chou fleur, œufs de hareng fumé et poutargue. Fraise des bois, cheese cake et sorbet citron (spring).
 ♦ A la mode ♦ Elegant ♦

Inside the hotel, this restaurant simply known as 'Le Restaurant' has a décor created by Jacques Garcia and a small indoor courtyard. Refined, modern cuisine.

XX **Atelier Maître Albert**   AC 🍴 VISA OO AE O

1 r. Maître Albert (5th) – **M** *Maubert Mutualité – ℰ 01 56 81 30 01*
– ateliermaitrealbert@guysavoy.com – Fax 01 53 10 83 23
– www.ateliermaitrealbert.com
– Closed 25 July-17 August, Christmas holidays, Saturday lunch and Sunday lunch   **U2**
Rest – Carte 45/55 €
 ♦ Traditional ♦ Bistro ♦

A huge medieval fireplace and spits for roast meat take pride of place in this handsome interior designed by J M Wilmotte. Guy Savoy is responsible for the mouth-watering menu.

FRANCE - PARIS

Alcazar   🕭 AC ⇔ VISA ◑◐ AE ⓞ

62 r. Mazarine (6th) – 🚇 Odéon – ℰ 01 53 10 19 99 – contact@alcazar.fr
– Fax 01 53 10 23 23 – www.alcazar.fr   **S2**
Rest – Menu 32 € bi (lunch), 35/43 € – Carte 40/66 €
♦ A la mode ♦ Trendy ♦

Sir Conrad's establishment attracts fans of electro-chic atmospheres and modern tastes. The glass wall, mezzanine and view of the kitchens give the location its individuality.

Fogon (Juan Alberto Herráiz)   AC ⌐Ⴌ (dinner) VISA ◑◐

45 quai des Grands-Augustins (6th) – 🚇 St-Michel – ℰ 01 43 54 31 33
– www.fogon.fr
– Closed 15-31 August and 23 December-3 January   **T2**
Rest – Menu 44/49 € – Carte 46/55 €
Spec. Jambon de porc Ibérique. Riz dans une paella aux langoustines. Tapas sucrés.
♦ Spanish ♦ Design ♦

Spanish cuisine (tapas, paëllas) revisited with flair and ingenuity, using top-quality produce and served in a contemporary designer setting.

L'Atelier de Joël Robuchon   AC ⇼ ⌐Ⴌ VISA ◑◐

5 r. Montalembert (7th) – 🚇 Rue du Bac – ℰ 01 42 22 56 56
– latelierdejoelrobuchon@wanadoo.fr – Fax 01 42 22 97 91
– www.joel-robuchon.com
– Reception open from 11.30am to 3.30pm and 6.30pm to midnight.
Reservations only possible for certain services: please enquire   **R1**
Rest – Menu 120 € – Carte 57/123 € ⌀
Spec. Langoustines en papillote croustillante au basilic. Caille caramélisée farcie de foie gras et pomme purée. Chocolat "sensation", sorbet ivoire et crémeux araguani.
♦ Innovative ♦ Design ♦

An original concept in a chic décor designed by Rochon: no tables, just high stools in a row facing the counter, where you can sample fine, modern cuisine, served tapas style.

Yen   AC VISA ◑◐ AE ⓞ

22 r. St-Benoît (6th) – 🚇 St-Germain des Prés – ℰ 01 45 44 11 18 – restau.yen@
wanadoo.fr – Fax 01 45 44 19 48 – Closed 2 weeks in August and Sunday
Rest – Menu 58 € – Carte 30/65 €   **S2**
♦ Japanese ♦ Minimalist ♦

Two dining rooms with highly refined Japanese decor, the one on the first floor is slightly warmer in style. Pride of place on the menu for the chef's speciality: soba (buckwheat noodles).

Gaya Rive Gauche par Pierre Gagnaire   AC VISA ◑◐ AE

44 r. Bac (7th) – 🚇 Rue du Bac – ℰ 01 45 44 73 73 – p.gagnaire@wanadoo.fr
– Fax 01 45 44 73 73 – www.pierre-gagnaire.com
– Closed Saturday lunch and Sunday   **R1**
Rest – Carte 70/95 €
Spec. Chair de tourteau à la gelée de fenouil au citron. Poêlée de langoustines à la coriandre fraîche. Gâteau au chocolat.
♦ Seafood ♦ Design ♦

In this delightful contemporary and relaxed bistro with a grey-blue décor designed by Christian Ghion, you are served a succession of creative seafood dishes.

L'Épi Dupin   VISA ◑◐

11 r. Dupin (6th) – 🚇 Sèvres Babylone – ℰ 01 42 22 64 56 – lepidupin@
wanadoo.fr – Fax 01 42 22 30 42 – www.epidupin.com
– Closed 1st-24 August, Monday lunch, Saturday and Sunday   **R2**
Rest – (number of covers limited, pre-book) Menu 34 €
♦ A la mode ♦ Friendly ♦

Beams and stonework for character, closely-packed tables for conviviality and delicious cuisine to delight the palate; this pocket-handkerchief-sized restaurant has captivated people in the Bon Marché area.

FRANCE - PARIS

Ze Kitchen Galerie (William Ledeuil)   ÅC VISA ⓐ AE ①

4 r. Grands Augustins (6th) – Ⓜ St-Michel – ℰ 01 44 32 00 32
– zekitchen.galerie@wanadoo.fr – Fax 01 44 32 00 33 – www.zekitchengalerie.fr
– Closed Saturday lunch and Sunday   **T2**
Rest – Menu 35 € (weekdays lunch)/76 € – Carte approx. 65 € ֍
Spec. Bouillon Thaï de crustacé, ravioli de langoustine. Saint Jacques grillées, condiment kumquat-citron caviar. Financier châtaigne, chocolat, coco et émulsion cacahuète.
 ♦ Fusion ♦ Design ♦
Tempting fusion menu influenced by Asia, refined interior with a loft atmosphere, contemporary paintings and visible kitchens: Ze Kitchen is 'ze' hip place to be on the Left Bank.

35 ° Ouest   ÅC ⇜ ⇦ VISA ⓐ AE

35 r. Verneuil (7th) – Ⓜ Rue du Bac – ℰ 01 42 86 98 88 – 35degresouest@
orange.fr – Fax 01 42 86 00 65 – Closed 2-24 August, Sunday and Monday
Rest – (number of covers limited, pre-book) Carte 45/85 €   **R1**
Spec. Friture d'éperlans sauce tartare. Saint-Pierre rôti aux girolles et pommes de terre ratte. Sablé breton aux pommes caramélisées.
 ♦ Seafood ♦
This modern, tastefully designed restaurant sports a grey and green colour scheme and a handsome bar. Inventive seafood cuisine full of flavour.

Itinéraires   VISA ⓐ

5 r. de Pontoise (5th) – Ⓜ Maubert Mutualité – ℰ 01 46 33 60 11 – Fax 01 40
26 44 91 – Closed 4-25 August, 20-29 December, Sunday and Monday
Rest – (booking essential) Menu 36 € ֍   **U2**
 ♦ A la mode ♦ Cosy ♦
Deservedly much-talked about bistro proposing fine modern cuisine in a contemporary setting. Charcuterie and tapas served at the counter in the evening.

La Maison du Jardin   ÅC VISA ⓐ AE ①

27 r. Vaugirard (6th) – Ⓜ Rennes – ℰ 01 45 48 22 31 – Fax 01 45 48 22 31
Rest – (pre-book) Menu 26/31 €   **S3**
 ♦ Traditional ♦ Bistro ♦
In a setting between bistro and provincial inn, this establishment serves tasty updated traditional dishes. Short, reasonably-priced wine list.

L'Épigramme   VISA AE

9 r. l'Éperon (6th) ⊠ 75006 – Ⓜ Odéon – ℰ 01 44 41 00 09
– Fax 01 44 41 00 09 – Closed for three weeks in August, one week at Christmas,
Sunday and Monday   **T2**
Rest – (number of covers limited, pre-book) Menu 28 € (lunch)/30 €
 ♦ Bistro ♦ Cosy ♦
The tasty updated bistro menu, nature inspired interior decoration (stone and bare beams) and moderate prices, explain the popularity of this often fully booked restaurant.

Papilles   ⇦ VISA ⓐ

30 r. Gay Lussac (5th) – Ⓜ Luxembourg – ℰ 01 43 25 20 79 – lespapilles@
hotmail.fr – Fax 01 43 25 24 35 – www.lespapillesparis.com
– Closed Easter holidays, 1st-21 August, 1st-8 January, Sunday and Monday
Rest – Menu 31 € – Carte lunch only 30/38 € ֍   **T3**
 ♦ South-western France ♦
Bistro, cellar and grocer's: on one side are wine racks, on the other shelves with jars of southwest specialities and in the middle…you can enjoy market-inspired food!

Mon Vieil Ami   VISA ⓐ AE ①

69 r. St-Louis-en-l'Île (4th) – Ⓜ Pont Marie – ℰ 01 40 46 01 35 – mon.vieil.ami
@wanadoo.fr – Fax 01 40 46 01 35 – www.mon-vieil-ami.com
– Closed 1st-20 August, 1st-20 January, Monday and Tuesday   **U2**
Rest – Menu 41 € – Carte lunch only 42/55 €
 ♦ Traditional ♦ Inn ♦
In this old house with a refurbished interior on Ile St Louis, sample tasty, traditional recipes infused with modern touches and Alsatian culinary influences.

Au Bourguignon du Marais ⬛ VISA ⓿ AE

52 r. François-Miron (4th) – **Ⓜ** *St-Paul* – 𝒞 *01 48 87 15 40* – *Fax 01 48 87 17 49*
– Closed 11-31 August, 19 January-1 February, Sunday and Monday
Rest – Carte 40/62 € ⛲ *Plan VII* **X2**
♦ De Terroir ♦ Bistro ♦

Located between the Hôtel de Ville and Saint Paul, the cuisine can be summed up in two words: regional and generous. Appealing setting and fine wine list.

Suan Thai ⬛ VISA ⓿ AE

41 r. Ste-Croix -de-la-Bretonnerie (4th) – **Ⓜ** *Rambuteau* – 𝒞 *01 42 77 10 20*
– suan.thai@yahoo.fr **U1**
Rest – Menu 18/28 € – Carte 37/61 €
♦ Thai ♦ Exotic ♦

An authentique taste of Thailand in a discreetly exotic setting. Reservations are often required, given the reasonable prices and good reputation of this local eatery.

MONTPARNASSE-DENFERT *Plan VI*

Méridien Montparnasse ⬛ ⬛ ⬛ rm ⬛ rm ⬛ ⬛ ⬛

19 r. Cdt Mouchotte (14th) VISA ⓿ AE ⓿
*– **Ⓜ** Montparnasse Bienvenüe – 𝒞 01 44 36 44 36*
– meridien.montparnasse@lemeridien.com – Fax 01 44 36 49 00
– www.lemeridien.com/montparnasse **V1**
918 rm – ♦159/600 € ♦♦159/600 €, ⬜ 25 € – 35 suites
Rest *Montparnasse'25* – see below
Rest *Justine* – 𝒞 01 44 36 44 00 – Menu 42 € – Carte 45/70 €
♦ Business ♦ Art Deco ♦

The spacious rooms in this glass and concrete building have been redone in a modern spirit with Art Deco details. Beautiful view of the capital from the top floors. At Justine's, winter garden decor, green terrace and buffet menus.

Concorde Montparnasse ⬛ ⬛ ⬛ ⬛ rm ⬛ rm ⬛ ⬛ ⬛ ⬛

40 r. Cdt Mouchotte (14th) – **Ⓜ** *Gaîté* VISA ⓿ AE ⓿
– 𝒞 01 56 54 84 00 – montparnasse-booking@concorde-hotels.com
– Fax 01 56 54 84 84 – www.concorde-montparnasse.com **V1**
354 rm – ♦150/500 € ♦♦150/500 €, ⬜ 21 € **Rest** – Carte 52/60 €
♦ Business ♦ Modern ♦

This hotel, on Place de Catalogne, was treated to a facelift recently. Calm and refined rooms, interior garden, fitness centre and bar. Exotic wood and colourful fabrics grace this modern, low-key restaurant, serving a modern menu.

Aiglon without rest ⬛ ⬛ ⬛ ⬛ ⬛ VISA ⓿ AE ⓿

232 bd Raspail (14th) – **Ⓜ** *Raspail* – 𝒞 *01 43 20 82 42* – *aiglon@*
espritfrance.com – *Fax 01 43 20 98 72* – *www.aiglon.com* **W1**
36 rm – ♦145/195 € ♦♦145/195 €, ⬜ 12 € – 10 suites
♦ Traditional ♦ Classical ♦

This one time home to Giacometti and Bunuel is gradually being modernised. Bright colours and stylish details (mosaic bathrooms, photos) set the scene for the new decor.

Ste-Beuve without rest ⬛ ⬛ ⬛ VISA ⓿ AE ⓿

9 r. Ste-Beuve (6th) – **Ⓜ** *Notre-Dame des Champs* – 𝒞 *01 45 48 20 07*
– saintebeuve@wanadoo.fr – Fax 01 45 48 67 52 – www.parishotelcharme.com
22 rm – ♦155/215 € ♦♦199/315 €, ⬜ 15 € **W1**
♦ Family ♦ Traditional ♦ Cosy ♦

The intimate atmosphere of this establishment makes it feel like a private home. The guestrooms have been renovated in a tasteful modern style; bathrooms in black and white.

TOUR EIFFEL INVALIDES (Plan IV)

ST-GERMAIN-DES-PRÉS / QUARTIER LATIN HÔTEL DE VILLE (Plan V)

Montparnasse, Denfert
(Plan VI)

Montparnasse Bienvenüe M

TOUR

Pl. du 18 Juin 1940

Bd du départ

Montparnasse M

6e

Ste-Beuve

Sensing X X

Des Académies et des Arts

Villa des Artistes

Cerisaie X

La Coupole X X

Le Dôme X X X

Vavin

Delambre

Lenox Montparnasse

Mercure Raspail Montparnasse

Montparnasse Bienvenüe M

Edgar Quinet M

GARE MONTPARNASSE 1

L'Aiglon

Raspail

JARDIN ATLANTIQUE

Méridien Montparnasse

Gaîté

Montparnasse 25

CIMETIÈRE DU MONTPARNASSE

Concorde Montparnasse

Pl. de Catalogne

Rue Jean Zay

Froidevaux

Apollon Montparnasse

Pernety

14e

L'Entêtée X

PL. DENFERT ROCHEREAU

La Cantine du Troquet X

Denfert Rochereau

Nouvel Orléans

● Hotel
● Restaurant

0   200 m

Mouton Duvernet M

15e

Des Académies et des Arts without rest   AC ⟷ SAT 🖫 VISA ⓿ AE

15 r. de la Grande-Chaumière (6th) – Ⓜ *Vavin* – ℰ *01 43 26 66 44*
– *reservation@hoteldesacademies.com* – *Fax 01 40 46 86 85*
– *www.hoteldesacademies.com*   **W1**
20 rm – ♦183/294 € ♦♦183/294 €, � 15 €
♦ Cosy ♦

The walls of this creative and artistic hotel are adorned with white figures painted by Jérôme Mesnager and sculptures by Sophie de Watrigant. Elegant, well-appointed guestrooms.

Villa des Artistes without rest ⌂   AC ⟷ SAT 🖫 VISA ⓿ AE ⓞ

9 r. Grande-Chaumière (6th) – Ⓜ *Vavin* – ℰ *01 43 26 60 86* – *hotel@villa-artistes.com* – *Fax 01 43 54 73 70* – *www.villa-artistes.com*   **W1**
55 rm – ♦109/270 € ♦♦129/350 €, ⊒ 15 €
♦ Family ♦ Traditional ♦ Stylish ♦

The name pays tribute to the artists who embellished the history of the Montparnasse district. Some rooms have been renovated on the theme of 20C artists.

225

FRANCE - PARIS

Lenox Montparnasse without rest   🖭 ⇔ 🖭 ⁿ⁄ⁿ 🖭 ⚫⚫ 🅰🅴 ⓞ
15 r. Delambre (14th) – Ⓜ Vavin – ℰ 01 43 35 34 50 – hotel@
lenoxmontparnasse.com – Fax 01 43 20 46 64 – www.hotellenox.com
52 rm – ♥150/310 € ♥♥150/310 €, ☑ 16 €   **W1**
♦ Business ♦ Classical ♦

Establishment noted for its elegance: plush, low-key bar and sitting rooms, personalised stylish rooms, pleasant suites on the sixth floor.

Nouvel Orléans without rest   🖭 ⇔ 🖭 ⁿ⁄ⁿ 🖭 ⚫⚫ 🅰🅴 ⓞ
25 av. Gén. Leclerc (14th) – Ⓜ Mouton Duvernet – ℰ 01 43 27 80 20
– nouvelorleans@aol.com – Fax 01 43 35 36 57 – www.hotelnouvelorleans.com
46 rm – ♥110/145 € ♥♥110/190 €, ☑ 12 €   **W2**
♦ Business ♦ Design ♦

The name comes from the Porte d'Orléans, 800m away. In this entirely renovated
hotel, modern furniture and warm colourful materials decorate the rooms.

Delambre without rest   🖭 🖭 ⁿ⁄ⁿ 🖭 ⚫⚫ 🅰🅴
35 r. Delambre (14th) – Ⓜ Edgar Quinet – ℰ 01 43 20 66 31 – delambre@
club-internet.fr – Fax 01 45 38 91 76 – www.hoteldelambre.com   **W1**
30 rm – ♥90/170 € ♥♥95/170 €, ☑ 11 €
♦ Business ♦ Functional ♦

André Breton stayed in this hotel located in a quiet street close to Montparnasse
railway station. The decor is modern, the rooms simple but bright, and many are
spacious.

Mercure Raspail Montparnasse without rest   ♿ 🖭 ⇔ 🖭 ⁿ⁄ⁿ
207 bd Raspail (14th) – Ⓜ Vavin – ℰ 01 43 20 62 94   🖭 ⚫⚫ 🅰🅴 ⓞ
– h0351@accor.com – Fax 01 43 27 39 69 – www.mercure.com   **W1**
63 rm – ♥170/220 € ♥♥175/220 €, ☑ 14 €
♦ Business ♦ Modern ♦

Enjoy an overnight stay in this Haussmann building near the famous Montparnasse brasseries. Fully refurbished, modern rooms graced with pale wood furniture.

Apollon Montparnasse without rest   🖭 ⇔ 🖭 ⁿ⁄ⁿ 🖭 ⚫⚫ 🅰🅴 ⓞ
91 r. Ouest (14th) – Ⓜ Pernety – ℰ 01 43 95 62 00 – apollonm@wanadoo.fr
– Fax 01 43 95 62 10 – www.apollon-montparnasse.com   **V2**
33 rm – ♥70/98 € ♥♥85/125 €, ☑ 11 €
♦ Traditional ♦ Functional ♦

Gradually renovated family hotel near the station. Tastefully decorated rooms, a
smiling welcome, and a quiet location in a side street.

XXXX   **Montparnasse'25** – Hôtel Méridien Montparnasse   🖭
☼   *19 r. Cdt Mouchotte (14th)*   🖭 ⚫⚫ 🅰🅴 ⓞ
– Ⓜ Montparnasse Bienvenüe – ℰ 01 44 36 44 25 – meridien.montparnasse@
lemeridien.com – Fax 01 44 36 49 03 – www.lemeridien.com/montparnasse
– Closed 1-10 May, 13 July-31 August, 22 December-4 January, Saturday,
Sunday and Bank Holidays   **V1**
Rest – Menu 50/110 € – Carte 110/133 € ⅋
Spec. Saint-Jacques et ormeaux, crème de chou-fleur au caviar. Sole au jus
d'étrilles. Gaufre, crème légère et châtaigne.
♦ A la mode ♦ Formal ♦

The modern setting based around black lacquer may surprise but this restaurant
turns out to be comfortable and warm. Contemporary cuisine, superb cheese
boards.

XXX   **Le Dôme**   🖭 ⇔ 🖭 ⚫⚫ 🅰🅴 ⓞ
108 bd Montparnasse (14th) – Ⓜ Vavin – ℰ 01 43 35 25 81
– Fax 01 42 79 01 19
– Closed Sunday and Monday in August   **W1**
Rest – Carte 85/150 €
♦ Seafood ♦ Elegant ♦

A temple of literary and artistic bohemian life in the Twenties has been turned into a
stylish and trendy Left-Bank brasserie, with its Art Deco style intact. Fish and seafood.

FRANCE - PARIS

XX **Sensing** &. AC 4/ VISA OO AE

19 r. Bréa (6th) – Ⓜ Vavin – ℰ 01 43 27 08 80 – contact@
restaurantsensing.com – Fax 01 43 26 99 27 – www.restaurant-sensing.com
– Closed August, Monday lunch and Sunday **W1**
Rest – Menu 55 € bi (lunch), 75 € bi/140 € bi – Carte 59/73 €
+ Innovative + Trendy +

A short menu with refined, contemporary dishes prepared using excellent produce
and served in an uncluttered, ultra-stylish setting. Run by the famous French chef,
Guy Martin.

XX **La Coupole** AC ⇔ VISA OO AE

102 bd Montparnasse (14th) – Ⓜ Vavin – ℰ 01 43 20 14 20 – jtosi@groupeflo.fr
– Fax 01 43 35 46 14 – www.flobrasseries.com **W1**
Rest – Menu 36 € – Carte 35/70 €
+ Brasserie + Brasserie +

The spirit of Montparnasse lives on in this immense Art Deco brasserie, opened in
1927. The 24 pillars were decorated by artists of the period, while the cupola sports
a new contemporary fresco.

X **La Cerisaie** VISA OO
ⓐ *70 bd E. Quinet (14th) – Ⓜ Edgar Quinet – ℰ 01 43 20 98 98 – Fax 01 43 20 98 98*
Closed 1-11 May, 11 July-17 August, 19 December-4 January, Saturday and Sunday
Rest – (pre-book) Menu 34/40 € ℬ **V1**
+ South-western France + Bistro +

A tiny restaurant in the heart of the Breton quarter. Every day, the owner chalks up
on a blackboard the carefully prepared south-western dishes.

X **La Cantine du Troquet** VISA OO
ⓐ *100 r. de l'Ouest (14th) – Ⓜ Pernety* **V2**
Rest – Menu 30 € – Carte 25/35 €
+ Bistro + Bistro +

This canteen breathes conviviality (no reservations, no telephone) and is the simpler, sister establishment to the Troquet. Red bench seating, wooden tables and
daily blackboard specials.

X **L'Entêtée** VISA OO
ⓐ *4 r. Danville (14th) – Ⓜ Denfert Rochereau – ℰ 01 40 47 56 81 – entetee@*
gmail.com – www.myspace.com/entetee
– Closed August, Saturday lunch, Sunday and Monday **W2**
Rest – (number of covers limited, pre-book) Menu 25 € (lunch)/30 €
+ A la mode +

"Entêtée" (stubborn) could be just the name of this discreet bistro or it could also
refer to the chef's character... Generous dishes, perfumed with herbs and spices.

MARAIS-BASTILLE-GARE DE LYON   *Plan VII*

🏨 **Pavillon de la Reine** without rest ⌂   AC ⁽¹⁾ ⅏ 🚗 VISA OO AE ①
28 pl. des Vosges (3rd) – Ⓜ Bastille – ℰ 01 40 29 19 19 – contact@
pavillon-de-la-reine.com – Fax 01 40 29 19 20 – www.pavillon-de-la-reine.com
41 rm – †380/480 € ††450/480 €, ⊂⊃ 30 € – 16 suites **Y2**
+ Luxury + Historic +

Behind one of the 36 brick houses lining the Place des Vosges stand two buildings,
one of which is 17C, housing elegant rooms on the courtyard or (private) garden
side. New spa.

🏨 **Les Jardins du Marais** 🛏 &. rm AC 4/ 📷 ⁽¹⁾ ⅏ VISA OO AE ①
74 r. Amelot (11th) – Ⓜ St-Sébastien Froissart – ℰ 01 40 21 20 00
– resabastille@homeplazza.com – Fax 01 47 00 82 40 – www.homeplazza.com
201 rm – †180/350 € ††180/350 €, ⊂⊃ 20 € – 64 suites **Y1**
Rest – (closed Sunday) Carte 36/60 €
+ Luxury + Art Deco +

Partly listed buildings overlooking an old cul-de-sac with small, private terraces.
Designer entrance hall and bar, and Art Deco touches in the bedrooms.

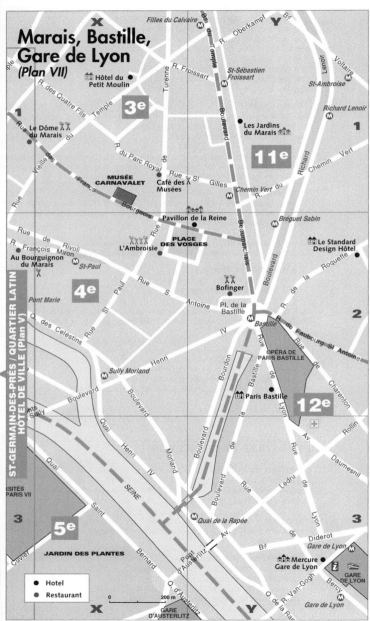

Mercure Gare de Lyon without rest

2 pl. Louis Armand (12th) – Ⓜ Gare de Lyon
– ✆ 01 43 44 84 84 – h2217@accor.com – Fax 01 43 47 41 94 – www.mercure.com
315 rm – 🚹160/294 € 🚹🚹175/310 €, ☕ 18 € **Y3**

◆ Chain hotel ◆ Functional ◆

The modern architecture of this hotel contrasts with the nearby belfry of the Gare de Lyon. The bedrooms are furnished in ceruse wood and have the benefit of good soundproofing. Wine bar.

Du Petit Moulin without rest

29 r. du Poitou (3rd) – Ⓜ St-Sébastien Froissart – ✆ 01 42 74 10 10 – contact@hoteldupetitmoulin.com – Fax 01 42 74 10 97 – www.hoteldupetitmoulin.com
17 rm – 🚹190/350 € 🚹🚹190/350 €, ☕ 15 € **X1**

◆ Luxury ◆ Personalised ◆

For this hotel in the Marais, Christian Lacroix has designed a unique and refined decor, playing on the contrasts between traditional and modern. Each room has a different design. Cosy bar.

Le Standard Design without rest

29 r. des Taillandiers (11th) – Ⓜ Bastille – ✆ 01 48 05 30 97 – reservation@standard-design-hotel-paris.com – Fax 01 47 00 29 26
– www.standard-design-hotel-paris.com **CZ**
36 rm – 🚹125/160 € 🚹🚹150/210 €, ☕ 15 €

◆ Traditional ◆ Cosy ◆

A contemporary interior in black and white with touches of colour in the bedrooms. Bright breakfast room under sloping ceilings.

Paris Bastille without rest

67 r. Lyon (12th) – Ⓜ Bastille – ✆ 01 40 01 07 17 – infosbastille@wanadoo.fr
– Fax 01 40 01 07 27 – www.hotelparisbastille.com **Y2**
37 rm – 🚹170/260 € 🚹🚹182/260 €, ☕ 13 €

◆ Business ◆ Functional ◆

Up-to-date comfort, modern furnishings and carefully chosen colour schemes characterise the rooms in this hotel facing the Opéra.

L'Ambroisie (Bernard Pacaud)

✿✿✿

9 pl. des Vosges (4th) – Ⓜ St-Paul – ✆ 01 42 78 51 45
– Closed August, 23 February-11 March, Sunday and Monday **X2**
Rest – Carte 240/360 €

Spec. Feuillantine de langoustines aux graines de sésame. Escalopines de bar à l'émincé d'artichaut, caviar "osciètre gold". Tarte fine sablée au chocolat, glace vanille.

◆ A la mode ◆ Luxury ◆

Under the arcades of the Place des Vosges, royal decor and subtle cuisine, close to perfection. The name is most appropriate: ambrosia was the food of the gods of Antiquity.

Bofinger (dinner)

5 r. Bastille (4th) – Ⓜ Bastille – ✆ 01 42 72 87 82 – eberne@groupeflo.fr
– Fax 01 42 72 97 68 – www.bofingerparis.com **Y2**
Rest – Menu 32 € – Carte 35/65 €

◆ Brasserie ◆ Retro ◆

The famous clients and remarkable decor have bestowed enduring renown on this brasserie created in 1864. The interior boasts a finely worked cupola, and a room on the first floor decorated by Hansi.

Le Dôme du Marais

53 bis r. Francs-Bourgeois (4th) – Ⓜ Rambuteau – ✆ 01 42 74 54 17
– ledomedumarais@hotmail.com – Fax 01 42 77 78 17 – www.ledomedumarais.fr
– Closed 2-27 August, 1-7 January, Sunday and Monday **X1**
Rest – Menu 25 € (lunch), 36/100 € bi – Carte approx. 58 €

◆ A la mode ◆ Romantic ◆

Tables are arranged under the pretty dome in the old sales room of the Crédit Municipal, and in a second dining room that resembles a winter garden. Modern cuisine.

FRANCE - PARIS

Café des Musées   AC VISA ⑩ AE

49 r. de Turenne (3rd) – Ⓜ *Chemin Vert – ℰ 01 42 72 96 17 – cafe.des.muses*
@orange.fr – Fax 01 44 59 38 68
– Closed 1-7 January and 7-27 August   **X1**
Rest – Menu 21 € – Carte 22/43 €
♦ Bistro ♦ Bistro ♦

Between the Carnavalet and Picasso museums, this bistro is Parisian through and
through and gets everything right: hearty seasonal cooking, served in a convivial
atmosphere.

MONTMARTRE, PIGALLE   *Plan VIII*

Terrass'Hôtel   ᾞ AC ⤢ rm 🖭 ℂℓ ⅀A VISA ⑩ AE ⑩

12 r. J. de Maistre (18th) – Ⓜ *Place de Clichy – ℰ 01 46 06 72 85 – reservation@*
terrass-hotel.com – www.terrass-hotel.com   **Z1**
98 rm – ♦280/330 € ♦♦280/330 €, ⅀ 17 €
Rest *Le Diapason* – ℰ 01 44 92 34 00 *(closed Sunday dinner16 September-30*
April and Saturday lunch) Menu 29/35 € bi – Carte 45/63 €
♦ Grand Luxury ♦ Traditional ♦ Classical ♦

Situated at the foot of the Sacré-Coeur basilica, this hotel has stunning views of
Paris from its upper-floor rooms and top-floor terrace. Elegant interior adorned
with ornaments and wood panelling. Plain, contemporary decor (in sands, greys
and black) at the Diapason. Cuisine in the same modern and refined style.

Mercure Montmartre *without rest*   ৬ AC ⤢ 🖭 ℣ ⅀A

3 r. Caulaincourt (18th) – Ⓜ *Place de Clichy*   VISA ⑩ AE ⑩
– ℰ 01 44 69 70 70 – h0373@accor.com – Fax 01 44 69 70 71
– www.mercure.com   **Z2**
305 rm – ♦205 € ♦♦215 €, ⅀ 15 €
♦ Chain hotel ♦ Business ♦ Minimalist ♦

A stone's throw from the famous Moulin Rouge, the hotel lobby is decorated on
the theme of Montmartre and its painters. The rooms on the top three floors
enjoy lovely views of the rooftops of Paris.

Holiday Inn Garden Court Montmartre *without rest*   ৬ AC

23 r. Damrémont (18th)   ⤢ 🖭 ℣ ⅀A VISA ⑩ AE ⑩
– Ⓜ *Lamarck Caulaincourt – ℰ 01 44 92 33 40 – hiparmm@aol.com*
– Fax 01 44 92 09 30 – www.holiday-inn.com/parismontmart   **Z1**
54 rm – ♦140/170 € ♦♦160/190 €, ⅀ 13 €
♦ Chain hotel ♦ Business ♦ Functional ♦

A recently built hotel with renovated, functional rooms on a typically steep Montmartre street. The breakfast room opens onto a small terrace.

Timhotel *without rest*   AC ⤢ 🖭 ℣ VISA ⑩ AE ⑩

11 r. Ravignan (18th) – Ⓜ *Abbesses – ℰ 01 42 55 74 79*
– montmartre.manager@timhotel.fr – Fax 01 42 55 71 01 – www.timhotel.com
59 rm – ♦85/130 € ♦♦85/210 €, ⅀ 8.50 €   **AA2**
♦ Chain hotel ♦ Traditional ♦ Modern ♦

Smart, functional hotel on one of the neighbourhood's most charming squares.
The rooms on the 4th and 5th floors have been renovated and offer superb views
of the capital.

Roma Sacré Coeur *without rest*   🖭 ℣ VISA ⑩ AE ⑩

101 r. Caulaincourt (18th) – Ⓜ *Lamarck Caulaincourt – ℰ 01 42 62 02 02*
– hotelroma@wanadoo.fr – Fax 01 42 54 34 92 – www.hotelromasacre.fr
57 rm – ♦80/120 € ♦♦95/145 €, ⅀ 8 €   **AA1**
♦ Traditional ♦ Family ♦ Classical ♦

This hotel has a charming location in Montmartre, with a garden to the front, typical flights of steps to the side and Sacré-Cœur above. Attractive, brightly coloured
guestrooms.

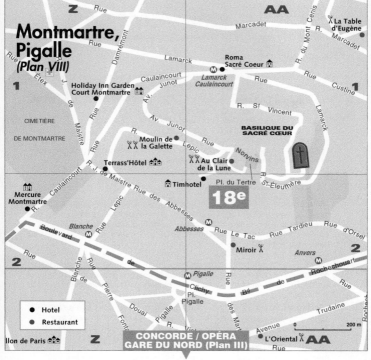

Montmartre,
Pigalle
(Plan VIII)

CIMETIÈRE
DE MONTMARTRE

18ᵉ

BASILIQUE DU
SACRÉ CŒUR

- Hotel
- Restaurant

Ilon de Paris

**CONCORDE / OPÉRA
GARE DU NORD (Plan III)**

XX **Le Moulin de la Galette**   AC VISA ③ AE

*83 r. Lepic (18th) – Ⓜ Abbesses – ℰ 01 46 06 84 77 – reservation@
lemoulindelagalette.fr – Fax 01 46 06 84 78 – www.lemoulindelagalette.fr*
Rest – Menu 25 € (lunch), 50/60 € – Carte 50/70 €   **Z1**
♦ A la mode ♦ Friendly ♦
A windmill in 1622, then a popular dance hall painted by Renoir and Toulouse-
Lautrec, this place has been remodelled and is now a bistro-style restaurant with
a plant filled terrace.

XX **Au Clair de la Lune**   VISA ③ AE ⓪

*9 r. Poulbot (18th) – Ⓜ Abbesses – ℰ 01 42 58 97 03 – herve.kerfant@free.fr
– Fax 01 42 55 64 74 – www.auclairdelalune.fr
– Closed 17 August-15 September, Monday lunch and Sunday*   **AA1**
Rest – Menu 32 € – Carte 37/65 €
♦ Traditional ♦ Rustic ♦
Situated behind Place du Tertre, this restaurant takes its name from a French nur-
sery rhyme. Classical cuisine served in a friendly atmosphere with frescoes of old
Montmartre on the walls.

X **L'Oriental**   AC ⇔ VISA ③

*47 av. Trudaine (9th) – Ⓜ Pigalle – ℰ 01 42 64 39 80 – Fax 01 42 64 39 80
– www.loriental-restaurant.com*   **AA2**
Rest – Menu 32 € – Carte 25/40 €
♦ Moroccan ♦
An oriental but more restrained decor for this restaurant transferred from the rue
des Martyrs to avenue Trudaine. Fragrant Moroccan cuisine.

231

✗ **Miroir**   *VISA* **©©** **AE**

94 r. des Martyrs (18th) – Ⓜ *Abbesses* – ✆ *01 46 06 50 73* – *miroir.restaurant@
gmail.com*
*– Closed 2-24 August, 23-28 December, Sunday dinner, Monday and Bank
Holidays*   **AA2**
Rest – Menu 32 €
♦ Bistro ♦ Bistro ♦

A young, professional team run this modern bistro. Contemporary dining room
with glass roof, seasonal offerings on the blackboard menu and fine wine list.

✗ **La Table d'Eugène**   *VISA* **©©**
🅐

18 r. Eugène-Süe (18th) – Ⓜ *Jules Joffrin* – ✆ *01 42 55 61 64*
– Closed 2-25 August, 20-29 December, Sunday and Monday   **AA1**
Rest – *(pre-book)* Menu 32 €
♦ A la mode ♦ Minimalist ♦

This simple bistro (mouldings and pastel tones) has a regularly changing menu
with intelligent and well-presented seasonal cuisine.

OUTSIDE CENTRAL AREA   *Plan I*

🏨 **Murano**   🔧 🕭 **AC** 🔁 rm 📶 *VISA* **©©** **AE** **①**

13 bd du Temple (3rd) – Ⓜ *Filles du Calvaire* – ✆ *01 42 71 20 00* – *paris@
muranoresort.com* – *Fax 01 42 71 21 01* – *www.muranoresort.com*
49 rm – ♗440/2500 € ♗♗440/2500 €, ⌸ 26 € – 2 suites   **C2**
Rest – Carte 49/151 €
♦ Luxury ♦ Design ♦

The Murano is a trendy hotel that stands out from the crowd with its immaculate
designer decor, play of colours, high-tech equipment and pop-art bar (150 types of
vodka). The restaurant has a colourful contemporary style, fusion cuisine and a DJ
at the decks.

🏨 **St-James Paris** 🌿   🚗 🕭 🔧 **AC** 🔁 rm 📺 📶 🛁 **P** *VISA* **©©** **AE** **①**

43 av. Bugeaud (16th) ✉ *75116* – Ⓜ *Porte Dauphine* – ✆ *01 44 05 81 81*
– contact@saint-james-paris.com – *Fax 01 44 05 81 82*
– www.saint-james-paris.com   **A2**
38 rm – ♗390/660 € ♗♗510/660 €, ⌸ 32 € – 10 suites
Rest – *(closed Saturday, Sunday and public holidays)* Carte 75/200 €
♦ Grand Luxury ♦ Personalised ♦

Beautiful private townhouse built in 1892 by Mrs. Thiers, in the heart of a shady
garden. Majestic staircase, spacious rooms and a bar-library with the atmosphere
of an English club.

🏨 **Paris Bercy Pullman**   🕭 🔧 🕭 rm **AC** 🔁 rm 📺 📶 🛁

1 r. Libourne (12th) – Ⓜ *Cour St-Emilion*   *VISA* **©©** **AE** **①**
– ✆ 01 44 67 34 00 – *h2192@accor.com* – *Fax 01 44 67 34 01*
– www.pullmanhotels.com   **D3**
395 rm – ♗410/490 € ♗♗410/490 €, ⌸ 27 €
Rest Café Ké – *(closed 4-25 August, 22-29 December, Saturday and Sunday)*
Menu 36 € – Carte 49/81 €
♦ Chain hotel ♦ Functional ♦

A beautiful glass façade, contemporary interior in shades of brown, beige and blue,
and modern facilities. Some of the rooms enjoy views across Paris. The elegant
Café Ké is a pleasant option in the Bercy village. Modern cuisine; Sunday brunch.

🏨 **Pullman Rive Gauche**   ≼ 🔧 🔳 🕭 rm **AC** 🔁 rm 📺 🕾 🛁 🚗

8 r. L. Armand (15th) – Ⓜ *Balard* – ✆ *01 40 60 30 30*   *VISA* **©©** **AE** **①**
– h0572@accor.com – *Fax 01 40 60 30 00* – *www.pullman-hotels.com*
606 rm – ♗141/430 € ♗♗141/430 €, ⌸ 27 € – 12 suites   **A3**
Rest Brasserie – ✆ *01 40 60 33 77* – Menu 28 € (weekdays lunch)
– Carte 39/66 €
♦ Chain hotel ♦ Business ♦ Modern ♦

Hotel opposite the heliport which has been refurbished with the business traveller
in mind. Modern, identical, soundproofed rooms. Upper floors have a lovely view
over western Paris. Simple cuisine in the brasserie, English style bar, panoramic
breakfast room.

FRANCE - PARIS

Square   🏨 rm 🅰️ 🈁 📶 🏋️ 🚗 💳 ⓿ 🄰🄴 ⓘ

3 r. Boulainvilliers (16th) ✉️ *75016 –* Ⓜ️ *Mirabeau –* 🕿 *01 44 14 91 90*
– reservation@hotelsquare.com – Fax 01 44 14 91 99 – www.hotelsquare.com
20 rm – 🛏320 € 🛏🛏320 €, ⌑ 25 € – 2 suites   **A2**
Rest Zébra Square – 🕿 *01 44 14 91 91* – Menu 32 € – Carte 45/60 €

♦ Luxury ♦ Business ♦ Design ♦

A jewel of contemporary architecture across from the Maison de la Radio. Curves, colours, high-tech facilities and abstract paintings: a hymn to modern art! Trendy decor with striped theme in the restaurant, a cellar-library and contemporary cuisine on the menu.

Kube *without rest*   🛗 🅰️ 🔌 🈁 📞 🏋️ 🚗 💳 ⓿ 🄰🄴 ⓘ

1 passage Ruelle (18th) – Ⓜ️ *La Chapelle –* 🕿 *01 42 05 20 00 – paris@*
kubehotel.com – Fax 01 42 05 21 01 – www.kubehotel.com   **C1**
41 rm – 🛏250/275 € 🛏🛏300/325 €, ⌑ 25 €

♦ Luxury ♦ Design ♦

The 19C façade belies this hotel's 21C high-tech designer interior. The bar – built entirely from ice (-10°C) – makes for an unusual and unforgettable experience.

Holiday Inn   🌳 🛗 & rm 🅰️ 🔌 rm 🈁 📞 🏋️ 🅿️ 💳 ⓿ 🄰🄴 ⓘ

216 av. J. Jaurès (19th) – Ⓜ️ *Porte de Pantin –* 🕿 *01 44 84 18 18 – hilavillette@*
alliance-hospitality.com – Fax 01 44 84 18 20
– www.holidayinn-parisvillette.com   **D1**
182 rm – 🛏240 € 🛏🛏240 €, ⌑ 18 €
Rest – *(closed Saturday and Sunday)* Menu 28 € – Carte 31/51 €

♦ Chain hotel ♦ Business ♦ Modern ♦

Modern construction across from the Cité de la Musique. Spacious and soundproofed rooms, offering modern comfort (mahogany furniture). Meeting rooms, auditorium and gym. Designer cafeteria décor and a brasserie menu: Small verdant terrace.

Novotel Tour Eiffel   ≼ 🛗 🌀 🖥 & rm 🅰️ 🔌 rm 🈁 📞 🏋️ 🚗

61 quai de Grenelle (15th) – Ⓜ️ *Charles Michels*   💳 ⓿ 🄰🄴 ⓘ
– 🕿 *01 40 58 20 00 – h3546@accor.com – Fax 01 40 58 24 44*
– www.novotel.com   **A2**
758 rm – 🛏260/450 € 🛏🛏260/450 €, ⌑ 22 € – 6 suites
Rest Benkay – see below
Rest Tour Eiffel Café – 🕿 *01 40 58 20 75* – Menu 40/48 € bi – Carte 29/55 €

♦ Chain hotel ♦ Business ♦ Modern ♦

A hotel overlooking the Seine with comfortable modern rooms (wood, light shades), most of which have views of the river. High-tech conference centre. Pleasant, minimalist decor and modern cuisine.

Océania *without rest*   🛗 🖥 & 🅰️ 🔌 🈁 📶 🏋️ 🚗 💳 ⓿ 🄰🄴 ⓘ

52 r. Oradour sur Glane (15th) – Ⓜ️ *Porte de Versailles –* 🕿 *01 56 09 09 09*
– oceania.paris@oceaniahotels.com – Fax 01 56 09 09 19
– www.oceaniahotels.com   **A3**
232 rm – 🛏270 € 🛏🛏285 €, ⌑ 17 € – 18 suites

♦ Business ♦ Modern ♦

Modern comfort in an elegant, contemporary setting. This new hotel offers well-equipped bedrooms, a relaxation centre and an exotic terrace-garden.

Novotel Bercy   🌳 & rm 🅰️ 🔌 rm 🈁 📶 🏋️ 💳 ⓿ 🄰🄴 ⓘ

85 r. Bercy (12th) – Ⓜ️ *Bercy –* 🕿 *01 43 42 30 00 – h0935@accor.com*
– Fax 01 43 45 30 60   **D3**
151 rm – 🛏110/255 € 🛏🛏110/255 €, ⌑ 15 €   **Rest** – Carte 26/47 €

♦ Business ♦ Functional ♦

The bright rooms in this Novotel are decorated in the chain's new "Novation" style. The nearby Parc de Bercy occupies the site of an old wine depot. Dining room/veranda and popular terrace in summertime. Traditional menu.

Novotel Gare de Lyon ₭ ◰ ⅍ rm 🄰🄲 ⟷ rm 🖂 🛜 🎿 ⇌
2 r. Hector Malot (12th) – **Ⓜ** *Gare de Lyon* — 🅅🅸🅂🄰 ⓿🄾 🄰🄴 ⓿
– ℰ 01 44 67 60 00 – h1735@accor.com – Fax 01 44 67 60 60
– www.novotel.com **D2**
253 rm – 🛉155/250 € 🛉🛉155/250 €, ⌲ 16 €   **Rest** – Carte 24/45 €
◆ Functional ◆

This modern hotel overlooking a tranquil square offers comfortable, typical Novotel-style guestrooms; those on the sixth floor have a terrace. 24-hour swimming pool and well-designed children's area. Brasserie style restaurant (modern decor, benches, bay windows) and traditional fare.

Mama Shelter ₺ 🄰🄲 ⟷ rm 🖂 🛜 ⇌ 🅅🅸🅂🄰 ⓿🄾 🄰🄴
109 r. de Bagnolet (20th) – **Ⓜ** *Gambetta* – ℰ 01 43 48 48 48
– paris@mamashelter.com – Fax 01 44 54 38 66 – www.mamashelter.com
171 rm – 🛉79/169 € 🛉🛉89/179 €, ⌲ 15 € – 1 suite **D2**
Rest – Carte 30/65 €
◆ Design ◆

This new hotel, built around the concept of shelter, is designed by architect Roland Castro and decorated by Philippe Starck. The rooms are 200% designer, with waxed concrete walls, chalk graffiti on the black ceilings, mask shaped bedside lights, and iMacs. Contemporary cuisine served in several original dining rooms.

Banville *without rest* 🄰🄲 ⟷ 🖂 🛜 🅅🅸🅂🄰 ⓿🄾 🄰🄴 ⓿
166 bd Berthier (17th) – **Ⓜ** *Porte de Champerret* – ℰ 01 42 67 70 16
– info@hotelbanville.fr – Fax 01 44 40 42 77 – www.hotelbanville.fr
38 rm – 🛉215/310 € 🛉🛉215/310 €, ⌲ 20 € **B1**
◆ Luxury ◆ Personalised ◆

Tastefully restored building from 1926. Elegant lobby and lounges and particularly refined rooms with personal (Provencal) touches. Live jazz on Tuesday evenings in the piano bar.

Windsor Home *without rest* ⟷ 🛜 🅅🅸🅂🄰 ⓿🄾 🄰🄴
3 r. Vital (16th) ⊠ *75016* – **Ⓜ** *La Muette* – ℰ 01 45 04 49 49
– whparis@wanadoo.fr – Fax 01 45 04 59 50 – www.windsorhomeparis.fr
8 rm – 🛉130/170 € 🛉🛉140/180 €, ⌲ 11 € **A2**
◆ Luxury ◆ Historic ◆ Personalised ◆

This charming, hundred-year-old residence with a garden in front is decorated like a private house: old furniture, mouldings, light colours and contemporary touches.

Le 20 Prieuré Hôtel *without rest* ₺ 🄰🄲 ⟷ 🛜 🅅🅸🅂🄰 ⓿🄾
20 r. Grand Prieuré (11th) – **Ⓜ** *Oberkampf* – ℰ 01 47 00 74 14
– gprieure@yahoo.fr – Fax 01 49 23 06 64 – www.hotelgrandprieure.fr
32 rm – 🛉150/169 € 🛉🛉169 €, ⌲ 8.50 € **C2**
◆ Design ◆

This hotel has been fully refurbished in a smart, contemporary urban style. Find a white colour scheme, woodwork, designer furniture and immense photos of Paris over the bed heads.

Pré Catelan 🍽 🍴 🄰🄲 ⍨ 🄿 🅅🅸🅂🄰 ⓿🄾 🄰🄴 ⓿
🕸🕸🕸 *rte Suresnes (16th)* ⊠ *75016* – ℰ 01 44 14 41 14
– leprecatelan-restaurant@lenotre.fr – Fax 01 45 24 43 25 – www.lenotre.fr
– Closed 2-24 August, 25 October-2 November, 21 February-8 March, Sunday
and Monday **A2**
Rest – Menu 85 € (weekdays lunch), 180/240 € – Carte 195/250 € 🕸
Spec. Homard breton rôti, pois gourmands au parfum d'ail, câpres et champignons. Bar poêlé recouvert de sésame doré acidulé et caviar d'Aquitaine. Pomme soufflée croustillante et crème glacée au carambar.
◆ Innovative ◆ Luxury ◆

Based on classic recipes that pay homage to the produce, Frédéric Anton's inventive cuisine is perfectly accomplished. Elegant Napoleon III pavilion with new décor by Pierre-Yves Rochon.

XXXX ⸙ **La Grande Cascade** 🛋 ⇔ 🍽 **P** 💳 ⓸ 🅰🅴 ⓞ

allée de Longchamp (16th) ✉ *75016 – 𝒞 01 45 27 33 51 – grandecascade@ wanadoo.fr – Fax 01 42 88 99 06 – www.grandecascade.com*
Rest – Menu 79/185 € – Carte 131/200 € 🍴
Spec. Fleurs de courgette ivres de girolles. Bar de ligne nacré aux algues et beurre demi-sel. Chaud-froid d'un chocolat pure origine "Praïa".
◆ A la mode ◆ Retro ◆
A Parisian paradise at the foot of the Grande Cascade (10m!) in the Bois de Boulogne. Delicately distinctive cuisine served in the 1850 pavilion or on the splendid terrace.

XXX **Benkay** – Novotel Tour Eiffel ≼ 🅰🅲 ⅃⁄ ⇔ 🍽 💳 ⓸ 🅰🅴 ⓞ

61 quai de Grenelle (15th) – **Ⓜ** *Bir-Hakeim – 𝒞 01 40 58 21 26 – reservations@ restaurant-benkay.com – Fax 01 40 58 21 30 – www.restaurant-benkay.com*
Rest – Menu 35 € (lunch), 55/150 € – Carte 84/162 € **A2**
◆ Japanese ◆ Exotic ◆
Elegant Japanese setting on the top floor of a hotel overlooking the Seine. Teppanyaki counter (prepared on the hot plate in front of guests) and kaiseki (table service).

XXX ⸙ **Relais d'Auteuil** (Patrick Pignol) 🅰🅲 🍽 💳 ⓸ 🅰🅴 ⓞ

31 bd. Murat (16th) ✉ *75016 – **Ⓜ** Michel Ange Molitor – 𝒞 01 46 51 09 54 – pignol-p@wanadoo.fr – Fax 01 40 71 05 03*
– Closed August, Christmas holidays, Monday lunch, Saturday lunch and Sunday **A2**
Rest – Menu 60 € (lunch), 110/149 € – Carte 120/185 € 🍴
Spec. Ravioles de Saint-Jacques à la truffe (season). Ris de veau rissolé au beurre de cardamome. Madeleines cuites minute, glace miel et noix.
◆ Classic ◆ Fashionable ◆
Intimate setting in neutral tones enhancing modern paintings and sculptures. Carefully-prepared classic cuisine and an excellent wine list (magnificent selection of Burgundy wines).

XX ⸙ **Au Trou Gascon** 🅰🅲 💳 ⓸ 🅰🅴 ⓞ

40 r. Taine (12th) – **Ⓜ** *Daumesnil – 𝒞 01 43 44 34 26 – trougascon@orange.fr – Fax 01 43 07 80 55 – www.autrougascon.fr*
– Closed August, Saturday and Sunday **D2**
Rest – Menu 36 € (lunch)/50 € – Carte 53/70 € 🍴
Spec. Gambas "plancha", royale de foie gras et émulsion de châtaignes (autumn-winter). Suprême de pigeonneau flanqué de foie gras et cuisse effilochée en cannelloni potager (spring-summer). Macaron à la rose, fraises des bois andalouses et litchis (winter-spring).
◆ South-western France ◆
The decor of this old 1900 bistro combines period mouldings, designer furniture and grey hues. On the menu: Landes and Chalosse produce and seafood southwestern wines.

XX ⊚ **Meating** 🍽 💳 ⓸ 🅰🅴

122 av.de Villiers (17th) – **Ⓜ** *Pereire – 𝒞 01 43 80 10 10 – chezmichelpereire@ wanadoo.fr – Fax 01 43 80 31 42 – www.meating.abemadi.com*
– Closed Sunday and Monday **B1**
Rest – Menu 34 € – Carte 50/75 €
◆ Grills ◆ Friendly ◆
A trendy steakhouse in a chic district where the chef sources the best cuts of meat and cooks them to your exact specifications. Classic dishes also available.

XX ⊚ **Chez Géraud** 💳 ⓸

31 r. Vital (16th) ✉ *75016 – **Ⓜ** La Muette – 𝒞 01 45 20 33 00 – Fax 01 45 20 46 60*
– Closed August, 23 December-5 January, Saturday and Sunday **A2**
Rest – Menu 32 € – Carte 48/75 €
◆ Traditional ◆ Bistro ◆
The façade and the inside mural, both in Longwy earthenware tiles, are most eyecatching. Stylish bistro setting for traditional cuisine that highlights game in season.

FRANCE - PARIS

XX 😳 Mansouria · AC ✦ VISA ⊕

11 r. Faidherbe (11th) – **Ⓜ** *Faidherbe Chaligny* – 𝒞 *01 43 71 00 16*
– lollisoraya@yahoo.fr – Fax 01 40 24 21 97 – www.fatemahalreceptions.com
– Closed 10-18 August, Monday lunch, Tuesday lunch and Sunday
Rest – *(pre-book)* Menu 30/46 € bi – Carte 30/50 €   **D2**

◆ Moroccan ◆ Exotic ◆

Run by a former ethnologist, well-known in Paris in the field of Moroccan cuisine. The delicate, aromatic dishes are prepared by women and served in a Moorish decor.

XX 😳 Caroubier · AC VISA ⊕ AE

82 bd Lefebvre (15th) – **Ⓜ** *Porte de Vanves* – 𝒞 *01 40 43 16 12*
– Fax 01 40 43 16 12 – www.restaurant-lecaroubier.com
– Closed 18 July-20 August and Monday   **B3**
Rest – Menu 19 € (weekdays lunch)/30 € – Carte 31/48 €

◆ Moroccan ◆

Modern decor enhanced with touches of the oriental. A family atmosphere and warm welcome presage generous helpings of sun-gorged Moroccan cuisine.

XX 😳 A et M Restaurant · · · · · · · · · · · 🛱 AC ☂ VISA ⊕ AE ⑩

136 bd Murat (16th) ✉ *75016* – **Ⓜ** *Porte de St-Cloud* – 𝒞 *01 45 27 39 60*
– am-bistrot-16@wanadoo.fr – Fax 01 45 27 69 71
– Closed August, Saturday lunch and Sunday   **A3**
Rest – Menu 30 €

◆ A la mode ◆ Fashionable ◆

Fashionable bistro close to the Seine. Tasteful contemporary décor in shades of cream and browns, designer lighting and carefully prepared up-to-date cuisine.

X 😳 La Marée Passy · · · · · · · · · · · · · · · · AC ☂ VISA ⊕ AE

71 av P. Doumer (16th) ✉ *75016* – **Ⓜ** *La Muette* – 𝒞 *01 45 04 12 81*
– paudou@orange.fr – Fax 01 45 04 00 50   **A2**
Rest – Carte 45/60 €

◆ Seafood ◆ Friendly ◆

The warm, red toned, wood-panelled dining room decorated with navigation tools is the perfect setting for the seafood-based menu (one daily special meat dish).

X 😳 La Régalade · AC VISA ⊕

49 av. J. Moulin (14th) – **Ⓜ** *Porte d'Orléans* – 𝒞 *01 45 45 68 58 – la_regalade@ yahoo.fr – Fax 01 45 40 96 74*
– Closed 25 July-20 August, 1st-10 January, Monday lunch, Saturday and Sunday   **B3**
Rest – *(pre-book)* Menu 32 € 🍃

◆ Bistro ◆ Bistro ◆

A welcoming smile, tasty country cuisine and a simple decor are the assets of this small bistro near the Porte de Châtillon.

X 😳 Jean-Pierre Frelet · · · · · · · · · · · · · · · · · AC VISA ⊕

25 r. Montgallet (12th) – **Ⓜ** *Montgallet* – 𝒞 *01 43 43 76 65 – jean-pierre.frelet@ orange.fr*
– Closed 3-31 August, Saturday lunch and Sunday   **D2**
Rest – Menu 28 € (dinner) – Carte 42/55 €

◆ Traditional ◆

This small neighbourhood restaurant has a friendly, authentic atmosphere. Minimalist decor, tightly packed tables; generous portions of seasonal cuisine.

X 😳 Urbane · VISA ⊕

12 r. Arthur-Groussier (10th) – **Ⓜ** *Goncourt* – 𝒞 *01 42 40 74 75 – urbane.resto@ gmail.com – www.myspace.com/urbaneparis*
– Closed 2 weeks in August, Saturday lunch, Sunday and Monday
Rest – Menu 20 € (lunch)/30 €   **C2**

◆ Innovative ◆ Trendy ◆

A trendy, yet simply decorated restaurant (white walls, bistro-style furniture, imitation leather banquettes and industrial lamps). Modern dishes with an emphasis on quality ingredients.

Auberge Pyrénées Cévennes

A/C VISA MC

106 r. Folie-Méricourt (11th) – M République – ✆ 01 43 57 33 78 – Closed 30 July-20 August, Saturday lunch and Sunday **C2**

Rest – Menu 30 € – Carte 33/81 €

◆ De Terroir ◆ Inn ◆

This establishment, popular with good food lovers, has hanging hams, sausages and peppers, as well as nourishing Lyon specialities (tripe). Frank, friendly welcome and a rustic decor.

Afaria

VISA MC

15 r. Desnouettes (15th) – M Convention – ✆ 01 48 56 15 36 – Fax 01 48 56 15 36 – Closed 23-28 December, 2-24 August, Sunday and Monday lunch

Rest – Menu 26 € (weekday lunch)/45 € – Carte 34/50 € **A-B3**

◆ Innovative ◆

Find tasty, well-prepared cuisine from southwest France in this bistro inspired restaurant (striped tablecloths and large mirrors). Drinks and tapas at the bar.

Beurre Noisette

VISA MC AE

68 r. Vasco de Gama (15th) – M Lourmel – ✆ 01 48 56 82 49 – Fax 01 48 28 59 38 – Closed 1st-24 August, 1st-7 January, Sunday and Monday **A3**

Rest – Menu 30 € (weekday lunch), 32/40 €

◆ A la mode ◆

Two contemporary-style rooms decorated in warm tones serving market-inspired cuisine (dishes chalked on a blackboard). Good choice of wines by the glass.

Le Bélisaire

VISA MC

2 r. Marmontel (15th) – M Vaugirard – ✆ 01 48 28 62 24 – Fax 01 48 28 62 24 – Closed 1-8 March, 2-23 August, 24 December-3 January, Saturday lunch and Sunday **B3**

Rest – Menu 22 € (weekday lunch), 32/42 €

◆ Bistro ◆

This well-presented bistro has built up a strong reputation in the neighbourhood thanks to its excellent contemporary-style cuisine and quality service.

Bistrot Paul Bert

VISA MC

18 r. Paul Bert (11th) – M Faidherbe Chaligny – ✆ 01 43 72 24 01 – Closed August, Sunday and Monday **D2**

Rest – *(pre-book)* Menu 23/34 €

◆ Bistro ◆ Bistro ◆

In addition to an intriguing wine list, this pleasant bistro is popular for its wholesome family cooking, full of flavour and generosity.

L'Auberge Aveyronnaise

A/C VISA MC AE

40 r. Lamé (12th) – M Cour St-Emilion – ✆ 01 43 40 12 24 – lesaubergistes@hotmail.fr – Fax 01 43 40 12 15 – Closed 2-18 August **D3**

Rest – Menu 24 € (weekdays lunch)/26 €

◆ De Terroir ◆ Rustic ◆

Modern bistro-cum-brasserie, and as the name suggests, specialities from Aveyron feature prominently. Large modern rustic dining rooms and pleasant terrace.

Le Grand Pan

VISA MC

20 r. Rosenwald (15th) – M Plaisance – ✆ 01 42 50 02 50 – Fax 01 42 50 02 66 – Closed 1 week in May, 10-30 August, Christmas holidays, Saturday and Sunday **B3**

Rest – Menu 28 € (lunch)/32 €

◆ Meat specialities ◆ Bistro ◆

Old-fashioned Parisian bistro (copper-topped bar, wood tables and blackboards) decorated in warm shades of brown. Meat specialities (game in season) and soup starter.

Le Dirigeable
`VISA` `MC` `AE`

37 r. d' Alleray (15th) – **M** *Vaugirard* – *𝒞 01 45 32 01 54*
– Closed 1ˢᵗ-24 August, 24-31 December, Sunday and Monday **B3**
Rest – Menu 22 € (lunch) – Carte 30/52 €
♦ Bistro ♦ Friendly ♦

Relaxed atmosphere, unpretentious setting and small traditional dishes at attractive prices: embark now for a cruise on the Dirigeable!

Pramil
`VISA` `MC` `AE`

9 r. Vertbois (3rd) – **M** *Temple* – *𝒞 01 42 72 03 60* – *apramil@free.fr*
– Closed 5-10 May, 17-31 August, Sunday lunch and Monday **C2**
Rest – Menu 31 € – Carte 30/40 €
♦ Bistro ♦

The simplicity of the decor (white orchids, artwork) in this family bistro contrasts with the warm welcome and the generous portions of market cuisine.

Les Cailloux
`VISA` `MC`

58 r. des Cinq-Diamants (13th) – **M** *Corvisart* – *𝒞 01 45 80 15 08* – *lescailloux@sljcohen.fr* – *Fax 01 45 80 96 36* – *www.lescailloux.fr*
– Closed for one week in August and at Christmas **C3**
Rest – (booking advisable) Menu 18 € bi (weekdays lunch) – Carte 23/46 €
♦ Italian ♦ Bistro ♦

The Butte des Cailles is home to many restaurants, including this laidback Italian bistro decorated in a monochrome of browns. Good food at good prices.

L'Ourcine
`VISA` `MC`

92 r. Broca (13th) – **M** *Les Gobelins* – *𝒞 01 47 07 13 65* – *Fax 01 47 07 18 48*
– Closed Sunday and Monday   **Rest** – Menu 32 € **C3**
♦ Bistro ♦ Bistro ♦

Simple, modern decor in this restaurant with a friendly atmosphere. Inspired, seasonal cuisine chalked up on a blackboard.

Jadis
`VISA` `MC` `AE`

208 r. de la Croix Nivert (15th) – **M** *Convention* – *𝒞 01 45 57 73 20*
– delageguillaume@wanadoo.fr – *Fax 01 45 57 18 67*
– Closed 3 weeks in August, Saturday and Sunday **A3**
Rest – Menu 32 €
♦ A la mode ♦ Bistro ♦

This restaurant with a bistro feel mirrors its promising and pleasant young chef-owner. Modern menu that changes with the season.

L'Os à Moelle
`🛖` `VISA` `MC` `AE`

3 r. Vasco-de-Gama (15th) – **M** *Lourmel* – *𝒞 01 45 57 27 27* – *th.faucher@laposte.net* – *Fax 01 45 57 28 00* – *Closed 3 - 25 August, Sunday and Monday*
Rest – Menu 28 € (weekdays lunch)/35 € **A3**
♦ Bistro ♦ Bistro ♦

Paradise for good food lovers. A small room painted in sunny colours and a menu on a slate. Delicious bistro-style, market-fresh cuisine.

Bigarrade (Christophe Pelé)
`VISA` `MC` `AE`

106 r. Nollet (17th) – **M** *Brochant* – *𝒞 01 42 26 01 02* – *restobigarrade@orange.fr* – *www.bigarrade.fr* – *Closed August, Christmas holidays, Monday lunch, Saturday and Sunday* **B1**
Rest – (number of covers limited, pre-book) Menu 35 € (lunch), 45/65 €
Spec. Menu du marché.
♦ Innovative ♦

No à la carte here but simply a choice of two set "surprise" menus composed of tasting-size portions. Seductive, creative cuisine and an open-plan kitchen with views of the chef at work.

Impérial Choisy
`AC` `VISA` `MC`

32 av. de Choisy (13th) – **M** *Porte de Choisy* – *𝒞 01 45 86 42 40* – *cdm13@free.fr* – *Fax 01 45 83 93 34*   **Rest** – Carte 25/50 € **C3**
♦ Chinese ♦ Minimalist ♦

Authentic and popular Chinese restaurant, much appreciated by regulars for its delicious Cantonese specialities.

FRANCE - PARIS

✗ **Le Bistrot des Soupirs "Chez les On"**   VISA ◯◯

49 r. Chine (20th) – Ⓜ *Gambetta* – ℰ *01 44 62 93 31* – Fax *01 44 62 77 83*
– *Closed 1-8 May, 5-25 August, 25 December-1 January, Sunday and Monday*
Rest – Menu 17 € (lunch) – Carte 29/43 € ⌘   **D2**
◆ De Terroir ◆ Bistro ◆

Next to the picturesque Soupirs lane, Auvergne and Lyons specialities take pride of
place in this pleasant countrified inn. Resolutely jovial in spirit.

✗ **Le Baratin**   VISA ◯◯
🍴
3 r. Jouye-Rouve (20th) – Ⓜ *Pyrénées* – ℰ *01 43 49 39 70*   **D2**
Rest – *(pre-book)* Menu 17 € – Carte 31/40 €
◆ Bistro ◆ Wine bar ◆

Enticing dishes chalked up on the blackboard, reasonable prices, choice of fine
wines... it's easy to understand the appeal of this neighbourhood bistro.

LA DÉFENSE   *Plan I*

🏨 **Pullman La Défense**   🛎 ⅃ẞ & rm 🆎 ⇔ rm 🖴 📞 ⌁ 🚗
11 av. Arche (Défense 6 exit) ✉ *92081*   VISA ◯◯ 🆎 ①
– ℰ *01 47 17 50 00* – h3013@accor.com – Fax *01 47 17 56 78*
– *www.pullman-hotels.com*
368 rm – ♦410 € ♦♦410 €, � 27 € – 16 suites
Rest *Avant Seine* – ℰ *01 47 17 50 99 (closed 7-30 August, 19 December-
3 January, Friday dinner, Saturday, Sunday and Bank Holidays)* Carte approx. 52 €
◆ Luxury ◆ Modern ◆

Beautiful architecture, resembling a ship's hull, a combination of glass and ochre
stonework. Spacious, elegant rooms, lounges and very well-equipped auditorium
(with simultaneous translation booths). The Avant Seine offers you quality designer
décor and spit-roast dishes.

🏨 **Renaissance**   ⅃ẞ & rm 🆎 ⇔ rm 🖴 ⌁ ⌁ 🚗 VISA ◯◯ 🆎 ①
60 Jardin de Valmy (on the circular road, exit La Défense 7) ✉ *92918*
– ℰ *01 41 97 50 50* – francereservation@mariott.com – Fax *01 41 97 51 51*
– *www.renaissancehotels.com/parld*
324 rm – ♦159/490 € ♦♦159/490 €, ⊟ 25 € – 3 suites
Rest – *(closed Saturday lunch, Sunday lunch and holidays lunch)* Menu 32 €
(weekdays lunch) – Carte 51/68 €
◆ Luxury ◆ Personalised ◆

Luxurious sophistication defines this contemporary hotel at the foot of the Grande
Arche: quality materials, flawless comfort and inviting, perfectly equipped guestrooms. In the restaurant, all wood features with a 1940s brasserie atmosphere
overlooking the gardens of Valmy.

🏨 **Hilton La Défense**   & rm 🆎 ⇔ rm 🖴 📞 ⌁ VISA ◯◯ 🆎 ①
2 pl. de la Défense ✉ *92053* – ℰ *01 46 92 10 10* – parldhirm@hilton.com
– *Fax 01 46 92 10 50* – www.hilton.com
142 rm – ♦255/360 € ♦♦255/360 €, ⊟ 27 € – 6 suites
Rest *Coté Parvis* – Carte 48/81 €
◆ Luxury ◆ Modern ◆

Hotel situated within the CNIT complex. Some of the rooms have been particularly
designed with the business traveller in mind: work, rest, relaxation and Jacuzzi tubs
in the bathrooms. At Côté Parvis, modern cuisine and a fine view of the Arch of La
Défense.

🏨 **Sofitel Centre**   & 🆎 ⇔ rm 🖴 ⌁ ⌁ 🚗 VISA ◯◯ 🆎 ①
34 cours Michelet (via ring road, La Défense 4 exit) ✉ *92060 Puteaux*
– ℰ *01 47 76 44 43* – h0912@sofitel.com – Fax *01 47 76 72 10*
– *www.sofitel-paris-ladefense.com*
150 rm – ♦140/495 € ♦♦140/495 €, ⊟ 27 € – 1 suite
Rest *L'Italian Lounge* – ℰ *01 47 76 72 40* – Menu 55/98 € bi – Carte 55/89 €
◆ Luxury ◆ Design ◆

The scalloped façade of this hotel blends in among the skyscrapers of La Défense.
Spacious, well-equipped rooms, which sport a fashionable look. A contemporary
setting for Mediterranean cuisine and a fine wine list.

Novotel La Défense   ⅙ rm 🅰 ⅙ rm 🆑 🛜 🛠 🚗 💳 ⊙⊙ 🅰🅴

2 bd Neuilly (Défense 1 exit) – ℰ *01 41 45 23 23* – *h0747@accor.com*
– Fax 01 41 45 23 24 – *www.novotel.com*   **A1**
280 rm – ♦290/390 € ♦♦290/490 €, � 16 €   **Rest** – Carte 22/45 €
♦ Business ♦ Modern ♦

This hotel is at the foot of La Défense, a genuine open-air museum. Some of the renovated rooms overlook Paris. Trendy new Novotel Café-style bar. Contemporary decor in the restaurant, whose cuisine evolves with the seasons.

PARIS AIRPORTS

Orly

Hilton Orly   🛁 🛀 & 🅰 ⅙ rm 🆑 🛜 🛠 🅿 💳 ⊙⊙ 🅰🅴 ⊙

(near Orly Sud airport) ⊠ *94544* – ℰ *01 45 12 45 12* – *rm.orly@hilton.com*
– Fax 01 45 12 45 00 – *www.hilton.fr*
351 rm – ♦130 € ♦♦130 €, ⊂ 19 €   **Rest** – Carte 41/64 €
♦ Chain hotel ♦ Functional ♦

A popular choice for corporate clients, this 1960s hotel has a designer interior, discreet yet elegant bedrooms and state of the art business facilities. Modern, entirely revamped decor and a classic menu.

Mercure   & 🅰 ⅙ rm 🆑 🛠 🅿 💳 ⊙⊙ 🅰🅴 ⊙

aérogare ⊠ *94547* – ℰ *01 49 75 15 50* – *h1246-re@accor.com*
– Fax 01 49 75 15 51 – *www.mercure.com*
192 rm – ♦110/220 € ♦♦120/230 €, ⊂ 15 €   **Rest** – Carte approx. 32 €
♦ Chain hotel ♦ Functional ♦

Convenient for travellers between flights. Smiling staff, pleasant verdant setting and above all, well-kept, gradually refurbished rooms. Bar snacks and traditional dishes adapted to the timetables of travellers in transit.

Roissy-en-France

Z. I. Paris Nord II

Hyatt Regency   🛁 🛀 ⅙ & rm 🅰 ⅙ rm 🆑 🛠 🅿 💳 ⊙⊙ 🅰🅴 ⊙

351 av. Bois de la Pie – ℰ *01 48 17 12 34* – *cdg@hyattintl.com*
– Fax 01 48 17 17 17 – *www.paris.charlesdegaulle.hyatt.com*
376 rm – ♦130/560 € ♦♦130/560 €, ⊂ 27 € – 12 suites
Rest – Menu 56 € – Carte 43/62 €
♦ Business ♦ Modern ♦

Spectacular, contemporary architecture in a good location close to the airport. Large, stylish bedrooms equipped with ultra-modern facilities for its predominantly corporate guests. Enjoy buffet cuisine or classic à la carte choices in the Hyatt Regency's glass-ceilinged restaurant.

à l'aérogare n° 2

Sheraton ⊗   ⩽ 🛀 🛁 & rm 🅰 ⅙ rm 🛠 🅿 💳 ⊙⊙ 🅰🅴 ⊙

– ℰ *01 49 19 70 70* – *Fax 01 49 19 70 71* – *www.sheraton.com/parisairport*
252 rm – ♦199/599 € ♦♦199/599 €, ⊂ 30 €
Rest *Les Étoiles* – ℰ *01 41 84 64 54 (closed 25 July-30 August, Saturday, Sunday and Bank Holidays)* Menu 57 € – Carte 60/86 €
Rest *Les Saisons* – Menu 35 € (weekdays lunch) – Carte 40/55 €
♦ Chain hotel ♦ Modern ♦

Leave your plane or train and take a trip on this "luxury liner" with its futuristic architecture. Decor by Andrée Putman, a view of the runways, absolute quiet and refined rooms. Les Étoiles offers modern cuisine and beautiful contemporary setting. Brasserie dishes at Les Saisons.

L'infini pluriel

Route du Fort-de-Brégançon - 83250 La Londe-les-Maures - Tél. 33 (0)4 94 01 53 53
Fax 33 (0)4 94 01 53 54 - domaines-ott.com - ott.particuliers@domaines-ott.com

à Roissypole

Hilton ⒣ 🔲 ⓹ 🆎 ↯ rm 📺 ⓕ ⓢ ⌂ 🗺 ⓜ 🅰🅴 ⓞ
– ✆ 01 49 19 77 77 – events.parischarlesdegaulleairport@hilton.com
– Fax 01 49 19 77 78 – www.hilton.fr
385 rm – ♥239/729 € ♥♥239/729 €, ⌒ 25 €
Rest Les Aviateurs – ✆ 01 49 19 77 95 – Carte 35/85 €
◆ Business ◆ Modern ◆
Daring architecture, space and light are the main features of this hotel. Its ultra-modern facilities make it an ideal place in which to work and relax. The Aviateurs offers a small choice of brasserie dishes.

Pullman ⒣ 🔲 ⓧ ⓹ rm ↯ rm 📺 ⓕ ⓢ 🅿 🗺 ⓜ 🅰🅴 ⓞ
Zone centrale Ouest – ✆ 01 49 19 29 29 – h0577-gm@accor.com
– Fax 01 49 19 29 00 – www.pullmanhotels.com
342 rm – ♥110/550 € ♥♥110/550 €, ⌒ 27 € – 8 suites
Rest L'Escale – Menu 31/45 € – Carte 30/72 €
◆ Business ◆ Classical ◆
A personal welcome, comfortable atmosphere, conference rooms, an elegant bar and well-looked-after rooms are the advantages of this hotel between two airport terminals. A pleasant port of call dedicated to travel, this restaurant offers a menu of world flavours.

à Roissy-Ville

Courtyard by Marriott ⌂ ⒣ ⓹ 🆎 ↯ rm 📺 ⓕ ⌂ 🅿 ⌂
allée du Verger – ✆ 01 34 38 53 53   🗺 ⓜ 🅰🅴 ⓞ
– mhrs.parmc.sales.mgr@marriott.com – Fax 01 34 38 53 54
– www.marriott.com
300 rm – ♥149/550 € ♥♥149/550 €, ⌒ 22 € – 4 suites
Rest – Menu 33 € – Carte 43/70 €
◆ Business ◆ Classical ◆
Behind its colonnaded white façade, this establishment has modern facilities perfectly in tune with the requirements of businessmen transiting through Paris. Themed brasserie menu served in a large and carefully decorated dining room.

Millennium ⌂ ⒣ 🔲 ⓹ rm 🆎 ↯ rm 📺 ⓕ ⓢ ⌂ 🗺 ⓜ 🅰🅴 ⓞ
allée du Verger – ✆ 01 34 29 33 33 – sales.cdg@mill-cop.com
– Fax 01 34 29 03 05 – www.millenniumhotels.com
239 rm – ♥380 € ♥♥380/500 €, ⌒ 20 €   **Rest** – Carte 28/46 €
◆ Business ◆ Modern ◆
Bar, Irish pub, fitness centre, attractive swimming pool, conference rooms, and spacious bedrooms with one floor specially equipped for businessmen: a hotel with good facilities. International cuisine and brasserie buffet or fast food served at the bar.

Novotel Convention et Wellness ⒣ 🌐 🔲 ⓹ 🆎 ↯ rm 📺 ⓕ
allée des Vergers – ✆ 01 30 18 20 00   ⓢ ⌂ 🗺 ⓜ 🅰🅴 ⓞ
– h5418-fo@accor.com – Fax 01 34 29 95 60 – www.novotel.com
282 rm – ♥109/350 € ♥♥109/350 €, ⌒ 19 € – 7 suites
Rest – Menu 25 € (weekdays) – Carte approx. 27 €
◆ Chain hotel ◆ Modern ◆
The latest arrival in the hotel zone at Roissy offers impressive services: extensive seminar facilities, kids' corner and comprehensive wellness centre. Lenôtre brasserie dishes available twenty-four hours a day at Novotel Café and Côté Jardin.

Mercure 🚑 🏠 👌 AC ⅙ rm 🖾 📞 🛁 🅿 VISA ⊚ AE ⓪

allée des Vergers – 📞 *01 34 29 40 00 –* h1245@accor.com
– Fax 01 34 29 00 18 – www.mercure.com
203 rm – ♥79/250 € ♥♥89/260 €, ☛ 18 €   **Rest** – Carte 28/42 €
◆ Business ◆ Classical ◆

This hotel has a meticulous decor comprising Provençal style in the hall, old-fashioned zinc in the bar and spacious rooms in light wood. A contemporary menu that changes with the seasons served in the pleasant dining room or on the terrace overlooking the garden.

Population (est.2007): 468 000 (conurbation 1 449 000) Altitude: 175m

Iconos/PHOTONONSTOP

Lyons is a city that needs a second look. The first may be to its disadvantage: from the outlying autoroute, passers speeding by get a vision of the petrochemical industry. But strip away that industrial façade and look what lies within: the gastronomic epicentre of France; a wonderfully characterful old town with medieval and Renaissance buildings plus a World Heritage Site stamp of approval; and the peaceful flow of not one but two great rivers, the Rhône and the Saône.

Lyons has been a wealthy place since the Roman Empire, but it really came of age in the sixteenth century thanks to its silk industry; many of the city's finest buildings were erected by Italian silk merchants who flocked here at the time. What they left behind was the largest Renaissance quarter in France, with glorious architecture and an imposing cathedral. Much of this character could have been lost when demolition of the old town was threatened, but an enlightened twentieth century mayor instead made it safe, sanitary and a living embodiment of the past. Nowadays it's an energised city whose modern industries give it a twenty first century buzz – on the outside. But that feeling hasn't pervaded the three-hour lunch ethos of the older quarters: there are more restaurants per square metre of the old town than anywhere else on earth. Step inside a Lyonnais bouchon for a real encounter with the city…

243

LIVING THE CITY

Two great waterways, the rivers **Saône** (west) and **Rhône** (east) have their confluence in Lyons, and provide the liquid heart of the city. Modern Lyons in the shape of the shiny new Villeurbanne and La Part Dieu districts are to the east of the Rhône. The medieval sector, the old town, is west of the Saône.

Between the two rivers is a peninsula, the **Presqu'ile**, which is indeed almost an island, and appears on maps like an extended tongue. This area is renowned for its red-roofed sixteenth and seventeenth century houses. Just north of here on a hill is the old silk-weavers' district, La Croix-Rousse.

PRACTICAL INFORMATION

ARRIVAL-DEPARTURE

Lyon-Saint-Exupéry Airport is 27km east of the city centre. The Express Bus takes 45min and runs every 20min. A taxi will cost around € 45.

TRANSPORT

The transport system in the city even includes the funicular, as well as bus, tram and metro. The 'Liberty' ticket is valid for one day for travel on the network. You can also buy single tickets and a carnet of ten tickets.

The Lyons City Card is available for one, two or three days, and grants unlimited access to the transport network, plus nineteen museums (including the Roman ruins in St-Romain-en-Gal), short river trips and guided city tours. The card is available from the tourist office and major public transport offices.

Lyons boasts one of Europe's biggest 'swipe a bike' schemes: with a smart card, you help yourself to a cycle at two hundred places around town, at a flat rate for every hour in which you're pedalling.

EXPLORING LYONS

So you've worked your way into the heart of Lyons past the not-so-endearing outskirts. Standing in the Presqu'ile, you can see why France's second biggest city made its name in history. The two rivers holding you in their grip ensured this old

Roman town evolved into an essential stopover for Renaissance merchants arriving from Italy and northern Europe. Lyons became the French land and river trade capital, and four annual fairs took place here, ensnaring merchants from all over the continent. But you'll need to take one of the city's twenty-eight bridges, and cross the Saône into the old town, to discover where Lyons' ancient heart really began to beat.

→ TRIPS ALONG THE TRABOULES

Old town is made up of three villages: **St-Georges,** **St-Jean**, and **St-Paul**. The characterful streets are pressed close together displaying a winning picture of medieval and Renaissance facades, interspersed with narrow alleys, paved courtyards, Italian built towers, and dozens of restaurants to settle into and absorb the atmosphere. Many diners will be enjoying the rest after taking on another element of the old town that's unique to Lyons: the traboules, or tunnelled passageways leading to courtyards open to the sky. There are more than three hundred of these shortcuts through ancient buildings, built in the 15C to make the transport of silk easier in rainy weather. Many traboules wind their way around the Croix-Rousse district as well as the old town, but you'll get lost trying to locate these fascinating medieval tunnels unless you've got a special traboule guide from the tourist office in your hand. The longest, by the way, is at number 27 in the old town's enchanting Rue du Boeuf.

→ OLD TREASURES

If you like your landmarks to be a little bit more familiar than the traboules, then you can't do much better than the old town's two massive churches. St Jean Cathedral is an imposing Gothic structure built from the 12C to the 15C, and boasts eight hundred year old stained glass above the altar and in the rose windows. Its main glory, though, is an astronomical clock built by 14C monks to calculate thousands of moveable feast days, such as Easter. Amazingly, it'll stop its workings in 2019 when its seven-hundred-year programme runs out! Up on Fourvière hill (reached by funicular) behind the Cathedral is an even more conspicuous pile: the **Notre-Dame Basilica** of Fourvière, built in the 19C. It's a monumental church with an outlandish interior that throws together marble and mosaics in an anarchic free for all, and the outside is a bit of a wedding cake, too. Best thing about your journey up here is the superb view you get of the city ranged below, showing the sweep of the rivers and the distinguishing marks of the different quartiers. Other highlights of the old town include the remains of two ruined Roman theatres, close to the basilica, and, from the other end of the cultural compass, an entertaining Marionnette Museum, whose biggest draw is the 18C Lyonnais creations Guignol and Madelon, the famous puppets who embody the spirit of the local people.

→ ALMOST PERFECT!

The Presqu'ile is dominated by its great red-sanded square Place Bellecour: it's a vast space, with good views across the Saône to the basilica. It has some interesting streets running off it: to the south the rue Auguste Comte is an antiquarian's heaven. This is the place to come if you're looking for a French Regency sideboard, Louis XVI armchair, tapestry or early edition of Voltaire. More than one hundred antiques shops are nestled around here. Meanwhile, running parallel is Rue Victor Hugo, renowned for its stylish, contemporary boutiques. North of the Place Bellecour, a leisurely stroll takes you to possibly Lyons' most beautiful square, **Place des Terreaux**, an arresting space with magnificent fountains and a mighty hôtel de ville. It also lays claim to the **Musée des Beaux-Arts**, which just happens to be rated the best art collection in France outside the Louvre. You name it: they've got it, from Tintoretto, El Greco and Rubens, to Picasso, Matisse, Canova and Rodin. The museum also includes an eye-catching collection of medieval woodcarvings, plus an eclectic range of objets d'art and antiquities.

→ A TISSUS

A more unexpected highlight of the Presqu'ile is to be found back south of Place Bellecour: the **Musée des Tissus** is considered by many - despite the competition - to be the best in Lyons. It tells the story of silk, with luxurious 17C to 19C hangings produced in Lyons, including those from a rather impressive client list that includes Marie-Antoinette, Empress Josephine, and Catherine the Great of Russia. It's not just local silks that are on display; there are also superb examples from Baghdad, as well as carpets from Iran, Turkey and India, and beautifully artistic decorative work from almost two thousand years ago. Afterwards, you'll probably be tempted to venture up to La Croix-Rousse, the old silk-weavers' district north of Place des Terreaux. Only a few looms still operate in the neighbourhood, but if you attempt the long ascent of Montée de la Grande Côte, you'll get a fair impression of what the area was like five hundred years ago. This is a quartier of many traboules and giant street murals depicting local life. At the top of **Croix-Rousse** (you can get there by metro) is a pleasant square of cafés and swaying trees, and, maybe best of all, grand city views.

→ **FOOD AND WATER**

Although Lyons is rightly renowned for its restaurants and bouchons, you can also grab your food on the hoof with confidence. A great bet is the bustling open-air market which runs along Quai des Célestins and St Antoine, two quays by the Saône in the heart of the Presqu'ile. Saunter along here and you can pick up any amount of French delicacies, including sausages, cakes, breads, hams, chocolates, fruits and jams. After lunch à pied, a good idea is to unwind on a river jaunt. Boats set off regularly along the Saône, travel around the southern end of the peninsula, and return by the Rhône. A night cruise is the top tip, when this beautifully illuminated city bathes its best bits in sumptuous light. If it's not too late, the ideal way to end the evening is a concert at Lyons' swanky Opera House, behind the hotel de ville. Its silver stairways are set off by a totally black interior, and its concerts range all the way from opera to jazz.

CALENDAR HIGHLIGHTS

As Lyons is famous for its gastronomy, what better than being here in October to celebrate Tasting Week? Chefs and cooks demonstrate their art, while markets and festivals bring the joys of Lyonnais' produce and recipes to one and all. The city's most time-honoured event occurs in December: it's the Festival of Lights, when a lantern lit procession, inaugurated in 1852, brings even more aura to the famously lauded illuminations of Lyons. Concerts and activities all add weight to this now four-day extravaganza. Also in December is the Vieux-Lyon Ancient Music Festival (at the Chapelle de la Trinité), which is one of the major events of its kind in

LYONS IN...

→ **ONE DAY**
Old town including funicular up Fourvière hill, Musée des Beaux-Arts, dining in a bouchon

→ **TWO DAYS**
Musée des Tissus, La Croix-Rousse, evening river trip, Opera House

→ **THREE DAYS**
Traboule hunting (map in hand), antique shops in rue Auguste Comte, meal in one of Lyons' famously starred restaurants

France, and features inspiring music by the likes of Mozart, Handel and Bach. On the same theme, Les Musicades (March) is an international chamber music festival which takes place in a number of venues around Lyons, while May's Nuits Sonores Panorama of Electronic Music is pretty much self-explanatory: electronic dance music through the night in various streets and squares. Les Estivales in May continues the musical thread, with a host of free events in outdoor spaces and parks; particularly noteworthy are the shows in the courtyard of the Hotel de Ville. Theatre and music dominates the Nuits de Fourvière Festival in June, when the two Roman amphitheatres on the hill provide an atmospheric setting. Day long street parties and fireworks (also on Fourvière Hill) provide the blistering backdrop to Bastille Day festivities in July. The action's fast and furious at September's Lyons Dance Biennial, with the dance traditions of twenty world cities being celebrated at twenty-three different venues, not to mention three hundred thousand parade-goers thronging the city streets. Things slow down to a more sedate air at the Red Carpet Antiques Festival (October) when a huge red carpet is thrown down on Rue Auguste Comte and all sorts of wonderful antiques are put on display for buyers and browsers.

EATING OUT

Lyons is a great place for eating. If your budget won't run to one of the smarter breed of restaurants, then pop into a local bouchon. These are the true gastronomic heart and soul of the city, atmospheric little establishments where the cuisine revolves round the sort of thing the silkworkers ate all those years ago: tripe, pigs' trotters, calf's head. Fish lovers will instead go for quenelles (fish dumplings); typical are quenelles de brochet of blended pike in a crayfish sauce. For the most atmospheric example of the bouchon, try and get to one in the tunnel-like recess inside a medieval building in the old town. Lyons also offers restaurants serving dishes from every region in France, as well as most places you can think of overseas. It's a city that loves its wine: it's said that Lyons is kept afloat on three rivers: the Saône, the Rhône, and the Beaujolais…Hours of repast in the city begin at 12.30 for lunch (and can continue for many an hour afterwards) and 7.30 in the evenings. With the reputation the city has for its restaurants, it's advisable to book ahead. The bill will include a service charge, but if you've been particularly happy with the service, then a tip of five to ten per cent is normal.

→ SPYING AS YOU'RE FRYING

On sunny summer days, the Lyonnais find their green relaxation in the Parc de la Tête d'Or, on the modern side of town east of the Rhône. Here there are ponds, botanical gardens, rose gardens and a small zoo. One curious interloper you can't miss: the spindly antennae overlooking the park that happens to be part of the international HQ of Interpol…

→ CORKING GOOD LUNCH

'Bouchon' is translated as 'cork'. The theory is that the buzzy local food hotspots acquired their name in the old days when corks from empty bottles were lined up along the bar and the waiter counted them to work out the bill. Earthy locals pour scorn on Parisians, who they believe have abandoned the concept of lunch. In Lyons, regulars at the bouchon embrace the three-hour midday meal with passion and flair.

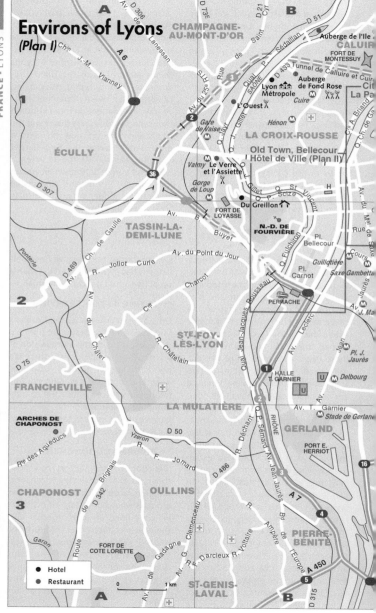

Environs of Lyons
(Plan I)

CHAMPAGNE-AU-MONT-D'OR

Auberge de l'Île

CALUIRE

FORT DE MONTESSUY

Tunnel de Calluire et Cuir

Lyon 🏨🏨 Métropole

Auberge de Fond Rose 🍴🍴🍴

Cuire

L'Ouest 🍴

Hénon

LA CROIX-ROUSSE

Old Town, Bellecour, Hôtel de Ville (Plan II)

ÉCULLY

Gare de Vaise

Valmy ● Le Verre et l'Assiette

Gorge de Loup

Du Greillon 🏨↑

FORT DE LOYASSE

N.-D. DE FOURVIÈRE

Pl. Bellecour

TASSIN-LA-DEMI-LUNE

Buyer

Av. du Point du Jour

Charcot

Pl. Carnot

Guillotière

Saxe Gambetta

PERRACHE

STE-FOY-LES-LYON

R. Châtelain

HALLE T. GARNIER

Pl. J. Jaurès

Delbourg

FRANCHEVILLE

LA MULATIÈRE

Av. T. Garnier

Stade de Gerlan

ARCHES DE CHAPONOST

Rte des Aqueducs

D 50

GERLAND

PORT E. HERRIOT

CHAPONOST

OULLINS

FORT DE COTE LORETTE

PIERRE-BÉNITE

A 450

● Hotel

● Restaurant

0   1 km

ST-GENIS-LAVAL

D 315

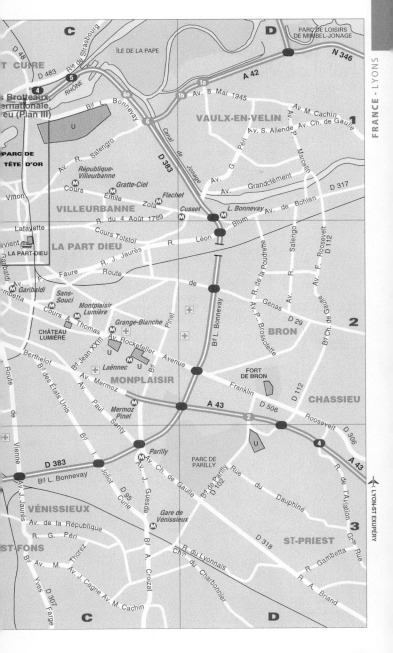

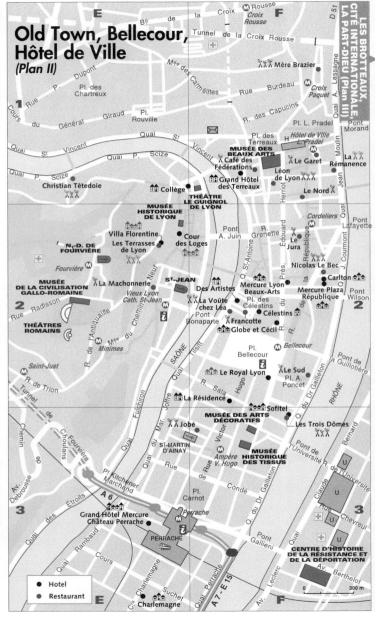

Old Town, Bellecour, Hôtel de Ville
(Plan II)

- Hotel
- Restaurant

Sofitel
≤ & rm 📺 ⅍ rm 📺 ⁕ 🖧 🚗 VISA ⓸ AE ⓪
20 quai Gailleton ⊠ 69002 – Ⓜ *Bellecour* – 𝒞 04 72 41 20 20 – h0553@
accor.com – Fax 04 72 40 05 50 – www.sofitel.com **F3**
164 rm – ▮230/380 € ▮▮230/380 €, � 27 € – 26 suites
Rest Les Trois Dômes – see below
Rest *Sofishop* – 𝒞 04 72 41 20 80 – Menu 28 € bi – Carte 37/51 €
 ♦ Luxury ♦ Modern ♦
The cuboid exterior contrasts with the luxurious interior: contemporary rooms in good taste, modern conference facilities, smart shops and a hair-dressing salon. Brasserie atmosphere and fare at the Sofishop (oyster bar).

Le Royal Lyon without rest
📺 ⅍ 📺 ⁕ VISA ⓸ AE ⓪
20 pl. Bellecour ⊠ 69002 – Ⓜ *Bellecour* – 𝒞 04 78 37 57 31 – H2952@
accor.com – Fax 04 78 37 01 36 – www.lyonhotel-leroyal.com **F2**
74 rm – ▮150/450 € ▮▮150/450 €, ⊇ 22 € – 10 suites
 ♦ Traditional ♦ Personalised ♦
After renovation, this 19C hotel run by the Paul Bocuse Institute, has regained its former splendour. Magnificent rooms. The breakfast room is decorated in the manner of a kitchen.

Carlton without rest
📺 ⅍ 📺 ⁕ VISA ⓸ AE ⓪
4 r. Jussieu ⊠ 69002 – Ⓜ *Cordeliers* – 𝒞 04 78 42 56 51 – h2950@accor.com
– Fax 04 78 42 10 71 – www.mercure.com **F2**
83 rm – ▮89/159 € ▮▮99/219 €, ⊇ 17 €
 ♦ Traditional ♦ Classical ♦
Purple and gold prevail in this traditional hotel, decorated in the manner of an old-fashioned luxury hotel. The period lift cage has a charm of its own. Comfortable rooms.

Globe et Cécil without rest
📺 ⅍ 📺 ⁕ 🖧 VISA ⓸ AE ⓪
21 r. Gasparin ⊠ 69002 – Ⓜ *Bellecour* – 𝒞 04 78 42 58 95 – accueil@
globeetcecilhotel.com – Fax 04 72 41 99 06 – www.globeetcecilhotel.com
60 rm ⊇ – ▮135/140 € ▮▮150/170 € **F2**
 ♦ Traditional ♦ Personalised ♦
One of the last silk-merchants of the town decorated the conference room of this hotel. Antique and modern furniture adorns the tastefully decorated rooms. Irresistible welcome.

Mercure Lyon Beaux-Arts without rest
📺 ⅍ 📺 ⁕ 🖧
75 r. Prés. E. Herriot ⊠ 69002 – Ⓜ *Cordeliers*
– 𝒞 04 78 38 09 50 – h2949@accor.com – Fax 04 78 42 19 19 VISA ⓸ AE ⓪
– www.mercure.com **F2**
75 rm – ▮94/219 € ▮▮104/229 €, ⊇ 16 € – 4 suites
 ♦ Chain hotel ♦ Modern ♦
Beautiful building from 1900, most of the bedrooms are furnished in Art Deco style. Four are more unusual and are decorated by contemporary artists.

Mercure Plaza République without rest
& 📺 ⅍ 📺 ⁕ 🖧
5 r. Stella ⊠ 69002 – Ⓜ *Cordeliers* – 𝒞 04 78 37 50 50
– h2951@accor.com – Fax 04 78 42 33 34 – www.mercure.com VISA ⓸ AE ⓪
78 rm – ▮99/209 € ▮▮109/219 €, ⊇ 17 € **F2**
 ♦ Business ♦ Modern ♦
19C architecture, central location, modern interior, full range of comforts and conference facilities: a hotel especially popular with its business clientele.

Grand Hôtel des Terreaux without rest
📺 ⅍ 📺 ⁕
16 r. Lanterne ⊠ 69001 – Ⓜ *Hôtel de ville* VISA ⓸ AE ⓪
– 𝒞 04 78 27 04 10 – ght@hotel-lyon.fr – Fax 04 78 27 97 75 – www.hotel-lyon.fr
53 rm – ▮85/90 € ▮▮115/157 €, ⊇ 12 € **F1**
 ♦ Traditional ♦ Personalised ♦
Personalised, tastefully decorated rooms, a pretty indoor pool and attentive service ensure that guests can relax to the full in this former 19C post house.

FRANCE - LYONS

Des Artistes without rest
AC "¹" VISA ©© AE ①

*8 r. G. André ⊠ 69002 – **Ⓜ** Cordeliers – ℰ 04 78 42 04 88 – reservation@*
hotel-des-artistes.fr – Fax 04 78 42 93 76 – www.hoteldesartistes.fr
45 rm – †85/100 € ††105/140 €, � 10 €   **F2**
♦ Traditional ♦ Personalised ♦

The hotel is named after the "artistes" of the neighbouring Célestins theatre. Stylish rooms; a Cocteau style fresco adorns the breakfast room.

La Résidence without rest
AC SAT "¹" VISA ©© AE ①

*18 r. V. Hugo ⊠ 69002 – **Ⓜ** Bellecour – ℰ 04 78 42 63 28 – hotel-la-residence@*
wanadoo.fr – Fax 04 78 42 85 76 – www.hotel-la-residence.com   **F2**
67 rm – †81 € ††81 €, ⊑ 7 €
♦ Business ♦ Functional ♦

In a pedestrian street near Bellecour square, this hotel provides rooms and a lounge in a 1970s style. A few rooms are more elegant and graced with wainscoting.

Célestins without rest
AC SAT "¹" VISA ©©

*4 r. Archers ⊠ 69002 – **Ⓜ** Guillotière – ℰ 04 72 56 08 98 – info@*
hotelcelestins.com – Fax 04 72 56 08 65 – www.hotelcelestins.com
25 rm – †69/110 € ††75/120 €, ⊑ 8.50 €   **F2**
♦ Traditional ♦ Cosy ♦

Hotel occupying several floors in a residential building. Light rooms with simple furnishings; those at the front have a view over the Fourvière hillside.

Nicolas Le Bec
⅄ AC ⊑ VISA ©© AE

*14 r. Grolée ⊠ 69002 – **Ⓜ** Cordeliers – ℰ 04 78 42 15 00 – restaurant@*
nicolaslebec.com – Fax 04 72 40 98 97 – www.nicolaslebec.com
– Closed 3-24 August, Sunday, Monday and Bank Holidays   **F2**
Rest – Menu 68 € (weekdays lunch), 118/158 € – Carte 90/130 € ⅛
Spec. Côtes de romaine et Saint-Jacques dorées (season). Pigeonneau cuit en croûte de moutarde. Tarte au caramel mou et pralines blanches.
♦ A la mode ♦ Design ♦

The more muted and intimate taupe and black decor of this restaurant is eminently suited to the cuisine, which is based on inventive products that are both subtle and delicate. Fine wine list.

Mère Brazier (Mathieu Viannay)
AC ⇆ VISA ©© AE

*12 r. Royale ⊠ 69001 – **Ⓜ** Hôtel de Ville – ℰ 04 78 23 17 20 – merebrazier@*
orange.fr – Fax 04 78 23 37 18 – www.lamerebrazier.fr
– Closed 1-23 August, 20-28 February, Saturday and Sunday   **F1**
Rest – Menu 35 € (weekdays lunch), 55/95 € – Carte 86/124 €
Spec. Pâté en croûte au foie gras. Volaille de Bresse et homard sauce suprême, jus de carapace. Paris-Brest et glace aux noisettes caramélisées.
♦ A la mode ♦ Elegant ♦

This iconic Lyonnais establishment has been taken over by a Master Craftsman of France. It has undergone a subtle refurbishment and the charming old-fashioned decor has returned. Culinary harmony combining classical and contemporary elements.

Les Trois Dômes – Hôtel Sofitel
≤ AC ⊑ **P** VISA ©© AE ①

*20 quai Gailleton ⊠ 69002 – **Ⓜ** Bellecour – ℰ 04 72 41 20 97 – reservation@*
les-3-domes.com – Fax 04 72 40 05 50 – www.les-3-domes.com
– Closed 1 July-30 September, 15-23 February, Sunday and Monday
Rest – Menu 56 € (weekdays lunch), 79/129 €   **F3**
– Carte 112/135 € ⅛
Spec. Millefeuille de crabe et avocat, huile parfumée au gingembre rose et citron jaune. Volaille de Bresse au citron et tomates séchées, courgette fleur et gnocchis au parmesan. Trois grands crus de chocolats.
♦ A la mode ♦ Formal ♦

Admire the matchless panorama from the top floor of the Sofitel hotel, where you can also enjoy delicious cuisine in keeping with current tastes. Flawless wine list.

XXX   **Léon de Lyon**   🏡 AC ⚡ ⇄ ⟳ VISA ©© AE

😊

1 r. Pleney (corner of r. du Plâtre) ✉ *69001 –* Ⓜ *Hôtel de ville*
– ℰ 04 72 10 11 12 – reservation@leondelyon.com – Fax 04 72 10 11 13
– www.leondelyon.com   **F1**
Rest – Menu 25/32 € – Carte 32/48 € ❀

     ◆ Brasserie ◆ Formal ◆

This institution in Lyons, treated to a lavish brasserie decor, has lost nothing of its
friendly, plush appeal. Excellent choice of produce that does full justice to local
gourmet specialities and delicacies.

XX   **La Rémanence**   VISA ©© AE ①

31 r. du Bât-d'Argent ✉ *69001 –* Ⓜ *Hôtel de Ville – ℰ 04 72 00 08 08*
– contact@laremanence.fr – Fax 04 78 39 85 10 – www.laremanence.fr
– Closed 2-24 August, Sunday and Monday   **F1**
Rest – Menu 27 € (weekdays lunch), 35/69 € – Carte 45/68 €

     ◆ Innovative ◆

Near the town hall, the golden stone vaulted rooms of this restaurant were once
the Jesuit refectory. Inventive cuisine rustled up by a talented young chef.

XX   **La Voûte - Chez Léa**   AC VISA ©© AE

11 pl. A. Gourju ✉ *69002 –* Ⓜ *Bellecour – ℰ 04 78 42 01 33*
– Fax 04 78 37 36 41 – Closed Sunday   **F2**
Rest – Menu 19 € (weekdays lunch), 30/40 € – Carte 30/56 €

     ◆ Traditional ◆ Friendly ◆

One of the oldest restaurants in Lyons, it continues to brilliantly uphold the region's
gastronomic traditions. Welcoming ambiance and decor. Game menu in autumn.

X   **Le Nord**   AC VISA ©© AE

18 r. Neuve ✉ *69002 –* Ⓜ *Hôtel de ville – ℰ 04 72 10 69 69 – commercial@*
brasseries-bocuse.com – Fax 04 72 10 69 68 – www.bocuse.fr   **F1**
Rest – Menu 23 € (weekdays)/33 € – Carte 26/50 €

     ◆ Brasserie ◆ Brasserie ◆

Authentic 1900s decor in the first of Bocuse's brasseries: banquettes, colourful tiled
floor, wood panelling and spherical lamps. Traditional cuisine.

X   **Le Sud**   🏡 AC VISA ©© AE

11 pl. Antonin-Poncet ✉ *69002 –* Ⓜ *Bellecour – ℰ 04 72 77 80 00*
– commercial@brasseries-bocuse.com – Fax 04 72 77 80 01 – www.bocuse.fr
Rest – Menu 23 € (weekdays)/28 € – Carte 33/45 €   **F2**

     ◆ Brasserie ◆ Brasserie ◆

"Le Sud" is another of chef Paul Bocuse's creations, with Mediterranean cuisine and
decor. Delightful summer terrace overlooking the square.

X   **Francotte**   AC VISA ©©

8 pl. Célestins ✉ *69002 –* Ⓜ *Bellecour – ℰ 04 78 37 38 64 – p.quarre@*
orange.fr – Fax 04 78 38 20 35 – www.francotte.fr
– Closed 1-17 August, Sunday and Monday   **F2**
Rest – Menu 24/32 € – Carte 33/50 €

     ◆ Traditional ◆ Neighbourhood ◆

Brasserie-style cuisine in a bistro/bouchon-inspired setting adorned with photos of
matriarchs and famous chefs from the region. Breakfasts served in the morning;
tea room in the afternoon.

BOUCHONS

X   **Daniel et Denise**   AC VISA ©© AE

😊

156 r. Créqui ✉ *69003 –* Ⓜ *Place Guichard – ℰ 04 78 60 66 53 – jviola@*
hotmail.fr – Fax 04 78 60 66 53 – www.daniel-et-denise.fr
– Closed 24 July-25 August, Saturday, Sunday and Bank Holidays
Rest – Carte 32/40 €   *Plan III* **G3**

     ◆ Lyons cuisine ◆ Bistro ◆

Attractive well-worn setting and a relaxed informal atmosphere in this welcoming
bistro, that serves traditionally prepared tasty Lyons specialities.

TOWN CENTER

✗ **Le Garet** ⬛ AC ⬛ VISA ⬤ ⬛ AE

7 r. Garet ✉ 69001 – Ⓜ Hôtel de ville – ✆ 04 78 28 16 94 – legaret@
wanadoo.fr – Fax 04 72 00 06 84
– Closed 24 July-24 August, 22 February-1 March, Saturday and Sunday
Rest – (pre-book) Menu 18 € (weekdays lunch)/23 € **F1**
– Carte 20/36 €
♦ Traditional ♦ Bistro ♦
This institution in Lyons is well-known to lovers of good cooking: calf's head, tripe,
quenelles and andouillettes served in a relaxed characteristic setting.

✗ **Café des Fédérations** ⬛ AC ⬛ VISA ⬤

8 r. Major Martin ✉ 69001 – Ⓜ Hôtel de ville – ✆ 04 78 28 26 00
– yr@lesfedeslyon.com – Fax 04 72 07 74 52 – www.lesfedeslyon.com
– Closed 24 December-4 January and Sunday **F1**
Rest – (pre-book) Menu 20 € (lunch)/25 €
♦ Lyons cuisine ♦ Bistro ♦
Checked tablecloths, tightly packed tables, giant sausages hanging from the cei-
ling and a relaxed informal atmosphere: a genuine "bouchon" for sure!

✗ **Le Jura** ⬛ AC ⬛ VISA ⬤

25 r. Tupin ✉ 69002 – Ⓜ Cordeliers – ✆ 04 78 42 20 57
– http://lejura.cartesurtables.com
– Closed August, Monday from September to April, Saturday from May to
September and Sunday **F2**
Rest – (pre-book) Menu 25 € – Carte 26/39 €
♦ Lyons cuisine ♦ Bistro ♦
This authentic "bouchon", in existence since 1864, has scrupulously preserved a
stylish 1930s decor. Traditional tasty dishes of Lyons.

OLD TOWN *Plan II*

🏨 **Villa Florentine** ❧ ⬤ ⬛ 🛁 🏊 ⬛ AC ⬛ 📶 ⬛ P ⬛ VISA ⬤ AE ⓪

25 montée St-Barthélémy ✉ 69005 – Ⓜ Fourvière – ✆ 04 72 56 56 56
– florentine@relaischateaux.com – Fax 04 72 40 90 56 – www.villaflorentine.com
24 rm – ♦230/470 € ♦♦230/470 €, ⬝ 25 € – 4 suites **E2**
Rest Les Terrasses de Lyon – see below
♦ Luxury ♦ Personalised ♦
On the Fourvière hill, this Renaissance-inspired abode commands a matchless
view of the town. The interior sports an elegant blend of old and new.

🏨 **Cour des Loges** ❧ ⬛ 🛁 AC ⬛ 📺 ⬛ 📶 ⬛ VISA ⬤ AE ⓪

6 r. Boeuf ✉ 69005 – Ⓜ Vieux Lyon Cathédrale Saint-Jean
– ✆ 04 72 77 44 44 – contact@courdesloges.com – Fax 04 72 40 93 61
– www.courdesloges.com **E2**
57 rm – ♦247/525 € ♦♦247/525 €, ⬝ 27 € – 4 suites
Rest Les Loges – (closed July, August, Sunday and Monday) (dinner only)
Menu 58/85 € – Carte 70/89 €
♦ Luxury ♦ Personalised ♦
An exceptional group of 14C-18C houses set around a splendid galleried courtyard
has been decorated by contemporary designers and artists. Creative cuisine and
decor with a personal touch.

🏨 **Collège** without rest ⬛ AC ⬛ 📺 ⬛ 📶 ⬛ VISA ⬤ AE

5 pl. St Paul ✉ 69005 – Ⓜ Vieux Lyon Cathédrale St -Jean
– ✆ 04 72 10 05 05 – contact@college-hotel.com – Fax 04 78 27 98 84
– www.college-hotel.com **E1**
39 rm – ♦115 € ♦♦115/145 €, ⬝ 12 €
♦ Business ♦ Minimalist ♦
Take a trip down memory lane: old-fashioned school desks, a pommel horse and
geography maps. The rooms are white, resolutely modern, with a balcony or
terrace.

XXX ⌖ **Les Terrasses de Lyon** – Hôtel Villa Florentine   ≤ 🚗 ⛲ 🗚 ⌁
25 montée St-Barthélémy ⌂ 69005 – Ⓜ *Fourvière*   **P.** 🚗 🅥🅘🅢🅐 ⓒ🅢 🅐🅔 ⓞ
– 𝒞 04 72 56 56 02 – lesterrassesdelyon@villaflorentine.com
– Fax 04 72 56 56 04 – www.villaflorentine.com
– Closed Sunday and Monday
Rest – Menu 48 € (weekdays lunch)/104 € – Carte 100/144 €   **E2**
Spec. Foie gras de canard façon "Melba". Filet mignon de veau rôti au lard fermier. Chocolat manjari à la fève de Tonka.
   ◆ A la mode ◆ Formal ◆
Breathtaking view of Lyons from the terrace. The interior and conservatory are stylish and the modern cuisine subtly enhances excellent produce.

XXX ⌖ **Christian Têtedoie**   🗚 🅥🅘🅢🅐 ⓒ🅢 🅐🅔
54 quai Pierre Scize ⌂ 69005 – 𝒞 04 78 29 40 10 – restaurant@tetedoie.com
– Fax 04 72 07 05 65 – www.tetedoie.com
– Closed Saturday lunch, Monday lunch and Sunday   **E1**
Rest – Menu 50/82 € – Carte 60/75 € 🕭
Spec. Quenelle de brochet farcie aux écrevisses. Homard et tête de veau confite au jus de carotte. Sablé breton en duo de framboise et poivron doux (March-November).
   ◆ Classic ◆ Formal ◆
This carefully decorated, elegant establishment (flowers, objects, paintings) is on the banks of the Saône. Modern cuisine complemented by a wine list of over 700 appellations.

X **La Machonnerie**   🗚 🅥🅘🅢🅐 ⓒ🅢 🅐🅔
36 r. Tramassac ⌂ 69005 – Ⓜ *Ampère Victor Hugo*
– 𝒞 04 78 42 24 62 – felix@lamachonnerie.com – Fax 04 72 40 23 32
– www.lamachonnerie.com
– Closed 15-30 July, 2 weeks in January, Sunday and lunch except Saturday
Rest – (dinner only) (pre-book) Menu 20 € (weekdays)/45 € bi   **E2**
– Carte 30/45 €
   ◆ Lyons cuisine ◆ Rustic ◆
The traditions of informal service, a friendly atmosphere and authentic regional cuisine are perpetuated in this typical neighbourhood *mâchon*. Attractive lounge devoted to jazz.

PERRACHE   *Plan II*

🏨 **Grand Hôtel Mercure Château Perrache**   🗚 ↩ rm 📺 ⁽¹⁾ 🕭
12 cours Verdun ⌂ 69002 – Ⓜ *Perrache*   **P.** 🚗 🅥🅘🅢🅐 ⓒ🅢 🅐🅔 ⓞ
– 𝒞 04 72 77 15 00 – h1292@accor.com – Fax 04 78 37 06 56
– www.mercure.com   **E3**
111 rm – ♦95/180 € ♦♦125/200 €, ⌂ 17 € – 2 suites
Rest Les Belles Saisons – (closed 25 July-25 August, weekends and public holidays) Carte 20/38 €
   ◆ Traditional ◆ Art Deco ◆
This hotel built in 1900 has partially conserved its Art Nouveau setting: intricate wood carving in the lobby and period furniture in some of the rooms and suites. The full effect of the Majorelle style is reflected in this superb restaurant.

🏨 **Charlemagne**   ⛲ 🗚 ↩ rm 📺 ⁽¹⁾ 🕭 **P** 🅥🅘🅢🅐 ⓒ🅢 🅐🅔 ⓞ
23 cours Charlemagne ⌂ 69002 – Ⓜ *Perrache – 𝒞 04 72 77 70 00*
– charlemagne@hotel-lyon.fr – Fax 04 78 42 94 84 – www.charlemagne-hotel.fr
116 rm – ♦80/125 € ♦♦85/135 €, ⌂ 10 €   **E3**
Rest – (closed Saturday and Sunday) Menu 19 € bi (weekdays)/50 € bi – Carte approx. 30 €
   ◆ Business ◆ Modern ◆
Two buildings home to renovated, comfortable and tastefully appointed rooms; a business centre; winter-garden style breakfast room. Modern restaurant with a pleasant terrace in summer and unpretentious, standard fare.

LES BROTTEAUX - CITÉ INTERNATIONALE - LA PART-DIEU

Plan III

Hilton 🛜 £₺ & rm 🔟 ↳ rm 🖭 ⁹⁄⁰ 🏖 🛜 VISA ◑◑ AE ⓪

70 quai Ch.-de-Gaulle ✉ *69006 –* ✆ *04 78 17 50 50*
– reservations.lyon@hilton.com – Fax 04 78 17 52 52
– www.hilton.com   **H1**
199 rm – ♦100/435 € ♦♦100/435 €, ⌂ 24 €
Rest *Blue Elephant* – ✆ *04 78 17 50 00 (closed 21 July-18 August, Saturday
lunch and Sunday)* Menu 28 €, 43/55 € – Carte 59/66 €
Rest *Brasserie* – ✆ *04 78 17 51 00* – Menu 24/42 € – Carte 40/60 €
♦ Chain hotel ♦ Modern ♦

This impressive modern hotel built in brick and glass is equipped with a comprehensive business centre. Fully equipped bedrooms and apartments facing the Tête
d'Or park and the Rhône. Thai specialities and decor at the Blue Elephant. Traditional
food is to be found at the Brasserie.

Radisson SAS 🌦   ⇐ & 🔟 ↳ rm 🖭 ⁹⁄⁰ 🏖 🛜 VISA ◑◑ AE ⓪

129 r. Servient ✉ *69003 –* Ⓜ *Part Dieu –* ✆ *04 78 63 55 00*
– info.lyon@radissonsas.com – Fax 04 78 63 55 20
– www.lyon.radissonsas.com   **H3**
245 rm – ♦125/285 € ♦♦125/285 €, ⌂ 21 €
Rest *L'Arc-en-Ciel* – *(closed 15 July-27 August, Saturday lunch and Sunday)*
Menu 44/89 € – Carte 79/120 € ✿
Rest *Bistrot de la Tour* – *(closed Saturday and Sunday) (lunch only)*
Menu 16 € bi/20 €
♦ Business ♦ Functional ♦

At the top of the "pencil" (100m high), interior layout inspired by the houses of old
Lyons: interior courtyards and superimposed galleries. Exceptional view from some
rooms. The Arc-en-Ciel is on the 32nd floor of the tower. Packed at lunchtime.

De la Cité   🛜 & 🔟 ↳ rm ⁹⁄⁰ 🏖 🛜 VISA ◑◑ AE ⓪

22 quai Ch.-de-Gaulle ✉ *69006 –* ✆ *04 78 17 86 86*
– hoteldelacite@concorde-hotels.com – Fax 04 78 17 86 99
– www.lyon.concorde-hotels.com   **H1**
164 rm – ♦95/280 € ♦♦95/345 €, ⌂ 20 € – 5 suites
Rest – *(closed 1-16 August)* Menu 29 € (weekdays lunch) – Carte 27/43 €
♦ Chain hotel ♦ Modern ♦

This modern building designed by Renzo Piano stands between the Tête d'Or park
and the Rhône. Bright rooms decorated in a contemporary vein. Traditional meals
(buffet lunch). Terrace overlooking the patio of the Cité Internationale. Cocktail bar.

Novotel La Part-Dieu   & rm 🔟 ↳ rm 🖭 ⁹⁄⁰ 🏖 VISA ◑◑ AE ⓪

47 bd Vivier-Merle ✉ *69003 –* Ⓜ *Part Dieu –* ✆ *04 72 13 51 51 – h0735@
accor.com – Fax 04 72 13 51 99 – www.novotel.com*   **H3**
124 rm – ♦120/165 € ♦♦120/165 €, ⌂ 15 €
Rest – Menu 25 € (weekdays) – Carte 24/48 €
♦ Business ♦ Functional ♦

Two minutes from the railway station. The rooms are being progressively revamped in line with latest Novotel standards. Lounge-bar with an Internet area. This
Novotel restaurant is practical for business travellers with a train to catch or between meetings.

Créqui Part-Dieu   & rm 🔟 ↳ rm 🖭 ⁹⁄⁰ 🏖 VISA ◑◑ AE ⓪

37 r. Bonnel ✉ *69003 –* Ⓜ *Place Guichard –* ✆ *04 78 60 20 47 – directeur@
hotel-crequi.com – Fax 04 78 62 21 12 – www.bestwestern-lyonpartdieu.com*
46 rm – ♦73/165 € ♦♦73/175 €, ⌂ 13 € – 3 suites   **G3**
Rest – *(closed August, Saturday and Sunday)* Menu 18/30 € – Carte 26/41 €
♦ Business ♦ Functional ♦

The establishment is located opposite the law courts district. The renovated rooms
are decorated in warm tones; those in the new wing are particularly modern in
style.

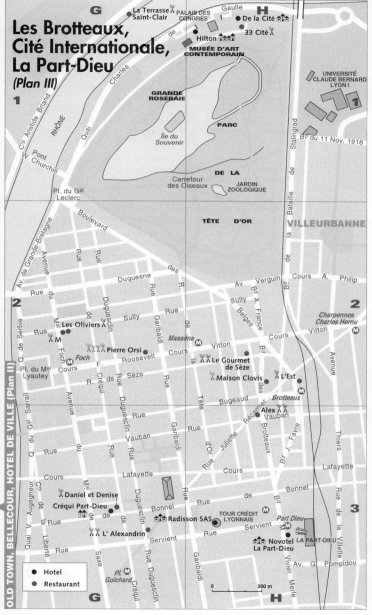

Les Brotteaux,
Cité Internationale,
La Part-Dieu
(Plan III)

La Terrasse 🍴 Saint-Clair — de Gaulle — PALAIS DES CONGRÈS — De la Cité 🏨

Hilton 🏨 — 33 Cité 🍴

MUSÉE D'ART CONTEMPORAIN

RHÔNE

Cⁱᵉ Aristide Briand

Pont W. Churchill

Quai — Charles

GRANDE ROSERAIE

Île du Souvenir

PARC

Pl. du Gᵃˡ Leclerc

Carrefour des Oiseaux

DE LA

JARDIN ZOOLOGIQUE

UNIVERSITÉ CLAUDE BERNARD LYON I

Bᵈ du 11 Nov. 1918

de Stalingrad

TÊTE D'OR

VILLEURBANNE

de la Bataille

Boulevard

Av. de Grande-Bretagne

Rue — Avenue

Rue — du

Duquesne

Rue — des

R.

Av. Verguin — Cours A. Philip

Charpennes Charles Hernu

Rue — Sully

Rue — Sully — Belges

Vitton

Les Oliviers 🍴 M

O. de Serbie

Rue

Mᵃˡ Foch

Duguesclin

Garibaldi

Masséna M

Bᵈ A. France

Cours — Vitton

Cours

Avenue

Pierre Orsi 🍴🍴🍴 ●

M Foch

Pl. du Mᵃˡ Lyautey

Cours — F. Roosevelt

R. Créqui — de — Sèze

Rue

Le Gourmet de Sèze 🍴🍴

Maison Clovis 🍴

🍴 L'Est M

Gᵃˡ Sarrail

Avenue — du

Rue — Rue — Duguesclin

Rue — Sèze

Garibaldi

Tête — Bugeaud

Rue — d'Or — Juliette — Récamier

Brotteaux

Alex 🍴🍴 Vauban

Q. — du — Gᵃˡ

Rue

Avenue — du

Rue — Duguesclin

Rue

Vauban

Rue

Brotteaux

Bᵈ J. Favre

Thiers

Cours — Lafayette

Rue — Mᵃˡ — Duguesclin

Lafayette

Cours — de

Bonnel

Rue — de — la — Villette

Lafayette

🍴 Daniel et Denise

Créqui Part-Dieu 🏨 ●

Rue — de — de

Bonnel

Rue — de

TOUR CRÉDIT LYONNAIS M

Part Dieu M

LA PART-DIEU

Quai — V. Augagneur

Crˢ — de — la — Liberté

🍴🍴 L' Alexandrin

Radisson SAS 🏨

Servient

Rue

Novotel 🏨 La Part-Dieu

PART-DIEU M

Rue — Saxe

Pl. M Guichard

Créqui

Rue — Duguesclin

Garibaldi

Servient

Rue — Vivier — Merle

Av. Gˡ Pompidou

0 — 300 m

● Hotel
● Restaurant

G — H

OLD TOWN, BELLECOUR, HOTEL DE VILLE (Plan II)

Pierre Orsi 🏮 & 🅰🅲 🛋 𝗩𝗜𝗦𝗔 ⓒⓞ 🅰🅴

3 pl. Kléber ⊠ 69006 – Ⓜ Masséna – ℰ 04 78 89 57 68 – orsi@
relaischateaux.com – Fax 04 72 44 93 34 – www.pierreorsi.com
– Closed Sunday and Monday except public holidays   **G2**
Rest – Menu 60 € (weekdays lunch), 85/115 € – Carte 70/135 € ⅜
Spec. Ravioles de foie gras de canard au jus de porto et truffes. Homard acadien en carapace "façon Pierre Orsi". Délice Geneviève (autumn).
 ◆ A la mode ◆ Formal ◆

This old house is home to elegant dining rooms and a rose garden terrace. Fine up-to-date cuisine and good wine list.

L' Alexandrin (Laurent Rigal) 🅰🅲 𝗩𝗜𝗦𝗔 ⓒⓞ

83 r. Moncey ⊠ 69003 – Ⓜ Place Guichard – ℰ 04 72 61 15 69
– laurent.rigal@lalexandrin.com – Fax 04 78 62 75 57 – www.lalexandrin.com
– Closed 2-25 August, 20-28 December, Sunday and Monday   **G3**
Rest – Menu 60 € bi/150 € ⅜
Spec. Terrine de foie gras de canard et coeur de pêche aux épices douces (15 June-15 September). Quenelle de brochet au crémeux d'écrevisse. Madeleine au chocolat à la marmelade d'orange.
 ◆ A la mode ◆ Cosy ◆

New management and new decor at this popular restaurant. Impressive choice of Côtes-du-Rhône, and regional dishes prepared with an original flair. Terrace.

Le Gourmet de Sèze (Bernard Mariller) 🅰🅲 ↯ 𝗩𝗜𝗦𝗔 ⓒⓞ 🅰🅴

129 r. Sèze ⊠ 69006 – Ⓜ Masséna – ℰ 04 78 24 23 42 – legourmetdeseze@
wanadoo.fr – Fax 04 78 24 66 81 – www.le-gourmet-de-seze.com – Closed 21-25
May, 25 July-20 August, 15-18 February, Sunday, Monday and Bank Holidays
Rest – (number of covers limited, pre-book) Menu 37 €   **H2**
(weekdays lunch), 47/100 €
Spec. Croustillants de pieds de cochon compotés à la moutarde. Saint-Jacques de la baie de Saint-Brieuc (October-March). Grand dessert du gourmet.
 ◆ A la mode ◆ Cosy ◆

Dining room in tones of white and chocolate, furnished with medallion chairs and well-spaced round tables. Classic cuisine that is skilfully modernised, and appeals well beyond the Rue de Sèze.

Alex 🅰🅲 ↯ 𝗩𝗜𝗦𝗔 ⓒⓞ 🅰🅴

44 bd des Brotteaux ⊠ 69006 – Ⓜ Brotteaux – ℰ 04 78 52 30 11 – chez.alex@
club-internet.fr – Fax 04 78 52 34 16 – Closed August, Sunday and Monday
Rest – Menu 23 € (weekdays lunch), 28/59 € – Carte approx. 52 €   **H3**
 ◆ A la mode ◆ Design ◆

Restaurant whose smart, refined setting boldly allies colour, designer furniture and contemporary artworks. Menu concocted by the owner-chef from market produce.

Maison Clovis 🅰🅲 𝗩𝗜𝗦𝗔 ⓒⓞ 🅰🅴

19 bd Brotteaux ⊠ 69006 – Ⓜ Brotteaux – ℰ 04 72 74 44 61
– ckcloviskhoury@yahoo.fr – Closed 10-31 August, Sunday and Monday
Rest – Menu 39/65 € bi – Carte 53/73 €   **H2**
 ◆ A la mode ◆ Design ◆

This new establishment is greatly appreciated for its contemporary decor (grey colour scheme and designer furniture) and its gourmet cuisine. Simpler midday slate menu.

L'Est 🏮 🅰🅲 𝗩𝗜𝗦𝗔 ⓒⓞ 🅰🅴

14 pl. J. Ferry ⊠ 69006 – Ⓜ Brotteaux – ℰ 04 37 24 25 26 – commercial@
brasseries-bocuse.com – Fax 04 37 24 25 25 – www.bocuse.fr   **H2**
Rest – Menu 24 € (weekdays)/29 € – Carte 32/50 €
 ◆ Traditional ◆ Brasserie ◆

Trendy brasserie with the locals. The kitchens can be seen from the dining room, miniature trains chug round above diners' heads and world cooking on the menu.

33 Cité 🏮 & 🅰🅲 𝗩𝗜𝗦𝗔 ⓒⓞ 🅰🅴

33 quai Charles de Gaulle ⊠ 69006 – ℰ 04 37 45 45 45 – 33cite.restaurant@
free.fr – Fax 04 37 45 45 46 **Rest** – Menu 23/27 € – Carte 35/53 €
 ◆ Traditional ◆ Design ◆   **H1**

Contemporary designer setting opposite the Salle 3000 at the Cité Internationale. View of the Parc de la Tête d'Or through the large windows. Choice of modern and classic dishes.

La Terrasse St-Clair
2 Grande Rue St-Clair ✉ 69300 Caluire-et-Cuire – ✆ 04 72 27 37 37
– clementboucher@wanadoo.fr – Fax 04 72 27 37 38 – www.terrasse-saint-clair.com
– Closed 5-22 August, 23 December-15 January, Sunday and Monday
Rest – Menu 30/40 €   **G1**
♦ Traditional ♦ Bistro ♦

There is a slight air of an open-air dance hall about the restaurant and especially the terrace shaded by plane trees. Pétanque pitch.

Les Oliviers
20 r. Sully ✉ 69006 – ⓜ Foch – ✆ 04 78 89 07 09 – Fax 04 72 43 03 32
– Closed 1-8 May, August, Saturday, Sunday and Bank Holidays   **G2**
Rest – Menu 24/33 € – Carte 34/45 €
♦ A la mode ♦ Friendly ♦

A tiny corner of Provence hidden in Paris' 6th district: intimate, low key dining room in warm colours and a tasty, sun-drenched cuisine, including bouillabaisse.

M
47 av. Foch ✉ 69006 – ⓜ Foch – ✆ 04 78 89 55 19 – restaurant.mviannay@
orange.fr – Fax 04 78 89 08 39
– Closed 1-23 August, 20-28 February, Saturday and Sunday   **G2**
Rest – Menu 25/35 €
♦ A la mode ♦ Trendy ♦

This establishment is very appealing with its open plan, minimalist, faintly psyche-delic interior dotted with orange arabesques. Updated cuisine steeped in flavour.

AROUND LYONS

Lyon Métropole
85 quai J. Gillet ✉ 69004 – ✆ 04 72 10 44 44
– metropole@lyonmetropole.com – Fax 04 72 10 44 42 – www.lyonmetropole.com
118 rm – ♦180/250 € ♦♦180/250 €, ⊑ 18 €   **B1**
Rest *Brasserie Lyon Plage* – ✆ 04 72 10 44 30 – Menu 27 € – Carte 34/53 €
♦ Business ♦ Modern ♦

This 1980s hotel, reflected in the Olympic swimming pool, offers a superb spa, fit-ness facilities, tennis and squash courts, as well as golf practice areas. Modern rooms. Seafood takes pride of place on the menu of the Brasserie Lyon Plage.

Du Greillon without rest ⟡
12 montée du Greillon ✉ 69009 – ✆ 06 08 22 26 33 – contact@legreillon.com
– Fax 04 72 29 10 97 – www.legreillon.com
– Closed 17-31 August and 18-24 February   **B1**
4 rm ⊑ – ♦78 € ♦♦110 €
♦ Traditional ♦ Personalised ♦

The former property of sculptor J. Chinard has been turned into a guesthouse. Pretty rooms, old furniture and ornaments, gorgeous garden and superb view of the Saône and Croix-Rousse.

Auberge de Fond Rose (Gérard Vignat)
23 quai G. Clemenceau ✉ 69300 Caluire-et-Cuire
– ✆ 04 78 29 34 61 – contact@aubergedefondrose.com – Fax 04 72 00 28 67
– www.aubergedefondrose.com
– Closed November school holidays, 16 February-3 March, Tuesday from
October to March, Sunday dinner and Monday except Bank Holidays
Rest – Menu 40 € bi (weekdays lunch), 55/85 € – Carte 75/85 € 🍷   **B1**
Spec. Rémoulade de grenouilles et minestrone de petits légumes. Pigeon-neau cuit dans la rôtissoire et jus aux olives. Fondant tiède au chocolat gua-naja et glace vanille.
♦ Classic ♦ Formal ♦

This handsome 1920s house features an idyllic terrace leading into the garden planted with ancient trees. Fine up-to-date menu and interesting wine list.

XX **Auberge de l'Ile** (Jean-Christophe Ansanay-Alex) ⅃⊬ ⊏ꝑ (dinner)

⊱⊱ *(On Barbe Island)* ⊠ 69009 – ℰ 04 78 83 99 49 **P** VISA ⦿ AE ⓞ
– info@aubergedelile.com – Fax 04 78 47 80 46 – www.aubergedelile.com
– Closed Sunday and Monday
Rest – Menu 95/125 € ⅋   **B1**
Spec. Velouté de cèpes dans l'esprit d'un cappuccino, lardons de foie gras à la
vapeur (autumn). Mignon d'agneau en croûte de sel, tomates "coeur de pigeon"
en aigre-doux (spring-summer). Glace à la réglisse, cornet de pain d'épice.
 ◆ Innovative ◆ Friendly ◆
Situated on Ile Barbe, this charming 17C inn is known for its fine cuisine made from
local, seasonal produce. The chef himself comes to your table to announce his
legendary dish of the day.

X **L'Ouest**   ⌂ AC VISA ⦿ AE

(⌣) *1 quai Commerce (North via the banks of the Saône (D 51))* ⊠ 69009
– ℰ 04 37 64 64 64 – commercial@brasseries-bocuse.com – Fax 04 37 64 64 65
– www.nordsudbrasseries.com   **B1**
Rest – Menu 24 € (weekdays)/29 € – Carte 35/56 €
 ◆ Brasserie ◆ Fashionable ◆
A distinctive modern building of wood, concrete and metal. Bar, giant screens,
open kitchen, river facing terrace and exotic dishes. Bocuse is on a western course!

X **Le Verre et l'Assiette**   VISA ⦿

(⌣) *20 Grande Rue de Vaise* ⊠ 69009 – ℰ 04 78 83 32 25 – leverreetlassiette@free.fr
– www.leverreetlassiette.com
– Closed 25 July-17 August, 6-15 February, Saturday and Sunday
Rest – Menu 28 € (weekdays)/42 €   **B1**
 ◆ A la mode ◆ Contemporary ◆
The talented chef reinvents and personalises traditional Lyons specialities as well as
a few French classics. Stone and wood prevail in the modern decor. Smiling service.

Collonges-au-Mont-d'Or

XXXXX **Paul Bocuse**   AC ⊏ꝑ **P** VISA ⦿ AE ⓞ

⊱⊱⊱ *40 r. de la Plage, at pont de Collonges* ⊠ 69660 – ℰ 04 72 42 90 90
– paul.bocuse@bocuse.fr – Fax 04 72 27 85 87 – www.bocuse.fr
Rest – Menu 125/210 € – Carte 111/188 € ⅋
Spec. Soupe aux truffes noires VGE. Volaille de Bresse en vessie. Gâteau "Le
Président".
 ◆ Classic ◆ Formal ◆
The culinary world beats a path to the colourful, elegant inn of the eponymous
"Monsieur Paul". His celebrated dishes in the dining room, murals of great chefs
in the courtyard.

Charbonnières-les-Bains

🏠🏠 **Le Pavillon de la Rotonde** without rest 🛏 ♨ ⦿ ⌧ & AC ⅃⊬
3 av. du Casino – ℰ 04 78 87 79 79 SAT ⦿ 🛁 **P** ⌤ VISA ⦿ AE ⓞ
contact@pavillon-rotonde.com – Fax 04 78 87 79 78 – www.pavillon-rotonde.com
16 rm – †295/495 € ††325/525 €, ⌸ 25 € **Rest La Rotonde** – see below
 ◆ Luxury ◆ Design ◆
A stone's throw from the casino, a luxurious hotel with contemporary decor and
discreet Art Deco touches. Spacious rooms with terrace giving onto the gardens.
Heated indoor swimming pool and spa.

XXXX **La Rotonde**   AC VISA ⦿ AE ⓞ

⊱⊱ *at casino Le Lyon Vert* ⊠ 69890 La Tour de Salvagny – ℰ 04 78 87 00 97
– restaurant-rotonde@g-partouche.fr – Fax 04 78 87 81 39 – www.restaurant-
rotonde.com – Closed 1-9 May, 1 August-2 September, Sunday and Monday
Rest – Menu 55 € bi (weekdays lunch), 110/155 € – Carte 101/192 € ⅋
Spec. Rouget barbet aux champignons iodés. Canard de Challans cuit à la
broche. Cannelloni de chocolat amer à la glace.
 ◆ Innovative ◆ Formal ◆
A renowned gourmet restaurant on the first floor of the casino. An elegant Art Deco-
style dining room opening onto the gardens and park, subtle cuisine and fine wine list.

STRASBOURG

STRASBOURG

Population (est. 2008): 272 700 (conurbation 451 240) – Altitude: 143m

J. Hampe/www.ot-strasbourg.fr

Would it be stretching things to call Strasbourg the ultimate European city? It can make an impressive claim: although in France, it sits just across the Rhine from Germany; it's home to the Court of Human Rights and the Council of Europe; its stunning Cathedral is the highest medieval building on the continent; and it's a major communications hub as it connects the Mediterranean with the Rhineland, Central Europe, the North Sea and the Baltic. Oh, and the Old Town is a UNESCO World Heritage Site.

What's more, there's a real cosmopolitan buzz here. A large student population, courtesy of the city's ancient university, helps generate a year-round feeling of liveliness. The name 'Strasbourg' translates as 'crossroads' and the city bounced back and forth between France and Germany for over three hundred years before its final acceptance as French over half a century ago. Its unique geographical position also lends the city a great gastronomic tradition, with two cuisine cultures colliding head on, and hungry visitors reaping the culinary benefits. Meantime, street signs in both French and Alsatian add to a gently teasing schizophrenia, enhanced by distinct areas of medieval French and German architecture. The final brushwork of this striking picture is the handsome waterway that completely encircles the Old Town, the ideal setting for a lingering boat journey on a summer's afternoon.

261

LIVING THE CITY

The **River Rhine** flows a short distance to the east of Strasbourg; the waterway that encircles the historical centre is the **River Ill** and the **Fossé des Remparts** canal. This effectively means that the heart of the city, the tourist epicentre, is an island: The Grande Ile. The **Petite France** neighbourhood is on the island's southwest tip, while the '**German district**' is northeast. The smart **European Parliament** zone is a couple of miles beyond this. Strasbourg's 'happening' district, **Krutenau**, lies near the university campus to the east of town. Right across from here, on the western fringes, is the main arrival point to the city, the central railway station.

PRACTICAL INFORMATION

ARRIVAL-DEPARTURE

Strasbourg-Entzheim International Airport is found 12km southwest of the city. The train to Central Station runs from Entzheim Station (a 5min walk from the terminal) and takes 15min. A taxi to the city centre will be about €30.

TRANSPORT

Strasbourg is covered by a bus and tram service. Tickets are valid for the whole transport network. You can buy a single ticket or carnets (multipass).

There's also a Tour-Pass which gives unlimited travel for 24hr.

The city has impressive green credentials. Buses run on natural gas, trams are slick and efficient, and there are 130,000 cyclists and 270 miles of cycle paths – hiring a bike is a great way of getting about here.

If you're staying longer, invest in a Strasbourg-Pass. This is a three-day pass which offers free travel, plus free admission (and numerous discounts) to city-wide monuments and visitor attractions.

EXPLORING STRASBOURG

Set on its island between the tree-lined embrace of the River Ill, Strasbourg's old town is a classic medieval gem, but the capital of Alsace is a lot more

than one-dimensional. The strikingly modern European Parliament building ensures the presence of smart shops; the large population of university students guarantees a youthful buzz; and what look like German wine taverns turn out to be cosy French bistros.

Visitors who arrive expecting a rather straight-laced city full of politicians are knocked out by its time-honed beauty and elegance. The World Heritage Site status is richly deserved: there are rows of half-timbered medieval buildings, glorious mansions and narrow pedestrianised streets dotted with leafy squares and lined with pavement cafés. The German quarter is the more northerly stretch of the old town, marked by sturdy public buildings and graceful gardens. Much of the architecture in these parts is of the grand nineteenth century neoclassical sort: witness a group of imposing structures such as the **Palace of the Rhine** and the **Strasbourg National Theatre** in the rather un-Germanic sounding Place de la Republique. Then a bit further down, on **Place Broglie**, nip inside the much-frequented **Rhine Opera** building to book tickets: performances here have earned Strasbourg a worldwide reputation for classical music.

➡ TRULY IN-SPIRED

The centre of the old town is also its busiest point. Many people here are making tracks to the magnificent **Notre-Dame Cathedral**. It's not hard to find, as its unmistakable single spire towers over crouching medieval roofs lying humbly in its wake. The cathedral's stark silhouette is visible from miles round, but on closer inspection, lace-like stonework softens its lines, though it won't do much to lessen the leering stares of countless gargoyles. This is a tremendous 11C sandstone confection that changes colour with the light, from dawn pink to afternoon ochre. Inside there's an elaborate astronomical clock that brings forth a parade of apostles when it chimes at 12.30pm. Crowning glory is the kaleidoscope of the rose window: on sunny days, the stained glass is a joy to behold. Two other medieval churches in the old town are worth visiting: **St-Pierre-le-Jeune** (in Place St-Pierre-Le-Jeune) is a superb Gothic pile from 1053, and you can still see the base of the bell tower and a number of walls from the original building, though what you might appreciate most are the church's wonderful 14C frescoes. Meantime, a similar reverie can be felt at the **Church of Saint Thomas** on the Quai Saint-Thomas. It dates back

to the 13C, and pride of place within goes to the organ that was played by Mozart and Albert Schweitzer.

➡ PETITE PLEASURES

The southern district of the old town (which contains St Thomas) is the predominantly Gallic part of Strasbourg – Petite France. This is the prettiest area of all, like a fairytale scene peopled by 21C tourists. It's made up of 15C black-and-white half-timbered houses, once the homes of tanners and dyers, with geranium-filled balconies. All around is a jumble of cobbled streets punctuated by canals and camel-back stone bridges. Stop at the characterful **Pont des Moulins** and listen to the gushing water as it's channelled through a narrow passageway. All around here you can take in memorable views. Climb to the top of the nearby **Vauban Dam**, which crosses the Ill at its widest point, and look across to the **Ponts Couverts**, covered bridges linked by grand medieval watchtowers that in turn provide an observation point for the four Ill canals.

➡ ART OF THE MATTER

Looking the other way from the dam you see the modish façade of the **Museum of Modern and Contemporary Art**. This is the crème de la crème of Strasbourg's museums, perhaps because of the striking steel-and-plate-glass structure in which it's housed as much as for the artworks themselves. Step inside and admire delightful floor-to-ceiling windows that enhance the powerful paintings on the walls…then finish your coffee in the Art Café and head on through to the actual permanent collection. This features Picasso, Braque, Ernst, Gauguin, Kandinsky and Magritte. The museum's upper gallery is a different concept altogether: an off-the-wall contemporary art ragbag that might have had even Picasso stroking his chin. If your taste in museums is a bit more conservative, check out the elegant **Rohan Palace**, in the shadow of the cathedral. Not only is this a fine eighteenth century building, it also boasts three museums, which delve into the worlds of archaeology, fine and applied arts. Across the water, on **quai Saint-Nicolas**, three adjoining sixteenth century houses make up the **Alsatian Museum**, dedicated to the history and traditions of the city and area you're visiting. If local history (or local signposts) have left you confused, this is the place to sort yourself out.

➜ MEET THE KRU

Strasbourg's 'playground' is Krutenau, a bohemian quarter that used to be occupied by 'water folk' such as fishermen and boatmen. It always had an alternative air, and it's kept that bohemian feel to this day, enhanced by the big student population that descends on its bars and clubs. This funky district has an eclectic mix of hole-in-the-wall restaurants serving everything from spicy Lebanese meals to rich Thai curries. If, however, your idea of playing is a gentle cruise on a boat, then it's simplicity itself to jump on one at the landing stage behind the Rohan Palace, and relax on a one-hour trip that does the classic circular trip taking in the grandiose European Parliament building to the north and the Ponts-Couverts to the south. Then again, a stroll along the banks of the Ill gives you a first-hand chance to appreciate the tastefully landscaped river-banks that typify a superior kind of European city.

CALENDAR HIGHLIGHTS

Alsatians look forward to September in the city, not for any particularly autumnal reasons, but because this is the month when Festival Musica comes to town, and wonderfully diverse works from the modern classical music genre are performed at venues throughout Strasbourg. This lights the blue touch paper for two more influential events in the city. November's St'Art at the Strasbourg Centre de Congrès is lauded as the second-biggest contemporary art fair in France (after the FIAC in Paris) and draws art-lovers from around Europe to the 'crossroads' of the continent. That same month sees Jazz d'Or, a highly popular jazz festival over two weeks with forty concerts spread across venues in the city. The main summer event here is the Route Romane Festival (August and September), when Strasbourg's shared Franco-German cultural heritage is celebrated with a feast of medieval and traditional music. Christmas markets in the city are worth a particular mention. They're amongst the oldest and the best in Europe, and have been

STRASBOURG IN...

➜ ONE DAY
Old Town, Notre-Dame Cathedral, Petite France

➜ TWO DAYS
Boat trip on the Ill, Museum of Modern and Contemporary Art, meal in a winstub

➜ THREE DAYS
Alsatian Museum (or Rohan Palace museums), European Parliament, Orangerie

held here since 1570. The market in Place Broglie, in the old town, is recognised as the one at the top of the tree.

EATING OUT

Strasbourg is generally considered one of the best cities in France for delicious cuisine and places in which to eat it. There's the attention to quality and detail that's the epitome of the French gourmet philosophy allied to bold and hearty Alsatian fare with its roots firmly set across the Rhine. A favourite of the region is choucroute (or sauerkraut if you're leaning towards Germany), which is a rumbustious mixture of cabbage, potatoes, pork, sausage and ham; then there's baeckoffe, a tasty Alsace stew, which translates as 'ovenbake' and blends pieces of stewing lamb, beef and pork with liberal dollops of Riesling. Talking of which, the fragrant wines of the area have a distinct character of their own: they're white, spicy and floral. The local fruit liquor, eau de vie, has a definite Alsatian kick, too – it's sweetened entirely by fruit without a hint of sugar. A good place in which to sample the local produce is a typical Strasbourg winstub. The smarter restaurants – highly prized and requiring advance reservation – are around the cathedral, in the Petite France quarter, and along the canal and river banks. As this is a eurocrat zone, expect a smart set to be at a table close to you. As in other parts of France, a fifteen per cent service charge is already added to your bill, but round it up for good service.

→ FOLLY IN THE PARK

The Orangerie is Strasbourg's most popular park, just across from the European Council offices. Not only is it full of people in serious suits – it also boasts a zoo and a bowling alley.

→ ARTY ANTHEM

Strasbourg can lay claim to three famous sons. Two of them, Gustave Dore and Jean Arp, became world renowned for their abilities with a paintbrush. The third, Frederic de Dietrich, was the mayor who commissioned the French national anthem, La Marseillaise.

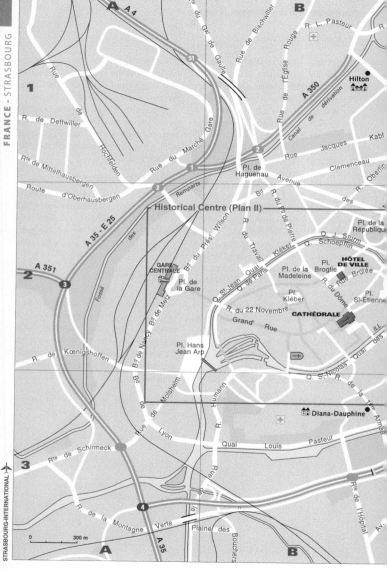

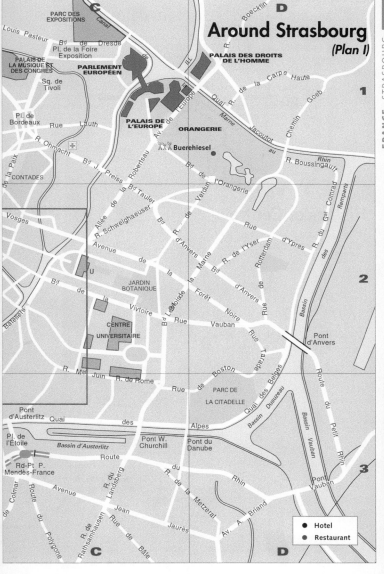

Around Strasbourg
(Plan I)

PARC DES
EXPOSITIONS

Louis Pasteur

Bd de Dresde
Pl. de la Foire
Exposition

PALAIS DE
LA MUSIQUE ET
DES CONGRÈS

PARLEMENT
EUROPÉEN

Sq. de
Tivoli

Pl. de
Bordeaux

Rue Lauth

R. Ohnacht

CONTADES

Bd J. Preiss

Allée de la Robertsau

R. Schweighaeuser

Vosges

Avenue de la

Bd de

Barefiers

JARDIN
BOTANIQUE

Vivtoire

CENTRE
UNIVERSITAIRE

R. Mai

Juin

R. de Rome

Pont
d'Austerlitz

Quai des

Pl. de
l'Étoile

Bassin d'Austerlitz

Route

Rd-Pt P.
Mendès-France

de Colmar

Route du Polygone

Avenue

R. du Landsberg

R. de Rathsamhausen

Rue de Bâle

Jean

Jaurès

Boecktin

PALAIS DES DROITS
DE L'HOMME

Pl. de la Carpe Haute

Quai Marne

Goeb

Jacoutot

Chemin

au

Rhin

R. Boussingault

PALAIS DE
L'EUROPE

ORANGERIE

XXX Buerehiesel

Bd de l'Orangerie

Bd Tauler

Bd de Verdun

Rue

R. du Gal Conrad

Remparts

des

Bassin

Rue d'Anvers

R. de l'Yser

d'Ypres

Rotterdam

Bd la Marne

Rue

d'Anvers

de

Pont
d'Anvers

Forêt

Noire

Rue

Vauban

Rue Tarade

Bd Leblois

Rue

de Boston

Rue de

PARC DE
LA CITADELLE

Quai des Belges

Bassin Dusuzeau

Route du Petit Rhin

Bassin Vauban

Alpes

Pont W.
Churchill

Pont du
Danube

du

R. de la Metzeral

Rhin

Av. A. Briand

Pont
Vauban

● Hotel
● Restaurant

C

D

1

2

3

FRANCE - STRASBOURG

Régent Petite France ⅏ ≼ ⌂ ⅃⅙ ⅙ ⅊ ⅏ ⅙ rm ⌨ ⁗ ⅍ ⌂
5 r. des Moulins – ⌀ *03 88 76 43 43 – rpf@* VISA ⅏⅌ ⅈ ⅀ ⅈ
regent-hotels.com – Fax 03 88 76 43 76 – www.regent-hotels.com
66 rm – ⅃265/395 € ⅃⅃287/417 €, ⌑ 22 € – 6 suites **F2**
Rest – *(closed Sunday, Monday and lunch October-May)* Menu 42 € *(dinner)*
– Carte 33/42 €
◆ Grand Luxury ◆ Business ◆ Design ◆
A modern hotel occupying an old ice-cream factory on the banks of the Ill. Bright,
spacious and comfortable bedrooms with high-tech equipment. Terrace and
sauna. Modern menu in keeping with the trendy feel of this restaurant with bar-
lounge and views of the river.

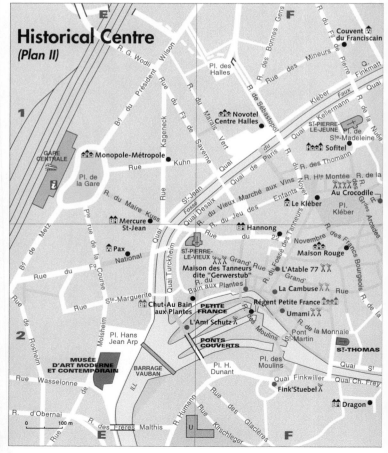

Historical Centre
(Plan II)

Sofitel 🛜 ⓘ 🆎 ⅋ rm 🆑 ⁽ᵖ⁾ ⅍ ⇔ 𝗩𝗜𝗦𝗔 ⓜ 🆎 ⓞ

pl. St-Pierre-le-Jeune – ℰ *03 88 15 49 00*
– *h0568@accor.com* – *Fax 03 88 15 49 99*
– *www.sofitel-strasbourg.com*
153 rm – 🛇140/380 € 🛇🛇140/380 €, ⌿ 25 €

F1

– 2 suites
Rest *Sofitel* – *(closed Saturday lunch, Sunday and holidays)* Carte 46/67 €
◆ Chain hotel ◆ Luxury ◆ Functional ◆

Two types of room – classic and those designed on a European political theme
on offer at this Sofitel. A full range of modern facilities, plus patio and fitness centre. Modern, Japanese-inspired design and luxury brasserie-style service at the
restaurant.

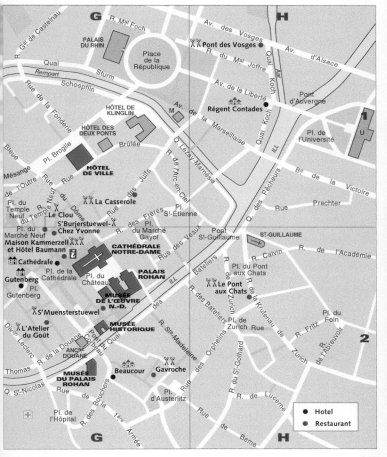

FRANCE - STRASBOURG

Hilton 🛰 ⅃ᵅ 🕸 ᵤᵉ rm 🔤 ⅃ᵉ rm 🖷 ᵠⁱ 🔏 🅿 🚗 ᵥₛₐ ⫸ 🄰🄴 ⓪
av. Herrenschmidt – ℰ *03 88 37 10 10* – *contact@hilton-strasbourg.com*
– *Fax 03 88 36 83 27* – *www.strasbourg.hilton.fr* Plan I **B1**
238 rm – ♦130/355 € ♦♦130/355 €, 🖃 23 € – 5 suites
Rest *La Table du Chef* – ℰ *03 88 37 41 42 (closed July-August, Monday dinner, Saturday lunch and Sunday)* Menu 35 €
Rest *Le Jardin du Tivoli* – ℰ *03 88 35 72 61* – Menu 30 € – Carte 34/46 €
This glass and steel hotel provides standardised comfort in its spacious guestrooms. Lobby with shops, a multimedia centre and bars. Traditional lunches and a British feel at La Table du Chef; wine bar in the evening. Buffet dining at the Jardin du Tivoli.

Régent Contades without rest 🕸 🔤 ⅃ᵉ 🖷 ᵠⁱ 🔏 ᵥₛₐ ⫸ 🄰🄴 ⓪
8 av. de la Liberté – ℰ *03 88 15 05 05* – *rc@regent-hotels.com*
– *Fax 03 88 15 05 15* – *www.regent-hotels.com* **H1**
45 rm – ♦195/325 € ♦♦215/345 €, 🖃 20 € – 2 suites
◆ Luxury ◆ Historic ◆ Classical ◆
A 19C hotel with an opulent and refined decor (wood panelling, paintings). Huge, renovated rooms, Belle Époque breakfast room. Sanarium/relaxation area.

Beaucour without rest ᵤᵉ 🔤 🖷 ᵠⁱ 🔏 ᵥₛₐ ⫸ 🄰🄴 ⓪
5 r. Bouchers – ℰ *03 88 76 72 00* – *info@hotel-beaucour.com*
– *Fax 03 88 76 72 60* – *www.hotel-beaucour.com* **G2**
49 rm – ♦110 € ♦♦135/165 €, 🖃 13 €
◆ Family ◆ Traditional ◆ Classical ◆
These two elegant 18C Alsatian buildings are linked by a flower-decked patio. The most pleasant guestrooms are decorated in local rustic style with wood panelling and exposed beams.

Maison Rouge without rest ᵤᵉ 🔤 ⅃ᵉ 🖷 ᵠⁱ 🔏 ᵥₛₐ ⫸ 🄰🄴 ⓪
4 r. des Francs-Bourgeois – ℰ *03 88 32 08 60* – *info@maison-rouge.com*
– *Fax 03 88 22 43 73* – *www.maison-rouge.com* **F2**
140 rm – ♦76/170 € ♦♦88/185 €, 🖃 14 € – 2 suites
◆ Luxury ◆ Business ◆ Stylish ◆
Behind the red stone façade is an elegant hotel with a cosy atmosphere. Well-designed bedrooms with a personal touch, and an attractively decorated lounge on each floor.

Monopole-Métropole without rest ⅃ᵅ 🔤 ⅃ᵉ 🖷 ᵠⁱ 🔏 🚗
16 r. Kuhn – ℰ *03 88 14 39 14* – *infos@* ᵥₛₐ ⫸ 🄰🄴 ⓪
bw-monopole.com – *Fax 03 88 32 82 55* – *www.bw-monopole.com*
86 rm 🖃 – ♦80/200 € ♦♦85/200 € **E1**
◆ Family ◆ Rustic ◆
Near the station, hotel split into two wings (one old and rustic, the other far more contemporary, featuring works by local artists). Lounges decorated with handicrafts.

Novotel Centre Halles ⅃ᵅ ᵤᵉ rm 🔤 ⅃ᵉ ᵠⁱ 🔏 ᵥₛₐ ⫸ 🄰🄴 ⓪
4 quai Kléber – ℰ *03 88 21 50 50* – *h0439@accor.com* – *Fax 03 88 21 50 51*
– *www.novotel.com* **F1**
96 rm – ♦87/198 € ♦♦87/198 €, 🖃 15 € **Rest** – Carte 22/47 €
◆ Chain hotel ◆ Modern ◆
Refurbished rooms in a pleasant, contemporary style at this hotel in the Les Halles shopping centre. Gym on the 8th floor with a view of the cathedral. A modern look in the bar and restaurant; simplified and practical menu.

Chut - Au Bain aux Plantes 🛰 ᵤᵉ rm 🔤 rm ⅃ᵉ ᵠⁱ ᵥₛₐ ⫸ 🄰🄴
4 r. Bain-aux-Plantes – ℰ *03 88 32 05 06* – *contact@hote-strasbourg.fr*
– *Fax 03 88 32 05 50* – *www.hote-strasbourg.fr* **E2**
8 rm – ♦90/100 € ♦♦100/160 €, 🖃 10 € – 1 suite
Rest – *(closed 26 April-5 May, 9-18 August, 21 December-7 January, Sunday and Monday)* Menu 18 € *(weekdays lunch)* – Carte 32/44 €
◆ Inn ◆ Luxury ◆ Personalised ◆
Designer or antique materials and furniture, spacious guestrooms and a relaxing, mini-malist feel are the hallmarks of this stylish hotel-cum-guesthouse. The varied menu, featuring the subtle use of myriad spices, changes daily. Charming courtyard terrace.

Diana-Dauphine without rest ⬛ 📶 🛜 📶 VISA 🅐🅔 ①

30 r. de la 1ère Armée – ℰ *03 88 36 26 61* – *info@hotel-diana-dauphine.com*
– *Fax 03 88 35 50 07* – *www.hotel-diana-dauphine.com*
– *Closed 22 December-2 January*   *Plan I* **B3**
45 rm – ✝90/150 € ✝✝90/150 €, ☐ 11 €
◆ Luxury ◆ Business ◆ Design ◆

Located by the tramline leading to the old town, this hotel has been treated to a
radical contemporary facelift. Modern comforts.

Hannong without rest ⬛ 📶 📶 🛜 VISA 🅐🅔 ①

15 r. du 22 Novembre – ℰ *03 88 32 16 22* – *info@hotel-hannong.com*
– *Fax 03 88 22 63 87* – *www.hotel-hannong.com* – *Closed 4-10 January*
72 rm – ✝65/157 € ✝✝75/197 €, ☐ 14 €   **F2**
◆ Family ◆ Business ◆ Classical ◆

A mix of styles (classic, cosy, modern) with parquet, wood panelling, sculptures
and paintings in this fine hotel built on the site of the Hannong earthenware factory (18C). Pleasant wine bar.

Du Dragon without rest ⬛ ⬛ 📶 🛜 VISA 🅐🅔 ①

2 r. Écarlate – ℰ *03 88 35 79 80* – *hotel@dragon.fr* – *Fax 03 88 25 78 95*
– *www.dragon.fr*   **32 rm** – ✝79/116 € ✝✝89/129 €, ☐ 12 €   **F2**
◆ Family ◆ Modern ◆

17C building around a small quiet courtyard with a clearly contemporary feel.
Shades of grey, designer furniture, rooms in a pared-down style and art exhibitions.

Mercure St-Jean without rest ⬛ ⬛ 📶 🛜 VISA 🅐🅔 ①

3 r. Maire Kuss – ℰ *03 88 32 80 80* – *h1813@accor.com* – *Fax 03 88 23 05 39*
52 rm – ✝69/125 € ✝✝69/125 €, ☐ 14 €   **E1**
◆ Chain hotel ◆ Business ◆ Design ◆

Chain hotel between the station and the "Petite France" quarter. Contemporary
decor; practical guestrooms in coffee-coloured tones. Patio with mini-fountains.

Gutenberg without rest ⬛ ⬛ 📶 VISA 🅐🅔

31 r. des Serruriers – ℰ *03 88 32 17 15* – *info@hotel-gutenberg.com*
– *Fax 03 88 75 76 67* – *www.hotel-gutenberg.com*   **G2**
42 rm – ✝74/113 € ✝✝74/113 €, ☐ 9 €
◆ Traditional ◆ Classical ◆

This building dating back to 1745 is now a hotel with an eclectic mix of spacious
guestrooms. The bright breakfast room is crowned by a glass roof.

Cathédrale without rest ⬛ ⬛ ⬛ 📶 🛜 VISA 🅐🅔 ①

12-13 pl. Cathédrale – ℰ *03 88 22 12 12* – *reservation@hotel-cathedrale.fr*
– *Fax 03 88 23 28 00* – *www.hotel-cathedrale.fr*   **G2**
47 rm – ✝55/140 € ✝✝65/150 €, ☐ 13 €
◆ Family ◆ Classic ◆

This century-old residence enjoys an ideal location opposite the cathedral, which is
visible from the breakfast room and some of the comfortable rooms. Religious
architecture-inspired decor in some rooms.

Le Kléber without rest ⬛ ⬛ 📶 VISA 🅐🅔 ①

29 pl. Kléber – ℰ *03 88 32 09 53* – *hotel-kleber-strasbourg@wanadoo.fr*
– *Fax 03 88 32 50 41* – *www.hotel-kleber.com*   **F1**
30 rm – ✝58/78 € ✝✝68/86 €, ☐ 9 €
◆ Family ◆ Personalised ◆

"Meringue", "Strawberry" and "Cinnamon" are just a few of the names of the rooms in
this comfortable hotel. Contemporary, colourful decor with a sweet-and-savoury theme.

Couvent du Franciscain without rest ⬛ ⬛ ⬛ 📶 🛜 📶 🅟

18 r. du Fg de Pierre – ℰ *03 88 32 93 93* – *info@*   VISA 🅐🅔 🅐🅔
hotel-franciscain.com – *Fax 03 88 75 68 46* – *www.hotel-franciscain.com*
– *Closed 24 December-3 January*   **F1**
43 rm – ✝40/64 € ✝✝68/74 €, ☐ 10 €
◆ Family ◆ Traditional ◆ Functional ◆

A simple yet comfortable hotel at the end of a cul-de-sac. Pleasant lounge; breakfast in a "winstub-style" basement (amusing mural).

Pax ⬆ ⓣ rm 🅰🅒 rest ⇆ rm 🖥 🕯 ⚙ 🆅🅸🆂🅰 ⓒⓞ 🅰🅴 ⓞ
24 r. Fg National – ℰ 03 88 32 14 54 – info@paxhotel.com – Fax 03 88 32 01 16
– www.paxhotel.com – Closed 1-10 January   **E2**
106 rm – ♦57/84 € ♦♦69/84 €, ⊐ 8.50 €
Rest – *(closed Sunday in January and February)* Menu 18/24 € – Carte 22/45 €
♦ Traditional ♦ Functional ♦
This hotel is on a street accessible only by the Strasbourg tramway. Some of the
rooms have been renovated and all are well kept. Common areas brightened by
antique objects reminiscent of the farm. On fine days, dining is outside on the
pretty terrace-patio under the Virginia creeper. Regional cuisine.

Au Crocodile (Emile Jung) 🅰🅒 🆅🅸🆂🅰 ⓒⓞ 🅰🅴 ⓞ
10 r. Outre – ℰ 03 88 32 13 02 – info@au-crocodile.com – Fax 03 88 75 72 01
– www.au-crocodile.com
– Closed 12 July-4 August, 24 December-6 January, Sunday and Monday
Rest – Menu 59 € (weekdays lunch), 89/128 € – Carte 108/164 € 🍴   **F1**
Spec. Foie de canard poêlé aux pommes et jus d'agrumes. Noisette de faon
de biche à l'écorce d'orange (season). Meringue glacée aux fruits chauds et
sorbet litchi.
♦ Classic ♦ Romantic ♦
Splendid wood panelling, paintings and the famous crocodile brought back from
the Egyptian campaign by an Alsatian captain adorn this restaurant. Refined classical cuisine.

Buerehiesel (Eric Westermann) ≼ 🅰🅒 🅿 🆅🅸🆂🅰 ⓒⓞ 🅰🅴 ⓞ
in parc de l'Orangerie – ℰ 03 88 45 56 65 – reservation@buerehiesel.fr
– Fax 03 88 61 32 00 – www.buerehiesel.fr
– Closed 1ˢᵗ-21 August, 31 December-21 January, Sunday and Monday
Rest – Menu 37 € (weekdays lunch), 67/96 € – Carte 55/110 € 🍴   *Plan I* **D1**
Spec. Schniederspaetle et cuisses de grenouille poêlées au cerfeuil. Pigeon
d'Alsace farci d'un tajine de céleri. Croustillant café-caramel au beurre salé.
♦ A la mode ♦ Formal ♦
Following on from his father Antoine, Éric Westermann creates reasonably priced
interesting cuisine in his own kitchen set in this pretty, half-timbered farmhouse at
the heart of the Parc de l'Orangerie.

Maison Kammerzell et Hôtel Baumann with rm 🅰🅒 🕯 🔒
16 pl. de la Cathédrale – ℰ 03 88 32 42 14 – info@ 🆅🅸🆂🅰 ⓒⓞ 🅰🅴 ⓞ
maison-kammerzell.com – Fax 03 88 23 03 92 – www.maison-kammerzell.com
– Closed 3 weeks in February   **G2**
9 rm – ♦75 € ♦♦110/125 €, ⊐ 10 €   **Rest** – Menu 31/46 € – Carte 32/59 €
♦ De Terroir ♦ Inn ♦
With its stained-glass windows, paintings, wood carvings and Gothic vaulting, this
16C construction retains the feel of the Middle Ages. Sober guestrooms. An excellent brasserie menu based around traditional local cuisine. Choucroute a speciality.

Maison des Tanneurs dite "Gerwerstub" 🆅🅸🆂🅰 ⓒⓞ 🅰🅴 ⓞ
42 r. Bain aux Plantes – ℰ 03 88 32 79 70 – maison.des.tanneurs@wanadoo.fr
– Fax 03 88 22 17 26 – www.maison-des-tanneurs.com
– Closed 27 July-11 August, 30 December-26 January, Sunday and Monday
Rest – Menu 25 € (weekdays lunch)/30 € – Carte 41/62 €   **F2**
♦ De Terroir ♦ Elegant ♦
Ideally located by the Ill, this typical Alsatian house in La Petite France district is the
place to go to if you love sauerkraut.

La Cambuse 🅰🅒 🆅🅸🆂🅰 ⓒⓞ
1 r. des Dentelles – ℰ 03 88 22 10 22 – Fax 03 88 23 24 99
– Closed 17-31 May, 2-24 August, 1-12 January, Sunday and Monday
Rest – *(number of covers limited, pre-book)* Carte 47/55 €   **F2**
♦ Fish ♦ Cosy ♦
Intimate dining room decorated in the style of a boat cabin. Fish and seafood are
the specialities here, prepared in a blend of French and Asian styles (herbs, spices
etc).

FRANCE • STRASBOURG

XX **L'Atable 77**   AC ⇆ VISA ⚫⚫ AE ⓘ

*77 Grand'Rue – ℰ 03 88 32 23 37 – latable77@free.fr – Fax 03 88 32 50 24
– www.latable77.com – Closed 1-11 May, 26 July-16 August, 10-24 January,
Sunday, Monday and Bank Holiday lunch*   **F2**
Rest – Menu 32/80 € bi – Carte 32/50 €
♦ À la mode ♦ Cosy ♦

A trendy restaurant with a resolutely contemporary feel throughout, from the paintings on the walls to the designer tableware and appetising modern cuisine. À table!

XX **Le Violon d'Ingres**   🍴 VISA ⚫⚫

*1 r. Chevalier Robert (at La Robertsau) – ℰ 03 88 31 39 50 – www.violondingres.com
– Closed 14-28 April, 25 July-12 August, 2-10 January, Saturday lunch, Sunday dinner
and Monday*
Rest – Menu 30/65 € – Carte 62/72 €
♦ À la mode ♦ Elegant ♦

Traditional Alsatian building in the residential district of Robertsau. Elegant dining area and shaded terrace; contemporary cuisine with a focus on fish.

XX **La Casserole** (Eric Girardin)   AC VISA ⚫⚫ AE
ⵜ
*24 r. des Juifs – ℰ 03 88 36 49 68 – Fax 03 88 24 25 12 – Closed 1-11 May,
2-24 August, 24 December-4 January, Saturday lunch, Sunday and Monday*
Rest – (pre-book) Menu 49/78 € 🍴   **G1**
Spec. Oeuf cassé à la truffe tuber mélanosporum et topinambours. Barbue,
"risotto" de céleri et sauce au curry. Mousse soufflée chaude au chocolat Guanaja.
♦ Innovative ♦ Neighbourhood ♦

The two sommeliers who run this restaurant carefully and passionately select the wines at reasonable prices, which they match to a refined and inventive menu. Original designer décor.

XX **Gavroche**   AC ⇆ VISA ⚫⚫ AE

*4 r. Klein – ℰ 03 88 36 82 89 – restaurant.gavroche@free.fr – Fax 03 88 36 82 89
– www.restaurant-gavroche.com
– Closed 27 July-14 August, 21 December-4 January, Saturday and Sunday*
Rest – Menu 36/56 € – Carte 52/72 €   **G2**
♦ À la mode ♦ Cosy ♦

The Gavroche has moved to a brand new space next door to the old restaurant. Plain, elegant and contemporary setting. Modern and creative market inspired cuisine.

XX **Umami** (René Fieger)   AC VISA ⚫⚫ AE
ⵜ
*8 r. des Dentelles – ℰ 03 88 32 80 53 – contact@restaurant-umami.com
– www.restaurant-umami.com – Closed 30 August-14 September, 25 December-
4 January, Sunday and Monday*   **F2**
Rest – Menu 42/60 €
Spec. Tartare de langoustines. Joue de bœuf braisée aux aromates et caca-
huètes. Le chocolat.
♦ Innovative ♦ Cosy ♦

According to a Japanese scientist, umami is the fifth flavour. The talented chef of this tiny establishment masterfully combines flavours and aromas, creating a delicious culinary score.

XX **Le Pont aux Chats**   🍴 ⇆ VISA ⚫⚫ AE

*42 r. de la Krutenau – ℰ 03 88 24 08 77 – le-pont-aux-chats.restaurant@
orange.fr – Fax 03 88 24 08 77 – Closed 3 weeks in August, for the Easter
holidays, Saturday lunch and Wednesday*   **H2**
Rest – Menu 48/60 €
♦ À la mode ♦ Friendly ♦

A charming interior featuring a successful fusion of ancient timbers and contemporary furniture, with an adorable courtyard terrace. Modern menu based around seasonal produce.

XX **Pont des Vosges**   🍴 VISA ⚫⚫ AE

*15 quai Koch – ℰ 03 88 36 47 75 – pontdesvosges@noos.fr – Fax 03 88 25 16 85
– Closed Sunday*   **H1**
Rest – Carte 30/55 €
♦ Brasserie ♦ Rétro ♦

Located on the corner of a stone building, this brasserie is renowned for its copious traditional cuisine. Antique advertising posters and mirrors decorate the dining room.

FRANCE - STRASBOURG

L'Atelier du Goût
17 r. des Tonneliers – ℰ *03 88 21 01 01* – *ateliergout.morabito@free.fr*
– Fax 03 88 23 64 36 – *www.atelier-du-gout.fr*
– Closed February holidays, 28 July-10 August, Saturday except dinner in
December, Sunday and holidays   **G2**
Rest – Menu 36 € (weekdays) – Carte 40/48 €
♦ Trendy ♦
A colourful designer decor sets the scene in this former winstub, turned into a laid-back restaurant devoted to good food. Appetising dishes made with organic and seasonal produce.

WINSTUBS

L'Ami Schutz
1 Ponts Couverts – ℰ *03 88 32 76 98* – *info@ami-schutz.com*
– Fax 03 88 32 38 40 – *www.ami-schutz.com*
– Closed Christmas holidays   **E-F2**
Rest – Menu 25/41 € – Carte 29/58 €
♦ Alsatian cuisine ♦ Rustic ♦
Between the meanders of the Ill, typical "winstub" with wood panelling and cosy banquettes (the smaller dining room has greater charm). Terrace beneath the lime trees.

S'Burjerstuewel - Chez Yvonne
10 r. Sanglier – ℰ *03 88 32 84 15* – *info@chez-yvonne.net* – *Fax 03 88 23 00 18*
– www.chez-yvonne.net   **G2**
Rest – *(pre-book)* Carte 30/60 €
♦ De Terroir ♦ Inn ♦
This winstub has become one of the city's institutions, witnessed by the photos and dedications of its famous guests. Regional cuisine with a modern twist.

Le Clou
3 r. Chaudron – ℰ *03 88 32 11 67* – *winstub.le.clou@wanadoo.fr*
– Fax 03 88 21 06 43 – *www.le-clou.com*
– Closed 27 July-8 August, Wednesday lunch, Sunday and Bank Holidays
Rest – Carte 26/55 €   **G1-2**
♦ Alsatian cuisine ♦ Rustic ♦
Traditional decor (a doll's house feel upstairs) and a friendly atmosphere characte-rise this well-known winstub situated near the cathedral. Generous portions.

Fink'Stuebel
26 r. Finkwiller – ℰ *03 88 25 07 57* – *finkstuebel@orange.fr* – *Fax 03 88 36 48 82*
– www.finkstuebel.free.fr
– Closed 1-8 March, Sunday and Monday   **F2**
Rest – Menu 10 € (weekdays lunch)/35 € – Carte 30/54 €
♦ Alsatian cuisine ♦ Family ♦
A half-timbered construction with bare floorboards, regional furniture and floral tablecloths, the Fink'Stuebel is the epitome of a traditional winstub. Local cuisine; foie gras to the fore.

S'Muensterstuewel
8 pl. Marché aux Cochons de Lait – ℰ *03 88 32 17 63* – *info@*
bateaux-strasbourg.fr – *Fax 03 88 32 96 02*
– Closed August, 25-31 December, 1-11 January, 1-8 March and Sunday
Rest – Menu 19/49 € – Carte 37/55 €   **G2**
♦ Alsatian cuisine ♦ Friendly ♦
Former butcher's shop transformed into a traditional winstub. Terrace overlooking the picturesque Place du Marché aux Cochons de Lait. Home-produced salted and cured meats.

TOULOUSE
TOULOUSE

Population (est. 2007): 437 100 (conurbation 936 800) – Altitude: 146m

S. Frances/HEMIS.fr

The first thing you notice about Toulouse is its pink buildings, leaving you in little doubt as to why France's fourth biggest city has the enchanting epithet 'La Ville Rose'. The rouge shade of brickwork lends the place a distinctly sunny charm, enhanced by a lovely old town infused with sixteenth century merchant houses and grand Romanesque churches.

It's here that the Toulousains throng, particularly at dusk when the town's bars and cafes are bathed in a sumptuous rosy glow. This is a confident, easy-going city whose rich architectural heritage is matched by an intellectual verve: its 115,000 students make it second only to Paris as a French university centre. You wouldn't think it to be sitting at a sunny bar with an Armagnac, but Toulouse is also at the heart of the European aerospace industry, and it's on the outskirts here that the space shuttle programme is based. Pre-eminence has come the way of this city before. From the tenth to the thirteenth centuries, the Counts of Toulouse ran a resplendent court populated by troubadours and poets whose works inspired the likes of Dante and Chaucer. Then in the sixteenth century, it flourished again through the cultivation of woad, and newly enriched merchants built the most magnificent town houses - *hotels particuliers* -which make up one of the best reasons to wander the streets on a sunny day.

275

Toulouse sits handsomely midway between the Mediterranean and the Atlantic. The visitor-friendly old town is bounded to the east by the Canal du Midi and to the west by the gently curving River Garonne. This charming area is even more tightly hemmed in by a ring of nineteenth-century boulevards (d'Arcole, Strasbourg, Lazare Carnot, Verdier and Jules Guesde). A sharply defined 'cross' of streets cuts the centre into four quarters (Rue d'Alsace Lorraine/Rue du Languedoc running north/south; Rue de Metz east/west). Over the river three kilometres to the northwest is Toulouse Blagnac airport, while the same distance southeast is the huge Cité de l'Espace centre.

PRACTICAL INFORMATION

ARRIVAL-DEPARTURE

Toulouse-Blagnac Airport is located 7km west of the city centre. The Express bus takes 20min while a taxi will cost about €26. High speed trains to Paris go from Gare Matabiau.

TRANSPORT

Toulouse offers a bus and metro system to get you around town. A one-trip red ticket allows you to travel anywhere on the network for an hour. There's a slightly more expensive round trip ticket, plus a Day ticket and 10-12 trip tickets.

The main railway station is situated in a picturesque setting by the Canal du Midi. It's a short five minute hop on the metro to the old town centre, but if you're not weighed down by luggage it's a pleasant twenty minute stroll over the canal on foot. On your walk into town, just before the central Place du Capitole, you'll find the main tourist office on the square Charles-de-Gaulle.

EXPLORING TOULOUSE

"Pink at dawn, red at noon and purple at dusk." How many cities can you say that about? At around the time of the colour purple, particularly in the summertime, you'll hear the sound of screeching chairs as everyone grabs a table at the bars around the capacious

Place du Capitole, and waits for the daily free light show. As the sun sets, the long, neoclassical facade of the city hall begins to glow. At first it's a soft blush, then a warm fiery light, as the sun works on the golden balconies of its eighteenth century, rose-coloured frontage. All this, and dinner too.

You don't have to go far to find another great treasure of old Toulouse. Just to the north of Capitole is **St-Sernin**, the largest Romanesque basilica in Europe and considered the finest in France. It was begun in 1080 as a stopping point for pilgrims on their way to Santiago de Compostela, and took another three centuries to complete. Nearly a thousand years after the first brick was laid it still has the power to knock you back in your stride. Its octagonal belfry is a masterpiece of its kind, while its cavernous, pale pink interior is full of soaring arches, and there's an array of ancient relics in the crypt. If St-Sernin is the towering landmark here, it's not the only church to impress. As the medieval streets spill out in a rich patchwork southwest of the basilica, you come across **Les Jacobins** on Rue Lakanal. A great Gothic pile built in the thirteenth century, it boasts elegant vaulting ribs like sprouting palm fronds, and lovingly maintained cloisters full of quiet, atmospheric splendour; beneath the altar lie the remains of the philosopher St Thomas Aquinas. Down Rue Gambetta from here is the baroque **Notre-Dame-de-la-Daurade**, whose dark and brooding interior is watched over by a black Madonna.

→ PARTICULIER-LY FINE

When the visitor's eye hasn't been taken by one of the churches, there's a good chance it's seized on the delights of a *hôtel particulier*. These are the superb Renaissance town houses and mansions which were built by the city's merchants from the wealth of the woad trade. Nearly all are built of red Toulousain brick, decorated with costly stone (brought over from the Pyrenees) in the form of ornate doorways, vaulted cloisters, statues, turrets and pillars. Most are closed, but you can peek at many by strolling casually into courtyards; particularly good is the elaborate **Hôtel de Bernuy** with its fine stone-galleried courtyard on Rue Gambetta. But the pick of les *particuliers* is **Hôtel d'Assezat**, on Rue de Metz, not least because it's open to the public. It's a superb twenty eight metre high building of brick and stone, enhanced by classic columns and a tower with octagonal lantern. Thanks to its Bemberg collection, there's a great assortment of artwork on view, including a roomful of Bonnards, and works by Monet, Canaletto, Dufy and Cranach the Elder. Eclectic is the word!

→ SCULPTURE, SPACE – AND A SLAUGHTERHOUSE

In keeping with its venerable surroundings, Toulouse's old town offers up a museum dedicated to the distant past. **Musée des Augustins** is itself a nineteenth-century building based round the cloisters of an Augustinian priory. Inside, the wonderful collections of Romanesque and medieval sculpture bring alive the fashions of the day; these are 'fleshed out' by sixteenth to nineteenth century European paintings. For the shock of the new, you have to head over the Garonne to the left bank and a mighty brick-built former nineteenth-century slaughterhouse – **Les Abattoirs**, opened in 2000 – which dives head first into the world of modern art from the 1950s onwards. It includes the head-turning La Depouille du Minotaure by Picasso – a stage curtain from 1936 (okay, not *everything* here is post-50s). Toulouse's up-to-the-minute face, however, is found in the southeastern suburbs at **Cité de l'Espace**, the science park that leaves earth to deal with all things galactic. This is the place to come if you want to dock your virtual capsule on a space station, or find out about weightlessness, satellite communications and planetary movements. You can also walk inside a mock-up of the Mir space station (but the bus back to Place du Capitole may seem a bit mundane afterwards).

→ KEEPING WATCH

Back on the old town's reassuring 'terra firma', fine detail appears in every nook and cranny; for somewhere apparently timeless, there's a fascination with the hours of the day, whether it's via the charming twenty-four hour clock on the face of an eighteenth-century townhouse, or in the absorbing **Musee Paul-Dupuy** (south of Capitole), which has an elegantly displayed collection of clocks and watches. All round this part of town are narrow lanes and pretty streets; the prettiest **is Rue Croix-Baragnon**, with its galleries and designer boutiques renowned for their chic interiors. Stroll about here to pick up interesting art and antiques or funky, bohemian one-offs. And when you've had your fill of street life, you'll be pleased to know that this is also the area where the city's best green spots are to be found. You can take your pick from either the enchanting formal gardens of the **Grand-Rond**, or the slightly larger and equally beguiling **Jardin des Plantes.**

→ MARKET FRESH

This is a city that makes the most of the outdoor life, and that includes its markets. The Place du Capitole is the place to be on a Wednesday, when a huge market sells food, clothes and bric-à-brac. And twice a week, they bring out the organic food, too: hang around and you'll be able to try all manner of breads, cheeses and cakes before you delve in your pocket for cash. Up at the Basilica St-Sernin on a Sunday, the antiques and bric-à-brac market is way too good to just call a flea-market – this is the place for gilded mirrors and chandeliers, so better keep some extra space in your rucksack. Market or not, the little squares dotted all over town are always humming with life, be it unicyclists or accordionists, roller-bladers or skateboarders. Or maybe just students. There are 115,000 of them here, not just adding to the weight of grey matter within the city walls, but, even more crucially if you're visiting, helping keep the prices down in the cafés and bars.

CALENDAR HIGHLIGHTS

La Ville Rose views its festivals and events through violet-tinted spectacles, even in the gloom of February, when it hosts the International Violet Meeting. Toulouse is the world capital of violets, and this celebration of the city's favourite flower includes exhibitions, markets, and various flower-based attractions. A month later, the Parc des Expositions de Toulouse is the venue for the Toulouse International Fair, when 150,000 visitors congregate for exhibitions and activities based around an international theme (in 2008 it's 'People of the Himalayas'). In June, the action moves down to the river. The Garonne Festival livens up the banksides with art happenings, music and parades, while also that month the Electronic Siestas Festival brings free afternoon concerts to the Garonne: it's innovative music to snooze-in-the-sun

TOULOUSE IN...

→ ONE DAY
Place du Capitole, St-Sernin, Les Jacobins, Hôtel d'Assezat, dusk back at Capitole

→ TWO DAYS
Musée des Augustins, Les Abattoirs (or Cité de l'Espace), the streets around rue Croix-Baragnon, a stroll along the banks of the Canal du Midi (or the Garonne)

→ THREE DAYS
Jardin des Plantes, Musée Paul-Dupuy, a boisterous market (if Sunday, at St-Sernin)

by. Toulouse is a cultural hothouse, and the Marathon des Mots, also in June, celebrates the written word, with more than three hundred writers and artists taking part in a series of readings and performances at more than forty venues. There's an eclectic air about the Toulouse d'Été Music Festival in July and August. International names rub shoulders with local musicians in a wide range of concerts at venues across the city, and the music ranges from flamenco to jazz to piano recital. Fans of the latter will be in seventh heaven, because September sees the Piano Aux Jacobins Festival, at the Church of the Jacobins, an atmospheric occasion with recitals by some of the world's best pianists in the cloisters of the ancient church. A huge contemporary art showpiece dominates the end of September and October: Printemps de Septembre is a free exhibition covering many artistic genres that takes place all over the city with special street lighting to enhance the effect. Alongside runs the Festival Occitania (also September) with more than fifty cultural events covering film, music, poetry, theatre, painting and more besides. To top it all off, November's Toulouse Antiques Fair, at the Parc des Expositions, has been voted France's premier event in its category by the trade press, so expect three impressive displays: Prestige, Antiques and Arts and Crafts.

EATING OUT

The food of the Toulousain is not for the faint-hearted. A lot of the city's favoured dishes concentrate on the parts of animals many prefer to forget. Neck, brain, ears and liver find their way onto the menu stuffed, slow-cooked or in eye-popping combinations. At the smart restaurants, it's possible to order the likes of pigeon stuffed with langoustines or foie gras with spiced fruits. Traditionally, the mainstay of the southwest is the cassoulet, a hearty stew with basic ingredients such as pork, duck fat, beans and garlic. You need to be hungry to take it on, so you'll be pleased to know that proper evening dining in Toulouse doesn't really start till at least 8.30 or 9 in the evening when your appetite should be well and truly whetted. Get there earlier and you'll be dining alone. This is a city that lives the late life: it's only sixty miles from the Spanish border, and its dining style is cheerily overseen as 'la mode espagnole'. There's a third element to the food scene here: wander down some of the narrower streets in the evening and you'll realise how close you are to North Africa. Exotic scents waft from darkened doorways and Moroccan restaurants – lots of them – tempt you inside. Wherever you decide to eat, the bill includes a service charge, but if you're happy with the service, it's usual to leave a tip of between five and ten per cent. And remember, if you've been excited by a particular ingredient then stock up at the farmers' markets that are popular in the city: these are the places for foie gras, sausages, creamy wads of goats' cheese, and bread the size of local rugby balls.

→ TOULOUSE L'EAU-TREK

If you get the chance, come into the city by the Canal du Midi. It's lined with plane trees and fine nineteenth-century houses, and winds its calm way up from the Mediterranean. The most atmospheric way to see it is by cycling, walking or just floating along its seductive course on a slow boat.

→ BIG ON OPERA

The city hall in the Place du Capitole is so big because it also contains Toulouse's main musical venue, the Opera House. This is a refurbished eighteenth century gem, with opulent gilt mouldings and painted cartouches. It's one of France's most prestigious homes of opera, but get along to see ballet, chamber music and recitals as well.

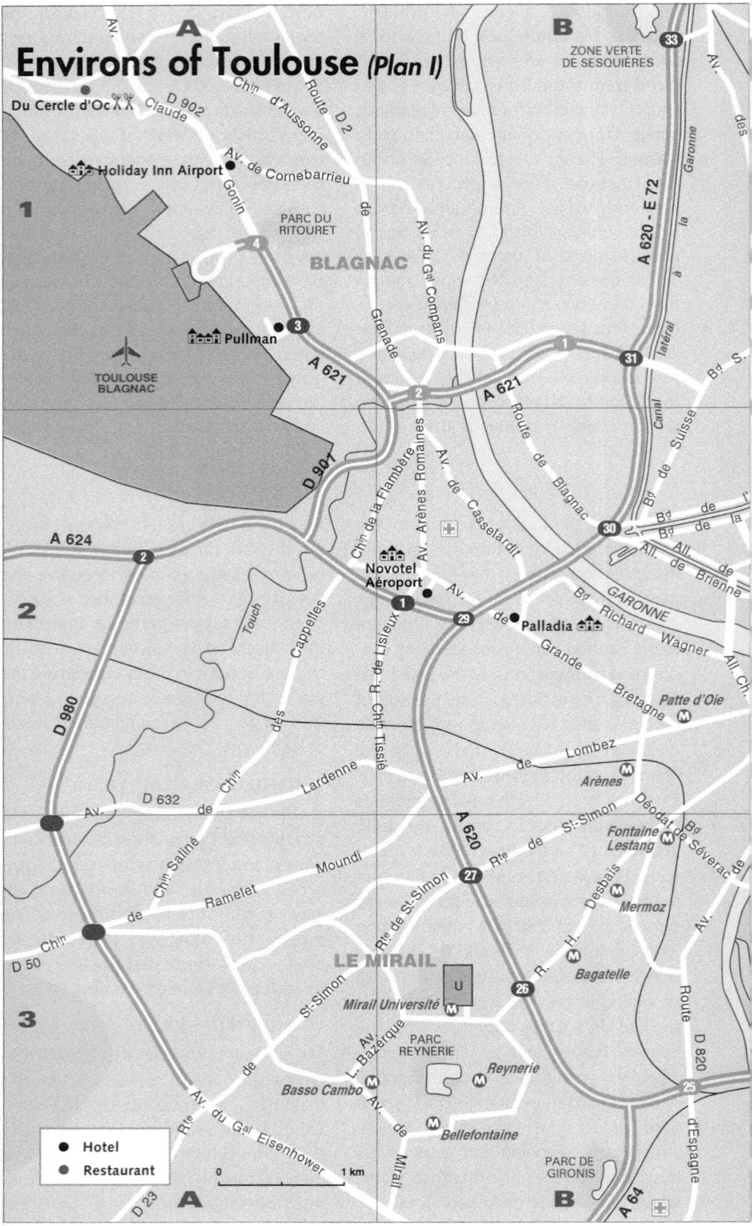

Environs of Toulouse (Plan I)
Du Cercle d'Oc
Holiday Inn Airport
Pullman
TOULOUSE BLAGNAC
BLAGNAC
PARC DU RITOURET
ZONE VERTE DE SESQUIÈRES
Novotel Aéroport
Palladia
GARONNE
A 621
A 624
A 620
A 620 - E 72
A 64
D 901
D 980
D 632
D 50
D 23
D 902
D 820
Route D 2
LE MIRAIL
PARC REYNERIE
PARC DE GIRONIS
Patte d'Oie
Arènes
Fontaine Lestang
Mermoz
Bagatelle
Mirail Université
Reynerie
Basso Cambo
Bellefontaine
Av. de Cornebarrieu
Av. du Gal Compans
Route de Blagnac
Av. de Casselardit
Av. Arènes Romaines
Chin de la Flambère
R. de Lisieux
Chin Tissié
Chin des Cappelles
Av. de Lardenne
Av. de Lombez
Av. de Grande Bretagne
Bd Richard Wagner
All. de Brienne
Rte de St-Simon
Chin Saliné
Chin de Ramelet Moundi
Av. du Gal Eisenhower
Av. L. Bazerque
Av. de Mirail
Route d'Espagne
R. H. Desbals
Bd Déodat de Séverac
Bd de Suisse
Canal latéral à la Garonne
Hotel
Restaurant
0
1 km

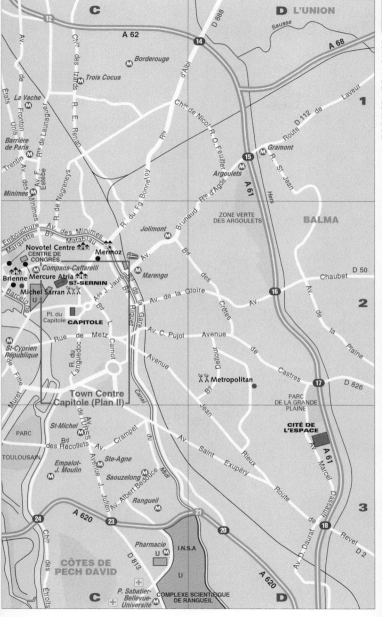

C   D   L'UNION

A 62

Borderouge

Trois Cocus

La Vache

Barrière
de Paris

Minimes

Embouchure

Marquette

Matabiau

Novotel Centre
CENTRE DE
CONGRÈS

Mermoz

Brienne

Compans-Caffarelli

Mercure Atria

Michel Sarran

ST-SERNIN

PL. du
Capitole

CAPITOLE

St-Cyprien
République

Rue   de   Metz

Av. C. Pujol

Town Centre
Capitole (Plan II)

PARC
TOULOUSAIN

St-Michel

Bd
des Récollets

Empalot-
J. Moulin

Ste-Agne

Saouzelong

Rangueil

A 620

CÔTES DE
PECH DAVID

Pharmacie

I.N.S.A

U

P. Sabatier-
Bellevue-
Université

COMPLEXE SCIENTIFIQUE
DE RANGUEIL

C   D

Chin   des Izards

Chin de Nicol-R. O. Feuiller

Gramont

Argoulets

Jolimont

Marengo

Av. de la Gloire

ZONE VERTE
DES ARGOULETS

BALMA

Chaubet

D 50

Metropolitan

PARC
DE LA GRANDE
PLAINE

CITÉ DE
L'ESPACE

Crampel

Av. Saint   Exupéry

Route   de

D 826

Sausse

A 68

Laveur

D 112 de

Av. de la Plaine

A 61

281

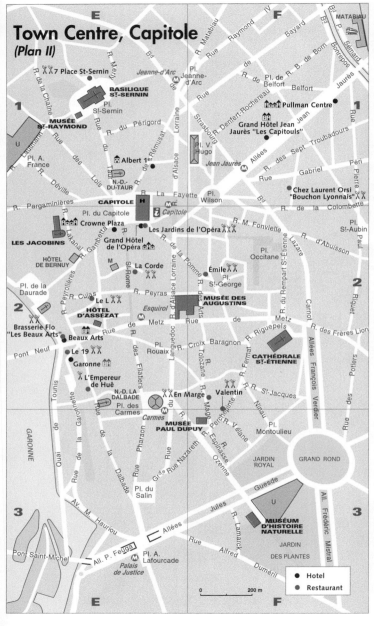

Sofitel Centre 🛜 ♿ rm 🎦 ⇙ rm 🕻 🕿 🚗 VISA ⚬⚬ AE ①

84 allées J. Jaurès – ℰ 05 61 10 23 10 – h1091@accor.com – Fax 05 61 10 23 20
– www.pullmanhotels.com **F1**
119 rm – ♦300/340 € ♦♦340/380 €, � 22 € – 14 suites
Rest *S W Café* – ℰ 05 61 10 23 40 – Menu 25 € bi (weekdays dinner)
– Carte 35/58 €
♦ Luxury ♦ Chain hotel ♦ Classical ♦

The hotel occupies an imposing red-brick and glass building. Discreetly luxurious rooms, with good soundproofing. Business centre and good seminar facilities. Modern setting and recipes combining regional products and foreign spices at the SW café.

Crowne Plaza 🛜 🛗 🍽 ♿ rm 🎦 ⇙ rm 🕿 🕻 🚗 VISA ⚬⚬ AE ①

7 pl. du Capitole – ℰ 05 61 61 19 19 – hicptoulouse@alliance-hospitality.com
– Fax 05 61 61 19 08 – www.crowne-plaza-toulouse.com **E2**
162 rm ⊐ – ♦130/390 € ♦♦145/405 € – 3 suites
Rest – *(closed August)* Menu 29/60 € bi – Carte 49/72 €
♦ Business ♦ Chain hotel ♦ Classical ♦

This luxury hotel enjoys a prestigious location on the famous Place du Capitole. Spacious, comfortable rooms, some of which overlook the town hall. Business centre. The restaurant opens onto a delightful Florentine-inspired patio.

Grand Hôtel de l'Opéra without rest ♿ 🎦 SAT 🕿 🕻

1 pl. du Capitole – ℰ 05 61 21 82 66 – hotelopera@ VISA ⚬⚬ AE ①
guichard.fr – Fax 05 61 23 41 04 – www.grand-hotel-opera.com **E2**
49 rm – ♦190/490 € ♦♦260/490 €, ⊐ 22 €
♦ Luxury ♦ Cosy ♦

This hotel in a 17C convent has an air of serenity and charm. Beautiful rooms with wood panels and velvet. Pleasant bar lounge and attractive vaulted reception hall.

de Brienne without rest ♿ 🎦 🕻 🕿 P 🚗 VISA ⚬⚬ AE ①

20 bd du Mar. Leclerc – ℰ 05 61 23 60 60 – brienne@hoteldebrienne.com
– Fax 05 61 23 18 94 – www.hoteldebrienne.com Plan I **C2**
70 rm – ♦70/95 € ♦♦70/95 €, ⊐ 11 € – 1 suite
♦ Chain hotel ♦ Classical ♦

Colourful and impeccably maintained rooms, numerous work and leisure areas (bar-library, patio): very popular with a business clientele.

Mercure Atria 🛜 ♿ 🎦 ⇙ rm 🕿 🕻 🚗 VISA ⚬⚬ AE ①

8 espl. Compans Caffarelli – ℰ 05 61 11 09 09 – h1585@accor.com
– Fax 05 61 23 14 12 – www.mercure.com Plan I **C2**
136 rm – ♦82/158 € ♦♦92/168 €, ⊐ 14 € – 2 suites
Rest – Carte 25/35 €
♦ Chain hotel ♦ Modern ♦

Modern comfortable furnishings, decorative wood panels and warm colours in rooms that have been recently refurbished in line with the chain's new look. Vast business area. The restaurant offers a soothing view of the public park, and another, busier one of the kitchen.

Novotel Centre 🐾 🛜 🏊 ♿ rm 🎦 ⇙ rm SAT 🕿 🚗

5 pl. A. Jourdain – ℰ 05 61 21 74 74 VISA ⚬⚬ AE ①
– h0906@accor.com – Fax 05 61 22 81 22
– www.novotel.com Plan I **C2**
135 rm – ♦103/175 € ♦♦103/175 €, ⊐ 15 € – 2 suites
Rest – Carte 25/45 €
♦ Chain hotel ♦ Modern ♦

This regional-style building adjacent to a Japanese garden and large park has spacious rooms renovated in a contemporary spirit, some with a terrace. A festival of colour in this dining room. Traditional and local cuisine.

283

Garonne without rest   💍 AC 🅂 📶 VISA 🆂 AE

*22 descente de la Halle aux Poissons – ℰ 05 34 31 94 80 – contact@
hotelgaronne.com – Fax 05 34 31 94 81 – www.hotelgaronne.com*
14 rm – †190/290 €, ††190/290 €, ⊡ 25 €   **E2**
♦ Traditional ♦ Modern ♦

An old building in one of the Old Town's narrow streets. A fine contemporary interior: stained-oak parquet flooring, design furniture, silk draperies and the odd Japanese touch.

Des Beaux Arts without rest   ≼ AC 🅂 📶 VISA 🆂 AE ①

*1 pl. du Pont-Neuf – ℰ 05 34 45 42 42 – contact@hoteldesbeauxarts.com
– Fax 05 34 45 42 43 – www.hoteldesbeauxarts.com*   **E2**
19 rm – †110/250 €, ††110/250 €, ⊡ 16 €
♦ Business ♦ Modern ♦

Tastefully done 18C establishment with cosy refined rooms, most with a view of the Garonne. Number 42 enjoys the additional benefit of a mini-terrace.

Les Capitouls without rest   💍 AC ⇎ 🅂 📶 ℥ VISA 🆂 AE ①

*29 allées J. Jaurès – ℰ 05 34 41 31 21 – reservation@hotel-capitouls.com
– Fax 05 61 63 15 17 – www.bestwestern-capitouls.com*   **F1**
55 rm – †130/181 €, ††130/181 €, ⊡ 14 € – 2 suites
♦ Chain hotel ♦ Classical ♦

Right by the Jean Jaurès metro station, this old town house has a distinctive foyer with pink brick vaulting. The rooms have Wifi access.

Mermoz without rest ⅏   💍 AC 🅂 📶 🛋 VISA 🆂 AE ①

*50 r. Matabiau – ℰ 05 61 63 04 04 – reservation@hotel-mermoz.com
– Fax 05 61 63 15 64 – www.hotel-mermoz.com*   *Plan I* **C2**
52 rm – †125/140 €, ††125/140 €, ⊡ 15 €
♦ Family ♦ Art Deco ♦

This hotel is undergoing gradual renovation. The decor recalls the Aeropostale's heroic pilots. Acid bright rooms, a conservatory and a tree-shaded terrace for breakfast.

Albert 1er without rest   AC 🅂 📶 ℥ VISA 🆂 AE

*8 r. Rivals – ℰ 05 61 21 17 91 – toulouse@hotel-albert1.com
– Fax 05 61 21 09 64 – www.hotel-albert1.com*   **E1**
47 rm – †55/115 €, ††65/123 €, ⊡ 10 €
♦ Family ♦ Functional ♦

A very practical base for discovering the "pink city" by foot. Ask for one of the refurbished rooms, or one at the rear for peace and quiet.

Les Jardins de l'Opéra   AC ⇎ ⇩ VISA 🆂 AE

*1 pl. du Capitole – ℰ 05 61 23 07 76 – contact@lesjardinsdelopera.com
– Fax 05 61 23 63 00 – www.lesjardinsdelopera.com
– Closed lunch Bank Holidays, Sunday and Monday*   **E2**
Rest – Menu 29 € (lunch), 44 € bi/110 € – Carte approx. 110 €
♦ A la mode ♦ Luxury ♦

The elegant dining rooms under a glass roof and separated by a fountain dedicated to Neptune. Unusually, the menu offers dishes in "trilogy": three dishes on the same plate.

Michel Sarran   🏠 AC ⇎ ⇩ ⊡ VISA 🆂 AE
ॐ ॐ

*21 bd A. Duportal – ℰ 05 61 12 32 32 – restaurant@michel-sarran.com
– Fax 05 61 12 32 33 – www.michel-sarran.com
– Closed August, 20-28 December, Wednesday lunch, Saturday and Sunday*
Rest – *(pre-book)* Menu 48 € bi (weekdays lunch), 98/165 € bi   *Plan I* **C2**
– Carte 86/127 €
Spec. Langoustines translucides sur un risotto glacé. Agneau allaiton de l'Aveyron rôti en viennoise aux dattes. Haricots tarbais en mousse légère au vieux rhum et lait de coco.
♦ Innovative ♦ Intimate ♦

This delightful 19C residence, with its friendly atmosphere that immediately makes one feel at home, and pretty, refined modern décor sets off the chef's inventive cuisine.

FRANCE - TOULOUSE

XX
£3 **En Marge** (Frank Renimel)   AC ⇔ VISA ◑ ⓞ
8 r. Mage – ℰ 05 61 53 07 24 – contact@restaurantenmarge.com
– www.restaurantenmarge.com
– Closed 6-12 April, 12 August-6 September, 21 December-3 January, Sunday,
Monday and Tuesday   **F2**
Rest – (number of covers limited, pre-book) Menu 55/80 €
Spec. Crème de potimarron aux Saint Jacques crues (December-February).
Suprême de pigeon rôti aux ravioles de foie gras. Parfait à la feuille de
tabac et "cigare" à la crème au rhum.
  ♦ Innovative ♦ Friendly ♦
A new restaurant with a homely atmosphere, friendly service and delicious, inno-
vative cuisine. Limited number of tables in a modern decor with a hint of Baroque.

XX
£3 **Metropolitan**   ⇱ & AC ⇔ P VISA ◑ AE
2 pl. Auguste-Albert – ℰ 05 61 34 63 11 – contact@metropolitan-restaurant.fr
– Fax 05 61 52 88 91 – www.metropolitan-restaurant.fr
– Closed 1ˢᵗ-21 August, 25-30 December, Saturday lunch, Sunday and Monday
Rest – Menu 30 € (weekdays lunch), 39/85 € – Carte 76/103 €   Plan I **D2**
Spec. Chair de crabe en barigoule de légumes à la coriandre. Calamars en
persillade, pressé de tomate au pesto. Framboises au naturel, croustillant de
chocolat au lait et thé (season).
  ♦ A la mode ♦ Design ♦
A modern restaurant which gets full marks for its delicious, contemporary cuisine,
designer-style dining room (with bar), small interior terrace adorned with vines,
and efficient, friendly service.

XX **Le L**   ⇱ AC ⇔ VISA ◑ AE
24 pl. de la Bourse – ℰ 05 61 21 69 05 – laurent.guillard@le-l.com
– Fax 05 61 21 61 79 – www.restaurantlel.com
– Closed 5-25 August, Sunday and Monday   **E2**
Rest – Menu 24 €, 48/75 € – Carte 32/64 €
  ♦ Innovative ♦ Fashionable ♦
This contemporary restaurant is in the heart of the old town. It features a regularly
renewed creative menu of Asian inspiration, more elaborate in the evenings. Sum-
mer terrace.

XX **Valentin**   VISA ◑
21 r. Perchepinte – ℰ 05 61 53 11 15 – contact@valentin-restaurant.fr
– www.valentin-restaurant.fr
– Closed Monday   **F2**
Rest – (dinner only) Menu 34/54 €
  ♦ Innovative ♦ Romantic ♦
A glass door crowned with an arch leads to this attractive restaurant, whose young
chef specialises in inventive cuisine. Elegant decor with period furniture, vaulted
cellar and brick walls.

XX **7 Place St-Sernin**   ⇱ AC ⇔ ⇔ VISA ◑ AE
7 pl. St-Sernin – ℰ 05 62 30 05 30 – restaurant@7placesaintsernin.com
– Fax 05 62 30 04 06 – www.7placesaintsernin.com
– Closed Saturday lunch and Sunday   **E1**
Rest – Menu 26 € (weekdays lunch), 34/75 € bi – Carte 49/68 €
  ♦ A la mode ♦ Fashionable ♦
This restaurant set in a typical Toulouse house boasts flamboyant colours and is
elegantly arranged and brightened with contemporary paintings. Modern dishes.

XX **La Corde**   AC ⇔ VISA ◑ AE
4 r. Chalande – ℰ 05 61 29 09 43 – Fax 05 62 15 25 88 – www.lacorde.com
– Closed Saturday lunch, Monday lunch and Sunday   **E2**
Rest – Menu 25 €, 37/110 € – Carte 70/110 €
  ♦ A la mode ♦ Fashionable ♦
This impressive 15C tower, all that remains of a mansion that used to belong to
prominent families of Toulouse, is home to the city's oldest restaurant (1881).
Updated regional dishes.

XX **Brasserie Flo "Les Beaux Arts"** 🏠 AC ⇄ 🛋 VISA ⬤⬤ AE
1 quai Daurade – ℰ 05 61 21 12 12 – Fax 05 61 21 14 80
– www.brasserielesbeauxarts.com   **E2**
Rest – Menu 31 € – Carte 33/50 €
◆ Brasserie ◆ Retro ◆
Popular with locals, this brasserie on the banks of the Garonne was once frequented by Ingres, Matisse and Bourdelle. Retro decor and a varied menu.

XX **Le 19** 🏠 AC ⇄ ⇕ VISA ⬤⬤ AE
19 descente de la Halle aux Poissons – ℰ 05 34 31 94 84 – contact@
restaurantle19.com – Fax 05 34 31 94 85 – www.restaurantle19.com
– Closed 11-17 August, 22 December-6 January, Monday lunch, Saturday lunch
and Sunday   **E2**
Rest – Menu 35 € (weekdays)/60 € bi – Carte 42/60 €
◆ De Terroir ◆ Trendy ◆
Welcoming, contemporary-style dining rooms (one with a superb 16C rib-vaulted ceiling), plus an open-view wine cellar. Hearty local cuisine.

XX **Chez Laurent Orsi "Bouchon Lyonnais"** 🏠 AC ⇄
13 r. de l'Industrie – ℰ 05 61 62 97 43   VISA ⬤⬤ ①
– orsi.le-bouchon-lyonnais@wanadoo.fr – Fax 05 61 63 00 71
– www.le-bouchon-lyonnais.com
– Closed Saturday lunch and Sunday except holidays
Rest – Menu 22/36 € – Carte 30/40 €   **F1**
◆ Bistro ◆ Brasserie ◆
A large bistro whose leather banquettes, closely-packed tables and mirrors are reminiscent of the brasseries of the 1930s. Dishes from the southwest and Lyon, as well as fish and seafood.

XX **Émile** 🏠 AC ⇄ VISA ⬤⬤ AE ①
13 pl. St-Georges – ℰ 05 61 21 05 56 – restaurant-emile@wanadoo.fr
– Fax 05 61 21 42 26 – www.restaurant-emile.com
– Closed 20 December-4 January, Monday except dinner from May to
September and Sunday   **F2**
Rest – Menu 20 € (lunch), 30/55 € – Carte 39/61 € 🏵
◆ De Terroir ◆ Friendly ◆
A restaurant with a popular terrace and a menu focused on local dishes and fish (cassoulet is the house speciality). Fine wine list.

X **L'Empereur de Huê** AC VISA ⬤⬤
17 r. Couteliers – ℰ 05 61 53 55 72 – www.empereurdehue.com
– Closed Sunday and Monday   **E2**
Rest – *(dinner only) (pre-book)* Menu 37 € – Carte 47/54 €
◆ Vietnamese ◆ Design ◆
If the decor of this family restaurant is contemporary, the cooking retains its Vietnamese roots.

AROUND TOULOUSE

Blagnac

🏨🏨🏨 **Pullman** 🏠 ⅃♨ ⓣ ✳ AC ⇄ rm 📺 ¶¶ 🧖 VISA ⬤⬤ AE ①
2 av. Didier Daurat (airport exit n° 3) – ℰ 05 34 56 11 11 – h0565@accor.com
– Fax 05 61 30 02 43 – www.pullmanhotels.com   **A1**
100 rm – ♦115/335 € ♦♦130/350 €, ⌣ 25 €
Rest *Le Caouec* – *(closed 27 July-23 August, Friday dinner, Saturday and Sunday)* Carte 51/67 €
◆ Chain hotel ◆ Business ◆ Modern ◆
1970s hotel being treated to a complete facelift. Contemporary style public areas, with some guestrooms updated in a similar vein. Free shuttle to the airport. Tapastype snacks served at the bar and more traditional menu in the dining room.

FRANCE - TOULOUSE

 Holiday Inn Airport 🛜 ⛶ ⤵ 🖐 rm 🆎 ⟷ rm 📺 📞 ♨ 🅿️
pl. Révolution – 🕾 *05 34 36 00 20 – tlsap@ihg.com* 💳 ⓒ 🅰️ ⓘ
– Fax 05 34 36 00 30 – www.holiday-inn.com/toulouse-apt **A1**
150 rm 🍴 – 📏99/240 € 📏📏99/240 €
Rest *– (closed Saturday lunch and Sunday lunch)* Menu 16 € (lunch), 22/38 €
– Carte 25/45 €
♦ Chain hotel ♦ Business ♦ Modern ♦
Both peaceful and warm shades adorn the rooms decorated with modern furniture. A well-appointed seminar area. A shuttle links the hotel to the airport. A pleasant brasserie-style restaurant decorated with frescoes depicting olive trees.

XX **Le Cercle d'Oc** 🚗 🛜 🆎 ⟷ 🅿️ 💳 ⓒ 🅰️ ⓘ
6 pl. M. Dassault – 🕾 *05 62 74 71 71 – cercledoc@wanadoo.fr*
– Fax 05 62 74 71 72
– Closed 3-24 August, 25 December-1st January, Saturday and Sunday
Rest – Menu 45 € bi/80 € bi – Carte 50/67 € **A1**
♦ A la mode ♦ Fashionable ♦
This pretty 18C farm is an island of greenery in the middle of a shopping area. English club atmosphere in the elegant dining rooms, billiards room and pleasant terrace.

Purpan

 Palladia 🛜 ⤵ 🖐 rm 🆎 ⟷ rm 📺 📶 ♨ 🅿️ 🚗 💳 ⓒ 🅰️ ⓘ
271 av. Grande Bretagne – 🕾 *05 62 12 01 20 – info@hotelpalladia.com*
– Fax 05 62 12 01 21 – www.hotelpalladia.com **B2**
90 rm – 📏109/215 € 📏📏109/215 €, 🍴 18 € – 3 suites
Rest *– (closed Sunday and public holidays)* Menu 25 € (lunch)/59 € bi
– Carte 40/65 €
♦ Business ♦ Modern ♦
An imposing building between the airport and city centre. Particularly well thought-out layout. The spacious and comfortable rooms are being progressively updated. Bright, modern dining room. Summer terrace shaded by parasols.

 Novotel Aéroport 🚗 🛜 ⤵ 🍴 🖐 rm 🆎 ⟷ rm 📺 📶 ♨ 🅿️
23 impasse Maubec – 🕾 *05 61 15 00 00 – h0445@* 💳 ⓒ 🅰️ ⓘ
accor.com – Fax 05 61 15 88 44 – www.novotel.com **B2**
123 rm – 📏81/160 € 📏📏81/160 €, 🍴 15 € **Rest** – Carte 33/50 €
♦ Chain hotel ♦ Functional ♦
The rooms of this chain hotel are fully soundproofed. Children's amusements, free shuttle to the airport, Wi-fi and plenty of green space. The restaurant and pleasant terrace offer a view of the pool. Updated menu, specials and diet meals.

Colomiers

XXX **L'Amphitryon** (Yannick Delpech) ⟵ 🛜 🆎 ⟷ 🅿️ 💳 ⓒ 🅰️ ⓘ
ⓢⓢ *chemin de Gramont –* 🕾 *05 61 15 55 55 – contact@lamphitryon.com*
– Fax 05 61 15 42 30 – www.lamphitryon.com
Rest – Menu 34 € (weekdays lunch), 64/105 € – Carte 95/113 € 🏵
Spec. Sardine fraîche taillée au couteau, crème de morue et caviar de hareng. Bar de ligne en deux cuissons, parfum de dulse et poutargue. Macaron moelleux au "cachou Lajaunie", tube givré au citron jaune et menthe.
♦ Innovative ♦ Fashionable ♦
A glass roof and fireplace have been added to this restaurant. It serves brilliantly inventive cuisine, which takes local produce to new heights.

GERMANY
DEUTSCHLAND

PROFILE

→ **AREA:**
356 733 km²
(137 735 sq mi).

→ **POPULATION:**
82 431 000
inhabitants (est.
2005), density = 231
per km².

→ **CAPITAL:**
Berlin (conurbation
3 761 000
inhabitants).

→ **CURRENCY:**
Euro (€); rate of
exchange: € 1 = US$
1.27 (Dec 2008).

→ **GOVERNMENT:**
Parliamentary federal
republic, comprising
16 states (Länder)
since 1990. Member
of European Union
since 1957 (one
of the 6 founding
countries).

→ **LANGUAGE:**
German.

→ **SPECIFIC PUBLIC
HOLIDAYS:**
Epiphany (6 January
– in Baden-
Württemberg, Bayern
and Sachsen-Anhalt
only); Good Friday
(Friday before
Easter); Corpus
Christi (in Baden-
Württemberg,
Bayern, Hessen,
Nordrhein-Westfalen,
Rheinland-Pfalz,
Saarland, Sachsen,
Thüringen and those
communities with
a predominantly
Roman Catholic
population only);
Day of German Unity
(3 October);
Reformation Day
(31 October – in new
Federal States only);
26 December.

→ **LOCAL TIME:**
GMT + 1 hour in
winter and GMT
+ 2 hours in summer.

→ **CLIMATE:**
Temperate
continental, with
cold winters and
warm summers
(Berlin: January: 0°C,
July: 20°C).

→ **INTERNATIONAL
DIALLING CODE:**
00 49 followed by
area code and then
the local number.
International
directory enquiries
☏ **11 834**.

→ **EMERGENCY:**
Police: ☏ **110**; Fire
Brigade: ☏ **112**.

→ **ELECTRICITY:**
220 volts AC,
50HZ; 2-pin round-
shaped continental
plugs.

→ **FORMALITIES**
Travellers from the
European Union
(EU), Switzerland,
Iceland and the main
countries of North
and South America
need a national
identity card or
passport (America:
passport required)
to visit Germany
for less than three
months (tourism or
business purpose).
For visitors from
other countries
a visa may be
required, in addition
to a passport,
especially for those
wishing to stay for
longer than three
months. We advise
you to check with
your embassy before
travelling.

Hamburg

BERLIN

Cologne

Frankfurt

Stuttgart

Munich

S. Guillot/MICHELIN

It's not every city parliament that has to scratch its head and decide where to put its centre, but that's the intriguing dilemma facing Berlin. Although homogeneous in many other ways, the east and the west of the city still lay claim to centres after their forty years of partition, and it may be that in time the exciting new – and central - Potsdamer Platz comes to be accepted as the city's hub. That's the thing about Germany's biggest metropolis – it's an invigorating mix of old and new, and constantly redefining itself.

After 1990, there were a tempestuous few years as Berlin sought to resolve its new identity, but it now stands proud as one of the most dynamic and forward thinking cities in the world. Alongside its idea of tomorrow, it's never lost sight of its bohemian past, and many parts of the city retain the arty sense of adventure that characterised downtown Berlin during the 1920s. Turn any corner and you might find a modernist art gallery, a tiny cinema or a cutting-edge club. Culture seeps through the very pores of life here.

LIVING THE CITY

The eastern side of the river Spree, around Nikolaiviertel, is the historic heart of the city, dating back to the 13C. Meanwhile, way over to the west of the centre lie Kurfürstendamm and Charlottenburg, smart districts which came to the fore after World War II as the heart of West Berlin. Between the two lie imposing areas which swarm with visitors:

Tiergarten is the green lung of the city, and just to its east is the great boulevard of Unter den Linden. Continuing eastward, the self-explanatory Museum Island sits snugly and securely in the tributaries of the Spree. The most southerly of Berlin's sprawling districts is **Kreuzberg**, renowned for its bohemian, alternative character.

PRACTICAL INFORMATION

ARRIVAL-DEPARTURE

Berlin is served by two airports : Berlin-Tegel Airport lies 12km northwest of the city centre and Berlin-Schönefeld is 21km to the southeast. U-Bahn and S-Bahn trains operate from all two.

TRANSPORT

Invest in a Berlin-Potsdam Welcome Card. It gives you unlimited travel on the S-Bahn (trains), and discounts for selected theatres, museums, attractions and city tours. Available at public transport ticket desks, many hotels, and tourist information offices.

To get from one side of Berlin to the other, you'll need to travel by public transport. The U- and S-Bahn are quick and efficient, but the bus is another good alternative. Routes 100 and 200 are special double-decker services ideal for the visitor, as they incorporate most of the top attractions. Trams operate mainly within East Berlin. A tram ticket can be used on buses, U- and S-Bahn trains. There are various ticketing options which prevail in the city: check with tourist information offices.

Cyclists are well looked after here, so a good idea might be to hire a bike. There are many cycling routes around the city: most of the main roads have separate cycling lanes and even special traffic lights at intersections.

EXPLORING BERLIN

Sooner or later, the visitor to Berlin will take a stroll down Unter den Linden. To all intents and purposes, this is the city's central avenue, and you'll find none more attractive. It's an imposing boulevard, and it begins at its western end with the symbol of German reunification, The Brandenburg Gate. This magnificent neo-classical structure was completed in 1795, and has borne witness to many of the city's momentous episodes, most recently the celebrations of 1989 when the detested Wall it overlooked was triumphantly torn down. Earlier this decade the Gate was painstakingly renovated to its original Acropolis-like glory.

The wide, tree-lined Unter den Linden contains many of the city's historic landmarks, with a high concentration of 18C buildings sporting a prestigious pedigree. There's a line of fine stop-off points a little way up, the highlight being the **German History Museum**, which is housed in a magnificent former arsenal of pink baroque built just over three hundred years ago. Its fascinating exhibits range from a stern looking Martin Luther to the jacket of a concentration camp prisoner. Close to here is the neo-classical façade of the **State Opera House**, home to some of Berlin's finest performances, and the **State Library**, which boasts a tranquil inner courtyard with fountain and snug café providing a welcome break from the bustling grandeur of the boulevard.

→ ON A SPREE

Crossing **Schlossbrücke**, the eye-catching bridge over the Spree, you're on Berlin's very own island, named after what's made it famous. There are five museums here, and they're all in a grand huddle to your left. Pick of the bunch is the **Pergamon Museum**, which has one of the best collections of antiquities in the world, impressive enough to draw thousands of art lovers from across the globe. The other museums are hardly put in the shade: the **Alte Nationalgalerie** has a fine collection of German Romantics and French Impressionists; the **Altes** and **Neues Museums** highlight intriguing collections of Greek and Roman antiquities, and Egyptian art respectively; and the **Bodemuseum** has an eclectic mix of sculpture and coins. Much-needed restoration to the museums may possibly limit your access; nevertheless, give yourself an hour in each to do them justice. Most visually arresting of the island's

buildings is the huge **Berliner Dom**, the city's cathedral, which has been painstakingly rebuilt since the War. Its impressive neo-Baroque exterior is modelled on St Peter's in Rome.

→ MEDIEVAL RECREATION

Just east from the island, across another bridge, lies the historic centre of Berlin, the Nikolaiviertel. By the time the city celebrated its seven hundred and fiftieth anniversary in 1987, the East German authorities of the time had rebuilt the area's pristine buildings: many of them having been lost in the War. What you see now is their attempt to recreate a medieval village. Centrepiece is the (originally) 13C **Nikolai Church**, which now includes a fascinating Berlin history exhibition. For true authenticity, make for the nearby **Knoblauchhaus**. This is the only house in Nikolaiviertel to escape War damage, and it's the oldest building still standing in Berlin. It's a beautiful mid-eighteenth century merchant's home, and its interior is now a household museum. For a radically different experience, head a little further east to the **TV Tower** – you're bound to have spotted it from practically any vantage point in the city. It's Berlin's tallest structure, like a giant toothpick that's bored its way up from the ground, and the view from its revolving café is spectacular: you'll see the whole of the city from up here, and you can enjoy a *Kaffee und Kuchen* while you're at it.

→ TOP OF THE POTS

Will **Potsdamer Platz** be recognised one day as the centrepoint of Berlin? It's ticking all the right boxes. Located just off the luxuriant Tiergarten, it was a mass of rubble not too many years ago. Now it's been developed as Germany's architectural showpiece, a shimmering zone of shiny new arcades and office buildings, where corporate domes merge with bright-as-a-button cafés and splashy fountains. This reborn area also does a nice line in irony: step out from one of its swish 21C entertainment complexes and spot the line of metal plaques thrusting from the street paving to denote where the Berlin Wall once stood. Potsdamer Platz also draws in a lot of visitors who've been to the nearby **Gemäldegalerie**, generally considered to be the best in Berlin. It contains nearly three thousand paintings covering five hundred years from the thirteenth to the eighteenth centuries, painstakingly acquired by experts whose task was to select high quality examples from all major European schools. Thus one can admire great works by Botticelli, Caravaggio, Rubens, Rembrandt, Bruegel, Vermeer and others. In keeping with the zeitgeist feel of Potsdamer Platz is the nearby **Reichstag** parliament building. Its wondrous late twentieth century glass beehive dome is visible for miles around, and adds another powerful visual statement to Berlin's modernist account. One more architectural wonder near the Gemäldegalerie is the 'circus tent' **Philharmonie** building, home to one of Europe's most renowned orchestras, the Berlin Philharmonic.

→ ALTERNATIVE CHECKPOINT

South of the centre is the 'alternative' highlight, Kreuzberg, the city's most bohemian quarter. Bizarrely enough, the 'entry point' to Kreuzberg could hardly be less bohemian (though it could possibly be termed 'alternative'): **Checkpoint Charlie** was the notorious crossing point between East and West Berlin during the Cold War. It's now marked by a single hut, but nearby is a fascinating Checkpoint Charlie museum full of weird ephemera relating to it. These days, this buzzing quarter is more renowned for its Turkish bazaars, arty boutiques, galleries and nightclubs: the latter often open in the early hours, not closing until long after the rising of the sun.

→ WEST SIDE STORY

Many tourists concentrate on the district that was East Berlin, where the origins of the city lie, but the western side also has much to commend it. Kurfürstendamm is a snazzy boulevard that runs through the heart of the area. It's not hard to realise that this was the 'free market' side of Berlin during the days of the Wall, as Ku'damm (the locals' name) runs the gamut of exclusive designer stores. The fashionable side-streets off it are also lined with boutiques and cafés tailor made to ensnare the *beau monde*. The area also boasts Europe's largest department store, **Kaufhaus des Westens** ('KaDeWe'), now over a hundred years old. The main attraction here is the gourmet's paradise, which has the largest collection of foodstuffs in the whole of Europe, including live fish and nearly two thousand five hundred different wines. Further west, Charlottenburg is possibly the most enchanting part of the city. It only became part of Berlin in 1920, and its heart is the seventeenth cen-

BERLIN IN...

→ **ONE DAY**
Unter Den Linden, Museum Island, Nikolaiviertel, coffee at TV Tower

→ **TWO DAYS**
Potsdamer Platz, Reichstag, Gemäldegalerie, concert at Philharmonie

→ **THREE DAYS**
KaDeWe, Kurfürstendamm, Charlottenburg Palace

tury former royal summer palace of Queen Sophie Charlotte. Its collection of richly decorated interiors is un-equalled in Berlin, and the beautifully picturesque park that surrounds it is a magnet for weekending locals.

CALENDAR HIGHLIGHTS

The importance of Berlin as a cultural centre begins early in the year with the world renowned Berlin Film Festival, which attracts top international movies and stars. Throughout the summer the city holds the Museumsinsel Festival, during which special music, theatre and film productions are held for the public: Potsdamer Platz's open-air cinema is a popular venue. At the beginning of summer, in May, Kreuzberg's hip streets play host to the Karneval der Kulturen, which is three days of singing and dancing in celebration of multicultural Berlin. Bach lovers are in their element in July with Bach Tage Berlin, which features nine days' worth of the maestro's music, performed throughout the city.

The same month, and on into August, World Music takes centre stage with open air concerts under the banner Heimatklange. The massive Global City celebration in August attracts up to three million visitors to Ku'damm. Now twenty years old, it hosts ten stages, featuring music of every description. A month later Musikfest Berlin offers two weeks of top classical performances in the Opera House and Philharmonie. The International Literary Festival (September) packs out Bebelplatz, as writers and poets from all over the world read to thousands. In October the focus is on a glittering metropolis when its top attractions are seductively illuminated in the Berlin Festival of Lights.

EATING OUT

Although by tradition Berlin hasn't been a gourmet stronghold, it does have a reputation for simple, hearty dishes, inspired by the long, hard winters. It's amazing how when the temperatures plummet, the city's comfort food can have an irresistible allure. Come the winter, who's for pork knuckle, Schnitzel, Bratwurst in mustard, chunky dumplings…or the real Berlin favourite Currywurst, which enjoins curry sauce and sausage. Be sure to try the local beer – Berliner Weisse mit Schuss – which is a light beer with a dash of raspberry or woodruff. Of course, that's not the whole story. Over the last fifteen years or so, Berlin has become so cosmopolitan that it can now claim a wider range of restaurants than any other German city. Many of the best restaurants are found within grand hotels and you only have to get to Savignyplatz near Ku'damm to realise how smart dining has taken off in a big way: the square is bursting with popular cafés and restaurants serving good food. There are lots too in Gendarmenmarkt. In the city as a whole there are almost unlimited options for the visitor: Asian restaurants of all kinds have sprung up in recent years. On the local front, bread and potatoes are ubiquitous – indeed Berlin has its own unique breads and rolls – but since reunification, the signature dishes have incorporated a global influence, so produce from the local forests, rivers and lakes may well have an Asian or Mediterranean twist. You can invariably eat late in Berlin: lots of places stay open until late, which can mean 2 or 3 in the morning. As dinner is the popular meal so there are plenty of inexpensive lunch menus available. Service is included in the price of your meal, but it's customary to round up the bill.

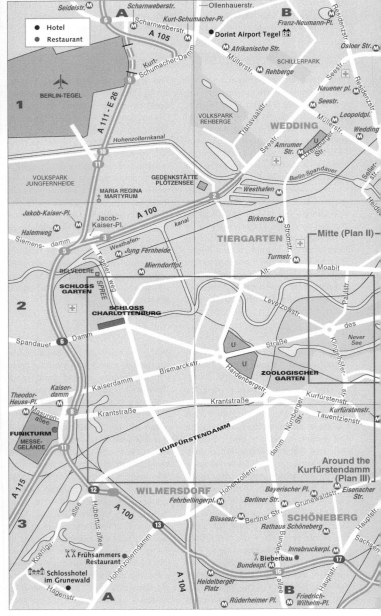

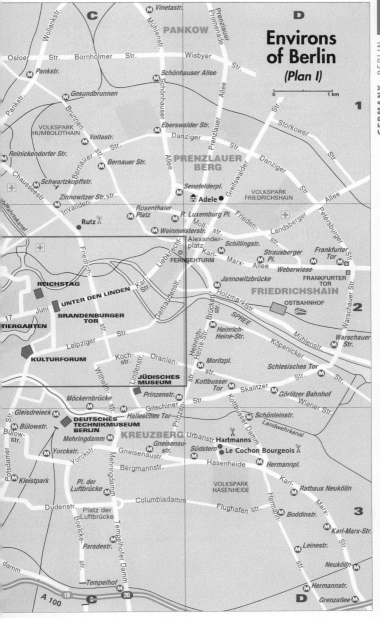

**Environs
of Berlin
(Plan I)**

0   1 km

PANKOW

Vinetastr.

Prenzlauer Promenade

Wollankstr.

Mühlenstr.

Wisbyer

Str.

Osloer   Str.   Bornholmer   Str.

Str.

Pankstr.

Schönhauser Allee

Storkower

Str.

Gesundbrunnen

Schönhauser

Allee

Eberswalder Str.

Prenzlauer

Danziger

Str.

Danziger

Str.

Allee

VOLKSPARK
HUMBOLDTHAIN

Brunnen

Voltastr.

PRENZLAUER
BERG

Greifswalder

Str.

Reinickendorfer Str.

Bernauer

Bernauer Str.

Allee

Chausseestr.

Schwartzkopffstr.

Senefelderpl.

Adele

VOLKSPARK
FRIEDRICHSHAIN

Petersburger

Zinnowitzer Str.

Str.

Invaliden-

Rosenthaler
Platz

R. Luxemburg Pl.

Frieden-

Landsberger

Allee

Rutz

Weinmeisterstr.

str.

Moll-

Friedrich-

Alexander-
platz

Schillingstr.

str.

Strausberger
Pl.

Frankfurter
Tor

REICHSTAG

Karl-

Liebknecht-

FERNSEHTURM

Marx-

Allee

Weberwiese

FRANKFURTER
TOR

Jannowitzbrücke

UNTER DEN LINDEN

Karl-

Str.

FRIEDRICHSHAIN

Warschauer Str.

17.

Juni

BRANDENBURGER
TOR

str.

Leipziger

Grenadierstr.

Holzmarktstr.

SPREE

OSTBAHNHOF

Str.

Brücken-

str.

Mühlenstr.

Köpenicker

Warschauer
Str.

TIERGARTEN

KULTURFORUM

Koch-
str.

Oranien-

Heinrich-
Heine-Str.

Moritzpl.

Heinrich-Heine-Str.

Schlesisches Tor

Wilhelm-

Lindenstr.

JÜDISCHES
MUSEUM

Prinzenstr.

str.

Kottbusser
Tor

Skalitzer

Görlitzer Bahnhof

Wiener Str.

Möckernbrücke

Gitschiner

Str.

Kottbusser Damm

Gleisdreieck

Str.

Bülowstr.

Bülow-
str.

Hallesches Tor

Prinzen-

Schönleinstr.

Landwehrkanal

DEUTSCHES
TECHNIKMUSEUM
BERLIN

Mehringdamm

Urbanstr.

Hartmanns

Potsdamer

Yorckstr.

Mehringdamm

Gneisenau-
str.

Südstern

Le Cochon Bourgeois

Kleistpark

Gneisenaustr.

Hasenheide

Hermannpl.

Bergmannstr.

KREUZBERG

VOLKSPARK
HASENHEIDE

Karl-

Rathaus Neukölln

Pl. der
Luftbrücke

Columbiadamm

Flughafen-str.

Hermann-

Boddinstr.

Dudenstr.

Platz der
Luftbrücke

Boelcke-

Karl-Marx-Str.

Paradestr.

str.

Tempelhofer Damm

Leinestr.

Neukölln

Tempelhof

damm

A 100

19

C

20

Hermannstr.

Grenzallee

D

🏨🏨🏨🏨 **Adlon Kempinski**   🛜 🗚 ⊕ ⋙ 🖾 ㄟ 🆔 📷 📡 🗚 🚗

Unter den Linden 77 ✉ *10117* – Ⓜ *Französische Str.*   VISA 🆖 AE ①
– 𝒞 *(030) 2 26 10 – hotel.adlon@kempinski.com – Fax (030) 22 61 22 22*
– *www.hotel-adlon.de*   **G1**
382 rm – 🛏315/620 € 🛏🛏315/620 €, ⌐ 36 €
– 29 suites
Rest *Lorenz Adlon* – see below
Rest *Quarré* – 𝒞 *(030) 22 61 15 55* – Menu 65/95 € – Carte 45/94 €
♦ Grand Luxury ♦ Historic ♦ Classic ♦
The magnificent Grand Hotel dating back to 1907 offers individual service and
high quality rooms and suites (all the Berlin suites have their own sauna). There is
an impressive wellness area with its elegant day spa. Attractive wine store. The
Quarré is classical in style with views over the Brandenburg Gate from the terrace.

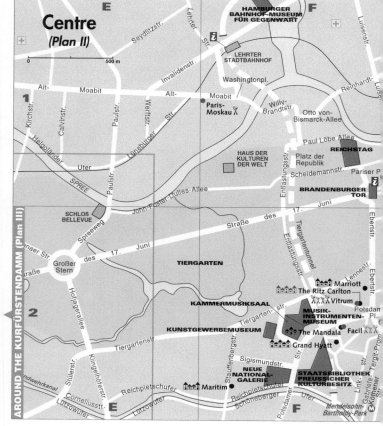

The Ritz-Carlton 🏨🏨🏨 📶 ⅃ᴙ 〆 🔲 ㄷ 🆎 🔤 📞 🛥 🚗 VISA ⓪ AE ①

Potsdamer Platz 3 ⊠ 10785 – Ⓜ *Potsdamer Platz –* 𝒞 *(030) 33 77 77*
– berlin@ritzcarlton.com – Fax (030) 3 37 77 55 55
– www.ritzcarlton.com

F2

302 rm – 🛇315/365 €, 🛇🛇345/445 €, ☁ 38 €
– 40 suites
Rest *Vitrum* – see below
Rest *Brasserie Desbrosses –* 𝒞 *(030) 3 37 77 63 41 –* Menu 43/76 €
– Carte 41/64 €

♦ Grand Luxury ♦ Chain hotel ♦ Classic ♦

An exclusive, elegant address. The splendid, lobby with its suspended marble stair-case also houses a stylish lounge where guests can meet for an afternoon tea. This original French brasserie, which was founded in 1875 and serves typical meals, has an informal atmosphere.

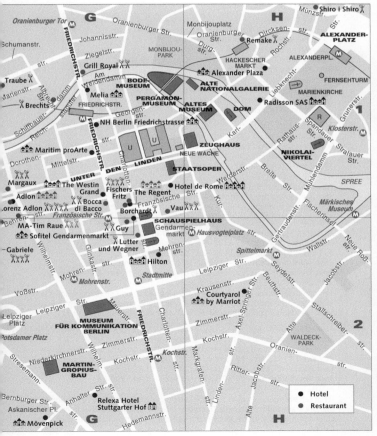

GERMANY - BERLIN

Grand Hyatt ⬛ 🍴 ⬛ 🛆 🔲 ⬛ 🛗 🅰 🛰 ⬛ 🛆 🚗 **VISA** ⬤ **AE** ⓪

Marlene-Dietrich-Platz 2 (Entrance Eichhornstraße) ✉ *10785*
– ⓜ Potsdamer Platz – ℰ (030) 25 53 12 34 – berlin.grand@hyatt.de
– Fax (030) 25 53 12 35 – www.berlin.grand.hyatt.com **F2**
342 rm – †255/490 € ††285/490 €, ⌂ 29 € – 16 suites
Rest *Vox* – *ℰ (030) 25 53 17 72 (closed Saturday lunch, Sunday lunch)*
Carte 42/65 €
♦ Grand Luxury ♦ Chain hotel ♦ Design ♦
This trapezoidal-shaped hotel on the Potsdamer Platz stands out for its modern, well-equipped rooms of purist design. Vox in Asian style.

Hotel de Rome 🛆 🍴 ⬛ 🔲 🛆 🅰 🛰 🕻 🛆 🚗 **VISA** ⬤ **AE** ⓪

Behrenstr. 37 ✉ *10117 – ⓜ Französische Str. – ℰ (030) 4 60 60 90*
– info.derome@roccofortecollection.com – Fax (030) 46 06 09 20 00
– www.roccofortecollection.com **G1**
146 rm – †395/595 € ††395/595 €, ⌂ 26 € – 9 suites
Rest *Parioli* – Menu 90 € – Carte 54/86 €
♦ Grand Luxury ♦ Classic ♦
A luxury hotel on the Bebelplatz in the impressive framework of a building dating from 1889, formerly used by the Dresdner Bank. Today, the old strongroom is a pool. The restaurant Parioli offers ambitious Italian cuisine.

The Regent 🛆 🍴 🛆 🅰 🛰 🕻 🛆 🚗 **VISA** ⬤ **AE** ⓪

Charlottenstr. 49 ✉ *10117 – ⓜ Französische Str. – ℰ (030) 2 03 38*
– info.berlin@rezidorregent.com – Fax (030) 20 33 61 19
– www.theregentberlin.com **G1**
195 rm – †260/430 € ††290/460 €, ⌂ 35 € – 39 suites
Rest *Fischers Fritz* – see below
♦ Grand Luxury ♦ Classic ♦
Excellent service and sophisticated elegance give this luxury hotel in the Gendarmenmarkt an exclusive feel. One of the many treats on offer is afternoon tea in English, Indian or Russian style.

Marriott 🍴 🛆 ⬛ 🔲 🛆 🅰 🛰 🕻 🛆 🚗 **VISA** ⬤ **AE** ⓪

Inge-Beisheim-Platz 1 ✉ *10785 – ⓜ Potsdamer Platz – ℰ (030) 22 00 00*
– berlin@marriotthotels.com – Fax (030) 2 20 00 10 00
– www.berlinmarriott.com **F2**
379 rm – †219/279 € ††219/299 €, ⌂ 28 € Rest – Carte 35/64 €
♦ Chain hotel ♦ Luxury ♦ Modern ♦
A business hotel in the modern style. Most of the rooms with American cherry fittings are laid out around the large atrium style lobby. Bistro style restaurant with open kitchen and large window façade.

Hilton 🍴 🛆 ⬛ 🔲 🔲 🛆 🅰 🛰 🕻 🛆 🚗 **VISA** ⬤ **AE** ⓪

Mohrenstr. 30 ✉ *10117 – ⓜ Stadtmitte – ℰ (030) 2 02 30 – info.berlin@*
hilton.com – Fax (030) 20 23 42 69 – www.hilton.de **G2**
591 rm – †145/365 € ††145/365 €, ⌂ 24 € – 14 suites
Rest *Mark Brandenburg* – *ℰ (030) 20 23 46 55 –* Carte 32/54 €
Rest *Trader Vic's* – *ℰ (030) 20 23 46 05 (dinner only)* Carte 28/54 €
♦ Chain hotel ♦ Luxury ♦ Functional ♦
This city hotel stands out for its impressive lobby, its wide range of wellness and fitness facilities and its rooms, some of which look onto the Gendarmenmarkt. Mark Brandenburg offers regional dishes. Trader Vic's: Polynesian cuisine.

Radisson SAS 🛆 🍴 🛆 🛆 🅰 🛰 🕻 🛆 🚗 **VISA** ⬤ **AE** ⓪

Karl-Liebknecht-Str. 3 ✉ *10178 – ⓜ Alexanderplatz – ℰ (030) 23 82 80*
– info.berlin@radissonsas.com – Fax (030) 2 38 28 10 – www.berlin.radissonsas.com
427 rm – †155/380 € ††155/380 €, ⌂ 25 € **H1**
Rest *HEat* – *ℰ (030) 2 38 28 34 72 –* Carte 35/53 €
Rest *Noodle Kitchen* – *ℰ (030) 2 38 28 34 64 –* Carte 29/38 €
♦ Business ♦ Chain hotel ♦ Modern ♦
What catches your eye when you look into the purist atrium lobby of this hotel is a cylindrical aquarium 25 m high. The rooms are light and stylish. HEat: international cuisine in a modern bistro ambience. The Noodle Kitchen offers Southeast Asian cuisine.

RAMOS PINTO

Est. 1880

You've got the right address !

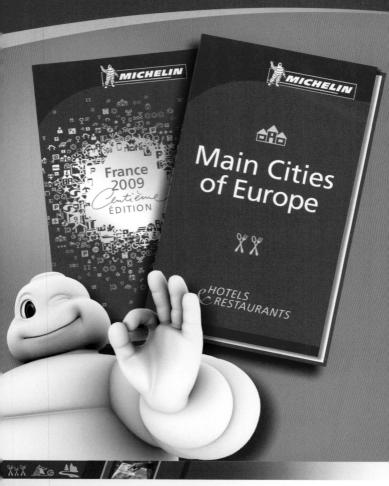

From palaces to bed and breakfast, from fine restaurants to small bistrots, the MICHELIN guide collection includes 45,000 hotels and restaurants selected by our inspectors in Europe and beyond. Wherever you may be, whatever your budget, you are sure you have the right address!

Maritim 🕸 🖾 ㄴ AC 📺 ⑪ 🙈 🚗 VISA ⚫ AE ⓪

Stauffenbergstr. 26 ✉ *10785 –* Ⓜ *Mendelssohn-Bartholdy-Park –* ℰ *(030)*
2 06 50 – info.ber@maritim.de – Fax (030) 20 65 10 00 – www.maritim.de
505 rm – ♦155/295 € ♦♦170/310 €, ⌁ 24 € **F2**
Rest *Grandrestaurant M – (closed Sunday lunch)* Carte 31/63 €
♦ Luxury ♦ Chain hotel ♦ Modern ♦
Stands out for its elegant setting, high-quality, well-equipped rooms and excellent
conference and event facilities. The Presidential Suite is 350 m2! A 1920s style
restaurant.

The Westin Grand 🎝 ⅙ 🕸 🖾 ㄴ AC 📺 ⑪ 🏊 VISA ⚫ AE ⓪

Friedrichstr. 158 ✉ *10117 –* Ⓜ *Französische Str. –* ℰ *(030) 2 02 70 – info@*
westin-grand.com – Fax (030) 20 27 33 62 – www.westin.com/berlin
400 rm – ♦139/495 € ♦♦159/520 €, ⌁ 28 € **– 14 suites G1**
Rest *Relish –* Carte 36/67 €
♦ Chain hotel ♦ Luxury ♦ Functional ♦
This hotel in the town centre greets guests with its magnificent hall and 30m-high
glass roof. Comfortable rooms in a modern style. The Relish restaurant serves contemporary, modern cuisine.

The Mandala ⅙ 🕸 ㄴ AC 📺 ⑪ 🏊 🚗 VISA ⚫ AE ⓪

Potsdamer Str. 3 ✉ *10785 –* Ⓜ *Potsdamer Platz –* ℰ *(030) 5 90 05 00 00*
– welcome@themandala.de – Fax (030) 5 90 05 05 00 – www.themandala.de
161 rm – ♦270/350 € ♦♦290/350 €, ⌁ 24 € **– 17 suites F2**
Rest *Facil –* see below
♦ Business ♦ ♦ Design ♦
This hotel, favourably positioned in Potsdamer Platz opposite the Sony Center,
boasts large, well-equipped, high-tech, modern rooms.

Mövenpick ⅙ 🕸 ㄴ AC 📺 ⑪ 🏊 🚗 VISA ⚫ AE ⓪

Schönebergerstr. 3 ✉ *10963 –* Ⓜ *Potsdamer Platz –* ℰ *(030) 23 00 60*
– hotel.berlin@moevenpick.com – Fax (030) 23 00 61 99
– www.moevenpick-berlin.com **G2**
243 rm – ♦94/190 € ♦♦104/210 €, ⌁ 21 € **Rest –** Carte 27/40 €
♦ Historic ♦ Design ♦
This former Siemens building attractively combines a trendy design with its old,
listed structure. The studio rooms at the top are particularly attractive. Restaurant
in an interior courtyard with a glass roof that can be opened in the summer.

Maritim proArte ⅙ 🕸 🖾 ㄴ AC 📺 ⑪ 🏊 🚗 VISA ⚫ AE ⓪

Friedrichstr. 151 ✉ *10117 –* Ⓜ *Friedrichstr. –* ℰ *(030) 2 03 35 – info.bpa@*
maritim.de – Fax (030) 20 33 40 90 – www.maritim.de **G1**
403 rm – ♦159/299 € ♦♦174/314 €, ⌁ 22 €
Rest *Atelier –* ℰ *(030) 20 33 45 20 (closed mid July - mid August and Sunday)*
(dinner only) Menu 49/55 € – Carte 38/54 €
Rest *Bistro media –* Carte 20/29 €
♦ Chain hotel ♦ Business ♦ Modern ♦
An avant-garde hotel near the lime tree-lined Pracht blvd. Providing well-appointed rooms with Jungen Wilden art on display. A modern designer style restaurant.

NH Berlin Friedrichstrasse 🎝 ⅙ 🕸 ㄴ AC 📺 ⑪ 🏊 🚗

Friedrichstr. 96 ✉ *10117 –* Ⓜ *Friedrichstr. –* ℰ *(030)* VISA ⚫ AE ⓪
2 06 26 60 – nhfriedrichstrasse@nh-hotels.com – Fax (030) 2 06 26 69 99
– www.nh-hotels.com **G1**
262 rm – ♦99/179 € ♦♦99/179 €, ⌁ 21 € **Rest –** Carte 35/45 €
♦ Business ♦ Modern ♦
When entering this modern, well-run hotel you will notice the spacious hall. High
quality wooden furniture and agreeable colours make the rooms a pleasant place
to stay. Light, open-plan restaurant with Italian cuisine.

Sofitel Gendarmenmarkt

Charlottenstr. 50 ✉ 10117 – Ⓜ Französische Str.
– ✆ (030) 20 37 50 – h5342@accor.com – Fax (030) 20 37 51 00
– www.sofitel.com **G1-2**
92 rm – 🚹175/250 € 🚹🚹175/250 €, ☕ 28 €
Rest *Aigner* – *✆ (030) 2 03 75 18 50* – Menu 26 € (lunch)/80 € – Carte 33/49 €
◆ Chain hotel ◆ Business ◆ Design ◆
Directly opposite the French cathedral in the Gendarmenmarkt. This hotel offers modern, designer-style rooms and a small leisure area on the top floor. The Aigner was built from original parts of a Viennese coffee house.

Courtyard by Marriott

Axel-Springer-Str. 55 ✉ 10117 – Ⓜ Spittelmarkt – ✆ (030) 8 00 92 80
– berlin.mitte@courtyard.com – Fax (030) 80 09 28 10 00
– www.courtyard.com/bermt **H2**
267 rm – 🚹139/189 € 🚹🚹139/189 €, ☕ 17 € – 4 suites **Rest** – Carte 19/29 €
◆ Chain hotel ◆ Business ◆ Functional ◆
A centrally located business hotel providing homely, well-equipped rooms with functional furnishings. A Mediterranean bistro style restaurant with bar.

Alexander Plaza

Rosenstr. 1 ✉ 10178 – Ⓜ Alexanderplatz – ✆ (030) 24 00 10 – info@hotel-alexander-plaza.de – Fax (030) 24 00 17 77
– www.hotel-alexander-plaza.de **H1**
92 rm – 🚹105/185 € 🚹🚹115/195 €, ☕ 17 €
Rest – *(closed Sunday) (dinner only)* Carte 25/35 €
◆ Business ◆ Functional ◆
Between the Marienkirche and the market, this restored old building provides modern rooms and apartments with small kitchen facilities. International dishes are served in the restaurant with conservatory.

Melia

Friedrichstr. 103 ✉ 10117 – Ⓜ Friedrichstr. – ✆ (030) 20 60 79 00
– melia.berlin@solmelia.com – Fax (030) 20 60 79 04 44 – www.meliaberlin.com
364 rm ☕ – 🚹163/310 € 🚹🚹163/310 € – 3 suites **G1**
Rest – Carte 33/52 €
◆ Business ◆ Functional ◆
Its central location and modern and functional decor are features of the first Berlin hotel of the Spanish Sol-Melia Group. Executive facilities on the seventh and eighth floors. Restaurant with an international range of food and a tapas bar.

relexa hotel Stuttgarter Hof

Anhalter Str. 8 ✉ 10963 – Ⓜ Kochstr. – ✆ (030) 26 48 30 – berlin@relexa-hotel.de – Fax (030) 26 48 39 00
– www.relexa-hotels.de **G2**
206 rm ☕ – 🚹157/237 € 🚹🚹177/257 € – 10 suites
Rest – Carte 31/46 €
◆ Business ◆ Functional ◆
This hotel has a large reception area, functional guestrooms and suites of different categories. The rooms in the annex are more spacious. Modern restaurant with a pleasant roofed courtyard terrace.

Adele without rest

Greifswalder Str. 227 ✉ 10405 – Ⓜ Alexanderplatz – ✆ (030) 44 32 43 10
– info@adele-berlin.de – Fax (030) 44 32 43 11 – www.adele-berlin.de
14 rm ☕ – 🚹110/145 € 🚹🚹160/176 € *Plan I* **D1**
◆ Townhouse ◆ Classic ◆
Great personal attention is lavished on guests in this small hotel near to Friedrichshain park. The rooms, furnished in a high quality, Art Deco style are captivating.

XXXXX £3
Lorenz Adlon – Hotel Adlon Kempinski 🗚 *VISA* ◑ 🗛 ⓞ

Unter den Linden 77 ⌧ *10117* – ◍ *Französische Str.* – ℰ *(030) 22 61 19 60*
– hotel.adlon@kempinski.com – Fax (030) 22 61 13 89 – www.hotel-adlon.de
– closed 4 - 19 January, 26 July - 17 August and Sunday
Rest *– (dinner only)* Menu 105/170 € – Carte 80/130 €   **G1**
Spec. Glasierte Jakobsmuschel mit Prunier St. James-Kaviar und Rindermark.
Scheiben vom Thunfisch mit Kartoffel-Curry-Stampf und Gewürz-Basilikum-
pesto. Caneton à la presse mit Pommes Maximes und Sauce Rouennaise.
   ◆ Classic ◆ Luxury ◆
This world-renowned, luxury hotel is rich in history. Classic dishes prepared in a
contemporary manner are served.

XXXX £3 £3
Fischers Fritz – Hotel The Regent 🗕 🗚 *VISA* ◑ 🗛 ⓞ

Charlottenstr. 49 ⌧ *10117* – ◍ *Französische Str.* – ℰ *(030) 20 33 63 63*
– fischersfritz.berlin@rezidorregent.com – Fax (030) 20 33 61 19
– www.fischersfritzberlin.com   **G1**
Rest *– (booking advisable)* Menu 39 € (lunch)/139 € – Carte 93/219 € 🕸
Spec. Terrine von Gänsestopfleber und geräuchertem Aal mit Pfefferkara-
mell. Homard à la presse (by arrangement for 2 people). Mispelconsommé
mit gerahmtem Cashmere-Curryreis.
   ◆ Inventive ◆ Elegant ◆
In this restaurant Christian Lohse and his team are famous for their fish dishes, whether classic or modern. The lunch menu is popular and very good value for money.

XXXX £3
Vitrum – Hotel The Ritz Carlton 🗕 🗚 *VISA* ◑ 🗛

Potsdamer Platz 3 ⌧ *10785* – ◍ *Potsdamer Platz* – ℰ *(030) 3 37 77 63 40*
– info@restaurant-vitrum.de – Fax (030) 3 37 77 53 41 – www.restaurant-vitrum.de
– closed Sunday - Monday   **F2**
Rest *– (dinner only) (booking advisable)* Menu 95/145 € – Carte 65/92 €
Spec. Carpaccio von der Dorade mit glasierten Flusskrebsschwänzen. Taube
mit Petersiliencreme und Trüffeljus. Tarte von Manjarie Schokolade mit Exotic Sorbet.
   ◆ Inventive ◆ Classic ◆
There is a noble and classically elegant atmosphere in this restaurant. It is decorated with alternating paintings by master scholars of various art schools.

XXXX £3
Gabriele 🗥 🗕 🗚 *VISA* ◑ 🗛 ⓞ

Behrenstr. 72 (at Adlon Palace) ⌧ *10117* – ◍ *Französische Str.* – ℰ *(030)*
20 62 86 10 – gabriele@gabriele-restaurant.de – Fax (030) 3 01 11 71 75
– www.gabriele-restaurant.de
– closed 1 - 12 January and Sunday - Monday   **G2**
Rest *– (dinner only)* Menu 62/110 € – Carte 66/88 €
Spec. Erbsenravioli mit Minzöl und Wachteleigelb. Kalbskotelett mit Gremo-
latajus und Sternanis-Tomatensugo. Pfirsich in Moscatogelee mit Himbeer-
schaum und Mascarponeeis.
   ◆ Italian ◆ Elegant ◆
Enjoy delicious Italian food in this very well furnished restaurant. The decor includes works by Harald Metzkes.

XXX £3
MA - Tim Raue 🗕 🗚 *VISA* ◑ 🗛

Behrenstr. 72 ⌧ *10117* – ◍ *Französische Str.* – ℰ *(030) 3 01 11 73 33*
– reservierung@ma-restaurants.de – Fax (030) 3 01 11 73 37
– www.ma-restaurant.de
– closed 2 weeks January, 2 weeks August and Sunday   **G1**
Rest *– (dinner only) (booking advisable)* Menu 78/118 € – Carte 64/144 €
Rest *Uma – (dinner only)* Carte 30/113 €
Spec. Heilbutt mit Spargel-beurre-blanc, Schildampfer, Champignons und
Trauben. Fish maw und Jakobsmuscheln mit grüner Paprika und Koriander.
Taube mit Artischocke, Haselnuss und Liebstöckel.
   ◆ Euro-asiatic ◆ Exotic ◆
This modern Asian-style restaurant has been fitted out with understated luxury.
The hand finished details and a valuable antique equestrian statue emphasise the
high quality ambience.Fine Chinese and European cuisine. Uma has a quality inte-
rior based on a Japanese theme.

GERMANY - BERLIN

XXX ✿ **Margaux** (Michael Hoffmann)   AC VISA ⊛ AE ①
Unter den Linden 78 (Entrance Wilhelmstraße) ✉ *10117*
– ℰ (030) 22 65 26 11 – hoffmann@margaux-berlin.de
– Fax (030) 22 65 26 12 – www.margaux-berlin.de
– closed Sunday   **G1**
Rest – *(dinner only)* Menu 80/140 € – Carte 83/130 € ⅏
Spec. Hummer und Melone mit Sauerampfer. Filet vom Wolfsbarsch mit Hühnerbouillon und Schnittlauch glaciert. Taube mit Oliven gefüllt und Rotwein-Thymianjus.
◆ Inventive ◆ Minimalist ◆
This restaurant in a prestigious location close to the Brandenburg Gate stands for modern elegance and professional service. Experience the cuisine at its best with the 'Voyage de Cuisine' menu.

XXX ✿ **FACIL** – Hotel The Mandala   ⇗ AC VISA ⊛ AE ①
Potsdamer Str. 3 (5th floor) ✉ *10785* – **Ⓜ** *Potsdamer Platz*
– ℰ (030) 5 90 05 12 34 – welcome@facil.de – Fax (030) 5 90 05 22 22
– www.facil.de
– closed 1 - 25 January, 25 July - 9 August and Saturday - Sunday
Rest – *(booking advisable)* Menu 39 € (lunch)/130 €   **F2**
– Carte 72/94 € ⅏
Spec. Saibling in Nussbutter konfiert mit Traubensenf und Artischockenmarmelade. Bisonfilet mit Pistoujus und Olivenravioli. Ziegenkäse mit Muscovadozucker und eingelegtem Weinbergpfirsich.
◆ Inventive ◆ Minimalist ◆
The restaurant is situated on the fifth floor in the landscaped inner courtyard of the building. Attractive, light architecture and contemporary style define the atmosphere. The cuisine is creative.

XXX ✿ **VAU** (Kolja Kleeberg)   ⇗ VISA ⊛ AE ①
Jägerstr. 54 ✉ *10117* – **Ⓜ** *Französische Str.* – ℰ *(030) 2 02 97 30*
– restaurant@vau-berlin.de – Fax (030) 20 29 73 11 – www.vau-berlin.de
– closed Sunday   **G1**
Rest – Menu 65 € (lunch)/110 € – Carte 77/98 € ⅏
Spec. Gerösteter Hummer mit Zwiebel-Pakora und geeistem Joghurt. Flüssige Gänseleberfagottini mit Morcheln und Spitzkohl. Zweierlei vom Maibock mit Mispeln und Kubebenpfeffer.
◆ Inventive ◆ Fashionable ◆
Located on the Gendarmenmark, this modern restaurant is decorated with large paintings and also has an inner courtyard terrace and cellar bar. The cuisine is characterised by its own style and classic roots – at midday a small lunchtime menu is also served.

XX **Grill Royal**   ⇗ VISA ⊛ AE
Friedrichstr. 105 b ✉ *10117* – **Ⓜ** *Oranienburger Tor*
– ℰ (030) 28 87 92 88 – office@grillroyal.com – Fax (030) 28 87 92 84
– www.grillroyal.com   **G1**
Rest – *(dinner only) (booking advisable)* Carte 38/90 €
◆ International ◆ Trendy ◆
A trendy restaurant with modern, high quality decor in earth colours. Diners select the meat themselves from a glass cool store!

XX **Bocca di Bacco**   AC ⇔ VISA ⊛ AE
Friedrichstr. 167 ✉ *10117* – **Ⓜ** *Französische Str.* – ℰ *(030) 20 67 28 28*
– info@boccadibacco.de – Fax (030) 20 67 29 29
– www.boccadibacco.de
– closed Sunday and bank holidays lunch   **G1**
Rest – *(booking advisable for dinner)* Menu 20 € (lunch) – Carte 34/48 €
◆ Italian ◆ Fashionable ◆
A restaurant in modern design with a bar and lounge area where good Italian cuisine. Very friendly atmosphere. Beautiful function room on the first floor.

GERMANY - BERLIN

XX **Guy** 🛜 *VISA* 🐽 🖭

Jägerstr. 59 ⊠ 10117 – **Ⓜ** *Französische Str. – 𝒞 (030) 20 94 26 00 – info@ guy-restaurant.de – Fax (030) 20 94 26 10 – www.guy-restaurant.de – closed Saturday lunch, Sunday* **G2**
Rest – Menu 59/79 € – Carte 57/72 €
♦ International ♦ Friendly ♦
This bright, friendly restaurant on three levels provides an informal atmosphere and serves contemporary international cuisine. There is also a lovely internal courtyard for dining.

X **Rutz** 🛜 *VISA* 🐽 🖭
⊗

Chausseestr. 8 ⊠ 10115 – **Ⓜ** *Oranienburger Tor – 𝒞 (030) 24 62 87 60 – info@ rutz-weinbar.de – Fax (030) 24 62 87 61 – www.rutz-weinbar.de – closed Sunday* **Plan I C2**
Rest – *(dinner only)* Menu 55/89 € – Carte 57/69 € 🈁
Spec. Geeistes Mozzarellasüppchen mit Jakobsmuschel, Pesto und Avocadoöl. Geschmorte Schulter vom Rind mit Schnippelbohnen und Trüffeljus. Rosa Schulter vom Joselito Schwein mit Poweraden und Manchego.
♦ Inventive ♦ Trendy ♦
This modern restaurant on the first floor serves Mediterranean style creative cuisine. In summer the vine covered outside seating area in the inner courtyard is very pleasant. There is also a wine bar on the ground floor.

X **Traube** 🛜 *VISA* 🐽 🖭

Reinhardtstr. 33 ⊠ 10117 – **Ⓜ** *Oranienburger Tor – 𝒞 (030) 27 58 26 08 – info@ferrari-ristorante.de – Fax (030) 27 58 26 10 – www.ferrari-ristorante.de – closed Saturday lunch, Sunday* **G1**
Rest – Menu 52/82 € *(dinner)* – Carte 37/46 €
♦ International ♦ Friendly ♦
This very attractive, classically modern restaurant has a bistro area. It also serves international dishes on the terrace in the inner courtyard. There is also a small midday menu.

X **Remake** 🛜 *VISA* 🐽 🖭

Große Hamburger Str. 32 ⊠ 10115 – 𝒞 (030) 20 05 41 02 – restaurantremake@aol.com – Fax (030) 97 89 48 60 – www.restaurant-remake.de **H1**
Rest – *(dinner only)* Menu 45/72 € – Carte 53/67 €
♦ International ♦ Fashionable ♦
Light, friendly atmosphere and modern ambience and a contemporary international menu are what make this décor restaurant.

X **Shiro i Shiro** 🛜 ♿ *VISA* 🐽 🖭

Rosa-Luxemburg-Str. 11 ⊠ 10178 – **Ⓜ** *Alexanderpl. – 𝒞 (030) 97 00 47 90 – info@shiroishiro.com – Fax (030) 97 00 47 95 – www.shiroishiro.com* **H1**
Rest – *(dinner only)* Carte 43/56 €
♦ International ♦ Minimalist ♦
The design of this gleaming white restaurant can be described as modern-purist. It has an extra long table and centre bar as a focal point and serves international cuisine and sushi.

X **Paris-Moskau** 🛜 *VISA* 🐽 🖭

Alt-Moabit 141 ⊠ 10557 – 𝒞 (030) 3 94 20 81 – restaurant@paris-moskau.de – Fax (030) 3 94 26 02 – www.paris-moskau.de – closed 1 - 4 January, Saturday lunch, Sunday lunch and bank holidays lunch
Rest – *(booking advisable)* Menu 72/81 € – Carte 38/53 € **F1**
♦ International ♦ Individual ♦
This old timber-framed hotel near where the Wall used to be not far from Lehrter station, offers international cuisine (reduced lunchtime menu).

Borchardt ❄ VISA ⊛ AE

Französische Str. 47 ⊠ 10117 – Ⓜ *Französische Str. – ℰ (030) 81 88 62 62
– Fax (030) 81 88 62 49* **G1**
Rest – Carte 32/50 €
♦ International ♦ Brasserie ♦

This trendy address can be found behind a classical townhouse façade. Meals are served in the restaurant, with its high ceilings and impressive pillars, or on the pleasant courtyard terrace.

Brechts ❄ VISA ⊛ AE

Schiffbauerdamm 6 ⊠ 10117 – Ⓜ *Oranienburger Tor – ℰ (030) 28 59 85 85
– info@brechts.de – Fax (030) 28 59 85 87 – www.brechts.de* **G1**
Rest – Carte 35/57 €
♦ Austrian ♦ Fashionable ♦

Named after Bertolt Brecht, this is a brasserie-style restaurant with a pleasant terrace overlooking the river Spree. Its guests can enjoy Austrian and international food.

Lutter und Wegner ❄ AC VISA ⊛

Charlottenstr. 56 ⊠ 10117 – Ⓜ *Französische Str. – ℰ (030) 2 02 95 40 – info@
l-w-berlin.de – Fax (030) 20 29 54 25 – www.l-w-berlin.de* **G2**
Rest – Carte 29/56 € 🍷
♦ Austrian ♦ Wine bar ♦

E T A Hoffmann used to live here. Three large columns painted by contemporary artists set the motto: Wine, women and song. Cosy wine bar.

Hartmanns ❄ VISA ⊛ AE

Fichtestr.31 ⊠ 10967 – Ⓜ *Südstern – ℰ (030) 61 20 10 03 – mail@
hartmanns-restaurant.de – Fax (030) 61 20 13 80
– www.hartmanns-restaurant.de
– closed Sunday, July - August: Sunday and Monday* Plan I **D3**
Rest – *(dinner only) (booking advisable)* Menu 40/61 € – Carte 46/54 €
♦ Modern ♦ Cosy ♦

This contemporary restaurant serves ambitious international food with regional influences. The works of two artists decorate the room.

Le Cochon Bourgeois ❄

Fichtestr. 24 ⊠ 10967 – Ⓜ *Südstern – ℰ (030) 6 93 01 01 – Fax (030)
6 94 34 80 – www.lecochon.de
– closed 1 - 19 January and Sunday - Monday* Plan I **D3**
Rest – *(dinner only)* Menu 35/74 €
♦ French ♦ Cosy ♦

A pleasant restaurant in a historical setting. French cuisine can be enjoyed in a very special, comfortable and rustic atmosphere. Live piano music.

AROUND THE KURFÜRSTENDAMM *Plan III*

Concorde ❄ 🛁 🏠 ♿ AC 🖂 🛜 🐾 🚗 VISA ⊛ AE ①

Augsburger Str. 41 ⊠ 10789 – Ⓜ *Kurfürstendamm – ℰ (030) 8 00 99 90
– info-berlin@concorde-hotels.com – Fax (030) 80 09 99 99
– www.berlin.concorde-hotel.com* **K2**
311 rm – ♟160/540 € ♟♟160/570 €, ☲ 26 € – 44 suites
Rest Le Faubourg – ℰ (030) 80 09 99 77 00 – Carte 36/62 €
♦ Business ♦ Grand Luxury ♦ Modern ♦

A luxury hotel in an outstanding location – generous and contemporary throughout. The rooms have all the latest technology, most suites offer beautiful views. VIP lounge. The Brasserie Le Faubourg is elegant and modern.

GERMANY - BERLIN

Palace
🏖 ⚙ 🏊 🅿 ♿ 🅰🅲 📠 📶 🛎 🚗 VISA 💳 AE 🅾

Budapester Str. 45 ✉ 10787 – **Ⓜ** *Zoologischer Garten –* 𝒞 *(030) 2 50 20*
– hotel@palace.de – Fax (030) 25 02 11 19 – www.palace.de **K2**
282 rm – ♦230/500 € ♦♦230/500 €, � 29 € – 19 suites
Rest First Floor – *see below*
◆ Grand Luxury ◆ Classic ◆
Guests enjoy modern, high-tech, smart rooms, luxurious suites and an elegant Mediterranean 800m2 spa area.

Grand Hotel Esplanade
🌳 🏖 ⚙ 🏊 🅿 ♿ 🅰🅲 📠 📶 🛎 🚗

Lützowufer 15 ✉ 10785 – 𝒞 *(030) 25 47 80 – info@* VISA 💳 AE
esplanade.de – Fax (030) 2 54 78 82 22 – www.esplanade.de **L2**
394 rm – ♦129/429 € ♦♦129/429 €, ⊒ 24 € – 24 suites
Rest – Carte 32/61 €
Rest Eckrestaurant – *(dinner only)* Carte 28/39 €
◆ Luxury ◆ Modern ◆
Modern design through and through marks this grand hotel on the Landwehr canal. Outside the building is the MS Esplanade yacht, a highlight for events of all kinds. The Ellipse Lounge offers international cuisine. Local specialities in the Eckrestaurant.

InterContinental
🌳 🏖 ⚙ 🏊 🅿 ♿ 🅰🅲 📠 📶 🛎 🚗

Budapester Str. 2 ✉ 10787 – **Ⓜ** *Wittenbergplatz* VISA 💳 AE 🅾
– 𝒞 *(030) 2 60 20 – berlin@ichotelsgroup.com – Fax (030) 26 02 26 00*
– www.berlin.intercontinental.com **L2**
584 rm – ♦145/330 € ♦♦145/330 €, ⊒ 29 € – 50 suites
Rest Hugos – see below
Rest L.A. Cafe – 𝒞 *(030) 26 02 12 50* – Carte 33/66 €
◆ Chain hotel ◆ Luxury ◆ Classic ◆
A good place to stay, with a large, quality Vitality Club and good conference and event facilities. The rooms are tastefully elegant or simple and modern. L.A. Cafe with international and Chinese dishes

Swissôtel
🏖 🏊 ♿ 🅰🅲 📠 📶 🛎 🚗 VISA 💳 AE 🅾

Augsburger Str. 44 ✉ 10789 – **Ⓜ** *Kurfürstendamm –* 𝒞 *(030) 22 01 00*
– berlin@swissotel.com – Fax (030) 2 20 10 22 22 – www.berlin.swissotel.com
316 rm – ♦140/290 € ♦♦155/310 €, ⊒ 21 € **K2**
Rest 44 – see below
◆ Luxury ◆ Modern ◆
This modern town hotel with its glass façade welcomes its guests with a spacious atrium hall. It has comfortable guestrooms, including business and executive rooms.

Pullman Schweizerhof
🌳 🏖 ⚙ 🏊 🅿 ♿ 🅰🅲 📠 📶 🛎 🚗

Budapester Str. 25 ✉ 10787 – **Ⓜ** *Zoologischer Garten* VISA 💳 AE 🅾
– 𝒞 *(030) 2 69 60 – h5347@accor.com – Fax (030) 26 96 10 00*
– www.pullmanhotels.com **L2**
383 rm – ♦135/320 € ♦♦135/320 €, ⊒ 23 € – 10 suites
Rest – Carte 32/42 €
◆ Chain hotel ◆ Business ◆ Design ◆
Designed specially for the business traveller, this hotel offers a light, generous reception area and functional rooms. Bistro-style restaurant

Steigenberger
🌳 🏊 🅿 ♿ 🅰🅲 📠 📶 🛎 VISA 💳 AE 🅾

Los-Angeles-Platz 1 ✉ 10789 – **Ⓜ** *Augsburger Str. –* 𝒞 *(030) 2 12 70 – berlin@*
steigenberger.de – Fax (030) 2 12 71 17 – www.berlin.steigenberger.de
397 rm – ♦165/355 € ♦♦165/355 €, ⊒ 23 € – 11 suites **K2**
Rest Berliner Stube – Carte 24/41 €
◆ Chain hotel ◆ Luxury ◆ Modern ◆
The Stadthotel has a large, modern lobby and functional rooms. Extra privacy can be enjoyed on the Executive level with the club lounge on the sixth floor. Rustic flair in the Berliner Stube.

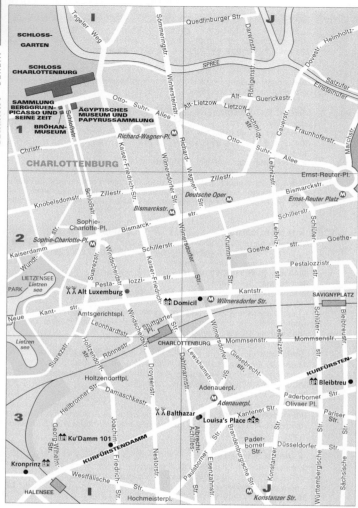

Kempinski Hotel Bristol

🍴 ⅃⅚ 🛁 🖼 🕭 🖵 ⟨⟨·⟩⟩ ⅍ 🚗 ⟨VISA⟩ ⟨∞⟩ ⟨AE⟩ ⟨①⟩

Kurfürstendamm 27 ⊠ *10719 –* Ⓜ *Uhlandstr.*
– 𝒞 (030) 88 43 40 – reservations.bristol@kempinski.com – Fax (030) 8 83 60 75
– www.kempinski-berlin.com

K2

301 rm – ♛185/349 € ♛♛185/349 €, ⌑ 25 € – 22 suites
Rest *Kempinski Grill* – Carte 43/74 €

◆ Luxury ◆ Classic ◆

The impressive building on the renowned Ku´damm is an elegant luxury hotel that has already welcomed many a distinguished guest. The Kempinski Grill has been a true Berlin institution since 1952.

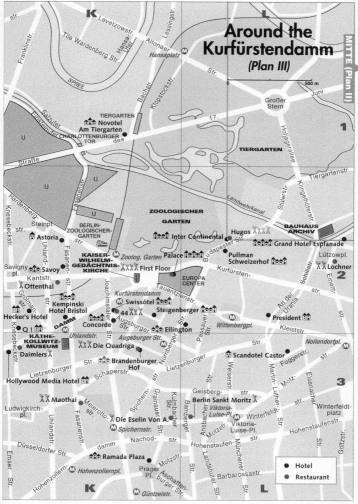

Around the Kurfürstendamm
(Plan III)

500 m

1

TIERGARTEN

2

3

Hotel

Restaurant

Brandenburger Hof

🛜 📠 📶 🧖 🚗 VISA 💳 AE ①

Eislebener Str. 14 ⊠ 10789 – Ⓜ Augsburger Str. – ℰ (030) 21 40 50 – info@ brandenburger-hof.com – Fax (030) 21 40 51 00 – www.brandenburger-hof.com
72 rm 🛏 – 🛏195/340 € 🛏🛏295/395 € – 8 suites   **K3**
Rest *Die Quadriga* – see below
Rest *Quadriga-Lounge* – ℰ (030) 21 40 56 51 – Menu 26/72 € – Carte 38/54 €
♦ Traditional ♦ Design ♦
Highly attractive and stylish, this beautiful nineteenth-century city palace combines historical elements with noble modern design. Pure elegance: the Quadriga Lounge extending into the Bar area.

309

GERMANY - BERLIN

Louisa's Place

Kurfürstendamm 160 ⊠ 10709 – Ⓜ Adenauerplatz – ℰ (030) 63 10 30
– info@louisas-place.de – Fax (030) 63 10 31 00
– www.louisas-place.de **J3**
47 suites – ♟155/595 € ♟♟155/595 €, ⌣ 20 €
Rest *Balthasar* – see below
♦ Business ♦ Personalised ♦
This hotel has a friendly service and offers tasteful, spacious suites with kitchens.
There is also a stylish breakfast room and library.

Ramada Plaza

Pragerstr. 12 ⊠ 10779 – Ⓜ Güntzelstr. – ℰ (030) 2 36 25 00 – berlin.plaza@
ramada.de – Fax (030) 2 36 25 05 50
– www.ramada-plaza-berlin.de **K3**
184 rm – ♟149/199 € ♟♟149/199 €, ⌣ 20 € – 60 suites
Rest – Carte 31/43 €
♦ Chain hotel ♦ Modern ♦
A business hotel providing elegant rooms and suites with American cherry wood
furnishings and the latest technical facilities. With executive suites on the sixth
floor. A classic style restaurant.

Ellington

Nürnberger Str. 50 ⊠ 10789 – Ⓜ Wittenbergplatz – ℰ (030) 68 31 50
– contact@ellington-hotel.com – Fax (030) 6 83 15 55 55
– www.ellington-hotel.com **L2**
285 rm – ♟108/238 € ♟♟118/248 €, ⌣ 17 €
Rest – Carte 31/53 €
♦ Business ♦ Modern ♦
Hause Nürnberg, built in 1928-31, now houses a hotel with a modern design. The
façade and many beautiful interior details preserve the historic charm. This restaurant has a straightforward, simple, elegant style with a pretty inner courtyard.

Novotel am Tiergarten

Straße des 17. Juni 106 ⊠ 10623 – Ⓜ Hansaplatz – ℰ (030) 60 03 50
– h3649@accor.com – Fax (030) 60 03 56 66 – www.accorhotels.com
274 rm – ♟90/219 € ♟♟105/234 €, ⌣ 18 € – 6 suites **K1**
Rest – Carte 23/35 €
♦ Chain hotel ♦ Modern ♦
Located near the Tiergarten station, this business hotel provides well-equipped
rooms in modern design.

Savoy

Fasanenstr. 9 ⊠ 10623 – Ⓜ Zoologischer Garten – ℰ (030) 31 10 30 – info@
hotel-savoy.com – Fax (030) 31 10 33 33
– www.hotel-savoy.com **K2**
125 rm ⌣ – ♟129/248 € ♟♟157/277 € – 18 suites
Rest – *(closed Sunday dinner)* Carte 31/49 €
♦ Business ♦ Modern ♦
This charming hotel, which has been mentioned in the writings of Thomas Mann
and where even today celebrities continually come and go, has been in existence
since 1928 and is the oldest in the city. Modern interior with red upholstered armchairs in the restaurant.

Q!

Knesebeckstr. 67 ⊠ 10623 – Ⓜ Uhlandstr. – ℰ (030) 8 10 06 60
– q-berlin@loock-hotels.com – Fax (030) 8 10 06 66 66
– www.loock-hotels.com **K2**
77 rm ⌣ – ♟149/269 € ♟♟165/269 €
Rest – *(dinner only for residents)* Carte 29/51 €
♦ Business ♦ Modern ♦
Design reigns supreme. The modern, technically well laid out rooms are minimalist
with their dark tones. Stylish restaurant with Euro-Asian fare.

GERMANY - BERLIN

President

An der Urania 16 ⊠ 10787 – **Ⓜ** Wittenbergplatz – ℰ (030) 21 90 30
– info@president.bestwestern.de – Fax (030) 2 18 61 20
– www.president.bestwestern.de

182 rm – ♦125/285 € ♦♦145/305 €, ⊑ 15 €   **Rest** – Carte 31/42 €   **L2**

♦ Business ♦ Functional ♦

As well as functional economy and business rooms, this hotel also has more comfortable club rooms, with extra-large desks and comfortable leather armchairs. Wicker chairs and contemporary design in the restaurant.

Hollywood Media Hotel without rest

Kurfürstendamm 202 ⊠ 10719 – **Ⓜ** Uhlandstr.
– ℰ (030) 88 91 00 – info@filmhotel.de – Fax (030) 88 91 02 80
– www.filmhotel.de

182 rm ⊑ – ♦99/169 € ♦♦119/189 € – 12 suites   **K3**

♦ Business ♦ Modern ♦

This residence is devoted to the world of film. The tasteful, contemporary rooms are decorated with numerous film posters and photos of stars. The hotel has its own small cinema.

Domicil

Kantstr. 111a ⊠ 10627 – **Ⓜ** Wilmersdorfer Str. – ℰ (030) 32 90 30
– info@hotel-domicil-berlin.de – Fax (030) 32 90 32 99
– www.hotel-domicil-berlin.de

70 rm ⊑ – ♦118/160 € ♦♦154/200 € – 3 suites   **Rest** – Carte 21/45 €   **J2**

♦ Business ♦ Modern ♦

In this hotel high above the city you will stay in attractive rooms in Italian style, in which the highlights are contemporary art and Tuscan fabrics. Rooftop restaurant with a roof garden. Cuisine with international influences.

Hecker's Hotel

Grolmanstr. 35 ⊠ 10623 – **Ⓜ** Uhlandstr. – ℰ (030) 8 89 00
– info@heckers-hotel.de – Fax (030) 8 89 02 60
– www.heckers-hotel.de

69 rm – ♦110/250 € ♦♦120/330 €, ⊑ 16 €   **K2**

Rest Cassambalis – ℰ (030) 8 85 47 47 (closed Sunday lunch) Carte 33/51 €

♦ Business ♦ Design ♦

A hotel which values individuality and service. The rooms, some cosy and functional, some in modern designer style or tastefully fitted out as themed rooms. Mediterranean flair and offer in the Cassambalis.

Bleibtreu

Bleibtreustr. 31 ⊠ 10707 – **Ⓜ** Uhlandstr. – ℰ (030) 88 47 40
– info@bleibtreu.com – Fax (030) 88 47 44 44 – www.bleibtreu.com

60 rm ⊑ – ♦130/195 € ♦♦140/227 €   **J3**

Rest – Carte 22/29 €

♦ Business ♦ Design ♦

This town house from the Gründerzeit [founders' era] has been carefully restored, creating an attractive modern style hotel. The restaurant offers sandwiches, steaks and burgers.

Ku' Damm 101 without rest

Kurfürstendamm 101 ⊠ 10711 – ℰ (030) 5 20 05 50
– info@kudamm101.com – Fax (030) 5 20 05 55 55
– www.kudamm101.com

170 rm – ♦99/205 € ♦♦101/222 €, ⊑ 15 €   **I3**

♦ Business ♦ Design ♦

Deliberately understated designer style. Rooms with modern colour schemes, large windows and modern facilities. The breakfast room on the seventh floor offers a view over the town.

GERMANY - BERLIN

Kronprinz without rest   ⤓ 🖭 ᴪ 🖧 🖾 🚗 VISA ⑩ AE ⑩

Kronprinzendamm 1 ⊠ 10711 – ℰ (030) 89 60 30 – reception@
kronprinz-hotel.de – Fax (030) 8 93 12 15 – www.kronprinz-hotel.de
78 rm � – ✝118/165 € ✝✝150/215 €   **I3**
♦ Traditional ♦ Cosy ♦

A late 19th century building is home to light, homely rooms and a charming
"Romantic room". Convention centre within walking distance. Terrace shaded by
chestnut trees.

Scandotel Castor without rest   🖭 ᴪ **P.** VISA ⑩ AE ⑩

Fuggerstr. 8 ⊠ 10777 – ⓜ Nollendorfplatz – ℰ (030) 21 30 30
– scandotel@t-online.de – Fax (030) 21 30 31 60
– www.scandotel-castor.de   **L3**
78 rm – ✝90/107 € ✝✝100/135 €
♦ Business ♦ Functional ♦

Whether it's the Ku'damm or KaDeWe, the cinema or the pub: this contemporary hotel with its functional rooms and good technical facilities is close to them
all.

Astoria without rest   ᴪ VISA ⑩ AE ⑩

Fasanenstr. 2 ⊠ 10623 – ⓜ Zoologischer Garten – ℰ (030) 3 12 40 67 – info@
hotelastoria.de – Fax (030) 3 12 50 27 – www.hotelastoria.de   **K2**
32 rm ⊑ – ✝74/170 € ✝✝94/198 €
♦ Townhouse ♦ Functional ♦

A small, well-kept town hotel in a central location. Its special service includes a sailing boat, which you can use to explore the Havel waters. Courtyard terrace.

XXXX   **First Floor** – Hotel Palace   🅰 ⇿ VISA ⑩ AE ⑩
ⵦ
Budapester Str. 45 ⊠ 10787 – ⓜ Zoologischer Garten – ℰ (030) 25 02 10 20
– hotel@palace.de – Fax (030) 25 02 11 19 – www.firstfloor.palace.de
– closed 19 July - 17 August   **K2**
Rest – *(Saturday - Sunday dinner only)* Menu 45 € (lunch)/118 €
– Carte 75/106 € 🏵

Spec. Carpaccio vom Pulpo mit weißem Tomatenmousse und Tomatensor-
bet. Jakobsmuschel im Nussmantel mit Curryspinat und Limonen. Rücken
und Schulter vom Lamm mit Oliven-Orangenemulsion.
♦ Classic ♦ Elegant ♦

Matthias Bochholz prepares classic dishes with finesse here. Suitable wines are
competently recommended from a wide range with many rarities.

XXXX   **Hugos** – Hotel InterContinental   ≼ 🅰 VISA ⑩ AE ⑩
ⵦ
Budapester Str. 2 (14th floor) ⊠ 10787 – ⓜ Wittenbergplatz
– ℰ (030) 26 02 12 63 – mail@hugos-restaurant.de – Fax (030) 26 02 12 39
– www.hugos-restaurant.de
– closed 15 July - 28 August and Sunday   **L2**
Rest – *(dinner only)* Menu 88/130 € – Carte 77/113 € 🏵

Spec. Seesaibling konfiert mit Topinambur und Estragon. Hecht mit Serrano
und Wildkräutern. Lammrücken mit Bohnen, Fenchel und Olivenjus.
♦ Classic ♦ Fashionable ♦

From atop the Hotel Inter-Continental take in a fantastic view of Berlin. Friendly and
competent staff serve modern creative cuisine and the matching wines.

XXX   **Die Quadriga** – Hotel Brandenburger Hof   VISA ⑩ AE ⑩

Eislebener Str. 14 ⊠ 10789 – ⓜ Augsburger Str. – ℰ (030) 21 40 56 51
– info@brandenburger-hof.com – Fax (030) 21 40 51 00
– www.brandenburger-hof.com
– closed 1 - 11 January, 20 July - 16 August and Saturday lunch, Sunday
- Monday lunch   **K3**
Rest – Menu 75/130 € – Carte 78/100 € 🏵
♦ Classic ♦ Elegant ♦

This hotel with its classical setting houses two stylish, tasteful restaurant rooms
where guests are served creative dishes.

GERMANY - BERLIN

XXX   **44** – Hotel Swissôtel   🛋 ⅙ AC VISA ⚫⚫ AE ①
Augsburger Str. 44 ⊠ *10789 –* Ⓜ *Kurfürstendamm –* 𝒞 *(030) 2 20 10 22 88*
– restaurant44.berlin@swissotel.com – Fax (030) 2 20 10 22 22
– www.restaurant44.de – closed 4 - 18 January, 26 July - 16 August and Sunday
Rest – Menu 62/84 €   **K2**
♦ Innovative ♦ Fashionable ♦
A modern, elegant style characterises the atmosphere in this restaurant. It offers its
guests a lovely outlook over the Ku'damm and a creative menu.

XX   **Alt Luxemburg**   AC VISA ⚫⚫ AE ①
Windscheidstr. 31 ⊠ *10627 –* Ⓜ *Wilmersdorfer Str. –* 𝒞 *(030) 3 23 87 30*
– info@altluxemburg.de – Fax (030) 3 27 40 03 – www.altluxemburg.de
– closed Sunday   **I2**
Rest – *(dinner only) (booking advisable)* Menu 67/73 € – Carte 48/69 €
♦ Classic ♦ Family ♦
Attractive, friendly colours mark the atmosphere of this restaurant. It offers classical
cuisine and has been traditionally run by the Wannemacher family since 1982.

XX   **Balthazar** – Hotel Louisa's Place   🛋 ⅙ AC VISA ⚫⚫ AE
Kurfürstendamm 160 ⊠ *10709 –* Ⓜ *Adenauerplatz –* 𝒞 *(030) 89 40 84 77*
– info@balthazar-restaurant.de – Fax (030) 89 40 84 78
– www.balthazar-restaurant.de   **J3**
Rest – *(dinner only)* Menu 40/44 € – Carte 33/50 €
♦ International ♦ Fashionable ♦
With its contemporary purist style, this restaurant on the 'Ku'damm' offers an inter-
national cuisine – it's nice to sit outside on the terrace, too.

XX   **Lochner**   🛋 VISA ⚫⚫ AE ①
Lützowplatz 5 ⊠ *10785 –* Ⓜ *Nollendorfplatz –* 𝒞 *(030) 23 00 52 20 – info@*
lochner-restaurant.de – Fax (030) 23 00 40 21 – www.lochner-restaurant.de
– closed 2 weeks July - August and Monday   **L2**
Rest – *(dinner only)* Menu 50/80 € – Carte 37/56 €
♦ International ♦ Friendly ♦
A pleasantly light, tastefully decorated restaurant offering an international menu.
There is a small terrace in front of the building.

XX   **Maothai**   🛋 VISA ⚫⚫ AE
Meierottostr. 1 ⊠ *10719 –* Ⓜ *Spichernstr. –* 𝒞 *(030) 8 83 28 23 – maothaiaf@*
aol.com – Fax (030) 88 67 56 58 – www.maothai-am-fasanenplatz.de
Rest – *(Monday - Friday dinner only)* Carte 20/48 €   **K3**
♦ Asian ♦ Exotic ♦
An intimate, candle-lit atmosphere in this restaurant near the Fasanen square, ser-
ving Thai cuisine. Charming terrace dining area.

X   **Bieberbau**   🛋
☺   *Durlacher Str. 15* ⊠ *10715 –* Ⓜ *Bundesplatz –* 𝒞 *(030) 8 53 23 90*
– webmaster@bieberbau-berlin.de – Fax (030) 81 00 68 65
– www.bieberbau-berlin.de
– closed 3 weeks July - August and Sunday - Monday   Plan I **B3**
Rest – *(dinner only) (booking advisable)* Menu 32/50 €
♦ International ♦ Cosy ♦
In the former workshop of the master stucco plasterer Richard Bieber, 19C crafts-
manship protected by a preservation order adorns the restaurant. Find well-trained personnel and tasty cuisine in a beautiful historical setting.

X   **Die Eselin von A.**   🛋 VISA ⚫⚫
Kulmbacher Str. 15 ⊠ *10777 –* Ⓜ *Spichernstr. –* 𝒞 *(030) 2 14 12 84*
– info@die-eselin-von-a.de – Fax (030) 21 47 69 48 – www.die-eselin-von-a.de
– closed 1- 20 January, 3 weeks August   **K3**
Rest – *(dinner only)* Menu 37/60 € – Carte 33/48 €
♦ International ♦ Friendly ♦
This friendly restaurant offers modern international cuisine, welcoming not just to
its many regular customers.

313

GERMANY - BERLIN

✗   **Berlin Sankt Moritz**   🛋 VISA ◎ AE

Regensburger Str. 7 ✉ 10777 – ⓜ Viktoria-Luise-Pl. – ℰ (030) 23 62 44 70
– anton.stenanov@email.de – Fax (030) 23 62 44 71
– www.restaurant-sankt-moritz.de – closed Sunday   **L3**
Rest *– (dinner only)* Menu 45/85 € – Carte 38/55 € ❀
  ◆ International ◆ Cosy ◆

A cosy restaurant with a lovely covered terrace. The wines to go with the international dishes are adeptly recommended from a list of over 200.

✗   **Ottenthal**   VISA ◎ AE
☺

Kantstr. 153 ✉ 10623 – ⓜ Uhlandstr. – ℰ (030) 3 13 31 62
– restaurant@ottenthal.com – Fax (030) 3 13 37 32 – www.ottenthal.com
Rest *– (dinner only) (booking advisable)* Carte 26/45 €   **K2**
  ◆ Austrian ◆ Bistro ◆

At this appealing establishment the owner and chef prepares Austrian dishes. He has named the restaurant after his hometown in Lower Austria – the old clock mechanism from the church tower there is part of the decor.

✗   **Daimlers**   🛋 ৬ AC VISA ◎ AE

Kurfürstendamm 203 ✉ 10719 – ⓜ Uhlandstr. – ℰ (030) 39 01 16 98
– info@daimlers.de – Fax (030) 39 01 44 66 – www.daimlers.de   **K3**
Rest *–* Menu 36/56 € – Carte 34/52 €
  ◆ International ◆ Bistro ◆

A car showroom gives this restaurant its unusual setting. Behind the glass façade sample international cuisine, and tapas in the afternoon, served in a pleasant bistro atmosphere.

ENVIRONS OF BERLIN

at Berlin-Grunewald

🏨   **Schlosshotel im Grunewald** ❀   🚗 ♨ 🛋 ⅙ ৯ ▤ AC SAT 📶

Brahmsstr. 10 ✉ 14193 – ℰ (030) 89 58 40 – info@   ঌ P VISA ◎ AE ⓞ
schlosshotelberlin.com – Fax (030) 89 58 48 00 – www.schlosshotelberlin.com
54 rm – ♦300/450 € ♦♦300/450 €, ⎵ 26 € – 12 suites   **A3**
Rest *Vivaldi – (closed Monday - Tuesday)* Menu 75 € – Carte 70/129 €
  ◆ Rural ◆ Luxury ◆ Design ◆

The glamorous setting of this wonderful historical manor is enhanced by its elegant interior. The combination of antique furniture and modern items is extremely successful. Diners can enjoy the elegant atmosphere of the Vivaldi or the pleasant terrace area.

✗✗   **Frühsammers Restaurant**   🛋 AE

Flinsberger Platz 8 ✉ 14193 – ℰ (030) 89 73 86 28 – info@fruehsammers-restaurant.de
– Fax (030) 89 73 86 28 – www.fruehsammers-restaurant.de
– closed 1 - 18 January and Sunday - Monday   **A3**
Rest *–* Menu 32/85 € – Carte 38/65 € ❀
  ◆ International ◆ Friendly ◆

Peter and Sonja Frühsammer serve good, international cuisine at this villa belonging to the Grunewalder tennis club. It has a courtside terrace. Simpler lunchtime selection and gourmet menu.

at Berlin-Tegel (Airport)

🏨   **Dorint Airport Tegel**   ৬ SAT 📶 ঌ P 🚗 VISA ◎ AE ⓞ

Gotthardstr. 96 ✉ 13403 – ℰ (030) 49 88 40 – info.berlin-tegel@dorint.com
– Fax (030) 49 88 45 55 – www.dorint.com/berlin-tegel   **B1**
303 rm – ♦59/171 € ♦♦59/181 €, ⎵ 14 €   **Rest** *–* Carte 20/33 €
  ◆ Chain hotel ◆ Functional ◆

A hotel with good transport connections and functional rooms. The luxury rooms on the top floors have air conditioning, newspapers and drinks free of charge, as well as a late check out service. Restaurant serving international cuisine.

COLOGNE
KÖLN

Population (est 2005) 976,000 - Altitude: 53m.

goodshoot.com

Based in the very centre of Europe on the banks of the Rhine, Cologne is Germany's oldest city (its name was instigated by the Romans, a 'colony' set up to fend off Barbarians). It became a Free City, and later fell under the rule of Napoleon and then the Prussians; all of which has given the locals a cosmopolitan, laid-back and sociable outlook. To illustrate the point, they have their own beer named after them, *Kölsch*, which enjoys the same regional status as Champagne, meaning it can't be brewed anywhere else in the country.

Although it may never be described as Europe's prettiest city, it has an eye-catching old town (largely rebuilt after World War II) and some world-class museums, with subjects ranging from modern art via sport and the Olympics to chocolate. It also boasts one of the finest collections of medieval churches in Europe (lovingly restored in the last half-century), and ploughs its own furrow by celebrating Carnival like it's Rio (no-one seems to care that there's no beach and not much sunshine). Most famously, Cologne has its Cathedral, a massive structure that stood tall during the War, and remains the biggest tourist attraction in Germany. Many of the people craning their necks to take in the exterior are also marvelling at the fact that the whole great edifice took over half a millennium to build…

315

LIVING THE CITY

The **River Rhine** cuts a swathe right through the heart of Cologne, with four central bridges allowing you plentiful passage from east to west. The main hub of the city is on the west bank, with the **Altstadt** (old town), dominated by its **Cathedral**, practically on the river bank itself. Out to the west, the old medieval walls are now a ring road, which neatly encircles the city centre. Just northwest of the ring road is **Mediapark**, a brash modern development, while to the east of the Rhine is the massive **Trade Fair Centre**, with its 80m-high tower. To its north is Cologne's biggest and most popular park, **Rheinpark.**

PRACTICAL INFORMATION

ARRIVAL-DEPARTURE

Cologne-Bonn Airport lies 17km southeast of the city centre. A taxi will cost approximately €30 or take the S13 train.

TRANSPORT

You can get around Cologne by bus, tram or metro. Validate (stamp) each ticket whenever you board. You can buy a single trip ticket for Cologne, which is valid for anywhere in the city. This is also valid for a journey to nearby Bonn. There are also day tickets covering the same area.

If you're in the city for a while, invest in a Köln Welcome Card. This offers almost ninety offers of reduced admission, ranging from art and culture, leisure facilities, shopping and eating establishments, to free travel on the public transport network. It's available from tourist information offices and many hotels.

EXPLORING COLOGNE

A lot of people come to Cologne for its trade fairs; this is a city renowned across Germany for people in suits making a beeline for the great redbrick Kölnmesse building on the Rhine's right bank. Any visitor not heading for this imposing Trade Fair Centre is invariably headed towards the city's other mighty landmark, rearing like a huge blackened monster over on the left bank. When Cologne **Cathedral** was completed in 1880, it was the tallest building in the world, a record it held for nine years until the rise of the Eiffel Tower. The massive Dom on the Rhine took an astonishing 632 years to complete, because its high Gothic style fell out of fashion in the mid-sixteenth century and tools were downed for another three hundred years, when it became popular again.

Two million visitors pass through its huge main door each year; the pluckier ones ascend the 509 steps that lead to an observation platform in one of the towers. Halfway up, many take a breather to look at the largest free-swinging bell in the world. At ground level, the massive oak stalls, now seven hundred years old, are the largest ever made in Germany; there's a beautiful fifteenth century altar painting of the patrons of Cologne, and a huge Romanesque reliquary, the Shrine of the Three Kings. After all this, the rest of the city might appear to suffer from an inferiority complex. Look closer, though, and you'll see the city's been fighting back.

→ ALL ROADS LEAD TO ROMANESQUE

Cologne was a powerful centre for the Church in medieval times and the result is the impressive circle of **Romanesque churches** huddled together in a circle in the old town. They were all badly damaged in the War, but the loving reparations carried out since have returned most to their former glory. Amongst the most startling are **St Ursula**, with a Baroque golden chamber full of ornate, gilded carving, wild-eyed busts and hundreds of skulls wearing sequinned caps, and **St Gereon**, with its massive, ten-sided dome making it one of the most distinctive and unusual buildings in Germany. The Romanesque church most identified with the city is **Great St Martin's**, mainly because its wonderful tower and steeple dominate the **Fischmarkt**, a popular tourist spot by the river. The houses and street layout around here have been rebuilt to historic designs, making it a romantically picturesque neighbourhood in which to wander.

→ DOM-MINIONS

Over the last few years, Cologne has rightly built itself a reputation as a cultural metropolis. Its museums are a byword for excellence, and two of them are within the shadow of the Dom. The **Romano-Germanic Museum** is essential viewing for anyone keen on 'what the Romans did for us'. Its centrepiece is a fabulous Dionysius mosaic discovered in 1941 during excavations for an air-raid shelter.

The mosaic features maids in flowing blue capes being attended by muscular satyrs, and it's made from over a million pieces of ceramic. On display elsewhere is a superb array of artefacts, including beautiful oil lamps, jewellery, sandals, snake thread glassware, dice and even bridge foundations. Almost next door, perfectly placed to provide a nice contrast, is the **Museum Ludwig**, which propels you forward two thousand years with a mind-blowing collection of twentieth century art. It's in a magically light, airy building that seems just right for the biggest collection of Pop Art outside the US. Over four floors, you cross continents and all sorts of borders and boundaries to take in Russian avant-garde, German Expressionism, surrealism, and contemporary installations. Expect the ubiquitous Picasso, Dali, Magritte and Chagall, and a whole lot more besides.

→ TASTY SELECTION

If your taste is for art from earlier, more classical, times, Cologne has that covered, too. A few minutes' walk south leads you to the **Wallraf-Richartz Museum**, a shiny edifice opened only in 2001. This should cater to most tastes, as the range of Western art from the thirteenth to the nineteenth centuries is pretty comprehensive. On the second floor is the very earliest depiction of Cologne – six hundred years old – in The Martyrdom of St Ursula at the City of Cologne. Go up a floor and you're face to face with a fantastic collection of works by the masters of Dutch and Flemish painting; up again and you'll find the Impressionists, plus the likes of Cezanne, Munch and Van Gogh. Nearby, on the banks of the Rhine, you'll find two more museum big hitters, rather incongruously plonked down next to each other. The **German Sport and Olympic Museum** gives you the chance to burn off energy by racing a cycle through a wind tunnel or playing football up on the roof, while at the **Chocolate Museum** you can put the pounds back on via a very tasty trip through three millennia's worth of the brown stuff.

→ OUT OF STEP?

Underground music takes on a very literal meaning in Cologne. Go down the steps of the Ludwig Museum and immediately underneath is the **Philharmonic Hall**, home to a wide range of concerts from classical to folk and pop. In the past, the Hall has also played host to the unwelcome sound of intrusive footsteps from pedestrians in the street above, so perhaps you should avoid performances with too many quiet passages. No such considerations at the city's classy **Opera House**, in the heart of the city centre, south west of the Dom. It's situated in Germany's largest theatre complex, and holds 1300, so you've a pretty good chance of getting a seat; as well

as classic and modern opera, ballet is featured heavily, too. One of the city's coolest musical venues is in the peaceful confines of the **Stadtgarten** (City Park) just beyond the ring road. **Stadtgarten** is set on the **Venloer Strasse** side of the park and has been the top jazz venue in the city for over thirty years. These days, it's widened its remit and features other strands of contemporary music. This is in general the 'cool' side of town, frequented by students and the media denizens who work in the nearby Mediapark. There are lots of fashionable restaurants and clubs, and, just to the west of the ring road, the **Belgian Quarter**, easily identified by its street names. This boasts handsome old buildings and chic apartments which make it one of the classiest places to live – and to stroll – in the city.

CALENDAR HIGHLIGHTS

As Cologne is a city of museums, it's fitting that one of its most acclaimed events is the Long Night of Cologne Museums (October). Around forty of them are open through most of the hours of darkness at a very low price. There's no real question, though, about what's the main festival in the city: Carnival. Unlike Rio or Venice, it begins on 11 November at 11.11am with a day of fancy dress and drinking in the old

town and goes on until it reaches its climax about three months later with five days of hard partying, culminating in a street parade on Rose Monday (just before Lent) watched by a million spectators. As a complete contrast, the city takes on a bookish air in March when it hosts Europe's largest international literature festival, lit.cologne, featuring a whole array of renowned authors. In June, half a million pairs of

COLOGNE IN...

→ ONE DAY
Altstadt, Dom, Romanesque churches

→ TWO DAYS
Museum Ludwig, Wallraf-Richartz Museum (or Chocolate Museum, depending on your taste), Stadtgarten (or Opera House, again depending on your taste)

→ THREE DAYS
Romano-Germanic Museum, Rheinpark

eyes look upwards as Cologne Lights illuminates the skies over the Rhine with the world's largest musically synchronised fireworks display; a convoy of boats adds to the spectacle. A month later, the Christopher Street Day gay pride gathering descends on an open-air stage in the old town for its off-the-wall parade; these days the event actually takes up a whole weekend. Also in July, the Summerjam (around the fields of Lake Fuhlinger) brings a Caribbean flair to Cologne in the shape of a reggae and world music jamboree. Not many cities can lay claim to concerts on their ring road, but Ringfest (August) sees a line of stages set up for two miles along the Ringstrassen (don't worry, it's closed to traffic) and two million rock fans descend on the area for a batch of free concerts.

EATING OUT

Cologne has a good variety of international restaurants, but before you consider eating, you should consider the local beer. The city is renowned throughout Germany for its Kölsch. It's the name of the local people and it's the name of their brew, a light beer with the yeast risen to the top rather than sunk to the bottom of the glass. There are twenty local breweries producing their own versions, and you can try them out in an old town brauhaus, atmospheric places with dark wood-panelled interiors and buzzy waiters always at hand to fill your empty stangen (small 0.2 litre glasses) whether you want them to or not. You haven't experienced Cologne properly till you've downed your Kölsch. That accomplished, you can make the most of the city's ethnic diversity by selecting a restaurant from an impressive global range; pick of the bunch are the fine Italian, Japanese and Turkish establishments. Seek out an Italian ice-cream parlour in the summertime, sit under a parasol and tuck into their renowned, full-on sundaes. If your preference is for something local, your best bet is not to be an animal lover. Favoured dishes include Himmer un Äad (bloodsausage and mash), Sauerbraten vom Pferd (braised horse) or Töttchen (ragout of brains and calf's head, cooked with herbs). As well as restaurants, cafés and bars stay open through the afternoon until late, maybe 11.00pm or midnight. Service charge is generally included but a tip of up to ten per cent is the norm.

ON THE RHEIN LINES

Pop over to the east bank for the city's biggest green space, Rheinpark. It's a whopping 125 acres and if you want to get from one end to the other you can climb aboard the park's very own miniature railway, or, if you fancy reaching it in dramatic fashion from the west bank, take a trip on the cable car that leaves from the zoo and crosses the river at head-spinning height.

Environs of Cologne
(Plan I)

0   2 km

PESCH

LONGERICH

WEIDENPESCH

MAUENHEIM

OSSENDORF

BICKENDORF

VOGELSANG

EHRENFELD

MÜNGERSDORF

WEIDEN

JUNKERSDORF

STADTWALD

Aachener   Str.

Aachener

MUSEUM FÜR
OSTASIATISCHE
KUNST

LINDENTHAL

SÜLZ

Dürener

Dürener

KLETTENBERG

HÜRTH

Venloer

Militärringstr.

Militärringstr.

Militärringstr.

Militärringstr.

Militärringstr.

Neusser Landstr.

Industriestr.

Neusser

Kempener Str.

Parkgürtel

Innere

Ehrenfeld-gürtel

Melatengürtel

Innere Kanalstr.

Äußere Kanalstr.

Kanalstr.

Venloer

Universitätsstr.

Sülzgürtel

Luxemburger

Klettenberg-gürtel

Zollstock-gürtel

Brühler

Bonn-

Holzstr.

str.

Kölner   Str.

Frechener   Str.

Horbeller   Str.

Horbeller

Str.

Luxemburger

Str.

Str.

Str.

Centre
(Plan II)

A 57-E 31

A 1-E 37

A 57

A 1-E 31

A 4-E 40

A 1-E 31

A 4-E 40

27

28

29

30

102

103

104

11

U

A   **B**

1

2

3

A   **B**

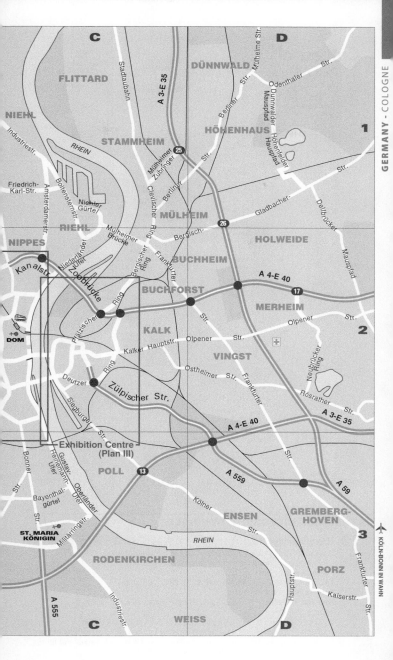

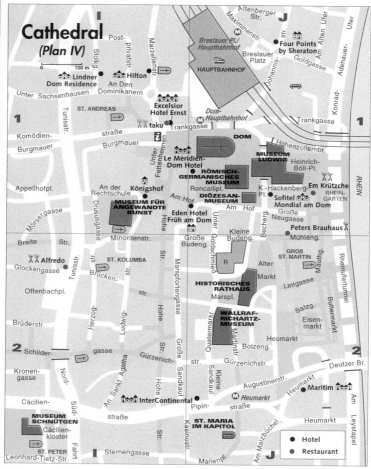

CATHEDRAL, HISTORIC TOWN HALL

Plan IV

Excelsior Hotel Ernst 🗠 ⌨ ⅙ ῗ AC SAT ⁇ ㎏ VISA ➋ AE ⓪

Domplatz/Trankgasse 1 ⌧ *50667* – Ⓜ *Dom-Hauptbahnhof* – ℰ *(0221) 27 01*
– *info@excelsior-hotel-ernst.de* – Fax *(0221) 2 70 33 33*
– *www.excelsior-hotel-ernst.de*   I1
142 rm – ♥245/325 € ♥♥325/440 €, ⌑ 25 € – 27 suites
Rest *Taku* – see below
Rest *Hanse Stube* – ℰ *(0221) 2 70 34 02* – Menu 29 € (lunch)/86 €
– Carte 61/84 €
♦ Grand Luxury ♦ Traditional ♦ Classic ♦
Tradition-rich grand hotel, in a central location by the cathedral, with its elegant
ambience from the lobby to the rooms. Piano bar. High-grade sauna and fitness
area. A stylish classical atmosphere prevails in the Hanse Stube.

GERMANY - COLOGNE

InterContinental   🛬 🚲 🏊 ⅃ 🍴 AC 🖨 ℡ ⚙ 🚗 VISA ⚛ AE ①
Pipinstr. 1 ⊠ *50667 –* Ⓜ *Heumarkt –* ℰ *(0221) 2 80 60 – cologne@ihg.com*
– Fax (0221) 28 06 11 11 – www.koeln.intercontinental.com   **J2**
262 rm ⊆ – †160/425 € ††190/455 € – 12 suites
Rest *Maulbeers* – ℰ *(0221) 28 06 12 70 (closed Sunday - Monday) (dinner only)*
Menu 49 € – Carte 48/60 € ☒
♦ Business ♦ Luxury ♦ Retro ♦

Modern design with '70s-revival elements are the key theme here. This hotel stands out for its generous setting and comfortable rooms with state of the art fittings. The Maulbeers restaurant on the first floor offers international cuisine.

Le Méridien-Dom Hotel   🍴 AC 🖨 ℡ ⅃ VISA ⚛ AE ①
Domkloster 2a ⊠ *50667 –* Ⓜ *Dom-Hauptbahnhof –* ℰ *(0221) 2 02 40*
– sales.domhotel@lemeridien.com – Fax (0221) 2 02 44 44 – www.domhotel.de
124 rm – †160/435 € ††200/450 €, ⊆ 25 € – 5 suites   **J1**
Rest – Menu 37 € (lunch) – Carte 43/75 €
♦ Traditional ♦ Luxury ♦ Classic ♦

This pleasant hotel right by the cathedral has been here since 1857. A successful combination of classical elegant and modern style. The rooms are very well equipped. Restaurant with bistro ambience, complemented by a large terrace looking onto the Roncalliplatz.

Maritim   🍴 ⅃ 🏊 🔲 AC 🖨 ℡ ⅃ VISA ⚛ AE ①
Heumarkt 20 ⊠ *50667 –* Ⓜ *Heumarkt –* ℰ *(0221) 2 02 70 – info.kol@*
maritim.de – Fax (0221) 2 02 78 26 – www.maritim.de   **J2**
454 rm – †143/339 € ††163/367 €, ⊆ 19 € – 24 suites
Rest *Bellevue* – Carte 42/54 €
♦ Chain hotel ♦ Functional ♦

This hotel, by the Deutz bridge, stands out for its impressive setting. The airy glass-roofed lobby with its boulevard flair is impressive. Functional rooms. The Bellevue offers classic ambience and views of the Rhine and Old Town.

Hilton   🛬 🏊 ⅃ AC 🖨 ℡ ⅃ 🚗 VISA ⚛ AE ①
Marzellenstr. 13 ⊠ *50668 –* Ⓜ *Dom-Hauptbahnhof –* ℰ *(0221) 13 07 10*
– info.cologne@hilton.com – Fax (0221) 13 07 20 – www.hilton.de/koeln
296 rm – †159/449 € ††189/509 €, ⊆ 24 €   **I1**
Rest – Carte 29/66 €
♦ Business ♦ Modern ♦

Located in a very central position in the town, a modern, purist design characterises this business hotel that used to be the post office. Linear ambience in the Konrad restaurant. Trendy: the Ice Bar.

Sofitel Mondial Am Dom   🍴 🛬 🏊 ⅃ AC 🖨 ℡ ⅃ 🚗
Kurt-Hackenberg-Platz 1 ⊠ *50667*
– Ⓜ *Dom-Hauptbahnhof –* ℰ *(0221) 2 06 30 – h1306@accor.com – Fax (0221)*   VISA ⚛ AE ①
2 06 35 27 – www.sofitel.com   **J1**
207 rm – †135/355 € ††155/375 €, ⊆ 22 €   **Rest** – Carte 32/45 €
♦ Business ♦ Modern ♦

This hotel is in an optimum position in the town centre near the cathedral. It provides modern, functional and well-furnished rooms. Spacious deluxe rooms also available. Contemporary restaurant with tapas bar.

Lindner Dom Residence   🍴 🛬 🏊 🔲 AC ℡ ⅃ 🚗
An den Dominikanern 4a (entrance Stolkgasse)   VISA ⚛ AE ①
⊠ *50668 –* Ⓜ *Dom-Hauptbahnhof –* ℰ *(0221) 1 64 40 – info.domresidence@*
lindner.de – Fax (0221) 1 64 44 40 – www.lindner.de
– closed 23 December-1 January
125 rm – †99/329 € ††129/359 €, ⊆ 20 €   **I1**
Rest *La Gazetta* – Carte 29/47 €
♦ Townhouse ♦ Functional ♦

This functional business hotel not far from the cathedral is a modern atrium building with large expanses of glass. The rooms on the seventh floor have a terrace. The large glass frontage of "La Gazetta" allows a view of the inner courtyard.

GERMANY - COLOGNE

Eden Hotel Früh am Dom 🛜 📺 📶 VISA 🐶

Sporergasse 1 ⊠ 50667 – ℰ (0221) 27 29 20 – hotel@frueh.de
– Fax (0221) 2 58 04 95 – www.hotel-eden.de **J1**
38 rm ⌷ – †117/253 € ††147/293 €
Rest *Hof 18* – ℰ (0221) 2 61 35 02 – Carte 28/42 €
♦ Townhouse ♦ Modern ♦
Close to the Domplatz is this hotel with modern rooms, some with views of the Dom. The breakfast room provides lovely views of the Heinzelmännchenbrunnen. This bistro-style restaurant is adorned with the works of Cologne artist HA Schult. International cuisine.

Four Points by Sheraton without rest 🗚 📺 📶 🏋 🅿

Breslauer Platz 2 ⊠ 50668 　　　　　　　VISA 🐶 🅰 ①
– Ⓜ Breslauer Pl. / Hauptbahnhof – ℰ (0221) 1 65 10 – reservierungfpk@
eurotels.de – Fax (0221) 1 65 13 33 – www.arabellastarwood.com
116 rm ⌷ – †105/485 € ††125/485 € – 6 suites **J1**
♦ Townhouse ♦ Business ♦
It's just a few minutes walk to the cathedral and the old town. The functional rooms are just right for business travellers.

Königshof without rest 📶 VISA 🐶 🅰 ①

Richartzstr. 14 ⊠ 50667 – Ⓜ Dom-Hauptbahnhof – ℰ (0221) 2 57 87 71
– hotel@hotelkoenigshof.com – Fax (0221) 2 57 87 62 – www.hotelkoenigshof.com
82 rm ⌷ – †90/198 € ††110/225 € **I1**
♦ Townhouse ♦ Functional ♦
This well-run hotel is situated a stone's throw away from Cologne Cathedral and the shopping mall. It has very clean, functionally furnished rooms.

taku – Excelsior Hotel Ernst 🗚 VISA 🐶 🅰 ①

Domplatz/Trankgasse 1 ⊠ 50667 – Ⓜ Dom-Hauptbahnhof – ℰ (0221)
2 70 39 10 – info@excelsior-hotel-ernst.de – Fax (0221) 2 70 33 33 – www.taku.de
– closed July - August 4 weeks **I1**
Rest – Carte 54/91 €
♦ Asian ♦ Minimalist ♦
Highly attentive service offering authentically prepared Japanese, Thai, Chinese and Vietnamese dishes, in a clean, purist setting.

Alfredo 🗚 🅰

Tunisstr. 3 ⊠ 50667 – ℰ (0221) 2 57 58 01 – info@ristorante-alfredo.com
– Fax (0221) 2 57 73 80 – www.ristorante-alfredo.com
– closed 3 weeks July - August, Saturday dinner - Sunday and bank holidays
Rest – *(booking advisable)* Carte 37/58 € **I2**
♦ Italian ♦ Friendly ♦
This bright, elegant restaurant is a second-generation family business. The high quality Italian dishes are recommended personally at the table, along with an attractive wine list.

Em Krützche 🛜 VISA 🐶 🅰

Am Frankenturm 1 ⊠ 50667 – ℰ (0221) 2 58 08 39 – info@em-kruetzche.de
– Fax (0221) 25 34 17 – www.em-kruetzche.de
– closed over Christmas, 7 - 14 April and Monday **J1**
Rest – Carte 33/48 €
♦ International ♦ Traditional ♦
This historical house in the old town is a traditional address with an elegant charm. Typical Rhineland and international dishes are served in the different rooms on two floors. Rhine terrace.

Peters Brauhaus 🛜

Mühlengasse 1 ⊠ 50667 – Ⓜ Dom-Hauptbahnhof – ℰ (0221) 2 57 39 50
– info@peters-brauhaus.de – Fax (0221) 2 57 39 62 – www.peters-brauhaus.de
– closed during Christmas **J1**
Rest – Carte 20/29 €
♦ Regional ♦ Cosy ♦
A rustic inn with a beautiful decorated façade. Worth a look around: each room has a character of its own. Serves good, solid food with fresh Kölsch beer on draught.

GERMANY - COLOGNE

Marriott 🖼️

*Johannisstr. 76 ⊠ 50668 – ⓜ Breslauer Pl. / Hauptbahnhof – ℰ (0221)
94 22 20 – cologne.marriott@marriotthotels.com – Fax (0221) 94 22 27 77
– www.koelnmarriott.com* **F1-2**
282 rm ⌿ – †139 € ††139 € – 11 suites   **Rest Fou** – Carte 26/41 €
♦ Business ♦ Modern ♦

A spacious lobby and "Plusch-Bar" greet you at this comfortable business hotel
near the cathedral. The rooms are comfortable and very modern. Fou: a restaurant
in French brasserie style.

Im Wasserturm 🖼️

*Kaygasse 2 ⊠ 50676 – ⓜ Poststr. – ℰ (0221) 2 00 80 – info@
hotel-im-wasserturm.de – Fax (0221) 2 00 88 88 – www.hotel-im-wasserturm.de*
78 rm – †215 € ††245 €, ⌿ 26 € – 7 suites   **F2**
Rest La Vision – see below
Rest d/\blju "W" – Menu 29 € – Carte 30/51 €
♦ Historic ♦ Business ♦ Design ♦

What is remarkable about this hotel is its unusual architecture – a former water
tower (a listed building) from the 19th century with an 11-m high lobby. Designer
style rooms. The d/\blju"W" has a clear, modern, elegant style. Regional and international cuisine.

Renaissance 🖼️

*Magnusstr. 20 ⊠ 50672 – ⓜ Friesenplatz – ℰ (0221) 2 03 40
– info.cologne@renaissancehotels.com – Fax (0221) 2 03 47 77
– www.renaissancekoeln.de* **E2**
236 rm – †125/495 € ††125/550 €, ⌿ 23 €
Rest Raffael – Carte 32/47 €
♦ Chain hotel ♦ Classic ♦

This city centre hotel is timelessly elegant, from the lobby to the comfortable
rooms. The Raffael restaurant serves international cuisine.

Savoy 🖼️

*Turiner Str. 9 ⊠ 50668 – ⓜ Breslauer Pl. / Hauptbahnhof – ℰ (0221) 1 62 30
– info@savoy.de – Fax (0221) 1 62 32 00 – www.savoy.de* **F1**
102 rm ⌿ – †140 € ††170 € – 6 suites   **Rest** – Carte 41/51 €
♦ Business ♦ Personalised ♦

The tasteful use of the themes of Africa, Asia, Italy and the Orient is what gives this
passionately managed hotel its individual tone. Extensive wellness area. A roof terrace completes this light, friendly restaurant.

Ascot *without rest* 🖼️

*Hohenzollernring 95 ⊠ 50672 – ⓜ Friesenplatz – ℰ (0221) 9 52 96 50
– info@ascot.bestwestern.de – Fax (0221) 9 52 96 51 00
– www.hotel-ascot.de
– closed 22 December-2 January* **E2**
44 rm ⌿ – †106/168 € ††122/188 €
♦ Townhouse ♦ Cosy ♦

This listed patrician house is now an elegant English-style hotel. Pretty hall with a
small library and an attractive courtyard terrace.

Santo *without rest* 🖼️

*Dagobertstr. 22 ⊠ 50668 – ⓜ Ebertplatz – ℰ (0221) 9 13 97 70 – info@
hotelsanto.de – Fax (0221) 9 13 97 77 77 – www.hotelsanto.de* **F1**
69 rm ⌿ – †138 € ††160 €
♦ Business ♦ Modern ♦

The modern, purist layout and the lighting concept (created by the light designer
Christian Türmer) create an appealing atmosphere in this hotel.

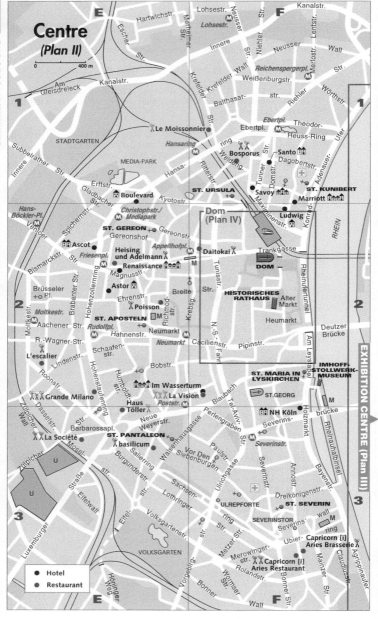

Centre
(Plan II)

0 400 m

GERMANY - COLOGNE

EXHIBITION CENTRE (Plan III)

Hartwichstr.
Lohsestr.
Neusser
Kanalstr.
Lohsestr.
Str.

Escher
Hartwichstr.
Merheimer Str.
Innere
Str.
Niehler
Neusser
Lentstr.

Am
Gleisdreieck
Kanalstr.
Krefelder
Wall
Reichenspergerpl.
Weißenburgstr.
Str.
Merlostr.
Wall

STADTGARTEN
Subbelrather Str.
Balthasar-
str.
Riehler
Wörthstr.

MEDIA-PARK
Hansaring
Le Moissonnier
Ebertpl.
Ebertpl.
Theodor-
Heuss-Ring
Ufer

Innere
Str.
Venloer
Erftstr.
Hansa
Ritterstr.
Weidng.
ring
Bosporus
Santo
Dagobertstr.
Theodor-
Adenauer-

Boulevard
Gladbacher Str.
Kyotostr.
ST. URSULA
Turiner
Domstr.
Savoy
Marriott
ST. KUNIBERT

Hans-
Böckler-Pl.
Spichernstr.
Christophstr./
Mediapark
Gereonstr.
Dom
(Plan IV)
Maximinenstr.
Ludwig
Konrad-
RHEIN

Ascot
Friesenpl.
ST. GEREON
Gereonshof
Appellhofpl.
Daitokai
Trankgasse
Rheinufertunnel

Bismarckstr.
Hohenzollernring
Heising
und Adelmann
Renaissance
Magnusstr.
Tunisstr.
DOM

Brüsseler
Pl.
Brabanter Str.
Astor
Ehrenstr.
Breite
Str.
HISTORISCHES
RATHAUS
Alter
Markt

Moltkestr.
Aachener Str.
Rudolfpl.
Poisson
ST. APOSTELN
Richmod-
str.
Neumarkt
N.-S.-Fahrt
Heumarkt
Deutzer
Brücke

R.-Wagner-Str.
Hahnenstr.
Neumarkt
Cäcilienstr.
Pipinstr.

L'escalier
Lindenstr.
Schaafen-
str.
Bobstr.

Roonstr.
Hohenstaufenring
Humboldt-
str.
Im Wasserturm
Blaubach
Tel-Aviv-
ST. MARIA IN
LYSKIRCHEN
IMHOFF-
STOLLWERK-
MUSEUM

Grande Milano
Haus
Töller
La Vision
Poststr.
ST. GEORG
Holzmarkt

Dasselst.
Zülpicher
Wall
Barbarossapl.
Neue
Weyerstr.
Perlengraben
NH Köln
brücke
Rheinauhalbinsel

La Société
Mosel-
str.
ST. PANTALEON
basilicum
Salierring
Walramstr.
Waisenhausgasse
Vor Den
Siebenburgen
Paulstr.
Severins-
str.
Severinstr.

Zülpicher Str.
U
U
Burgunderstr.
Sachsen-
ring
Ulrichgasse
Severinstr.
Annostr.
Bayenstr.

Straße
Eifelwall
Lothringer
str.
ULREPFORTE
Dreikönigenstr.
ST. SEVERIN
SEVERINSTR.
Severins-
ring

Luxemburger
Str.
Volksgartenstr.
Metzer
Str.
Ubier-
str.
Capricorn [i]
Aries Brasserie
Mainzer
Str.

VOLKSGARTEN
Vorgebirg-
str.
Merowinger-
str.
Capricorn [i]
Aries Restaurant
Rolandstr.
Bonner
Str.
Agrippinaufer

Höninger
Weg
Bonner
Str.
Wormser
Str.
Wall
Claudiusstr.

● Hotel
● Restaurant

326

NH Köln

Holzmarkt 47 ⊠ 50676 – Ⓜ Severinstr. – ℰ (0221) 2 72 28 80
– nhkoeln@nh-hotels.com – Fax (0221) 2 72 28 81 00
– www.nh-hotels.com   **F3**
204 rm – ♥99/212 € ♥♥116/236 €, � 18 €   **Rest** – Carte 22/40 €
◆ Chain hotel ◆ Modern ◆

The hotel is right beside the Severin bridge, not far from the Stollwerck chocolate museum. Functional, contemporary rooms with relaxation chairs and marble desks. The modern restaurant has a small conservatory facing the courtyard.

Astor without rest

Friesenwall 68 ⊠ 50672 – Ⓜ Friesenplatz – ℰ (0221) 20 71 20 – mail@
hotelastor.de – Fax (0221) 25 31 06 – www.hotelastor.de
– closed 24 December-3 January   **E2**
50 rm � – ♥95/115 € ♥♥115/138 €
◆ Townhouse ◆ Functional ◆

This highly personally managed hotel consists of two houses which have been joined together. Some of the rooms are particularly comfortable and modern.

Ludwig without rest

Brandenburger Str. 24 ⊠ 50668 – Ⓜ Breslauer Pl. / Hauptbahnhof – ℰ (0221)
16 05 40 – hotel@hotelludwig.com – Fax (0221) 16 05 44 44
– www.hotelludwig.de
– closed 23 December-1 January   **F2**
55 rm � – ♥85/195 € ♥♥110/255 €
◆ Townhouse ◆ Functional ◆

This hotel is close to the city centre, not far from the station, and offers contemporary, functionally equipped rooms and a reception staffed around the clock.

Boulevard without rest

Hansaring 14 ⊠ 50670 – Ⓜ Christophstr./Mediapark – ℰ (0221) 3 55 84 40
– hotel@hotelboulevard.de – Fax (0221) 13 83 07 – www.hotelboulevard.de
– closed 23 December-2 January   **E1**
27 rm � – ♥88/220 € ♥♥109/280 €
◆ Townhouse ◆ Functional ◆

This hotel benefits from its convenient location near the ring road and its well looked after, functional rooms.

La Vision – Hotel Im Wasserturm

Kaygasse 2 (11th floor) ⊠ 50676 – Ⓜ Poststr. – ℰ (0221) 2 00 80 – info@
hotel-im-wasserturm.de – Fax (0221) 2 00 88 88 – www.hotel-im-wasserturm.de
– closed 2 weeks January, 4 weeks July - August and Sunday - Monday
Rest – Menu 70/130 € – Carte 61/83 € 🌿   **F2**
Spec. Kaisergranat und Fenchel in Anisbrot gebacken mit Estragon. Gebratene Schulter vom Schwarzen Schwein mit Krustel, Spinat und Sauce Charcutière. Drei kleine aromatische Schokoladenkuppeln.
◆ Inventive ◆ Elegant ◆

Elegant restaurant atop the historical water tower. Enjoy creative, classic cuisine with a fantastic view over Cologne. There is also a fabulous panoramic roof terrace.

Grande Milano

Hohenstaufenring 29 ⊠ 50674 – Ⓜ Rudolfpl. – ℰ (0221) 24 21 21 – info@
grandemilano.com – Fax (0221) 24 48 46 – www.grandemilano.com
– closed 1 week January, Saturday lunch, Sunday and bank holidays
Rest – Menu 58/78 € – Carte 38/75 €   **E2**
Rest *Pinot di Pinot* – Menu 13 € (lunch) – Carte 23/40 €
◆ Italian ◆ Elegant ◆

Elegant Italian restaurant with fine service. Menu features a truffle specialty. A relaxed, typically bistro-style atmosphere in the Pinot di Pinot.

XX
🕄 **Capricorn [i] Aries Restaurant**

Alteburger Str. 34 ⊠ 50678 – ℰ (0221) 32 31 82 – Fax (0221) 32 31 82
– www.capricorniaries.com
– closed 18 - 25 February, 8 - 14 April and Monday - Tuesday, except trade fairs
Rest *– (dinner only) (booking essential)* Menu 75/99 € **F3**
Spec. Steinbutt mit Zitronennage. Kalbsfilet mit Ragout von Kalbsbäckchen und
Kalbsbries. Parfait vom Montélimar-Nougat mit Nougateis und Blutorangen.
◆ Inventive ◆ Intimate ◆

Take your seat at one of the four tables in this intimate restaurant decorated entirely in white. Friendly and competent personnel serve classic cuisine with a creative touch.

XX
🕄 **La Société** *VISA AE*

Kyffhäuser Str. 53 ⊠ 50674 – ℰ (0221) 23 24 64 – kueche@lasociete.info
– Fax (0221) 21 04 51 – www.lasociete.info
– closed 2 weeks July - August **E3**
Rest *– (dinner only) (booking advisable)* Menu 60/90 € – Carte 52/86 € 🕸
Spec. Fünf Suppen mit Kondimenten. Gebratener Seeteufel (2 people). Mari-
nierte Tamarillo und Kiwi mit Ziegenquarkmousse im Knusper.
◆ Inventive ◆ Individual ◆

This externally rather non-descript townhouse accommodates a pleasant small restaurant with friendly service. Mr Kotaska prepares creative dishes accompanied by
some rather good wines.

XX
Bosporus *🛖 AC ⇔ VISA ⬤ AE ⬤*

Weidengasse 36 ⊠ 50668 – ⓜ Hansaring – ℰ (0221) 12 52 65 – info@
bosporus.de – Fax (0221) 9 12 38 29 – www.bosporus.de **F1**
Rest *–* Carte 27/34 €
◆ Turkish ◆ Classic ◆

A classically designed restaurant with a pleasant terrace and an attractive function
room on the first floor. Authentic Turkish cuisine served in the open kitchen.

X
🕄🕄 **Le Moissonnier** *AC VISA ⬤*

Krefelder Str. 25 ⊠ 50670 – ⓜ Hansaring – ℰ (0221) 72 94 79 – Fax (0221)
7 32 54 61 – www.lemoissonnier.de
– closed 24 December - early January, 2 weeks over Easter, 3 weeks July
- August and Sunday - Monday **F1**
Rest *– (booking essential)* Menu 58/91 € – Carte 59/85 €
Spec. Foie gras de canard Maison. Saint-Jacques aux artichauts et jus de
paella. Suprême de pigeonneau.
◆ Inventive ◆ Bistro ◆

A charming, lively restaurant created with style and taste to fully emulate a Parisian
bistro. A friendly and very well trained service team will attend to you with creative
French cuisine.

X
Poisson *🛖 AC VISA ⬤*

Wolfstr. 6 ⊠ 50667 – ⓜ Neumarkt – ℰ (0221) 27 73 68 83 – menue@
poisson-restaurant.de – Fax (0221) 27 73 68 84 – www.poisson-restaurant.de
– closed Sunday and bank holidays **E3**
Rest *– (booking advisable)* Carte 42/72 €
◆ Fish ◆ Bistro ◆

This trendy restaurant is right in the centre and has a relaxed atmosphere and
open kitchen. The modern fish dishes are simple and produce specific.

X
🕄 **L'escalier** (Jens Dannenfeld) *🛖 AC ⇔ VISA ⬤ AE*

Brüsseler Str. 11 ⊠ 50674 – ⓜ Moltkestr. – ℰ (0221) 2 05 39 98
– info@lescalier-restaurant.de – Fax (0221) 5 69 12 80 – www.lescalier-restaurant.de
– closed 19 - 25 February, 6 - 16 April, 12 - 22 October and Sunday - Monday
lunch, Saturday lunch **E2**
Rest *–* Menu 42/60 € – Carte 44/61 €
Spec. Dreierlei vom Felchen und gebratenen Endivien. Heidschnucke mit
Pastinakenpüree. Vanillesoufflé mit gepfefferter Ananas.
◆ Classic ◆ Fashionable ◆

A cosy and pleasantly casual atmosphere reigns in this bistro-style restaurant.
Modern international and surprise dishes are served.

328

GERMANY - COLOGNE

⅍ **Capricorn [i] Aries Brasserie**
Alteburgerstr. 31 ⊠ *50678 – ℰ (0221) 3 97 57 10 – Fax (0221) 32 31 82*
– www.capricorniaries.com
– closed Carnival and Saturday lunch, Sunday **F3**
Rest – Menu 55 € – Carte 23/49 €
♦ International ♦ Bistro ♦
A slightly more casual variation of the restaurant opposite (which shares the same name). This friendly, contemporary brasserie has a comfortable, informal atmosphere and attentive service.

⅍ **Heising und Adelmann** 🍃 ⇆
Friesenstr. 58 ⊠ *50670 –* Ⓜ *Friesenplatz – ℰ (0221) 1 30 94 24 – info@ heising-und-adelmann.de – Fax (0221) 1 30 94 25*
– www.heising-und-adelmann.de
– closed Sunday and bank holidays **E2**
Rest – *(dinner only)* Menu 35 € – Carte 33/50 €
♦ International ♦ Bistro ♦
A lively restaurant in the popular bistro-style with a delightful terrace. Modern, international cuisine is served in a relaxed atmosphere. Large bar area.

⅍ **basilicum** 🍃 *VISA* ◍◐
Am Weidenbach 33 ⊠ *50676 –* Ⓜ *Poststr. – ℰ (0221) 32 35 55 – info@ basilicum.org – Fax (0221) 16 89 61 33 – www.basilicum.org*
– closed 19 - 25 February and Sunday **E3**
Rest – *(dinner only)* Menu 30/36 € – Carte 32/45 €
♦ International ♦ Friendly ♦
Small, bistro-style restaurant offering international cuisine, which is also served on the attractive inner courtyard terrace.

⅍ **Daitokai** AC *VISA* ◍◐ AE ◍
Kattenbug 2 ⊠ *50667 –* Ⓜ *Appellhofpl. – ℰ (0221) 12 00 48 – Fax (0221) 13 75 03 – www.daitokai.de*
– closed Monday - Tuesday lunch **F2**
Rest – *(booking advisable for dinner)* Menu 24 € (lunch)/53 € – Carte 37/61 €
♦ Japanese ♦ Friendly ♦
The cooks demonstrate their dexterity at teppanyaki tables in this typical Japanese restaurant in the town centre.

⅍ **Haus Töller** 🍃 ⇆
Weyerstr. 96 ⊠ *50676 –* Ⓜ *Poststr. – ℰ (0221) 2 58 93 16 – Fax (0211) 3 97 50 67 – www.haus-toeller.de*
– closed July, Sunday and bank holidays **E3**
Rest – *(dinner only) (booking advisable)* Carte 18/25 €
♦ Regional ♦ Traditional ♦
A Cologne pub like no other. Everything is still the same as when it opened back in 1889 – including a 'confessional' – creating a really cosy atmosphere.

AT THE EXHIBITION CENTRE *Plan III*

🏨 **Hyatt Regency** ⟨ 🍃 ⅙ ⌂ ▥ ♿ AC 🖳 📶 ᴪ **P** ⇆
Kennedy-Ufer 2a ⊠ *50679 –* Ⓜ *Deutzer Freiheit* *VISA* ◍◐ AE ◍
– ℰ (0221) 8 28 12 34 – cologne.regency@hyatt.com – Fax (0221) 8 28 13 70
– www.cologne.regency.hyatt.de **G2**
306 rm – †160/360 € ††185/385 €, � 23 € – 18 suites
Rest *Graugans* – *(closed Sunday - Monday) (Tuesday - Saturday dinner only)* Menu 69/99 € – Carte 57/78 €
Rest *Glashaus* – Carte 43/62 €
♦ Chain hotel ♦ Luxury ♦ Classic ♦
The Grand Hotel located on the banks of the Rhine is a luxurious address. It has a large atrium hall, elegant guestrooms and a lovely view of the city. A classical atmosphere and European/Asian cuisine in the Graugans. The Glashaus offers Italian cuisine.

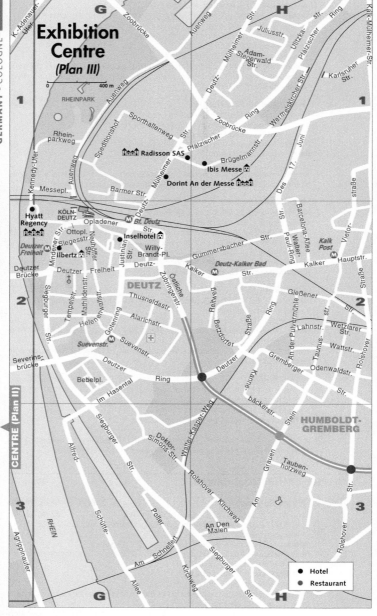

Exhibition Centre
(Plan III)

GERMANY - COLOGNE

CENTRE (Plan II)

RHEINPARK

Rheinparkweg

Radisson SAS

Ibis Messe

Dorint An der Messe

Hyatt Regency

KÖLN-DEUTZ

Inselhotel

Deutzer Freiheit

Ilbertz

Deutzer Brücke

DEUTZ

Severinsbrücke

Kalk Post

Deutz-Kalker Bad

HUMBOLDT-GREMBERG

RHEIN

● Hotel
● Restaurant

Dorint An der Messe

Deutz-Mülheimer-Str. 22 ✉ *50679* – Ⓜ *Bf. Deutz*   *VISA* **OO** **AE** **①**
– ✆ *(0221) 80 19 00 – info.koeln-messe@dorint.com – Fax (0221) 80 19 08 00*
– www.dorint.com/koeln   **G1**
313 rm ⌷ – ♦128/294 € ♦♦200/384 € – 32 suites
Rest *L'Adresse* *– (closed 4 weeks August and Sunday - Tuesday) (dinner only)*
Carte 47/74 €
Rest *Bell Arte* *– (lunch only)* Carte 36/49 €
Rest *Düx* *–* Carte 29/49 €
♦ Chain hotel ♦ Business ♦ Modern ♦

Find modern elegance and well-equipped rooms in this hotel close to the conference centre. The hotel also has a 650m2 spa and a pleasant bar. Upmarket dishes are served at L'Adresse. The Düx is a typical Cologne restaurant.

Radisson SAS

Messe Kreisel 3 ✉ *50679* – Ⓜ *Bf. Deutz* – ✆ *(0221) 27 72 00*
– reservations.cologne@radissonsas.com – Fax (0221) 2 77 20 10
– www.radissonsas.com   **G1**
393 rm – ♦115/210 € ♦♦115/210 €, ⌷ 23 €   **Rest** – Carte 36/54 €
♦ Chain hotel ♦ Stylish ♦

This business hotel next to the exhibition centre is extremely modern. There is an impressive 15m/50ft high glass hall and rooms with top quality technical fittings. The Paparazzi serves as an a la carte restaurant, with its large pizza oven.

Inselhotel *without rest*

Constantinstr. 96 ✉ *50679* – Ⓜ *Bf. Deutz* – ✆ *(0221) 8 80 34 50 – mail@*
inselhotel-koeln.de – Fax (0221) 8 80 34 90 – www.inselhotel-koeln.de
42 rm ⌷ – ♦79/185 € ♦♦109/275 €   **G2**
♦ Townhouse ♦ Functional ♦

The hotel offers well-maintained, functional guestrooms. It faces Deutz station and is not far from the trade fair site and the Köln Arena.

Ibis Messe

Brügelmannstr. 1 ✉ *50679* – Ⓜ *Bf. Deutz* – ✆ *(0221) 98 93 10 – h3744@*
accor.com – Fax (0221) 98 93 15 55 – www.ibishotel.com   **H1**
180 rm – ♦74/149 € ♦♦74/179 €, ⌷ 10 €   **Rest** – Carte 18/36 €
♦ Chain hotel ♦ Functional ♦

Ideal for business travellers, this hotel near the conference centre provides modern, well-furnished rooms. A pub-style restaurant with much wooden décor.

Ilbertz *without rest*

Mindener Str. 6 (corner Siegesstraße) ✉ *50679* – Ⓜ *Deutzer Freiheit*
– ✆ (0221) 8 29 59 20 – hotel@hotel-ilbertz.de – Fax (0221) 8 29 59 21 55
– www.hotel-ilbertz.de   **G2**
26 rm ⌷ – ♦95/135 € ♦♦115/185 €
♦ Family ♦ Functional ♦

Appealing particularly to business travellers, this pleasant, spotlessly clean hotel has contemporary, technically well-equipped guestrooms.

ENVIRONS OF COLOGNE

at the airport South-East: 17 km by A59 **D3**

Holiday Inn Airport

Waldstr. 255 (at airport Köln/Bonn) ✉ *51147* – ✆ *(02203) 56 10*
– reservation.hi-cologne-bonn-airport@queensgruppe.de – Fax (02203) 56 19
– www.koeln-bonn-airport-holiday-inn.de
177 rm – ♦119/350 € ♦♦150/390 €, ⌷ 19 €   **Rest** – Carte 28/45 €
♦ Chain hotel ♦ Functional ♦

This business hotel provides functional, well-equipped rooms and has easy access to the airport. An elegant restaurant with mainly international cuisine.

at Köln - Porz-Langel South : 17 km by Hauptstraße **D3**

XXX **Zur Tant** (Franz und Alexander Hütter) ≤ 🍴 **P** VISA ⚫ AE ①

Rheinbergstr. 49 ✉ *51143 – ℰ (02203) 8 18 83 – info@zurtant.de – Fax (02203)
8 73 27 – www.zurtant.de
– closed 2 weeks by Carnival and Thursday*
Rest – Menu 65/85 € – Carte 50/68 €
Rest *Hütter's Piccolo* – Carte 29/40 €
Spec. Sautierte Jakobsmuscheln mit Aromen von weißer Schokolade. Steinbutt in asiatischer Würze mit Basmatireis. Crépinette vom Reh mit Holunder-
sauce und Rahmspitzkohl.
 ♦ Classic ♦ Friendly ♦
This elegant restaurant offers classic cuisine, which guests can enjoy while taking
in the lovely view of the Rhine. Hütter's Piccolo is a friendly bistro-style restaurant
with a Mediterranean touch.

Population (est.2005) 649 000 (conurbation 1 489 000) – Altitude:40m

Sime/PHOTONONSTOP

European travellers might feel there's no need to go all the way to New York when they've got Frankfurt. After all, it's earned itself the nickname 'Mainhattan' what with all those slinky, shiny skyscrapers reaching up from the banks of the river Main. This may be a city of brash towers housing big corporations (hence its other nickname 'Bankfurt') but you'll also find half-timbered medieval houses (admittedly rebuilt), and a blistering array of museums along the south bank of the river.

Located at the crossing point of Germany's north-south and east-west roads, Frankfurt is the financial powerhouse of the country, but a city that takes its cultural scene very seriously. It's said that it spends more money on the arts per year than any other European city, and from being something of a gastronomic back water, it's become a gourmet hotspot with its cuisine range becoming more eclectic by the month. The city has also joined the recent trend in turning local venues into summer beach clubs, complete with palm trees and sand. One man who wouldn't believe his eyes if he saw Frankfurt today is Germany's great poet, novelist and dramatist Johann Wolfgang von Goethe...he was born and bred here.

LIVING THE CITY

The centre of Frankfurt is **Cathedral Hill**, where the cathedral has stood for eight hundred years. It towers over **Römerberg**, the medieval square, rebuilt following the War. To the west, amongst the mighty skyscrapers of international banks and corporations, lies the main railway station and **Exhibition Centre**, while south of the **river Main**, which cuts east-west through the city, is the famous **'museum embankment'** and Frankfurt's oldest area, **Sachsenhausen**, full of bars, cafés and restaurants.

PRACTICAL INFORMATION

ARRIVAL-DEPARTURE

Frankfurt Airport is only 9km southeast from the city centre. A taxi will cost around €25. S-Bahn trains S8 and S9 leave every 15min for Frankfurt station and the journey takes just over 10min.

TRANSPORT

Frankfurt runs an efficient bus, metro and tram system. You can buy a day ticket for one person or a group (maximum five), which is valid until the last ride of the day. Tickets are available at vending machines and from bus drivers, but not on trams, the U-Bahn or S-Bahn.

Be a smart Frankfurter and invest in a Frankfurt Card. This entitles you to free public transport and discounts at a variety of museums and attractions. There are also reductions of up to thirty per cent on selected boat trips. You can buy the Card at many travel agencies, at tourist information offices and in both terminals at the airport. It's valid for 24 or 48 hours.

EXPLORING FRANKFURT

During Germany's post-war economic miracle, Frankfurt soon re-established itself as the economic hub of the country. As part of a big drive to show that there was more to the city than Deutschmarks, the authorities poured millions into invigorating its cultural life, using old plans to faithfully rebuild key parts of the war-torn old town and at the same time launch a succession of exciting opera companies, museums and theatres. The city was reborn, and is now the closest thing western Germany has to a high-rise metropolis. To view its skyline from the south bank at night is to see a twinkling fairyland of light, its resemblance to Manhattan evident to all.

Just to the north of the curving River Main is a compact area that speaks of a far older Frankfurt, where once Holy Roman Emperors were crowned, and where market fairs rang to the cries of traders over a thousand years ago. The dominant feature of the district is the Römerberg, the old centre with its eye-catching half-timbered buildings lovingly rebuilt in 1986 with the aid of historical plans. Römerberg is a cobbled, octagonal square known locally as the 'Great Parlour', and its most striking landmark is the **town hall**, originally three 14C town houses linked by a Gothic triple-gabled frontage. It's not just pretty façades around here, there's a great gallery on the square – the **Kunsthalle Schirn**, opened little more than twenty years ago. It hosts a range of high-powered art, archaeology and cultural exhibitions, and in a short period has become one of Europe's most prestigious spaces. As a contrast, the twin-naved church of **St Nicholas**, just west of the Schirn, dates back to 1290, and twice a day reverberates to the sound of German folk songs. On the eastern side of the old town is the Kaiserdom, the city's thirteenth century cathedral, which remained standing throughout Allied bombing, and boasts stunning views from its Gothic tower: you'll have to climb 324 steps first, though.

➜ BANKING ON CULTURE

Visitors don't have to travel far to find out more about the centuries long, incident-filled history of Frankfurt. Close by St Nicholas is the **History Museum**, finished in 1972, which includes a fascinating model of the medieval town, and colourful fragments of buildings that were lost in World War II. By now, you're just about at the water's edge. Cross the river and you'll face to face with one of the best cultural neighbourhoods in Europe: the Museum Embankment. Along here, strung out like pearls, are nine exhibition buildings, enough to keep an art lover engrossed for many hours, if not days. Some of the museums are quite new (such as those looking at **German Film**, or **World Cultures**), but the **Stadel Art Institute** – perhaps the jewel in the crown – is nearly two hundred years old. The imposing neo-renaissance building boasts work by the likes of

Vermeer, Rembrandt, Botticelli, Bosch and van Eyck. If Old Masters are not to your taste, then you can try your luck at other exhibitions around here, which deal with architecture, icons, sculpture, communications, applied art, or – the newest baby on the block – local artists from the Rhine-Main area. In terms of sheer novelty, head back over the Main for the **Modern Art Museum**: the collections from the 1960s onwards are innovative enough, but just gazing at the building itself is an absorbing experience – it looks like a rather tasty slice of cake.

➜ MAIN PLAYERS

You can't avoid looking at buildings in this city. In the centre, the now emblematic skyscrapers tower endlessly up to the clouds; if you're of a mind, you could even call them gigantic works of art themselves. One of them, the **Commerzbank Tower**, just happens to be the tallest office building in Europe. Slightly dwarfed, but still very large indeed, is the **Main Tower**, and this is the one that's of interest to visitors. It's the only one in Frankfurt with a public viewing platform, which can be located up on the roof. It hardly needs saying that the vista from here is astounding.

The contrast between the new and the old is thrown up again back in the old town where, a short way up from the north bank of the Main, stands the **Goethe house**. The great man was born here in 1749, and it's where he lived for the next twenty-six years. It's a fascinating example of a mid-eighteenth century home of the upper middle classes, lovingly restored with an interior that includes his writing desk and an astronomical clock. Next door is the decade-old **Goethemuseum**, which includes a collection of items related to Goethe, and an absorbing library with his writings. Another cultural highlight of the area is the **Opera House**, completely rebuilt in a compelling Italian Renaissance style. What happens inside, too, is of a high order: this is Frankfurt's top venue for a wide range of concerts, which take place in either the Great Hall or the Mozart Hall – expect anything from chamber and symphony concerts to jazz, pop and comedy.

Frankfurt is home to some of the country's best shopping streets. Number one on the list is the pedestrianised **Zeil Promenade**, which is lined with department stores. There are more specialised streets dotted around: the nearby **Goethestrasse** (for exclusive designer boutiques); **Berger Strasse** (for trendy fashion); **Schillerstrasse** (for shoes). Seek out the **Kleinmarkthalle,** the city's huge indoor grocery market, for some superbly fresh German foodstuffs. A slightly more out of the way quarter to hit is Sachsenhausen, which is over the river and to the southeast of Museum

Embankment. It's a leafy, laidback area, very popular for chilling out, so, after checking its quirky little specialist shops (and Saturday flea market), locals like to sip beer or coffee in one of the neighbourhood's many bars and restaurants.

Of course, if relaxing by a beach is more your thing, then even somewhere seriously landlocked like Frankfurt can come up with a solution. In the summer, many of the city's venues set up outdoor beach clubs, complete with sand and palm trees. The rooftops of some city centre buildings are fair game to double as the faux-seaside; for instance, the roof of the car park of the **Frankfurt Stock Exchange** boasts two pools and a five-hundred strong capacity, while **City Beach Frankfurt**, on the roof of the car park of (this time) a department store, goes that extra mile with a pool and sand, open air cinema, beach volley ball, and salsa evenings.

CALENDAR HIGHLIGHTS

Practically everyone in Europe's heard of Frankfurt's main event, and with good reason. The Book Fair (in October) is a major jamboree for publishers and book lovers, and reflects the latest trends in global literature. Not by any means is every celebration in the city so cerebral. Frankfurt's Carnival in February is a riot of colour, music and festivities, and it kick-starts an impressive array of spring and summer events. The

Forest Folk Festival (May) in Niederrad Forest, a stone's throw from the city, boasts a fairground, bustling market and traditional festivities. A month later, the Opernplatz Festival (in the square with the Opera House) has a stage with music, a motley collective of cabaret artists and a fine range of international gourmet treats (enough to bring local bankers down from their towers). The Rose and Light Festival (also June) transforms the city's Palm

FRANKFURT IN...

→ ONE DAY
Old Town, Römerberg, the view from Main Tower

→ TWO DAYS
Goethe House, Museum Embankment (take your pick of one or two museums), a restaurant in Sachsenhausen

→ THREE DAYS
Boat trip on the Main, window shopping (Zeil), concert at Opera House

Garden into a wonderland of lanterns and candles, which complement the music going on all around. Zeil's inner-city pavements are shaken in July by the Sound of Frankfurt, when the likes of techno, rock and pop throb round the pedestrian zones. Refuge may be sought with Frankfurt Cinema Week, where you can lose yourself watching films in unusual places (don't expect a cinema!). The river hosts two big entertainments in August: the River Main Festival, and the Museum Quay Festival. Both rejoice in Frankfurt's waterway, with music, fireworks, a regatta, the museums, and local concert halls all playing a big part. The end of summer is announced with Autumn Dippe Fair, at Festplatz am Ratsweg in September. The last big open-air fair before winter is a riot of old-fashioned fun, with carousels, rollercoasters, and fireworks to set it all off and close it down.

EATING OUT

Not so long ago, Frankfurt's gastronomic fame came courtesy of its Apfelwein (a sweet or dry variant of cider) and Handkäs mit Musik (small yellow cheese with vinegar, oil and onions). Not forgetting Grüne Sauce (a mixture of various herbs and sour cream served with boiled eggs). That's not the case now. Head along to the Fressgass (near Opernplatz) and you've got a pedestrian mile of fine eateries – food on the hoof or to graze over at good prices. Fressgass, by the way, translates as 'Eatery Alley' or 'Glutton's Lane', so you get the picture. Nearly thirty per cent of Frankfurt's citizens have come to live here from overseas, so a wealth of eating possibilities has been opened up and it's now no problem to 'eat globally' all round the city. Foreign communities have added a real touch of spice to the culinary landscape, which is full of the likes of Turkish, Italian and Chinese establishments. Nevertheless, a visit to this city wouldn't be complete without a trip to the äppelwoilokale in Sachsenhausen, the casual but lively cafés where tradition is the key, and Apfelwein served up in ceramic mugs is the drink. Any down sides to eating here? In a city full of bankers, it can prove a bit difficult locating good but inexpensive food, but if in doubt (or potential penury) - hit the Fressgass!

→ EXPRESS DELIVERY

For a leisurely trip round Frankfurt, try the Ebbelwei Express. This colourful tram takes visitors all over the city from Römer to the zoo, across the river to Sachsenhausen and back – and you get a free bottle of cider. But it only runs at weekends and on public holidays.

→ A RIVER RUNS

Taking to the water makes a great day out here. Only a few steps away from the Römerberg is the Main quay at the Eiserner Steg, from where you can catch boats up and down the river. You can choose between day trips up to the Rhine or shorter journeys taking in the amazing skyline of the city.

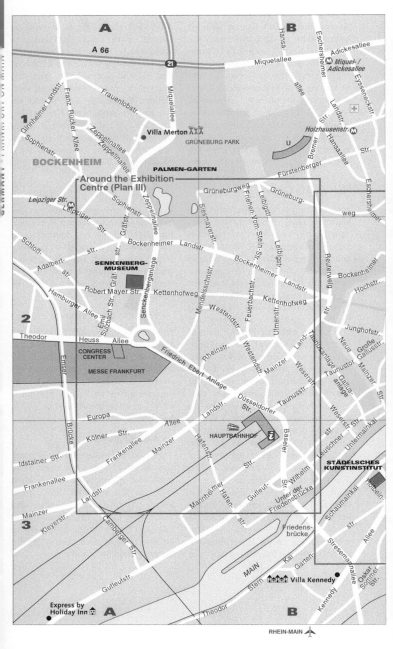

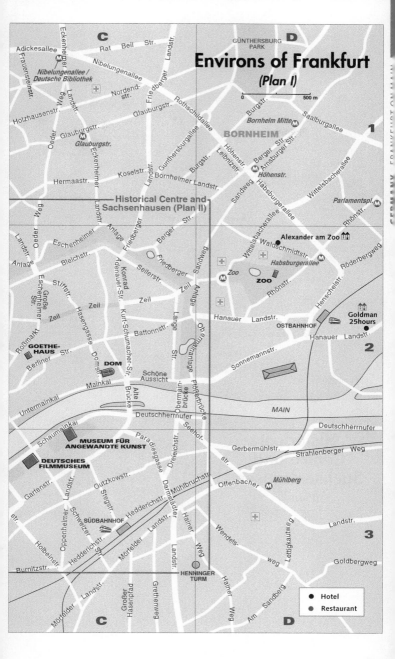

Environs of Frankfurt
(Plan I)

Historical Centre and Sachsenhausen (Plan II)

GÜNTHERSBURG PARK

BORNHEIM

Bornhelm Mitte

ZOO

Alexander am Zoo

OSTBAHNHOF

Goldman 25hours

MAIN

GOETHE-HAUS

DOM

MUSEUM FÜR ANGEWANDTE KUNST

DEUTSCHES FILMMUSEUM

SÜDBAHNHOF

HENNINGER TURM

Nibelungenallee / Deutsche Bibliothek

Parlamentspl.

●	Hotel
●	Restaurant

0   500 m

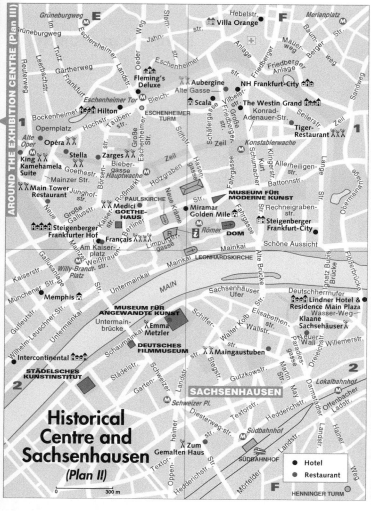

Historical
Centre and
Sachsenhausen
(Plan II)

0 — 300 m

- ● Hotel
- ● Restaurant

340

Steigenberger Frankfurter Hof 🖼 🏵 👤 🅰🅲 🖳 📶 ♨

Am Kaiserplatz ✉ *60311 –* 🅜 *Willy-Brandt-Platz* **VISA 🅜🅞 🅐🅔 🅞**
– ✆ *(069) 2 15 02 – frankfurter-hof@steigenberger.de – Fax (069) 21 59 00*
– www.frankfurter-hof.steigenberger.de **E1**
321 rm – ⬩290/669 € ⬩⬩290/669 €, ☐ 28 € – 20 suites
Rest *Français* – see below
Rest *Oscar's* – ✆ *(069) 21 51 50 (booking advisable)* Menu 30 €
– Carte 39/61 €
Rest *Iroha* – ✆ *(069) 21 99 49 30 (closed 8 - 16 August, Sunday and bank*
holidays, except trade fairs) Menu 55/120 € *(dinner)* – Carte 55/73 €
♦ Grand Luxury ♦ Business ♦ Classic ♦
Steigenberger's traditional flagship dates back to 1876. This impressive, comprehensively refurbished building conveys exclusiveness. Cosmetics and massage facilities. Oscar's, with its light bistro atmosphere. Far East cuisine in the Iroha.

Villa Kennedy 🖼 🗗 🏵 🏵 🖻 👤 🅰🅲 🖳 📶 ♨ 🚗 VISA 🅜🅞 🅐🅔 🅞

Kennedyallee 70 ✉ *60596 –* 🅜 *Schweizer Platz –* ✆ *(069) 71 71 20*
– info.villakennedy@roccofortecollection.com – Fax (069) 71 71 22 00
– www.roccofortecollection.com *Plan I* **B3**
163 rm – ⬩220/590 € ⬩⬩220/590 €, ☐ 28 € – 25 suites
Rest – Carte 46/81 €
♦ Grand Luxury ♦ Villa ♦ Classic ♦
The former Villa Speyer (1904) has now been extended to give an impressive hotel complex in the historical style, with a tasteful atmosphere and elegant spa area. Restaurant in charming inner courtyard, with Italian-influenced international cuisine.

The Westin Grand 🗗 🏵 🏵 🖻 👤 🅰🅲 🖳 ♨ 🚗 VISA 🅜🅞 🅐🅔 🅞

Konrad-Adenauer-Str. 7 ✉ *60313 –* 🅜 *Konstablerwache –* ✆ *(069) 2 98 10*
– grandhotel.frankfurt@arabellastarwood.com – Fax (069) 2 98 18 10
– www.starwoodhotels.com/frankfurt **F1**
371 rm – ⬩199/525 € ⬩⬩199/525 €, ☐ 30 € – 18 suites
Rest *aquaterra* – *(closed Saturday lunch and Sunday lunch)* Carte 42/59 €
Rest *san san* – ✆ *(069) 91 39 90 50 (closed Sunday)* Menu 16 €
– Carte 25/36 €
Rest *Sushimoto* – , ✆ *(069) 2 98 11 87 (closed end July - early August 2 weeks,*
end December 2 weeks and Monday, except trade fairs) (Sunday and bank
holidays dinner only) Menu 40/82 € – Carte 27/56 €
♦ Luxury ♦ Chain hotel ♦ Modern ♦
In the centre of town, the rooms in the Grand Hotel are tasteful, modern, extremely cosy and high-tech. Old-timer exhibition in the lobby. aquaterra with its Mediterranean cuisine. san san: Thai and Indo-Chinese flavours. Japanese in the Sushimoto.

Hilton 🖼 🗗 🏵 🖻 👤 🅰🅲 🖳 📶 ♨ 🚗 VISA 🅜🅞 🅐🅔 🅞

Hochstr. 4 ✉ *60313 –* 🅜 *Eschenheimer Tor –* ✆ *(069) 1 33 80 00*
– sales.frankfurt@hilton.com – Fax (069) 13 38 20 – www.hilton.de/frankfurt
342 rm – ⬩195/349 € ⬩⬩195/349 €, ☐ 33 € – 3 suites **E1**
Rest – Carte 43/81 €
♦ Chain hotel ♦ Luxury ♦ Modern ♦
A generous, airy atrium takes you into this green-surrounded hotel in the centre. The "Wave, Health & Fitness Club" includes a 25 m indoor pool. Restaurant with an international and American menu.

InterContinental 🖼 🗗 👤 🅰🅲 🖳 📶 ♨ 🚗 VISA 🅜🅞 🅐🅔 🅞

Wilhelm-Leuschner-Str. 43 ✉ *60329 –* ✆ *(069) 2 60 50 – frankfurt@ihg.com*
– Fax (069) 25 24 67 – www.frankfurt.intercontinental.com **E2**
469 rm – ⬩237/287 € ⬩⬩237/287 €, ☐ 29 € – 28 suites
Rest *Signatures* – Carte 39/58 €
♦ Luxury ♦ Chain hotel ♦ Functional ♦
The guestrooms in this hotel on the Main are marked by a timeless elegance. The Club level, located on the 21st floor, has fantastic views over Frankfurt. A restaurant in warm tones, with a modern conservatory.

Lindner Hotel & Residence Main Plaza

Walther-von-Cronberg Platz 1
⊠ 60594 – **Ⓜ** *Lokalbahnhof* – *℘ (069) 66 40 10* – *info.mainplaza@lindner.de*
– Fax (069) 6 64 01 40 04 – www.lindner.de **F2**
118 rm – **†**179/209 € **††**209/239 €, ⊇ 23 € – 20 suites
Rest *New Brick* – Carte 40/51 €
♦ Business ♦ Luxury ♦ Modern ♦

Behind its red brick façade, this high rise building on the banks of the Main houses a luxurious hotel. It offers a modern, elegant interior, views of the skyline, and a 450m2 beauty spa. The New Brick offers Californian cuisine, prepared before your eyes.

NH Frankfurt-City

Vilbelerstr. 2 ⊠ 60313 – **Ⓜ** *Konstablerwache* – *℘ (069) 9 28 85 90*
– nhfrankfurtcity@nh-hotels.com – Fax (069) 9 28 85 91 00
– www.nh-hotels.com **F1**
256 rm – **†**149/240 € **††**149/240 €, ⊇ 24 € – 8 suites **Rest** – Carte 35/53 €
♦ Chain hotel ♦ Functional ♦

This hotel is located in the town centre around the corner from the pedestrian zone. The modern comfort of the rooms is combined with a high level of technical facilities. Restaurant on the first floor with a large buffet.

Fleming's Deluxe

Eschenheimer Tor 2 ⊠ 60318 – **Ⓜ** *Eschenheimer Tor* – *℘ (069) 4 27 23 20*
– frankfurt-city@flemings-hotels.com – Fax (069) 4 27 23 29 99
– www.flemings-hotels.com **E1**
106 rm ⊇ – **†**128/199 € **††**147/250 € – 6 suites **Rest** – Carte 32/56 €
♦ Chain hotel ♦ Modern ♦

A contemporary-style hotel especially designed for business guests, in the centre opposite the Eschenheimer Tor. Bar and lounge above the rooftops of the city. Dine with a view of the skyline in the rooftop restaurant with its open kitchen or on the terrace.

Villa Orange *without rest*

Hebelstr. 1 ⊠ 60318 – *℘ (069) 40 58 40* – *contact@villa-orange.de – Fax (069) 40 58 41 00 – www.villa-orange.de* **F1**
38 rm ⊇ – **†**125/145 € **††**145/165 €
♦ Family ♦ Modern ♦

This hotel has a striking orange façade. The owner is extremely committed to her guests and the rooms are presented in a friendly, cosy, modern style. Some of the bathrooms have free-standing baths.

Steigenberger Frankfurt-City

Lange Str. 5 ⊠ 60311 – *℘ (069) 21 93 00*
– frankfurt-city@steigenberger.de – Fax (069) 21 93 05 99
– www.frankfurt-city.steigenberger.de **F1**
149 rm – **†**105/166 € **††**119/182 €, ⊇ 18 € **Rest** – Carte 21/35 €
♦ Business ♦ Functional ♦

This hotel is particularly popular with business people. It offers tasteful rooms with a hint of an Italian style; some have views over the skyline. Restaurant with a visible kitchen and an international menu.

Alexander am Zoo *without rest*

Waldschmidtstr. 59 ⊠ 60316 – **Ⓜ** *Habsburgerallee* – *℘ (069) 94 96 00* – *info@alexanderamzoo.de – Fax (069) 94 96 07 20 – www.alexanderamzoo.de*
66 rm ⊇ – **†**108/130 € **††**128/155 € – 9 suites *Plan I* **D2**
♦ Business ♦ Classic ♦

Modern angularity with a homely, elegant atmosphere in the rooms. Spend conference intervals on the terraces, admiring the views of the Main metropolis' rooftops.

Goldman 25hours 🚡 ⁽ᵗ⁾ ⅍ 𝘝𝘐𝘚𝘈 ⓄⓄ ᴀᴇ

Hanauer Landstr. 127 ☒ 60314 – ℰ *(069) 40 58 68 90*
– frankfurt@25hours-hotels.com – Fax (069) 40 58 68 98 90
– www.25hours-hotels.com 　　　　　　　　　　　　　　*Plan I* **D2**
49 rm – ♦115/135 € ♦♦115/135 €, ⌂ 15 €
Rest – *(closed Sunday)* Menu 42/56 € – Carte 38/56 €
♦ Business ♦ Design ♦
An unusual hotel in which modern design and interesting details of different styles come together to create a very attractive and comfortable décor and ambience. Restaurant with a maritime feel.

Memphis without rest ⁽ᵗ⁾ 🄿 𝘝𝘐𝘚𝘈 ⓄⓄ ᴀᴇ ①

Münchener Str. 15 ☒ 60329 – Ⓜ *Willy-Brandt-Platz*
– ℰ *(069) 2 42 60 90 – memphis-hotel@t-online.de – Fax (069) 24 26 09 99*
– www.memphis-hotel.de 　　　　　　　　　　　　　　　　　　　　　　**E2**
42 rm ⌂ **–** ♦110/140 € ♦♦130/170 €
♦ Business ♦ Functional ♦
In the centre of town, in a lively arts scene, is this charming hotel with its pleasant rooms in contemporary colours. The rooms on the inner courtyard are quiet.

Miramar Golden Mile without rest ᴀᴄ ⌨ ⁽ᵗ⁾ 𝘝𝘐𝘚𝘈 ⓄⓄ ᴀᴇ ①

Berliner Str. 31 ☒ 60311 – ℰ *(069) 9 20 39 70*
– info@miramar-frankfurt.de – Fax (069) 92 03 97 69
– www.miramar-frankfurt.de
– closed 23-31 December 　　　　　　　　　　　　　　　　　　　　　**E-F1**
39 rm ⌂ **–** ♦100/130 € ♦♦130/150 €
♦ Business ♦ Functional ♦
Between the Zeil and the Römer, with well-tended, functional rooms and a friendly breakfast room.

Scala without rest ⌨ ⁽ᵗ⁾ 𝘝𝘐𝘚𝘈 ⓄⓄ ᴀᴇ ①

Schäfergasse 31 ☒ 60313 – Ⓜ *Konstablerwache –* ℰ *(069) 1 38 11 10*
– info@scala.bestwestern.de – Fax (069) 13 81 11 38
– www.scala.bestwestern.de 　　　　　　　　　　　　　　　　　　　　**F1**
40 rm – ♦107/147 € ♦♦132/187 €, ⌂ 13 €
♦ Business ♦ Functional ♦
Its central location in the centre of the city and its modern, functionally equipped rooms are what make this hotel. The reception and drinks service is staffed 24 hours a day.

XXXX Français – Hotel Steigenberger Frankfurter Hof 🚡 㐂 ᴀᴄ
🕸 　　　　　　　　　　　　　　　　　　　　　　　　　　　　 𝘝𝘐𝘚𝘈 ⓄⓄ ᴀᴇ ①

Am Kaiserplatz ☒ 60311 – Ⓜ *Willy-Brand-Platz*
– ℰ *(069) 21 51 38 – frankfurter-hof@steigenberger.de*
– Fax (069) 21 51 19
– www.frankfurter-hof.steigenberger.de
– closed 1 - 12 January, 10 - 27 April, 3 - 24 August, Saturday - Sunday and bank holidays, except trade fairs 　　　　　　　　　　　　　　　　**E1**
Rest – Menu 45 € (lunch)/125 € (dinner) – Carte 66/94 € 舘
Spec. Steinbutt mit Tomate und Ciabatta. Milchlamm mit bunten Linsen, Paprika und Kreuzkümmel. Guanaja 85% mit Zwergorange, Ingwer und Rosmarin.
♦ French ♦ Elegant ♦
Enjoy Patrick Bittner's French inspired cuisine, as well as some classics. Dishes are professionally served at the table in the refined restaurant featuring a fireplace, or in the bright conservatory. In summer dine in the beautiful Ehrenhof.

XXX · ⁂

Tiger-Restaurant

[AC] [VISA] [CO] [AE] [D]

Heiligkreuzgasse 20 ⊠ *60313 –* Ⓜ *Konstablerwache –* ℰ *(069) 92 00 22 25*
– info@tigerpalast.de – Fax (069) 92 00 22 17 – www.tigerpalast.de
– closed 22 - 24 February, 26 July - 25 August and Sunday - Monday
Rest *– (dinner only) (booking essential)* Menu 68/110 €   **F1**
– Carte 67/81 € ⅋
Rest *Palast-Bistrot –* ℰ *(069) 92 00 22 92 (closed 22 - 24 February, 26 July -*
25 August and Monday) (dinner only) Menu 49/54 € *–* Carte 39/53 €
Spec. Pochierte Austern mit Schwarzwälder Speck gebraten auf Kräuter-
creme. Etouffé Taube in zwei Gängen. Pistazienschnitte und marinierte Himbeeren mit Gelee von Matcha Tee und Kaffir-Limetten-Sorbet.
◆ Classic ◆ Elegant ◆
In addition to the variety theatre, the Tiger Palace accommodates this modern restaurant in the basement. It serves classic cuisine with a Mediterranean influence,
accompanied by a good selection of French wines. An historic, brick vaulted ceiling in the Palast-Bistrot restaurant.

XX · ⁂

Zarges

[AC] [VISA] [CO] [AE]

Kalbächer Gasse 10 ⊠ *60311 –* Ⓜ *Hauptwache –* ℰ *(069) 29 90 30*
– gourmet@zarges-frankfurt.com – Fax (069) 29 90 33 88
– www.zarges-frankfurt.com
– closed 23 December - 9 January, 19 July - 21 August, Sunday - Monday
and bank holidays   **E1**
Rest *–* Menu 59 € (lunch)/125 € *–* Carte 81/119 € ⅋
Rest *Bistro – (closed 25 December - 1 January)* Carte 35/53 €
Spec. Taubenbrust mit Pfifferlingen und Saubohnen im Kräutersud. Rücken
vom Rind mit weißem Zwiebelkompott. Geeiste Champagner-Praline mit
Himbeeren.
◆ International ◆ Cosy ◆
In addition to the Confiserie the townhouse in the Fressgass' is also home to this
restaurant. It is very tastefully designed in a French salon style. There is also a bistro
and a club lounge on the first floor.

XX · ⁂

King Kamehameha Suite

[AC] [CO] [AE]

Taunusanlage 20 ⊠ *60235 –* Ⓜ *Alte Oper –* ℰ *(069) 71 03 52 77 – suite@*
king-kamehameha.de – Fax (069) 71 03 59 80 – www.king-kamehameda.de
Rest *– (closed 1 - 11 January, 13 - 19 April, 4 weeks July*   **E1**
- August, Sunday and bank holidays) (dinner only) (booking essential)
Menu 79/99 € *–* Carte 66/78 €
Rest *Atrium – (closed Saturday lunch, Sunday dinner and bank holidays)*
Carte 35/53 €
Spec. Schellfisch mit Stielmus und Schinkennage. Hummer mit Rhabarber
Beurre monté und Curry. Banane mit Orange, Karamell und Mandel.
◆ Inventive ◆ Trendy ◆
A stylish and popular meeting place within a classical building. The trendy restau-
rant and bar offers creative cuisine. Atrium serves international cuisine.

XX

Aubergine

[VISA] [CO] [AE]

Alte Gasse 14 ⊠ *60313 –* Ⓜ *Konstablerwache –* ℰ *(069) 9 20 07 80 – info@*
aubergine-frankfurt.de – Fax (069) 9 20 07 86 – www.aubergine-frankfurt.de
– closed 3 weeks July - August and Saturday lunch, Sunday   **F1**
Rest *– (booking advisable)* Menu 28 € (lunch)/57 € (dinner) *–* Carte 50/64 € ⅋
◆ International ◆ Elegant ◆
Guests enjoy the friendly, familiar atmosphere of this restaurant. It serves ambitious cuisine on Versace dishes accompanied by a wide selection of Tuscan wines.

XX

Opéra

[VISA] [CO] [AE]

Opernplatz 1 (level 3) ⊠ *60313 –* Ⓜ *Alte Oper –* ℰ *(069) 1 34 02 15 – info@*
opera-restauration.de – Fax (069) 1 34 02 39 – www.opera-restauration.de
Rest *–* Menu 32 € *–* Carte 38/58 €   **E1**
◆ International ◆ Classic ◆
Restaurant in the former foyer of the Old Opera House with elaborate wall decorations and original Art Nouveau candlesticks. Terrace with lovely views. Saturday
snacks and Sunday brunch.

XX **Maingaustuben** VISA ⓒⓢ AE ⓪

Schifferstr. 38 ✉ *60594 – ℰ (069) 61 07 52 – info@maingau.de – Fax (069)*
61 99 53 72 – www.maingau.de
– closed Saturday lunch, Sunday dinner - Monday F2
Rest – Menu 17 € (lunch)/75 € (dinner) – Carte 34/56 €
♦ International ♦ Friendly ♦

Tasteful decor and stylish ambience characterise this restaurant, which offers international and some classic cuisine. Simpler menu at lunchtime.

XX **Stella** VISA ⓒⓢ AE ⓪

Große Bockenheimer Str. 52 (Gallerie Fressgass) ✉ *60313 –* ⓜ *Alte Oper*
– ℰ (069) 90 50 12 71 – info@stella-ffm.de – Fax (069) 90 50 16 69
– www.stella-ffm.de
– closed Sunday, except trade fairs E1
Rest – Menu 29 € (lunch)/72 € (dinner) – Carte 45/58 €
♦ Italian ♦ Friendly ♦

Friendly, family-run restaurant serving classic Italian food, with Tuscan wines featuring strongly. Large pictures of cars add to the bright décor. Glass-roofed outside dining.

XX **Medici** 🍴 AC VISA ⓒⓢ AE

Weißadlergasse 2 ✉ *60311 –* ⓜ *Hauptwache – ℰ (069) 21 99 07 94 – info@*
restaurantmedici.de – Fax (069) 21 99 07 95 – www.restaurantmedici.de
– closed Sunday and bank holidays E1
Rest – Menu 35/59 € – Carte 37/59 €
♦ International ♦ Formal ♦

The centrally located restaurant run by two brothers is modern in style and serves international cuisine.

XX **Main Tower Restaurant** ≤ VISA ⓒⓢ AE

Neue Mainzer Str. 52 (53th floor, charge) ✉ *60311 –* ⓜ *Alte Oper – ℰ (069)*
36 50 47 77 – maintower.restaurant@compass-group.de – Fax (069) 36 50 48 71
– www.maintower-restaurant.de
– closed Sunday - Monday E1
Rest – (dinner only) (booking essential) Menu 57/98 €
♦ Mediterranean ♦ Fashionable ♦

The modern restaurant and bar are 187 m up, and stand out for their fantastic views over the city. Contemporary Mediterranean cuisine in menu form.

XX **Emma Metzler** 🍴 P VISA ⓒⓢ AE

Schaumainkai 17 ✉ *60594 –* ⓜ *Schweizer Platz – ℰ (069) 61 99 59 06*
– office@emma-metzler.com – Fax (069) 61 99 59 09 – www.emma-metzler.com
– closed 27 December-5 January and Sunday dinner - Monday, except trade fairs
Rest – Menu 25 € (lunch)/89 € (dinner) – Carte 52/64 € E2
♦ Modern ♦ Fashionable ♦

The bright, simple and modern restaurant in the museum of applied art offers contemporary dishes with a creative touch and views over the park

X **Klaane Sachsehäuser** 🍴

Neuer Wall 11 ✉ *60594 – ℰ (069) 61 59 83 – klaanesachse@web.de*
– Fax (069) 62 21 41 – www.klaanesachsehaeuser.de
– closed 22 - 31 December and Sunday F2
Rest – Carte 12/22 €
♦ Regional ♦ Rustic ♦

The home-brewed "Stöffche" and good Frankfurt food have been served in this traditional pub since 1876. And no one ever has to sit alone!

X **Zum gemalten Haus** 🍴 VISA

Schweizer Str. 67 ✉ *60594 –* ⓜ *Schweizer Platz – ℰ (069) 61 45 59 – Fax (069)*
6 03 14 57 – www.zumgemaltenhaus.de
– closed 3 weeks July and Monday F2
Rest – Carte 13/20 €
♦ Regional ♦ Rustic ♦

Huddle up, talk shop and chat in the midst of these wall murals and mementos from bygone days. The main thing is the "Bembel" is always full!

Hessischer Hof   AC · SAT · ⁽ᵗ⁾ · ♨ · 🚗 · VISA · MO · AE · O

Friedrich-Ebert-Anlage 40 ✉ *60325 –* ☎ *(069) 7 54 00 – info@hessischer-hof.de
– Fax (069) 75 40 29 24 – www.hessischer-hof.de*   **G2**
117 rm – ♦243/571 € ♦♦291/571 €, ☐ 26 € – 3 suites
Rest – Menu 51/60 € – Carte 55/70 €

♦ Luxury ♦ Classic ♦

Combines classic hotel style with the latest standards in luxury, devoting itself to its guests with exemplary commitment. A display of Sèvres porcelain decorates this elegant restaurant.

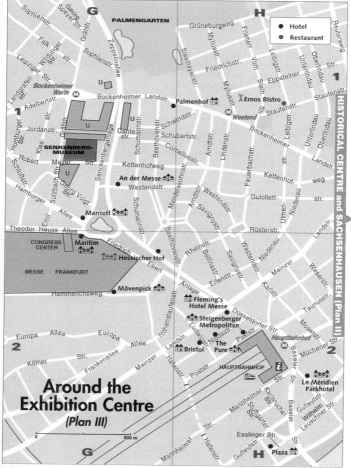

Around the Exhibition Centre
(Plan III)

Radisson SAS   🛏 𝐿𝔟 🕉 ▢ ⅙ 🄰🄲 🄶🄰 ⁽¹⁾ 🕸 🍴 𝖵𝖨𝖲𝖠 ⦾ 🄰🄴

Franklinstr. 65 (by Theodor Heuss Allee **A2)** *⊠ 60486 – ℰ (069) 7 70 15 50*
– info.frankfurt@radissonsas.com – Fax (069) 77 01 55 10
– www.frankfurt.radissonsas.com
428 rm – 🛉195/225 € 🛉🛉195/225 €, ⊊ 26 € – 10 suites
Rest *Gaia* – ℰ (069) 77 01 55 22 00 – Carte 29/45 €
Rest *Coast* – ℰ (069) 77 01 55 21 00 (closed Sunday - Monday and bank
holidays) (dinner only) Carte 32/56 €
♦ Business ♦ Chain hotel ♦ Design ♦
Very modern and trendy, this is not your average hotel, with its designer rooms "At
home", "Chic", "Fashion" and "Fresh". The upper floors offer inspiring views. Gaia
with Mediterranean cuisine. Sample the seafood at Coast Brasserie and Oyster Bar.

Marriott   ≤ 𝐿𝔟 🕉 🄰🄲 🄶🄰 ⁽¹⁾ 🕸 🍴 𝖵𝖨𝖲𝖠 ⦾ 🄰🄴 ⓞ

Hamburger Allee 2 ⊠ 60486 – ℰ (069) 7 95 50 – info.frankfurt@
marriotthotels.com – Fax (069) 79 55 24 32 – www.frankfurt-marriott.com
588 rm – 🛉179/259 € 🛉🛉179/259 €, ⊊ 27 € – 11 suites   **G1**
Rest – *(closed Saturday lunch and Sunday dinner)* Carte 32/57 €
♦ Luxury ♦ Chain hotel ♦ Modern ♦
Opposite the exhibition centre, this hotel stands out for its well-equipped rooms in
an elegant classical style – all looking onto the city. Restaurant with a pleasant
brasserie ambience and French cuisine.

Maritim   𝐿𝔟 🕉 ▢ ⅙ 🄰🄲 🄶🄰 ⁽¹⁾ 🕸 🍴 𝖵𝖨𝖲𝖠 ⦾ 🄰🄴 ⓞ

Theodor-Heuss-Allee 3 ⊠ 60486 – ℰ (069) 7 57 80 – info.fra@maritim.de
– Fax (069) 75 78 10 00 – www.maritim.de   **G2**
543 rm – 🛉140/315 € 🛉🛉170/345 €, ⊊ 26 € – 24 suites
Rest *Classico* – *(dinner only)* Carte 50/66 €
Rest *SushiSho* – ℰ (069) 75 78 11 48 (closed 23 December - 10 January,
5 weeks July-August and Saturday - Sunday, except trade fairs) Menu 38/95 €
– Carte 32/73 €
♦ Business ♦ Chain hotel ♦ Modern ♦
This hotel, by the exhibition centre, offers modern, spacious rooms and a generous
wellness area on the sixth floor. The elegant "Classico" offers international cuisine.
SushiSho, Japanese style

Le Méridien Parkhotel   🛏 𝐿𝔟 🕉 🄰🄲 🄶🄰 ⁽¹⁾ 🕸 🍴 𝖵𝖨𝖲𝖠 ⦾ 🄰🄴 ⓞ

Wiesenhüttenplatz 28 ⊠ 60329 – Ⓜ Hauptbahnhof – ℰ (069) 2 69 70
– info.frankfurt@lemeridien.com – Fax (069) 2 69 78 84
– www.lemeridien.com/frankfurt   **H2**
297 rm – 🛉145/485 € 🛉🛉155/505 €, ⊊ 25 €
Rest – Menu 39 € – Carte 34/61 €
♦ Luxury ♦ Chain hotel ♦ Design ♦
This comfortable town hotel comprises a historical palace and a modern business-
like extension. The elegant Casablanca Bar in the old building is attractive. Le Parc
bistro-style restaurant.

Steigenberger Metropolitan   𝐿𝔟 🕉 ⅙ 🄰🄲 🄶🄰 ⁽¹⁾ 🕸 🍴

Poststr. 6 ⊠ 60329 – Ⓜ Hauptbahnhof – ℰ (069)
5 06 07 00 – metropolitan@steigenberger.de – Fax (069) 5 06 07 05 55   𝖵𝖨𝖲𝖠 ⦾ 🄰🄴 ⓞ
– www.metropolitan.steigenberger.de   **H2**
131 rm – 🛉169/229 € 🛉🛉189/294 €, ⊊ 21 € – 3 suites   **Rest** – Carte 34/58 €
♦ Chain hotel ♦ Modern ♦
This beautiful city palace by the main station dates from the 19th century, and is
fitted out in a modern style which is both functional and elegant. The Brasserie M
restaurant is kept in contemporary style

The Pure *without rest*   𝐿𝔟 🕉 🄰🄲 🄶🄰 ⁽¹⁾ 🍴 𝖵𝖨𝖲𝖠 ⦾ 🄰🄴 ⓞ

Niddastr. 86 ⊠ 60329 – Ⓜ Hauptbahnhof – ℰ (069) 7 10 45 70 – info@
the-pure.de – Fax (069) 7 10 45 71 77 – www.the-pure.de   **H2**
50 rm ⊊ – 🛉180/300 € 🛉🛉210/360 €
♦ Business ♦ Design ♦
Minimalist, modern elegance. The interior of this hotel is exclusively in white. Close
to the railway station. Dark furnishings create an interesting contrast.

347

Mövenpick

Den Haager Str. 5 ✉ 60327 – ☎ (069) 7 88 07 50 – hotel.frankfurt.city@moevenpick.com – Fax (069) 7 88 07 58 88 – www.moevenpick-frankfurt-city.com **G2**

288 rm – 🚹185/235 € 🚹🚹215/255 €, ☕ 22 € **Rest** – Carte 25/53 €

◆ Chain hotel ◆ Modern ◆

Located directly next to the exhibition centre is this business hotel with conspicuous red-green facade. The rooms feature clean, modern and functional design. Fitness area with roof terrace. Bistro-style restaurant with international menu.

An der Messe without rest

Westendstr. 104 ✉ 60325 – ☎ (069) 74 79 79 – info@hotel-an-der-messe.de – Fax (069) 74 83 49 – www.hotel-an-der-messe.de **G1**

45 rm ☕ – 🚹130/330 € 🚹🚹155/350 €

◆ Business ◆ Classic ◆

This hotel is located near the exhibition centre. It is characterised by its individually designed rooms ranging from rustic to elegant, as well as a number of interesting thematic rooms.

Palmenhof without rest

Bockenheimer Landstr. 89 ✉ 60325 – Ⓜ Westend – ☎ (069) 7 53 00 60 – info@palmenhof.com – Fax (069) 75 30 06 66 – www.palmenhof.com – closed 23 December - 2 January **G1**

46 rm – 🚹109/149 € 🚹🚹149/179 €, ☕ 16 €

◆ Business ◆ Classic ◆

In this hotel in the banking district spend the night in an individually furnished room with beautiful, stylish bureaux and brass beds.

Fleming's Hotel Messe

Mainzer Landstr. 87 ✉ 60329 – Ⓜ Hauptbahnhof – ☎ (069) 8 08 08 00 – frankfurt-messe@flemings-hotels.com – Fax (069) 8 08 08 04 99 – www.flemings-hotel.com **H2**

96 rm – 🚹175 € 🚹🚹175 €, ☕ 16 € **Rest** – Carte 22/42 €

◆ Business ◆ Functional ◆

A business hotel in the town centre with modern, functional rooms with all technical facilities. Bistro style restaurant with international cuisine.

Bristol

Ludwigstr. 15 ✉ 60327 – Ⓜ Hauptbahnhof – ☎ (069) 24 23 90 – info@bristol-hotel.de – Fax (069) 25 15 39 – www.bristol-hotel.de **H2**

145 rm ☕ – 🚹95/130 € 🚹🚹160/170 € **Rest** – *(dinner only for residents)*

◆ Business ◆ Modern ◆

This contemporary hotel building with its modern, functional facilities is close to the main station and the town centre. Summer lounge, bar and reception with 24-hr service.

Plaza without rest

Esslinger Str. 8 ✉ 60329 – ☎ (069) 2 71 37 80 – info@plaza-frankfurt.bestwestern.de – Fax (069) 23 76 50 – www.plaza-frankfurt.bestwestern.de **H2**

45 rm – 🚹98/125 € 🚹🚹125/135 €, ☕ 13 €

◆ Business ◆ Modern ◆

A quieter hotel located in a side street near the station. It has a functional, modern interior made from light beech wood and warm, welcoming materials and colours.

Express by Holiday Inn without rest

Gutleutstr. 296 ✉ 60327 – ☎ (069) 50 69 60 – express.frankfurtmesse@whgeu.com – Fax (069) 50 69 61 00 – www.hiexpress.com/exfrankfurtmes Plan I **A3**

175 rm ☕ – 🚹95/115 € 🚹🚹95/115 €

◆ Chain hotel ◆ Functional ◆

Ideal for business travellers, this modern well-equipped hotel is conveniently located near the exhibition centre and the local station.

XXX   **Villa Merton**   🛱 ⟷

Am Leonhardsbrunn 12 ✉ 60487 – ℰ (069) 70 30 33
– villa-merton@koflerkompanie.com – Fax (069) 7 07 38 20
– www.koflerkompanie.com
– closed 22 December - 13 January and Saturday - Sunday   *Plan I* **A1**
Rest *– (booking advisable)* Menu 64/118 € – Carte 64/76 €
Spec. Pochiertes Ei mit schwarzem Trüffel. Seeteufel mit Gewürzemulsion
und Couscous. Dreimal Zicklein mit rotem Mangoldsalat und mildem Knob-
lauch.
  ◆ Inventive ◆ Classic ◆
A lovely elegant villa in the diplomatic quarter. Served at very well set tables is
competent, creative, classically based cuisine. Simpler business lunch at midday.

X   **Ernos Bistro**   🛱 **VISA ◯ AE**

Liebigstr. 15 ✉ 60323 – Ⓜ Westend – ℰ (069) 72 19 97
– Fax (069) 17 38 38
– closed 20 December - 5 January, 10 - 20 April, 25 July - 16 August, Saturday
- Sunday and bank holidays   **H1**
Rest *– (booking advisable)* Menu 36 € (lunch)/115 € – Carte 67/106 € 🕸
Spec. Hausgemachte Gänsestopfleber. Steinbutt mit Petersilien-Nuss-Kruste
und Steinpilzen. Kalbskotelett mit Pfifferlingen und Salbeijus (2 people)
  ◆ French ◆ Bistro ◆
Cosy restaurant in the west end where guests can enjoy classic cuisine and good
quality French wines.

ENVIRONS OF FRANKFURT

at Frankfurt-Fechenheim   by Hanauer Landstraße **D2**

XX   **Silk** (Mario Lohninger)   **VISA ◯ AE**

Carl-Benz-Str. 21 ✉ 60386 – ℰ (069) 90 02 00
– reservierung@cocoonclub.net – Fax (069) 90 02 02 90
– www.silk-restaurant.de
– closed 1 - 15 January, 20 July - 20 August and Sunday - Monday
Rest *– (dinner only)* Menu 109 €
Rest Micro Fine Dining *– (dinner only)* Carte 50/77 €
Spec. Melonensalat, Ziegenkäse, Traminer Balsamico und Melonenkaviar. Ein
Stunden Bio Ei mit Champignonfond und Ingwer. Lauwarm geräucherter
"Black Cod" mit Tomate und Steinpilzen.
  ◆ Innovative ◆ Minimalist ◆
The trendy Cocoon Club includes this modern, purist restaurant with a harmo-
nious lounge-type atmosphere and a slightly unconventional dining code.
Guests are served innovative dishes in bite-sized morsels on white upholstered
loungers. Micro features an open kitchen serving fusion cuisine. The disco is
next door.

at Frankfurt-Rödelheim   by Theodor Heuss Allee **A2**

XX   **Osteria Enoteca**   🛱 **VISA ◯ AE**

Arnoldshainer Str. 2 ✉ 60489 – ℰ (069) 7 89 22 16 – Fax (069) 7 89 22 16
– www.osteria-enoteca.de
– closed 22 December - 7 January, Saturday lunch, Sunday and bank holidays
Rest – Menu 68/118 € – Carte 48/56 €
Spec. Langostinos in Rinderfiletscheiben gebraten mit Parmesanpolenta.
Taglierini im Krustentierfond. Fritto Misto mit Senfschaum.
  ◆ Italian ◆ Friendly ◆
Find well-trained service and interesting Italian cuisine prepared with taste and
finesse here.

349

at the Rhein-Main Airport by Kennedy Allee **B3**

GERMANY - FRANKFURT ON MAIN

Kempinski Hotel Gravenbruch

Graf zu Ysenburg und Büdingen-Platz 1
✉ *63263 –* ℰ *(069) 38 98 80 – reservations.gravenbruch@kempinski.com*
– Fax (069) 38 98 89 00 – www.kempinski-frankfurt.com
284 rm – ♦147/446 € ♦♦147/473 €, ☑ 25 € – 20 suites
Rest – Menu 69 € – Carte 44/67 €
Rest *L'olivo* – *(closed Saturday - Sunday) (dinner only)* Carte 32/58 €
♦ Chain hotel ♦ Classic ♦

With the charm of a country house villa, this hotel lies in the countryside with its own lake. The rooms are classic, and the suites generous. Leisure area etc. with beauty farm. A fine restaurant with garden views. L'Olivo with Italian cuisine.

Steigenberger Airport

Unterschweinstiege 16 ✉ *60549 –* ℰ *(069) 6 97 50*
– info@airporthotel.steigenberger.de – Fax (069) 69 75 25 05
– www.airporthotel.steigenberger.de
570 rm – ♦179/239 € ♦♦179/239 €, ☑ 28 € – 10 suites
Rest *Unterschweinstiege* – Carte 35/70 €
Rest *Faces* – ℰ *(069) 69 75 24 00 (closed 20 July - 24 August and Saturday - Sunday) (dinner only)* Carte 45/83 €
♦ Chain hotel ♦ Modern ♦

This hotel is characterised by its elegant hall, comfortable rooms (in particular the modern Tower room) and the 'Open Sky' leisure area with fantastic views. A cosy atmosphere in the Unterschweinstiege. Faces has a fine bistro atmosphere.

HAMBURG
HAMBURG

Sime/PHOTONONSTOP

With a maritime role stretching back centuries, Germany's second largest city has a lively and liberal ambience. Hamburg's motto is 'The Gateway to the World', and there's certainly a visceral feel here, particularly around the big, buzzy and bustling port area. Locals enjoy a long-held reputation for their tolerance and outward looking stance, cosmopolitan to the core. This tolerance extends famously to the city's nightlife, which in the St Pauli area is renowned for its racy characteristics.

But there's another side to Hamburg. Despite its northerly position, it sits easily with a Mediterranean style café culture, and boasts waterside areas that have seen a significant amount of renovation and restyling in recent years. This is a big city for culture; it's where you come for the Long Theatre Night and the Art Mile Day. And, of course, it's where the Beatles paid their dues: the Reeperbahn is a classic first stop for many visitors. Eight hundred years' worth of trading with the world has left another favourable legacy: Hamburg's cuisine scene touches on all four corners of the globe. And space to breathe is seen as very important here: the city authorities have paid much attention to green spaces, and Hamburg can proudly claim an enviable amount of parks, lakes and tree-lined canals.

351

LIVING THE CITY

There's no cathedral in Hamburg (at least not a standing one, as war-destroyed St Nikolai remains a ruin) so the **Town Hall** acts as the central landmark. Just north of here is the Binnenalster (inner) and Aussenalster (outer) lake. The old walls of the city, dating back over eight hundred years, are delineated by a distinct semicircle of boulevards that curve attractively in a wide arc south of the lakes. Further south from here is the port and harbour area, defined by Landungsbrücken to the west, and Speicherstadt to the east. The district to the west of the centre is **St Pauli**, famed for its clubs and bars, particularly along the notorious Reeperbahn, which pierces the district from east to west. The contrastingly smart **Altona** suburb and delightful **Blankenese** village are west of St Pauli.

PRACTICAL INFORMATION

ARRIVAL-DEPARTURE

Hamburg Airport is 15km from the city centre. A taxi costs approximately €20. Airport buses leave for Hamburg Hauptbahnhof every 15-20min and Altona Station every 30min, with a journey time for both of 20min.

TRANSPORT

Hamburg Transport Authority controls all bus routes, S-Bahn and U-Bahn underground lines, and several river and ferry services. Tickets are available for single journeys, or for one day or three day duration. Buy from vending machines or bus drivers. Information available from many underground stations and the main railway station (Hauptbahnhof).

The Hamburg Card is valid for the transport network, and offers free entrance to eleven state-run museums, discounts on other activities, and on tours on water and land. Buy it from Tourist Information offices, vending machines, hotels and travel agents.

EXPLORING HAMBURG

If it weren't for the **Elbe**, there would be no Hamburg, so why not get the feel of the place by heading down to the water and sniffing the salty harbour air? An endless

stream of ships calls at the twenty-seven miles of quayside to transport goods to and from ports far and wide. Take a boat yourself from the Landungsbrücken pier for an invigorating harbour tour. The views of the Elbe are wonderful, and you can pick and choose how you want to travel, either by basic boat or slinky cruiser. These will carry you upriver towards the huge modern container docks or eastwards through a network of canals, leading to the fascinating **Speicherstadt**. This is a wondrous place to be, the biggest warehouse complex in the world – the 'City of Warehouses'. It's a hauntingly Hanseatic dark-red brick complex from the mid-nineteenth century, and it's no ghost building: wholesalers still keep a range of goods here. It's also alive with museums (four in total) relating to the Speicherstadt's history. Close to here, in Deichstrasse, and the nearby old Cremon road, stand charmingly romantic merchants' houses, dating back to the seventeenth and eighteenth centuries. As much of the city was rebuilt after the War, this nugget of old Hamburg offers a tantalising flavour of what the port quarter must once have been like.

→ WATER, WATER EVERYWHERE

Water dominates this city. Go up through the old town, and the liquid quality takes on a different feel altogether, as you arrive at the shimmering **Alster**. Locals proudly ask a rhetorical question: what other bustling metropolis can boast such a wondrous lake in its centre? Surrounded by cafés, promenades and invigorating lungfuls of greenery, you can actually walk around the entire 160-hectare lake without having to cross a single road. For the energetically challenged, steamboats leave from the Jungfernstieg pier, pass under two bridges connecting the outer lake from the inner, and take in a view which incorporates elaborate nineteenth century merchants' villas and delightful parks full of poplars, chestnuts and oaks. If the chance arises, hop off your boat and down a coffee at one of the tempting lakeside cafés: memorable views of the Hamburg skyline, with its dominant spires and steeples, are guaranteed. The third watery option is a cruise along inner-city canals, where weeping willows bow down gracefully and grand-looking villas offer a haughty eye as you make your stately procession between Alster and Elbe.

→ PICTURE PERFECT

Not only can Hamburgers crow about the glory of their lake, they can also lay claim to the most important art gallery in northern Germany. The **Kunsthalle** is made up of three interconnected buildings and the paintings and artworks contained within make an entrance in the fifteenth century and an exit at the present day, taking in the likes of Master Bertram of Minden, Friedrichs, Runge, Monet, Manet, Renoir, Warhol and Beuys. A refuelling point well worth a look round itself is the Café Liebermann, where you can enjoy cake and coffee in the rarefied splendour of marble-columned surroundings. If your appreciation of art isn't quite yet sated, then continue south along the boulevard arc, past the railway station, and very soon you'll reach the Arts and Crafts Museum. This is an eclectic wonderland, with exhibits ranging from the Orient, ancient Greece and Rome right through to musical instruments down the ages and handsome examples of Art Nouveau.

You have to go right across to the inner city's west side to locate the third in Hamburg's winning triumvirate of galleries and museums, and many think this is the most satisfying of the three. The **Hamburg History Museum** covers just about every aspect of the city; particularly impressive are the models of Hamburg showing the stark differences over a five hundred year period. It's interesting, too, to enter into the elegant seventeenth century merchant's home, or see just what the medieval authorities did with huge nails and the skulls of pirates who dared terrorise the port.

→ CONVERSION OF ST PAULI

Of course, lots of tourists come to Hamburg and make a beeline for the St Pauli district, just up from the western docks, and it's safe to say that visiting churches and opera houses is probably not top of their tour agenda. St Pauli is the district where the Beatles cut their teeth in the early 60s, and its pulsating nightlife is still a big draw.

The Reeperbahn has kept its reputation as the street where you wouldn't bring your great aunt: the sex shows and strip clubs are as lurid as ever, but times are a–changing. Tourists are making for the area because in recent years it's become a lively theatre and restaurant quarter in its own right. Hip young Hamburgers come here too because the bars and clubs have taken on a trendy, rather than garish, aspect. It's now a well-regulated area, and the nightlife is multi-layered, rather than notoriously one-dimensional as of old. In fact, your great aunt may demand to be taken there.

➜ FOR FISH

If early starts are your thing, then St Pauli's world-famous **fishmarket**, down by the Elbe, is the ideal destination. A Sunday stalwart for three hundred years, it kicks off at five in the morning, and is often frequented by revellers unwilling to draw a line under their Saturday night. It's a cross between a rock concert and a flea-market with an impressive sideline in exotic fruit and smoked fish. There are great bargains to be had in plants and vegetables, too, and the salty-sounding vendors are an integral part of the experience. A cavernous steel and glass hall, on two floors, is given over for the morning to eating, drinking and live bands belting out a fine collection of old favourites to sing along with. For anyone still in the mood to savour the delights of St Pauli, just up the road is the Erotic Art Museum, which has nearly two thousand exhibits spanning five hundred years.

➜ TOP PERFORMERS

Performance venues of another shade are high on Hamburg's cultural hit-list. In fact, they're the best of their kind in northern Germany. Just west of the inner Alster lake is the **Hamburg State Opera** and Ballet, where the best international names regularly perform. Meanwhile, The Musikhalle, which is by the Wallanlagen Gardens on aptly named Johannes-Brahms-Platz, celebrated its hundredth birthday in 2008. It's one of the most beautiful concert venues in Germany, an ornate building with three fine halls offering a wide range of orchestral and vocal performances. Hamburg can even boast two local orchestras of high renown, and the Musikhalle is their home.

CALENDAR HIGHLIGHTS

The event that really puts Hamburg on the map is the **Dom Festival**, which happens three times a year (usually March, July and August). It goes back to the fourteenth century, and translates as the Cathedral Festival. Basically, it's a huge funfair, with thrill rides, live music and beer tents – it attracts a phenomenal nine million visitors a year. The city's other major annual event

HAMBURG IN...

➜ ONE DAY
Boat trip from Landungsbrücken, Speicherstadt, Kunsthalle, Fishmarket (if it's a Sunday morning!)

➜ TWO DAYS
Steamboat on the Alster, Hamburg History Museum, St Pauli by night

➜ THREE DAYS
Arts and Crafts Museum, canal trip between lake and harbour, concert at Musikhalle

is the harbour's birthday celebration every May – Hafengeburtstag - fun and games (and tug boats dancing) happen all along the harbour. There's a month-long market to celebrate the arrival of Spring, every March and April, in St Pauli's Heiligengeistfeld. Fiery entertainment lights up the Bürgerhaus Wilhelmsburg, when the Flamenco Festival hits town in April, while in September movie fans wallow in a glut of celluloid at the Film Festival Hamburg. May's Long Night of Hamburg Museums and November's Art Mile Day cement the city's reputation as a cultural behemoth: on both occasions arty hothouses are kept open deep into the night.

EATING OUT

Being a city immersed in water, it's no surprise to find Hamburg is pretty hot on fish. Though its fishing industry isn't the powerhouse of old, the city still boasts a giant trawler's worth of seafood places to eat. Eel dishes are mainstays of the traditional restaurant's menu, as is the herring stew with vegetables called Labskaus. Also unsurprisingly, considering it's the country's gateway to the world, this is somewhere that offers a vast range of international dishes. As good restaurants tend to open where the media gathers, and Hamburg is Germany's media capital, you're assured of a range of smart and swanky places to dine. Wherever you eat here, the portions are likely to be generous. There's no problem with finding somewhere early: cafes are often open at seven, with the belief that it's never too early for coffee and cake. Bakeries, too, believe in an early start, and the calorie content here, too, can be pretty high. Bistros and restaurants, usually open by midday, are proud of their local ingredients, so keep your eyes open for Hamburgisch on the menu. Service charges are always included in the bill, so tipping is not compulsory, although most people will round it up to the next euro, and possibly add five to ten per cent.

➜ TIME FOR THE TOWN HALL

Hamburg's nineteenth-century town hall, in **Rathausplatz**, is an eye-catching place with nearly six hundred and fifty rooms. It does battle as the city's main landmark with 'Michel' – St Michael's Church – which stands proudly over the port as a centuries-old guide to sailors. Its massive clock face is the biggest in Germany, and at midday every day its three organs put on an awesome, ear-piercing show.

➜ VIEW FROM A BRIDGE

Hamburg's a great place to look at the world from a bridge. You won't have trouble finding one. There are a whopping 2,247 of them around the city. Bear in mind that Venice has a measly 450, and you might begin to get the picture.

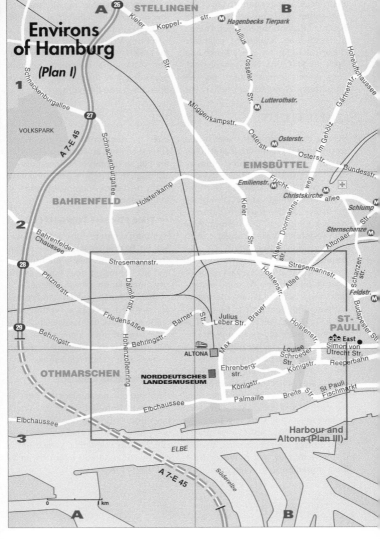

Environs of Hamburg
(Plan I)

STELLINGEN

A 26

Kieler Koppel- str.

Hagenbecks Tierpark

Julius Vosseler Str.

Lutterothstr.

Schnackenburgallee

1

VOLKSPARK

27

A 7-E 45

Schnackenburgallee

Müggenkampstr.

Osterstr.

Osterstr.

Im Gehölz

Osterstr.

Hoheluftchaussee

Gärtnerstr.

EIMSBÜTTEL

Bundesstr.

Emilienstr.

Frucht-

Doormanns- weg

Christskirche allee

BAHRENFELD

Holstenkamp

Kieler

Str.

Schlump

Sternschanze

2

Bahrenfelder Chaussee

Altonaer

Str.

28

Stresemannstr.

Stresemannstr.

Schanzen- str.

Pfitznerstr.

Daimlerstr.

Holstenstr.

Allee

Feldstr.

Budapester Str.

29

Friedensallee

Barner Str.

Julius Leber Str.

Brauer

Str.

Holstenstr.

ST-PAULI

East

Simon von Utrecht Str.

Behringstr.

Behringstr.

Hohenzollernring

ALTONA

Max

Louise Schroeder Str.

Reeperbahn

Königstr.

OTHMARSCHEN

Ehrenberg- str.

Königstr.

NORDDEUTSCHES LANDESMUSEUM

Palmaille

Breite st.

St Pauli Fischmarkt

Elbchaussee

Elbchaussee

Harbour and Altona (Plan III)

3

ELBE

A 7-E 45

Süderelbe

0   1 km

A

B

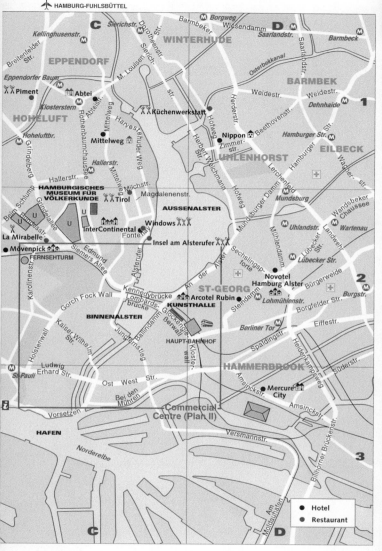

Sierichstr. · Barmbeker · Borgweg · Wiesendamm · Saarlandstr. · Barmbeck
Kellinghusenstr. · Drohnenstr. · WINTERHUDE
Breitenfelder Str. · M. Louisen str. · Sierich · Osterbekkanal · BARMBEK
EPPENDORF
Eppendorfer Baum · Weidestr. · Weidestr. · Dehnhaide
✗✗ Piment · 🏠 Abtei · ✗✗ Küchenwerkstatt · Herderstr. · Beethovenstr.
Klosterstern · Hotweg · Nippon 🏠 · Hamburger Str. · EILBECK
HOHELUFT
Hoheluftbr. · Mittelweg 🏠 · Zimmer-str. · Hamburger
Grindelberg · Rothenbaumchaussee · Harvestehuder Weg · UHLENHORST · Wagner Str.
Hallerstr. · Herbert Weichmann Str. · Lerchenfeld · ➕
Hallerstr. · Milchstr. · Hotweg · Mundsburg
Beim Schlump · HAMBURGISCHES MUSEUM FÜR VÖLKERKUNDE · ✗✗ Tirol · Magdalenenstr. · AUSSENALSTER · Mundsburger Damm · Wandsbeker Chaussee
U · U · U · U · Windows ✗✗✗ · Mühlendamm · Uhlandstr. · Landwehr · Wartenau
La Mirabelle · InterContinental 🏠 · Fonte · An der Alster · Lübecker Str.
Mövenpick 🏠🏠 · Insel am Alsterufer ✗✗✗ · Sechslingspr · Lübecker Str.
FERNSEHTURM · forte · Novotel · Bürgerweide
Karolinenstr. · Alsterufer · Edmund Siemers Allee · ➕ · Hamburg Alster 🏠🏠 · Burgstr.
Kennedybrücke · An der Alster · Steindamm · Lohmühlenstr. · Borgfelder Str.
Gorch Fock Wall · Lombards-brücke · ST-GEORG · Arcotel Rubin 🏠 ●
BINNENALSTER · Glockengie berwall · KUNSTHALLE · Berliner Tor · Eiffestr.
Kaiser Wilhelm Str. · Ballindamm · HAUPT-BAHNHOF · Spaldingstr. · Heidenkampsweg · Süderstr.
Holstenwall · Jungfernstieg · Kloster-wall · HAMMERBROOK
Ludwig Erhard Str. · St-Pauli · Ost · West · den · Amsinckstr. · Mercure 🏠🏠 City
Vorsetzen · Bei den Mühren · Commercial Centre (Plan II) · Amsinckstr. · Billhorner Brückenstr.
HAFEN · Versmannstr.
Norderelbe · Am Moldauhafen

● Hotel
● Restaurant

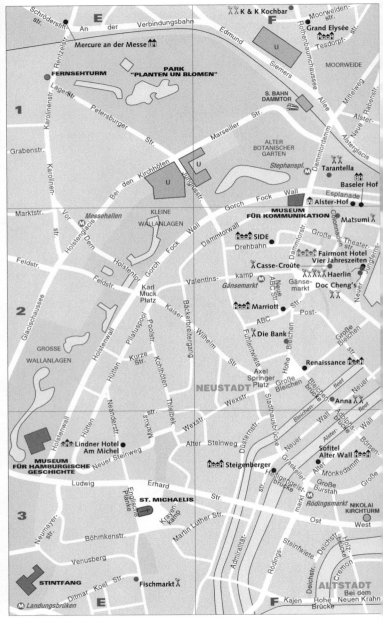

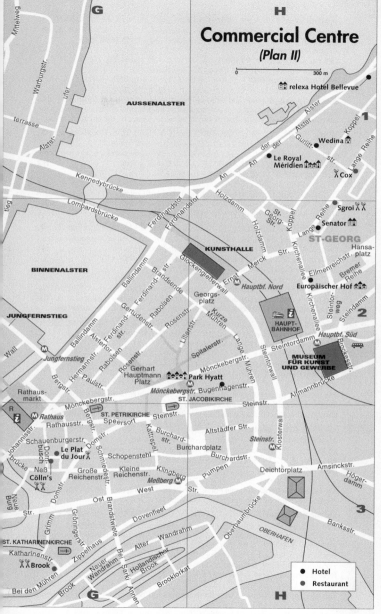

Commercial Centre
(Plan II)

0   300 m

relexa Hotel Bellevue

AUSSENALSTER

Wedina

Le Royal
Méridien

Cox

Sgroi

Senator

ST-GEORG

KUNSTHALLE

Hansa-
platz

BINNENALSTER

Georgs-
platz

Hauptbf. Nord

Europäischer Hof

JUNGFERNSTIEG

HAUPT-
BAHNHOF

Hauptbf. Süd

Jungfernstieg

Gerhart
Hauptmann
Platz

Park Hyatt

**MUSEUM
FÜR KUNST
UND GEWERBE**

Rathaus-
markt

Rathaus

ST. JACOBIKIRCHE

Le Plat
du Jour

ST. PETRIKIRCHE

Cölln's

Steinstr.

Burchardplatz

Steinstr.

Deichtorplatz

Höger-
damm

West

ST. KATHARINENKIRCHE

Banksstr.

OBERHAFEN

Brook

| ● | Hotel |
| ● | Restaurant |

Fairmont Hotel Vier Jahreszeiten ⟨≼ 🛱 🖪 🕸 🖪 🖾 📶 🕸⟩

Neuer Jungfernstieg 9 ⊠ 20354 – **Ⓜ** *Jungfernstieg* 🖭 📶 **②** 🗚 **①**
– *⌀ (040) 3 49 40* – *hamburg@fairmont.com* – *Fax (040) 34 94 26 08*
– *www.fairmont-hvj.de*   **F2**
156 rm – ♦250/350 € ♦♦300/650 €, ⊑ 28 € – 19 suites
Rest *Haerlin* and **Rest *Doc Cheng's*** – see below
Rest *Jahreszeiten Grill* – *⌀ (040) 34 94 33 12* – Carte 35/81 €
  ♦ Grand Luxury ♦ Traditional ♦ Classic ♦
Understated luxury through and through. Perfect service, exclusive design and the ideal
location make this the flagship of Hamburg hotels. International dishes are served in the
Jahreszeiten Grill restaurant. There is also an attractive terrace on the Binnenalster lake.

Park Hyatt   🛱 🖪 ⊛ 🕸 🔄 🖪 🖾 📶 🛱 🖭 📶 **②** 🗚 **①**

Bugenhagenstr. 8 ⊠ 20095 – **Ⓜ** *Mönckebergstr.* – *⌀ (040) 33 32 12 34*
– *hamburg.park@hyatt.de* – *Fax (040) 33 32 12 35* – *www.hamburg.park.hyatt.com*
252 rm – ♦175/325 € ♦♦205/355 €, ⊑ 30 € – 21 suites   **H2**
Rest *Apples* – *⌀ (040) 33 321511* – Carte 38/63 €
  ♦ Grand Luxury ♦ Chain hotel ♦ Modern ♦
This former office building is a luxurious hotel, with quality materials and warm
colours creating an elegant modern ambience. Rooms with Philippe Starck baths.
The Apples open kitchen offers international cuisine.

Le Royal Méridien   🖪 🕸 🔄 ₺ 🖪 🖾 🕲 🛱 🖭 📶 **②** 🗚 **①**

An der Alster 52 ⊠ 20099 – *⌀ (040) 2 10 00* – *info.lrmhamburg@lemeridien.com*
– *Fax (040) 21 00 11 11* – *www.lemeridien.com/hamburg*   **H1**
284 rm – ♦199/399 € ♦♦219/419 €, ⊑ 28 € – 19 suites
Rest – Menu 60 € (dinner) – Carte 43/57 €
  ♦ Chain hotel ♦ Luxury ♦ Modern ♦
This modern hotel have an attractive, clear style extending from the brightly furnis-
hed rooms (with specially designed therapeutic beds) to the wellness area. The
restaurant on the ninth floor offers a fantastic view over the Außenalster lake.

Grand Elysée   🛱 🖪 ⊛ 🕸 🔄 ₺ 🖪 🖾 📶 🛱 🖭 📶 **②** 🗚 **①**

Rothenbaumchaussee 10 ⊠ 20148 – *⌀ (040) 41 41 20* – *info@elysee.de*
– *Fax (040) 41 41 27 33* – *www.elysee.de*   **F1**
511 rm – ♦137/177 € ♦♦157/197 €, ⊑ 20 € – 13 suites
Rest *Piazza Romana* – *⌀ (040) 41 41 27 34* – Carte 30/51 €
Rest *Brasserie* – *⌀ (040) 41 41 27 24* – Carte 24/35 €
  ♦ Luxury ♦ Classic ♦
The generous hotel lobby with its café greets you in boulevard style. Classic, elegant
rooms, quiet garden courtyard rooms and south-facing rooms on the Moorweiden
park. Italian cuisine in the Piazza Romana. Brasserie and oyster bar with seafood

Sofitel Alter Wall   🛱 🖪 ⊛ 🕸 🔄 ₺ 🖪 🖾 🕲 🛱 🖚

Alter Wall 40 ⊠ 20457 – **Ⓜ** *Rödingsmarkt* – *⌀ (040)*   🖭 📶 **②** 🗚 **①**
36 95 00 – *h5395@accor.com* – *Fax (040) 36 95 10 00* – *www.sofitel.com*
241 rm – ♦165/349 € ♦♦185/369 €, ⊑ 26 € – 10 suites   **F3**
Rest – Carte 41/68 €
  ♦ Chain hotel ♦ Luxury ♦ Design ♦
The last word in trendy designer hotels, with its own landing direct on one of the Alster
canals. The rooms offer an interesting mix of materials. A restaurant in a purist style.

Steigenberger   🛱 🖪 ⊛ 🕸 ₺ 🖪 🖾 📶 🛱 🖚 🖭 📶 **②** 🗚 **①**

Heiligengeistbrücke 4 ⊠ 20459 – **Ⓜ** *Rödingsmarkt* – *⌀ (040) 36 80 60*
– *hamburg@steigenberger.de* – *Fax (040) 36 80 67 77* – *www.hamburg.steigenberger.de*
233 rm – ♦209/249 € ♦♦229/269 €, ⊑ 23 € – 6 suites   **F3**
Rest *Calla* – (closed 22 December - 2 January, 16 July - 26 August, Sunday
- Monday and bank holidays) (dinner only) Menu 39/75 € – Carte 49/79 €
Rest *Bistro am Fleet* – Menu 27 € – Carte 26/46 €
  ♦ Luxury ♦ Classic ♦
This elegant establishment with the Hanseatic red brick façade is in a wonderful
location on the Alsterfleet. Conference rooms overlooking the town's rooftops are
available to the guests. Calla with its Euro-Asian menu, looking onto the Alster
International cuisine from the open bistro kitchen

SIDE
🛗 ⊛ 🕥 🔄 ⅙ 🆎 🖳 📡 🛎 🚗 VISA ⸺ AE ①

Drehbahn 49 ⊠ 20354 – Ⓜ Stephansplatz – ℰ (040) 30 99 90
– info@side-hamburg.de – Fax (040) 30 99 93 99 – www.side-hamburg.de
178 rm – ♦170/325 € ♦♦170/325 €, ⌑ 23 € – 10 suites   **F2**
Rest – *(Saturday, Sunday and bank holidays dinner only)* Carte 31/64 €
♦ Luxury ♦ Design ♦

Part of the "Design hotels" partnership, designed to be modern and attractive accordingly. Generous rooms and suites. The Fusion restaurant is linear and minimalist.

Renaissance
🕼 🛗 🕥 🔄 🆎 🖳 📡 🛎 P VISA ⸺ AE ①

Große Bleichen ⊠ 20354 – Ⓜ Jungfernstieg – ℰ (040) 34 91 80
– renaissance.hamburg@renaissancehotels.com – Fax (040) 34 91 89 69
– www.renaissance-hamburg.com   **F2**
205 rm – ♦159/239 € ♦♦179/259 €, ⌑ 24 €   **Rest** – Carte 27/42 €
♦ Luxury ♦ Classic ♦

In typical renaissance style, this classic, tastefully designed hotel with its functional, comfortable rooms. Sauna on the sixth floor with beautiful views. The restaurant has a bar and an open kitchen.

Marriott
🕼 🛗 🕥 🔄 ⅙ 🆎 🖳 📡 🛎 🚗 VISA ⸺ AE ①

ABC-Str. 52 ⊠ 20354 – Ⓜ Gänsemarkt – ℰ (040) 3 50 50 – hamburg.marriott@
marriotthotels.com – Fax (040) 35 05 17 77 – www.hamburgmarriott.com
278 rm – ♦179/269 € ♦♦179/269 €, ⌑ 26 € – 5 suites   **F2**
Rest – Carte 28/48 €
♦ Chain hotel ♦ Luxury ♦ Modern ♦

Close to the Gänsemarkt is this classic hotel, with a hint of America, with its tasteful, functional rooms, a wellness area, hair salon and beauty studio. Modern designs and an abundance of light wood in Restaurant Speicher 52.

Europäischer Hof
🛗 ⊛ 🕥 🔄 🆎 rest 🖳 🛎 🚗 VISA ⸺ AE ①

Kirchenallee 45 ⊠ 20099 – Ⓜ Hauptbahnhof Süd – ℰ (040) 24 82 48 – info@
europaeischer-hof.de – Fax (040) 24 82 47 99 – www.europaeischer-hof.de
275 rm ⌑ – ♦115/195 € ♦♦145/232 € – **Rest** *Paulaner's* – Carte 19/35 €   **H2**
♦ Business ♦ Classic ♦

A large, dignified hall welcomes you to this hotel located opposite the main station. The highlight of the leisure area is the water slide on six different levels. Paulaner's: rustic and relaxed.

Novotel Hamburg Alster
🛗 🕥 🆎 🖳 📡 🛎 🚗 VISA ⸺ AE ①

Lübecker Str. 3 ⊠ 22087 – Ⓜ Lübecker Str. – ℰ (040) 39 19 00 – h3737@
accor.com – Fax (040) 39 19 02 72 – www.novotel.com   *Plan I* **D2**
210 rm – ♦99/199 € ♦♦99/199 €, ⌑ 18 €   **Rest** – Carte 29/52 €
♦ Chain hotel ♦ Modern ♦

A modern hotel providing well-equipped rooms in comfortable, modern style. Conferences facilities available. Restaurant accessed from the hotel lobby.

Mövenpick
🕼 🕼 🛗 ⅙ 🆎 🖳 📡 🛎 P 🚗 VISA ⸺ AE ①

Sternschanze 6 ⊠ 20357 – Ⓜ Sternschanze – ℰ (040) 3 34 41 10 – hotel.hamburg@
moevenpick.com – Fax (040) 33 44 11 33 33 – www.moevenpick-hamburg.com
226 rm – ♦150/340 € ♦♦170/340 €, ⌑ 21 € – **Rest** – Carte 26/55 €   *Plan I* **C2**
♦ Chain hotel ♦ Historic ♦ Functional ♦

The beautiful old water tower from 1907 has been extended with an annex. It houses rooms in warm tones with very good technical facilities and views over Hamburg. International cuisine is served in the restaurant with a terrace facing the park.

Arcotel Rubin
🛗 🕥 ⅙ 🆎 🖳 📡 🛎 🚗 VISA ⸺ AE ①

Steindamm 63 (access via Danzingerstraße) ⊠ 20099 – Ⓜ Lohmühlenstr.
– ℰ (040) 2 41 92 90 – rubin@arcotel.at – Fax (040) 24 19 29 25 50
– www.arcotel.at   *Plan I* **D2**
217 rm – ♦125/250 € ♦♦125/250 €, ⌑ 17 € – 7 suites
Rest *Facette* – Carte 28/42 €
♦ Chain hotel ♦ Business ♦ Design ♦

In this hotel in St Georg, not far from the main railway station, ruby red tones are in keeping with the hotel's name. There is a pretty themed 'Red Room' and 'Gateway to the World' room. The Facette is a bright restaurant with a room high glass frontage.

Lindner Hotel Am Michel 🛜 ⅃ᴪ 🐾 ♿ 🗚 🖾 📶 🕍 🚗

Neanderstr. 20 ⊠ *20459 –* ☎ *(040) 3 07 06 70*   🆅🅸🆂🅰 ⓒⓔ 🅰🅴 ⓞ
– info.hamburg@lindner.de – Fax (040) 3 07 06 77 77
– www.lindner.de/hotel-hamburg   **E3**
259 rm – ♥139/579 € ♥♥159/599 €, ⊆ 20 € – 8 suites
Rest *Sonnin* – Carte 31/47 €
Rest *Hamburger Stube* – *(dinner only)* Menu 42/145 € – Carte 43/55 €
◆ Business ◆ Chain hotel ◆ Modern ◆
A brick building in a relatively quiet and central location close to the 'Michel'. It offers modern, well-appointed rooms in warm colours. The restaurant Sonnin serves international cuisine. Creative cuisine and classic dishes are served in the Hamburger Stube.

relexa Hotel Bellevue 🖾 📶 🕍 🅿 🚗 🆅🅸🆂🅰 ⓒⓔ 🅰🅴 ⓞ

An der Alster 14 ⊠ *20099 –* ☎ *(040) 28 44 40 – hamburg@relexa-hotel.de*
– Fax (040) 28 44 42 22 – www.relexa-hotels.de   **H1**
85 rm ⊆ – ♥93/120 € ♥♥123/140 €   **Rest** – Carte 28/42 €
◆ Business ◆ Functional ◆
Classic white hotel building. The rooms are very pretty and some of them in the main building have views over the Alster. Smaller single rooms in the St Georg. During the day diners are served in the restaurant on the Außenalster lake and in the evening in the UG restaurant with its tasteful, comfortable atmosphere.

Mercure an der Messe ♿ 🗚 🖾 📞 🕍 🚗 🆅🅸🆂🅰 ⓒⓔ 🅰🅴 ⓞ

Schröderstiftstr. 3 ⊠ *20146 –* ☎ *(040) 45 06 90 – h5394@accor.com – Fax (040)*
4 50 69 10 00 – www.mercure.com   **E1**
180 rm – ♥93/143 € ♥♥93/143 €, ⊆ 17 €
Rest – *(closed Sunday dinner)* Carte 24/45 €
◆ Business ◆ Functional ◆
Business hotel next door to the exhibition centre and a few minutes walk from the TV tower. Rooms with a modern design and functional equipment.

Mercure City 🐾 ♿ 🗚 🖾 📞 🕍 🅿 🚗 🆅🅸🆂🅰 ⓒⓔ 🅰🅴 ⓞ

Amsinckstr. 53 ⊠ *20097 –* ☎ *(040) 23 63 80 – h1163@accor.com – Fax (040)*
23 42 30 – www.mercure.com   *Plan I* **D3**
187 rm – ♥99/159 € ♥♥99/159 €, ⊆ 18 €   **Rest** – Carte 24/37 €
◆ Chain hotel ◆ Modern ◆
Modern functional rooms in this inner city hotel, ideal for business guests.

Senator without rest 🖾 📶 🚗 🆅🅸🆂🅰 ⓒⓔ 🅰🅴 ⓞ

Lange Reihe 18 ⊠ *20099 –* Ⓜ *Hauptbahnhof Nord –* ☎ *(040) 24 19 30 – info@*
hotel-senator-hamburg.de – Fax (040) 24 19 31 09 – www.hotel-senator-hamburg.de
56 rm ⊆ – ♥99/129 € ♥♥109/179 €   **H2**
◆ Townhouse ◆ Functional ◆
Pale wood and pastel tones create a harmonious atmosphere in the rooms, some of which have a waterbed for a perfect night's sleep.

Baseler Hof 🐾 🖾 📶 🕍 🆅🅸🆂🅰 ⓒⓔ 🅰🅴 ⓞ

Esplanade 11 ⊠ *20354 –* Ⓜ *Stephansplatz –* ☎ *(040) 35 90 60 – info@*
baselerhof.de – Fax (040) 35 90 69 18 – www.baselerhof.de   **F1**
168 rm ⊆ – ♥89/125 € ♥♥149/159 €
Rest *Kleinhuis* – ☎ *(040) 353399* – Carte 26/38 €
◆ Traditional ◆ Functional ◆
This hotel is located between the Außenalster lake and the Botanical Gardens and is a member of the Association of Christian Hotels. Rooms with different types of furnishing including rattan. The Kleinhuis is a nice bistro-style restaurant.

Wedina without rest (with guesthouses) 🚃 🖾 📞 🚗

Gurlittstr. 23 ⊠ *20099 –* ☎ *(040) 2 80 89 00 – info@*   🆅🅸🆂🅰 ⓒⓔ 🅰🅴 ⓞ
wedina.de – Fax (040) 2 80 38 94 – www.wedina.de – closed over Christmas
59 rm ⊆ – ♥88/155 € ♥♥108/175 €   **H1**
◆ Family ◆ Cosy ◆
The different buildings which make up this hotel are aglow in Bauhaus colours. The interior is also attractively designed featuring natural materials.

🏠 **Alster-Hof** without rest _Lʃ ⁿⁱ VISA ⚹ AE ①_
Esplanade 12 ⊠ 20354 – Ⓜ Stephansplatz – ℰ (040) 35 00 70
– info@alster-hof.de – Fax (040) 35 00 75 14 – www.alster-hof.de
– closed 21 December-2 January **F1**
113 rm ⌓ – ♥85/100 € ♥♥120/136 €
♦ Traditional ♦ Functional ♦
This centrally located hotel provides functional rooms with a refined atmosphere.

XXXXX **Haerlin** – Fairmont Hotel Vier Jahreszeiten _≼ AK VISA ⚹ AE ①_
☸ *Neuer Jungfernstieg 9 ⊠ 20354 – Ⓜ Jungfernstieg – ℰ (040) 34 94 33 10*
– hamburg@fairmont.com – Fax (040) 34 94 26 08 – www.fairmont-hvj.de
– closed 2 - 15 January, 21 July - 17 August and Sunday - Monday
Rest – *(dinner only)* Menu 82/115 € – Carte 70/90 € ⅏ **F2**
Spec. Pochiertes Entenleberparfait mit Kaisergranat und Grapefruit. Zweierlei vom Kalb mit Wermutschaum und Gemüsecroûtons. Mandeltarte mit glacierten Früchten und Cheese-Cake-Eis.
♦ Classic ♦ Luxury ♦
An elegant restaurant featuring attentive and competent service as well as impeccably and harmoniously prepared classic dishes. Diners have an excellent view of the Binnenalster.

XXX **Insel am Alsterufer** _🏠 ⇵ VISA ⚹ AE ①_
Alsterufer 35 (1st floor) ⊠ 20354 – ℰ (040) 4 50 18 50 – info@insel-am-alsterufer.de
– Fax (040) 45 01 85 11 – www.insel-am-alsterufer.de
– closed Saturday lunch, Sunday *Plan I* **C2**
Rest – Carte 30/113 €
♦ Classic ♦ Elegant ♦
This little white jewel of a villa houses an elegant restaurant with warm tones, offering its guests international cuisine. Some of the tables look out on the Aussenalster.

XX **Cölln's** _🏠 ⇵ VISA ⚹ AE ①_
Brodschrangen 1 ⊠ 20457 – Ⓜ Rathaus – ℰ (040) 36 41 53
– coellns-restaurant@web.de – Fax (040) 37 22 01 – www.coellns-restaurant.de
– closed Saturday lunch, Sunday and bank holidays **G3**
Rest – *(booking advisable)* Carte 35/79 €
♦ Classic ♦ Cosy ♦
This tastefully renovated historic establishment offers classic and regional dishes. Details such as old tiles and wood panelling feature within their comfortable rooms.

XX **Sgroi** _🏠 VISA ⚹_
☸ *Lange Reihe 40 ⊠ 20099 – ℰ (040) 28 00 39 30 – Fax (040) 28 00 39 31*
– www.sgroi.de
– closed Saturday lunch, Sunday - Monday **H1-2**
Rest – Menu 35 € (lunch)/70 € – Carte 54/69 €
Spec. Gratinierte gefüllte Artischocken mit Kartoffelblättern und Rotweinjus. Safranrisotto mit gebackenem Kalbsmark. Rindsnuss in Lardo mit Fonduta von Chicoree.
♦ Italian ♦ Minimalist ♦
The clean-cut modern design and equally straightforward Italian cuisine are the key features of this restaurant. There is also a very pleasant lounge.

XX **Anna** _🏠 VISA ⚹ AE_
Bleichenbrücke 2 ⊠ 20354 – Ⓜ Rathaus – ℰ (040) 36 70 14 – Fax (040)
37 50 07 36 – closed Sunday and bank holidays **F2**
Rest – Carte 31/41 €
♦ International ♦ Friendly ♦
Mediterranean tones set the ambience of this two-floor restaurant with its wide range of international cuisine. Pleasant terrace on the Fleet.

XX **Tarantella** _🏠 ♿ ⇵ VISA ⚹ AE_
Stephanspl. 10 (at Casino Esplanade) ⊠ 20354 – Ⓜ Stephanspl. – ℰ (040)
65 06 77 90 – info@tarantella.cc – Fax (040) 65 06 77 87 – www.tarantella.cc
Rest – Carte 31/66 € **F1**
♦ International ♦ Fashionable ♦
This modern style restaurant with a bistro area is located in the casino building. International dishes are prepared in the open kitchen.

GERMANY - HAMBURG

Brook ⚄

🙂 *Bei den Mühren 91* ✉ *20457 –* ✆ *(040) 37 50 31 28 – lschablinski@web.de*
– Fax (040) 37 50 31 27 – www.restaurant-brook.de – closed Sunday
Rest – Menu 31/35 € – Carte 31/50 €   **G3**
♦ International ♦ Fashionable ♦

A modern restaurant with friendly service and high quality international cuisine. In
the evening there is a pretty view of the illuminated Speicherstadt (warehouses)
opposite.

Doc Cheng's – Fairmont Hotel Vier Jahreszeiten   🏧 VISA ◯◯ ⚄ ◉

Neuer Jungfernstieg 9 ✉ *20354 –* Ⓜ *Jungfernstieg –* ✆ *(040) 3 49 43 33*
– hamburg@fairmont.com – Fax (040) 34 94 26 08 – www.fairmont-hvj.de
– closed Saturday lunch, Sunday   **F2**
Rest – *(July - August dinner only)* Carte 40/59 €
♦ Asian ♦ Individual ♦

The Far East inspires both the stylish design and cuisine here. Euro-Asian cuisine,
with reduced lunch menu.

Die Bank   🏠 VISA ⚄

Hohe Bleichen 17 ✉ *20354 –* Ⓜ *Gänsemarkt –* ✆ *(040) 2 38 00 30 – info@*
diebank-brasserie.de – Fax (040) 23 80 03 33 – www.diebank-brasserie.de
– closed Sunday and bank holidays   **F2**
Rest – Carte 38/61 €
♦ International ♦ Brasserie ♦

A lively brasserie and bar in the imposing cashiers' hall on the first floor of what
used to be a bank, offers contemporary cuisine.

La Mirabelle   VISA ⚄ ⚄

Bundesstr. 15 ✉ *20146 –* ✆ *(040) 4 10 75 85 – Fax (040) 4 10 75 85*
– www.la-mirabelle-hamburg.de – closed Sunday   *Plan I* **C2**
Rest – *(dinner only)* Menu 38/45 € – Carte 39/56 €
♦ French ♦ Cosy ♦

In this small, friendly restaurant with its relaxed atmosphere and French flair, Pierre
Moissonnier serves his guests in friendly but passionate style.

Fischmarkt   🏠 VISA ⚄ ⚄

Ditmar-Koel-Str. 1 ✉ *20459 –* Ⓜ *Landungsbrücken –* ✆ *(040) 36 38 09*
– Fax (040) 36 21 91 – www.restaurant-fischmarkt.de
– closed Saturday lunch   **E3**
Rest – *(booking advisable)* Menu 30/48 € – Carte 31/64 €
♦ Fish ♦ Bistro ♦

At the Schaarmarkt close to the harbour, this bistro on two levels has a Mediterranean decor. It serves many fish specials and the fish display is very appetising.

Le Plat du Jour   🏧 VISA ⚄ ⚄ ◉

🙂 *Dornbusch 4* ✉ *20095 –* Ⓜ *Rathaus –* ✆ *(040) 32 14 14 – Fax (040)*
32 52 63 93 – www.leplatdujour.de   **G3**
Rest – *(booking advisable)* Menu 27 € (dinner) – Carte 26/36 €
♦ French ♦ Bistro ♦

A pleasant French bistro decorated with black and white photographs. For Hamburg prices very good value French dishes!

Casse-Croûte   🏧 VISA ⚄ ⚄

🙂 *Büschstr. 2* ✉ *20354 –* Ⓜ *Gänsemarkt –* ✆ *(040) 34 33 73*
– info@cassecroute.de – Fax (040) 3 58 96 50 – www.cassecroute.de
– closed over Christmas, Sunday lunch and bank holidays lunch   **F2**
Rest – *(booking advisable)* Menu 27 € – Carte 31/43 € 🌿
♦ International ♦ Bistro ♦

This popular bistro with its relaxed atmosphere is in a side street near the Gänsemarkt. From the open kitchen, tasty fare ranging from good traditional to international dishes, finds its way to the table.

✗ **Cox** AE

Lange Reihe 68 ⊠ *20099 –* ✆ *(040) 24 94 22 – info@restaurant-cox.de*
– Fax (040) 28 05 09 02 – www.restaurant-cox.de
– closed Saturday lunch, Sunday lunch **H1**
Rest – Carte 30/42 €
♦ International ♦ Bistro ♦

This lovely bistro restaurant is extremely comfortable. The service is friendly and informal and the food is international with a Mediterranean influence. Simpler lunchtime menu.

✗ **Matsumi** 🖧 VISA ⓒ AE ①

Colonnaden 96 (1st floor) ⊠ *20354 –* Ⓜ *Stephansplatz*
– ✆ *(040) 34 31 25 – Fax (040) 34 42 19 – www.matsumi.de*
– closed 22 December - 7 January, Sunday and bank holidays lunch
Rest – Menu 43/50 € – Carte 20/54 € **F2**
♦ Japanese ♦ Minimalist ♦

You will find this classic Japanese restaurant in the pedestrian zone. The authentic fare is served at the table, at the sushi bar or in the tatami rooms (for groups).

NORTH OF THE CENTRE *Plan I*

🏨 **InterContinental** ≤ 🏤 ⅃⅚ 🏊 🖾 🖾 🖾 ✆ 🖼 🅿 🚗

Fontenay 10 ⊠ *20354 –* ✆ *(040) 4 14 20 – hamburg@ihg.com* VISA ⓒ AE ①
– Fax (040) 41 42 22 99 – www.hamburg.intercontinental.com **C2**
281 rm – ♗139/389 € ♗♗139/389 €, � 23 € – 12 suites
Rest *Windows* – see below
Rest *Signatures* – Carte 28/48 €
♦ Chain hotel ♦ Luxury ♦ Functional ♦

This hotel is located on the Alster. It will charm guests with its extravagant appearance and the technically perfect design of the rooms. The Signatures conservatory restaurant has an international menu and is bright and pleasant.

🏠 **Abtei** 🕭 🚗 🏤 🖾 🖾 VISA ⓒ AE
⁂
Abteistr. 14 ⊠ *20149 –* ✆ *(040) 44 29 05 – info@abtei-hotel.de*
– Fax (040) 44 98 20 – www.abtei-hotel.de – closed 24-27 December
11 rm �⊋ – ♗155/210 € ♗♗190/270 € **C1**
Rest – *(closed Sunday - Monday) (dinner only) (booking essential)*
Menu 69/95 €
Spec. St. Pierre mit Koriandersauce und Croustillant von Chicoree. Taubenbrust mit Ingwer und Rauchmandeln. Schokoladendessert mit milden Pfefferaromen.
♦ Villa ♦ Personalised ♦

This extremely charming patrician's villa dates back to 1897. It is a lovely residence that offers individual rooms. Located in a beautiful, quiet district surrounded by mature trees. An intimate atmosphere reigns in this restaurant with its stylish salon. A bistro offers a small range of dishes.

🏠 **Mittelweg** without rest 🚗 🖾 🖾 🅿 VISA ⓒ AE ①

Mittelweg 59 ⊠ *20149 –* Ⓜ *Klosterstern –* ✆ *(040) 4 14 10 10*
– hotel.mittelweg@gmx.de – Fax (040) 41 41 01 20 – www.hotel-mittelweg.de
30 rm ⊋ – ♗95/148 € ♗♗135/168 € **C1**
♦ Villa ♦ Cosy ♦

Built by a Bremen merchant as his town house in 1890, this hotel stands out for its friendly, private atmosphere and old-style charm and classic, comfortable rooms.

🏠 **Nippon** 🖾 🖾 🖾 🅿 🚗 VISA ⓒ AE ①

Hofweg 75 ⊠ *22085 –* ✆ *(040) 2 27 11 40 – reservations@nipponhotel.de*
– Fax (040) 22 71 14 90 – www.nipponhotel.de – closed 23 Dec. - 1 Jan.
42 rm – ♗101/124 € ♗♗119/153 €, ⊋ 13 € **D1**
Rest – *(closed Monday) (dinner only)* Carte 26/47 €
♦ Townhouse ♦ Minimalist ♦

Furnished in a modern, purist Japanese style with light colours and clear shapes: tatami floors, shoji walls and futons. Wa-Yo: a Japanese restaurant and sushi bar.

GERMANY - HAMBURG

XXXX **Windows** – Hotel InterContinental   ≤ AC P VISA ©© AE ①

*Fontenay 10 ⊠ 20354 – ℰ (040) 4 14 20 – hamburg@ihg.com – Fax (040)
41 42 22 99 – www.hamburg.intercontinental.com
– closed 1 - 21 January, mid July - mid August and Sunday - Monday*
Rest – *(dinner only)* Carte 47/65 € ♨   **C2**
• Classic • Elegant •

This restaurant high above the city offers an elegant atmosphere and fabulous
views over Hamburg and the Alster. French cuisine.

XX **Poletto**   ⇔ VISA ©© AE
☺ *Eppendorfer Landstr. 145 (by Breidenjelder Straße C1) ⊠ 20251
– ℰ (040) 4 80 21 59 – Fax (040) 41 40 69 93 – www.poletto.de
– closed 2 weeks July - August, Saturday lunch, Sunday - Monday and bank holidays*
Rest – *(booking advisable)* Menu 35 € (lunch)/120 € – Carte 68/97 €
Spec. Handgemachte Pasta. Weißer Heilbutt an der Gräte gegart mit Arti-
schocken und Kapernäpfeln. Variation vom Lamm.
• Mediterranean • Friendly •

In the nicely relaxed atmosphere of this pleasant restaurant, Cornelia Poletto serves Italian-Mediterreanean dishes.

XX **Piment** (Wahabi Nouri)   ⇔ VISA ©© AE
☺ *Lehmweg 29 ⊠ 20251 – ℰ (040) 42 93 77 88 – info@restaurant-piment.de
– Fax (040) 42 93 77 89 – www.restaurant-piment.de
– closed Sunday*   **C1**
Rest – *(dinner only) (booking advisable)* Menu 65/88 € – Carte 57/72 €
Spec. Gänsestopfleberterrine mit gebeizter Zitrone und grünem Apfel. B'Stilla von
der Taube mit Honig-Ingwerjus. Banane und Passionsfrucht mit Pomelosauce.
• Inventive • Friendly •

The native-born Moroccan, Wahabi Nouri gives his cuisine a very individual touch with
North African influences. The lovely Art Nouveau building provides a cosy setting.

XX **Küchenwerkstatt**   ⇔ ⇔ P AE
*Hans-Henny-Jahnn-Weg 1 (entrance Hofweg) ⊠ 22085 – ℰ (040) 22 92 75 88
– mail@kuechenwerkstatt-hamburg.de – Fax (040) 22 92 75 99
– www.kuechenwerkstatt-hamburg.de
– closed 2 weeks early January, Sunday - Monday and bank holidays lunch*
Rest – Menu 22 € (lunch)/69 € (dinner) – Carte 43/54 €   **D1**
• Inventive • Trendy •

This former ferry building has been done out in an attractive cool modern style.
Here you'll find committed service and creative cuisine. Short lunchtime menu.

XX **K & K Kochbar**   ⇔ VISA ©© AE ①
*Rothenbaumchaussee 11 (at the Curio-Haus) ⊠ 20148 – ℰ (040) 36 11 16 36
– kochbar@koflerkompanie.com – Fax (040) 36 11 16 11 – www.koflerkompanie.com
– closed 24 December - 5 January and Sunday*   Plan II **F1**
Rest – *(dinner only)* Menu 59 € – Carte 38/63 €
• Innovative • Trendy •

The restaurant is decorated with modern art work and sits within a beautiful historic Curio House of 1911 at a trendy address. The centrally positioned show kitchen
is an eye catcher.

HARBOUR AND ALTONA   *Plan III*

🏠🏠🏠 **Empire Riverside Hotel**   ≤ ⅙ 🐾 & AC ℀ 🛁 🍽 VISA ©© AE
*Bernhardt-Nocht-Str. 97 ⊠ 20359 – Ⓜ Reeperbahn – ℰ (040) 31 11 90
– empire@hotel-hamburg.de – Fax (040) 31 11 97 06 01 – www.empire-riverside.de*
328 rm – †169/279 € ††169/279 €, ⊆ 18 €   **J1**
Rest Waterkant – Carte 32/67 €
• Business • Conference hotel • Design •

Star architect David Chipperfield has designed this modern hotel close to the landing
stages. The rooms overlook the harbour, the Elbe and the city – as does the bar on the
20th floor. International cuisine is served in the contemporary designed Waterkant.

East
🛐 🕍 ♿ 🖨 📶 🏋 VISA 🟠 AE

Simon-von-Utrecht-Str. 31 ⊠ 20359 – Ⓜ St. Pauli – ℰ (040) 30 99 30
– info@east-hamburg.de – Fax (040) 30 99 32 07 – www.east-hamburg.de
128 rm – †155/180 € ††175/220 €, ⊃ 17 € – 3 suites   *Plan I* **B2**
Rest – Carte 33/59 €
◆ Business ◆ Design ◆

In an old foundry, this pleasant designer hotel with the latest word in rooms and bar/lounge occupies two floors. Cinema, indoor golf, putting green in the garden. Not your average restaurant, in an old factory.

XXXX   Landhaus Scherrer (Heinz Wehmann)
AC ⇿ P VISA 🟠 AE ⓪

ξ3   *Elbchaussee 130 ⊠ 22763 – ℰ (040) 8 80 13 25 – info@landhausscherrer.de*
– Fax (040) 8 80 62 60 – www.landhausscherrer.de – closed Sunday
Rest – Menu 79/109 € – Carte 55/97 € ㅤ   **I1**
Rest Bistro – Menu 33 € – Carte 35/41 €
Spec. Steinbutt an der Gräte gebraten. Krosser Ferkelbauch mit Graupen-Hummerrisotto und Balsamico-Senf. Topfensoufflé mit glasierten Kirschen.
◆ Classic ◆ Elegant ◆

This 19C country house is an elegant restaurant that for over 30-years has been synonymous with excellent cuisine. An extensive range of wines accompanies the classic dishes. Nice friendly bistro with its light wood panelling

XXX   Le Canard nouveau (Ali Güngörmüs)
← 🛐 P VISA 🟠 AE

ξ3   *Elbchaussee 139 ⊠ 22763 – ℰ (040) 88 12 95 31 – info@lecanard-hamburg.de*
– Fax (040) 88 12 95 33 – www.lecanard-hamburg.de
– closed 1 week early January, Sunday - Monday   **I1**
Rest – Menu 33 € (lunch) – Carte 66/73 € ㅤ
Spec. Ziegenkäse-Feigentortellini mit Pancetta und Lorbeerjus. Maibockrücken mit Sellerie-Gänseleberravioli und karamellisiertem Pfefferpfirsich. Schokoladenkuchen mit marinierten Himbeeren.
◆ International ◆ Fashionable ◆

Dine in the semi-circular restaurant above the Elbe with a view of the harbour. The decor is modern and simpler, value for money dishes are served at lunchtime.

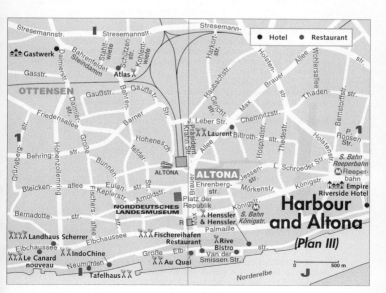

XXX **Fischereihafen Restaurant** ⟨ 🛱 ❁ **P** 𝘝𝘐𝘚𝘈 ⓪ 🅰🅴 ⓪

Große Elbstr. 143 ⊠ *22767 –* ✆ *(040) 38 18 16 – info@fischereihafenrestaurant.de*
– Fax (040) 3 89 30 21 – www.fischereihafenrestaurant.de **J1**
Rest *– (booking advisable)* Menu 20 € (lunch)/50 € – Carte 32/74 €
◆ Fish ◆ Classic ◆
This Hamburg institution is a restaurant serving regional cuisine specialising in fish.
Terrace overlooking the Elbe.

XX **Au Quai** ⟨ 🛱 𝘝𝘐𝘚𝘈 ⓪ 🅰🅴

Grosse Elbstr. 145 b ⊠ *22767 –* ✆ *(040) 38 03 77 30 – info@au-quai.com*
– Fax (040) 38 03 77 32 – www.au-quai.com
– closed 20 December - 8 January and Saturday lunch, Sunday **J1**
Rest *–* Menu 18 € (lunch)/49 € – Carte 34/61 €
◆ Fusion ◆ Trendy ◆
This popular establishment is situated close to the harbour and has a terrace facing
the water. The modern interior is complemented by designer items and holographs.

XX **IndoChine** ⟨ 🛱 ❁ **P** 𝘝𝘐𝘚𝘈 ⓪ 🅰🅴

Neumühlen 11 ⊠ *22763 –* ✆ *(040) 39 80 78 80 – info@indochine.de – Fax (040)*
39 80 78 82 – www.indochine.de **I1**
Rest *–* Menu 40/59 € – Carte 37/72 €
◆ Asian ◆ Trendy ◆
Great views, especially from the window seats, in this elegant modern restaurant on
the Elbe. Cambodian, Laotian and Vietnamese cuisine. The IceBar is worth seeing.

XX **Laurent** 🛱

Max-Brauer-Allee 80 ⊠ *22765 –* ✆ *(040) 41 30 62 72 – tim@*
restaurant-laurent.de – Fax (040) 41 30 62 82 – www.restaurant-laurent.de
– closed 2 weeks early January, Saturday lunch and Sunday **J1**
Rest *–* Menu 18 € (lunch)/85 € (dinner) – Carte 32/59 €
◆ Inventive ◆ Friendly ◆
Tasty regional dishes with a local touch are served. Frescos and stucco ornamentation are focal points in this cheerful restaurant.

XX **Tafelhaus** (Christian Rach) ⟨ 🛱 𝘝𝘐𝘚𝘈 ⓪ 🅰🅴
❀ *Neumühlen 17* ⊠ *22763 –* ✆ *(040) 89 27 60 – anfrage@tafelhaus.de*
– Fax (040) 8 99 33 24 – www.tafelhaus.de
– closed Saturday lunch, Sunday - Monday **I1**
Rest *– (booking advisable)* Menu 40 € (lunch)/82 € – Carte 78/86 € 🍸
Spec. Steinbutt im Ganzen gebraten. Geschmorte Rehschulter mit gebrate-
nem Crêpe und Erdbeer-Lorbeer-Marmelade. Schokoladencannelloni mit
Rohrzuckereis und Rum.
◆ Inventive ◆ Minimalist ◆
This simple and modern style restaurant with a view of passing ships serves crea-
tive French cuisine. There is also a view of the Elbe from the terrace.

X **Henssler Henssler** 🛱 🅰🅴

Große Elbstr. 160 ⊠ *22767 –* Ⓜ *Königstr. –* ✆ *(040) 38 69 90 00*
– Fax (040) 38 69 90 55 – www.hensslerhenssler.de
– closed 4 weeks July - August, Sunday and bank holidays **J1**
Rest *– (booking advisable)* Carte 30/55 €
◆ Japanese ◆ Minimalist ◆
Father and son run this Far East-inspired simple modern restaurant in an old fish-
monger's hall: Japanese cuisine with the Californian touch. Sushi bar.

X **Rive Bistro** ⟨ 🛱 🅰🅴
❀ *Van-der-Smissen-Str. 1 (at Cruise-Centre)* ⊠ *22767 –* Ⓜ *Königstr.*
– ✆ *(040) 3 80 59 19 – info@rive.de – Fax (040) 3 89 47 75 – www.rive.de*
Rest *– (booking advisable)* Carte 29/57 € **J1**
◆ Fish ◆ Trendy ◆
This modern restaurant with a wonderful view of the Elbe is directly by the har-
bour, not far from the fish market. The emphasis of the international cuisine is
very much on fish, and fresh oysters are available at the bar.

GERMANY - HAMBURG

Louis C. Jacob ⟨⟩ 🕸 🅰️ 📺 ⁿ↑ 🛁 🚗 **VISA** 🔵 🅰️🅴 ⓪

Elbchaussee 401 (by Elbchaussee A3) ⊠ *22609 –* ☏ *(040) 82 25 50*
– jacob@hotel-jacob.de – Fax (040) 82 25 54 44
– www.hotel-jacob.de
85 rm – ▪195/245 € ▪▪255/485 €, ⊐ 26 € – 8 suites
Rest Jacobs Restaurant *and* **Rest Weinwirtschaft Kleines Jacob** – see below
♦ Luxury ♦ Traditional ♦ Classic ♦

The successful management and competent services in this elegant hotel on the Elbe are exemplary. The rooms are characterised by an attractive mix of modern and classical styles.

Gastwerk 🕭 🕸 📺 ⁿ↑ 🛁 🅿️ 🚗 **VISA** 🔵 🅰️🅴 ⓪

Beim Alten Gaswerk 3 (corner of Daimlerstraße) ⊠ *22761 –* ☏ *(040) 89 06 20*
– info@gastwerk-hotel.de – Fax (040) 8 90 62 20 – www.gastwerk-hotel.de
141 rm – ▪136/182 € ▪▪146/192 €, ⊐ 18 € – 3 suites   **I1**
Rest *– (closed Saturday lunch, Sunday lunch)* Carte 34/50 €
♦ Business ♦ Design ♦

A successful combination of imposing industrial architecture and modern design. Pleasant rooms, lofts and suites – two of the suites have room terraces. A modern restaurant serving Italian cuisine.

Landhaus Flottbek 🚗 🕭 📺 ⁿ↑ 🛁 🅿️

Baron-Voght-Str. 179 (by Stresemannstraße A2) ⊠ *22607 –* ☏ *(040) 8 22 74 10*
– info@landhaus-flottbek.de – Fax (040) 82 27 41 51 – www.landhaus-flottbek.de
25 rm – ▪90/120 € ▪▪120/150 €, ⊐ 16 €
Rest *– (closed Saturday lunch, Sunday lunch)* Carte 33/55 €
♦ Family ♦ Cosy ♦

A group of 18C farmhouses with a beautiful garden. The lovely, individually furnished, country-style rooms are rustic and elegant. This restaurant offers international cuisine from good produce. Friendly terrace on the garden.

XXXX Jacobs Restaurant – Hotel Louis C. Jacob ⟨⟩ 🕭 🅰️ **VISA** 🔵 🅰️🅴 ⓪
ॐ

Elbchaussee 401 (by Elbchaussee A3) ⊠ *22609 –* ☏ *(040) 82 25 50*
– jacob@hotel-jacob.de – Fax (040) 82 25 54 44 – www.hotel-jacob.de
Rest *– (booking advisable)* Menu 62 € (lunch)/106 € – Carte 71/98 € 🍷
Spec. Rotbarbe mit orientalischer Würze und Gemüsebeignets. Geschmorte Ochsenschulter mit Baroloessigjus und Kartoffelschaum. Delice von Himbeeren mit Schokolade und Minze.
♦ Classic ♦ Formal ♦

Enjoy Thomas Martin's contemporary, classic based cuisine at this elegant restaurant. It has a delightful terrace under lime trees from which you have a fantastic view of the Elbe.

XXXX Süllberg - Seven Seas (Karlheinz Hauser) with rm ⟨⟩ 🕭 🅰️ 📺
ॐ

Süllbergsterrasse 12 (by Elbchaussee A3) ⊠ *22587*   ⁿ↑ 🚗 **VISA** 🔵 🅰️🅴
– ☏ *(040) 8 66 25 20 – info@suellberg-hamburg.de – Fax (040) 86 62 52 13*
– www.suellberg-hamburg.de
10 rm – ▪170/190 € ▪▪190/210 €, ⊐ 8 €
Rest *– (closed 1 - 28 January and Monday - Tuesday) (Wednesday - Saturday dinner only)* Menu 72/122 € – Carte 68/95 € 🍷
Rest Bistro – Carte 35/58 €
Spec. Rotbarbe und Jakobsmuschel mit Ravioli von sonnengetrockneten Tomaten und Parmesanschaum. Petersfisch unter der Pinienkruste mit Bouillabaisse-Infusion und Muscheln. Rücken und Geschmortes vom Lamm mit Zitronenthymianfond und gefüllten Poweraden.
♦ Mediterranean ♦ Luxury ♦

Overlooking the Elbe the Süllberg buildings form an extremely imposing architectural ensemble from Kaiser Wilhelm's time. The ambience is modern and elegant, the cuisine Mediterranean. Tasteful rooms and beauty facilities await guests in the hotel area.

GERMANY - HAMBURG

XX **Abendroth**   🛋 _VISA_ ⓜ AE

Statthalterplatz 5 (by Behringstraße A2) ✉ *22605 –* ✆ *(040) 89 72 67 22*
– info@restaurant-abendroth.de – Fax (040) 89 72 67 23
– www.restaurant-abendroth.de
– closed Monday, Saturday lunch
Rest – Menu 15 € (lunch)/49 € (dinner) – Carte 37/64 €
  ◆ International ◆ Trendy ◆
This restaurant with a lounge and sunny terrace is close to Othmarschen station.
The cuisine is international with classic influences.

X **Atlas**   🛋 **P** _VISA_ ⓜ

Schützenstr. 9a (entrance Phoenixhof) ✉ *22761 –* ✆ *(040) 8 51 78 10*
– atlas@atlas.at – Fax (040) 8 51 78 11 – www.atlas.at
– closed Saturday lunch   **I1**
Rest – Menu 17 € (lunch)/28 € (dinner) – Carte 27/41 €
  ◆ International ◆ Bistro ◆
This old fish smokery is now a restaurant in a modern bistro style. Short menu at
lunchtimes, Sunday brunch. Nice ivy-wreathed terrace.

X **Weinwirtschaft Kleines Jacob** – Hotel Louis C. Jacob   🛋

Elbchaussee 404 (by Elbchaussee A3) ✉ *22609*   _VISA_ ⓜ AE ⓪
– ✆ *(040) 82255510 – kleines-jacob@hotel-jacob.de – Fax (040) 82 25 54 44*
– www.hotel-jacob.de
– closed mid July - mid August and Tuesday
Rest – *(Monday - Saturday dinner only)* Carte 29/41 € 🈸
  ◆ Mediterranean ◆ Wine bar ◆
A very cosy wine bar atmosphere prevails in this little house opposite the Louis C.
Jacob Hotel. Mediterranean-style cuisine.

AT THE AIRPORT

🏨 **Courtyard by Marriott**   🛋 🛗 🕸 🔲 🅰🅲 🛰 🍸 🛃 🚗

Flughafenstr. 47 ✉ *22415 –* ✆ *(040) 53 10 20*   _VISA_ ⓜ AE ⓪
– service@airporthh.com – Fax (040) 53 10 22 22
– www.courtyard.com/hamcy
159 rm – ♦139/179 € ♦♦139/179 €, ⥤ 18 €
Rest – Carte 27/50 €
  ◆ Business ◆ Chain hotel ◆ Functional ◆
This country house style hotel is just 500 m from the airport, and stands out for its
functional but classic elegant design. Restaurant with international menu.

MUNICH
MÜNCHEN

Population: 1 205 000 (conurbation 1 656 000) – Altitude: 520m

Sime/PHOTONONSTOP

Situated in a stunning position not far north of the Alps, Munich is a cultural titan, rather unfairly overshadowed in publicity terms by its world-famous Oktoberfest bier extravaganza. Famously described as the 'village with a million inhabitants', its mix of German organisation and Italian lifestyle makes for a magical merge, with an enviable amount of Italian restaurants to seek out and enjoy.

This capital of Southern Germany boasts over forty theatres and dozens of museums, temples of culture that blend charmingly with the Bavarian love of folklore and lederhosen – the cliché actually does ring true, and locals will proudly don their traditional garb at the drop of a green hat (with jauntily set feather). Perhaps in no other world location – certainly not in Western Europe – is there such an enjoyable abundance of folk festivals and groups dedicated to playing the local music. And there's an abundance of places to see them, too: Munich is awash with Bierhallen, Bierkeller, and Biergarten. Surrounded by green fields and rolling hills (on good days, you can see across to the Alps) it's not difficult to see why Munich is currently seen as one of – if not the most – liveable city in the world.

LIVING THE CITY

The heart of Munich is the Old Town, and its epicentre the **Marienplatz** in the south and **Residenz** to the north: there are many fine historic buildings around here. Running to the east is the **River Isar**, with fine urban thoroughfares and green areas for walks. Head north for the area dissected by the **Ludwigstrasse** and **Leopoldstrasse** – **Schwabing** – which is full of students as it's the University district. To the east is the **English Garden**, a denizen of peace. West of here, the Museums district, dominated by the **Pinakothek**, is characterised by bookshops, antique stores and galleries.

PRACTICAL INFORMATION

ARRIVAL-DEPARTURE

A taxi from Airport Frank-Josef Strauss, which is 28km northeast of the city, will cost around €55. Alternatively, take the Munich S-Bahn Lines S1 or S8 to the centre, which will take 45 minutes.

TRANSPORT

On buses and trams, Munich's not the most straightforward city to travel around. It's divided into four ring-shaped price zones; zone 1 (the white zone) is the most important for visitors, as it covers the city centre. Prices rise in accordance with the amount of zones you intend to travel. If you plan to make several journeys, invest in a strip card, which costs ten euros. You can also buy a one- or three-day Tageskarte, which are good value for tourists. Available from tourist information offices, hotel receptions, travel agents and newsagents.

The underground network (U-Bahn) opened in 1971, and some stretches of the network are still not finished. It operates the same fare system as on Munich's buses and trams.

The München Welcome Card is valid for use on public transport in the city centre and for discounts of up to fifty per cent for more than thirty sights, museums, castles and palaces, city tours and bicycle hire. The card is available for one or three days.

EXPLORING MUNICH

There's really only one building you can identify as your marker for a tour of Munich, and that's the **Frauenkirche**,

the largest Gothic church in Southern Germany. Its distinctive onion domes, standing high and mighty on twin towers, have been an impressive sight since the mid-fifteenth century. Around them sits snugly the old town, a tourist mecca with an intimacy and warmth enhanced by fine historic architecture and an absence of modern buildings zooming to the sky. Aesthetically, this looks great, but the reason for it is more prosaic: if the top rung of the city's fire engines can't reach, then it won't get built...

Marienplatz is the focal point for visitors. It's the central square, just a stone's throw from Frauenkirche, and Munich life emanates from this busy, bustling hub. In its immediate vicinity stand three other distinctive churches: **Peterskirche**, built in the twelfth century, is the oldest in Munich; **Michaelskirche** is famous for its magnificent barrel vaulting; and **Asamkirche** is a riot of colourful frescoes and gold leaf. Marienplatz's town hall – the **Rathaus** – took over fifty years to build at the end of the 19C, and is a testimony to Gothic splendour, with Glockenspiel marionettes performing a daily dance high up the façade. Just up the road (or, more precisely, medieval street) from here is the majestic Residenz, the grand palatial home of the Wittelsbach dynasty who ruled over Bavaria for seven hundred years, right up until the end of the First World War. It boasts the jaw-dropping **Antiquarium** – a great hall built in the 17C – and a Rococo theatre (the **Cuvilliés**) just bursting with grand operatic pomp.

→ DRINK, ANYONE?

You might feel the need to balance all this civic glory with something a little more down-to-earth: a drink maybe. Well, just a hop, skip and jump away from Residenz, across the luxurious boulevard **Maximilianstrasse,** is what locals modestly call the most famous pub in the world. **Hofbräuhaus** was opened in 1830, and, perhaps unsurprisingly, it's the city's greatest tourist attraction. It can seat around 2,500 drinkers. There's a hall with long tables for a thousand on the ground floor, and a vaulted hall for thirteen hundred on the first. Side rooms make up the number. Every day, nearly eighteen thousand pints of beer are drunk, but Muncheners rather turn their noses up at it as a tourist honeypot. They have their more cherished and authentic bierhallen to keep them in liquid company.

If induced to claustrophobia at the thought of all that humanity reaching for a frothing litre of ale, then head to the **Viktualienmarkt**. It's another great landmark of the old town, and it celebrated its two hundredth birthday in 2007. Here you can get your beer and wine on the hoof, along with fruit and vegetables, meat and fish, cheese and flowers, sausages and salamis. This is Munich's oldest and most picturesque market, where you'll find fellow shoppers knocking back mugs of beer and tots of schnapps under canvas awnings.

→ PICTURE THIS

Head north and you hit the newer part of Munich, much of it built in the 19C. This part of town is famous for its stylish art galleries, and they don't come much more stylish than the Pinakothek, which boasts no less than three completely individual galleries each with its own distinctive allure. The oldest is the **Alte Pinakothek**, now considered one of the world's most important art galleries, with an outstanding collection of work from the 14C and 18C. Cross the road to the **Neue Pinakothek**, opened in 1853 and home to an impressive range of European art from the 19C. Most recent addition to this revered grouping is the **Pinakothek der Moderne**, opened only in 2002. As you might have guessed from the name, this is a temple to the world of modern art, architecture and design, housed in a spacious, three-floor structure of glass and concrete just demanding to be noticed by the passing public. Museums abound in this district; jostling for your attention in one compact and classy area are grand buildings with collections that include ancient classical antiquities, dazzling mineral formations, Greek and Roman sculpture, fossilised palm trees (and a mastodon), and artworks by Kandinsky, Klee, Beuys and Warhol. A respite from cultural overload can be taken at the **Old Botanical Gardens**, a short walk south from the museums. It has a delightful café garden, shaded by exotic trees.

→ IN AN ENGLISH CITY GARDEN

Mind you, when it comes to green spaces, there's nothing in the city to compare with the **English Garden**, so called because of its naturalistic landscaped style. It's one of Europe's largest city parks, and, looked at on a map, resembles a great green lung breathing life into the surrounding *strassen*. It's in a favourable position on the east side of Munich, close to the river Isar, and is a huge attraction in the summer months. You can, if you so wish, sunbathe naked here, or go for a swim in the winding streams that weave their way amongst the trees and shrubs. Many head for the 18C **Chinese Tower**, not for the view it offers (though that's good) but because it proffers a famous biergarten in its shadow. This is the university quarter: there are sixty thousand students, and the streets in the vicinity are full of life and noise. A grand boulevard runs right through, south to north. Ludwigstrasse, at the southern end, is elegantly neo-Classical in style, but as you walk northwards along Leopoldstrasse, the ambience becomes much less formal. The students come into their own, and there are pubs and swish boutiques lining the way. This is the famous Schwabing area, renowned since the late nineteenth century as a bohemian hang out, populated in its pre-World War I heyday by the likes of Thomas Mann, Kandinsky and Klee.

→ BEER IN BAVARIA

One of the main attractions of Munich lies in wait in a most fortuitous spot between the English Garden and the Isar. It's the **Bavarian National Museum** and it covers all aspects of life in this part of Germany from classical antiquity until the nineteenth century. It's laid out over three fascinating floors, and leaves barely a stone unturned if that stone may reveal an interesting nugget of Bavarian life. What it doesn't feature, ironically, is the one subject great hordes come exclusively to Munich for…the Oktoberfest. The largest beer orgy in the world takes up two weeks of September (and a little bit of October) and welcomes six million (yes, six million) visitors, who quaff around six million litres of golden stuff in fourteen giant tents. Sausages, ox meat and roast chickens are devoured in frightening proportions, and the songs hammered out with much gusto are invariably of the Bavarian kind. The Oktoberfest began life in 1810 to celebrate royal nuptials, so in two years' time it'll be putting on its two hundredth anniversary party. Imagine what *that's* going to be like…

CALENDAR HIGHLIGHTS

Festivals, many of them free, come thick and fast in Munich. The beer festivals (unfortunately, not free) kick off in March with Starkbierfest

MUNICH IN…

→ ONE DAY

The old town, Frauenkirche, English Garden, Wagner (if possible!) at the National Theatre

→ TWO DAYS

Schwabing, Pinakothek, Hofbräuhaus

→ THREE DAYS

Olympic Park, Schloss Nymphenburg, last night 'hurrah' at a traditional Bavarian inn

(The Festival of Strong Beer), carry on with the Maibockausschank at the Hofbräuhaus in May, and end with a quiet little affair in September and October…A few measures will probably be raised at the Biennale in April; this is Germany's largest contemporary music festival, heralding a host of musical events in the city. The Tollwood Festival in June, in the Olympic Park, features jazz and rock, while in July the Münchner Opernfestspiele is for opera and ballet lovers. Jazz Summer, also in July, lights up the swish Hotel Bayerischer Hof; meanwhile, rock and jazz fans are catered for in August's Theatron Music Summer in the Olympic Park's open-air theatre. The dramatic sounding Long Night of Museums is a dream for culture vultures, with over seventy museums and galleries staying open till 2am (October). Runners can get their hit also in October with the Munich Media Marathon, not a long-distance run for journos, but a twenty-six miler for one and all – over six thousand 'ordinary' runners took part in 2006.

EATING OUT

Munich is a city in which you can eat well (especially if you're not vegetarian), and in large quantities. The local specialities are meat and potatoes, with large dollops of cabbage on the side ; you won't have trouble finding roast pork and dumplings or meatloaf and don't forget the local white veal sausage or weisswurst. The meat is invariably succulent, and cabbage is often adorned with the likes of juniper berries. Potatoes, meanwhile, have a tendency to evolve into soft and buttery dumplings. And sausage? Take your pick from over 1,500 recognised species. Other specialities include Schweinshaxe (knuckle of pork) or Leberkäs (meat and offal pâté). Eating out in Munich, or anywhere in Bavaria, is an experience in itself, with the distinctive background din of laughter, singing and the clinking of mugs of Bavarian Weissbier. It's famous for the Brauereigaststätten or brewery inns. When you've found your inn, be prepared for much noise, and don't be afraid to 'muck in' on a long bench, i.e. fall into conversation of a kind with fellow diners and drinkers. If that's not your idea of a good night out, then the many Italian restaurants in the city provide an excellent alternative. Most restaurants stay open until midnight or 1am. Service is included in the bill, but it's customary to leave an extra 10 per cent tip.

→ BAROQUE

Head west from the city for the baroque palace to beat all baroque palaces. The Schloss Nymphenburg – the Nymphs' Castle - was once the home of Bavaria's monarchs, and it boasts wondrous landscaping with canals, a gallery of thirty-six beautiful women, and a museum that includes 'mad' king Ludwig's coronation coach.

→ RING FIRST

If you want a night at the opera, then head to the National Theatre, right next to the Residenz. Modelled on a Greek temple, it specialises in the work of Wagner; in fact, it's where the great man actually made his name. He would have loved the latest version of the auditorium: its décor is sky blue, ivory, purple and gold.

→ PARK LIFE

Munich's most arguably famous sight is actually a few miles to the northwest of the city itself. The Olympic Park, and its iconic Olympic Tower, was built for the 1972 Games. The hills around the park aren't natural…they were made from rubble taken away from the city at the end of World War II.

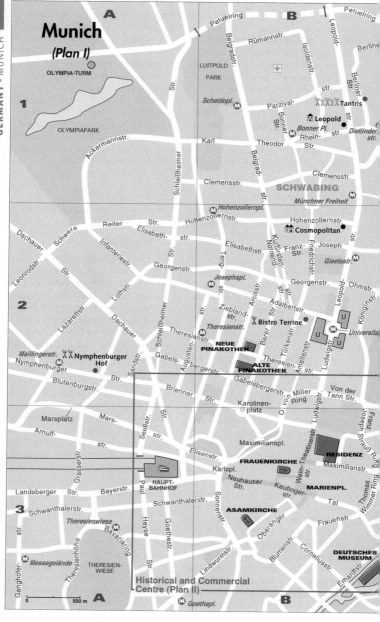

Munich
(Plan I)

OLYMPIA-TURM

OLYMPIAPARK

1

Petuelring

Belgradstr.

Rümannstr.

Petuelring

Leopold-

Berline

LUITPOLD

PARK

Scheidpl.

Parzival-

str.

Tantris

Bonner
Str.

Leopold

Bonner Pl.

Dietlinder
str.

Rhein-
Str.

Karl

Theodor
Str.

Clemensstr.

Clemensstr.

SCHWABING

Münchner Freiheit

Hohenzollernpl.

Hohenzollernstr.

Hohenzollernstr.

Cosmopolitan

Elisabethstr.

Franz-
Str.

Joseph

Giselastr.

Josephspl.

Georgenstr.

Ohmstr.

Königinstr.

Adalbertstr.

Ziebland-
str.

Theresienstr.

Bistro Terrine

Universita

**NEUE
PINAKOTHEK**

**ALTE
PINAKOTHEK**

Theresien-
str.

Maillingerstr.

Nymphenburger
Hof

Nymphenburger

Gabels-
bergerstr.

Gabelsbergerstr.

Von der
Tann Str.

Blutenburgstr.

Brienner

Str.

Karolinen-
platz

Miller

Marsplatz

Mars-

str.

Maximilianspl.

RESIDENZ

Arnulf-

FRAUENKIRCHE

Maximilianstr.

Landsberger

Str.

Bayerstr.

**HAUPT-
BAHNHOF**

Karlspl.

Neuhauser
Str.

MARIENPL.

Tal

2

3

Schwanthalerstr.

Schwanthalerstr.

ASAMKIRCHE

Frauenstr.

Theresienwiese

Bavariaring

**DEUTSCHES
MUSEUM**

Messegelände

**THERESIEN-
WIESE**

Blumenstr.

Cornelusstr.

Historical and Commercial
Centre (Plan II)

0   500 m

Goethepl.

Dachauer

Schwere

Reiter

Str.

Infanteriestr.

Leonrodstr.

Str.

Lothstr.

Lazarettstr.

Dachauer

Schleißheimer

Str.

Schleißheimer
str.

Augusten-
str.

Seidlstr.

Str.

Elisenstr.

Paul

Goethestr.

Heyse

Str.

Lindwurmstr.

Sonnenstr.

Erhardtstr.

Belgrad-
str.

Kurfürsten-
Nordend

Friedrichstr.

Leopold-

Türkenstr.

Amalienstr.

Ludwigstr.

Wein-Theatinerstr.

Ludwigstr.

Franz
Joseph Straub Ring

Thomas
Wimmer Ring

Teng-
str.

Arcisstr.

Barer
Str.

Ackermannstr.

Str.

376

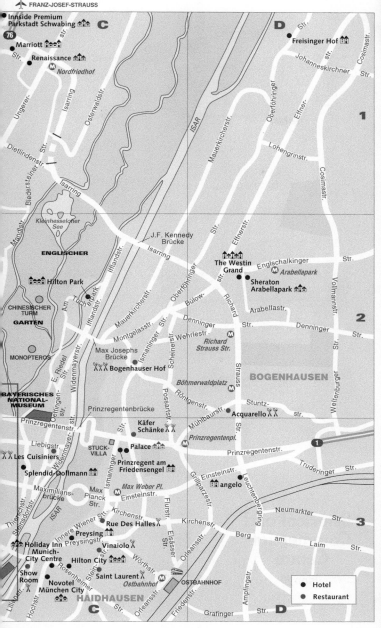

Innside Premium
Parkstadt Schwabing ᆱᆱ C

76

Marriott ᆱᆱ

Renaissance ᆱᆱ
Ⓜ Nordfriedhof

Str.

D

Freisinger Hof ᆱ

Str.
Johanneskirchner
Oberföhringer
Elfenstr.
Cosimastr.

1

Ungerer-
Str.
Isaring
Osterwaldstr.
ISAR
Mauerkircherstr.
Cosimastr.
Lohengrinstr.

Dietlindenstr.
Biedersteiner Str.
Isarring

Kleinhesseloher
See

J.F. Kennedy
Brücke
Isarring
Elfenstr.
Str.
Englschalkinger Str.

The Westin
Grand ᆱᆱᆱᆱ
Ⓜ Arabellapark

Sheraton
Arabellapark ᆱᆱ

Volmannstr.

ENGLISCHER

Hilton Park ᆱᆱ

Ifflandstr.
Am Tucherpark
Iffandstr.
Oberföhringer str.
Bülow-
Arabellastr.
Richard
Denninger Str.
Denninger Str.

2

CHINESISCHER
TURM

GARTEN

Mauerkircherstr.
Montgelasstr.
Ismaninger Str.
Scheinerstr.
Wehrlestr.
Richard
Strauss Str.

MONOPTEROS

E. Riedel Str.
Widenmayerstr.
Max Josephs
Brücke
Bogenhauser Hof ✗✗✗
Böhmerwaldplatz
Ⓜ

Strauss
BOGENHAUSEN
Wellenburgerstr.

BAYERISCHES
NATIONAL-
MUSEUM

Oettingen- str.
Prinzregentenbrücke
Possartstr.
Röntgenstr.
Stuntz-
str.

Prinzregentenstr.
Liebigstr.

Käfer
Schänke ✗✗
Mühlbaurstr.
Acquarello ✗✗

1

✗✗ Les Cuisiniers
Widenmayer str.
Ismaninger str.
STUCK-
VILLA
Palace ᆱᆱ
Prinzregentpl.
Prinzregentenstr.
Truderinger Str.

Splendid-Dollmann ᆱ

Prinzregent am
Friedensengel ᆱᆱ
Einsteinstr.
ᆱ angelo
Leuchtenbergring
Neumarkter Str.

Maximilians-
brücke
ISAR
Thierschstr.
Seitzdorfstr.
Max
Planck
Str.
Max Weber Pl.
Ⓜ
Einsteinstr.
Gillparzstr.

3

Kirchenstr.
Flurstr.
Berg
am
Laim
Str.

Innere Wiener Str.
Rue Des Halles ✗
Kirchenstr.
Elsässer Str.
Orleansstr.

Preysing ᆱ
Preysingstr.

Holiday Inn ᆱᆱ
Munich-
City Centre
Vinaiolo ✗
Hilton City ᆱᆱ
Rosenheimer Str.
Steinstr.
Wörthstr.
Ⓜ
OSTBAHNHOF

Show
Room

Novotel
München City ᆱᆱ
Saint Laurent ✗
Ostbahnhof
Orleansstr.
Friedenstr.
Amplingstr.

Hochstr.
Lilienstr.
HAIDHAUSEN
Grafinger Str.

C

D

● Hotel
● Restaurant

377

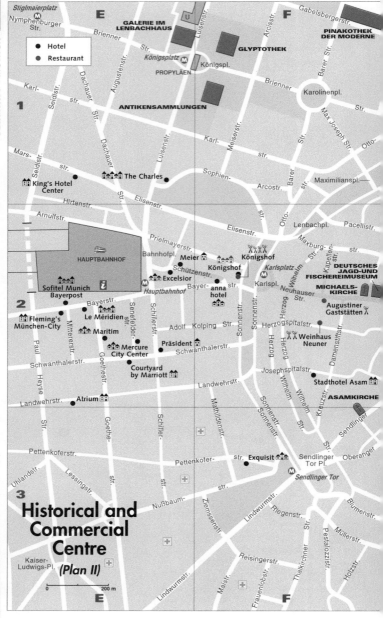

- ● Hotel
- ● Restaurant

Stiglmaierplatz
Nymphenburger Str.
GALERIE IM
LENBACHHAUS
PINAKOTHEK
DER MODERNE
Brienner Str.
GLYPTOTHEK
Königsplatz
Königspl.
PROPYLÄEN
Karolinenpl.
ANTIKENSAMMLUNGEN
Maximilianspl.
King's Hotel
Center
The Charles
Lenbachpl.
Pacellistr.
HAUPTBAHNHOF
DEUTSCHES
JAGD-UND
FISCHEREIMUSEUM
Meier
Königshof
Königshof
Karlsplatz
Schützenstr.
Excelsior
Karlspl.
MICHAELS-
KIRCHE
Sofitel Munich
Bayerpost
Hauptbahnhof
Bayer-
anna
hotel
str.
Augustiner
Gaststätten
Fleming's
München-City
Le Méridien
Weinhaus
Neuner
Maritim
Mercure
City Center
Präsident
Courtyard
by Marriott
Stadthotel Asam
Landwehrstr.
ASAMKIRCHE
Atrium
Exquisit
Sendlinger
Tor Pl.
Oberanger
Pettenkoferstr.
Sendlinger Tor

Historical and
Commercial
Centre
(Plan II)

Kaiser-
Ludwigs-Pl.

0   200 m

E   F

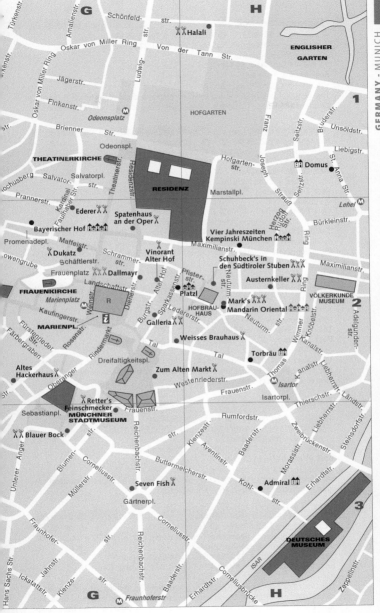

Türkenstr.

G Schönfeld- str.

× × Halali

Amalienstr.

Oskar von Miller Ring Von der Tann Str.

H

ENGLISHER GARTEN

Jägerstr.

Ludwigstr.

Seitzstr.

Bruderstr.

1

Finkenstr.

Odeonsplatz

HOFGARTEN

Franz

Unsöldstr.

Liebigstr.

Brienner Str.

Odeonpl.

St. Anna Str.

THEATINERKIRCHE

Salvator- str.

Salvatorpl.

Hofgarten- str.

Joseph

Domus

Hochusberg

Kardinal-Faulhaber Str.

Theatinerstr.

Residenzstr.

RESIDENZ

Marstallpl.

Strauß

Seitzstr.

Lehel M

Prannerstr.

Ederer × ×

Spatenhaus an der Oper ×

Vier Jahreszeiten Kempinski München

Herzog Rudolf Str.

Bürkleinstr.

Bayerischer Hof

Maffeistr.

Maximilianstr.

Promenadepl.

× Dukatz

Schäftlerstr.

Schrammer- str.

Vinorant Alter Hof

Schuhbeck's in den Südtiroler Stuben × × ×

Ring

Maximilianstr.

owengrube

Frauenplatz × × × Dallmayr

Landschaftstr.

Weinstr.

Dienerstr.

Alter Hof

Pfister- str.

Sparkassenstr.

Neuturm- str.

Austernkeller × ×

FRAUENKIRCHE

Marienplatz

R

Platzl

VÖLKERKUNDE MUSEUM

Kaufingerstr.

Fürstenfelder Str.

MARIENPL.

Rosenstr.

Burgstr.

Ledererstr.

HOFBRÄU-HAUS

Mark's × × ×

Mandarin Oriental

Neuturm- str.

Wimmer

Knöbelstr.

2

Färbergraben

Rindermarkt

Galleria × ×

Weisses Brauhaus ×

Kanalstr.

Adelgunden- str.

Dreifaltigkeitspl.

Tal

Tal

Torbräu

Thomas

Liebherrstr.

Ländstr.

Altes Hackerhaus ×

Oberanger

Zum Alten Markt ×

Westenriederstr.

Frauenstr.

M Isartor

Isartorpl.

Kanalstr.

Steinsdorfstr.

Sebastianpl.

Retter's Feinschmecker

MÜNCHNER STADTMUSEUM

Frauenstr.

Rumfordstr.

Zweibrückenstr.

Liebherrstr.

× × Blauer Bock

str.

Reichenbachstr.

str.

Klenzestr.

Baaderstr.

Aventinstr.

Morassistr.

Thierschstr.

Unterer Anger

Blumen-

Corneliusstr.

Buttermelcherstr.

Müllerstr.

Seven Fish ×

Kohl-

Admiral

Erhardtstr.

3

Gärtnerpl.

Corneliusstr.

Fraunhoferstr.

str.

Reichenbachstr.

Baaderstr.

DEUTSCHES MUSEUM

Hans Sachs Str.

Jahnstr.

Ickstattstr.

Klenze- str.

G

Fraunhoferstr M

Erhardtstr.

Corneliusbrücke

ISAR

H

Zeppelinstr.

GERMANY - MUNICH

Mandarin Oriental   🔨 AC 📺 ᵗ⁰ 🏄 🚗 VISA ⚫ AE ⓪

Neuturmstr. 1 ✉ *80331* – 🔵 *Isartor* – ✆ *(089) 29 09 80*
– *momuc-reservations@mohg.com* – *Fax (089) 22 25 39*
– *www.mandarinoriental.com*   **H2**
73 rm – ❕345/545 € ❕❕395/595 €, ⏥ 32 € – 8 suites
Rest *Mark's* – see below
♦ Grand Luxury ♦ Historic ♦ Classic ♦
This beautiful palace in the old town combines a classical, historical flair with a luxurious ambience. The unique service gives this address its exclusive nature.

Bayerischer Hof   ☂ ⅃ਠ 🌐 🏊 ◧ ⅄ 占 AC 📺 ᵗ⁰ 🏄 🚗 VISA ⚫ AE ⓪

Promenadeplatz 2 ✉ *80333* – 🔵 *Marienplatz* – ✆ *(089) 2 12 00* – *info@*
bayerischerhof.de – *Fax (089) 2 12 09 06* – *www.bayerischerhof.de*
                                                                G2
373 rm – ❕221/480 € ❕❕338/480 €, ⏥ 27 € – 21 suites
Rest *Garden-Restaurant* – ✆ *(089) 2 12 09 93 (booking advisable)* Menu 38 €
(lunch)/78 € – Carte 52/81 €
Rest *Trader Vic's* – ✆ *(089) 2 12 09 95 (dinner only)* Menu 40/77 €
– Carte 30/63 €
Rest *Palais Keller* – ✆ *(089) 2 12 09 90* – Carte 19/35 €
♦ Grand Luxury ♦ Traditional ♦ Classic ♦
The Grand Hotel dating back to 1841 is very imposing. The rooms on the VIP floor are extremely comfortable. Lovely views can be enjoyed from the spa area on three floors. International Garden Restaurant. South Sea flair in Trader Vic's. Palais-Keller: truly Bavarian

The Charles   ☂ ⅃ਠ 🌐 🏊 ◧ 占 AC 📺 📞 🏄 🚗 VISA ⚫ AE ⓪

Sophienstr. 28 ✉ *80333* – 🔵 *Hauptbahnhof* – ✆ *(089) 5 44 55 50*
– *reservations.charles@roccofortecollection.com* – *Fax (089) 54 45 55 20 00*
– *www.roccofortecollection.com*   **E1**
160 rm – ❕495/550 € ❕❕495/550 €, ⏥ 28 € – 20 suites
Rest *Davvero* – ✆ *(089) 54 45 55 12 00* – Carte 42/68 €
♦ Grand Luxury ♦ Elegant ♦
This luxury hotel is situated in the old botanic garden. The tasteful, modern furnishing impart a timeless elegance. Some rooms have a fine view of the town. Italian food is served at Davvero.

Königshof   ⅃ਠ 🏊 AC 📺 ᵗ⁰ 🏄 🚗 VISA ⚫ AE ⓪

Karlsplatz 25 ✉ *80335* – 🔵 *Karlsplatz (Stachus)* – ✆ *(089) 55 13 60*
– *koenigshof@geisel-privathotels.de* – *Fax (089) 55 13 61 13*
– *www.geisel-privathotels.de*   **F2**
87 rm – ❕245/370 € ❕❕320/485 €, ⏥ 26 € – 11 suites
Rest *Königshof* – see below
♦ Luxury ♦ Traditional ♦ Elegant ♦
This hotel right on Karlsplatz is a very pleasant address. It conceals a classical, elegant atmosphere behind its very simple façade.

Vier Jahreszeiten Kempinski   ⅃ਠ 🌐 🏊 ◧ AC 📺 📞 🏄 🚗

Maximilianstr. 17 ✉ *80539* – 🔵 *Lehel* – ✆ *(089)*   VISA ⚫ AE ⓪
2 12 50 – *reservations.vierjahreszeiten@kempinski.com* – *Fax (089) 21 25 20 00*
– *www.kempinski-vierjahreszeiten.de*   **H2**
303 rm – ❕238/460 € ❕❕279/465 €, ⏥ 34 € – 30 suites
Rest *Vue Maximilian* – Menu 49 € (lunch)/82 € – Carte 45/67 €
♦ Luxury ♦ Traditional ♦ Classic ♦
This hotel has been one of the classic grand hotels in Munich since it opened in 1858. Combines historical charm with contemporary comfort in a most attractive way. Diners in the Vue Maximilian restaurant have a view over the Maximilian-straße.

Sofitel Munich Bayerpost 🕍 🈸 🈺 🔲 ⚗ 🅰️ 🈸 📞 🎿 🚗

Bayerstr. 12 ⊠ 80335 – Ⓜ Hauptbahnhof – ☎ (089) 　　　　　　　ⅤⅠⅤⅠⅤⅠ 📀 📧 ⓪
59 94 80 – h5413@accor.com – Fax (089) 5 99 48 10 00 – www.sofitel.com
396 rm – ♦229/399 € ♦♦229/399 €, ⊆ 28 € – 14 suites 　　　　　　　　**E2**
Rest – *(closed Sunday) (dinner only)* Carte 51/65 €
Rest Suzie W. – Carte 34/37 €
　◆ Chain hotel ◆ Luxury ◆ Design ◆
This hotel with its beautiful sandstone facade is impressive with its generous framework. Tasteful avant-garde design, from the atrium lobby to the rooms. The restaurant offers an international menu. Suzie W. with its Asian-influenced cuisine.

Hilton Park 　　　　🈺 🏠 🔲 ⚗ 🅰️ 🈸 🍴 🎿 🚗 ⅤⅠⅤⅠ 📀 📧 ⓪

Am Tucherpark 7 ⊠ 80538 – ☎ (089) 3 84 50 – info.munich@hilton.com
– Fax (089) 38 45 25 88 – www.hilton.de 　　　　　　　　　　　*Plan I* **C2**
482 rm – ♦169/227 € ♦♦169/227 €, ⊆ 27 € – 3 suites
Rest Tivoli & Club – Carte 27/45 €
　◆ Chain hotel ◆ Luxury ◆ Modern ◆
Besides being located on the Englischer Garten, the benefits of this hotel also include its contemporary, well-equipped rooms. Business and executive rooms also available

Le Méridien 　　　🈺 🕍 🈸 🈺 🔲 🅰️ 🈸 📞 🎿 🚗 ⅤⅠⅤⅠ 📀 📧 ⓪

Bayerstr. 41 ⊠ 80335 – Ⓜ Hauptbahnhof – ☎ (089) 2 42 20
– info.muenchen@lemeridien.com – Fax (089) 24 22 11 11
– www.lemeridien.com/munich 　　　　　　　　　　　　　　　**E2**
381 rm – ♦199/299 € ♦♦199/299 €, ⊆ 26 € – 9 suites　　**Rest** – Carte 44/68 €
　◆ Chain hotel ◆ Luxury ◆ Design ◆
Opposite the main station, this hotel offers a contemporary, understated ambience. The rooms are furnished in high-quality rectangular style. The restaurant looks onto the pleasant courtyard garden.

Excelsior 　　　　　🈺 🏠 🔲 🅰️ 🈸 📞 🎿 🚗 ⅤⅠⅤⅠ 📀 📧 ⓪

Schützenstr. 11 ⊠ 80335 – Ⓜ Hauptbahnhof – ☎ (089) 55 13 70 – excelsior@
geisel-privathotels.de – Fax (089) 55 13 71 21 – www.geisel-privathotels.de
112 rm – ♦155/290 € ♦♦260/295 €, ⊆ 18 € 　　　　　　　　　**E2**
Rest Geisel's Vinothek – *(closed Sunday lunch)* Menu 19 € (lunch)/38 € (dinner) – Carte 31/40 €
　◆ Business ◆ Classic ◆
The rooms are individual and elegant in this hotel in the city centre. Guests can use the Königshof leisure area. Nice, rustic-style vinotheque offering a wide range of wines.

Maritim 　　　　　🈺 🏠 🔲 🅰️ 🈸 📞 🎿 🚗 ⅤⅠⅤⅠ 📀 📧 ⓪

Goethestr. 7 ⊠ 80336 – Ⓜ Hauptbahnhof – ☎ (089) 55 23 50 – info.mun@
maritim.de – Fax (089) 55 23 59 00 – www.maritim.de 　　　　　　**E2**
339 rm – ♦162/313 € ♦♦187/338 €, ⊆ 22 € – 6 suites 　　**Rest** – Carte 29/45 €
　◆ Business ◆ Functional ◆
Close to the Deutsches Theater, the Stachus and the Theresienwiese, with its tastefully elegant rooms, is where this hotel wins out. The grill-room and bistro restaurants serve international cuisine.

Exquisit 　　　　　🏠 ⚗ 🔲 🍴 🎿 🚗 ⅤⅠⅤⅠ 📀 📧 ⓪

Pettenkoferstr. 3 ⊠ 80336 – Ⓜ Sendlinger Tor – ☎ (089) 5 51 99 00 – info@
hotel-exquisit.com – Fax (089) 55 19 94 99 – www.hotel-exquisit.com
50 rm ⊆ – ♦145/230 € ♦♦175/285 € – 5 suites 　　　　　　　　**F3**
Rest – *(closed August, Saturday - Sunday and bank holidays lunch only)*
Menu 13 € (buffet) – Carte 20/30 €
　◆ Business ◆ Classic ◆
This well-managed hotel not far from the Sendlinger Tor is characterised by a classical style and high quality facilities. Modern bistro with a small menu.

anna hotel

Schützenstr. 1 ⊠ 80335 – Ⓜ Karlsplatz (Stachus) – ℰ (089) 59 99 40
– anna@geisel-privathotels.de – Fax (089) 59 99 43 33
– www.geisel-privathotel.de **F2**
73 rm ⊑ – ♥175/230 € ♥♥195/370 €   **Rest** – Menu 33 € – Carte 30/44 €
♦ Business ♦ Modern ♦

Modern design is what marks the atmosphere of this comfortable hotel, right on the Stachus. The rooms have state of the art technology, with panoramic views on the top floor. Bistro-style restaurant and sushi bar

Mercure City Center

Senefelder Str. 9 ⊠ 80336 – Ⓜ Hauptbahnhof
– ℰ (089) 55 13 20 – h0878@accor.com – Fax (089) 59 64 44
– www.mercure.com **E2**
167 rm – ♥164/189 € ♥♥164/189 €, ⊑ 19 €   **Rest** – Carte 29/43 €
♦ Chain hotel ♦ Modern ♦

A modern-style and warm colours surround you from the reception area to the well-equipped rooms in this hotel. Located near the main station. Opening off the lobby, the restaurant features international fare.

Platzl

Sparkassenstr. 10 ⊠ 80331 – Ⓜ Marienplatz – ℰ (089) 23 70 30 – info@
platzl.de – Fax (089) 23 70 38 00 – www.platzl.de **G2**
167 rm ⊑ – ♥99/232 € ♥♥192/244 €
Rest Pfistermühle – ℰ (089) 23 70 38 65 (closed Sunday) Carte 36/49 €
Rest Ayingers – ℰ (089) 23 70 36 66 – Carte 20/38 €
♦ Traditional ♦ Cosy ♦

Hotel in the centre of the Old Town, with rooms very successfully combining classic and modern style. Recreation area in the style of Ludwig II's Moorish Kiosk. Old Munich flair awaits you under the vaults of the Pfistermühle. Ayingers offers tavern tradition

Stadthotel Asam without rest

Josephspitalstr. 3 ⊠ 80331 – Ⓜ Sendlinger Tor – ℰ (089) 2 30 97 00
– info@hotel-asam.de – Fax (089) 23 09 70 97 – www.hotel-asam.de
– closed over Christmas **F2**
25 rm – ♥142/160 € ♥♥173/190 €, ⊑ 17 € – 8 suites
♦ Business ♦ Personalised ♦

A small hotel with a touch of luxury in the city centre. The rooms are stylish and tasteful with very carefully chosen details.

Courtyard by Marriott

Schwanthalerstr. 37 ⊠ 80336 – Ⓜ Hauptbahnhof – ℰ (089) 54 88 48 80
– Fax (089) 54 88 48 83 33 – www.courtyardmunichcitycenter.com
248 rm – ♥149/189 € ♥♥149/189 €, ⊑ 19 € **E2**
Rest – Carte 23/38 €
♦ Business ♦ Modern ♦

Located in the city centre, not far from the railway station, is this hotel with contemporary rooms and studios aimed at business travellers. Good breakfast buffet.

Torbräu

Tal 41 ⊠ 80331 – Ⓜ Isartor – ℰ (089) 24 23 40 – info@torbraeu.de – Fax (089)
24 23 42 35 – www.torbraeu.de **H2**
91 rm ⊑ – ♥149/272 € ♥♥189/381 € – 3 suites
Rest La Famiglia – ℰ (089) 22 80 75 33 – Carte 35/48 €
♦ Traditional ♦ Classic ♦

Built in the 15C, this hotel must be the oldest in the city. Pleasant spacious rooms, all with air conditioning. Tuscan flair and Italian cuisine in the terracotta-tiled "La Famiglia".

GERMANY - MUNICH

Admiral without rest
`SAT` `📡` `🚗` `VISA` `◎◎` `AE` `①`

Kohlstr. 9 ✉ *80469 –* **Ⓜ** *Isartor –* ℰ *(089) 21 63 50 – info@hotel-admiral.de*
– Fax (089) 29 36 74 – www.hotel-admiral.de **H3**
32 rm ⌂ – 🛏170/220 € 🛏🛏200/250 €
♦ Business ♦ Functional ♦

Just a few minutes by foot from the City Centre this hotel has functional rooms, some of which are extremely quiet. In fine weather you can enjoy breakfast in the small garden.

King's Hotel Center without rest
`&` `SAT` `📡` `VISA` `◎◎` `AE` `①`

Marsstr. 15 ✉ *80335 –* ℰ *(089) 51 55 30 – center@kingshotels.de – Fax (089) 51 55 33 00 – www.kingshotels.de* **E1**
90 rm – 🛏99/140 € 🛏🛏140/160 €, ⌂ 12 €
♦ Business ♦ Cosy ♦

A wooden lobby welcomes guests in this hotel located close to the centre of town. Carefully worked canopy beds make the rooms particularly cosy.

Atrium without rest
`🦢` `SAT` `📡` `🏋` `🚗` `VISA` `◎◎` `AE` `①`

Landwehrstr. 59 ✉ *80336 –* **Ⓜ** *Theresienwiese –* ℰ *(089) 51 41 90 – info@atrium-hotel.de – Fax (089) 53 50 66 – www.atrium-hotel.de* **E2**
160 rm ⌂ – 🛏129/159 € 🛏🛏159/189 €
♦ Business ♦ Functional ♦

This hotel with its contemporary, functional rooms and small green courtyard is located between the main station and Theresienwiese.

Splendid-Dollmann without rest
`📡` `VISA` `◎◎` `AE`

Thierschstr. 49 ✉ *80538 –* **Ⓜ** *Lehel –* ℰ *(089) 23 80 80 – splendid-muc@t-online.de – Fax (089) 23 80 83 65 – www.hotel-splendid-dollmann.de*
36 rm – 🛏130/170 € 🛏🛏160/200 €, ⌂ 13 € *Plan I* **C3**
♦ Historic ♦ Personalised ♦

This 19C middle class house has a stylish lobby, presented as a library. Find individually decorated rooms, some with antiques, and a pretty breakfast room with an arched ceiling.

Fleming's München-City
`🛗` `🦢` `&` `AC` `SAT` `📡` `🏋` `🚗`

Bayerstr. 47 ✉ *80335 –* **Ⓜ** *Hauptbahnhof –* ℰ *(089)* `VISA` `◎◎` `AE` `①`
4 44 46 60 – muenchen-city@flemings-hotels.com – Fax (089) 4 44 46 69 99
– www.flemings-hotels.com **E2**
112 rm ⌂ – 🛏115/206 € 🛏🛏141/242 € **Rest** – Carte 19/41 €
♦ Business ♦ Modern ♦

Centrally located near the main railway station, this hotel offers functional, modern rooms. Bistro-style restaurant with bar and delicatessen.

Domus
`SAT` `📞` `🚗` `VISA` `◎◎`

St.-Anna-Str. 31 ✉ *80538 –* **Ⓜ** *Lehel –* ℰ *(089) 2 17 77 30 – reservation@domus-hotel.de – Fax (089) 2 28 53 59 – www.domus-hotel.de*
– closed over Christmas **H1**
45 rm ⌂ – 🛏110/165 € 🛏🛏145/200 €
Rest *facile* – ℰ *(089) 21 77 73 67 (closed Saturday lunch, Sunday and bank holidays)* Carte 26/36 €
♦ Business ♦ Functional ♦

Embedded between the Maximilianstrasse and Prinzregentenstrasse, this tastefully furnished establishment is ideal as a base from which to explore the town's art, culture and shopping. Modern atmosphere and Italian cuisine served.

Präsident without rest
`SAT` `📡` `🏋` `VISA` `◎◎` `AE` `①`

Schwanthalerstr. 20 ✉ *80336 –* **Ⓜ** *Hauptbahnhof –* ℰ *(089) 5 49 00 60*
– hotel.praesident@t-online.de – Fax (089) 54 90 06 28
– www.hotel-praesident.de **E2**
42 rm – 🛏79/151 € 🛏🛏95/194 €
♦ Business ♦ Functional ♦

The location of this fairly central hotel is ideal for theatre-goers and is diagonally opposite is the Deutsche Theater. Contemporary rooms with light-coloured wooden furniture.

GERMANY - MUNICH

Meier without rest ☺ 🛜 💳 ⚏ 🄰🄴 ⓘ
Schützenstr. 12 ⊠ 80335 – Ⓜ Hauptbahnhof – 𝒞 (089) 5 49 03 40 – info@
hotel-meier.de – Fax (089) 5 49 03 43 40 – www.hotel-meier.de
– closed 24 - 27 December **E2**
50 rm ⊊ – ✝98/108 € ✝✝128/138 €
 ♦ Business ♦ Functional ♦
This multi-floored hotel between the main station and Stachus offers visitors uniform, functional rooms.

🗙🗙🗙🗙 **Könighof** – Hotel Königshof ≤ 🄰🄲 🛜 💳 ⚏ 🄰🄴 ⓘ
❀ *Karlsplatz 25 (1st floor) ⊠ 80335 – Ⓜ Karlsplatz (Stachus) – 𝒞 (089)*
55 13 61 42 – koenigshof@geisel-privathotels.de – Fax (089) 55 13 61 13
– www.geisel-privathotels.de
– closed 1 - 11 January, 27 July - 7 September and Sunday - Monday, October
- December: Sunday only **F2**
Rest – *(booking advisable)* Menu 42 € (lunch)/130 € – Carte 64/82 € 🍴
Spec. Marinierte Königsmakrele mit Couscous und Curry. Medaillon vom Reh
mit Hagebuttenpovesen und Sellerie. Gâteau vom Kaffee mit Himbeeren
und Carripoulé.
 ♦ Classic ♦ Elegant ♦
Contemporary cuisine based on classical recipes is served at the impeccably set
tables of this refined restaurant. The window seats afford an interesting view of
the Stachus.

🗙🗙🗙 **Dallmayr** 🄰🄲 🛜 💳 ⚏ 🄰🄴
❀❀ *Dienerstr. 14 (1st floor) ⊠ 80331 – Ⓜ Marienplatz – 𝒞 (089) 2 13 51 00*
– gastro@dallmayr.de – Fax (089) 2 13 54 43 – www.dallmayr.de
– closed 1 week January, 3 weeks August, Sunday - Monday and bank holidays
Rest – *(booking advisable)* Menu 59 € (lunch)/125 € **G2**
– Carte 68/96 € 🍴
Spec. Gâteau von Gänseleber mit Bitterschokolade und als geeiste Crème
mit Melone. Confierte Rotbarbe mit Spargel und Bottarga-Tomatenjus. Tau-
benbrust im Champignonkopf mit Poweraden und Sommertrüffeljus.
 ♦ Innovative ♦ Elegant ♦
On the first floor of the tradition-rich delicatessen in the town centre is a top qua-
lity restaurant. Find a very pleasant atmosphere and innovative cuisine.

🗙🗙🗙 **Mark's** – Hotel Mandarin Oriental 🄰🄲 🛜 💳 ⚏ 🄰🄴 ⓘ
❀ *Neuturmstr. 1 (1st floor) ⊠ 80331 – Ⓜ Isartor – 𝒞 (089) 29 09 88 75*
– Fax (089) 22 25 39 – www.mandarinoriental.com
– closed Monday **H2**
Rest – Menu 65/155 € – Carte 61/84 €
Spec. Komposition von Kaninchen mit schwarzem Olivenöl und gefüllter
Gemüse-Chartreuse. St. Pierre und Hummer auf Safran-Erbsenrisotto mit wei-
ßer Tomatenbutter. Suprême von der Taube auf Blumenkohl-Schnittlauch-
mousseline mit Rotweinschalotten und Brandteigtascherl.
 ♦ Classic ♦ Elegant ♦
In the gallery above the hotel foyer contemporary cookery on a classic basis can be
enjoyed in elegant surroundings. Friendly and competent personnel.

🗙🗙🗙 **Schuhbecks in den Südtiroler Stuben** ⇆ 🛜 💳 ⚏ 🄰🄴 ⓘ
❀ *Platzl 6 ⊠ 80331 – Ⓜ Isartor – 𝒞 (089) 2 16 69 00 – info@schuhbeck.de*
– Fax (089) 21 66 90 25 – www.schubeck.de
– closed 2 weeks early January, Sunday - Monday lunch and bank holidays
Rest – *(booking essential)* Menu 78/113 € 🍴 **H2**
Spec. Scheiben von der Rinderhaxe mit Sellerie-Trüffelmarinade und geba-
ckenem Kalbskopf. Gebratenes und Pochiertes vom "Alpenlachs" mit Kopfsa-
latherzen und Schinken-Grießravioli. Karamellisierter Rhabarber-Grießstrudel
mit Mandelgebäck und Rhabarbereis.
 ♦ Regional ♦ Rustic ♦
In his elegant, wood-panelled restaurant on the little square Alfons Schuhbeck serves very tasty and uncomplicated regional dishes.

XX **G** 🛱 AC VISA ⊙⊙ AE

Geyerstr. 52 (by Lindwurmstraße A3 and Kapuzinerstraße) ✉ *80469 – ℰ (089) 74 74 79 99 – info@g-munich.de – Fax (089) 74 74 79 29 – www.g-munich.de – closed 24 December - 6 January and Sunday - Monday*
Rest *– (dinner only) (booking advisable)* Menu 74/98 € – Carte 58/81 €
♦ Inventive ♦ Fashionable ♦
A purist contemporary restaurant offering guests creative cuisine. Sit back on elegant leather-upholstered seats in the stylish lounge.

XX **Blauer Bock** 🛱 AE

Sebastiansplatz 9 ✉ *80331 –* Ⓜ *Marienplatz – ℰ (089) 45 22 23 33 – mail@ restaurant-blauerbock.de – Fax (089) 45 22 23 30 – www.restaurant-blauerbock.de – closed 1 week August, Sunday and bank holidays* **G3**
Rest – Menu 25 € (lunch)/63 € (dinner) – Carte 54/71 €
♦ International ♦ Minimalist ♦
This modern restaurant is just a few steps from the Viktualienmarkt. It offers international cuisine and a pleasant terrace.

XX **Halali** VISA ⊙⊙ AE

Schönfeldstr. 22 ✉ *80539 –* Ⓜ *Odeonsplatz – ℰ (089) 28 59 09 – halali-muenchen@t-online.de – Fax (089) 28 27 86 – www.restaurant-halali.de – closed Saturday lunch, Sunday and bank holidays* **H1**
Rest *– (booking advisable)* Menu 25 € (lunch)/56 € – Carte 34/55 €
♦ International ♦ Cosy ♦
This 19C guesthouse has a comfortable, elegant, rustic restaurant that is highly regarded by many regulars.

XX **Ederer** 🛱 AC VISA ⊙⊙ AE

Kardinal-Faulhaber-Str. 10 (1st floor) ✉ *80333 –* Ⓜ *Odeonsplatz – ℰ (089) 24 23 13 10 – restaurant-ederer@t-online.de – Fax (089) 24 23 13 12 – www.restaurant-ederer.de – closed 1 week during Christmas, Sunday and bank holidays* **G2**
Rest *– (booking advisable)* Menu 37 € (lunch)/70 € (dinner) – Carte 42/78 € ♨
♦ International ♦ Fashionable ♦
This restaurant decorated with modern art is located in a historical townhouse. The international cuisine is also served in the inner courtyard.

XX **Austernkeller** VISA ⊙⊙ AE ⓪

Stollbergstr. 11 ✉ *80539 –* Ⓜ *Isartor – ℰ (089) 29 87 87 – Fax (089) 22 31 66 – www.austernkeller.de – closed 23 - 26 December* **H2**
Rest *– (dinner only) (booking advisable)* Carte 32/52 €
♦ Fish ♦ Cosy ♦
Guests particularly enjoy fish and seafood in this listed cellar vault decorated with porcelain plates.

XX **Nymphenburger Hof** 🛱 AC VISA ⊙⊙ AE

Nymphenburger Str. 24 ✉ *80335 –* Ⓜ *Maillingerstr. – ℰ (089) 1 23 38 30 – Fax (089) 1 23 38 52 – www.nymphenburgerhof.de – closed 24 December - 8 January, Saturday lunch, Sunday and bank holidays*
Rest *– (booking advisable)* Menu 22 € (lunch)/78 € (dinner)   *Plan I* **A2**
– Carte 36/58 €
♦ International ♦ Friendly ♦
International cuisine with Austrian influences is served in this restaurant. Dining is also on the pleasant terrace in front of the restaurant.

XX **Galleria** AC VISA ⊙⊙ AE ⓪

Sparkassenstr. 11 (corner Ledererstraße) ✉ *80331 –* Ⓜ *Marienplatz – ℰ (089) 29 79 95 – ristorantegalleria@yahoo.de – Fax (089) 2 91 36 53 – closed Sunday* **G2**
Rest *– (booking advisable)* Menu 25 € (lunch)/55 € – Carte 38/45 €
♦ Italian ♦ Cosy ♦
A small, cosy restaurant in the inner city with Italian cuisine. Temporary art displays in the dining area.

GERMANY - MUNICH

XX **Weinhaus Neuner** ⇔ 𝘝𝘐𝘚𝘈 ⓒⓢ Æ

Herzogspitalstr. 8 ✉ *80331* – Ⓜ *Karlsplatz (Stachus)* – ℰ *(089) 2 60 39 54*
– info@weinhaus-neuner.de – Fax (089) 26 69 33 – www.weinhaus-neuner.de
– closed Sunday and bank holidays **F2**
Rest – Menu 18 € (lunch)/37 € – Carte 33/48 €
♦ International ♦ Traditional ♦
This comfortable, elegant address is steeped in tradition and dates back to the
16C. The lovely cross-shaped vaults, old panelling and impressive carvings have
been maintained in their original style.

XX **Les Cuisiniers** 🍴 𝘝𝘐𝘚𝘈 ⓒⓢ

Reitmorstr. 21 ✉ *80538* – Ⓜ *Lehel* – ℰ *(089) 23 70 98 90 – Fax (089)*
23 70 98 91 – www.lescuisiniers.de
– closed Saturday lunch, Sunday - Monday *Plan I* **C3**
Rest – Carte 32/45 €
♦ Mediterranean ♦ Bistro ♦
This friendly, bistro type restaurant is light with modern pictures adorning the
walls. Uncomplicated Mediterranean cuisine.

X **Seven Fish** 🍴 𝘝𝘐𝘚𝘈 ⓒⓢ Æ

Gärtnerplatz 6 ✉ *80469* – Ⓜ *Fraunhoferstr.* – ℰ *(089) 23 00 02 19 – info@*
seven-fish.de – Fax (089) 48 95 21 81 – www.sevenfish.de
Rest – Menu 49 € – Carte 40/55 € **G3**
♦ Fish ♦ Fashionable ♦
Creative fish dishes prepared from quality produce and served by friendly staff in a
modern atmosphere. A selection of Greek wines. More modest menu at lunch.

X **Dukatz** 🍴 𝘈𝘊 𝘝𝘐𝘚𝘈 ⓒⓢ

Maffeistr. 3a (1st floor) ✉ *80333* – Ⓜ *Marienplatz* – ℰ *(089) 7 10 40 73 73*
– info@dukatz.de – Fax (089) 7 10 40 73 74 – www.dukatz.de
– closed Sunday and bank holidays **G2**
Rest – (booking advisable) Carte 24/49 €
♦ French ♦ Bistro ♦
Pleasant bistro-style atmosphere in this restaurant centrally located in the Schäff-
lerhof. Friendly staff serving French cuisine.

X **Show Room** 🍴

Lilienstr. 6 ✉ *81669* – ℰ *(089) 44 42 90 82 – info@schweiger2.de – Fax (089)*
44 42 90 82 – www.schweiger2.de
– closed 17 - 30 August, 24 December - 6 January, Sunday and bank holidays
Rest – (dinner only) (booking advisable) Menu 45/99 € *Plan I* **C3**
– Carte 39/50 €
♦ Inventive ♦ Friendly ♦
The chef recommends his creative dishes to guests at the table in this small,
modern restaurant.

X **Vinorant Alter Hof** 🍴 𝘝𝘐𝘚𝘈 ⓒⓢ Æ

Alter Hof 3 ✉ *80331* – Ⓜ *Marienplatz* – ℰ *(089) 24 24 37 33 – mail@*
alter-hof-muenchen.de – Fax (089) 24 24 37 34 – www.alter-hof-muenchen.de
Rest – Carte 26/38 € **G2**
♦ Regional ♦ Rustic ♦
At the former Wittelsbach residence, one of the oldest buildings in Munich, guests
dine in two halls with attractive vaulted ceilings and simple modern decoration.
Downstairs there is a vinotheque and bar.

X **Retter's Feinschmecker** 𝘝𝘐𝘚𝘈 ⓒⓢ

Frauenstr. 10 ✉ *80469* – Ⓜ *Isartor* – ℰ *(089) 23 23 79 23 – info@retters.de*
– Fax (089) 23 23 79 21 – www.retters.de
– closed 1 - 6 January, 1 - 15 June, Sunday - Monday and bank holidays
Rest – Menu 27 € (lunch)/50 € (dinner) **G3**
♦ Seasonal cuisine ♦ Cosy ♦
Facing the market is this appealing bistro-like restaurant with its antique pine
panelling. Seasonal dishes are served in the form of daily changing menus.

GERMANY - MUNICH

Zum Alten Markt

Dreifaltigkeitsplatz 3 ✉ *80331* – **M** *Marienplatz* – ☎ *(089) 29 99 95*
– lehner.gastro@zumaltenmarkt.de – Fax (089) 2 28 50 76
– www.zumaltenmarkt.de
– closed Sunday and bank holidays **G2**
Rest – Menu 39 € – Carte 22/36 €
◆ Regional ◆ Cosy ◆

This establishment on the Viktualienmarkt is very cosy. It has lavish wood panelling
in the style of a South Tyrolean councillor's parlour, part of which is authentic and
over 400-years-old.

Spatenhaus an der Oper

Residenzstr. 12 ✉ *80333* – **M** *Marienplatz* – ☎ *(089) 2 90 70 60* – *spatenhaus@*
kuffler.de – Fax (089) 2 91 30 54 – www.kuffler.de **G2**
Rest – Carte 23/44 €
◆ Bavarian specialities ◆ Traditional ◆

This townhouse, which is more than 100-years-old, is home to a pleasant, traditional-style restaurant. The different rooms on the first floor are particularly pleasant.

Weisses Bräuhaus

Tal 7 ✉ *80331* – **M** *Isartor* – ☎ *(089) 2 90 13 80* – *info@weisses-brauhaus.de*
– Fax (089) 29 01 38 15 – www.weisses-brauhaus.de **G2**
Rest – Carte 18/33 €
◆ Bavarian specialities ◆ Cosy ◆

This house in the Old Town, built around 1900, has a fine façade and cosy furnishings. The restaurant serves authentic regional specialities.

Augustiner Gaststätten

Neuhauser Str. 27 ✉ *80331* – **M** *Karlsplatz (Stachus)* – ☎ *(089) 23 18 32 57*
– mail@augustiner-restaurant.com – Fax (089) 2 60 53 79
– www.augustiner-restaurant.com **F2**
Rest – Carte 16/37 €
◆ Bavarian specialities ◆ Traditional ◆

Until 1885, beer was still brewed in the Augustinians' "headquarters" on the Neuhauser Strasse. An arcaded garden and a "Muschelsaal" are among the monuments of Munich's Art Nouveau period. Lovely beer garden.

Altes Hackerhaus

Sendlinger Str. 14 ✉ *80331* – **M** *Marienplatz* – ☎ *(089) 2 60 50 26*
– hackerhaus@aol.com – Fax (089) 2 60 50 27 – www.hackerhaus.de **G2**
Rest – Carte 18/51 €
◆ Bavarian specialities ◆ Cosy ◆

The lovingly decorated rooms of this inn are really cosy with their rustic panelling
and sturdy seating. Extremely pretty inner courtyard terrace. Good home cooking.

ENVIRONS
Plan I

The Westin Grand

Arabellastr. 6 ✉ *81925* – **M** *Arabellapark* – ☎ *(089)*
9 26 40 – grandhotel.muenchen@arabellastarwood.com – Fax (089) 92 64 86 99
– www.sheraton.com/grandmunich **D2**
629 rm – †139/493 € ††139/493 €, ⌷ 27 € – 28 suites
Rest – *(closed Sunday) (lunch only)* Carte 31/41 €
Rest *Die Ente vom Lehel* – ☎ *(089) 92 64 81 12 (closed August- early September, 25 December - 7 January and Sunday - Monday) (dinner only)*
Menu 66/96 € – Carte 51/66 €
Rest *Paulaner's* – ☎ *(089) 92 64 81 15 (closed Saturday lunch, Sunday and
bank holidays lunch)* Carte 24/46 €
◆ Business ◆ Luxury ◆ Contemporary ◆

A luxurious hotel with an impressive lobby and large conference area. The top four
floors convey an atmosphere of exclusivity, with the Towers rooms and their own
lounge. A lively atmosphere welcomes you in the elegant Ente vom Lehel, which is
open to the foyer.

GERMANY - MUNICH

Marriott 🔥 📶 🖥 ⅙ 🅰 📺 📞 🛎 🚗 VISA ⚙ 🅰🅴 ⓪

Berliner Str. 93 ✉ *80805 –* ⓜ *Nordfriedhof*
– 🌐 *(089) 36 00 20 – muenchen.marriott@marriotthotels.com*
– Fax (089) 36 00 22 00 – www.marriott-muenchen.de   **C1**
348 rm – 🛏119/199 € 🛏🛏119/199 €, ⌷ 24 € – 4 suites   **Rest** – Carte 29/40 €
♦ Luxury ♦ Chain hotel ♦ Contemporary ♦
A comfortable business hotel in a generous, elegant setting with cosy rooms offering high-tech fittings. Massage and beauty treatments also available. Modern restaurant with an international menu.

Hilton City 🔥 🕌 🅰 📺 📞 🛎 🚗 VISA ⚙ 🅰🅴 ⓪

Rosenheimer Str. 15 ✉ *81667 –* 🌐 *(089) 4 80 40 – info.munich@hilton.com*
– Fax (089) 48 04 48 04 – www.hilton.de   **C3**
480 rm – 🛏215/470 € 🛏🛏215/470 €, ⌷ 28 € – 4 suites   **Rest** – Carte 28/44 €
♦ Chain hotel ♦ Contemporary ♦
This hotel is next to the Philharmonie and the Gasteig Cultural Centre. It has
contemporary, functional rooms and is tailored primarily to the needs of the
business traveller. Regional and international cuisine is served in this rustic
restaurant.

Palace 🚗 🕌 📶 📺 📞 🛎 🚗 VISA ⚙ 🅰🅴

Trogerstr. 21 ✉ *81675 –* ⓜ *Prinzregentenplatz –* 🌐 *(089) 41 97 10 – palace@*
kuffler.de – Fax (089) 41 97 18 19 – www.muenchenpalace.de   **C3**
74 rm – 🛏185/320 € 🛏🛏230/350 €, ⌷ 24 €   **Rest** – Carte 34/49 €
♦ Business ♦ Classic ♦
The friendly service and extremely homely rooms with Louis XVI style furniture
make this an extremely pleasant address. The pretty garden and roof terrace are
perfect places to relax. Timelessly elegant Palace restaurant.

Innside Premium Parkstadt Schwabing 🕌 🔥 📶 🅰 📺 📞

Mies-van-der-Rohe-Str. 10 ✉ *80807 –* 🌐 *(089)* 🛎 🚗 VISA ⚙ 🅰🅴 ⓪
35 40 80 – muenchen.schwabing@innside.de – Fax (089) 35 40 82 99
– www.innside.de   **C1**
160 rm ⌷ – 🛏190/220 € 🛏🛏220/250 €
Rest – *(closed Saturday lunch, Sunday lunch and bank holidays)* Carte 33/46 €
♦ Business ♦ Functional ♦
This hotel has a thoroughly modern design, from the fully glazed façade through
to the reception area and the pleasant, bright rooms. Bistro-style restaurant with
interesting lighting. International cuisine is served.

Renaissance 🕌 🔥 📶 📺 📞 🛎 🚗 VISA ⚙ 🅰🅴 ⓪

Theodor-Dombart-Str. 4 (corner Berliner Straße) ✉ *80805 –* ⓜ *Nordfriedhof*
– 🌐 *(089) 36 09 90 – rhi.mucbr.fom@renaissancehotels.com – Fax (089)*
3 60 99 65 00 – www.marriott.com/mucbr   **C1**
261 rm – 🛏149/199 € 🛏🛏149/199 €, ⌷ 24 € – 40 suites
Rest – Carte 24/41 €
♦ Chain hotel ♦ Contemporary ♦
This business hotel close to the English Garden offers cosy, spacious rooms and
extremely roomy, elegant suites and junior suites. This restaurant, known as 46°-
47°, is in a modern bistro-style and has an internal courtyard terrace.

Novotel München City 🕌 🔥 📶 🖥 ⅙ 🅰 📺 📞 🛎 🚗

Hochstr. 11 ✉ *81669 –* 🌐 *(089) 66 10 70 – h3280@* VISA ⚙ 🅰🅴 ⓪
accor.com – Fax (089) 66 10 79 99 – www.novotel.com   **C3**
307 rm – 🛏119/169 € 🛏🛏142/192 €, ⌷ 19 €   **Rest** – Carte 27/46 €
♦ Business ♦ Modern ♦
The well-equipped rooms of this business hotel are presented in pleasant tones
and with smart design, some with a lovely view of the inner city. Light, contemporary restaurant.

Holiday Inn Munich - City Centre

Hochstr. 3 ⊠ 81669 – ℰ (089) 4 80 30 – hi.muenchen@
whgen.com – Fax (089) 4 48 71 70 – www.munich-meeting-centre.de   VISA ◯◯ AE ◯
582 rm – †149/249 € ††169/269 €, ⊆ 20 €   **C3**
Rest – Carte 19/28 €
◆ Conference hotel ◆ Contemporary ◆
A modern hotel intended for business guests with functional guestrooms and a spacious conference area.

Sheraton Arabellapark

Arabellastr. 5 ⊠ 81925 – Ⓜ Arabellapark – ℰ (089)   VISA ◯◯ AE ◯
9 23 20 – sheraton.arabellapark.muenchen@arabellastarwood.com – Fax (089)
92 32 44 49 – www.sheraton.com/arabellapark   **D2**
446 rm – †175/328 € ††175/328 €, ⊆ 23 € – 37 suites
Rest – Carte 32/58 €
◆ Business ◆ Modern ◆
This high rise building near the English Garden offers a comfortable ambience and fantastic view. A clean, modern, multifunctional style sets the scene here. Restaurant serving international cuisine.

Cosmopolitan without rest

Hohenzollernstr. 5 ⊠ 80801 – Ⓜ Münchner Freiheit – ℰ (089) 38 38 10
– cosmopolitan@geisel-privathotels.de – Fax (089) 38 38 11 11
– www.geisel-privathotels.de   **B2**
71 rm ⊆ – †125/190 € ††135/200 €
◆ Business ◆ Functional ◆
Two annexed houses in the heart of Schwabing provide contemporary rooms with functional furnishings and modern, technical equipment.

Prinzregent am Friedensengel without rest

Ismaninger Str. 42 ⊠ 81675
– Ⓜ Prinzregentenplatz – ℰ (089) 41 60 50 – friedensengel@prinzregent.de
– Fax (089) 41 60 54 66 – www.prinzregent.de
– closed 23 December-5 January
65 rm – †139/219 € ††164/270 €   **C3**
◆ Business ◆ Cosy ◆
This hotel, with its comfortable Alpine-style rooms is just five minutes from the Englischer Garten. Breakfast room with fine settings and conservatory.

Freisinger Hof

Oberföhringer Str. 189 ⊠ 81925 – ℰ (089) 95 23 02 – office@freisinger-hof-de
– Fax (089) 9 57 85 16 – www.freisinger-hof.de   **D1**
51 rm ⊆ – †115/125 € ††145/150 €   **Rest** – Carte 28/49 €
◆ Country house ◆ Cosy ◆
This old tavern from 1875 has been extended with a hotel annex. Look forward to good, homely country-style rooms. Regional cuisine is served in a cosy, rustic ambience.

angelo

Leuchtenbergring 20 ⊠ 81677 – Ⓜ Prinzregentenpl. – ℰ (089) 1 89 08 60
– info@angelo-munich.com – Fax (089) 1 89 08 61 74 – www.angelo-munich.com
146 rm ⊆ – †165/315 € ††225/315 €   **Rest** – Carte 24/38 €   **D3**
◆ Business ◆ Contemporary ◆
This well-appointed business hotel with a modern style has direct access to the rapid transit network. Pictures of jazz legends adorn the lobby and bar. Bistro-style restaurant.

Preysing without rest

Preysingstr. 1 / Stubenvollstr. 2 ⊠ 81667 – ℰ (089) 45 84 50 – info@
hotel-preysing.de – Fax (089) 45 84 54 44 – www.hotel-preysing.de
– closed 20 December - 6 January   **C3**
62 rm ⊆ – †145/220 € ††198/280 € – 5 suites
◆ Townhouse ◆ Cosy ◆
This extremely well kept hotel has contemporary granite floors in the guestrooms. Particularly suited to business travellers.

GERMANY - MUNICH

Leopold ⌂ 🖵 📶 SAT 📡 🚆 P 🚗 VISA ⓜ AE

Leopoldstr. 119 ✉ 80804 – Ⓜ Dietlindenstr. – ℰ (089) 36 04 30
– hotel-leopold@t-online.de – Fax (089) 36 04 31 50 – www.hotel-leopold.de
– closed 22 - 31 December **B1**
63 rm ⊇ – †108/159 € ††132/195 € **Rest** – *(dinner only)* Carte 22/32 €
♦ Family ♦ Contemporary ♦

Hotel rich in tradition, family-run, with a wide range of rooms furnished in different styles. Ask for a room with a view of the idyllic garden. Rustic restaurant with international menu.

XXXX Tantris 🖵 AC P VISA ⓜ AE ⓞ
🕸 🕸

Johann-Fichte-Str. 7 ✉ 80805 – Ⓜ Dietlindenstr. – ℰ (089) 3 61 95 90 – info@tantris.de – Fax (089) 36 19 59 22 – www.tantris.de
– closed 2 - 12 January, Sunday - Monday and bank holidays **B1**
Rest – *(booking advisable)* Menu 65 € (lunch)/145 € – Carte 66/109 € 🍴
Spec. Ausgelöste Flusskrebse mit Kohlrabi und Arganölmarinade. Geräucherte Taubenbrust mit getrüffelter Polenta und Artischocken-Olivenfond. Ravioli vom Wollschwein mit eingelegtem Radi in Buttermilch.
♦ Classic ♦ Retro ♦

For more than 35-years now Tantris has been an institution in Munich. It is famous for its unusual 1970s style atmosphere, charming service and excellent wines, and last but not least, the fabulous classic cuisine of Hans Haas.

XXX Bogenhauser Hof 🖵 ⇄ VISA ⓜ AE ⓞ

Ismaninger Str. 85 ✉ 81675 – ℰ (089) 98 55 86 – info@bogenhauser-hof.de
– Fax (089) 9 81 02 21 – www.bogenhauser-hof.de
– closed 24 December - 6 January, 10 - 19 April, Sunday and bank holidays
Rest – *(booking advisable)* Menu 73/116 € – Carte 46/74 € **C2**
♦ Classic ♦ Traditional ♦

This inn dating from 1825 is a classic of Munich gastronomy. Superior classical cuisine, which can also be enjoyed in the idyllic summer garden.

XX Acquarello (Mario Gamba) 🖵 ⓜ AE
🕸

Mühlbaurstr. 36 ✉ 81677 – Ⓜ Böhmerwaldplatz – ℰ (089) 4 70 48 48 – info@acquarello.com – Fax (089) 47 64 64 – www.acquarello.com
– closed 1 - 4 January, Saturday lunch, Sunday lunch and bank holiday lunch
Rest – Menu 39 € (lunch)/98 € – Carte 42/76 € **D2**
Spec. Vitello Tonnato. Von Kopf bis Fuß vom Kalb. Schokoladenravioli mit Minzeis und Orangensauce.
♦ Italian ♦ Friendly ♦

In this restaurant with Mediterranean flair guests are served Italian inspired dishes in a very friendly and attentive manner.

XX Käfer Schänke 🖵 ⇄ VISA ⓜ AE ⓞ

Prinzregentenstr. 73 (1st floor) ✉ 81675 – Ⓜ Prinzregentenplatz – ℰ (089)
4 16 82 47 – kaeferschaenke@feinkost-kaefer.de – Fax (089) 4 16 86 23
– www.feinkost-kaefer.de
– closed Sunday and bank holidays **C3**
Rest – *(booking essential)* Carte 48/88 €
♦ International ♦ Cosy ♦

The restaurant is comfortable, and the small rooms have been lovingly decorated, from the "Cutlery Parlour" to the "Tobacco Parlour".

X Acetaia 🖵 VISA ⓜ AE

Nymphenburger Str. 215 (A2) ✉ 80639 – ℰ (089) 13 92 90 77 – info@restaurant-acetaia.de – Fax (089) 13 92 90 78 – www.restaurant-acetaia.de
– closed Saturday lunch
Rest – Menu 27 € (lunch)/68 € – Carte 39/60 € 🍴
♦ Italian ♦ Cosy ♦

A friendly atmosphere prevails in this restaurant, with its tasteful art nouveau décor, serving Italian and Mediterranean dishes.

Terrine

Amalienstr. 89 (Amalien-Passage) ✉ 80799 – Ⓜ *Universität* – ℰ (089) 28 17 80
– geniessen@terrine.de – Fax (089) 2 80 93 16 – www.terrine.de
– closed 1 - 13 January and Saturday lunch, Sunday - Monday and bank
holidays   **B2**
Rest – Menu 37 € (lunch)/95 € (dinner) – Carte 58/75 €
Spec. Weißer Heilbutt mit Rote-Bete-Kruste und Brunnenkresseschaum. Taubenbrust mit karamellisiertem Chicoree und Koriandersauce. Rehrücken mit
Rahmkohlrabi und Kaffeejus.
 ♦ Seasonal cuisine ♦ Bistro ♦
Dine on seasonal and contemporary cuisine in this Art Nouveau style bistro or on
the pleasant terrace on the inner courtyard of the arcade. Cheaper à la carte menu
at lunchtime.

Vinaiolo

Steinstr. 42 ✉ 81667 – Ⓜ *Ostbahnhof* – ℰ (089) 48 95 03 56 – Fax (089)
48 06 80 11 – www.vinaiolo.de
– closed Saturday lunch   **C3**
Rest – Menu 48 € – Carte 42/53 €
 ♦ Italian ♦ Cosy ♦
A comfortable Italian restaurant. Part of the structure was a grocery shop dating
back to 1904. Wines are displayed in beautiful old cabinets.

Saint Laurent

Steinstr. 63 ✉ 81667 – Ⓜ *Ostbahnhof* – ℰ (089) 47 08 40 00 – Fax (089)
47 08 40 00
– closed 3 - 18 August and Monday   **C3**
Rest – *(dinner only)* Menu 54 € – Carte 34/51 €
 ♦ French ♦ Cosy ♦
Enjoy the French inspired atmosphere and cuisine in this dark wood panelled restaurant. The terrace is approximately 50m away.

Rue Des Halles

Steinstr. 18 ✉ 81667 – Ⓜ *Max Weber Platz* – ℰ (089) 48 56 75 – Fax (089)
44 45 10 76   **C3**
Rest – *(dinner only) (booking advisable)* Menu 23/52 € – Carte 27/46 €
 ♦ French ♦ Bistro ♦
Experience the typical French flair of this town house restaurant in the bistro style,
with both classic and regional French dishes on the menu.

AT THE EXHIBITION CENTRE

Schreiberhof

Erdinger Str. 2 ✉ 85609 – ℰ (089) 90 00 60 – info@schreiberhof.de – Fax (089)
90 00 64 59 – www.schreiberhof.de
87 rm ☲ – †98 € ††118 €   **Rest** – Carte 25/46 €
 ♦ Inn ♦ Conference hotel ♦ Functional ♦
This centrally located hotel is an extended former guesthouse with functional
rooms. The light flooded conservatory is one of the areas used for conferences.
The restaurant is divided between different rooms whose styles range from comfortably rustic to stylish.

Prinzregent an der Messe

Riemer Str. 350 ✉ 81829 – ℰ (089) 94 53 90 – messe@prinzregent.de
– Fax (089) 94 53 95 66 – www.prinzregent.de
91 rm ☲ – †120/175 € ††140/205 €   **Rest** – Carte 35/44 €
 ♦ Business ♦ Country house ♦ Cosy ♦
This hotel close to the exhibition centre is in an 18C building extended with a
modern annexe. The guestrooms with their Italian furnishings are elegant and
cosy. The cosy restaurant with a touch of elegance is located in the historical part
of the building.

GERMANY - MUNICH

Innside Premium Neue Messe

Humboldtstr. 12 (Industrialpark-West) ⊠ *85609 – ℰ (089)*
94 00 50 – muenchen@innside.de – Fax (089) 94 00 52 99 – www.innside.de
– closed 24 December - 1 January
134 rm – ♦166/186 € ♦♦196/216 €, ⊇ 16 €
Rest – *(closed Saturday lunch, Sunday lunch)* Carte 29/35 €
♦ Business ♦ Modern ♦

A modern design characterises this hotel, from the light hall area in atrium style,
through to the cosy guestrooms. Unusual features include the freestanding glass
showers. Bistro-style restaurant with international cuisine.

Novotel München Messe

Willy-Brandt-Platz 1 ⊠ *81829 – ℰ (089) 99 40 00 – h5563@accor.com*
– Fax (089) 99 40 01 00 – www.novotel.com
278 rm – ♦85/165 € ♦♦105/185 €, ⊇ 19 €   **Rest** – Carte 28/42 €
♦ Chain hotel ♦ Business ♦ Modern ♦

Located in the former airport grounds next to the convention centre, this hotel is
modern and functional. Good transport connections with the motorway and
underground. Light, friendly restaurant with glass frontage.

AT THE AIRPORT

Kempinski Airport München

Terminalstraße Mitte 20 ⊠ *85356 Munich – ℰ (089)*
9 78 20 – info@kempinski-airport.de – Fax (089) 97 82 26 10
– www.kempinski-airport.de
389 rm – ♦208/500 € ♦♦208/500 €, ⊇ 29 € – 43 suites
Rest – Carte 32/52 €
Rest Safran – *(closed August and Sunday - Monday) (dinner only)*
Menu 45/82 € – Carte 43/66 €
♦ Business ♦ Contemporary ♦

Helmut Jahn designed this hotel at the airport. It is accessed through an imposing
glazed atrium hall with 18m-high palms. Excellent conference facilities. The Safran
restaurant serves Thai and Mediterranean cuisine.

Population: 589,170 – Altitude: 245m

R. Brayan/Arcaid/CORBIS

Baden-Württemberg, in Germany's south west, is one of the country's most popular tourist destinations, defined by superb castles, delectable resorts, and renowned wine-growing areas. The capital of the region, Stuttgart, sits easily within this framework. Its valley location, surrounded by steeply rising slopes, has allowed vineyards to approach the city centre from all around: the twisting branches of grapes are as much a part of the inner city picture as the sleek museums for Mercedes or Porsche.

There's an enviable amount of open space in Stuttgart. Parks, forests and orchards cover more than half of its area. It seems appropriate that the city started life as a horse stud farm in the tenth century, growing to become Germany's most prosperous metropolis by way – incongruously or not - of its association with the world's sleekest cars. This is also a city of fine squares, majestic palaces, architecturally diverse buildings and cultural vigour. Three years ago a spectacular glass cube announced itself as the city's new museum of art, while theatre, ballet and opera are housed together in the largest 'three function' building in Europe. Meanwhile, many visitors keep an eye open for Stuttgart's Beer Festival, which gives Munich's Oktoberfest a run for its money.

LIVING THE CITY

Stuttgart is enviably situated amongst picturesque hills. It's surrounded on three sides by wooded elevations, while to the east it's open to the river **Neckar.** The old town is bounded to the east by the district of **Obertürkheim**, a popular destination as it's the home of the Mercedes-Benz Museum. The city is in the heart of Germany's most scenic state (with the possible exception of Bavaria), and to its northwest lies Heidelberg, and to its west is Baden-Baden.

PRACTICAL INFORMATION

ARRIVAL-DEPARTURE

The Airport is 13km south of the city centre. S-Bahn commuter trains S2 and S3 run to Central Station in 30min, while a taxi will cost around € 20.

TRANSPORT

There's an impressively integrated public transport system in Stuttgart, which covers nearby towns as well as the city itself. Once you've bought a ticket, you can switch between buses, trams, U-Bahns, and mainline and S-Bahn trains.

There are three types of ticket you might need. If you're only in town for a short time, buy a day ticket. If you're around for longer, invest in either a city explorer Stuttcard or Stuttcard plus; these give free admission to most museums, reduced entry to theatres, and free travel on public transport for three days, including transport to the airport (the Stuttcard plus is more expensive, but offers a few more benefits).

EXPLORING STUTTGART

Stuttgart breathes well-being and good living. Even its neighbours are of the very top drawer, in the shape of nearby Heidelberg and Baden-Baden. It's a city that was always favoured by the local bigwigs, becoming first ducal, then royal, capital of Württemberg. Its beautiful position, cosseted by rolling hills, may have had something to do

with this, but the local hierarchy of the past would have been bamboozled at the source of Stuttgart's current success: fast cars. Both Mercedes-Benz and Porsche have made their names in this city, and both manufacturers boast slinky museums devoted to their pride and joy.

→ SQUARE DEAL

Visitors here invariably make for **Schlossplatz,** the imposing square at the centre of the city. Its huge dimensions are breath-taking, especially when you take in the proportions of the vast **Neues Schloss**, the palace that eats up the whole of the square's east side. It was the last Baroque castle-residence to be built in Germany, and its construction lasted throughout much of the eighteenth century's latter half. The idea was to make it a second Versailles, and a pretty good job they made of it. The only part you can visit are the cellars, but it's worth it to see the **Römisches Lapidarium**, a collection of Roman stone fragments dating back to 200AD. The grandeur of the square extends still further: opposite the Neues Schloss is **Königsbau**, a fine Neo-Classical structure from the mid-nineteenth century, which has been turned to modern day use by lining it with glitzy shops.

→ STATE OF PERFECTION

You get a clue to Stuttgart's cultural import a short stroll from Schlossplatz, by arriving at the nineteenth century **Staatsgalerie**, or Old State Gallery. Reckoned to be one of the top art museums in the country, it boasts a fantastic collection of old masters and a fascinating inventory of graphics, which includes illustrated books, posters and photographs. Its stature was enhanced in 1984 when a dazzling new extension was added – the New State Gallery – which contains works from the twentieth century by the likes of Modigliani, Picasso and Beuys. This is now one of Germany's most visited museums, but its status has been challenged in the past couple of years by the new kid on the block, The **Kunstmuseum**, just off Schlossplatz. Maybe that should read the new *block* on the block, because this twenty first century upstart is in the shape of a cube made of glass, and even if you don't intend going in, you'll want to stop and look at it. It features the work of German artists, including Otto Dix and Swabian Impressionists, and its hidden tunnels of art are an unexpected delight for the first-time visitor.

→ SCHILL-OUT ZONE

You only have to cross the smart shopping street, **Königstrasse,** to indulge in a bit more of Stuttgart's cultural scene. On the beautiful **Schillerplatz**, the remains of a fourteenth century castle were given a sixteenth century makeover, and the **Altes Schloss** got its Renaissance look with atmospheric arcaded cloisters encircling a spooky inner courtyard. You might not expect to find a museum here, but this is the home of the **Württembergisches Landesmuseum**, which has an eclectic mix of Italian sculptures, Renaissance curios, and – on the top floor – the nineteenth century crown jewels.

Hang around a bit on Schillerplatz. It's the city's one example of a truly historic square, as it was here that the stud farm that gave Stuttgart its name is said to have stood. It's surrounded by historic buildings: apart from the Altes Schloss, there's the sixteenth century **Old Chancellery**, which is now a restaurant; a **gabled granary**, also from the sixteenth century, where you can find a museum of musical instruments and the elegant seventeenth century **Prinzenbau**.

→ GET YOUR MOTOR RUNNING

You often read about somewhere being a 'city of contrasts', but in Stuttgart they really mean it. To the east of the centre, away from the charms of the past, lies the roaring glory of the **Mercedes-Benz Museum**, a must for petrol-heads. Here you can see the first cars in the world, Carl Benz's three-wheeled automobile from 1886, and Gottlieb Daimler's horseless carriage. There are over seventy vehicles on display, all in mint condition, from the earliest models to today's state-of-the-art cars. One of the most impressive exhibits is the Blitzen Benz, which was driven at 228mph to set the world record at Daytona Beach nearly one hundred years ago. Of course, where there's Merc, there's **Porsche,** and Stuttgart's other legendary car manufacturer has its own museum, too, ranging from the 356 Roadster of 1948 to the latest models. A spectacular new Porsche Museum is opening in the city, and it promises to be even more comprehensive than its predecessor.

If you like to see a play, or you're a bit partial to the opera or the ballet, it's possible to combine all three at Stuttgart's **State Theatre**. It's big enough and it's bold enough to house all three within the same premises, either in the **Playhouse** or the **Opera house.** The foyer, with its busts of writers and composers, is an imposing place to gather, and there should be a special buzz about the place this year (2009) as it's the hundredth anniversary of the theatre's construction.

→ GREEN U-TURN

Stuttgart cherishes its verdant surroundings. Not only swathed in hills and vineyards, it also boasts an enviable amount of parks and green space. In fact, this has a collective name, The Green U, named after the rough shape this 'natural trail' takes. It's eight kilometres in length, starting at the Schlossplatz, and heading away via magnificent gardens (the Schlossgarten) north of Neues Schloss, before taking in the glorious Rosenstein Park, with its lake, rose garden, grand old trees, and showy Schloss Rosenstein, the former country house of the Württemberg kings. If it sounds rather idyllic from ground level, get bird's eye confirmation by heading nearly 220m up the city's famous TV Tower. Now over fifty years old, it stands on top of a wooded hill, and from either its observation platform or crows nest café you can indulge uninterrupted, jaw-dropping views of Stuttgart, the vineyards of the Neckar Valley, the Black Forest and the Alps.

CALENDAR HIGHLIGHTS

As the home to two of the world's most famous marques, it's not surprising that Stuttgart should honour the motor car. It does this in March with Retroclassics (at the Messe Stuttgart), which is a show full of vintage favourites, such as Aston Martins, Rolls Royces and Porsches, alongside a 'history of classic cars' exhibit. A month earlier, the year gets a stately opening with the Stuttgart Bach Week, at the Liederhalle, during which international artists celebrate the great man's music over a ten-day festival. The art world comes to the fore in March with Long Art Night at the Staatsgalerie: the idea is to enjoy an evening meal, then head to the museum and get into the unique experience of taking on Picasso and Munch till the midnight hour. The coming of summer is a good time to be a beer drinker in this city. The Stuttgart Spring Beer Festival (April/May), at Cannstatter Wasen, is a three-week ale celebration, with the distraction of hot-air balloon flights and fireworks. July sees three big events. Schlossplatz hosts the Viva

STUTTGART IN...

→ ONE DAY
Schlossplatz, Staatsgalerie, Mercedes-Benz Museum

→ TWO DAYS
Kunstmuseum, Altes Schloss, amble through Schlossgarten, Porsche Museum, State Theatre Stuttgart

→ THREE DAYS
Stroll in Rosenstein park, outing to Heidelberg or Baden-Baden

AfroBrasil Festival, Europe's biggest and longest-running Latino event, with samba, salsa, reggae and funk, while the Jazz Open features many international artists giving it their all for a week at the Liederhalle or on the adjacent open-air stage. Meanwhile, the Stuttgart Christopher Street Day parade is a gay pride event lasting a week, with special events running alongside stage and cabaret shows. The elegant Summer Festival (August) shimmers across three days of white pavilions, fairy lights and lanterns, with music, food and entertainment keeping thousands happy outside Neues Schloss and the Opera House.

The grape and the grain hit the forefront again with the city's final two big festivals of the year. The Stuttgarter Weindorf (Aug/Sep) attracts a million wine lovers to the Marktplatz and Schlossplatz for twelve days of serious imbibing. Fifty local wineries create the famous "wine village", with over one hundred lovingly-decorated arbours. A month later, the Stuttgart Beer Festival at Cannstatter Wasen has almost two hundred years of history behind it. 'Fleshed out' with a giant Ferris wheel and numerous fairground attractions, it's the world's second biggest beer extravaganza, behind Munich's Oktoberfest.

EATING OUT

Württemberg's viniculture has a tradition of more than a thousand years and the most popular variety amongst the locals is the ruby red Trollinger. You might be surprised how it's served to you: in quarter litre glasses with handles. You won't be surprised that the 'Schwäbische Weinstuben' (local wine taverns) are rollicking good places to go. Beer is a flourishing trade too, with large Stuttgart breweries vying for your palate. That's not to say that food takes a back seat. On the contrary, this south western city isn't far from the French border, and prides itself on accomplished French inspired menus. Italian restaurants, and lots of them, jostle for position as well. There's a renowned 'local kitchen', with *Gaisburger Marsch* the pick of the dishes: it's a tasty stew made of *Spätzle* (the staple Stuttgart noodle), potatoes, beef pieces, vegetables, broth and roasted onions. *Spätzles* turn up everywhere, and are very popular '*mit Linsen*' (lentils), especial-

ly when they're teamed up and served with warm sausages, or accompanying a Swabian roast, another hearty dish featuring roasted slices of beef with lots of roasted onions, served with Sauerkraut and *Maultaschen* (square dumplings with a savoury filling). There's an impressive range of international restaurants in the city, so if you want to eat good cuisine from beyond European borders, you won't have a problem. Prices include service, but it's usual to leave a tip of around ten per cent of the bill.

➔ NATURAL MAGNETISM

Plant and animal lovers in Stuttgart will want to head for the Wilhelma, Europe's largest zoological/botanical gardens. Not only can you gaze at more than ten thousand animals, you can also take in the glory of rare orchids, a large magnolia grove, and all kinds of exotic plants. It can get rather crowded: nearly two million visitors turn up each year, so be prepared to have your space invaded.

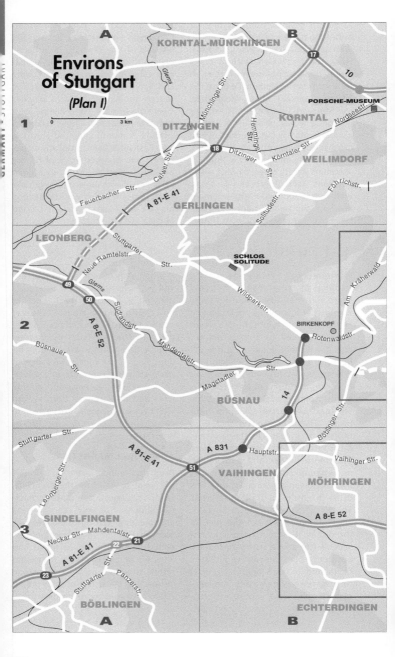

Environs
of Stuttgart
(Plan I)

0   3 km

A

B

KORNTAL-MÜNCHINGEN

17

10

PORSCHE-MUSEUM

Nordseestr.

KORNTAL

1

Glems

Münchinger Str.

DITZINGEN

Hemminger Str.

18

Ditzinger

Körntaler Str.

WEILIMDORF

Calwer Str.

Feuerbacher Str.

A 81-E 41

GERLINGEN

Solitudestr.

Fröhlichstr.

LEONBERG

Stuttgarter

Neue Ramtelstr.

Str.

SCHLOß SOLITUDE

Am Krähenwald

2

49

Glems

50

Südrandstr.

A 8-E 52

Wildparkstr.

BIRKENKOPF

Rotenwaldstr.

Büsnauer Str.

Mahdentalstr.

Str.

14

BÜSNAU

Böblinger Str.

Magstadter

Stuttgarter Str.

A 81-E 41

A 831

Hauptstr.

51

VAIHINGEN

Vaihinger Str.

MÖHRINGEN

A 8-E 52

Leonberger Str.

SINDELFINGEN

3

Neckar Str.

Mahdentalstr.

22

21

A 81-E 41

23

Stuttgarter Str.

Panzerstr.

BÖBLINGEN

ECHTERDINGEN

A

B

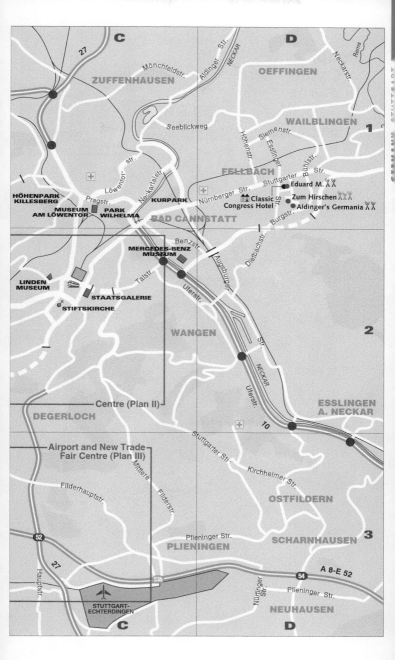

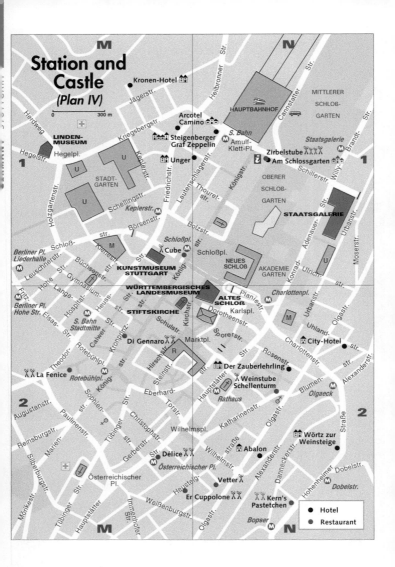

Station and Castle
(Plan IV)

0   300 m

M

N

Kronen-Hotel 🏨

Jägerstr.

Herdweg

Heilbronner Str.

Cannstatter Str.

Str.

HAUPTBAHNHOF

MITTLERER
SCHLOSS-
GARTEN

Arcotel
Camino 🏨

Kriegsbergstr.

S. Bahn

Staatsgalerie

LINDEN-
MUSEUM

Steigenberger
Graf Zeppelin 🏨

Amulf-
Klett-Pl.

Zirbelstube ✗✗✗✗

Hegelstr.

Hegelpl.

Keplerstr.

Friedrichstr.

🏨 Unger

Königstr.

Am Schlossgarten 🏨

Schillerstr.

Willy

Brandtstr.

1

1

U

U

STADT-
GARTEN

Schellingstr.

Lautenschlagerstr.

Thouret-
str.

OBERER

SCHLOSS-

GARTEN

Adenauer-

Str.

Holzgartenstr.

U

Keplerstr.

Börsenstr.

Bolzstr.

STAATSGALERIE

Urbanstr.

Moserstr.

Berliner Pl.,
Liederhalle

Schloß-
str.

M

Kienestr.

Schloßpl.

✗ Cube

M

Schloßpl.

NEUES

U

Büchsenstr.

KUNSTMUSEUM
STUTTGART

König-

SCHLOSS

AKADEMIE

Konrad-

Ulrich-

Leuschnerstr.

Hohe

Gymnasiumstr.

str.

GARTEN

Fritz-
Berliner Pl.,
Hohe Str.

Lange-

str.

Heusteigstr.

WÜRTTEMBERGISCHES
LANDESMUSEUM

Planiestr.

Charlottenpl.

Elsas-

Hospital-

str.

ALTES
SCHLOSS

M

Urbanstr.

Olgastr.

Str.

S. Bahn
Stadtmitte

Calwerstr.

STIFTSKIRCHE

Schulstr.

Kirchstr.

Dorotheenstr.

Karlspl.

🏨 City-Hotel

Uhland-

str.

Kronprinzstr.

Di Gennaro ✗ 🏨

Marktpl.

Sporerstr.

Charlottenstr.

Alexanderstr.

✗✗ La Fenice

Rotebühlpl.

Hirschstr.

Str.

Rosenstr.

🏨 Der Zauberlehrling

Theodor-

König-

str.

Steinstr.

Eberhard-

✗ Weinstube
Schellenturm

Blumen-

Olgaeck

Augustenstr.

Sophien-

str.

Tübingerstr.

Christophstr.

Torstr.

Rathaus

Katharinenstr.

Olgastr.

Straße

2

2

Reinsburgstr.

Paulinenstr.

Marien-

Gerberstr.

Wilhelmspl.

Wilhelmstraße

🏨 Wörtz zur
Weinsteige

Alexanderstr.

Danneckerstr.

Hohenheimer

Dobelstr.

Silberburgstr.

Mörikestr.

str.

Österreichischer
Pl.

Heigeistr.

Délice ✗✗

Österreichischer Pl.

🏨 Abalon

Str.

Dobelstr.

Vetter ✗

Olgastr.

Tübingerstr.

Hauptstätterstr.

Immenhofstr.

Weißenburgstr.

Er Cuppolone ✗✗

Kern's
Pastetchen ✗✗

Bopser

● Hotel
● Restaurant

M

N

Steigenberger Graf Zeppelin

Arnulf-Klett-Platz 7 ✉ _70173 –_ **M** _S. Bahn –_ 𝒞 _(0711)_
2 04 80 – stuttgart@steigenberger.de – Fax (0711) 2 04 85 42
– www.stuttgart.steigenberger.de **N1**
189 rm – †155/235 €, ††180/260 €, ⊡ 22 €
Rest _Olivo_ – 𝒞 _(0711) 2 04 82 77 (closed Sunday - Monday and bank holidays)_
Menu 42 € (lunch)/119 € – Carte 44/70 €
Rest _Zeppelin Stüble_ – 𝒞 _(0711) 2 04 83 63 (closed Sunday dinner)_
Carte 24/40 €
Rest _Zeppelino's_ – 𝒞 _(0711) 2 04 83 63 –_ Menu 39/49 € – Carte 36/56 €
♦ Chain hotel ♦ Classic ♦

This business hotel in its lavish setting is centrally located opposite the station. The rooms are divided into Classic, Elegance and Avant-garde categories. Olivo has a modern atmosphere and serves Italian cuisine. Try the Zeppelin-Stüble with its rustic atmosphere. The cuisine at Zeppelino's is Italian.

Am Schlossgarten

Schillerstr. 23 ✉ _70173 –_ **M** _S. Bahn –_ 𝒞 _(0711) 2 02 60 – info@_
hotelschlossgarten.com – Fax (0711) 2 02 68 88 – www.hotelschlossgarten.com
116 rm – †222/311 €, ††279/311 €, ⊡ 21 € – 4 suites **N1**
Rest _Zirbelstube_ – see below
Rest _Schlossgarten-Restaurant_ – 𝒞 _(0711) 2 02 68 30 (closed Friday lunch_
and Saturday lunch) Carte 40/59 €
Rest _Vinothek_ – 𝒞 _(0711) 2 02 68 36 (closed Sunday - Monday)_ Menu 25 €
– Carte 30/35 €
♦ Townhouse ♦ Classic ♦

This carefully managed hotel is popular for its friendly service and cosy atmosphere. Some of the rooms have views over the Schlossgarten. The Schlossgarten-Restaurant has an elegant atmosphere. Vinothek: Mediterranean style.

Arcotel Camino

Heilbronner Str. 21 (access via Im Kaisemer) ✉ _70191 –_ **M** _S. Bahn –_ 𝒞 _(0711)_
25 85 80 – camino@arcotel.at – Fax (0711) 25 85 82 20 – www.arcotel.at
168 rm – †117/270 €, ††117/270 €, ⊡ 17 € – 3 suites **M1**
Rest _Weissenhof_ – 𝒞 _(0711) 2 58 58 42 00 –_ Carte 31/48 €
♦ Business ♦ Design ♦

This centrally located, beautifully restored 1890 sandstone building has modern rooms and very pleasant leisure facilities. The gabled junior suites are particularly appealing. Restaurant decorated in shades of brown and ochre.

Kronen-Hotel without rest ⌂

Kronenstr. 48 ✉ _70174 –_ **M** _S. Bahn –_ 𝒞 _(0711) 2 25 10 – info@_
kronenhotel-stuttgart.de – Fax (0711) 2 25 14 04
– www.kronenhotel-stuttgart.de
– closed 22 December-2 January **M1**
80 rm ⊡ **–** †108/145 €, ††138/185 €
♦ Business ♦ Functional ♦

This hotel, which is particularly suited to business guests with its cosy, functional rooms, is near the centre of town. In summer, the sunny, green terrace is a perfect place to enjoy breakfast.

Wörtz zur Weinsteige

Hohenheimer Str. 30 ✉ _70184 –_ **M** _Dobelstr. –_ 𝒞 _(0711) 2 36 70 00 – info@_
zur-weinsteige.de – Fax (0711) 2 36 70 07 – www.zur-weinsteige.de
33 rm ⊡ **–** †95/135 €, ††110/155 € **N2**
Rest – _(closed 1 - 15 January, 10 - 28 August, Sunday - Monday and bank_
holidays) Menu 30/75 € – Carte 30/60 € ⌘
♦ Townhouse ♦ Rustic ♦

The Scherle family really look after their guests in their hotel. The rooms in the little Schloss are particularly comfortable and elegant; or there's the stylish Louis-XVI Junior suite. Rustic décor defines the character of this restaurant.

Der Zauberlehrling   AC rm 🎛 📶 🚗

Rosenstr. 38 ⊠ *70182 –* Ⓜ *Olgaeck –* 𝒞 *(0711) 2 37 77 70 – kontakt@*
zauberlehrling.de – Fax (0711) 2 37 77 75 – www.zauberlehrling.de
17 rm 🛏 *–* 🛏135/250 € 🛏🛏185/350 € *– 4 suites*   **N2**
Rest *– (Saturday, Sunday and bank holidays dinner only) Menu 35/115 €*
– Carte 54/70 €
  ♦ Townhouse ♦ Personalised ♦
This small hotel consists of two townhouses. The themed rooms are designed individually, have great attention to detail and offer high-tech fittings. A modern restaurant in white, gold and pink tones serving international cuisine.

Unger without rest   🎛 📞 🔧 🚗 VISA ⓪ 🅐🅔 ⓪

Kronenstr. 17 ⊠ *70173 –* Ⓜ *S. Bahn –* 𝒞 *(0711) 2 09 90 – info@hotel-unger.de*
– Fax (0711) 2 09 91 00 – www.hotel-unger.de   **N1**
114 rm 🛏 *–* 🛏121/149 € 🛏🛏168/212 €
  ♦ Townhouse ♦ Functional ♦
This hotel with its functional guestrooms is situated just off the pedestrian zone.
The rooms on the sixth and seventh floors are particularly attractive.

City-Hotel without rest   📶 🅿 VISA ⓪ 🅐🅔 ⓪

Uhlandstr. 18 ⊠ *70182 –* Ⓜ *Olgaeck –* 𝒞 *(0711) 21 08 10 – ch@bbv-hotels.de*
– Fax (0711) 2 36 97 72 – www.cityhotel-stuttgart.de   **N2**
31 rm 🛏 *–* 🛏79/89 € 🛏🛏99/115 €
  ♦ Townhouse ♦ Functional ♦
This contemporary hotel is right in the city centre. It has a nice friendly breakfast
room with a conservatory – or you can breakfast on the terrace in summer.

Abalon without rest   📶 📶 🚗 VISA ⓪ 🅐🅔 ⓪

Zimmermannstr. 7 (access via Olgastr. 79) ⊠ *70182 –* Ⓜ *Olgaeck –* 𝒞 *(0711)*
2 17 10 – info@abalon.de – Fax (0711) 2 17 12 17 – www.abalon.de
42 rm 🛏 *–* 🛏79/86 € 🛏🛏99/112 €   **N2**
  ♦ Business ♦ Functional ♦
This modern hotel building has a roof terrace garden in the upper part of the centre and offers functional rooms with laminate floors. Juice and water are part of the
service.

Zirbelstube – Hotel Am Schlossgarten   🍴 🌳 VISA ⓪ 🅐🅔 ⓪

Schillerstr. 23 ⊠ *70173 –* Ⓜ *S. Bahn –* 𝒞 *(0711) 2 02 68 28 – info@*
hotelschlossgarten.com – Fax (0711) 2 02 68 88 – www.hotelschlossgarten.com
– closed 1 - 13 January, 10 August - 1 September and Sunday - Monday
Rest *– (booking advisable) Menu 58 € (lunch)/118 €*   **N1**
– Carte 78/122 € 🍴
Spec. Cannelloni von Gänsestopfleber und Aprikose. Medaillon vom Seeteufel mit Speckschaum und Kräuternudeln. Mousse von Herzkirschen auf Can-
tuccini-Praliné im Schokoladenmantel mit knusprigen Mandeln.
  ♦ Classic ♦ Elegant ♦
The pine panelled restaurant provides an elegant setting for Bernhard Diers'
modern, classic cuisine. Excellent professional and attentive service and a pleasant
terrace with a view of the park.

Kern's Pastetchen   ⇔

Hohenheimer Str. 64 ⊠ *70184 –* Ⓜ *Bopser –* 𝒞 *(0711) 48 48 55 – info@*
kerns-pastetchen.de – Fax (0711) 48 75 65 – www.kerns-pastetchen.de
– closed 1 week during Carnival, 2 weeks June and Sunday
Rest *– (dinner only) (booking essential) Menu 52/64 € – Carte 46/59 €* 🍴   **N2**
  ♦ Classic ♦ Friendly ♦
Attentively looked after by the Kern family with pleasant, professional service. This
restaurant has a tasteful, rustic atmosphere and serves French-style cuisine. Excellent selection of wines recommended by the owner.

XX
🕸️ **Délice** (Friedrich Gutscher)

Hauptstätter Str. 61 ⌧ *70178 –* Ⓜ *Österreichischer Pl. –* ☏ *(0711) 6 40 32 22*
– www.restaurant-delice.de
*– closed 23 December - 6 January, 6 - 13 April, Saturday - Sunday and bank
holidays* **M2**
Rest *– (dinner only) (booking essential)* Menu 70/95 € – Carte 48/72 € 🍷
Spec. Jakobsmuschel im Tempurateig mit lauwarmem Gemüsesalat und Cur-
ryschaum. Gebratene Attersee-Reinanke mit Estragon-Kartoffelpüree und
Kohlrabi. Topfeneisparfait mit Kürbiskernkrokant und Kürbiskernöl.
♦ Classic ♦ Friendly ♦
Cosy, intimate, vaulted restaurant with an open kitchen. Selected wines, including
some Riesling rarities, are served to accompany the classic cuisine.

XX **La Fenice** 🌳 🅥🅘🅢🅐

Rotebühlplatz 29 ⌧ *70178 –* Ⓜ *Rotebühlpl.*
– ☏ *(0711) 6 15 11 44 – g.vincenzo@t-online.de – Fax (0711) 6 15 11 46*
– www.ristorante-la-fenice.de
– closed Saturday lunch, Sunday and bank holidays **M2**
Rest *–* Menu 18 € (lunch)/60 € – Carte 41/60 €
♦ Italian ♦ Cosy ♦
A light, friendly restaurant with the elegant touch, where the Gorgoglione sisters
offer Italian cuisine.

XX **Di Gennaro** 🅥🅘🅢🅐 🅒🅞 🅐🅔 ①

Kronprinzstr. 11 ⌧ *70173 –* Ⓜ *Rotebühlpl. –* ☏ *(0711) 22 29 60 51*
– gourmet-haus@digennaro.de – Fax (0711) 22 29 60 40
– www.digennaro.de
– closed Sunday and bank holidays **M2**
Rest *–* Menu 34/84 € – Carte 47/67 €
♦ Italian ♦ Bistro ♦
An Italian restaurant under the same roof as a delicatessen. Dine in a contemporary bistro atmosphere or in an elegant wine cellar.

XX **Er Cuppolone** 🌳 🅥🅘🅢🅐 🅒🅞 🅐🅔 ①

Heusteigstr. 45 ⌧ *70180 –* Ⓜ *Österreichischer Pl. –* ☏ *(0711) 6 07 18 80*
– sante@schwaben.de – Fax (0711) 6 20 83 66 – www.santedesantis.de
– closed 2 weeks August and Sunday **M2**
Rest *– (dinner only)* Menu 69/71 € – Carte 44/55 € 🍷
♦ Italian ♦ Individual ♦
The old state parliament walls hide a cookery school, wine bar and an elegant restaurant, offering authentic Italian cuisine.

X **Cube** ⪕ 🅰🅒 🅥🅘🅢🅐 🅒🅞 🅐🅔 ①

Kleiner Schlossplatz 1 (at the Kunstmuseum, 4th floor) ⌧ *70173*
– Ⓜ *Schloßpl. –* ☏ *(0711) 2 80 44 41 – info@cube-restaurant.de*
– Fax (0711) 2 80 44 42 – www.cube-restaurant.de **M1**
Rest *–* Menu 30 € (lunch) – Carte 43/58 €
♦ Mediterranean ♦ Fashionable ♦
A modern restaurant in the art museum. Simple design with unique view and
Mediterranean/Asian cuisine. Simple menus available at midday.

X **Vetter** 🍽️

Bopserstr. 18 ⌧ *70180 –* Ⓜ *Österreichischer Pl. –* ☏ *(0711) 24 19 16*
– Fax (0711) 60 18 96 40
– closed 10 - 23 August, Christmas - New Year, Sunday and bank holidays
Rest *– (dinner only) (booking advisable)* Carte 25/48 € **N2**
♦ Regional ♦ Cosy ♦
This comfortable establishment is down a side street in the town centre. Modern
interior and a selection of regional and international dishes.

✗ **Weinstube Schellenturm** 🍴 VISA

Weberstr. 72 ✉ *70182* – Ⓜ *Olgaeck* – ✆ *(0711) 2 36 48 88*
– *info@weinstube-schellenturm.de* – *Fax (0711) 2 26 26 99*
– *www.weinstube-schellenturm.de*
– *closed 24 December - 7 January, Sunday and bank holidays*   **N2**
Rest – *(dinner only)* Carte 20/31 €
♦ Regional ♦ Cosy ♦

This 16th century fortified tower offers real local Swabian atmosphere. There is good wine, large Swabian ravioli (Maultaschen), and cheese spaetzle (noodles).

CENTRE   *Plan II*

🏨 **Le Méridien** 🖪 ⊕ 🐾 🔲 ﴾ 🗚 🖾 ℣ 🏊 🚗 VISA ⦾ AE ⓞ

Willy-Brandt-Str. 30 ✉ *70173* – ✆ *(0711) 2 22 10*
– *info.stuttgart@lemeridien.com* – *Fax (0711) 22 21 25 99*
– *www.lemeridien.com/stuttgart*   **G1**
291 rm – †195/370 € ††195/370 €, ☲ 24 € – 12 suites
Rest *Le Cassoulet* – ✆ *(0711) 22 21 22 70* – Carte 45/60 €
♦ Luxury ♦ Business ♦ Classic ♦

A luxurious hotel beside the Schlossgarten. It offers a spacious lobby, modern, elegant rooms with top quality, high-tech fittings and a pleasant spa area. Le Cassoulet provides a range of international dishes.

🏨 **Maritim** 🍴 🖪 🐾 🔲 ﴾ 🗚 🖾 ℣ 🏊 🚗 VISA ⦾ AE ⓞ

Seidenstr. 34 ✉ *70174* – Ⓜ *Rosenberg-/Seidenstr.* – ✆ *(0711) 94 20*
– *info.stu@maritim.de* – *Fax (0711) 9 42 10 00*
– *www.maritim.de*   **F1**
555 rm – †159/290 € ††196/330 €, ☲ 18 € – 12 suites
Rest – Carte 35/41 €
♦ Chain hotel ♦ Functional ♦

With the 'Alte Stuttgarter Reithalle' built in 1885 and the connection to the Liederhalle, this hotel is ideal for conferences. Relaxation is guaranteed in the rooms with the 'In-Room Spa'. As well as the Reuchlin restaurant, there is the rotisserie and buffet.

🏨 **Mercure City-Center** ﴾ 🗚 🖾 ℣ 🏊 🚗 VISA ⦾ AE ⓞ

Heilbronner Str. 88 ✉ *70191* – Ⓜ *Türlenstr.* – ✆ *(0711) 25 55 80*
– *h5424@accor.com* – *Fax (0711) 25 55 81 00*
– *www.mercure.com*   **G1**
174 rm – †89/199 € ††99/209 €, ☲ 17 €
Rest – Carte 19/42 €
♦ Chain hotel ♦ Functional ♦

This hotel is popular with business guests. It offers modern, functional rooms in a convenient location close to the main station and the motorway.

🏨 **Central Classic** *without rest* ℣° VISA ⦾ AE ⓞ

Hasenbergstr. 49a ✉ *70176* – Ⓜ *Schwab-Bebelstr.*
– ✆ *(0711) 6 15 50 50* – *cc@bbv-hotels.de* – *Fax (0711) 61 55 05 30*
– *www.central-classic.de*
– *closed 23 December-3 January*   **F2**
34 rm ☲ – †73/79 € ††89/99 €
♦ Townhouse ♦ Functional ♦

Business travellers appreciate this little hotel by the Feuersee with its practical, well looked-after rooms.

STUTTGART - GERMANY

XXX
&

Wielandshöhe

≤ ⌂ VISA ◑◐ AE ⓞ

Alte Weinsteige 71 ⊠ 70597 – ⓜ Weinsteige – 𝒞 (0711) 6 40 88 48
– Fax (0711) 6 40 94 08 – www.wielandshoehe.com
– closed Sunday-Monday   **F3**
Rest – *(booking advisable)* Menu 74/98 € – Carte 52/84 € 🌿
Spec. Saibling mit Champagnerkraut. Rehragout mit Dinkelspätze. Quark-
soufflé mit Kirschenkompott.
   ◆ Classic ◆ Fashionable ◆
Classic dishes with a strong regional influence are the highlights of this restaurant.
In summer you get a particularly good view of the town from the terrace.

XX
☺

Fässle

⌂ ⇔ VISA ◑◐ AE ⓞ

Löwenstr. 51 ⊠ 70597 – ⓜ Degerloch – 𝒞 (0711) 76 01 00 – info@faessle.de
– Fax (0711) 7 65 21 56 – www.faessle.de
– closed Sunday - Monday lunch   **F3**
Rest – *(booking advisable)* Menu 34/52 € – Carte 26/46 €
   ◆ International ◆ Traditional ◆
Guests are well looked after in this pretty old sandstone house. Tasty international
and regional cuisine is served.

XX
&

Breitenbach

⌂ ⇔ VISA ◑◐ AE ⓞ

Gebelsbergstr. 97 ⊠ 70199 – ⓜ Bihlpl. – 𝒞 (0711) 6 40 64 67
– restaurantbreitenbach@t-online.de – Fax (0711) 6 74 42 34
– www.restaurant-breitenbach.de
– closed 2 weeks January, August, Sunday - Monday and bank holidays
Rest – *(dinner only) (booking advisable)* Menu 65/80 €   **E3**
– Carte 65/82 €
Spec. Carpaccio von Jakobsmuscheln und Thunfisch mit Meerrettichschaum.
Seeteufel im Zucchinimantel mit Venusmuschelsauce und Safran-Kartoffel-
püree. Medaillon vom Rinderfilet mit Kalbsbrieskruste und Trüffelsauce.
   ◆ Inventive ◆ Friendly ◆
A pleasant dining experience is assured in these elegant surroundings. Find char-
ming and competent service directed by the manageress and creative cuisine on a
classic basis.

X

Augusten Stüble

⌂

Augustenstr. 104 ⊠ 70197 – ⓜ Schwab-Bebelstr. – 𝒞 (0711) 62 12 48
– spaetburgunder@netic.de – www.augustenstueble.de
– closed Sunday and bank holidays   **F2**
Rest – *(dinner only) (booking advisable)* Menu 38/48 € – Carte 29/39 €
   ◆ Regional ◆ Cosy ◆
The décor of this bistro-style restaurant on the edge of the centre features lots of
dark wooden detail. Regional fare and a good selection of wines. Open until midnight.

X

Weinstube Klink

⌂

Epplestr. 1b (Degerloch) ⊠ 70597 – ⓜ Degerloch – 𝒞 (0711) 7 65 32 05
– Fax (0711) 7 87 42 21 – www.weinstube-klink.de
– closed Sunday and bank holidays   **F3**
Rest – *(dinner only) (booking advisable)* Carte 24/49 €
   ◆ Regional ◆ Rustic ◆
The restaurant is nestling in a courtyard. The simple Swabian menu is supplemen-
ted with specials presented on a slate. Very good selection of wines.

X

Weinstube Träuble

⌂

Gablenberger Hauptstr. 66 (entrance on Bussenstraße) ⊠ 70186 – 𝒞 (0711)
46 54 28 – Fax (0711) 4 20 79 61
– closed 24 August - 7 September, Sunday and bank holidays   **H2**
Rest – *(open from 5 pm)* Carte 17/36 €
   ◆ Regional ◆ Wine bar ◆
The panelled dining room of this tiny 200-year-old house is extremely cosy. Snacks
and daily specials are available.

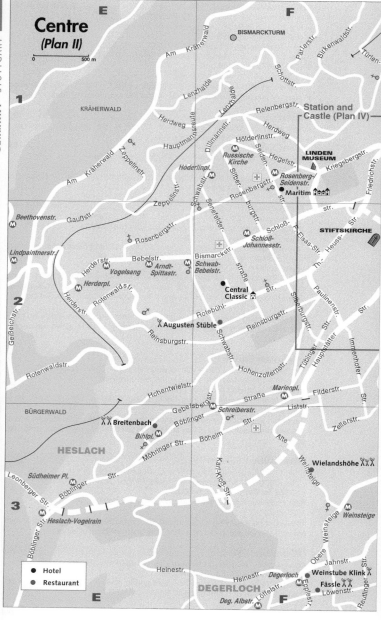

Centre
(Plan II)

0   500 m

BISMARCKTURM

Am Kräherwald

KRÄHERWALD

Lenzhalde

Schottstr.

Pat.str.

Birkenwaldstr.

Türlen-

Herdweg

Relenbergstr.

Station and
Castle (Plan IV)

Hölderlinstr.

Hegelstr.

Herdweg

Hauptmannsreute

Zeppelinstr.

Hölderlinpl.

Russische
Kirche

Silber-

Seiden-

LINDEN
MUSEUM

Kriegsbergstr.

Friedrichstr.

Am Kräherwald

Schwabstr.

Rosenbergstr.

Rosenberg-
Seidenstr.

Maritim

Beethovenstr.

Gaußstr.

Zeppelinstr.

burgstr.

Schloß-

STIFTSKIRCHE

Lindpaintnerstr.

Rosenbergstr.

Seefelder-

Schloß-
Johannesstr.

F.-Elsas-Str.

Th.-Heuss-Str.

Herderstr.

Bebelstr.

Bismarckstr.

Schwab-

straße

Geißeichstr.

Herderstr.

Vogelsang

Arndt-
Spittastr.

Bebelstr.

Paulinenstr.

Str.

Herderpl.

Rotenwaldstr.

Central
Classic

Str.

Immenhofer

Rotenwaldstr.

Reinsburgstr.

Augusten Stüble

Rotebühl-

Schwab-

Reinsburgstr.

Hohenzollernstr.

Tübinger

Hauptstätter

Str.

Hohentwielstr.

Gebelsbergstr.

Straße

Marienpl.

Filderstr.

Str.

BÜRGERWALD

Breitenbach

Böblinger

Schreiberstr.

Str.

Liststr.

Zelterstr.

Bihlpl.

Böheim-

HESLACH

Mörhinger Str.

Alte

Weinsteige

Wielandshöhe

Südheimer Pl.

Böblinger

Str.

Karl-Kloß-Str.

Leonberger Str.

Böblinger

Obere Weinsteige

Weinsteige

Böblinger Str.

Heslach-Vogelrain

Weinsteige

Jahnstr.

Str.

● Hotel
● Restaurant

Heinestr.

Heinestr.

Degerloch

Löffelstr.

Weinstube Klink

Fässle

Epplestr.

Reutlinger

DEGERLOCH

Deg. Albstr.

Löwenstr.

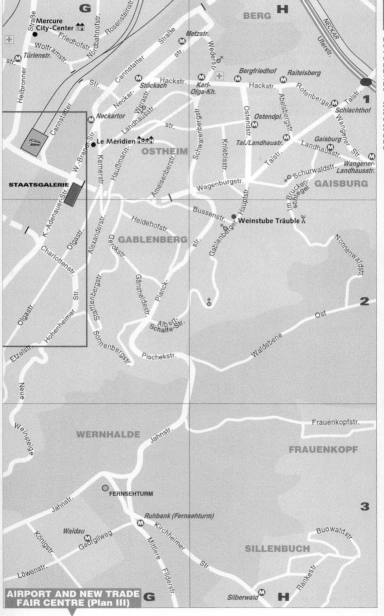

G

BERG H

NECKAR

Mercure
City-Center

Straße

Rosensteinstr.

Friedhofstr.

Nordbahnhofstr.

Wolframstr.

Türlenstr.

str.

Heilbronner

Cannstatter

Straße

Metzstr.

Weder-str.

Uferstr.

Bergfriedhof

Raitelsberg

Schlachthof

1

Hackstr.

Stöckach

Karl-
Olga-Kh.

Hackstr.

Rotenbergstr.

Abelsbergstr.

Talstr.

Neckar-
tor-str.

Wagastr.

Schwarenbergstr.

Ostendpl.

Gaisburg

Wangener Str.

Neckartor

Landhausstr.

Ostendstr.

Tal./Landhaustr.

Landhausstr.

Wangener-
Landhausstr.

str.

OSTHEIM

Knieblsstr.

Talstr.

Le Méridien

Kernerstr.

Haußmann

Ameisenbergstr.

Wagenburgstr.

Schurwaldstr.

Im Brucken-
schlegel

GAISBURG

STAATSGALERIE

K.-Adenauer-Str.

W.-Brandt-Str.

Olgastr.

Charlottenstr.

Alexanderstr.

Heidehofstr.

GABLENBERG

Gerokstr.

Bussenstr.

Gablenberger

Hauptstr.

str.

Weinstube Träuble

Nonnenwaldstr.

Olgastr.

Hohenheimer

Str.

Staffelbergstr.

Gänsheidstr.

Planck-

str.

Albert-
Schäffle-Str.

Ost

2

Etzelstr.

Sonnenbergstr.

Pischekstr.

Waldebene

Neue

Weinsteige

WERNHALDE

Jahnstr.

Frauenkopfstr.

FRAUENKOPF

Jahnstr.

FERNSEHTURM

Ruhbank (Fernsehturm)

3

Königstr.

Waldau

Georgiiweg

Kirchheimer

Mittlere

Buowaldstr.

Löwenstr.

Filder-

Str.

SILLENBUCH

Rankestr.

**AIRPORT AND NEW TRADE
FAIR CENTRE (Plan III)** G

Silberwald

H

407

Mövenpick Hotel Stuttgart Airport

Flughafenstr. 50 ✉ *70629 –* ☎ *(0711) 55 34 40*
– hotel.stuttgart.airport@moevenpick.com – Fax (0711) 5 53 44 90 00
– www.moevenpick-stuttgart-airport.com

L2

326 rm – ♦130/285 € ♦♦155/310 €, ⊑ 20 €
Rest – Carte 29/49 €

♦ Conference hotel ♦ Business ♦ Design ♦

An ultra-modern business hotel directly at the airport. It is tastefully and simply designed, from the spacious lobby via the rooms to the sauna and fitness facilities. From the clean-lined grey and white restaurant there is a view of the terminals.

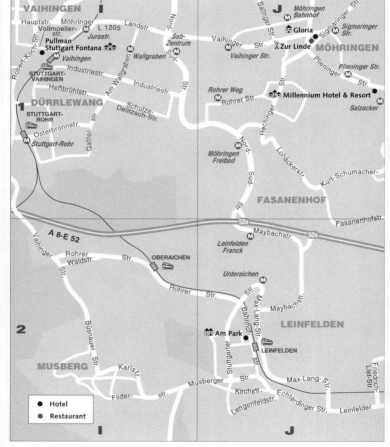

Mövenpick-Hotel Messe

Flughafenstr. 51 ⊠ *70629*

– ℰ *(0711) 7 90 70 – hotel.stuttgart.messe@moevenpick.com*

– *Fax (0711) 79 35 85*

– *www.moevenpick-stuttgart-messe.com*

229 rm – ♣131/245 € ♣♣131/270 €, ⌷ 19 €

Rest – Carte 24/44 €

L2

◆ Conference hotel ◆ Business ◆ Functional ◆

The hotel is just 200 m from the airport terminals. Very well sound-proofed, homely rooms. S-Bahn train access nearby. A restaurant serving international cuisine and a popular Sunday brunch.

GERMANY - STUTTGART

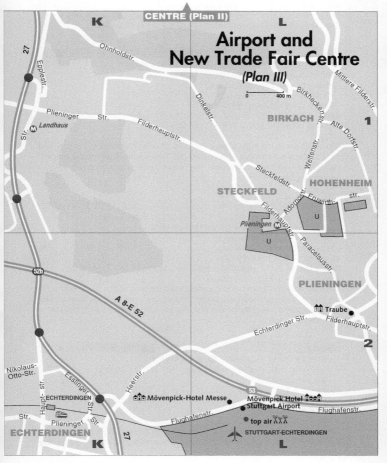

GERMANY - STUTTGART

Millennium Hotel & Resort

Plieninger Str. 100 ✉ 70567 – ⓜ Salzacker
– ☏ (0711) 72 10 – sales.stuttgart@milleniumhotels.com
– Fax (0711) 7 21 29 50 – www.si-centrum.de **J1**
454 rm – ♟109/234 € ♟♟109/234 €, ⌷ 20 € – 22 suites
Rest – Carte 27/56 €
♦ Conference hotel ♦ Personalised ♦
A large, modern hotel with rooms of various categories. The SI experience centre and its Musical Theatre are right on the doorstep. Access to the Swabian springs. Choose between 19 different restaurants, bars and cafés.

Pullman Stuttgart Fontana

Vollmoellerstr. 5 ✉ 70563 – ⓜ Vaihingen – ☏ (0711)
73 00 – h5425@accor.com – Fax (0711) 7 30 25 25
– www.pullmanhotels.com **I1**
252 rm – ♟119/169 € ♟♟139/189 €, ⌷ 19 € – 5 suites   **Rest** – Carte 23/46 €
♦ Chain hotel ♦ Business ♦ Classic ♦
This comfortable hotel offers homely, elegant rooms with high quality technical fittings. The restaurant is divided into an elegant and a rustic section.

Traube

Brabandtgasse 2 ✉ 70599 – ☏ (0711) 45 89 20 – info@
romantik-hotel-traube.com – Fax (0711) 4 58 92 20
– www.romantik-hotel-traube.com
– closed 23 December-4 January **L2**
19 rm ⌷ – ♟109/149 € ♟♟129/199 €
Rest – *(closed 2 weeks August and Saturday lunch, Sunday - Monday lunch)*
(booking advisable) Menu 52 € – Carte 33/61 €
♦ Country house ♦ Rustic ♦
This small, family-run hotel offers a range of different rooms: from the cosy and rustic to those with a more refined feel. They are divided between a historical half-timbered house and an inn. The pleasantly decorated restaurant lounges are comfortable.

Am Park

Lessingstr. 4 (Leinfelden) ✉ 70771 – ☏ (0711) 90 31 00 – info@
hotelampark-leinfelden.de – Fax (0711) 9 03 10 99
– www.hotelampark-leinfelden.de
– closed 23 December-8 January **J2**
42 rm ⌷ – ♟90/112 € ♟♟120 €
Rest – *(closed 3 - 21 August and Saturday - Sunday)* Carte 21/43 €
♦ Business ♦ Functional ♦
This hotel with its blue and white façade is in a quiet location in a cul-de-sac beside the park. A family-run hotel with bright, contemporary rooms. Enjoy carefully prepared regional dishes in the comfortable dining rooms. In summer it is pleasant to sit in the beer garden.

Gloria

Sigmaringer Str. 59 ✉ 70567 – ⓜ Sigmaringer Str.
– ☏ (0711) 7 18 50 – info@hotelgloria.de – Fax (0711) 7 18 51 21
– www.hotelgloria.de **J1**
90 rm ⌷ – ♟88/105 € ♟♟95/125 €
Rest Möhringer Hexle – ☏ (0711) 7 18 51 17 *(closed Sunday dinner, bank holidays dinner)* Carte 27/37 €
♦ Business ♦ Functional ♦
This conveniently located hotel has been managed for over 20 years by the proprietary family. The largest, most attractive rooms are the attic rooms. The friendly Möhringer Hexle also has a conservatory.

XXX

top air   [AC] **P** [VISA] ⊕ [AE] ①

at the airport (Terminal 1, Level 4) ✉ *70629 –* ✆ *(0711) 9 48 21 37 – info@restaurant-top-air.de – Fax (0711) 7 97 92 10 – www.restaurant-top-air.de – closed end December - mid January, August, Saturday - Sunday and bank holidays*   **L2**

Rest – Menu 74/112 €

Spec. Warmer Taschenkrebs mit Petersilienmousseline und confiertem Schweinebauch. Filet und Geschmortes vom Bison mit Erbsencreme. Fondant von Schokolade und Rosmarin mit Mango.

◆ Inventive ◆ Friendly ◆

Creative French cuisine and friendly professional service characterise this modern restaurant at Stuttgart airport. Some of the seats afford an interesting view of the runway.

X

Zur Linde   ☆ ⇔ [VISA] ⊕ [AE]

Sigmaringer Str. 49 ✉ *70567 –* Ⓜ *Sigmaringer Str. –* ✆ *(0711) 7 19 95 90 – info@gasthauszurlin.de – Fax (0711) 7 19 95 92 – www.joergmink.com – closed Saturday lunch*   **J1**

Rest – *(booking advisable)* Carte 28/49 €

◆ Regional ◆ Inn ◆

Lovers of Swabian food will certainly feel at home in this listed restaurant. The menu in the cosy dining rooms includes homemade Maultaschen, a local speciality. Cosy vaulted cellar for events.

ENVIRONS OF STUTTGART   *Plan I*

at Fellbach

Classic Congress Hotel   [symbols] [VISA] ⊕ [AE] ①

Tainer Str. 7 ✉ *70734 –* ✆ *(0711) 5 85 90 – info@cch-bw.de – Fax (0711) 5 85 93 04 – www.cch-bw.de – closed 21-31 December*   **D1**

149 rm � – †129/179 € ††153/203 €

Rest *Eduard M.* – see below

◆ Business ◆ Conference hotel ◆ Functional ◆

This hotel next to the Schwabenlandhalle has a lavish, glazed atrium hall. It offers functional rooms, some of which are situated beside the park, and a good capacity for conferences.

XXX

Zum Hirschen (Armin Karrer) with rm   ☆ ⁉ [VISA] ⊕ ①

Hirschstr. 1 ✉ *70734 –* ✆ *(0711) 95 79 37 10 – info@zumhirschen-fellbach.de – Fax (0711) 95 79 37 10 – www.zumhirschen-fellbach.de – closed 1 - 12 January, 9 - 13 June and 21 July - 1 August*   **D1**

9 rm ⊆ – †80/95 € ††95/130 €

Rest – *(closed Sunday - Monday) (dinner only) (booking advisable)* Menu 68/138 € ❀

Rest *Zum kleinen Hirschen* – *(closed Sunday - Monday) (lunch only)* Menu 65 € – Carte 48/64 €

Spec. Ravioli von Auberginen im Pestosud mit Calamaretti. Gebratener Seeteufel mit Bohnen und Zitronen-Senfsauce. Lammkarree mit Knoblauchjus und Kartoffeltarte.

◆ Classic ◆ Elegant ◆

This 16C building has an attractive modern interior. In the evening enjoy two set menus offering classic and Mediterranean dishes. At lunchtime the restaurant Zum kleinen Hirschen offers a simplified menu.

XX

Eduard M. – Classic Congress Hotel   ☆ [AC] ⇔ **P** [VISA] ⊕ [AE] ①

Tainer Str. 7 ✉ *70734 –* ✆ *(0711) 5 85 94 11 – restaurant@eduardm.de – Fax (0711) 5 85 94 20 – www.eduardm.de – closed 21 - 30 December*   **D1**

Rest – Menu 52 € – Carte 28/56 €

◆ International ◆ Friendly ◆

This restaurant on two levels is characterised by a friendly atmosphere. Guests can enjoy international cuisine served at attractive tables.

Aldinger's Germania

XX

Schmerstr. 6 ⊠ 70734 – ℰ (0711) 58 20 37 – aldingers@t-online.de
– Fax (0711) 58 20 77 – www.aldingers-germania.de
– closed 15 February - 2 March and Sunday - Monday **D1**
Rest – *(booking advisable)* Menu 32/42 € – Carte 23/44 €

♦ Regional ♦ Cosy ♦

For three generations the Aldinger family has been attending to its guests with tasty regional and international dishes. There is a cosy vaulted cellar available for celebrations.

PROFILE

→ **AREA:**
131 944 km²
(50 944 sq mi).

→ **POPULATION:**
10 668 000
inhabitants (est.
2005), density = 81
per km².

→ **CAPITAL:**
Athens (conurbation
3 368 000
inhabitants).

→ **CURRENCY:**
Euro (€); rate of
exchange: € 1 =
US$ 1.32 (Jan 2009).

→ **GOVERNMENT:**
Parliamentary
republic (since 1974).
Member of European
Union since 1981.

→ **LANGUAGE:**
Greek.

→ **SPECIFIC PUBLIC
HOLIDAYS:**
Epiphany (6 January);
Orthodox Shrove
Monday (late
February-March);
Independence Day
(25 March); Orthodox

Good Friday (Friday
before Easter);
Orthodox Easter
Monday; Day of
the Holy Spirit (late
May-June); Ochi
Day (28 October);
Boxing Day
(26 December).

→ **LOCAL TIME:**
GMT + 2 hours in
winter and GMT +
3 hours in summer.

→ **CLIMATE:**
Temperate
Mediterranean, with
mild winters and
hot, sunny summers
(Athens: January:
10°C, July: 27°C).

→ **INTERNATIONAL
DIALLING CODE:**
00 30 followed by
local number.

→ **EMERGENCY:**
General Police:
☏ **100**, Tourist Police:
☏ **171**, Ambulance:
☏ **166.**

→ **ELECTRICITY:**
220 volts AC, 50Hz;
2-pin round-shaped
continental plugs.

ATHENS

→ **FORMALITIES**
Travellers from the
European Union
(EU), Switzerland,
Iceland and the main
countries of North
and South America
need a national
identity card or
passport (America:
passport required) to
visit Greece for less
than three months
(tourism or business
purpose). For visitors
from other countries
a visa may be
required, in addition
to a passport,
especially for those
wishing to stay for
longer than three
months. We advise
you to check with
your embassy before
travelling.

ATHENS
ATHÍNA

Population: 732 000 (conurbation 3 368 000) – Altitude: 156m

Sime/PHOTONONSTOP

So what did the Greeks ever do for us? Apart from inventing democracy, the theatre and the Olympic Games, that is… and planting the seeds of philosophy and Western Civilisation, of course… Athens was central to all of these, a city that became a byword for glory and learning, a place whose golden reputation could inspire such awe in later centuries that just the mention of its name was enough to turn people misty-eyed and reverential: the poets Lamartine and Byron are just two who waxed lyrical over its splendours.

It's a truly magical place, built upon eight hills and plains, with a recorded history stretching back at least 3,000 years. Its short but highly productive golden age (roughly 470BC to 430BC) resulted in the architectural glory of The Acropolis, while the likes of Plato, Aristotle and Socrates were in the business of changing the mindset of society. In more recent times, Athens suffered at the hands of the motor car, the heat and the mountains, a notorious cocktail producing a fog that would hang over the city like a heavy hand, reaching such gruesome levels that even tourists stayed away. But since the 1980s and up to and beyond the 2004 Olympics, the city has made great efforts to regenerate itself with imaginative planning and a much-needed metro. Hip clubs and restaurants have sprung up. Quaint inner city areas have been restored. Could the glory days of Athens be returning?

LIVING THE CITY

No one could possibly argue with the fact that **The Acropolis** dominates Athens. It can be seen peeking through alleyways and turnings all over the city. Beneath it lies a teeming metropolis, part urban melting pot, part uber-buzzy neighbourhood. **Plaka**, below the Acropolis, is the old quarter, and the most visited, a mixture of great charm and cheap gift shops. North and west, **Monastiraki** and **Psirri** has become a trendy zone after decades of decay; to the east,

Syntagma and Kolonaki are notably modern and smart, home to the Greek parliament and the rich and famous; you can look down on them – literally and metaphorically, if you wish – from the glorious green heights of Lykkavittos Hill. The most northerly districts of central Athens are **Omonia** and **Exarcheia**, distinguished by their rugged appearance, and steeped in history; much of the life in these parts is centred round the polytechnic and the central marketplace.

PRACTICAL INFORMATION

ARRIVAL-DEPARTURE

If you're coming to the city by sea, or intending to visit the islands, then your port of call is Piraeus, a few miles from Athens. Piraeus is now the third largest port in the Mediterranean.

Athens International Airport is 33km east of the city. A taxi can take a while so your best bet is to hop on the metro and take Line 3 to Monastiraki.

TRANSPORT

Because of that traffic, the sensible way of getting around town is by the metro. Two new lines were opened in 2001 and accessibility round Athens is now markedly better than a decade ago.

Buses and trolley-buses run an excellent service (though hampered by traffic). Carnets of 10 tickets are available from newsstands, OASA booths and kiosks and at metro or subway stations.

EXPLORING ATHENS

Where can you start exploring Athens other than at the **Acropolis**? The world's most famous hill shows evidence of settlements as far back as Neolithic times,

but the reign of Pericles in the fifth century BC produced buildings so stylistically perfect that they're considered, 2,500 years later, the most important monuments in the Western world and the greatest-ever influence on our architecture. These great marble masterpieces were mostly temples built to honour **Athena**, the city's patron goddess. Their scale and breathtaking proportion manage to triumph on both a majestic and a human level, a testament to the ancient architects Iktinos and Kallikrates and the unerring eye of their supervising sculptor Phidias. The **Parthenon**, much of which still stands before us today, was completed in just 10 years, an amazing achievement. When you're up at the summit of the sacred rock of Athens, take your pick of the temples around you: The Parthenon (a must), Propyleia (the grand entrance temple), the small Temple of Athena Nike, or the exceptional Ionic structure of the Erechtheion. There are two ancient theatres also on the Acropolis, including one still used for the Athens Festival (Herodes Atticus Theatre). The other is the Dionysus Theatre, the world's oldest, where plays by Sophocles and Euripedes were staged. When visiting the Acropolis, try to get there in the early morning or evening, because crowds and midday heat can sap even the most enthusiastic classicist.

If it's just too damn hot up there at the summit, you don't have to walk far to find shady relief…and buildings dating back even further than the Parthenon. The ancient **Agora** is a grassy haven at the base of the hill, the one-time marketplace founded in the sixth century BC where the likes of Socrates would make impassioned speeches to interested passers-by. Its rambling and varied remains can confuse the unwary visitor, but it doesn't take much to fall into a reverie about the lively events that once happened here (it was the centre for civic activities such as commerce, politics, arts and athletics) and it's also where you come face-to-face with the best-preserved Classical temple in Greece, the **Temple of Hephaestus**. Stroll across to the area east of this at the bottom of the Acropolis and you're in **Plaka**, the old town section that's become the gathering place for tourists and travellers, especially in the warm Athenian evenings. Its charming ambience is captured in winding alleyways haunted by a medieval air (and touts in midsummer). Seek out nuggets of sheer delight, such as the irresistible Byzantine courtyards, and the delightful hidden neighbourhood of **Anafiotika**, which clings to the foot of the Acropolis, and contains idyllic blue-and-white houses

built in the 19 C by Cycladic workmen. Just up from here stands The Tower of the Winds, built in 50 BC by a Syrian astronomer, with personifications of the winds on each of its eight sides – there's no other building like it in the ancient world.

→ THE PAST AND THE PRESENTS

You can go from one end of the retail extreme to the other in central Athens; if you favour the cheaper option, then get up early on a Sunday and head for the **Monastiraki flea market**. Fabled throughout the Hellenic world, it takes place right next to the Agora, with traders and buyers filling the surrounding streets. Everything's for sale, from tat to things like antique furnishings and rare books. Just remember to haggle. At the other end of the shopping scale are the designer boutiques of **Kolonaki**, where haggling is most definitely not an option. This is the area where you can find the Parliament building, adjacent to which, along the avenue of Vassilissis Sofias, is the renowned **Museum Row**, home to four of Athens' finest. Nearest the Parliament building, The **Benaki Museum** is one of the best in Greece. It contains a fabulously all-encompassing range of prehistoric to 20 C Greek art, and its lovely rooftop garden restaurant is worth the visit in itself. Next along is the Museum of Cycladic Art, featuring elegant female figures carved 2,000 years before the Parthenon; the Byzantine Museum chronicles the rise and fall of the great Byzantine Empire from the third to the nineteenth century; and finally, the War Museum, on two huge floors, tells the history of conflict in Greece from prehistoric to modern times. Trumping all these fine collections, though, is the **National Archaeological Museum**, up in Exarcheia. Not only is this the number one museum in Greece, it's also one of the best in the world, containing a week's worth of ancient wonders to discover. Chief of these are arguably the treasures of the Mycenaean civilization, including hoards of gold and fantastical golden swords.

→ TECHNO ART

So, where does an Athenian go for the edgy, the arty and the gallery-strewn? Answer: a one-time toxin-spewing foundry in the Gaslands ('Gazi' in Greek), a former dingy neck of the woods just northwest of the Agora. This old foundry has been converted into a huge arts centre called **Technopolis**, where concerts, exhibits and arts spaces, generally of the first order, come together under one gargantuan roof with coloured lights illuminating the old chimneys. Some of the city's sleekest restaurants now nestle in the surrounding streets, while the neighbouring quarters of Thissio and Psirri have benefitted too, with grungy Greek music dives and squares dotted with bars and cafés sidling in alongside the industrial behemoths of yesteryear.

Athens is a hot and steamy place in the summer, so areas of green refuge are not just welcome but essential. South of the Acropolis is **Filopappou Hill**, the highest point in southern Athens, boasting superb views out to sea and, on its pathway up to the peak, a small cave that's said to be where Socrates was held after being sentenced to death for corrupting the youth of the city. The hill is full of shade and interesting paths. Back down to earth, you can escape the traffic in the rather wonderful National Gardens, next to the Parliament Building in Syntagma. These are full of exotic plants and winding paths, statuary and fountains. You may feel so intoxicated by this abundantly verdant oasis that you get lost (it has been known). Lykkavittos Hill, to the east of town, is accessible by foot, but most people take the funicular. It boasts stupendous views over the city from its Chapel of St George at the peak. There are a few little cafés dotted around the hill, great places to sip a drink or two as the sun goes down.

CALENDAR HIGHLIGHTS

Summer time is party time for Athenians. The Hellenic Festival runs from June to September and performances take place in a wonderful setting - the awe-inspiring Odeon of Herodes Atticus, which is backed by the floodlit Acropolis: other events featuring music, theatre and dance take place at venues around town. During the same months, The International Petra Festival at Petra Theatre gives it a good run for its money with an eclectic variety of music and theatre. The European Jazz Festival blasted off in Athens in 2001 and is now a renowned event for

ATHENS IN...

→ ONE DAY
Acropolis, Parthenon, Agora and Temple of Hephaestus, Plaka

→ TWO DAYS
Kolonaki, National Archaeological Museum, Filopappou Hill

→ THREE DAYS
Monastiraki flea-market (on Sunday), Benaki Museum, Technopolis, National Gardens, Lykkavittos Hill

international names – it takes place in June at Gazi's Technopolis. Rock fans, meanwhile, should make for Terravibe in June for Rockwave Festival, the best in Greece. It's a full-on rock celebration and includes bungee jumping and a skate park. The Dora Stratou Theatre is home to a renowned program of Greek folk dances from May to September, while The Greek Orthodox calendar highlight occurs at Easter, when a most impressive looking candlelit procession climbs Lykavittos Hill to the chapel of Agios Georgos. Talking of atmosphere: every August all Athens' monuments and archaeological sights are open to the public for free for moonlit classical performances under the title 'Nights Under The Full Moon'.

EATING OUT

In recent times, Michelin has been busy in Athens awarding stars for the smart new wave of restaurants that has hit the city. With many chefs now going abroad to train and returning home to put their nifty skills to good use, this is a fine time to eat out in the shadow of the Acropolis. If you want to get the full experience and dine with the locals (rather than the tourists), make your reservation for late evening, as Greeks rarely go out for dinner before 10pm. There's a good range of flavours in vogue, as ethnic menus have come to the fore, highlighted by Asian and Moroccan dishes. Sushi is now a big fish in Athens, too. And the trend towards a more eclectic restaurant scene now means that classic French and Italian cuisine is easily found. New modern tavernas offer good attention to detail, but this doesn't mean they're replacing the wonderfully traditional old favourites. These tavernas, along with mezedopoleia, are the backbone of Greek dining, and most visitors wouldn't think their trip was complete without eating in at least one or two. Often the waiter will just tell you what's cooking today, and you're often very welcome to go into the kitchen and make your selection. Greece is a country where it is customary to tip good service; ten per cent is the normal rate.

➜ UNIFORM APPEAL

A time-honoured tourist ritual is having a gander at the changing of the guard outside the Parliament Building, on the hour every hour. Individual soldiers perform an eye-catching high kicking march, wearing mini skirts, white stockings, and red clogs with pom-poms. Selected from the ranks of Greek military conscripts, they're chosen these days not because of any war-like efficiency, but because of crowd-pleasing height and good looks.

➜ MARBLES RE-FOUND

The exciting, brand new Acropolis Museum in Makrigianni, at the foot of Acropolis hill, is more than just a stunning, all-glass showpiece for its fabulous treasures. It's a sharp reminder that Greece now has a safe and adequate home for its **Marbles**, purloined by the Earl of Elgin in 1799 and sold to the British Museum where they remain to this day. After gazing at them for hours, Keats summed up the beauty of the Marbles when he famously wrote: 'Beauty is truth, truth beauty – that is all ye know on earth, and all ye need to know.'

➜ A LONG WAIT FOR THE METRO

If you fancy a trip to a museum, you could do worse than nip down into the metro. During construction, many of the stations unearthed ancient remains, and these have been put on display for travellers or curious tourists; expect to find the likes of pottery and gravestones, even a skeleton still entombed. Two of the best stations are Syntagma and Akropoli. Catching a train afterwards is optional.

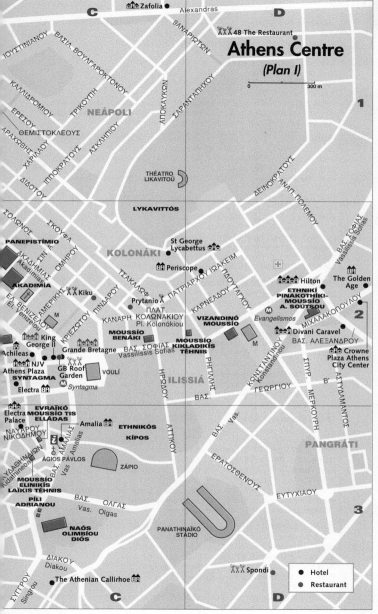

Zafolia ●

Alexandras

9ANAPIΩTΩN

✗✗✗48 The Restaurant

Athens Centre
(Plan I)

0   300 m

1

ΙΟΥΣΤΙΝΙΑΝΟΥ

ΒΑΣΙΛ. ΒΟΥΛΓΑΡΟΚΤΟΝΟΥ

ΚΑΛΛΙΔΡΟΜΙΟΥ

ΕΡΕΣΟΥ

ΤΡΙΚΟΥΠΗ

ΑΠΟΚΑΥΚΩΝ

ΣΑΡΑΝΤΑΠΗΧΟΥ

NEÁPOLI

ΘΕΜΙΣΤΟΚΛΕΟΥΣ

ΑΡΑΧΩΒΗΣ

ΧΑΡΙΛΑΟΥ

ΙΠΠΟΚΡΑΤΟΥΣ

ΑΣΚΛΗΠΙΟΥ

ΔΙΔΟΤΟΥ

THÉÁTRO LIKAVITOÚ

ΔΕΙΝΟΚΡΑΤΟΥΣ

ΑΝΑΠ. ΠΟΛΕΜΟΥ

ΒΑΣ. ΣΟΦΙΑΣ
Vassilissis Sofias

LYKAVITTÓS

ΣΟΛΩΝΟΣ

ΣΚΟΥΦΑ

PANEPISTÍMIO

ΣΙΝ

ΟΜΗΡΟΥ

KOLONÁKI ●

St George Lycabettus ▲▲

ΑΚΑΔΗΜΙΑΣ
Akadimías

▲▲ Periscope

ΠΑΤΡΙΑΡΧΟΥ ΙΩΑΚΕΙΜ

✚ Hilton

The Golden Age ●

AKADIMÍA

ΕΛ. ΑΜΕΡΙΚΗΣ

✗✗ Kiku

ΠΙΝΔΑΡΟΥ

ΤΣΑΚΑΛΩΦ

ΚΑΡΝΕΑΔΟΥ

ΠΛΟΥΤΑΡΧΟΥ

ETHNIKÍ PINAKOTHÍKI-MOUSSÍO A. SOÚTSOU

ΜΙΧΑΛΑΚΟΠΟΥΛΟΥ

ΕΛ. ΒΕΝΙΖΕΛΟΥ
El. Venizélou

M

Prytanío ✗

ΚΑΝΑΡΗ

ΠΛΑΤ.
ΚΟΛΩΝΑΚΙΟΥ
Pl. Kolonákiou

Evangelismos

M

Divani Caravel ▲▲

VIZANDINÓ MOUSSÍO

ΚΡΙΕΖΩΤΟΥ

MOUSSÍO BENÁKI

ΒΑΣ. ΣΟΦΙΑΣ
Vassilissis Sofias

MOUSSÍO KIKLADIKIS TÉHNIS

ΒΑΣ. ΑΛΕΞΑΝΔΡΟΥ

▲▲ Crowne Plaza Athens City Center

▲▲ King George II

▲▲ Grande Bretagne

ΡΗΓΙΛΛΗΣ

ΚΩΝΣΤΑΝΤΙΝΟΥ
Konstandínou

M

ΣΠΥΡ.

Β΄.

ΑΤΤΥΔΑΜΑΝΤΟΣ

Achíleas ●

▲▲ NJV Athens Plaza

SYNTAGMA

GB Roof Garden

VOULÍ

ΗΡΩΔΟΥ

ILISSIÁ

ΓΕΩΡΓΙΟΥ

ΜΕΡΚΟΥΡΗ

PANGRÁTI

Electra ▲▲

Syntagma

ΒΑΣ.

ΒΑΣ. Vas.

▲▲ Electra Palace

EVRAÏKÓ MOUSSÍO TIS ELLÁDAS

ΝΑΥΑΡΟΥ
ΝΙΚΟΔΗΜΟΥ

Amalía ▲▲

ETHNIKÓS KÍPOS

ΑΤΤΙΚΟΥ

ΕΡΑΤΟΣΘΕΝΟΥΣ

ΧΥΔΑΘΗΝΑΙΩΝ
Kidathíneon

ÁGIOS PÁVLOS

✚

ΒΑΣ. ΑΜΑΛΙΑΣ
Vas. Amalías

ZÁPIO

ΕΥΤΥΧΙΑΟΥ

3

MOUSSÍO ELINIKÍS LAIKÍS TÉHNIS

PÍLI ADRIÁNOU

ΒΑΣ. ΟΛΓΑΣ
Vas. Olgas

NAÓS OLIMBÍOU DIÓS

PANATHINAÏKÓ STADIO

ΔΙΑΚΟΥ
Diákou

ΣΥΓΓΡΟΥ
Singroú

● The Athenian Callirhoe ▲▲

✗✗✗ Spondi

●	Hotel
●	Restaurant

C   **D**

Grande Bretagne

≤ ⅃⅚ ⊕ ⅏ ⅂ ⅃ ⅙ ᴀ⦿ ⅟ rm ⅏ ⊠ ⅍

Constitution Sq ⊠ *105 63* – 🅜 *Syntagma* – ℰ *(210)* VISA ⦿ 🄰🄴 ⓞ
3330 000 – *info@grandebretagne.gr* – *Fax (210) 3228 0 34*
– *www.grandebretagne.gr* **C2**
265 rm – †656/700 € ††828 €, � 35 € – 56 suites
Rest *GB Roof Garden* – see below
Rest *GB Corner* – ℰ *(210) 3330 750* – Carte 65/99 €
♦ Grand Luxury ♦ Palace ♦ Stylish ♦

Stylish 19C hotel with classic, modernised interior overlooking Constitution Square. Splendid spa and pool. Luxuriously-appointed bedrooms; 2 floors offer a butler service. GB Corner offers an international à la carte menu.

Hilton

≤ ⅏ ⅃⅚ ⊕ ⅏ ⅂ ⅃ ⅙ ᴀ⦿ ⅟ rm ⅏ ⊠ ⅍ ⅚ VISA ⦿ 🄰🄴 ⓞ

46 Vas. Sofias Ave ⊠ *115 28* – 🅜 *Evangelismos* – ℰ *(210) 7281 000*
– *sales.athens@hilton.com* – *Fax (210) 7281 2 41* – *www.athens.hilton.com*
506 rm – †229 € ††359 €, ⊠ 33 € – 18 suites **D2**
Rest *The Byzantine* – ℰ *(210) 7281 400 (Buffet lunch)* Menu 42/44 €
– Carte 55/75 €
Rest *Galaxy Roof* – ℰ *(210) 7281 402 (May to October) (dinner only)*
Carte 62/86 €
Rest *Milo's* – ℰ *(210) 7244 400* – Menu 20 € – Carte 85/150 €
♦ Grand Luxury ♦ Modern ♦

Luxurious modern hotel close to city centre, near shops and Kolonaki Square. Bedrooms similar in size; all are well-equipped with every modern comfort. Informal Byzantine with an international menu. Rooftop Galaxy with terrace and lounge/bar is the place to be seen. Milo's is large seafood restaurant with open-plan kitchen.

Athenaeum Inter-Continental

≤ ⅏ ⅃⅚ ⊕ ⅏ ⅂ ⅙ ᴀ⦿ ⅟ rm

89-93 Singrou (Southwest : 2 ¾ km) ⊠ ⅟ ⅍ ⅚ VISA ⦿ 🄰🄴 ⓞ
⊠ *117 45* – ℰ *(210) 9206 000* – *attha.hotel@ihg.com* – *Fax (210) 9206 5 00*
– *www.athensintercontinental.com*
543 rm – †150/260 € ††150/260 €, ⊠ 32 € – 60 suites
Rest *Première (9th floor)* – ℰ *(210) 9206 981 (Closed Sunday and Monday)*
(dinner only) Menu 52 € – Carte 63/86 €
Rest *Cafezoe* – ℰ *(210) 9206 655 (buffet lunch)* Carte 46/65 €
♦ Grand Luxury ♦ Business ♦ Modern ♦

Modern, top class corporate hotel, close to business district, with modern artwork displayed throughout. Luxuriously-appointed club floor rooms with exclusive lounge. Roof-top gourmet restaurant; splendid views. Informal all day café near swimming pool; international menu, some Greek specialities.

King George Palace

⅏ ⅃⅚ ⊕ ⅏ ⅂ ⅙ ᴀ⦿ ⅟ rm ⅏ ⅟ ⅍

3 Vasileos Georgiou A, Syntagma (Constitution) Sq VISA ⦿ 🄰🄴 ⓞ
⊠ *105 64* – 🅜 *Syntagma* – ℰ *(210) 3222 210* – *info@kinggeorge.gr*
– *Fax (210) 3250 5 04* – *www.classicalhotels.com* **C2**
89 rm ⊠ – †490 € ††490 € – 13 suites
Rest *Tudor Hall* – *(Closed January-March and Sunday)* Carte 70/116 €
♦ Luxury ♦ Classic ♦

Elegant converted mansion in Syntagma Square. Luxurious bedrooms with handmade French furniture; rooftop suite with own pool and panoramic views. Stylish 7th floor restaurant with chandeliers, large terrace and good views. Eclectic menu.

Divani Caravel

≤ ⅃⅚ ⅏ ⅂ ⅙ ᴀ⦿ ⅟ ⊠ ⅍ ⅚ VISA ⦿ 🄰🄴 ⓞ

2 Vas. Alexandrou ⊠ *161 21* – 🅜 *Evangelismos* – ℰ *(210) 7207 000* – *info@*
divanicaravel.gr – *Fax (210) 7236 6 83* – *www.divanis.com* **D2**
427 rm – †370/470 € ††370/470 €, ⊠ 32 € – 44 suites
Rest *Brown's* – *(Closed Sunday) (dinner only)* Carte 58/75 €
Rest *Café Constantinople* – Carte 38/58 €
♦ Business ♦ Classic ♦

Modern hotel with spacious, marbled lobby. Attractive roof terrace with far-reaching views. Well-equipped, classically furnished rooms. Brown's for stylish dining and elegant cigar lounge; international cuisine with Asian influences. Café Constantinople is open all day and serves buffet lunch.

GREECE - ATHENS

Metropolitan 🛏️ 🗼 ⛹️ 🏊 ⛷️ 🔲 ⚐ rm 🔲 📞 🛁 **P** 🔲 🔲 🔲 🔲

385 Singrou Ave (Southwest : 7 km) ✉️ *175 64 –* ☏ *(210) 9471 000*
– metropolitan@chandris.gr – Fax (210) 9471 0 10 – www.chandris.gr
350 rm – †545 € ††545 €, ⛲ 22 € – 25 suites
Rest Trocadero – Menu 35 € – Carte 34/46 €
◆ Business ◆ Modern ◆
Striking, modern corporate hotel with easy access into and out of the city. Spacious, comfortable rooms with state-of-the-art facilities. Popular for business conventions. International or Italian fare can be taken overlooking the garden or beside the pool.

Ledra Marriott 🗼 🌐 🛏️ 🏊 ⛷️ 🔲 ⚐ rm 🔲 🛁 🛏️

115 Singrou (Southwest : 3 km) ✉️ *117 45 –* ☏ *(210)* 🔲 🔲 🔲 🔲
9300 000 – athensledramarriott@marriotthotels.com – Fax (210) 9559 1 53
– www.athensledramarriott.com
296 rm – †199/249 € ††199/249 €, ⛲ 26 € – 18 suites
Rest Kona Kai – *(Closed Sunday) (dinner only)* Menu 55 € – Carte 68/87 €
Rest Zephyros – ☏ *(210) 9300 060 (buffet lunch)* Carte 38/42 €
◆ Business ◆ Modern ◆
Commercial hotel with panoramic views from rooftop terrace. Executive rooms have exclusive lounge and high-tech extras. Ornate Kona Kai for authentic Polynesian dishes and teppan-yaki. Zephyros on 1st floor for traditional and international buffet.

NJV Athens Plaza 🔲 ⚐ rm 🔲 🛁 🛏️ 🔲 🔲 🔲 🔲

2 Vas. Georgiou A, Syntagma Sq ✉️ *105 64 –* Ⓜ *Syntagma –* ☏ *(210) 3352 400*
– sales_njv@classicalhotels.com – Fax (210) 3235 8 56
– www.classicalhotels.com **C2**
159 rm – †260/300 € ††280/320 €, ⛲ 25 € – 23 suites
Rest The Parliament – Carte 41/60 €
◆ Business ◆ Classic ◆
Modern hotel handy for the shopping and business districts. Local stone adorns the contemporary lobby and bar. Boldly decorated, hi-tech bedrooms and luxurious suites. Modern menu of international dishes served in stylish first floor restaurant.

Athens Imperial 🗼 🛏️ 🏊 ⛷️ 🔲 ⚐ rm 🔲 🛁 🛏️ 🔲 🔲 🔲 🔲

Karaiskaki Sq ✉️ *104 37 –* Ⓜ *Metaxourghio –* ☏ *(210) 5201 600 – ai@*
classicalhotels.gr – Fax (210) 5225 5 21 – www.classicalhotels.com
235 rm – †530 € ††530 €, ⛲ 23 € – 25 suites **A2**
Rest – Carte 33/58 €
◆ Business ◆ Modern ◆
Modern hotel, its impressive atrium boasting opulent lounge and bar with suspended arboreal artwork. Lovely rooftop decked pool area with superb views to Acropolis. Mod cons match smart, stylish rooms. Views over the square from restaurant; international cuisine served.

St George Lycabettus ⟨ 🛏️ 🗼 🌐 🛏️ 🏊 🔲 🛁 🛏️ 🛏️

2 Kleomenous St ✉️ *106 75 –* ☏ *(210) 7290 711* 🔲 🔲 🔲 🔲
– info@sglycabettus.gr – Fax (210) 7290 4 39 – www.sglycabettus.gr
148 rm – †455 € ††522 €, ⛲ 29 € – 6 suites **C2**
Rest Le Grand Balcon – *(Closed Sunday and Monday) (dinner only)*
Carte 28/48 €
Rest Frame – Menu 28 €
◆ Business ◆ Modern ◆
Elevated position on Lycabettus Hill. Greek artwork and artefacts throughout. Rooftop pool. South-facing rooms with balconies, view of Acropolis and Athens skyline. Le Grand Balcon roof-top restaurant for international menu. All day Frame for Greek dishes.

Divani Palace Acropolis 🔊 AC ↔ rm 🖭 ℃ 🖋 VISA ⨾ AE ⓘ

19-25 Parthenonos ⊠ 117 42 – Ⓜ Akropolis – ℰ (210) 9280 100 – divanis@ divaniacropolis.gr – Fax (210) 9214 9 93 – www.divaniacropolis.gr
242 rm – †275/325 € ††275/325 €, ⊆ 20 € – 8 suites **B3**
Rest *Aspassia* – Menu 30 € – Carte 36/68 €
Rest *Roof Garden* – *(Closed Tuesday) (dinner only)* Carte 60/90 €
◆ Traditional ◆ Classic ◆

Near the Parthenon yet fairly quiet with parts of Themistocles' wall in the basement. Particularly comfortable suites. All day Aspassia for international and Greek meals. Roof Garden for summer barbecue buffet with live music.

Electra Palace ⩽ 𝄞 ⋒ 🔊 ⛶ AC ↔ rm 🖭 ℃ 🖋 ⨾

18-20 Nikodimou St ⊠ 105 57 – Ⓜ Syntagma VISA ⨾ AE ⓘ
– ℰ (210) 3370 000 – salesepath@electrahotels.gr – Fax (210) 3241 8 75
– www.electrahotels.gr **C3**
135 rm ⊆ – †226/360 € ††298/360 € – 20 suites
Rest – *(dinner only)* Carte 51/63 €
◆ Business ◆ Classic ◆

Modern interior behind a classical façade on a quiet street in Plaka. Ultra-modern bedrooms and suites with classical décor; some with view of the Acropolis. Electra rooftop restaurant with beautiful terrace and superb view. Creative Greek cuisine.

Park H. Athens ⩽ 𝄞 ⋒ 🔊 ⅙ AC ↔ rm 🖭 ℡ 🖋 ⨾

10 Alexandras Ave ⊠ 106 82 – Ⓜ Victoria – ℰ (210) VISA ⨾ AE ⓘ
8894 500 – sales@athensparkhotel.gr – Fax (210) 8238 4 20
– www.athensparkhotel.gr **B1**
140 rm – †320/360 € ††380/420 €, ⊆ 18 € – 10 suites
Rest *Park Café* – Carte 18/40 €
Rest *St'Astra* – *(Closed Sunday) (dinner only)* Menu 55 € – Carte 60/110 €
◆ Business ◆ Traditional ◆ Classic ◆

Modern, family-owned hotel between the archaeological museum and Pedio Areos Park. Smartly fitted rooms, suites with spa baths. Enjoy view from St'Astra by rooftop pool. Mediterranean menu and live jazz in evenings.

Crowne Plaza Athens City Center ⩽ 𝄞 ⋒ 🔊 ⛶ ↔ rm 🖭

50 Mihalakopoulou ⊠ 115 28 ℡ 🖋 ⨾ VISA ⨾ AE ⓘ
– Ⓜ Megaro Moussikis – ℰ (210) 7278 000 – info@cpathens.com – Fax (210) 7278 6 00 – www.cpathens.com **D2**
191 rm – †184/244 € ††184/244 €, ⊆ 27 € – 2 suites
Rest *Ambrosia* – Carte 40/70 €
◆ Chain hotel ◆ Business ◆ Modern ◆

Centrally located corporate hotel. 17 new bedrooms boast sitting areas, large desks and mod cons; smart bathrooms have TVs in the mirrors. Excellent conference facilities. casual dining in 1st floor Ambrosia.

Holiday Suites *without rest* AC ℡ VISA ⨾ AE ⓘ

4 Arnis St (by Mihalakopoulou) ⊠ 115 28 – Ⓜ Megaro Moussikis – ℰ (210) 7278 500 – info@hiathens.com – Fax (210) 7278 6 96 – www.holiday-suites.com
16 rm – †167/237 € ††167/247 € – **18 suites**, ⊆ 21 €
◆ Business ◆ Modern ◆

Converted apartments in quiet residential area. Spacious rooms each with kitchenette, sofa and work area, superbly equipped with CD/DVD/fax. Breakfast here or at the Crowne Plaza Athens City Center.

Zafolia ⩽ 𝄞 ⋒ 🔊 ⅙ AC ↔ rm 🖭 ℃ 🖋 ⨾ VISA ⨾ AE ⓘ

87-89 Alexandras Ave ⊠ 114 74 – Ⓜ Ambelokipi – ℰ (210) 6449 002 – info@ zafoliahotel.gr – Fax (210) 6442 0 42 – www.zafoliahotel.gr **C1**
185 rm ⊆ – †138/180 € ††145/180 € – 7 suites **Rest** – Menu 25/42 €
◆ Business ◆ Modern ◆

Privately-owned, commercial hotel on east side of city. Well-equipped rooms with modern amenities, some with private balcony. Excellent views from rooftop bar and pool. Shop-fitted mezzanine level restaurant. Greek and international menu.

Eridanus 🛋 ᵻ₅ 🕸 AC CAT ⁽¹⁾ 🏊 🚙 VISA ⓪ AE ⓪

78 Pireaus Ave, Keramikos ✉ *104 35* – Ⓜ *Thissio* – 𝒞 *(210) 5205 360*
– eridanus@eridanus.gr – Fax (210) 5200 5 50 – www.eridanus.gr
35 rm 🖙 – 🛉170/245 € 🛉🛉170/245 € – 3 suites   **A2**
Rest *Perea* *– (closed Sunday) (dinner only)* Carte 36/56 €
♦ Business ♦ Stylish ♦

Contemporary design hotel on a busy main road. Luxurious bedrooms with high-tech equipment and hydro massage showers; some with views of the Acropolis. Contemporary French cuisine in Perea; dinner is served on the rooftop terrace in summer.

The Athenian Callirhoe *without rest* ᵻ₅ 🕸 AC ⁴⁄⁻ CAT ⁽¹⁾ 🏊

✉ *117 43* VISA ⓪ AE ⓪
32 Kallirois Ave and Petmeza ✉ *117 43*
– Ⓜ *Singrou-Fix* – 𝒞 *(210) 9215 353 – hotel@tac.gr – Fax (210) 9215 3 42*
– www.tac.gr   **C3**
84 rm 🖙 – 🛉130/190 € 🛉🛉150/200 €
♦ Business ♦ Stylish ♦

A bright, contemporary boutique hotel with subtle art deco styling. City views from the rooftop terrace and balconies of the smartly fitted executive rooms.

Alexandros 🏡 ᵻ₅ 🕸 �&. AC ⁴⁄⁻ rm CAT ⁽¹⁾ 🏊 🚙 VISA ⓪ AE ⓪

8 Timoleontos Vassou St (via Vas. Sofias off Soutsou D.) ✉ *115 21*
– Ⓜ *Megaro Moussikis* – 𝒞 *(210) 6430 464 – alexandros@airotel.gr – Fax (210)*
6441 0 84 – www.airotel.gr
92 rm 🖙 – 🛉86/146 € 🛉🛉96/156 € – 3 suites
Rest *Don Giovanni* – Carte 25/75 €
♦ Business ♦ Modern ♦

A relaxed, commercial hotel off a busy avenue in residential area. Simple accommodation is offered in comfortably appointed bedrooms. Don Giovanni is an elegant little restaurant offering mostly Greek cuisine, with some Italian dishes too.

Electra AC ⁴⁄⁻ CAT ⁽¹⁾ 🏊 VISA ⓪ AE ⓪

5 Ermou ✉ *105 63* – Ⓜ *Syntagma* – 𝒞 *(210) 3378 000 – saleselath@*
electrahotels.gr – Fax (210) 3220 3 10 – www.electrahotels.gr   **C2**
106 rm 🖙 – 🛉195/312 € 🛉🛉252/312 € – 3 suites
Rest – Menu 27 € – Carte 43/51 €
♦ Business ♦ Modern ♦

Popular tourist hotel within the lively pedestrianised shopping area. Soundproofed, refurbished bedrooms are thoughtfully equipped and well maintained, some have spa baths. International dishes in mezzanine restaurant.

Art AC ⁴⁄⁻ CAT ⁽¹⁾ 🏊 VISA ⓪ AE

27 Marni St ✉ *104 32* – Ⓜ *Omonia* – 𝒞 *(210) 5240 501 – info@*
arthotelathens.gr – Fax (210) 5243 3 84 – www.arthotelathens.gr
30 rm 🖙 – 🛉69/129 € 🛉🛉105/129 €   **Rest** – Carte 40/60 €   **B1**
♦ Family ♦ Personalised ♦

The name's the clue: artwork in all areas of this family-owned 21C boutique hotel behind a classic 1930s façade on busy central street. Simply furnished bedrooms; some with balcony. Classically-styled restaurant; short international menu.

Baby Grand AC ⁴⁄⁻ CAT ⁽¹⁾ 🏊 VISA ⓪ AE ⓪

65 Athens St ✉ *105 52* – Ⓜ *Omonia* – 𝒞 *(210) 3250 900 – bg@*
classicalhotels.com – Fax (210) 3743 9 20 – www.classicalhotels.com
70 rm – 🛉490 € 🛉🛉490 €, 🖙 21 € – 6 suites   **B2**
Rest *Baby Grand* – Carte 25/40 €
♦ Business ♦ Modern ♦

Eclectically-furnished city centre hotel featuring Mini Cooper reception desks. Relax in colourful lounge with squashy sofas. Individually designed rooms are well equipped. Ground floor restaurant serves international and Greek dishes.

Amalia

AC ☐ 📞 🏄 VISA ⑳ AE ①

10 Amalia Ave ⊠ 105 57 – Ⓜ Syntagma – ℰ (210) 3237 300 – reserve@ amaliahotels.com – Fax (210) 3237 3 09 – www.amaliahotels.com
97 rm – ♦150/200 € ♦♦220/280 €, � 20 € – 1 suite   **C3**
Rest – Carte 29/49 €

♦ Chain hotel ♦ Modern ♦

Well located just in front of the National Gardens. Spacious, modern bedrooms, refurbished in 2007; those in front have balconies overlooking the gardens. First floor restaurant serves Mediterranean and Greek cuisine.

Periscope without rest

AC ↩ ☐ 📞 🏄 VISA ⑳ AE ①

22 Haritos St, Kolonaki ⊠ 106 75 – Ⓜ Evangelismos – ℰ (210) 7297 200 – info@periscope.gr – Fax (210) 7297 2 06 – www.periscope.gr   **D2**
21 rm ⊆ – ♦165 € ♦♦225 €

♦ Business ♦ Modern ♦

Minimalism in quiet area; trendy bar has plasma screens and reconditioned Mini Cooper seats! Uniquely-styled rooms boast balconies; executive rooms are quietest and have enlarged Athenian images on ceiling.

The Golden Age

AC ↩ rm ☐ 📞 🏄 VISA ⑳ AE ①

57 Michaelakopoulou ⊠ 115 28 – Ⓜ Megaro Moussikis – ℰ (210) 7240861 – goldenage@ath.forthnet.gr – Fax (210) 7 21 39 65 – www.goldenage.gr
115 rm – ♦192 € ♦♦234 €, ⊆ 31 € – 7 suites   **D2**
Rest – Carte 41 €

♦ Business ♦ Functional ♦

This refurbished hotel boasts a new steely high-tech façade and good-sized bedrooms with up-to-date facilities; those at the front have balconies, while those at the back are quieter. International cuisine.

Hermes without rest

AC ☐ 📞 VISA ⑳ AE ①

19 Apollonos St ⊠ 105 57 – Ⓜ Syntagma – ℰ (210) 3235 514 – hermes@ tourhotel.gr – Fax (210) 3211 8 00 – www.hermeshotel.gr   **B3**
45 rm ⊆ – ♦90/145 € ♦♦95/145 €

♦ Family ♦ Modern ♦

Small modern hotel near the shops in Plaka. Stylish lobby and breakfast room. Tidy bedrooms have all mod cons; those at the front have balconies.

O & B

☐ 📞 VISA ⑳ AE

7 Leokoriou St ⊠ 105 54 – Ⓜ Thissio – ℰ (210) 331 2940 – info@ oandbhotel.com – Fax (210) 331 29 42 – www.oandbhotel.com   **A2**
11 rm – ♦150/250 € ♦♦150/250 €   **Rest** – Menu 26/40 € – Carte 33/64 €

♦ Townhouse ♦ Design ♦

Boutique hotel in up and coming part of town. Good sized bedrooms boast ochre and brown colour schemes, quality furnishings and attention to detail; suite has terrace and views. Restaurant offers all day café-style fare, including pasta, Greek and Mediterranean dishes.

Museum without rest

AC ↩ 📞 🏄 VISA ⑳ AE ①

16 Bouboulinas St ⊠ 106 82 – Ⓜ Victoria – ℰ (210) 3805 611 – museum@ hotelsofathens.com – Fax (210) 3800 5 07 – www.hotelsofathens.com
93 rm ⊆ – ♦65/150 € ♦♦70/230 €   **B1**

♦ Family ♦ Functional ♦

Overlooking the National Archaeological Museum and offering comfy facilities. Extension rooms are spacious, stylish and modern. Others are classically-furnished, with balcony views.

Arion without rest

AC ☐ VISA ⑳ AE

18 Aglou Dimitriou St ⊠ 105 54 – Ⓜ Monastiraki – ℰ (210) 3240 415 – arion@tourhotel.gr – Fax (210) 3222 4 19 – www.arionhotel.gr   **B2**
51 rm ⊆ – ♦70/110 € ♦♦80/135 €

♦ Family ♦ Modern ♦

A sensibly priced tourist hotel in a lively part of city. Roof-top terrace with superb views. Compact, impressive rooms - ask for one that overlooks Acropolis.

Plaka without rest ≼ AC ⁽ᵗ⁾ VISA ⵯ AE ①

7 Kapnikareas and Mitropoleos St ⊠ *105 56 –* Ⓜ *Monastiraki –* ℰ *(210)*
3222 096 – plaka@tourhotel.gr – Fax (210) 3211 8 00 – www.plakahotel.gr
67 rm � – †90/145 € ††95/145 €   **B3**
♦ Traditional ♦ Family ♦

Privately owned hotel among shops and tavernas, with a rooftop bar overlooking
the old town. Spotless, sensibly priced modern rooms; ask for one with a view of
the Acropolis.

Achilleas without rest AC CAT VISA ⵯ AE

21 Lekka St ⊠ *105 54 –* Ⓜ *Syntagma –* ℰ *(210) 3233197 – marilena@*
tourhotel.gr – Fax (210) 3 21 67 79 – www.achilleashotel.gr   **C2**
34 rm ⊠ – †70/110 € ††80/135 €
♦ Family ♦ Functional ♦

In small street known for its silversmiths, near Constitution Square. Spacious
bedrooms, ideal for families. Clean compact bathrooms. Mezzanine for self-service
breakfast.

XXX Spondi ⏢ AC ⇔ P VISA ⵯ AE ①
⁂ ⁂

5 Pyronos, off Varnava Sq, Pangrati ⊠ *116 36 –* ℰ *(210) 7564 021 – spondi@*
relaischateaux.com – Fax (210) 7567 0 21 – www.spondi.gr
– Closed 1 week Easter   **D3**
Rest – *(dinner only)* Menu 70/115 € – Carte 87/112 € ⊞
Spec. Tandoori-roasted scallops with cabbage and candied lemon butter.
Duck coated in aniseed with candied peaches and sweet potato. Half-coo-
ked Guanaja chocolate brownie and coffee ice cream.
♦ French ♦ Formal ♦

Attractive converted villa creating an intimate atmosphere in its elegant rooms
and external courtyard and terraces. Outstanding modern French cooking; well
crafted, balanced and precise.

XXX Varoulko (Lazarou Lefteris) ⏢ AC VISA ⵯ AE ①
⁂

80 Pireaus Ave, Keramikos ⊠ *104 35 –* Ⓜ *Thissio –* ℰ *(210) 5228 400 – info@*
varoulko.gr – Fax (210) 5228 8 00 – www.varoulko.gr
– Closed Christmas, Easter, 13-18 August and Sunday   **A2**
Rest – *(booking essential) (dinner only)* Carte 54/64 €
Spec. Fresh squid with basil pesto and nest of fries. White grouper with por-
cini mushrooms and truffle paste. Sautéed apples with pear streusel and
caramel ice cream
♦ Seafood ♦ Fashionable ♦

Modern, stylish restaurant in converted house with roof terrace and view of the
Acropolis. Daily-changing menu of freshest and finest local seafood. Accomplished
cooking.

XX GB Roof Garden – at Grande Bretagne Hotel ≼ ⏢ AC

– ℰ *(210) 3330 876 – info@grandebretagne.gr*   VISA ⵯ AE ①
– Fax (210) 3228 0 34 – www.grandbretagne.gr   **C2**
Rest – *(booking essential)* Carte 57/86 €
♦ Mediterranean ♦ Friendly ♦

Very comfortable, popular roof-top dining room with lively bar and spectacular
views. Elegantly dressed tables. Mediterranean and Greek menu. Relaxed, informal ambience.

XX Hytra AC VISA ⵯ AE ①

Navarhou Apostoli 7, Psirri ⊠ *105 54 –* Ⓜ *Monastiraki –* ℰ *(210) 3316 767*
– info@hytra.gr – Fax (210) 3316 7 67 – www.hytra.gr
– Closed April-October and Monday   **B2**
Rest – *(dinner only)* Carte 47/60 €
♦ Inventive ♦ Trendy ♦

Refurbished, vibrant modern restaurant in trendy Psirri. Modish Greek menus,
innovative in places; reworking of Greek classics. Friendly, knowledgeable service.

GREECE - ATHENS

XX **Luna Rossa** ⟺ 𝑉𝐼𝑆𝐴 ◐● 𝐀𝐄

213 Sokratous, Kallithea (Southwest : 4 km) ✉ *176 74*
– 𝒞 (210) 942 3777 – info@lunarossa.gr – Fax (210) 9328 1 46
– www.lunarossa.gr
– Closed August
Rest *– (lunch by arrangement)* Menu 45/60 €
– Carte 60/90 € ❧
♦ Italian ♦ Family ♦
Delightful and intimate converted house which still feels like a family home. Divided into four dining rooms and small terrace. Authentic Italian cooking with Roman base. Comprehensive and impressive wine list.

XX **Kiku** 𝐀𝐂 𝑉𝐼𝑆𝐴 ◐● 𝐀𝐄 ◑

12 Dimokritou St, Kolonaki ✉ *106 73 –* Ⓜ *Syntagma*
– 𝒞 (210) 3647 033 – athenskiku@yahoo.gr – Fax (210) 3626 2 39
– www.kiku.com
– Closed August, Easter, Christmas, New Year and Sunday **C2**
Rest *–* Menu 35/71 € *–* Carte 62/71 €
♦ Japanese ♦ Minimalist ♦
Authentic Japanese restaurant hidden away in a quiet side street. Clean, crisp, minimalist interior and large sushi counter with mood changing lighting.

X **Kuzina** 🍴 𝐀𝐂 𝑉𝐼𝑆𝐴 ◐● ◑

9 Adrianou St ✉ *105 55 –* Ⓜ *Thissio – 𝒞 (210) 3240 133*
– Fax (210) 3240 1 35 – www.kuzina.gr **B3**
Rest *–* Carte 32/45 €
♦ Modern ♦ Bistro ♦
Modern taverna-style restaurant in the Thissio area, with large front terrace, open kitchen and lively atmosphere. Contemporary cooking makes good use of local produce.

X **Psarra's** 🍴 𝑉𝐼𝑆𝐴 ◐● 𝐀𝐄

16 Erehtheos and Erotokritou St, Plaka ✉ *105 56 –* Ⓜ *Monastiraki*
– 𝒞 (210) 3218 733 – Fax (210) 3218 7 34
– www.psaras-taverna.gr **B3**
Rest *–* Menu 15/40 € *–* Carte 19/31 €
♦ Traditional ♦ Rustic ♦
Just below the Acropolis; has been a taverna since 1898. Refurbished rustic style within two yellow-washed houses with terrace. Fresh ingredients enhance classic taverna menus.

X **Prytaneion** 🍴 𝐀𝐂 𝑉𝐼𝑆𝐴 ◐● 𝐀𝐄 ◑

7 Milioni St, Kolonaki ✉ *106 73 – 𝒞 (210) 3643 353 – info@prytaneion.gr*
– Fax (210) 8082 5 77 – www.prytaneion.gr **C2**
Rest *–* Carte 22/64 €
♦ Mediterranean ♦ Bistro ♦
Watch the fashionable shoppers go by from a table on the terrace or choose the more intimate interior or the garden. Pleasant service and modern Mediterranean-influenced menu.

X **Oraia Penteli** 🍴 𝐀𝐂 𝑉𝐼𝑆𝐴 ◐●

Iroon Sq, Psirri ✉ *105 54 –* Ⓜ *Monastiraki – 𝒞 (210) 3218 627*
– Fax (210) 3218 6 27 **B2**
Rest *–* Carte 16/39 €
♦ Traditional ♦ Rustic ♦
Historic building converted into rustic café-restaurant with terrace on lively square in the centre of the Psirri district. Traditional Greek cooking; menu changes daily.

at Kifissia Northeast : 15 km by Vas. Sofias

Pentelikon ⚜️ 🚪 🛍 🕯️ 🕸 ⛄ ⚑ 🏧 ⅔ rm 🛋 📞 👗 🅿️ 🚗

66 Diligianni St, Kefalari (off Harilaou Trikoupi, follow *VISA* 🔵🟠 🆎 ⓪
signs to Politia) ✉️ 145 62 – Ⓜ️ Kifissia – 𝒞 (210) 6230 650 – sales@
pentelikon.gr – Fax (210) 8019 2 23 – www.pentelikon.gr
101 rm – 🛏280/340 € 🛏🛏390 €, 🍽 30 € – 11 suites
Rest *Vardis* – see below
Rest *La Terrasse* – Carte 38/67 €

♦ Grand Luxury ♦ Traditional ♦ Classic ♦

Imposing mansion in affluent residential suburb. Opulence and antiques throughout. Most charming and tranquil rooms overlook the gardens. Traditional service. La Terrasse offers a full range of dishes with piano music nightly.

Theoxenia Palace   🏧 🕸 ⛄ 🏧 ⅔ rm 🛋 📞 👗 🚗 *VISA* 🔵🟠 🆎 ⓪

2 Filadelfeos St ✉️ 145 62 – Ⓜ️ Kifissia – 𝒞 (210) 6233 622 – reservations@
theoxeniapalace.com – Fax (210) 6231 6 75 – www.theoxeniapalace.com
67 rm 🍽 – 🛏302/426 € 🛏🛏354/448 € – 4 suites
Rest – (dinner only) Carte 50/57 €

♦ Business ♦ Classic ♦

Renovated 1920s hotel with imposing façade. Spacious well-equipped rooms. Good leisure and large conference/banqueting facilities. Shogun for Asian cuisine, with sushi bar.

Theoxenia House without rest   🏧 🛋 📞 👗 🚗 *VISA* 🔵🟠 🆎 ⓪

42 Charilaou Trikoupi St and 9 Pentelis St ✉️ 145 62 – Ⓜ️ Kifissia – 𝒞 (210)
6233 622 – reservations@theoxeniapalace.com – Fax (210) 6231 6 75
– www.theoxeniapalace.com
11 rm 🍽 – 🛏352/373 € 🛏🛏374/395 € – 1 suite

♦ Business ♦ Classic ♦

Stylish house in pleasant suburb converted to provide very large, well-equipped rooms, each with lounge area and cooking facilities, plus full use of Theoxenia Palace hotel.

The Kefalari Suites without rest   🏧 ⅔ rm 🛋 📞 *VISA* 🔵🟠 🆎 ⓪

1 Pentelis and Kolokotroni St, Kefalari ✉️ 145 62 – Ⓜ️ Kifissia – 𝒞 (210)
6233 333 – info@kefalarisuites.gr – Fax (210) 6233 3 30 – www.kefalarisuites.gr
12 rm – 🛏215 € 🛏🛏230 €, 🍽 15 € – 1 suite

♦ Townhouse ♦ Stylish ♦

Early 20C villa set in a smart, quiet suburb; stylish, airy, thoughtfully appointed rooms, each on a subtle, imaginative theme, including one with Arabian arch, palm tree and terrace.

Semiramis   🕯️ 🛍 🕸 ⛄ 🏧 ⅔ rm 🛋 📞 👗 🚗 *VISA* 🔵🟠 🆎 ⓪

48 Charilaou Trikoupi St, Kefalari ✉️ 145 62 – Ⓜ️ Kifissia – 𝒞 (210) 6284 400
– info@semiramisathens.com – Fax (210) 6284 4 99
– www.semiramisathens.com
50 rm 🍽 – 🛏210/250 € 🛏🛏225/305 € – 1 suite   **Rest** – Carte 38/53 €

♦ Business ♦ Design ♦

Striking 1930s conversion accentuated by lime green balconies, boldly hued public areas and organic shaped pool. Rooms with no numbers on the doors and stunning interiors. Spacious restaurant serving Italian cuisine, with view of pool and terrace and music from DJ.

Twenty One   🚪 🏧 ⅔ rm 🛋 📞 *VISA* 🔵🟠 🆎 ⓪

21 Kolokotroni and Mykonou St, Kefalari ✉️ 145 62 – Ⓜ️ Kifissia – 𝒞 (210)
6233 521 – info@twentyone.gr – Fax (210) 6233 8 21 – www.twentyone.gr
16 rm – 🛏200/215 € 🛏🛏215 €, 🍽 15 € – 5 suites   **Rest** – Carte 28/39 €

♦ Business ♦ Modern ♦

Converted slate grey 19C former watermill in pleasant suburb. Flowing minimalistic interior. Standard rooms are well designed, some with balconies; five trendy loft suites. Informal dining room and expansive terrace; Italian menus.

GREECE - ATHENS

XXX ✿
Vardis – at Pentelikon Hotel 🍴 AK P VISA ⊙◎ AE ①
66 Diligianni St, Kefalari (off Harilaou Trikoupi, follow signs to Politia)
✉ 145 62 – **Ⓜ** *Kifissia* – ℰ *(210) 6230 660* – *sales@pentelikon.gr* – *Fax (210) 8019 2 23* – *www.pentelikon.gr*
– Closed Sunday
Rest – *(booking essential) (dinner only)* Carte 56/81 € ⅌
Spec. Spinach risotto with grilled cuttlefish and squid ink chips. Suckling pork cutlets with polenta, leek and baked quince. Halva soufflé with mandarin marmalade and halva cream.
  ◆ Traditional ◆ Formal ◆
Contemporary restaurant with terrace, offering classical French cuisine which uses native produce and influences; excellent olives, bread, sweets and desserts. Knowledgeable sommelier.

at Ekali Northeast : 20 km by Vas. Sofias

🏠
Life Gallery 🍴 🍴 ₤₅ ⊕ 🀄 ⌁ ⌁ AK ⌁ rm 🆒 ℰ 🕍 P
103 Thisseos Ave ✉ 145 78 – ℰ *(210) 6260 400* VISA ⊙◎ AE ①
– info-lifegallery@bluegr.com – *Fax (210) 6229 3 53* – *www.bluegr.com*
30 rm ⌂ – ♦222/284 € ♦♦245/305 € **Rest** – Carte 48/77 €
  ◆ Luxury ◆ Design ◆
Strikingly smart 'glass cube' with discreet yet eye-catchingly contemporary décor at every turn: don't miss the modern library. Sleek, stylish bedrooms all boast balconies. Bright, spacious restaurant with capacious outdoor terrace. Mediterranean-influenced menus.

at Athens International Airport East : 35 km by Vas. Sofias

🏨
Sofitel Athens Airport 🍴 ₤₅ ⊕ 🀄 ⌁ & AK ⌁ rm 🆒 🕍 ⇲
✉ 190 19 – **Ⓜ** *Airport* – ℰ *(210) 3544 000* – *h3167@* VISA ⊙◎ AE ①
accor.com – *Fax (210) 3544 4 44* – *www.sofitel.com*
332 rm – ♦300/430 € ♦♦360/430 €, ⌂ 24 € – 13 suites
Rest Karavi – *(dinner only, brunch Saturday and Sunday)* Menu 50/65 €
– Carte 60/96 €
Rest Mesoghaia – ℰ *(210) 3544 920* – Menu 32 € – Carte 32/74 €
  ◆ Business ◆ Modern ◆
First hotel at the new airport. Modern and very well equipped, from comfy library bar to exclusive leisure club. Spacious, soundproofed rooms and impressive bathrooms. French menus on the 9th floor in Karavi. Informal brightly decorated Mediterranean-themed Mesoghaia.

at Vouliagmeni South : 18 km by Singrou

🏨
The Westin Athens ⇲ 🍴 ◑ 🍴 ₤₅ ⊕ 🀄 ⌁ ⌁ ❀ 🆒 ℰ 🕍
40 Apollonos St ✉ 166 71 – ℰ *(210) 8902 000* VISA ⊙◎ AE ①
– reservation@astir.gr – *Fax (210) 8962 5 82* – *www.westin.com/athens*
153 rm ⌂ – ♦395 € ♦♦425 € – 9 suites
Rest Blue Hytra – *(closed Monday April-October) (dinner only)* Carte 60/90 €
Rest Kymata – *(lunch only)(buffet only)* Carte 39/55 €
  ◆ Luxury ◆ Palace ◆ Modern ◆
Recently transformed vast 75 acre resort complex on its own peninsula. Supremely comfortable hotel with private beaches and extensive facilities. Delightful bedrooms are spacious with sea views. Fusion cooking in Sao with its own terrace. Buffet menu in Kymata.

🏨
Arion Resort & Spa ⇲ 🍴 ◑ 🍴 ₤₅ ⊕ 🀄 ⌁ ⌁ ❀ & AK 🆒 ℰ
40 Apollonos St ✉ 166 71 – ℰ *(210) 8902 000* 🕍 P VISA ⊙◎ AE ①
– reservation@astir.gr – *Fax (210) 8960 7 58* – *www.luxurycollection.com/arion*
107 rm ⌂ – ♦395 € ♦♦425 € – 16 suites
Rest Alia – Carte 30/50 €
Rest Grill Room – Menu 70 € – Carte 60/90 €
  ◆ Luxury ◆ Modern ◆
Next door to the Westin on private peninsula and sharing many of the wide-ranging facilities. Bedrooms are large, contemporary in style and most have balconies. Relaxed sophistication and a Mediterranean menu at Alia. International cuisine and local seafood in the Grill Room.

Divani Apollon Palace & Spa

10 Ag. Nikolaou and Iliou St
(Kavouri) off Athinas ⊠ 166 71 – ℰ (210) 8911 100 – info@divaniapollon.gr
– Fax (210) 9658 0 10 – www.divanis.com
279 rm � – ♟440/580 € ♟♟480/620 € – 7 suites
Rest Mythos – (dinner only) Carte 56/140 €
Rest Anemos – Carte 51/71 €
◆ Luxury ◆ Classic ◆
Modern hotel in fashionable resort. Poolside lounge. Spa and thalassotherapy centre. Every bedroom boasts balcony overlooking the Saronic Gulf. Small private beach. Dine in Mythos on the beach with local dishes. Anemos is modern with global fare.

Apollon Suites without rest

11 Nikolaou St ⊠ 166 71 – ℰ ((210)) 8911 100 – suites@divaniapollen.gr
– Fax ((210)) 9658 0 10 – www.divanis.gr
56 rm – ♟390/490 € ♟♟410/510 €
◆ Luxury ◆ Modern ◆
New annex for the Divani Apollon Palace, whose facilities it shares, with the added benefit of a slightly quieter atmosphere. Well-equipped, luxury suites with modern style.

The Margi

11 Litous St, off Athinas by Apollonos ⊠ 166 71 – ℰ (210) 8929 000
– themargi@themargi.gr – Fax (210) 8929 1 43 – www.themargi.gr
88 rm � – ♟200/260 € ♟♟210/280 € – 7 suites   **Rest** – Carte 42/59 €
◆ Business ◆ Stylish ◆
A stylish hotel that combines contemporary elegance with a colonial feel. Breakfast can be taken on the poolside terrace. Bedrooms have antique pieces and smart marble bathrooms. Bistro restaurant serving Mediterranean menu.

Matsuhisa

40 Opollonos St ⊠ 16671 – ℰ (210) 8960 510 – contact@matsuhisaathens.com
– Fax (210) 896 25 20 – www.matsuhisaathens.com
– Dinner only and Sunday lunch, and closed Monday in winter
Rest – (booking essential) Menu 98 € – Carte 70/100 €
◆ Japanese ◆ Fashionable ◆
Bustling destination restaurant boasting sushi counter, stone wood-oven, robata grill, large terrace and sea views. Concise à la carte or chef's choice menu with appealing range of dishes.

Pireas Southwest: 8 km by Singrou

 Theoxenia

23 Karaol St and Dimitriou St ⊠ 185 31 – Ⓜ Pireaus – ℰ (210) 4112 550
– piraeus@theoxeniapalace.com – Fax (210) 4125 5 65
– www.theoxeniaplace.com
72 rm – ♟257/304 € ♟♟300/324 € – 4 suites
Rest Incognito – Menu 35/45 € – Carte 46/50 €
◆ Business ◆ Functional ◆
Corporate hotel in the heart of town, close to the markets and harbour. Good size bedrooms boast sitting and working areas at the higher end of the range. Business centre also available. Simple restaurant offers a mix of Greek and Italian dishes.

at Kalamaki Southwest : 14 km by Singrou

Akrotiri

Vas. Georgiou B5, Agios Kosmas, Helliniko ⊠ 167 77 – ℰ (210) 9859 147
– akrotiri@enternet.gr – Fax (210) 9859 1 49 – www.akrotirilounge.gr
– Friday and Saturday only November-April
Rest – (dinner only) Menu 80 € – Carte 59/90 €
◆ French ◆ Fashionable ◆
A trendy seaside restaurant combining simplicity and luxury. Candlelit dinners on the pool terrace; DJ music. Menu of good quality international cuisine with French influence.

HUNGARY
MAGYARORSZÁG

PROFILE

→ **AREA:**
93 032 km²
(35 920 sq mi).

→ **POPULATION:**
10 007 000
inhabitants (est.
2005), density
= 108 per km².

→ **CAPITAL:**
Budapest
(conurbation
2 232 000
inhabitants).

→ **CURRENCY:**
Forint (Ft or HUF);
rate of exchange:
HUF 100 = € 0.38
= US$ 0.48
(Dec 2008).

→ **GOVERNMENT:**
Parliamentary
republic (since 1989).
Member of European
Union since 2004.

→ **LANGUAGE:**
Hungarian; many
Hungarians also
speak English and
German.

→ **SPECIFIC PUBLIC
HOLIDAYS:**
1848 Revolution Day
(15 March); National
Day-St. Stephen Day
(20 August); Republic
Day-1956 Uprising

Remembrance Day
(23 October);
All Saints' Day
(1 November);
Boxing Day (25-26
December).

→ **LOCAL TIME:**
GMT + 1 hour in
winter and GMT
+ 2 hours
in summer.

→ **CLIMATE:**
Temperate
continental with cold
winters and warm
summers (Budapest:
January: -1°C, July:
22°C).

→ **INTERNATIONAL
DIALLING CODE:**
00 36 followed by
area code (1 for
Budapest) and local
number, international
enquiries: ℘ 199.

→ **EMERGENCY:**
Central emergency
line: ℘ 112;
Ambulance: ℘ 104,
Fire Brigade: ℘ 105,
Police: ℘ 107,
Roadside breakdown
service: ℘ 188.

→ **ELECTRICITY:**
220 volts, 50 Hz;

BUDAPEST

2-pin round-shaped
continental plugs.

→ **FORMALITIES**
Travellers from the
European Union
(EU), Switzerland,
Iceland and the main
countries of North
and South America
need a national
identity card or
passport (America:
passport required) to
visit Hungary for less
than three months
(tourism or business
purpose). For visitors
from other countries
a visa may be
required, in addition
to a passport,
especially for those
wishing to stay for
longer than three
months. We advise
you to check with
your embassy before
travelling.

BUDAPEST

BUDAPEST

Population: 1 702 000 (conurbation 2 232 000) – Altitude: 102m

J. Warbuton-Lee/PHOTONONSTOP

No one knows quite where the Hungarian language came from. It's not quite Slavic, not quite Turkic, and its closest relatives appear to be in Finland and Siberia. In much the same way, Hungary's capital is a bit of an enigma. A lot of what you see is not as old as it appears. Classical and Gothic buildings are mostly Neoclassical and neo-Gothic, and the fabled Baroque of the city is of a more recent vintage than in other European capitals. That's because Budapest's frequent invaders and conquerors, from all compass points of the map, left little but rubble behind them when they left; the grand look of today took shape for the most part no earlier than the mid 19C.

It's still a beautiful place to look at, with hilly Buda keeping watch via eight great bridges over sprawling Pest on the other side of the lilting, bending Danube. These were formerly two separate towns, united in 1873 to form a capital city. It reached its heyday around that time, a magnificent city that was the hub of the Austro-Hungarian Empire. Defeats in two world wars and fifty years behind the Iron Curtain put paid to the glory, but battered Budapest is used to rising from the ashes, and now it's Europe's most earthily beautiful capital, particularly when winter mists rise from the river to shroud it in a thick white cloak. The spas are good, too.

LIVING THE CITY

It's not easy to get lost in Budapest. Despite its size, it's split asunder by the great **Danube**, whose ubiquitous liquid pathway helps you keep your bearings. **Buda**, on the west bank, is very hilly and provides constant views of the river. Its southern quarter, Gellert and Taban, is smartly residential, while northern Buda is dominated by visitor hotspot The Royal Palace. This stares across to the imposing Parliament Building in **Pest**, around which large squares and wide avenues offer reminders of the Austro-Hungarian Empire. South of here is the commercial hub of Belvaros, or inner city, full of shops, cafes and summer tourists. The northeast quarter of the city, furthest from the river, is Varosliget, which translates as City Park, and it's the place the locals come to play and lounge around in the sun; this is also an area renowned for its grand buildings and monuments. In the middle of the Danube, as the city reaches its northern boundary, stands the green oasis of Margaret Island.

PRACTICAL INFORMATION

ARRIVAL-DEPARTURE

Ferihegy Budapest National Airport is 24km southeast of the city. A taxi will take about 45min and cost around 4000 HUF ; there are Shuttle Mini-buses doing the rounds of the hotels or, from Terminal 1, a train will take you to the Western train station for 300 HUF.

TRANSPORT

Budapest has an extensive public transport system: its metro, with three lines, is second oldest in the world after the London Underground. Above ground, you can take your pick of buses, trolley buses or trams. Tickets must be bought in advance and validated in the ticket stampers at the start of the journey. Buy your tickets at metro stations, ticket machines, newsagents or tobacconists.

If you're in town for more than a day, then the Budapest Card is a sound investment. It includes unlimited travel on public transport, free or reduced price admission to many museums and sights, cultural and folklore programmes, as well as discounts in some shops, restaurants and thermal baths. The Card is valid for two or three days, and can be bought at the airport, main metro stations, tourist offices and some hotels.

If you're going shopping on the weekend, make sure you do it on Saturday morning. Most high street shops are shut on Saturday afternoons, and there is almost no Sunday opening, apart from the shopping malls.

EXPLORING BUDAPEST

Budapest offers a thick slice of East European charm that hasn't been ruined by monotonously grey communist architecture. It's grander in scale than Vienna and Prague, the other two members of the 'Habsburg triumvirate', and you can't help but get the feeling that its art nouveau delights are modelled on nineteenth century Paris (which indeed they are, at least in Pest). Ask two locals to tell you the city's defining tourist location – its unmissable sight - and one will probably say "The Royal Palace", the other "The Parliament Building". The **Royal Palace** can certainly stake a strong claim. There's been a dominant castle or palace overlooking Buda since 1255. The latest incarnation was built in the eighteenth century after the Habsburg Empire claimed it from the Ottomans in a bloody siege. They developed not one palace but an amalgamation of buildings, spreading out along the hill. These took a big hit during World War II, and what we see today has been healthily patched up over the past sixty years: the dome, for instance, was entirely rebuilt. The **Hungarian National Gallery** was inaugurated at the Palace just over fifty years ago, in 1957, and nowhere in the city is there more treasure than here; it displays art from medieval times to the present day in six permanent exhibitions which lavish upon the visitor the very best of Hungarian creativity. Fans of the Secession (the nineteenth century arts movement devoted to bright colours and fantastical designs) will be in their element. There are actually more than 10,000 exhibits spread over much of the Royal Palace, making it one of the greatest collections in the world.

→ PARLIAMENTARY PRIVILEGE

So how does the **Parliament building** compare with all that? It's certainly nowhere near as old, as it was only completed in 1902 after two decades of construction. A symbol of Hungarian self-confidence at the beginning of the twentieth century, it certainly looks the part. It's one of Europe's finest neo-Gothic buildings and when you gaze at it from across the water its dazzling symmetry imbues it with a real sense of magnificence. Inside, its two biggest 'vote catchers' are its sweeping Grand Staircase and its Domed Hall, which houses the Crown Jewels. To see them, you'll have to join a guided tour, but as our imaginary second

local would tell you, that's something well worth doing.

→ GET YOUR THERMALS ON

If you're in Budapest in the summer, you'll very likely be hot; this is a place that swelters. The good news is you won't have any trouble finding somewhere to cool down. The city is renowned for its therapeutic **thermal baths**, and when the weather's hot it can seem like the whole of Budapest is immersed. The Ottomans loved the natural springs and built some wonderful domed baths with steam rooms, hot and cold pools and peaceful chambers in which to relax. Enough original Turkish baths remain to give you (something like) the full Oriental experience. It was when spa bathing became a craze across central Europe in the nineteenth and early twentieth century that Budapest's two most famous bathing complexes opened, and they remain top visitor attractions: the Gellert Baths, in Buda, are part of the Secessionist Gellert Hotel and the stunning neo-classical main pool is surrounded by high galleries and marble columns, and studded with colourful mosaics. Meanwhile, to say Central Park's Szechenyi baths are big is like saying that Paris does some nice food and Athens has one or two interesting relics. Szechenyi is vast, the biggest in Europe, its neo-Baroque façade more like a Grand Central rail station than a bathing complex. There are splendid Belle Epoque foyers, an all-weather mixed swimming area, which includes Hungary's deepest thermal baths, single sex steam baths, and chess-players who congregate around stone chessboards in one of the expansive open-air pools.

→ PEST CONTROL

You'll know you're in the heart of Pest when you get to **Vaci Utca**. A teeming street in two parts (one for eating and drinking, one for hitting the shops) this is the city's buzziest thoroughfare, running parallel to the Danube. At the top end is Gerbeaud Cukraszda, the smartest and most famous coffee house in Budapest, at the bottom end the bustling Central Market Hall, where the locals go for their fruit and veg from local allotments on one side, and more exotic global fare on the other. Vaci Utca is the true hub of the city, lined with many types of store, though perhaps lacking the 'designer' glamour of more fashion-conscious cities.

Staying in Pest, go for a wonderful cultural hit at two of its most stunning buildings. The **State Opera House**, inland from the Parliament building, is a neo-Renaissance masterpiece, its interior so full of opulent splendour, you'll feel you're back at the height of the Austro-Hungarian Empire. Best of all, though: take in a concert there. Further south, beyond Vaci Utca, is the outstanding **Museum of Applied Arts**, its appearance a fitting tribute to the Secessionist movement and its stunning green domes worth the trip alone. Inside, dazzling Oriental artefacts complement the graceful white architecture. The creative genius behind the building was Odon Lechner, who, in the late nineteenth century, was to Budapest what Gaudi was to Barcelona. Lechner's designs adorn many structures in the city.

→ THE GREAT ESCAPE

If you need a break from the crowds, there's one very visible, and another not so visible, refuge. **Margaret Island** (the visible one) is a tranquil oasis plonked down in the middle of the Danube. Locals sprawl around during high summer, but there's enough room for anyone to find a cool spot and relax under a tree. In the winter, with the wind gushing through the swirling branches and not a soul to be seen, it takes on a distinctly romantic feel. 2008 is its one hundredth anniversary as a public park. And as for the hidden escape? Well, you won't discover it anywhere above ground. North of the Royal Palace, walk up Uri Utca (Lords' Street) till you get to number nine, which is the entrance to the bizarre but wonderful Buda Castle Labyrinth, an underground maze of tunnels and chambers formed by hot springs half a million years ago. In the seventeenth century, a part of these catacombs was used to store wine, and there's a room today where fruity red wine gushes from a fountain – but you'll have to find it! (Your best bet is to join a guided tour). Incidentally, Úri Utca itself is something to see with its Gothic and Baroque façades lining the way, but spare a thought that much of this fine street was rebuilt in the 1950s after that great shadow over Budapest – war – had once more taken its heavy toll.

BUDAPEST IN...

→ ONE DAY
Royal Palace, the Parliament Building, a trip on the Danube

→ TWO DAYS
Gellert Baths, a stroll down Váci Utca, a concert at the State Opera House

→ THREE DAYS
Museum of Applied Arts, Margaret Island, coffee and cake at Gerbeaud Cukrazda

Music is high on the list of Hungarian passions: this is the country that gave us Liszt and Bartok. Winter is the time for high calibre concerts at great prices in venues like the Opera House, Franz Liszt Music Academy, and the National Concert Hall. The Spring Festival, in March, is the city's largest cultural jamboree, with a heady mixture of ballet, opera and chamber music fusing with the likes of jazz and folk dance. An entire Danube island is taken over by rock fans in August for the huge Sziget Festival, which goes on for a week and features roots music as well as ubiquitous four/four rhythms. World music takes centre stage at July's WoMuFe, where musicians from Central, Eastern Europe and beyond join forces for a fine old mash-up. The Autumn Festival, in October, is a kind of counterbalance to the Spring Festival: this one acts as a showcase for cutting edge theatre, dance and media arts, as well as music and film.

EATING OUT

The city is most famous for its coffee houses so before you dive into a restaurant tuck into a cream cake with a double espresso in, say, the Ruszwurm on Castle Hill, the city's oldest, and possibly cosiest, café. In tourist areas, it's not difficult to locate goulash on your menu, and you never have to travel far to find beans, dumplings and cabbage in profusion. Having said that, Budapest's culinary scene has moved on apace since the fall of communism, and Hungarian chefs have become inventive with their use of local seasonal produce. Pest is where you'll find most choice but even in Buda there are plenty of worthy restaurants in among the tourist traps. Lots of locals like to eat sausage on the run and if you fancy the idea, buy a pocket knife. Sunday brunch is popular in Budapest, especially at the best hotels. If you're in a restaurant, it might well include a service charge. Don't feel obliged to pay it, as tipping is entirely at your own discretion but you may find that the persistence of the little folk groups that pop up in many of the restaurants hard to resist.

➔ WAITING FOR THE DAY

There are two outstanding places of worship in the city. The **Matyas Church**, towering over Buda, dates from 1255, but its most recent addition, the multi-coloured tiled roof, was built as recently as 1970. The magnificent **St Stephen's Basilica,** in the heart of Pest and seen from all over the city, was only completed in 1905, fifty-five years after it was begun. The great length of time in construction led to the local equivalent of 'pigs might fly' – 'when the basilica is finished'.

➔ CHAIN REACTION

Budapest's most magnificent bridge is **The Chain Bridge**, linking the towns since 1848. It was designed by an Englishman, built by a Scotsman, and loved by the world: its huge towers are superbly lit at night, making it one of the city's most photographed sights.

➔ TERROR TRIP

Fancy a trip to the House of Terror? You might not when you get there. Based in **Andrassy Street**, it's the former HQ of the fascist, then communist, secret police who ran the city for much of the twentieth century. Now a museum, it's dedicated to those who perished under both dictatorships. This is the place where confessions were extracted and victims sentenced to death. A sobering experience.

HUNGARY - BUDAPEST

Four Seasons Gresham Palace

Roosevelt tér 5-6 ✉ *1051*
– **Ⓜ** *Vörösmarty tér* – ✆ *(01) 268 6000* – *budapest.reservations@
fourseasons.com* – *Fax (01) 268 50 00* – *www.fourseasons.com/budapest*
165 rm – ♦67000/108500 HUF ♦♦73500/108500 HUF,   **E2**
⚅ 8500 HUF – 14 suites
Rest *Páva* – *(Closed Sunday) (dinner only)* Carte 13500/18100 HUF
Rest *Gresham Kávénáz* – ✆ *(01) 268 5110* – Carte 10250/12500 HUF
♦ Grand Luxury ♦ Palace ♦ Art Deco ♦

Art Nouveau palace on the Danube converted into an elegant, modern hotel
with excellent service; stunning atrium. Riverside Páva restaurant and terrace
offers a menu of seasonal Italian-influenced dishes with modish twist. Kávénáz is
a coffee house renowned for traditional dishes - and its cakes.

Corinthia Grand H. Royal

Erzsébet krt 43-49 ✉ *1073* – **Ⓜ** *Oktogon* – ✆ *(01)*
479 4000 – *royal@corinthia.hu* – *Fax (01) 479 43 33* – *www.corinthia.hu*
383 rm – ♦87500 HUF ♦♦87500 HUF, ⚅ 5500 HUF – 31 suites   *Plan I* **B2**
Rest *Brasserie Royale* – ✆ *(01) 479 4850* – Carte 7500/12800 HUF
Rest *Rickshaw* – *(Closed Monday) (dinner only)* Menu 5500 HUF – Carte 6600/
10700 HUF
♦ Grand Luxury ♦ Business ♦ Modern ♦

Early 20C grand hotel with impressive atrium. Well-appointed bedrooms - particularly Executive - with modern décor in warm colours. Stylish new spa. Brasserie
Royale for pleasant atrium dining, with family brunch on Sundays. Wok dishes
and sushi bar in Rickshaw.

New York Palace

Erzsébet Krt 9-11 ✉ *1073* – **Ⓜ** *Blaha Tér* – ✆ *(01) 886 6111* – *reservations@
newyork.boscolo.com* – *Fax (01) 886 61 99* – *www.boscolohotels.com*
108 rm – ♦130000 HUF ♦♦130000 HUF, ⚅ 6500 HUF – 4 suites   *Plan I* **B2**
Rest *Deep Water* – ✆ *(01) 886 6166 (dinner only)* Carte 12700/15050 HUF
Rest *New York Cafe* – Carte 7000/9000 HUF
♦ Grand Luxury ♦ Business ♦ Classic ♦

This stunning 1894 former insurance company building opened as a hotel in
2006. Sympathetic renovation has created impressive levels of comfort. Deep
Water, with wood panelling and formal settings, for Hungarian and Italian dishes.
The New York Cafe is rightly celebrated for its striking baroque style and long
history.

Kempinski H. Corvinus

Erzsébet tér 7-8 ✉ *1051* – **Ⓜ** *Deák tér* – ✆ *(01)*
429 3777 – *hotel.corvinus@kempinski.com* – *Fax (01) 429 47 77*
– *www.kempinski-budapest.com*   **E2**
335 rm – ♦42600/85400 HUF ♦♦51000/96000 HUF, ⚅ 8000 HUF – 31 suites
Rest *Ristorante Giardino* – Carte 10000/12500 HUF
Rest *Bistro Jardin* – Carte 8600/11600 HUF
♦ Grand Luxury ♦ Business ♦ Modern ♦

Modern hotel in the heart of the city. Spa boasts panoply of up-to-date treatments.
Rooms provide top class comforts and facilities. Italian Ristorante Giardino. Bistro
Jardin buffet restaurant.

Sofitel Budapest

Roosevelt tér 2 ✉ *1051* – **Ⓜ** *Vörösmarty tér* – ✆ *(01) 266 1234* – *h3229-re@
accor.com* – *Fax (01) 235 91 01* – *www.sofitel-budapest.com*   **E2**
328 rm – ♦30195/66795 HUF ♦♦30195/88450 HUF, ⚅ 7250 HUF – 22 suites
Rest *Paris Budapest Café* – Carte 8600/13400 HUF
♦ Business ♦ Chain hotel ♦ Modern ♦

Modern hotel near Chain Bridge. 'Bibliotheque' and coffee lounge; plane suspended in mid-air. Comfortable, well-equipped rooms. Contemporary restaurant with
open kitchen offers modern fusion cooking with Thai influences.

Le Meridien

Erzsébet tér 9-10 ⊠ 1051 – Ⓜ Deák tér – ☏ (01) 429 5500
– concierge.budapest@le-meridien.hu – Fax (01) 429 55 55
– www.lemeridien.com/budapest

203 rm – ♦115000 HUF ♦♦115000 HUF, ⊊ 7500 HUF – 15 suites
Rest Le Bourbon – (closed Saturday lunch) Carte 8300/14100 HUF

E2

♦ Business ♦ Traditional ♦ Modern ♦

Top class hotel, ideally located for both business and leisure. Classically furnished, very comfortable bedrooms and particularly smart bathrooms. Atrium styled restaurant with Art Deco glass dome and impressive French-influenced desserts.

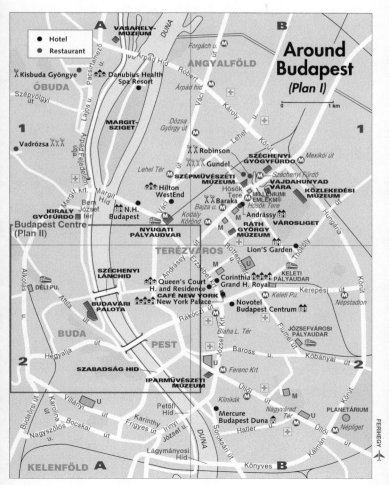

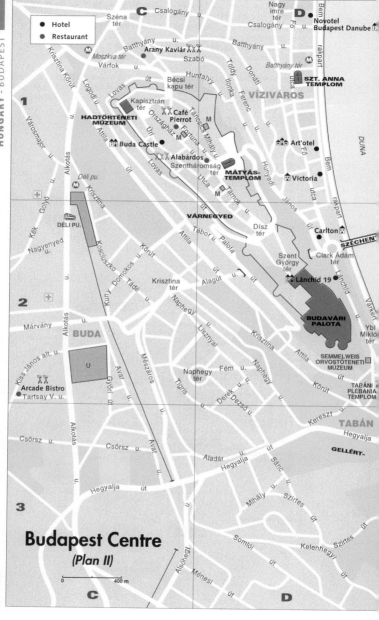

Budapest Centre
(Plan II)

0 ——— 400 m

Legend:
● Hotel
● Restaurant

Labels on map:

Nagy imre tér
Novotel Budapest Danube
Csalogány u.
Széna tér
Csalogány u.
Batthyány u.
Batthyány
Arany Kaviár
Szabó
Moszkva tér
Várfok
Bécsi kapu tér
Hunfalvy
Toldy
Donáti
Ilona
Ferenc
SZT. ANNA TEMPLOM
Batthyány tér
VÍZIVÁROS
Krisztina Körút
Logodi u.
Lovas
út
Kapisztrán tér
Café Pierrot
HADTÖRTÉNETI MÚZEUM
Attila
Országház
Úri
Táncsics Mihály u.
Fortuna
Art'otel
Fő
DUNA
Városmajor u.
Buda Castle
Alabárdos
Szentháromság tér
MÁTYÁS-TEMPLOM
Hunyadi
Victoria
Alkotás
Déli pu.
Kriszttina
DÉLI PU.
Tárnok
VÁRNEGYED
Tábor u.
Palota
Dísz tér
János
Carlton
SZÉCHEN
Kék
Győrő
Nagyenyed u.
Kosciuszko
Körút
Kuny Domokos Tádé u.
Krisztina tér
Attila
út
Alagút
Szent György tér
Clark Ádám tér
Lánchíd 19
Várken
Márvány
BUDA
Naphegy
Liszayal u.
Krisztina
Attila
BUDAVÁRI PALOTA
Ybl Miklós tér
Kiss János alt. u.
Arcade Bistro
Tartsay V. u.
U
Avar
Győri
Mészáros
Naphegy tér
Fém u.
Naphegy
Derék Dezső u.
SEMMELWEIS ORVOSTÖRTÉNETI MÚZEUM
út
Körút
TABÁNI PLÉBÁNIA TEMPLOM
TABÁN
Csörsz u.
Alkotás u.
Csörsz u.
Avar u.
Aladár u.
Hegyalja út
Sánc u.
Kereszt u.
Hegyalja
GELLÉRT-
Tigris
Hegyalja út
Mihály
Szirtes út
Somlói út
Kelenhegyi út
Szirtes út
Alsóhegy
Ménesi út

442

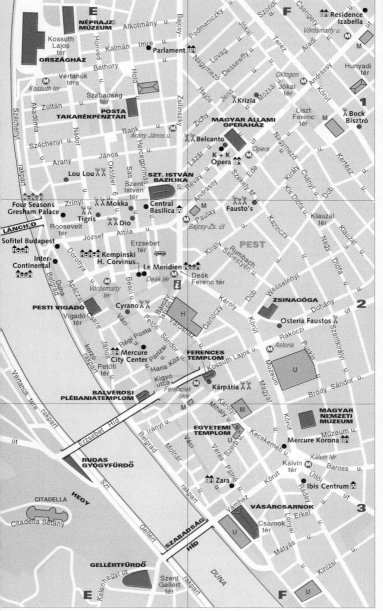

NÉPRAJZI MÚZEUM

Kossuth Lajos tér

ORSZÁGHÁZ

Parlament

Vértanúk tere

Kossuth tér

Szabadság tér

POSTA TAKARÉKPÉNZTÁR

MAGYAR ÁLLAMI OPERAHÁZ

Krizia

Liszt Ferenc tér

Bock Bisztró

Belcanto

K + K Opera

Lou Lou

SZT. ISTVÁN BAZILIKA

Four Seasons Gresham Palace

Mokka

Central Basilica

Fausto's

Tigris

LÁNCHÍD

Roosevelt tér

Dio

Sofitel Budapest

Inter-Continental

Kempinski H. Corvinus

Le Meridien

PEST

Erzsébet tér

Deák Ferenc tér

ZSINAGÓGA

PESTI VIGADÓ

Cyrano

Vörösmarty tér

Osteria Faustos

Vigadó tér

Mercure City Center

FERENCES TEMPLOM

Rákóczi

Astoria

Régi Posta

Kárpátia

Haris Köze

BALVÉROSI PLÉBÁNIATEMPLOM

Ferenciek tere

EGYETEMI TEMPLOM

MAGYAR NEMZETI MÚZEUM

Mercure Korona

RUDAS GYÓGYFÜRDŐ

Zara

Kálvin tér

Ibis Centrum

CITADELLA

Citadella Sétány

HEGY

VÁSÁRCSARNOK

Vámház

Csarnok tér

GELLÉRTFÜRDŐ

SZABADSÁG HÍD

Szent Gellért tér

DUNA

Residence Izabella

Hunyadi tér

443

Inter-Continental 🛜 ⚡ 🏊 🖥 ♿ 🅰 🤸 rm 🆔 📞 🛄 🚗

Apáczai Csere János útca 12-14 ✉ *1052*   🆅🆂🅰 🆅🅾 🅰🅴 ⓘ
– Ⓜ *Vörösmarty tér* – ⚐ *(01) 327 6333* – *budapest@intercontinental.com*
– *Fax (01) 327 63 57* – *www.intercontinental.com*   **E2**
383 rm – ♥74850 HUF ♥♥74850 HUF, � 7000 HUF – 15 suites
Rest – Carte 5700/10300 HUF
◆ Business ◆ Modern ◆

Large hotel tower on river bank with good views from most rooms which have modern décor and all mod cons. Popular with business travellers. Viennese-style coffee house. The pleasant modern restaurant offers popular fare.

Danubius Health Spa Resort ⚓ 🚗 ⚡ 🏊 🖥 ♿ 🅰

Margitsziget ✉ *1138*   ⚡ rm 🆔 🤸 🅿 🚗 🆅🆂🅰 🖥 🅰🅴 ⓘ
– Ⓜ *Árpád híd* – ⚐ *(01) 889 4700* – *msz.reservation@danubiushotels.com*
– *Fax (01) 889 49 88* – *www.danubiushotels.com/margitsziget*   *Plan I* **A1**
267 rm – ♥29400/58950 HUF ♥♥33500/63000 HUF, ☐ 3630 HUF
Rest *Platan* – Menu 4800/5200 HUF – Carte 4200/10800 HUF
◆ Business ◆ Modern ◆

Concrete hotel set in island gardens on the Danube. Conference facilities. Huge thermal spa: heat, massage and water treatments. Modern bedrooms with a view. Buffet meals available alongside à la carte menu in the restaurant.

Queen's Court Hotel & Residence 🚗 ⚡ 🏊 🅰 ⚡ 🆔 🤸

Dob u. 63 ✉ *1074* – Ⓜ *Oktogon* – ⚐ *(01)*   🤸 🚗 🆅🆂🅰 🖥 🅰🅴
878 0300 – *welcome@queenscourt.hu* – *Fax (01) 878 03 99*
– *www.queenscourt.hu*   **B2**
70 suites – ♥♥29850/38400 HUF, ☐ 4150 HUF
Rest *Chess* – Carte 3800/5800 HUF
◆ Business ◆ Modern ◆

Smart apartment hotel with relaxation area, pool and garden. Good sized bedrooms, all suites, boast comfy sitting areas, smart bathrooms and fully equipped kitchens; some have balconies. Named after its chessboard tiling, the small restaurant offers international menus.

Hilton WestEnd 🛜 ⚡ 🏊 ♿ 🅰 ⚡ rm 🆔 🤸 🚗 🆅🆂🅰 🖥 🅰🅴 ⓘ

Váci útca 1-3 ✉ *1062* – Ⓜ *Nyugati pályaudvar* – ⚐ *(01) 288 5500*
– *info.budapest-westend@hilton.com* – *Fax (01) 288 55 52*
– *www.budapest-westend.hilton.com*   *Plan I* **A1**
230 rm – ♥22000/43500 HUF ♥♥22000/43500 HUF, ☐ 7500 HUF
Rest *Arrabona* – Menu 1990 HUF (lunch) – Carte 7500/9500 HUF
◆ Business ◆ Chain hotel ◆ Modern ◆

21C hotel incorporated in large adjoining indoor shopping centre. Comprehensive business facilities. Very comfortable modern bedrooms with roof garden as bonus. A bright and contemporary dining room on the first floor of the hotel, serving Hungarian and international cuisine.

Andrássy 🅰 ⚡ 🖥 🆔 🤸 🅿 🆅🆂🅰 🖥 🅰🅴 ⓘ

Andrássy útca 111 ✉ *1063* – Ⓜ *Bajza u.* – ⚐ *(01) 462 2100* – *reservation@*
andrassyhotel.com – *Fax (01) 322 94 45* – *www.andrassyhotel.com*
65 rm – ♥53130 HUF ♥♥59455 HUF, ☐ 5060 HUF – 5 suites   *Plan I* **B1**
Rest *Baraka* – see below
◆ Business ◆ Stylish ◆

A classical Bauhaus building converted into a hotel in 2001. Stylish lobby of glass and metal filigree, plus stylish water feature. Bright and contemporary bedrooms, most with balconies.

N. H. Budapest ⚡ 🏊 ♿ 🅰 ⚡ rm 🆔 🤸 🚗 🆅🆂🅰 🖥 🅰🅴 ⓘ

Vigszinház u. 3 ✉ *1137* – Ⓜ *Nyugati pályaudvar* – ⚐ *(01) 814 0000*
– *nhbudapest@nh-hotels.com* – *Fax (01) 814 01 00* – *www.nh-hotels.com*
160 rm – ♥27000/53000 HUF ♥♥27000/53000 HUF, ☐ 4500 HUF   *Plan I* **A1**
Rest – Menu 4600 HUF – Carte 6440/9150 HUF
◆ Business ◆ Modern ◆

Modern hotel in city suburbs. Conference facilities; gym and sauna. Bright, modern, well-furnished rooms in bold colours with extra touches; some with balconies. Simple restaurant; dishes show modern Hungarian style, with some Spanish influences.

Residence Izabella 🚗 ⓕ 🕸 Ꮺ ᏯᏟ ⤴ ⱝ 📶 🚗 🆅🆂🅰 ⓜ🅾 ⱯⒺ

Izabella u 61 ✉ *1064* – ⓜ *Vörösmarty ucta* – ℰ *(01) 4755900* – *reservation@ residenceizabella.com* – *Fax (01) 4 75 59 02* – *www.residence-izabella.com*
38 suites – 🛏30000 HUF 🛏🛏65000 HUF   **F1**
Rest – *(Room service only)* Carte 5000/10450 HUF
♦ Business ♦ Modern ♦

Impressive mansion, formerly a police station, with comfy lounge and Mediterranean style reception. Modern bedrooms – all suites – boast quality furniture, high level facilities and kitchens. Extensive room service menu offers soups, pastas and pizzas to the fore.

Parlament without rest 🕸 ⱝ ᏯᏟ ⤴ 📟 ☏ 🦽 🆅🆂🅰 ⓜ🅾 ⱯⒺ

Kálmán Imre U. 19 ✉ *1054* – ℰ *(01) 3746000* – *reservation@ parlament-hotel.hu* – *Fax (01) 3 73 08 43* – *www.parlament-hotel.hu*
65 rm ⌕ – 🛏25000/36000 HUF 🛏🛏28000/39000 HUF   **E1**
♦ Business ♦ Design ♦

Stylish modern interior contrasts with the classic 19C exterior. Open plan atrium with display of famous Hungarians. Identical bedrooms have a clean and crisp design.

Novotel Budapest Centrum ᏪᏟ 🕸 ⱝ ᏯᏟ ⤴ rm 📟 ☏ 🦽 🚗

Rákóczi útca 43-45 ✉ *1088* – ⓜ *Blaha tér* – ℰ *(01)* 🆅🆂🅰 ⓜ🅾 ⱯⒺ ⓄⒹ
477 5300 – *h3560@accor.com* – *Fax (01) 477 53 53* – *www.novotel.com*
227 rm – 🛏33700/88200 HUF 🛏🛏33700/88200 HUF, ⌕ 4410 HUF   *Plan I* **B2**
Rest *Palace* – ℰ *(01) 477 5400* – Carte 5300/9800 HUF
♦ Business ♦ Chain hotel ♦ Functional ♦

Early 20C Art Deco hotel with extensions, in the business district. Conference facilities; basement leisure club. Spacious, well-fitted and modern bedrooms. The ornate, classic Palace restaurant serves an international menu.

K + K Opera 🦢 ᏪᏟ 🕸 ᏯᏟ ⤴ rm 📟 ☏ 🦽 🚗 🆅🆂🅰 ⓜ🅾 ⱯⒺ ⓄⒹ

Révay útca 24 ✉ *1065* – ⓜ *Opera* – ℰ *(01) 269 0222* – *kk.hotel.opera @kkhotels.hu* – *Fax (01) 269 02 30* – *www.kkhotels.com*   **F1**
202 rm ⌕ – 🛏50600 HUF 🛏🛏63250 HUF – 2 suites
Rest – *(room service only)* Carte 5313/8855 HUF
♦ Business ♦ Modern ♦

Well run hotel in quiet street of business district near opera. Stylish modern interior design. Good size rooms smartly furnished and well equipped. Informal dining in bar with bright modern décor and pale wood furniture; bistro-style menu.

Lion's Garden 🚗 ᏪᏟ 🕸 📺 ⱝ ᏯᏟ ⤴ 📟 ☏ 🦽 🚗 🆅🆂🅰 ⓜ🅾 ⱯⒺ

Cházár András 4 ✉ *1146* – ℰ *(01) 2732070* – *info@lions-garden.com*
– *Fax (01) 2 21 42 74* – *www.lions-garden.com*   *Plan I* **B1**
107 rm ⌕ – 🛏26000/33740 HUF 🛏🛏31150/38933 HUF
Rest – Carte 4770/6770 HUF
♦ Business ♦ Modern ♦

Set in a residential area, a modern, open-plan hotel with smart leisure club. Contemporary bedrooms boast wooden flooring, modern furniture and good facilities. Ideal for corporate guests. Restaurant with terrace offers international menu.

Mercure Korona 🕸 📺 ⱝ ᏯᏟ ⤴ rm 📟 ☏ 🦽 🚗 🆅🆂🅰 ⓜ🅾 ⱯⒺ ⓄⒹ

Kecskeméti útca 14 ✉ *1053* – ⓜ *Kálvin tér* – ℰ *(01) 486 8825* – *h1765@ accor.com* – *Fax (01) 66 88 71* – *www.mercure-korona.hu*   **F3**
412 rm – 🛏33700/42800 HUF 🛏🛏33700/42800 HUF, ⌕ 4410 HUF – 8 suites
Rest – Carte approx. 6850 HUF
♦ Business ♦ Chain hotel ♦ Modern ♦

Well-equipped modern business hotel close to Hungarian National Museum. Contemporary rooms with all mod cons. Coffee bar and modish lounge. Buzzy restaurant above lobby; informal, modern with original lighting and contemporary local menus. Hungarian wine by the glass.

Zara
Só U. 6 ⊠ 1056 – ℰ (01) 3576170 – info@zarahotels.com – Fax (01) 3 57 61 71
– www.zarahotels.com **F3**
74 rm ☞ – †45600/51000 HUF †¶56000/61000 HUF
Rest – Carte 2580/5060 HUF
♦ Townhouse ♦ Modern ♦

Adjacent to the river and the main shopping street, this purpose-built hotel opened in 2006. Mirrored glass façade; compact but comfortable bedrooms with modern fabrics. Atrium bar and a simple dining room with an easy menu.

Mercure City Center without rest
Váci utca 20 ⊠ 1052 – Ⓜ Ferenciek tere – ℰ 485 3100
– h6565@accor.com – Fax 485 31 11 – www.mercure.com/6565 **E2**
223 rm – †46700 HUF †¶46700 HUF, ☞ 4400 HUF – 4 suites
♦ Traditional ♦ Business ♦ Functional ♦

Business and tourist hotel on main pedestrianised shopping street. Extensive facilities offer something for everyone. Comfortable, refurbished rooms; suites have own sauna.

Central Basilica without rest
Hercegprímás u. 8 ⊠ 1051 – Ⓜ Bajcsy-Zs. út – ℰ (01) 328 5010 – info@hotelcentral-basilica.hu – Fax (01) 328 50 19 – www.central-basilica.hu
37 rm ☞ – †25740/28340 HUF †¶28340/30940 HUF **E2**
♦ Traditional ♦ Functional ♦

Brand new hotel located downtown, close to the basilica. Functional bedrooms have wood furniture, double glazed windows and well-equipped bathrooms. Buffet breakfast.

Ibis Centrum without rest
Raday útca 6 ⊠ 1092 – Ⓜ Kálvin tér – ℰ (01) 456 4100 – h2078@accor.com
– Fax (01) 456 41 16 – www.ibis-centrum.com **F3**
126 rm – †17130/23100 HUF †¶17130/23100 HUF, ☞ 2336 HUF
♦ Business ♦ Chain hotel ♦ Functional ♦

Modern hotel well located for city and national museum. Good functional accommodation with all necessary facilities. Lounge, small bar, bright breakfast room and roof garden.

Mercure Budapest Duna without rest
Soroksári útca 12 ⊠ 1095 – ℰ (01) 455 8300
– h2025@accor.com – Fax (01) 455 83 85 – www.mercure.com *Plan I* **B2**
130 rm – †29900/52000 HUF †¶29900/52000 HUF, ☞ 3300 HUF
♦ Business ♦ Chain hotel ♦ Functional ♦

Modern hotel catering well for business people and tourists, close to river and city. Fair-sized bedrooms offer simple but modern comforts and reasonable level of mod cons.

Gundel
Állatkerti útca 2 ⊠ 1146 – Ⓜ Hösök tere – ℰ (01) 468 4040 – info@gundel.hu
– Fax (01) 363 19 17 – www.gundel.hu
– Closed 24 December *Plan I* **B1**
Rest – (booking essential) Menu 3800 HUF (lunch) – Carte 9070/15400 HUF
♦ Traditional Hungarian ♦ Elegant ♦

Hungary's best known restaurant, an elegant classic. Spacious main room with walnut panelling and ornate ceiling. Traditional cuisine. Summer terrace and live music at dinner.

Fausto's
Székely Mihály u.2 ⊠ 1061 – Ⓜ Opera – ℰ (01) 8776210 – faustos@fausto.hu
– www.fausto.hu
– Closed Christmas and New Year, 2 weeks August, 23 October, Saturday lunch and Sunday **F1/2**
Rest – Menu 4500/1200 HUF – Carte 6700/12500 HUF
♦ Italian ♦ Design ♦

Stylish, well run restaurant hidden behind a discreet façade. Sophisticated, comfortable interior is divided in two. The owner and his team deliver refined, flavoursome Italian cooking.

XX **Lou Lou** AC VISA OO AE

Vigyázó Ferenc Útca 4 ⊠ 1051 – 𝒞 (01) 3124505 – loulou@
loulourestaurant.com – Fax (01) 4 72 05 95 – www.loulourestaurant.com
– Closed Saturday lunch, Sunday and Bank Holidays **E1**
Rest – Menu 4900/13900 HUF – Carte 7000/11200 HUF
♦ Hungarian ♦ Fashionable ♦

Elegant restaurant with chocolate coloured walls, vaulted ceiling and intimate atmosphere. Modern Hungarian cooking displays good flavours and a refined edge. The place to be seen.

XX **Tigris** AC VISA OO AE

Mérleg útca 10 ⊠ 1052 – Ⓜ Bajcsy-Zs. út – 𝒞 (01) 317 3715 – info@
tigrisrestaurant.hu – www.tigrisrestaurant.hu – Closed Sunday **E2**
Rest – (booking essential) Carte 5000/8000 HUF
♦ Hungarian ♦ Brasserie ♦

Originally the city's first luxury hotel, now a smart restaurant with a French brasserie feel. Cooking is almost exclusively Hungarian in both produce and style; dishes are rustic, tasty and flavoursome.

XX **Robinson** 🛋 ⇄ VISA OO AE

Városligeti tó ⊠ 1146 – Ⓜ Széchenyi Fürdö – 𝒞 (01) 422 0222
– robinson@t-online.hu – Fax (01) 422 00 72 – www.robinsonrestaurant.hu
– closed 24-26 December *Plan I* **B1**
Rest – Menu 4500/11200 HUF – Carte 4000/8500 HUF
♦ Traditional ♦ Friendly ♦

Pavilion on tiny island in park; plenty of ducks to watch in lake with fountains. Spacious conservatory with terrace. Extensive menu of traditional and modern fare. Guitar music at dinner.

XX **Cyrano** 🛋 AC ⇄ VISA OO AE

Kristóf tér 7-8 ⊠ 1052 – Ⓜ Vörösmarty tér – 𝒞 (01) 266 4747 – cyrano@
citynet.hu – Fax (01) 266 68 18 – www.cyranorestaurant.info **E2**
Rest – Carte 7250/9700 HUF
♦ Contemporary ♦ Trendy ♦

Popular informal restaurant just off main shopping street with unusual dramatic modern designer-style décor. Serves selection of good modern European and Hungarian food.

XX **Dio** 🛋 AC VISA OO AE

Sas u. 4 ⊠ 1051 – Ⓜ Bajcsy-Zs. út – 𝒞 (01) 328 0360 – dio@diorestaurant.com
– Fax (01) 328 03 61 – www.diorestaurant.com
– Closed 31 December and 1 January **E2**
Rest – Menu 6800/8400 HUF – Carte 5200/8300 HUF
♦ Hungarian ♦ Fashionable ♦

Trendy, modern restaurant set close to the Basillica, with colourful décor, frosted mirrors and pleasant pavement terrace. Traditional Hungarian dishes have a light, refined edge.

XX **Mokka** AC VISA OO AE

Sas u. 4 ⊠ 1051 – Ⓜ Bajcsy-Zs. út – 𝒞 (01) 328 0081 – mokkar@
mokkarestaurant.hu – Fax (01) 328 00 82 – www.mokkarestaurant.hu
Rest – (booking essential) Carte 6550/10140 HUF **E2**
♦ Fusion ♦ Trendy ♦

Trendy, warm and buzzy destination close to the Basilica; booking essential. Décor changing in 2008. Eclectic menus offer a mix of Hungarian, Italian and Asian dishes.

XX **Kárpátia** ⇄ VISA OO AE

Ferenciek tere 7-8 ⊠ 1053 – Ⓜ Ferenciek tere – 𝒞 (01) 317 3596 – restaurant@
karpatia.hu – Fax (01) 318 05 91 – www.karpatia.hu – Closed 24 December
Rest – Carte 6800/13300 HUF **F2**
♦ Traditional Hungarian ♦ Rustic ♦

One of the city's oldest restaurants with characterful vaulted renaissance-style interior, beautifully painted walls and works of art. Extensive menu of traditional cuisine.

XX **Belcanto**   AC ⇔ VISA ◎ AE ①

Dalszínház útca 8 ⊠ 1062 – ⓜ Opera – ℰ (01) 269 2786 – restaurant@
belcanto.hu – Fax (01) 311 95 47 – www.belcanto.hu
– Closed 25 December   **F1**
Rest – *(booking essential)* Menu 7800/8200 HUF – Carte 11000/15200 HUF
   ♦ Traditional Hungarian ♦ Musical ♦

Next to the opera and famous for classical and operatic evening recitals, including impromptu performances by waiters! Atmosphere is lively and enjoyable. Hungarian food.

XX **Baraka** – at Andrássy Hotel   🛏 P VISA ◎ AE ①

Andrássy útca 111 ⊠ 1063 – ⓜ Bajza u. – ℰ (01) 462 2100
– reservation@andrassyhotel.com – Fax (01) 322 94 45 – www.andrassyhotel.com
Rest – Carte 5313/12903 HUF   *Plan I* **B1**
   ♦ Innovative ♦ Fashionable ♦

Chic restaurant with smart black tables, velvet armchairs and terrace. Cooking is original and uses interesting combinations; dishes are modern, or classical with an innovative twist.

X **Bock Bisztró**   AC VISA ◎

Erzsébet Krt 43-49 ⊠ 1073 – ⓜ Oktogon – ℰ (01) 321 0340 – bockbisztro@
t-online.hu – Fax (01) 321 03 40 – www.bockbistro.hu
– Closed Sunday and Bank Holidays   **F1**
Rest – Carte 5600/9650 HUF 🍷
   ♦ Traditional ♦ Bistro ♦

Stylish décor with Art Deco lighting, though the feel is informal bistro. Classic local recipes with a 21C lift; tapas and cheese/ham plates available too.

X **Osteria Fausto's**   AC ♿ VISA ◎ AE

Dohány U.5 ⊠ 1072 – ⓜ Astoria – ℰ (01) 2696806 – faustos@fausto.hu
– Fax (01) 2 69 68 06 – www.osteria.hu
– Closed 24-26 December, 1 January, 23 October and Sunday   **F2**
Rest – Menu 2500/6000 HUF – Carte 4200/8400 HUF
   ♦ Italian ♦ Bistro ♦

Informal Italian restaurant and wine bar serving simple, rustic Italian food supplemented by blackboard specials, and Hungarian and Italian wines. Expect a friendly welcome.

X **Krizia**   AC VISA ◎ AE

Mozsár útca 12 ⊠ 1066 – ⓜ Oktogon – ℰ (01) 331 8711
– ristorante.krizia@axelero.hu – Fax (01) 331 87 11 – www.ristorantekrizia.hu
– Closed 3 weeks July-August, 2 weeks New Year, 24-26 December, Easter and
Sunday   **F1**
Rest – Menu 2600/8000 HUF – Carte 3210/9840 HUF
   ♦ Italian ♦ Cosy ♦

Dining room in vaulted cellar with a pleasant intimate atmosphere and friendly service. Carefully-prepared Italian cooking, supplemented by regularly changing specials.

BUDA   *Plan II*

🏨 **Art'otel**   ≤ 🛏 🛋 🌙 ⅙ AC ♿ rm 🖭 ⁽ᵗ⁾ 🧖 🚗 VISA ◎ AE

Bem Rakpart 16-19 ⊠ 1011 – ⓜ Batthyány tér – ℰ (01) 487 9487
– budapest@artotel.hu – Fax (01) 487 94 88 – www.artotels.com   **D1**
156 rm – ♥26500/80000 HUF ♥♥26500/80000 HUF, � 3115 HUF – 9 suites
Rest *Chelsea* – Carte 4600/7900 HUF
   ♦ Business ♦ Design ♦

Half new building, half converted baroque houses. Stylish and original interior in cool shades and clean lines. Features over 700 pieces of original art by Donald Sultan. Bright dining room with vaulted ceiling topped with glass and modern artwork.

Lánchíd 19 ≤ 🏠 ᓂ 🄰🄲 ⅏ 🖃 ⅏ 🛁 🆅🆂🅰 ⊕⊕ 🄰🄴 ⊕

Lánchíd u 19 ⊠ 1013 – ℰ (01) 4191900 – rooms@lanchid19hotel.hu – Fax (01) 4 19 19 19 – www.lanchid19hotel.hu **D2**
48 rm � – ♗31894 HUF ♗♗49291 HUF **Rest** *L19* – Carte 6000/8700 HUF
◆ Business ◆ Design ◆

Trendy design hotel overlooking the Danube and Castle. Glass floored lounge looks down onto 14C ruins. Bedrooms boast modern facilities and designer chairs; front rooms have river views. Colourful restaurant offers an international menu and good outlook.

Buda Castle *without rest* 🚗 🄰🄲 ⅏ 🖃 ⅏ 🆅🆂🅰 ⊕⊕ 🄰🄴

Úri utca 39 ⊠ 1014 – ⓂMoszkva tér – ℰ (01) 2247900 – info@budacastlehotel.eu – Fax (01) 2 01 49 03 – www.budacastlehotel.eu
21 rm ⊆ – ♗22000/26500 HUF ♗♗28500/50000 HUF – 4 suites **C1**
◆ Townhouse ◆ Modern ◆

On a quiet street in old Buda – previously the Hunting Association HQ. Spacious bedrooms boast modern décor and quality furniture. Comfy breakfast room doubles as a bar lounge; pleasant garden terrace.

Novotel Budapest Danube 🛗 🏠 ᓂ 🄰🄲 ⅏ 🖃 ⅏ 🛁 🅿

Bem Rakpart 33-34 ⊠ 1027 – ⓂBatthyány tér 🆅🆂🅰 ⊕⊕ 🄰🄴 ⊕
– ℰ (01) 458 4900 – h6151@accor.com – Fax (01) 458 49 09
– www.novotel.com **D1**
175 rm – ♗26000/70200 HUF ♗♗26000/70200 HUF, ⊆ 4500 HUF
Rest – Menu 7300 HUF – Carte 5400/17200 HUF
◆ Chain hotel ◆ Business ◆ Modern ◆

Well located, modern hotel boasting basement gym and sauna, meeting rooms for the business traveller and well equipped bedrooms, with a choice of 'Novation' or 'Executive.' Enjoy panoramic views of the river and the Parliament building from Café Danube, which serves international cuisine.

Uhu Villa ⌂ ≤ 🚗 🏠 🏠 🖵 🄰🄲 ⅏ 🖃 ⅏ 🅿 🆅🆂🅰 ⊕⊕ 🄰🄴

Keselyü l/a (Northwest : 8 km by Szilágyi Erzsébet fasor) ⊠ 1025 – ℰ (01) 275 1002 – uhuvilla@uhuvilla.hu – Fax (01) 398 05 71 – www.uhuvilla.hu
13 rm ⊆ – ♗28550/38900 HUF ♗♗38900/44100 HUF – 1 suite
Rest – *(Closed Sunday) (dinner only)* Carte 6000/10100 HUF
◆ Traditional ◆ Cosy ◆

Friendly, discreet, personally-styled early 20C villa with gardens in peaceful Buda Hills. Smart, contemporary bedrooms with neat décor, some with balconies. Restaurant with terrace and view serving Italian dishes; Hungarian and Italian wine list.

Carlton *without rest* 🄰🄲 ⅏ 🖃 ⅏ 🛁 🚗 🆅🆂🅰 ⊕⊕ 🄰🄴 ⊕

Apor Péter útca 3 ⊠ 1011 – ⓂBatthyány tér – ℰ (01) 224 0999
– carltonhotel@t-online.hu – Fax (01) 224 09 90 – www.carltonhotel.hu
95 rm ⊆ – ♗20100/25500 HUF ♗♗22800/29500 HUF **D2**
◆ Traditional ◆ Classic ◆

Usefully-located hotel on Buda side of river, offering straightforward accommodation for the cost-conscious traveller. Rooms are functional and comfortable. Small bar.

Victoria *without rest* ≤ 🏠 🄰🄲 ⅏ 🖃 ⅏ 🅿 🆅🆂🅰 ⊕⊕ 🄰🄴

Bem Rakpart 11 ⊠ 1011 – ⓂBatthyány tér – ℰ (01) 457 8080
– victoria@victoria.hu – Fax (01) 457 80 88
– www.victoria.hu **D1**
27 rm ⊆ – ♗21160/31400 HUF ♗♗23000/32950 HUF
◆ Traditional ◆ Functional ◆

Family-run hotel, popular with tourists, in a row of town houses below the castle. Spacious rooms, equipped with good range of facilities, offer fine views. Refreshing sauna.

XXX **Alabárdos** 🛏 AC ½ ⇔ VISA ⊙ AE

Országház útca 2 ✉ *1014 –* Ⓜ *Moszkva tér –* ✆ *(01) 356 0851 – alabardos@*
t-online.hu – Fax (01) 214 38 14 – www.alabardos.hu – Closed Sunday
Rest *– (booking essential) (dinner only and Saturday lunch)* **D1**
Carte 8900/10200 HUF 🍴
  ♦ Traditional ♦ Formal ♦

Well-run restaurant in vaulted Gothic interior of characterful 17C building with covered
courtyard in castle square. Extensive menu of good traditional Hungarian classics.

XXX **Arany Kaviár** 🛏 AC VISA ⊙ AE ⊙

Ostrom u. 19 ✉ *1015 –* Ⓜ *Moszkva tér –* ✆ *(01) 2016737 – reservation@*
aranykaviar.hu – www.aranykaviar.hu – Closed 24 December **C1**
Rest *– Menu 5000/10000 HUF – Carte 7550/10600 HUF*
  ♦ Russian ♦ Intimate ♦

Elegant Russian restaurant boasting heavy fabrics and lovely terrace. Choice of tasting menu, gourmet caviar or extensive Russian/Eastern European/international à
la carte; refined, flavoursome cooking.

XXX **Vadrózsa** 🛏 AC ⇔ VISA ⊙ AE

Pentelei Molnár útca 15 (via Rómer Flóris útca) ✉ *1025 –* ✆ *(01) 326 5817*
– vadrozsa@hungary.net – Fax (01) 326 58 09 – www.vadrozsa.hu
– Closed 24-26 December *Plan I* **A1**
Rest *– Menu 5000 HUF – Carte 7630/10840 HUF*
  ♦ Traditional Hungarian ♦ Formal ♦

Pleasant villa just out of town. Spacious wood panelled dining room with piano.
Display of raw ingredients presented with the menu. Attractive summer terrace.
Detailed service.

XX **Café Pierrot** 🛏 AC ½ VISA ⊙ AE

Fortuna u. 14 ✉ *1014 –* Ⓜ *Moszkva tér –* ✆ *(01) 375 6971 – info@pierrot.hu*
– Fax (01) 375 69 71 – www.pierrot.hu **C1**
Rest *– Menu 4300 HUF (lunch) – Carte 5370/9570 HUF*
  ♦ Modern ♦ Friendly ♦

Trees in pots, twinkling fairy lights, Pierrot clown theming with original artwork
by local artists. Hungarian base underpins dishes skilfully concocted with Gallic
finesse. Live jazz piano.

XX **Arcade Bistro** 🛏 AC VISA ⊙ AE

Kiss Janos Alt u. 38 ✉ *1126 –* Ⓜ *Déli pu. –* ✆ *(01) 225 1969*
– arcade@freestart.hu – Fax (01) 225 19 68 – www.arcadebistro.hu
– Closed 24 December, 1 January and Sunday dinner **C2-3**
Rest *– (booking essential) Carte 4610/9130 HUF*
  ♦ Traditional ♦ Bistro ♦

Small and friendly local restaurant in drab residential area, with central column
water feature and colourful modern art décor. Traditional Hungarian cooking.

X **Kisbuda Gyöngye** 🛏 AC ½ ⇔ VISA ⊙ AE

Kenyeres útca 34 ✉ *1034 –* Ⓜ *Árpád híd –* ✆ *(01) 368 9246 – gyongye@*
remiz.hu – Fax (01) 368 92 27 – www.remiz.hu
– Closed 24 December, 1 January and Sunday *Plan I* **A1**
Rest *– (booking essential) (music at dinner) Carte 6500/8500 HUF*
  ♦ Traditional Hungarian ♦ Rustic ♦

Neighbourhood restaurant in a residential street. Rustic wood panelling created by
old wardrobes. Attentive service. Good choice menu; international and authentic
food. Live piano.

X **Náncsi Néni** 🛏 VISA ⊙ AE

Ördögárok útca 80, Hüvösvölgy (Northwest : 10 km by Szilágyi Erzsébetfasor)
✉ *1029 –* ✆ *(01) 397 2742 – info@nancsineni.hu – Fax (01) 397 27 42*
– www.nancsineni.hu – Closed dinner 24 and 31 December
Rest *– Carte 3940/6830 HUF*
  ♦ Traditional Hungarian ♦ Minimalist ♦

Interior similar to a Swiss chalet with gingham tablecloths, convivial atmosphere and
large terrace. Well-priced home-style Hungarian cooking. Worth the drive from the city.

Republic of IRELAND
ÉIRE

→ **AREA:**
70 284 km²
(27 137 sq mi).

→ **POPULATION:**
4 016 000 inhabitants
(est. 2005), density =
57 per km².

→ **CAPITAL:**
Dublin (population
1 004 614).

→ **CURRENCY:**
Euro (€); rate of
exchange: € 1 =
US$ 1.32 (Jan 2009).

→ **GOVERNMENT:**
Parliamentary
republic (since 1921).
Member of European
Union since 1973.

→ **LANGUAGES:**
Irish and English.

→ **SPECIFIC PUBLIC
HOLIDAYS:**
St. Patrick's
Day (17 March)
Good Friday (Friday
before Easter);
May Bank Holiday
(first Monday in May);
June Bank Holiday
(first Monday in June);
August Bank Holiday
(first Monday in
August); October
Bank Holiday (last
Monday in October);

St. Stephen's
Day (26 December).

→ **LOCAL TIME:**
GMT in winter and
GMT + 1 hour in
summer.

→ **CLIMATE:**
Temperate maritime,
with cool winters and
mild summers, fairly
high rainfall (Dublin :
January: 5°C, July:
15°C).

→ **INTERNATIONAL
DIALLING CODE:**
00 353 followed
by area code and
then the local
number.

→ **EMERGENCY:**
☎ **999** for all
emergency services
– Fire Brigade,
Police, Ambulance,
Mountain, Cave,
Coastguard and Sea
rescue.

→ **ELECTRICITY:**
230 volts AC, 50Hz;
3 pin flat or 2-pin
round-shaped
wall sockets are
standard.

→ **FORMALITIES**
Travellers from the
European Union

DUBLIN●

(EU), Switzerland,
Iceland and the main
countries of North
and South America
need a national
identity card or
passport (except
for British nationals
travelling from the
UK; America: passport
required)
to visit Ireland for
less than three
months (tourism or
business purpose).
For visitors from
other countries
a visa may be
required, in addition
to a passport,
especially for those
wishing to stay for
longer than three
months. We advise
you to check with
your embassy before
travelling.

DUBLIN
BAILE ÁTHA CLIATH

Population: 495 101 (conurbation 1 004 614) – Altitude: sea level

R. Kord PHOTONONSTOP

For somewhere touted as the finest Georgian city in the British Isles, Dublin enjoys a very young image. As the 'Celtic Tiger' roared to prominence in the 1990s, Ireland's old capital took on a youthful expression, and for the first time revelled in the epithets 'chic' and 'trendy'. Nowadays it's not just the bastion of Guinness drinkers and those here for the 'craic', but a twenty-first century city with smart restaurants, grand new hotels, modern architecture, impressive galleries and ethnic diversity (and yes, the Guinness still tastes perfect).

Dublin hasn't known a period of such economic prosperity and growth for 250 years, when its handsome squares and façades took shape, designed by the finest architects of the time. In the intervening years, it's gone through uprising, civil war and independence from Britain, and the last decade or so has seen the Irish economy grow ever stronger so that now the city holds a strong fascination for foreign visitors – people are going to Dublin rather than leaving it, as was traditionally the case. Mind you, the locals don't always take too kindly to their guests: invading hordes of stag and hen parties crossing the Irish Sea for intense liquid refreshment, mostly in the Temple Bar area alongside the Liffey, put a strain on even a Dubliner's amiability. At least it leaves all those other fascinating parts of the city ripe for the rest of us to explore.

LIVING THE CITY

Dublin can be pretty well divided into three parts. The area southeast of the river is the classiest, defined by the glorious **Trinity College, St Stephen's Green**, and **Grafton Street's** smart shops. Just west of here is the second area, dominated by **Dublin Castle** and **Christ Church Cathedral** – ancient buildings abound, but it doesn't quite match the sleek aura of the city's Georgian quarter. Cross the **Liffey** to reach the third area. This northern section was the last part of Dublin to be developed during the eighteenth century. Although it lacks the glamour and affluence of its southern neighbours, it does boast the city's grandest avenue, **O'Connell Street,** as well as its most celebrated theatres, a fact that counts in a city which has been home to four Nobel Prize winning writers.

PRACTICAL INFORMATION

ARRIVAL-DEPARTURE

Dublin Airport is just over 7 miles north of the city and a taxi will cost around €20. There is no rail link to the airport but a number of coaches and buses, including Airlink and Aircoach, will take you to the city centre in approximately 30mins.

TRANSPORT

The bus network covers the whole city from the Central Bus Station in Store Street. The price of a single ticket varies depending on the number of stages you've travelled, but it's a cheap and efficient service.

The exciting LUAS (meaning 'speed') light rail network rushes you to areas of the city and suburbs previously only connected to the centre by bus. LUAS was introduced in 2004; like the buses, you pay more as you travel further by zones.

If you want to get out to the coast, then jump on a Dublin Area Rapid Transport (DART) train. They operate at regular intervals, are awesomely efficient, and leave central Dublin from Connolly, Tara Street and Pearse stations. They're as quick as they sound. Buy tickets at any station.

Get along to a Tourist Information Office for the Dublin Pass, which gains you access to just about anywhere in the city. Well, to over thirty attractions, anyway. Passes range from one to six days.

EXPLORING DUBLIN

Despite its twenty-first century gloss, Dublin still enjoys a meandering pace of life with an emphasis on the slow and relaxed. Locals will advise you to take your time over a visit; this is not the biggest metropolis on the planet, so why hurry to get around it? With almost a thousand pubs inside the city limits (never mind the new bars and cafés which have sprung up) there's certainly no problem in interrupting your sightseeing schedule. Most of the tourist hotspots are in the area to the south of the Liffey, but there's a lot of fun to be had in turning into inconspicuous alleyways and seeing what shadowy hidden gem might be giving you the nod.

➜ BROUGHT TO BOOK

If you did happen to be in a rush, you could walk from the top of O'Connell Street over the river to the smart southern suburb of **Ballsbridge** in an hour. But then what would be the point of coming to Dublin? The best place to linger is the area around Trinity College, leading down Grafton Street. This section of the city was pretty much undeveloped until the college was founded in 1592, but it was another hundred years before St Stephen's Green, just to the south, was created. As we say, around here no-one's in a particular hurry. It's not difficult to see why people flock to the college. The alma mater of Samuel Beckett, Oliver Goldsmith and Edmund Burke, it's populated with attractive squares, an Old Library with a spectacular Long Room, and a dominant thirty metre high Campanile. Its main attraction, though, is in the Treasury, where the magnificent **Book of Kells** is housed. Dated from around AD 800, it's one of the oldest books in the world, a lavishly illustrated manuscript produced by monks on the remote Scottish island of Iona. It features superbly decorated opening letters of each chapter and dyes supposedly imported from the Middle East.

By way of a complete contrast to the intense intellectualism of Trinity College, step outside and there'll find the fancy shops lining Grafton Street, the city's most fashionable thoroughfare. Its most exclusive store, Brown Thomas, is also one of its oldest, and locals look upon it as a Londoner might look upon Harvey Nichols. Grafton Street certainly pulls in the crowds, and for those heading south, there's the reward of a ver-

dant sanctuary: St Stephen's Green. Landscaped with flowerbeds, trees, a lake and a fountain, it likes to remind you exactly where you are by displaying numerous memorials to eminent Dubliners: Joyce, Yeats and Wolfe Tone are all here.

➜ MAKING MERRION

This is where Georgian architecture really makes its impact felt; head north along **Merrion Street Upper** and you'll find **Merrion Square,** twelve swanky acres of mid-eighteenth century splendour, bordered on three sides by attractive town-houses featuring wrought-iron balconies and brightly painted doors. The area's sophisticated appeal is enhanced by a rash of museums and galleries, chief of these being the **National Museum** on Kildare Street, which announces itself with an eye-catching domed rotunda and beautiful jewellery from the Bronze Age. In the **National Gallery** on Clare Street, the major schools of European art are represented alongside Irish painting. One of the benefactors here was George Bernard Shaw (his own birthplace, a twenty minute walk south from here, is itself now a museum). Truly worth a visit when you're in the Georgian quarter is the **National Library**, fascinating because it contains first editions of every major Irish writer, and you don't have to think too hard to come up with an awesome list. But museum lovers need not yet feel sated, as also in the area are the **Heraldic Museum** and the **Natural History Museum**, or 'the Dead Zoo' as it's known to the locals.

➜ TEMPLE WORSHIP

You don't really feel you're strolling into a radically different area when you venture south-west of the Liffey: after all, it's just a hop, skip and jump across from Trinity College and Grafton Street. But this is an even older part of town, with **Temple Bar** boasting a wealth of attractive cobbled streets. The area is alive during the daytime as well, particularly around Temple Bar Square, which buzzes with little gallery shops, designer boutiques and a thriving book market at weekends. With its now legendary number of bars, pubs and restaurants jostling for your attention, you might feel the only way to find sanctuary is in a big church or even a castle. Wouldn't you know it, there are two on the doorstep. Christ Church Cathedral, in Christchurch Place, was established nearly a thousand years ago, making it Ireland's oldest. Its history continues right up to 2000, when the vast and fascinating twelfth century crypt was restored. Just across the way is Dublin Castle, first built in the thirteenth century, but with the **Record Tower** the only survivor from that time; luxurious state apartments and a throne presented by William of Orange can be found here, but the star turn is the **Chester Beatty Library**, in the Castle's Clock Tower Building. This outstanding collection of ancient works of art from around the world includes hundreds of illuminated manuscripts with exquisite calligraphy, and almost 300 copies of the Koran spread over a thousand years (considered to be the best example of illuminated Islamic texts in the world). There are striking Buddhist paintings, clay tablets and detailed miniatures. Not surprisingly, it was named European Museum of the Year in 2002. Oh, and the rooftop garden's a great place to eat your lunch if it's a sunny day.

→ NOT WRITTEN OFF

North of the Liffey has for many years been considered a bit of an Achilles Heel, an area 'down on its uppers' and in need of a facelift, an urban botox. That said, there are good reasons to cross the river in a northwards direction, not least a stroll along Dublin's grandest thoroughfare, O'Connell Street. This imposing avenue's mid-eighteenth century glory days may be long gone, but meandering along its central mall you can still get a feel for its heyday as you sample its mix of monuments, fine department stores and historic public buildings. At either end of O'Connell Street stand Dublin's two most famous theatres: **The Abbey** to the south is Ireland's national theatre where Irish playwrights are proudly to the fore; while **The Gate** in Parnell Square to the north has a great reputation for contemporary drama. Slipping very conveniently into this creative mix is the absorbing **Dublin Writers' Museum**, also in Parnell Square, which pays tribute to the city's long history as a literary giant, and includes letters, photos and other memorabilia. Fans of Joyce can then pop along a few streets east to the **James Joyce Cultural Centre**, housed neatly in a Georgian townhouse.

DUBLIN IN...

→ ONE DAY
Trinity College, Grafton Street, St Stephen's Green, Merrion Square, a drink and a meal in Temple Bar

→ TWO DAYS
Christ Church Cathedral, Dublin Castle, Chester Beatty Library, the quayside, a play at one of Dublin's theatres

→ THREE DAYS
A further amble round the alleyways of Temple Bar, O'Connell Street, Parnell Square, Dublin Writers' Museum, a DART train to the coast

CALENDAR HIGHLIGHTS

Some people think Dubliners celebrate a special event every day of the year – the moment the first pint of Guinness goes down. Well, that apart, there are many events and calendar highlights of an official kind in the city. St Patrick's Day in March is, surprise surprise, taken rather seriously here. It's a national holiday given over to music and carnival-style merriment. Around the same time, Celtic Flame lets rip, a citywide festival of traditional and modern music. Don't get this mixed up with the Temple Bar Fleadh, another mid-March mash-up, which resounds to traditional rhythms all around the Temple Bar area. On a more refined scale, April hosts the Colours Boat Race along the Liffey between Trinity College and University College teams, while a little later in the month Feis Ceoil is one of Europe's most well-established and prestigious classical music festivals. Temple Bar again plays host to Diversions right through the summer, an umbrella title for loads of free concerts and open-air theatre shows. The sixteenth of June is a sacred day for fans of Joyce's Ulysses, because it's Bloomsday, when walks, pub talks and lectures take place all over the city. Dublin's premier social event, the Horse Show, trots along in August and gives people a chance to dress in funny hats. Drama's back centre-stage in September with the Fringe Theatre Festival, and then in October with the Dublin Theatre Festival, where new plays are put under the spotlight. A different kind of traditional music sees Opera Ireland make its mark for a week in November at the Gaiety Theatre.

EATING OUT

It's still possible to indulge in Irish stew, but nowadays in Dublin you can also dine out on everything from Thai to tacos and Malaysian to Middle-Eastern. The last decade has seen a boom in global cuisine, often in the Temple Bar area. The city makes the most of its bay proximity, and seafood and fish are used abundantly ; in particular, smoked salmon and oysters. The latter is a staple diet of Dubliners, who love nothing better than to wash them down with Guinness. Portions here are generous, especially in pubs: a plate of roast meat and vegetables is invariably good value for money. For decades vegetables were seen as a bit of a curse in Ireland: a mere decoration, over-boiled to death. Now they're treated with the respect they deserve, and local chefs insist on the best seasonal produce, cooked for just the right amount of time to savour all the taste and goodness. There's never been a better time to be a vegetarian in Dublin, as every type of veg from asparagus to spinach and seaweed is used liberally in dishes. Meat is particularly tasty in Ireland, due to healthy livestock and a wet climate: Irish beef is world famous for its fulsome flavour. Dinner here is usually served till about 10pm, though many ethnic and city-centre restaurants stay open later. If you make your main meal at lunchtime, you'll pay considerably less than in the evening: the menus are often similar, but the bill in the middle of the day will probably be about half the price. Good restaurants nowadays include a fifteen per cent service charge, so there's no need to add a tip.

IRELAND - DUBLIN

The Shelbourne   🚿 ⚙ ↯ 🛈 🛁 💳 💳 💳

27 St Stephen's Green ✉ _D2 –_ ℰ _(01) 663 4500_
– info@renaissancehotels.com – Fax (01) 661 60 06
– www.theshelbourne.ie   **E3**
265 rm – 🛏219/289 € 🛏🛏219/289 €, ⌓ 29 € – 19 suites
Rest _The Saddle Room_ – see below
♦ Grand Luxury ♦ Classic ♦
A delightful refit of a grand old hotel, with elegant meeting rooms and sumptuous bedrooms offering a host of extras. The historic Horseshoe Bar and Lord Mayor's Room remain.

The Merrion   🚗 🛗 🖥 ⚙ 🛰 🛈 🛁 🚗 💳 💳 💳 🌀

Upper Merrion St ✉ _D2 –_ ℰ _(01) 603 0600 – info@merrionhotel.com_
– Fax (01) 603 07 00 – www.merrionhotel.com   **F3**
133 rm – 🛏480 € 🛏🛏510 €, ⌓ 29 € – 10 suites
Rest The Cellar and **The Cellar Bar** – see below
♦ Grand Luxury ♦ Cosy ♦
Classic hotel in series of elegantly restored Georgian town houses; many of the individually designed grand rooms overlook pleasant gardens. Irish art in opulent lounges.

The Westin   🛗 ⚙ rm 🛗 ⚙ 🛈 🛁 💳 💳 💳 🌀

College Green, Westmoreland St ✉ _D2 –_ ℰ _(01) 645 1000_
– reservations.dublin@westin.com – Fax (01) 645 12 34
– www.westin.com/dublin   **E2**
150 rm – 🛏179/489 € 🛏🛏179/489 €, ⌓ 28 € – 13 suites
Rest _The Exchange_ – _(Closed Sunday dinner and Monday)_ Menu 26 € (lunch)
– Carte dinner 34/59 €
Rest _The Mint_ – Carte approx. 30 €
♦ Luxury ♦ Classic ♦
Immaculately kept and consummately run hotel in a useful central location. Smart, uniform interiors and an ornate period banking hall. Excellent bedrooms with marvellous beds. Elegant, Art Deco 1920s-style dining in Exchange. More informal fare at The Mint.

The Westbury   🛗 ⚙ rm 🛗 ⚙ 🛈 🛁 🚗 💳 💳 💳 🌀

Grafton St ✉ _D2 –_ ℰ _(01) 679 1122 – westbury@jurysdoyle.com_
– Fax (01) 679 70 78 – www.jurysdoyle.com   **E2**
179 rm – 🛏209/309 € 🛏🛏209/309 €, ⌓ 28 € – 8 suites
Rest _The Wilde_ – Menu 35/50 € – Carte 51/83 €
Rest _Café Novo_ – Carte 32/47 €
♦ Luxury ♦ Modern ♦
Imposing marble foyer and stairs lead to lounge famous for afternoon teas. Stylish Mandarin bar. Luxurious bedrooms offer every conceivable facility. Modern grill restaurant serves carefully sourced produce; Black Angus steak a speciality. Café Novo offers more international brasserie menu.

Conrad Dublin   🛗 ⚙ rm 🛗 ⚙ 🛈 🛁 🚗 💳 💳 💳 🌀

Earlsfort Terrace ✉ _D2 –_ ℰ _(01) 602 8900_
_– dubhc_rs@conradhotels.com – Fax (01) 676 54 24_
– www.conradhotels.com/dublin   **E3**
191 rm – 🛏185/380 € 🛏🛏200/380 €, ⌓ 15 €
Rest _Alex_ – Menu 30/40 € – Carte 38/68 €
♦ Luxury ♦ Modern ♦
Smart, business oriented international hotel opposite the National Concert Hall. Popular, pub-style bar. Spacious rooms with bright, modern décor and comprehensive facilities. Modern, bright and airy restaurant offers seafood specialities.

Dylan
                                       க rm 🏧 ↳ 🖭 🎙 🚰 VISA ⑤ AE ①

Eastmoreland Place ✉ D2 – ℰ *(01) 660 3000 – justask@dylan.ie*
– Fax (01) 660 30 05 – www.dylan.ie
– Closed Christmas   *Plan III* **H1**
44 rm – ♦395 €, ♦♦395 €, ⇆ 30 €
Rest *Still* – *(Closed Saturday lunch)* Carte 45/74 €
  ♦ Luxury ♦ Modern ♦

Modern boutique hotel with vibrant use of colour. Supremely comfortable, individually decorated bedrooms boast an opulent feel and a host of unexpected extras. Modern Irish cooking served in elegant, white-furnished dining room.

The Clarence
                                   ⫷ ௴ க 🖭 ℭ 🕍 🅿 VISA ⑤ AE ①

6-8 Wellington Quay ✉ D2 – ℰ *(01) 407 0800 – reservations@theclarence.ie*
– Fax (01) 407 08 20 – www.theclarence.ie
– Closed 24-26 December   **D2**
44 rm – ♦390 €, ♦♦390 €, ⇆ 28 € – 5 suites
Rest *The Tea Room* – see below
  ♦ Luxury ♦ Design ♦

Discreet, stylish former warehouse overlooking river boasting 21C interior design. Small panelled library. Modern, distinctive rooms: quietest face courtyard on fourth floor.

The Fitzwilliam
                                   ⫷ ௴ 🏧 🖭 🎙 🕍 🚗 VISA ⑤ AE ①

St Stephen's Green ✉ D2 – ℰ *(01) 478 7000 – enq@fitzwilliamhotel.com*
– Fax (01) 478 78 78 – www.fitzwilliamhotel.com   **E3**
136 rm – ♦220/380 €, ♦♦220/380 €, ⇆ 24 € – 3 suites
Rest *Thornton's* – see below
Rest *Citron* – Carte 28/50 €
  ♦ Business ♦ Classic ♦

Rewardingly overlooks the Green and boasts a bright contemporary interior. Spacious, finely appointed rooms offer understated elegance. Largest hotel roof garden in Europe. Very trendy, informal brasserie.

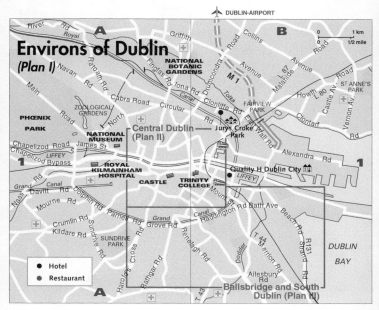

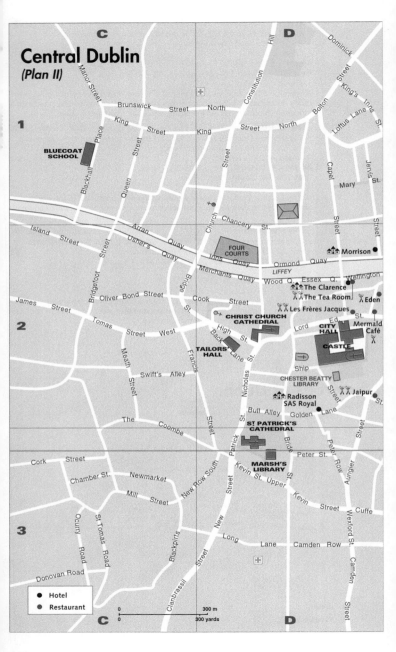

Central Dublin
(Plan II)

C **D**

Dominick Street

Manor Street

Constitution Hill

King's Inns St.

Brunswick Street North

Loftus Lane

Bolton Street

1

King Street

King Street North

Jervis St.

Capel Street

BLUECOAT SCHOOL

Blackhall Place

Queen Street

Church Street

Mary Street

Chancery St.

Arran Quay

Island Street

Usher's Quay

FOUR COURTS

Ormond Quay

⚓ Morrison ●

Bridgefoot Street

Inns Quay

Merchants Quay

LIFFEY

Wood Quay

Essex Q.

Wellington

⚓♨ The Clarence

James Street

Oliver Bond Street

Cook Street

Bridge St.

XX Les Frères Jacques

X Eden ●

Tomas Street West

High St.

Back Lane

CHRIST CHURCH CATHEDRAL

Lord Ed. St.

CITY HALL

Mermaid Café ●

2

Meath Street

TAILORS' HALL

Francis Street

Nicholas St.

CASTLE

X

Ship St.

CHESTER BEATTY LIBRARY

Swift's Alley

⚓ Radisson SAS Royal ●

XX Jaipur St.

The Coombe

Bull Alley

Golden Lane

Peter Row

ST PATRICK'S CATHEDRAL

Patrick Street

Bride St.

Peter St.

Aungier Street

Cork Street

Chamber St.

Newmarket

New Row South

MARSH'S LIBRARY

Kevin St. Upper

Kevin Street

Cuffe Street

Mill Street

St Tomas Road

Kevin St.

Wexford St.

Ocurry Road

Blackpitts

New Street

Long Lane

Camden Row

3

Camden Street

Donovan Road

Clanbrassil Street

● Hotel
● Restaurant

0 ____ 300 m
0 ____ 300 yards

C **D**

460

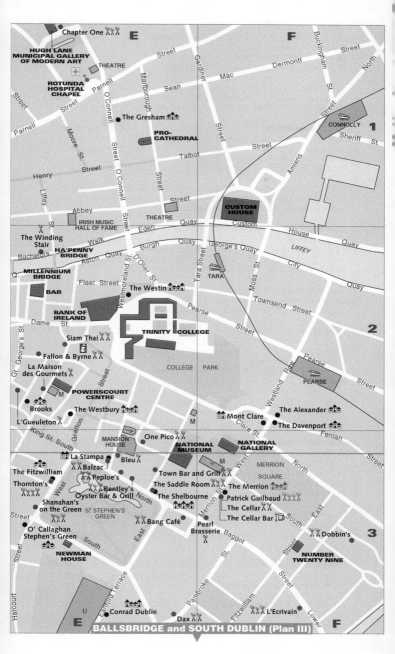

BALLSBRIDGE and SOUTH DUBLIN (Plan III)

Brooks   _Lb_ 🕭 AC 🛁 🕸 _VISA_ ⓒ AE

Drury St ✉ _D2 – ℰ (01) 670 4000 – reservations@brookshotel.ie – Fax (01)_
670 44 55 – www.brookshotel.ie   **E2**
98 rm – ♦170/200 € ♦♦200/240 €, ⌸ 20 €
Rest _Francesca's_ – _(dinner only)_ Carte 19/44 €
 ♦ Business ♦ Stylish ♦

Commercial hotel in modish, boutique, Irish town house style. Smart lounges and
stylish rooms exude contemporary panache. Extras in top range rooms, at a sup-
plement. Fine dining with open kitchen for chef-watching.

Stephen's Green   _Lb_ AC 🛁 🕸 ⌂ _VISA_ ⓒ AE

Cuffe St, off St Stephen's Green ✉ _D2 – ℰ (01) 607 3600 – info@_
ocallaghanhotels.com – Fax (01) 478 14 44 – www.ocallaghanhotels.com
67 rm – ♦150/480 € ♦♦150/480 €, ⌸ 17 € – 11 suites   **E3**
Rest _The Pie Dish_ – _(Closed lunch Saturday and Sunday)_ Carte 35/60 €
 ♦ Business ♦ Modern ♦

This smart modern hotel housed in an originally Georgian property frequented by
business clients; popular Magic Glass bar. Bright bedrooms offer a good range of
facilities. Bright and breezy bistro restaurant.

Radisson SAS Royal   🕸 🛁 P _VISA_ ⓒ AE

Golden Lane ✉ _8 – ℰ (01) 898 2900 – info.royal.dublin@radissonsas.com_
– Fax (01) 898 29 01 – www.dublin.radissonsas.com   **D2**
146 rm – ♦170/180 € ♦♦170/180 €, ⌸ 22 € – 4 suites
Rest _Verres en Vers_ – Menu 20 € (lunch) – Carte 36/58 €
 ♦ Business ♦ Modern ♦

Modern, purpose-built hotel in the heart of the city, geared to the corporate market. Bedrooms get bigger, the higher the floor - Executive rooms have lots of extras; some with balconies. Classic French brasserie cooking.

The Morrison   AC 📞 🛁 _VISA_ ⓒ AE ⓞ

Lower Ormond Quay ✉ _D1 – ℰ (01) 887 2400 – reservations@morrisonhotel.ie_
– Fax (01) 874 40 39 – www.morrisonhotel.ie
– closed 24-26 December   **D2**
135 rm – ♦355 € ♦♦355 €, ⌸ 21.50 € – 3 suites
Rest _Halo_ – Lower Ormond Quay, – Carte 33/46 €
 ♦ Luxury ♦ Design ♦

Modern riverside hotel with ultra-contemporary interior by acclaimed fashion
designer John Rocha. New rooms are particularly stylish. Relaxed dining room con-
centrates on Irish produce in modish and home-cooked blend of dishes.

The Gresham   _Lb_ & rm AC 📺 🛁 🛁 P _VISA_ ⓒ AE

23 Upper O'Connell St ✉ _D1 – ℰ (01) 874 6881 – info@thegresham.com_
– Fax (01) 878 71 75 – www.gresham-hotels.com   **E1**
282 rm – ♦150/600 € ♦♦150/600 €, ⌸ 23 € – 6 suites
Rest _23_ – _(dinner only)_ Carte 40/50 €
Rest _The Gallery_ – Menu 30 € – Carte 40/50 €
 ♦ Business ♦ Modern ♦

Long-established restored 19C property in a famous street offers elegance tinged
with luxury. Some penthouse suites. Well-equipped business centre, lounge and
Toddy's bar. 23 is named after available wines by glass. The Gallery boasts formal
ambience.

Jurys Croke Park   🕭 _Lb_ & rm AC 🛁 🛁 ⌂ _VISA_ ⓒ AE ⓞ

Jones's Rd ✉ _D3 – ℰ (01) 871 4444 – crokepark@jurysdoyle.com – Fax (01)_
871 44 00 – www.jurysdoyle.com
– Closed 24-26 December   _Plan I_ **B1**
230 rm ⌸ – ♦450 € ♦♦450 € – 2 suites   **Rest** – _(bar lunch)_ Carte 38/56 €
 ♦ Business ♦ Modern ♦

Corporate styled hotel opposite Croke Park Stadium. Stylish 'Side Line' bar with terrace. Rooms are a strong point: spacious with good business amenities. Bistro
boasts the Canal terrace and modern/Mediterranean influenced menus.

IRELAND • DUBLIN

 O'Callaghan Alexander   Fᴙ ᴋ rm 🅰🅲 🆀 ¶ 🔊 🚗 𝑽𝑰𝑺𝑨 ⓸⓸ 🅰🅴
Fienian St, Merrion Sq ⊠ *D2* – 𝒞 *(01) 607 3700 – info@ocallaghanhotels.com*
– Fax (01) 661 56 63 – www.ocallaghanhotels.com   **F2**
98 rm – ♟150/480 € ♟♟150/480 €, ⊊ 17 € – 4 suites
Rest *Caravaggio's* – *(bar lunch Saturday and Sunday)* Carte 38/45 €
♦ Business ♦ Modern ♦
This bright corporate hotel, well placed for museums and Trinity College, has a sty-
lish contemporary interior. Spacious comfortable rooms and suites with good faci-
lities. Stylish contemporary restaurant with wide-ranging menus.

 O'Callaghan Davenport   Fᴙ 🅰🅲 🆀 ¶ 🔊 🚗 𝑽𝑰𝑺𝑨 ⓸⓸ 🅰🅴
Lower Merrion St, off Merrion Sq ⊠ *D2* – 𝒞 *(01) 607 3500 – info@*
ocallaghanhotels.com – Fax (01) 661 56 63 – www.ocallaghanhotels.com
113 rm – ♟150/480 € ♟♟150/480 €, ⊊ 17 € – 2 suites   **F2**
Rest *Lanyons* – Carte 40/47 €
♦ Business ♦ Modern ♦
Sumptuous Victorian gospel hall façade heralds elegant hotel popular with business clientele. Tastefully furnished, well-fitted rooms. Presidents bar honours past
leaders. Dining room with fine choice menu.

 La Stampa   ⓸⓸ 🕷 🅰🅲 🆀 ¶ 𝑽𝑰𝑺𝑨 ⓸⓸ 🅰🅴 ⓿
35-36 Dawson St ⊠ *D2* – 𝒞 *(01) 677 4444 – hotel@lastampa.ie – Fax (01)*
677 44 11 – www.lastampa.ie
– Closed 25-27 December and Good Friday   **E3**
27 rm – ♟200/300 € ♟♟220/300 €, ⊊ 14.95 € – 1 suite
Rest *Balzac* – see below
Rest *Tiger Becs* – *(dinner only)* Carte approx. 40 €
♦ Business ♦ Personalised ♦
Silks and oriental furnishings give an Eastern feel to this substantial Georgian
house. Elegant bar, beautiful spa and individually appointed, well-equip-
ped bedrooms. Basement restaurant Tiger Becs serves an authentic Thai menu.

 O'Callaghan Mont Clare   🅰🅲 🆀 ¶ 🔊 🚗 𝑽𝑰𝑺𝑨 ⓸⓸ 🅰🅴
Lower Merrion St, off Merrion Sq ⊠ *D2* – 𝒞 *(01) 607 3800 – info@*
ocallaghanhotels.com – Fax (01) 661 56 63 – www.ocallaghanhotels.com
– Closed 23-28 December   **F2**
74 rm – ♟130/300 € ♟♟130/300 €, ⊊ 17 €
Rest *Goldsmiths* – *(dinner only)* Carte 30/40 €
♦ Business ♦ Classic ♦
Classic property with elegant panelled reception and tasteful comfortable rooms
at heart of Georgian Dublin. Corporate suites available. Traditional pub style Gallery
bar. Informal restaurant with tried-and-tested menus.

 Maldon   Fᴙ 🕷 🔲 🅰🅲 rest 🆀 📞 🔊 𝑽𝑰𝑺𝑨 ⓸⓸ 🅰🅴 ⓿
Sir John Rogerson's Quay, Cardiff Lane ⊠ *D2* – 𝒞 *(01) 643 9500*
– info.cardifflane@maldonhotels.com – Fax (01) 643 95 10
– www.maldonhotels.com   *Plan I* **B1**
213 rm – ♟99/359 € ♟♟99/359 €, ⊊ 15 €
Rest – *(bar lunch)* Menu 35 € – Carte 30/46 €
♦ Business ♦ Modern ♦
Based in 'new generation' quayside area. Sleek Vertigo bar named after U2 song.
Impressive health club with large pool. Spacious, modern rooms, 48 boasting bal-
conies. Irish and European mix of dishes in open plan restaurant.

 Kilronan House without rest   🅲🅰🆃 𝑽𝑰𝑺𝑨 ⓸⓸ 🅰🅴
70 Adelaide Rd ⊠ *D2* – 𝒞 *(01) 475 5266 – info@kilronanhouse.com – Fax (01)*
478 28 41 – www.kilronanhouse.com
– Closed Christmas   *Plan III* **G1**
12 rm ⊊ – ♟55/170 € ♟♟89/170 €
♦ Traditional ♦ Classic ♦
In the heart of Georgian Dublin, a good value, well-kept town house run by knowledgeable, friendly couple. Individually styled rooms; sustaining breakfasts.

XXXX ⁂⁂

Patrick Guilbaud (Guillaume Lebrun) AC ⇄ VISA ⬤ AE ⓞ

21 Upper Merrion St ⊠ D2 – ℰ (01) 676 4192 – restaurantpatrickguilbaud@
eircom.net – Fax (01) 661 00 52 – www.restaurantpatrickguilbaud.ie
– Closed 25-26 December, 17 March, Good Friday, Sunday and Monday
Rest – Menu 50 € (lunch) – Carte 93/135 € ⅋   **F3**
Spec. Crubeen with crispy pork, quail egg, cream and Meaux mustard. Turbot with sweet onion, white asparagus and tomato caramel. Lime soufflé
with honey and Yuzu lemon.
♦ French ♦ Formal ♦
Run by consummate professional offering accomplished and acclaimed Irish-influ-
enced dishes in redesigned Georgian town house. Contemporary Irish art; glass-
roofed terrace.

XXXX ⁂

Thornton's – at The Fitzwilliam Hotel AC VISA ⬤ AE ⓞ

128 St Stephen's Green ⊠ D2 – ℰ (01) 478 7008 – thorntonsrestaurant@
eircom.net – Fax (01) 478 70 09 – www.thorntonsrestaurant.com
– Closed Sunday and Monday   **E3**
Rest – Menu 55 € (lunch) – Carte 104/108 € ⅋
Spec. Bacon and cabbage terrine, celeriac purée and pea sorbet. Fillet of
turbot, white onion and samphire. Prune and armagnac soufflé with pear
sorbet.
♦ Modern ♦ Formal ♦
Sample canapés in spacious lounge; dine at linen-clad tables in restaurant, hung
with the chef's striking photos. Luxury ingredients are prepared with balance and
knowledge.

XXXX

Shanahan's on the Green AC VISA ⬤ AE ⓞ

119 St Stephen's Green ⊠ D2 – ℰ (01) 407 0939 – sales@shanahans.ie
– Fax (01) 407 09 40 – www.shanahans.ie
– Closed Christmas and Good Friday   **E3**
Rest – *(dinner only and lunch Friday and Sunday) (booking essential)*
Menu 45 € (lunch) – Carte 76/122 €
♦ Beef specialities ♦ Formal ♦
Sumptuous Georgian town house; upper floor window tables survey the Green.
Supreme comfort enhances your enjoyment of strong seafood dishes and choice
cuts of Irish beef.

XXX ⁂

L'Ecrivain (Derry Clarke) ⇱ AC ⇄ VISA ⬤ AE

109A Lower Baggot St ⊠ D2 – ℰ (01) 661 1919 – enquiries@lecrivain.com
– Fax (01) 661 06 17 – www.lecrivain.com
– Closed 10 days Christmas, Easter, Saturday lunch and Sunday   **F3**
Rest – *(booking essential)* Menu 50/85 € – Carte dinner 86/100 €
Spec. Scallops with frog's leg beignet, morels and garlic foam. Suckling pig
with tortellini and baby vegetable salad. Lemon tart, raspberry granite, rasp-
berry and basil mascarpone.
♦ Contemporary ♦ Formal ♦
Well-established restaurant serving well prepared, modern Irish menus with
emphasis on fish and game. Attentive service from well-versed team. Delightful
private dining room.

XXX ⁂

Chapter One (Ross Lewis) AC ⇄ ♨ VISA ⬤

The Dublin Writers Museum, 18-19 Parnell Sq ⊠ D1 – ℰ (01) 873 2266 – info@
chapteronerestaurant.com – Fax (01) 873 23 30
– www.chapteronerestaurant.com
– Closed first 2 weeks August, 24 December-8 January, Sunday, Monday and
Saturday Lunch   **E1**
Rest – Menu 38 € (lunch) – Carte dinner 62/74 €
Spec. White pudding with horseradish, lentils, and poached egg hollandaise.
Sea bream with fennel, squid, tomato and shellfish sauce. Hazelnut parfait,
citrus jelly and espresso sauce.
♦ Modern ♦ Formal ♦
Stylish restaurant in basement of historic building; rustic walls filled with contem-
porary art. Seasonal, classically-based cooking demonstrates skill and understan-
ding.

XXX **The Saddle Room** – at The Shelbourne Hotel AC ⇔
27 St Stephen's Green ⊠ *D2* – ℰ *(01) 663 4500* VISA ⚭ AE ①
– info@renaissancehotels.com – Fax (01) 651 60 66 – www.theshelbourne.ie
Rest – Menu 30/55 € – Carte 51/69 € **E3**
♦ Grills ♦ Formal ♦

Smart restaurant in heart of hotel with delightful seafood bar. Grill/seafood menu offers quality Irish produce including superior 21 day hung steaks. Two private dining rooms.

XXX **Bentley's Oyster Bar & Grill** AC VISA ⚭ AE ①
22 St. Stephen's Green ⊠ *D 2* – ℰ *(01) 6383939 – info@bentleysdublin.com*
– Fax (01) 6 38 39 00 – www.bentleysdublin.com
– closed 25-27 December **E3**
Rest – *(booking advisable)* Carte 39/80 €
♦ Seafood ♦ Brasserie ♦

Imposing Georgian house in main city square. Large formally laid dining room and marble topped oyster bar with stools. Menus display tasty dishes crafted from quality produce.

XX **Balzac** – at La Stampa Hotel VISA ⚭ AE
35-36 Dawson St ⊠ *D2* – ℰ *(01) 677 8611 – hotel@lastampa.ie – Fax (01) 677 44 11*
– closed 25-26 December, Good Friday and Sunday **E3**
Rest – *(closed Sunday lunch)* Carte 34/65 €
♦ French ♦ Fashionable ♦

Elegant yet spacious restaurant with high ceiling, blond wood bar, mirrors, banquette seating and a real bistro feel. Tasty, classical French cooking from an appealing menu.

XX **Locks** ⇔ VISA ⚭ AE
Number 1, Windsor Terrace ⊠ *D8* – ℰ *(01) 454 3391 – info@locksrestaurant.ie*
– Fax (01) 453 83 52 – www.locksrestaurant.ie
– closed 25, 26 and 31 December, 1 January and Sunday dinner
Rest – Carte 35/59 € *Plan III* **G1**
♦ French ♦ Fashionable ♦

Quirky modern restaurant by the canal boasting stylish inner with wooden floor, comfy leather seating and dining split over 2 floors. French menu includes some regional dishes.

XX **The Tea Room** – at The Clarence Hotel VISA ⚭ AE ①
6-8 Wellington Quay ⊠ *D2* – ℰ *(01) 407 0813 – tearoom@theclarence.ie*
– Fax (01) 407 08 26
– Closed 24-26 December and Saturday lunch **D2**
Rest – *(booking essential)* Menu 31/39 € (lunch) – Carte 44/74 €
♦ Modern ♦ Fashionable ♦

Spacious elegant ground floor room with soaring coved ceiling and stylish contemporary décor offers interesting modern Irish dishes with hint of continental influence.

XX **Dax** ⇎ VISA ⚭ AE
23 Pembroke Street Upper ⊠ *D2* – ℰ *(01) 676 1494 – olivier@dax.ie – www.dax.ie*
– Closed Christmas and New Year, Easter, Saturday lunch, Sunday and Monday
Rest – *(booking essential)* Menu 29 € (lunch) – Carte 52/91 € **E3**
♦ French ♦ Rustic ♦

Hidden away in basement of Georgian terrace, with rustic inner, immaculately laid tables, wine cellar and bar serving tapas. Knowledgable staff serve French influenced menus.

XX **Fallon & Byrne** ⇎ VISA ⚭ AE
First Floor, 11-17 Exchequer St ⊠ *D2* – ℰ *(01) 472 1000 – Fax (01) 472 10 16*
– www.fallonandbyrne.com
– Closed 25-26 December,1 January and Good Friday **E2**
Rest – Menu 23 € (lunch) – Carte 33/57 €
♦ French ♦ Bistro ♦

Food emporium boasting vast basement wine cellar, ground floor full of fresh quality produce, and first floor French style bistro with banquettes, mirrors and tasty bistro food.

XX **The Cellar** – at The Merrion Hotel ⬛ *VISA* ⬤⬤ ⬛ ⬤

Upper Merrion St ✉ *D2* – ✆ *(01) 603 0630* – *info@merrionhotel.com*
– Fax (01) 603 07 00 – www.merrionhotel.com
– Closed Saturday lunch **F3**
Rest – Menu 27 € (lunch) – Carte dinner 40/58 €
 ◆ Mediterranean ◆ Formal ◆

Smart open-plan basement restaurant with informal ambience offering well-prepared formal style fare crossing Irish with Mediterranean influences. Good value lunch menu.

XX **One Pico** ⬛ ⬄ ⬛ *VISA* ⬤⬤ ⬛ ⬤

5-6 Molesworth Pl ✉ *D2* – ✆ *(01) 676 0300* – *eamonnoreilly@ireland.com*
– Fax (01) 676 04 11 – www.onepico.com
– Closed 25 December-February, Sunday and Bank Holidays **E3**
Rest – Menu 37 € (lunch) – Carte dinner 57/67 €
 ◆ Modern ◆ Fashionable ◆

Wide-ranging cuisine, classic and traditional by turns, always with an original, eclectic edge. Décor and service share a pleasant formality, crisp, modern and stylish.

XX **Rhodes D7** ⬛ ⬛ *VISA* ⬤⬤ ⬛ ⬤

The Capel Buildings, Mary's Abbey ✉ *D7* – ✆ *(01) 804 4444* – *info@*
rhodesd7.com – Fax (01) 804 44 45 – www.rhodesd7.com
– Closed Sunday and Monday *Plan III* **J1**
Rest – Menu 18 € (lunch) – Carte 36/47 €
 ◆ Modern ◆ Brasserie ◆

Cavernous restaurant: take your pick from four dining areas. Bright, warm décor incorporating bold, colourful paintings accompanies classic Rhodes menus given an Irish twist.

XX **Les Frères Jacques** ⬛ *VISA* ⬤⬤ ⬛

74 Dame St ✉ *D2* – ✆ *(01) 679 4555* – *info@lesfreresjacques.com*
– Fax (01) 679 47 25 – www.lesfreresjacques.com
– Closed 24 December-2 January, Saturday lunch, Sunday and Bank Holidays
Rest – Menu 38 € – Carte 34/65 € **D2**
 ◆ French ◆ Bistro ◆

Smart and well established, offering well prepared, classic French cuisine with fresh fish and seafood a speciality, served by efficient French staff. Warm, modern décor.

XX **Peploe's** ⬛ *VISA* ⬤⬤ ⬛

16 St Stephen's Green ✉ *D2* – ✆ *(01) 676 3144*
– reception@peploes.com – Fax (01) 676 31 54
– www.peploes.com
– Closed 25-29 December and Good Friday **E3**
Rest – Carte 40/56 €
 ◆ Mediterranean ◆ Fashionable ◆

Fashionable restaurant - a former bank vault - by the Green. Irish wall mural, Italian leather chairs, suede banquettes. Original dishes with pronounced Mediterranean accents.

XX **Town Bar and Grill** ⬛ ⬛ *VISA* ⬤⬤ ⬛

21 Kildare St ✉ *D2* – ✆ *(01) 662 4800* – *reservations@townbarandgrill.com*
– Fax (01) 662 38 57 – www.townbarandgrill.com
– Closed 25-26 December, 1 January and Good Friday **E3**
Rest – Menu 30 € (lunch) – Carte dinner 45/58 €
 ◆ Italian influences ◆ Rustic ◆

Located in wine merchant's old cellars: brick pillars divide a large space; fresh flowers and candles add a personal touch. Italian flair in bold cooking with innovative edge.

XX **Dobbin's** 🏠 AC ⇔ P VISA ☺☺ AE ①

15 Stephen's Lane, (off Stephen's Place) off Lower Mount St ⊠ D2 – ℰ (01) 661 9536 – dobbinsbistro@g.mail.com – Fax (01) 661 33 31 – www.dobbins.ie – Closed 1 week Christmas-New Year, Good Friday, Saturday lunch, Sunday dinner and Bank Holidays **F3**

Rest – *(booking essential)* Menu 24 € (lunch) – Carte 53/81 €
♦ Traditional ♦ Retro ♦

In the unlikely setting of a former Nissen hut, and now with contemporary styling, this popular restaurant, something of a local landmark, offers good food to suit all tastes.

XX **Siam Thai** AC VISA ☺☺ AE

14-15 Andrew St ⊠ D2 – ℰ (01) 677 3363 – siam@eircom.net – Fax (01) 670 76 44 – www.siamthai.ie – Closed 25 December, Good Friday and lunch Saturday and Sunday

Rest – Menu 18/36 € – Carte 28/37 € **E2**
♦ Thai ♦ Exotic ♦

Invariably popular, centrally located restaurant with a warm, homely feel, embodied by woven Thai prints. Daily specials enhance Thai menus full of choice and originality.

XX **Jaipur** VISA ☺☺ AE ①

41 South Great George's St ⊠ D2 – ℰ (01) 677 0999 – dublin@jaipur.ie – Fax (01) 677 09 79 – www.jaipur.ie **D2**

Rest – *(dinner only and lunch in December)* Menu 50 € – Carte 35/45 €
♦ Indian ♦ Minimalist ♦

Vivid modernity in the city centre; run by knowledgeable team. Immaculately laid, linen-clad tables. Interesting, freshly prepared Indian dishes using unique variations.

XX **Bang Café** 🏠 AC VISA ☺☺ ①
😊
11 Merrion Row ⊠ D2 – ℰ (01) 676 0898 – bangcafe@eircom.net – Fax (01) 676 08 99 – www.bangrestaurant.com – Closed 2 weeks late December-early January, Sunday and Bank Holidays

Rest – *(booking essential)* Menu 30 € (lunch) – Carte 28/43 € **E3**
♦ Modern ♦ Fashionable ♦

Stylish feel, closely set tables and an open kitchen lend a lively, contemporary air to this established three-tier favourite. Menus balance the classical and the creative.

X **The Winding Stair** ⇔ VISA ☺☺
😊
40 Lower Ormond Quay ⊠ D1 – ℰ (01) 872 7320 – www.winding-stair.com – Closed 25 December - 4 January **E2**

Rest – *(booking essential)* Carte 39/47 €
♦ Modern ♦ Rustic ♦

Delightfully rustic restaurant on banks of River Liffey, unusually set above a bookshop. Open dining room with wooden tables; frequently-changing menu has strong organic base.

X **Pearl Brasserie** AC VISA ☺☺ AE

20 Merrion St Upper ⊠ D2 – ℰ (01) 661 3572 – info@pearl-brasserie.com – Fax (01) 661 36 29 – www.pearl-brasserie.com – Closed 25 December and Sunday **F3**

Rest – Carte 31/59 €
♦ French ♦ Brasserie ♦

A metal staircase leads down to this intimate, newly refurbished, vaulted brasserie where Franco-Irish dishes are served at smart, linen-laid tables. Amiable, helpful service.

X **Eden** 🏠 AC ⇔ 🐧 VISA ☺☺ AE

Meeting House Sq, Temple Bar ⊠ D2 – ℰ (01) 670 5372 – eden@ edenrestaurant.ie – Fax (01) 670 33 30 – www.edenrestaurant.ie – Closed 25 December-4 January **D2**

Rest – Menu 27 € (lunch) – Carte dinner 36/51 €
♦ Modern ♦ Minimalist ♦

Modern minimalist restaurant with open plan kitchen serves good robust food. Terrace overlooks theatre square, at the heart of a busy arty district. The place for pre-theatre.

✗ **Mermaid Café**   AC ⇔ VISA ⊙⊙ AE

69-70 Dame St ⊠ *D2 – 𝒞 (01) 670 8236 – info@mermaid.ie – Fax (01)
670 82 05 – www.mermaid.ie*
– Closed 24-26 December, 1 January and Good Friday   **D2**
Rest *– (Sunday brunch) (booking essential)* Carte 34/52 €
♦ Modern ♦ Minimalist ♦

This informal restaurant with unfussy décor and bustling atmosphere offers an
interesting and well cooked selection of robust modern dishes. Efficient service.

✗ **L'Gueleton**   VISA ⊙⊙

1 Fade St ⊠ *D2 – 𝒞 (01) 675 3708*
– closed 25-26 and 31 December, 1 January   **E2**
Rest *– (bookings not accepted)* Carte 30/49 €
♦ French ♦ Bistro ♦

Busy, highly renowned recent arrival. Rustic style: mish-mash of roughed-up chairs
and tables with candles or Parisian lamps. Authentic French country dishes full of
flavour.

✗ **Bleu**   AC ⊗⊘ VISA ⊙⊙ AE

Joshua House, Dawson St ⊠ *D2 – 𝒞 (01) 676 7015 – Fax (01) 676 70 27
– www.bleu.ie*
– Closed 25-26 December, Sunday and Bank Holidays   **E3**
Rest *– Menu 25 € (lunch) –* Carte 30/49 €
♦ Modern ♦ Fashionable ♦

Black leather and polished wood provide a modern feel to this friendly all-day restaurant. The appealing, varied menu is well executed and very tasty. Good wine
selection.

✗ **La Maison des Gourmets**   🛌 VISA ⊙⊙ AE ⓪
🕙

15 Castlemarket ⊠ *D2 – 𝒞 (01) 672 7258 – info@la-maison.ie – Fax (01)
672 72 38*
– Closed 25-27 December and Bank Holidays   **E2**
Rest *– (lunch only) (bookings not accepted)* Carte 19/26 €
♦ French ♦ Cosy ♦

Neat, refurbished eatery on first floor above an excellent French bakery. Extremely
good value Gallic meals with simplicity the key. Get there early or be prepared to
wait!

🍴 **The Cellar Bar** – *at The Merrion H.*   VISA ⊙⊙ AE ⓪

Upper Merrion St ⊠ *D2 – 𝒞 (01) 603 0600 – info@merrionhotel.com – Fax (01)
603 07 00 – www.merrionhotel.com*
– Closed 25 December   **F3**
Rest *– (Closed Sunday) (carvery lunch)* Carte 29/43 €
♦ Traditional ♦ Pub ♦

Characterful stone and brick bar-restaurant in the original vaulted cellars with large
wood bar. Popular with Dublin's social set. Offers wholesome Irish pub lunch fare.

BALLSBRIDGE and SOUTH DUBLIN   *Plan III*

🏨🏨 **Four Seasons**   🚗 🛁 ⊕ ⋔ 🔲 ⅛ rm AC 🖥 ⑂ 🈂 🅿 ⌂
                                                VISA ⊙⊙ AE ⓪

Simmonscourt Rd ⊠ *D4 – 𝒞 (01) 665 4000*
– reservations.dublin@fourseasons.com – Fax (01) 665 40 99
– www.fourseasons.com/dublin   **J2**
157 rm – †225/610 € ††225/610 €, ⌷ 32 € – 40 suites
Rest Seasons *– Menu 40 € (lunch) –* Carte dinner 62/84 €
Rest The Cafe *– (lunch only)* Carte 38/75 €
♦ Grand Luxury ♦ Modern ♦

Every inch the epitome of international style - supremely comfortable rooms with
every facility; richly furnished lounge; a warm mix of antiques, oils and soft piano
études. Dining in Seasons guarantees luxury ingredients. Good choice menu in The
Café.

Herbert Park 🛜 ᵳ᷉ 🄰🄲 🄳🄳 ⁽ᵗ⁾ 🄰 🄿 🆅🅸🆂🅰 🅾🅾 🄰🄴 ⓞ

✉ D4 – ℰ (01) 667 2200 – reservations@herbertparkhotel.ie – Fax (01)
667 25 95 – www.herbertparkhotel.ie **J2**
151 rm – ♦135/300 € ♦♦150/385 €, ⊊ 23.50 € – 2 suites
Rest *The Pavilion* – Menu 26 € – Carte 36/72 €
♦ Business ♦ Modern ♦

Stylish contemporary hotel. Open, modern lobby and lounges. Excellent, well-
designed rooms with tasteful décor: fifth floor Executive rooms boast several
upgraded extras. French-windowed restaurant with alfresco potential; oyster/lobs-
ter specialities.

Merrion Hall without rest 🚗 🅂🄰🅃 ⁽ᵗ⁾ 🄿 🆅🅸🆂🅰 🅾🅾 🄰🄴 ⓞ

54-56 Merrion Rd ✉ D4 – ℰ (01) 668 1426 – merrionhall@iol.ie – Fax (01)
668 42 80 – www.halpinsprivatehotels.com **J2**
34 rm ⊊ – ♦99/119 € ♦♦139/169 € – 2 suites
♦ Business ♦ Minimalist ♦

Manor house hotel has comfy sitting rooms with Georgian feel and some original
features plus rear breakfast room with conservatory. Minimalist bedrooms boast
quality feel.

The Schoolhouse 🚗 🄰🄲 ⁽ᵗ⁾ 🄿 🆅🅸🆂🅰 🅾🅾 🄰🄴 ⓞ

2-8 Northumberland Rd ✉ D4 – ℰ (01) 667 5014 – reservations@
schoolhousehotel.com – Fax (01) 667 50 15 – www.schoolhousehotel.com
– Closed 24-27 December **H1**
31 rm ⊊ – ♦169/500 € ♦♦199/500 €
Rest *The Schoolhouse* – (brunch Saturday and Sunday) Menu 31 € (lunch)
– Carte 28/48 €
♦ Business ♦ Historic ♦

Spacious converted 19C schoolhouse, close to canal, boasts modernity and charm.
Inkwell bar exudes a convivial atmosphere. Rooms contain locally crafted furniture.
Old classroom now a large restaurant with beamed ceilings.

Ariel House without rest 🄿 🆅🅸🆂🅰 🅾🅾

50-54 Lansdowne Rd ✉ D4 – ℰ (01) 668 5512 – reservations@ariel-house.net
– Fax (01) 668 58 45 – www.ariel-house.net
– Closed 23-28 December **J1**
37 rm ⊊ – ♦99/130 € ♦♦130/180 €
♦ Business ♦ Classic ♦

Restored, listed Victorian mansion in smart suburb houses personally run, traditional small hotel. Rooms feature period décor and some antiques; comfy four poster
rooms.

Bewley's 🛜 ᵹ rm 🄰🄲 rest ⁽ᵗ⁾ 🄰 🚗 🆅🅸🆂🅰 🅾🅾 🄰🄴 ⓞ

Merrion Rd ✉ D4 – ℰ (01) 668 1111 – ballsbridge@bewleyshotels.com
– Fax (01) 668 19 99 – www.bewleyshotels.com
– closed 24-26 December **J2**
304 rm – ♦119/199 € ♦♦119/199 €, ⊊ 12 €
Rest *The Brasserie* – (carvery lunch) Menu 28 € – Carte 27/37 €
♦ Business ♦ Functional ♦

Huge hotel offers stylish modern accommodation behind sumptuous Victorian
façade of former Masonic school. Location, facilities and value for money make
this a good choice. Carvery lunch served in The Brasserie.

Aberdeen Lodge 🚗 🅂🄰🅃 ⁽ᵗ⁾ 🄿 🆅🅸🆂🅰 🅾🅾 🄰🄴 ⓞ

53-55 Park Ave ✉ D4 – ℰ (01) 283 8155 – aberdeen@iol.ie – Fax (01) 283 78 77
– www.halpinsprivatehotels.com **J2**
17 rm ⊊ – ♦99/119 € ♦♦139/169 €
Rest – (residents only, light meals) Carte 25/34 €
♦ Townhouse ♦ Classic ♦

Neat red brick house in smart residential suburb. Comfortable rooms with Edwardian style décor in neutral tones, wood furniture and modern facilities. Some garden views. Comfortable, traditionally decorated dining room.

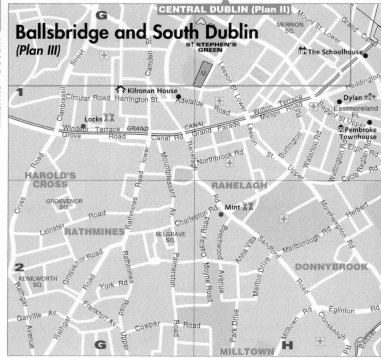

Ballsbridge and South Dublin
(Plan III)

Pembroke Townhouse without rest   🛜 P VISA ⊚ AE ①

90 Pembroke Rd ⊠ D4 – ℰ (01) 660 0277
– info@pembroketownhouse.ie – Fax (01) 660 02 91
– www.pembroketownhouse.ie
– closed 21 December- 4 January   **H1**
48 rm – †145/190 € ††190/220 €, ☲ 14 €
◆ Townhouse ◆ Classic ◆
Period-inspired décor adds to the appeal of a sensitively modernised Georgian terrace town house in the smart suburbs. Neat, simple accommodation.

Glenogra House without rest   SAT 🛜 P VISA ⊚ AE ①

64 Merrion Rd ⊠ D4 – ℰ (01) 668 3661
– info@glenogra.com – Fax (01) 668 36 98
– www.glenogra.com
– Closed 23 December-10 January   **J2**
13 rm ☲ – †79/109 € ††120/190 €
◆ Family ◆ Cosy ◆
Neat and tidy bay-windowed house in smart suburb. Personally-run to good standard with bedrooms attractively decorated in keeping with a period property. Modern facilities.

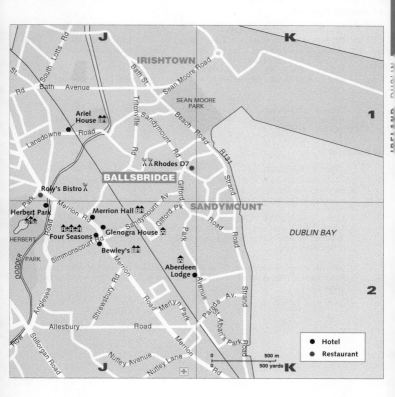

✗ **Roly's Bistro**　　　　　[AK] ⟳ 🐦 *VISA* ⓿ [AE] ①

7 Ballsbridge Terrace ✉ D4 – ✆ (01) 668 2611 – ireland@rolysbistro.ie
– Fax (01) 660 33 42 – www.rolysbistro.ie
– Closed Christmas　　　　　　　　　　　　　　　　　　**J1**
Rest – (booking essential) Menu 22/42 € – Carte 41/54 €
♦ Traditional ♦ Intimate ♦

A Dublin institution: this roadside bistro is very busy and well run with a buzzy, fun
atmosphere. Its two floors offer traditional Irish dishes and a very good value lunch.

---

at DUBLIN AIRPORT

🏨 **Hilton Dublin Airport**　　　[F&] [&] rm [AK] 🔲 🌐 [&] [P] *VISA* ⓿ [AE] ①

Northern Cross, Malahide Rd (East : 3 km by A 32) ✉ D17 – ✆ (01) 8661800
– reservations.dublinairport@hilton.com – Fax (01) 8 66 18 66
– www.hilton.com/dublinairport
– Closed 24-29 December
162 rm – ♟100/240 € ♟♟100/260 €, � 21.50 € – 4 suites
Rest *Barnell Bar and Grill* – Menu 22 € (lunch) – Carte 31/51 €
♦ Business ♦ Modern ♦

Opened in 2005, just five minutes from the airport, adjacent to busy shopping centre.
Modish feel throughout. State-of-the-art meeting facilities. Airy, well-equipped rooms.
Spacious bar and grill serve modern dishes with Irish and international flavours.

Carlton H. Dublin Airport ≤ ㋐ rm AC ⁙ ㋑ P̄ VISA ⓒⓞ AE

Old Airport Rd, Cloughran (on R 132 Santry rd) – ℰ (01) 866 7500 – info@ carltondublinairport.com – Fax (01) 862 31 14 – www.carlton.ie/dublinairport – Closed 24-26 December
117 rm – ♥165 € ♥♥330 €, ☞ 16.50 € – 1 suite
Rest *Carlton Dublin Airport* – Old Airport Rd, Cloughran, – Carte /dinner 35/53 €
◆ Business ◆ Modern ◆
Purpose-built hotel on edge of airport. State-of-the-art conference rooms. Impressive bedrooms, though many a touch compact, in warm colours with high level of facilities.

at Ranelagh

XX **Mint** (Dylan McGrath) AC VISA ⓒⓞ AE

ξ3 *47 Ranelagh ⊠ D6 – ℰ (01) 497 8655 – info@mintrestaurant.ie – Fax (01) 497 90 35 – www.mintrestaurant.ie*
– Closed 23 December-6 January, 6-17 April, Sunday, Monday and Saturday lunch **H2**
Rest – Menu 30/75 € – Carte 37/75 € ℬ
Spec. Salmon, beetroot, lemon and avocado mousse. Smoked loin and belly of pork, sweetcorn, polenta and pearl barley. Pear and chocolate frangipan, chocolate sorbet.
◆ Inventive ◆ Intimate ◆
Intimate, pastel-hued restaurant in up and coming area of the city. Ambitious, confident kitchen serving uncompromisingly rich and elaborate dishes with French influences.

ITALY
ITALIA

PROFILE

→ **AREA:**
301 262 km² (116 317 sq mi).

→ **POPULATION:**
59 131 287 inhabitants (est. 2007), density = 196 per km².

→ **CAPITAL:**
Rome (conurbation 2 867 000 inhabitants).

→ **CURRENCY:**
Euro (€); rate of exchange: € 1 = 1.32 US$ (Jan 2009).

→ **GOVERNMENT:**
Parliamentary republic with two chambers (since 1946). Member of European Union since 1957 (one of the 6 founding countries).

→ **LANGUAGE:**
Italian.

→ **SPECIFIC PUBLIC HOLIDAYS:**
Epiphany (6 January); Liberation Day (25 April); Anniversary of the Republic (2 June); Immaculate Conception (8 December); St. Stephen's Day (26 December). Each town also celebrates the feast day of its patron saint (Rome: 29 June St. Peter, Milan: 7 December St. Ambrose, etc details from the local tourist offices).

→ **LOCAL TIME:**
GMT + 1 hour in winter and GMT + 2 hours in summer.

→ **CLIMATE:**
Temperate Mediterranean, with mild winters and hot, sunny summers (Rome: January: 8°C, July: 25°C).

→ **INTERNATIONAL DIALLING CODE:**
00 39 followed by area or city code and then the local number.

→ **EMERGENCY:**
Police: ✆ **112**; Fire Brigade: ✆ **115**; Health services: ✆ **118**.

→ **ELECTRICITY:**
220 volts AC, 50Hz; 2-pin round-shaped continental plugs.

→ **FORMALITIES**
Travellers from the European Union (EU), Switzerland, Iceland and the main countries of North and South America need a national identity card or passport (America: passport required) to visit Italy for less than three months (tourism or business purpose). For visitors from other countries a visa may be required, in addition to a passport, especially for those wishing to stay for longer than three months. We advise you to check with your embassy before travelling.

ROME
ROMA

Population (est. 2007): 2 705 000 (conurbation 4 013 000) – Altitude: about 100m above sea level

R. Mattès/HEMIS.fr

Rome wasn't built in a day, and it's pretty hard to do it justice in less than three. The Italian capital is so richly layered in Imperial, Renaissance, Baroque and modern architecture that it takes on the appearance of a sprawling stew, its ingredients stirred together into a spicy and multi-ingredient feast. Its broad piazzas, hooting traffic and cobbled thoroughfares all lend their part to the heady fare: a theatrical stage cradled within seven famous hills.

Being Eternal, Rome never ceases to feel like a lively, living city, while at the same time a scintillating monument to Renaissance power and an epic centre of antiquity. Nowhere else offers such a wealth of classical remains, strung together alongside palaces and churches, and bathed in the soft, golden light for which it is famous. Even when taking time off from exploring the famous sights, you can hardly fail to come across ochre-coloured façades hiding a little square with a bustling market, or stairways that lead you down to a gushing fountain. You're always aware of the steady drip of history here: over 2,700 years of it. When Augustus became the first Emperor of Rome, he could hardly have imagined the impact his city's language, laws and calendar would have upon the world.

475

LIVING THE CITY

The **River Tiber** snakes its way north to south through the heart of Rome. On its west bank lies the characterful and 'independent' neighbourhood of **Trastevere**, while north of here is Vatican City. Over the river the **Piazza di Spagna** area to the north has Rome's smartest shopping streets, while the southern boundary is mar-

ked by the **Aventine** and **Celian** hills, the latter overlooking the **Colosseum**. **Esquiline**'s teeming quarter is just to the east of the city's heart; that honour goes to the **Capitol,** which gave its name to the concept of a 'capital' city. Rome is surrounded by the **Lazio** countryside, beautiful in the spring and autumn months.

PRACTICAL INFORMATION

ARRIVAL-DEPARTURE

Leonardo da Vinci Airport at Fiumicino is 32km southwest of Rome ; a taxi will be around €40. The Fiumicino Leonardo Express train runs every 30min and takes 32min. Every 30min the Cotral bus travels to the Anagnina Station of Metro Line A.

TRANSPORT

Rome is served by a metro, bus and tram system. Tickets are available from metro stations, bus terminals, ticket machines, tobacconists, newsagents, cafés and tourist information centres. Choose your ticket type: a single tic-

ket, which must be time stamped on board, or travelcards for one, three or seven days.

By the very nature of its hills and piazzas, Rome is best seen on foot, so make sure you have a good pair of walking shoes. A pair of binoculars is useful to have slung round your neck, too, as lots of sights are on ceilings or the top of columns.

Remember not to overdo the dressing down if you're visiting the religious sights around the city. You won't be allowed in if you think walking into a Roman church is akin to stepping onto an Italian beach – so avoid the likes of sleeveless tops, shorts and mini skirts.

EXPLORING ROME

To get to the very heart of Rome, you need to climb stairs. But these stairs

are by Michelangelo, and once you've reached the top of the **Cordonata**, you arrive at the great man's **Piazza dei Campidoglio**, a spectacular setting for Rome's city hall, whose bell tower offers incomparable views far and wide. You are now at the Capitol, which, for Romans, has been the centre of their world and the seat of municipal government for centuries. Around the piazza are two of the city's best museums, the **Capitoline Museums**, home to a fantastic collection of Classical statues and artworks by the likes of Tintoretto, Titian and Rubens. The grandeur of these two late Middle Age temples to culture sets the tone for an even more awe-inspiring art show: the one featuring the old city's remarkable buildings themselves.

→ FORUM…HERE TO ETERNITY

Just south of the Capitol is quite simply one of the world's great sights. It doesn't matter from which angle you come at it, there's little to compare with the drama afforded by the **Forum's** weary old bones backed up by the brooding presence of the Colosseum. What remains of the Forum gives only a hint of its former imperial pomp, but even this relative handful of columns, temples and basilicas, scattered in a great drunken maze around you, offers a moving impression of what was once the centre of Rome's political and commercial life. Imagine it…over two thousand years ago, on this spot, Julius Caesar was building his very own temple to vanity, setting the template for future emperors from Augustus onwards. Even in its ruined state, the Colosseum, arching up in the background, is a sight to take the breath away. Rome's greatest amphitheatre was built in AD80 for over fifty thousand spectators to gawp at gladiatorial contests, but was plundered in Renaissance times for its stone. Nevertheless, it still remains an awesome presence; venture inside to the top row seats for head-spinning views.

→ PLEASURE DOME

If you turn north from the Capitol, rather than south, you'll find not only the best-preserved ancient temple in Rome, but also one of the finest buildings in European architectural history – **The Pantheon**. This beautifully proportioned 'Temple of all the Gods' boasts a portico with granite columns, but these offer no clue as to the beauty and elegance of the building's main highlight, its vast dome. Go inside and marvel at it. The hole at the top provides the only light, and is a constant talking point for architects, who never cease to wonder just why the unreinforced dome has never come crashing to the ground!

→ THREE COINS

A little way northeast of here is another of Rome's star turns: The **Trevi Fountain**, on the Quirinal Hill. It was only built in 1762, which makes it almost modern by the city's standards, and its theatrical figures of Neptune and two tritons take up most of the tiny **Piazza di Trevi**. The fountain resembles a stage set, and was suitably employed as the shimmering, splashy backdrop to Anita Ekberg's cavortings during Fellini's ground-breaking movie *La Dolce Vita* in 1960. Nowadays, visitors chuck coins in the Trevi, just like the secretaries in another famous 'Rome' movie, *Three Coins In the Fountain*. In the back streets around here are lots of hidden churches – neat, mysterious and charming - while further down Quirinal Hill, fine palaces built for the ancient and powerful families of the city are a splendid sight.

→ SPANISH STROLL

Carry on northwards and you reach one of Rome's smartest areas, around Piazza di Spagna. This neighbourhood offers superb Renaissance and Baroque art in its churches, as well as one of the city's most prized ancient monuments (the **Ara Pacis**) repackaged in a 21C glass hangar. There's also fine art in the **Villa Medici**, and wonderful views of the city from the **Pincio Gardens**. But most people come up here to loll around awhile on the **Spanish Steps**. Built in 1726, the steps curve around terraces, richly flowered at Easter, to create one of the city's most famously distinctive landmarks. At their base, rather incongruously, is the **Keats-Shelley Memorial House**, a small museum dedicated to the two poets who are both buried in Rome. Latin sophistication is very much restored when you cross the Piazza di Spagna to take in the shadowy chic of **Via Condotti**. This is the home of Rome's smartest shops where early evening strollers come to gaze at the windows of the coolest designer names in the city. Another favourite is the nearby **Via del Babuino**, along which hushed art galleries and fascinating antique shops combine to create a smart feel.

Along the curving Tiber a little way south west is Rome's most handsome, most theatrical piazza – **Piazza Navona**. It's shaped like a huge oval lozenge because it was once a great athletics stadium, originally built in AD86. Today the entertainment comes from its three grandiose fountains, and the little human dramas being enacted in the pedestrian areas day and night. The eye-catching Baroque churches here provide a spectacle of their own. Close by is the fascinating **Via del Governo Vecchio**, full of 15C and 16C Renaissance houses interspersed with charming antique shops.

The east bank, just across from Trastevere, boasts a down-to-earth shrine of its own in the bustling market place of **Campo de' Fiori**, which has been in existence since medieval times when it was surrounded by inns for pilgrims; these days the lively ambience lives on and the teeming stalls of fruit and vegetables are used to supply many of the nearby restaurants. Of course, in this city you're never far from a majestic building or two to set alight the flame of inspiration. Close by is the grandiose baroque church of **Sant' Andrea della Valle**, renowned for its beautiful dome. Praying in here one day, with the cries of the market stall vendors in the distance, Puccini came up with the idea for the first act of *Tosca*.

→ THE TRASTEVERE

To get the feel for a different Rome, one that gives the impression of proletarian life in bygone times, cross the Tiber by any of the five bridges in the area, and soak up the atmosphere of **Trastevere**. It's one of the most picturesque old neighbourhoods of the city, with a distinctly laidback feel in contrast to the frenetic world over the river. The narrow cobbled alleyways here have a charm all their own and are a great place to escape to for a quiet lunch or early evening drink. The only threat to Trastevere's earthy character is the steady growth of fashionable bars, clubs and boutiques which have arrived in recent years, but in high summer the proximity of its densely packed buildings offers a welcomingly cool experience when the rest of Rome feels like a spit roast.

CALENDAR HIGHLIGHTS

You could say that Rome is an event in itself, but the city still likes to down tools for a bit of a celebration. February, for example, sees the historical thoroughfares of the city come alive for the annual Carnival. When

ROME IN...

→ ONE DAY
Capitol, Forum, Colosseum, Pantheon, Trevi Fountain, Spanish Steps

→ TWO DAYS
Via Condotti, Piazza Navona and churches in surrounding area, Capitoline museums

→ THREE DAYS
A day on the west bank of the Tiber at Trastevere and Vatican City

the azaleas appear in March, three thousand vases of them are arranged dramatically on the Spanish Steps for the Spring Festival. That same month, film fans celebrate the first of Rome's two big festivals with the Independent Film Festival, featuring more than sixty innovative movies from around the globe at a variety of cinemas. Also at that time, the city boasts its Cultural Heritage Week, with museums and monuments opening up to the public without charge. April is a big month here: Rome celebrates its birthday on the twenty-first (it was 'born' in 753BC) and the Campidoglio is the centre of activity with illuminated hillside palazzi and monster fireworks. There's also the Parklife festival at Fiera di Roma, which celebrates environmental culture with exhibits, films and installations promoting protected areas and natural parks in Italy. The Roman Summer is renowned for its oppressive heat, but the festival bearing that name (June-September) is hot in another way: the city's piazzas, palaces, parks and courtyards host a wide array of pop and jazz concerts (the outdoor film screenings late into the night may be a cooler choice). Tiberina Island is lit up like a film set for Cinema Isle (June-August) with retrospectives and blockbusters high on its agenda, while July's Festa de Noantri has two weeks' worth of art and street performances in honour of Trastevere's earthy proletarian beginnings. Also in July get cool on both banks of the Tiber at the Tevere Expo, when stalls full of arts and crafts, food and wine tempt you to buy. Two other summer highlights for music lovers: Secret Passages (July-August) boasts classical concerts and theatre performances at various locations in the city, while New Operafestival (July-September) at Basilica di San Clemente, just behind the Colosseum, is an operatic feast, featuring the likes of Mozart, Verdi and Donizetti. Autumn's Roma Europa Festival is a big one, with music, dance and theatre at stunning locations across Rome. Museums, galleries and theatres stay open till the early hours during White Night (September), while film from every angle is highlighted at the Rome Film Festival, at important movie venues, in October.

EATING OUT

Despite being Italy's capital, Rome largely favours a local, traditional cuisine to be found in typically unpretentious trattorie or osterie. Although not far from the sea, the city doesn't go in much for fish, and food is often connected to the rural, pastoral life with products coming from the surrounding Lazio hills, which also produce good wines. Pasta, of course, is not to be missed – mainly spaghetti, bucatini or rigatoni – combined with sauces such as amatriciana (prepared with tomatoes and unsmoked bacon), carbonara (eggs and unsmoked bacon) or arrabbiata (chilli). Lamb is favoured among meats for the main course; so too, the 'quinto quarto', which is another example of Roman cuisine's links to popular traditions based on rural tastes. The quinto quarto is a long-established way of indicating those parts of the beef (tail, tripe, liver, spleen, lungs, heart, kidney) left over after the best bits had gone to the richest families. Trastevere and the historical centre are full of restaurants featuring quinto quarto. For international, or more classic, cuisine combined with a more refined setting, head for the elegant hotels: very few other areas of Italy have such an increasing number of good quality restaurants within a hotel setting. Locals like to dine later in Rome than, say, Milan, with 1pm, or 8pm the very earliest you'd dream of appearing for lunch or dinner. In the famous tourist hotspots, of course, owners are only too pleased to open that bit earlier.

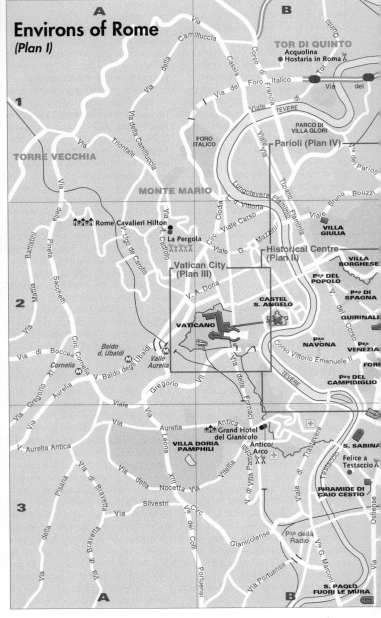

Environs of Rome
(Plan I)

A

B

TOR DI QUINTO
Acquolina
● Hostaria in Roma

1

Via della Camilluccia

Via Cassia

Corso di Francia

Foro Italico

Via del Foro Italico

TEVERE

Viale Via

TORRE VECCHIA

Via della Camilluccia

Via Trionfale

FORO ITALICO

PARCO DI VILLA GLORI

Parioli (Plan IV)

Via dei Parioli

MONTE MARIO

Lungotevere Flaminio

V. d. Vittoria

Circ. Viale Carso

Via Clodia

Viale Tiziano

Via Flaminia

Bruno Bouzzi

Viale

VILLA GIULIA

2

Via della Pineta Sacchetti

Via Battistini

🏨🏨🏨 Rome Cavalieri Hilton

Via A. Cadlolo

● La Pergola
✕✕✕✕✕

V. Ugo de Carolis

Viale G. Mazzini

Historical Centre (Plan II)

VILLA BORGHESE

Vatican City (Plan III)

V. A. Doria

Pza DEL POPOLO

Pza DI SPAGNA

VATICANO

CASTEL S. ANGELO

QUIRINALE

Via Mattia Battistini

Via di Boccea

Circ. Cornelia

Baldo d. Ubaldi

Cornelia Ⓜ

Ⓜ V. Baldo degli Ubaldi

Ⓜ Valle Aurelia

Via Gregorio VII

Via Aurelia

Viale Gregorio VII

Via delle Fornaci

Via d. Corso

Corso Vittorio Emanuele II

Pza NAVONA

Pza VENEZIA

FORI

TEVERE

Pza DEL CAMPIDIGLIO

3

Via Gregorio XI

V. Aurelia Antica

Via Aurelia

Via Leona

Via Aurelia Antica

VILLA DORIA PAMPHILI

🏨🏨 Grand Hotel del Gianicolo

Antico Arco ✕✕

Viale di Trastevere

Via di Traspontina

S. SABINA

● Felice a Testaccio

PIRAMIDE DI CAIO CESTIO

Via della Pisana

Via di Bravetta

Via della Nocetta

Via XIII Silvestri

V. d. Villa Pamphili

Via dei Colli

Pza della Radio

Via Portuense

Vle G. Marconi

Via Ostiense

Via Gianicolense

S. PAOLO FUORI LE MURA

A

B

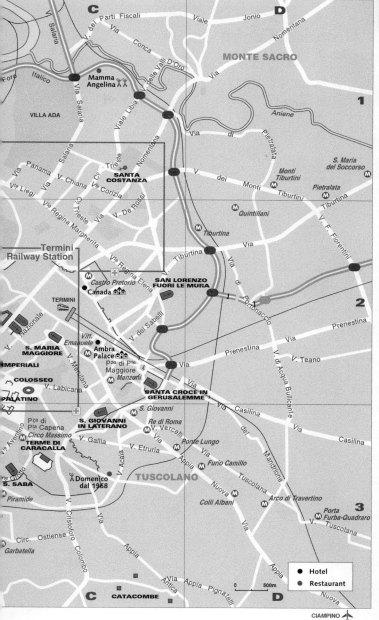

C

D

V. dei Parti Fiscali

Viale

Jonio

Nomentana

MONTE SACRO

1

V. Salaria

Foro Italico

V. Salaria

Via

Conca

Delle Valli D'Oro

Mamma Angelina

VILLA ADA

Viale Libia

Via

Aniene

Via

di

Pietralata

S. Maria del Soccorso

Via Panama

V. Chiana

C. Corizia

Trieste

Nomentana

SANTA COSTANZA

Monti Tiburtini

Pietralata

Monti

Tiburtini

Tiburtina

Via Liegi

V.le Trieste

Via

V. De Rossi

V.le Regina Margherita

Quintiliani

V. F. Fiorentini

Termini Railway Station

V.le Regina Elena

Tiburtina

Tiburtina

Via

Via

di

Portonaccio

2

Castro Pretorio

Canada

SAN LORENZO FUORI LE MURA

Prenestina

TERMINI

Nazionale

V. dei Sabelli

Prenestina

Via

V. di Teano

V. di Acqua Bullicante

S. MARIA MAGGIORE

Vitt. Emanuele

Ambra Palace

Via Merulana

P.za di P.ta Maggiore

Manzoni

Via

IMPERIALI

COLOSSEO

V. Labicana

SANTA CROCE IN GERUSALEMME

Via

Casilina

Casilina

PALATINO

P.za di P.ta Capena

S. GIOVANNI IN LATERANO

S. Giovanni

Re di Roma

Via

Via

del

Circo Massimo

V. Vercelli

V. Gallia

Ponte Lungo

TERME DI CARACALLA

V. Acaia

V. Etruria

Appia

Furio Camillo

Tuscolana

Mandrione

V.le Aventino

V.le Giotto

Domenico dal 1968

TUSCOLANA

Nuova

Colli Albani

Arco di Travertino

S. SABA

Piramide

V. Cristoforo Colombo

Via

Appia

Porta Furba-Quadraro

Tuscolana

3

Circ. Ostiense

Garbatella

Appia

V. Appia Pignatelli

Nuova

● Hotel

● Restaurant

0   500m

C

CATACOMBE

D

CIAMPINO ✈

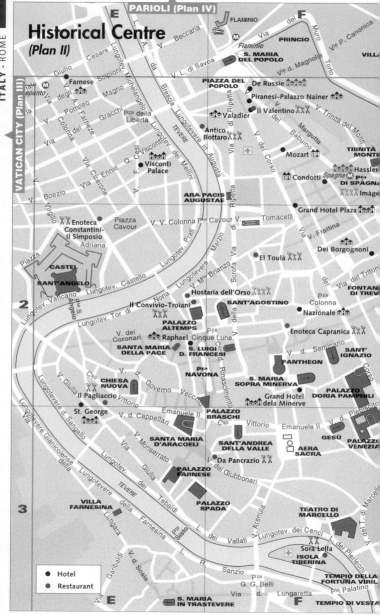

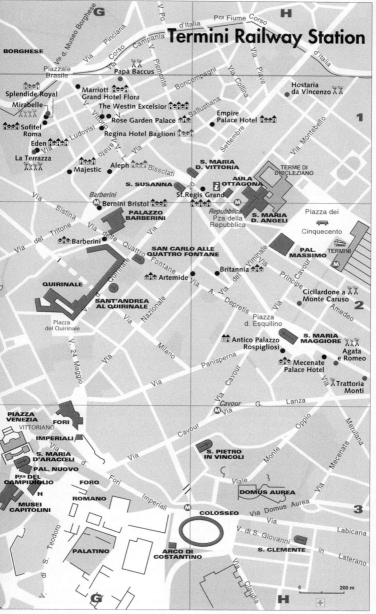

Termini Railway Station

BORGHESE

Pza Fiume

Corso d'Italia

Pinciana

V. d. Museo Borghese

Campania

V. Po

Corso d'Italia

Piazzale Brasile

Papà Baccus

Piemonte

Boncompagni

Via Plave

Via Collina

Hostaria da Vincenzo

Splendide Royal

Marriott Grand Hotel Flora

The Westin Excelsior

Sallustiana

Mirabelle

Sofitel Roma

Rose Garden Palace

Empire Palace Hotel

Via Montebello

Eden

Regina Hotel Baglioni

Ludovisi

Via Veneto

Settembre

La Terrazza

Majestic

Aleph

Bissolati

S. MARIA D. VITTORIA

TERME DI DIOCLEZIANO

AULA OTTAGONA

S. SUSANNA

St.Regis Grand

Barberini

Bernini Bristol

PALAZZO BARBERINI

Republica

Pza della Repubblica

S. MARIA D. ANGELI

Piazza dei Cinquecento

Via del Tritone

Via Sistina

Via delle Quattro Fontane

Barberini

SAN CARLO ALLE QUATTRO FONTANE

Artemide

Britannia

Viminale

PAL. MASSIMO

TERMINI

QUIRINALE

SANT'ANDREA AL QUIRINALE

Via Nazionale

A. Depretis

Via del Quirinale

Principe Amedeo

Via Cavour

Cicilardone a Monte Caruso

Piazza del Quirinale

Milano

Piazza d. Esquilino

Antico Palazzo Rospigliosi

S. MARIA MAGGIORE

Agata e Romeo

Via Panisperna

Mecenate Palace Hotel

V. 24 Maggio

Via Cavour

Via

Cavour

G. Lanza

Trattoria Monti

Merulana

PIAZZA VENEZIA

FORI IMPERIALI

VITTORIANO

S. MARIA D'ARACŒLI

PAL. NUOVO

Pza DEL CAMPIDOGLIO

FORO

S. PIETRO IN VINCOLI

Oppio

Mecenate

MUSEI CAPITOLINI

ROMANO

Fori Imperiali

DOMUS AUREA

Viale

V. di S. Teodoro

PALATINO

ARCO DI COSTANTINO

COLOSSEO

Via Domus Aurea

Via

V. di S. Giovanni

S. CLEMENTE

Labicana

in

Laterano

V. Claudia

0   200 m

ITALY - ROME

Hassler   ⅃ 🕭 AC 📶 ⅃ VISA ⊚ AE ⓪

piazza Trinità dei Monti 6 ✉ *00187* – ⓜ *Spagna*
– ℰ *06 699340* – *booking@hotelhassler.it* – *Fax 06 6 78 99 91*
– *www.hotelhassler.com*   **F1**
95 rm – ♥450/520 €, ♥♥550/660 €, � 42 € – 8 suites
Rest Imago – see below
◆ Grand Luxury ◆ Classic ◆
With its superb location at the top of the Spanish Steps, this hotel combines elegance, luxury and tradition. Unusual interpretation of the classical style on the fifth
floor.

De Russie   🚗 🕭 ⅃ 🕭 ⅙ AC ⅃ rm 📞 ⅃ VISA ⊚ AE ⓪

via del Babuino 9 ✉ *00187* – ⓜ *Flaminio* – ℰ *06 328881*
– *reservations.derussie@roccofortecollection.com* – *Fax 06 32 88 88 88*
– *www.roccofortecollection.com*   **F1**
97 rm – ♥350/540 € ♥♥470/1030 €, � 33 € – 25 suites
Rest Le Jardin de Russie – ℰ *06 32888870* – Carte 72/122 €
◆ Grand Luxury ◆ Modern ◆
Designed by Valadier during the early 19C, this hotel has hosted many famous
artists and writers over the years. It is now furnished in a simple, modern and minimalist style. The restaurant overlooks the attractive terraced garden, where meals
are served in summer.

St. George   🕭 🕭 ⅙ AC 📞 ⅃ VISA ⊚ AE ⓪

via Giulia 62 ✉ *00186* – ℰ *06 686611* – *stgeorge@hotel-invest.com*
– *Fax 06 6 86 61 30* – *www.stgeorgehotel.it*   **E2**
64 rm – ♥230/570 € ♥♥280/620 €
Rest I Sofà di Via Giulia – *(closed Sunday)* Carte 59/101 €
Rest Terrazza Rosé – *(June-September; closed Sunday and Monday) (booking
advisable)* Carte 64/97 €
◆ Grand Luxury ◆ Modern ◆
Opened in 2007, this hotel is decorated with luxurious, comfortable furnishings in
its bedrooms and public lounges. Refined, elegant atmosphere. I Sofà di Via Giulia
serves a good selection of typical Italian dishes alongside a range of international
specialities. Enjoy generous portions of shellfish in the delightful roof garden of
the Terrazza Rosé.

Grand Hotel de la Minerve   🕭 ⅃ ⅙ AC ⅃ rm 📞 ⅃

piazza della Minerva 69 ✉ *00186* – ⓜ *Colosseo*   VISA ⊚ AE ⓪
– ℰ *06 695201* – *minerva@hotel-invest.com* – *Fax 06 6 79 41 65*
– *www.grandhoteldelaminerve.it*   **F2**
131 rm – ♥290/420 € ♥♥340/470 €, � 31 € – 4 suites
Rest La Cesta – ℰ *06 69520704* – Carte 52/95 €
◆ Luxury ◆ Stylish ◆
An historic building surrounded by ancient monuments. Elegant atmosphere and
an imaginative menu of traditional cuisine. Attractive views from the terrace.

Grand Hotel Plaza   ⅙ rm AC 📶 ⅃ VISA ⊚ AE ⓪

via del Corso 126 ✉ *00186* – ⓜ *Spagna* – ℰ *06 67495*
– *plaza@grandhotelplaza.com* – *Fax 06 69 94 15 75*
– *www.grandhotelplaza.com*   **F1**
200 rm � – ♥450 € ♥♥750 € – 5 suites
Rest Bistrot-Mascagni – ℰ *06 69921111* – Carte 43/65 €
◆ Luxury ◆ Stylish ◆
This attractive hotel, restored during the Art Nouveau period, was once an important social and cultural meeting-place. The ornate Baroque-style reading room is
particularly attractive. The atmosphere of bygone times can also be found in the
evocative restaurant

ITALY - ROME

Visconti Palace without rest 🖪 ♿ 🔟 ⇆ 🕻 🖽 🆚 🆚 🆚 ⓘ
via Federico Cesi 37 ⊠ 00193 – ❶ Lepanto – ℰ 06 3684
– info@viscontipalace.com – Fax 06 3 20 05 51
– www.viscontipalace.com   E1
242 rm ⌱ – ♦300/320 € ♦♦350/380 €
◆ Business ◆ Design ◆
A large building, dating from the 1970s, which has gradually been modernised, this hotel is elegant and functional, whether for the business traveller or the tourist visitor; its spacious rooms are equipped with every comfort.

Raphaël 🏯 🖪 "𝓲" 🍴 🖽 🆚 🆚 ⓘ
largo Febo 2 ⊠ 00186 – ℰ 06 682831 – info@raphaelhotel.com
– Fax 06 6 87 89 93 – www.raphaelhotel.com   E2
55 rm – ♦230/600 € ♦♦250/800 €, ⌱ 28 €   **Rest** – Carte 59/101 €
◆ Traditional ◆ Classic ◆
With its collection of porcelain, antiquarian artefacts and sculptures by famous artists, the entrance to this hotel resembles a museum. The guestrooms are elegantly furnished in traditional style. The menu in this modern restaurant focuses mainly on Italian cuisine, with some French dishes. Meals are served on the panoramic terrace in summer.

Piranesi-Palazzo Nainer without rest 🖪 🏯 🔟 "𝓲" 🖽 🆚 🆚 ⓘ
via del Babuino 196 ⊠ 00187 – ❶ Flaminio – ℰ 06 328041
– info@hotelpiranesi.com – Fax 06 3 61 05 97
– www.hotelpiranesi.com   F1
32 rm ⌱ – ♦168 € ♦♦220/290 €
◆ Traditional ◆ Classic ◆
The lobby, guestrooms and corridors of this hotel are decorated with marble, elegant furnishings and an unusual exhibition of old fabrics. The hotel also boasts a roof garden and sun terrace.

Valadier 🔟 ⇆ "𝓲" 🖽 🆚 🆚 ⓘ
via della Fontanella 15 ⊠ 00187 – ❶ Flaminio – ℰ 06 3611998
– info@hotelvaladier.com – Fax 06 3 20 15 58
– www.hotelvaladier.com   F1
66 rm ⌱ – ♦120/350 € ♦♦160/600 € – 4 suites
Rest Il Valentino – see below
◆ Luxury ◆ Personalised ◆
Elegant hotel close to Piazza del Popolo with a dark and stylish interior decor. The guestrooms have period touches such as tapestries and coffered ceilings. Panoramic roof-garden.

Dei Borgognoni without rest 🔟 🕻 🖽 🚗 🆚 🆚 ⓘ
via del Bufalo 126 ⊠ 00187 – ❶ Spagna – ℰ 06 69941505 – info@
hotelborgognoni.it – Fax 06 69 94 15 01 – www.hotelborgognoni.it
51 rm ⌱ – ♦210/240 € ♦♦240/340 €   F2
◆ Traditional ◆ Classic ◆
Occupying a 19C palazzo, this smart hotel has an elegant atmosphere, spacious, modern public rooms and comfortable, traditional-style bedrooms. Attractive winter garden.

Nazionale 🔟 🕻 🖽 🆚 🆚 ⓘ
piazza Montecitorio 131 ⊠ 00186 – ❶ Barberini – ℰ 06 695001 – info@
hotelnazionale.it – Fax 06 6 78 66 77 – www.hotelnazionale.it   F2
100 rm ⌱ – ♦200/280 € ♦♦350 € – 1 suite
Rest 31 Al Vicario – ℰ 06 69925530 (closed August and Sunday)
Carte 34/51 €
◆ Traditional ◆ Classic ◆
Situated on Piazza di Montecitorio, this hotel occupies an 18C building which was once a private residence. Elegant, classical interior decor. Guests will enjoy traditional Italian cuisine in this elegant, comfortable restaurant.

Barberini without rest 🌾 AC 🏷 VISA ⊚ AE ①

via Rasella 3 ✉ *00187* – ⓜ *Barberini* – ℰ *06 4814993* – *info@
hotelbarberini.com* – *Fax 06 4 81 52 11* – *www.hotelbarberini.com*
35 rm ☲ – ♦187/250 € ♦♦244/344 €   **G2**
♦ Traditional ♦ Classic ♦

This elegant hotel near the Palazzo of the same name is decorated with fine marble,
stylish fabrics and wood furnishings. The roof garden is perfect for a breakfast with a
view or an atmospheric evening aperitif. Well-being centre with a sauna and Jacuzzi.

Grand Hotel del Gianicolo without rest 🚗 ⅃ AC ⅍ ⅍ ⅏

viale Mura Gianicolensi 107 ✉ *00152*   VISA ⊚ AE ①
– ⓜ *Cipro Musei Vaticani* – ℰ *06 58333405* – *info@grandhotelgianicolo.it*
– *Fax 06 58 17 94 34* – *www.grandhotelgianicolo.it*   Plan I **B3**
48 rm ☲ – ♦160/320 € ♦♦200/360 €
♦ Traditional ♦ Classic ♦

Located in an elegant villa with a well-maintained garden and swimming pool, this
hotel has comfortable, spacious rooms and refined public spaces.

Mozart without rest AC ⅍ VISA ⊚ AE ①

via dei Greci 23/b ✉ *00187* – ⓜ *Spagna* – ℰ *06 36001915* – *info@
hotelmozart.com* – *Fax 06 36 00 17 35* – *www.hotelmozart.com*   **F1**
66 rm ☲ – ♦114/190 € ♦♦165/275 €
♦ Traditional ♦ Classic ♦

Housed in a 19C palazzo, this restored hotel has simple rooms with elegant furnishings. More modern rooms are available in a nearby annex. Pleasant roof garden.

Condotti without rest AC ⅍ VISA ⊚ AE ①

via Mario dè Fiori 37 ✉ *00187* – ⓜ *Spagna* – ℰ *06 6794661* – *info@
hotelcondotti.com* – *Fax 06 6 79 04 57* – *www.hotelcondotti.com*   **F1**
16 rm ☲ – ♦139/215 € ♦♦179/299 €
♦ Traditional ♦ Classic ♦

The lobby of this hotel is decorated in marble and adorned with elegant chandeliers. Small guestrooms furnished in traditional style; some are in a separate building nearby. Quiet breakfast room in the basement.

XXXX Imàgo – Hotel Hassler 🍴 AC VISA ⊚ AE ①

❀ *piazza Trinità dei Monti 6* ✉ *00187* – ⓜ *Spagna* – ℰ *06 69934726* – *imago@
hotelhassler.it* – *Fax 06 6 78 99 91* – *www.imagorestaurant.com*   **F1**
Rest – *(dinner only in August)* Menu 100/130 € – Carte 73/136 €
Spec. Fusilloni con ragù di quaglia alla carbonara. Coda di rospo fiammata
con zabaione al marsala e cous cous ai funghi misti. Coscia d'agnello al
forno con mais, ricotta salata e santoreggia.
♦ Modern ♦ Luxury ♦

A perennial favourite, this restaurant boasts large windows with delightful views of
Rome. Excellent contemporary cuisine.

XXXX Hostaria dell'Orso 🍴 AC ⇔ VISA ⊚ AE ①

via dei Soldati 25/c ✉ *00186* – ⓜ *Spagna* – ℰ *06 68301192* – *info@hdo.it*
– *Fax 06 68 21 70 63* – *www.hdo.it*
– *closed from 10 to 25 August and Sunday*   **E-F2**
Rest – *(dinner only) (booking advisable)* Menu 75/145 € – Carte 64/102 € ⅜
♦ Modern ♦ Luxury ♦

Housed in an historic building, this restaurant has intimate, romantic dining rooms
decorated in a simple, elegant style. The elegant cuisine is based around the highest quality ingredients.

XXX Il Convivio-Troiani AC ⇔ VISA ⊚ AE ①

vicolo dei Soldati 31 ✉ *00186* – ⓜ *Spagna* – ℰ *06 6869432* – *info@
ilconviviotroiani.com* – *Fax 06 6 86 94 32* – *www.ilconviviotroiani.com*
– *closed from 13 to 17 August and Sunday*   **E2**
Rest – *(dinner only)* Carte 89/104 € ⅜
♦ Inventive ♦ Formal ♦

Hidden in the alleyways of the historical centre, this restaurant serves modern
innovative cuisine, with an emphasis on meat and fish dishes. Simple, elegant
decor in the three dining rooms.

ITALY - ROME

✗✗✗ El Toulà
AC ⇄ VISA ⓞ AE ①

via della Lupa 29/b ⊠ 00186 – Ⓜ Spagna – ℰ 06 6873498 – roma@toula.it
– Fax 06 6 87 11 15 – www.toula.it
– closed from 24 to 26 December, August, Sunday, Monday and Saturday
lunchtime   **F2**
Rest – Carte 60/85 €
♦ Modern ♦ Intimate ♦
This quiet, elegant restaurant comprises a series of small dining rooms furnished
with comfortable chairs and separated by arches. The restaurant specialises in
Italian and Venetian cuisine.

✗✗✗ Antico Bottaro
AC VISA ⓞ AE ①

Passeggiata di Ripetta 15 ⊠ 00186 – Ⓜ Flaminio – ℰ 06 3236763
– anticobottaro@anticobottaro.it – Fax 06 3 23 67 63 – www.anticobottaro.it
– closed from 4 to 31 August and Wednesday   **E-F1**
Rest – *(dinner only)* Carte 67/94 €
♦ Classic ♦ Formal ♦
This smart private residence is adorned with fine stucco and elegant fabrics. The
restaurant here serves innovative cuisine with a French flavour, using the best
ingredients.

✗✗✗ Enoteca Capranica
AC ⇄ VISA ⓞ AE ①

piazza Capranica 99/100 ⊠ 00186 – Ⓜ Spagna – ℰ 06 69940992
– Fax 06 69 94 09 89 – www.enotecacapranica.it
– closed Saturday lunchtime and Sunday   **F2**
Rest – *(dinner only in August)* Menu 65/75 € – Carte 50/78 € 🏵
♦ Mediterranean ♦ Formal ♦
This wine bar near Montecitorio has been transformed into an elegant restaurant
serving Mediterranean cuisine. Colourful vaulted ceiling and a small exhibition of
wine bottles on display.

✗✗✗ Il Valentino – Hotel Valadier
AC ⇄ VISA ⓞ AE ①

via della Fontanella 14 ⊠ 00187 – Ⓜ Flaminio – ℰ 06 3610880 – info@
ilvalentino.com – Fax 06 3 20 15 58 – www.ilvalentino.com   **F1**
Rest – Carte 60/78 €
♦ Mediterranean ♦ Intimate ♦
Light wood panelling and warm colours decorate this elegant restaurant, which
serves traditional Italian dishes, often with an innovative twist. Meals may be
enjoyed on the roof garden in summer.

✗✗ Il Pagliaccio (Anthony Genovese)
AC VISA ⓞ AE ①
🏵 🏵

via dei Banchi Vecchi 129 ⊠ 00186 – ℰ 06 68809595 – info@
ristoranteilpagliaccio.it – Fax 06 68 21 75 04 – www.ristoranteilpagliaccio.it
– closed 9 to 17 January, 6 to 25 August, Sunday, Monday, Tuesday midday
Rest – Menu 85/150 € – Carte 75/99 €   **E2**
Spec. Gnocchi d'acqua di patate, ostriche, caviale e crema di burrata alle
spezie. San Pietro al forno al profumo di vaniglia, semola e avocado. Sigari
di cioccolato amaro con gelato di limone e cannella.
♦ Inventive ♦ Friendly ♦
The young, enthusiastic team at this restaurant offers a varied menu, including
Mediterranean, Eastern and traditional French dishes.

✗✗ Da Pancrazio
🏠 ⇄ VISA ⓞ AE ①

piazza del Biscione 92 ⊠ 00186 – ℰ 06 6861246 – info@dapancrazio.it
– Fax 06 97 84 02 35 – www.dapancrazio.it
– closed from 12 to 16 August, Christmas and Wednesday   **F3**
Rest – Carte 32/57 €
♦ Classic ♦ Formal ♦
Da Pancrazio offers two different styles and two thousand years of history: one of
its dining rooms is decorated in the style of a typical 19C tavern; the other is built
over a section of the ruins of Pompey's Theatre.

ITALY - ROME

XX **Sora Lella**   AK VISA ⊗ AE
via di Ponte Quattro Capi 16 (Tiber Island) ⊠ *00186 –* Ⓜ *Circo Massimo*
– ☏ 06 6861601 – soralella@soralella.com – Fax 06 6 86 16 01
– www.soralella.com
– closed 2 weeks in August, Sunday, Tuesday midday   **F3**
Rest *– Carte 44/78 €*
♦ Roman ♦ Family ♦
'Gastronomic' globalisation has not affected this traditional restaurant on the Isola
Tiberina, which specialises in authentic regional cuisine with an innovative touch.
A delightful statue of the Madonna can be seen in one of the restaurant's
windows.

XX **Antico Arco**   AK ⇔ VISA ⊗ AE ①
piazzale Aurelio 7 ⊠ *00152 – ☏ 06 5815274 – info@anticoarco.it*
– Fax 06 5 81 52 74 – www.anticoarco.it
– closed Sunday   *Plan I* **B3**
Rest *– (dinner only) Carte 44/62 €* ❀
♦ Inventive ♦ Fashionable ♦
Situated in a fashionable and popular location, this restaurant has been refurbished in minimalist style. The wine-bar is near the entrance and the restaurant occupies two floors. Attentive service.

X **Felice a Testaccio**   AK VISA ⊗ AE
(⊜) *via Mastrogiorgio 29* ⊠ *00153 – ☏ 06 5746800 – Fax 06 5 74 68 00*
– www.feliceatestaccio.com
– closed August and Sunday evening   *Plan I* **B3**
Rest *– (booking advisable) Carte 30/35 €*
♦ Roman ♦ Family ♦
With its opaque windows, brick walls and wooden tables, this restaurant has an
authentic turn of the century atmosphere. The charming owners, Franco and Fla-
vio, have a host of anecdotes and information on the restaurant and its fine cuisine, which showcases specialities from Rome and the Lazio region.

TERMINI RAILWAY STATION   *Plan II*

🏨 **St. Regis Grand**   ¿å 🦢 ᴕ AK ⁽ᵉᵖ⁾ 🖐 VISA ⊗ AE ①
via Vittorio Emanuele Orlando 3 ⊠ *00185 –* Ⓜ *Repubblica – ☏ 06 47091*
– stregisgrandrome@stregis.com – Fax 06 47 09 28 31
– www.stregis.com/grandrome
– closed for 2 weeks in August   **H1**
153 rm *–* ♦855/950 € ♦♦995/1195 €, � 33 € – 8 suites
Rest *Vivendo – ☏ 06 47092736 (closed Saturday lunchtime and Sunday)*
Carte 62/96 € ❀
♦ Grand Luxury ♦ Classic ♦
Frescoes, valuable furnishings and Empire-style antiques in the luxurious
bedrooms and the magnificent lounges of a hotel restored to its original antique
splendours (1894). The restaurant has a modern, eclectic decor.

🏨 **The Westin Excelsior**   ¿å ⊛ ᴕ 🖵 AK ⁽ᵉᵖ⁾ 🖐 VISA ⊗ AE ①
via Vittorio Veneto 125 ⊠ *00187 –* Ⓜ *Barberini – ☏ 0647081*
– excelsiorrome@westin.com – Fax 0 64 82 62 05
– www.westin.com/excelsiorrome   **G1**
316 rm *–* ♦545 € ♦♦895 €, ⊆ 42 € – 35 suites
Rest *Doney – Carte 52/121 €*
♦ Luxury ♦ Classic ♦
Spoil yourself with a stay in the royal suite (the largest in Europe) or choose one of
the luxurious guestrooms, where elegant and comfortable furnishings are complemented by the very latest technology. The 'dolce vita' at its best!

Eden

via Ludovisi 49 ✉ 00187 – Ⓜ Barberini – ☎ 06 478121 – 1872.resevations@lemeridien.com – Fax 06 4 82 15 84 – www.lemeridien.com/eden **G1**

121 rm – 528/550 € 880/1067 €, ☕ 54 € – 13 suites

Rest La Terrazza – see below

◆ Luxury ◆ Business ◆ Stylish ◆

This large, top-end hotel has a formal atmosphere but the service is warm and friendly. Some of the rooms on the upper floors have what is perhaps the best view of Rome.

Regina Hotel Baglioni

via Vittorio Veneto 72 ✉ 00187 – Ⓜ Barberini – ☎ 06 421111 – regina.roma@baglionihotels.com – Fax 06 42 01 21 30 – www.baglionihotels.com

128 rm – 240/330 € 308/462 €, ☕ 29 € – 8 suites **G1**

Rest *Brunello Lounge & Restaurant* – Carte 48/64 €

◆ Luxury ◆ Stylish ◆

This building restructured in Art Nouveau style is home to an historic hotel with Art Deco interiors and excellent facilities. The attractive guestrooms are striking for their marble decor. Restaurant with a warm, elegant atmosphere and a hint of the Far East. International cuisine.

Majestic without rest

via Vittorio Veneto 50 ✉ 00187 – Ⓜ Barberini – ☎ 06 421441 – info@hotelmajestic.com – Fax 06 4 88 09 84 – www.hotelmajestic.com **G1**

98 rm – 410/510 € 540/675 €, ☕ 40 €

◆ Traditional ◆ Classic ◆

Although space is limited in the hotel lobby, this is compensated for by the elegant lounge areas adorned with late-19C frescoes on the first floor. Splendid lift and charming guestrooms.

Sofitel Rome e Villa Borghese

via Lombardia 47 ✉ 00187 – Ⓜ Barberini – ☎ 06 478021 – h1312-re@accor.com – Fax 06 4 82 10 19 – www.sofitel.com **G1**

108 rm – 400 € 540 €, ☕ 25 € – 3 suites **Rest** – Carte 61/82 €

◆ Luxury ◆ Classic ◆

The neo-classical style of the Imperial Roman period dominates in this hotel, with statues and sculptures dotted around the historic palazzo. Attractive terrace with panoramic views of Rome. An elegant restaurant with vaulted ceilings, housed in the former stables of the palazzo.

Splendide Royal

via di porta Pinciana 14 ✉ 00187 – Ⓜ Barberini – ☎ 06 421689 – reservations@splendideroyal.com – Fax 06 42 16 88 00 – www.splendideroyal.com **G1**

60 rm – 260/480 € 300/800 €, ☕ 35 € – 9 suites

Rest Mirabelle – see below

◆ Luxury ◆ Classic ◆

Gilded stucco, damask fabrics and sumptuous antique furnishings contribute to the Roman Baroque style of this hotel, which is in sharp contrast to the contemporary trend for minimalist design.

Aleph

via San Basilio 15 ✉ 00187 – Ⓜ Barberini – ☎ 06 422901 – reception@aleph.boscolo.com – Fax 06 42 29 00 00 – www.boscolohotels.com

96 rm – 307/670 €, ☕ 25 € **G1**

Rest *Maremoto* – Carte 46/58 €

◆ Luxury ◆ Design ◆

The architecture of this hotel is inspired by Dante's 'Divine Comedy'. The lobby and public rooms painted in red evoke 'Hell', 'Paradise' is symbolised by the blues and whites of the small fitness centre, and 'Purgatory' is the theme of the bedrooms decorated in light and dark tones. The Maremoto restaurant has a minimalist decor and specialises in fish dishes.

ITALY - ROME

Bernini Bristol 🏠🏠🏠 ⚏ ⻏ 🜲 ⅍ rm ⯍ ⅄ rm ⮑ 🔊 VISA ⓪ 🜂 ⓪

piazza Barberini 23 ✉ *00187* – 🅜 *Barberini* – ✆ *06 488931* – *reservationsbb@*
sinahotels.it – *Fax 06 4 82 42 66* – *www.berninibristol.com*   **G2**
117 rm – ❌490 € ❌❌616 €, ⊊ 28 € – 10 suites
Rest *L'Olimpo* – ✆ *06 488933288* – Carte 90/130 €
◆ Traditional ◆ Classic ◆
This stylish period hotel dating from 1870 has rooms with both classic and contemporary furnishings. The rooms with a view on the upper floors are perhaps preferable. Roof garden restaurant serving modern cuisine. It has outdoor dining in
the summer and a marvellous view of the Eternal City.

Marriott Grand Hotel Flora 🏠🏠🏠 ⻏ 🜲 rest ⯍ ⅄ rm ⮑ 🔊

via Vittorio Veneto 191 ✉ *00187* – 🅜 *Spagna*   VISA ⓪ 🜂 ⓪
– ✆ *06 489929* – *info@grandhotelflora.net* – *Fax 06 4 82 03 59*
– *www.grandhotelflora.net*   **G1**
153 rm – ❌280/485 € ❌❌387/760 €, ⊊ 30 € – 3 suites   **Rest** – Carte 48/99 €
◆ Traditional ◆ Modern ◆
Situated at the end of the Via Veneto, this recently renovated hotel is a functional
yet harmonious building of classical simplicity with modern touches. Elegant furnishings in the spacious bedrooms. Parquet flooring and wooden touches evoke
a warm decor in the elegant restaurant dining room. Mediterranean cuisine.

Empire Palace Hotel 🏠🏠🏠 ⚏ ⻏ 🜲 ⯍ ⅄ rm ⯍ 🔊 VISA ⓪ 🜂 ⓪

via Aureliana 39 ✉ *00187* – ✆ *06 421281* – *gold@empirepalacehotel.com*
– *Fax 06 42 12 84 00* – *www.empirepalacehotel.com*   **H1**
110 rm ⊊ – ❌455 € ❌❌512 €
Rest *Aureliano* – *(closed Sunday)* Carte 46/80 €
◆ Personalised ◆
Sophisticated combination of 19C architecture and contemporary design with simple, classic bedrooms. There is a collection of modern art in the public areas. An
interesting selection of Mediterranean dishes are served in a dining room decorated with cherry wood furnishings and multi-coloured table lamps.

Rose Garden Palace 🏠🏠 ⻏ 🜲 🜲 ⯍ ⅄ rm ⯍ 🔊 VISA ⓪ 🜂 ⓪

via Boncompagni 19 ✉ *00187* – 🅜 *Barberini* – ✆ *06 421741* – *info@*
rosegardenpalace.com – *Fax 06 4 81 56 08* – *www.rosegardenpalace.com*
65 rm ⊊ – ❌368 € ❌❌440 €   **G1**
Rest – *(closed Sunday)* Carte 48/61 €
◆ Traditional ◆ Modern ◆
A modern, minimalist design in muted colours is the inspiration behind the furnishing of this hotel housed in an early-20C palazzo. The à la carte restaurant, located in an unexpected rose garden, specialises in dishes inspired by fine contemporary cuisine.

Mecenate Palace Hotel without rest 🏠🏠 🜲 ⯍ ⅄ ⯍ 🔊

via Carlo Alberto 3 ✉ *00185* – 🅜 *Vittorio Emanuele*   VISA ⓪ 🜂 ⓪
– ✆ *06 44702024* – *info@mecenatepalace.com* – *Fax 06 4 46 13 54*
– *www.mecenatepalace.com*   **H2**
72 rm ⊊ – ❌120/330 € ❌❌200/390 € – 1 suite
◆ Traditional ◆ Stylish ◆
The warm and elegant period-style interiors are in perfect keeping with the spirit
of the 19C building which houses this new hotel. Fine views of Santa Maria Maggiore from the upper floors.

Artemide without rest 🏠🏠 ⻏ 🜲 🜲 ⯍ ⅄ ⮑ 🔊 VISA ⓪ 🜂 ⓪

via Nazionale 22 ✉ *00184* – 🅜 *Repubblica* – ✆ *06 489911* – *info@*
hotelartemide.it – *Fax 06 48 99 17 00* – *www.hotelartemide.it*   **G-H2**
85 rm ⊊ – ❌150/370 € ❌❌150/450 €
◆ Business ◆ Classic ◆
This classically elegant hotel is a delightful restored Art Nouveau building. It offers
a full range of modern facilities, including well-organised conference areas and a
small fitness centre.

Canada without rest   AC ❝¶❞ VISA ⦾ AE ①

via Vicenza 58 ✉ *00185* – Ⓜ *Castro Pretorio* – ℰ *06 4457770*
– *info@hotelcanadaroma.com* – *Fax 06 4 45 07 49*
– *www.hotelcanadaroma.com*   Plan I **C2**
73 rm ☲ – ♥128/164 € ♥♥146/225 €
◆ Traditional ◆ Classic ◆
In period style building near the Termini railway station, a simple but elegant hotel, with period style furnishings; luxurious rooms: some with four poster beds available on request.

 Ambra Palace without rest   ⅙ AC ⅘ ❝¶❞ ⅚ VISA ⦾ AE ①

via Principe Amedeo 257 ✉ *00185* – Ⓜ *Vittorio Emanuele* – ℰ *06 492330*
– *info@ambrapalacehotel.com* – *Fax 06 49 23 31 00*
– *www.ambrapalacehotel.com*   Plan I **C2**
78 rm ☲ – ♥109/230 € ♥♥129/430 €
◆ Traditional ◆ Classic ◆
Professional and attentive management is the key to this functional, welcoming hotel housed in a 19C palazzo. Its many facilities and high level of comfort make this an ideal address for both business travellers and visitors to Rome.

 Britannia without rest   AC ❝¶❞ VISA ⦾ AE ①

via Napoli 64 ✉ *00184* – Ⓜ *Repubblica* – ℰ *06 4883153*
– *info@hotelbritannia.it* – *Fax 06 48 98 63 16*
– *www.hotelbritannia.it*   **H2**
33 rm ☲ – ♥100/200 € ♥♥120/240 €
◆ Traditional ◆ Classic ◆
This small hotel has reasonable facilities, comfortable guestrooms and an English-style bar. Marble decor, neo-Classical reproductions and attention to detail.

 Antico Palazzo Rospigliosi without rest   ⅙ AC ⅘ ❝¶❞ ⅚ Ⓟ

via Liberiana 22 ✉ *00185* – Ⓜ *Cavour*   VISA ⦾ AE ①
– ℰ *06 48930495* – *info@hotelrospigliosi.com* – *Fax 06 4 81 48 37*
– *www.hotelrospigliosi.com*   **G2**
39 rm ☲ – ♥120/240 € ♥♥150/295 €
◆ Historic ◆ Classic ◆
This 16C mansion has retained much of its period elegance in its large lounges, as well as in the fine detail of its beautiful bedrooms. The cloister-garden, with its bubbling fountain and splendid 17C chapel, is particularly delightful.

ХХХХ **La Terrazza** – Hotel Eden   AC ⇆ VISA ⦾ AE ①

via Ludovisi 49 ✉ *00187* – Ⓜ *Barberini* – ℰ *06 47812752*
– *laterrazzadelleden.roma@lemeridien.com* – *Fax 06 4 81 44 73*   **G1**
Rest – Menu 110 € – Carte 99/148 € 🕮
◆ Classic ◆ Formal ◆
Situated on the top floor of the building (lift), and enclosed by a glass wall, this restaurant boasts magnificent views of the entire historical centre of the city.

ХХХХ **Mirabelle** – Hotel Splendide Royal   🍴 ⅙ AC ⇆ VISA ⦾ AE ①
ⵛⵛ
via di porta Pinciana 14 ✉ *00187* – Ⓜ *Barberini*
– ℰ *06 42168838* – *mirabelle@splendideroyal.com* – *Fax 06 42 16 88 70*
– *www.mirabelle.it*   **G1**
Rest – Carte 89/127 €
Spec. Crudo di spigola e scampi marinati al pompelmo rosa con insalata di sedano. Scaloppa di fegato d'oca con pere caramellate e gelatina al Sauternes. Soufflé serviti con le loro salse.
◆ Mediterranean ◆ Formal ◆
This restaurant has one of the most spectacular roof gardens in Rome with views as far as the Vatican gardens. Choose from a range of local and international dishes, all beautifully presented with real attention to detail.

491

ITALY - ROME

XXX ⭐ Agata e Romeo (Agata Parisella) | AE VISA ⊕ AE ⓪

*via Carlo Alberto 45 ⊠ 00185 – **Ⓜ** Vittorio Emanuele – ℰ 06 4466115*
– ristorante@agataeromeo.it – Fax 06 4 46 58 42 – www.agataeromeo.it
– closed 1 - 24 January, 7 - 29 August, Saturdays and Sundays **H2**
Rest – Menu 110/160 € – Carte 90/125 € ⅋
Spec. Cinque modi di cucinare il baccalà. Paccheri all'amatriciana. Il millefoglie di Agata.
♦ Roman ♦ Friendly ♦
Despite its location in a district which is becoming more and more multicultural, this restaurant continues to specialise in inventive Roman and Italian cuisine.

XX Cicilardone a Monte Caruso | AE ⇔ VISA ⊕ AE ⓪

*via Farini 12 ⊠ 00185 – **Ⓜ** Termini – ℰ 06 483549 – cicilardone@tiscali.it*
– www.montecaruso.com
– closed August, Christmas, Mondays at lunchtime and Sundays **H2**
Rest – Carte 31/39 €
♦ Regional ♦ Rustic ♦
The flavours of the South in a warm and welcoming family-run establishment, with a menu based on Lucanian specialities, achieved in a simple and genuine manner.

XX Papà Baccus | 🏡 AE ⇔ VISA ⊕ AE ⓪

*via Toscana 32/36 ⊠ 00187 – **Ⓜ** Barberini – ℰ 06 42742808 – papabaccus@papabaccus.com – Fax 06 42 01 00 05 – www.papabaccus.com*
– closed 15 days in August, Saturday lunch and Sunday **G1**
Rest – Carte 47/62 €
♦ Regional ♦ Formal ♦
This pleasant restaurant situated on the elegant Via Veneto has a friendly ambience. Delicious Tuscan cuisine is the order of the day (Chianina beef and Sienese pork), as well as fish specialities.

XX Hostaria da Vincenzo | 🏡 ⇔ VISA ⊕ AE ⓪

via Castelfidardo 6 ⊠ 00185 – ℰ 06 484596 – Fax 06 4 87 00 92
– closed August and Sunday **H1**
Rest – Carte 23/41 €
♦ Fish ♦ Friendly ♦
With its traditional, friendly atmosphere and typical regional and Italian dishes, this restaurant has a loyal following and is particularly popular with business clientele.

X 🛆 Trattoria Monti | AE VISA ⊕ ⓪

*via di San Vito 13/a ⊠ 00185 – **Ⓜ** Cavour – ℰ 06 4466573 – Fax 06 4 46 65 73*
– closed 10 days at Christmas, 1 week at Easter, August, Sunday evening and Monday **H2**
Rest – (booking advisable) Carte 35/43 €
♦ Regional ♦ Cosy ♦
As a result of renovation work completed a few years ago, this trattoria is resolutely contemporary in style with wooden chairs, copper piping and low-hanging lamps. Specialities include dishes from Lazio and the Marche, the owner's birthplace.

ST-PETER'S BASILICA | *Plan II*

🏨 Rome Cavalieri | ← 🏊 🏡 🛁 🕙 🛝 🖎 🗔 🍴 🛗 AE ↯ rm 🛎️ 🛢 P

via Cadlolo 101 ⊠ 00136 – ℰ 06 35091 | 🕬 VISA ⊕ AE ⓪
– sales.rome@hilton.com – Fax 06 35 09 22 41 – www.hilton.com
370 rm – ♦380/855 € ♦♦405/910 €, � 38 € – 25 suites | *Plan I* **A2**
Rest La Pergola – see below
Rest L'Uliveto – Carte 82/121 €
♦ Luxury ♦ Classic ♦
This imposing building overlooks the entire city of Rome. The hotel has excellent facilities, including extensive gardens, an outdoor swimming pool, plus a fine art collection. Restaurant with an informal atmosphere by the edge of the swimming pool for dining with live music.

Farnese without rest   AC ⟨ᵗ⟩ P VISA ⑳ AE ①

via Alessandro Farnese 30 ⊠ 00192 – Ⓜ Lepanto – 𝒞 06 3212553 – info@hotelfarnese.com – Fax 06 3 21 51 29 – www.hotelfarnese.com   **E1**

23 rm ⌑ – †140/210 € ††190/300 €

♦ Traditional ♦ Classic ♦

Decorated in period style, this hotel has elegant rooms and an attractive lobby housing a 17C polychrome marble frontal. Fine views of St Peter's from the terrace.

Dei Consoli without rest   ⟨ᵗ⟩ AC ⟨⁄⟩ VISA ⑳ AE ①

via Varrone 2/d ⊠ 00193 – Ⓜ Ottaviano-San Pietro – 𝒞 06 68892972 – info@hoteldeiconsoli.com – Fax 06 68 21 22 74 – www.hoteldeiconsoli.com

28 rm ⌑ – †100/220 € ††150/320 €   *Plan III* **K1**

♦ Traditional ♦ Stylish ♦

Housed in an old palazzo, this hotel caters for a discerning clientele, with its rich decor, careful attention to detail and elegant rooms furnished in Empire style.

Hotel Alimandi Vaticano without rest   AC ⟨ᵗ⟩ VISA ⑳ AE ①

viale Vaticano 99 ⊠ 00165 – Ⓜ Ottaviano-San Pietro – 𝒞 06 39745562 – hotelali@hotelalimandie.191.it – Fax 06 39 73 01 32 – www.alimandi.it

24 rm – †140/170 € ††160/200 €, ⌑ 15 €   *Plan III* **J1**

♦ Family ♦ Classic ♦

This pleasant hotel enjoys an excellent location directly opposite the Vatican Museums. The marble and wood decor in the well-appointed guestrooms adds to their elegant atmosphere.

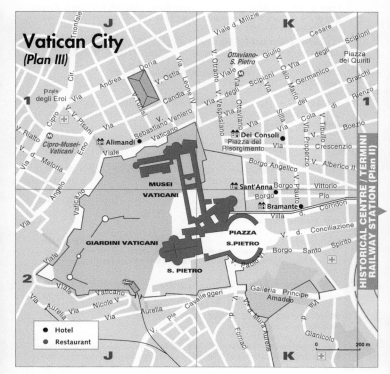

ITALY - ROME

Sant'Anna without rest $\overline{AC}$ $^{(1)}$ $\overline{VISA}$ $\textcircled{00}$ $\overline{AE}$ $\textcircled{0}$

borgo Pio 133 ⊠ *00193 –* Ⓜ *Ottaviano-San Pietro –* ℰ *06 68801602*
– santanna@travel.it – Fax 06 68 30 87 17 – www.hotelsantanna.com
20 rm ☐ *–* ♦100/150 € ♦♦150/230 € *Plan III* **K1-2**
♦ Traditional ♦ Classic ♦
An original coffered ceiling and pleasant interior courtyard add a decorative touch
to this small, welcoming hotel occupying a 16C building a short distance from
St Peter's.

Bramante without rest $\overline{AC}$ $^{(1)}$ $\overline{VISA}$ $\textcircled{00}$ $\overline{AE}$ $\textcircled{0}$

vicolo delle Palline 24 ⊠ *00193 –* Ⓜ *Ottaviano-San Pietro –* ℰ *06 68806426*
– hotelbramante@libero.it – Fax 06 68 13 33 39 – www.hotelbramante.com
16 rm ☐ *–* ♦100/160 € ♦♦150/240 € *Plan III* **K2**
♦ Traditional ♦ Classic ♦
This small, comfortable hotel situated a stone's throw from St Peter's is ideal for
visitors wishing to stay in the heart of the Vatican district.

XXXXX La Pergola (Heinz Beck) – Hotel Rome Cavalieri Hilton ≤ 🎇 & $\overline{AC}$
😚😚😚

via Cadlolo 101 ⊠ *00136 –* ℰ *06 35092152* ⇧ $\overline{P}$ $\overline{VISA}$ $\textcircled{00}$ $\overline{AE}$ $\textcircled{0}$
– lapergola.rome@hilton.com – Fax 06 35 09 21 65 – www.cavalieri-hilton.it
– closed from 1 to 26 January, from 9 to 24 August, Sunday and Monday
Rest *– (dinner only) (booking essential) Menu 170/195 €* *Plan I* **A2**
– Carte 121/183 € 🍴
Spec. Uovo poché in consommé di asparagi verdi con tartufo bianco d'Alba.
Spalla di maialino iberico alla liquirizia con puré di patate alle erbe e salsa di
olive taggiasche. Gelatina di arancia con sorbetto al bergamotto e fiori.
♦ Inventive ♦ Luxury ♦
Enjoy an unforgettable view of Rome and its surrounding hills from the roof-gar-
den of this restaurant. Quiet, elegant atmosphere, impeccable service, and excel-
lent Mediterranean cuisine.

XX Enoteca Costantini-Il Simposio $\overline{AC}$ $\overline{VISA}$ $\textcircled{00}$ $\overline{AE}$ $\textcircled{0}$

piazza Cavour 16 ⊠ *00193 –* Ⓜ *Lepanto –* ℰ *06 32111131 – ilsimposio@*
pierocostantini.it – Fax 06 32 11 11 31
– closed August, Christmas, Saturday at midday and Sunday **E2**
Rest *– Carte 43/60 €* 🍴
♦ Classic ♦ Formal ♦
An evocative wrought-iron vine marks the entrance to this restaurant-cum-wine
bar, which serves specialities such as foie gras, as well as a selection of different
cheeses, accompanied by a glass of wine.

PARIOLI *Plan IV*

Grand Hotel Parco dei Principi ≤ 🐾 🎇 𝄙 ☒ & $\overline{AC}$ ⇼ rm

via Gerolamo Frescobaldi 5 ⊠ *00198 –* ℰ *06 854421* $^{(1)}$ 🔊 $\overline{VISA}$ $\overline{AE}$ $\textcircled{0}$
– principi@parcodeiprincipi.com – Fax 06 8 84 51 04
– www.parcodeiprincipi.com **M2**
165 rm ☐ *–* ♦400/450 € ♦♦550/600 € *– 15 suites*
Rest *Pauline Borghese – Carte 64/115 €*
♦ Grand Luxury ♦ Classic ♦
Overlooking the Villa Borghese gardens, this hotel is a veritable oasis of tranquillity
in the heart of Rome. Warm and elegant interiors, with wood panelling and neo-
Classical decor in the lobby. Exclusive restaurant serving well-prepared, varied cuisine.

Aldrovandi Palace Villa Borghese 🏊 𝄙 ☒ & $\overline{AC}$ ⇼ $^{(1)}$ 🔊

via Ulisse Aldrovandi 15 ⊠ *00197 –* ℰ *06 3223993* $\overline{P}$ $\overline{VISA}$ $\textcircled{00}$ $\overline{AE}$ $\textcircled{0}$
– hotel@aldrovandi.com – Fax 06 3 22 14 35 – www.aldrovandi.com
96 rm *–* ♦600/800 € ♦♦650/850 €, ☐ 33 € *– 12 suites* **M2**
Rest *Baby – see below*
♦ Luxury ♦ Classic ♦
In an elegant palazzo dating from the late 19C, this hotel has luxurious period-style
interiors, stylish bedrooms and a delightful internal garden to the rear of the building.

Lord Byron 🕭   AC 🛜 VISA ◉ AE ⓘ
via G. De Notaris 5 ✉ *00197 –* Ⓜ *Flaminio –* ℰ *06 3220404 – info@
lordbyronhotel.com – Fax 06 3 22 04 05 – www.lordbyronhotel.com*
26 rm ⌂ – ♦335/425 € ♦♦374/567 € – 6 suites   **L-M1**
Rest *Sapori del Lord Byron – (closed Sunday)* Carte 53/71 €
♦ Luxury ♦ Art Deco ♦
Elegant Art Deco furnishings, luxurious guestrooms and modern facilities make
this hotel near the Villa Borghese gardens an excellent base. Impeccable service.
This stylish restaurant adorned with mirrors, marble and fine paintings has its
own entrance. Ideal for quiet, intimate dinners.

 The Duke Hotel   👌 rm AC ↔ 🛜 🕭 🚗 VISA ◉ AE ⓘ
via Archimede 69 ✉ *00197 –* ℰ *06 367221 – theduke@thedukehotel.com
– Fax 06 36 00 41 04 – www.thedukehotel.com*   **L1**
78 rm ⌂ – ♦305/410 € ♦♦410/515 €   **Rest** – Carte 46/74 €
♦ Traditional ♦ Classic ♦
Situated in a quiet residential area, this hotel has the discreet, muted atmosphere
of an elegant English club. Decorated in typical period style, but with all the latest
modern comforts. Afternoon tea is served in front of the fireplace. Italian and international dishes are reinterpreted with a creative flair at this restaurant.

 Mercure Roma Corso Trieste without rest   ♨ 🕭 👌 AC 🛜 🕭
via Gradisca 29 ✉ *00198 –* Ⓜ *Bologna*   🚗 VISA ◉ AE ⓘ
– ℰ 06 852021 – h3320-re@accor.com – Fax 06 8 41 24 44 – www.accor.com
97 rm – ♦145/165 € ♦♦185/200 €, ⌂ 13 €   **O1**
♦ Business ♦ Modern ♦
A modern, comfortable hotel with a hint of Art Deco in a predominantly residential
district. The tastefully furnished rooms vary in size. Gym, terrace and solarium on
the top floor.

 Fenix   🚗 🕭 AC ↔ rm 🛜 🕭 VISA ◉ AE ⓘ
viale Gorizia 5 ✉ *00198 –* Ⓜ *Bologna –* ℰ *06 8540741 – info@fenixhotel.it
– Fax 06 8 54 36 32 – www.fenixhotel.it*   **O1**
73 rm ⌂ – ♦110/180 € ♦♦150/250 €
Rest – *(closed August, Saturday evening and Sunday)* Carte 28/52 €
♦ Traditional ♦ Personalised ♦
Situated near the Villa Torlonia gardens, this hotel has an modern, elegant atmosphere and is tastefully furnished with original, colourful decor. Pleasant internal
garden. Soft, elegant colours dominate the dining room of the restaurant.

 Villa Morgagni without rest   🕭 👌 AC ↔ 🛜 P 🚗 VISA ◉ AE ⓘ
via G.B. Morgagni 2 ✉ *00161 –* Ⓜ *Policlinico –* ℰ *06 44202190 – info@
villamorgagni.it – Fax 06 44 20 21 90 – www.villamorgagni.it*   **O2**
34 rm ⌂ – ♦80/150 € ♦♦110/230 €
♦ Luxury ♦ Classic ♦
Private and quiet in an elegant Art Nouveau setting with comfortable rooms. In
summer or winter, the first meal of the day is prepared in the panoramic roof
garden.

 Degli Aranci   🕭 £ô 👌 rm AC 🛜 🕭 VISA ◉ AE ⓘ
via Oriani 11 ✉ *00197 –* Ⓜ *Flaminio –* ℰ *06 8070202 – info@
hoteldegliaranci.com – Fax 06 8 07 07 04 – www.hoteldegliaranci.com*
58 rm ⌂ – ♦100/200 € ♦♦180/300 € – 2 suites   **M1**
Rest – Carte 35/55 €
♦ Traditional ♦ Stylish ♦
This elegant hotel occupies a fine early 20C building. Situated in a quiet residential
street, the hotel has a peaceful ambience and is decorated in gentle pastel colours.
Polite, attentive service. The restaurant has an English feel, with windows overlooking the garden.

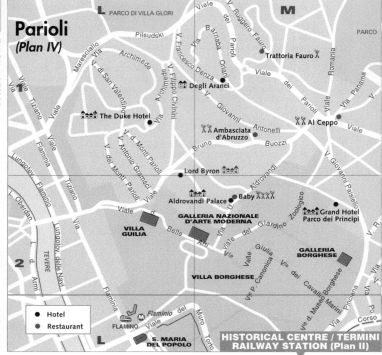

Parioli
(Plan IV)

PARCO DI VILLA GLORI

Pilsudski

Trattoria Fauro ✗

Degli Aranci ⛪⛪

The Duke Hotel 🏨🏨🏨

✗✗ Al Ceppo

✗✗ Ambasciata d'Abruzzo

Lord Byron 🏨🏨🏨

Aldrovandi Palace 🏨🏨🏨 ● Baby ✗✗✗✗

Grand Hotel 🏨🏨🏨 Parco dei Principi

GALLERIA NAZIONALE D'ARTE MODERNA

VILLA GUILIA

GALLERIA BORGHESE

VILLA BORGHESE

Flaminio

FLAMINO

● Hotel
● Restaurant

S. MARIA DEL POPOLO

HISTORICAL CENTRE / TERMINI RAILWAY STATION (Plan II)

✗✗✗✗ 🟢   **Baby** (Alfonso Iaccarino) – Hotel Aldrovandi Palace   🛋 AC P VISA 🔴 AE ①
via Ulisse Aldrovandi 15 ✉ *00197 –* ✆ *06 3216126*
– baby@aldrovandi.com – Fax 06 3 22 14 35 – www.aldrovandi.com
– closed Monday
Rest – Menu 115 € – Carte 90/115 €   **M2**
Spec. Macedonia di astice con gelatina di pomodoro e basilico. Ravioli di caciotta fresca e maggiorana con pomodorini vesuviani e basilico. Pesce spada con pangrattato alla lavanda, asparagi e misticanza.
♦ Inventive ♦ Luxury ♦
The result of a partnership with a well-known chef from Sant'Agata, this restaurant specialises in dishes from the Campania region. Belonging to the elegant Aldovrandi Palace hotel, the restaurant is decorated in bright minimalist style.

✗✗   **Al Ceppo**   AC VISA 🔴 AE ①
via Panama 2 ✉ *00198 –* ✆ *06 8551379 – info@ristorantealceppo.it*
– Fax 06 85 30 13 70 – www.ristorantealceppo.it
– closed from 8 to 24 August and Monday   **M1**
Rest – Carte 51/68 €
♦ Classic ♦ Formal ♦
Innovative Mediterranean cuisine served in an elegantly rustic setting. Main courses include meat and fish grilled in the dining room.

496

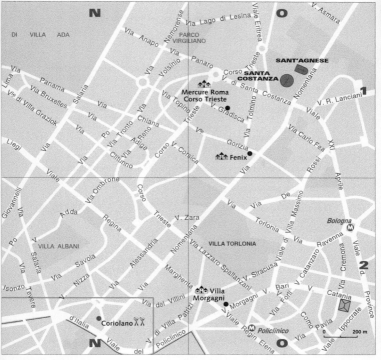

Mamma Angelina 🛋 AC VISA ✆ AE ①

viale Arrigo Boito 65 ✉ *00199* – 🕿 *06 8608928* – *mammangelina@libero.it*
– *Fax 06 97 61 56 68*
– *closed August and Wednesday*   *Plan I* **C1**
Rest – Carte 20/32 € 🍴

♦ Fish ♦ Formal ♦

Traditional Italian cuisine is the hallmark of this friendly restaurant. Specialities include an excellent buffet of antipasti, fish and seafood dishes and typical Roman delicacies.

Acquolina Hostaria in Roma (Giulio Terrinoni) 🛋 AC ↔

via Antonio Serra 60 ✉ *00191* – 🕿 *06 3337192* – *info@*   VISA ✆ AE
acquolinahostaria.com – *Fax 06 3 33 71 92* – *www.acquolinahostaria.com*
– *closed Christmas, Sunday from April to September and Monday the rest of
the year*   *Plan I* **B1**
Rest – *(dinner only except Sunday from October to March)* Carte 59/77 €
Spec. Gran crudo Acquolina. Vermicelli alla carbonara di mare. Torta di baccalà e patate con bagna caoda moderna e cipolla fritta.

♦ Fish ♦ Cosy ♦

The young and enthusiastic managers of this elegant restaurant have built an excellent reputation for fish dishes. There is an emphasis on traditional favourites, as well as lighter, more contemporary cuisine.

%% **Coriolano**   AC VISA ⓪ AE ①

via Ancona 14 ✉ *00198 –* ⓜ *Castro Pretorio –* ℰ *06 44249863*
– Fax 06 44 24 97 24
– closed 8 August-1 September   **N2**
Rest *–* Carte 34/71 €
♦ Fish ♦ Formal ♦
A well-maintained, family-run restaurant with a pleasant and elegant atmosphere.
The menu here is varied, featuring different types of cuisine including fish dishes
and traditional Roman specialities.

%% **Ambasciata d'Abruzzo**   🛖 VISA ⓪ AE ①

via Pietro Tacchini 26 ✉ *00197 –* ⓜ *Euclide –* ℰ *06 8078256 – info@*
ambasciatadiabruzzo.com – Fax 06 8 07 49 64
– www.ambasciatadiabruzzo.com   **M1**
Rest *– (pre-book)* Carte 28/45 €
♦ Abruzzian specialities ♦ Rustic ♦
The location of this family-run trattoria in the middle of a residential district comes
as something of a surprise. Good selection of antipasti, fish dishes and specialities
from the Lazio and Abruzzi regions.

%% **Trattoria Fauro**   🛖 AC VISA ⓪ AE ①
☺

via R. Fauro 44 ✉ *00197 –* ℰ *06 8083301 – Fax 06 8 08 33 01*
– closed Sunday   **M1**
Rest *–* Carte 26/34 €
♦ Fish ♦ Friendly ♦
A stone's throw from the Teatro Parioli, this friendly trattoria serves delicious fish
dishes, as well as specialities from Rome and Mantua, the owners' home town.

%% **Domenico dal 1968**   🛖 AC VISA ⓪ AE ①
☺

via Satrico23/25 ✉ *00183 –* ℰ *06 70494602 – info@domenicodal1968.it*
– Fax 06 70 49 46 02 – www.domenicodal1968.it
– closed 20 days in August, Sunday and Monday midday from May to
September, Sunday evening and Monday the rest of the year   *Plan I* **C3**
Rest *– (number of covers limited, pre-book)* Menu 25/30 € *–* Carte 34/46 €
♦ Roman ♦ Family ♦
Roman cuisine and hearty dishes full of flavour are the specialities of this friendly,
family-run trattoria. The wood furnishings in the two small dining rooms add to the
warm atmosphere.

FLORENCE
FIRENZE

Population (est. 2008): 364 700 – Altitude: 50m

C. Belloli/MICHELIN

Never one to sully itself with a political or economic role, Florence has instead always stood for beauty, and represents Italy's greatest contribution to the world of arts: the Renaissance. The city itself is much like an open air museum, with churches and squares alongside the most precious of marbles. You may have read about Florence in Forster's books or see it in Ivory's film, yet nothing prepares you for the real thing, with its works of art of unparalleled beauty. The Duomo, Michelangelo's David, Botticelli's Venere and Ponte Vecchio: the postcard becomes reality. It is said that Cupid lives in Florence and it's hard to imagine a city more romantic than this; lovers visit from around the world while those not yet in love are thought to find their match here.

Tuscany is home to one of Italy's most celebrated cuisines, as well as gorgeous olive oil and those famous Super Tuscan red wines. They form part of the fiorentini's taste for life and pursuit of excellence. It's not by chance that the Italian language originated here and that the country's national poet, Dante, was born here too. Many suggest that this brilliance must be connected to the local diet, most notably the local white cannellini beans; try them for yourself and see…

LIVING THE CITY

Florence is surrounded by a ring of hills, the **'colli'**, and winding streets flanked with cypress and olive trees lead you to the heart of Dante's beloved hometown. The city centre and many of its monuments lie on the northern side of the **Arno**, a river closely connected with Florence's history and celebrated by poets throughout the years. The river is crossed by many beautiful bridges, **Ponte Vecchio** being the most famous, but, despite its beauty, the Arno has in the past wreaked havoc in the form of regular flooding which has caused huge amounts of damage to parts of the city.

In each area of Florence, civic and religious powers each occupy their own distinct site. **Piazza della Signoria** is home to the town hall, while the **Duomo** sits in the piazza of the same name at the end of **Via Calzaiuoli**, the city's most famous shopping street and home to some Italy's well-known brands. This area also boasts many magnificent churches. Cross one of the bridges to the south side of the city for a more relaxed, village-like atmosphere. Here you will find the **Palazzo Pitti** and the **Gardino di Boboli**. Walking eastwards will bring you to the **Piazzale Michelangelo**, which boasts probably the best views in Florence.

PRACTICAL INFORMATION

ARRIVAL-DEPARTURE

Amerigo Vespucci, Florence's airport, lies 5km outside of the city and a taxi to the centre will cost approximately €15-20. Alternatively, you can opt for a bus, which takes you to the Santa Maria Novella railway station, for €3-4.

TRANSPORT

If you are staying in the city centre the best and most interesting way to see Florence is by foot: most of the sights are within easy walking distance. Alternatively, one of the municipal orange buses will take you everywhere you need; €1,50 will buy you a 60 minute ride.

There are two main tourist offices in Florence; one is in Piazza Stazione (Santa Maria Novella), 4/a (tel. 055 212245), the other is close to Ponte alle Grazie in Borgo Santa Croce, 29r (tel. 055 2340444). More information can be obtained on the web at www.comune.fi.it or www.firenzeturismo.it.

EXPLORING FLORENCE

With so many things to see and do in Florence, it's hard to even scratch the surface in just a couple of days

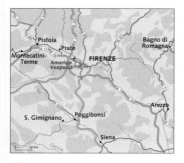

and a complete list of what's relevant would run into several pages. If you have the time, then just walk around and explore by yourself – you'll find yourself surrounded by art and beauty everywhere you go.

→ DIVINE BEAUTY & POWER

Piazza del Duomo, the city's religious heart, is a masterpiece of marble, technical audacity and unadulterated beauty. It's composed of three parts: the Duomo, the Baptistery and the bell-tower. The Duomo itself is a magnificent example of the interpretation of Gothic style that was popular in Florence at one time and its masterpiece, Brunelleschi's Dome, is a feat that defied the rules and limits of architecture of the age. The Baptistery epitomises Florence's taste for harmony and balance and the bas-relief on its doors are one of the city's greatest treasures. Last but by no means least is Giotto's bell tower which, aside from its impressive construction, will reward you for climbing those 414 steps with breathtaking views.

In Piazza della Signoria, a 13C square, sits the stone-built Palazzo Vecchio, from where the secular powers of Florence make decisions that govern the city. Via Calzaiuoli connects Piazza della Signoria to Piazza del Duomo and it is here where you'll find all those glamorous designer shops.

Italy's most famous museum, the Uffizi, is located within a 16C Vasari Palazzo – a masterpiece of beauty with its two parallel wings – and started life as offices (uffizi) for the Medicean administration. The beauty of the construction along with the family's love for art, later convinced Francesco I to open it to the public in 1591. Today, a unique collection of artwork is on display to the public, distributed throughout 45 halls. Don't miss the three 'Madonne in Maestà' by Cimabue, Giotti and Duccio (room 2); the 'Nascita di Venere' and the 'Primavera' in Botticelli's Rooms (10-14); Leonardo da Vinci's 'L'Annunciazione' and 'L'Adorazione dei Magi' (room 15); or Tiziano's 'Venere d'Urbino' (room 28). If Florence is the heart of the Renaissance, then the Uffizi museum is the heart of Florence.

The city's most famous bridge – Ponte Vecchio – is also its oldest, dating back to 1345 and the only bridge to survive the German bombings of World War II. It stands unique, with shops and sellers flanking both sides. Butchers once occupied these shops but now they've been replaced mostly by goldsmiths. Even if the jewellery is a little too rich for your taste, then at least it's free to enjoy the romantic atmosphere that has seduced lovers over the years.

"Another Renaissance Palazzo" you may say…but this one is special; across the Ponte Vecchio towards the southern bank of the Arno, it's one of the most imposing in Florence. Its story starts with the Pitti family, ranked in the 15C among the city's most influential families together with the Medici. In an endless struggle to prove their wealth, the Pitti's ambition to build a bigger house than their rivals' brought them to financial ruin. Ironically, the Palazzo they built was then bought by the Medici themselves, who amassed an astonishing collection of works of art. Housed in the Galleria Palatina inside the Palazzo, the collection comprises paintings from the 16C to the 18C, including pieces by Raffaello and Tiziano.

→ MAGNIFICENT LORENZO

If there is one person who truly represents the city it is Lorenzo il Magnifico. Part of the Medici family who ruled Florence for more than three centuries, Lorenzo was only 20 years old when he took on the role of governing the city. Refusing every sort of official power he became a true principe and his ability as a diplomat became famous throughout Europe. The people loved him and he was hailed as a saviour after he saved Florence from invasion during the Guerra de' Pazzi. Two years after his death in 1492, Italy was invaded by Carlo VIII and one of the most magnificent periods in Florence came to an end.

No one ever matched his love for the arts and during his reign Florence became one of Europe's most influential intellectual and artistic centres. Lorenzo himself was a writer and poet, and throughout his reign he was surrounded by the best painters and sculptors of the time. He famously invited people to 'perché di doman non c'è certezza' – enjoy the best of life – because no one knows what the future holds. He also opened a school for artists that saw the young Michelangelo amongst its scholars. The legacy of this golden age has made Florence world famous: Santa Maria Novella and San Lorenzo's 'Cappelle' and 'Biblioteca Medicea Laurenziana' are only a few examples of this magnificent era.

CALENDAR HIGHLIGHTS

Florence's calendar revolves mainly around events connected with the city's rich past, many of which will be particularly appreciated by those looking to gain a deeper insight into its history. For example, The Piazza del Duomo plays host to a spectacular Easter celebration, which includes a procession of Renaissance costumes. Still going strong every April after 70 years is the handicraft exposition; while May sees the Trofeo Marzocco,

a flag-waving competition. Those interested in more sporting activities should come in mid June to witness the passions engendered by a vital football match. Firework displays in Piazzale Michelangelo happen on the 24th June; while October is usually dedicated to various theatrical events. Towards the end of the year, Pitti Immagine attracts thousands of fashion lovers, so make sure you book your hotel well in advance.

EATING OUT

Tuscan food is one of the most famous and highly regarded of Italy's regional cuisines and it will come as no surprise to learn that some of the best examples are to be found here in Florence. Soups are particularly renowned and often combine popular ingredients; don't miss pappa col pomodoro – made with bread and tomatoes – or ribollita – made from cannellini, a local variety of beans, black cabbage, bread and other vegetables. You will no doubt have noticed that bread is an important feature of the Tuscan cuisine but don't be surprised if it comes with no salt, as they still follow age old traditions dating back to a time when salt was too expensive to be used lavishly.

Pasta can certainly not be ignored; pappardelle con la lepre (with hare) and pici (a sort of spaghetti) are two of the most popular. Meat is a favourite for second courses : the fiorentina, a grilled T-bone steak which takes its name from the city, has now become a favourite nationwide. Beware, restaurants in tourist areas can be very pricey – for a quick, inexpensive meal you're better off opting for a pizza.

Wines are equally important in Florence as the cooking. Buying a Super Tuscan will obviously mean digging deep into the wallet ; however, you can find good value for money with a Chianti, a Morellino di Scansano or a Nobile di Montepulciano – the Brunello di Montepulciano is usually more expensive and ranked amongst the best red wines. If price is not an issue, then opt for a Ornellaia, Sassicaia, Solaia or Tignanello.

FLORENCE IN...

→ **ONE DAY**
  Piazza della Signoria, Via Calzaiuoli, the Duomo, Santa Croce, Ponte Vecchio, the Galleria dell'Accademia

→ **TWO DAYS**
  The Uffizi, Santa Maria Novella, San Lorenzo

→ **THREE DAYS**
  Palazzo Pitti and the Galleria Palatina, Giardino di Boboli, Santa Maria del Carmine, Piazzale Michelangelo

Don't worry too much about the time that you go to the restaurant. Although locals may lunch around 1pm and dine around 8pm, the great number of tourists and visitors to the city has encouraged restaurants to be very flexible about timings.

Tipping has become less and less customary amongst Italians, so don't feel obliged to leave anything extra. Prices have to be displayed outside the restaurant so you'll know what to expect ; a cover charge may occasionally be added.

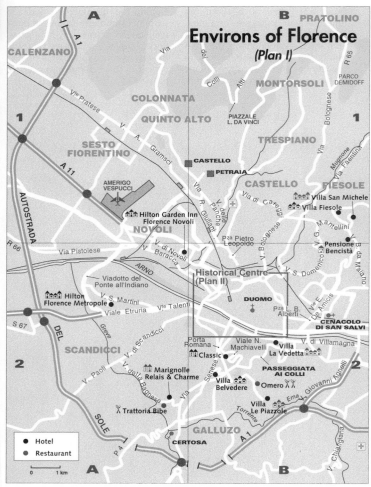

HISTORICAL CENTRE

Plan II

The Westin Excelsior

👪 ⚓ rm 🆎 ↤ rm 🕻 🖴 VISA ⦿ AE ⓪

piazza Ognissanti 3 ⊠ 50123 – ℰ 055 27151 – excelsiorflorence@westin.com
– Fax 055 21 02 78 – www.westin.com/excelsiorflorence **C2**

171 rm – ♥650/938 € ♥♥900/1108 €, ☲ 39 € – 9 suites

Rest Orvm – ℰ 055 27152785 – Carte 54/70 €

♦ Grand Luxury ♦ Palace ♦ Historic ♦

The lounge areas of this aristocratic palazzo overlooking the Arno are bright and elegant. Comfortable, stylish bedrooms decorated in shades of purple. This magnificent dining room is adorned with paintings on the walls, coffered ceilings and Carrara marble. Florentine specialities.

Grand Hotel 　　🔷 ♨ 🅰🄺 ⅘ rm 📞 💳 💵 🄰🄴 📴

piazza Ognissanti 1 ✉ *50123* – 🕾 *055 27161* – *grandflorence@luxurycollection.com* – *Fax 055 21 74 00*
– *www.luxurycollection.com/grandflorence*　　　**C2**
94 rm – ♛680/1023 € ♛♛930/1153 €, ⌂ 39 € – 13 suites
Rest *Incanto Café Restaurant* – 🕾 *055 27163767* – Carte 70/110 €
♦ Grand Luxury ♦ Historic ♦ Personalised ♦
Perfect for visitors in search of discreet elegance, this 19C hotel recreates the sumptuous atmosphere of the Florentine Renaissance. The restaurant, which specialises in Mediterranean cuisine, has a more modern atmosphere. The terrace overlooking the piazza is perfect for warm summer evenings.

Four Seasons Hotel Firenze 　🔷 ♨ 🅰🕥 🝧 🈷 🄰🄺 ⅘ rm 📴

borgo Pinti 99 ✉ *50121* – 🕾 *055 26261*　　🅂🄰 💳 💵 🄰🄴 📴
– *concierge.firenze@fourseasons.com* – *Fax 055 2 62 65 00*
– *www.fourseasons.com/florence*　　　**F2**
117 rm – ♛♛550/850 €, ⌂ 32 € – 46 suites　　**Rest *Pelagio*** – Carte 74/120 €
♦ Chain hotel ♦ Luxury ♦ Historic ♦
Surrounded by delicious botanical gardens, the hotel is composed of two buildings: "Palazzo della Gherardesca" and the "Conventino". You'll find elegance in both options: frescoes, bas-reliefs, stuccoes and walls covered with oriental silk paper. It's an exclusive stay leading you through a journey of art.

Savoy 　　🔷 🅰🃸 🄺 🝧 🅂🄰 💳 💵 🄰🄴 📴

piazza della Repubblica 7 ✉ *50123* – 🕾 *055 27351* – *reservations.savoy@roccofortecollection.com* – *Fax 055 2 73 58 88* – *www.roccofortecollection.com*
102 rm – ♛440 € ♛♛561 €, ⌂ 32 € – 14 suites　　　**D2**
Rest *L'Incontro* – 🕾 *055 2735891* – Carte 60/100 €
♦ Luxury ♦ Palace ♦ Historic ♦
This elegant, historical hotel is situated near the Duomo, museums and main fashion boutiques. The rooms here are spacious and comfortable, with attractive mosaics in the bathrooms.　Specialising in Florentine cuisine, this restaurant, which opens on to the piazza in summer, has a lovely atmosphere.

Montebello Splendid 　🔷 🔷 🅰🄺 ⅘ rm 🝧 🅂🄰 💳 💵 🄰🄴 📴

via Garibaldi 14 ✉ *50123* – 🕾 *055 27471* – *info@montebellosplendid.com*
– *Fax 055 2 74 77 00* – *www.montebellosplendid.com*　　**C2**
60 rm ⌂ – ♛190/320 € ♛♛230/580 €　　**Rest** – Carte 43/75 €
♦ Traditional ♦ Functional ♦
Surrounded by typical narrow streets and historical buildings, this sumptuous palazzo is adorned with different types of marble. Elegant internal garden.

Relais Santa Croce 　　🄺 ⅘ rm 📞 💳 💵 🄰🄴 📴

via Ghibellina 87 ✉ *50122* – 🕾 *055 2342230* – *info@relaisantacroce.com*
– *Fax 055 2 34 11 95* – *www.relaisantacroce.com*　　**E3**
20 rm ⌂ – ♛414/545 € ♛♛460/605 € – 4 suites　　**Rest** – Menu 70 €
♦ Luxury ♦ Palace ♦
Luxury and elegance are the hallmarks of this centrally located hotel. It offers a blend of the traditional and modern with its period furniture, luxurious fabrics and contemporary design.

Helvetia e Bristol 　　🄺 🝧 💳 💵 🄰🄴 📴

via dei Pescioni 2 ✉ *50123* – 🕾 *055 26651* – *information.hbf@royaldemeure.com* – *Fax 055 28 83 53* – *www.royaldemeure.com*　　**D2**
52 rm – ♛212/352 € ♛♛278/638 €, ⌂ 26 € – 15 suites
Rest *Hostaria Bibendum* – Carte 49/63 €
♦ Palace ♦ Luxury ♦ Personalised ♦
Situated near the Duomo and Palazzo Strozzi, this elegant 19C residence has retained its traditional atmosphere with authentic antiques and period Florentine paintings. Guestrooms with charming individual touches. Imaginative Tuscan cuisine is the hallmark of this small, elegant restaurant.

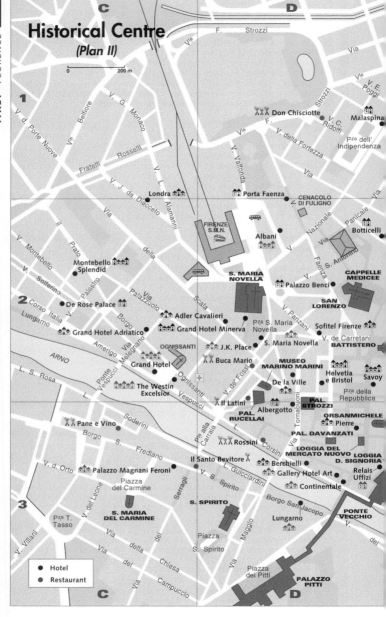

Historical Centre
(Plan II)

ITALY - FLORENCE

0   200 m

F. Strozzi

Via

V.le V. E. Poggi

Don Chisciotte   Malaspina

V. C. Ridolfi

V. della Fortezza

Pza dell' Indipendenza

Via

V.le Belfiore

V. G. Monaco

Rosselli

Fratelli

V. J. da Diacceto

Alamanni

Londra   Porta Faenza

CENACOLO DI FULIGNO

Nazionale

Panicale

Botticelli

FIRENZE S.M.N.

Albani

S. Antonino

Via

Faenza

CAPPELLE MEDICEE

della

Scala

S. MARIA NOVELLA

Palazzo Benci

SAN LORENZO

V. d. Porte Nuove

V. Montebello

Prato

Il

Palestro

Via Palazzuolo

Montebello Splendid

V. Sollerino

Corso Italia

De Rose Palace

Lungarno

Borgo

Amerigo

Grand Hotel Adriatico

Adler Cavalieri

Grand Hotel Minerva

Pza S. Maria Novella

V. Panzani

Sofitel Firenze

V. de Carretani

BATTISTERO

ARNO

L. S. Rosa

Ponte Vespucci

Via Melegnano

OGNISSANTI

J.K. Place

S. Maria Novella

MUSEO MARINO MARINI

Grand Hotel

Buca Mario

Ognissanti

Vespucci

De la Ville

Helvetia e Bristol

Savoy

The Westin Excelsior

V. de' Fossi

Il Latini

Albergotto

PAL. STROZZI

Pza della Repubblica

Tornabuoni

ORSANMICHELE

Pierre

Pane e Vino

Soderini

Borgo

S. Frediano

Pte alla Carraia

PAL. RUCELLAI

Corsini

PAL. DAVANZATI

LOGGIA DEL MERCATO NUOVO

LOGGIA D. SIGNORIA

Rossini

Via

V. d. Orto

Palazzo Magnani Feroni

Piazza del Carmine

Serragli

V. S. Spirito

Il Santo Bevitore

L. Guicciardini

Berchielli

Gallery Hotel Art

Continentale

Relais Uffizi

Borgo San Jacopo

S. MARIA DEL CARMINE

Pza T. Tasso

V. Villani

Via

della

Chiesa

S. SPIRITO

Piazza S. Spirito

Maggio

Lungarno

PONTE VECCHIO

V.

del

Via

del

Campuccio

Piazza dei Pitti

PALAZZO PITTI

● Hotel
● Restaurant

E

F

Lorenzo II Magnifico

Pza della
Libertà

V. L. da Vinci

Levagnini

Spartaco

V. Duca d'Aosta

V. S. Caterina d'A.

Cavour

Gallo

Vie

Pza
Savonarola

Pza G.
Vasari

1

V. d. Ruote

Zanobi

San

Taverna del Bronzino ✕✕✕

Lamarmora

Giacomo

V. d. Artisti

Matteotti

Via

V. d.

Cellai 🏨

V. - P. - A. Micheli

Venezia

Capponi

Via d.

27

Aprile

S. APOLLONIA

Piazza
S. Marco

CONVENTO
E MUSEO
DI S. MARCO

Via

Della

Guelfa

GALLERIA
D. ACCADEMIA

U

C. Battisti

SS. ANNUNZIATA

V. G.

Pinti

Piazzale
Donatello

V. G. La Farina

Robbia

Il Guelfo
Bianco

V. Cavour

OPIFICIO DELLE
PIETRE DURE 🏨

Ricasoli

Loggiato
dei Serviti

Giusti

Borgo

Alfieri

Viale

Four Seasons
Hotel Firenze 🏨🏨🏨

OSPEDALE
D. INNOCENTI

MUSEO
ARCHEOLOGICO

V. dei Servi

degli

Regency 🏨🏨

V. Martelli

PALAZZO
MEDICI-RICCARDI

V. della

Alfani

V. Colonna

Pergola

Pinti

Pza

d' Azeglio

2

V. G. B.
Niccolini

della

Mattonaia

Gramsci

DUOMO

MUSEO
DELL'OPERA
DEL DUOMO 🏨

Monna Lisa 🏨🏨

Via

Fiesolana

CROCIFISSIONE
DEL PERUGINO

V. Farini

V. dei Pilastri

SINAGOGA 🕍

CAMPANILE

Via dell' Oriuolo

Borgo

V. dei Pepi

Via di Mezzo

V. dei Calzaiuoli

Brunelleschi 🏨🏨

Alle Murate ✕✕✕

V. d. Corso

Borgo d. Albizi

V. Pietrapiana

la

Croce

Trattoria
Cibrèo-Cibreino ✕

V. Marzoni

🛈

Pza
Beccaria

V.D.Alighieri

✕✕
dei Frescobaldi

Borghese
Palace Art Hotel 🏨

Via

V. Verdi

✕✕✕ Cibrèo

Borgo

V. F. Paolieri

BARGELLO 🏨

Relais
Santa Croce 🏨

Allegri

CASA
BUONARROTI

Piazza
L. Ghiberti

V. F. Paolieri

PZA D.
SIGNORIA 🏨

Inpiazzadellasignoria

Osteria ✕
Caffè Italiano

V. dei Macci

V. dell'Agnolo

Giovine Italia

PALAZZO
VECCHIO

Enoteca
Pinchiorri
✕✕✕✕

Pza di
S. Croce

Baccarossa ✕✕

Ghibellina

GALLERIA
DEGLI UFFIZI

de' Benci

Borgo

Via S.
Giuseppe

✕✕✕ Ora D'Aria ●

V. Pietro Thouar

G. Amendola

MUSEO DI STORIA
DELLA SCIENZA

MUSEO
HORNE

V. dei Malcontenti

3

L. Gen. Diaz

Del Fagioli ✕

S. CROCE

Via d.

L.
Torrigiani

Pte alle
Grazie

L. delle Grazie

L. della Zecca
Vecchia

L.
Bardi

MUSEO
BARDINI

Serristori

Pza G.
Poggi

Pte S. Niccolò

E

F

ITALY - FLORENCE

Regency 🚐 🛋 AC 📶 VISA 🅾 AE ①

piazza Massimo D'Azeglio 3 ✉ *50121* – ✆ *055 245247* – *info@
regency-hotel.com* – *Fax 055 2 34 67 35* – *www.regency-hotel.com*
31 rm ⌑ – 📱334/424 € 📱📱350/566 € – 3 suites **F2**
Rest *Relais le Jardin* – Carte 51/70 €
♦ Luxury ♦ Personalised ♦
Originally opened to offer accommodation to the Florentine political classes, this
comfortable hotel has a tranquil, elegant ambience with a charming old-world
feel. This restaurant has two dining rooms: one elegant room overlooks the garden; the other is more ornately furnished with warm wooden panelling.

Albani 🎿 🛏 🕭 AC 📶 rm 📶 🚿 VISA 🅾 AE ①

via Fiume 12 ✉ *50123* – ✆ *055 26030* – *info.flo@albanihotels.com*
– *Fax 055 21 10 45* – *www.albanihotels.icom* **D2**
103 rm ⌑ – 📱150/365 € 📱📱200/450 € **Rest** – *(residents only)* Carte 34/54 €
♦ Traditional ♦ Functional ♦
Situated near the station, this hotel occupies an imposing yet elegant early 20C
palazzo. It has a stylish neo-classical atmosphere, a colourful decor and contemporary artistic touches.

Grand Hotel Minerva 🏊 🕭 AC ↳ rm 📶 🚿 VISA 🅾 AE ①

piazza Santa Maria Novella 16 ✉ *50123* – ✆ *055 27230* – *info@
grandhotelminerva.com* – *Fax 055 26 82 81* – *www.concertohotels.com*
102 rm – 📱145/300 € 📱📱155/500 €, ⌑ 15 € – 14 suites **D2**
Rest *I Chiostri* – *(closed Sunday)* Carte 40/75 €
♦ Palace ♦ Modern ♦
This hotel, one of the oldest in Florence, has a cosy atmosphere and elegantly furnished bedrooms. Works of art adorn the hotel, which also has a terrace with a
pool and splendid views of the city. Huge windows overlook the garden in the
main room of this restaurant, which serves traditional Mediterranean cuisine.

Lungarno 🕭 AC ↳ rm 📶 🚿 VISA 🅾 AE ①

borgo San Jacopo 14 ✉ *50125* – ✆ *055 27261* – *lungarnohotels@
lungarnohotels.com* – *Fax 055 26 84 37* – *www.lungarnohotels.com*
73 rm – 📱📱341/660 €, ⌑ 25 € **D3**
Rest *Borgo San Jacopo* – ✆ *055 281661 (closed from 29 July to 3 September
and Tuesday) (dinner only)* Carte 57/70 €
♦ Business ♦ Personalised ♦
In addition to its superb location right on the Arno, this hotel has elegant rooms
decorated with individual touches, as well as a valuable collection of modern paintings. A bright, modern restaurant with splendid views of the river and Ponte Vecchio.

J.K. Place without rest 🕭 AC 📶 VISA 🅾 AE ①

piazza Santa Maria Novella 7 ✉ *50123* – ✆ *055 2645181* – *info@jkplace.com*
– *Fax 055 2 65 83 87* – *www.jkplace.com* **D2**
19 rm ⌑ – 📱250/350 € 📱📱250/500 € – 1 suite
♦ Luxury ♦ Personalised ♦
This luxury hotel is more like a private house with its lovely fireplaces and quiet
atmosphere. In the contrasting, yet harmonious decor find wooden flooring in
the corridors, soft armchairs, English style comfort and a hint of the 1970s.

Continentale without rest 🎿 🛏 🕭 AC ↳ 📶 VISA 🅾 AE ①

vicolo dell'Oro 6 r ✉ *50123* – ✆ *055 27262* – *continentale@
lungarnohotels.com* – *Fax 055 28 31 39* – *www.lungarnohotels.com*
42 rm ⌑ – 📱📱340/640 € – 1 suite **D3**
♦ Traditional ♦ Design ♦
This modern, elegant hotel built around a medieval tower has a fine view of the
Ponte Vecchio. Brightly coloured, contemporary style interior.

ITALY - FLORENCE

Santa Maria Novella without rest ≤ 🕭 🗚 ¶º 𝘝𝘐𝘚𝘈 ⚅ 𝖠𝖤 𝖔

piazza Santa Maria Novella 1 ✉ *50123 –* ☏ *055 271840 – info@*
hotelsantamarianovella.it – Fax 055 27 18 41 99
– www.hotelsantamarianovella.it **D2**
71 rm ⊇ – ♛150/290 € ♛♛178/450 €
♦ Traditional ♦ Functional ♦

Overlooking the piazza of the same name, this hotel has a cosy atmosphere. There
are large public areas divided into smaller lounges, and elegant bedrooms decorated in different colours and styles.

Gallery Hotel Art 🕭 🗚 ⇔ rm ¶º 𝘝𝘐𝘚𝘈 ⚅ 𝖠𝖤 𝖔

vicolo dell'Oro 5 ✉ *50123 –* ☏ *055 27263 – gallery@lungarnohotels.com*
– Fax 055 26 85 57 – www.lungarnohotels.com **D3**
69 rm ⊇ – ♛♛330/517 € – 5 suites
Rest *The Fusion Bar-Shozan Gallery* – ☏ *055 27266987 (closed August)*
Carte 39/67 €
♦ Business ♦ Design ♦

African wood in the bedrooms, bathtubs covered with Middle Eastern stone, and
views of Florence on the walls give this hotel a museum-like atmosphere. The cosmopolitan art creates a highly contemporary feel. Contemporary style restaurant
serving 'fusion' cuisine. The emphasis is on creative and innovative dishes.

Brunelleschi ≤ 🗚 ⇔ rm 🕭 🐾 𝘝𝘐𝘚𝘈 ⚅ 𝖠𝖤 𝖔

piazza Santa Elisabetta 3 ✉ *50122 –* ☏ *055 27370 – info@hotelbrunelleschi.it*
– Fax 055 21 96 53 – www.hotelbrunelleschi.it **E2**
96 rm ⊇ – ♛145/255 € ♛♛215/400 €
Rest *– (closed Sunday) (residents only)* Menu 35/50 €
♦ Historic ♦ Functional ♦

This hotel is housed in the Torre della Pagliazza, a Byzantine tower that is one of
the oldest buildings in the city. The hotel is also home to a small museum with
exhibits dating from the Roman period.

Monna Lisa without rest 🚗 ᵮᵃ 🕭 🗚 🐾 𝘝𝘐𝘚𝘈 ⚅ 𝖠𝖤 𝖔

via Borgo Pinti 27 ✉ *50121 –* ☏ *055 2479751 – hotel@monnalisa.it*
– Fax 055 2 47 97 55 – www.monnalisa.it **E2**
45 rm ⊇ – ♛152/250 € ♛♛226/380 €
♦ Luxury ♦ Historic ♦

This medieval palazzo in the historic centre has an impressive staircase, terracotta
flooring and coffered ceilings. The bedrooms and public areas are furnished in
Renaissance style.

Palazzo Magnani Feroni without rest ᵮᵃ 🗚 ⇔ ¶º 🚗

borgo San Frediano 5 ✉ *50124 –* ☏ *055 2399544* 𝘝𝘐𝘚𝘈 ⚅ 𝖠𝖤 𝖔
– info@florencepalace.it – Fax 055 2 60 89 08 – www.palazzomagnaniferoni.it
12 suites ⊇ – ♛♛450/750 € **C3**
♦ Luxury ♦ Historic ♦

Only suites are available in this 16C palazzo, which in the past hosted lavish receptions during the French occupancy of Florence. Splendid panoramic views from
the terrace, which is transformed into a bar in summer.

Borghese Palace Art Hotel without rest ᵮᵃ 🕊 🕭 🗚 ℡

via Ghibellina 174/r ✉ *50122 –* ☏ *055 284363* 𝘝𝘐𝘚𝘈 ⚅ 𝖠𝖤 𝖔
– hotelmanager@borghesepalace.it – Fax 055 2 30 20 99
– www.borghesepalace.it **E3**
25 rm ⊇ – ♛110/200 € ♛♛120/350 €
♦ Historic ♦ Functional ♦

In the 19C mansion that was the residence of Carolina Bonaparte, this recently
opened hotel blends classical elegance and modern furnishings. The relaxation
area is pretty and full of character.

ITALY - FLORENCE

Londra 　 Là 🕸 & 🕮 ⫲ rm ℉ 🗼 🗟 VISA ⚼ AE ①
via Jacopo da Diacceto 18 ⊠ 50123 – ℰ 055 27390 – info@hotellondra.com
– Fax 055 21 06 82 – www.concertohotels.com 　 C1-2
166 rm ⫴ – ♥170/280 € ♥♥210/395 € 　 **Rest** – Carte 34/62 €
♦ Palace ♦ Design ♦
A stone's throw from Florence's congress and exhibition centres, as well as the
city's main sights of interest, this hotel has comfortable rooms with balconies.
Good conference facilities. Contemporary style dining room, plus a small lounge
for smokers.

Sofitel Firenze 　 & 🕮 ⫲ rm ℉ VISA ⚼ AE ①
via de' Cerretani 10 ⊠ 50123 – ℰ 055 2381301 – h1539-re1@accor.com
– Fax 055 2 38 13 12 – www.sofitel.com 　 D2
83 rm – ♥♥206/432 €, ⫴ 23 € – 1 suite 　 **Rest** *Il Patio* – Carte 36/56 €
♦ Traditional ♦ Functional ♦
Attention to detail and elegance are the hallmarks of this 18C palazzo situated
near the Duomo. Modern, well-soundproofed bedrooms and attentive service.
Good, traditional cuisine is served in this glass-roofed dining room whose walls
are adorned with painted landscapes.

De la Ville without rest 　 🕮 ℉ 🗼 VISA ⚼ AE ①
piazza Antinori 1 ⊠ 50123 – ℰ 055 2381805 – info@hoteldelaville.it
– Fax 055 2 38 18 09 – www.hoteldelaville.it 　 D2
68 rm ⫴ – ♥145/300 € ♥♥160/570 € – 4 suites
♦ Historic ♦ Functional ♦
This luxury hotel is situated in an elegant shopping street. It offers guests spacious,
completely renovated bedrooms decorated in period style and in shades of blue.

Adler Cavalieri without rest 　 Là 🕸 & 🕮 ℉ 🗼 ⚼ AE ①
via della Scala 40 ⊠ 50123 – ℰ 055 277810 – info@hoteladlercavalieri.com
– Fax 055 27 78 15 09 – www.hoteladlercavalieri.com 　 D2
60 rm ⫴ – ♥115/255 € ♥♥150/340 €
♦ Traditional ♦ Functional ♦
This elegant hotel is located in the immediate vicinity of the station. Excellent
soundproofing, bright guestrooms and cosy public lounges with wood furnishings.

Grand Hotel Adriatico 　 🚗 & rm 🕮 ⫲ rm ℃ 🗼 🅿
via Maso Finiguerra 9 ⊠ 50123 – ℰ 055 27931 – info@ 　 VISA ⚼ AE ①
hoteladriatico.it – Fax 055 28 96 61 – www.hoteladriatico.it 　 C2
126 rm ⫴ – ♥130/230 € ♥♥150/350 €
Rest – *(closed Sunday)* Carte 33/45 €
♦ Traditional ♦ Functional ♦
The hotel is conveniently located in the city centre. Large lobby and modern, functional guestrooms furnished in a simple yet elegant style. Private parking. Tuscan
and Italian specialities are served in two quiet, cosy dining rooms and an attractive
garden.

Pierre without rest 　 & 🕮 ℃ VISA ⚼ AE ①
via Dè Lamberti 5 ⊠ 50123 – ℰ 055 216218 – pierre@remarhotels.com
– Fax 055 2 39 65 73 – www.remarhotels.com 　 D3
44 rm ⫴ – ♥150/265 € ♥♥205/410 €
♦ Traditional ♦ Classic ♦
This recently enlarged hotel in the historic centre has elegant, comfortable and
fully equipped rooms furnished in period style.

Berchielli without rest 　 ≼ 🕮 ⫲ ℉ 🗼 VISA ⚼ AE ①
lungarno Acciaiuoli 14 ⊠ 50123 – ℰ 055 264061 – info@berchielli.it
– Fax 055 21 86 36 – www.berchielli.it 　 D3
76 rm ⫴ – ♥140/285 € ♥♥180/390 €
♦ Traditional ♦ Classic ♦
This hotel is a comfortable base from which to explore the centre of historic Florence. It has artistic coloured glass, magnificent views of the Arno and Ponte Vecchio, as well as cosy rooms decorated in warm, bright tones.

Il Guelfo Bianco without rest
via Cavour 29 ✉ 50129 – ✆ 055 288330 – info@ilguelfobianco.it – Fax 055 29 52 03 – www.ilguelfobianco.it **E2**
40 rm ☕ – 🚹120/155 € 🚹🚹150/250 €
◆ Family ◆ Traditional ◆ Personalised ◆
Situated in the heart of Medici Florence, this hotel is suitable for tourists and business travellers alike. It has comfortable bedrooms, some of which have frescoed ceilings. Public rooms decorated in contemporary style.

Cellai without rest
via 27 Aprile 14 ✉ 50129 – ✆ 055 489291 – info@hotelcellai.it – Fax 055 47 03 87 – www.hotelcellai.it **E1**
68 rm ☕ – 🚹110/160 € 🚹🚹129/235 €
◆ Family ◆ Traditional ◆ Classic ◆
Conveniently situated near the main cultural sights, this hotel has a cosy atmosphere, period furniture and magnificent views of the Florentine hills. Temporary exhibitions are occasionally held here.

Porta Faenza without rest
via Faenza 77 ✉ 50123 – ✆ 055 284119 – info@hotelportafaenza.it – Fax 055 21 01 01 – www.hotelportafaenza.it **D1-2**
25 rm ☕ – 🚹70/220 € 🚹🚹90/230 €
◆ Business ◆ Classic ◆
A small, elegant hotel in an 18C palazzo just a stone's throw from the Palazzo dei Congressi. Attractive, well-maintained rooms and impeccable, attentive service.

Inpiazzadellasignoria without rest
via de' Magazzini 2 ✉ 50122 – ✆ 055 2399546 – info@inpiazzadellasignoria.com – Fax 055 2 67 66 16 – www.inpiazzadellasignoria.com **E3**
12 rm ☕ – 🚹160/220 € 🚹🚹220/290 €
◆ Luxury ◆ Historic ◆ Personalised ◆
Elegant and full of character, this small hotel offers its guests a taste of the magic of Renaissance Florence. Excellent location near Piazza della Signoria.

Palazzo Benci without rest
piazza Madonna degli Aldobrandini 3 ✉ 50123 – ✆ 055 213848 – info@palazzobenci.com – Fax 055 28 83 08 – www.palazzobenci.com **D2**
35 rm ☕ – 🚹83/140 € 🚹🚹130/195 €
◆ Traditional ◆ Classic ◆
The 16C residence of the Benci family has been converted into an elegant hotel with modern, comfortable bedrooms and a delightful internal courtyard.

Botticelli without rest
via Taddea 8 ✉ 50123 – ✆ 055 290905 – info@hotelbotticelli.it – Fax 055 29 43 22 – www.hotelbotticelli.it **D2**
34 rm ☕ – 🚹70/150 € 🚹🚹120/240 €
◆ Traditional ◆ Classic ◆
This hotel is housed in a 16C palazzo near San Lorenzo market and the cathedral. It has retained many of its frescoed vaulted ceilings in its public areas. Elegant bedrooms and a small covered terrace.

Albergotto without rest
via Dè Tornabuoni 13 ✉ 50123 – ✆ 055 2396464 – info@albergotto.com – Fax 055 2 39 81 08 – www.albergotto.com **D3**
22 rm ☕ – 🚹81/270 € 🚹🚹155/335 €
◆ Historic ◆ Personalised ◆
In 1860 the English novelist George Eliot chose this hotel during her trip to Italy. Located in a mansion in the town centre, it offers peaceful and elegant rooms.

Relais Uffizi without rest 🕭   🔟 ⁱⁱ VISA ⚙ AE

chiasso de' Baroncelli-chiasso del Buco 16 ⊠ *50122* – ☎ *055 2676239* – *info@
relaisuffizi.it* – *Fax 055 2 65 79 09* – *www.relaisuffizi.it*   **D3**
12 rm ⊆ – ♦80/120 € ♦♦160/250 €
♦ Historic ♦ Personalised ♦

This medieval palazzo has a warm atmosphere and many historical features. Simple yet cosy rooms boasting large windows with views of the Piazza della Signoria. Recently extended.

Loggiato dei Serviti without rest   ᵢₕ 🔟 ⁱⁱ VISA ⚙ AE ⓞ

piazza strada statale Annunziata 3 ⊠ *50122* – ☎ *055 289592* – *info@
loggiatodeiservitihotel.it* – *Fax 055 28 95 95* – *www.loggiadeiservitihotel.it*
36 rm ⊆ – ♦75/150 € ♦♦95/240 € – 2 suites   **E2**
♦ Historic ♦ Personalised ♦

Built by the Servite monks in 1527, this building now houses a discreetly elegant, comfortable hotel. It has retained many of its original architectural features and has a tranquil atmosphere.

De Rose Palace without rest   🔟 ⁱⁱ VISA ⚙ AE ⓞ

via Solferino 5 ⊠ *50123* – ☎ *055 2396818* – *firenze@hotelderose.it*
– *Fax 055 26 82 49* – *www.hotelderose.it*   **C2**
18 rm ⊆ – ♦90/200 € ♦♦120/220 €
♦ Traditional ♦ Classic ♦

Housed in a Florentine palazzo near the Teatro Comunale, this hotel has large, elegant bedrooms, some of which are decorated with period style furnishings. Pleasant family atmosphere.

Malaspina without rest   ᵢₕ 🔟 ⁱⁱ VISA ⚙ AE ⓞ

piazza dell'Indipendenza 24 ⊠ *50129* – ☎ *055 489869* – *info@
malaspinahotel.it* – *Fax 055 47 48 09* – *www.malaspinahotel.it*   **D1**
31 rm ⊆ – ♦60/155 € ♦♦70/235 €
♦ Traditional ♦ Classic ♦

In the 13C the Malaspina family are said to have hosted Dante in the Castello di Fosdinovo. This tradition of hospitality continues today in a 19C building decorated in period style.

Enoteca Pinchiorri (Annie Féolde)   ᵢₕ 🔟 ⇆ VISA ⚙ AE
🌼🌼🌼

via Ghibellina 87 ⊠ *50122* – ☎ *055 242777* – *ristorante@enotecapinchiorri.com*
– *Fax 055 24 49 83* – *www.enotecapinchiorri.com*
– *closed from 15 to 27 December, 3 weeks in August, Sunday and Monday*
Rest – *(dinner only except Thursday-Friday-Saturday)*   **E3**
Menu 200/300 € – Carte 225/295 €
Spec. Agnolotti di polenta con code di scampi, pomodorini canditi, olive nere e origano. Spalla d'agnello gratinata alle erbe con scalogni in agrodolce e patate glassate. Spirale di limone, purea di more su disco di cocco e sorbetto al limone ricoperto di perle alle more.
♦ Modern ♦ Luxury ♦

Spectacular from the entrance, it is Florence's gastronomic treasure. Art blends in the cuisine into a combination of Tuscan and creative twists. Legendary wine cellar.

Don Chisciotte   🔟 ⇆ VISA ⚙ AE ⓞ

via Ridolfi 4 r ⊠ *50129* – ☎ *055 475430* – *info@ristorantedonchisciotte.it*
– *Fax 055 48 53 05* – *www.ristorantedonchisciotte.it*
– *closed August, Sunday, Monday at midday*   **D1**
Rest – Carte 41/68 €
♦ Modern ♦ Formal ♦

Situated near the lower fortress, this simple and elegant restaurant specialises in creative interpretations of traditional Tuscan dishes. Good wine list.

ITALY • FLORENCE

Cibrèo
XXX   🔥 AC ⇔ VISA ☺☺ AE ①

via A. Del Verrocchio 8/r ✉ *50122 – ℰ 055 2341100 – cibreo.fi@tin.it*
– Fax 055 24 49 66
*– closed from 31 December to 7 January, from 29 July to 3 September, Sunday
and Monday*   **F3**
Rest – Menu 71 €
♦ Tuscany ♦ Formal ♦
This restaurant is a perennial favourite due to its informal, elegant atmosphere,
friendly young staff and excellent, imaginative dishes based on traditional cuisine.

Rossini
XXX   🔥 AC VISA ☺☺ AE ①

lungarno Corsini 4 ✉ *50123 – ℰ 055 2399224 – info@ristoranterossini.it*
– Fax 055 2 71 79 90 – www.ristoranterossini.it
– closed Wednesday   **D3**
Rest – Menu 100 € – Carte 86/122 €
♦ Modern ♦ Formal ♦
The short distance from Ponte Vecchio and the historic literary background are the
cornerstones of this refined restaurant where the traditional cuisine meets new
approaches.

Alle Murate
XXX   AC VISA ☺☺ AE ①

via del Proconsolo 16 r ✉ *50122 – ℰ 055 240618 – info@allemurate.it*
– Fax 055 28 89 50 – www.allemurate.it
– closed Christmas, 16 February - 10 March and Monday   **E2-3**
Rest – *(dinner only)* Menu 60/90 € – Carte 66/101 €
♦ Modern ♦ Intimate ♦
Vaulted, frescoed ceilings, archaeological remains and modern, refined elegance:
the perfect place for a candle lit dinner. Contemporary cuisine.

Ora D'Aria
XXX   AC VISA ☺☺ AE

Via Ghibellina 3/C r ✉ *50126 – ℰ 055 2001699 – prenotazioni@
oradariaristorante.com – www.oradariaristorante.com*
– closed from 1 to 7 January, August and Sunday   **F3**
Rest – *(dinner only) (booking essential)* Menu 50/65 € – Carte 52/68 €
♦ Modern ♦ Formal ♦
The name explains its position and evokes the intention of its cuisine. Near the old
gaol, it offers a relaxing and peaceful break from the everyday hustle and bustle.

Taverna del Bronzino
XXX   AC VISA ☺☺ AE

via delle Ruote 25/27 r ✉ *50129 – ℰ 055 495220 – tavernadelbronzino@
rabottiumberto.191.it – Fax 055 4 62 00 76*
– closed Christmas, Easter, August and Sunday   **E1**
Rest – Carte 53/68 € ⊞
♦ Tuscany ♦ Family ♦
Housed in a 16C palazzo, this restaurant specialises in traditional Tuscan cuisine.
Elegant setting, friendly, attentive service and a real passion for good food.

Baccarossa
XX   AC VISA ☺☺ AE

via Ghibellina 46/r ✉ *50122 – ℰ 055240620 – info@baccarossa.it*
– Fax 055 2 00 99 56 – www.baccarossa.it
– closed 25-26 December and Mondays   **F3**
Rest – *(dinner only)* Carte 58/85 €
♦ Fish ♦ Family ♦
This elegant bistro-style wine bar serves delicious Mediterranean cuisine centred
entirely on fish. It is decorated in bright colours and furnished with wooden tables.

Buca Mario
XX   VISA ☺☺ AE ①

piazza Degli Ottaviani 16 r ✉ *50123 – ℰ 055 214179 – bucamario@
bucamario.it – Fax 055 2 64 73 36 – www.bucamario.it*
– closed 11 - 22 December and 18 - 30 August   **D2**
Rest – *(dinner only except Saturday and Sunday)* Carte 45/68 €
♦ Tuscany ♦ Family ♦
Housed in the cellars of the Palazzo Niccolini, this typical Florentine restaurant was
opened in 1886. It is popular with tourists who come here to sample the traditional
Tuscan cuisine.

XX
😊
Pane e Vino
AC VISA ᴏᴼ ᴼ

piazza di Cestello 3 rosso ⊠ *50125 –* ☏ *055 2476956 – paneevino@yahoo.it*
– Fax 055 2 47 69 56 – www.ristorantepaneevino.it
– closed from 10 to 24 August and Sunday   **C3**
Rest – *(dinner only)* Carte 34/48 €
♦ Tuscany ♦ Family ♦
Friendly, well maintained and furnished with a curious wooden mezzanine. This
pleasant establishment offers creatively reinterpreted traditional regional
cuisine.

XX
dei Frescobaldi
AC VISA ᴏᴼ

via dè Magazzini 2/4 r ⊠ *50122 –* ☏ *055 284724*
– ristorantefirenze@frescobaldi.it – Fax 055 2 65 65 35
– www.deifrescobaldi.it
– closed from 1 to 7 January, from 10 to 31 August, Sunday and Monday
lunchtime   **E3**
Rest – *(booking essential)* Carte 38/51 € ᵇᵇ
♦ Tuscany ♦ Friendly ♦
For this wine producer the jump to restaurant services has been an adventure.
The result is two inviting rooms of stone and wood to savour regional and other
dishes.

X
😊
Il Santo Bevitore
⇔ VISA ᴏᴼ

via Santo Spirito 64/66 r ⊠ *50125 –* ☏ *055 211264 – info@ilsantobevitore.com*
– Fax 055 21 12 64 – www.ilsantobevitore.com
– closed from 10 to 20 August and Sunday at midday   **C3**
Rest – Carte 24/45 €
♦ Tuscany ♦ Wine bar ♦
Young and welcoming establishment, in a prominent position in the Sanfrediano
quarter. The cuisine is in the Tuscan tradition with some interesting touches of
creativity. Good value for money.

X
Osteria Caffè Italiano
AC ⇔ VISA ᴏᴼ

via Isola delle Stinche 11 ⊠ *50122 –* ☏ *055 289368 – info@caffeitaliano.it*
– Fax 055 28 89 50 – www.caffeitaliano.it
– closed Monday   **E3**
Rest – Carte 34/45 € ᵇᵇ
♦ Italian ♦ Friendly ♦
Housed in the 14C Palazzo Salviati, this typical, informal restaurant has a number of
small dining rooms. Regional and Italian cuisine, accompanied by a fine choice of
wines.

X
😊
Trattoria Cibrèo-Cibreino
AC VISA ᴏᴼ AE ᴼ

via dei Macci 122/r ⊠ *50122 –* ☏ *055 2341100 – cibreo.fi@tin.it*
– closed from 31 December to 7 January, from 29 July to 3 September, Sunday
and Monday   **F3**
Rest – Carte 26/33 €
♦ Modern ♦ Friendly ♦
Once past the queue at the entrance, you will find a charming dining room. It is
very simple and informal and furnished with small tables. Extravagant traditional
cuisine at competitive prices is served.

X
😊
Il Latini
AC VISA ᴏᴼ ᴼ

via dei Palchetti 6 r ⊠ *50123 –* ☏ *055 210916 – info@illatini.com*
– Fax 055 28 97 94 – www.illatini.com
– closed from 24 December to 5 January and Monday   **D2**
Rest – Carte 35/45 €
♦ Tuscany ♦ Family ♦
Tourists and locals queue at midday in order to eat in this trattoria, which is appre-
ciated as much for the cuisine as for the exuberant and informal atmosphere.

Del Fagioli   AC

corso Tintori 47 r ⊠ *50122 –* ℰ *055 244285 – Fax 055 24 42 85*
– www.localistorici.it
– closed August, Saturday and Sunday   **E3**
Rest – Carte 22/26 €
♦ **Tuscany** ♦ **Family** ♦

A typical Tuscan trattoria serving homemade, traditional Florentine cuisine. As well as the usual menu, the restaurant offers daily specials. The warm welcome and reasonable prices here make this an excellent choice.

ON THE HILLS   *Plan I*

Villa La Vedetta   ← 🚗 🛎 ᕯ AC ⁽ᵗ⁾ P VISA 🅾🅾 AE ⓪

viale Michelangiolo 78 ⊠ *50125 –* ℰ *055 681631*
– info@villalavedettahotel.com – Fax 055 6 58 25 44
– www.concertohotels.com   **B2**
11 rm – ♦♦299/980 €, � 25 € – 7 suites
Rest *Onice Lounge & Restaurant* – *(closed 2 weeks in January and Monday)*
Carte 85/146 € 🍴
♦ **Grand Luxury** ♦ **Design** ♦

Situated on top of a hill, this patrician villa has a large terrace with splendid views of the city. The interior is elegant and spacious and all the bedrooms have individual touches. Two large windows open onto the garden of this elegant restaurant, which has satin covered chairs and glass tables.

Villa Belvedere *without rest* 🌿   ← 🕭 🛏 🍴 AC P VISA 🅾🅾 AE ⓪

via Benedetto Castelli 3 ⊠ *50124 –* ℰ *055 222501*
– reception@villabelvederefirenze.it – Fax 055 22 31 63
– www.villabelvederefirenze.it
– March-20 November   **B2**
26 rm ⊊ – ♦80/130 € ♦♦100/200 €
♦ **Historic** ♦ **Personalised** ♦

This elegant yet comfortable villa is the perfect base for a quiet stay: It stands in lovely gardens with a swimming pool, and has splendid views of the town and surrounding hills.

Villa Le Piazzole 🌿   ← 🚗 🛎 🛏 AC ⁽ᵗ⁾ 🅢 P VISA 🅾🅾 AE ⓪

via Suor Maria Celeste 28 – ℰ *055 223520 – lepiazzole@gmail.com*
– Fax 055 22 34 95 – www.lepiazzole.com
– closed from 20 December to 8 January   **B2**
14 rm ⊊ – ♦140/200 € ♦♦190/270 €
Rest – *(booking essential) (residents only)* Menu 35/95 €
♦ **Traditional** ♦ **Personalised** ♦

This 16C villa has been lovingly restored to recreate the elegant atmosphere of an old mansion. The guestrooms here are spacious and comfortable, providing all the facilities you would expect of a modern luxury hotel. There is also the feel of the peace and quiet of a private residence. Lovely views of the Chianti hills.

Classic *without rest*   🚗 AC ⁽ᵗ⁾ P VISA 🅾🅾 AE

viale Machiavelli 25 ⊠ *50125 –* ℰ *055 229351*
– info@classichotel.it – Fax 055 22 93 53
– www.classichotel.it   **B2**
20 rm – ♦110/125 € ♦♦160 €, ⊊ 8 €
♦ **Historic** ♦ **Classic** ♦

This small 19C villa behind the Boboli Gardens has been converted into a cosy hotel with elegant rooms furnished in period style. Surrounded by 100-year-old trees, the villa has an attractive breakfast room with a vaulted ceiling painted with flowers.

ITALY - FLORENCE

Marignolle Relais & Charme without rest ⚜   ← 🚗 🌲 AC ♿ 🛜 P VISA ⑤ AE ①

via di San Quirichino 16, Marignolle
– ℰ 055 2286910 – info@marignolle.com – Fax 055 2 04 73 96
– www.marignolle.com   **A2**
7 rm ⌂ – ♦115/225 € ♦♦130/275 €
♦ Family ♦ Personalised ♦
This elegant residence in a delightful location in the hills boasts stylish rooms, each with individual touches and fine fabrics. Panoramic swimming pool surrounded by greenery.

Omero   ← 🌿 VISA ⑤ AE ①

via Pian de' Giullari 49 – ℰ 055 220053
– omero@ristoranteomero.it – Fax 055 2 33 61 83
– www.ristoranteomero.it
– closed 11 - 31 August and Tuesday   **B2**
Rest – Carte 39/49 € ❀
♦ Tuscany ♦ Friendly ♦
Enjoy typical Italian dishes in this traditional restaurant, which has been run by the same family for 30-years. Summer dining on the outdoor terrace with views of the surrounding hills.

Trattoria Bibe   🌿 P VISA ⑤ AE

via delle Bagnese 15 – ℰ 055 2049085
– trattoriabibe@freemail.it – Fax 055 2 04 71 67
– www.trattoriabibe.com
– closed from 21 January to 8 February, from 10 to 25 November
Rest – *(dinner only except Saturday and Sunday)* Carte 22/34 €   **A2**
♦ Tuscany ♦ Family ♦
Mentioned by the Italian poet Montale, this rustic trattoria serving traditional Italian cuisine has been run by the same family for almost two centuries. Outdoor tables in summer.

AT BAGNO A RIPOLI

Villa La Massa ⚜   ← 🚗 🌿 ₭ 🌲 ⚹ AC 🛜 ⚙ P VISA ⑤ AE ①

via della Massa 24 – ℰ 055 62611 – reservations@villalamassa.it
– Fax 055 63 31 02 – www.villalamassa.it
– 6 March-15 November
23 rm ⌂ – ♦270/455 € ♦♦425/505 € – 12 suites
Rest *Il Verrocchio* – Carte 64/125 €
♦ Luxury ♦ Palace ♦ Historic ♦
Standing in a tranquil setting surrounded by green hills, this 17C Medici villa enjoys spectacular views of the River Arno. The attractive interior has period furnishings and a charming old world atmosphere. A stylish restaurant with vaulted ceilings, columns and a large fireplace. The cuisine is traditional with special menus for children.

Villa Olmi Resort   🚗 ₭ 🌲 ⚹ AC 🛜 ⚙ P VISA ⑤ AE ①

via degli Olmi 4/8 – ℰ 055 637710
– info@villaolmiresort.com – Fax 055 63 77 16 00
– www.villaolmiresort.com
59 rm ⌂ – ♦265/330 € ♦♦325/410 € – 3 suites
Rest – Carte 62/80 €
♦ Business ♦ Modern ♦
An 18C villa with a recent addition, connected via an underground passage. Offers elegant and personalised rooms, furnished with antique pieces. In the dining room find antique chandeliers on the ceiling, a natural finish on the walls and fanciful Italian cuisine.

Villa San Michele ⌖ ◁ 🚗 🍴 L᷃ ☐ AC 📶 P VISA ◉◉ AE ①
via Doccia 4 – ℰ 055 5678200 – info@villasanmichele.net
– Fax 055 5 67 82 50 – www.villasanmichele.com
– 3 April-15 November   B1
46 rm ⌑ – 🛉737 € 🛉🛉946/1177 € – 6 suites   **Rest** – Carte 82/149 €
♦ Grand Luxury ♦ Historic ♦
This is a fine 15C building standing in its own park and garden. The atmosphere
has the special charm of a former monastery, the façade is very beautiful and the
landscape impressive. Cooking lessons are available. Splendid dining room with
views of Florence from the summer terrace. In low season, meals are served in
the internal cloister.

Villa Fiesole ◁ 🚗 🍴 ☐ & AC ☏ P VISA ◉◉ AE ①
via Beato Angelico 35 – ℰ 055 597252 – info@villafiesole.it – Fax 055 59 91 33
– www.villafiesole.it   B1
32 rm ⌑ – 🛉100/290 € 🛉🛉110/350 €
Rest – *(residents only)* Carte 43/87 €
♦ Traditional ♦ Classic ♦
A typical 19C Tuscan villa, a restructured hothouse and interiors featuring frescoed
ceilings combine to make this a particularly attractive hotel. One can also participate in cooking lessons.

Pensione Bencistà ⌖ ◁ 🚗 ↩ rm P VISA ◉◉
via Benedetto da Maiano 4 – ℰ 055 59163 – info@bencista.com
– Fax 055 5 91 63 – www.bencista.com
– March-November   B1
40 rm ⌑ – 🛉110/120 € 🛉🛉143/158 € – 2 suites   **Rest** – Menu 20/35 €
♦ Family ♦ Historic ♦
14th Century origins, an old villa among the olive groves, surrounded by large park
gardens and a terrace with a view over the town; family atmosphere and period
style furnishings. This simple, spotless restaurant serves typical Tuscan cuisine at
breakfast, lunch and dinner.

✂
🕲 **Tullio a Montebeni** 🍴 VISA ◉◉ AE ①
via Ontignano 48 – ℰ 055 697354
– closed August, Monday
Rest – *(dinner only in November)* Carte 26/54 €
♦ Tuscany ♦ Family ♦
Everything started in a village shop, as some warm dish to restore farmers and
hunters in the area. Today, the cuisine reproposes the same flavours and home
produced wines.

AT SAN CASCIANO IN VAL DI PESA

Villa il Poggiale ◁ 🚗 🍴 ☐ AC 📶 ṡÁ P VISA ◉◉ AE
via Empolese 69 (North-West: 1 km) – ℰ 055 828311
– villailpoggiale@villailpoggiale.it – Fax 055 8 29 42 96
– www.villailpoggiale.it
– closed February
20 rm – 🛉130/200 € 🛉🛉150/240 € – 4 suites
Rest – *(April-1 November) (dinner only) (residents only)* Menu 28 €
♦ Family ♦ Historic ♦
Historic 16th century inn nestled in the wonderfully attractive hills of the Tuscan
countryside. A dream vacation in original surroundings at a very fair price. Elegant
restaurant where the emphasis is on delicious regional cuisine.

XXXX   **La Tenda Rossa** (Salcuni e Santandrea)   AC VISA OO AE OD
☘
piazza del Monumento 9/14 – *☎ 055 826132* – *info@latendarossa.it*
– Fax 055 82 52 10 – *www.latendarossa.it*
– closed Christmas, 9 to 24 August, Sunday and Monday midday
Rest – Menu 65/120 € – Carte 78/100 € ℮
Spec. Mattonella di capasanta in vellutata di carciofo alla maggiorana con
squacquerone e polvere di pane nero tostato. Petto di piccione farcito con
le sue rigaglie con tartufo nero e coscetta croccante in foglia di spinaci.
Crema di gianduia bruciata con cannoli al mandarino e salsa di cioccolato
bianco al ginepro.
♦ Modern ♦ Luxury ♦
Italian restaurants are traditionally family-run, and three families run this one! Its
quality of service and the food is three times as good.

AT THE AIRPORT   *Plan I*

   Hilton Florence Metropole   ♿ AC ↛ rm ☎ ⚼ P ⛰
via del Cavallaccio 36 ✉ *50142* – *☎ 055 78711*   VISA OO AE OD
– res.florencemetropole@hilton.com – *Fax 055 78 71 80 20*
– www.florencemetropole.hilton.com   **A2**
208 rm – ♟130/340 € ♟♟150/370 €, ∢ 15 € – 4 suites
Rest – *(residents only)*
♦ Business ♦ Chain hotel ♦ Modern ♦
A modern hotel with easy access to the airport. The bedrooms and public areas
here are furnished in minimalist style. Spacious conference centre. Situated on
the first floor, this spacious modern restaurant has large windows and pleasant
natural lighting.

  Hilton Garden Inn Florence Novoli   ♿ AC ↛ rm 🖥 ☏
via Sandro Pertini 2/9, Novoli ✉ *50127* – *☎ 055 42401*   VISA OO AE OD
– flrnv-salesadm@hilton.com – *Fax 055 42 40 20 20*
– www.florencenovoli.stayhgi.com   **A2**
121 rm – ♟110/210 € ♟♟130/210 €, ∢ 12 €   **Rest** *City* – Carte 45/57 €
♦ Business ♦ Chain hotel ♦ Modern ♦
A modern building near the motorway, ideal for a business clientele, offers bright
and airy common areas. Comfortable rooms furnished in an exquisite modern
style. Equipped with all the latest accessories.

MILAN
MILANO

Population (est. 2007): 1 303 000 (conurbation 3 884 000) – Altitude: 122m

Ph. Renault/HEMIS.fr

If it's the romantic charm of places like Venice, Florence or Rome you're looking for, then best avoid Milan. If you're hankering for a permanent panorama of Renaissance chapels, palazzi, shimmering canals and bastions of fine art, then you're in the wrong place. What Milan does is relentless fashion, churned out with oodles of attitude and style. Italy's second largest city is constantly reinventing itself, and when Milan does a makeover, it invariably does it with flair and panache.

That's not to say that Italy's capital of fast money and fast fashion doesn't have an eye for its past. The centrepiece of the whole city is the magnificent gleaming white Duomo, which took five hundred years to complete, while up *la via* a little way, La Scala is quite simply the world's most famous opera house. But this city is known primarily for its sleek and modern towers, many housing the very latest threads from the very latest fashion gurus. There are cutting-edge art galleries here, rubbing shoulders with space-age spas and bars, some of them opened by exclusive high-street designers. You know you've arrived in Milan not so much when you stare at a Renaissance piece of art as when you take an *aperitivo* at cocktail hour in a snazzy bar.

519

LIVING THE CITY

When you see the great bulk of the **Duomo**, you know you're in the centre of landlocked Milan. Just north lies **Brera,** with its much prized old-world charm, and **Quadrilatero d'Oro**, with no little new-world glitz. The popular **Giardini Pubblici** are a little way fur-ther north east from here. South of the centre is the **Navigli** quarter, home to rejuvenated Middle Age canals, while to the west are the green lungs of the **Parco Sempione.** The artily trendy neighbourhood of **Lambrate** is way up to the north east of Milan.

PRACTICAL INFORMATION

ARRIVAL-DEPARTURE

Malpensa Airport is 48km northwest of the city and Linate Airport 7km east. A train connects Malpensa with Stazione Cadorna every 30min which takes 40min, while a taxi will cost around €70. From Linate take the Airport bus no. 73 to Piazza San Babila metro station (every 10min, time 25min).

TRANSPORT

The best way to get about Milan is by bus, tram or metro. Tickets are valid for one metro ride, or seventy five minutes of travel on buses or trams. You can also purchase books of ten tickets, or unlimited one-day or two-day passes. Buy them at metro stations, kiosks, bars or tobacconists.

The metro provides a fast and efficient service, with frequent trains running on three different coloured lines. If you don't fancy waiting around for public transport, then walking is also advised: although Milan may seem too big to conquer on foot, most of its attractions are based in the small and compact centre.

EXPLORING MILAN

Milan's fashion designers pride themselves on peering into the future and dreaming up the garments of tomorrow. But high up in the city centre you get the chance to project your own vision even further than them. Just climb to the roof of the mighty Duomo and take in the spectacular

views, which, on a clear day, will let you gaze on the Alps sixty miles away. Come back down to comprehend the wonders of a building which took half a millennium to complete. This immense Gothic cathedral, begun in 1387, reflects the whims of fashion over the centuries and is a surreal amalgam of architectural styles. The spires are capped by thousands of sculptures in an awesome embrace of High Gothic. Much of the building is marble, but the interior highlight, La Madonnina, is pure gold. It doesn't take very long to realise that this is the shade of choice for much of Milan: you'll see it in the glitter of handbags and the flash of credit cards. Cross the piazza and the sight of gold will be much in evidence at the **Galleria Vittorio Emanuele II**. Built in 1878, this fabulous salotto (drawing room) lays claim to being the first shopping arcade in Europe. For much more than a century, stylish Milanese have browsed in this elegant neoclassical structure with its landmark glass roof.

→ FADING GLORY

Head west for the city's most lauded artistic experience (but make sure you've booked first). Invariably most visitors will find their way to see Leonardo da Vinci's **The Last Supper**. It's not in a cathedral or church, but is painted on the wall of a convent dining hall at the **Santa Maria delle Grazie**, half a mile west of the Duomo. The effect of the years (over six hundred of them) and damp Milan winters has resulted in the masterpiece literally fading in front of the onlookers' eyes. But you can still read the apostles' reactions in their movements and positions; you can still admire the brilliant colours used in the original. Your appetite for high culture whetted, head a short distance north east to the city's very own castle stronghold, **Castello Sforzesco**. Built in the fourteenth century to protect Milan's assets, over the centuries its use was adapted to showcase what the city does best: creativity. Now it's the home to no less than ten museums, and some are well worth a visit. Particularly impressive is the **Museo d'Arte Antica**, which includes a fresco believed to be by Leonardo -Sala delle Asse - and Michelangelo's extraordinary, unfinished final work, Rondanini Pieta, which he toiled over for years until his death in 1564. There's also the **Photographic Archive**, full of fascinating pictures of Italian life dating back to 1840, and the **Achille Bertarelli Prints Collection**, which seems to show that before Milan was obsessed with fashion it was rather partial to postcards, maps and all kinds of printed ephemera.

→ PARK ART

Step out of Castello Sforzesco, and you're in one of the city's top green spaces - the Parco Sempione. It's a rambling quadrangle of grassy hillocks and leafy avenues named after philosophers and writers. Because this is Milan, there's also a temple to design here, **The Triennale,** where the way the temporary exhibitions are presented is often as impressive as the subject matter. More evidence that they like to mix relaxation and up-to-the-minute art can be found in the city's other main park, Giardini Publicci, northeast of the centre, where a double dose of culture lies in wait amongst the rose bushes and pebble paths. The **Galleria d'Arte Moderna** is chock full of Futurists and twentieth century Realists; next door the **Padiglione d'Arte Contemporanea** puts on the gutsiest and most daring exhibitions in town. Afterwards step back outside and enjoy an ice cream in the park.

The city's best art collection is in the Brera quarter, the one neighbourhood of Milan that breathes old-style Italian charm, with its low stucco buildings and cobblestone streets. This is the ideal setting for **Pinacoteca Brera**, which celebrates its two hundredth birthday in 2009. It contains over seven hundred years' worth of Italian art, including Raphael's Marriage of the Virgin, Piero della Francesca's Brera Altarpiece and Veronese's Last Supper (a very different take to Leonardo's!). Throw in the likes of Caravaggio, Canaletto, Titian, Tintoretto, Botticelli and Mantegna, and you may well convince yourself that, despite its best efforts, Milan does appreciate things other than shopping and fashion.

→ FOOLS' GOLD?

Mind you, if that really is the reason you're here, then you'll certainly have no trouble striking gold – quite literally, in the quarter north east of the Duomo, which the locals call Quadrilatero d'Oro, or 'Golden Quad'. This is the part of town where plastic is the only currency, and if you're here on a tight budget, then a visit will be for anecdotal or research purposes only. The 'Quad' lies along and between four lengthy streets, and has earned its gold status because of the outlandishly expensive boutiques all around here. The big design names are gathered in clusters; many are so exclusive they don't bother with price tags. The good news for those financially challenged is that it isn't really necessary to shop here: the primary pastime is to perfect your strutting.

For a complete contrast, go to the south of the city centre where, in Navigli, you'll find canals from the Middle Ages. This is a rather shabby but fascinating district; artists and designers are taking over the old warehouses, particularly in **Zona Tortona**, where you can pick up well-priced trinkets from the refashioned artisans' studios. A leisurely stroll along the main drag of Ripa di Porta Ticinese brings you into contact with antiques shops during the day and trendy bars by night.

→ DIVA

To 'do' Milan properly, there's only one way to finish the evening, and that's to take in a performance at **La Scala**. The legendary venue was completely refurbished in 2004, but the history lives on: in the eighteenth and nineteenth centuries it was normal practice for the audience to chat, gamble and walk in and out during shows, while up to the middle of the last century even Italy's top divas would shy away from performing here because of the cat calls and whistles that could come their way courtesy of the nation's harshest critics located in the upper tiers. Nowadays, the diva is safe: aficionados reserve their thoughts until the bar at intermission.

CALENDAR HIGHLIGHTS

Some locals would say that the Milan calendar means nothing until early December, when the opera season at La Scala gets underway. But if you can't grab a seat for a performance for love or money, you can instead get all at sea at the Milan Aquarium's The Sea In Milan (also in December), a series of aquatic activities with marine related exhibitions and art-based events. The Fiera Milano plays host to MiArt in March, an international modern art fair that gives you the chance to check out four fascinatingly different sections: Preview, Modern, Contemporary, and Art&Co. April is the time to head down to the canals for the Naviglio Grande Flower Market, when two hundred 'flower pros' from all over Italy set up a beautiful carnival of flowers and fragrance along the wharf complex. Something completely different in June: the Gods of Metal Festival at Idropark Fila, when heavy metal music reigns for two days. In the same month, the rhythms are of a very different nature at the Festival Latino Americando, in

MILAN IN...

→ ONE DAY
Duomo, The Last Supper (remember to book first), Brera, Navigli

→ TWO DAYS
Pinacoteca Brera, Castello Sforzesco, Parco Sempione, a night at La Scala

→ THREE DAYS
Giardini Publicci and its museums, trendy Lambrate district

the grounds of Datchforum: a South American village is set up to host not only top musicians from that continent, but also literature, art and films. June's a busy month in Milan: there's the Festa del Naviglio, with music, food and special events around the canals, and also Notte Bianca (on the third Saturday of the month) when a variety of concerts and performances go on right through the night. During September Music, they continue right through a whole month, and feature the work of famous composers, as well as the world's regional music.

Panoramica (also in September) is a top film festival featuring a selection of the best movies from the Venice and Locarno Festivals: get along to the Anteo or Multisala Plinius cinemas for the reel deal. More than twenty thousand visitors jog along to the Fiera Milano in October for a fitness fiesta at the Wellness World Exhibition, while the ambience is more on the decadent side the same month for the Celtic New Year celebrations, when the Castello Sforzesco is turned into a medieval north European site for traditional music and revelry.

EATING OUT

For a taste of Italy's regional cuisines, Milan is a great place to be. The city is often the goal of those leaving their home regions in the south or centre of the country; many open trattoria or restaurants with the result that Milan offers a wide range of provincial menus. Excellent fish restaurants, inspired by recipes from the south, are a big draw despite the fact that the city is a long way from the sea. Going beyond the local borders, that emphasis on really good food continues and the quality (if not always the number) of ethnically diverse places to eat is better in Milan than just about anywhere else in Italy, including Rome. Japanese restaurants are all the rage now and they're having a growing influence on menus here: raw fish is very popular. You'd expect avant-garde eating destinations to be the thing in this city of fashion and style, and you'd be right: there are some top-notch cutting-edge restaurants, thanks to Milan's famous tendency to reshape and experiment as it goes. For those who want to try out the local gastronomic traditions, risotto allo zafferano is not to be missed, nor either the cotoletta alla Milanese (veal cutlet), or the casoeula (a winter special made with pork and cabbage). Then, of course, there's the ubiquitous panettone, to be enjoyed at Christmas. Milanesi tend to eat earlier than diners in Rome, starting the evening meal at roughly eight o'clock. If you want to stay up that much later lingering with the beautiful people, your best bet is the bohemian Navigli quarter, with its unique atmosphere created by old fashioned houses and laidback canal side eateries. The bill will always include service charge.

→ HAVING A BALL AT THE GALLERIA

A couple of things you should know about the oh-so-stylish Galleria Vittorio Emanuele II. Architect Giuseppe Mengoni spent fourteen years working on this, his pet project, but died falling from the roof the day before it opened in 1878. Bring yourself good luck by rubbing your feet on the genitals of the bull in the central mosaic. Decades of grinding stilettos meant the bull required a recent touch up.

If you can't get enough of this century's art scene, then head out of town (fifteen minutes on the metro) to the suburb of Lambrate. The provocative and highly singular gallerias beckon you inside for audacious artworks and flights of fancy with a technological twist. What would Leonardo have made of it all?

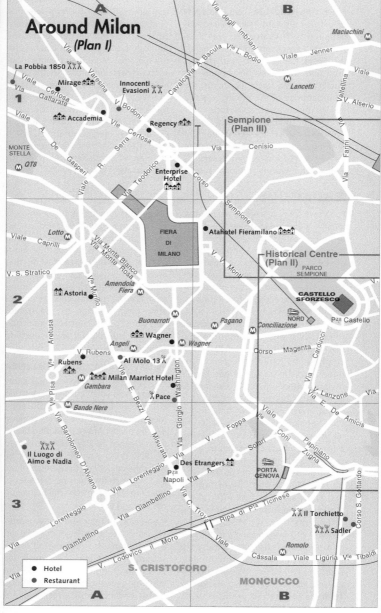

Around Milan
(Plan I)

La Pobbia 1850

Mirage

Innocenti Evasioni

Accademia

Regency

Enterprise Hotel

Sempione (Plan III)

MONTE STELLA

QT8

Lotto

Atahotel Fieramilano

FIERA DI MILANO

Historical Centre (Plan II)

PARCO SEMPIONE

Astoria

Amendola Fiera

CASTELLO SFORZESCO

NORD

Pza Castello

Buonarroti

Pagano

Conciliazione

Wagner

Angeli

Wagner

Rubens

Al Molo 13

Rubens

Milan Marriot Hotel

Gambara

Pace

Bande Nere

Il Luogo di Aimo e Nadia

Des Etrangers

Pza Napoli

PORTA GENOVA

Il Torchietto

Sadler

Romolo

S. CRISTOFORO

MONCUCCO

● Hotel
● Restaurant

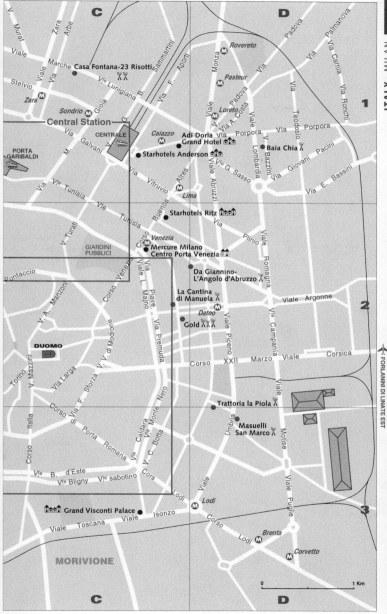

FORLANINI DI LINATE EST

525

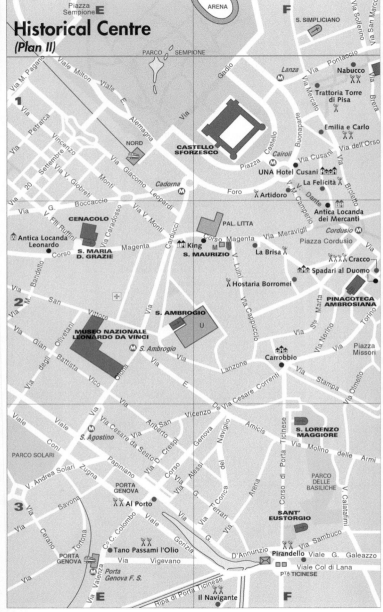

Historical Centre
(Plan II)

Piazza
Sempione **E**

F

ARENA

S. SIMPLICIANO

Via San Marco

Via Solferino

PARCO SEMPIONE

Viale Milton

Viale Pagano

Via M. Pagano

Gadio

Lanza

Via Pontaccio

Nabucco

Via Mercato

Buonaparte

Via Castello

Trattoria Torre
di Pisa

Via Petrarca

Via Vincenzo

Settembre Via V. Giobetti

Viale E.

Alemagna

NORD

Via Giacomo

Leopardi

CASTELLO
SFORZESCO

Cairoli

Emilia e Carlo

Via dell'Orso

Via Cusani

UNA Hotel Cusani

La Felicità

Via Dante

Via Brioletto

Via 20

Via G.

V. F.lli Ruffini

Boccaccio

Cadorna

Piazza

Foro

Artidoro

Camperio

Antica Locanda
dei Mercanti

CENACOLO

Via Caradosso

PAL. LITTA

Via Meravigli

Cordusio

Antica Locanda
Leonardo

S. MARIA
D. GRAZIE

Magenta

Corso

Via V. Monti

Carducci

Corso Magenta

King

S. MAURIZIO

La Brisa

Piazza Cordusio

Bandello

Via

San

Vittore

Oliveti

MUSEO NAZIONALE
LEONARDO DA VINCI

S. AMBROGIO

S. Ambrogio

V. Lanzi

Via Capuccio

Hostaria Borromei

Cracco

Spadari al Duomo

PINACOTECA
AMBROSIANA

Via S.ta Marta

Via Nerino

Via Torino

Via Gian

Via degli

Battista

Vico

Via E.

Via

Lanzone

Carrobbio

Via Stampa

Piazza
Missori

Via Olmetto

Via

Vicenzo

De Via Cesare Correnti

Amicis

Viale

Viale

S. Agostino

Via Cesare da Sesto

Crespi

Ariberto San

Genova

Naviglio

del

Corso di Porta Ticinese

S. LORENZO
MAGGIORE

Via Molino

delle

Armi

PARCO SOLARI

V. Andrea Solari

Coni

Zugna

Papiniano

Via

Corso Via

Alessi

G.

Via Conca

Ferrari

Arena

PARCO
DELLE
BASILICHE

V. Calatafimi

PORTA
GENOVA

Savona

Al Porto

C.C. Colombo

Viale

SANT'
EUSTORGIO

Via Cerano

Via Tortona

PORTA
GENOVA

Tano Passami l'Olio

Via

Vigevano

D'Annunzio

Pirandello

Via Sambuco

Viale G. Galeazzo

Via Valenza

Porta
Genova F. S.

Viale Col di Lana

PTA TICINESE

Ripa di Porta Ticinese

Il Navigante

E

F

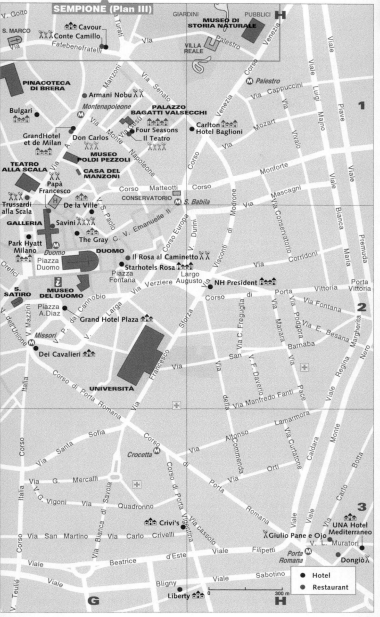

SEMPIONE (Plan III)

GIARDINI PUBBLICI

MUSEO DI STORIA NATURALE

V. Goito

S. MARCO

🏠🏠 Cavour
✗✗✗ Conte Camillo
Fatebenefratelli

V. Turati

Via

VILLA REALE

Palestro

Via

Venezia

Viale

Viale Luigi Majno

Plave

1

PINACOTECA DI BRERA

Via Manzoni

Via Senato

Ⓜ Palestro

Via Cappuccini

Via Mozart

Via Vivaio

Bulgari

Armani Nobu ✗✗

Montenapoleone

Ⓜ

Via

Monte

Via Tivoli

PALAZZO BAGATTI VALSECCHI

Four Seasons
Il Teatro
✗✗✗✗

Carlton 🏠🏠
Hotel Baglioni

Via

Corso

Monforte

Viale

Viale

GrandHotel et de Milan
🏠🏠

Don Carlos
✗✗✗

Napoleone

Don Carlos

MUSEO POLDI PEZZOLI

Mascagni

Via Conservatorio

Bianca

Premuda

Maria

TEATRO ALLA SCALA

CASA DEL MANZONI

Corso Matteotti
CONSERVATORIO Ⓜ S. Babila

Corso

Via

Papà Francesco

Ⓗ

Via Monte di Pietà

Via di Modrone

Porta

✗✗✗ Trussardi alla Scala

De la Ville

V. S. Paolo

Corso Europa

V. Durini

Via

Corridoni

Via Conservatorio

Porta Vittoria

2

GALLERIA

Savini ✗✗✗

C. V. Emanuelle II

Visconti di

Park Hyatt Milano 🏠🏠

The Gray

Duomo Ⓜ

DUOMO

Piazza Duomo

Il Rosa al Caminetto ✗✗
Starhotels Rosa 🏠🏠

Largo Augusto

NH President 🏠🏠

Via Fontana

Orefici

Piazza Fontana

Piazza Verziere

Corso

di

Porta

Via E. Besana

Margherita

S. SATIRO

MUSEO DEL DUOMO

Cannobio

V. Mazzini

V. dell'Unione

Piazza A. Diaz

Larga

Grand Hotel Plaza 🏠🏠

Storza

San

V. C. Freguglia

V. E. Daverio

Manara

Via Podgora

Barnaba

Via

della

Via Manfredo Fanti

Pace

Regina

Nero

Missori Ⓜ

V. P. da Cannobio

Dei Cavalieri 🏠🏠

Italia

Corso di Porta Romana

Francesco

Via

UNIVERSITÀ

Lamarmora

Corso

Sofia

Corso

Alfonso

Via Curtatone

Monte

Caldara

Botta

Sarfa

Via

Crocetta Ⓜ

di

Orti

Via

Via G. Mercalli

V. V. G. Vigoni

Via

Savoia

Quadronno

Porta

Romana

Viale

Carlo

Corso

Via San Martino

Via Bianca di Savoia

Via Carlo Crivelli

Via cassolo

Crivi's 🏠🏠

UNA Hotel Mediterraneo 🏠🏠

Via

d'Este

Beatrice

Giulio Pane e Ojo ✗
V. L. Muratori

Porta Romana Ⓜ

Dongiò ✗

Viale

Filipetti

Sabotino

Bligny

Viale

Liberty 🏠🏠

V. Teulié

Viale

● Hotel
● Restaurant

0   300 m

3

G   **H**

527

Four Seasons 🛗 ♨ ᵬ rm 🅰🅲 ⇙ rm ⁽ᵞ⁾ 🏋 🚗 VISA ⓒⓑ 🅰🅴 ⑩

via Gesù 6/8 ✉ 20121 – ⓜ Montenapoleone – ☎ 02 77088
– res.milano@fourseasons.com – Fax 02 77 08 50 00
– www.fourseasons.com/milan G1
93 rm – ♦638/726 € ♦♦759/869 €, � 36 € – 25 suites
Rest Il Teatro – see below
Rest La Veranda – Carte 67/134 €
♦ Grand Luxury ♦ Stylish ♦

This hotel, housed in a 15C monastery in Milan's "Golden Triangle", is one of the most elegant and exclusive places to stay in the city. The hotel has retained some of the building's original decorative features. Restaurant facing the interior garden. Refined atmosphere.

Park Hyatt Milano ᵬ ᵬ 🅰🅲 ⇙ rm ⁽ᵞ⁾ 🏋 VISA ⓒⓑ 🅰🅴 ⑩

via Tommaso Grossi 1 ✉ 20121 – ⓜ Duomo – ☎ 02 88211234
– milano@hyattintl.com – Fax 02 88 21 12 35
– www.milan.park.hyatt.com G2
109 rm – ♦510/660 € ♦♦630/780 €, � 35 € – 8 suites
Rest The Park – (closed from 3 to 24 August, Saturday at midday, Sunday) Carte 71/101 €
♦ Luxury ♦ Modern ♦

A lounge area crowned with a large cupola, public rooms decorated in light tones and a relaxing spa with a gym and Turkish bath are some of the features of this hotel housed in a late-19C building.

Grand Hotel et de Milan ᵬ 🅰🅲 ⁽ᵞ⁾ 🏋 VISA ⓒⓑ 🅰🅴 ⑩

via Manzoni 29 ✉ 20121 – ⓜ Montenapoleone – ☎ 02 723141
– concierge@grandhoteletdemilan.it – Fax 02 86 46 08 61
– www.grandhoteletdemilan.it G1
95 rm – ♦589/677 € ♦♦649/737 €, � 35 € – 7 suites
Rest Don Carlos – see below
Rest Caruso – (closed in the evening) Carte 47/62 €
♦ Luxury ♦ Traditional ♦ Stylish ♦

This hotel opened over 150 years ago. Big names in the field of music, theatre and politics have stayed in its elegant rooms that are full of charm. Bright restaurant dedicated to the great tenor, who recorded his first record in this hotel.

Carlton Hotel Baglioni ᵬ ᵬ rm 🅰🅲 ⇙ rm ⁽ᵞ⁾ 🏋 🚗

via Senato 5 ✉ 20121 – ⓜ San Babila – ☎ 02 77077 VISA ⓒⓑ 🅰🅴 ⑩
– reservations.carltonmilano@baglionihotels.com – Fax 02 78 33 00
– www.baglionihotels.com H1
83 rm – ♦560/660 € ♦♦610/970 €, � 34 € – 9 suites
Rest Il Baretto al Baglioni – Carte 75/90 €
♦ Grand Luxury ♦ Classic ♦

Refined features and period furniture, valuable fabrics with warm tones in the public rooms and in the bedrooms of a most elegant "bomboniera" in the heart of fashion conscious Milan. The restaurant has several, wood-panelled rooms, creating an air of quality and distinction.

Bulgari 🛗 ᵬ 🍴 🖥 ᵬ ⇙ rm ⁽ᵞ⁾ 🚗 VISA ⓒⓑ 🅰🅴 ⑩

via privata Fratelli Gabba 7/b ✉ 20121 – ⓜ Montenapoleone – ☎ 02 8058051
– milano@bulgarihotels.com – Fax 02 8 05 80 52 22 – www.bulgarihotels.com
49 rm – ♦550/690 € ♦♦650/790 €, � 30 € – 9 suites G1
Rest – Carte 58/118 €
♦ Luxury ♦ Stylish ♦

This recent addition to Milan's luxury hotels is decorated with the finest materials, creating an atmosphere of simple, discreet elegance. A charming garden comes as a pleasant surprise. This is an exclusive restaurant surrounded by greenery.

Starhotels Rosa

piazza Fontana 3 ⊠ *20122* – Ⓜ *Duomo* – ℰ *02 8831* – *rosa.mi@starhotels.it*
– Fax 02 8 05 79 64 – *www.starhotels.it*   **G2**
320 rm ☲ – ♥♥165/1300 € – 7 suites
Rest Il Rosa al Caminetto – see below
♦ Chain hotel ♦ Classic ♦
Just a short walk from the Duomo, this establishment offers a discreet elegance. It
has a spacious ground floor lounge with marble and stucco décor, well-designed
rooms, a conference centre, and health centre.

Grand Visconti Palace

viale Isonzo 14 ⊠ *20135* – Ⓜ *Lodi TIBB*
– ℰ 02 540341 – *info@grandviscontipalace.com* – *Fax 02 54 06 95 23*
– www.grandviscontipalace.com   Plan I **C3**
166 rm ☲ – ♥300/800 € ♥♥400/900 € – 6 suites
Rest Al Quinto Piano – Carte 42/86 €
♦ Business ♦ Classic ♦
This elegant hotel is housed in the extensive buildings of an old industrial mill.
Facilities include conference rooms, a delightful garden and a first-class fitness cen-
tre. As its name suggests, this restaurant is situated on the fifth floor. Creative, imaginative cuisine.

NH President

largo Augusto 10 ⊠ *20122* – Ⓜ *San Babila* – ℰ *02 77461*
– jhmilanopresident@nh-hotels.it – *Fax 02 78 34 49* – *www.nh-hotels.it*
253 rm ☲ – ♥130/430 € ♥♥150/480 € – 12 suites   **H2**
Rest Il Verziere – Carte 43/62 €
♦ Chain hotel ♦ Modern ♦
An international standard hotel for business travellers or tourists. It has attractive,
spacious lounge areas as well as facilities for fashion shows, business lunches and
conferences. The restaurant serves specialities from Lombardy, as well as Mediterranean-style dishes.

UNA Hotel Cusani

via Cusani 13 ⊠ *20121* – Ⓜ *Cairoli* – ℰ *02 85601* – *una.cusani@unahotels.it*
– Fax 02 8 69 36 01 – *www.unahotels.it*   **F1**
87 rm ☲ – ♥154/374 € ♥♥154/440 € – 5 suites   **Rest** – Carte 45/72 €
♦ Business ♦ Classic ♦
Located in the heart of the historic town centre, this hotel is in an ideal location for
business and sightseeing. It has simple and modern, very large attractive rooms.
Choose from classic Italian or international dishes at this cosy restaurant.

De la Ville

via Hoepli 6 ⊠ *20121* – Ⓜ *Duomo* – ℰ *02 8791311* – *reservationsdlv@*
sinahotels.it – *Fax 02 86 66 09* – *www.sinahotels.com*   **G2**
109 rm ☲ – ♥396/418 € ♥♥429/440 €
Rest L'Opera – ℰ *02 8051231* – Carte 45/70 €
♦ Luxury ♦ ♦ Classic ♦
Located near the Duomo, this chic hotel with warm surroundings is decorated with
marble and colourful silk. It has a relaxing swimming pool on the top floor covered
with a transparent dome. Ideal for after theatre dinner, this restaurant serves Mediterranean cuisine reinterpreted with a creative flair.

The Gray

via San Raffaele 6 ⊠ *20121* – Ⓜ *Duomo* – ℰ *02 7208951* – *info.thegray@*
sinahotels.it – *Fax 02 86 65 26* – *www.sinahotels.com*   **G2**
21 rm – ♥418 € ♥♥605/792 €, ☲ 37 €   **Rest** – Carte 63/78 €
♦ Luxury ♦ Design ♦
Near the Galleria, this elegant hotel's modern design has rooms with stylish touches. There is also a fitness centre. This cosy restaurant with a creative décor offers
a gourmet menu.

Spadari al Duomo without rest 🏨 ↔ ¶¹ VISA ⊕ AE ①

*via Spadari 11 ⊠ 20123 – **M** Duomo – ☎ 02 72002371 – reservation@*
spadarihotel.com – Fax 02 86 11 84 – www.spadarihotel.com **F2**
40 rm � – ¶178/368 € ¶¶198/368 €
♦ Business ♦ Design ♦
With its extensive collection of contemporary art, this small hotel combines comfort with a penchant for new and exciting forms of artistic expression.

Cavour 🏨 ↔ 🕭 🛎 VISA ⊕ AE ①

*via Fatebenefratelli 21 ⊠ 20121 – **M** Turati – ☎ 02 620001 – booking@*
hotelcavour.it – Fax 02 6 59 22 63 – www.hotelcavour.it
– closed August **G1**
113 rm ⊑ – ¶128/257 € ¶¶147/295 € **Rest Conte Camillo** – see below
♦ Business ♦ Functional ♦
This traditional, family-run hotel is situated near the city's main cultural sights, cafés and restaurants. It offers guests well-furnished, soundproofed rooms and excellent service.

Dei Cavalieri without rest 🏨 ↔ ¶¹ 🛎 VISA ⊕ AE ①

*piazza Missori 1 ⊠ 20123 – **M** Missori – ☎ 02 88571 – info@*
hoteldeicavalieri.com – Fax 02 8 85 72 41 – www.hoteldeicavalieri.com
177 rm ⊑ – ¶¶720 € **G2**
♦ Traditional ♦ Business ♦
Housed in an historical palazzo dating from the late 19C, this hotel has a relaxing atmosphere and attentive, efficient service. The elegant, comfortable rooms are furnished in contemporary style.

Grand Hotel Plaza without rest 🖪 🏨 ¶¹ 🛎 VISA ⊕ AE ①

*piazza Diaz 3 ⊠ 20123 – **M** Duomo – ☎ 02 8555 – info@*
grandhotelplazamilano.it – Fax 02 86 72 40 – www.grandhotelplazamilano.it
136 rm ⊑ – ¶160/370 € ¶¶160/400 € **G2**
♦ Business ♦ Traditional ♦ Classic ♦
A traditional hotel in the heart of the city, with large, tastefully furnished rooms, a lobby with a bar and piano, and a new fully-equipped gym.

Carrobbio without rest 🏨 🛎 VISA ⊕ AE ①

*via Medici 3 ⊠ 20123 – **M** Duomo – ☎ 02 89010740 – info@*
hotelcarrobbiomilano.com – Fax 02 8 05 33 34
– www.hotelcarrobbiomilano.com
– closed August and 22 December-2 January **F2**
56 rm ⊑ – ¶198 € ¶¶356 €
♦ Business ♦ Classic ♦
This recently renovated hotel is in a quiet district near the historic town centre and the Borsa. It offers rooms of different styles and sizes. Delightful winter garden.

Liberty without rest 🏨 🕭 VISA ⊕ AE ①

viale Bligny 56 ⊠ 20136 – ☎ 02 58318562 – reserve@hotelliberty-milano.com
– Fax 02 58 31 90 61 – www.hotelliberty-milano.com
– closed August **G3**
58 rm ⊑ – ¶100/300 € ¶¶100/400 €
♦ Traditional ♦ Stylish ♦
Near to the Bocconi University, an elegant hotel, with public areas inspired by the style from which they take their name and some antique furniture; many bedrooms with hydromassage unit.

Crivi's without rest 🏨 ¶¹ 🛎 🚗 VISA ⊕ AE ①

*corso Porta Vigentina 46 ⊠ 20122 – **M** Crocetta – ☎ 02 582891 – crivis@tin.it*
– Fax 02 58 31 81 82 – www.crivis.com
– closed Christmas and August **G3**
86 rm ⊑ – ¶130/250 € ¶¶190/350 €
♦ Business ♦ Modern ♦
In a convenient location near the metro, this comfortable hotel has pleasant public areas and traditionally furnished, reasonably comfortable and spacious guestrooms.

UNA Hotel Mediterraneo　　　AC ⁴⁄₊ rm ⁽ᵠ⁾ ⅜ VISA ⓭ AE ①
via Muratori 14 ⊠ 20135 – ⓜ *Porta Romana*
– ℰ 02 550071 – una.mediterraneo@unahotels.it – Fax 02 5 50 07 22 17
– www.unahotels.it　　　　　　　　　　　　　　　　　**H3**
93 rm ⌴ – ⁑108/268 € ⁑⁑108/315 €　　**Rest** *– (residents only)* Carte 32/42 €
◆ Business ◆ Functional ◆
This business hotel, situated near the metro in the Porta Romana district, is modern in style, with functional, comfortable and sound-proofed guestrooms.

King without rest　　　AC ⁽ᵠ⁾ VISA ⓭ AE ①
corso Magenta 19 ⊠ 20123 – ⓜ *Cadorna F.N.M. – ℰ 02 874432*
– info@hotelkingmilano.com – Fax 02 89 01 07 98
– www.mokinba.it　　　　　　　　　　　　　　　　**F2**
48 rm ⌴ – ⁑70/290 € ⁑⁑80/395 €
◆ Business ◆ Classic ◆
Housed in a six-storey building not far from the Duomo, this hotel has been renovated with opulent and elegant furnishings. The guestrooms, although not that spacious, are very comfortable.

Antica Locanda dei Mercanti without rest　　　⁽ᵠ⁾ VISA ⓭
via San Tomaso 6 ⊠ 20121 – ⓜ *Cordusio – ℰ 02 8054080*
– locanda@locanda.it – Fax 02 8 05 40 90
– www.locanda.it　　　　　　　　　　　　　　　　**F2**
14 rm – ⁑155/215 € ⁑⁑185/500 €, ⌴ 15 €
◆ Townhouse ◆ Family ◆ Personalised ◆
A small, cosy hotel, simple and elegant in style, and furnished with antique furniture. Many of the light and spacious guestrooms have a small terrace.

Mercure Milano Centro Porta Venezia without rest　　　よ AC
piazza Oberdan 12 ⊠ 20129　　　　　　　⁴⁄₊ ⁽ᵠ⁾ ⅜ VISA ⓭ AE ①
– ⓜ *Porta Venezia – ℰ 02 29403907 – booking@hotelmercuremilanocentro.it*
– Fax 02 29 52 61 71 – www.mercure.com　　　　　　　　*Plan I* **C2**
30 rm ⌴ – ⁑130/349 € ⁑⁑130/399 €
◆ Chain hotel ◆ Stylish ◆
The hotel is a few steps away from the cultural heart of the city. Set in a 19C house, it has Art Nouveau furnishings and elegant, comfortable rooms.

Cracco　　　AC VISA ⓭ AE ①
via Victor Hugo 4 ⊠ 20123 – ⓜ *Duomo – ℰ 02 876774 – info@*
ristorantecracco.it – Fax 02 86 10 40 – www.peck.it
– closed from 22 December to 10 January, 3 weeks in August, Saturday at
midday (all day from June to August), Sunday, Monday at midday
Rest *–* Menu 130/160 € *–* Carte 95/133 € ⅜　　　　**F2**
Spec. Marinara di pesce in foglie con verdure croccanti. Spaghetti d'uovo, aglio, olio e peperoncino. Rognone di vitello con ricci di mare e spugnole.
◆ Inventive ◆ Fashionable ◆
Decorated in a simple, modern style, this restaurant serves excellent contemporary cuisine with a focus on innovative and inventive dishes.

Il Teatro *– Hotel Four Seasons*　　　AC ⇆ VISA ⓭ AE ①
via Gesù 6/8 ⊠ 20121 – ⓜ *Montenapoleone – ℰ 02 77081435*
– luca.simbaldi@fourseasons.com – Fax 02 77 08 50 00
– www.fourseasons.com/teatro
– closed August and Sunday　　　　　　　　　　　　**G1**
Rest *– (dinner only)* Carte 78/103 €
◆ Modern ◆ Formal ◆
The restaurant, contained in the splendid premises of the Four Seasons hotel, is characterised by exclusiveness and class. The cuisine highlights interpretive creativity.

531

ITALY - MILAN

Savini
🍽️ 🔥 AC ⟷ P VISA ⊕ AE ⓪

galleria Vittorio Emanuele II ⊠ 20121 – Ⓜ *Duomo – 𝒞 02 72003433*
– prenotazioni@savinimilano.it – Fax 02 72 02 28 88 – www.savinimilano.it
– closed 10 days in January and 20 days in August **G2**
Rest – *(closed Saturday midday, Sunday)* Menu 95/125 € – Carte 75/113 € ⅋⅋
Rest *Caffetteria* – Carte 35/80 € ⅋⅋
♦ Inventive ♦ Luxury ♦
This perennial Milanese favourite has benefited from a recent facelift. The new
menu focuses on a fusion of innovative flavours and traditional regional specialities. Enjoy the informal atmosphere by the bar in the Caffetteria, which serves
pizza, salads and a range of specialities from Lombardy.

Don Carlos – Grand Hotel et de Milan
AC VISA ⊕ AE ⓪

via Manzoni 29 ⊠ 20121 – Ⓜ *Montenapoleone – 𝒞 02 72314640 – info@*
ristorantedoncarlos.it – Fax 02 86 46 08 61 – www.ristorantedoncarlos.it
– closed August and Sunday **G1**
Rest – *(dinner only)* Carte 58/82 €
♦ Lombard-piedmontese ♦ Formal ♦
A charming restaurant with a quiet atmosphere and elegant decor, including
wood panelling, red appliqué and pictures and photos dating from the time of
Verdi. Fine seasonal and regional cuisine with a creative touch.

Conte Camillo – Hotel Cavour
AC VISA ⊕ AE ⓪

via Fatebenefratelli 21 ⊠ 20121 – Ⓜ *Turati – 𝒞 02 6570516 – booking@*
hotelcavour.it – Fax 02 6 59 22 63 – www.hotelcavour.it
– closed August and Saturdays and Sundays at lunchtime **G1**
Rest – Carte 29/58 €
♦ Classic ♦ Formal ♦
This discreetly stylish restaurant in the centre of Milan offers traditional dishes with
a modern touch.

Sadler
AC ⟷ VISA ⊕ AE ⓪
🏵️ 🏵️

via Ascanio Sforza 77 ⊠ 20136 – Ⓜ *Romolo – 𝒞 02 58104451 – sadler@*
sadler.it – Fax 02 58 11 23 43 – www.sadler.it
– closed from 1 to 10 January, from 10 to 29 August and Sunday
Rest – *(dinner only)* Menu 130/160 € – Carte 76/112 € ⅋⅋ *Plan I* **B3**
Spec. Carpaccio di astice, maionese di pomodoro bianco e riccioli croccanti
di puntarelle. Ravioli di mozzarella liquida, crema di broccoletti e olio di alici.
Mondeghili (polpette) di vitello alla milanese, punte d'asparagi, uovo di
quaglia e tartufo nero.
♦ Inventive ♦ Formal ♦
The new premises of the renowned Sadler restaurant has large windows opening
on to the street, offering views of the kitchen. Inventive contemporary cuisine with
real attention to detail.

Trussardi alla Scala *(Andrea Berton)*
🔥 AC VISA ⊕ AE ⓪
🏵️ 🏵️

piazza della Scala 5 ((Trussardi palace)) ⊠ 20121 – Ⓜ *Duomo*
– 𝒞 02 80688201 – ristorante@trussardiallascala.com – Fax 02 80 68 82 87
– www.trussardiallascala.com
– closed from 22 December to 6 January, from 9 to 31 August, Saturday at
lunchtime and Sunday **G1**
Rest – Menu 110/135 € – Carte 78/104 €
Spec. Seppie arrosto con salsa alla liquirizia. Risotto alle erbe, olive taggiasche, polvere di cappero e noce di capasanta alla plancia. Tiramisù cremoso
nel bicchiere.
♦ Modern ♦ Trendy ♦
Housed in a beautiful palazzo in the square of the same name, this restaurant serves the best of Italian cuisine. The dining room is modern and spacious, with pleasant views from some of the tables.

532

XX **Il Rosa al Caminetto** – Starhotels Rosa   AC ⇔ VISA ⏣ AE ⏣
via Beccaria 4 ✉ *20122* – Ⓜ *Duomo* – *ℰ 02 89095235* – *info@ilrosa.it*
– Fax 02 89 01 68 93 – *www.ilrosa.it*   **G2**
Rest – Carte 46/68 € ⌂
♦ Classic ♦ Intimate ♦
This restaurant under new management features fast and attentive service with a
menu of regional and Italian dishes. A lavish buffet lunch is also served.

XX **Armani/Nobu**   AC ⇔ VISA ⏣ AE ⏣
via Pisoni 1 ✉ *20121* – Ⓜ *Montenapoleone* – *ℰ 02 62312645*
– armani.nobu@giorgioarmani.it – *Fax 02 62 31 26 74*
– www.armaninobu.it
– closed 25 December to 7 January, August, Sunday midday   **G1**
Rest – Carte 45/73 €
♦ Japanese ♦ Trendy ♦
An exotic union between fashion and gastronomy: Japanese "fusion" cuisine with
South American influences in a simple, refined atmosphere inspired by Japanese
design.

XX **Nabucco**   AC VISA ⏣ AE ⏣
via Fiori Chiari 10 ✉ *20121* – Ⓜ *Cairoli* – *ℰ 02 860663*
– info@nabucco.it – *Fax 02 8 69 25 76*
– www.nabucco.it   **F1**
Rest – Carte 40/66 €
♦ Classic ♦ Intimate ♦
Located in a typical alleyway in the Brera district with interesting inspired cuisine,
both fish and meat dishes, evening meals by candlelight.

XX **Emilia e Carlo**   AC ⇔ VISA ⏣ AE ⏣
via Sacchi 8 ✉ *20121* – Ⓜ *Lanza* – *ℰ 02 875948*
– emiliaecarlosas@virgilio.it – *Fax 02 86 21 00*
– www.ristoranteemiliaecarlo.it
– closed Christmas, Easter, August, Saturday midday and Sunday
Rest – Carte 49/64 € ⌂   **F1**
♦ Classic ♦ Formal ♦
Set in an early 19th-century palazzo, this traditional-looking trattoria serves creative contemporary cuisine, and has a fine choice of wines.

XX **Papà Francesco**   ⌂ & AC ⇔ VISA ⏣
via Marino 7 angolo piazza della Scala ✉ *20121* – Ⓜ *Duomo*
– ℰ 02 862177 – *info@papafrancesco.com* – *Fax 02 45 40 91 12*
– www.papafrancesco.com
– closed Monday   **G2**
Rest – Carte 47/63 €
♦ Classic ♦ Formal ♦
This successful restaurant, conveniently located near the Scala, has been
recently extended. In spring, enjoy lunch outdoors with lovely views of the
opera house.

XX **Al Porto**   AC VISA ⏣ AE ⏣
piazzale Generale Cantore ✉ *20123* – Ⓜ *Porta Genova FS*
– ℰ 02 89407425 – *alportodimilano@acena.it*
– Fax 02 8 32 14 81
– closed 24 December - 3 January, August, Sunday, Monday midday
Rest – Carte 45/60 €   **E3**
♦ Fish ♦ Formal ♦
There is a definite maritime flavour to this restaurant, which occupies the old 19C
Porta Genova toll house. Always busy, Al Porto specialises exclusively in fresh fish
dishes, including raw fish.

XX
✿

Tano Passami l'Olio (Gaetano Simonato) [AC] [VISA] [CO] [AE] [O]

via Villoresi, 16 ⊠ *20143 –* Ⓜ *Porta Genova FS –* ✆ *02 8394139 – info@ tanopassamilolio.it – Fax 02 83 24 01 04 – www.tanopassamilolio.it*

– closed from 24 December to 6 January, August, Sunday **E3**

Rest *– (dinner only) (booking advisable)* Carte 73/97 €

Spec. Petto di piccione laccato in lardo d'oca affumicato e tartufo, purea di cavoletti di Bruxelles e mousse di piccione in verza croccante. Maccheroncini di pasta fresca con ragù d'agnello all'anice stellato in crema di mozzarella di bufala. Dal pesce alla carne ed il suo arcobaleno.

♦ Inventive ♦ Intimate ♦

The key features here are the soft lighting, romantic atmosphere and creative fish and meat dishes, flavoured with a choice of extra-virgin olive oils on display in the dining room. Smoking lounge with a sofa.

XX
Il Torchietto [AC] [VISA] [CO] [AE]

via Ascanio Sforza 47 ⊠ *20136 –* Ⓜ *Porta Genova FS –* ✆ *02 8372910 – info@ iltorchietto.net – Fax 02 8 37 20 00 – www.iltorchietto.net*

– closed 26 December - 3 January, August, Monday, Saturday midday

Rest *–* Carte 35/49 € *Plan I* **B3**

♦ Mantuan ♦ Friendly ♦

Specialising in regional cuisine using seasonal ingredients, with a particular emphasis on dishes from Mantua, this large, traditional trattoria is situated on the Naviglio Pavese canal.

XX
Il Navigante [AC] [P] [VISA] [CO] [AE] [O]

via Magolfa 14 ⊠ *20143 –* Ⓜ *Porta Genova FS –* ✆ *02 89406320 – info@ navigante.it – Fax 02 89 42 08 97 – www.navigante.it*

– closed August, Sunday and Monday **F3**

Rest *– (dinner only)* Carte 37/60 €

♦ Fish ♦ Intimate ♦

On a road at the back of the waterway, live music every evening in an establishment, managed by an ex-ship's cook, with an unusual aquarium on the floor; seafood cuisine.

XX
Pirandello [AC] [VISA] [CO] [AE]

viale Gian Galeazzo 6 ⊠ *20136 –* ✆ *02 89402901 – Fax 02 89 40 29 01*

– closed from 7 to 30 August, Christmas, Saturday at midday and Sunday

Rest *–* Carte 40/52 € **F3**

♦ Sicilian ♦ Formal ♦

This restaurant has a decidedly Sicilian atmosphere, management and cuisine. Sample the tasty fish dishes and traditional Sicilian cuisine in both dining rooms.

XX
Hostaria Borromei [🍴] [✿] [VISA] [CO] [AE]

via Borromei 4 ⊠ *20123 –* Ⓜ *Cordusio –* ✆ *02 86453760 – Fax 02 86 45 21 78*

– closed from 24 December to 7 January, from 8 to 31 August, Saturday lunchtime and Sunday **F2**

Rest *–* Carte 39/54 €

♦ Mantuan ♦ Family ♦

Housed in an 18C palazzo in the heart of the historic centre, this small restaurant serves traditional, regional cuisine, with the accent on dishes from Mantua. Outdoor dining in the courtyard in summer.

X
La Felicità [&] [AC] [VISA] [CO] [AE] [O]

via Rovello 3 ⊠ *20121 –* Ⓜ *Cordusio –* ✆ *02 865235 – fanglei@cebichina.cn*

– Fax 02 86 52 35 **F1**

Rest *–* Carte 17/25 €

♦ Chinese ♦ Family ♦

This simple, well-run Chinese restaurant also serves Vietnamese, Thai and Korean cuisine. Elegant furnishings which are broadly Oriental in style.

Artidoro
AC ⇄ VISA ◎ AE ①

via Camperio 15 ⊠ 20123 – ⑩ Cairoli – ℰ 02 8057386 – info@artidoro.it
– Fax 02 85 91 04 10 – www.artidoro.it
– closed 6 to 19 August and Christmas **F1**
Rest – Carte 41/78 € 錦
♦ Emilian specialities ♦

Situated in the heart of Milan, this tavern offers cuisine from Emilia and Lombardy. It has a contemporary decor and young management with international experience. A pleasant combination of tradition and innovation.

Trattoria Torre di Pisa
AC ⇄ VISA ◎ AE ①

via Fiori Chiari 21/5 ⊠ 20121 – ⑩ Lanza – ℰ 02 874877 – Fax 02 87 63 22
– www.trattoriatorredipisa.it
– closed 3 weeks in August and Saturday midday **F1**
Rest – Carte 37/45 €
♦ Tuscany ♦ Rustic ♦

A family-type Tuscan restaurant located at the heart of the characterful quarter of Brera. Enjoy the cuisine of Dante's homeland at particularly attractive prices.

Masuelli San Marco
AC ⇄ VISA ◎ AE ①

viale Umbria 80 ⊠ 20135 – ⑩ Lodi TIBB – ℰ 02 55184138 – prenotazioni@ masuellitrattoria.it – Fax 02 54 12 45 12 – www.masuellitrattoria.it
– closed 25 December - 6 January, 3 weeks in August, Sunday, Monday midday
Rest – Carte 34/46 € *Plan I* **D3**
♦ Lombard specialities ♦ Friendly ♦

A rustic atmosphere with a luxurious feel in a typical trattoria, with the same management since 1921; cuisine strongly linked to traditional Lombardy and Piedmont recipes.

Giulio Pane e Ojo
AC ⇄ VISA ◎ AE ①

via Muratori 10 ⊠ 20135 – ⑩ Porta Romana – ℰ 02 5456189 – info@ giuliopaneojo.com – Fax 02 36 50 46 03 – www.giuliopaneojo.com
– closed 24 - 26 December, Mid-August holiday and Sunday except December
Rest – Menu 10 € bi (lunch) – Carte 25/30 € **H3**
♦ Roman ♦ Friendly ♦

This rustic, informal osteria, with its young managers, is very popular with locals. The emphasis here is on typically Roman cuisine, with simpler, less expensive options at lunchtime. Visitors are advised to book in advance for dinner.

Dongiò
AC VISA ◎ AE ①

via Corio 3 ⊠ 20135 – ⑩ Porta Romana – ℰ 02 5511372 – tosame@ dongio.com – Fax 02 54 01 18 69
– closed 2 weeks in Christmas, Easter, August, Saturday at midday and Sunday
Rest – Carte 23/35 € **H3**
♦ Calabrian specialities ♦ Family ♦

This typical, family-run trattoria has a simple decor and friendly atmosphere. Specialities on the menu include fresh pasta, meat and dishes from Calabria.

Trattoria la Piola
AC VISA ◎ AE

via Perugino 18 ⊠ 20135 – ℰ 02 55195945 – info@lapiola.it
– Fax 02 55 19 59 45 – www.lapiola.it
– closed 24 December-2 January, Easter, August, Saturday lunch and Sunday
Rest – Carte 34/59 € *Plan I* **D2**
♦ Fish ♦ Family ♦

At this well-run trattoria, the variety of the enticing fish menus is the key to their continued success.

La Brisa
⇞ VISA ◎ AE ①

via Brisa 15 ⊠ 20123 – ℰ 02 86450521 – pedrochiara@infinito.it
– Fax 02 86 45 05 21
– closed 23 December-3 January, 8 August-8 September, Saturday, Sunday midday
Rest – Carte 31/67 € **F2**
♦ Classic ♦ Regional ♦

Opposite an archaeological site dating from Roman times, this trattoria serves modern, regional cuisine. Summer dining on the veranda overlooking the garden.

Principe di Savoia ⓘ ⓘ ⓘ ⓘ ⓘ ⓘ rm ⓘ ⓘ *VISA* ⓘ ⓘ ⓘ
piazza della Repubblica 17 ⊠ *20124 –* Ⓜ *Repubblica – ℰ 02 62301*
– principe@hotelprincipedisavoia.com – Fax 02 6 59 58 38
– www.hotelprincipedisavoia.com   **M2**
269 rm – ♜610/890 € ♜♜680/960 €, ⌷ 35 €
– 64 suites
Rest *Acanto – ℰ 02 62302026 – Carte 80/100 €*
♦ Grand Luxury ♦ Palace ♦ Stylish ♦
Period furniture, luxury, and sophistication predominate in this 19th-century building with an international appeal. There are also sports facilities and a health centre. This recently renovated restaurant occupies a modern, elegant building with
large windows overlooking a garden. Classic, contemporary cuisine.

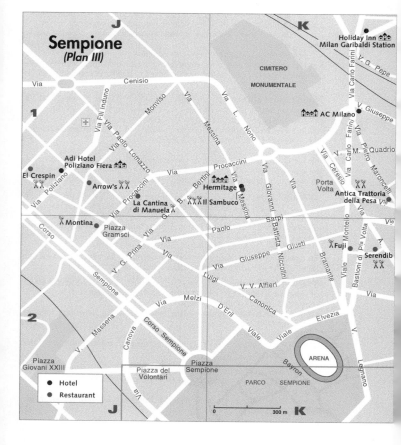

The Westin Palace ⌂ 🅙 🅰🅚 ⚡ rm 📞 🚿 🍽 🆅🅸🆂🅰 ⓜⓞ 🅰🅴 ⓓ

piazza della Repubblica 20 ✉ *20124*
– Ⓜ *Repubblica* – 𝒞 *02 63361*
– *palacemilan@westin.com* – *Fax 02 65 44 85*
– *www.westin.com/palacemilan*
215 rm – 🛏234/791 € 🛏🛏263/1023 €, ⊑ 36 €
– 13 suites
Rest – Carte 65/83 € ⌁

♦ Grand Luxury ♦ Stylish ♦

A luxury hotel housed in a modern tower block. It has spacious public lounges and attractive bedrooms furnished with delightful touches. Elegant fitness and wellness centre. Innovative Mediterranean cuisine is the hallmark of this elegant restaurant with a private dining section.

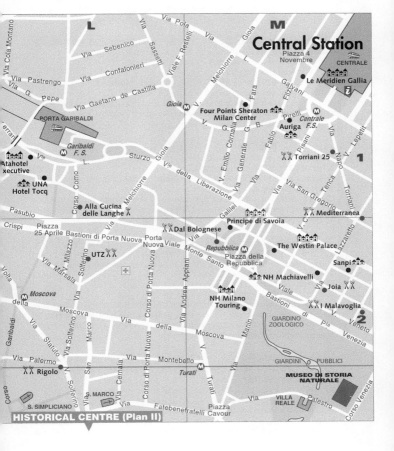

Le Meridien Gallia   🔥 AC 🏧 rm 🕪 🔊 VISA 🐵 AE ⑩

piazza Duca d'Aosta 9 ⊠ *20124* – **Ⓜ** *Centrale F.N.M.* – 🖋 *02 67851*
– *reservations.gallia@lemeridien.com* – *Fax 02 66 71 32 39*
– *www.lemeridien.com/milan*   **M1**
224 rm – ♦125/553 € ♦♦156/795 €, ⊡ 35 € – 13 suites
Rest – Carte 65/83 €
♦ Grand Luxury ♦ Stylish ♦
Spacious public areas furnished in warm tones, elegant guestrooms, a beauty centre and gym are some of the features of this luxury hotel, which has long been a
favourite with politicians and celebrities. An elegant and professionally run restaurant specialising in cuisine from the Lombardy region and the Mediterranean.

NH Milano Touring   🔥 AC 🏧 rm 🕪 🔊 VISA 🐵 AE ⑩

via Tarchetti 2 ⊠ *20121* – **Ⓜ** *Repubblica* – 🖋 *02 63351* – *jhmilanotouring@*
nh-hotels.com – *Fax 02 6 59 22 09* – *www.nh-hotels.com*   **M2**
282 rm ⊡ – ♦152/459 € ♦♦182/509 €   **Rest** – Carte 40/53 €
♦ Chain hotel ♦ Functional ♦
This hotel caters mostly to business travellers and has recently refurbished the
lounge areas. Friendly reception and excellent service. Very near the centre of
town. Typical regional dishes are served in these cosy, stylish surroundings.

Atahotel Executive   🔥 AC 🏧 rm 🕪 🔊 VISA 🐵 AE ⑩

viale Luigi Sturzo 45 ⊠ *20154* – **Ⓜ** *Porta Garibaldi FS* – 🖋 *02 62941*
– *booking.executive@atahotels.it* – *Fax 02 29 01 02 38*
– *www.executive.atahotels.it*   **L1**
414 rm ⊡ – ♦199/399 € ♦♦209/479 € – 6 suites   **Rest** – Carte 35/80 €
♦ Chain hotel ♦ Business ♦ Classic ♦
Situated opposite the Garibaldi railway station, this large hotel with its well-equipped conference centre is ideal for business clients and meetings. The guestrooms
are attractive and comfortable.

Starhotels Ritz   🔥 🕉 AC 🏧 rm 🍴 🔊 VISA 🐵 AE ⑩

via Spallanzani 40 ⊠ *20129* – **Ⓜ** *Lima* – 🖋 *02 2055* – *ritz.mi@starhotels.it*
– *Fax 02 29 51 86 79* – *www.starhotels.com*   *Plan I* **C2**
191 rm ⊡ – ♦♦120/800 € – 6 suites   **Rest** – (residents only)
♦ Chain hotel ♦ Classic ♦
Centrally located in a quiet area, this simple and elegant hotel is now equipped
with a health centre with gym and spa facilities. A large dining room for banquets,
and wall paintings are the features of this restaurant.

Four Points Sheraton Milan Center   🔥 🔥 AC 🏧 rm 🍴 🔊

via Cardano 1 ⊠ *20124* – **Ⓜ** *Gioia* – 🖋 *02 667461*   VISA 🐵 AE ⑩
– *info@fourpointsmilano.it* – *Fax 02 6 70 30 24* – *www.fourpoints.com/milan*
254 rm – ♦370 € ♦♦420 €, ⊡ 25 €   **M1**
Rest *Nectare* – Carte 37/63 €
♦ Business ♦ Classic ♦
Housed in a modern building in the centre of Milan, this hotel offers relaxing public
areas furnished in a simple, elegant style, as well as pleasant and comfortable
guestrooms. An attractive restaurant full of light, serving simple dishes at lunchtime and more elaborate meals in the evening.

UNA Hotel Tocq   AC 🏧 rm 🍴 🔊 VISA 🐵 AE ⑩

via A. de Tocqueville 7/D ⊠ *20154* – **Ⓜ** *Porta Garibaldi FS* – 🖋 *02 62071*
– *una.tocq@unahotels.it* – *Fax 02 6 57 07 80* – *www.unahotels.it*   **L1**
109 rm ⊡ – ♦116/302 € ♦♦116/355 € – 13 suites   **Rest** – Carte 38/50 €
♦ Business ♦ Chain hotel ♦ Design ♦
Modern design is the key feature of this hotel, with its subtle, minimalist furnishings. Fully equipped with all the facilities expected of a contemporary hotel.
Main dining room of the restaurant with summer colours and natural Danish oak
parquet flooring.

Holiday Inn Milan Garibaldi Station

via Farini angolo via Ugo Bassi ⊠ *20159*
– **Ⓜ** *Porta Garibaldi FS* – ℰ *02 6076801*
– *reservations@himilangaribaldi.com* – *Fax 02 6 88 07 64*
– *www.himilangaribaldi.com*   **K1**
129 rm – †79/499 € ††99/499 €, ⌓ 20 €   **Rest** – Carte 39/59 €
♦ Chain hotel ♦ Classic ♦

The hotel has undergone a complete restructuring. It is bright and welcoming and particularly attractive thanks to its minimalist decor. The pleasant lunch-room has a glass cupola. Modern decor and contemporary cuisine.

Starhotels Anderson

piazza Luigi di Savoia 20 ⊠ *20124* – **Ⓜ** *Centrale FS* – ℰ *02 6690141*
– *anderson.mi@starhotels.it* – *Fax 02 6 69 03 31* – *www.starhotels.com*
106 rm ⌓ – ††109/750 €   **Rest** – *(residents only)*   *Plan I* **C1**
♦ Chain hotel ♦ Classic ♦

There is a distinctly exclusive air to this hotel, which is decorated with elegant fabrics and traditional ethnic furnishings. The guestrooms here are modern, light and spacious. Have dinner in the elegant lounges in this small restaurant.

NH Machiavelli

via Lazzaretto 5 ⊠ *20124* – **Ⓜ** *Repubblica* – ℰ *02 631141* – *jhmachiavelli@ nh-hotels.com* – *Fax 02 6 59 98 00* – *www.nh-hotels.it*   **M2**
103 rm ⌓ – †200/409 € ††240/460 €   **Rest** *Caffè Niccolò* – Carte 37/51 €
♦ Chain hotel ♦ Business ♦ Modern ♦

This recently built hotel has simple, bright rooms and a large open lounge area. A small restaurant serving à la carte and buffet meals.

Adi Doria Grand Hotel

viale Andrea Doria 22 ⊠ *20124* – **Ⓜ** *Caiazzo* – ℰ *02 67411411*
– *info.doriagrandhotel@adihotels.com* – *Fax 02 6 69 66 69*
– *www.adihotels.com*   *Plan I* **C1**
124 rm ⌓ – †201/299 € ††265/419 € – 2 suites
Rest – *(closed from 24 December to 6 January and from 28 July to 26 August)*
Carte 40/67 €
♦ Chain hotel ♦ Classic ♦

A classical building with an elegant lobby furnished in early-20C style and large, comfortable guestrooms. Cultural and musical events are occasionally held in the spacious public areas. This small, bright restaurant serves fine Italian and international cuisine in elegant surroundings.

Sanpi without rest

via Lazzaro Palazzi 18 ⊠ *20124* – **Ⓜ** *Porta Venezia* – ℰ *02 29513341* – *info@ hotelsanpimilano.it* – *Fax 02 29 40 24 51* – *www.hotelsanpimilano.it*
– *closed from 24 December to 2 January*   **M2**
79 rm ⌓ – †95/350 € ††119/480 €
♦ Business ♦ Design ♦

Comprising three buildings in the heart of the city, this quiet hotel has well-lit public areas and guestrooms decorated in pastel shades. There is a small garden in the internal courtyard.

Auriga without rest

via Giovanni Battista Pirelli 7 ⊠ *20124* – **Ⓜ** *Centrale FS* – ℰ *02 66985851*
– *auriga@auriga-milano.com* – *Fax 02 66 98 06 98* – *www.auriga-milano.com*
– *closed from 21 to 31 December, from 1 to 7 January and from 3 to 26 August*
52 rm ⌓ – †90/250 € ††120/340 €   **M1**
♦ Business ♦ Modern ♦

The mix of styles, unusual façade and bright colours of this hotel combine to create a striking exterior. Comfortable facilities and efficient service for tourists and business travellers alike.

XXX **Gold** [AC] [⇄] [VISA] [◉◉] [AE] [◉]

via Poerio 2/A ✉ 20129 – ℰ 02 7577771 – Fax 02 75 77 77 73
– www.dolcegabbanagold.it
– closed Christmas, New Year, Easter and twenty days in August
Rest – *(dinner only)* Carte 60/90 € ⅛   Plan I **C2**
Rest *Bistrot Gold* – Carte 42/48 €
◆ Modern ◆ Italian ◆

This modern, contemporary-style restaurant furnished with large round tables is
the creation of two leading names in the fashion world. Smoking room. The Bistrot
Gold specialises in simple dishes served in an informal, yet elegant atmosphere.

XX **Dal Bolognese** [♨] [&] [AC] [⇄] [VISA] [◉◉] [AE]

piazza della Repubblica 13 ✉ 20124 – Ⓜ Repubblica – ℰ 02 62694845
– dalbolognesemilano@virgilio.it – Fax 02 62 02 71 28
– closed Saturday lunchtime and Sunday   **M2**
Rest – Carte 54/72 €
◆ Classic ◆ Formal ◆

Find muted colors and a lively atmosphere in this deluxe bistrot-style bar. Classic
cuisine is served, and outside dining is available in the summer.

XX **Mediterranea** [AC] [VISA] [◉◉] [AE] [◉]

piazza Cincinnato 4 ✉ 20124 – Ⓜ Porta Venezia – ℰ 02 29522076 – info@
ristorantemeditteranea.eu – Fax 02 20 11 56 – www.ristorantemediterranea.it
– closed Sunday and Monday lunchtime   **M1-2**
Rest – Menu 35/50 € ⅛
◆ Fish ◆ Formal ◆

This friendly restaurant with walls decorated with picturesque views of Italy, serves
fish dishes and has a good selection of wines.

XX **Joia** (Pietro Leemann) [AC] [⇄] [VISA] [◉◉] [AE]
🕸

via Panfilo Castaldi 18 ✉ 20124 – Ⓜ Repubblica – ℰ 02 29522124 – joia@
joia.it – Fax 02 2 04 92 44 – www.joia.it
– closed from 25 December to 8 January, from 4 to 25 August, Saturday
lunchtime and Sunday   **M2**
Rest – Menu 60/100 € – Carte 64/84 € ⅛
Spec. Il quinto gusto che mi piace (cannelloni grigliati con ricotta siciliana affu-
micata, zucchine e coste novelle). Oltre il giardino (verdure con yogurt della
casa). La mia charlotte (bavarese con contrasto di caramello ed albicocche).
◆ Inventive ◆ Formal ◆

One of the most unusual and distinctive restaurants in Milan, the Joia serves
mainly vegetarian food, with some fish dishes. Creative, innovative cuisine.

XX **Torriani 25** [AC] [⇄] [VISA] [◉◉] [AE] [◉]

via Napo Torriani 25 ✉ 20124 – Ⓜ Centrale FS – ℰ 02 67078183
– torriani25@tiscali.it – Fax 02 67 47 95 48 – www.torriani25.it
– closed from 25 December to 1 January, from 9 to 26 August, Saturday at
midday, Sunday   **M1**
Rest – Carte 40/56 €
◆ Fish ◆ Formal ◆

This modern restaurant is decorated in warm colours with plenty of natural light.
Choose from the buffet's wide selection of fish dishes (the house speciality) or
meat cooked on the grill.

XX **I Malavoglia** [AC] [VISA] [◉◉] [AE] [◉]

via Lecco 4 ✉ 20124 – Ⓜ Porta Venezia – ℰ 02 29531387
– www.ristorante-imalavoglia.com
– closed from 24 December to 7 January, Easter, 1 May, August, Sunday
Rest – *(dinner only)* Carte 46/59 €   **M2**
◆ Sicilian ◆ Formal ◆

This classic restaurant has been run by the same team for over thirty years. They
serve typical Sicilian dishes in Lombardy's capital.

MICHELIN ATLASES
Let your imagination take you away.

Get the most from your traveling with Michelin atlases
• Detailed road network coverage, updated annually
• Unique atlas format designed for the way you drive
• Route-planning made easy for business and leisure

www.michelin.co.uk

ITALY - MILAN

XX **Rigolo**   🛇 AC ⇄ VISA ⚫ AE ⓪

largo Treves ang. via Solferino 11 ✉ 20121 – **Ⓜ** *Moscova –* ℰ *02 804589
– ristorante.rigolo@tiscalinet.it – Fax 02 86 46 32 20 – www.rigolo.it
– closed August and Monday*   **L2**
Rest – Carte 32/47 €
◆ Classic ◆ Retro ◆
Managed by the same family for over 40 years, this traditional restaurant situated in a fashionable part of the city centre is popular with locals. Meat and fish dishes are served in the elegant dining rooms.

XX **Casa Fontana-23 Risotti**   AC VISA ⚫ AE

piazza Carbonari 5 ✉ 20125 – **Ⓜ** *Sondrio –* ℰ *02 6704710 – trattoria@
23risotti.it – Fax 02 66 80 04 65 – www.23risotti.it
– closed 1 - 12 January, 13 - 15 April, 27 June - 20 July, 1 week in August,
Monday, Saturday midday, also Saturday evening and Sunday in July and
August*   *Plan I* **C1**
Rest – Carte 38/60 €
◆ Lombard specialities ◆ Family ◆
Despite its location in the suburbs and the obligatory 25-minute wait for your food, this small, friendly restaurant is well worth a visit for its excellent risottos.

XX **UTZ**   🍴 AC VISA ⚫ AE

via Solferino 48 ✉ 20121 – **Ⓜ** *Moscova –* ℰ *02 6551180 – parla@
utz-foodemotion.net – Fax 02 31 52 22 – www.utzrestaurant.it
– closed 2 weeks at Christmas, 2 weeks in August, Saturday at midday and
Monday*   **L2**
Rest – Carte 21/45 €
◆ Inventive ◆ Friendly ◆
The young, dynamic management at this restaurant offers an eclectic cuisine. The colourful decor recalls Iberian folklore. It also serves pizzas and Sunday brunch.

XX **Antica Trattoria della Pesa**   🛇 AC VISA ⚫ AE ⓪

viale Pasubio 10 ✉ 20154 – **Ⓜ** *Porta Garibaldi FS –* ℰ *02 6555741
– Fax 02 29 01 51 57
– closed August and Sunday*   **K1**
Rest – Carte 42/64 €
◆ Lombard specialities ◆ Rustic ◆
This Milanese trattoria with a delightfully old-fashioned atmosphere specialises in dishes from Lombardy. A plaque in the entrance commemorates a brief visit by Ho Chi Min to the building that the restaurant occupies.

XX **Serendib**   AC VISA ⚫

😊 *via Pontida 2 ✉ 20121 –* **Ⓜ** *Moscova –* ℰ *02 6592139
– surange@email.it – Fax 02 6 59 21 39
– www.serendib.it
– closed from 10 to 20 August*   **K2**
Rest – *(dinner only)* Carte 18/29 €
◆ Indian ◆ Friendly ◆
Loyal to its origins both in the decoration and in the Indian and "cingalese" cuisine, is a pleasant establishment which bears the old name of Sri Lanka ("to make people happy").

X **La Cantina di Manuela**   🍴 AC VISA ⚫ AE

😊 *via Poerio 3 ✉ 20129 –* **Ⓜ** *Porta Venezia –* ℰ *02 76318892
– info@lacantinadimanuela.it – Fax 02 76 31 29 71
– www.lacantinadimanuela.it
– closed Sunday*   *Plan I* **C2**
Rest – Carte 33/42 € 🏵
◆ Classic ◆ Wine bar ◆
This restaurant has an especially interesting wine list that accompanies its excellent cooking. A few tables are put on the path outside during summer.

❌ 😊 Da Giannino-L'Angolo d'Abruzzo ⬜ AC VISA ⬧ AE ⬧

via Pilo 20 ✉ *20129* – **Ⓜ** *Porta Venezia* – *☏ 02 29406526*
– Fax 02 29 40 65 26
– closed August and Monday **Plan I D2**
Rest – Carte 21/31 €
◆ Abruzzian specialities ◆ Neighbourhood ◆
Visitors can expect a warm welcome in this simple, cheerful and popular restaurant. Generous portions of typical Abruzzi cuisine.

❌ 😊 Baia Chia ⬜ 🍴 AC ⬧ VISA ⬧

via Bazzini 37 ✉ *20131* – **Ⓜ** *Piola* – *☏ 02 2361131* – *fabrizio.papetti@*
fastwebnet.it – *Fax 02 2 36 11 31*
– closed from December 24 to January 2, Easter, 3 weeks in August, Sundays
and Mondays at lunchtime **Plan I D1**
Rest - Carte 26/37 €
◆ Sardinian specialities ◆ Rustic ◆
This is a pleasant establishment with a family atmosphere that is divided into several dining areas. Sample delicious fish dishes, savoury specialities and Sardinian wines.

❌ Fuji ⬜ AC VISA ⬧ AE ⬧

viale Montello 9 ✉ *20154* – **Ⓜ** *Moscova* – *☏ 02 29008349*
– Fax 02 29 00 35 92
– closed 24 December - 2 January, Easter, 1 - 23 August, Saturday midday and
Sunday **K2**
Rest – Carte 40/53 €
◆ Japanese ◆ Minimalist ◆
Jointly managed by Italian and Japanese owners, this simple Japanese restaurant is a popular choice in the city. Sushi bar next door.

❌ Alla Cucina delle Langhe ⬜ ♿ AC ⬧ VISA ⬧ AE ⬧

corso Como 6 ✉ *20154* – **Ⓜ** *Porta Garibaldi FS* – *☏ 02 6554279*
– Fax 02 29 00 68 59
– closed August, Sunday, Saturday also in July **L1**
Rest – Carte 34/49 €
◆ Piedmontese specialities ◆ Friendly ◆
The typical atmosphere of this beautiful trattoria is in keeping with the traditional Lombard and Piedmontese specialities served here. Comprehensive salad buffet.

FIERA-SEMPIONE **Plan I**

🏨 Hermitage ⬜ ♿ AC ⬧ 📞 🛁 🚗 VISA ⬧ AE ⬧

via Messina 10 ✉ *20154* – **Ⓜ** *Porta Garibaldi FS* – *☏ 02 318170*
– hermitage.res@monrifhotels.it – *Fax 02 33 10 73 99* – *www.monrifhotels.it*
– closed August **Plan III K1**
131 rm ⬩ – 🛏169/280 € 🛏🛏199/310 € – 10 suites
Rest Il Sambuco – see below
◆ Business ◆ Classic ◆
Style and comfort are the trademarks of this hotel which combines the atmosphere of elegant period-style interiors with modern facilities; popular with models and other celebrities.

🏨 Milan Marriott Hotel ⬜ 🛁 AC ⬧ rm 📞 🛁 🚗 VISA ⬧ AE ⬧

via Washington 66 ✉ *20146* – **Ⓜ** *Wagner* – *☏ 02 48521* – *mhrs.milit.booking*
@marriotthotel.com – *Fax 02 4 81 89 25* – *www.marriott.com/milit*
322 rm – 🛏🛏240/800 €, ⬩ 26 € **A2**
Rest La Brasserie de Milan – *☏ 02 48522834* – Carte evenings only 47/92 €
◆ Business ◆ Classic ◆
Original contrast between the modern building and the imposing classic interiors of a hotel clearly geared towards Conference and Trade Fair business clientele; functional period style bedrooms. The dining room in this brasserie has a kitchen in full view of customers. Open from 12.30pm to 11pm.

Enterprise Hotel 🏨🏨🏨 ♨ ♿ 🆑 ↩ 🎧 ♨ 📶 🆚 ⓒ 🆎 ⓞ

corso Sempione 91 ✉ *20149 –* 🕿 *02 318181 – info@enterprisehotel.com*
– Fax 02 31 81 88 11 – www.enterprisehotel.com **A1**
123 rm 🍽 – 🛏129/608 € 🛏🛏139/648 € **Rest Sophia's** – see below
♦ Business ♦ Design ♦
Attention to detail and design is evident in every aspect of this elegant modern hotel, from the marble and granite exterior to its bespoke furnishings and pleasing geometrical lines.

Atahotel Fieramilano 🏨🏨 ♨ 🆑 ↩ rm 🎧 ♨ 🆚 ⓒ 🆎 ⓞ

viale Boezio 20 ✉ *20145 –* 🕿 *02 336221 – meeting.fieramilano@atahotels.it*
– Fax 02 31 41 19 – www.fieramilano.atahotels.it
– closed August **B2**
238 rm 🍽 – 🛏104/260 € 🛏🛏139/340 € – 2 suites
Rest *Ambrosiano* – Carte 31/62 €
♦ Chain hotel ♦ Classic ♦
This tastefully furnished hotel opposite the Fiera Milano offers modern and comfortable rooms. In summer, breakfast is served in a gazebo in the garden. Quiet, elegant dining room.

AC Milano 🏨🏨🏨 ♨ 🛉 🆑 🆑 🎧 🍽 🆚 ⓒ 🆎 ⓞ

via Tazzoli 2 ✉ *20154 –* 🕿 *02 2042411 – www.ac-hotels.com* *Plan III* **K1**
160 rm 🍽 – 🛏125/500 € 🛏🛏125/650 € **Rest** – *(residents only)* Carte 47/76 €
♦ Business ♦ Design ♦
This modern, designer-style hotel is popular with an upmarket business clientele. Spacious, well-appointed bedrooms in keeping with the high standards of this hotel chain.

Regency *without rest* 🏨🏨 ♨ 🆑 🎧 ♨ 🆚 ⓒ 🆎 ⓞ

via Arimondi 12 ✉ *20155 –* 🕿 *02 39216021 – regency@regency-milano.com*
– Fax 02 39 21 77 34 – www.regency-milano.com
– closed from 24 December to 6 January and from 1 to 23 August
71 rm 🍽 – 🛏150/230 € 🛏🛏180/350 € **A1**
♦ Business ♦ Classic ♦
This charming mansion dating from the late 19C is built around a delightful courtyard. Stylish interior furnishings, including an elegant living room with a real open fire.

Adi Hotel Poliziano Fiera *without rest* 🆑 🆑 ↩ 🎧 ♨

via Poliziano 11 ✉ *20154 –* 🕿 *02 3191911* 🆚 ⓒ 🆎 ⓞ
– info.hotelpolizianofiera@adihotels.com – Fax 02 3 19 19 31
– www.adihotels.com
– closed 1 - 6 January and 25 July - 24 August
98 rm 🍽 – 🛏220/320 € 🛏🛏265/360 € – 2 suites *Plan III* **J1**
♦ Business ♦ Classic ♦
Friendly, attentive service and spacious guestrooms furnished in light green and sand-coloured tones compensate for the rather small public areas in this modern hotel.

Wagner *without rest* 🆑 🎧 ♨ 🆚 ⓒ 🆎 ⓞ

via Buonarroti 13 – Ⓜ *Wagner –* 🕿 *02 463151 – wagner@roma-wagner.com*
– Fax 02 48 02 09 48 – www.roma-wagner.com
– closed from 12 to 19 August **A2**
48 rm 🍽 – 🛏119/398 € 🛏🛏169/519 € – 1 suite
♦ Business ♦ Personalised ♦
Elegant, well-maintained hotel with attentive service. Striking decor and warm, cosy, comfortable bedrooms.

Rubens 🏨🏨 ♨ 🆑 ↩ rm 🎧 ♨ 🅿 🆚 ⓒ 🆎 ⓞ

via Rubens 21 ✉ *20148 –* Ⓜ *Gambara –* 🕿 *02 40302 – rubens@*
antareshotels.com – Fax 02 48 19 31 14 – www.hotelrubensmilano.it
87 rm 🍽 – 🛏90/299 € 🛏🛏110/370 € **A2**
Rest – *(residents only)* Carte 33/52 €
♦ Business ♦ Personalised ♦
The spacious, comfortable guestrooms in this elegant hotel are adorned with frescoes by contemporary artists and furnished in stylish purple and cobalt-blue tones.

Accademia 〔AC〕 ⇔ rm ⁽ᵗᵖ⁾ ⅍ VISA ⓜⓞ ⒜ⓔ ⓞ

viale Certosa 68 ⊠ 20155 – ℰ 02 39211122
– accademia@antareshotels.com – Fax 02 33 10 38 78
– www.antareshotels.com
– closed from 8 to 23 August   **A1**
65 rm � – **†**300 € **††**400 € – 1 suite   **Rest** – *(residents only)* Menu 19/38 €
♦ Business ♦ Classic ♦

Recently refurbished, the attractive Accademia has a modern feel with relaxing public areas and contemporary guestrooms with designer furnishings.

Mirage Ⅰ₆ & rm 〔AC〕 ⇔ rm ⁽ᵗᵖ⁾ ⅍ ⌂ VISA ⓜⓞ ⒜ⓔ ⓞ

viale Certosa 104/106 ⊠ 20156 – ℰ 02 39210471 – mirage@gruppomirage.it
– Fax 02 39 21 05 89 – www.gruppomirage.it
– closed from 24 December to 3 January and from 31 July to 19 August
86 rm � – **†**106/214 € **††**150/282 €   **A1**
Rest – *(closed Friday and Saturday) (dinner only) (residents only)* Carte 34/44 €
♦ Business ♦ Classic ♦

Not far from the Trade Fair complex, this hotel offers simply furnished public areas and guestrooms renovated in classical style; the bathrooms are decorated with large tiles or mosaics.

Astoria *without rest* 〔AC〕 ⇔ ⁽ᵗᵖ⁾ ⅍ VISA ⓜⓞ ⒜ⓔ ⓞ

viale Murillo 9 ⊠ 20149 – ⓜ Lotto – ℰ 02 40090095 – info@
astoriahotelmilano.com – Fax 02 40 07 46 42 – www.astoriahotelmilano.com
68 rm ⊝ – **†**50/250 € **††**70/420 € – 1 suite   **A2**
♦ Chain hotel ♦ Modern ♦

This hotel that caters mostly to business travellers is located along a ring road. The rooms are modern and soundproof.

Des Etrangers *without rest* & 〔AC〕 ⇔ ⁽ᵗᵖ⁾ ⅍ ⌂ VISA ⓜⓞ ⒜ⓔ ⓞ

via Sirte 9 ⊠ 20146 – ℰ 02 48955325 – info@hde.it – Fax 02 48 95 53 59
– www.hoteldesetrangers.it
– closed from 7 to 23 August   **A3**
94 rm ⊝ – **†**60/150 € **††**80/190 €
♦ Business ♦ Classic ♦

This well-maintained hotel in a quiet street offers its guests functional and comfortable public areas and guestrooms, as well as convenient underground parking.

Antica Locanda Leonardo *without rest* ⇔ 〔AC〕 ⓒ VISA ⓜⓞ ⒜ⓔ ⓞ

corso Magenta 78 ⊠ 20123 – ⓜ Conciliazione – ℰ 02 48014197 – info@
anticalocandaleonardo.com – Fax 02 48 01 90 12
– www.anticalocandaleonardo.com
– closed from 31 December to 6 January and from 5 to 25 August
16 rm ⊝ – **†**95/120 € **††**165/245 €   *Plan II* **E2**
♦ Townhouse ♦ Personalised ♦

This smart hotel occupies an elegant palazzo on Corso Magenta, and is popular with an international clientele. It is a stone's throw from the museum where Leonardo da Vinci's 'Last Supper' is housed

Il Luogo di Aimo e Nadia *(Aimo Moroni)* 〔AC〕 ⇔ VISA ⓜⓞ ⒜ⓔ ⓞ

via Montecuccoli 6 ⊠ 20147 – ⓜ Primaticcio – ℰ 02 416886
– info@aimoenadia.com – Fax 02 48 30 20 05 – www.aimoenadia.com
– closed 12 to 15 April, 1 to 25 August, 1 to 8 January, Saturday lunch and
Sunday   **A3**
Rest – Carte 87/129 €
Spec. Baccalà marinato al miele di erica, melissa e coriandolo, le sue trippette su panzanella di sedano verde. Trenette di semola con julienne di seppie, fave fresche, pomodori canditi ed erbe aromatiche. Dolci ortaggi
♦ Contemporary ♦ Formal ♦

A leading light of the city's culinary scene, this restaurant, with an impressive display of modern works of art, has cuisine memorable for its creativity.

ITALY - MILAN

XXX La Pobbia 1850   🚫 AC ⟺ VISA 🅆 AE ①

via Gallarate 92 ✉ 20151 – 𝒞 02 38006641 – lapobbia@lapobbia.com
– Fax 02 38 00 07 24 – www.lapobbia.com
– closed August and Sunday **A1**
Rest – Carte 46/76 €
♦ Lombard specialities ♦ Formal ♦
This 19C tavern is now an elegant restaurant with an interior garden. It serves tra-
ditional Lombard and international cuisine. There is also an area set aside for smo-
kers.

XXX Il Sambuco – Hotel Hermitage   AC VISA 🅆 AE ①

via Messina 10 ✉ 20154 – 🄼 Porta Garibaldi FS – 𝒞 02 33610333 – info@
ilsambuco.it – Fax 02 33 61 18 50 – www.ilsambuco.it
– closed 25 December-3 January, Easter, 1-20 August, Saturday lunch and
Sunday   *Plan III* **K1**
Rest – Menu 40/65 € – Carte 54/82 € ❄
♦ Fish ♦ Formal ♦
Like the hotel of which it is a part, this restaurant is characterised by elegant decor
and attentive service. The cuisine is renowned for its seafood specialities and, on
Mondays, for its dishes of boiled meat.

XXX Sophia's – Enterprise Hotel   🍴 🚫 AC ⟺ rm VISA 🅆 AE ①

corso Sempione 91 ✉ 20149 – 🄼 Lotto – 𝒞 02 31818855
– sophiasrestaurant@enterprisehotel.com – Fax 02 31 81 88 11
– www.sophiasrestaurant.com
Rest – Carte 39/64 €
♦ Classic ♦ Design ♦
A pleasant and original restaurant for lunch and dinner. Outdoor dining in summer.

XX Innocenti Evasioni (Arrigoni e Picco)   🚗 🍴 AC ⟺ VISA 🅆 AE ①

❄

via privata della Bindellina ✉ 20155 – 𝒞 02 33001882 – ristorante@
innocentievasioni.com – Fax 02 89 05 55 02 – www.innocentievasioni.com
– closed from 3 to 9 January, August and Sunday **A1**
Rest – *(dinner only)* Menu 65 € – Carte 45/59 € ❄
Spec. Terrina di foie gras con marmellata di rabarbaro e pan brioche. Cappe-
sante caramellate con insalata cremosa di piselli. Costoletta di maialino iberico con pesche caramellate all'aceto balsamico.
♦ Innovative ♦ Formal ♦
This pleasant establishment, with large windows facing the garden, offers classic
cuisine reinterpreted with imagination. Enjoyable outdoor summer dining.

XX Arrow's   🍴 🚫 AC ⟺ VISA AE ①

via Mantegna 17/19 ✉ 20154 – 𝒞 02 341533 – Fax 02 33 10 64 96
– closed August, Sunday, Monday at midday   *Plan III* **J1**
Rest – Carte 42/57 €
♦ Fish ♦ Formal ♦
Packed, even at midday, the atmosphere becomes cosier in the evening but the
seafood cuisine, prepared according to tradition, remains the same.

XX El Crespin   AC ⟺ rm ⟺ VISA 🅆 AE ①

via Castelvetro 18 ✉ 20154 – 𝒞 02 33103004 – info@elcrespin.it
– Fax 02 33 10 30 04 – www.elcrespin.it
– closed from 26 December to 7 January, August, Saturday and Sunday
Rest – *(dinner only)* Carte 36/48 €   *Plan III* **J1**
♦ Classic ♦ Formal ♦
The entrance of this restaurant is decorated with period photos, while the dining
room is tastefully furnished in a simple, modern style. Both meat and fish dishes
feature on the menu.

ITALY - MILAN

La Cantina di Manuela [AC] [VISA] [CO] [AE]

via Procaccini 41 ✉ *20154 –* ℰ *02 31056235 – Fax 02 3 45 20 34*
– www.lacantinadimanuela.it
– closed from 8 to 28 August and Sunday   *Plan III* **J1**
Rest – Carte 32/43 € 🕸

♦ Traditional ♦ Formal ♦

Not far from Fiera/Milano City, it's a wine-bar restaurant made of two communicating dining rooms with an original display of bottles.The cuisine is traditional and personalized at the same time and takes pride in the quality of the products.

Trattoria Montina [AC] [VISA] [CO] [AE] [O]

via Procaccini 54 ✉ *20154 –* Ⓜ *Porta Garibaldi FS –* ℰ *02 3490498*
– closed 25 December - 5 January, August, Sunday, Monday midday
Rest – Carte 27/36 €   *Plan III* **J2**

♦ Classic ♦ Intimate ♦

Twin brothers manage this elegant restaurant. It has an attractive, French style bistro atmosphere with soft lighting and tables close together. Italian and Milanese dishes made from seasonal ingredients.

Pace [AC] [VISA] [CO] [AE] [O]

via Washington 74 ✉ *20146 –* Ⓜ *Wagner –* ℰ *02 468567 – Fax 02 46 85 67*
– closed from 24 December to 5 January, Easter, 1-24 August, Saturdays at
lunchtime and Wednesdays   **A2-3**
Rest – Carte 24/37 €

♦ Classic ♦ Family ♦

This very popular family-run trattoria has been providing cordial hospitality for over 30 years. The surroundings are simple and the menu traditional.

Al Molo 13 [AC] [VISA] [CO] [AE] [O]

via Rubens 13 ✉ *20148 –* Ⓜ *De Angelis –* ℰ *02 4042743 – info@molo13.it*
– Fax 02 40 07 26 16 – www.molo13.it
– closed 26 December - 5 January, August, Sunday, Monday midday
Rest – Carte 45/83 €   **A2**

♦ Fish ♦ Friendly ♦

The two colourful dining rooms of this restaurant are adorned with paintings and ceramics which give a Sardinian flavour to the decor. Specialities include seafood dishes and typical Sardinian cuisine. Generous portions.

Targa/Age Fotostock/Hoa-Qui

If there's ever been a time to visit Turin, that time is now. In the past, the city was associated with the car industry and its somewhat sombre atmosphere never really attracted many tourists. All this changed dramatically in 2006 when the Winter Olympic Games took place and Turin underwent a complete renewal. Once the skiing and ice-skating were over an even greater transformation took place. The result was complex and fascinating, and Turin's name as a destination now ranks alongside Italy's more famous cities.

Turin has also had a glorious past. The city played a big part in the country's history, while at the same time opening many new doors to the future. Few know that the *Regno delle due Sicilie*, the little state Turin was head of, paved the way to Italy's unification in 1861 and that the city itself became Italy's first capital. Turin's royal family, the Savoia (later to be Italy's monarchs), moulded the city with their monuments and taste for grandeur, creating the squares and avenues that are now celebrated in this rediscovered capital.

LIVING THE CITY

Piazza Castello, the square from which some of the city's most celebrated avenues start, may well be considered the heart of Turin; while the city's landmark building has to be the **Mole Antonelliana** – originally designed as a Jewish synagogue – the city's tallest building and Turin's answer to the 'Tour Eiffel'. Named after an ancient Roman settlement, the **Quadrilatero Romano** is now the most fashionable quarter of Turin and boasts some of its most elegant shops ; its narrow medieval streets are a fascinating interlude to the city's orthogonal plan. Less fashionable but equally interesting is **Borgo Dora**, the quarter north of the **Piazza della Repubblica**; it's a popular area that has recently been given a facelift but still retains its old,

bohemian atmosphere. Don't miss the **Cortile del Maglio**, inside the arsenal in Piazza Borgo Dora, with its markets and art. At the other end of the scale, **la Collina** provides some of Turin's poshest addresses, while crossing the River Po – the longest in Italy – at Piazza Vittorio Veneto will lead you to Turin's luxurious period houses. Those interested in residential architecture can also find some of Turin's most beautiful houses – dating back to the 19C – in the Via Galileo Ferraris area of the Crocetta quarter. For a more vibrant atmosphere, head for the embankment between Piazza Vittorio Veneto and Corso Vittorio Emanuele and you will find the 'murazzi', where you will get the best of Turin's nightlife with its bars and clubs.

PRACTICAL INFORMATION

ARRIVAL-DEPARTURE

Better known as Caselle – after the town near which you land – Turin's airport, Sandro Pertini, is located 11km north of the city. It will cost you between €25 and €40 to reach the city centre by taxi, or €5 by bus. The best bet, however, is to use the train, which runs every 30mins and brings you into Torino Dora railway station in just 19mins. The price of €3,40 also

includes a 70 minute bus ride of your choice once in Turin.

TRANSPORT

Bus tickets range from a good value €1 for 70mins travel and up to €3,50 for unlimited daily use. In recent years the underground has been progressively extending its reach throughout Turin and provides a quick and easy way of getting around.

EXPLORING TURIN

The best way to discover the city is to walk along its arcades - 18 pleasurable kilometres of shops and cafés - and all without having to worry about the weather. Famous for its long, wide avenues which interconnect at imposing squares, it's hard to get lost here. Mirroring the torinesi themselves, the city combines an air of thoroughness and order with a sense of discretion and understatement. Even baroque style churches and monuments have been reinterpreted with the native desire for measured composure; a long way from the opulence of Rome.

→ INDUSTRY & ART

Turin's love for cinema dates back to the beginning of the 20C, when the city was used as the backdrop for some of Italy's first shoots. This love affair continues today, with the Torino Film Festival having grown into one of the most interesting film events. The Mole Antonelliana plays host to the Museo del Cinema which recounts the history of cinema and displays thousands of objects relating to its birth and concluding with some spectacular recreations of famous films.

Turin has always been closely associated with Italy's car industry and in particular FIAT, a move which contributed largely to the 'miracolo economio' – the rapid economic growth that Italy experienced during the '50s and '60s. The car factories have moved on but the historical 1920s **Lingotto** plant still remains and has been ingeniously converted into a business and shopping centre, with cinemas, a picture gallery, concert hall and even two hotels. Cleverly transformed by architect Renzo Piano, it retains most of its original architectural features which lead Le Corbusier to define it as "one of the most remarkable sights industry has given us". It can be found in Via Nizza 280. Car enthusiasts should also head for the **Museo dell'Automobile Biscaretti di Ruffia**, in Corso Unità d'Italia 40, which tells the story of the car and boasts an impressive display of motor vehicles.

Turin wouldn't be the city we know today without its newspapers, bookshops and publishing houses. Those who are at ease with the Italian language will find all they need to know about what's hot in town in 'La Stampa', the daily newspaper; while book lovers will queue at the 'Fiera Internazionale del Libro' in the Lingotto, a yearly exhibition and one of Italy's most important publishing seminars. Even more unique and definitely more intriguing, is the 'Portici di Carta', which takes place in via Roma sometime in the autumn. Around 120 companies participate in the event, creating possibly the biggest ever bookshop, spread over 2 kilometres of Turin's most beautiful avenues.

→ WALK LIKE AN EGYPTIAN

As the city has never had any links with the Egyptian civilization, it may surprise you to find that Turin is home to one of the world's most important Egyptian museums. It has recently been revamped and is definitely worth a visit to view the vast range of archaeological finds. The main attraction is the collection of statues dating back to the New Reign Period, the golden age of ancient Egypt. You'll find the museum in Via Accademia delle Scienze 6, close the central Via Roma.

If you feel like a stroll in the park then **Valentino** is the most popular choice for visitors and locals alike. Relatively close to the city centre, it offers over a kilometre of pleasant walks along the Po embankment. More than just green space, it is also home to a theatre, the 17C Valentino Castle and the Borgo Medioevale – a 19C reproduction of a historic local village.

If you have the time and fancy going a little further afield, the **'corona di delizie'** deserves your attention. This refers to a series of royal palaces around Turin – hence the name 'corona' or 'crown' – built from as early as the 17C by the Savoia Royal Family. The best architects of the time contributed to these palaces and at least three deserve particular mention. Firstly, the recently restored Reggia di Venaria, once dedicated to royal hunting and now home to the richly decorated Grande Galleria; secondly, the Palazzina di Caccia di Stupingi, Juvarra's imposing 19C masterpiece;

and finally, the Castello e Museo d'Arte Contemporanea, perched on a hill 15km outside of Turin in Rivoli and host to a famous modern art museum. This last collection contributes to Turin's growing name as the capital of modern design. If you're passionate about art, don't miss the Galleria Civica di Arte Moderne e Contemporanea (GAM).

CALENDAR HIGHLIGHTS

Turin is busy throughout the year, courtesy of a multitude of business and tourist events. The Lingotto building with its post-industrial architecture, is the centre of many of these, such as Italy's most important book exhibition, the Fiera Internazionale del Libro, which usually takes place in May. Later in the year, September sees music fans flock to Turin for the annual Mito, a collection of over 200 music events lasting almost a month. Every two years in late October, food lovers can queue at the Salone del Gusto, an immense event organised by the Slow Food Movement, which gathers the best Italian producers and their products, as well as running conferences and debates. Autumn, usually November, has been attracting cinema-goers since 1982 with the Torino Film Festival (TFF) and, thanks to the quality of its selected films, it has really made a name for itself.

EATING OUT

Turin can rightly boast of being one of Italy's gastronomic centres. Faithful to its ancient role as capital, the city displays the best food the Piemonte region has to offer. Not to be missed are the fresh egg pastas (usually in the form of the very fine tajarin or as ravioli del Plin), the local braised beef (fassone), lamb and pigeons. The locals definitely have a taste for meat and most recipes use it in one form or another. Indeed, meat may keep you company throughout your meal: as an entrée such as vital tonnato, as a filling for ravioli in your second course, as well as for the main course itself. White truffles deserve a special mention, although they've become so rare and world famous that prices are often incredibly high. Picked on the Langhe Hills between October and December, they are usually served with pasta (most commonly grated over tajarin with butter) or fonduta (cheese cream with yolks).

With some of the best Italian chocolate being produced in Turin, desserts are a real treat. You might find bonèt (chocolate pudding with almond biscuits), torta di nocciole (hazelnut

TURIN IN...

→ **ONE DAY**
  Piazza Castello, Via Roma, Piazza San Carlo, the Mole Antonelliana, Piazza Vittorio Veneto, the Duomo and the Sacra Sindone Chapel

→ **TWO DAYS**
  The Egyptian Museum, the Sabaudia Gallery, Palazzo Carignano, Palazzo Madama and its Museum of Ancient Arts

→ **THREE DAYS**
  The Valentino Park, the Reggia di Venaria and the Museum of the Cinema

cake) or panna cotta (cooked cream). Alongside Tuscany, Piemontes's red wines are indisputably the best in Italy; to accompany your meal try a local Barbera, a reliable Nebiolo or a world famous Barbaresco or Barolo – the 'king of wines'.

Cafés have a long tradition in Turin and stopping at one can be a good way of getting a little closer to local life. Dating back to 1763, *Al Bicerin* is one of the best known, and prime minister Cavour – one of the founders of Italian unity – used to be a frequent visitor here at piazza della Consolata 5. Café *San Carlo* in the elegant San Carlo Square is equally famous, as it was as the meeting point for patriots fighting for Italian independence; those more into art nouveau usually meet at Baratti & Milano, 29 Piazza Castello. Wherever you go, make sure you try a *bicerin* – a drink made from coffee, cream and chocolate – and a *gianduiotti* – added chocolate and 'tonda gentile', a famous variety of hazelnut from the Piemonte region.

The region's love for food recently paved the way to the opening of the world's biggest food market, 'Eataly': 2,500 square metres of Italy's most famous delicacies brought to you by local producers, who pride themselves of the quality of their excellent, and often rare, ingredients. The choice ranges from pasta and wine through to special varieties of rice, olive oil, cheese and all that Italy is known for. Set in via Nizza 230, close to the Lingotto, it offers a good number of restaurants too.

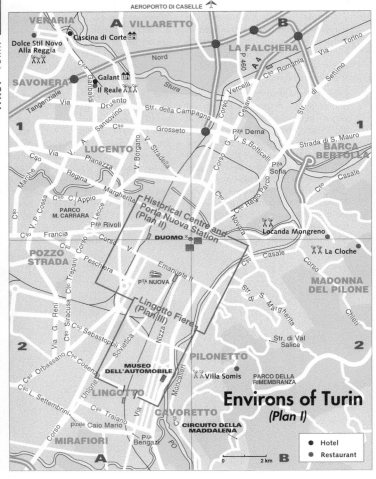

AEROPORTO DI CASELLE

Environs of Turin
(Plan I)

● Hotel
● Restaurant

0 ____ 2 km

HISTORICAL CENTRE

Plan II

Golden Palace 🛜 Ĺẟ 🕒 ≫ 🏊 ⅓ 🅰🅒 🕐 🅰 ⅤⅠⅤ ∞ 🅰🄴 ⓐ
via dell'Arcivescovado 18 ✉ *10121* – ℰ *011 5512111* – *goldenpalace@thi.it*
– Fax 011 5 51 28 00 – *www.goldenpalace.thi.it* **D2**
195 rm ⌸ – ♦185/475 € ♦♦205/475 € – 12 suites
Rest *Winner* – *(closed August)* Carte 53/80 €
♦ Grand Luxury ♦ Art Deco ♦
This luxury hotel in the heart of the city is decorated in Art Deco and minimalist style. The gold, silver and bronze tones evoke the colours of the three Olympic medals.

Principi di Piemonte

via Gobetti 15 ✉ *10123 –* ☎ *011 55151 – prenotazione@*
principidipiemonte.com – Fax 011 5 18 58 70 – www.atahotels.it **E2**
81 rm ☕ **– ♥♥** 280/450 € – 18 suites
Rest *Casa Savoia* – Carte 50/88 €

♦ Chain hotel ♦ Luxury ♦ Modern ♦

A stone's throw from the town centre, this historic building from the 30s boasts spacious rooms that are rich in marble. They have been renovated in homage to luxury and comfort in order to create an elegant modern atmosphere. The magnificence is also taken up in the dining room, where no detail has been left to chance, so that this gastronomic stop stays in the memory.

Grand Hotel Sitea

via Carlo Alberto 35 ✉ *10123 –* ☎ *011 5170171 – sitea@thi.it*
– Fax 011 54 80 90 – www.sitea.thi.it **E2**
120 rm ☕ **– ♥** 135/294 € **♥♥** 171/320 € – 1 suite
Rest *Carignano* – Carte 53/71 €

♦ Palace ♦ Traditional ♦ Classic ♦

Founded in 1925, the period furnishings in this traditional hotel add to the building's stylish, elegant atmosphere. This beautiful, elegant restaurant boasts large windows with views of the surrounding greenery. International cuisine and Piedmontese specialities take pride of place here.

Starhotels Majestic

corso Vittorio Emanuele II 54 ✉ *10123 –* ☎ *011 539153 – majestic.to@*
starhotels.it – Fax 011 53 49 63 – www.starhotels.com **E2**
159 rm ☕ **– ♥♥** 99/340 € – 2 suites
Rest *Le Regine – (closed Sunday)* Carte 40/60 €

♦ Chain hotel ♦ Traditional ♦ Classic ♦

This elegant hotel is located beneath the portico opposite the central station. It has large, well-appointed and cosy rooms with individual touches. A large dome of coloured glass dominates the beautiful dining room. International cuisine is served in the à la carte restaurant.

Turin Palace Hotel without rest

via Sacchi 8 ✉ *10128 –* ☎ *011 5625511 – palace@thi.it – Fax 011 5 61 21 87*
– www.thi.it
– closed August **E2**
122 rm ☕ **– ♥** 140/230 € **♥♥** 190/295 € – 2 suites

♦ Palace ♦ Traditional ♦ Classic ♦

Tradition and elegance are the hallmarks of this historic hotel, which has undergone major renovation. Cosy atmosphere and restrained elegance in the guestrooms and public areas.

Victoria without rest

via Nino Costa 4 ✉ *10123 –* ☎ *011 5611909 – reservation@*
hotelvictoria-torino.com – Fax 011 5 61 18 06 – www.hotelvictoria-torino.com
106 rm ☕ **– ♥** 150/200 € **♥♥** 220/260 € **E2**

♦ Traditional ♦ Personalised ♦

Antique furniture, colourful decor and attention to detail make this warm, elegant residence a popular choice. New fitness centre in Egyptian style. Attentive service.

NH Santo Stefano

via Porta Palatina 19 ✉ *10122 –* ☎ *011 5223311 – info.nhsantostefano@*
nh-hotels.com – Fax 011 5 22 33 13 – www.nh-hotels.com **E1**
125 rm ☕ **– ♥** 99/270 € **♥♥** 129/360 €
Rest *– (closed from 25 July to 24 August)* Menu 28 €

♦ Chain hotel ♦ Minimalist ♦

Built from scratch in the elegant and tranquil district of Quadrilatero Romano. It boasts comfortable rooms in a minimalist style, which are reached via the old staircase at the entrance. Warm and inviting lighting gives a modern air to the dining room that serves Piedmontese and national dishes.

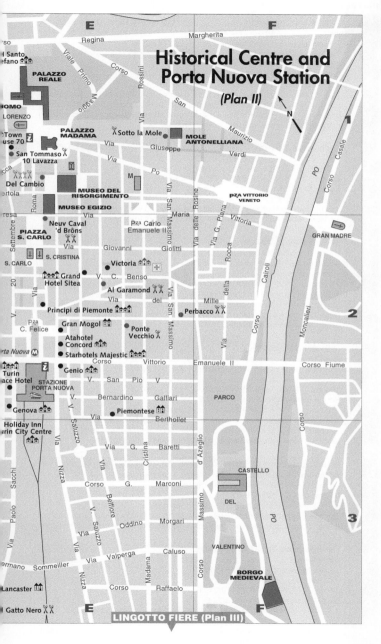

ITALY - TURIN

Historical Centre and Porta Nuova Station

(Plan II)

N

E · F

Regina · Margherita

Corso · Rossini · San · Maurizio

Viale Primo Maggio

l Santo
efano

PALAZZO
REALE

IOMO

LORENZO

Town
use 70

PALAZZO
MADAMA

Sotto la Mole

MOLE
ANTONELLIANA

Via · Giuseppe · Verdi

San Tommaso
10 Lavazza

Via

Del Cambio

ertola

Roma

MUSEO DEL
RISORGIMENTO

Po

Via San Maria

PZA VITTORIO
VENETO

MUSEO EGIZIO

Via

teresa

Neuv Caval
'd Brôns

Pza Carlo
Emanuele II

Via delle Rosine

Via G. Plana

Vittoria

GRAN MADRE

PIAZZA
S. CARLO

Settembre

Via

Giovanni · Giolitti

Rocca

Caroli

S. CARLO · S. CRISTINA

Victoria

della

Grand
Hotel Sitea

V. C. Benso

Al Garamond

Via del

Mille

Via San Massimo

Moncalieri

Principi di Piemonte

Perbacco

20

Via

Pza
C. Felice

Gran Mogol

Ponte
Vecchio

Corso

Atahotel
Concord

Starhotels Majestic

rta Nuova

Corso · Vittorio · Emanuele II

Corso Fiume

Turin
ace Hotel

Genio

STAZIONE
PORTA NUOVA

V. San Pio V

Bernardino · Galliari

PARCO

Genova

Via

Piemontese

Berthollet

PO

Holiday Inn
urin City Centre

Via G. Cristina · Baretti

d'Azeglio

Corso

Sacchi

Via Nizza

Corso G. Marconi

CASTELLO

Massimo

Via Belfiore

V. Saluzzo

Oddino · Morgari

DEL

PO

Paolo

Via

ermano Sommeiller

Via Valperga

Caluso

Madama

VALENTINO

Corso

Lancaster

Nizza · Corso · Raffaelo

BORGO
MEDIEVALE

Gatto Nero

E · F

LINGOTTO FIERE (Plan III)

Atahotel Concord ♿ 🅰🅲 ⁇ 🏖 VISA 💳 AE ①

via Lagrange 47 ✉ *10123 –* ✆ *011 5176756*
– booking.concord@atahotels.it – Fax 011 5 17 63 05
– www.hotelconcorde.com **E2**
139 rm ☑ – †138/280 € ††158/340 €
Rest – *(dinner only)* Carte 41/63 €
♦ Chain hotel ♦ Traditional ♦ Classic ♦
Very centrally situated and just a short distance from Porta Nuova, this hotel is popular with conference delegates. Large public rooms and comfortable bedrooms. This elegant restaurant next to an American bar specialises in Italian cuisine. Lighter meals available at lunchtime.

Art Hotel Boston 🍽 🅰🅲 ↯ rm ⁇ 🏖 VISA 💳 AE ①

via Massena 70 ✉ *10128 –* ✆ *011 500359 – info@hotelbostontorino.it*
– Fax 011 59 93 58 – www.hotelbostontorino.it **D3**
86 rm ☑ – †80/160 € ††105/195 € – 1 suite
Rest – Carte 25/60 €
♦ Business ♦ Design ♦
This modern hotel offers comfortable rooms adorned with works of contemporary art. Good location not far from the main museums of the city.

Town House 70 without rest 🅰🅲 📞 🏖 VISA 💳 AE ①

via XX Settembre 70 ✉ *10122 –* ✆ *011 19700003*
– townhouse70@townhouse.it – Fax 011 19 70 01 88
– www.townhouse.it **E1**
47 rm ☑ – †95/410 € ††106/459 € – 1 suite
♦ Business ♦ Minimalist ♦
A new hotel in light colours with pretty rooms that are spacious and straightforward. There is a single large table in the small breakfast room, on which guests can start the morning together.

NH Ambasciatori 🅰🅲 ↯ rm ⁇ 🏖 VISA 💳 AE ①

corso Vittorio Emanuele II 104 ✉ *10121 –* ✆ *011 57521*
– jhtorinoambasciatori@nh-hotels.com – Fax 011 54 49 78
– www.nh-hotels.it **C2**
195 rm – †145/260 € ††169/270 €, ☑ 22 € – 4 suites
Rest *Il Diplomatico* – Carte 32/65 €
♦ Business ♦ Chain hotel ♦ Classic ♦
This modern hotel in a square shaped building is ideal for conferences, shows and receptions. Elegant, comfortable bedrooms decorated in the style of the 1980s. Large windows bathe the elegant and refined dining room in light.

City without rest ♿ 🅰🅲 ↯ ⁇ 🏖 🍽 VISA 💳 AE ①

via Juvarra 25 ✉ *10122 –* ✆ *011 540546 – city.to@bestwestern.it*
– Fax 011 54 81 88 – www.bwhotelcity-to.it **C1**
61 rm ☑ – †115/280 € ††149/320 €
♦ Business ♦ Chain hotel ♦ Design ♦
The wood furnishings in this hotel contrast with the building's modern, functional design. Comfortable bedrooms in a convenient location near Porta Susa station.

Holiday Inn Turin City Centre ♿ rm 🅰🅲 ↯ rm ⁇ 🏖

via Assietta 3 ✉ *10128 –* ✆ *011 5167111* VISA 💳 AE ①
– hi.torit@libero.it – Fax 011 5 16 76 99
– www.holiday-inn.it **E2**
57 rm ☑ – †92/119 € ††110/249 €
Rest – *(dinner only)* Menu 18/22 €
♦ Chain hotel ♦ Traditional ♦ Modern ♦
Situated near the station, this hotel in a 19C palazzo offers guests well-maintained rooms equipped with the very latest technology. Convenient garage. This restaurant is modern in both tone and layout. À la carte dining in the evening.

Genio without rest   🅰🅒 ⅙ ⁝⁰⁰ 🕍 💳 ⦿ 🄰🄴 ⓞ

corso Vittorio Emanuele II 47 ⊠ 10125 – 𝒫 011 6505771 – info@hotelgenio.it
– Fax 011 6 50 82 64 – www.hotelgenio.it   **E2**
128 rm � – †90/140 € ††140/200 € – 3 suites
♦ Chain hotel ♦ Traditional ♦ Classic ♦
Extended for the Olympics, this hotel has attractive bedrooms decorated with real attention to detail. The artistic flooring in the rooms and corridors provides a touch of elegance.

Genova without rest   ⅙ 🅰🅒 ⅙ ⁝⁰⁰ 🕍 💳 ⦿ 🄰🄴 ⓞ

via Sacchi 14/b ⊠ 10128 – 𝒫 011 5629400
– info@albergogenova.it – Fax 011 5 62 98 96
– www.albergogenova.it   **E2**
78 rm ⊆ – †75/160 € ††100/230 €
♦ Chain hotel ♦ Traditional ♦ Personalised ♦
An elegant hotel in a 19C building, where classical style goes hand in hand with comfortable modern facilities. Ten of the bedrooms are adorned with frescoes on the ceiling.

Piemontese without rest   ⅙ 🅰🅒 ⅙ ⁝⁰⁰ 🅿 💳 ⦿ 🄰🄴 ⓞ

via Berthollet 21 ⊠ 10125 – 𝒫 011 6698101
– info@hotelpiemontese.it – Fax 011 6 69 05 71
– www.hotelpiemontese.it   **E2**
39 rm ⊆ – †65/140 € ††80/160 €
♦ Chain hotel ♦ Traditional ♦ Personalised ♦
This hotel situated between Porta Nuova and the River Po has been renovated with elegant, colourful furnishings and individual touches in the bedrooms. Breakfast is served on the veranda.

Lancaster without rest   🅰🅒 ⁝⁰⁰ 🕍 💳 ⦿ 🄰🄴 ⓞ

corso Filippo Turati 8 ⊠ 10128 – 𝒫 011 5681982 – hotel@lancaster.it
– Fax 011 5 68 30 19 – www.lancaster.it
– closed from 5 to 20 August   **E3**
83 rm ⊆ – †73/95 € ††101/137 €
♦ Traditional ♦ Personalised ♦
Each floor of this hotel is decorated in a different colour. Attractive furnishings add a contemporary touch to the public rooms, a more traditional feel to the bedrooms and a more rustic atmosphere in the breakfast room.

Gran Mogol without rest   🅰🅒 ⅙ ⁝⁰⁰ 💳 ⦿ 🄰🄴 ⓞ

via Guarini 2 ⊠ 10123 – 𝒫 011 5612120
– info@hotelgranmogol.it – Fax 011 5 62 31 60
– www.hotelgranmogol.it
– closed 23 December to 1 January and 30 July to 25 August   **E2**
45 rm ⊆ – †70/140 € ††90/200 €
♦ Chain hotel ♦ Traditional ♦ Classic ♦
Situated near the Egyptian Museum, this luxury hotel has a relaxing atmosphere and is suitable for tourists and business travellers alike. Comfortable bedrooms furnished in classical style.

Del Cambio   🍴 🅰🅒 ✦ 💳 ⦿ 🄰🄴 ⓞ

piazza Carignano 2 ⊠ 10123 – 𝒫 011 543760 – cambio@thi.it
– Fax 011 53 52 82 – www.thi.it
– closed 1 - 6 January and Sunday except January-February   **E1**
Rest – *(booking advisable)* Menu 75 € – Carte 64/89 € ✧
♦ Regional ♦ Luxury ♦
Over the past 250 years this restaurant has hosted a number of famous guests, including Cavour, Rattazzi and Lamarmora. Rich velvet decor provides the backdrop for innovative and traditional cuisine.

ITALY - TURIN

XXX   **Vintage 1997** (Pierluigi Consonni)   AC VISA ∞ AE ①
£3

piazza Solferino 16/h ⊠ *10121 –* ℰ *011 535948 – info@vintage1997.com
– Fax 011 53 59 48 – www.vintage1997.com
– closed from 1 to 7 January, from 6 to 31 August, Saturday lunchtime and
Sunday*   **D2**
Rest – Carte 45/82 € 🕸
Spec. Risotto con gamberi rossi crudi. Trittico di baccalà. Igloo (semifreddo
di gianduja).
♦ Italian ♦ Formal ♦
Scarlet fabric, lampshades and elegant wood panelling soften the interior of this
elegant restaurant. While the creativity takes its cue from tradition in order to
whirl round in multiple forms.

XXX   **Marco Polo**   AC ⇔ VISA ∞ AE ①

via Marco Polo 38/40 ⊠ *10129 –* ℰ *011 500096 – ristorantemarcopolo@
libero.it – Fax 011 59 99 00 – www.ristorantemarcopolo.to.it
– closed Saturday lunchtime*   **C3**
Rest – Carte 44/70 € 🕸
Rest Flù – ℰ *011 503333 (closed 11 to 26 August and Monday)* Carte 35/58 €
♦ Fish ♦ Formal ♦
The dining rooms of this restaurant are on two floors and offer a variety of culinary
specialities - Japanese dishes, grilled meats, shellfish and seafood.

XX   **Neuv Caval 'd Brôns**   AC ⇔ VISA ∞ AE ①

piazza San Carlo 151 ⊠ *10123 –* ℰ *011 539030 – info@cavallodibronzo.it
– Fax 011 5 92 04 85 – www.cavallodibronzo.it
– closed 10 days in mid-August and Sunday evening*   **E2**
Rest – Carte 62/76 €
♦ Fish ♦ Formal ♦
Located under the portico of a 19C mansion, this elegant, prestigious restaurant
specialises in traditional Piedmontese cuisine. Fish dishes also available.

XX   **Al Garamond**   AC ⇔ VISA ∞ AE

via Pomba 14 ⊠ *10123 –* ℰ *011 8122781 – info@algaramond.it
– www.algaramond.it
– closed Saturday lunchtime and Sunday*   **E2**
Rest – Carte 45/72 € 🕸
♦ Modern ♦ Formal ♦
Named after a lieutenant in Napoleon's dragoons, this restaurant serves creative,
modern cuisine. Young, enthusiastic staff.

XX   **Al Gatto Nero**   AC ∞ AE ①

corso Filippo Turati 14 ⊠ *10128 –* ℰ *011 590414 – info@gattonero.it
– Fax 011 50 22 45 – www.gattonero.it
– closed Sunday*   **E3**
Rest – Carte 45/62 € 🕸
♦ Tuscany ♦ Retro ♦
Piedmontese and Tuscan dishes with a Mediterranean flavour take pride of place
in this established restaurant. Excellent wine list with over 1,000 different wines. An
unusual cat themed decor.

XX   **Galante**   AC VISA ∞ AE ①

corso Palestro 15 ⊠ *10122 –* ℰ *011 537757 – didomax@hotmail.it
– Fax 011 5 17 82 07 – www.ristorantegalante.it
– closed 3 weeks in August, Saturday lunch and Sunday*   **E1**
Rest – Carte 35/50 €
♦ Fish ♦ Formal ♦
A classical, elegant restaurant, attractively furnished with upholstered chairs, soft
shades, columns and mirrors. The cuisine focuses on Piedmont specialities and
fish dishes.

XX **Babette**   AC VISA ⚫⚫ AE ①

via Alfieri 16/F ⊠ 10121 – ℰ 011 547882
– info@ristorantebabette.it – Fax 011 19 50 34 12
– www.ristorantebabette.it
– closed from 8 to 31 August, Saturday lunchtime and Sunday   **D2**
Rest – Carte 37/47 € ※
  ◆ Inventive ◆ Fashionable ◆
Amazement and elegance immediately spring to the fore: a modern establishment, furnished with refined and minimalist taste in stone and wood. The cuisine
is also between classical and creative, and it has an excellent wine cellar.

XX **Perbacco**   AC ⟷ VISA ⚫⚫ AE ①

via Mazzini 31 ⊠ 10123 – ℰ 011 882110 – Fax 011 83 75 17
– www.ristoranteperbacco.torino.it
– closed August and Sunday   **E2**
Rest – *(dinner only)* Menu 35 €
  ◆ Regional ◆ Family ◆
Open late into the evening, this modern restaurant, run by the same family for
over a century, is popular with actors and theatre goers. Four-course menu with
various options.

XX **Solferino**   AC VISA ⚫⚫ AE

piazza Solferino 3 ⊠ 10121 – ℰ 011 535851 – Fax 011 53 51 95
– www.ristorantesolferino.com
– closed 25 December-2 January, Easter, August, Saturday lunch and Sunday
Rest – Carte 33/42 €   **D2**
  ◆ Regional ◆ Family ◆
This restaurant has been serving traditional Italian cuisine for almost 30 years. The
house specialities are homemade dishes from the Piedmont region.

X **San Tommaso 10 Lavazza**   AC VISA ⚫⚫ AE ①

via San Tommaso 10 ⊠ 10122 – ℰ 011 534201 – f.sgura@lavazza.it
– Fax 011 54 93 04 – www.lavazza.it
– closed August and Sunday   **E1**
Rest – Carte 38/73 €
  ◆ Regional ◆ Trendy ◆
Right behind the bar, beauty is the element that characterises every creation. The
pleasure of looking out at the view and tempting the palate with Italian cuisine
that reinterprets fantasy into delicate and intriguing recipes.

X **Sotto la Mole**   AC VISA ⚫⚫

via Montebello 9 ⊠ 10124 – ℰ 011 8179398
– info@sottolamole.eu – Fax 011 8 17 93 98
– www.sottolamole.eu
– closed Sunday from June to September, Wednesday and at midday (except
Sunday) the rest of the year   **E1**
Rest – Carte 31/47 €
  ◆ Regional ◆ Friendly ◆
This small, attractive restaurant looks directly onto the quayside. The interior is
decorated with old-fashioned advertising posters. The cuisine is traditional.

X **Ponte Vecchio**   AC VISA ⚫⚫ AE ①

via San Francesco da Paola 41 ⊠ 10123 – ℰ 011 835100 – Fax 011 88 38 79
– www.ristorantino.net
– closed August, Monday and Tuesday lunchtime   **E2**
Rest – Carte 26/50 €
  ◆ Regional ◆ Family ◆
The same family has run this partially renovated restaurant for three generations.
Classical early 20C decor and traditional Italian and regional cuisine.

ITALY - TURIN

✗ **Taverna delle Rose**   AC VISA ⓒⓐ AE ①
via Massena 24 ⊠ 10128 – 𝒞 011 538345 – tavernadellerose@gmail.com
– Fax 011 53 83 45
– closed August, Saturday lunchtime and Sunday   **D3**
Rest – Carte 25/43 €
♦ Italian ♦ Friendly ♦
Pleasant, informal atmosphere and a wide selection of traditional and classical
Italian dishes. Romantic dining room with exposed brickwork and soft lighting in
the evening.

LINGOTTO FIERE   *Plan III*

Le Meridien Turin Art+Tech   �&ं AC ⇆ rm ¶¶ ♨ P
via Nizza 230 ⊠ 10126 – 𝒞 011 6642000   VISA ⓒⓐ AE ①
– reservations_turin@lemeridien.com – Fax 011 6 64 20 04
– www.lemeridien.com
– closed August
140 rm – ¶¶150/410 €, ⊇ 13 € – 1 suite   **H2**
Rest – Carte 36/52 €
♦ Palace ♦ Design ♦
A panoramic lift takes guests from the small lobby to the top floor, where a
balcony provides access to the bedrooms. A sister hotel to the Hotel Lingotto,
although the layout here is more modern. This bright, spacious restaurant
furnished in cherry wood has an elegant yet informal atmosphere. Traditional
cuisine.

Le Meridien Lingotto   🚗 ☷ �&ं AC ⇆ rm ¶¶ ♨ P VISA ⓒⓐ AE ①
via Nizza 262 ⊠ 10126 – 𝒞 011 6642000
– reservations_turin@lemeridien.com – Fax 011 6 64 20 01
– www.lemeridien.com   **H2**
240 rm ⊇ – ¶110/300 € ¶¶125/300 € – 14 suites
Rest *Torpedo* – Carte 36/52 €
♦ Palace ♦ Design ♦
This modern hotel in the Palazzo del Lingotto has been successfully converted
from an old industrial building. Contemporary bedrooms designed by Renzo
Piano, plus a tropical garden. Comfortable armchairs at the tables of this bright
and elegant restaurant, which serves high quality cuisine.

AC Torino   ☝ं �& AC ⇆ rm ¶¶ ♨ P VISA ⓒⓐ AE ①
via Bisalta 11 ⊠ 10126 – 𝒞 011 6395091
– actorino@ac-hotels.com – Fax 011 6 67 78 22
– www.ac-hotels.com   **H2**
89 rm ⊇ – ¶¶110/330 € – 6 suites
Rest – *(residents only)* Menu 35/70 €
♦ Chain hotel ♦ Luxury ♦ Minimalist ♦
Once a pasta factory, this typical industrial building dates from the early 20C.
It is now an up-to-date, minimalist style hotel offering comfortable, modern
facilities.

Giotto without rest   AC ¶¶ ♨ VISA ⓒⓐ AE ①
via Giotto 27 ⊠ 10126 – 𝒞 011 6637172
– info@hotelgiottotorino.it – Fax 011 6 63 71 73
– www.hotelgiottotorino.it   **H1**
50 rm ⊇ – ¶80/125 € ¶¶90/162 €
♦ Traditional ♦ Modern ♦
This modern hotel is situated in a residential area near the River Po close to the
Valentino park. It has spacious, well-appointed bedrooms, many of which have
baths or hydromassage showers.

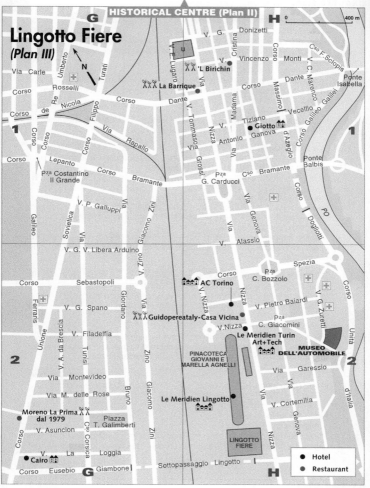

Lingotto Fiere
(Plan III)

HISTORICAL CENTRE (Plan II)

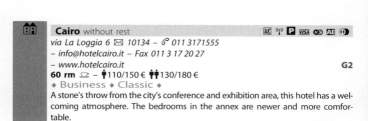

Cairo without rest   AC ░ P VISA ⓜ AE ⓪

via La Loggia 6 ⊠ 10134 – ℰ 011 3171555
– info@hotelcairo.it – Fax 011 3 17 20 27
– www.hotelcairo.it   **G2**
60 rm ⌑ – ♦110/150 € ♦♦130/180 €
♦ Business ♦ Classic ♦

A stone's throw from the city's conference and exhibition area, this hotel has a welcoming atmosphere. The bedrooms in the annex are newer and more comfortable.

561

XXX
ٷ
Guidopereataly-Casa Vicina (Claudio Vicina Mazzaretto) &
via Nizza 224 ✉ *10126 –* ✆ *011 19506840* 🅰🅒 🆅🅸🆂🅰 ⓞⓞ 🅰🅴
– casavicina@libero.it – Fax 011 19 50 68 95 – www.casavicina.it
*– closed during Christmas period, 10 August - 8 September, Sunday evening
and Monday* **H1**
Rest – Menu 50/100 € – Carte 61/83 € 🍴
Spec. Tonno di coniglio grigio con giardiniera in agrodolce. Agnolotti pizzi-
cati a mano al sugo d'arrosto. Rognone "à la coque" con vellutata di senape
e aglio in camicia.
◆ Modern ◆ Minimalist ◆
Inside Eatitaly, the first Italian supermarket with 'niche' foodstuffs, the minimalist
style restaurant offers a wide range of creative cuisine.

XXX
ٷ
La Barrique (Stefano Gallo) 🅰🅒 ⇄ 🆅🅸🆂🅰 ⓞⓞ
corso Dante 53 ✉ *10126 –* ✆ *011 657900 – labarriquedigallostefano@virgilio.it
– Fax 011 65 79 95 – www.labarriqueristorante.it
– closed Sunday and Monday* **H1**
Rest – Menu 85 € – Carte 68/92 € 🍴
Spec. Fagottini al nero di seppia con sugo di pescatrice (spring-summer).
Riso mantecato ai gamberi rossi, funghi porcini secchi e seppie (autumn).
Hamburger di coda di vitella piemontese brasata al vino nebbiolo.
◆ Modern ◆ Formal ◆
Friendly, family management in this restaurant that blends classical regional
dishes, fresh pastas, fish, meat and the inevitable triumph of chocolate, for more
creative fare.

XX
ٷ
Moreno La Prima dal 1979 🅰🅒 ⇄ 🆅🅸🆂🅰 ⓞⓞ 🅰🅴 ⓞ
corso Unione Sovietica 244 ✉ *10134 –* ✆ *011 3179191 – info@
laprimamoreno.it – Fax 011 3 14 34 23 – www.laprimamoreno.it
– closed twenty days in August and Monday midday* **G2**
Rest – Carte 60/70 €
◆ Modern ◆ Formal ◆
This elegant restaurant stands in an unusual location surrounded by greenery. In
the dining room, attractive tables are set out next to the large windows overlooking the garden. The cuisine is a blend of the modern and traditional.

XX
ٷ
'L Birichin 🅰🅒 ⇄ 🆅🅸🆂🅰 ⓞⓞ 🅰🅴 ⓞ
via Vincenzo Monti 16/A ✉ *10126 –* ✆ *011 657457 – batavia@birichin.it
– Fax 011 65 74 57 – www.birichin.it
– closed August and Sunday* **H1**
Rest – Carte 46/76 € 🍴
◆ Modern ◆ Formal ◆
The young chef in this light suffused establishment offers a creative cuisine. Offering mainly fish, embellished in turn with produce from the south but never forgetting Piedmont.

AT THE HILLS *Plan I*

XX
ٷ
Locanda Mongreno (Pier Bussetti)
*strada comunale di Mongreno 50 (will move to Govone-CN- in the second half
of 2009)* ✉ *10132 –* ✆ *011 8980417 – info@locandamongreno.it
– Fax 011 8 22 73 45 – www.locandamongreno.it
– closed from 26 December to 10 January, from 25 August to 10 September
and Mondays* **B1**
Rest – *(dinner only)* Menu 60/85 € – Carte 61/83 € 🍴
Spec. Insalata russa in due versioni. Risotto al té con calamaretti e profumo
di lime (spring-summer). Succo di fragole con fragole, gelato al fior di panna
e gelatina di limone (spring-summer).
◆ Inventive ◆ Formal ◆
The enthusiastic management has refined this establishment outside Turin over
time. From the kitchen emerge masterpieces of fish and meat, which tirelessly
play between tradition and creativity.

XX   **Villa Somis**   ← 🚗 🏠 🏡 ⅍ AC ⇦ P VISA ∞ AE ①
strada Val Pattonera 138 ⊠ 10133 – ℰ 011 6312617 – info@villasomis.it
– Fax 011 6 31 23 36 – www.villasomis.it
– closed from 10 to 20 August, 1 week in January, Sunday evening and
Monday   **B2**
Rest – *(dinner only)* Menu 35/100 € – Carte 58/76 € 🕸
◆ Modern ◆ Formal ◆
Set amid the hills, this 18C residence of the eponymous musician is now an elegant restaurant. The menu shows modern inspiration.

XX   **La Cloche**   🏠 AC ⇦ P VISA ∞ AE ①
strada al Traforo del Pino 106 ⊠ 10132 – ℰ 011 8994213 – lacloche@
tiscalinet.it – Fax 011 8 98 15 22 – www.lacloche.it
– closed three weeks in July, Sunday evening and Monday   **B2**
Rest – Carte 32/44 €
◆ Regional ◆ Formal ◆
Funghi and truffles in the autumn, country produce in the spring. Whatever your choice, this charming establishment offers its guests the passion for traditional Piedmontese cuisine.

AT CASELLE TORINESE

    Jet Hotel   AC 🛈 ⅍ P VISA ∞ AE ①
via Della Zecca 9 – ℰ 0119913733 – info@jet-hotel.com – Fax 011 9 96 15 44
– www.jet-hotel.com
– closed from 6 to 20 August
79 rm ⊏⊐ – ♦70/195 € ♦♦120/240 €
Rest Antica Zecca – ℰ 0119961403 *(closed Monday)* Carte 32/50 €
◆ Business ◆ Traditional ◆ Classic ◆
Housed in a beautiful, renovated 16C building this hotel has an elegant atmosphere, good standard of service and well-equipped bedrooms. Conveniently located near the airport. Elegant restaurant serving creative dishes inspired by traditional, regional cuisine.

AT RIVOLI   *Plan 22*

XXX   **Combal.zero** (Davide Scabin)   ← AC VISA ∞ AE ①
😣 😣   *piazza Mafalda di Savoia – ℰ 011 9565225 – combal.zero@combal.org*
– Fax 011 9 56 52 48 – www.combal.org
– closed from 24 December to 7 January, from 3 to 26 August, Sunday and
Monday
Rest – Carte 80/115 € 🕸
Spec. Uovo affogato con salsa d'acciughe e misticanza di stagione. Cybereggs. Lingua di vitello brasata al Barolo con purè di patate ratte e cuori di sedano bianco brasato.
◆ Inventive ◆ Design ◆
Near the museum of contemporary art, from which it draws the modern and essentialist forms, is this kingdom of gastronomic eclecticism. Savour cuisine from classical Piedmontese to more imaginative dishes.

AT VENARIA REALE   *Plan I*

    Galant without rest   AC 🛈 P VISA ∞ AE ①
corso Garibaldi 155 – ℰ 011 4551021 – info@hotelgalant.it – Fax 011 4 55 12 19
– www.hotelgalant.it   **A1**
39 rm ⊏⊐ – ♦91/139 € ♦♦133/190 €
◆ Family ◆ Classic ◆
This modern hotel situated less than a kilometre from the Stadio delle Alpi is ideal for business clients. Attractive public rooms and simple, comfortable bedrooms.

ITALY - TURIN

Cascina di Corte

via Amedeo di Castellamonte 2 – ℰ 011 4593278 – info@cascinadicorte.it
– Fax 011 4 59 83 95 – www.cascinadicorte.it
– closed from 10 to 23 August   **A1**
10 rm – ♦130/220 € ♦♦160/280 € – 2 suites   **Rest** – Carte 29/54 €
♦ Historic ♦ Rustic ♦

Not far from the famous palace, this 19C farmhouse with adjoining ice-cream parlour has a simple architectural style that is typical of the region. A rustic interior with exposed brickwork in the bedrooms goes hand-in-hand with modern, comfortable furnishings and facilities.

Dolce Stil Novo alla Reggia (Alfredo Russo)

piazza della Repubblica 4 – ℰ 011 4992343 – info@
dolcestilnovo.com – Fax 01 14 99 23 42 – www.dolcestilnovo.com
– closed 2 weeks January, 2 weeks August, Sunday dinner and Monday
Rest – *(number of covers limited, pre-book)* Menu 70/90 €   **A1**
– Carte 66/90 €
Spec. Fritto ipercroccante di pesce e verdure. Coscia d'anatra morbida profumata agli agrumi. Crema di pan di spezie con mandarino e yogurt naturale (inverno).
♦ Inventive ♦ Formal ♦

Inside the Torrione del Garove, the restaurant offers a fascinating terrace facing the gardens of the Reggia di Venaria. Two spacious dining rooms and minimalist furniture will welcome you inside. Traditional cuisine with some seafood suggestions.

Il Reale

corso Garibaldi 153 – ℰ 011 4530413 – info@ilreale.it – Fax 011 4 54 09 35
– www.ilreale.it
– closed from 10 to 25 August   **A1**
Rest – Menu 30/40 € – Carte 35/45 € ॐ
♦ Regional ♦ Formal ♦

Opened in 2000, this relatively new restaurant has two elegant, modern dining rooms. The menu here focuses on creative regional cuisine and fish specialities.

LUXEMBOURG
LËTZEBUERG

PROFILE

→ **AREA:**
2 586 km²
(998 sq mi).

→ **POPULATION:**
468 600 inhabitants
(est. 2005) nearly
62% nationals,
38% resident
foreigners (mostly
Belgian, French,
German, Italian and
Portuguese); Density
= 181 per km².

→ **CAPITAL:**
Luxembourg
(conurbation
125 000 inhabitants).

→ **CURRENCY:**
Euro (€); rate of
exchange: € 1 =
US$ 1.32 (Jan 2009).

→ **GOVERNMENT:**
Constitutional
parliamentary
monarchy (since
1868). Member of
European Union since
1957 (one of the 6
founding countries).

→ **LANGUAGES:**
The official language
is Lëtzebuergesch, a
variant of German,
similar to the Frankish
dialect of the Moselle
valley; High German
is used for general
purposes and is the
first language for
teaching; French
is the literary and

administrative
language.

→ **SPECIFIC PUBLIC
HOLIDAYS:**
Carnival (Late
February-
March); National
Day (23 June);
Luxembourg City
Kermesse (early
September, applies to
the Luxembourg City
only); St. Stephen's
Day (26 December).

→ **LOCAL TIME:**
GMT + 1 hour in
winter and GMT
+ 2 hours in summer.

→ **CLIMATE:**
Temperate
continental with
cold winters and
mild summers
(Luxembourg:
January: 1°C, July:
17°C).

→ **INTERNATIONAL
DIALLING CODE:**
00 352 followed by
the local number of 5
or 6 or (exceptionally)
8 figures. Online
telephone directory:
www.editus.lu

→ **EMERGENCY NUMBERS:**
Police : ☎ 113 ;
Medical Assistance :
☎ 112.

→ **ELECTRICITY:**
220 volts AC, 50Hz;

LUXEMBOURG

2-pin round-shaped
continental plugs.

→ **FORMALITIES**
Travellers from the
European Union
(EU), Switzerland,
Iceland and the main
countries of North
and South America
need a national
identity card or
passport (America:
passport required)
to visit the
Grand Duchy of
Luxembourg for less
than three
months (tourism or
business purpose).
For visitors from
other countries
a visa may be
required, in addition
to a passport,
especially for those
wishing to stay for
longer than three
months. We advise
you to check with
your embassy before
travelling.

LUXEMBOURG
LËTZEBUERG

Population: 85 467 – Altitude: 300m

N. Rung/Author's Image/PHOTONONSTOP

uxembourg may be small but it's perfectly formed. And perfectly situated. It stands high above two rivers on a sandstone bluff, looking composedly back on a thousand year history that's been anything but composed. Its commanding position over sheer gorges may be a boon to modern day visitors, but down the centuries that very setting of enviable altitude has rendered it the subject of conquest on many occasions.

ts eye-catching geography makes it a city of distinctive districts, linked by spectacular bridges spanning lush green valleys. The city squares boast elegant façades painted in pastel colours, ideally suited as the backdrop to café culture on a warm afternoon. UNESCO liked what they saw, and in 1994 conferred World Heritage Status on the old town. It may not be instantly apparent, but Luxembourg is also a hub of activity for the European Union, with new buildings and offices mushrooming in recent years – thankfully, some way from the old centre. Most visitors head in the opposite direction for wonderful walks in the valleys and across the fine bridges, finding this the best way to appreciate the capital's uniquely charming aura.

LIVING THE CITY

The absolute heart of the city is the **old town**, unmistakable at the top of its surrounding valleys, its most prominent landmark the **cathedral** spires. Winding its way deep below to the south west is the river **Pétrusse**, which has its confluence with the river **Alzette** in the south east. Directly to the south of the old town is the rather sleazy **railway station** quarter, while down at river level to the east is the altogether more attractive **Grund** district, which has northerly neighbours **Clausen** and **Pfaffenthal**. Up in the north east, connected by the grand sounding **Pont Grand-Duchesse Charlotte**, is the EU institution quarter of **Kirchberg Plateau**.

PRACTICAL INFORMATION

ARRIVAL-DEPARTURE

Luxembourg-Findel Airport is 6km from the city centre ; a taxi should cost about €25. Alternatively, take city bus Number 16 which runs every 20min and takes 25min.

TRANSPORT

There's a good bus service in Luxembourg City, but no metro or tram. Buses run from 5am to 10pm each day, and there's an additional late night service on Fridays and Saturdays only. The most convenient bus stations for visitors are at the exit of Gare Centrale and on Place Hamilius in the old town. The fare system (valid for trains too) is simple enough: for trips of 10km or less you buy a 'short' ticket; for an unlimited day ticket (valid till 8am the next day) you buy a Billet Reseau.

You can also opt for the Luxembourg Card. This is valid for one, two or three days and, apart from giving you unlimited use of public transport, also offers free admission to lots of attractions, not just in the city but in other parts of the country too. Available from tourist offices, it's valid throughout the summer. In winter, the Stater Museeskaart offers three days of free admission to important sights in Luxembourg City.

EXPLORING LUXEMBOURG CITY

It's not every city that can boast 'Europe's Most Beautiful Balcony' in its blurb. But Luxembourg can. Along the stunning pedestrian promenade called **Chemin de la Corniche** there are scintillating views over the sheer-sided gorges that give this elegantly compact city a natural aesthetic advantage over so many others. Luxembourg City has taken a battering over the centuries. It's been taken by the Burgundians, Spanish, French, Austrians and Prussians; the stately old defensive walls that remain around the edges of the centre add an extra layer of historic charm to the place.

→ TAKING UP D'ARMES

The old town, nestled above the gorges, is a true delight. Its narrow streets are home to arty residents, while quirky shops, traditional cafés and fine restaurants enhance the general feel of a city contented in its skin. At the centre is the slightly formal Place Guillaume II, where you'll find the town hall. Most people, though, make a beeline for the **Place d'Armes**, the 'Parlour of the City', lined with sunny pavement terraces in the summer. The feeling of informality is enhanced when you stroll a little way east and come across the **Ducal Grand Palace**. No pomp or circumstance here, despite the fact that Louis XIV and Napoleon called in. Nowadays, with the royals having left some time ago, the Moorish-style palace, built by the Spanish in 1570, is used for functions on the inside, and as a tourist spot for photos on the outside. You're not bothered by traffic or blaring horns, and there's just a single guard on duty. All very peaceful. If you *are* searching out more life, the area right behind the Ducal Palace has several restaurants.

→ HISTORY LESSON

There's a great museum here too, just round the corner from the palace. It's the **National Museum of History and Art**, and its show-stopping white contours come as quite a surprise after the Ducal Grand Palace. It's a state-of-the-art affair, with a glass atrium and exhibits housed over several levels. They range from the 13C to the present day and highlights include a superb Roman mosaic, absorbing works by Luxembourg's Expressionist artist Joseph Kutter, paintings by Cézanne, Picasso and Magritte, and a watercolour of the city by Turner. South from here, you can indulge a comprehensive primer on the life and times of this underestimated city at the impressive **Luxembourg City History Museum**, which, over six floors, does pretty much what it says on the label.

Luxembourg City has raised itself above the museum parapet and shone

a light into the 21C with its brand new **Museum of Modern Art,** opened in 2006. Located in the Kirchberg district, it's a stunning white concrete-and-glass palace and home to an eclectic mix of work, including photography, painting, multimedia, fashion, design and graphic arts. Close by, another new building has seen the light of day: the **Luxembourg Philharmonic Hall** is now *the* place to catch a concert in the city. It's not just home to the Philharmonic Orchestra, but also caters to a wide range of styles including jazz and world music. There are three separate concert halls, and you can squeeze in any number from 120 to 1,500.

→ ON THE CASE

From the modern to the extremely ancient – at the end of the wonderful Chemin de la Corniche you arrive at the cliff on which the very first castle was built in 963. It's called **The Bock**, and though its mighty fort and fortifications are now no more than ruins, that's not the case with the **Casemates**. This is a labyrinth of 17C-18C underground defences carved out beneath the Bock by the Spaniards. These rock thoroughfares have known a number of uses down the years. They've seen action as slaughterhouses and bakeries and housed garrisons of soldiers. Many of the locals used them as bomb shelters during the two world wars. Further west, there are more casemates at Pétrusse, but these are slightly less accessible than those at Bock.

→ A GRUND LIFE

Another little world exists below the Bock, and it's called the Grund, or the lower town. It's an attractive area, where the cluster of cafés, bars and restaurants sits easily alongside the meandering Alzette. Its characterful charm is enhanced by clumps of ruins offset by groups of terrace houses, once home to artisans who needed the river waters to assist them in their crafts. There's an easy way to get down here: just take the elevator from the **Plateau du St Esprit**, a hilltop bluff that itself offers stunning views over the valleys and the Grund. Although it pretty much exists in its very own green heaven, Luxembourg has fashioned itself a lovely **park,** and very moreish it is too. It's down in the valley on the same level as the Grund, but west of it in the vicinity of the Pétrusse. Get down to it from the Old Bridge, or Viaduc and, if you're here in the spring, take in the stunning display of magnolias.

CALENDAR HIGHLIGHTS

For a small place, Luxembourg packs a big festive punch. From the end of November until early January, the Winter Lights Festival uses Christmas as the excuse to let rip with street art, theatre, concerts and fireworks. Spring is celebrated with the Printemps Festival, which lasts from March until June. At concert venues throughout the city, internationally acclaimed world music and jazz musicians hold centre stage. The spotlight moves to the city's great outdoors in May with the running of the Luxembourg Marathon. This is a marathon with a difference, held in the evening and to the accompaniment of revellers soaking up the atmosphere at mini festivals in the narrow streets of the old town. Locals keep the evening of 22 June clear in their diaries: this is the eve before National Day, when fireworks are set off from the bridge over the Pétrusse Valley, and there's much partying with music and dancing on Place d'Armes and Place Guillaume II. One of Europe's biggest funfairs has evolved over the centuries from an ancient shepherd's market – it's called Schueberfouer, and it lasts two weeks from the end of August, when seemingly most of the city comes along to watch the lavish fireworks that finish it all off.

EATING OUT

The taste buds of Luxembourg have been very much influenced by French classical cuisine and the results are there for all to savour, particularly around and about the old town, an area that in the summer becomes one smart open-air terrace. The centre of town is in fact an eclectic place to eat. It runs the gauntlet from fast-style pizzeria (there are lots of Italians in the

LUXEMBOURG CITY IN...

→ **ONE DAY**
Place d'Armes, Ducal Grand Palace, National Museum of History and Art, Chemin de la Corniche

→ **TWO DAYS**
Leisurely coffee back on Place d'Armes, Luxembourg City History Museum, Bock Casemates, afternoon and evening in the Grund, including a meal in one of its restaurants

→ **THREE DAYS**
Kirchberg Plateau, Museum of Modern Art, concert at Luxembourg Philharmonic Hall

city), taverns, cafés and brasseries up to expense account restaurants favoured by bankers and businessmen. On winter evenings, though, this part of town can be a bit quiet. A good bet for atmosphere, certainly in the darker months, is the Grund, which offers a variety of restaurants with a wide range of prices. It's certainly the area that boasts the most popular cafés and pubs. A few trendy places have sprouted over recent times near the Casemates, and these too are proving to be pretty hot with the younger crowd. On the menus here look out for the local speciality *Judd mat Gaardebounen*, which is a very hearty smoked neck of pork with broad beans. The Grand Duchy produces its own white and sparkling wines on the borders of the Moselle. These didn't have much of a reputation at first, but over the last decade a number of young winemakers have produced some interesting wines. You'll rarely find these abroad, as they're bought locally by business people and smart restaurants. At the end of your meal, a service charges is included in your bill, but if you want to tip, ten per cent is a reasonable amount.

→ NOTRE DAMNED

The city's Notre Dame Cathedral is unmissable, what with its black spires reaching up above the rooftops. And inside it has Luxembourg's most revered icon, The Lady Comforter of the Afflicted. But you won't see the city's greatest church in many 'must-see' lists. That's because the rest of the interior is full of renovations and mismatching styles, creating a none to inspiring mishmash. You're better off heading by on your way to the grand views of the Viaduc.

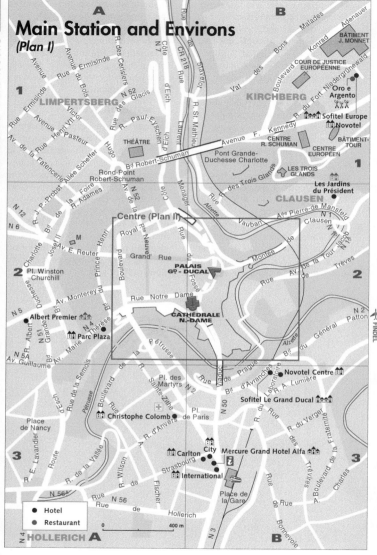

Main Station and Environs
(Plan I)

LIMPERTSBERG

KIRCHBERG

BÂTIMENT J. MONNET

COUR DE JUSTICE EUROPÉENNE

Oro e Argento

Sofitel Europe
Novotel

BÂTIMENT-TOUR

CENTRE R. SCHUMAN

CENTRE EUROPÉEN

THÉÂTRE

Avenue F. Kennedy

Pont Grande-Duchesse Charlotte

LES TROIS GLANDS

Les Jardins du Président

Rond-Point Robert-Schuman

CLAUSEN

Centre (Plan II)

PALAIS Gᵈ - DUCAL

Pl. Winston Churchill

Albert Premier

Parc Plaza

CATHÉDRALE N.-DAME

FINDEL

Novotel Centre

Sofitel Le Grand Ducal

Pl. des Martyrs

Christophe Colomb

Pl. de Paris

Place de Nancy

Carlton
City
Mercure Grand Hotel Alfa

International

Place de la Gare

● Hotel
● Restaurant

0 ————— 400 m

HOLLERICH

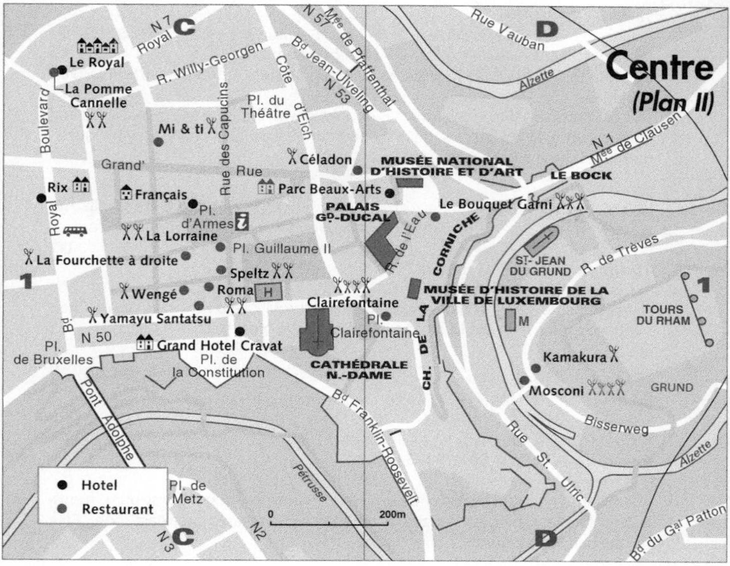

CENTRE
Plan II

Le Royal
rest

bd Royal 12 ✉ *2449 –* ✆ *241 61 61 – reservations@leroyalluxembourg.com – Fax 22 59 48 – www.leroyalluxembourg.com*

190 rm – 🚹380/510 € 🚹🚹380/510 €, ☕ 27 € – 20 suites **C1**

Rest *La Pomme Cannelle* – see below

Rest *Le Jardin* – ✆ *0 4 161 67 37* – Carte 37/61 €

◆ Palace ◆ Personalised ◆

A modern, luxury hotel with extremely comfortable bedrooms in the main building. The Royal Club wing is home to several types of suites. Spa, piano bar and a high level of service. The Le Jardin restaurant serves classic brasserie-style dishes. Lunch buffet every Sunday.

Sofitel Le Grand Ducal

bd d'Avranches 40 ✉ *1160 –* ✆ *24 87 71 – h5555@accor.com – Fax 26 48 02 23 – www.sofitel.com* *Plan I* **B3**

126 rm – 🚹550/1500 € 🚹🚹550/1500 €, ☕ 30 € – 2 suites

Rest *Top Floor* – *(open until 11pm)* Carte 64/78 €

◆ Chain hotel ◆ Business ◆ Modern ◆

Luxury, comfort and a designer decor are the hallmarks of this new hotel in which half of the guestrooms enjoy views of the city.

Parc Belair

av. du X Septembre 111 (by N5) ✉ *2551 Belair –* ✆ *442 32 31 – reception.belair@goeres-group.com – Fax 44 44 84 – www.goeres-group.com*

52 rm ☕ – 🚹280/360 € 🚹🚹302/382 € – 1 suite

Rest – *(closed Saturday lunch and Sunday lunch)* Menu 30/50 € – Carte 29/47 €

◆ Luxury ◆ Personalised ◆

A modern building offering comfortable guestrooms and junior suites, some with a themed decor. Quieter rooms with more attractive park views to the rear. Pleasant lounge bar. A bistro with a menu focusing on traditional cuisine.

Albert Premier 🛜 ᵬ 🕸 🕸 ᵬ rest 🅰 ᵬ 🖼 🖧 ✎ 🚗

r. Albert Iᵉʳ 2a ✉ *1117 Belair –* ℰ *442 44 21 – hotel@*   VISA ⓒⓞ 🆎 ⓘ
albertpremier.lu – Fax 44 74 41 – www.albertpremier.lu   Plan I **A2**
39 rm – 🛏255/465 € 🛏🛏255/465 €, � 18 € – 1 suite   **Rest** – Carte 43/70 €
◆ Luxury ◆ Modern ◆

This old house on the edge of town is endowed with English-style public areas and
lounges, as well as cosy, traditional bedrooms. Excellent contemporary guestrooms in the new wing.

Parc Beaux-Arts without rest   ᵬ 🕸 🖧 ✎ VISA ⓒⓞ 🆎 ⓘ

r. Sigefroi 1 ✉ *2536 –* ℰ *26 86 76 – reception.beauxarts@goeres-group.com*
– Fax 26 86 76 36 – www.goeres-group.com   **D1**
10 rm ⊷ – 🛏360/425 € 🛏🛏382/447 €
◆ Luxury ◆

A well-restored series of old houses adjoining the Musée d'Histoire et d'Art. Charming, neo-retro style public areas and suites. Good breakfast.

Rix without rest   ᵬ 🕸 **P** VISA ⓒⓞ

bd Royal 20 ✉ *2449 –* ℰ *47 16 66 – info@hotelrix.lu – Fax 22 75 35*
– www.hotelrix.lu
– closed 1ˢᵗ - 4 January and 2 - 16 August   **C1**
22 rm ⊷ – 🛏180 € 🛏🛏180/195 €
◆ Functional ◆

A family-run hotel set back from a busy road. Somewhat sober guestrooms furnished in a variety of styles. Attractive, traditionally decorated breakfast room. Free
private parking for guests.

Novotel Centre   ᵬ ᵬ 🅰 ᵬ 🖼 🕸 🖧 VISA ⓒⓞ 🆎 ⓘ

r. Laboratoire 35 ✉ *1911 –* ℰ *24 87 81 – h5556@accor.com*
– Fax 26 48 02 24   Plan I **B3**
150 rm – 🛏85/275 € 🛏🛏85/275 €, ⊷ 20 €
Rest – *(closed Saturday lunch and Sunday lunch) (open until 11pm)*
Carte 36/54 €
◆ Business ◆ Functional ◆

Opened in May 2007, this chain hotel stands midway between the railway station
and old town. Modern façade, designer-styled public areas, functional guestrooms,
and seminar facilties. Contemporary dining in this restaurant with its fashionable
decor of claret, black and white.

Grand Hôtel Cravat   🅰 rest ᵬ 🕸 🖧 VISA ⓒⓞ 🆎 ⓘ

bd Roosevelt 29 ✉ *2450 –* ℰ *22 19 75 – contact@hotelcravat.lu*
– Fax 22 67 11 – www.hotelcravat.lu   **C1**
61 rm ⊷ – 🛏260/280 € 🛏🛏380/395 €   **Rest** – Menu 42 € – Carte 45/57 €
◆ Retro ◆

This long-standing hotel is located on a square with panoramic views of the Pétrusse valley. Comfortable, classically furnished guestrooms of varying size. This
old style building located on the square with views of the Pétrusse valley is home
to a hotel with comfortable, classic style rooms of various sizes.

Parc Plaza 🌶   🛜 ᵬ 🖧 **P** ✎ VISA ⓒⓞ 🆎 ⓘ

av. Marie-Thérèse 5 ✉ *2132 –* ℰ *456 14 11 – reception.plaza@*
goeres-group.com – Fax 0 5 614 12 22 – www.goeres-group.com   Plan I **A2**
89 rm ⊷ – 🛏205/230 € 🛏🛏223/248 €
Rest – *(closed Saturday lunch and Sunday lunch)* Menu 32 € – Carte 26/45 €
◆ Business ◆ Classical ◆

A modern complex divided into three sections: the Parc Plaza, with a reception
area and close to 90 bedrooms, the Parc Belle-Vue, with some 60 bedrooms, and
the wing set aside for dining and meetings. Traditional cuisine served in the
tavern-style interior or on the outdoor terrace.

Parc Belle-Vue 🏠

av. Marie-Thérèse 5 ✉ 2132 – ℰ 456 14 11 – reception.bellevue@goeres-group.com
– Fax 0 5 614 12 22 – www.goeres-group.com
58 rm ⚏ – ♦145 € ♦♦163 €
♦ Business ♦ Functional ♦

Français

pl. d'Armes 14 ✉ 1136 – ℰ 47 45 34 – info@hotelfrancais.lu
– Fax 46 42 74 – www.hotelfrancais.lu
C1
21 rm ⚏ – ♦99/120 € ♦♦125/140 €
Rest – *(open until 11pm)* Menu 25/70 € bi – Carte 33/66 €
♦ Functional ♦

Run by the same family since 1970, this hotel overlooks the city's liveliest square. Works of art on display throughout. Superbly maintained guestrooms. A tavern-style restaurant serving classic traditional cuisine.

Clairefontaine (Arnaud Magnier)

pl. de Clairefontaine 9 ✉ 1341 – ℰ 46 22 11 – clairefo@pt.lu – Fax 47 08 21
– www.restaurantclairefontaine.lu
– closed first week January, 1 week at Easter, 15 August - 6 September,
23 - 31 December, Saturday and Sunday
D1
Rest – Menu 78/98 € bi – Carte 68/102 € 🍴
Spec. Tartare de langoustines, haricots verts à la crème de truffe, carpaccio tiède de tête de veau, vinaigrette truffée. Poularde de Bresse cuite en vessie, farce au foie gras, sauce Albufera. Assiette autour du chocolat grand cru "Los Ancones", glace moka blanc.
♦ Contemporary ♦

An attractive restaurant with a terrace on an elegant square. Traditional decor with old wood panelling and contemporary furnishing. Creative modern cuisine and astute wine pairings.

Mosconi (Ilario Mosconi)

r. Münster 13 ✉ 2160 – ℰ 54 69 94 – mosconi@pt.lu – Fax 54 00 43
– www.mosconi.lu
– closed 1 week at Easter, last 3 weeks August, 24 December
– early January, Saturday lunch, Sunday and Monday
D1
Rest – Menu 44/110 € – Carte 81/148 € 🍴
Spec. Pâté de foies de poulet à la crème de truffes blanches, polenta, câpres caramélisées, sauce au vin rouge. Risotto aux truffes blanches (October-December). Porcelet, tortino de pommes de terre et poireaux.
♦ Italian ♦ Cosy ♦

An old manor house on the banks of the Alzette. Romantic, discreetly luxurious lounge and dining rooms where the focus is on fine Italian cuisine and an excellent wine list. Attractive terrace by the water.

Le Bouquet Garni (Thierry Duhr)

r. Eau 32 ✉ 1449 – ℰ 26 20 06 20 – bouquetgarni@pt.lu – Fax 26 20 09 11
– www.lebouquetgarni.lu
– closed 15 August – early September, late December
– early January, Sunday, Monday and bank holidays
D1
Rest – Menu 85 € – Carte 76/100 €
Spec. Tartare de thon Blue Fine, huîtres Gillardeau, gelée de concombre, jeunes pousses. Civet de homard rôti au vin rouge de Graves, mousseline de rattes légèrement fumée. Croquant de tiramisu, crème brûlée moka, gelée d'amaretto.
♦ Traditional ♦ Rustic ♦

Restaurant in an 18C house next to the Grand Duke's Palace. Refined classic cuisine with a modern touch served in an elegant, rustic setting. Small, wood-decked summer terrace.

575

XXX **Yves Radelet**   🛏 ⇔ 𝚅𝙸𝚂𝙰 ⦿ 🄰🄴

av. du X Septembre 44 (by N5) ✉ *2550 Belair –* 🕾 *22 26 18 – info@yvesradelet.lu – Fax 46 24 40 – www.yvesradelet.lu*
– closed 22 August - 8 September, Christmas, New Year, Sunday and Monday
Rest – Menu 48/80 € – Carte 66/83 €
♦ Cosy ♦

This restaurant moved to a completely refurbished mansion in 2008. Fusion of traditional and contemporary cuisine by the inventive chef who makes his own cheeses and prepares his own cured meats.

XX **Speltz**   🛏 🄰🄲 ⇔ 𝚅𝙸𝚂𝙰 ⦿ 🄰🄴 ⦿

r. Chimay 8 (corner Rue Louvigny) ✉ *1333 –* 🕾 *47 49 50*
– info@restaurant-speltz.lu – Fax 47 46 77
– www.restaurant-speltz.lu
– closed 12 - 20 April, 2 - 17 August, 24 December - 1ˢᵗ January, Sunday, Monday and bank holidays   **C1**
Rest – Menu 57/114 € bi – Carte approx. 70 €
♦ Family ♦

A gastronomic restaurant serving contemporary cuisine enhanced by a superb cheese trolley. Brasserie with a terrace on a pedestrianised street. Afternoon tea room.

XX **La Lorraine**   🛏 🄰🄲 ⇔ 𝚅𝙸𝚂𝙰 ⦿ 🄰🄴 ⦿

pl. d'Armes 7 ✉ *1136 –* 🕾 *47 14 36 – reservation.lorraine-luxembourg@blanc.net – Fax 47 09 64 – www.lalorraine-restaurant.lu*
– closed Sundays and bank holidays   **C1**
Rest – Carte 46/72 €
Rest *Bistrot de La Lorraine (on the ground floor)* – Carte 45/63 €
♦ Seafood ♦

Two types of cuisine are on offer within the walls of this fine building on Place d'Armes. A predominance of fish and seafood plus an excellent wine list in the restaurant. A bistro with a display of fresh oysters and a front terrace.

XX **La Pomme Cannelle** – H. Le Royal   ⛴ 🄰🄲 ⇔ ⇄ 𝚅𝙸𝚂𝙰 ⦿ 🄰🄴 ⦿

bd Royal 12 ✉ *2449 –* 🕾 *0 4 161 67 36 – restauration@leroyalluxembourg.com*
– Fax 22 29 85 – www.leroyalluxembourg.com
– closed 8 - 30 August, Saturday and Sunday   **C1**
Rest – Menu 49/79 € bi – Carte 67/84 € ⅏

♦ Contemporary ♦

Contemporary cuisine inspired by products of noble origin, and wines and spices from the New World. Elegant and warm interior reminiscent of the Indian Empire.

XX **Roma**   🛏 ⇔ 𝚅𝙸𝚂𝙰 ⦿ 🄰🄴 ⦿

r. Louvigny 5 ✉ *1946 –* 🕾 *22 36 92 – Fax 26 20 34 70*
– closed Monday   **C1**
Rest – Carte 45/58 € ⅏
♦ Italian ♦ Family ♦

One of the doyens of Luxembourg's 'ristoranti'. Relaxed atmosphere and attractive furnishings. Traditional and contemporary à la carte choices, as well as an excellent selection of Italian wines.

X **Wengé**   🛏 ⇔ 𝚅𝙸𝚂𝙰 ⦿ 🄰🄴

r. Louvigny 15 ✉ *1946 –* 🕾 *26 20 10 58 – contact@wenge.lu – Fax 26 20 12 59*
– www.wenge.lu
– closed 15 - 31 August and Sunday   **C1**
Rest – *(lunch only)* Menu 50/70 € – Carte 48/77 € ⅏
♦ Contemporary ♦

A contemporary restaurant with a mezzanine located behind a patisserie/delicatessen. A tranquil atmosphere pervades the designer dining room adorned with Wenge panelling. Carefully selected wine list.

✗ **Mi & ti** ⛩ AC ⇔ VISA ⓒⓢ

av. de la Porte-Neuve 8 ⊠ 2227 – ℰ 26 26 22 50 – mieti@pt.lu
– Fax 26 26 22 51
– closed Easter week, last 3 weeks August, Christmas – New year, Saturday
dinner, Sunday and Monday dinner. **C1**
Rest – Menu 36/51 € bi – Carte 39/54 €
♦ Italian ♦

A trendily decorated Italian restaurant occupying the first floor of a modern building. Authentic produce imported directly from Italy. Simplified menu at the
downstairs Bottega. Busy street terrace.

✗ **La Fourchette à droite** ⛩ AC ⇔ VISA ⓒⓢ AE ⓞ

av. Monterey 5 ⊠ 2163 – ℰ 22 13 60 – Fax 22 24 95
– closed Sunday lunch and bank holidays **C1**
Rest – Menu 38/66 € bi – Carte 44/66 €
♦ Traditional ♦

A modern bistro in a pedestrianised area teeming with restaurants. Dining rooms
on two floors with tables packed tightly together. Copious cuisine popular with a
business clientele.

✗ **Yamayu Santatsu** ⇔ VISA ⓒⓢ AE ⓞ

r. Notre-Dame 26 ⊠ 2240 – ℰ 46 12 49 – Fax 46 05 71
– closed first 3 weeks August, 23 December – first week January and Sunday
and Monday except bank holidays **C1**
Rest – Menu 28 € – Carte 28/47 €
♦ Japanese ♦ Family ♦

A minimalist-style Japanese restaurant just 200m from the cathedral. Varied, traditional dishes including a set menu. Sushi is freshly prepared behind the counter in
the restaurant.

✗ **Kamakura** VISA ⓒⓢ AE ⓞ
😊
r. Münster 4 ⊠ 2160 – ℰ 47 06 04 – kamakura@pt.lu – Fax 46 73 30
– www.kamakura.lu
– closed 2 weeks at Easter, 3 weeks late August, Saturday lunch, Sunday and
bank holidays lunch **D1**
Rest – Menu 29/68 € bi – Carte 35/53 €
♦ Japanese ♦ Minimalist ♦

Kamakura has a minimalist decor and a 'zen'-like ambience. Behind the restaurant's success for the past 20 years are the good menus/à la carte choices that
remain loyal to Japanese culinary tradition.

✗ **Céladon** ⇔

r. Nord 1 ⊠ 2229 – ℰ 47 49 34 – Fax 26 38 38 27 – www.thai.lu
– closed Saturday lunch and Sunday **C1**
Rest – Menu 48 € – Carte approx. 40 €
♦ Thai ♦

This exotic city centre restaurant is named after a precious varnish used by Thai
potters. Restrained contemporary decor in the Céladon's dining rooms. Thai cuisine with vegetarian options.

MAIN STATION *Plan I*

 Mercure Grand Hotel Alfa AC ⇄ ⁽ⁱ⁾ ⅍ VISA ⓒⓢ AE ⓞ

pl. de la Gare 16 ⊠ 1616 – ℰ 490 01 11 – H2058@accor.com – Fax 49 00 09
– www.mercure.com **B3**
140 rm – †210 € ††210 €, � 18 € – 1 suite **Rest** – Carte 30/63 €
♦ Business ♦ Modern ♦

A chain hotel offering spacious guestrooms behind the typical 1930s-style façade.
A practical address for rail passengers, who are guaranteed a good night's sleep
here. A restaurant in attractive Art Deco style with a typical Parisian brasserie
atmosphere.

577

International   🖽 ↳ ℣ 🚗 💳 ⓒ 🅰🅴 ⓞ
pl. de la Gare 20 ✉ *1616* – ☏ *48 59 11* – *info@hotelinter.lu* – *Fax 49 32 27*
– *www.hotelinter.lu* **B3**
69 rm ⊡ – ♦95/170 € ♦♦110/390 € – 1 suite
Rest *Am Inter* – *(closed 19 December - 5 January, Saturday and Sunday)*
Menu 30/70 € bi – Carte 33/59 €
♦ Classical ♦

A recently renovated building located opposite the railway station. Well-maintained guestrooms, the best of which – the new junior suites – are at the front of the building. A bright and airy corner restaurant with large bay windows. An extensive menu of traditional, classic cuisine.

Carlton without rest   ↳ 🖾 ℣ 🚿 💳 ⓒ 🅰🅴 ⓞ
r. Strasbourg 9 ✉ *2561* – ☏ *29 96 60* – *carlton@pt.lu* – *Fax 29 96 64*
– *www.carlton.lu* **B3**
48 rm ⊡ – ♦95/105 € ♦♦110/120 €
♦ Business ♦ Functional ♦

A delightful Art Deco building dating from 1930. Comfortable guestrooms, public areas that recall the roaring twenties, plus a retro-style lounge. Friendly staff and excellent service throughout.

City without rest   🖪 🕉 ℣ 🚿 🚗 💳 ⓒ 🅰🅴 ⓞ
r. Strasbourg 1 ✉ *2561* – ☏ *29 11 22* – *mail@cityhotel.lu* – *Fax 29 11 33*
– *www.cityhotel.lu* **B3**
35 rm ⊡ – ♦94/140 € ♦♦129/172 €
♦ Business ♦ Functional ♦

This corner building dates from the inter-war period. It offers a choice of reasonably spacious guestrooms in varying decor from the 1980s.

Christophe Colomb without rest   ↳ 🖾 ℣ 🚿 🚗 💳 ⓒ 🅰🅴 ⓞ
r. Anvers 10 ✉ *1130* – ☏ *408 41 41* – *mail@christophe-colomb.lu*
– *Fax 40 84 08* – *www.christophe-colomb.lu* **A3**
24 rm ⊡ – ♦80/170 € ♦♦90/185 €
♦ Functional ♦

Located just 500m from the station, this small hotel is ideal for rail travellers. Standard, reasonably spacious guestrooms with modern furnishings.

ENVIRONS OF LUXEMBOURG   *Plan I*

NH   📶 🖽 ↳ ℣ 🚿 🅿 💳 ⓒ 🅰🅴 ⓞ
rte de Trèves 1 (Airport) ✉ *1019* – ☏ *34 05 71* – *nhluxembourg@nh-hotels.com*
– *Fax 34 02 17* – *www.nh-hotels.com*
148 rm – ♦75/350 € ♦♦75/350 €, ⊡ 22 €
Rest – *(closed Sunday dinner) (open until 11.30 pm)* – Menu 32/77 € bi
– Carte 32/60 €
♦ Business ♦ Modern ♦

A recently renovated 1970s-style building offering superbly appointed guestrooms, triple glazing and discreet luxury. Views over the airport. Impeccable service.

Sofitel Europe 🌊   🖪 ♿ rm 🖽 ↳ ℣ 🚿 🅿 🚗 💳 ⓒ 🅰🅴 ⓞ
r. Fort Niedergrünewald 6 (European Centre) ✉ *2015 Kirchberg* – ☏ *43 77 61*
– *H1314@accor.com* – *Fax 42 50 91* – *www.sofitel.com* **B1**
105 rm – ♦240/450 € ♦♦240/450 €, ⊡ 25 € – 4 suites
Rest *Oro e Argento* – see below
Rest *Le Stübli* – ☏ *43 77 68 83 (closed July, Saturday lunch and Sunday)* Carte approx. 40 €
♦ Business ♦ Personalised ♦

A bold, oval shaped hotel at the heart of the European Institutions district. Central atrium and spacious, extremely comfortable guestrooms. The attentive, friendly service you would expect from this upmarket chain. A typical restaurant serving regional cuisine. A warm atmosphere enhanced by the staff in traditional costume.

🏨 **Les Jardins du President** 🦢   🚙 🛜 AC rm ⇄ 🥋 P

pl. Ste-Cunégonde 2 ✉ *1367 Clausen –* 𝒞 *260 90 71*   VISA ⓪ AE ①
– jardins@president.lu – Fax 26 09 07 73 – www.jardinspresident.lu
– closed 21 December - 4 January
7 rm ⌂ – 🛏200 € 🛏🛏250/350 €   **B2**
Rest – *(closed Saturday lunch and Sunday)* Menu 53/123 € bi
– Carte 52/68 €
♦ Family ♦ Stylish ♦

An elegant hotel and restaurant in a verdant setting. Cosy interior and superb, individually furnished guestrooms. Garden with ornamental ponds, a waterfall, vines, ducks and rabbits. Enjoy classic cuisine with a modern twist in the welcoming and elegant dining room or on the attractive summer terrace.

🏨 **Novotel** 🦢   🛜 ♿ rm AC ⇄ 🖥 🥋 🏋 P VISA ⓪ AE ①

r. Fort Niedergrünewald 6 (European Centre) ✉ *2226 Kirchberg*
– 𝒞 *429 84 81 – h1930@accor.com – Fax 43 86 58*
– www.novotel.com   **B1**
260 rm – 🛏170/220 € 🛏🛏170/220 €, ⌂ 18 €   **Rest** – Carte 36/52 €
♦ Business ♦ Functional ♦

A neighbour to its larger sister hotel, this hotel run by the same group offers excellent facilities for business meetings and seminars. Recently refurbished guestrooms.

🏠 **Ibis**   🛜 ♿ AC ⇄ 🥋 🏋 P VISA ⓪ AE ①

rte de Trèves (Airport) ✉ *2632 –* 𝒞 *43 88 01 – H0974@accor.com*
– Fax 43 88 02 – www.accorhotels.com
167 rm – 🛏66/95 € 🛏🛏66/95 €, ⌂ 12 €
Rest – *(closed Saturday lunch and Sunday lunch)* Menu 18 €
– Carte approx. 30 €
♦ Business ♦ Functional ♦

A chain hotel with welcoming public areas and lounge. Although lacking space, the guestrooms offer the Ibis' usual standard of comfort. Low budget annexe. A restaurant occupying a glass rotunda.

XXX **Oro e Argento** – H. Sofitel Europe   AC P VISA ⓪ AE ①

r. Fort Niedergrünewald 6 (European Centre) ✉ *2015 Kirchberg*
– 𝒞 *43 77 61 – h1314@accor.com – Fax 42 50 91 – www.sofitel.com*
– closed August and Saturday   **B1**
Rest – Carte 56/70 €
♦ Italian ♦

An attractive Italian restaurant in a luxury hotel. Contemporary cuisine served to a backdrop of plush interior decor with a Venetian touch. Intimate atmosphere and stylish service.

XXX **Hostellerie du Grünewald** with rm   🚙 🛜 AC rest ⇄ ↔ P

rte d'Echternach 10 ✉ *1453 Dommeldange*   VISA ⓪ AE ①
– 𝒞 *43 18 82 – hostgrun@pt.lu – Fax 42 06 46*
– www.hotel-romantik.com
24 rm ⌂ – 🛏80/150 € 🛏🛏90/175 €
Rest – *(closed Saturday lunch, Monday lunch and Sunday)* Menu 60/72 €
– Carte approx. 80 €
♦ Traditional ♦ Family ♦

A delightful restaurant with a romantic and refined atmosphere. Fine, classic cuisine and highly attentive service. For overall charm, the tables in the middle dining room are recommended. Two generations of guestrooms in this small, comfortable inn. Breakfast in an attractive conservatory.

579

XXX **Le Grimpereau**

r. Cents 140 (Airport) ✉ *1319* – ✆ *43 67 87* – *bridard@pt.lu*
– Fax 42 60 26 – *www.legrimpereau.lu*
– closed 1 week at Easter, first 3 weeks August, Saturday lunch,
Sunday dinner and Monday lunch
Rest – Menu 40/80 € – Carte 68/80 €
♦ Traditional ♦

Enjoy contemporary cuisine in the intimate and cosy neo-rustic dining room with its wooden beams, stone fireplace and Lloyd Loom chairs. Decked terrace for summer dining.

LUXEMBOURG - LUXEMBOURG

NETHERLANDS
NEDERLAND

PROFILE

→ **AREA:**
41 863 km² (16 163 sq mi).

→ **POPULATION:**
16 407 000 inhabitants (est. 2005), density = 392 per km².

→ **CAPITAL:**
Amsterdam (conurbation) 193 000 inhabitants); The Hague is the seat of government and Parliament.

→ **CURRENCY:**
Euro (€); rate of exchange: € 1 = US$1.32 (Jan 2009).

→ **GOVERNMENT:**
Constitutional parliamentary monarchy (since 1815). Member of European Union since 1957 (one of the 6 founding countries).

→ **LANGUAGE:**
Dutch; many Dutch people also speak English.

→ **SPECIFIC PUBLIC HOLIDAYS:**
Good Friday (Friday before Easter);

Queen's Day Liberation Day (5 May); Boxing Day (26 December).

→ **LOCAL TIME:**
GMT + 1hour in winter and GMT + 2 hours in summer.

→ **CLIMATE:**
Temperate maritime with cool winters and mild summers (Amsterdam: January: 2°C, July: 17°C), rainfall evenly distributed throughout the year.

→ **INTERNATIONAL DIALLING CODE:**
00 31 followed by area code without the initial **0** and then the local number. International Directory enquiries: ☏ **06 0418**.

→ **EMERGENCY:**
Fire Brigade: ☏ **112**; Police, Ambulance, Roadside assistance: ☏ **0900 8418**.

→ **ELECTRICITY:**
220 volts AC, 50Hz; 2-pin round-shaped continental plugs.

Formalities Travellers from the European Union (EU), Switzerland, Iceland and the main countries of North and South America need a national identity card or passport (America: passport required) to visit the Netherlands for less than three months (tourism or business purpose). For visitors from other countries a visa may be required, in addition to a passport, especially for those wishing to stay for longer than three months. We advise you to check with your embassy before travelling.

AMSTERDAM
AMSTERDAM

Population: 747 093 – Altitude: sea level

R. Mazin/PHOTONONSTOP

Once visited, never forgotten. That's Amsterdam's great claim to fame. Its endearing horseshoe shape - defined by 17C canals cut to drain land for a growing population – allied to finely detailed gabled houses, has produced a compact city centre of aesthetically splendid symmetry and matchless consistency. Exploring the city on foot or by bike is the real joy here; visitors rarely need to jump on a tram or bus.

Amsterdam, 'the world's biggest small city', displays a host of distinctive characteristics ranging from the red light district to the brown cafés, from the wonderful art galleries to the tree-lined waterways. There's the feel of a northern Venice, but without the hallowed and revered atmosphere. It exists on a human scale, small enough to walk from one end to the other. Those who might moan that it's just *too* small should stroll along to the former derelict docklands on the east side and contemplate the shiny new apartments giving the waterfront a sleek twenty-first century feel. Most people who come here, though, are just happy to cosy up to old Amsterdam's sleepy, relaxed vibe. No European city does snug bars better: this is the place to go for cats kipping on beat-up chairs and candles flickering on wax-encrusted tables…

LIVING THE CITY

Arrive at the **Central station**, at the top end of Amsterdam's centre, and you really do have the city laid out in front of you. How many other famous European destinations can you say that about? You're in the **New Side**, although 'new' in this case refers to the medieval period. Just to your east is the **Old Side,** which began to develop in the 12C as a thriving village of fisher-folk on the River **Amstel**. Keeping these two ancient areas in a vice-like grip and fanning out beneath them in a kind of watery spider's web is the **Grachtengordel**, the superb semicircle of three canals lined by elegant gabled houses and connec-

ted by pretty bridges: the Western Canal ring includes the lively, bohemian **Jordaan** district. Just beyond the Grachtengordel lies the museum quarter, a tourist must-see, as it features two of the world's most prestigious museums. There's the lovely **Vondelpark** here, too. The most easterly quarter of the city is Plantage, or 'Plantation', a name mirroring its historically green qualities. This area was once parkland, and seventeenth century Amsterdammers would come here to spend leisure time. Nowadays it's elegant and tree lined, but seems strangely undiscovered by many visitors.

PRACTICAL INFORMATION

ARRIVAL-DEPARTURE

Schipol International Airport is 18km southwest of the city and trains run regularly to Amsterdam Central Station, a journey that takes about 20 minutes. A taxi costs around €38 and there are also Airport Shuttles available.

TRANSPORT

To get around Amsterdam – take a hike. Of all Europe's main cities, this is the one most geared to walking, what with its narrow streets and canals.

Avoid any thoughts of driving a car here. Word of warning: trams can be pretty silent and can move pretty fast, so look both ways when crossing tram routes. If you venture inadvertently onto a cycle path (there are many), you'll soon hear the frantic ringing of bicycle bells.

The Amsterdam Card entitles the holder to free public transport, free admission to major museums, a canal cruise and discounts in some restaurants. It's valid for 24hr, 48hr, or 72hr, and available from the Tourist Information Office opposite the central station.

Trams and buses run mostly from the central station; the metro has four short lines, mostly used by commuters. Modern white and blue trams are the most popular form of public transport; they operate from 6am on weekdays, finish just after midnight and tickets are available from the Tourist Information office or vending machines. Bus routes mainly complement the tram network.

It's safe to say you won't experience the like of Amsterdam anywhere else in Europe. The city appears so well planned that it's possible to look at it on a map and sense in your head that you've got the measure of it. Most visitors arrive at the Central Railway station and get their bearings from here. Just down the road they will find two veritable old churches steeped in medieval history, a red light district famous throughout the world and a museum devoted to the history of marijuana. Such is the city they've arrived in. Central to all the action is **Dam Square** – simply 'The Dam' to locals – built on the very spot where the city's roots lie. Now somewhat faded, it nevertheless boasts the glorious Nieuwe Kerk and the Classical seventeenth century Koninklijk Palace, once the city's town hall. The Dam's size makes it a great place for markets and all shade of al fresco events. As a complete contrast to the area's seedier elements, and not far west of the Red Light district, is the beguiling Begijnhof, an enchanting sanctuary of gabled houses (including Amsterdam's oldest) overlooking a tranquil green. Its hushed atmosphere allows for no large tour groups.

→ CANAL PLUS

Amsterdam's first canal, the **Singel**, is the tight boundary for the Old and New sides, and it is just beyond here that the Grachtengordel's concentric arrangement of canals begins. They're called Herengracht, Keizersgracht and Prinsengracht, and were cut in two stages through the seventeenth century. There's no better way of getting a feel for Amsterdam's charms than taking a slow boat along one of them, taking in the timeless appeal of the narrow houses and the steady progress of bike riders on the little waterside streets, making the most of this, the flattest country on the planet. A jaunt along the canals is best in the spring or summer, when the city blooms into a café society. Chairs and tables spill outdoors to welcome the sun, and taking in the tree-lined banks here is one of Europe's greatest pleasures. A super vantage point is from the bridge at the crossing of the Herengracht with Reguliersgracht (another pretty canal in the eastern canal ring, dug after those in the Grachtengordel): this is called the 'golden curve' and gives a view of fifteen bridges all at one time.

→ THE COLOUR BROWN

If any part of the city can claim the title of the 'real' Amsterdam, that accolade belongs to the **Jordaan**. This delightful maze of canals and backstreets on the western canal ring is a short stroll from the main visitor hotspots, yet it doesn't quite draw the same crowds. Losing yourself here is all part of the fun, idling amongst the seventeenth century workers' houses and quirky shops. This is where to stop and enjoy Amsterdam's best brown cafés, so called not just because their interiors are characterised by dark wooden panelling, but also because they've turned that rather inviting nutty colour with age and cigarette smoke. They're cosy and convivial, and often form the social hub of the neighbourhood.

At the heart of the Jordaan are two of the city's most famous sights, standing within a stone's throw of each other. The **Westerkerk** is the tallest church in Amsterdam, its spire rewarding climbers with stunning views. Rembrandt, who lived close by, is buried here, though his grave has never been found. Just along Prinsengracht is a humble abode that attracts nine hundred thousand visitors a year – **Anne Frank House**. For two years during

World War II, this was where the now-famous young diarist lived with her family in a little upstairs apartment hidden behind a revolving bookcase. You can visit her room, empty except for pin-ups of wartime film stars. It's advisable, for obvious reasons, to get here either early or late in the day.

➜ SEMINAL MUSEUMS

If the weather's inclement, you can easily spend a day in the museums and galleries of this city. In fact, whatever the elements are doing, be sure to head just beyond the limits of the Grachtengordel and pay homage to the district around **Museumplein**. Here you will find the **Rijksmuseum** and the **Van Gogh Museum**, two of Europe's cultural landmarks. The Rijksmuseum has been undergoing extensive renovation which began five years ago, and the reopened in 2008. This neo-Gothic titan is a powerhouse of art, possessing nearly seven million works, with only a fraction on display at any one time. Over two hundred years, it's built an unrivalled collection of Dutch art; try not to miss the paintings of the 17C, the Golden Age, adorned by the likes of Rembrandt, Vermeer and Hals. There are also tremendously impressive sections on Asiatic art and sculpture/applied art. It can be quite overpowering to take in this museum in a single day; best do some planning beforehand. The Van Gogh museum, on the other hand, is on a more human scale, and includes two hundred of the great man's paintings and five hundred of his drawings. There are hundreds of letters to his brother Theo, too. As if all this wasn't enough, practically opposite the homage to Van Gogh is the Stedelijk Museum, the national Museum of Modern Art, now seventy years old. Inside are works by the likes of Chagall, Cézanne and Picasso, plus, naturally enough, a fascinating insight into the Dutch De Stijl movement, iconic in the world of twentieth century abstract art.

HIPPY TRAIL

There's only one place to head after a gallery trawl, and that's the nearby **Vondelpark**. This former hippie haven boasts about eight million visitors a year. They come for the landscaped delights, the meandering footpaths, rose gardens and waterways, the parakeets which home in on the pavilion every morning, and the sheep, goats and cows which graze lazily in the pastures. They come for the free summer musical concerts and plays which the park is famous for, and they come too for its film museum, where classic movies are shown each day, either in the lovingly restored interior, or, in the summer, out on the terrace during summer. These are free to watch as well.

In recent decades Amsterdam has been famous for its enjoyment of plant life (mainly the sort you inhale in a brown café), but the city has been cultiva-

AMSTERDAM IN...

➜ ONE DAY
A trip on a canal boat; evening atmosphere of a brown café ; a stroll around the red light district

➜ TWO DAYS
Begijnhof. Rijksmuseum, Vondelpark,

➜ THREE DAYS
The Jordaan, Van Gogh museum, Plantage and Entrepotdok

ting medicinal herbs for about three hundred and twenty five years in the **Botanical Gardens** in the Plantage district to the east of town. These are amongst the oldest in the world, and include a three-climate greenhouse with tropical, sub-tropical and desert sections. There's an Orangery, too, with museum and terrace, which is a great place to take afternoon tea, while art shows with a botanical theme are a common sight. Plantage as a whole boasts attractively wide, tree-lined streets, and offers a vivid new take on the past: at Entrepotdok, the grand old warehouses have been redeveloped, and this dockland quarter buzzes with colour, café tables and shiny houseboats. Twenty-first century Amsterdam's evolution on water continues apace.

CALENDAR HIGHLIGHTS

Summertime is a cultural big-hit in Amsterdam. The highlight comes in the middle of August with Uitmarkt, a weekend of theatrical and musical shows on Leidseplein and Museumplein, which launches a season of dance, opera, music and drama in the city. This is also the month of the Grachtenfestival, which sees classical concerts along all sections of the Grachtengordel. September's third weekend is the time to be in Jordaan to check out its annual festival, when musical shows and fairs light up Westerkerk and its surrounding quarter. Earlier in the summer, during three weeks of June, look out for the Holland Festival, a three-week long jamboree, featuring theatrical drama in Amsterdamse Bos, southwest of the city, and a host of other plays, concerts and ballets around town: Vondelpark puts on some renowned shows al fresco. This is also the month for the Amsterdam Roots Festival, a celebration of global music and dance, and Open Garden Days, when picturesque private gardens are free for public perusal. Modern art is up for inspection in May at the Kunst RAI, a huge exhibition held in Amsterdam RAI, just southeast of the city. Every July, classical music fans make for the Concertgebouw for summer concerts, which continue throughout August. Brave Amsterdammers leave the comfort of cosy brown cafés on the first Saturday of November for Museumnacht, when many museums stay open during the night, with musical events and guided tours to keep eyelids from drooping.

EATING OUT

Amsterdam is a vibrant and multicultural city and, as such, offers a wide proliferation of restaurants offering a varied choice of cuisines where you can eat well without paying too much. Head for an eetcafe, and you'll get satisfying three-course menus at a reasonable price. The Dutch consider the evening to be the time to eat your main meal, so some restaurants shut at lunchtime. Aside from the eetcafe, you can top up your middle-of-day fuel levels at a bruin (brown) café, or one specialising in coffee and cake. If you wish to try local specialities, number one on the hit list could be rijsttafel or rice table, as the Dutch have imported much from their former colonies of Indonesia. Fresh raw herring from local waters is another nutritious local favourite, as are apple pies and pancakes of the sweet persuasion. Restaurants are never too big but are certainly atmospheric and busy so it's worth making reservations.

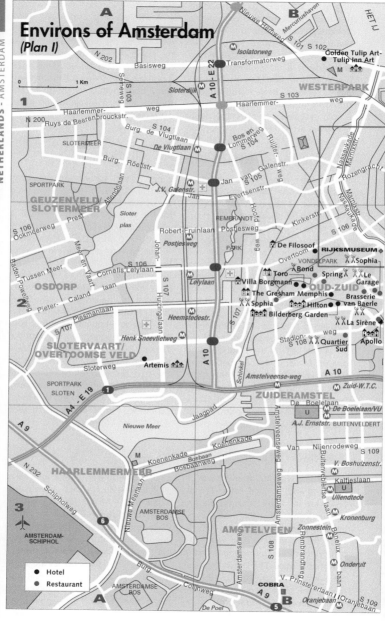

Environs of Amsterdam
(Plan I)

0   1 Km

A   **B**

HET IJ

Nieuwe Hemweg   S 101   S 102   Mercuriushaven

N 202

Isolatorweg

Golden Tulip Art-
Tulip Inn Art

Basisweg

Transformatorweg

WESTERPARK

Sloterdijk

S 103   weg

Seneweg   S 103

1

Haarlemmer-
weg   Haarlemmer-

N 200   Ruys de Beerenbrouckstr.

Burg. de Vlugtlaan   S 104

Nassaukade   Marnixstr.

SLOTERMEER

De Vlugtlaan

Bos en
Lommerweg
S 104

Ruiter-   weg

Rozengracht

Burg. Röetstr.

Jan   van   Galenstr.
S 105

Galenstr.

J.V. Galenstr.

Jan

Evertsenstr.

GEUZENVELD/
SLOTERMEER

SPORTPARK

Allardlaan

Sloter
plas

Robert-Fruinlaan   Postjesweg

REMBRANDT
PARK

Hoofd

Kinkerstr.

S 106

Pres.

Postjesweg

Johan-

De Filosoof

RIJKSMUSEUM

S 106   Ookmeerweg

Baden Powellweg

Meer en Vaart

S 106

Cornelis Lelylaan

Lelylaan

Overtoom

VONDELPARK

Sophia

Bend

Spring   Le
Garage

OUD-ZUID

Baden Powellweg

OSDORP

Tussen Meer

Pieter-

Caland   laan

Plesmanlaan

Huizingalaan

S 107

Villa Borgmann

Toro

The Gresham Memphis

Sophia

Hilton

Bilderberg Garden

Brasserie
van Baerle

La Sirène

SLOTERVAART/
OVERTOOMSE VELD

S 107

Heemstedestr.

Henk Sneevlietweg

Stadion-
S 108   Quartier
Sud

Apollo

Sloterweg

Artemis

A 10

Amstelveense-weg   A 10

SPORTPARK
SLOTEN

A4 - E 19

Schinkel

Zuid-W.T.C.

ZUIDERAMSTEL

De Boelelaan

De Boelelaan/VU

BUITENVELDERT

A 9

N 232

Schipholweg

Jaagpad

Nieuwe Meer

Amstelveenseweg

A.J. Ernststr.

Van

Nijenrodeweg   S 109

V. Boshuizenstr.

Buitenveldertselaan

Kalfjeslaan

Ullendtede

HAARLEMMERMEER

Koenenkade   Bosbaan
Bosbaanweg

Koenenkade

Amsterdamseweg

Kronenburg

Nieuwe Meerlaan

AMSTERDAMSE
BOS

AMSTELVEEN

Zonnestein

S 108

Rembrandtweg

Benelux-   baan

Onderuit

3

AMSTERDAM-
SCHIPHOL

Burg.

Collijnweg

AMSTERDAMSE
BOS

V. Prinsterenlaan   Oranjebaan

COBRA

S 109

Oranjebaan

● Hotel
● Restaurant

De Poel

A   **B**

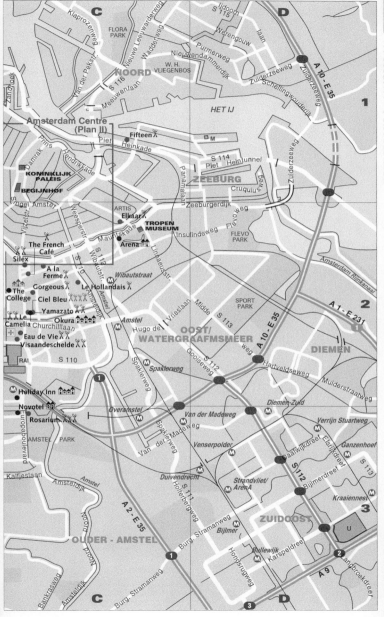

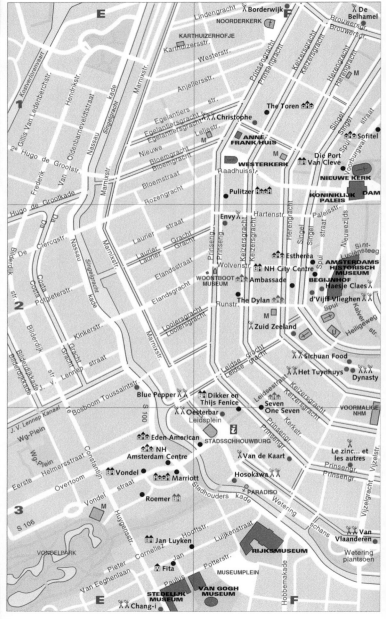

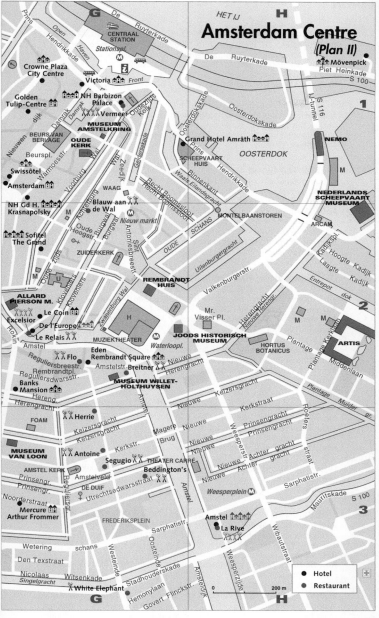

Amsterdam Centre
(Plan II)

HET IJ

Hotel ●
Restaurant ●

0   200 m

591

Amstel ⟨ 🍴 ℔ 🐾 🖥 🅰🅒 🛗 🖾 📶 🖧 📡 🅿 🅅🅸🅂🅰 ⓒ🅐🅴 ⓘ

Prof. Tulpplein 1 ✉ *1018 GX* – ℰ *(0 20) 622 60 60* – *amstel@ihg.com*
– *Fax (0 20) 622 58 08* – *www.amstel.intercontinental.com* **H3**
62 rm – ♦430/725 € ♦♦430/725 €, ☕ 28 € – 17 suites
Rest *La Rive* – see below
Rest *The Amstel Bar and Brasserie* – ℰ *(0 20) 520 32 69 (open until 11.30pm)*
Carte 58/95 €
◆ Palace ◆ Luxury ◆ Classical ◆
A veritable haven of luxury and good taste in this grand hotel on the banks of the
Amstel. The vast rooms are decorated with attention to detail and stylish furnishings. Complete, efficient service. A cosy library-bar, with an appetising cosmopolitan-influenced menu.

Sofitel The Grand ⤳ 🚗 ℔ 🐾 🖥 🛗 🅰🅒 🛗 🖾 📶 🖧 📡 🚗

O.Z. Voorburgwal 197 ✉ *1012 EX* – ℰ *(0 20) 555 31 11* 🅅🅸🅂🅰 ⓒ🅐🅴 ⓘ
– *h2783@accor.com* – *Fax (0 20) 555 32 22* – *www.sofitel.com* **G2**
170 rm – ♦250/450 € ♦♦250/450 €, ☕ 30 € – 12 suites
Rest – Menu 43/55 € – Carte 54/73 €
◆ Palace ◆ Luxury ◆ Historic ◆
Maria de Medici once stayed in this superb historic building, once Amsterdam's
town hall. Authentic Art Nouveau lounges, exquisite rooms and a beautiful indoor
garden await you.

NH Grand Hotel Krasnapolsky ℔ & 🅰🅒 🛗 🖾 📶 🖧 📡 🚗

Dam 9 ✉ *1012 JS* – ℰ *(0 20) 554 91 11* 🅅🅸🅂🅰 ⓒ🅐🅴 ⓘ
– *nhkrasnapolsky@nh-hotels.com* – *Fax (0 20) 622 86 07* – *www.nh-hotels.com*
467 rm – ♦169/444 € ♦♦169/444 €, ☕ 29 € – 1 suite **G1**
Rest *Reflet* – ℰ *(0 20) 554 61 14 (closed 27 July - 16 August) (dinner only)*
Menu 36/104 € bi – Carte 60/79 €
◆ Traditional ◆ Luxury ◆ Classical ◆
Large, historic hotel on the Dam with various categories of rooms, apartments for
rent by the week and buffet breakfast served under a magnificent glass roof dating
from 1879. Classic menu, chic décor and well-heeled ambiance at the Reflet, founded in 1883.

De l'Europe ⟨ ℔ 🐾 🖥 🅰🅒 🛗 📶 🖧 📡 🅿 🅅🅸🅂🅰 ⓒ🅐🅴 ⓘ

Nieuwe Doelenstraat 2 ✉ *1012 CP* – ℰ *(0 20) 531 17 77* – *hotel@leurope.nl*
– *Fax (0 20) 531 17 78* – *www.leurope.nl* **G2**
95 rm – ♦360/440 € ♦♦445/535 €, ☕ 25 € – 5 suites
Rest *Excelsior* and *Le Relais* – see below
◆ Palace ◆ Luxury ◆ Classical ◆
Luxury hotel dating from late 19th century with charm and tradition. Tastefully
decorated rooms. A collection of Dutch landscape paintings displayed. Beautiful
water views.

NH Barbizon Palace ℔ 🐾 & 🅰🅒 🛗 🖾 📶 🖧 📡 🚗

Prins Hendrikkade 59 ✉ *1012 AD* – ℰ *(0 20) 556 45 64* 🅅🅸🅂🅰 ⓒ🅐🅴 ⓘ
– *nhbarbizonpalace@nh-hotels.com* – *Fax (0 20) 624 33 53* – *www.nh-hotels.com*
266 rm – ♦129/299 € ♦♦129/299 €, ☕ 25 € – 3 suites **G1**
Rest *Vermeer* – see below
Rest *Hudson's Terrace and Restaurant* – ℰ *(0 20) 556 49 75* – Menu 43/48 €
– Carte approx. 47 €
◆ Chain hotel ◆ Business ◆ Modern ◆
Modern hotel adjoining the station. Huge, light-filled foyer, various types of rooms
available (some with sloping ceilings). A converted church provides a multipurpose
room for groups. Vaguely nautical atmosphere, international menu and interior
terrace at Hudson's.

Marriott 🛠 🏋 ⛗ & rm 🔳 ↔ 🈹 ◻️ 🚗 VISA ⦿ AE ①

Stadhouderskade 12 ⊠ *1054 ES* – 🕾 *(0 20) 607 55 55* – *amsterdam.guest@ marriott.com* – *Fax (0 20) 607 55 11* – *www.amsterdammarriotthotel.com*
387 rm – 🛏199/354 € 🛏🛏199/354 €, ⌑ 26 € – 5 suites   **E3**
Rest – *(closed Sunday and Monday) (dinner only)* Menu 33 € – Carte 28/54 €
• Chain hotel • Business • Cosy •

A high-class, American-style hotel on a major thoroughfare. The rooms are vast and well-equipped. A good seminar infrastructure and business centre. Internatio-nal menu served in the restaurant; grilled meats, salads and pizza in the brasserie.

Pulitzer ☕ 🍴 🛠 & 🔳 ↔ 🈹 🛜 🈹 ◻️ 🚗 VISA ⦿ AE ①

Prinsengracht 323 ⊠ *1016 GZ* – 🕾 *(0 20) 523 52 35* – *pulitzer.amsterdam@ luxurycollection.com* – *Fax (0 20) 627 67 53* – *www.luxurycollection.com*
227 rm – 🛏239/489 € 🛏🛏264/514 €, ⌑ 27 € – 3 suites   **F1**
Rest *Pulitzers* – Menu 37/100 € bi – Carte 43/63 €
• Chain hotel • Business • Classical •

A group of 25 admirably-restored houses, dating from the 17th and 18th centuries set around a well-tended garden. Public areas filled with works of art; refined, indi-vidualized bedrooms. Modern restaurant with novel décor (including an amusing reference to the painter, Frans Hals). Intimate bar.

Grand Hotel Amrâth 🛠 🏋 🔳 & rm 🔳 ↔ 🈹 🛜 🈹 P

Prins Hendrikkade 108 ⊠ *1011 AK* – 🕾 *(0 20) 552 00 00*   VISA ⦿ AE ①
– *info@amrathamsterdam.com* – *Fax (0 20) 552 09 00* – *www.amrathamsterdam.com*
155 rm – 🛏270 € 🛏🛏270/690 €, ⌑ 25 € – 10 suites   **G1**
Rest – *(dinner only)* Menu 43 € – Carte 48/83 €
• Chain hotel • Business • Stylish •

The hotel opened in 2007, in the monumental Shipping House (1916), characteris-tic of the Amsterdam School. Stunning Art Deco interior. Contemporary cuisine served in a large, delightfully old-fashioned dining room.

Crowne Plaza City Centre 🛠 🏋 🔳 & 🔳 ↔ 🈹 🛜 🈹 ◻️ 🚗

N.Z. Voorburgwal 5 ⊠ *1012 RC* – 🕾 *(0 20) 620 05 00*   VISA ⦿ AE ①
– *amsnl.gsc@ihg.com* – *Fax (0 20) 620 11 73*
– *www.amsterdam-citycentre.crowneplaza.com*   **G1**
268 rm – 🛏159/340 € 🛏🛏159/340 €, ⌑ 24 € – 2 suites
Rest *Dorrius* – 🕾 *(0 20) 420 22 24 (closed Sunday) (dinner only until 11pm)*
Menu 35/45 € – Carte 33/51 €
• Chain hotel • Business • Classical •

Chain hotel near the station. Functional bedrooms. Town roofscape view from the top-floor "lounge club". A restaurant featuring reconstructed 19th century décor. Classic menu accompanied by local dishes.

Eden American 🍴 🛠 🏋 & 🔳 rm ↔ 🈹 🛜 🈹 VISA ⦿ AE

Leidsekade 97 ⊠ *1017 PN* – 🕾 *(0 20) 556 30 00* – *info@edenamsterdamamerican.com*
– *Fax (0 20) 556 30 01* – *www.edenamsterdamamerican.com*   **F3**
174 rm – 🛏120/300 € 🛏🛏120/300 €, ⌑ 20 € – 1 suite
Rest *Café Americain* – 🕾 *(0 20) 556 30 10* – Menu 25/38 € – Carte approx. 50 €
• Palace • Business • Art Deco •

Near a lively square, this hotel with its imposing historic façade is a bit of a local institution. Bedrooms are gradually being updated. Bar popular with artists and people watchers. Elegant vaulted Art Deco café. International menu; high tea ser-ved in the afternoon.

The Dylan 🍴 🛠 🔳 rm ↔ 🈹 🛜 🈹 ◻️ VISA ⦿ AE ①

Keizersgracht 384 ⊠ *1016 GB* – 🕾 *(0 20) 530 20 10* – *info@ dylanamsterdam.com* – *Fax (0 20) 530 20 30* – *www.dylanamsterdam.com*
38 rm – 🛏285 € 🛏🛏455/960 €, ⌑ 25 € – 3 suites   **F2**
Rest – *(closed 24 December - 4 January, Sunday and bank holidays) (dinner only)* Carte 61/81 €
• Grand Luxury • Design • Stylish •

"Order and beauty; luxury, peace and delight." Discover the secret harmony of the excep-tional interior design of this unique hotel. Exquisite rooms by Anouska Hempel. Inventive traditional cuisine served in a former bakery or in a fashionable courtyard terrace.

Ambassade without rest 🔲 AC 🔲 CAB 🔲 VISA ⬤ AE ⬤

Herengracht 341 ⊠ 1016 AZ – ℰ (0 20) 555 02 22 – info@ambassade-hotel.nl
– Fax (0 20) 555 02 77 – www.ambassade-hotel.nl **F2**
53 rm – †185/195 € ††185/245 €, ⊑ 16 € – 6 suites
♦ Family ♦ Luxury ♦ Stylish ♦

Beautiful rooms and suites with a personal touch, spread over ten 17C houses overlooking the canal. Modern art and interesting library. Float and massage centre. Breakfast served in an elegant dining room.

Sofitel 🔲 🔲 🔲 AC 🔲 CAB 🔲 🔲 🔲 VISA ⬤ AE ⬤

N.Z. Voorburgwal 67 ⊠ 1012 RE – ℰ (0 20) 627 59 00 – h1159-gm@accor.com
– Fax (0 20) 623 89 32 – www.sofitel.com **F1**
148 rm – †150/299 € ††150/299 €, ⊑ 23 € **Rest** – Carte 39/53 €
♦ Chain hotel ♦ Traditional ♦ Classical ♦

Chain hotel near a main road, made up of three 17th to 19th century houses. Various types of bedrooms, including about ten modern junior suites. Orient-Express atmosphere and brasserie-style cuisine in the restaurant.

Seven One Seven without rest AC 🔲 CAB 🔲 🔲 VISA ⬤ AE ⬤

Prinsengracht 717 ⊠ 1017 JW – ℰ (0 20) 427 07 17 – info@
hotelsevenoneseven.nl – Fax (0 20) 423 07 17 – www.hotelsevenoneseven.nl
8 rm ⊑ – †410 € ††435/665 € **F2-3**
♦ Grand Luxury ♦ Traditional ♦ Classical ♦

Small, attractive 18th century house converted into an intimate and select place to stay. The guestrooms are veritable gems. Romantic lounges; leafy courtyard where breakfast is served in summer.

Victoria 🔲 🔲 🔲 🔲 rm AC 🔲 CAB 🔲 🔲 VISA ⬤ AE ⬤

Damrak 1 ⊠ 1012 LG – ℰ (0 20) 623 42 55 – ppvares@pphe.com – Fax (0 20)
625 29 97 – www.parkplaza.com **G1**
296 rm – †99/600 € ††99/600 €, ⊑ 22 € – 10 suites
Rest – *(open until 11pm)* Menu 30/38 € – Carte approx. 30 €
♦ Chain hotel ♦ Traditional ♦ Classical ♦

Neo-classical 19C luxury hotel and extension dating from the 1980s near the station. Domed lobby with modern stained glass. Refurbished rooms. Tavern-restaurant with traditional menu.

Eden Rembrandt Square 🔲 🔲 AC 🔲 VISA ⬤ AE ⬤

Amstelstraat 17 ⊠ 1017 DA – ℰ (0 20) 890 47 47 – info.rembrandtsquare@
edenhotelgroup.com – Fax (0 20) 890 47 40 – www.edenrembrandtsquare.com
165 rm – †165/335 € ††165/335 €, ⊑ 20 € – 1 suite **G2**
Rest *Flo* – see below
♦ Chain hotel ♦ Functional ♦

Old hotel building with modernised interior, set on a lively square. High-tech bedrooms with contemporary minimalist décor.

Banks Mansion without rest AC 🔲 🔲 VISA ⬤ AE ⬤

Herengracht 519 ⊠ 1017 BV – ℰ (0 20) 420 00 55 – desk@banksmansion.nl
– Fax (0 20) 420 09 93 – www.banksmansion.nl **G2**
51 rm ⊑ – †159/319 € ††189/349 €
♦ Chain hotel ♦ Business ♦ Modern ♦

Building dating from 1923 whose interior combines the styles of Dutch architect Hendrik Petrus Berlage and American architect Frank Lloyd Wright. Modern rooms with retro touches. Attractive, intimate lounge.

Mövenpick 🔲 🔲 🔲 🔲 🔲 rm AC 🔲 CAB 🔲 🔲 🔲 VISA ⬤ AE ⬤

Piet Heinkade 11 ⊠ 1019 BR – ℰ (0 20) 519 12 00
– hotel.amsterdam@moevenpick.com – Fax (0 20) 519 12 49
– www.moevenpick-amsterdam.com **H1**
407 rm – †159/359 € ††159/359 €, ⊑ 23 € – 1 suite
Rest – *(open until 11pm)* Carte 28/52 €
♦ Chain hotel ♦ Business ♦ Modern ♦

Modern chain hotel inaugurated in 2006 in a modern district. The rooms have panoramic views. Concert hall, jazz club and congress centre next door. Restaurant serving Asian cuisine: Chinese, Thai and Indonesian.

Estheréa without rest

Singel 305 ⊠ 1012 WJ – 𝒞 (0 20) 624 51 46 – info@estherea.nl
– Fax (0 20) 623 90 01 – www.estherea.nl
F2
71 rm – †190/261 € ††203/333 €, ⊇ 16 €
♦ Family ♦ Traditional ♦ Personalised ♦

The same family have run this hotel since 1942 set in a row of old merchants' houses with refined, neoclassical communal areas, personalised rooms and characterful breakfast room.

Swissôtel

Damrak 96 ⊠ 1012 LP – 𝒞 (0 20) 522 30 00
– harold.kluit@swissotel.com – Fax (0 20) 522 32 25
– www.swissotel-amsterdam.com
G1
104 rm – †99/580 € ††99/580 €, ⊇ 20 € – 5 suites
Rest – (open until 11pm) Carte 21/52 €
♦ Chain hotel ♦ Business ♦ Functional ♦

Renovated chain hotel in a centrally-located traditional-looking building. Modern public areas, functional bedrooms and good reception. Contemporary brasserie-restaurant. International menu.

The Toren without rest

Keizersgracht 164 ⊠ 1015 CZ – 𝒞 (0 20) 622 63 52 – info@thetoren.nl
– Fax (0 20) 626 97 05 – www.thetoren.nl
F1
38 rm – †180/280 € ††190/300 €, ⊇ 12 €
♦ Traditional ♦ Classical ♦

A charming hotel composed of several old houses, near the Anne Frank House. Neo-baroque bedrooms, elegant breakfast room with an attractive bar.

NH Amsterdam Centre

Stadhouderskade 7 ⊠ 1054 ES – 𝒞 (0 20) 685 13 51
– nhamsterdamcentre@nh-hotels.com – Fax (0 20) 685 16 11
– www.nh-hotels.com
E3
228 rm – †129 € ††129 €, ⊇ 25 € – 2 suites
Rest Sogno – 𝒞 (0 20) 589 88 70 (closed 13 July - 4 August and Sunday)
(dinner only) Carte approx. 45 €
♦ Chain hotel ♦ Business ♦ Modern ♦

Renovated chain hotel built to host athletes attending the Amsterdam Olympic Games in 1928. Designer public areas. Large modern bedrooms. Italian menu, contemporary décor and view over the Leidseplein at the Sogno.

Amsterdam

Damrak 93 ⊠ 1012 LP – 𝒞 (0 20) 555 06 66
– info@hotelamsterdam.nl – Fax (0 20) 620 47 16
– www.hotelamsterdam.nl
G1
79 rm – †100/265 € ††120/325 €, ⊇ 14 €
Rest De Roode Leeuw – Carte 34/54 €
♦ Traditional ♦ Classical ♦

This traditional Amsterdam hotel is on a very central section of the busy Damrak. Very comfortable rooms. Public car parks nearby. A brasserie offering traditional Dutch dishes in a modernised setting with red decor.

Die Port van Cleve

N.Z. Voorburgwal 178 ⊠ 1012 SJ – 𝒞 (0 20) 714 20 00 – info@
dieportvancleve.com – Fax (0 20) 714 20 01 – www.dieportvancleve.com
120 rm – †150/285 € ††150/285 €, ⊇ 20 € – 1 suite
F1
Rest – (open until 11pm) Carte 36/49 €
♦ Traditional ♦ Functional ♦

The first Dutch brewers started work in the 19th century behind the flamboyant façade of this building (1864). Tidy rooms. Dutch gin bar decorated with Delft china and panelling. Restaurant-grill where they keep a tally of the number of steaks served since 1870.

Dikker en Thijs Fenice without rest   AC ⇄ 📺 💬 VISA ⓪ AE

Prinsengracht 444 ⊠ 1017 KE – ℰ (0 20) 620 12 12 – info@dtfh.nl – Fax (0 20)
625 89 86 – www.dtfh.nl   **F3**
42 rm – †125/245 € ††150/345 €, ⌚ 13 €
♦ Traditional ♦ Business ♦ Classical ♦

A building dating from 1921 on the corner of a shopping street, opposite the Princes Canal, where an assistant of Escoffier once owned a food shop. Large guestrooms, studio and penthouse.

Golden Tulip-Centre without rest   AC ⇄ 📺 💬 VISA ⓪ AE ⓪

Nieuwezijdskolk 19 ⊠ 1012 PV – ℰ (0 20) 530 18 18 – infoamsterdam@
goldentulipinntel.com – Fax (0 20) 422 19 19 – www.goldentulipinntel.com
239 rm – †99/450 € ††99/450 €, ⌚ 20 €   **G1**
♦ Chain hotel ♦ Modern ♦

A modern glass-fronted establishment in the heart of the busy Nieuwe Zijde, the
shopping area next to the station. Well sound-proofed rooms. Breakfast area entirely surrounded by glass.

NH City Centre without rest   ⇆ & ⇄ 💬 ☇ VISA ⓪ AE ⓪

Spuistraat 288 ⊠ 1012 VX – ℰ (0 20) 420 45 45 – nhcitycentre@nh.hotels.com
– Fax (0 20) 420 43 00 – www.nh-hotels.com   **F2**
209 rm – †139/359 € ††139/359 €, ⌚ 19 €
♦ Chain hotel ♦ Business ♦ Functional ♦

Slotted between the Singel canal and the Béguine convent, this hotel has neutral,
contemporary-style bedrooms typical of the NH chain. Spacious and comfortable
lounge.

Mercure Arthur Frommer without rest   AC ⇄ 💬 P

Noorderstraat 46 ⊠ 1017 TV – ℰ (0 20) 622 03 28   VISA ⓪ AE ⓪
– h1032@accor.com – Fax (0 20) 620 32 08 – www.accorhotels.com
92 rm – †95/219 € ††115/239 €, ⌚ 16 €   **G3**
♦ Chain hotel ♦ Traditional ♦ Classical ♦

A group of houses (including a former wool factory) in a quiet residential street,
close to the Rijksmuseum. Public areas and bedrooms with Dutch decorative touches.

Le Coin without rest   ⇄ 💬 VISA ⓪ AE

Nieuwe Doelenstraat 5 ⊠ 1012 CP – ℰ (0 20) 524 68 00 – hotel@lecoin.nl
– Fax (0 20) 524 68 01 – www.lecoin.nl   **G2**
42 rm – †119 € ††139/154 €, ⌚ 12 €
♦ Traditional ♦ Functional ♦

Seven houses next to the University of Amsterdam make up this hotel. Rooms of
various shapes and sizes, but all decorated in a contemporary style and equipped
with a kitchenette.

Roemer without rest   ☇ Ⅰ⑤ AC ⇄ 📺 💬 VISA ⓪ AE ⓪

Roemer Visscherstraat 10 ⊠ 1054 EX – ℰ (0 20) 589 08 00 – info@
hotelroemer.com – Fax (0 20) 589 08 01 – www.vondelhotels.com
23 rm ⌚ – †169 € ††169 €   **E3**
♦ Business ♦ Design ♦

This small designer-decorated hotel is located in an early 20C house not far from
the Vondelpark. Well-equipped pleasant rooms. Town garden.

Vondel without rest ⑤   ☇ ⇄ 📺 💬 ☇ⓐ VISA ⓪ AE ⓪

Vondelstraat 26 ⊠ 1054 GD – ℰ (0 20) 612 01 20
– info@hotelvondel.com – Fax (0 20) 685 43 21
– www.hotelvondel.com   **E3**
82 rm – †89 € ††99 €, ⌚ 20 €
♦ Luxury ♦ Business ♦ Design ♦

Hotel occupying several late-19th century houses. Trendy communal areas in
Italian designer style, works of modern art, contemporary bedrooms and ornamental garden.

Jan Luyken without rest   AC ⚡ °¹ VISA ⊕ AE ⓪

Jan Luykenstraat 58 ⌧ 1071 CS – ℰ (0 20) 573 07 30
– jan-luyken@bilderberg.nl – Fax (0 20) 676 38 41
– www.janluyken.nl   **E3**
62 rm – ♦119/199 € ♦♦169/289 €, ⌘ 20 €
◆ Chain hotel ◆ Traditional ◆ Cosy ◆

Three 1900s houses make up this hotel with contemporary interior décor. Modern bedrooms, designer bar with a few period touches and small courtyard terrace.

Fita without rest   ⚡ SAT °¹ VISA ⊕ AE ⓪

Jan Luykenstraat 37 ⌧ 1071 CL – ℰ (0 20) 679 09 76 – info@fita.nl
– Fax (0 20) 664 39 69 – www.hotelfita.com
– closed 20 December - 15 January   **E3**
15 rm ⌘ – ♦105/150 € ♦♦135/165 €
◆ Family ◆ Classical ◆

This typical family-run hotel has functional rooms in three different sizes with the added advantage of being near Amsterdam's most prestigious museums. Friendly welcome.

La Rive – H. Amstel   ⇐ 🏠 AC ⇕ ⇗ P VISA ⊕ AE ⓪
⊗

Prof. Tulpplein 1 ⌧ 1018 GX – ℰ (0 20) 520 32 64 – larive@ihg.com
– Fax (0 20) 520 32 66 – www.restaurantlarive.com
– closed 1 - 12 January, 19 July - 10 August, Saturday lunch, Sunday and Monday   **H3**
Rest – Menu 85/192 € bi – Carte 101/138 €
Spec. Langoustines in kadaifi deeg gebakken, buikspek, ui en bospeen vinaigrette. Gegratineerde tarbot, aardappel krokant en zacht, schaaldieren béarnaise. Gebraden Wagyu rund, geroosterde artisjok en Nebiolo jus.
◆ Contemporary ◆ Formal ◆

A fine atmosphere with refined décor, a prestigious wine collection and high level of comfort characterize this gastronomic restaurant on the Amstel. Views of the river from the dining area at the front.

Excelsior – H. De l'Europe   ⇐ 🏠 AC ⇕ ⇗ P VISA ⊕ AE ⓪

Nieuwe Doelenstraat 2 ⌧ 1012 CP – ℰ (0 20) 531 17 05 – restaurant@
leurope.nl – Fax (0 20) 531 17 78 – www.restaurantexcelsior.nl
– closed 1 - 16 January, Saturday lunch and Sunday lunch   **G2**
Rest – Menu 55/90 € – Carte 64/97 € ▨
◆ Contemporary ◆ Formal ◆

Up-to-date cuisine served in the deluxe setting of a 100-year-old luxury hotel or on the attractive waterside terrace. Knowledgeable sommelier. Fixed lunch menu.

Vermeer – H. NH Barbizon Palace   � AC ⇕ ⇗ P VISA ⊕ AE ⓪

Prins Hendrikkade 59 ⌧ 1012 AD – ℰ (0 20) 556 48 85 – vermeer@
nh-hotels.com – Fax (0 20) 624 33 53 – www.restaurantvermeer.nl
– closed 5 July - 8 August, 24 - 31 December, Saturday lunch and Sunday
Rest – Menu 70/85 € bi – Carte 80 € ▨   **G1**
◆ Innovative ◆ Classical ◆

Hotel restaurant where the chef creates inventive dishes with a bold personal touch. Fine à la carte menu offered at five sittings, magnificent cellar, expert sommelier and chic classical setting.

Christophe   AC ⇕ VISA ⊕ AE

Leliegracht 46 ⌧ 1015 DH – ℰ (0 20) 625 08 07 – info@restaurantchristophe.nl
– Fax (0 20) 638 91 32 – www.restaurantchristophe.nl
– closed 1 January, Sunday and Monday   **F1**
Rest – *(dinner only)* Menu 45/95 € bi – Carte 59/80 €
◆ French traditional ◆ Formal ◆

This low-key, refined restaurant in a traditional building on the banks of the canal Lys serves good classic to modern cuisine.

NETHERLANDS - AMSTERDAM

XXX Dynasty 🏠 AC ⇔ VISA ⓞ AE ⑩

Reguliersdwarsstraat 30 ⊠ 1017 BM – ℰ (0 20) 626 84 00 – dynasty@hetnet.nl
– Fax (0 20) 622 30 38 – www.fer.nl
– closed 27 December - 1 February and Tuesday **F2**
Rest – *(dinner only)* Menu 43/66 € – Carte 35/69 €
♦ Exotic ♦

A pleasant, longstanding restaurant featuring cuisine from around Asia. The 'trendy exotic' décor is warm and colourful. Lovely terrace in the back and attentive service.

XX d'Vijff Vlieghen AC ⇔ VISA ⓞ AE ⑩

Spuistraat 294 (via Vlieghendesteeg 1) ⊠ 1012 VX – ℰ (0 20) 530 40 60
– vijffvlieghen@nh-hotels.com – Fax (0 20) 623 64 04 – www.vijffvlieghen.com
Rest – *(dinner only)* Menu 36 € – Carte 50/65 € **F2**
♦ Contemporary ♦ Rustic ♦

Modern cuisine prepared using typically Dutch produce and served in a restaurant taking up five 17th century townhouses. Maze of fully-renovated rustic dining rooms.

XX Breitner ⇐ VISA ⓞ AE

Amstel 212 ⊠ 1017 AH – ℰ (0 20) 627 78 79 – info@restaurant-breitner.nl
– Fax (0 20) 330 29 98 – www.restaurant-breitner.nl
– closed 20 July - 2 August, 25 December - 2 January and Sunday
Rest – *(dinner only)* Menu 44/58 € – Carte 48/74 € **G2**
♦ Contemporary ♦ Cosy ♦

Creative and elaborate meals served in a classical modern setting. There are views over the Amstel with sightseeing boats and monuments (drawbridges, Amstelhof) in the background.

XX Het Tuynhuys 🏠 AC ⇔ VISA ⓞ AE ⑩

Reguliersdwarsstraat 28 ⊠ 1017 BM – ℰ (0 20) 627 66 03 – info@tuynhuys.nl
– Fax (0 20) 423 59 97 – www.tuynhuys.nl
– closed 28 December - 4 January, Saturday lunch and Sunday lunch
Rest – Menu 33/65 € – Carte 43/69 € **F2**
♦ Contemporary ♦ Fashionable ♦

Mediterranean-inspired menu, attractive modern décor (white walls, wrought iron chairs, azulejo tiles) and courtyard-garden with a fine view of the baroque façade.

XX Van Vlaanderen 🏠 AC ⇔ VISA ⓞ AE

Weteringschans 175 ⊠ 1017 XD – ℰ (0 20) 622 82 92
– closed last 3 weeks in August, 25 December - 1 January, Sunday and Monday
Rest – *(dinner only)* (set menu only) Menu 43/50 € **F3**
♦ Contemporary ♦

Bow window façade, discreet and polished dining rooms, trendy atmosphere and modern cuisine. Balcony-terrace overlooking the water and sidewalk terrace.

XX Hosokawa AC ⇔ VISA ⓞ AE ⑩

Max Euweplein 22 ⊠ 1017 MB – ℰ (0 20) 638 80 86 – info@hosokawa.nl
– Fax (0 20) 638 22 19 – www.hosokawa.nl
– closed 27 July - 9 August and Sunday lunch
Rest – Menu 59/78 € – Carte 45/71 € **F3**
♦ Japanese ♦

A sober, modern Japanese restaurant with cooking tables, worth a detour to watch the entertaining show of food rotating past your eyes! At lunchtimes, only sushi is available.

XX Beddington's 🏠 VISA ⓞ AE

Utrechtsedwarsstraat 141 ⊠ 1017 WE – ℰ (0 20) 620 73 93 – Fax (0 20) 620 01 90
– closed 20 December - 5 January, 19 July - 10 August, Sunday and Monday
Rest – *(dinner only)* Menu 45/52 € **G3**
♦ Contemporary ♦

A British chef runs the open kitchen of this modern restaurant serving contemporary cuisine in her adopted home of Amsterdam. Black and white décor.

Sichuan Food   AC ⇔ VISA ☻ AE

*Reguliersdwarsstraat 35 ⊠ 1017 BK – ℰ (0 20) 626 93 27 – Fax (0 20)
627 72 81*   **F2**
Rest – *(dinner only)* Menu 31/43 € – Carte 35/55 €
♦ Chinese ♦ Exotic ♦

Small oriental restaurant with good local reputation situated in a lively area. Typical
local Chinese restaurant décor. Peking Duck prepared and served in the dining
room.

Le Relais – H. De l'Europe   AC ⇨₣ VISA ☻ AE ⊙

*Nieuwe Doelenstraat 2 ⊠ 1012 CP – ℰ (0 20) 531 17 04 – concierge@leurope.nl
– Fax (0 20) 531 17 78 – www.leurope.nl*   **G2**
Rest – *(open until 11pm)* Menu 28/33 € – Carte approx. 39 €
♦ Brasserie ♦

Despite the grand hotel location, stylish welcome and waiters in tails, this restaurant is far from stuffy! Blackboard lunchtime specials, set menus and local specialities.

Blauw aan de Wal   🛋 AC ⇔ VISA ☻ AE

*O.Z. Achterburgwal 99 ⊠ 1012 DD – ℰ (0 20) 330 22 57 – Fax (0 20) 330 20 06
– closed 25 December - 1 January, Sunday and Monday*   **G2**
Rest – *(dinner only until 11.30 pm) (booking advisable)* Menu 55 €
– Carte 60/72 € 🏵
♦ Contemporary ♦ Friendly ♦

A popular restaurant at the end of a cul-de-sac in the lively red district. Discreet
décor, simple and tasty modern cuisine, good wine selection and a shady terrace.

Herrie   ⇔ VISA ☻ AE

*Utrechtsestraat 30a ⊠ 1017 VN – ℰ (0 20) 622 08 38 – herrie@engel.nl
– Fax (0 20) 626 80 93 – www.engelgroep.com
– closed 25 - 31 December and Sundays*   **G3**
Rest – *(dinner only) (booking advisable)* Menu 65/90 € – Carte approx. 75 €
♦ Contemporary ♦

Cocktail bar-lounge downstairs, and a discreet modern restaurant upstairs. Here
the walls are covered with fabric and dark panels with two gas stoves. Kitchen
visible in the entrance.

Oesterbar   AC ⇔ VISA ☻ AE ⊙

*Leidseplein 10 ⊠ 1017 PT – ℰ (0 20) 623 29 88 – info@oesterbar.nl – Fax (0 20)
623 21 99 – www.oesterbar.nl*   **F3**
Rest – *(open until 11pm)* Carte 43/91 €
♦ Seafood ♦

A seafood restaurant with a new twist, featuring classic (Oude school) and evolving
(Nieuwe school) cuisine served on three levels. Aquariums and fish tanks.

Antoine   AC ⇔ VISA ☻ AE

*Kerkstraat 377 ⊠ 1017 HW – ℰ (0 20) 422 27 66 – info@restaurantantoine.nl
– Fax (0 20) 423 41 09 – www.restaurantantoine.nl
– closed 1 - 15 January*   **G3**
Rest – *(dinner only)* Menu 40/55 € – Carte approx. 50 €
♦ Contemporary ♦

Up-to-date cuisine served in two modern rooms, one a mezzanine, the other with
a view outside. Neat tables, banquettes and comfortable chairs.

Flo – H. Eden Rembrandt Square   VISA ☻ AE ⊙

*Amstelstraat 9 ⊠ 1017 DA – ℰ (0 20) 890 47 57 – info@floamsterdam.com
– Fax (0 20) 890 47 40 – www.floamsterdam.com
– closed Saturday lunch and Sunday lunch*   **G2**
Rest – *(open until midnight)* Menu 30/50 € – Carte 33/68 €
♦ Brasserie ♦ Brasserie ♦

Brasserie/oyster bar with a chic Parisian look featuring red velvet banquettes,
sparkling brass, retro lighting and white apron service. Typical brasserie fare and
good set menus.

XX **Segugio**   🅰️🔲 ⇦⇨ VISA ⚏ AE ①

Utrechtsestraat 96 ✉️ *1017 VS –* ℰ *(0 20) 330 15 03 – adriano@segugio.nl*
– Fax (0 20) 330 15 16 – www.segugio.nl
– closed 25, 26 and 31 December - 1 January and Sunday   **G3**
Rest – *(dinner only until 11pm)* Menu 52/96 € bi – Carte 47/71 €
♦ Italian ♦ Design ♦
This establishment with three modern dining rooms on several levels features sunny Italian cuisine made right before your eyes. Good selection of regional wines.

XX **Blue Pepper**   🅰️🔲 VISA ⚏ AE

Nassaukade 366h ✉️ *1054 AB –* ℰ *(0 20) 489 70 39 – info@*
restaurantbluepepper.com – www.restaurantbluepepper.com
– closed 30 April and 24, 25, 26 and 31 January - 1 January   **E2**
Rest – *(dinner only)* Menu 55/80 € – Carte 52/60 €
♦ Indonesian ♦ Romantic ♦
An intimate modern setting and up-to-date Indonesian cuisine are featured at this establishment popular with romantic diners. Three menus. Attentive service.

X **Bordewijk**   � 🅰️🔲 VISA ⚏ AE ①

Noordermarkt 7 ✉️ *1015 MV –* ℰ *(0 20) 624 38 99*
– www.restaurantbordewijk.nl
– closed mid July - mid August, late December, Sunday and Monday
Rest – *(dinner only)* Menu 39/59 € – Carte 46/62 €   **F1**
♦ Contemporary ♦ Minimalist ♦
Popular restaurant due to its modern menu with inventive touches and minimalist décor: bare floorboards, Formica tables and designer chairs. Noisy atmosphere when busy.

X **Envy**   🅰️🔲 VISA ⚏ AE

😊

Prinsengracht 381 ✉️ *1016 HL –* ℰ *(0 20) 344 64 07 – info@envy.nl – Fax (0 20)*
344 64 05 – www.envy.nl   **F2**
Rest – *(dinner only except weekend until 11 pm)* Carte approx. 30 €
♦ Design ♦ Contemporary ♦
Contemporary-style brasserie where guests eat on both sides of a long wenge wood bar lit by modern globe-shaped lights or at one of the neighbouring tables. Open kitchen.

X **Le zinc... et les autres**   ⇦⇨ VISA ⚏ AE ①

Prinsengracht 999 ✉️ *1017 KM –* ℰ *(0 20) 622 90 44 – info@lezinc.nl*
– Fax (0 20) 639 02 70 – www.lezinc.nl
– closed last 2 weeks in July, 27 December - 1 January and Sunday
Rest – *(dinner only until 11pm)* Menu 33/82 € bi   **F3**
– Carte 41/58 €
♦ Contemporary ♦ Rustic ♦
Former 17C warehouse located off the tourist trail opposite the Prinsengracht. Superb zinc bar with rustic dining room upstairs. Classic contemporary cuisine.

X **Haesje Claes**   🌂 🅰️ ⇦⇨ VISA ⚏ AE ①

Spuistraat 275 ✉️ *1012 VR –* ℰ *(0 20) 624 99 98 – info@haesjeclaes.nl*
– Fax (0 20) 627 48 17 – www.haesjeclaes.nl
– closed 30 April and 25, 26 and 31 December   **F2**
Rest – Menu 21/29 € – Carte 26/53 €
♦ Dutch regional ♦
A popular restaurant reflecting the town's atmosphere. Simple and copious Dutch cuisine served in a cheerful setting. Historical museum nearby.

X **Fifteen**   🌂 🅰️ VISA ⚏ AE

Jollemanhof 9 ✉️ *1019 GW –* ℰ *(0 900) 343 83 36 – info@fifteen.nl – Fax (0 20)*
509 50 12 – www.fifteen.nl – closed 31 December - 1 January and Sunday
Rest – *(open until 11pm)* Menu 46 € – Carte approx. 40 €   *Plan I* **C1**
♦ Contemporary ♦ Brasserie ♦
Jamie Oliver is behind the concept of this popular restaurant with a mission to give disadvantaged youngsters opportunities. Parking at the Passengers Terminal.

✗ ☺ Zuid Zeeland   🍴 VISA ⦿ AE

Herengracht 413 ✉ *1017 BP* – ℰ *(0 20) 624 31 54* – *mail@zuidzeeland.nl*
– *Fax (0 20) 428 31 71* – *www.zuidzeeland.nl*   **F2**
Rest – *(open until 11 pm)* Menu 36/63 € bi – Carte 47/64 €
♦ Traditional ♦ Friendly ♦
This old establishment gives onto an attractive section of the Herengracht canal on
one side and a patio on the other. Good, reasonably priced menu. Sidewalk terrace
on the canal.

✗ Van de Kaart   🍴 VISA ⦿ AE

Prinsengracht 512 ✉ *1017 KH* – ℰ *(0 20) 625 92 32* – *info@vandekaart.com*
– *www.vandekaart.com*   **F3**
Rest – *(dinner only)* Menu 40/55 € – Carte 53/67 €
♦ Contemporary ♦ Friendly ♦
Friendly service, streamlined décor, chef on view in the kitchen, terrace on the
canal, up-to-date cuisine and Atlantic crab speciality in season.

✗ ☺ De Belhamel   ≼ 🍴 AC ⟷ VISA ⦿ AE

Brouwersgracht 60 ✉ *1013 GX* – ℰ *(0 20) 622 10 95* – *info@belhamel.nl*
– *Fax (0 20) 623 88 40* – *www.belhamel.nl*   **F1**
Rest – Menu 35/45 € – Carte approx. 50 €
♦ Bistro ♦ Retro ♦
A local brasserie at the confluence of several delightful canals. A small classical
choice plus a blackboard menu. Belle Époque style dining room with a mezzanine.

SOUTH and WEST QUARTERS   *Plan I*

🏨🏨🏨🏨🏨 Okura ⊗   ₤ ⊛ ♨ ▢ ⅃ rm AC ⇘ 🖙 🖤 🏊 P ⌂ VISA ⦿ AE ⓘ

Ferdinand Bolstraat 333 ✉ *1072 LH* – ℰ *(0 20) 678 71 11* – *sales@okura.nl*
– *Fax (0 20) 671 23 44* – *www.okura.nl*   **C2**
293 rm – ♦260/410 € ♦♦260/410 €, ⇱ 33 € – 8 suites
Rest *Ciel Bleu* and *Yamazato* and *Le Camelia* – see below
Rest *Sazanka* – *(dinner only)* Menu 73/93 € – Carte 49/113 €
♦ Grand Luxury ♦ Business ♦ Modern ♦
A luxury Japanese style hotel set in a modern tower block. Various types of rooms
and suites, superb wellness centre, extensive conference facilities and a full range
of services. Japanese culinary expertise displayed in dishes such as teppanyaki.

🏨🏨🏨🏨 Hilton   ≼ 🚗 🍴 ₤ ♨ ⅃ rm AC ⇘ 🖙 🖤 🏊 P VISA ⦿ AE ⓘ

Apollolaan 138 ✉ *1077 BG* – ℰ *(0 20) 710 60 00* – *info.amsterdam@hilton.com*
– *Fax (0 20) 710 60 80* – *www.amsterdam.hilton.com*   **B2**
268 rm – ♦215/445 € ♦♦215/445 €, ⇱ 27 € – 3 suites
Rest *Roberto's* – ℰ *(0 20) 710 60 25* – Menu 55/60 € – Carte 41/66 €
♦ Chain hotel ♦ Business ♦ Modern ♦
This modern and spacious hotel belonging to a chain has a terrace and garden
with a water feature. Rooms and suites with superb views, one on a 1969 theme
of 'John Lennon and Yoko Ono'. Italian menu served in a contemporary setting at
Roberto's restaurant.

🏨🏨🏨 Apollo   ≼ ₤ AC ⇘ 🖙 🖤 🏊 P VISA ⦿ AE ⓘ

Apollolaan 2 ✉ *1077 BA* – ℰ *(0 20) 673 59 22* – *info@gtaa.nl* – *Fax (0 20)*
570 57 44 – *www.goldentulipapolloamsterdam.com*   **B2**
223 rm – ♦110/350 € ♦♦110/350 €, ⇱ 23 € – 2 suites
Rest *La Sirène* – see below
♦ Chain hotel ♦ Business ♦ Stylish ♦
An international chain hotel located at the intersection of five canals. Guestrooms
designed with the business traveller in mind. Waterside bar, terrace and landing
stage.

Bilderberg Garden

Dijsselhofplantsoen 7 ✉ 1077 BJ – 𝒞 (0 20) 570 56 00 – garden@bilderberg.nl
– Fax (0 20) 570 56 54 – www.bilderberg.nl **B2**
120 rm – ♦189/309 € ♦♦189/309 €, ⌑ 22 € – 2 suites
Rest *De Kersentuin* – *(closed Saturday lunch and Sunday)* Menu 43/50 €
– Carte 47/62 €
♦ Luxury ♦ Business ♦ Stylish ♦
Chain hotel catering mainly to corporate customers in the business district. Fully renovated interior and bedrooms. Meals in line with current tastes, modern brasserie décor, pavement terrace.

Holiday Inn

De Boelelaan 2 ✉ 1083 HJ – 𝒞 (0 20) 646 23 00 – Fax (0 20) 517 25 34
– www.holidayinn.com/amsterdam **C2**
264 rm – ♦90/295 € ♦♦90/335 €, ⌑ 20 €
Rest – *(open until 11pm)* Carte 36/56 €
♦ Chain hotel ♦ Business ♦ Functional ♦
Chain hotel close to the RAI. Enjoy the discreet luxury and spaciousness of the communal areas and the comfortable guestrooms. Lounge-bar and restaurant in a modern setting evocative of New England. International and American cuisine.

Golden Tulip Art-Tulip Inn Art

Spaarndammerdijk 302 (Westerpark) ✉ 1013 ZX
– 𝒞 (0 20) 410 96 70 – art@westcordhotels.nl – Fax (0 20) 681 08 02
– www.westcordhotels.nl **B1**
187 rm – ♦205/225 € ♦♦225/250 €, ⌑ 18 € – 3 suites
Rest – *(closed Sunday dinner) (open until 11pm)* Menu 25 € – Carte 33/50 €
♦ Chain hotel ♦ Business ♦ Stylish ♦
Near a slip road off the ring, a modern hotel with very contemporary guestrooms, available in two sizes. Exhibition of modern paintings in the public areas. Modern meals served in a trendy atmosphere; simpler set menu in the "eetcafé".

The College

Roelof Hartstraat 1 ✉ 1071 VE – 𝒞 (0 20) 571 15 11 – info@
thecollegehotel.com – Fax (0 20) 571 15 13 – www.steinhotels.com/college
40 rm – ♦230 € ♦♦260/310 €, ⌑ 20 € **C2**
Rest – *(closed Sunday dinner)* Menu 41/55 €
♦ Grand Luxury ♦ Design ♦
This hotel is located in a former 19C "college", redecorated with refinement. Chic and fashionable lounge bar and rooms in the same style. Modern restaurant installed in a former gym. Serves modern cuisine.

Toro without rest

Koningslaan 64 ✉ 1075 AG – 𝒞 (0 20) 673 72 23 – info@hoteltoro.nl
– Fax (0 20) 675 00 31 – www.hoteltoro.nl **B2**
22 rm – ♦75/300 € ♦♦95/325 €, ⌑ 15 €
♦ Luxury ♦ Stylish ♦
Villa set in a diplomatic/residential neighbourhood; half the rooms overlook the Vondelpark, as does the pretty breakfast room. Convenient street parking.

Novotel

Europaboulevard 10 ✉ 1083 AD – 𝒞 (0 20) 541 11 23 – h0515@accor.com
– Fax (0 20) 646 28 23 – www.novotel.com **C3**
611 rm – ♦99/399 € ♦♦99/399 €, ⌑ 20 €
Rest – *(open until midnight)* Menu 34 € – Carte 35/53 €
♦ Chain hotel ♦ Business ♦ Functional ♦
Imposing hotel block, with one of the largest guest capacities in Benelux. Fully-renovated interior. Bright, modern and functional bedrooms. Functional tavern-restaurant serving traditional classic cuisine.

NETHERLANDS - AMSTERDAM

The Gresham Memphis without rest   🗼 🛗 📺 ⁽ᵠ⁾ 🏄
De Lairessestraat 87 ⊠ *1071 NX – ℰ (0 20) 673 31 41*   𝚅𝙸𝚂𝙰 ⓩ 🝔 ❶
– info@gresham-memphishotel.com – Fax (0 20) 673 73 12 – www.memphishotel.nl
74 rm – †85/295 € ††95/345 €, ⊇ 22 €   **B2**
  ◆ Chain hotel ◆ Business ◆ Classical ◆
The tram line to the city centre runs in front of this ivy-covered hotel. Modern and intimate lounge bar with hushed atmosphere. Fresh bedrooms and pleasant breakfast area.

Arena   🚗 🛖 🄰🄲 rest ⇆ 📺 ⁽ᵠ⁾ 🏄 🅿 𝚅𝙸𝚂𝙰 ⓩ 🄰🄴 ❶
's-Gravesandestraat 51 ⊠ *1092 AA – ℰ (0 20) 850 24 00*
– info@hotelarena.nl – Fax (0 20) 850 24 25 – www.hotelarena.nl
116 rm – †139/305 € ††139/305 €, ⊇ 19 €   **C2**
Rest – Menu 27 € – Carte 36/69 €
  ◆ Minimalist ◆
Formerly an orphanage (1890), now an ultra-trendy hotel. Fantastic old staircase, designer bar and guestrooms of various styles and levels of comfort. Weekend nightclub (separate access). Designer setting and modern cuisine in the restaurant.

De Filosoof without rest 🦶   🚗 ⇆ 📺 ⁽ᵠ⁾ 🏄 𝚅𝙸𝚂𝙰 ⓩ 🄰🄴
Anna van den Vondelstraat 6 ⊠ *1054 GZ – ℰ (0 20) 683 30 13 – reservations@*
hotelfilosoof.nl – Fax (0 20) 685 37 50 – www.hotelfilosoof.nl   **B2**
38 rm – †90/130 € ††100/165 €, ⊇ 15 €
  ◆ Family ◆ Personalised ◆
The originality of this hotel in a one-way street alongside the Vondelpark is in the decor of its rooms, based on cultural or philosophical themes. Garden.

Villa Borgmann without rest 🦶   ⇆ 📺 ⁽ᵠ⁾ 𝚅𝙸𝚂𝙰 ⓩ 🄰🄴 ❶
Koningslaan 48 ⊠ *1075 AE – ℰ (0 20) 673 52 52 – info@hotel-borgmann.nl*
– Fax (0 20) 676 25 80 – www.hotel-borgmann.nl   **B2**
15 rm – †79/115 € ††89/155 €, ⊇ 12 €
  ◆ Family ◆ Functional ◆
A Russian couple play host in this large red-brick 1900s villa near the Vondelpark. Uncluttered rooms, simple breakfasts, quiet neighbourhood and easy car parking (paying).

Ciel Bleu – H. Okura, 23rd floor   ≤ 🄰🄲 ⇄ 🅿 𝚅𝙸𝚂𝙰 ⓩ 🄰🄴 ❶
✗✗✗✗
✿✿
Ferdinand Bolstraat 333 ⊠ *1072 LH – ℰ (0 20) 678 74 50 – restaurants@*
okura.nl – Fax (0 20) 678 77 88 – www.okura.nl
– closed late December and for the 3 weeks of the construction industry holidays
Rest – *(dinner only)* Menu 73/235 € bi – Carte 90/110 € 🏵   **C2**
Spec. Tartaar van moerkalf, salade en croque madam van koningscrab, bouillabaisesaus.Tarbot met Pata Negra en lardo di colonnata, geglaceerde asperges en dressing van sherry. Krokante Gianduja met aardnoot, creme van chocolade, roomijs van wiskey en gezouten karamel.
  ◆ Contemporary ◆ Fashionable ◆
A chic restaurant at the top of the Okura Hotel with a superb contemporary décor, and fascinating urban panorama. Experience stylish service, delicious creative cuisine with exotic touches, a fine wine list and sunset views from the lounge.

Visaandeschelde   🛖 🄰🄲 ⇄ *(dinner)* 𝚅𝙸𝚂𝙰 ⓩ 🄰🄴 ❶
✗✗
Scheldeplein 4 ⊠ *1078 GR – ℰ (0 20) 675 15 83 – info@visaandeschelde.nl*
– Fax (0 20) 471 46 53 – www.visaandeschelde.nl
– closed 30 April, 24, 25, 26 and 31 December, 1 January, Saturday lunch and
Sunday lunch   **C2**
Rest – *(open until 11pm)* Menu 37/54 € – Carte 47/91 €
  ◆ Seafood ◆
Opposite the RAI congress centre, this restaurant is popular with Amsterdammers for its dishes full of the flavours of the sea, contemporary brasserie décor and lively atmosphere.

La Sirène – H. Apollo   ≤ 🛖 🄰🄲 ⇄ 🅿 𝚅𝙸𝚂𝙰 ⓩ 🄰🄴 ❶
✗✗
Apollolaan 2 ⊠ *1077 BA – ℰ (0 20) 673 59 22 – esther.rookhuijzen@*
apollohotelsressorts.com – Fax (0 20) 570 57 44 – www.goldentulipapolloamsterdam.com
Rest – Menu 40/50 € – Carte 51/85 €   **B2**
  ◆ Seafood ◆
Cuisine which comes in with the tide, served either in the large, bright dining room with views over the point where five canals meet or on the panoramic waterside terrace.

XX **Le Garage**   AC ⟺ ⌁ (dinner) VISA ◑ AE

Ruysdaelstraat 54 ✉ *1071 XE – ℰ (0 20) 679 71 76 – info@*
restaurantlegarage.nl – Fax (0 20) 662 22 49 – www.restaurantlegarage.nl
– closed 20 July - 2 August, Saturday lunch and Sunday lunch   **B2**
Rest – *(open until 11pm)* Menu 37/48 € – Carte 40/75 €
 ♦ Brasserie ♦
Excellent up-to-date establishment with an original décor. The entertainment and
business clientele come to see and be seen as well as to enjoy the great food.

XX **Brasserie van Baerle**   ⌂ ⟺ VISA ◑ AE ◉

Van Baerlestraat 158 ✉ *1071 BG – ℰ (0 20) 679 15 32 – info@*
brasserievanbaerle.nl – Fax (0 20) 671 71 96 – www.brasserievanbaerle.nl
– closed 30 April, 25, 26 and 31 December - 1 January and Saturday lunch
Rest – *(open until 11pm)* Menu 35/57 € – Carte 51/64 €   **B2**
 ♦ Brasserie ♦
This retro brasserie attracts regular customers, mainly from the local area because of
its attractive menu, tasty steak tartare and well-matched wines. Courtyard terrace.

XX **Sophia**   ⌂ AC ⟺ VISA ◑ AE

Sophialaan 55 ✉ *1075 BP – ℰ (0 20) 305 27 60 – info@restaurantsophia.nl*
– Fax (0 20) 305 27 67 – www.restaurantsophia.nl
– closed Saturday lunch and Sunday lunch   **C2**
Rest – *(open until 11pm)* Menu 50/103 € bi
 ♦ Design ♦
Very trendy establishment where the well dressed clientele samples the cuisine in
a stylish setting. Small portions of several dishes served on one plate. Cocktail bar.
Professional service.

XX **Quartier Sud**   ⌂ AC VISA ◑ AE

Olympiaplein 176 ✉ *1076 AM – ℰ (0 20) 675 39 90 – info@quartiersud.nl*
– Fax (0 20) 675 42 60 – www.quartiersud.nl
– closed 24 December - 2 January, Saturday and Sunday   **B2**
Rest – *(open until 11.30pm)* Menu 42/65 € bi – Carte 43/57 €
 ♦ Contemporary ♦ Fashionable ♦
Their 10th anniversary is in 2009! Denise, courted by the media, has turned the kit-
chen over to her second in command. Fashionable décor and sidewalk terrace.
Very crowded at lunchtime.

XX **Eau de Vie**   ⌂ AC VISA ◑ AE

Maasstraat 20 ✉ *1078 HK – ℰ (0 20) 662 95 88 – info@restaurant-eaudevie.nl*
– Fax (0 20) 423 44 78 – www.restaurant-eaudevie.nl
– closed 30 April, 25 and 31 December - 1 January and Saturday lunch
Rest – Menu 38/55 € – Carte 46/55 €   **C2**
 ♦ Contemporary ♦ Friendly ♦
This establishment run by a dynamic and motivated young team has lived up to its gast-
ronomic promise. Surprise set menus, modern paintings on display and urban terrace.

XX **Silex**   ⟺ VISA ◑ AE ◉

Daniël Stalpertstraat 93 ✉ *1072 XD – ℰ (0 20) 620 59 59 – info@*
restaurantsilex.nl – Fax (0 20) 620 89 01 – www.restaurantsilex.nl
– closed Sunday   *Plan II* **G3**
Rest – *(dinner only)* Menu 33/48 € – Carte approx. 45 €
 ♦ Contemporary ♦ Fashionable ♦
In an up-and-coming working class neighbourhood near a lively square. Up-to-
date menu based on the chef's inspiration, warm modern setting, conservatory.

XX **Chang-i**   AC ⟺ VISA ◑ AE

Jan Willem Brouwersstraat 7 (adjacent to the artists' entrance to the
Concertgebouw) ✉ *1071 LH – ℰ (0 20) 470 17 00 – info@chang-i.nl*
– Fax (0 20) 470 81 18 – www.chang-i.nl – closed Sunday   *Plan II* **E3**
Rest – *(dinner only until 11pm) (booking advisable)* Menu 35/59 € – Carte 45/77 €
 ♦ Asian ♦ Trendy ♦
The 'I' in the name highlights the innovative nature of this chef's Asian cuisine.
Trendy and intimate lounge style atmosphere. Near a theatre.

XX **Rosarium**   ≼ ⍩ 🎧 ⇔ **P** 🚾 ☯ 🄰🄴

Amstelpark 1 ⊠ *1083 HZ –* ℰ *(0 20) 644 40 85 – info@rosarium.net*
– Fax (0 20) 646 60 04 – www.rosarium.net – closed Saturday and Sunday
Rest – Menu 40 € – Carte 44/55 €   **C3**
♦ French traditional ♦ Fashionable ♦
Modern restaurant on the edge of the Amstelpark, located in a modern circular
building with two wings. Spacious and bright designer setting, wine bar and ver-
dant terrace.

XX **Yamazato** – H. Okura   🄰🄲 ⇔ **P** 🚾 ☯ 🄰🄴 ⓞ
🐾
Ferdinand Bolstraat 333 ⊠ *1072 LH –* ℰ *(0 20) 678 83 51 – restaurants@*
okura.nl – Fax (0 20) 678 77 88 – www.okura.nl   **C2**
Rest – Menu 68/145 € bi – Carte 35/84 €
Spec. Tokusen sushi. Gegrilde zeebaars met Japans zeezout. Wagyu rib-eye
met seizoensgroenten.
♦ Japanese ♦
Good Japanese restaurant featuring authentic Kaiseki cuisine in a Sukiya décor.
Sushi bar. Meticulous service. Simplified lunch menu (lunchbox).

XX **Le Camelia** – H. Okura   ⅙ rm 🄰🄲 ⁴⁄≠ **P** 🚾 ☯ 🄰🄴
😊
Ferdinand Bolstraat 333 ⊠ *1072 LH –* ℰ *(0 20) 678 71 11 – sales@okura.nl*
– Fax (0 20) 671 23 44 – www.okura.nl   **C2**
Rest – *(open until 11 pm)* Menu 27/34 € – Carte approx. 40 €
♦ Classical ♦ Brasserie ♦
Hotel restaurant popular with locals, featuring a deluxe French brasserie atmo-
sphere, elegant and reasonably priced set menus and an enthusiastic young staff.

X **Le Hollandais**   🎧 🄰🄲 ⇔ 🚾 ☯ 🄰🄴
Amsteldijk 41 ⊠ *1074 HV –* ℰ *(0 20) 679 12 48 – info@lehollandais.nl*
– www.lehollandais.nl – closed first 3 weeks in August, Sunday and Monday
Rest – *(dinner only)* Menu 36/53 € bi – Carte 44/54 €   **C2**
♦ Traditional ♦ Trendy ♦
The 1970s furniture and lighting, wooden floors and panelling create a charming
setting. The menu features traditional simmered dishes, offal, blood sausage and
homemade cold meats.

X **Gorgeous**   🎧 🚾 ☯ 🄰🄴 ⓞ
2de v.d. Helststraat 16 ⊠ *1072 PD –* ℰ *(0 20) 379 14 00 – info@gorgeousrestaurant.nl*
– www.gorgeousrestaurant.nl – closed 25 December - 1 January and Monday
Rest – *(dinner only)* Menu 31/75 € bi – Carte 30/56 €   **C2**
♦ Bistro ♦
Near Sarphati Park, with a blue tiled façade and terrace overlooking a lively neighbourhood. Normal or reduced size portions. Menu read aloud.

X **White Elephant**   🎧 🚾 ☯ 🄰🄴 ⓞ
Van Woustraat 3 ⊠ *1074 AA –* ℰ *(0 20) 679 55 56 – info@whiteelephant.nl*
– Fax (0 20) 679 55 58 – www.whiteelephant.nl   Plan II **G3**
Rest – *(dinner only until 11pm)* Carte 32/50 €
♦ Thai ♦ Exotic ♦
Thai restaurant with matching décor: panelling, orchids, bar in a traditional "hut",
exotic terrace and friendly waiters in traditional costume. Authentic cuisine.

X **Spring**   🎧 🄰🄲 ⇔ 🚾 ☯ 🄰🄴 ⓞ
Willemsparkweg 177 ⊠ *1071 GZ –* ℰ *(0 20) 675 44 21 – info@*
restaurantspring.nl – Fax (0 20) 676 94 14 – www.restaurantspring.nl
– closed 25, 26 and 31 December - 1 January, Saturday lunch and Sunday
Rest – *(booking advisable)* Menu 39/71 € bi – Carte 45/64 €   **B2**
♦ Contemporary ♦ Minimalist ♦
Contemporary dining room with minimalist tubular décor, divided in two by a long
leather bench. Mediterranean inspired cuisine. Set lunchtime menu; a la carte in
the evening.

Elkaar

🏠 ⇆ *VISA* ⓪ AE

Alexanderplein 6 ⊠ 1018 CG – ℰ (0 20) 330 75 59 – info@etenbijelkaar.nl
– Fax (0 20) 423 44 78 – www.etenbijelkaar.nl
– closed 30 April, 25 and 31 December, 1 January and Saturday lunch
Rest – Menu 35/55 € – Carte 37/50 €　　　　　　　　　　　　**C2**
♦ Taverne / Bistrot ♦ Cosy ♦

Refined lunches and menus are offered at this restaurant in a large townhouse. Enthusiastic young team, bistro comforts, modern paintings and a teak terrace facing the Tropenmuseum.

Bond

AC *VISA* ⓪ AE ⓪

Valeriusstraat 128b ⊠ 1075 GD – ℰ (0 20) 676 46 47 – info@
restaurant-bond.nl – Fax (0 20) 379 01 39 – www.restaurant-bond.nl
– closed Saturday lunch and Sunday
Rest – Carte 36/55 €　　　　　　　　　　　　　　　　　　**B2**
♦ Brasserie ♦ Trendy ♦

Located in a rather up-market district, this modern restaurant has a trendy bistro-style décor, a pastiche of the characteristic atmosphere of a chic hotel lobby of the 1950s.

The French Café

🏠 AC *VISA* ⓪ AE

Gerard Doustraat 98 ⊠ 1072 VX – ℰ (0 20) 470 03 01 – info@thefrenchcafe.nl
– Fax (0 20) 670 57 02 – www.thefrenchcafe.nl
– closed 1-12 January, 27 July - 10 August, bank holidays and Sunday
Rest – (dinner only until 11 pm) Menu 32 € – Carte 39/76 €　　*Plan II* **G3**
♦ French traditional ♦ Friendly ♦

A tasteful modern setting with neo-retro wallpaper, a summer terrace overlooking the lively neighbourhood, and a French chef who cooks with Gallic flair.

A la Ferme

🏠 ⇆ *VISA* ⓪

Govert Flinckstraat 251 ⊠ 1073 BX – ℰ (0 20) 679 82 40 – info@alaferme.nl
– www.alaferme.nl – closed 25 December - 2 January and Monday
Rest – (dinner only) Menu 34/50 € – Carte 41/56 €　　　　*Plan II* **G3**
♦ Contemporary ♦ Friendly ♦

Monthly menus featured in the contemporary dining room, in one of the smaller, more intimate rooms in the back, or under the grape arbour in summer.

AT SCHIPHOL AIRPORT

Plan I

Sheraton Airport

🔊 ⋙ & rm AC ⇆ 📠 📶 🔊 ➾ *VISA* ⓪ AE ⓪

Schiphol bd 101 ⊠ 1118 BG Schiphol – ℰ (0 20) 316 43 00 – sales.amsterdam@
sheraton.com – Fax (0 20) 316 43 99 – www.sheraton.com/amsterdamair
– closed 1 - 12 January, 27 July - 10 August, bank holidays and Sunday
400 rm – †160/419 € ††185/444 €, ⊡ 27 € – 6 suites
Rest *Voyager* – (closed Saturday lunch and Sunday lunch) (open until 11pm)
Menu 40 € – Carte 46/68 €
♦ Chain hotel ♦ Business ♦ Modern ♦

Modern hotel complex near the airport, designed for a globe-trotting business clientèle. Guestrooms offer every comfort. Fine atrium. Full service. Modern brasserie with a bluish dome reminiscent of the Paris Zénith concert hall. International menu and buffets.

Hilton Schiphol

🔊 ⋙ & rm AC ⇆ 📠 🔊 P *VISA* ⓪ AE ⓪

Schiphol Bd 701 ⊠ 1118 BN Schiphol – ℰ (0 20) 710 40 00 – hilton.schiphol@
hilton.com – Fax (0 20) 710 40 80 – www.hilton.com
278 rm – †145/365 € ††160/380 €, ⊡ 27 € – 2 suites
Rest *East West* – (open until 11pm) Menu 33/68 € – Carte 46/60 €
♦ Chain hotel ♦ Business ♦ Functional ♦

A chain hotel, located near the airport and popular with business clientele. Modern, well-equipped guestrooms and meeting rooms. Meals combining Asian and Western flavours at the East West restaurant (Japanese cooking table during the week).

Radisson SAS Airport 🐾   🛋 ᏝᏏ ᠗ᠣ ᏚᏏ rm 🎬 ᏪᏪ ᠍ᠣ 🏰 🅿 ᧕
Boeing Avenue 2 (Rijk) (South: 4 km via N201)   **VISA** **👁** **ΑΕ** **①**
⊠ *1119 PB Schiphol* – ℰ *(0 20) 655 31 31*
– *reservations.amsterdam.airport@radissonsas.com*
– *Fax (0 20) 655 31 00* – *www.radissonsas.com*
278 rm – †121/221 € ††121/221 €, ⟑ 20 € – 1 suite
Rest – Carte 35/48 €
◆ Chain hotel ◆ Business ◆
This hotel is ideal for business trips. It is spacious, close to the airport and motor-way, with a convivial bar, meeting rooms and modern guestrooms which want for nothing. The restaurant menu offers international cuisine, dominated by Mediterranean dishes.

 Courtyard by Marriott - Amsterdam Airport   🛋 ᏝᏏ ᠗ᠣ ᏚᏏ
Bosweg 15 ⊠ *2131 LX Hoofddorp*   🎬 ᏪᏪ 🖾 ᠍ᠣ 🏰 🅿 **VISA** **👁** **ΑΕ** **①**
– ℰ *(0 23) 556 90 00* – *courtyard@claus.nl* – *Fax (0 23) 556 90 09*
– *www.courtyardamsterdamairport.nl*
148 rm – †79/245 € ††79/245 €, ⟑ 18 €   **Rest** – Carte 29/40 €
◆ Chain hotel ◆ Business ◆ Modern ◆
A modern-style business hotel next to a wooded area and lake. Spacious and contemporary guestrooms with king-size beds. Designer fireside lounge. Brasserie in a modern setting serving intercontinental cuisine and pizzas.

 Artemis   🛋 ᏝᏏ ᏚᏏ 🎬 ᏪᏪ ᠍ᠣ 🏰 🅿 ᧕ **VISA** **👁** **ΑΕ**
John M. Keynesplein 2 (exit ① Sloten) ⊠ *1066 EP* – ℰ *(0 20) 714 10 00*
– *info@artemisamsterdam.com* – *Fax (0 20) 714 10 01*
– *www.artemisamsterdam.com*   **A2**
256 rm – †150/285 € ††150/285 €, ⟑ 20 €
Rest – *(open until 11pm)* Carte 35/54 €
◆ Luxury ◆ Design ◆
This modern building of original design in the business district features Dutch designer-style décor. There is an art gallery for exploring the subject in more detail. A large restaurant with ultra-modern décor and a big waterside terrace. Contemporary menu.

Crowne Plaza Amsterdam-Schiphol   ᏝᏏ ᠗ᠣ 🖾 ᏚᏏ rm 🎬 ᏪᏪ
Planeetbaan 2 ⊠ *2132 HZ Hoofddorp*   🖬 ᠍ᠣ 🏰 🅿 **VISA** **👁** **ΑΕ** **①**
– ℰ *(0 23) 565 00 00* – *reservations.amsap@whgeu.com* – *Fax (0 23) 565 05 21*
– *www.crowneplaza.com/ams-schiphol*
241 rm – †119/349 € ††119/349 €, ⟑ 20 € – 1 suite
Rest – *(open until 11pm)* Menu 35/43 € – Carte 36/52 €
◆ Chain hotel ◆ Business ◆ Functional ◆
Establishment in a modern building, popular with business and conference clientele. Huge lobby, superb swimming pool, health club, large guestrooms and suites with lounges. Restaurant offering an international menu in several rooms.

XX **De Herbergh** with rm   🛋 🎬 rest ᏪᏪ ᠍ᠣ ⇔ 🅿 **VISA** **👁** **ΑΕ**
Sloterweg 259 ⊠ *1171 CP Badhoevedorp* – ℰ *(0 20) 659 26 00* – *info@herbergh.nl* – *Fax (0 20) 659 83 90* – *www.herbergh.nl*
24 rm – †90/120 € ††90/130 €, ⟑ 14 €
Rest – *(closed Sunday)* Menu 30/40 €
◆ Contemporary ◆ Cosy ◆
A new lease of life for this 100-year-old family-run inn: two generous, up-to-date menus delight food lovers in an airy and cosy setting. Attractive modern rooms. Facilities available for receptions and small executive seminars.

XX **Marktzicht**   🛋 ⇔ **VISA** **👁** **ΑΕ** **①**
Marktplein 31 ⊠ *2132 DA Hoofddorp* – ℰ *(0 23) 561 24 11* – *info@restaurant-marktzicht.nl* – *Fax (0 23) 563 72 91* – *www.restaurant-marktzicht.nl*
– *closed 25 and 26 December, 1 January and Sunday*
Rest – Menu 39/48 € – Carte 43/66 €
◆ Contemporary ◆
A wind of change is blowing through this old 19C inn on the Markt, built when the polder was erected. Up-to-date menu and welcoming terrace.

THE HAGUE
DEN HAAG – 'S GRAVENHAGE'

Population: 475 681 – Altitude: 3m

Iconotec/PHOTONONSTOP

The Hague appears to be a city of anomalies. Although the seat of Dutch government, it's not the capital of the Netherlands (which is Amsterdam); although a city of Europe wide importance, it's just as famous for its kiss-me-quick resort of Scheveningen; and although populated for hundreds of years by the well-to-do, its canal-side houses share little of Amsterdam's flamboyance.

The Hague earned its nickname 'the biggest village in Europe' because of its relatively small population sprawled about a large area: that 'village' is marked by an aristocratic charm, which is why it's rightly obtained another title – Holland's most elegant town. There are signs, though, that The Hague is doffing its neatly tailored cap to the 21C. Parts of the centre now shoot skywards courtesy of shiny government high-rises, while at ground level a rash of reasonably priced and buzzy restaurants and bars has brightened the streets. An outward-thinking city council has helped loosen the staid image with a lively programme of concerts and events, and there's an enticing range of museums clustered in the centre. A village, however large, wouldn't be a village without its sections of green and pleasant land, and The Hague doesn't disappoint with a kaleidoscope of leafy lanes and large parks.

609

LIVING THE CITY

Arrive at **Den Haag Centraal Station**, and you're only a five-minute walk from the centre of town (to your west). This is a compact quarter dominated by the **Binnenhof** parliament buildings. To the northeast of the centre are numerous green spaces and parks, while to the east and southeast lie the suburbs **Leidschendam, Voorburg** and **Rijswijk**. A couple of miles northwest of the centre is the **North Sea** and the popular beach resort of **Scheveningen**.

PRACTICAL INFORMATION

ARRIVAL-DEPARTURE

Rotterdam Airport is 16km southeast of The Hague which translates as a €45 taxi ride. Alternatively, there are shuttle and train services to Central Station which take 45 and 30min respectively.

TRANSPORT

A bus and tram system will whisk you around The Hague. Single tickets can be purchased from the bus driver but saver tickets must be bought in advance from the tourist information office, post offices, tobacconists, newsagents and hotels.

You can buy good value stripcards for your journeys. These are in two varieties; as a 15-stripcard or 45-stripcard and are valid throughout the country on buses, trams and metro. A one-day pass is also available for travel in The Hague, with price dependent on the amount of zones to be covered.

Once in The Hague, the only rail travel within the city is the line linking the two stations, Den Haag Centraal Station and Den Haag Hollands Spoor, which is a kilometre to the south of the centre, and is connected to it by frequent trams.

EXPLORING THE HAGUE

Although it gives the impression of being charmingly laid back and provincial, The Hague is a truly international city. It's home to over eighty embassies, as well as the International Court of Justice, and, of course, the Dutch Parliament. The Queen lives here too, albeit quite modestly. Not as modestly as the Crown Prince, though. His palace door opens on to the street. The air of gentle manners and 1950s calm is all-pervasive, as though the bureaucrats and bankers know that in a few minutes they can be sitting in a deckchair on the sandy beach.

→ LOUNGING ALONG THE LANGE

For all the new generation of eateries in the city, a stroll along **Lange Voorhout,** slap bang in the centre, even on a Saturday evening, can still be a serenely still experience. From here The Hague spreads through several square miles of art galleries and bistros. In the summer, the sun casts long shadows over leafy avenues and you can hear birds singing in the lime trees. A suitably bucolic spot to head for is the **Court Pond**, a dreamy lake which reflects the low-slung brick buildings of the Binnenhof – the Dutch Parliament. This is an impressive complex whose focal point is the thirteenth-century **Knights Hall**, a striking oak-roofed building in which the state opening of parliament takes place.

The tone is set for a visit to the adjacent **Mauritshuis**, not only The Hague's most important gallery, but one of the top art spaces in the world. What makes it so special is its size, or rather its lack of it. This is a compact and intimate gallery over just two floors, with around a hundred paintings on show. But what paintings! The core of the collection consists of masterpieces from the Dutch Golden Age, including works by Vermeer (yes, 'Girl With A Pearl Earring' is here), Rembrandt (the museum holds no less than twelve of his paintings), Hals and Potter. There are also stunning Flemish works from the sixteenth and seventeenth centuries by the likes of Rubens and van Dyck. Look out too for Holbein the Younger and some stark Flemish lowlife from the seventeenth century painter Brouwer, a man who knew his subject well, as he spent most of his short life in either a tavern or a prison.

→ PURE TORTURE

The feeling of cool sophistication continues as you regain Lange Voorhout. This is the main street in the city, a wide cobblestoned thoroughfare that becomes a leafy square. It boasts neoclassical mansions whose grand façades lead into foreign embassies and consulates. There's a museum on the square devoted to the vibrant works of the Dutch artist **M.C.Escher**, while two minutes' walk away yet more beautiful paintings are on offer at the **Museum Bredius**. These are packed tight like a splendid species in confinement, their setting enhanced by a sumptuous interior. The pick of the bunch are two works by Rembrandt. Just a short stroll west of the Museum Bredius, things take a darker turn as you arrive at a venue proud of its branding irons, execution swords and axes, elbow and thumb screws, racks and pillory boards: the **Prison Gate** museum, which occupies the old town prison, has a special section devoted to instruments of torture and interrogation. The tourist office people are quick to remind you that times have changed and the International Court of Justice really is based a few blocks from here.

→ LOOK AT THE VIEW!

If you head north past the **Noordeinde Palace**, home of the royals, you arrive, quite literally, at the Netherlands' biggest panorama. **Panorama Mesdag** was painted over the space of four months in 1880 by Hendrik Mesdag of the Hague School. It's a vast, cylindrical painting of Scheveningen, measuring 120m in circumference and standing 14m tall: it covers an amazing square mile of canvas (Mesdag did get assistance with his task!). From the viewing platform, the vista is endless in all directions: to the fishing village and its lighthouse, over the beach and the North Sea with its flat-bottomed fishing boats, to the fashionable seaside resort where bathing carriages are being rolled into the sea, over the dune landscape and on to The Hague. You can look three hundred and sixty degrees around you, and, to add to the illusion, the canvas itself blends into a 'virtual terrain' of seemingly abandoned objects on the floor. Real tufts of grass poke through the artificial beach that holds scraps of driftwood and a rusty anchor. Nearby, a weathered wooden chair lies next to a solitary clog. It all seems so real, you wonder why you can't sniff the seaweed or hear the swoosh of the waves.

→ A TRUE GEM

Heading inexorably towards the seaside, visitors are waylaid by another artistic gem – **The Gemeentemuseum**, the largest and most diverse of the city's exhibition spaces. Over seventy years old, it displays a rotated selection from a vast permanent collection. Nip down to the basement and you'll find eclectic sections on fashion and old musical instruments; upstairs the modern art section reflects changes from the early nineteenth century onwards. Many visitors are drawn to the impressive section on the De Stijl movement, which flourished between the two world wars, while others come because the museum boasts the world's largest collection of paintings by Holland's most famous twentieth century artist, Piet Mondrian. In his honour, an entire section is devoted to his early works. Trumping these, though, is his last (unfinished) painting 'Victory Boogie Woogie', a visual feast for the eye that's considered by many to be his best.

→ RATHER FRED THAN DEAD

Back in the centre of town, The Hague has some rather interesting shopping streets. First and foremost, hit the Fred, or, to be more precise, get along to **De Frederik Hendriklaan**, one of the city's most beautiful retail thoroughfares. It's lined with high-end boutiques and galleries, with a particular penchant for home furnishings and good food. There are charming streetside cafes here too. In **Hofweg,** right next to the Binnenhof, is **The Passage**, a restored covered arcade – the only one in the city – with a good selection of small boutiques and special interest shops. Meanwhile, Noordeinde is the place to go for elegant and imposing modern art galleries and boutiques, while the best antiques dealers can be found on **Denneweg**. The ideal way to round off your day is to take in a concert at the **Lucent Dans Theater**, a spankingly modern building near the Binnenhof, home to the National Dance Theatre. Their choreographed productions are of world renown and immense colour, a shimmering contrast to the coolly sedate charms of their home 'big village'.

CALENDAR HIGHLIGHTS

The Hague knows how to loosen its stays and flaunt itself when it comes to annual festivals. For instance, in April the Queen's Night Festival sees the city lighten up with five outdoor stages for a mammoth free music show…in honour of Beatrix. The focus turns seawards in May with the North Sea Regatta, which has sailing competitions between Scheveningen and Harwich in the UK. The sand stays in your eyes between April and June at the International Sand Sculpture Festival, as teams from around the

THE HAGUE IN…

→ ONE DAY
Binnenhof, Mauritshuis, Panorama Mesdag

→ TWO DAYS
Gemeentemuseum, 'The Fred', a stroll around Noordeinde, a show at Lucent Dans Theater

→ THREE DAYS
A day out at Scheveningen by the sea, Madurodam

world come up with magical creations made out of Scheveningen's shifting stuff. June's Music In My Head takes place at the Hague's Paard Van Troje over a couple of cutting-edge days: established rock acts line up alongside up-and-coming names. The city really throws off its ambassadorial trappings with July's De Parade, a travelling festival which alights in Westbroekpark with ten days of fairground rides, music, theatre, film, dance and opera. Tasty world cuisine's on offer too. Back at Scheveningen in August, the Van der Valk pier lights up twice every evening for the three nights of the International Fireworks Festival, while a month later the Todaysart Festival puts on a whole range of performing arts shows at twenty indoor and outdoor venues across the Hague. Fans of that event should also make a beeline for the Theater aan het Spui in November for the Crossing Border Festival which is, quite simply, Europe's biggest literature, music and visual arts all-in-one celebration, with over eighty acts taking part.

EATING OUT

Locals like to think that their 'biggest village in Europe' is the result of a lot made from a little. They call it the Hague Bluff. But what's that got to do with food? Well, the Hague Bluff is also a local pudding, made with eggs and sugar, representing the idea that something grand can be made from humble ingredients (in its finished state the Hague Bluff becomes a gooseberry fool). There's nothing bluff, though, about the city's restaurant scene. It's first rate in every respect, and although some are targeted full-on at the embassy army, many more are very affordable, with main courses set between fifteen and twenty euros. With the cuisine of more than twenty nationalities on offer, the choice is broad and pleasingly sophisticated: the number of exotic restaurants reflects the many cultures found here. Asian influences are everywhere, but in particular, the Indonesian connection is clear. There's a host of first-rate restaurants in the area just beyond Lange Voorhout around Denneweg and Frederikstraat. If you can't find what you want there, then head to Molenstraat, near the Noordeinde Palace, for another exciting cluster.

➜ PEACE BE WITH YOU

The Peace Palace, to the north of the city, was the result of a donation by American millionaire Andrew Carnegie at the turn of the twentieth century. In turn, nations donated stained glass, marble, tapestries, urns, and a Swiss clock in the bell tower. Despite the onset of World War I, the Peace Palace's reputation went from strength to strength…today, this is where you'll find the International Court of Justice.

➜ SCULPTURE BY THE SEA

If you decide to go to Scheveningen, you won't be alone. The resort is Holland's most popular seaside location and is visited by nine million a year. Its most fascinating attraction is the Museum Beelden-aan-Zee, which features modern sculptures in an old pavilion. Many leading sculptors are represented, including Fritz Koenig and Man Ray.

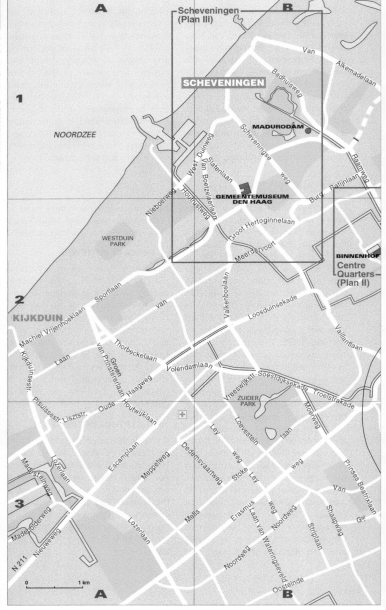

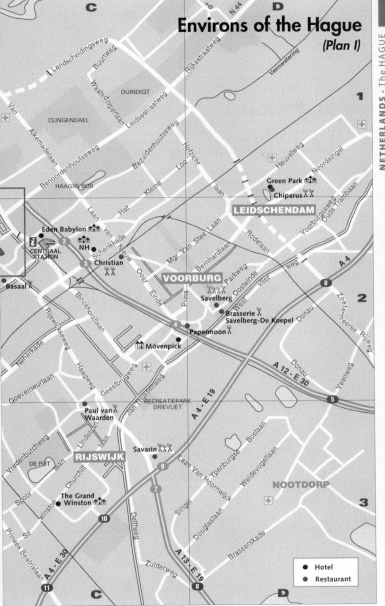

Environs of the Hague
(Plan I)

N 44

C

D

1

Landscheidingsweg

Buurtweg

Waalsdorperlaan

DUINDIGT

Leidsestraatweg

Rijksstraatweg

Veenwatering

Van

CLINGENDAEL

Alkemadelaan

Benoordenhoutseweg

Bezuidenhoutseweg

Hofzicht

Loo

Heuveweg

Noordsingel

HAAGSE BOS

Kleine

Laan

Green Park

Chiparus

LEIDSCHENDAM

Voorburgseweg

Oude Tranbaan

Eden Babylon

2

NH

CENTRAAL STATION

3

Christian

Schenkkade

Nieuw

Oost - Einde

Mgr. Van Stee Laan

VOORBURG

Bernhardlaan

Parkweg

Oosteinde

Rodelaan

weg

A 4

8

2

Basaal

Rijswickseweg

Blinckhorstlaan

Prins

Savelberg

West

Vliet

Brasserie
Savelberg-De Koepel

Donau

Zoetermeerse Rijweg

Nenerkade

Haagweg

Gesslbrgweg

4

Papermoon

Mövenpick

Donau

A 12 - E 30

Veenweg

5

Goeverneurlaan

Jan Thijssenweg

RECREATIEPARK
DRIEVLIET

A 4 - E 19

Paul van
Waarden

Lindelaan

laan

Savarin

Laan Van Ypenburgse

Boslaan

Weidevogellaan

NOOTDORP

Vredenburchweg

DE PUT

Churchill

9

Laan Van Hoornwijck

RIJSWIJK

Spoor

Winston

7

Singel

Douglaslaan

3

The Grand
Winston

10

Deltweg

Prinss Beatrixlaan

Sir

Winston

A 4 - E 30

11

Zuiderweg

A 13 - E 19

8

C

D

| | Hotel |
| | Restaurant |

CENTRE

Plan II

Le Méridien Hotel des Indes

Lange Voorhout 54 ✉ 2514 EG – ✆ (0 70) 361 23 45 – info.hague@lemeridien.com – Fax (0 70) 361 23 50 – www.hoteldesindes.nl

VISA MC AE

89 rm – 490 € 415/490 €, 27 € – 2 suites **F1**

Rest *Des Indes* – see below

◆ Luxury ◆ Design ◆

Following a renovation by J. Garcia, this 1858 luxury hotel has been restored to its former glory. Refined, modern comforts and facilities; splendid well-being centre.

Carlton Ambassador

Sophialaan 2 ✉ 2514 JP – ✆ (0 70) 363 03 63 – info@ambassador.carlton.nl – Fax (0 70) 360 05 35 – www.carlton.nl/ambassador

VISA MC AE

77 rm – 149/360 € 149/385 €, 23 € – 1 suite **E1**

Rest *Henricus* – *(closed Sunday)* Menu 43 € – Carte 47/57 €

◆ Palace ◆ Classical ◆

Dozens of ancient oak trees protect this small luxury hotel, in the Mesdag diplomatic district. Dutch- and English-style bedrooms. Whisky bar in the basement. Up-to-date cuisine served in a light, modern dining room, and outdoors in summertime.

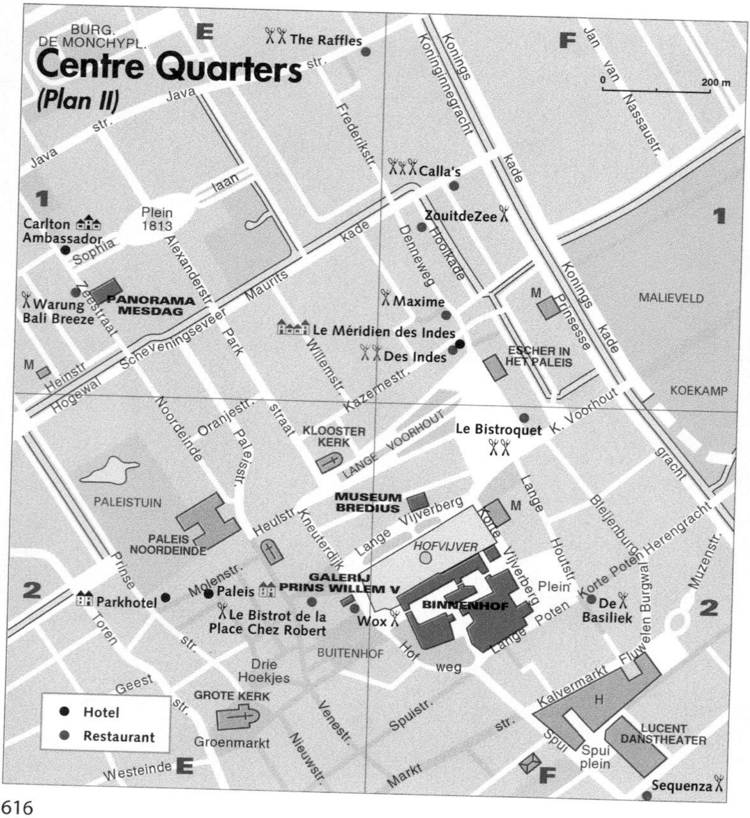

THE HAGUE - NETHERLANDS

Eden Babylon   🔥 AC ⇄ 🛰 ⸙ 🏋 🅿 🚗 VISA ⑩ AE ①

Koningin Julianaplein 35 ✉ 2595 AA – ℰ (0 70) 381 49 01 – info@
edenhotelgroup.com – Fax (0 70) 382 59 27 – www.edencityhotels.com
142 rm – ♦129/305 € ♦♦129/305 €, ⊇ 18 € – 1 suite   *Plan I* **C2**
Rest – Menu 38/58 € – Carte 43/56 €
♦ Chain hotel ♦ Business ♦ Design ♦

Next-door to the station, the interior of this modern hotel was redesigned by
Miguel Cancio Martins (responsible for the Paris Buddha Bar). Designer-style
rooms. Trendy lounge-bar and designer-style dining room, whose large bay
windows overlook the park.

Bel Air   ≼ 🍴 🔥 AC ⇄ 🛰 ⸙ 🅿 VISA ⑩ AE ①

Johan de Wittlaan 30 ✉ 2517 JR – ℰ (0 70) 352 53 54 – info@
goldentulipbelairhotel.nl – Fax (0 70) 352 53 53 – www.goldentulipbelairhotel.nl
326 rm – ♦145/210 € ♦♦145/210 €, ⊇ 20 €   *Plan III* **H3**
Rest – Carte 36/53 €
♦ Chain hotel ♦ Classical ♦

Immense hotel whose spacious comfortable rooms overlook the park or the
museum. Spacious public area, conference and fitness facilities and long-stay studios. Immense contemporary-inspired restaurant in a brasserie style.

Crowne Plaza Promenade   ≼ 🍴 🔥 🕅 🔥 AC ⇄ 🛰 ⸙ 🏋 🅿

van Stolkweg 1 ✉ 2585 JL – ℰ (0 70) 352 51 61 – info@   🅿 VISA ⑩ ①
crowneplazadenhaag.nl – Fax (0 70) 354 10 46 – www.crowneplazadenhaag.nl
92 rm – ♦120/285 € ♦♦120/300 €, ⊇ 23 € – 2 suites   *Plan III* **H2**
Rest – Menu 37/69 € – Carte 40/68 €
♦ Chain hotel ♦ Functional ♦

Chain hotel overlooking a vast park that is home to the Madurodam (Miniature
Holland). Standard rooms and junior suites. Fine collection of modern artwork.
Relaxed brasserie offering a simple meal.

NH   🔥 🕅 🔥 AC ⇄ 🛰 ⸙ 🏋 🚗 VISA ⑩ AE ①

Prinses Margrietplantsoen 100 ✉ 2595 BR – ℰ (0 70) 381 23 45 – nhdenhaag@
nh-hotels.com – Fax (0 70) 381 23 33 – www.nh-hotels.com   *Plan I* **C2**
205 rm – ♦85/275 € ♦♦85/275 €, ⊇ 18 €
Rest – *(closed Saturday lunch and Sunday lunch)* Carte 35/49 €
♦ Chain hotel ♦ Business ♦ Modern ♦

Three modern tower blocks, inaugurated in 2005 in the heart of the local Manhattan, are home to various categories of contemporary rooms. Glass-roofed atrium
shopping centre. Trendy lounge restaurant, with culinary concept to match, appreciated for its versatility.

Parkhotel   🍴 ⇄ 🛰 ⸙ 🏋 🚗 VISA ⑩ AE ①

Molenstraat 53 ✉ 2513 BJ – ℰ (0 70) 362 43 71 – info@parkhoteldenhaag.nl
– Fax (0 70) 361 45 25 – www.parkhoteldenhaag.nl   **E2**
120 rm – ♦89/170 € ♦♦99/335 €, ⊇ 18 €
Rest – Menu 23/48 € – Carte 34/51 €
♦ Traditional ♦ Classical ♦

Contemporary dining room, dotted with "neo-retro" influences in a hotel founded in
1912, overlooking a park. Cosy lounge, period staircase, modernised rooms and garden.

Paleis without rest ⸙   🔥 ⇄ 🛰 ⸙ 🕅 VISA ⑩ AE ①

Molenstraat 26 ✉ 2513 BL – ℰ (0 70) 362 46 21 – info@paleishotel.nl
– Fax (0 70) 361 45 33 – www.paleishotel.nl   **E2**
20 rm – ♦195/285 € ♦♦199/295 €, ⊇ 17 €
♦ Luxury ♦ Classical ♦

Plush boutique hotel noted for its personalised welcome. Louis XVI-style rooms adorned with rich fabrics by French designer Pierre Frey. Sumptuous breakfast room.

Hampshire without rest   ⇄ 🅿 VISA ⑩ AE

Laan van Meerdervoort 108 ✉ 2517 AS – ℰ (0 70) 360 53 85 – denhaag@
hampshire-hotels.com – Fax (0 70) 360 54 07 – www.hampshirehotels.nl/denhaag
47 rm – ♦89/185 € ♦♦99/195 €, ⊇ 16 €   *Plan III* **H3**
♦ Chain hotel ♦ Business ♦ Modern ♦

Renovated in a restrained modern style in 2005, the hotel is on a busy street (tramway) into the centre. Quieter rooms at the rear. Free car parking for early birds.

NETHERLANDS - The HAGUE

XxXxXx **Calla's** (Marcel van der Kleijn)   *VISA* ✪ **AE**

*Laan van Roos en Doorn 51a ☒ 2514 BC – 𝒞 (0 70) 345 58 66 – info@
restaurantcallas.nl – Fax (0 70) 345 57 10 – www.restaurantcallas.nl
– closed 1 - 5 January, 26 July - 17 August, Saturday lunch, Sunday and
Monday*   **F1**

Rest – Menu 75/152 € bi – Carte 84/107 €

Spec. Tartelette van Jacobsmosselen, parmezaanse kaas en seizoenstruffel
(October-April). Gebakken tarbot met soufflé van aardappel en look, saus
van kreeft en rode wijn. Crêpe soufflé met vanille en citroen.

♦ Contemporary ♦ Fashionable ♦

A former warehouse turned into a smart contemporary-style restaurant. Lounge,
chef's table and a view of the kitchen below. Main room is upstairs.

XxXx **Des Indes** – H. Le Méridien Hotel des Indes   ⇔ ⇱ **P**

Lange Voorhout 54 ☒ 2514 EG – 𝒞 (0 70) 361 23 45   *VISA* ✪ **AE ①**
– info.hague@lemeridien.com – Fax (0 70) 361 23 50 – www.hoteldesindes.nl

Rest – *(open until 11.30pm)* Menu 45 € – Carte 53/85 €   **F1**

♦ Contemporary ♦ Luxury ♦

Tasty up-to-date cooking oozing with oriental spices and flavours; smart lounge
ambience signed by J. Garcia. Cosmopolitan and affluent. Afternoon high teas.

XxXx **Le Bistroquet**   ⇱ **AC** *VISA* ✪ **AE**

*Lange Voorhout 98 ☒ 2514 EJ – 𝒞 (0 70) 360 11 70 – info@bistroquet.nl
– Fax (0 70) 360 55 30 – www.bistroquet.nl
– closed 24 December - 1 January, Saturday lunch and Sunday*   **F2**

Rest – Menu 43/65 € bi – Carte 54/74 €

♦ Contemporary ♦ Cosy ♦

This plush bistro is popular with the diplomatic-parliamentary crowd. Up-to-date
cuisine served in a warm, intimate atmosphere or outdoors in the shade of the
square's trees.

XxXx **Rousseau**   ⇱ ⇔ *VISA* ✪

*Van Boetzelaerlaan 134 ☒ 2581 AX – 𝒞 (0 70) 355 47 43 – info@
restaurantrousseau.com – www.restaurantrousseau.com
– closed 14 - 23 February, 26 July - 19 August, 20 December - 4 January,
Saturday lunch, Sunday and Monday*   *Plan III* **G3**

Rest – Menu 33/94 € bi – Carte 52/78 €

♦ Traditional ♦ Intimate ♦

Well-thought out, traditional, seasonal menu served in front of a naïve fresco in the
style of Douanier Rousseau, (the chef-owner shares his surname), or in the courtyard with pergola.

XxXx **Christian**   ⇱ ⇔ *VISA* ✪ **AE**

*Laan van Nieuw Oost Indië 1f ☒ 2593 BH – 𝒞 (0 70) 383 88 56 – info@
restaurantchristian.nl – Fax (0 70) 385 59 32 – www.restaurantchristian.nl
– closed first week in January, last week in July - first 2 weeks in August,
Saturday lunch, Tuesday and Wednesday:*   *Plan I* **C2**

Rest – Menu 35/125 € bi – Carte 53/65 €

♦ Contemporary ♦ Trendy ♦

Excellent cuisine served in this modern restaurant enhanced by a tasteful grey and
orange colour scheme. Chef's table for 8 to 10 guests to the rear; courtyard terrace.

XxXx **The Raffles**   **AC** *VISA* ✪ **AE ①**

*Javastraat 63 ☒ 2585 AG – 𝒞 (0 70) 345 85 87 – info@restaurantraffles.com
– Fax (0 70) 356 00 84 – www.restaurantraffles.com
– closed during carnival, late July - early August, 25 December - 2 January,
Sunday and Monday*   **E1**

Rest – *(dinner only)* Menu 38/78 € bi – Carte 37/63 €

♦ Indonesian ♦ Exotic ♦

Located on the fittingly-named Javastraat, restaurant serving authentic, flavoursome Indonesian cooking, served in a suitably exotic setting, enhanced with Colonial touches.

Maxime ⚔ 😊 AC VISA 🞮 AE

Denneweg 10b ✉ 2514 CG – ☎ (0 70) 360 92 24 – info@restaurantmaxime.nl
– www.restaurantmaxime.nl
– closed 25, 26, 31 December - 2 January and Saturday lunch **F1**
Rest *– (booking essential)* Menu 32 €
  ◆ Contemporary ◆ Bistro ◆
Small hip bistro offering two set four-course menus - "links" and "rechts". Cosy designer décor. Book for the first (6-8pm) or second (8-10pm) sitting.

Shirasagi ⚔ 🛏 ⇆ VISA 🞮 AE

Stadhouderslaan 76 R ✉ 2517 JA – ☎ (0 70) 346 47 00 – shirasagi@planet.nl
– Fax (0 70) 346 26 01 – www.shirasagi.nl
– closed 31 December - 3 January and Sunday *Plan III* **G3**
Rest – Menu 40/85 € – Carte 31/63 €
  ◆ Japanese ◆ Minimalist ◆
Japanese restaurant out of the town centre in an attractive old house. Minimalist décor, teppanyaki (evenings), sushi bar, open kitchens and inviting rear terrace.

Sequenza ⚔ 🛏 VISA 🞮 AE

Spui 224 ✉ 2511 BX – ☎ (0 70) 345 28 53
– closed 1 week in May, 3 weeks in September, Sunday and Monday
Rest *– (dinner only until 11pm) (set menu only)* Menu 43 € **F2**
  ◆ Contemporary ◆ Friendly ◆
Mediterranean-inspired cusine, daily changing menu depending on the season. Wooden floorboards and rustic chairs indoors, ivy-covered walled terrace outdoors.

Wox ⚔ AC ⇆ VISA 🞮 AE

Buitenhof 36 ✉ 2513 AH – ☎ (0 70) 365 37 54 – info@woxgoodfood.nl
– Fax (0 70) 364 83 79 – www.wox.nl
– closed August, late December, Saturday lunch, Sunday and Monday
Rest – Carte 41/76 € 🏱 **E2**
  ◆ Contemporary ◆ Fashionable ◆
Fashionable brasserie located on the main square offering three rooms, including a mezzanine. Menu with a strong Asian influence. Excellent wine list, particularly by the glass.

De Basiliek ⚔ 🛏 ⇆ VISA 🞮 AE

Korte Houtstraat 4a ✉ 2511 CD – ☎ (0 70) 360 61 44 – info@debasiliek.nl
– www.debasiliek.nl
– closed Sunday dinner and Monday dinner **F2**
Rest – Menu 39/50 € – Carte approx. 45 €
  ◆ Contemporary ◆ Bistro ◆
World cuisine, modern bistro atmosphere and muted lighting (tealight holders and lanterns on the tables, designer chandeliers and wall lighting), tiny city terrace.

Warung Bali Breeze ⚔ VISA 🞮

Zeestraat 58 ✉ 2518 AB – ☎ (0 70) 360 06 50 – info@balibreeze.nl – Fax (0 70) 362 97 00 – www.balibreeze.nl
– closed Monday and Tuesday **E1**
Rest *– (dinner only)* Menu 40/53 € – Carte 40/55 €
  ◆ Indonesian ◆ Exotic ◆
Balinese cuisine served in an attractive exotic setting: Buddhist statues, bamboo tables, woks and spatulas recycled into wall lights and menu boards!

Basaal ⚔ 🛏 ⇆ VISA 🞮

Dunne Bierkade 3 ✉ 2512 BC – ☎ (0 70) 427 68 88 – info@basaal.net
– Fax (0 70) 363 42 35 – www.basaal.net
– closed late December - first week in January, Monday and Tuesday
Rest *– (dinner only)* Carte 39/48 € *Plan I* **C2**
  ◆ Contemporary ◆ Bistro ◆
Up-to-the-minute menu served in a minimalist designer décor or on a pavement terrace overlooking the canal and house barges. Friendly service. Bistro style.

NETHERLANDS - The HAGUE

⚴ **ZouitdeZee** ⬛ ⬦ _VISA_ ⬤ ⬛

Hooikade 14 ⊠ 2514 BH – ℰ (0 70) 346 26 03 – info@restaurantzouitdezee.nl
– Fax (0 70) 365 40 76 – www.restaurantzouitdezee.nl **F1**
Rest – *(dinner only)* Menu 39/82 € bi – Carte 45/61 €
♦ Seafood ♦ Intimate ♦

In a lively neighbourhood, this canal-side restaurant is cosy and contrasted: old Delft tiles, bricks, beams, designer lighting, modern artwork, white walls and red seating.

⚴ **Le Bistrot de la Place Chez Norbert** ⬛ ⬦ _VISA_ ⬤

Plaats 27 ⊠ 2513 AD – ℰ (0 70) 364 33 27 – info@bistrotdelace.nl – Fax (0 70)
365 19 36 – www.bistrotdelaplace.nl
– closed 15 - 24 August, 27 December - 4 January, Saturday lunch and Sunday
Rest – Menu 40/45 € – Carte 41/57 € **E2**
♦ French traditional ♦ Bistro ♦

Upmarket bistro reputed for its traditional range of classic dishes and setting inspired by bistros of Lyons in France. Meat cut in front of you. Terrace on the square.

SCHEVENINGEN *Plan III*

🏨 **Steigenberger Kurhaus** ⟨ _Lb_ ⬤ ⬔ ⬛ ⬛ ↩ 🔧 ☞ **P**

Gevers Deynootplein 30 ⊠ 2586 CK – ℰ (0 70) _VISA_ ⬤ ⬛ ⬤
416 26 36 – info@kurhaus.nl – Fax (0 70) 416 26 46
– www.kurhaus.nl **G1**
245 rm – †295/415 € ††295/415 €, ⊡ 24 € – 8 suites
Rest *Kandinsky* – see below
Rest *Kurzaal* – ℰ (0 70) 416 27 13 – Menu 28/33 €
♦ Palace ♦ Luxury ♦ Classical ♦

This beachside luxury hotel frequently hosts upmarket seminars. Extensive facilities, full spa service and sophisticated rooms equipped with modern comforts. Extensive modern menu served under the dome of a splendid period concert hall.

🏨 **Carlton Beach** ⟨ 🍽 _Lb_ ⬔ ⬛ ⬛ rm ↩ 🔧 **P** _VISA_ ⬤ ⬛ ⬤

Gevers Deynootweg 201 ⊠ 2586 HZ – ℰ (0 70) 354 14 14 – info@
beach.carlton.nl – Fax (0 70) 352 00 20 – www.carlton.nl/beach **H1**
178 rm – †210/300 € ††240/330 €, ⊡ 21 € – 4 suites
Rest – Menu 30/53 € – Carte 24/40 €
♦ Business ♦ Modern ♦

1980s building standing at the end of the dyke offering rooms that overlook the beach, dunes or street. Generous buffet and fine sea-view at breakfast time. Two restaurants: pirate-inspired grill room and modern brasserie-style dining room.

🏨 **Europa** 🍽 _Lb_ ⬔ ⬛ ⬛ rest ↩ ⬗ 🔧 ☁ _VISA_ ⬤ ⬛ ⬤

Zwolsestraat 2 ⊠ 2587 VJ – ℰ (0 70) 416 95 95 – europa@bilderberg.nl
– Fax (0 70) 416 95 55 – www.bilderberg.nl **H1**
174 rm – †120/215 € ††145/235 €, ⊡ 19 €
Rest – Menu 35 € – Carte 38/52 €
♦ Chain hotel ♦ Functional ♦

This modern hotel, 300m from the jetty, overlooks a busy street. Ask for one of the quieter rooms at the back to avoid the noise. The restaurant features an up-to-date menu, smart brasserie style and city terrace.

🏨 **Badhotel** ⬛ ↩ ⬛ ⬗ 🔧 **P** _VISA_ ⬤ ⬛ ⬤

Gevers Deynootweg 15 ⊠ 2586 BB – ℰ (0 70) 351 22 21 – info@
badhotelscheveningen.nl – Fax (0 70) 355 58 70
– www.badhotelscheveningen.nl **G1**
90 rm – †130/190 € ††130/190 €, ⊡ 17 €
Rest – *(dinner only)* Menu 33 € – Carte 31/45 €
♦ Traditional ♦ Classical ♦

On the main street (tramway), this building offers tastefully decorated rooms in a nautical style. Those to the rear and on the top floors are larger and quieter. Spruced up restaurant; classic, traditional dishes.

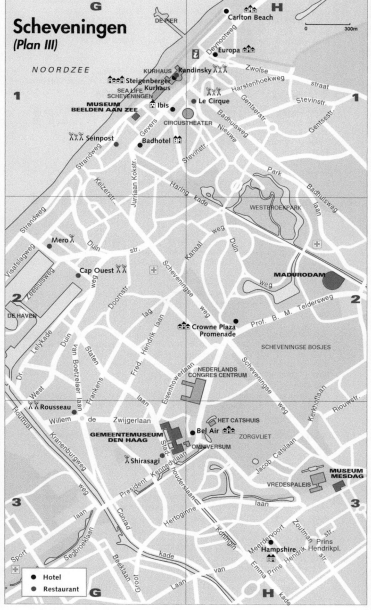

Scheveningen
(Plan III)

NETHERLANDS - The Hague

NOORDZEE

G — DE PIER

H — Carlton Beach

Deynootweg — Europa

KURHAUS — Kandinsky
Steigenberger
Kurhaus
SEA LIFE
SCHEVENINGEN
MUSEUM
BEELDEN AAN ZEE
Ibis — Le Cirque
CIRCUSTHEATER

Zwolse
Harstenhoekweg
Stevinstr.
Gentserstr.
Badhuisweg
Gentsestr.

1

Seinpost
Badhotel
Gevers
Strandweg
Keizerstr.
Juriaan Kokstr.
Haring — kade
Stevinstr.
Nieuwe

Park
Badhuisweg
laan
WESTBROEKPARK

Mero
Duin
str.
Cap Ouest
Doornstr.
Scheveningse
weg
Kanaal
weg
Duin
weg

2

DE HAVEN
Visafslagweg
Zeesluisweg
Strandweg
Duin
van Boetzelaer laan
Staten
laan
Frankens
Fred. Hendrik laan
Jag

MADURODAM

Prof. B. M. Teldersweg

Crowne Plaza
Promenade

SCHEVENINGSE BOSJES

Scheveningse
weg
Kerkhoflaan
Riouwstr.

Rousseau
Willem de Zwijgerlaan
Dr. West — Lelykade
Kranenburgweg
GEMEENTEMUSEUM
DEN HAAG
Shirasagi
President Kennedylaan
Stad houderslaan

NEDERLANDS
CONGRES CENTRUM
Eisenhowerlaan

HET CATSHUIS
Bel Air
ZORGVLIET
OMNIVERSUM
Jacob Catslaan

MUSEUM
MESDAG
VREDESPALEIS

3

Sport
laan
Segbroeklaan
Conrad
kade
Groot
Beeklaan
Hertoginne
laan
Koningin
van
Meerdervoort
Hampshire
Emma
Prins Hendrik str.
Prins
Hendrikpl.
Zoutman str.
Koningin
Laan

G — **H**

0 — 300m

Legend:
- ● Hotel
- ● Restaurant

621

🏠

Ibis
                         🔥 rm ⚤ 🛜 🛜 P VISA ⓒⓞ AE ①
Gevers Deynootweg 63 ⊠ 2586 BJ – ℘ (0 70) 354 33 00 – h1153@accor.com
– Fax (0 70) 352 39 16 – www.ibishotel.com   **G1**
88 rm – ♦85/110 € ♦♦95/125 €, ⊑ 14 €
Rest – *(closed Saturday and Sunday) (dinner only)* Menu 24/35 €
– Carte 26/36 €
♦ Chain hotel ♦ Business ♦ Functional ♦

Centrally located and close to all the resort's main amenities, this chain hotel stands on a main street parallel with the dyke (Strandweg). Two sizes of rooms. Restaurant in the lobby; simple menu with pasta and pizzas.

XXX

Kandinsky – H. Steigenberger Kurhaus
    ≤ 🍴 AC ⇔ ⊸ P
Gevers Deynootplein 30 ⊠ 2586 CK – ℘ (0 70)   VISA ⓒⓞ AE ①
416 26 34 – info@kurhaus.nl – Fax (0 70) 416 26 46 – www.kurhaus.nl
– closed Saturday lunch and Sunday
Rest – Menu 55/93 € bi – Carte 57/91 €   **G1**
♦ Contemporary ♦ Formal ♦

Elegant, modern restaurant in the resort's flagship hotel. Comfortable dining area, tasty inventive cuisine, pleasant seaside view and terrace overlooking the dyke.

XXX
🏵

Seinpost
    ≤ AC VISA ⓒⓞ AE ①
Zeekant 60 ⊠ 2586 AD – ℘ (0 70) 355 52 50 – mail@seinpost.nl – Fax (0 70)
355 50 93 – www.seinpost.nl
– closed Saturday lunch and Sunday
Rest – Menu 59/89 € – Carte 73/110 € 🍴   **G1**
Spec. Kreeft en piepkuiken met zeewier, appel en amandelen. Met brood gebakken schelvis en gekonfijte ganzenlever. Frambozensoufflé met karne-melkijs.
♦ Seafood ♦ Elegant ♦

Book a table with a sea view in this modern rotunda where seafood takes pride of place in the elaborate modern cuisine. Fine wine list. The owner supervises with care.

XXX

Le Cirque
    AC ⇔ ⊸ VISA ⓒⓞ AE ①
Circusplein 50 ⊠ 2586 CZ – ℘ (0 70) 416 76 76 – info@restaurantlecirque.com
– Fax (0 70) 416 75 37 – www.restaurantlecirque.com
– closed 20 July - 3 August, Sunday dinner and Monday
Rest – Menu 40/100 € bi – Carte 39/66 € 🍴   **H1**
♦ Innovative ♦ Design ♦

A designer restaurant next to the Circustheater. Veranda and rear dining area with red and black décor contrasts. Classic and creative cuisine served. Very popular pre-theatre menu.

XX

Cap Ouest
    ≤ 🍴 VISA ⓒⓞ AE
Schokkerweg 37 (1st floor) ⊠ 2583 BH – ℘ (0 70) 306 09 35 – info@capouest.nl
– Fax (0 70) 350 84 54 – www.capouest.nl
– closed 28 December - 4 January, Saturday lunch and Sunday lunch
Rest – Menu 40/63 € – Carte 55/77 €   **G2**
♦ Seafood ♦ Intimate ♦

Establishment opposite the harbour that supplies the kitchen with fresh North Sea produce. New modern décor, spacious mezzanine and terrace overlooking the docks.

X

Mero
    🍴 AC VISA ⓒⓞ AE
Vissershavenweg 61e ⊠ 2583 DL – ℘ (0 70) 352 36 00 – info@merovis.nl
– Fax (0 70) 306 34 97 – www.merovis.nl
– closed Saturday lunch, Sunday and Monday
Rest – Menu 35 € – Carte 47/78 €   **G2**
♦ Seafood ♦ Friendly ♦

Harbour-side fish restaurant in keeping with the times, both by its post-industrial loft-style, and by its cuisine, where the daily catch of fish and seafood takes pride of place.

NETHERLANDS - The HAGUE

🏨 Grand Winston   ↳ ⅙ rm 🆎 ⇄ 🔲 📶 ⚙ 🅿 🆚 ⓪ 🅰 ⓪

Generaal Eisenhowerplein 1 ⊠ 2288 AE Rijswijk – ℰ (0 70) 414 15 00
– info@grandwinston.nl – Fax (0 70) 414 15 10 – www.grandwinston.nl
245 rm ⌂ – ♦98/230 € ♦♦124/256 € – 7 suites   **C3**
Rest Leds – ℰ (0 70) 414 15 14 *(closed 19 July - 17 August, 21 December -*
4 January, Sunday and Monday) Menu 42/106 € bi – Carte 64/95 € ॐ
Rest The Grand Canteen – Menu 28/49 € bi – Carte approx. 40 €
♦ Business ♦ Modern ♦
A designer hotel next to the Rijswijk station with Winston Churchill watching over
the lobby! Rooms in two modern blocks. Futuristic décor, modern menu and
attractive selection of wines. Flamboyantly modern canteen; international menu.

🏨 Green Park   ⇐ ↳ ⅗ 🆎 ⇄ 🔲 📶 ⚙ 🆚 ⓪ 🅰 ⓪

Weigelia 22 ⊠ 2262 AB Leidschendam – ℰ (0 70) 320 92 80
– info@greenpark.nl – Fax (0 70) 327 49 07 – www.greenpark.nl   **D1**
92 rm ⌂ – ♦85/199 € ♦♦111/225 € – 4 suites
Rest Chiparus – see below
♦ Chain hotel ♦ Business ♦ Classical ♦
Lakeside hotel built on piles not far from an immense shopping centre. The lobby
is under the glass roof of an atrium and the best rooms enjoy a lake-view balcony.

🏨 Mövenpick   🏠 ⅙ 🆎 ⇄ 🔲 ⚙ 🚗 🆚 ⓪ 🅰 ⓪

Stationsplein 8 ⊠ 2275 AZ Voorburg – ℰ (0 70) 337 37 37 – hotel.voorburg@
moevenpick.com – Fax (0 70) 337 37 00 – www.moevenpick-voorburg.com
125 rm – ♦146/161 € ♦♦166/181 €, ⌂ 17 €   **C2**
Rest – *(open until 11pm)* Menu 25/45 € – Carte 26/41 €
♦ Chain hotel ♦ Functional ♦
Modern chain hotel, whose semi-circular façade overlooks the station. Functional
rooms, the best ones at the rear. Designer-style bar. Modern brasserie with an
Italian-Asian focus: pasta and wok-cooked dishes. Front terrace.

🍴 Savelberg with rm ⌂   ⇐ 🍸 🏠 ⅙ rest ⇄ 📶 ⇄ 🅿 🆚 ⓪ 🅰 ⓪
ॐ
Oosteinde 14 ⊠ 2271 EH Voorburg – ℰ (0 70) 387 20 81
– info@restauranthotelsavelberg.nl – Fax (0 70) 387 77 15
– www.restauranthotelsavelberg.nl – closed 1 - 11 January   **D2**
14 rm – ♦150/350 € ♦♦150/350 €, ⌂ 16 €
Rest – *(closed Saturday lunch, Sunday and Monday)* Menu 58/110 €
– Carte 78/110 € ॐ
Spec. Salade van kreeft met artisjok en groene boontjes, eendenlever met
zwarte truffel. Gegrilde tarbot met kappertjes en ansjovis, auberginecrème.
Gebraden duif met ravioli van ui, groene linzen en jus van duif.
♦ Contemporary ♦ Luxury ♦
This luxurious 18C abode is a real treat for the eyes! Good quality seasonal produce,
extensive wine cellar, well-informed wine waiter and splendid terrace facing the
park. Elegant rooms and suites with balcony, personalised in a plush classical register.

🍴 Savarin   🏠 ⅙ ⇄ 🅿 🆚 ⓪ 🅰 ⓪

Laan van Hoornwijck 29 ⊠ 2289 DG Rijswijk – ℰ (0 70) 307 20 50
– info@savarin.nl – Fax (0 70) 307 20 55 – www.savarin.nl
– closed Saturday lunch and Sunday   **C3**
Rest – Menu 38/48 €
♦ Contemporary ♦ Formal ♦
Former farm dating from 1916 where inventive cuisine is served in a designer
inspired rustic-contemporary dining room. Modern conference room with whitewashed beams. Terrace.

🍴 Chiparus – H. Green Park   ⇐ 🏠 🆎 ⇄ 🆚 ⓪ 🅰 ⓪

Weigelia 22 ⊠ 2262 AB Leidschendam – ℰ (0 70) 320 92 80
– info@greenpark.nl – Fax (0 70) 327 49 07 – www.greenpark.nl   **D1**
Rest – Menu 33/45 € bi – Carte 40/51 €
♦ Contemporary ♦
This restaurant, named after a 20th century Romanian sculptor, offers a dining
room with a water view. Modern Mediterranean cuisine. Lakeside terrace.

NETHERLANDS - The HAGUE

XX **Papermoon**
Herenstraat 175 ⊠ 2271 CE Voorburg – ℰ (0 70) 387 31 61 – info@
papermoon.nl – www.papermoon.nl
– closed 27 December - 2 January and Monday   **C2-3**
Rest – *(dinner only)* Menu 30/34 € – Carte approx. 40 €
  ♦ Contemporary ♦ Friendly ♦
An appealing modern menu with several set menus at this friendly restaurant
where the dining room has a refined atmosphere.

X **Paul van Waarden**
ॐ *Tollensstraat 10 ⊠ 2282 BM Rijswijk – ℰ (0 70) 414 08 12 – info@*
paulvanwaarden.nl – Fax (0 70) 414 03 91 – www.paulvanwaarden.nl
– closed 2 weeks in August, 2 weeks after Christmas, Saturday lunch, Sunday
and Monday   **C3**
Rest – Menu 35/78 € bi – Carte 51/72 €
Spec. Vier bereidingen met lever. Krokant gebakken kabeljauw, erwtensoep
met gerookte paling (21 September-21 March). Tarte tatin van rabarber met
gemberroomijs (march-August).
  ♦ Contemporary ♦ Brasserie ♦
Paul van Waarden hosts you in one of the series of rooms which make up the restaurant, designed in the style of a modern brasserie. Modern cuisine. Walled terrace.

X **Brasserie De Koepel**
Oosteinde 1 ⊠ 2271 EA Voorburg – ℰ (0 70) 369 35 72 – brasseriedekoepel@
telfort.nl – Fax (0 70) 369 32 14 – www.brasseriedekoepel.nl   **D2**
Rest – *(dinner only except Sundays; open until 11pm)* Menu 35/49 €
– Carte 39/49 €
  ♦ French traditional ♦ Brasserie ♦
Upmarket brasserie in an immense rotunda, topped by a cupola and adorned by
modern frescoes. Lush summer terrace. Reasonably priced, tasty dishes.

Simeone/PHOTONONSTOP

Rotterdam trades on its earthy appeal, on a rough-and-ready grittiness tied in with its status as the largest seaport in the world, handling 350 million tonnes of goods a year, with over half of all goods that are heading into Europe passing through it. Flattened during the Second World War, Rotterdam was rebuilt on a grand scale, jettisoning the idea of streets full of terraced houses in favour of a modern cityscape of concrete and glass.

The city is located on the Nieuwe Maas, but is centred round a maze of other rivers - most importantly the Rhine and the Maas - and is only a few dozen kilometres inland from the North Sea. It spills over both banks of its river, and is linked by tunnels, bridges and the metro; the most stunning connection across the water is the modern Erasmusbridge, whose sleek design has come to embody the Rotterdam of the new millennium. It's mirrored on the southern banks by the development of the previously run-down Kop Van Zuid area into a zone of new build and sleek promise.

LIVING THE CITY

Rotterdam is a sprawling city that's eaten up both banks of the **Nieuwe Maas River**. Its northern extremity is bounded by the **Zestienhoven airport,** while to the south, over the water, shimmers the modernist, once industrialised, area of **Kop Van Zuid**. Central Rotterdam's main rail station, **Centraal**, is to the north of the river; immediately to its east is a complex array of modern high-rises with the focus on the pedestrianized **Lijnbaan**. The culture zone of **Museumpark** is close to the water, and it's bounded on either side by two old harbours, **Delfshaven** and **Oude Haven**. The latter is in the compact and interesting district of **Blaak**, another of the city's modernist shrines.

PRACTICAL INFORMATION

ARRIVAL-DEPARTURE

The Airport is 6km northwest of the city, with a taxi costing about €23. Shuttle buses no.33 and 43 run every 10min and take 20min to Central Railway Station.

TRANSPORT

Metro, bus, tram and train combine to delve into every little corner of the city. There are a variety of stripcards to ease your way around: from two-strip right up to forty-five strip tickets. That could entail a lot of fiddling about and franking. A better bet could be to invest in a one-day, two-day, or three-day card, which give you unlimited travel on any form of transport.

Another good idea is to buy a Rotterdam Card, which provides unlimited use of the transport network as well as free admission to most attractions. It's available for either 24 or 72 hours.

You can hire bicycles from the Centraal station cycle shop. These work out at good value, and can be hired for either a day or a week.

EXPLORING ROTTERDAM

Whatever else anyone may say about Rotterdam, no-one denies that it has edge. Pacy, big and brash, it barged its way into the European zeitgeist earlier

Noordwijk aan Zee
Katwijk aan Zee
Leiden
NOORDZEE
Scheveningen
DEN HAAG
('S-GRAVENHAGE)
Hoek van Holland
Delft
Gouda
Rotterdam
Europoort
Schiedam
ROTTERDAM
Vlaardingen
Oude Maas
Dordrecht

this decade when it was European City of Culture. It lived – and still lives – easily with that term. Constructed anew after 1945, the bustling port city on the Nieuwe Maas introduced to Europe the concept of modern building, for good or bad. Walk down the Lijnbaan, and you're face to face with the continent's first pedestrianized shopping precinct. It's now fifty-five years old, and on no-one's list for an architecture award – but it's a fascinating prototype, all the same; back in 1953, this was very much the shape of things to come.

A different kind of modernity confronts you just a half mile to the east. The district of Blaak was a working-class stronghold until it was destroyed in World War II. The phoenix that arose took everyone by surprise. For starters, a space-age metro station rose from the ashes, alongside apartments that are shaped like cubes, up-ended on one corner and perched on tall stalks. They're called **Cube Houses**, and were built to the bemusement of locals a quarter of a century ago. One of them, the **Kijk-Kubus**, is open to visitors, but beware if you're unbalanced at the thought of an 'upside-down' house. The city's trademark melding of functional and eccentric is further enhanced just a bit to the southwest with the fabulous sounding **Boompjestorens**, three dice-shaped apartment blocks in a seventeenth century double row of lime trees turned into a modish boulevard.

→ BUILDING SIGHTS

The more you wander the city, the more you realise that Blaak isn't the sole preserve of architectural innovation. Whatever your take on it all, there's no getting away from the fact that there are few places in the world that have such an eclectic range of buildings to keep you entertained (or bewildered). Try these for size: the **Euromast Space Tower** (which, at 185m, really is a size), a spire with super-fast automatic lifts which zoom you up for awesome views of the city; the **Groothandelsgebouw** (which translates as large business building) and is, well, a large business building with a stunning post-war design; the **Witte Huis**, a twelve-storey high-rise dating from 1897, making it Europe's first skyscraper; **Willemswerf**, the sparkling global HQ of shipping giant Nedlloyd; **Huis Sonnenfeld**, a modernist house from the 1930s that sets off the adjacent **Architectuur Instituut** a treat; the soaring **KPN Telekom Building**, built by Renzo Piano in 2000, and looking in its precarious way as if it's about to topple over; and the city's two iconic bridges, the **Willemsbrug**,

and **Erasmusbrug**, whose graceful, angular lines of silver tubing have earned it the nickname 'The Swan'.

→ HAVENS OF PEACE

If you're looking for a more picturesque aspect of Rotterdam – something that might give a clue to its long lost past – then bits of the Nieuwe Maas harbourside area can nudge you in the right direction. A couple of kilometres southwest of Centraal Station is Delfshaven, an antique harbour that managed to stay pretty much intact as the bombs fell. It has history: the Pilgrim Fathers set sail from here in 1620 en route to the New World, and its quiet waterways lend it a feel of decorous charm. Way off to the east at the other end of the central waterfront is Oude Haven, the city's oldest harbour dating from 1325, and sympathetically redeveloped after the War. A tiny inlet, it adds another dimension to the 'cube house'/Witte Huis area - it's lined with peaceful cafes and houses whose origins stretch back seven hundred years. The antique boats and barges that mill around just add to the feeling of a different city at a different time.

→ DAM CULTURED

There's no problem locating the area where culture is the name of the game – the authorities found a wide, open area not far up from the waterfront and called it Museumpark. Chief amongst its glories is Rotterdam's number one attraction, The **Museum Boijmans Van Beuningen,** which covers a mighty span of art history and holds a continuing cycle of temporary exhibitions. The permanent collection ranges across all major schools of Dutch and continental art from old masters (Bosch, Breugel, Rembrandt) through the Impressionists (Van Gogh, Degas, Gaugin, Monet), to the modernists (Dali, Duchamp, Magritte). As a perfect foil, the nearby **Kunsthal** is a great place to look at premier league exhibitions of contemporary art, design and photography, while there's the **Natuurmuseum** next door, a pure joy for lovers of taxidermy. Outside, the nature's pretty good, too, as Museumpark gives you the chance for a good stroll, with a fountain, a lake and enough benches for you to sit and ruminate on the meaning of the giant rabbit sculptures that dot the lawn.

Finding out more about the history of Rotterdam itself is the preserve of two museums east of Museumpark near the old **Leuvehaven** harbour. The **Maritiem Museum** is a salty dog of a gallery, full of the sights and sounds of the city as seaport, and with an absorbing look at what it was like to be a seafarer in the seventeenth and eighteenth centuries. Up the road, past Churchillplein metro station, the **Museum het Schielandshuis** is housed in one of the city's few preserved seventeenth century mansions, and it paints a broader brush over Rotterdam's history, with original footage of World War II bombing, and, on a lighter note, social history in photographs.

The story of modern Rotterdam is embodied in the tale of the neighbourhood to the south of the river – Kop Van Zuid. Historically, a predominantly working class area with docks, a shipyard and a terminal for ocean-going liners, its stock plummeted in the 1960s and 70s when most of the heavy waterfront industry packed up and moved way out west to **Europoort** by the North Sea. Kop Van Zuid, poorly connected to the north bank, was abandoned. Then, in 1986, development started to turn the area around, and by 2010 it's expected that fifteen thousand residents will be living in the hard-edged modern urban apartments that have helped earn the south bank its new reputation as a high quality zone with eye-catching architecture and smart cafés and bars. The icing on the cake for this, the city's most heralded up-and-coming quarter, came with the arrival of the **Luxor Theatre**, a stunning modern building that's brought a real touch of culture – through concerts, musicals and dance – to the 'other side' of the Nieuwe Maas.

CALENDAR HIGHLIGHTS

Holland's most prestigious jazz event, The North Sea Jazz Festival, has moved its base from The Hague to Rotterdam's Ahoy centre in Kop Van Zuid, a sure sign of the city's emergence on the cultural map. It attracts many of the world's top musicians and, held in mid-July, it's just part of a vibrant summer in the city. May's Dunya Festival presents a wealth of arts and culture from across the globe, with several stages around Euromast and Parklaan hosting music, storytelling and performance. The streets

ROTTERDAM IN...

→ **ONE DAY**
Blaak area, including Kijk-Kubus and Boompjestorens, Oude Haven, Museum Boijmans Van Beuningen

→ **TWO DAYS**
A fuller investigation of Museumpark, Delfshaven, the view from Euromast, a cruise along the Nieuwe Maas

→ **THREE DAYS**
Kop Van Zuid, including a meal at one of its restaurants, a show at the Luxor Theatre

come alive with colour at two spectacular events, one in July and one in August. The first – the Summer Carnival – matches the spirit of more exotic climes, a great street parade enlivened by ethnic groups from the likes of Cape Verde, the Antilles and Surinam. Then along comes Dance Parade, during which around forty decorated trucks wind their way through the centre, to the sound of pulsing drums, eventually arriving at Schiehaven's Lloydpier. As a complete contrast, the Municipal Theatre hosts the Poetry International Festival in June – the largest gathering of global poets in Europe; there are Dutch and English translations of their work. The action moves back outside again for September's World Port Festival, when, over three days, the secrets of the city's huge harbour are revealed: there are ship tours, rescue and aviation demos, boat cruises and bus trips. In the same month, The Kunsthal hosts Chocolad' Amour (can there *be* a more enticing name?), which does pretty much what it says on the label, with tasting sessions – surprise, surprise – a huge draw. Sticking to the food theme, the Kunsthal is also home base and kitchen for KunsthalCOOKING, a three-day food jamboree with tastings, again in September. January is the month for movie buffs with the twelve-day International Film Festival, renowned for its innovative aspect, while in March you can stay up late for Museum Night, when more than forty galleries and museums have extended opening hours – a great time for a guided tour.

EATING OUT

Rotterdam is a hot place for dining, in the literal and metaphorical sense. There are lots of places to tuck into the flavours of Holland's colonial past, in particular the spicy delicacies of Indonesia and Surinam. The long east/west stretch of Oude and Nieuwe Binnenweg is not only central and handy for many of the sights, it's also chock-full of good cafes, café-bars and restaurants. The recently smartened up canal district of Oudehaven has also introduced to the city a good selection of places to eat while taking in the relaxed vibe. Along the waterfront, various warehouses have been transformed into mega-restaurants, particularly around the Noordereiland isle in the middle of the river, while in Kop Van Zuid the Wilhelminapier quay is spot-on for a brand new area with good restaurants and tasty views to go with it. Many establishments in the city are closed at lunchtime, except business restaurants and those that set a high gastronomic standard and like to show it off in the middle of the day as well as in the evening. The bill includes service charge, and tipping is optional: round up the total if you're pleased with the service.

→ LIQUID REFRESHMENT

A satisfying – and speedy – way to get a duck's eye view of the intriguing architecture here is to take a water taxi. Introduced to the harbour just a few years ago, they whisk you along at nearly 30mph past the cranes, warehouses and giant cargo ships. They skim towards the harbour mouth, then spin round and bring you back, so that what you missed on the way out, you can catch on the return.

→ BINNEN THERE, BOUGHT IT

You may think you've *seen* a few oddities in Rotterdam, but the place to buy them is the massive Binnenrotte market, open three days of the week. It's not inconceivable to think you can get anything here, from antique dolls and Turkish bread to 1930s bikes and secondhand fishing rods.

Environs of Rotterdam
(Plan I)

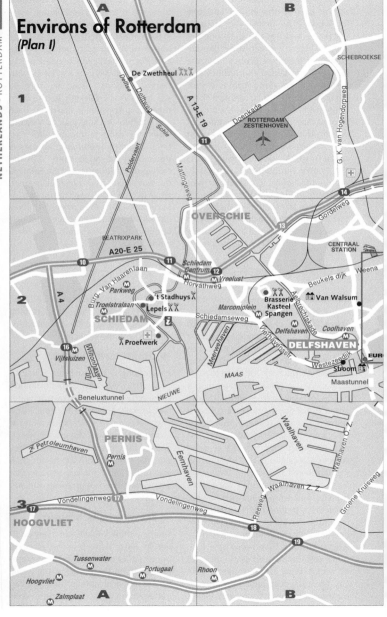

C

D

BERGSE BOS

N 209

PARK

De Tochten

Wilsonweg

Nieuw Verlaat

Ambachtsland

HILLEGERSBERG

Pres. Romeynshof

Hesseplaats

Jasonweg

Grindweg

Molen

Laan

Binnenhof

SCHIEBROEK

Pres. Rooseveltweg

Graskruid

16

Hoofdweg

1

Ringdijk

Straatweg

Borgse

Voorplas

A 20 - E 25

Bergse

Achterplas

Bosdreef

27

Hoofdweg

Alexander

Prins Alexander

Oosterflank

Capelseweg

15

Gordelweg

Boezemlaan

KRALINGSEBOS

Prinsenlaan

Prinsenlaan

N 219

Bergweg

KRALINGSE

Prins Alexander Laan

Schenkel

PLAS

Kralingseweg

Slotlaan

Crown

Kralingseweg

CAPELLE A/D
IJSSEL

Rotterdam-
Centre
(Plan II)

Gerdesiaweg

Voorschoterlaan

26

Coolsingel

Oostplein

In den
Rustwat

Kralingse
Zoom

Capelseburg

Rickevorselweg

N 210

KRIMPEN A/D IJSSEL

Blaak

Maasboulevard

U

N 210

Fred

Abraham

25

van

N 210

Vasteland

Rosestr.

MAAS

OMAST

Laan op Zuid

NIEUWE

MAASHAVEN

Rijnhaven

Putse laan

Maashaven

Stadionweg

24

Pleinweg

Marathonweg

Dorpsweg

Zuidplein

Olympiaweg

Klein
Nieuwland

Dordtsestraatweg

Reyerdijk

AHOY

Vaanweg

Slinge

Oldegaarde

Spinozaweg

IJsselmondse Randweg

3

Slinge

20

A 16-E19

A 15

0   1 Km

A 29

BARENDRECHT

● Hotel

● Restaurant

C

D

631

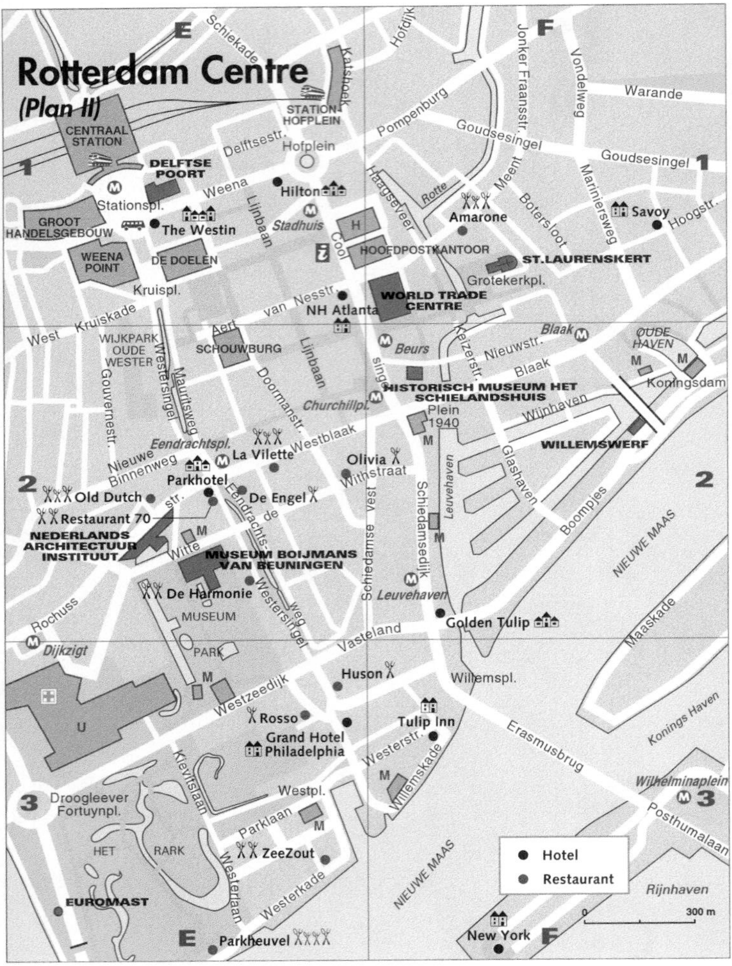

CENTRE *Plan II*

🏨 **The Westin** ⋞ 🛗 ♿ AC ⊘ SAT 📶 🏋 🖧 VISA MC AE Ⓓ

Weena 686 ✉ 3012 CN – ✆ (0 10) 430 20 00 – westin.rotterdam@westin.com – Fax (0 10) 430 20 01 – www.westin.com/rotterdam **E1**

227 rm – 🚹159/365 € 🚹🚹184/390 €, ☕ 27 € – 4 suites

Rest – Menu 40 € – Carte 43/117 €

♦ Business ♦ Luxury ♦ Modern ♦

A huge skyscraper built across from the station, featuring large bedrooms with all modern comforts, conference rooms and a business centre. Striking urban view from the upper floors. Up-to-date cuisine in a panoramic dining room with a streamlined contemporary décor.

NETHERLANDS - ROTTERDAM

Parkhotel ≤ ƒ6 🕥 🏧 ⇎ 📺 ⁙ 🛅 🅿 🆚 ⓪ 🆎 ⓪

Westersingel 70 ⊠ *3015 LB – ℰ (0 10) 436 36 11 – parkhotel@bilderberg.nl*
– Fax (0 10) 436 42 12 – www.parkhotelrotterdam.nl **E2**
187 rm – ♥89/325 € ♥♥99/345 €, ☲ 21 € – 2 suites
Rest Restaurant 70 – see below
♦ Business ♦ Personalised ♦
Hotel established in 1922 and modernised over the years, which explains the mixed architecture. Recently-renovated interior. Several types of guestroom.

Hilton ƒ6 ὅ 🏧 ⇎ 📺 ⁙ 🛅 ⇎ 🆚 ⓪ 🆎 ⓪

Weena 10 ⊠ *3012 CM – ℰ (0 10) 710 80 00 – info-rotterdam@hilton.com*
– Fax (0 10) 710 80 80 – www.rotterdam.hilton.com **E1**
246 rm – ♥99/249 € ♥♥99/269 €, ☲ 25 € – 8 suites
Rest – *(open until 11pm)* Menu 27/35 € – Carte approx. 45 €
♦ Chain hotel ♦ Business ♦ Classical ♦
Close to the WTC, the hotel was designed by the architect of the Euromast tower. Immense lobby, varying categories of rooms, business center and fine conference facilities. Lounge-restaurant offering a modern menu and choice of wines by the glass.

Golden Tulip ≤ ƒ6 ὅ 🖼 🔅 rest 🏧 ⇎ 📺 ⁙ 🛅 🅿 🆚 ⓪ 🆎 ⓪

Leuvehaven 80 ⊠ *3011 EA – ℰ (0 10) 413 41 39 – inforotterdam@*
goldentuliphotelinntel.com – Fax (0 10) 413 32 22
– www.goldentuliprotterdamcentre.com **F2**
263 rm – ♥255 € ♥♥255 €, ☲ 24 €
Rest – *(open until 11.30pm)* Carte 33/46 €
♦ Chain hotel ♦ Business ♦ Modern ♦
Chain hotel, lining a harbour museum dock, just one stride away from the majestic Erasmus Bridge (Erasmusbrug). Top-floor pool and panoramic bar.

NH Atlanta ƒ6 🔅 ⇎ 📺 ⁙ 🛅 ⇎ 🆚 ⓪ 🆎 ⓪

Aert van Nesstraat 4 ⊠ *3012 CA – ℰ (0 10) 206 78 00 – nhatlantarotterdam@*
nh-hotels.com – Fax (0 10) 413 53 20 – www.nh-hotels.com **E1**
215 rm – ♥85/310 € ♥♥85/310 €, ☲ 19 € – 2 suites
Rest – *(closed Saturday and Sunday) (dinner only until 11pm)* Menu 25/50 € bi
– Carte 31/45 €
♦ Chain hotel ♦ Classical ♦
Next-door to the WTC, this hotel is comprised of three buildings, the oldest of which dates from the 1930s. Suites, junior suites, studios and new modern rooms. Art deco public areas. Up-to-date cuisine and bar ambience.

Savoy without rest ƒ6 🏧 ⇎ 📺 🛅 🆚 ⓪ 🆎 ⓪

Hoogstraat 81 ⊠ *3011 PJ – ℰ (0 10) 413 92 80 – info.savoy@*
edenhotelgroup.com – Fax (0 10) 404 57 12 – www.edencityhotels.com
94 rm – ♥89/275 € ♥♥89/275 €, ☲ 17 € **F1**
♦ Business ♦ Classical ♦
A 7-storey building, just a stone's throw from Blom's famous "cube houses". Modern rooms adorned with Burberry-style fabrics, fitness facilities and a nautical-style bar.

Stroom ⛲ ƒ6 🔅 rest ⇎ ⁙ 🛅 🆚 ⓪ 🆎 ⓪

Lloydstraat 1 ⊠ *3024 EA – ℰ (0 10) 221 40 60 – info@stroomrotterdam.nl*
– Fax (0 10) 221 40 61 – www.stroomrotterdam.nl *Plan I* **B2**
21 rm – ♥165 € ♥♥255 €, ☲ 15 €
Rest – Menu 20/45 € – Carte approx. 40 €
♦ Business ♦ Minimalist ♦
In a newly-developed district near the docks, former power station now an ultra-trendy hotel. Remains of its industrial past displayed in the lobby. Bright minimalist-style designer rooms. Uber-trendy lounge-bar setting for this restaurant with modern, international menu.

NETHERLANDS - ROTTERDAM

New York
⟨ 🛎 & ↩ 🗺 ¶ ⚒ 🚗 🆚🅰 ⓪ 🅰🅴 ⓪

Koninginnenhoofd 1 (Wilhelminapier) ✉ *3072 AD – 𝒞 (0 10) 439 05 00 – info@*
hotelnewyork.nl – Fax (0 10) 484 27 01 – www.hotelnewyork.nl **F3**
72 rm – ♦110/240 € ♦♦110/240 €, ⌂ 14 €
Rest – Menu 28 € – Carte 19/55 €
♦ Traditional ♦ Retro ♦

The former HQ of the Holland-America shipping line is now a hotel with character.
Rooms overlooking the port, town or river. Vintage New York-style barbershop. Spacious historic café in a "post-industrial" style. Modern menu printed on placemats.

Crown without rest
& 🅰🅲 ↩ ¶ ⚒ 🚗 🆚🅰 ⓪ 🅰🅴

Schiekade 658 ✉ *3032 AK – 𝒞 (0 10) 466 33 44*
– info@crownrotterdam.nl – Fax (0 10) 467 52 78
– www.crownrotterdam.nl *Plan I* **C2**
124 rm ⌂ – ♦119/139 € ♦♦139/159 €
♦ Traditional ♦ Functional ♦

On a busy main street, the hotel is made up of three old houses and a modern
wing at the rear, where rooms are just as comfortable, but quieter.

Grand Hotel Philadelphia
🅰🅲 ↩ 🗺 ¶ ⚒ 🆚🅰 ⓪ 🅰🅴

Van Vollenhovenstraat 48 ✉ *3016 BJ – 𝒞 (0 10) 240 04 25*
– grandhotel@philadelphia.nl – Fax (0 10) 270 97 35
– www.grandhotelphiladelphia.nl – closed 24 December - 3 January
20 rm – ♦95/140 € ♦♦95/140 €, ⌂ 10 € **E3**
Rest – *(closed Saturday and Sunday) (lunch only , small restaurant)* Menu 13 €
♦ Inn ♦ Modern ♦

The maritime past of this period house (1900) can still be seen in some of the interior decoration. Three types of modern rooms; opt for one at the rear. Snacks and
simple lunchtime menu served in the bistro whose décor mixes old with new.

Van Walsum without rest
↩ ¶ 🅿 🆚🅰 ⓪ 🅰🅴 ⓪

Mathenesserlaan 199 ✉ *3014 HC – 𝒞 (0 10) 436 32 75*
– info@hotelvanwalsum.nl – Fax (0 10) 436 44 10 – www.hotelvanwalsum.nl
– closed 23 December - 1 January *Plan I* **B2**
28 rm ⌂ – ♦85/110 € ♦♦110/145 € **Rest** – *(resident only)*
♦ Family ♦ Classical ♦

This 1895 abode has been run by the same family since 1955. The rooms, of
varying appeal, are gradually being renovated. Dining room-veranda opening
onto a terrace-garden.

Parkheuvel (Erik van Loo)
⟨ 🛎 ⇄ 🅿 🆚🅰 ⓪ 🅰🅴
ⰅⰅ ⰅⰅ

Heuvellaan 21 ✉ *3016 GL – 𝒞 (0 10) 436 07 66 – info@parkheuvel.nl*
– Fax (0 10) 436 71 40 – www.parkheuvel.nl
– closed 27 July - 16 August, 27 December - 5 January, Saturday lunch and
Sunday **E3**
Rest – Menu 100/135 € – Carte 73/115 € 🍃
Spec. Ravioli van Bresse kip met gebakken nieroogkreeftjes. Koningskrab op
een risotto van buikspek, olijvenjus en witte chocolade. Aardbei "anders"
met granité van gin en dragon, cocktail Romanov.
♦ Innovative ♦ Formal ♦

A semi-circular modern pavillion located on the Maas by a park with bay windows
and a terrace overlooking the harbour. Lovely remodelled Art Deco interior, extensive menu and wine list, as well as impeccable service.

Old Dutch
🛎 ⇄ ⌑ 🅿 🆚🅰 ⓪ 🅰🅴

Rochussenstraat 20 ✉ *3015 EK – 𝒞 (0 10) 436 03 44 – info@olddutch.net*
– Fax (0 10) 436 78 26 – www.olddutch.net
– closed Saturday, Sunday and bank holidays **E2**
Rest – Menu 50/60 € – Carte 49/77 €
♦ Traditional ♦ Retro ♦

Founded in 1932, the restaurant serves traditional fare in a conventional classical
décor: stained glass, beams, period furniture, wood panelling and carving. Meat
carved on the spot.

XXX **La Vilette** $\boxed{AC}$ $\leftrightarrows$ ¶ (dinner) $\boxed{VISA}$ $\boxed{CO}$ $\boxed{AE}$ $\boxed{①}$

Westblaak 160 $\boxtimes$ *3012 KM –* $\mathscr{C}$ *(0 10) 414 86 92 – lavilette@cistron.nl*
– Fax (0 10) 414 33 91 – www.lavillete.nl
– closed 20 July - 10 August, 21 December - 5 January, Saturday lunch, Sunday
and Monday **E2**
Rest – Menu 53/80 € – Carte 60/79 €
 ♦ Contemporary ♦ Intimate ♦
Comfortable restaurant in a business district. Discreet welcome and service, smart, intimate setting, open kitchen and up-to-date menu composed by the new chef.

XXX **Amarone** (Gert Blom) $\boxed{AC}$ $\boxed{VISA}$ $\boxed{CO}$ $\boxed{AE}$
ξ^3_3

Meent 72a $\boxtimes$ *3011 JN –* $\mathscr{C}$ *(0 10) 414 84 87 – info@restaurantamarone.nl*
– Fax (0 10) 413 36 73 – www.restaurantamarone.nl
– closed 20 July - 10 August, 28 December - 4 January, Saturday lunch and
Sunday **F1**
Rest – Menu 40/72 € bi – Carte 52/64 € $\boxed{\&}$
Spec. Dungesneden coquilles met truffel, hazelnoot en schuim van pecori-
nokaas. Gebakken makreel met polenta en vinaigrette van gember en ker-
rie. Eend in eigen jus met winters stoofpotje verrijkt met eendenlever.
 ♦ Contemporary ♦ Fashionable ♦
Close to the WTC, a tasty updated menu and fashionable setting: large mirrors reflecting the open kitchen, striped chairs, grey benches and a fine glass-fronted wine cellar.

XXX **In den Rustwat** $\boxed{\widehat{m}}$ $\boxed{AC}$ $\leftrightarrows$ $\boxed{VISA}$ $\boxed{CO}$ $\boxed{AE}$

Honingerdijk 96 $\boxtimes$ *3062 NX Kralingen –* $\mathscr{C}$ *(0 10) 413 41 10 – info@*
indenrustwat.nl – Fax (0 10) 404 85 40 – www.indenrustwat.nl
– closed 26 July - 17 August, Saturday lunch, Sunday and Monday
Rest – Menu 43/60 € – Carte 48/64 € *Plan I* **C2**
 ♦ Contemporary ♦ Intimate ♦
Near an arboretum, lovely old (1597) thatched-roof inn with a new wing. Old-fashioned, tastefully refreshed interior, up-to-date cuisine and terrace garden.

XXX **Fred** $\boxed{AC}$ $\leftrightarrows$ ¶ (dinner) $\boxed{VISA}$ $\boxed{CO}$ $\boxed{AE}$

Honingerdijk 263 $\boxtimes$ *3063 AM Kralingen –* $\mathscr{C}$ *(0 10) 212 01 10 – info@*
restaurantfred.nl – Fax (0 10) 212 40 09 – www.restaurantfred.nl
– closed 20 July - 10 August, Saturday lunch and Sunday *Plan I* **C2**
Rest – Menu 48/58 € – Carte 65/78 €
 ♦ Inovative ♦ Design ♦
Creative meals in an ultra-fashionable décor with an unusual painted ceiling, LED lighting, and purple velvet Empire chairs. Business clientele for lunch and a bit more glamorous in the evening.

XX **Brasserie Kasteel Spangen** $\boxed{\widehat{m}}$ $\boxed{AC}$ $\leftrightarrows$ $\boxed{P}$ $\boxed{VISA}$ $\boxed{CO}$ $\boxed{AE}$
$\odot$

Spartastraat 7 (Sparta stadion) $\boxtimes$ *3027 ER –* $\mathscr{C}$ *(0 10) 238 03 00 – brasserie@*
kasteelspangen.nl – Fax (0 10) 238 03 09 – www.kasteelspangen.nl
– closed 30 April, 26 December, Saturday lunch, Sunday lunch and Monday
Rest – Menu 33/99 € bi – Carte 40/57 € $\boxed{\&}$ *Plan I* **B2**
 ♦ Contemporary ♦ Brasserie ♦
Modern brasserie underneath the Sparta stadion stands, overlooking a castle where banquets are held. Up-to-the-minute menu and fine choice of well-recom-
mended wines.

XX **De Harmonie** $\boxed{\widehat{m}}$ $\leftrightarrows$ $\boxed{VISA}$ $\boxed{CO}$ $\boxed{AE}$ $\boxed{①}$

Westersingel 95 $\boxtimes$ *3015 LC –* $\mathscr{C}$ *(0 10) 436 36 10 – deharmonie@*
deharmonie.demon.nl – Fax (0 10) 436 36 08 – www.restaurantdeharmonie.nl
– closed 25 December - 1 January, Saturday lunch and Sunday **E2**
Rest – Menu 43/83 € bi – Carte 66/96 €
 ♦ Contemporary ♦ Fashionable ♦
A modern restaurant opposite the Museumpark in a chic avenue of fine houses. A modern, refined dining area opening onto the charming garden terrace.

NETHERLANDS - ROTTERDAM

XX **Restaurant 70** – H. Parkhotel ⤣ 🛋 ⟷ ⚠ ✳ **P** *VISA* 🅾 **AE** ⓪
😊

Westersingel 70 ✉ *3015 LB – 𝒞 (0 10) 436 36 11*
– restaurant70@bilderberg.nl – Fax (0 10) 436 42 12
– www.restaurant70.nl   **E2**
Rest – *(dinner only)* Menu 34 €
  ◆ Contemporary ◆ Intimate ◆

Tasteful modern restaurant within the Parkhotel. Comfy beige armchairs, blue benches and light wooden floors. Inner garden with terrace in summertime.

XX **Zeezout** 🛋 ⚠ *VISA* 🅾 **AE** ⓪

Westerkade 11b ✉ *3016 CL – 𝒞 (0 10) 436 50 49*
– zeezout1@hetnet.nl – Fax (0 10) 225 18 47
– www.engelgroep.com
– closed Saturday lunch, Sunday and Monday   **E3**
Rest – *(booking essentiel)* Menu 44/58 € – Carte 46/62 €
  ◆ Seafood ◆ Trendy ◆

The chic and trendy atmosphere, fish and seafood menu and waterside terrace are this modern brasserie's assets, whose name – "Sea Salt" – gives the game away.

X **Huson** 🛋 ⚠ *VISA* 🅾 **AE**
😊

Scheepstimmermanslaan 14 ✉ *3011 BS – 𝒞 (0 10) 413 03 71*
– lunch@huson.info – Fax (0 10) 412 49 38 – www.huson.info
– closed first 2 weeks in January, last week July-first 2 weeks August, Saturday lunch and Sunday   **E3**
Rest – *(booking essentiel)* Menu 32 € – Carte approx. 40 €
  ◆ Contemporary ◆ Brasserie ◆

Trendy atmosphere in a modern dining room in aubergine and peppermint tones. Nice leather benches. Serving a small menu of a variety of dishes from noon till 9.30pm.

X **De Engel** ⚠ ⟷ 🍽 (dinner) *VISA* 🅾 **AE** ⓪

Eendrachtsweg 19 ✉ *3012 LB – 𝒞 (0 10) 413 82 56*
– restaurant@engel.nl – Fax (0 10) 412 51 96
– www.engelgroep.com
– closed Saturday lunch and Sunday   **E2**
Rest – Menu 43 € – Carte 45/62 €
  ◆ Contemporary ◆

Opulent house set in a lively neighbourhood. World cuisine, relaxed atmosphere, decorative mixture of old and new and collection of photographs illustrating the culinary arts..

X **Oliva** 🛋 ⟷ *VISA* 🅾

Witte de Withstraat 15a ✉ *3012 BK – 𝒞 (0 10) 412 14 13*
– info@restaurantoliva.nl – Fax (0 10) 412 70 69
– www.restaurantoliva.nl   **E2**
Rest – *(dinner only)* Menu 34/49 € bi – Carte 28/43 €
  ◆ Italian ◆ Bistro ◆

Lively Italian restaurant and a lively loft-inspired ambience. Open kitchen, simple menu and daily specials chalked on a board.

X **Rosso** 🛋 ⚠ ⟷ *VISA* 🅾 **AE**

Van Vollenhovenstraat 15 (access via Westerlijk Handelsterrein) ✉ *3016 BE*
– 𝒞 (0 10) 225 07 05 – hans-veerman@hetnet.nl
– Fax (0 10) 436 95 04 – www.rossorotterdam.nl
– closed last week in July and Sunday   **E3**
Rest – *(dinner only until 11pm)* Menu 38 € – Carte 46/57 €
  ◆ Contemporary ◆

Bar-restaurant in a renovated 19th century warehouse, with dining area in vibrant red tones. Chic clientele and ambience. Très à la mode!

XXX
£3 £3

De Zwethheul   ⪡ 🌿 AC ⇔ P VISA ⑩ AE ⓪

Rotterdamseweg 480 (beside the canal in Zweth) ⊠ *2636 KB Schipluiden*
– 𝒞 (0 10) 470 41 66 – info@zwethheul.nl – Fax (0 10) 470 65 22
– www.zwethheul.nl
– closed 24 December - 3 January, Saturday lunch, Sunday lunch and Monday
Rest – Menu 75/220 € bi – Carte 80/145 € 🕸   **A1**
Spec. "Rosbief" van tonijn met zwarte peper, chaud-froid van krab. Gevuld briochebrood met ganzenlever en truffel. Zwartpoot kip gepocheerd met gesmolten ganzenlever en morieltjes.
◆ Innovative ◆ Design ◆
This remodelled former inn (1865) serves fine meals to be enjoyed while observing the boats come and go, either from the dining room or the shaded, waterside terrace.

XX

Lepels   🌿 AC VISA ⑩ AE

Korte Haven 5 ⊠ *3111 BH Schiedam – 𝒞 (0 10) 246 73 58 – info@lepels.net*
– Fax (0 10) 246 73 59 – www.lepels.net
– closed Monday   **A2**
Rest – Menu 42/88 € bi – Carte 43/60 €
◆ Contemporary ◆ Brasserie ◆
Trendy restaurant between the covered market and the windmill. Central open kitchen, black and white designer décor, soft lighting, plates on display, lounge music and floating terrace on the canal.

X

't Stadhuys   🌿 ⇔ VISA ⑩ AE

Grote Markt 1a ⊠ *3111 NG Schiedam – 𝒞 (0 10) 426 55 33 – info@*
restauranthetstadhuys.nl – www.restauranthetstadhuys.nl   **A2**
Rest – Menu 33/85 € bi – Carte approx. 55 €
◆ Traditional ◆ Brasserie ◆
Restaurant located in Schiedam's former town hall: a splendid baroque building with voluted gables and a pinnacle on the roof. Summer terrace on the Grote Markt.

X

Proefwerk   AC ⇔ VISA ⑩ AE

Schoolstraat 1 ⊠ *3116 HJ Schiedam – 𝒞 (0 10) 426 09 90 – info@*
restaurantproefwerk.nl – Fax (0 10) 426 52 92 – www.restaurantproefwerk.nl
– closed last week in July - first week in August, 27 December - 2 January,
Saturday lunch, Sunday lunch and Monday   **A2**
Rest – Menu 38 € – Carte 44/59 €
◆ Contemporary ◆ Brasserie ◆
Set in an old juniper distillery. Black walls contrast with the visible red kitchen open onto the dining room. Modern menu. Trendy loft-lounge ambience.

NORWAY
NORGE

PROFILE

→ **AREA:**
323 878 km²
(125 049 sq mi).

→ **POPULATION:**
4 640 000 inhabitants
(est. 2006), density =
14 per km².

→ **CAPITAL:**
Oslo (conurbation
731 600 inhabitants).

→ **CURRENCY:**
Krone (kr or NOK)
divided into 100 øre;
rate of exchange:
NOK 1 = € 0.11 = US$
0.14 (Dec 2008).

→ **GOVERNMENT:**
Constitutional
parliamentary
monarchy with
single-chamber
Parliament (since
1945).

→ **LANGUAGES:**
Norwegian has two
written variants:
Bokmål (influenced
by Danish) spoken
by 80% of the
population
and Nynorsk
(New Norwegian).
Sami is the language
of the Sami people in
the far north. English
is widely spoken.

→ **SPECIFIC PUBLIC
HOLIDAYS:**
Maundy Thursday
and Good Friday
(Thursday and Friday
before Easter);
Constitution
Day (17 May); Boxing
Day (26 December).

→ **LOCAL TIME:**
GMT + 1 hour in
winter and GMT
+ 2 hours in summer.

→ **CLIMATE:**
Temperate northern
maritime, with cold
winters and mild
summers (Oslo:
January: -4°C,
July: 16°C). Colder
interior, fairly high
precipitation in the
coastal regions.

→ **INTERNATIONAL
DIALLING CODE:**
00 47 followed by full
local number.

→ **EMERGENCY:**
Police: ☏ **112**;
Ambulance service:
☏ **113**; Fire Brigade:
☏ **110**.

→ **ELECTRICITY:**
220 volts AC, 50Hz;
2-pin round-shaped
continental plugs.

→ **FORMALITIES**
Travellers from the
European Union
(EU), Switzerland,
Iceland and the main
countries of North
and South America
need a national
identity card or
passport (America:
passport required) to
visit Norway for less
than three months
(tourism or business
purpose). For visitors
from other countries
a visa may be
required, in addition
to a passport,
especially for those
wishing to stay for
longer than three
months. We advise
you to check with
your embassy before
travelling.

Population: 538 411 (conurbation 731 600) – Altitude: 96m

Sime/PHOTONONSTOP

Oslo has a lot going for it and one particularly striking downside. Let's get that out of the way first: it's currently the world's most expensive city, above even Tokyo, London and Paris. So don't expect the cheapest trip you've ever made. But it also rates as the city with the world's best standard of living, and its position, at the head of Oslofjord and surrounded by steep forested hills, is hard to match for drama and beauty. It's mellow and elegant, and though it can make as much of an impression on your wallet as on your memory, it's a charmingly compact place to stroll round, particularly in the summer, when the daylight hours practically abolish the night.

Oslo is rather underrated in that it lacks the urban cool of other Scandinavian cities like Copenhagen or Stockholm, but it boasts its fair share of trendy clubs and a raft of Michelin starred restaurants. Oh, and a real raft, too: Thor Hyerdahl's famous balsawood Kon-Tiki, which is one of the star turns in a city that loves its museums. You won't feel claustrophobic here; there's an uncluttered feel enhanced by parks and wide streets and, in the winter, there are times when you feel you have the whole place to yourself!

LIVING THE CITY

It's almost impossible for Oslo to live up to its lovely setting, but somehow it manages it. Drift into the city by boat down the Oslofjord and land at the smart harbour of **Aker Brygge**. To the west lies the charming **Bygdøy** peninsula, home, naturally enough, to museums permeated with the smell of the sea. North-west of your arrival point is **Frogner**, with its famous sculpture park, the place where locals hang out on long summer days. The centre of town, the commercial hub, is Karl Johans Gate, bounded at one end by the Royal Palace and at the other by the Cathedral, while further east lie two trendy multi-cultural areas, Grunerlokka and Grønland, which have taken on a vibrant edge over the last decade. This area is also home to the Edvard Munch Museum.

PRACTICAL INFORMATION

ARRIVAL-DEPARTURE

A taxi from Oslo International Airport, Gardermoen, which is 47km north of the city, will cost around NOK600. The train station is located beneath the terminal and the high speed Flytoget train takes 19 minutes to Oslo's central station. Alternatively, take the Express Bus to Galleri bus terminal – it leaves every 20min and takes 45min.

TRANSPORT

Serious sightseeing is enhanced with the Oslo Pass, which covers the transport system and entry to all those museums. It's valid for one to three days. Get it from the Information Centre next to Oslo Central Station.

Oslo is proud of its green credentials, and you'll have to pay a toll if you arrive by car. The integrated transport system within the city is efficient, comprising bus, tram or metro. You can obtain single or day tickets. For a small deposit, you can tap into the green-friendly Citybike scheme in Oslo. Go to a tourist information office, get your electronic 'Tourist Card', and hire one of the many free bicycles parked at different points around the city.

EXPLORING OSLO

Step ashore from your ferry at Akker Brygge - the swishly redeveloped harbour area of Oslo - in the summer months and it seems that the population of Norway is your escort. Locals cherish this time of year, when the sun never apparently sets, and they spend long hours in the streets and parks of the city. This is when restaurants, bars and museums stay open that much longer, and concert halls and theatres move their productions outdoors; in mid-summer bonfires are lit and the clink of glasses rustles the still air in celebration of life al fresco.

Akker Brygge itself is a bustling waterfront area and a fine place to make the acquaintance of Oslo. It used to be a full-on shipyard, but has been re-born as a trendy glass-and-chrome shopping and entertainment quarter, more Fisherman's Wharf of San Francisco than Docklands of London. It's a lovely place to settle down with a glass of wine and look at the fishing boats, and there are some snazzy eating places, but be warned that lots of them weigh in with a hefty bill. Best bet is to stroll the waterfront down to one of the most striking buildings of the city, the **Akershus Fortress**, an imposing building that has acted as Oslo's guardian since the thirteenth century. In those seven hundred plus years, Akershus has been under siege nine times, but has never fallen except during World War II.

→ OPEN GATE

Back up behind the harbour a coterie of colourful streets leads to the grand boulevard of Oslo: **Karl Johans Gate.** Aside from the shops, this is where many of Norway's most important buildings are based, including **Slottet** (the Royal Palace) and **Stortinget** (the Parliament building). Culture lovers need only pop round the corner to get a fix of Ibsen at the National Theatre, where his plays are a staple, and for good measure enjoy one of the country's finest art collections, which is included in the price of a ticket. It won't take long before you stumble on a museum. In this part of the capital alone, near the Royal Palace, are the Historical Museum, documenting Norwegian history, and the Stenersen Museum, named after the art collector who donated his entire collection to the city of Oslo. Wandering around further, you'll find museums dedicated to…well, you name it. Think architecture and zoology, and just about everything in between. Some of them have become especially well renowned. Modern art lovers, for instance, like to sniff out a couple in the

streets behind Akershus, and with good reason. The Astrup Fearnley Museum of Modern Art is relatively new on the block (opened in 1993), housing recent works by Norwegian and critically acclaimed international artists in a strikingly modern building whose main entrance is two massive steel doors. Nearby is the National Museum for Art, Architecture and Design, full of disturbing works by post-war Norwegians in a rather eye-catching art nouveau building.

→ SCREAM OF THE CROP

Edvard Munch is a national institution in Norway. Though his fellow countrymen aren't particularly maudlin by nature, Munch revelled in despair, depression, disease and death. Or at least his paintings did. In the 1880s and 90s, when he was at his creative height, many people were outraged at his take on the national psyche, but now his work is lauded the length and breadth of the land, and features in two Oslo museums – The National Gallery, which contains a number of his most famous works, and the Munch Museum, out in Grunerlokka, an exhibition which is constantly changing, due to the huge amount of paintings, prints, drawings, plates and letters he produced. There are versions of The Scream in both galleries (dependent on the adroitness of thieves, of course…)

→ MARITIME MUSEUMS

A short ferry trip across the Oslofjord takes you to the **Bygdøy** peninsula, a favoured summer retreat with its meadows, groves, beaches and watery views (you can take a bus here, too, but it's not quite as spectacular). Bygdøy is home to some of the best attractions in the city (and yes, when we say attractions, we really mean – you've guessed it – museums). Being right alongside the fjord, these rightly take on a maritime quality. The **Kon-Tiki** Museum gives an evocatively vivid account of the exploits of the famed explorer Thor Heyerdahl, who sailed his balsawood raft across the South Pacific in 1947. It's there, looking remarkably flimsy, as is Ra II, in which he sailed the Atlantic in 1970. Next door, in the Fram Museum, proudly sits the Fram, 'the world's strongest ship' which sailed the North Pole and Antarctica a century ago: board her and see the preserved objects from those remarkable trips.

Hit land again and breathe in the fragrant pine before reaching the final piece of this triumvirate, the Viking Ship Museum, a church-like building containing three ancient oak ships (ancient here meaning the ninth century) whose sweeping lines are simple but elegant; their ornate prows having been preserved in the clay of chieftains' graves. However, it's not all homage to derring-do in Bygdøy. Up the road from the Viking ships stands Europe's largest open-air museum, the **Norwegian Folk Museum** – more than 150 buildings from across Norway which you can wander around to your heart's content. Exhibits range from a twelfth century stave church to a petrol station from the 1920s.

→ PARK AND GLIDE

Despite the user-friendly appeal of its other attractions, the two most popular places to visit in Oslo are a park and a ski jump. The park, in the Frogner quarter, is **Vigeland Park**, named after the sculptor Gustav Vigeland, and the thousands who flock here throughout the year add to the permanent numbers already present, resolutely naked and constructed from granite or weathered bronze. Inevitably, there's a museum on hand, with nearly 3000 sculptures and 10,000 drawings, all by Vigeland. Meanwhile, the ski jump is a metro ride away at Holmenkollen. If you visit in winter you might be lucky and catch a competition, but if you're here in the summer, go to the top of the jump and get the best view of Oslo imaginable. Yes, there's a ski museum too, located at the foot of the jump.

It *is* possible to stroll a part of Oslo without an exhibit in sight, unless you count the blond-highlighted cool cats of Grunerlokka and Grønland as exhibits. This is the east end part of the city which has evolved from worn-out working-class area to creative boho quarter and boasts a quirky range of cafés and restaurants frequented by local artists and photographers. It's by the Aker River, and the many small shops and delis are a febrile hunting ground, enhanced by many immigrant nationalities creating a buzzy, eclectic atmosphere.

OSLO IN...

→ ONE DAY
Aker Brygge, Karl Johans Gate, a central museum, a meal in Grunerlokka

→ TWO DAYS
Akershus, Astrup Fearnley Museum, ferry trip to Bygdøy, museum and picnic there

→ THREE DAYS
Vigeland Park, Holmenkollen Ski Jump, a stroll round Grunerlokka, Munch Museum, supper in Akker Brygge

CALENDAR HIGHLIGHTS

Oslo's cultural highlights are obviously dependent on the time of year. If you're a ski fancier, then go in the winter months for competitions at Holmenkollen. At Christmas, the Folk Museum on Bygdøy and the seventeenth century former foundry at Baerums Verk with its workers' houses converted into small shops are magical places to be. February and March are the months for the Winter Night Festival, a classical music extravaganza, and the Oslo International Church Music Festival, held at the cathedral and other churches within the city. Summer is welcomed with St Hallvard's Day in May, when a host of concerts and theatre productions pronounce curtain-up; a month later, the Norwegian Wood rock festival is a three-day jamboree with mostly Norwegian bands. Bonfires are lit on Midsummer Night, and in July/August the Folk Museum has daily folk dancing and helpings of traditional food. Mid-August is given over to an International Jazz Festival, while the Oslo World Music Festival blasts out from various city venues in November. The Nobel Peace Prize, awarded in December, is celebrated with parades and festivities across town.

EATING OUT

Oslo has a very vibrant dining scene, albeit one that is somewhat expensive, particularly if you drink wine. The cooking is generally quite refined and classical, although some innovative menus are beginning to appear. France has always exerted the greatest influence on the cuisine but now younger chefs are looking also to Italy and Spain for inspiration and, these days, there is generally a broader choice of food styles. What is in no doubt is the quality of the produce used, whether that's the ever-popular game or the superlative shellfish which comes from very cold water, giving it a clean and fresh flavour. Classic Norwegian dishes often include fruit, such as lingonberries with venison. Lunch is not a particularly major affair ; most prefer just a snack or sandwich at midday while making dinner the main event of the day. You'll find most diners seated by 7pm and are offered a 6,7,or 8 course menu which they can reduce at their will, with a paired wine menu alongside. Service is another great strength of the restaurants ; staff are generally very polite, speak English and are fully versed in the menu.

It doesn't have to be expensive, though. Look out for konditoris (bakeries) where you can pick up sandwiches and pastries, while kafeterias serve substantial meals, traditional and simple, at reasonable prices.

➜ TAKE THE TRAIN TO THE TRAIL

One of the reasons there aren't many people about in Oslo in the winter is that they're making use of the cross-country ski trails that encircle the city. There are 1,250 miles of them and they're floodlit at night. A local train ride gets you to them.

➜ A FRIEND OF THE PEOPLE

Henrik Ibsen would walk every day from Oslo's Grand Café to the apartment in Arbiens Gate where he spent the last years of his life. He was so punctual with this sortie that the people of the city would set their watches by him.

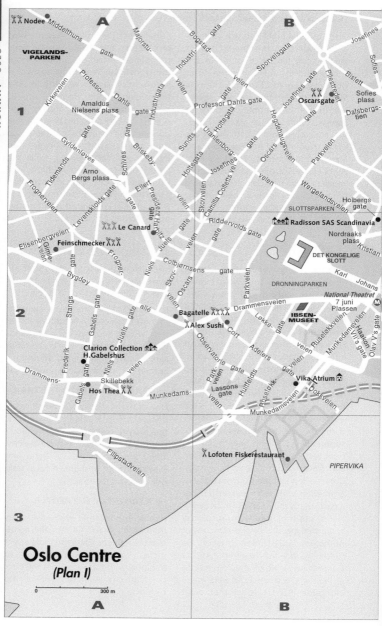

Oslo Centre
(Plan I)

0   300 m

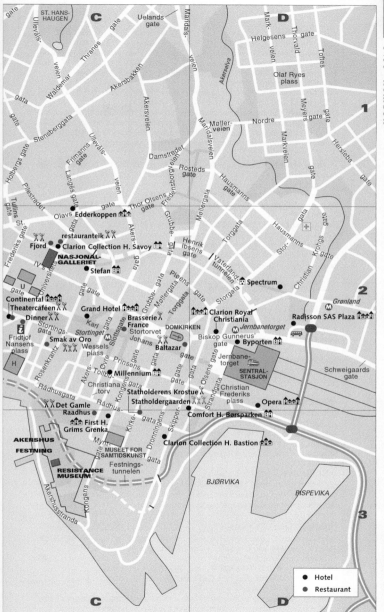

C

ST. HANS-
HAUGEN

Uelands gate

Maridals-

D

Mark-
veien

Thorvald

gate

Helgesens gate

gate

Ullevåls-
veien

Thranes

gate

Waldemar

Akersbakken

Akerselva

Olaf Ryes
plass

Toftes

gate

Meyers gate

Herslebs gate

1

Stensberggata

gate

Frimanns gate

Ullevåls-
veien

Langes gate

Akersveien

Damstreder

Møller-
veien

Maridalsveien

Nordre

Markveien

Holbergs gate

Pilestredet

Tullins
gate

Frederiks gate

St.

Olavs gate

Rosteds
gate

Thor Olsens gate

Fredensborgveien

Grubbe gata

Møllergata

Hausmanns
gate

Hausmanns gate

Stor-
gata

Kongs gate

2

Edderkoppen

restauranteik

Fjord

Olavs gate

Akers

Clarion Collection H. Savoy

NASJONAL-
GALLERIET

Stefan

IV's

Universitets

Henrik
Ibsens
gate

Pleens

Grubbe- gata

Vaterland
tunnelen

Spectrum

Storgata

Grønland

Continental

gate

gate

gate

Theatercafeen

Dinner

Grand Hotel

Brasserie
France

Møllergata

Torggata

gate

Clarion Royal
Christiania

Radisson SAS Plaza

Karl

Stortinget

Slottsgate

Johans

DOMKIRKEN

Stortorvet

Bispok Gunnerus'

Jernbanetorget

Byporten

Smak av Oro

Wessels
plass

Baltazar

gate

Jernbane-
torget

Schweigaards
gate

Fridtjof
Nansens
plass

Rosenkrantz

Øvre

Prinsens

gata

Akers

gate

Millennium

Prinsens

gate

Olsens gata

Strandgata

SENTRAL-
STASJON

Christiania
torv

Rådhus-

gata

Christian
Frederiks
plass

Det Gamle
Raadhus

Stotholderens Krostue

Statholdergaarden

Comfort H. Børsparken

Opera

First H.
Grims Grenka

Kirke-

Dronningens

gata

Clarion Collection H. Bastion

AKERSHUS
FESTNING

Myntgata

MUSEET FOR
SAMTIDSKUNST

Festnings-
tunnelen

Skipper-

RESISTANCE
MUSEUM

Kongens

Akershusstranda

Tollbu- gata

BJØRVIKA

BISPEVIKA

3

● Hotel

● Restaurant

C

D

647

Continental   🛗 ♿ 🅰🅺 ↲ 📺 ⁇ 🚿 🚗 🆅🅸🆂🅰 ☺ 🅰🅴 ⓿

Stortingsgaten 24-26 ✉ *0117* – ⓜ *National Theatret* – ℰ *22 82 40 00*
– booking@hotel-continental.no – Fax 22 42 96 89 – www.hotel-continental.no
– Closed 23 December - 2 January   **C2**
152 rm – ♥2085/2480 NOK ♥♥2495/4360 NOK, ☲ 175 NOK – 3 suites
Rest *Theatercaféen* – see below
Rest *Continental* – *(dinner only)* Menu 640/1400 NOK – Carte 605/795 NOK
♦ Grand Luxury ♦ Traditional ♦ Classic ♦
De luxe hotel, run by the same family for 100 years. Comfortable bedrooms in
varying sizes; some classically furnished, others more contemporary. Art collection
includes Edvard Munch. Elegant formal dining room decorated in early 1920s style.
Gourmet menu offers interesting range of contemporary cuisine.

Grand Hotel   🛗 🕸 🛇 🅰🅺 ↲ rm 📺 ⁇ 🚿 ♿ 🆅🅸🆂🅰 ☺ 🅰🅴 ⓿

Karl Johans Gate 31 ✉ *0101* – ⓜ *Stortinget* – ℰ *23 21 20 00* – *grand@rica.no*
– Fax 23 21 21 00 – www.grand.no   **C2**
290 rm ☲ – ♥1185/2580 NOK ♥♥1435/2580 NOK – 9 suites
Rest *Julius Fritzner* – *(Closed Sunday) (dinner only)* Menu 645 NOK – Carte
733/891 NOK
Rest *Grand Café* – Menu 295/445 NOK – Carte 445/615 NOK
♦ Grand Luxury ♦ Traditional ♦ Classic ♦
Opulent 1874 hotel, in prime location. De luxe well furnished rooms. Swimming
pool on roof. Inventive cooking served in wood-panelled Julius Fritzner. Informal
brasserie-style in Grand Café.

Radisson SAS Scandinavia   ≤ 🛗 🕸 🛇 ♿ 🅰🅺 ↲ rm 📺 ⁇ 🚿

Holbergsgate 30 ✉ *0166* – ⓜ *National Theatret*   🚗 🆅🅸🆂🅰 ☺ 🅰🅴 ⓿
– ℰ 23 29 30 00 – reservations.scandinavia.oslo@radissonsas.com
– Fax 23 29 30 01 – www.scandinavia.oslo.radissonsas.com   **B2**
479 rm ☲ – ♥995/2195 NOK ♥♥995/2195 NOK – 1 suite
Rest *Enzo* – Carte 330/550 NOK
♦ Luxury ♦ Modern ♦
Modern hotel block offering spectacular views. Vast international lobby with
variety of shops and good conference facilities. Spacious comfortable rooms. Pano-
ramic bar. Small and simple Enzo offers popular international dishes.

Radisson SAS Plaza   ≤ 🕸 🛇 ♿ 🅰🅺 ↲ rm 📺 ⁇ 🚿 🚗

Sonja Henies Plass 3 ✉ *0134* – ⓜ *Jernbanetorget*   🆅🅸🆂🅰 ☺ 🅰🅴 ⓿
– ℰ 22 05 80 00 – sales.plaza.oslo@radissonsas.com – Fax 22 05 80 30
– www.plaza.oslo.radissonsas.com   **D2**
673 rm ☲ – ♥1295/2295 NOK ♥♥1595/2595 NOK
Rest *34* – *(Closed Sunday) (tapas buffet lunch)* Menu 495 NOK (dinner) – Carte
495/675 NOK
♦ Business ♦ Modern ♦
Business-oriented hotel block, the tallest in Norway, with footbridge link to congress centre. Well furnished modern rooms. Panoramic bar. 34th floor restaurant offers a Mediterranean menu and spectacular views.

Clarion Royal Christiania   🛗 🕸 🛇 ♿ 🅰🅺 ↲ ⁇ 🚿 🚗

Biskop Gunnerus' Gate 3 ✉ *0106* – ⓜ *Jernbanetorget*   🆅🅸🆂🅰 ☺ 🅰🅴 ⓿
– ℰ 23 10 80 00 – clarionroyal.christiania@choice.no – Fax 23 10 80 80
– www.clarionroyal.christiania.no   **D2**
448 rm ☲ – ♥1095/2495 NOK ♥♥1395/2695 NOK – 60 suites
Rest – Menu 365 NOK (lunch) – Carte 395/665 NOK
♦ Luxury ♦ Business ♦ Modern ♦
Imposing conveniently located hotel built around a vast atrium. Spacious lobby.
Large rooms with pleasant décor; the quietest overlook the atrium. Excellent con-
ference facilities. Pleasantly decorated restaurant in atrium with a varied international menu.

NORWAY - OSLO

Opera ⇐ 🛴 🕷 🔥 🎓 ↩ rm 🖾 ⁽ᵖ⁾ 🏋 🟥 ⚫ 🄰🄴 ⓘ

Christian Frederiks plass 5 ⊠ *0103 –* Ⓜ *Jernbanetorget –* ✆ *24 10 30 00*
– opera@thonhotels.no – Fax 24 10 30 10 – www.thonhotels.no/opera
– Closed Christmas-New Year   **D2**
432 rm ⌑ – 🛉1295/1995 NOK 🛉🛉2095/2295 NOK – 2 suites
Rest *– (buffet lunch)* Carte 505/655 NOK
♦ Business ♦ Modern ♦

Located next to the railway station and in front of the new opera house, with an
imposing hall and functional yet contemporary furnishings; the best
bedrooms overlook the sea. Restaurant with huge windows affording panoramic
views. Elaborate traditional cooking.

First H. Grims Grenka 🛴 🕷 🄰🄲 🖾 ⁽ᵖ⁾ 🟥 ⚫ 🄰🄴 ⓘ

Kongensgate 5 ⊠ *0153 –* Ⓜ *Stortinget –* ✆ *23 10 72 00 – grims.grenka@*
firsthotels.no – Fax 23 10 72 10 – www.grimsgrenka.no   **C3**
65 rm ⌑ – 🛉1550/6000 NOK 🛉🛉1550/6000 NOK – 1 suite
Rest *Madu – (closed Sunday and Monday) (light lunch)* Carte 404/1023 NOK
♦ Business ♦ Stylish ♦

Boutique hotel with trendy bar and smart summer terrace. Split between Summer
and Winter (atrium/outside views), with colours to match, bedrooms boast wi-fi,
iPod docks and stylish glass shower rooms. Modern Asian restaurant specialises in
dim sum.

Clarion Collection H. Bastion without rest 🛴 🕷 🄰🄲 ↩ ⁽ᵖ⁾

Skippergaten 7 ⊠ *0152 –* Ⓜ *Jernbanetorget* 🏋 🄿 🟥 ⚫ 🄰🄴 ⓘ
– ✆ *22 47 77 00 – cc.bastion@choice.no – Fax 22 33 11 80 – www.hotelbastion.no*
– Closed Christmas and Easter
94 rm ⌑ – 🛉995/2450 NOK 🛉🛉1195/2450 NOK – 5 suites   **C3**
♦ Business ♦ Modern ♦

Comfortable, modern hotel handily placed for motorway. Welcoming rooms with
good facilities; the best in the new wing. Furniture and paintings reminiscent of
English style.

Edderkoppen 🛴 🕷 ↩ 🖾 ⁽ᵖ⁾ 🏋 🍽 🟥 ⚫ 🄰🄴 ⓘ

St Olavs Plass 1 ⊠ *0165 –* ✆ *23 15 56 00 – edderkoppen@scandichotels.com*
– Fax 23 15 56 66 – www.scandichotels.no/edderkoppen
– Closed 21 December-4 January   **C2**
235 rm ⌑ – 🛉2550/2750 NOK 🛉🛉2750 NOK – 6 suites
Rest *– (Closed Sunday) (dinner only)* Menu 375 NOK – Carte 375/455 NOK
♦ Business ♦ Modern ♦

550 photographs of Norway's famous actors adorn the walls of this renovated building, incorporating a theatre. Modern, functional, well-equipped bedrooms.
Modern restaurant offering dishes with Mediterranean and international flavours.

Clarion Collection H. Gabelshus without rest ⤬ 🕷 ↩ ⁽ᵖ⁾

Gabelsgate 16 ⊠ *0272 –* ✆ *23 27 65 00* 🏋 🄿 🟥 ⚫ 🄰🄴 ⓘ
– cc.gabelshus@choice.no – Fax 23 27 65 60 – www.choicehotels.no/no094
– Closed 1 week Christmas
113 rm ⌑ – 🛉895/2095 NOK 🛉🛉1095/2095 NOK – 1 suite   **A2**
♦ Traditional ♦ Classic ♦

Attractive early 20C vine-clad hotel with extension in quiet district. Modern public
rooms. Large well-fitted bedrooms; some on front with balconies, quieter at the rear.

Millennium 🔥 ↩ 🖾 ⁽ᵖ⁾ 🍽 🟥 ⚫ 🄰🄴 ⓘ

Tollbugaten 25 ⊠ *0157 –* Ⓜ *Stortinget –* ✆ *21 02 28 00 – millennium@*
firsthotels.no – Fax 21 02 28 30 – www.firsthotels.com   **C2**
102 rm – 🛉850/1895 NOK 🛉🛉1050/2095 NOK, ⌑ 95 NOK – 10 suites
Rest *– (Closed Saturday lunch and Sunday)* Menu 159/470 NOK – Carte approx.
420 NOK
♦ Business ♦ Functional ♦

Functional modern hotel near harbour and restaurants. Internet access. Spacious
well-equipped rooms; top floor with balconies; quietest on inside although overlooked. Simple restaurant on different levels serving global cuisine, from pizza to tapas.

Stefan   ♿ 🅰🅲 ⇔ 📶 🛰 📱 🌐 VISA ⓪ 🅰🅴 ⓪

Rosenkrantzgate 1 ⊠ 0159 – Ⓜ Stortinget – 𝒞 23 31 55 00
– stefan@thonhotels.no – Fax 23 31 55 55
– www.thonhotels.no/stefan
– Closed 3-14 April and 20 December-4 January   **C2**
150 rm – ☐ 1445/1745 NOK ♥♥1745/2045 NOK
Rest – *(Closed Sunday and 3 weeks July)* Carte approx. 176 NOK
♦ Business ♦ Functional ♦
Modern hotel on convenient corner site. Rooms are well equipped with functional furniture and good facilities; top floor recently refurbished. Families and groups catered for. Comfortable ground floor restaurant with fireplace.

Clarion Collection H. Savoy   ⇔ 🛰 📱 VISA ⓪ 🅰🅴 ⓪

Universitetsgata 11 ⊠ 0164 – Ⓜ National Theatret – 𝒞 23 35 42 00
– cc.savoy@choice.no – Fax 23 35 42 01
– www.choice.no/hotels/no060
– Closed 22 December-4 January   **C2**
93 rm ☐ – ♥995/2350 NOK ♥♥1395/3150 NOK
Rest *restauranteik* – see below
♦ Business ♦ Classic ♦
Classic early 20C hotel in the city centre behind the museum. Spacious well-kept bedrooms with good facilities. Free dinner buffet in elegant attic room.

Byporten without rest   ♿ ⇔ 🛰 📱 🌐 VISA ⓪ 🅰🅴 ⓪

Jernbanetorget 6 ⊠ 0154 – Ⓜ Jernbanetorget – 𝒞 23 15 55 00 – byporten@
scandic-hotels.com – Fax 23 15 55 11 – www.scandic-hotels.com/byporten
235 rm ☐ – ♥1090/2590 NOK ♥♥1290/2790 NOK – 4 suites   **D2**
♦ Business ♦ Modern ♦
Modern hotel in vast office/commercial centre block by station. Functional sound-proofed rooms with environmentally friendly decor. Breakfast in nearby public restaurant.

Comfort H. Børsparken without rest   ♿ ⇔ 🛰 📱 🆒

Tollbugaten 4 ⊠ 0152 – Ⓜ Jernbanetorget   VISA ⓪ 🅰🅴 ⓪
– 𝒞 22 47 17 17 – co.borsparken@choice.no – Fax 22 47 17 18
– www.choicehotels.no   **C-D2**
198 rm ☐ – ♥1995 NOK ♥♥2195 NOK
♦ Business ♦ Functional ♦
Modern functional chain hotel on corner site in city centre. Pleasant lobby opening onto tree-lined square. Compact practical rooms, well equipped for business clientele.

Vika Atrium without rest   🏋 ⇔ 🛰 📱 🆒 VISA ⓪ 🅰🅴 ⓪

Munkedamsveien 45 ⊠ 0121 – Ⓜ National Theatret – 𝒞 22 83 33 00
– vika.atrium@thonhotels.no – Fax 22 83 09 57
– www.thonhotels.no/vikaatrium   **B2**
79 rm ☐ – ♥1495/1795 NOK ♥♥1795/2095 NOK
♦ Business ♦ Functional ♦
Located in large office block built around an atrium. Comfortable lobby lounge. Well-serviced rooms with functional modern fittings. Good conference facilities.

Spectrum without rest   ♿ ⇔ 🛰 📱 VISA ⓪ 🅰🅴 ⓪

Brugata 7 ⊠ 0133 – Ⓜ Jernbanetorget – 𝒞 23 36 27 00
– spectrum@thonhotels.no – Fax 23 36 27 50
– www.thonhotels.no/spectrum
– Closed 18 December-3 January   **D2**
151 rm ☐ – ♥810/1010 NOK ♥♥1075 NOK
♦ Business ♦ Functional ♦
Conveniently located, basic hotel not far from station, in area full of grocery stores. Some bedrooms are fairly functional; others have more interesting décor and furniture.

XXXX **Bagatelle** (Eyvind Hellstrøm)   `AK` `VISA` `OO` `AE` `OO`
$$ $$ Bygdøy Allé 3 ⊠ 0257 – 𝒞 22 12 14 40 – bagatelle@relaischateaux.com
– Fax 22 43 64 20 – www.bagatelle.no
– Closed July,1 week Christmas-New Year, 1 week Easter, Sunday and Bank
Holidays **A2**
Rest – (booking essential) (dinner only) Menu 850 NOK
– Carte 840/1030 NOK ⅛
Spec. Caesar salad with salmon. Crayfish tails with wild mushroom fricassee.
Grand dessert 'creation'.
 ◆ Contemporary ◆ Design ◆
Renowned restaurant with tasteful styling and engaging, professional service. Tra-
ditional menus are kept simple and flavours are sublime. 14 course 'Creation'
menu can be tailored.

XXX **Le Canard**   `🔥` `AK` `⇔` `P` `VISA` `OO` `AE` `OO`
$$ President Harbitz Gate 4 ⊠ 0259 – 𝒞 22 54 34 00 – lecanard@lecanard.no
– Fax 22 54 34 10 – www.lecanard.no
– Closed Easter, Christmas-New Year, 16-20 February, 3 weeks July, Sunday and
Bank Holidays **A2**
Rest – (dinner only) Menu 495/1145 NOK ⅛
Spec. Scallops with pumpkin gnocchi and sage. Duck with fig jam, salsify
and jus rôti. Apple terrine with brown butter ice cream and brioche.
 ◆ Inventive ◆ Intimate ◆
Vast villa with subtle contemporary styling and relaxed, intimate atmosphere.
Menus display classical, seasonal dishes and some well-judged modern interpreta-
tions; fine Norwegian produce.

XXX **Statholdergaarden** (Bent Stiansen)   `VISA` `OO` `AE` `OO`
$$ Rådhusgate 11, (entrance by Kirkegate) ⊠ 0151 – Ⓜ Stortinget
– 𝒞 22 41 88 00 – post@statholdergaarden.no – Fax 22 41 22 24
– www.statholdergaarden.no
– Closed 5-13 April, 1 and 21 May, 1 June, 12 July-3 August, 23 December-
3 January and Sunday **C2**
Rest Statholderens Krostue – see below
Rest – (booking essential) (dinner only) Menu 875 NOK – Carte 755/875 NOK ⅛
Spec. Scallops coated in capers with horseradish and parsley velouté. Lamb
with creamed rissoni and bell pepper sauce. Cloudberry soufflé with hazel-
nut ice cream.
 ◆ Traditional ◆ Formal ◆
Attractive 17C house in the heart of the city boasting chandeliers and superb 18C
stucco ceiling. Accomplished, flavoursome dishes arrive well presented and display
a contemporary edge.

XXX **Feinschmecker**   `AK` `⇔` `VISA` `OO` `AE` `OO`
$$ Balchensgate 5 ⊠ 0265 – 𝒞 22 12 93 80 – kontakt@feinschmecker.no
– Fax 22 12 93 88 – www.feinschmecker.no
– Closed Easter, 4 weeks Summer and Sunday **A2**
Rest – (dinner only) Menu 695 NOK – Carte 740/850 NOK ⅛
Spec. King scallops with Jerusalem artichokes. Roast suckling pig with apples
and mustard jus. Passion fruit charlotte with raspberries.
 ◆ Traditional ◆ Formal ◆
Well established restaurant in the suburbs, offering flexible set menus and an à la
carte. Unashamedly classical dishes use good ingredients in well-presented, fla-
voursome combinations.

XXX **Smak av Oro**   `AK` `⇔` `VISA` `OO` `AE` `OO`
$$ Tordenskioldsgate 6A ⊠ 0160 – Ⓜ Stortinget – 𝒞 23 01 02 40 – kontakt@
smakavororestaurant.no – Fax 23 01 02 48 – www.smakavorestaurant.no
– Closed Christmas-New Year, July and Sunday **C2**
Rest – (booking essential) (dinner only) Menu 570/590 NOK
Rest *Smak av Oro bar* – Menu 200/300 NOK – Carte 100/150 NOK
 ◆ International ◆ Trendy ◆
Elegant, modern designer décor in muted tones with an informal atmosphere.
Open-plan kitchen offers inventive cuisine with French influences. Booking a
must. Adjoining tapas bar with large counter displays cold and some warm dishes.

NORWAY - OSLO

NORWAY - OSLO

XX **Haga** (Terje Ness)   🛣 AC ⇔ VISA ⓪ AE ⓪
🕸
*Griniveien 315 (Baerum, Northwest: 11 km) – 𝒞 67157515 – post@
hagarestaurant.no – Fax 67 15 75 16 – www.hagarestaurant.no*
*– Closed Christmas-New Year, Easter and 12 July-4 August, Sunday and
Monday*
Rest – *(booking essential) (dinner only)* Menu 585 NOK 𝄢
Spec. Cod with black truffles. Roasted pigeon with sauce 'Marco Polo'. Pas-
sion fruit soufflé
  ♦ Inventive ♦ Design ♦
Angular glass building on a suburban golf course, with pleasant country views.
Classical French cooking is modern in style and presentation; daily changing
7 course menu can be tailored.

XX **Oscarsgate** (Bjorn Svensson)   AC VISA ⓪ AE ⓪
🕸
*Pilestredet 63 ✉ 0350 – 𝒞 22465906 – mail@restarantoscargate.no
– Fax 22 46 59 07 – www.restaurantoscargate.no*
– Closed July, Christmas-New Year, Sunday and Monday   **B1**
Rest – *(booking essential) (dinner only)* Menu 695 NOK
– Carte 740/1200 NOK 𝄢
Spec. Salmon with carpaccio and a coconut and lime sorbet. Reindeer with
foie gras, juniper berry and blackcurrant sauce. Apple yoghurt and lemon
curd with white chocolate Chiboust.
  ♦ Innovative ♦ Fashionable ♦
Small but popular restaurant just outside the city centre. À la carte offers Norwe-
gian, French and Italian influences; 8 course set menu boasts some innovative
combinations.

XX **Det Gamle Raadhus**   🛣 VISA ⓪ AE ⓪
*Nedre Slottsgate 1 ✉ 0157 – Ⓜ Stortinget – 𝒞 22 42 01 07 – gamle.raadhus@
gamle-raadhus.no – Fax 22 42 04 90 – www.gamle-raadhus.no*
– Closed Easter, 3 weeks July, 1 week Christmas, Saturday lunch and Sunday
Rest – Menu 425 NOK (dinner) – Carte 412/618 NOK   **C3**
  ♦ Traditional ♦ Rustic ♦
Well-run restaurant operating for over a century located in Oslo's original City Hall,
dating from 1641. Elegant rustic interior décor and English-style atmosphere in bar.

XX **Fjord**   AC VISA ⓪ AE ⓪
*Kristian Augusts gt. 11 ✉ 0164 – Ⓜ National Theatret – 𝒞 (0045) 22 98 21 50
– fjord@restauranteik.no – www.restaurantfjord.no*
– Closed Christmas-New Year, Monday (except December) and Sunday
Rest – *(dinner only)* Menu 375/495 NOK   **C2**
  ♦ Seafood ♦ Design ♦
Bold and quirky design, from blue glass walls to buffalo horns, atmospheric ligh-
ting and strikingly displayed wines. Seafood the speciality; dishes are quite elabo-
rate in content.

XX **Dinner**   AC VISA ⓪ AE ⓪
*Stortingsgata 22 ✉ 0161 – Ⓜ National Theatret – 𝒞 23 10 04 66 – dinner@
online.no – Fax 23 10 04 65 – www.dinner.no*
– Closed Christmas, Easter and Sunday lunch   **C2**
Rest – Menu 390 NOK (dinner) – Carte 358/766 NOK
  ♦ Chinese ♦ Design ♦
Smart restaurant with comfy sofas and plush banquettes, set on a central square
close to the National Theatre. Authentic Chinese cooking offers interesting Canto-
nese and Sichuan dishes.

XX **Nodee**   🛣 AC ⇔ VISA ⓪ AE ⓪
*Middelthunsgt 25 ✉ 0368 – Ⓜ Majorstuen – 𝒞 22 93 34 50 – nodee@
nodee.no – Fax 22 93 34 55 – www.nodee.no*
– Closed Christmas, Easter and Sunday lunch   **A1**
Rest – Menu 220/435 NOK – Carte 353/515 NOK
  ♦ Asian ♦ Fashionable ♦
Neat, modern restaurant with spacious pavement terrace, stylish lounge and all
day sushi bar. Light lunch. Choice of Japanese, Malaysian, Thai, Cantonese and
Sichuan dishes at dinner.

restauranteik – Clarion Collection H. Savoy   🄰🄲 🆅🅸🆂🅰 ⓒ🄰🄴 ⓞ

Universitetsgata 11 ⊠ 0164 – Ⓜ *National Theatret –* ℰ *22 36 07 10*
– eikefjord@restauranteik.no – Fax 22 36 07 11 – www.restauranteik.no
– Closed Easter, 4 weeks Summer, Christmas, Sunday and Monday
Rest *– (set menu only)(dinner only)* Menu 355 NOK   **C2**
♦ Contemporary ♦ Fashionable ♦
Restaurant in striking minimalist style; open-plan kitchen with chef's table. Good value set menu of 3 or 5 courses of interesting dishes.

Baltazar   🄰🄲 🆅🅸🆂🅰 ⓒ🄰🄴 ⓞ

Dronningensgt 27 ⊠ 0154 – Ⓜ *Jernbanetorget –* ℰ *23 35 70 60 – baltazar@*
baltazar.no – Fax 23 35 70 61 – www.baltazar.no
– Closed 6 July-10 August, Easter, Christmas, 17 May and Sunday
Rest *– (dinner only)* Menu 535 NOK 🍃   **C2**
Rest Enoteca *– (closed lunch 17 June-1 September and Sunday)* Carte 380/
540 NOK
♦ Italian ♦ Friendly ♦
Behind cathedral, under arcades of 1852 brick market. Serious Italian wine list; small à la carte or concise chef's menu: home-made pasta, fine Italian produce and local fish. The rustic décor of the wine bar is just right for an informal lunch.

Theatercaféen – at Continental Hotel   🆅🅸🆂🅰 ⓒ🄰🄴 ⓞ

Stortingsgaten 24-26 ⊠ 0117 – Ⓜ *National Theatret –* ℰ *22 82 40 50*
– theatercafeen@hotel-continental.no – Fax 22 41 20 94
– www.hotel-continental.no
– Closed 23 December - 2 January   **C2**
Rest *– (light lunch)* Carte 384/755 NOK
♦ Traditional ♦ Brasserie ♦
An institution in the city and the place to see and be seen. Elaborate lunchtime sandwiches make way for afternoon/evening brasserie specials.

Hos Thea   🆅🅸🆂🅰 ⓒ🄰🄴 ⓞ

Gabelsgate 11 ⊠ 0272 – ℰ *22 44 68 74 – post@hosthea.no – www.hosthea.no*
– Closed Easter, 24-26 December and 1 January   **A2**
Rest *– (dinner only)* Menu 435 NOK – Carte 390/555 NOK
♦ Italian influences ♦ Family ♦
Discreet black façade in residential area conceals this typical little restaurant fitted out with simple, Scandinavian-style décor. Appealing menu boasts Italian influences.

Brasserie France   🆅🅸🆂🅰 ⓒ🄰🄴 ⓞ

Øvre Slottsgate 16 ⊠ 0157 – Ⓜ *Stortinget –* ℰ *23 10 01 65 – bord@*
brasseriefrance.no – Fax 23 10 01 61 – www.brasseriefrance.no
– Closed Easter, 23 December-3 January   **C2**
Rest *– (dinner only and light lunch Saturday)* Menu 385 NOK – Carte 385/
495 NOK
♦ French ♦ Brasserie ♦
Set over 3 floors plus a dining cellar, with French brasserie-style on ground floor. Wall benches, bistro chairs and open kitchen. Interesting dishes from all areas of France.

Statholderens Krostue – at Statholdergaarden   🆅🅸🆂🅰 ⓒ🄰🄴 ⓞ

Rådhusgate 11, 1st floor ⊠ 0151 – Ⓜ *Stortinget –* ℰ *22 41 88 00 – post@*
statholdergaarden.no – Fax 22 41 22 24 – www.statholdergaarden.no
– Closed 5-13 April, 1 and 21 May, 1 June, 5 July-4 August, 23 December-
4 January, Sunday and Monday   **C2**
Rest – Menu 569 NOK (dinner) – Carte 510/560 NOK
♦ International ♦ Rustic ♦
Vaulted basement restaurant with bistro-style décor and warm candle-lit ambience. Each dish on the 10 course menu represents a nation. Unusually for Oslo, it also offers an à la carte.

NORWAY - OSLO

✗ **Lofoten Fiskerestaurant** ≤ 🏠 VISA ⓒⓞ AE ⓞ

Stranden 75 ✉ 0250 – ℰ 22 83 08 08 – lofoten@fiskerestaurant.no
– Fax 22 83 68 66 – www.lofoten-fiskerestaurant.no
– Closed 23 December-4 January **B3**
Rest – Menu 250/395 NOK – Carte 438/490 NOK
◆ Seafood ◆ Brasserie ◆
Attractive, modern fjord-side restaurant at Aker Brygge. Owner-chef offers a tempting array of seafood and shellfish. Ask for a table on the terrace so you can enjoy the view.

✗ **Alex Sushi** VISA ⓒⓞ AE ⓞ

Cort Adelers Gate 2 ✉ 0254 – ℰ 22 43 99 99 – alex@alexsushi.no
– Fax 22 43 99 98 – www.alexsushi.no
– Closed Christmas, New Year and Easter **B2**
Rest – (dinner only) Carte 390/725 NOK
◆ Japanese ◆ Design ◆
Swish Japanese restaurant features central oval sushi bar shaped like small boat with metallic roof. Dining room enlivened by modern art. Appealing tempura and miso dishes.

ENVIRONS OF OSLO

at Holmenkollen Northwest : 10 km by Bogstadveien, Sørkedalsveien and Holmenkollveien

🏨🏨🏨 **Holmenkollen Park** ⌂ ≤ ♨ 🌐 🛁 🔲 🕭 АС ⅙ rm 🛏 🍸 🕌 ℙ

Kongeveien 26 ✉ 0787 – ⓜ Holmenkollen ☕ VISA ⓒⓞ AE ⓞ
– ℰ 22 92 20 00 – holmenkollen.park.hotel.rica@rica.no – Fax 22 14 61 92
– www.holmenkollenparkhotel.no
– Closed 22 December-2 January
222 rm ☐ – ✝835/2275 NOK ✝✝1085/2525 NOK – 11 suites
Rest De Fem Stuer – (buffet lunch) Menu 565 NOK
Rest Galleriet – (Closed Saturday lunch and Sunday) (buffet lunch)
Menu 350 NOK
◆ Traditional ◆ Personalised ◆
Smart hotel near Olympic ski jump; superb views. Part built (1894) in old Norwegian "dragon style" decorated wood. Chalet-style rooms, some with balconies or views or saunas. Norwegian cuisine with global influences in De Fem Stuer. Informal Galleriet for a more popular menu.

at Oslo Airport Northeast : 45 km by E 6 at Gardermoen

🏨🏨 **Radisson SAS Airport** 🏠 ♨ 🌐 АС ⅙ 🛏 🍸 🕌 ℙ

✉ 2061 – ℰ 63 93 30 00 – sales.airport.oslo
@radissonsas.com – Fax 63 93 30 30 – www.gardermoen.radissonsas.com
503 rm ☐ – ✝2095/2295 NOK ✝✝2395/2595 NOK **Rest** – Carte 380/545 NOK
◆ Business ◆ Modern ◆
Ultra-contemporary business hotel on a semi-circular plan overlooking runway but well soundproofed. Rooms are a good size, well equipped and have varied décor. Modern restaurant offering a variety of international dishes to appeal to all comers.

🏨🏨 **Clarion Oslo Airport** ♨ 🌐 АС ⅙ rm 🛏 🍸 🕌 ℙ

(West : 6 km) ✉ 2060 – ℰ 63 94 94 94 – cl.oslo.airport VISA ⓒⓞ AE ⓞ
@choice.no – Fax 63 94 94 95 – www.clarionosloairport.no
358 rm ☐ – ✝1095/2095 NOK ✝✝1295/2295 NOK – 2 suites
Rest – (buffet lunch) Carte 415/480 NOK
◆ Business ◆ Functional ◆
Modern hotel with Norwegian design of wood and red tiles, a few minutes from airport by bus shuttle. Newly renovated rooms; elegant furnishings. Well equipped for conferences. Vast restaurant offers a standard range of international dishes to cater for all tastes.

POLAND
POLSKA

PROFILE

→ **AREA:**
312 677 km²
(120 725 sq mi).

→ **POPULATION:**
38 635 000
inhabitants (est.
2005), density =
124 per km².

→ **CAPITAL:**
Warsaw (conurbation
2 135 000
inhabitants).

→ **CURRENCY:**
Złoty (zl or PLN); rate
of exchange: PLN 1 =
€ 0.26 = US$ 0.33
(Dec 2008).

→ **GOVERNMENT:**
Parliamentary
republic (since 1990).
Member of European
Union since 2004.

→ **LANGUAGE:**
Polish.

→ **SPECIFIC PUBLIC
HOLIDAYS:**
National 3rd of May
Holiday, Corpus
Christi (9th Thursday
after Easter),
Independence Day
(11 November).

→ **LOCAL TIME:**
GMT + 1 hour in
winter and GMT +
2 hours in summer.

→ **CLIMATE:**
Temperate
continental with
cold winters and
warm summers
(Warsaw: January:
-2°C; July: 20°C).

→ **INTERNATIONAL
DIALLING CODE:**
00 48 followed
by the area code
and then the local
number. Directory
enquiries:
☎ 118 912.

→ **EMERGENCY:**
Ambulance: ☎ 999;
Fire Brigade: ☎ 998;
Police: ☎ 997;
Police from mobile:
☎ 112.

→ **ELECTRICITY:**
230V AC, 50Hz;
2 pin round-shaped
continental plugs.

→ **FORMALITIES**
Travellers from the

European Union
(EU), Switzerland,
Iceland and the main
countries of North
and South America
need a national
identity card or
passport (America:
passport required) to
visit Poland for less
than three months
(tourism or business
purpose). For visitors
from other countries
a visa may be
required, in addition
to a passport,
especially for those
wishing to stay for
longer than three
months. We advise
you to check with
your embassy before
travelling.

WARSAW
WARSZAWA

Population: 1 593 000 (conurbation 2 135 000) - Altitude: 106m.

Office National Polonais du Tourisme

When UNESCO added Warsaw to its World Heritage list a few years ago, it was a fitting seal of approval for an inspired refit and rebuild: eighty per cent of the city had been destroyed during World War II, with over half the city's population either killed or displaced. Using plans of the old city, architects painstakingly rebuilt the shattered Polish capital throughout the 1950s until it became an admirable mirror image of its former self. Strolling around the renovated Old Town, it's hard to believe that most of it is barely fifty years old.

The city still has its grey communist era apartment blocks, and these pall desperately when up against the old-style buildings with their pastel prettiness and aristocratic swagger, their architecture spanning a whole range of movements from Gothic to Baroque, Rococo to Secession. It's a vibrant place to be, and the locals are well known for their exuberance and warmth: chat briefly to a Varsovian at bar or bus stop and you'll soon be given a phone number and an invitation to meet up and share a vodka. Throw in the charming river views, superb parkland, and hearty cuisine now on offer, and you have a city confidently reclaiming its glories of old.

LIVING THE CITY

Warsaw sidles up along the left bank of the River Vistula; its opposite side, the district of **Praga**, is mostly marshy banks fronting a district of tower blocks. The main area for visitors is the **Old Town**, nestling against the river, which was established at the end of the thirteenth century around what is now the Royal Castle. A century later the **New Town**, to the north, began to take shape. To the south of Old Town runs 'The Royal Route', so named because from the late middle ages wealthy citizens built summer residences with lush gardens along these rural thoroughfares. Continue southwards and you're in Lazienki Park with its palaces and pavilions. To the west lie the more commercial areas of Marshal Street and Solidarity Avenue, once the commercial heart of the city. The northwest of Warsaw was traditionally the Jewish district, destroyed during World War II, and today redeveloped with housing estates and the sobering Monument to the Ghetto Heroes.

PRACTICAL INFORMATION

ARRIVAL-DEPARTURE

Warsaw Frederic Chopin Airport in Okecie is 10km from the city. Bus 179 or 188 will take you to the centre in 20 mins. Ensure you take a taxi from the rank outside arrivals.

TRANSPORT

Warsaw's metro is under development, and the best way to get about town is bus or tram (beyond the centre) or on foot for the central attractions.

Buy a pack of ten tickets for travelling on Warsaw's public transport system.

Most single tickets are bought from RUCH kiosks, but as these are often closed in evenings and at weekends, it's best to get them in a pack. A flat rate fare for all single journeys applies. One-day and family tickets are also available.

It's well worth buying a Warsaw Tourist Card. Available from tourist information offices, it entitles you to free travel on public transport, free admission to 21 museums, and discounts in some shops, restaurants and leisure centres.

EXPLORING WARSAW

Warsaw is one of the youngest capital cities of Europe. It only assumed the mantle in 1596, after the royal castle in Cracow was destroyed by fire. It's been destroyed twice since then: by the Swedes in 1655 and the Germans in 1944. Visitors today are taken aback at how superbly the centre was rebuilt, using old documents and plans. The Old Town (Stare Miasto) is a masterclass of **Baroque** style in a smart geometric grid of little streets, swarming with delighted onlookers in summer.

→ ROYAL FAMILIAR

The heartbeat of this quarter is **The Royal Castle**, the rebuild of which wasn't actually completed until 1988. It's now a museum and a focal point for formal ceremonies; it had once been the official residence of the Polish monarchs. Its interior is lavish, with many original furnishings and *objets d'art*: the Poles managed to hide many treasured statues and paintings from the Nazis. Check out the ballroom, Marble Room and Canaletto Room, each an opulent treat. Just north of Castle Square stands **Old Town Market Square**, which for centuries was the city's most important public meeting place. Here, everything from fairs to executions was carried out. The square's town hall was demolished nearly two hundred years ago, and its distinctive four sides are each named after parliamentarians of the eighteenth century; the houses grandly surrounding you were designed in the seventeenth. The Dekert side of the square is really worth discovering: all the houses are interconnected and form the Warsaw History Museum, which includes paintings, illustrations, archaeological finds, sculpture and photographs – a chronological odyssey through the city's troubled history. The cultural thrust of the square doesn't end here. On the Barss side stand two burghers' houses, a popular location for swarms of Varsovians, for this is the home of the Literature Museum, and in particular, first editions and original manuscripts of Poland's best-loved Romantic poet Adam Mickiewicz.

→ NATIONAL TREASURE

Warsaw's real cultural gem is **The National Museum**: travel due south from Old Town Market Square for a mile to find it. Founded in 1862 with just 36 paintings, the museum now holds a mesmerising 780,000 exhibits. But you shouldn't suffer too much cultural overload: many are only on show at special exhibitions. Nevertheless, you might well feel like a park break when you stumble from the National's hallowed portals. You're in luck. A few minutes' walk and you're in **Lazienki Park,** Warsaw's green jewel, a luscious, peacock-strewn wonderland of old palaces and an orangerie with an eighteenth century court theatre. There's a second theatre here, too, on an island with a moat separating the auditorium from the stage. And a neoclassical Temple based on ancient Greek design. Not forgetting the Chopin Monument, sculpted one hundred years ago (1908) depicting the great man sitting under a willow tree in search of inspiration. In summer, the park is packed with visitors to the lakeside Palace on the Water, one of the finest examples of neoclassical architecture in Poland. There's another glorious park with palaces further south in Wilanow: again this is a lovely place to visit, with a stunning Baroque Park hiding behind the palace and, fascinatingly, a poster museum in a former stable: it includes posters by Picasso, Warhol and Mucha.

→ GRAND TOUR

Warsaw has earned a reputation as a centre of cultural tourism thanks to numerous theatrical and musical venues. Top of the list is the grand sounding, grand looking...**Grand Theatre**, just south of Solidarity Avenue. Badly damaged during World War II, it was enlarged during reconstruction and its modern interiors have brought it bang up to date. This is where to go if you want to see top-class opera or ballet. Before going in, incidentally, you could stroll over to the nearby **Saxon Gardens**, Warsaw's first public park and another leafy oasis. Modelled on Versailles, it boasts statues, fountains, mature trees and, more sombrely, the Tomb of the Unknown Soldier, a constant reminder of the city's anguished 20C history. Mozart lovers, meanwhile, often make a beeline for the Philharmonic Hall, near prestigious Marshal Street, where his music is a well-established attraction. And the Royal Castle is a great place to go for Renaissance and Baroque music (but remember it's only on a Sunday!)

Going shopping in Warsaw, as you might imagine, is a rather different experience than it was in 1989. From famine to feast might be putting it a bit strongly, but you get the picture. An expanding number of department stores and shopping arcades have arrived in the centre of the city with the Marshal Street area being the hub. For many locals, though, markets are what this city is really all about. Muffled up against the wind and snow, doing business with a street trader is part and parcel of Warsaw life. And for market lovers there's only one place to go – the **'Russian Market'**, across the river, in the Praga district. Quite simply, it's Europe's largest open-air market, a daily hotch-potch on a massive scale, the home of thousands of traders from Russia (hence the name) to the sub-Sahara, hawking everything from mobiles to counterfeit clothes, hunting knives to rifles. It encircles a vast disused stadium, and as you get off the number 12 tram, there are stalls as far as the eye can see. A bizarre bazaar, the like of which you won't have encountered before.

→ MOVING MEMORIALS

In the northwest of the city there are a lot of memorials: they tell the sombre story, in small part, of the many thousands of Jews who lived here before 1939, and who were murdered during World War II. One of the most affecting is the Monument to the Ghetto Heroes in **Zamenhofa**. It was erected in 1948, when the city was still in ruins, and powerfully commemorates the Ghetto Uprising of 1943, with men, women and children surrounded by the burning ghetto. Other monuments in the area include the **Umschlagplatz** Monument, to denote an old railway siding where Jews were sent to concentration camps, and the Monument to 300 Victims, a small 'funeral pyre' at the location where the remains of 300 Jews and Poles were unearthed during building works. Both the last two monuments were completed just twenty years ago.

CALENDAR HIGHLIGHTS

Warsaw's a hot spot for events, particularly in spring and autumn when the weather's at neither extreme. On Easter Monday, the first public holiday of the year, don't be surprised if you get doused, or at least sprinkled, with water by a total stranger. Amid much jollity, this has become something

WARSAW IN...

→ ONE DAY
Royal Castle, Warsaw History Museum, National Museum, Lazienki Park

→ TWO DAYS
Russian Market, Monument to the Ghetto Heroes, Saxon Gardens, top-class concert at Grand Theatre or Philharmonic Hall

→ THREE DAYS
The Royal Route, Marshal Street, Solidarity Avenue, Wilanow

of an institution for Varsovians. Also around this time is the Drowning of Marzanna, symbolizing the death of winter, when children throw a raggy doll into the Vistula (don't worry, they don't pick on visitors). In May, the cultural season really gets under way: there's an International Book Fair at the Palace of Culture and Science, while the Festival of Latin American Culture lasts a week and displays art from all over that continent. Also in June is the International Street Arts Festival, which literally brings art to the streets, plus the tunnels, bus and tram stops, and subway stations of Warsaw. Music plays a special place in Varsovians' lives – Chopin, their favourite son, is celebrated in concerts on Sunday afternoons in June in Lazienki Park, while the Chopin International Piano Competition, held every five years in October, is one of the most important in the world, and only music by Chopin is performed. Another summer favourite, meanwhile, is the Mozart Festival, where all of his operas are performed. Or you can mosey on over to the Royal Castle courtyard in July and August, where you'll join forty thousand others for the Musical Gardens festival, featuring films depicting opera, ballet and art. As the leaves turn to rich autumnal tones, Warsaw hosts a plethora of fine festivals, including Warsaw Autumn (September) featuring top composers from around the world, the Film Festival (October) which blends new and classic movies in cinemas around the city, and, also that month, the Jazz Jamboree, one of Europe's most prestigious, celebrating its fiftieth year in 2008.

EATING OUT

There's an old Polish proverb that says: "Eat, drink and loosen your belt." It rather lost its edge during the communist era, but in the near twenty years since democracy returned, the quality and quantity of Warsaw's restaurants has moved unerringly northwards. New venues seem to open weekly, and long gone are the days when a waiter would tell the hapless diner that none of the items on the menu were actually available. A visitor arriving for the first time since 1989 would be astonished at the proliferation of eateries, everything from veggie to Vietnamese, with fast food joints on most corners, as well as stalls selling falafel and noodles. A large Italian business community has encouraged a boom in the amount of good Italian restaurants. Asian food is also well represented, with Japanese restaurants particularly plentiful. What about Polish food? The centuries-old traditional cuisine of Warsaw was influenced by neighbouring countries, such as Russia, Ukraine and Germany, while Jewish dishes were also added to the mix. Time-honoured classics, such as the ubiquitous pierogi (turnovers with various fillings) and assorted pork dishes, have been updated with flair by Poland's finest chefs. Accompanied, of course, by Polish vodka, which covers a bewildering range of styles and brands, but tastes like no other vodka on earth: it has a distinct character, and should be served chilled. A good number of restaurants and cafés in central Warsaw provide stylised settings, such as a burgher's house, vaulted cellar, or Secessionist sophistication. Wherever you eat, check that VAT has been included with prices (it's not always) and add ten per cent for a tip, which is customary.

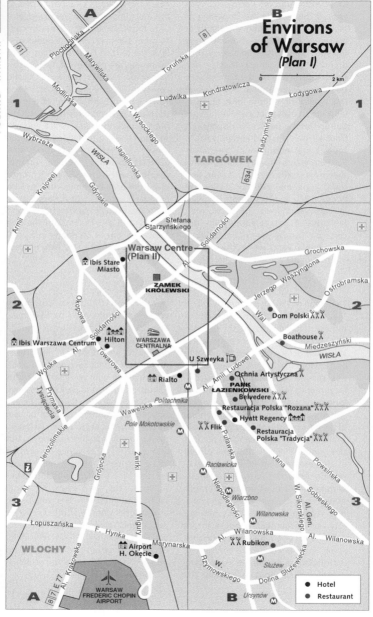

Environs
of Warsaw
(Plan I)

0   2 km

TARGÓWEK

Stefana
Starzyńskiego

**Warsaw Centre
(Plan II)**

**ZAMEK
KRÓLEWSKI**

Ibis Stare
Miasto

Dom Polski ✗✗✗

Ibis Warszawa Centrum

Hilton

**WARSZAWA
CENTRALNA**

Boathouse ✗

U Szweyka

Rialto

Ochnia Artystyczna ✗

**PARK
ŁAZIENKOWSKI**

Belvedere ✗✗

Restauracja Polska "Rozana" ✗✗✗

Hyatt Regency

✗✗ Flik

Restauracja
Polska "Tradycja" ✗✗✗

Racławicka

Wierzbno

Wilanowo

Wilanowska

Łopuszańska

WŁOCHY

Airport
H. Okęcie

Marynarska

✗✗ Rubikon

Służew

Dolina Służewiecka

Ursynów

**WARSAW
FREDERIC CHOPIN
AIRPORT**

● Hotel
● Restaurant

662

POLAND - WARSAW

Intercontinental ← ⅃ⅉ ⊕ ☵ ☒ ⅋ ㏎ ⅌ rm 🆒 ⅋ ⅃ ⊿

Ul. Emilii Plater 49 ⊠ *00 125 –* **Ⓜ** *Centrum* 🆅🅸🅂🅰 ⓪⓪ 🅰🅴 ⓪
– 𝒞 (022) 328 88 88 – warsaw@ihg.com – Fax (022) 328 88 89
– www.warsaw.intercontinental.com **C2**
328 rm ⊑ – 📍480/600 PLN 📍📍600/800 PLN – 76 suites
Rest *Frida* – Carte 110/350 PLN
Rest *Downtown* – *(buffet dinner)* Carte lunch 42/84 PLN
♦ Grand Luxury ♦ Business ♦ Modern ♦

Striking high-rise hotel with large atrium. Modern bedrooms are spacious and well-equipped; some boast beautiful views. Smart, state-of-the-art wellness centre. Brasserie-style Frida is famous for its steaks; Downtown offers an international menu.

Le Meridien Bristol ⌂ ⅃ⅉ ☵ ☒ ⅋ ㏎ ⅌ rm 🆒 ⅋ ⅃

Krakowskie Przedmieście 42-44 ⊠ *00 325* 🆅🅸🅂🅰 ⓪⓪ 🅰🅴 ⓪
– **Ⓜ** *Świętokrzyska – 𝒞 (022) 551 10 00 – bristol@lemeridien.com*
– Fax (022) 625 25 77 – www.lemeridien.com/warsaw **D1**
169 rm – 📍490/680 PLN 📍📍490/680 PLN, ⊑ 110 PLN – 36 suites
Rest *Marconi* – 𝒞 *(022) 551 11 832* – Menu 75/99 PLN – Carte 84/179 PLN
Rest *Malinowa* – 𝒞 *(022) 55 11 832 (Closed Sunday and Monday) (dinner only)* Menu 125 PLN – Carte 117/235 PLN
♦ Grand Luxury ♦ Classic ♦

Established hotel close to the old town, with classical 19C façade and art nouveau styling. Spacious, elegant bedrooms, some with views of the Presidential Palace. Small fitness/relaxation centre. Modern Italian cuisine in Marconi, contemporary Polish dishes in Malinowa.

Hyatt Regency ← ⌂ ⅃ⅉ ⊕ ☵ ☒ ⅋ ㏎ ⅌ rm 🆒 ⅋ ⅃ 🅿 ⊿

Belwederska Ave 23 ⊠ *00 761 – 𝒞 (022) 558 12 34*
– warsaw.regency@hyatt.com – Fax (022) 558 12 35 🆅🅸🅂🅰 ⓪⓪ 🅰🅴 ⓪
– www.warsaw.regency.hyatt.com *Plan I* **B3**
231 rm – 📍905/959 PLN 📍📍996 PLN, ⊑ 77 PLN – 19 suites
Rest *Venti Tre* – 𝒞 *(022) 558 10 94* – Carte 107/179 PLN
Rest *Q Club* – 𝒞 *(022) 558 1054 (Closed Saturday and Sunday) (dinner only)* Carte 109/158 PLN
♦ Luxury ♦ Business ♦ Modern ♦

Imposing glass-fronted hotel near Lazienski Park. Spacious, modern bedrooms – some with park and skyline views – furnished in an Italian style; luxury bathrooms. Excellent sports/wellness facilities. Italian cuisine served in Venti Tre and on its summer terrace; contemporary Asian fare in Q Club.

The Westin ← ⅃ⅉ ☵ & ㏎ ⅌ rm 🆒 ⅋ ⅃ ⊿ 🆅🅸🅂🅰 ⓪⓪ 🅰🅴 ⓪

Al. Jana Pawła II 21 ⊠ *00 854 –* **Ⓜ** *Świętokrzyska – 𝒞 (022) 450 80 00*
– warsaw@westin.com – Fax (022) 450 81 11 – www.westin.com/warsaw
348 rm – 📍691/901 PLN 📍📍691/901 PLN, ⊑ 111 PLN – 13 suites **C2**
Rest *Fusion* – Carte 101/260 PLN
♦ Luxury ♦ Business ♦ Modern ♦

Two glass towers joined by a huge glazed tube with high-speed, panoramic lifts. Modern bedrooms boast huge windows and many have pleasant skyline outlooks. Smart executive lounge with views. International cuisine in Fusion.

Hilton ← ⅃ⅉ ⊕ ☵ & ㏎ ⅌ 🆒 ⅋ ⅃ ⊿ 🆅🅸🅂🅰 ⓪⓪ 🅰🅴 ⓪

Grzybowska 63 ⊠ *00-844 – 𝒞 (022) 356 55 55 – info.warsaw@hilton.com*
– Fax (022) 356 55 56 – www.hilton.com *Plan I* **A2**
314 rm – 📍475/1100 PLN 📍📍475/1100 PLN, ⊑ 100 PLN – 11 suites
Rest *Meza* – Carte 125/210 PLN
♦ Business ♦ Modern ♦

Contemporary hotel with well-equipped modern bedrooms, smart executive lounge, huge fitness centre and fantastic views. Vast atrium houses shops and a lounge bar. Conference centre is the biggest in Poland. Brasserie-style Meza offers international cuisine.

Sheraton

🖺 🏠 🕭 🔀 AC 🦽 rm 🖭 ⅏ 🖾 🚗 VISA ◑ AE ①

Ul. B. Prusa 2 ⊠ 00493 – 🅜 *Centrum* – 𝒞 *(022) 450 61 00* – *warsaw@
sheraton.com* – *Fax (022) 450 62 00* – *www.sheraton.com/warsaw*
350 rm – 🛏782 PLN 🛏🛏782 PLN, � 99 PLN   **D2**
Rest *The Oriental* – 𝒞 *(022) 450 67 05 (Closed lunch Monday and Saturday,
and Sunday dinner)* Carte 124/208 PLN
Rest *Olive* – *(buffet lunch)* Carte 147/199 PLN
◆ Luxury ◆ Business ◆ Classic ◆

Classical hotel set on a large square, close to a smart shopping street. Spacious
bedrooms display a classic-contemporary style. The hotel is in the process of
being modernised. Olive offers a buffet lunch and international/Mediterranean
dishes; Oriental provides Asian fare, mainly Thai.

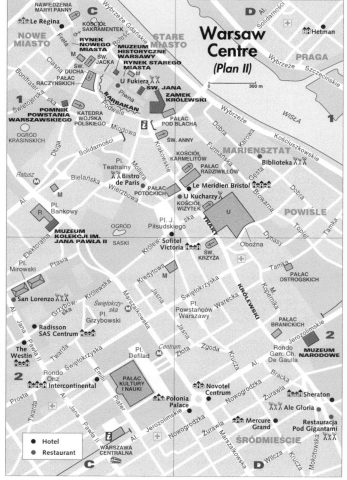

POLAND - WARSAW

Sofitel Victoria
🏨🏨🏨 🕸 🖥 🕭 🔟 🎧 rm 🖼 📞 🔧 🅿 🚁 VISA ⓿ 🅰🅴 ⓪

Ul. Krŏlewska 11 ✉ *00 065* – Ⓜ *Świętokrzyska* – ☏ *(022) 657 80 11*
– sof.victoria@orbis.pl – Fax (022) 657 80 57 – www.sofitel.com   **C1-2**
290 rm – ♦385/770 PLN ♦♦385/770 PLN, ⌘ 88 PLN – 53 suites
Rest *Canaletto* – Menu 70/100 PLN – Carte 110/160 PLN
♦ Business ♦ Classic ♦

Large corporate hotel by Saski gardens; a popular choice for conferences. Spacious lobby with coffee bar and meeting rooms. Modernisation currently underway: new pool, relaxation and fitness facilities being built. Mix of Polish and European dishes in Canaletto.

Polonia Palace
🏨🏨🏨 🖫 🕸 🕭 🔟 🎧 rm 🖼 📞 🔧 VISA ⓿ 🅰🅴 ⓪

Al. Jerozolimskie 45 ✉ *00 692* – Ⓜ *Centrum* – ☏ *(022) 318 2800*
– poloniapalace@syrena.com.pl – Fax (022) 318 28 89 – www.poloniapalace.com
206 rm – ♦268/901 PLN ♦♦268/901 PLN, ⌘ 69 PLN – 3 suites   **D2**
Rest *Strauss* – Carte 73/175 PLN
♦ Business ♦ Classic ♦

Set in the heart of town and boasting an early 20C façade, marble staircases and a magnificent ballroom; one of the few buildings of its kind to have survived. Well-maintained bedrooms display modern facilities; fantastic top floor suite. Strauss serves Polish and international cuisine.

Radisson SAS Centrum
🏨🏨🏨 🖫 🕸 🖥 🕭 🔟 🎧 rm 🖼 📞 🔧 🚁

Grzybowska 24 ✉ *00 132* – Ⓜ *Świętokrzyska*   VISA ⓿ 🅰🅴 ⓪
– ☏ (022) 321 88 88 – reservations.warsaw@radissonsas.com
– Fax (022) 321 88 89 – www.warsaw.radissonsas.com   **C2**
292 rm – ♦440/1482 PLN ♦♦440/1482 PLN, ⌘ 95 PLN – 19 suites
Rest *Latino Brasserie at Ferdy's* – ☏ *(022) 321 88 22* – Menu 79 PLN (lunch)
– Carte 80/150 PLN
♦ Business ♦ Modern ♦

Modern, corporate hotel set in the business district, close to the central park. Check-in 'islands' in the lobby and three choices of bedroom: Italian, Scandinavian or Maritime. Brasserie-style restaurant with South American influences.

Le Régina
🏨🏨🏨 🚿 🕸 🕭 🔟 🎧 rm 🖼 📞 🔧 🚁 VISA ⓿ 🅰🅴 ⓪

U. Kościelna 12 ✉ *00 218* – Ⓜ *Ratusz* – ☏ *(022) 531 60 00*
– info@leregina.com – Fax (022) 531 60 01 – www.leregina.com   **C1**
59 rm – ♦1194/1849 PLN ♦♦1194/1849 PLN, ⌘ 78 PLN – 2 suites
Rest *La Rotisserie* – Menu 120/224 PLN – Carte 183/231 PLN
♦ Luxury ♦ Design ♦

Set outside the city walls in a quiet, old town street; a boutique hotel hidden behind a classical façade. Bedrooms, ranging in size, display modern furnishings and smart bathrooms. Intimate restaurant offers classical à la carte and contemporary set menus.

Mercure Grand
🏨🏨🏨 🖫 🕸 🕭 🔟 🎧 rm 🖼 📞 🔧 🅿 🚁 VISA ⓿ 🅰🅴 ⓪

Ul. Krucza 28 ✉ *00-522* – ☏ *(022) 583 21 00*
– h3384@accor.com – Fax (022) 583 21 21 – www.orbisonline.pl   **D2**
293 rm – ♦850/920 PLN ♦♦990 PLN, ⌘ 70 PLN – 6 suites
Rest *Grand's Brasserie* – ☏ *(022) 583 21 32* – Menu 65 PLN (lunch)
– Carte 125/200 PLN
♦ Business ♦ Modern ♦

Set on a wide avenue close to the city centre; formerly the meeting place of the Olympic Games Committee. Modern bedrooms boast smart bathrooms; spacious corner rooms are luxury level or suites. Brasserie-style restaurant serves Polish dishes with a European touch.

Rialto
🏨🏨 🖫 🕸 🕭 🔟 🎧 rm 🖼 📞 🔧 🅿 VISA ⓿ 🅰🅴 ⓪

Ul. Wilcza 73 ✉ *00 670* – Ⓜ *Politechnika* – ☏ *(022) 584 87 00*
– reservation@hotelrialto.com.pl – Fax (022) 584 87 01
– www.hotelrialto.com.pl   *Plan I* **A2**
33 rm – ♦690/926 PLN ♦♦807/926 PLN, ⌘ 98 PLN – 11 suites
Rest – Menu 98 PLN (lunch) – Carte 120/182 PLN
♦ Business ♦ Art Deco ♦

Boutique hotel with art nouveau features, set south of the city centre by the University and Constitution Square. Bedrooms boast DVD players and high-speed internet access. Restaurant serves contemporary Polish cuisine.

POLAND - WARSAW

Novotel Centrum ← 🏋 🕉 🛦 🕅 ↳ rm 📺 📞 🟥 VISA ⚫ AE

Ul. Marszalkowska 94/98 ✉ *00 510 –* **🅜** *Centrum –* ☏ *(022) 621 02 71*
– rez.nov.warszawa@orbis.pl – Fax (022) 625 04 76 – www.accor.com
730 rm ☁ *–* 🛉306/547 PLN 🛉🛉306/547 PLN – 10 suites **D2**
Rest *Essencia* – Carte 85/117 PLN
   ◆ Business ◆ Functional ◆

Set on a busy crossroads, a white high-rise hotel that dominates the city centre and boasts the largest number of bedrooms in the city. Colourful lobby leads to 4 floors of conference rooms. International cuisine and vibrant bar and lounge.

Hetman 🕉 ↳ rm 📺 🟥 🛦 🚗 VISA ⚫ AE ⓪

Klopotowskiego 36 ✉ *03 717 –* ☏ *(022) 511 98 00 – rez@hotelhetman.pl*
– Fax (022) 618 51 39 – www.hotelhetman.pl **D1**
68 rm ☁ *–* 🛉360/380 PLN 🛉🛉430 PLN   **Rest** – Carte 65/76 PLN
   ◆ Business ◆ Functional ◆

Accessed via a bridge over the river, a modern hotel in converted 19C apartment block, just a short walk from the old town and city centre. Spacious, well-kept bedrooms display good bathrooms. Small restaurant serves international cuisine.

Ibis Warszawa Centrum 🕉 🕅 ↳ rm 📺 🟥 🛦 🚗 VISA ⚫ AE

Al. Solidarności 165 ✉ *00 876 –* ☏ *(022) 520 30 00 – h2894@accor.com*
– Fax (022) 520 30 30 – www.ibishotel.com Plan I **A2**
189 rm *–* 🛉209/329 PLN 🛉🛉209/329 PLN, ☁ 29 PLN
Rest – Menu 51 PLN – Carte 65/134 PLN
   ◆ Chain hotel ◆ Functional ◆

Functional hotel set on a big avenue outside the city centre; popular with business-people. Modern bedrooms boast wooden floors, open wardrobes, flat screen TVs and free wi-fi. Café-style French bistro serves international and a few Polish dishes.

Ibis Stare Miasto 🕉 🕅 ↳ rm 📺 🟥 🛦 🚗 VISA ⚫ AE

Ul. Muranowska 2 ✉ *00 209 –* ☏ *(022) 310 10 00 – h3714@accor.com*
– Fax (022) 310 10 10 – www.ibishotel.com Plan I **A2**
333 rm *–* 🛉289/339 PLN 🛉🛉289/339 PLN, ☁ 33 PLN
Rest – Menu 51 PLN – Carte 65/134 PLN
   ◆ Chain hotel ◆ Functional ◆

Set near the old town and close to the football stadium, a chain hotel with 24hr bar and business centre. Clean, simple bedrooms; 6th floor are most spacious and have balconies. French bistro-style restaurant serves international dishes and a few Polish offerings.

🍴🍴🍴🍴 Pod Gigantami 🕅 ⇄ VISA ⚫ AE

Al. Ujazdowskie 24 ✉ *00 478 –* **🅜** *Centrum –* ☏ *(022) 629 23 12*
– podgigantami@zapart.pl – Fax (022) 621 30 59 – www.podgigantami.pl
Rest – Carte 81/147 PLN **D2**
   ◆ Contemporary ◆ Formal ◆

Classical interior boasts marble fireplaces, historic parquetry and period chairs. Contemporary à la carte offers Polish and Mediterranean influences; they someti-mes cater for the Presidential Palace.

🍴🍴🍴 Polska "Tradycja" 🍴 🕅 ↳ ⇄ 🅿 VISA ⚫ AE ⓪

Belwederska Ave 18A ✉ *00 762 –* ☏ *(022) 840 09 01 – Fax (022) 840 09 50*
– www.restauracjatradycja.pl Plan I **B3**
Rest – *(booking essential)* Carte 64/130 PLN
   ◆ Traditional ◆ Family ◆

Villa with warm, homely dining areas spread over two floors and enclosed terrace to the rear. 'Summer' and 'Winter' menus present traditional, home-cooked Polish cuisine.

🍴🍴🍴 AleGloria 🕅 ↳ ⇄ VISA ⚫ AE ⓪

Pl. Trzech Krzyzy 3 ✉ *00 535 –* **🅜** *Centrum –* ☏ *(022) 584 70 80*
– alegloria@alegloria.pl – Fax (022) 584 70 81 – www.alegloria.pl
Rest – Carte 87/192 PLN **D2**
   ◆ Modern ◆ Design ◆

Set in the basement of an early 20C house, in what was once the stables. Modern Polish dishes use local ingredients that are prepared in a fresh, uncomplicated, contemporary manner.

XXX **Polska "Rozana"** 🛋 AC ᐧ⁄ᐧ ⟲ VISA ⊙ AE ①

Chocimska 7 ✉ 00 791 – ⓜ *Pole Mokotowskie –* 𝒞 *(022) 848 12 25*
– Fax (022) 848 15 90 – www.restauracjapolska.com.pl   *Plan I* **B3**
Rest *– (booking essential)* Carte 64/130 PLN
  ◆ Traditional ◆ Friendly ◆

Hidden in a quiet street, this spacious restaurant boasts four dining rooms over 2 levels and a splendid rear terrace. Traditional, home-cooked Polish dishes displayed on 'Summer' and 'Winter' menus.

XXX **Belvedere** ⇐ 🍸 🛋 AC ⟲ P VISA ⊙ AE ①

Ul. Agrykoli 1 (entry from Parkowa St) ✉ 00 460 – 𝒞 *(022) 841 22 50*
– restauracja@belvedere.com.pl – Fax (022) 841 71 35 – www.belvedere.com.pl
– Closed 24 December-6 January   *Plan I* **B2**
Rest *– (booking essential)* Carte 101/205 PLN
  ◆ International ◆ Formal ◆

Large 19C orangery with pleasant summer terrace, set in Lazienki Park. Tables are hidden amongst foliage and trailing plants; intimate atmosphere at night. Polish and international cuisine.

XXX **San Lorenzo** 🛋 AC VISA ⊙ AE ①

AL. Jana Pawla II 36 (1st floor) ✉ 00-141 – 𝒞 *(022) 652 16 16*
– sanlorenzo@sanlorenzo.pl – www.sanlorenzo.pl   **C2**
Rest *–* Carte 125/200 PLN
  ◆ Italian ◆ Formal ◆

Large classical building with veranda, set near the business centre. Ground floor bistro with marble tables; elegant 1st floor restaurant. Italian cooking. Be sure to order the tasty bread.

XXX **Michel Moran - Bistro de Paris** AC ⟲ VISA ⊙ AE ①

Pl. Piłsudskiego 9 ✉ 00-073 – ⓜ *Ratusz –* 𝒞 *(022) 826 01 07*
– michelmoran@02.pl – Fax (022) 827 08 08 – www.restaurantbistrodeparis.com
– Closed Sunday and Bank Holidays   **C1**
Rest *–* Menu 65 PLN (lunch) *–* Carte 121/178 PLN
  ◆ French ◆ Elegant ◆

Set in the old opera house close to the park and displaying modern-retro styling. Large central counter with glass-separated mezzanine levels and two intimate inner rooms. Classical French cuisine.

XXX **Biblioteka** AC VISA ⊙ AE ①

Ul. Dobra 56/66 – 𝒞 *(022) 552 71 95 – biblioteka@hotel.com.pl*
– www.biblioteka.hotel.com.pl
– Closed 24 December, Easter, 1-3 May and Sunday   **D1**
Rest *–* Carte 113/143 PLN   **Rest** *Presto –* Carte 60/150 PLN
  ◆ Italian ◆ Formal ◆

Contemporary restaurant in the University library, with roof top garden and river views. Spacious loft-style room with well-spaced tables and leather seating. Italian menu with French influences.

XX **Dom Polski** 🛋 AC ᐧ⁄ᐧ ⟲ VISA ⊙ AE ①

Ul. Francuska 11 ✉ 03 906 – 𝒞 *(022) 616 24 32 – restauracjadompolski@wp.pl*
– Fax (022) 616 24 88 – www.restauracjadompolski.pl   *Plan I* **B2**
Rest *–* Carte 61/169 PLN
  ◆ Traditional ◆ Friendly ◆

Spacious restaurant with rear terrace, set on a wide avenue on the west bank of the River Wisla. Five rooms are arranged over 2 floors; intimate atmosphere. Traditional Polish cuisine.

XX **Rubikon** 🛋 AC ᐧ⁄ᐧ ⟲ VISA ⊙ AE ①

Ul. Wróbla 3/5 ✉ 02 736 – ⓜ *Słuzew –* 𝒞 *(022) 847 66 55*
– info@rubikon.waw.pl – www.rubikon.waw.pl   *Plan I* **B3**
Rest *–* Menu 90 PLN (dinner)/155 PLN *–* Carte 94/144 PLN
  ◆ Italian ◆ Neighbourhood ◆

Large, white, columned villa, with several rooms set over 2 levels, a canopy-covered garden terrace and a 1st floor balcony. Italian menu has been adapted to suit Polish tastes.

POLAND - WARSAW

POLAND - WARSAW

XX   **U Fukiera**   🛜 ⤄ ⟳ 𝗩𝗜𝗦𝗔 ⦿⦿ 𝗔𝗘 ⓪

Rynek Starego Miasta 27 ✉ *00 272* – **Ⓜ** *Ratusz* – 𝒞 *(022) 831 10 13*
– fukier@tlen.pl – Fax (022) 831 58 08 – www.ufukiera.pl – Closed 24-25 and 31 December
Rest – Carte 101/200 PLN   **C1**
   ◆ Traditional ◆ Rustic ◆

Set in an ancient market square in the old town, with a beautiful façade and rear
courtyard. Three rooms boast painted ceilings and historical pictures; 17C vaulted
cellar. Traditional Polish cuisine.

XX   **Flik**   🛜 𝗔𝗖 𝗩𝗜𝗦𝗔 ⦿⦿ 𝗔𝗘 ⓪

Ul. Puławska 43 ✉ *02 508* – **Ⓜ** *Pole Mokotowskie* – 𝒞 *(022) 849 44 34*
– restauracja@flik.com.pl – Fax (022) 849 44 06 – www.flik.com.pl
Rest – Menu 69/75 PLN – Carte 58/89 PLN   *Plan I* **B3**
   ◆ Traditional ◆ Neighbourhood ◆

Contemporary neighbourhood restaurant set near the park, with modern Polish
art adorning the walls and tent-covered garden terrace. All-afternoon buffet
lunch; à la carte dinner.

X   **Boathouse**   🛜 𝗔𝗖 ⤄ ⟳ 𝗣 𝗩𝗜𝗦𝗔 ⦿⦿ 𝗔𝗘 ⓪

Wat Miedzeszynski 389a ✉ *03-975* – 𝒞 *(022) 616 32 23* – *boathouse@boathouse.pl*
– Fax (022) 616 33 32 – www.boathouse.pl – Closed 29-31 December
Rest – Carte 121/212 PLN 🍷   *Plan I* **B2**
   ◆ Italian ◆ Rustic ◆

Old wooden boathouse with garden terrace, set near a bridge on the west side of
the river. Ground floor wine bar; 1st floor restaurant with huge wooden tables.
Contemporary French and Italian cooking.

X   **Qchnia Artystyczna**   🛜 ⤄ 𝗩𝗜𝗦𝗔 ⦿⦿ 𝗔𝗘 ⓪

Al. Ujazdowskie 6 (Ujazdowski Castle) ✉ *00 461* – **Ⓜ** *Politechnika*
– 𝒞 (022) 625 76 27 – qchnia@qchnia.pl – Fax (022) 625 76 27 – www.qchnia.pl
– Closed 25 December and New Year – **Rest** *– Carte 60/100 PLN*   *Plan I* **B2**
   ◆ Modern ◆ Fashionable ◆

Simply furnished restaurant in Ujazdowski Castle – home to the Museum of
Modern Art – with a big terrace overlooking the city. Each course comes in 7 different styles – pick and choose between them.

X   **U Kucharzy**   𝗔𝗖 ⤄ ⟳ 𝗩𝗜𝗦𝗔 𝗔𝗘 ⓪
😊

Ul. Ossolinskich 7 ✉ *00-087* – 𝒞 *(022) 826 79 36* – *reserwacje@gessler.pl*
– Fax (022) 826 79 36 – www.gessler.pl   **D1**
Rest *– (booking essential) (open until midnight)* Menu 30/100 PLN – Carte 81/126 PLN
   ◆ Polish ◆ Neighbourhood ◆

Set in an old 19C hotel, where the former hotel kitchen defines the space, creating
seven different areas. Concise, twice daily-changing menu uses organic produce
sourced from within 50km.

🍴   **U Szwejka**   🛜 𝗔𝗖 ⤄ ⟳ 𝗩𝗜𝗦𝗔 ⦿⦿ 𝗔𝗘

Pl. Konstytucji 1 ✉ *00-647* – 𝒞 *(022) 339 17 10* – *restauracja@uszwejka.pl*
– Fax (022) 621 87 55 – www.uszwejka.pl   *Plan I* **B2**
Rest – Carte 46 PLN
   ◆ Polish ◆ Pub ◆

Pleasant pub with spacious cellar and heated terrace. Menu is supplemented by
seasonal specials, which are described by staff in Polish costumes. Owner seeks
out small, local producers.

at Warsaw Frederick Chopin Airport Southwest : 10 km by Zwirki i Wigury

🏨   **Airport H. Okęcie**   ⛲ ☾ 🍴 ♿ 𝗔𝗖 ⤄ rm ☎ 📞 🧖 𝗣 🚗

Ul. 17 Stycznia 24 ✉ *02 146* – 𝒞 *(022) 456 80 00*   𝗩𝗜𝗦𝗔 ⦿⦿ 𝗔𝗘 ⓪
– reservation@airporthotel.pl – Fax (022) 456 80 29 – www.airporthotel.pl
158 rm 🛏 – 📞342/638 PLN 📞📞342/638 PLN – 7 suites   **A3**
Rest *Mirage* *– (buffet lunch)* Carte 93/145 PLN
   ◆ Business ◆ Classic ◆

Set 800m from the airport, with a shuttle running from 5-1am. Mainly standard rooms, with
one suite on each floor. 400 person conference centre for business; tennis court for pleasure. Snacks served in the lobby bar or Polish and international cuisine in the restaurant.

CRACOW
KRAKÓW

Population: 760 000 (conurbation 1 500000) - Altitude: 219m

R. Mauritius/PHOTONONSTOP

Cracow has often been referred to as the 'new Prague', which is both good and bad news for the locals. They don't want the stag-party brigade who've recently been latching on to Poland's third biggest city as the place to go for cheap vodka. But they do want visitors who'll appreciate the superb cultural atmosphere and artistic treasures which abound here. Not for nothing was Cracow included in the very first UNESCO World Heritage List.

Unlike much of Poland, this beautiful old city - the country's capital from the eleventh to the seventeenth centuries - was spared Second World War destruction because the German Governor had his HQ here. So Cracow is still able to boast a hugely imposing market square that was the biggest in medieval Europe, and a hill that's crowned with not just a castle, but a cathedral too. And not far away there's even a glorious chapel made of salt one hundred metres underground! It's a city famous for its links with Judaism and its visitor-friendly Royal Route, but also for its cultural inheritance. During the Renaissance, Cracow became a centre of new ideas that drew the most outstanding writers, thinkers and musicians of the day. It has literally thousands of architectural monuments and millions of artefacts collected and displayed in its museums and churches. But it's very much a modern city, too, with an eye on the twenty first century.

669

LIVING THE CITY

The heart and soul of Cracow is its **old quarter**, which received its charter in 1257. This area is dominated by the imposing **Market Square**, and almost completely encircled by the restful green embrace of the **Planty** gardens. A short way to the south, briefly interrupted by the curving streets of **Okol** neighbourhood, is **Wawel Hill**, the second major tourist destination of the city. Further south from here is the characterful Jewish quarter of **Kazimierz.** The smartly residential areas of **Piasek** and **Nowy Swiat** are to the west of the old quarter.

PRACTICAL INFORMATION

ARRIVAL-DEPARTURE

John Paul II International Airport-Balice is 13km west of the city centre. A taxi will cost around 65PLN and take 20min. There's a free shuttle to the train station which is located 200m from the terminal building ; trains to the centre take 15min. Bus 192 goes to the central Bus station.

TRANSPORT

The historic centre of the city is a largely pedestrian precinct, so getting about on foot here is a traffic-free pleasure. The streets in the old quarter are laid out in a grid pattern, which makes orientation even easier.

The public transport system in Cracow is made up of an extensive network of buses and trams (there's no metro here). You can use your tickets on both bus or tram, and there are four different types available: timed (valid for one hour from the moment of punching), daily (from punching till midnight), weekly and family. Buy your tickets from MPK outlets or newspaper kiosks.

EXPLORING CRACOW

The sound of music has rasped out from Cracow's Market Square for centuries without a break. On the hour, every hour, for six hundred years a bugler has climbed one of the towers of **St Mary's Church**, and sounded a two-and-a-half minute bugle call across the square, day and night. It's just one of the quirks that gives this city its special appeal. The church itself, a Gothic basilica, is the proud owner of two towers, one taller than the other, making it the slightly uneven and easily distinguishable main landmark of Cracow. Inside, St Mary's is pretty impressive too, boasting Baroque and Renaissance finery (in the shape of the pulpit and the tombs), but most people who come here make for the **High Altar**, because this is the scene of daily theatre. At 11.45am, on the dot, a nun arrives and, in front of an expectant gallery, peels away the outer panels of Veit Stoss's 15C 39-ft. high, 36-ft long wood-carved polyptych. The inner cabinet is dazzling, a whole array of exquisite carvings tracing the death

Map showing area around KRAKÓW with locations: Olkusz, Słomniki, Trzebinia, Krzeszowice, Chrzanów, Kraków-Balice, Skawina, Zator, Niepołomice, Wieliczka, Wadowice, Kalwaria Zebrzydowska, Myślenice.

of Mary and her Assumption in a blaze of golden sunbeams. Catch it if you can: the whole 'show' only lasts ten minutes each day.

→ CLOTHED IN HISTORY

Another notable – and ancient – building on the Market Square is the **Cloth Hall**, which dates back to the days of the original charter. Naturally enough, it once dealt in the trade of cloth, but now plays host to a colourful parade of souvenir stalls. More interestingly, inside its much remodelled walls is the impressive **Gallery of 19th Century Polish Painting.** Outside, in the huge arena of the square, there are churches, palaces, town houses, eye-catching modern sculptures, a sprinkling of designer clothes stores, and a whole al fresco jumble (at least in summer) of café tables and chairs. Near the Cloth Hall is one of the city's most beautiful palaces, **Christopher Palace**, which boasts a spectacular arcaded courtyard to dazzle the eye. You actually get double the value here, because it's also home to the **Museum of Cracow**, a fascinating treasure trove of goodies dug up from the city's rich history.

→ WAWEL

Jostling Market Square in the fame stakes is Wawel Hill. It's attached to the old quarter by the umbilical cord that is **Gródzska Street**, a lovely old cobbled thoroughfare with varying styles of architecture that are a delight to stroll past. Medieval kings made Wawel the seat of their political power, and a royal residence was built here, overlooking the city below. It went through much chopping and changing before evolving into the castle you see today, sprawling nonchalantly across the hill, its mishmash of styles representing Poland's turbulent history. Various captors have given it a style makeover down the centuries: in Renaissance times it was one of the most thrilling royal residences in

Central Europe. Just to add more lustre, the 14C kings added a cathedral to the castle complex, and this is the final resting place of Poland's national heroes and royalty, making it the number one symbol of the country's statehood. There are beautifully carved tombs here, as well as important works of art, and the largest bell in Poland, weighing in at a mighty eleven tons.

→ KAZIMIERZ

The neighbourhood of Kazimierz is the most southerly quarter of Cracow. It feels like a different place, which isn't surprising because, until 1791, it was an independent town in its own right. It's a characterful area of narrow streets lined with low buildings, and has been a major centre of Jewish culture for over five hundred years. It's the ideal place to discover more about the story of the Jews in Poland and contains seven synagogues and a number of Jewish cemeteries. But it's also a magnet for Cracow's young, as many of the old buildings here have been reborn as cafés and bars. Steven Spielberg's epic drama *Schindler's List* was filmed around Kazimierz and the actors were regulars in the eating establishments around here, appreciating the blasts of live klezmer that periodically ring out from many of the neighbourhood's restaurants. Klezmer is Jewish folk music, and you'd have to have feet of clay for its infectious rhythms not to get you up and dancing.

→ SALT OF THE EARTH

The winters can get mighty cold in Cracow, and if you want to dive into a museum for cover, you'll find there are dozens hiding in all sorts of alleyways and corners. The main building of the **National Museum** takes some beating. A modern construction finished less than twenty years ago, it's west in Nowy Swiat. Suitably enough, it's full of 20C and contemporary Polish art; the Modernist section is a real stand out.

Meanwhile, back in the old quarter, the **Czartoryski Museum** is for lovers of Western art. There are works by the likes of Leonardo Da Vinci and Rembrandt on display in three houses which exude a warm and homely feel. As a complete contrast, head out on a bus to the **Wieliczka salt mine** for a truly one-off experience. The mine has been operating for over nine hundred years, and has two hundred miles of underground corridors. Down the years miners have carved out hundreds of statues, and the most awe-inspiring is the **Chapel of St Kinga**. It took three miners sixty seven years to eke out this masterpiece, which lies over a hundred metres underground, and is fifty four metres long and twelve metres high. Everything in the chapel is made from rock salt, from the statue of Christ on the cross to the chandeliers, and it all makes for a spectacular experience. Should you get hungry down there, you can go for a meal at the deepest underground restaurant in the world.

→ DIG THE PLANTY

Very much back on terra firma, don't forget a stroll around the Planty, the 'green belt' that embraces the old quarter. It replaced the medieval walls of the city early in the nineteenth century, and its gardens were landscaped to make the most of the superb vistas on offer. The Planty has always been a popular venue for strolling and socialising, and for the last twenty years it's been getting lots of tender loving care, courtesy of period fencing and street lamps that give it the look it once knew two hundred years ago.

→ OVERWHELMING VISIT

An hour's journey from Cracow is Auschwitz, now a UNESCO World Heritage site. The grounds and buildings are open to visitors as a museum and poignant memorial; many of the inhabitants of Kazimierz were sent here by the Nazis. Remember that Auschwitz can be an emotionally draining experience.

CALENDAR HIGHLIGHTS

Cracow can get so cold in the winter that it pretty much shuts down on the festival front (though it looks beautiful under a blanket of snow). Things pick up in the spring with the arrival of the first crocuses and the first visitors drawing up chairs at al fresco tables in the old quarter. Two events in June highlight the city's love of myths: The Lajkonik Festival recalls an age-old victory for the citizens of Cracow over Tartar invaders. A procession of musicians and merrymakers takes three hours to pass from the 12C Convent of St.Norbet to Market Square. Meanwhile, Wianki is based on a pagan festival, as wreaths of flowers are floated down

CRACOW IN...

→ **ONE DAY**
St Mary's Church, Cloth Hall, Wawel, main building of National Museum

→ **TWO DAYS**
Kazimierz, Czartoryski Museum, stroll round Planty

→ **THREE DAYS**
Trip either to Auschwitz or Wieliczka salt mine

the Vistula river, lit by huge bonfires as midsummer is celebrated to the sound of music and fireworks. The Kazimierz neighbourhood comes under the spotlight for the Cracow Jewish Culture Festival (June/July) when the quarter's lively streets, with their synagogues, cafés and pubs, celebrate Yiddish traditions with a whole range of concerts and recitals. The infectious sound of klezmer is a highlight. A month later, many of the beautiful buildings of the old quarter double as venues for Music in Old Cracow, a seventeen-day event featuring classical music from Baroque to Romantic to Modern. The sounds here will be familiar to most ears, but for those looking for something a bit different, October's intriguingly named International Festival of Forgotten Music is a treat. It features archaic songs from the Baltic region performed by country folk groups, and a good time is a cast-iron guarantee.

EATING OUT

Cracow has long had a reputation as a good place to go and eat. Even during the Communist era it kept its end up, with busy cafés serving good food unknown at the time in the rest of Poland. In the 1990s, hundreds of new restaurants opened their doors, often in pretty locations with medieval or Renaissance interiors. Other restaurateurs chose to go into ancient cellars, restored and furnished to give just the right intimate feel. As for the food itself, many Poles go misty-eyed at the thought of Bigos (Hunter's stew) on a cold winter's day. It's a game, sausage and cabbage stew that comes with sauerkraut, onion, potatoes, herbs and spices. It's reputed to get better with reheating on successive days, and lots of Cracow restaurants claim to serve the tastiest version. Pierogi is another local favourite: crescent-shaped dumplings which you can eat either in savoury or sweet style. Barszcz is a lemon and garlic flavoured beetroot soup that's invariably good value, while in Kazimierz, specialities include Jewish dumpling, filled with onion, cheese and potatoes, and Berdytchov soup, which imaginatively mixes honey and cinnamon with beef. Global grub is also on the menu here. Look around and you won't be short-changed on restaurants specialising in French, Greek, Vietnamese, Middle Eastern, Indian, Italian and Mexican food. You can eat quite late in Cracow: most restaurants don't close until around midnight, and there's no pressure on customers to rush their final drinks and leave. A tip of about ten per cent is the norm.

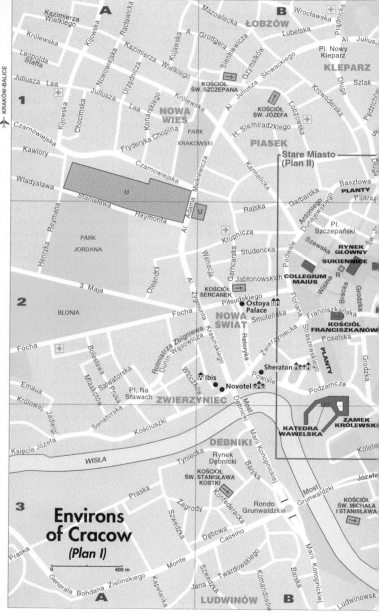

Environs of Cracow
(Plan I)

0 ——— 400 m

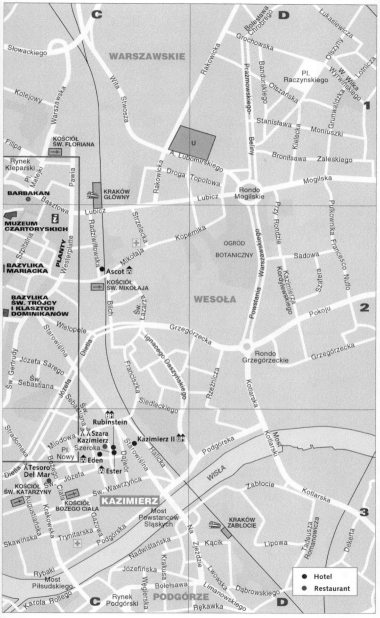

Łukasiewicza
Bolesława Chrobrego
Grochowska
Słowackiego
WARSZAWSKIE
Kolejowy
Warszawska
Willa Stwosza
Rakowicka
Olszyny
W. Wilka Wyrwińskiego
Lotnicza
Pl. Raczynskiego
Bandurskiego
Prażmowskiego
Olszańska
Stanisława
Grunwaldzka
Kielecka
Moniuszki

Filipa
KOŚCIÓŁ ŚW. FLORIANA
Pawia
A. Lubomirskiego
U
Bellny
Bronisława
Zaleskiego

Rynek Kleparski
Matejki
Rakowicka
Droga Topolowa
Mogilska

BARBAKAN
Baszfowa
KRAKÓW GŁÓWNY
Rondo Mogilskie
Przy Rondzie
Pułkownika Francesco Nullo

MUZEUM CZARTORYSKICH
Szpitalna
Lubicz
Lubicz

Radziwiłłowska
Strzelecka
Kopernika
OGRÓD BOTANICZNY
Sadowa
Szafera

BAZYLIKA MARIACKA
PLANTY
Westerplatte
Mikołaja
Powstania Warszawskiego
Kazimierza Kordylewskiego

Ascot
KOŚCIÓŁ ŚW. MIKOŁAJA
WESOŁA
Pokoju

BAZYLIKA ŚW. TRÓJCY I KLASZTOR DOMINIKANÓW
Blich
Św. Łazarza

Wielopole
Dietla
Grzegórzecka
Rondo Grzegórzeckie
Grzegórzecka

Starowiślna
Ignacego Daszyńskiego

Św. Gertrudy
Józefa Sarego
Józefa
Franciszka
Siedleckiego
Rzeźnicza
Kotlarska

Św. Sebastiana
Św. Sebastiana

Stradomska
Rubinstein
Kazimierz
Szara
Kazimierz II
Most Kotlarski

Miodowa
Szeroka
Podgórska

Pl. Nowy
Eden
Dajwór
Halicka

Dietla
Tesoro Del Mar
Brzozowa
Józefa
Starowiślna
WISŁA
Zabłocie
Kotlarska

KOŚCIÓŁ ŚW. KATARZYNY
Ester
Św. Wawrzyńca

Augustiańska
Krakowska
Skawińska
KOŚCIÓŁ BOŻEGO CIAŁA
KAZIMIERZ
Most Powstańców Śląskich
KRAKÓW ZABŁOCIE
Lipowa
Dekerta
Tadeusza Romanowicza

Trynitarska
Podgórska
Gazowa
Na Zjeździe
Kącik
Lwowska
Dąbrowskiego

Rybaki
Most Piłsudskiego
Nadwiślańska
Krakusa
Limanowskiego

Karola Rollego
Rynek Podgórski
Józefińska
Bolesawa
PODGÓRZE
Węgierska
Rękawka

● Hotel
● Restaurant

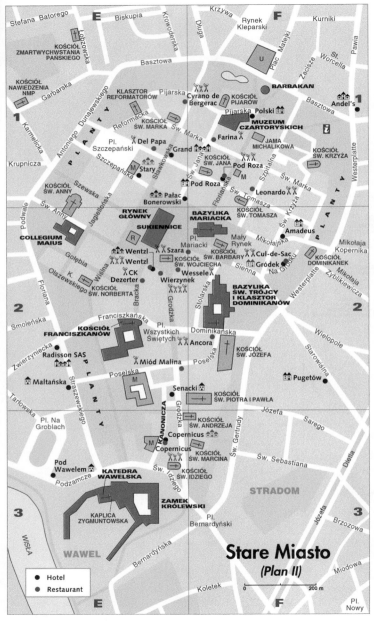

Stare Miasto
(Plan II)

Hotel
Restaurant

0   200 m

Sheraton ⩽ ⅃ᵴ 🕸 ☒ ⅃ᵴ ⒜ ⅃⁄ rm 🖥 ⁽ᵗ⁾ 🏋 🅿 🛋 ⱅₛₐ ⓪⓪ 🄰🄴 ⓪

Ul. Powiśle 7 ⊠ 31 101 – ℰ (12) 662 10 00 – krakow@sheraton.com
– Fax (12) 6 62 11 00 – www.sheraton.com/krakow *Plan I* | **B2**
229 rm ☒ – ⅋910 PLN ⅋⅋984 PLN – 3 suites
Rest *The Olive* – ℰ (12) 662 1662 – Carte 150/220 PLN
♦ Business ♦ Modern ♦

Purpose-built hotel near the castle, with views of the Wisła river. Well-equipped bedrooms come with all mod cons. Qube bar serves over 200 different vodkas. Mediterranean/international menu served at The Olive; relaxed open plan restaurant situated in huge glass-roofed atrium.

Radisson SAS ⅃ᵴ ⅃ᵴ 🔟 ⅃⁄ 🖥 ⁽ᵗ⁾ 🏋 🛋 ⱅₛₐ ⓪⓪ 🄰🄴 ⓪

Ul. Straszewskiego 17 ⊠ 31 101 – ℰ (12) 618 88 88 – reservations.krakow@
radissonsas.com – Fax (12) 6 18 88 89 – www.radissonsas.com **E2**
177 rm – ⅋515/710 PLN ⅋⅋515/710 PLN, ☒ 70 PLN – 19 suites
Rest – *(buffet lunch)* Carte 115/175 PLN
♦ Business ♦ Modern ♦

Well run chain hotel, five minutes from the main square. Large open plan lobby and stylish bar. Generously proportioned, comfortable and warmly decorated bedrooms with a high level of facilities. International and Polish cuisine served in bright restaurant; regular buffets and themed evenings.

Grand ⅃ᵴ 🕸 🔟 🖥 ⁽ᵗ⁾ 🏋 ⱅₛₐ ⓪⓪ 🄰🄴 ⓪

Ul. Sławkowska 5/7 ⊠ 31 014 – ℰ (12) 424 08 00 – hotel@grand.pl
– Fax (12) 4 21 83 60 – www.grand.pl **E1**
55 rm ☒ – ⅋819/1000 PLN ⅋⅋915/1076 PLN – 9 suites
Rest *Mirror Hall* – Carte 107/163 PLN
♦ Traditional ♦ Historic ♦

Historic hotel, formerly the palace of the Duke Czartoryski, now restored to its former glory, with gold leaf, high ceilings and stained glass windows. Sumptuous, spacious suites. Formal dining under chandeliers in the Mirror Hall.

Copernicus ⅃ᵴ 🕸 🔟 🖥 ⁽ᵗ⁾ ⱅₛₐ ⓪⓪ 🄰🄴

Ul. Kanonicza 16 ⊠ 31 002 – ℰ (12) 424 34 00 – copernicus@hotel.com.pl
– Fax (12) 4 24 34 05 – www.hotel.com.pl **E3**
29 rm ☒ – ⅋800/900 PLN ⅋⅋900/980 PLN – 4 suites
Rest *Copernicus* – see below
♦ Historic ♦ Stylish ♦

Set on one of the oldest streets in the city, restoration of this intimate, atmospheric hotel revealed 15C ceiling inscriptions and ornaments. Handmade furniture, velvet bedspreads, silk drapes. Attentive service.

Wentzl ⩽ 🔟 ⅃⁄ 🖥 ⁽ᵗ⁾ ⱅₛₐ ⓪⓪ 🄰🄴

Rynek Główny 19 ⊠ 31 008 – ℰ (12) 430 26 64 – hotel@wentzl.pl
– Fax (12) 4 30 26 65 – www.wentzl.pl **E2**
18 rm ☒ – ⅋169/179 PLN ⅋⅋179/199 PLN **Rest** *Wentzl* – see below
♦ Townhouse ♦ Historic ♦

15C house overlooking splendour of main square. Charming, antique-furnished bedrooms bedecked with art offer high level of facilities; those on top floor are contemporary in the style, others more traditional.

Stary ⅃ᵴ 🕸 🔟 🖥 ⁽ᵗ⁾ 🏋 ⱅₛₐ ⓪⓪ 🄰🄴

Ul. Szczepańska 5 ⊠ 31 011 – ℰ (12) 384 08 08 – stary@hotel.co.pl
– Fax (12) 3 84 08 09 – www.hotel.com.pl **E1**
46 rm ☒ – ⅋680/900 PLN ⅋⅋765/900 PLN – 7 suites
Rest *Trzy Rybki* – Carte 123/159 PLN
♦ Townhouse ♦ Stylish ♦

Stylish hotel, its oldest part dating from 15C, with original frescos on the walls. Atmospheric, antique-furnished rooms with marble bathrooms. Good levels of service. European menu with strong Italian influences served in Trzy Rybki.

POLAND - CRACOW

Pałac Bonerowski   🛏 🕸 AC 🛗 rm SAT 🛜 ☝ 🛋 VISA ⓪ AE ⓪

Ul. Św. Jana 1 ✉ *31 013 –* ✆ *(12) 374 13 00 – rezerwacja@palacbonerowski.pl*
– Fax (12) 3 74 13 05 – www.palacbonerowski.pl   **E1**
8 rm ⊊ – ♦720/820 PLN ♦♦820/920 PLN – 6 suites
Rest *Pod Winogronomi* – Menu 75/109 PLN – Carte 63/119 PLN
♦ Palace ♦ Personalised ♦

Characterful hotel overlooking the main square, whose historic features include medieval portals and restored 17C polychrome and ceilings. Suite 201 is probably the biggest in the city. Italian cuisine served in restaurant, with fresh fish a feature.

Andel's   🕸 🛏 🕸 & AC 🛗 rm SAT 🛜 ☝ 🛋 ☕ VISA ⓪ AE

Ul. Pawia 3 ✉ *31 154 –* ✆ *(12) 660 01 00 – info@andelscracow.com*
– Fax (12) 6 60 00 01 – www.andelscracow.com   **F1**
153 rm – ♦180/210 PLN ♦♦205/235 PLN, ⊊ 15 PLN – 6 suites
Rest – Menu 12 PLN (lunch) – Carte 31/40 PLN
♦ Business ♦ Modern ♦

Opened in 2007, this hotel opposite main station boasts bright, open plan public areas with original design features. Stylishly lit rooms feature flat screen TVs and DVD players. Cool lobby bar. Light, spacious restaurant opens out onto terrace and plaza and serves international and Polish cuisine.

Novotel   🕸 🛏 🕸 🗗 & AC 🛗 rm SAT 🛜 ☝ 🛋 ☕ VISA ⓪ AE ⓪

Ul. Tadeusza Kościuszki 5 ✉ *30 105 –* ✆ *(12) 299 29 00 – H3372@accor.com*
– Fax (12) 2 99 29 99 – www.novotel.com   *Plan I* **B2**
192 rm – ♦444/665 PLN ♦♦444/665 PLN, ⊊ 58 PLN – 6 suites
Rest – Carte 55/136 PLN
♦ Chain hotel ♦ Functional ♦

Geared towards corporate customers, with simple, bright rooms over six floors, some with terrific views of Wawel castle. Large gym and pool. Children under 16 are free. Light and airy restaurant serving an international menu.

Gródek   🕸 & AC 🛗 rest SAT 🛜 ☝ VISA ⓪ AE ⓪

Ul. Na Gródku 4 ✉ *31 028 –* ✆ *(12) 431 90 30 – grodek@donimirski.com*
– Fax (12) 4 31 90 40 – www.donimirski.com   **F2**
21 rm – ♦520/650 PLN ♦♦750/850 PLN, ⊊ 50 PLN – 2 suites
Rest *Cul-de-Sac* – see below
♦ Townhouse ♦ Personalised ♦

Charming boutique hotel with bright, comfortable feel, cosy wood-panelled bar and pleasant roof terrace. Individually decorated, immaculately kept bedrooms. Pleasing service.

Pod Różą   🛏 🕸 AC SAT 🛋 VISA ⓪ AE

Ul. Floriańska 14 ✉ *31 021 –* ✆ *(12) 424 33 00 – pod-roza@hotel.com.pl*
– Fax (12) 4 24 33 51 – www.hotel.com.pl   **F1**
53 rm ⊊ – ♦552/720 PLN ♦♦612/720 PLN – 4 suites
Rest *Pod Różą* – see below
Rest *Amarone* – Carte 99/139 PLN
♦ Traditional ♦ Classic ♦

16C building - reputedly the oldest hotel in the city - whose past guests include such luminaries as Balzac and Liszt. Traditional rooms with antique furnishings. Atmospheric conference facilities in cellars. Amarone offers a wide selection of Italian dishes.

Amadeus   🛏 🕸 & AC 🛗 SAT 🛜 ☝ 🛋 VISA ⓪ AE ⓪

Ul. Mikolajska 20 ✉ *31 027 –* ✆ *(12) 429 60 70 – amadeus@janpol.com.pl*
– Fax (12) 2 49 60 62 – www.hotel-amadeus.pl   **F2**
18 rm ⊊ – ♦615/846 PLN ♦♦653/884 PLN – 2 suites
Rest – Carte 64/166 PLN
♦ Traditional ♦ Classic ♦

Charming 16C house with subtle baroque character, a short stroll from main square. Characterful bedrooms boast cosy, warm feel. Intimate dining in former cellars; the vaulted ceilings brightened with paintings and frescoes. Mostly European menu; many Polish dishes.

Ostoya Palace 🏠 ⅙ AC SAT ⁹⁰ VISA ⁰⁰ AE ①

Ul. Pilsudskiego 24 ⊠ 31 109 – ℰ (12) 430 90 00 – hotel@ostoyapalace.pl
– Fax (12) 4 30 90 01 – www.ostoyapalace.pl   Plan I **B2**
24 rm ☐ – †570/680 PLN ††640/730 PLN   **Rest** – Carte 69/144 PLN
◆ Historic ◆ Stylish ◆

Discreet, comfortable and characterful hotel whose bedrooms reflect its 19C origins, with high ceilings and original stove heaters. Popular pub in basement. Restaurant features original 15C ceiling and serves international menu.

Polski *without rest* ⅙ SAT VISA ⁰⁰ AE ①

Ul.Pijarska 17 ⊠ 31 015 – ℰ (12) 422 11 44 – hotel.polski@podorlem.com.pl
– Fax (12) 4 22 14 26 – www.podorlem.com.pl   **F1**
54 rm ☐ – †295/375 PLN ††355/525 PLN – 3 suites
◆ Family ◆ Classic ◆

Friendly hotel located next door to the Czartoryski Museum, which houses da Vinci's 'Lady with an Ermine.' Comfy rooms range from singles to triples. Friendly service; pleasant atmosphere.

Pugetów *without rest* AC SAT ⁣ℂ⁾ P VISA ⁰⁰ AE ①

Ul. Starowiślna 15a ⊠ 31 038 – ℰ (12) 432 49 50 – pugetow@donimirski.com
– Fax (12) 3 78 93 25 – www.donimirski.com   **F2**
5 rm – †350/510 PLN ††480/510 PLN, ☐ 30 PLN – 3 suites
◆ Traditional ◆ Historic ◆

Cosy 19C house set alongside the Pugetów Palace, away from main street, with the intimate feel of a private residence. Spacious rooms include 2 huge antique-furnished suites.

Maltański *without rest* ⅙ ↤ SAT ⁣ℂ⁾ P VISA ⁰⁰ AE ①

Ul. Straszewskiego 14 ⊠ 31 101 – ℰ (12) 431 00 10
– maltanski@donimirski.com – Fax (12) 3 78 93 12 – www.donimirski.com
16 rm – †350/440 PLN ††420/480 PLN, ☐ 40 PLN   **E2**
◆ Traditional ◆ Personalised ◆

Charming little hotel - a former stable block - set back from the road. Ground floor rooms are best, with doors onto small terraces, but all rooms are equally comfortable.

Senacki SAT ⁣ℂ⁾ VISA ⁰⁰ AE ①

Ul. Grodzska 51 ⊠ 31 001 – ℰ (12) 421 11 61 – recepcja@senacki.krakow.pl
– Fax (12) 4 22 79 34 – www.senacki.krakow.pl   **E2**
18 rm ☐ – †315/500 PLN ††420/540 PLN – 2 suites
Rest – Menu 45/65 PLN – Carte 57/93 PLN
◆ Townhouse ◆ Functional ◆

Well located, simple hotel close to the castle and opposite the 17C Church of Saint Peter and Paul. Atmospheric bar and café in converted cellars. Neat bedrooms over 3 floors. Concise menu of Polish and Italian dishes served in restaurant.

Pod Wawelem 🏠 ℒ๖ 🏠 AC ⁣ℂ⁾ rm SAT ˢᴬ VISA ⁰⁰ AE ①

PL. Na Groblach 22 ⊠ 31 101 – ℰ (12) 426 26 26 – rezerwacja@
hotelpodwawelem.pl – Fax (12) 4 22 33 99 – www.hotelpodwawelem.pl
47 rm ☐ – †250/423 PLN ††365/519 PLN – 1 suite   **E3**
Rest – Carte 48/100 PLN
◆ Family ◆ Functional ◆

Small, sensibly-priced hotel in the shadow of the Royal Castle and close to the river; purpose built, but sympathetically so. Terrific rooftop café in summer. Functional bedrooms. Bright and airy café-style restaurant serving international and Polish dishes.

Ascot *without rest* ⅙ ↤ SAT ⁣ℂ⁾ VISA ⁰⁰ AE ①

Ul. Radziwillowska 3 ⊠ 31 026 – ℰ (12) 384 06 06 – rezerwacja@hotelascot.pl
– Fax (12) 3 84 06 07 – www.hotelascot.pl   Plan I **C2**
49 rm ☐ – †270/340 PLN ††390/430 PLN
◆ Family ◆ Functional ◆

Purpose-built hotel, a 5 minute walk from the centre, opened in 2007. Small lobby with corner bar. Functional downstairs breakfast room. Clean, compact, fairly priced bedrooms.

Ibis
AC ⚹ rm 🖥 📶 🚗 VISA 🅾️ AE

Ul. Syrokomli 2 – ℰ (12) 2993300 – h3710@accor.com – Fax (12) 2 99 33 33
– www.ibishotel.com   Plan / **B2**
175 rm – ♦249/329 PLN ♦♦249/329 PLN, ⌷ 29 PLN
Rest – Menu 51 PLN – Carte 50/104 PLN
◆ Chain hotel ◆ Functional ◆

Chain hotel five minutes walk from the Castle and old town centre. Simple, functional bedrooms offer wi-fi, good disabled access and the expected mod cons. Café-style French bistro serves mainly international and a few local dishes.

XXXX   Wierzynek
🍴 AC ⚹ VISA 🅾️ AE ⓘ

Rynek Główny 15 ⊠ 31 008 – ℰ (12) 424 96 00 – rezerwacja@wierzynek.pl
– Fax (12) 4 24 96 01 – www.wierzynek.pl   **E2**
Rest – Menu 71/110 PLN – Carte 103/200 PLN
◆ Polish ◆ Elegant ◆

Ornately decorated restaurant occupying commanding position in main square; past guests include George Bush and Steven Spielberg. Polish specialities carefully prepared using top quality ingredients. Well-organised, formal service.

XXX   Wentzl – at Wentzl Hotel
AC VISA 🅾️ AE ⓘ

Rynek Główny 19 ⊠ 31 008 – ℰ (12) 429 57 12 – restauracja@wentzl.pl
– Fax (12) 431 92 20 – www.wentzl.pl   **E2**
Rest – Carte 128/159 PLN
◆ International ◆ Formal ◆

Hotel restaurant exuding palpable sense of history; impressive Renaissance interiors include original wood ceilings and 15C triptych. Menu adds an international note to Polish dishes.

XXX   Cyrano de Bergerac with rm
🍴 VISA 🅾️ AE ⓘ

Ul. Sławekowska 26 ⊠ 31 014 – ℰ (12) 411 72 88 – rest@cyranodebergerac.pl
– Fax (12) 4 12 15 72 – www.cyranodebergerac.pl – Closed Bank Holidays
4 rm – ♦288/404 PLN – 1 suite   **E/F 1**
Rest – (Closed Sunday) (booking essential) Carte 101/198 PLN
◆ French ◆ Romantic ◆

Characterful cellar restaurant; antique furniture, tapestries and candlelight create a romantic atmosphere. Ground floor art deco piano bar; robust classical French cooking. Individually styled bedrooms; each reflect a different decade.

XXX   Copernicus – at Copernicus Hotel
AC VISA 🅾️ AE

Ul. Kanonicza 16 ⊠ 31 002 – ℰ (12) 424 43421 – copernicus@hotel.com.pl
– Fax (12) 4 24 34 05 – www.hotel.com.pl   **E3**
Rest – (booking essential) Carte 123/157 PLN ⚜
◆ Polish ◆ Formal ◆

Charming restaurant specialising in seasonal Polish cooking, artfully presented and full of flavour. A table on the gallery allows one to fully appreciate the ornate Renaissance ceiling.

XXX   Pod Różą – at Pod Różą Hotel
AC VISA 🅾️ AE

Ul. Floriańska 14 ⊠ 31 021 – ℰ (12) 424 33 00 – pod-roza@hotel.com.pl
– Fax (12) 4 24 33 51 – www.hotel.com.pl   **F1**
Rest – Carte 119/177 PLN ⚜
◆ International ◆ Friendly ◆

Capacious restaurant; its large glass roof supported by a row of columns, giving the room a proud feel. Appealing European cooking with a heavy Italian accent. Formal service.

XX   Cul-de-Sac – at Gródek Hotel
VISA 🅾️ AE ⓘ

Ul. Na Gródku 4 ⊠ 31 028 – ℰ (12) 431 90 30 – Fax (12) 4 31 90 40
– www.donimirski.com   **F2**
Rest – Carte 85/139 PLN
◆ International ◆ Design ◆

Bright restaurant in basement of Gródek hotel, decorated with objects found during the building's renovation. International menu; its base rooted in Italy. Imaginative, ambitious cooking.

POLAND - CRACOW

XX **Ancora**   AC VISA OO AE OD

Ul. Dominikánska 3 ✉ *31 043 –* 𝒞 *(12) 357 33 55*
– restauracja@ancora-restaurant.com – www.ancora-restaurant.com
– Closed 25 December and Easter Sunday   **F2**
Rest – Carte 72/122 PLN 🦞
♦ International ♦ Fashionable ♦
Large, contemporary corner restaurant with open kitchen and photos of the chef in action; equally cavernous converted cellars downstairs. Cooking is rooted in Poland with modern, international sensibilities.

XX **Leonardo**   AC VISA OO AE OD

Ul. Szpitalna 20-22 ✉ *31 024 –* 𝒞 *(12) 429 68 50 – rezerwacja@leonardo.com.pl*
– Fax (12) 4 32 22 56 – www.leonardo.com.pl – Closed 24-25 December
Rest – Carte 62/193 PLN   **F1**
♦ Italian ♦ Neighbourhood ♦
Leonardo room decorated with da Vinci's etchings and musings; cosy Wine room takes the grapevine as its motif; produce hangs from ceiling in Spice room. Italian menu features plenty of fresh fish. Friendly service.

XX **Szara**   🍴 AC VISA OO AE OD

Rynek Główny 6 ✉ *31 042 –* 𝒞 *(12) 421 66 69 – restauracja@szara.pl*
– www.szara.pl   **E/F2**
Rest – Carte 85/126 PLN
♦ Polish ♦ Friendly ♦
Two rooms with original Gothic vaulted ceilings, situated on main square. Elaborately presented, flavourful European cuisine, with Polish and Swedish dishes to the fore. Friendly service.

X **Wesele**   🍴 AC VISA OO AE

Rynek Główny 10 ✉ *31 042 –* 𝒞 *(12) 422 74 60 – restauracja@*
weselerestauracja.pl – www.weselerestauracja.pl
– Closed 25 December and Easter   **E2**
Rest – Carte 56/102 PLN
♦ Polish ♦ Intimate ♦
Proudly Polish restaurant set on the market square, boasting large windows, rustic wood panelling and summer terrace. Traditional Polish menu also offers some more modern dishes.

X **Farina**   AC VISA OO AE OD

Ul. Św. Marka 16 ✉ *31 017 –* 𝒞 *(12) 422 16 80 – restauracja@farina.com.pl*
– Fax (12) 4 21 37 30 – www.farina.com.pl – Closed 24-25 December
Rest – Carte 56/122 PLN   **F1**
♦ Seafood ♦ Rustic ♦
Attractive candlelit corner restaurant divided into 2 rooms with wood floors and a bright rustic style. Menu specialises in seafood with a hint of Italy. Warm, friendly service.

X **Miód Malina**   🍴 AC VISA OO AE OD

Ul. Grodzka 40 ✉ *31 044 –* 𝒞 *(12) 430 04 11 – restauracja@miodmalina.pl*
– Fax (12) 430 04 11 – www.miodmalina.pl
– Closed 24-25 December and Easter Sunday   **E2**
Rest – *(booking essential)* Carte 46/99 PLN
♦ Italian ♦ Neighbourhood ♦
Busy restaurant with pleasant atmosphere serving a mix of Polish and Italian dishes, some cooked in wood fired oven. Larger, no-smoking room with vaulted ceiling is best place to sit.

X **Del Papa**   AC VISA OO AE OD

Ul. Św. Tomasza 6 ✉ *31 014 –* 𝒞 *(12) 421 83 43 – delpapa@vp.pl*
– Fax (12) 429 52 62 – www.delpapa.pl – Closed 24-25 December and 12 April
Rest – Carte 48/115 PLN   **E1**
♦ Italian ♦ Rustic ♦
Characterful and popular with locals. Café style front room; distressed brick walls in middle; bright room with glass roof at back. Friendly staff. Simple Italian food with homemade pasta a speciality.

✕ **C. K. Dezerter** 🅰🄲 VISA ⊙⊙ 🄰🄴 ⓪

Ul. Bracka 6 ✉ 31 005 – 𝒞 (12) 422 79 31 – ckdezerter.bracka6@wp.pl
– Fax (12) 422 79 31 – www.ck-dezerter.pl **Rest** *– Carte 36/90 PLN*
◆ Polish ◆ Neighbourhood ◆
                                                                     E2
Decorated in a homely farmhouse style, with a warm, friendly atmopshere. Menu
offers specialities from Austria-Hungary and the Galicia region of Poland, and inclu-
des a full page of pork dishes.

at KAZIMIERZ

🏨 **Rubinstein** 🛜 ⅃⑤ ⅏ 🅰🄲 ⅙ rm 🄶🄰 𝄞 VISA ⊙⊙ 🄰🄴 ⓪

Ul. Szeroka 12 ✉ 31 053 – 𝒞 (12) 384 00 00 – recepcja@hotelrubinstein.com
– Fax (12) 3 84 00 01 – www.hotelrubinstein.com   **C3**
23 rm ⌑ – †560/640 PLN ††640/700 PLN – 4 suites
Rest – Carte 53/149 PLN
◆ Historic ◆ Modern ◆
Well run, characterful hotel in in the Jewish quarter, converted from 15C tenement
buildings and named after Helena, of cosmetics fame, who grew up in this street.
Comfortable rooms reflect the age of the house. Glass-roofed restaurant, ser-
ving Jewish and Polish specialities.

🏨 **Kazimierz II** *without rest* ⅙ 🄶🄰 𝄞 VISA ⊙⊙ 🄰🄴 ⓪

Ul. Starowiślna 60 ✉ 31 035 – 𝒞 (12) 426 80 70 – rezerwacja@hk.com.pl
– Fax (12) 4 26 80 71 – www.hk.com.pl   **C3**
23 rm ⌑ – †240/320 PLN ††300/380 PLN
◆ Family ◆ Functional ◆
Purpose-built hotel on busy street, opened in 2006. Decently-sized blue and yellow
bedrooms boast a fresh feel; those at the front are the largest. Bright breakfast room.

🏠 **Ester** 🛜 ⅏ 🅰🄲 🄶🄰 𝄞 🆊 VISA ⊙⊙ 🄰🄴

Ul. Szeroka 20 ✉ 31 053 – 𝒞 (12) 429 11 88 – biuro@hotel.ester.krakow.pl
– Fax (12) 4 29 12 33 – www.hotel-ester.krakow.pl   **C3**
32 rm ⌑ – †423/673 PLN ††480/673 PLN **Rest** – Carte 62/118 PLN
◆ Townhouse ◆ Personalised ◆
Friendly hotel in the heart of the Jewish quarter. Clean, functional, decently-
sized bedrooms include five triple rooms. Café-style restaurant with outside summer terrace. Menu focuses on Jewish and Polish cuisine, with a few international
dishes. Live music at weekends.

🏠 **Eden** *without rest* ⅏ ⅄ ⅙ 🄶🄰 𝄞 VISA ⊙⊙ 🄰🄴 ⓪

Ul. Ciemna 15 ✉ 31 053 – 𝒞 (12) 430 65 65 – eden@hoteleden.pl
– Fax (12) 4 30 67 67 – www.hoteleden.pl   **C3**
27 rm ⌑ – †200/280 PLN ††280/380 PLN
◆ Traditional ◆ Personalised ◆
Friendly hotel whose idiosyncratic bedrooms reflect its 15 and 16C history. Characterful cellar pub and pleasant breakfast room with hot and cold buffet. Hotel has
own Mikveh.

✕✕ **Szara Kazimierz** 🛜 VISA ⊙⊙

Ul. Szeroka 39 ✉ 31 053 – 𝒞 (12) 429 12 19 – kazimierz@szara.pl – Fax (12) 426 88 56
– www.szarakazimierz.pl – Closed 24 December **Rest** – Carte 62/94 PLN
◆ Polish ◆ Brasserie ◆
                                                                     C3
Relaxed, brasserie style restaurant; sister to Szara in the old town, with wood burning stoves, pillars and a secluded back terrace. European cooking with a nod
towards Italy. Courteous service.

✕ **Tesoro del Mar** 🅰🄲 VISA ⊙⊙ 🄰🄴 ⓪

Ul. Józefa 6 ✉ 31 056 – 𝒞 (12) 430 60 13 – info@tesorodelmar.pl
– Fax (12) 430 60 13 – www.tesorodelmar.pl **Rest** – Carte 100/165 PLN
◆ Seafood ◆ Neighbourhood ◆
                                                                     C3
Trendy new restaurant opened in late 2007, with cellar-like appearance; sit in the war-
mer, more inviting back room. Artful seafood menu with Mediterranean influences.

PORTUGAL

PROFILE

→ **AREA:**
92 391 km² .

→ **POPULATION:**
11 317 192
(est. 2008), density
= 123 per km².

→ **CAPITAL:**
Lisbon (conurbation
2 900 000
inhabitants).

→ **CURRENCY:**
Euro (€); rate
of exchange: € 1
= US$ 1.27 (Dec 2008).

→ **GOVERNMENT:**
Parliamentary
republic (since 1976).
Member of European
Union since 1986.

→ **LANGUAGE:**
Portuguese.

→ **SPECIFIC PUBLIC
HOLIDAYS:**
Shrove Tuesday
(February);
Good Friday (Friday
before Easter);
Freedom Day
(25 April), Corpus
Christi (May or
June); Portugal Day
(10 June); Republic
Day (5 October);
Restoration of

Independence
Day (1 December);
Immaculate
Conception
(8 December).

→ **LOCAL TIME:**
GMT in winter and
GMT + 1 hour in
summer.

→ **CLIMATE:**
Temperate
Mediterranean with
warm winters and
hot summers (Lisbon:
January 15°C, July
26°C).

→ **INTERNATIONAL DIALLING
CODE:**
00 351 followed by
a nine-digit number.
International
directory enquiries :
℘ **098**.

→ **EMERGENCY:**
Dial ℘ **112**.

→ **ELECTRICITY:**
230-240 volts AC,
50 Hz; 2-pin round-
shaped continental
plugs.

→ **FORMALITIES**
Travellers from the
European Union

LISBON

(EU), Switzerland,
Iceland and the main
countries of North
and South America
need a national
identity card or
passport (America:
passport required)
to visit Portugal
for less than three
months (tourism or
business purpose).
For visitors from
other countries
a visa may be
required, in addition
to a passport,
especially for those
wishing to stay for
longer than three
months. We advise
you to check with
your embassy before
travelling.

LISBON
LISBOA

Population (est. 2007): 662782 (conurbation 2 900 000) – Altitude: at sea level

Simeone/PHOTONONSTOP

Lisbon wears a time-worn look of fading grandeur sitting as it does beneath huge open skies and within an amphitheatre of seven hills. Sited on the north bank of the River Tagus as it feeds into the Atlantic, it boasts an atmosphere that few cities can match; an enchanting walk around the streets of the Bairro Alto, Alfama, the Baixa or Graça has an old-time ambience all its own, matched only by a jaunt on the trams and funiculars that run up and down the steep hills.

At first sight Lisbon is all flaky palaces, meandering alleyways and castellated horizon quarried from medieval stone. But there's a 21C element to the city, kick-started with Expo 98 and carried on with the Euro 2004 football tournament. Slinky new developments line the riverside to east and west, linking the old and the new in a kind of glorious jumble spilling down the slopes to the water's edge. It's the views of that water from various vantage points all over Lisbon that continually draw the visitor: the vistas of the 'Straw Sea', so named because of the golden reflections of the sun on the Tagus, are an inspiration whatever time of year. So too are the sounds of fado, the city's alluring folk music. Fado conjures up a melancholic yearning, and can be heard in taverns and dives all over town. They are the songs of fate, and they add another layer of intrigue to Lisbon's absorbing patchwork.

LIVING THE CITY

Lisbon is strung out along the north bank of the curving **River Tagus**. The compact heart of the city is the **Baixa**, the flat eighteenth century grid of streets flanked by seven hills. Just to the west of the Baixa is the elegant commercial district of **Chiado** and the funky hilltop **Bairro Alto**, while imme-diately to the east is **Alfama**, a tightly packed former Moorish quarter with kasbah-like qualities. North of here is the working-class neighbourhood of **Graça**. Way out west lies the spacious riverside suburb of **Belém**, while up the river to the east can be found the ultra modern **Parque das Nações.**

PRACTICAL INFORMATION

ARRIVAL-DEPARTURE

The airport is just 7km from the city centre and a taxi will cost about €14. Alternatively, take the Aerobus which runs every 20min.

TRANSPORT

Lisbon's an easy city to get around. Four metro lines cover much of the central part of the city, with three different ticket types: single ticket, one-day ticket, or ten tickets.

There's also a good network of trams, buses and funiculars, with six main bus routes and three funiculars. Buses and trams operate every 11-15 minutes; tram routes 15 and 28 serve the main sights. Tickets for buses and trams can be bought as a single fare, a one-day or a three-day ticket. For bus, trams and funiculars: 4-day and 7-day passes are available.

The Lisboa Card is valid for unlimited travel on public transport (except trams 15 and 28) and for free or reduced admission to most museums and cultural sites. Valid for 24, 48 or 72hr.

EXPLORING LISBON

Lisbon takes the best elements of other big cities and blends them together: the winding alleyways of Venice, the wide boulevards of Paris, the trams of Amsterdam, the cobbled streets of Brussels. And it doesn't end there: the **Ponte 25 de Abril**, slung out across the Tagus, looks just like San Francisco's Golden Gate, while the 80ft-high **statue of Christ**, on the river's far bank, is a spitting image of the original overlooking Rio. Despite all this, Lisbon is very much its own city with a distinct melancholy charm. Just wander up and down the slopes of its central core and you'll get the vibe.

→ SO MOORISH

The Alfama district is the oldest bit of Lisbon still standing. It survived the 1755 earthquake which knocked out the rest of the city, but by then its Moorish population had moved further west. They left behind a myriad of tightly packed alleyways and steep streets lined with compact houses which exist to this day; the medieval layout has a humble allure, its alleys so narrow that the balconies on opposite sides of the street almost meet in greeting. There are local grocery stores hidden in corners, and cosy, cellar-like tavernas announcing themselves like a conspiratorial secret. Above Alfama is the city's most distinctive landmark: the **Castelo São Jorge**. The castle was built by the Moors on the site of a Roman fort, but was left in ruins for centuries until it was reconstructed in the Twentieth. Hang around the ramparts for gorgeous views of the Tagus estuary and the city lining its northern bank. Then head further north to the neighbourhood of Graça for more super views - mostly a panorama of rooftops - enjoyed best of all in the early evening at a café table beneath the swaying pines.

→ CENTRAL PLANNING

Looked down upon from the castle, bustling Baixa was totally destroyed in the earthquake, but, under the guidance of the Marquês de Pombal, this sea-level centre of town was reborn with neo-classical buildings and a symmetrically laid out grid of elegant, broad boulevards – it was one of Europe's first examples of town planning. This is the heart of the city, where the smart shops are. They're book-ended by two imposing squares, the buzzing **Praça do Comércio** down by the river, and the **Rossio** further north. A favourite way of coming into Lisbon is by ferry from the southern bank, alighting at the Praça do Comércio, and admiring the impressive triumphal arch which towers over the north side of the square. From here, you stroll into **Rua Augusta**, Lisbon's main tourist thoroughfare, lined with open-air cafés and smart boutiques. Handsomely adorned with mosaic pavements, it's lively, bustling and pedestrianized, and it's flanked on either side by **'Goldsmiths' Street'** and **'Silversmiths' Street'**, just to give

you an idea of the kind of retail going on in this compact part of town. By day, it seems all of Lisbon is here, but as soon as darkness descends, Baixa becomes a ghost town.

Not so the adjacent quarter of Bairro Alto, high up the hill to the west of Baixa. It's a raffish, bohemian warren of streets that by day is peaceful enough, with hippie shops and sedate viewpoints. When the sun goes down, though, the shutters go up, hundreds of local restaurants open their doors, and the clubs and bars pulsate to the sounds of African and samba rhythms. This is a nightlife zone that doesn't let up till the dawn. When the day does come, shopping around Bairro Alto can be a very personalised and social occasion, where bars sell clothes, hairdressers flip open a beer bottle (for the customer, that is) and the cosy neighbourhood store boasts a DJ. The nearby district of Chiado exudes a different feel again: it's an area of elegant shops and old-style cafés, typified by the century-old **Café A Brasileira** with its carved and panelled wood interior set off by gleaming, gilded mirrors.

→ SEA THE PAST

Jump on a tram, head out west for half an hour, and you're in Belém, the riverside neighbourhood of Lisbon most in thrall to its seafaring past. When Vasco da Gama and Ferdinand Magellan were at the height of their medieval adventures, the city was celebrating their fame by building exuberant late-Gothic churches and monuments in Belem, from where they'd set sail. The real showstopper here is the **Jerónimos monastery**, an exotic structure with a richly carved cloister and portal. Vasco da Gama is buried here in a tomb of seafaring symbols; lying next to him is Portugal's most famous poet, Luis de Camões. Outside, Belém is a suburb of pocket-sized parks and gardens, a snazzy promenade with cafés and, when the sun's shining, a distinctly seaside vibe.

→ PARQUE AND TIDE

You have to take a trip about eight kilometres east of the centre to find the glittering twenty first century face of Lisbon. You'll find it at Parque das Nações. Just fifteen years ago, this area was a wasteland, but it was developed for Expo 98, and is now a riot of modern attractions. Chief amongst these is the Portugal Pavilion, which boasts a stunning concrete canopy floating over its forecourt. There's also a science museum and an Oceanarium vying for your attention, but what might *really* grab it lies further along the riverside promenade: the **Vasco da Gama bridge** stretches for 10 miles across the wide river, making it the longest bridge in Europe.

→ ACROSS THE RANGE

Not many art collections can claim to span 4,000 years of exhibits, but Lisbon boasts one, and it's not to be missed. The **Calouste Gulbenkian Museum**, north of the city centre, is a private collection that happens to be one of the finest in Europe. It ranges from ancient Egyptian statuettes to works by Turner, Rembrandt and Manet. There's also a stunning display of Oriental and Islamic pieces, as colourful as anything else on display here. The other hot museum of art to head for is down near the river at the western end of Bairro Alto. It's the **Museu Nacional de Arte Antiga**, which translates as the National Museum of Ancient Art. It houses a phenomenal range of Portuguese national art ranging from the twelfth to the nineteenth centuries, and it's the largest collection of paintings in the country, complemented by many works from other parts of Europe and the Orient. One look round here, taking in Portugal's historic links with so many other countries around the globe, gives another hint as to why Lisbon has bolted on all those parts of other world cities to create its magical whole.

CALENDAR HIGHLIGHTS

Despite their reputation as being more reserved than their Spanish neighbours, the Portuguese do love a party, particularly if there's a saint involved. Which means that Festas dos Santos Populares, (or Feast Days of the Popular Saints), in June, is Lisbon's biggest party. The city streets are decorated with paper lanterns, streamers and coloured lights, and balconies and railings are festooned, creating a magical sight. Another big celebration that month is Portugal's National Day, which marks the anniversary of the death of the country's greatest poet, Luis de Camões: when the city hosts various cultural events. On the theme of writing, June's Lisbon Book Fair, in Parque Eduardo VII, has been a great event since the 1930s, and you can browse old tomes, new books and comics at your leisure

LISBON IN...

→ ONE DAY
Alfama, Castelo São Jorge, Bairro Alto

→ TWO DAYS
Baixa, Calouste Gulbenkian Museum, Parque das Nações

→ THREE DAYS
Museu Nacional de Arte Antiga, Belém

as you stroll amongst the trees. Also that month, the Alkantara Festival is a seventeen-day jamboree which includes theatre, dance and performance art, but which may be even more notable for its fascinating walk through Alfama, or its all-night marathon! The Parque do Tejo in Parque das Nações blasts to life in July when top names in rock give it their all at the Super Bock Super Rock Festival. Later that month, a slightly more refined air accompanies the Almada International Theatre Festival, during which various city venues host plays and exhibitions from across the globe. November's Arte Lisboa is an important event in the city's art world, with contempo-rary works filling sixty-six galleries at the FIL. In the spring, the Belém Cultural Centre hosts two important events: the Spring Festival (March), which puts on various shows, concerts and exhibitions, and then, in April, the CCB Music Festival: at this one, seven different stages are home to baroque orchestras, choirs and soloists in an intense three-day event. On the same theme, and running right through the winter and spring (November-May), Great Orchestras of the World, at the Coliseu dos Recreios, is presented by the influential Calouste Gulbenkian Foundation, and features various internationally renowned conductors and soloists.

EATING OUT

The cuisine of the Lisbon region can be characterised by its simplicity. *Lisboetas* love their local agricultural produce, prepared naturally, without the addition of a large number of extra ingredients. The city has an age-old maritime tradition and is open to the sea, so it's home to a range of dishes based on fish and seafood. There are a number of fishing ports nearby which supply it with ocean-fresh produce. Gastronomically, Lisbon doesn't disappoint, with all the country's regional cuisine represented: it might not be strikingly original, but there's a clear commitment to values such as simplicity and honesty. Having said that, the locals love *bacalhau* (cod), and it's said that there's a different way to prepare it each day for a year, while a Lisbon academy has identified over a thousand cod recipes. Eating in either a humble *tasca* (tavern with a few tables), *casa de pasto* (large dining room) or *restaurante*, there are some specialities to keep an eye open for. *Bacalhau* may come oven baked, slow cooked or cooked in milk, and served wrapped in cabbage, with tocino belly pork, a topping of mayonnaise or in a myriad other ways. *Amêijoas à bulhão pato* (clams cooked with garlic and coriander), *cozido à Portuguesa* (traditional stew with beef, chicken and sausage cooked with vegetables and rice), *feijao à Portuguesa* (bean casserole with tocino belly pork), or *arroz de lamprea* (lamprey eel with rice) are all mainstays of the Lisbon menu. Enjoy them with a *vinho verde*, the wine of the region. A service charge will be included on your bill, but it's customary to leave a tip of about ten per cent.

➜ A BAKER'S SECRET

Belém has always been famous for its tarts; in this case, they're warm, creamy, and dripping with custard. They're made at the legendary Antiga Confeitaria de Belém, and the secret recipe used in their production is known only to three bakers. Ten thousand *pastéis de Belém* are sold on an average weekday, and eaten, time permitting, in the café's rooms, which are famous far and wide for their colourful tiles depicting the area four hundred years ago.

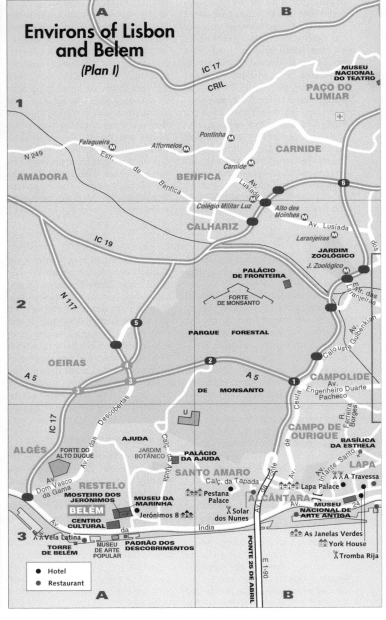

Environs of Lisbon and Belem
(Plan I)

A · B

MUSEU NACIONAL DO TEATRO

IC 17
CRIL

PAÇO DO LUMIAR

1

N 249

Falagueirs · Afornelos · Pontinha

CARNIDE

Estr. de Benfica

AMADORA

BENFICA

Carnide

Av. Lusíada

Colégio Militar Luz

Alto des Moinhes

CALHARIZ

Av. Lusíada

IC 19

Laranjeiras

N 117

JARDIM ZOOLÓGICO

J. Zoológico

6

PALÁCIO DE FRONTEIRA

FORTE DE MONSANTO

Estr. das Laranjeiras

2

OEIRAS

PARQUE FORESTAL

Av. Calouste Gulbenkian

A 5

5

2

A 5

CAMPOLIDE

4

3

DE MONSANTO

1

Av. Engenheiro Duarte Pacheco

3

IC 17

Av. das Descobertas

R. Ferreira Borges

CAMPO DE OURIQUE

BASÍLICA DA ESTRELA

ALGÉS

FORTE DO ALTO DUQUE

AJUDA

JARDIM BOTÂNICO

U

Calç. da Ajuda

PALÁCIO DA AJUDA

SANTO AMARO

Av. Infante Santo

LAPA

Av. Dom Vasco da Gama

RESTELO

MOSTEIRO DOS JERÓNIMOS

BELÉM

MUSEU DA MARINHA

Calç. da Tapada

Pestana Palace

Jerónimos 8

Solar dos Nunes

Lapa Palace

ALCÂNTARA

A Travessa

MUSEU NACIONAL DE ARTE ANTIGA

CENTRO CULTURAL

3

Vela Latina

TORRE DE BELÉM

MUSEU DE ARTE POPULAR

PADRÃO DOS DESCOBRIMENTOS

da Índia

E 1-90

As Janelas Verdes

York House

Tromba Rija

PONTE 26 DE ABRIL

A · B

● Hotel
● Restaurant

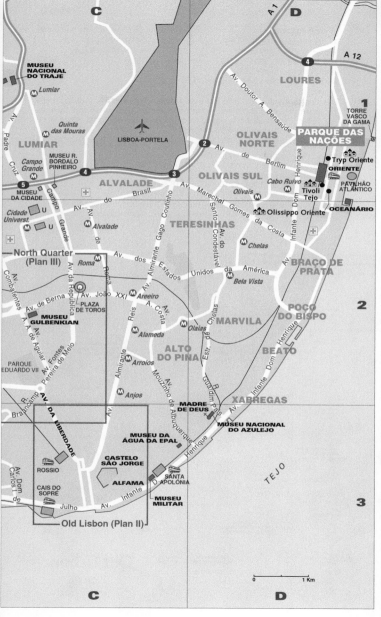

C   D

A 1

A 12

Ⓐ

TORRE
VASCO
DA GAMA

LOURES

**MUSEU
NACIONAL
DO TRAJE**

Ⓜ Lumiar

Av. Doutor A. Bensaude

1

Av. Padre Cruz

Quinta
das Mouras

Ⓜ

LISBOA-PORTELA

OLIVAIS
NORTE

Ⓐ Av. de Berlim

**PARQUE DAS
NAÇÕES**

● Tryp Oriente

ORIENTE

Ⓜ

PAVILHÃO
ATLÂNTICO

LUMIAR

MUSEU R.
BORDALO
PINHEIRO

Ⓜ

Ⓐ

OLIVAIS SUL

Cabo Ruivo

Tivoli
Tejo

Campo
Grande

Ⓐ

ALVALADE

Olivais Ⓜ

OCEANÁRIO

Ⓜ Olissippo Oriente

Av. do Brasil

Av. Marechal Gomes da Costa

Ⓜ
MUSEU
DA CIDADE

Ⓜ

Cidade
Universt.

Ⓤ

Av. de

Santo Condestável

Av. do Infante Dom Henrique

Ⓤ

Ⓜ Alvalade

TERESINHAS

Campo Grande

Av. Almirante Gago Coutinho

Ⓜ Chelas

BRAÇO DE
PRATA

—North Quarter
(Plan III)—

Ⓜ Roma

Av. dos Estados Unidos da América

2

Av. da República

Rocha

Bela Vista

POÇO
DO BISPO

Av. de Berna

Ⓜ
Areeiro

Av. João XXI

PLAZA
DE TOROS

A. Costa

MARVILA

BEATO

**MUSEU
GULBENKIAN**

Reis

Ⓜ Olaias

Av. Infante Dom Henrique

Av. A. A. de Aguiar

Ⓜ Alameda

PARQUE
EDUARDO VII

Av. Fontes Pereira de Melo

Almirante

ALTO
DO PINA

Estr.

Ⓜ Arroios

R. Braancamp

AV. DA LIBERDADE

Ⓜ Anjos

Av. Mouzinho de Albuquerque

XABREGAS

R. Guadiana

**MADRE
DE DEUS**

Av. Infante Dom Henrique

**MUSEU DA
ÁGUA DA EPAL**

**MUSEU NACIONAL
DO AZULEJO**

Av. Dom Carlos de

ROSSIO

**CASTELO
SÃO JORGE**

Ⓜ

SANTA
APOLÓNIA

T E J O

CAIS DO
SOPRÉ

ALFAMA

D.

**MUSEU
MILITAR**

Av. Infante

Av. 24 de Julho

—Old Lisbon (Plan II)—

3

0   1 Km

C   D

OLD LISBON (Alfama, Castelo de São Jorge, Rossio, Baixa, Chiado, Bairro Alto)
Plan II

Tivoli Lisboa ⟨ 🛏 ⽔ ⼿ rm 🅿 🛜 🕭 🛜 🆚 🔵 🅰🅴 🔘

Av. da Liberdade 185 ⊠ 1269-050 – ⓜ Avenida – ℰ 213 19 89 00
– htlisboa@tivolihotels.com – Fax 213 19 89 50 – www.tivolihotels.com
260 rm – 🛉🛉160/500 €, ⊊ 25 € – 48 suites **E1**
Rest *Terraço* – Carte 50/58 €
Rest *Brasserie Flo Lisboa* – Carte 41/51 €
◆ Urban ◆ Modern ◆
This elegant, comfortable hotel has a delightful lounge area. The well-appointed guestrooms are cosy and stylish. Attractive swimming pool surrounded by trees. The Terraço restaurant has a dining room enclosed by large glass windows on the top floor, with stunning views of the city.

Avenida Palace without rest 🛏 🅿 🕭 🔼 🆚 🔵 🅰🅴 🔘

Rua 1° de Dezembro 123 ⊠ 1200-359 – ⓜ Restauradores – ℰ 213 21 81 00
– reservas@hotelavenidapalace.pt – Fax 213 42 28 84
– www.hotelavenidapalace.pt **E1**
64 rm ⊊ – 🛉150/190 € 🛉🛉180/400 € – 18 suites
◆ Historic building ◆ Elegant ◆
An elegant, prestigious building dating from 1892. This hotel has a magnificent lounge area, delightful English-style bar and well-maintained, classical-style guestrooms.

Sofitel Lisbon Liberdade 🛦 ⛬ 🛜 ♨ 🖨 🚗 VISA ⓿ AE ①

Av. da Liberdade 127 ✉ *1269-038 –* Ⓜ *Avenida –* ☏ *213 22 83 00*
– h1319@accor.com – Fax 213 22 83 60 – www.sofitel-lisboa.com
167 rm ⌑ – ♦285/365 € ♦♦325/365 € – 4 suites   **E1**
Rest Ad Lib – see below
♦ Chain hotel ♦ Modern ♦

This hotel is decorated in contemporary-style with numerous designer details. It has fully equipped guestrooms furnished with top-quality materials.

Bairro Alto H 🛦Totally no smoking ⛬ 🛜 ♨ VISA ⓿ AE ①

Praça Luis de Camões 2 ✉ *1200-243 –* Ⓜ *Baixa-Chiado –* ☏ *213 40 82 88*
– info@bairroaltohotel.com – Fax 213 40 82 99 – www.bairroaltohotel.com
51 rm ⌑ – ♦205/315 € ♦♦240/620 € – 4 suites   **E2**
Rest – Menu 45 €
♦ Historic building ♦ Modern ♦

An attractively restored building in the city's historic quarter. Contemporary decor with minimalist touches, and a roof terrace with views. A simple restaurant with large windows overlooking the square.

Lisboa Plaza ⛬ 🛜 ♨ Ⓟ VISA ⓿ AE ①

Travessa do Salitre 7 ✉ *1269-066 –* Ⓜ *Avenida –* ☏ *213 21 82 18*
– plaza.hotels@heritage.pt – Fax 213 47 16 30 – www.heritage.pt
94 rm – ♦190/226 € ♦♦198/248 €, ⌑ 14 € – 12 suites   **E1**
Rest – Menu 35 €
♦ Urban ♦ Classical ♦

Classic-style hotel with an attractive small lounge area and elegant guestrooms. Good facilities and high quality furnishings. The Lisboa Plaza's restaurant offers an attractive menu and a substantial buffet.

Lisboa Regency Chiado without rest ← ⛬ 🛜 🚗 VISA ⓿ AE ①

Rua Nova do Almada 114 ✉ *1200-290 –* Ⓜ *Baixa-Chiado –* ☏ *213 25 61 00*
– reservations.chiado@madeiraregency.pt – Fax 213 25 61 61
– www.regency-hotels-resorts.com   **E2**
40 rm ⌑ – ♦163/412 € ♦♦184/412 €
♦ Urban ♦ Contemporary ♦

A hotel with well-appointed guestrooms in the heart of the Chiado district. Those on the seventh floor have private balconies with splendid views of the city.

Heritage Av Liberdade without rest ⛬ 🛜 VISA ⓿ AE ①

Av. da Liberdade 28 ✉ *1250-145 –* Ⓜ *Avenida –* ☏ *213 40 40 40*
– avliberdade@heritage.pt – Fax 213 40 40 44 – www.heritage.pt
42 rm – ♦230/295 € ♦♦240/325 €, ⌑ 14 €   **E1**
♦ Business ♦ Contemporary ♦

The Heritage has a classic façade and a multipurpose public area, which also serves as the breakfast room. Well-appointed guestrooms that are contemporary in style.

NH Liberdade ⅃ ↯ rm ⛬ 🛜 🛦 🚗 VISA ⓿ AE ①

Av. da Liberdade 180-B ✉ *1250-146 –* Ⓜ *Avenida –* ☏ *213 51 40 60*
– nhliberdade@nh-hotels.com – Fax 213 14 36 74 – www.nh-hotels.com
58 rm ⌑ – ♦90/170 € ♦♦105/185 € – 25 suites   **E1**
Rest – *(closed Saturday, Sunday and Bank Holidays)* Carte approx. 27 €
♦ Chain hotel ♦ Modern ♦

Located in the city's main business district this comfortable, functional hotel is decorated in the typical style of this chain. Modern guestrooms in tones of grey. The restaurant menu features a combination of Spanish and Portuguese cuisine.

Tivoli Jardim ⅃ ⛬ 🛜 🛦 Ⓟ 🚗 VISA ⓿ AE ①

Rua Julio Cesar Machado 7 ✉ *1250-135 –* Ⓜ *Avenida –* ☏ *213 59 10 00*
– htjardim@tivolihotels.com – Fax 213 59 12 45 – www.tivolijardim.com
119 rm – ♦100/250 € ♦♦110/290 €, ⌑ 10 €   **E1**
Rest – Carte 28/45 €
♦ Business ♦ Functional ♦

Modern and functional facilities aimed at the business traveller. Large lobby and warmly decorated guestrooms in contemporary-style, half of which have their own terrace. This restaurant, with its bright, attractively lit dining room, specialises in traditional cuisine.

Britania without rest

Rua Rodrigues Sampaio 17 ✉ 1150-278 – Ⓜ Avenida – ✆ 213 15 50 16 – britania.hotel@heritage.pt – Fax 213 15 50 21 – www.heritage.pt

33 rm – †198/230 € ††215/255 €, ☕ 14 € **E1**

◆ Urban ◆ Classical ◆

The only public area in this hotel is the bar with its lovely wood floor and paintings of Portugal's former colonies. Spacious guestrooms with an Art Deco feel.

Olissippo Castelo without rest

Rua Costa do Castelo 126 ✉ 1100-179 – Ⓜ Rossio – ✆ 218 82 01 90 – info.oc@olissippohotels.com – Fax 218 82 01 94 – www.olissippohotels.com

24 rm ☕ – †135/175 € ††155/195 € **F2**

◆ Relax ◆ Classical ◆

Located on a hill next to the San Jorge castle, part of this hotel is built up against the castle ramparts. Very comfortable guestrooms, a dozen of which have their own garden terrace and magnificent views.

Veneza without rest

Av. da Liberdade 189 ✉ 1250-141 – Ⓜ Avenida – ✆ 213 52 26 18 – hotelveneza@viphotels.com – Fax 213 52 66 78 – www.viphotels.com

37 rm – ††87/103 €, ☕ 8.50 € **E1**

◆ Mansion ◆ Classical ◆

Housed in an elegant small mansion with limited public areas. Perfect blend of old-world charm and functional modern style in the lounge area and guestrooms.

Solar do Castelo without rest

Rua das Cozinhas 2 ✉ 1100-181 – ✆ 218 80 60 50 – solar.castelo@heritage.pt – Fax 218 87 09 07 – www.heritage.pt **F2**

14 rm – †230/310 € ††240/340 €, ☕ 14 €

◆ Mansion ◆ Contemporary ◆

Small 18C mansion with a comfortable, completely renovated interior. The guestrooms here are modern and decorated with striking designer touches.

Metropole without rest

Praça Don Pedro IV-30 (Rossio) ✉ 1100-200 – Ⓜ Rossio – ✆ 213 21 90 30 – metropole@almeidahotels.com – Fax 213 46 91 66 – www.almeidahotels.com

36 rm ☕ – †130/185 € ††145/210 € **E2**

◆ Urban ◆ Classical ◆

Early 20C building in the heart of old Lisbon. Traditional, comfortable guestrooms, the best of which have a balcony overlooking the Praça do Rossio.

Solar dos Mouros without rest

Rua do Milagre de Santo António 6 ✉ 1100-351 – Ⓜ Baixa-Chiado – ✆ 218 85 49 40 – reservation@solardosmouros.com – Fax 218 85 49 45 – www.solardosmouros.com **F2**

13 rm – †122/215 € ††149/248 €, ☕ 13.90 €

◆ Vacation ◆ Urban ◆ Contemporary ◆

A traditional-style hotel with an original decor, a somewhat irregular layout and a modern interior. Colourful guestrooms, some enjoying excellent views.

Lisboa Tejo without rest

Rua dos Condes de Monsanto 2 ✉ 1100-159 – Ⓜ Rossio – ✆ 218 86 61 82 – evidencia.tejo@evidenciahoteis.com – Fax 218 86 51 63 – www.evidenciahoteis.com **F2**

51 rm ☕ – †80/110 € ††87/128 € – 7 suites

◆ Urban ◆ Functional ◆

The Lisboa Tejo's overriding feature, both on the façade and inside, is the predominant use of the colour blue. Modernist-style lobby and well-appointed guestrooms.

PORTUGAL - LISBON

XXX **Tavares**   Totally no smoking 🚭 VISA ⊙⊙ AE ①
Rua da Misericórdia 37 ⊠ 1200-270 – ⓜ Baixa-Chiado – ℰ 213 42 11 12
– reservas@tavaresrico.pt – Fax 213 47 81 25 – www.tavaresrico.pt
Rest – Carte approx. 80 € 🎎   **E2**
♦ Inventive ♦ Formal ♦
Founded in 1784, this emblematic restaurant is renowned for its aristocratic
elegance and history. Lavish decor, creative cuisine and an excellent wine list.

XXX **Gambrinus**   ⇪ VISA ⊙⊙ AE
Rua das Portas de Santo Antão 25 ⊠ 1150-264 – ⓜ Restauradores
– ℰ 213 42 14 66 – rest.gambrinus@mail.telepac.pt – Fax 213 46 50 32
Rest – Carte 47/70 €   **E1**
♦ Traditional ♦ Formal ♦
This renowned Lisbon restaurant has an attractive bar and a dining room with a
fireplace. Traditional Portuguese specialities, international cuisine and seafood.

XXX **Casa do Leão**   ≼ 🌡 VISA ⊙⊙ AE ①
Castelo de São Jorge ⊠ 1100-129 – ⓜ Rossio – ℰ 218 87 59 62
– guest@pousadas.pt – Fax 218 87 63 29 – www.pousadas.pt   **F2**
Rest – Carte approx. 48 €
♦ Traditional ♦ Formal ♦
A unique location inside the defensive walls of the Castle of São Jorge. Typical Por-
tuguese style dining room with a fireplace and vaulted roof, as well as a terrace
with spectacular views.

XX **Vírgula**   ≼ VISA AE
Rua da Cintura do Porto 16 - Armazém B - Cais de Santos ⊠ 1200-109
– ⓜ Cais do Sodré – ℰ 213 43 20 02 – restvirgula@sapo.pt – Fax 213 43 20 08
– www.restaurantevirgula.com
– closed Sunday   **E2**
Rest – Carte 40/54 € 🎎
♦ Inventive ♦ Modern ♦
Situated in the heart of the port area, this restaurant occupies a former metal-struc-
tured salt warehouse. Attractive bar, contemporary-style dining room and innova-
tive cuisine.

XX **Ad Lib** – Hotel Sofitel Lisbon Liberdade   VISA ⊙⊙ AE ①
Av. da Liberdade 127 ⊠ 1269-038 – ⓜ Avenida – ℰ 213 22 83 50
– h1319@accor.com – Fax 213 22 83 60 – www.sofitel-lisboa.com
– closed Saturday lunch and Sunday lunch   **E1**
Rest – Carte approx. 45 €
♦ Traditional ♦ Modern ♦
The entrance to the Ad Lib is separate from the hotel. Small reception area, and a
glass-enclosed wine display. Modern decor with oriental touches in the dining
room. Traditional cuisine.

XX **Solar dos Presuntos**   VISA ⊙⊙ AE ①
Rua das Portas de Santo Antão 150 ⊠ 1150-269 – ⓜ Avenida
– ℰ 213 42 42 53 – restaurante@solardospresuntos.com – Fax 213 46 84 68
– www.solardospresuntos.com
– closed August, Christmas, Sunday and Bank Holidays   **E1**
Rest – Carte 35/41 € 🎎
♦ Traditional ♦ Contemporary ♦
Run by its owners, this pleasant restaurant has an attractive counter of fresh pro-
duce on display. Large selection of traditional dishes and seafood specialities, as
well as an excellent wine list.

X **La Paparrucha**   ≼ 🌡 VISA ⊙⊙ AE ①
Rua D. Pedro V 18-20 ⊠ 1250-094 – ⓜ Baixa-Chiado – ℰ 213 42 53 33
– reservas@lapaparrucha.com – Fax 214 25 31 09 – www.lapaparrucha.com
Rest – Carte 21/29 €   **E1**
♦ International ♦ Functional ♦
A popular, functional Argentinean restaurant that specialises in top quality grilled
meats. Good views, and a busy outdoor terrace.

NORTH QUARTER (Av. da Liberdade, Parque Eduardo VII, Museu Gulbenkian) *Plan III*

Four Seasons H. Ritz Lisbon

Rua Rodrigo da Fonseca 88 ✉ *1099-039*
– **Ⓜ** *Marquês de Pombal* – ☎ *213 81 14 00* – *fsh.lisbon@fourseasons.com*
– *Fax 213 83 17 83* – *www.fourseasons.com* **G3**
262 rm – ✝360/465 € ✝✝385/490 €, ⊊ 29 € – 20 suites
Rest *Varanda* – Carte approx. 73 €
♦ Grand Luxury ♦ Classical ♦
Luxurious, exquisite guestrooms, some of which are truly spectacular. Magnificent lounge areas and high quality furnishings. A wonderful place to stay! An attractive traditional restaurant. It offers à la carte options and a buffet at lunchtime, and more sophisticated dining in the evening.

Tiara Park Atlantic Lisboa

Rua Castilho 149 ✉ *1099-034* – **Ⓜ** *Marquês de Pombal* – ☎ *213 81 87 00*
– *reservas.lisboa@tiara-hotels.com* – *Fax 213 89 05 05* – *www.tiara-hotels.com*
314 rm – ✝370/390 € ✝✝445/465 €, ⊊ 23 € – 17 suites **G3**
Rest *L'Appart* – Carte 41/51 €
♦ Business ♦ Contemporary ♦
Excellent facilities and professional staff in this well-maintained hotel with modern guestrooms and suites. Marble bathrooms and quality furniture. An attractively decorated restaurant with four different dining areas. Options include a buffet, à la carte menu and daily specials.

Sheraton Lisboa H.

Rua Latino Coelho 1 ✉ *1069-025* – ☎ *213 12 00 00* – *sheraton.lisboa@*
sheraton.com – *Fax 213 54 71 64* – *www.sheraton.com/lisboa* **H2**
358 rm – ✝400/470 € ✝✝420/505 €, ⊊ 25 € – 11 suites **Rest** – Menu 65 €
♦ Luxury ♦ Business ♦ Modern ♦
A modernised luxury hotel with spacious public areas and lounges. Extremely comfortable guestrooms and a full range of treatments available in the spa centre. The Sheraton's gastronomic restaurant, located on the top floor of the hotel, enjoys magnificent views of the city.

Real Palacio

Rua Tomás Ribeiro 115 ✉ *1050-228* – **Ⓜ** *São Sebastião* – ☎ *213 19 95 00*
– *realpalacio@hoteisreal.com* – *Fax 213 19 95 01* – *www.hoteisreal.com*
143 rm ⊊ – ✝130/240 € ✝✝140/260 € – 4 suites **G2**
Rest *Guarda Real* – Carte 30/35 €
♦ Luxury ♦ Urban ♦ Stylish ♦
Decorated with a profusion of marble and hardwoods, this classic-contemporary hotel has attractive guestrooms, the most striking of which are housed in a 17C mansion. This elegant restaurant serves traditional and international cuisine.

Villa Rica

Av. 5 de Outubro 295 ✉ *1600-035* – ☎ *210 04 30 00* – *villarica@fibeira.pt*
– *Fax 210 04 34 99* – *www.hotelvillarica.com* **H1**
166 rm – ✝190/200 € ✝✝210/220 €, ⊊ 12 € – 5 suites
Rest *Ouro Preto* – Carte approx. 50 €
♦ Business ♦ Urban ♦ Modern ♦
Original architectural design with cutting-edge furnishings and decor. Attractive, brightly lit lounge areas. The Ouro Preto restaurant offers guests a high quality à la carte menu.

Holiday Inn Lisbon Continental

Rua Laura Alves 9 ✉ *1069-169* – **Ⓜ** *Campo Pequeno*
– ☎ *210 04 60 00* – *hic@grupo-continental.com* – *Fax 217 97 36 69*
– *www.holiday-inn.com* **H1**
210 rm – ✝95/180 € ✝✝105/205 €, ⊊ 12.50 € – 10 suites **Rest** – Menu 18 €
♦ Business ♦ Contemporary ♦
Popular with business travellers, the hotel has a contemporary façade and attractive public areas. The welcoming guestrooms are well appointed with good attention to detail. The hotel's dining room is somewhat lacking in charm.

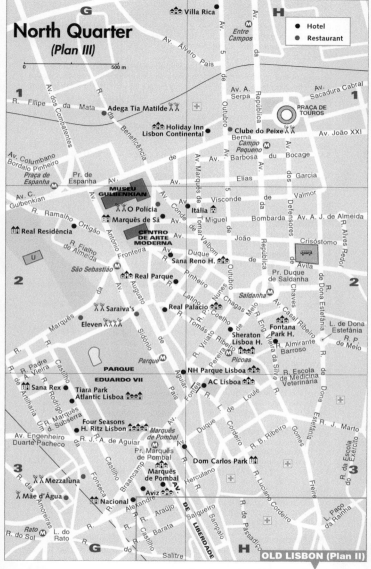

North Quarter
(Plan III)

0   500 m

Legend:
- ● Hotel
- ● Restaurant

Villa Rica

Entre Campos

Av. Alvaro Pais

R. Filipe

da Mata

R. dos Combatentes

Av. da Beneficência

Adega Tia Matilde

Holiday Inn
Lisbon Continental

Clube do Peixe

Av. A. Serpa

Av. Sacadura Cabral

PRAÇA DE
TOUROS

Av. João XXI

Berna

Campo
Pequeno

Av. Barbosa du Bocage

Av. Columbano
Bordalo Pinheiro

Praça de
Espanha

Av. C. Gulbenkian

R. Ramalho Ortigão

Real Residência

R. Fialho
de Almeida

Elias

Garcia

MUSEU
GULBENKIAN

O Polícia

Marquês de Sá

Itália

Visconde

Miguel

Bombarda

Av. A. J. de Almeida

Valmor

Defensores

de Tomar

São Sebastião

CENTRO
DE ARTE
MODERNA

Duque

Sana Reno H.

João

Crisóstomo

Pr. Duque
de Saldanha

Real Parque

Av. Augusto

Saraiva's

Eleven

Pinheiro

Latino

Nunes Chagas

Coelho

Real Palácio

Saldanha

Av. Casal Ribeiro

Av. da República

L. de Dona
Estefânia

R. P.
de Melo

Tomás o Ribeiro

Sheraton
Lisboa H.

Fontana
Park H.

R. Almirante
Barroso

PARQUE

Parque

Picoas

NH Parque Lisboa

AC Lisboa

R. Escola
de Medicina
Veterinária

EDUARDO VII

Sana Rex

Tiara Park
Atlantic Lisboa

Four Seasons
H. Ritz Lisbon

Marquês
de Pombal

Av. Engenheiro
Duarte Pacheco

R. J. A. de Aguiar

Pr. Marquês
de Pombal

Dom Carlos Park

R. da Escola
do Exército

Mezzaluna

Mãe d'Água

Marquês
de Pombal

Aviz

Nacional

DE LIBERDADE

L. do Paço
da Rainha

Rato

R. do Sol

L. do
Rato

OLD LISBON (Plan II)

697

Real Parque

Av. Luís Bívar 67 ✉ *1069-146 –* Ⓜ *Picoas –* ℰ *213 19 90 00*
– realparque@hoteisreal.com – Fax 213 57 07 50 – www.hoteisreal.com
147 rm ⌣ – ∮80/240 € ∮∮100/260 € – 6 suites   **G2**
Rest *Cozinha do Real* – Carte 24/30 €
♦ Urban ♦ Classical ♦

A popular choice for both business travellers and tourists, this hotel is furnished in an elegant and tasteful style. Contemporary-classic interior with a modern façade and a charming lounge area. A welcoming restaurant with an attractive, elegant appearance.

Aviz

Rua Duque de Palmela 32 ✉ *1250-098 –* Ⓜ *Marquês de Pombal*
– ℰ 210 40 20 00 – geral@hotelaviz.com – Fax 210 40 21 98
– www.hotelaviz.com   **G3**
56 rm ⌣ – ∮170 € ∮∮240/350 € – 14 suites   **Rest** – Carte 32/57 €
♦ Traditional ♦ Classical ♦

The name Aviz pays homage to one of Lisbon's small luxury hotels, which no longer exists. Elegant lobby and well-appointed bedrooms with marble bathrooms. The restaurant is classical in style and decorated with objects from the old Aviz hotel.

Fontana Park H.

Rua Engenheiro Vieira da Silva 2 ✉ *1050-105 –* Ⓜ *Saldanha –* ℰ *213 57 62 12*
– geral@fontanaparkhotel.com – Fax 213 57 92 44
– www.fontanaparkhotel.com   **H2**
138 rm ⌣ – ∮170/200 € ∮∮185/215 €   **Rest** – Menu 35 €
♦ Business ♦ Modern ♦

This hotel is decorated in a contemporary, minimalist style. It has spacious lounge areas, various meeting rooms and comfortable, well-appointed guestrooms. The style and decor of this restaurant is similar to that of the hotel. International cuisine.

AC Lisboa

Rua Largo Andaluz 13 - B ✉ *1050-121 –* Ⓜ *Marquês de Pombal*
– ℰ 210 05 09 30 – aclisboa@ac-hotels.com – Fax 210 05 09 31
– www.ac-hotels.com   **H3**
81 rm ⌣ – ∮∮160/184 € – 2 suites   **Rest** – Menu 21 €
♦ Chain hotel ♦ Modern ♦

Occupying the rear of the Palacio Sottomayor, this chain hotel has a modern façade and extensive public areas. Fully equipped guestrooms, some with a terrace. A pleasant dining room offering à la carte and buffet choices.

Marquês de Pombal

Av. da Liberdade 243 ✉ *1250-143 –* Ⓜ *Marquês de Pombal –* ℰ *213 19 79 00*
– info@hotel-marquesdepombal.pt – Fax 213 19 79 90
– www.hotel-marquesdepombal.pt   **G3**
120 rm ⌣ – ∮138/172 € ∮∮150/184 € – 3 suites   **Rest** – Carte 22/32 €
♦ Business ♦ Contemporary ♦

This hotel has a contemporary, functional feel. It features elegant furnishings, modern technology, a modular conference room and good levels of comfort throughout. The restaurant is connected to the cafeteria and serves a varied selection of traditional dishes.

NH Parque Lisboa

Av. Antonio Augusto de Aguiar 12 ✉ *1050-016 –* Ⓜ *Parque –* ℰ *213 51 50 00*
– nhparquelisboa@nh-hotels.com – Fax 213 57 99 99 – www.nh-hotels.com
148 rm ⌣ – ∮80/237 € ∮∮85/250 €   **G2-3**
Rest – *(dinner only)* Carte 33/42 €
♦ Business ♦ Functional ♦

This hotel has a modern façade and a lobby typical of the NH chain. Comfortable sofas in the cafeteria, three meeting rooms, and functional guestrooms painted in bright colours.

Sana Reno H. without rest 　　🛒 🅰️ 🎙️ 🏋️ 🚗 🆚🅰️ 🆚🅰️ 🆎 🅾️

Av. Duque d'Ávila 195-197 ⊠ 1050-082 – Ⓜ *São Sebastião –* ✆ *213 13 50 00*
– sanareno@sanahotels.com – Fax 213 13 50 01 – www.sanahotels.com
89 rm ⚏ **–** ♦180 € ♦♦200 € – 3 suites 　　　　　　　　　　G2
◆ Urban ◆ Classical ◆
The hotel's elegant lobby provides a taste of the comfortable facilities on offer
here. Well-appointed guestrooms with carpeted floors, as well as a small swimming pool and sauna.

Dom Carlos Park without rest 　　　🛒 🎙️ 🏋️ 🆚🅰️ 🆚🅰️ 🆎 🅾️

Av. Duque de Loulé 121 ⊠ 1050-089 – Ⓜ *Marquês de Pombal*
– ✆ *213 51 25 90 – comercial@domcarloshoteis.com – Fax 213 52 07 28*
– www.domcarlospark.com 　　　　　　　　　　　　　　　G-H3
76 rm ⚏ **–** ♦84/147 € ♦♦100/196 €
◆ Urban ◆ Classical ◆
This classic, elegant hotel enjoys an excellent location, and provides the perfect
setting for a relaxing break. Charming guestrooms with marble bathrooms. Limited public areas and lounges.

Marquês de Sá 　　🏋️ rm 🛒 🎙️ 🏋️ 🚗 🆚🅰️ 🆚🅰️ 🆎 🅾️

Av. Miguel Bombarda 130 ⊠ 1050-167 – Ⓜ *São Sebastião –* ✆ *217 91 10 14*
– reservas@olissippohotels.com – Fax 217 93 69 83 – www.olissippohotels.com
163 rm ⚏ **–** ♦110/150 € ♦♦130/170 € 　**Rest** *–* Menu 17 € 　　G2
◆ Urban ◆ Functional ◆
A functional hotel with an attractive lobby and spacious bar-lounge area. The
guestrooms are well appointed, albeit relatively simple in style. The classic-style
dining room offers a simple traditional menu.

Sana Rex H. without rest 　　　　🛒 🎙️ 🏋️ 🆚🅰️ 🆚🅰️ 🆎 🅾️

Rua Castilho 169 ⊠ 1070-051 – Ⓜ *Marquês de Pombal –* ✆ *213 88 21 61*
– sanarex@sanahotels.com – Fax 213 88 75 81 – www.sanahotels.com
68 rm ⚏ **–** ♦78/190 € ♦♦88/200 € 　　　　　　　　　　　G3
◆ Chain hotel ◆ Functional ◆
This hotel enjoys an attractive location opposite the Eduardo VII park, which is
overlooked by many of the guestrooms. The lobby-bar, with its delightful paved
floor, is particularly striking.

Real Residência without rest 　　🏋️ 🛒 🎙️ 🏋️ 🅿️ 🆚🅰️ 🆚🅰️ 🆎 🅾️

Rua Ramalho Ortigão 41 ⊠ 1070-228 – Ⓜ *São Sebastião –* ✆ *213 82 29 00*
– realresidencia@hoteisreal.com – Fax 213 82 29 30 – www.realresidencial.com
24 suites ⚏ **–** ♦♦100/260 € 　　　　　　　　　　　　　G2
◆ Urban ◆ Classical ◆
Small classic-style apartment-hotel situated in the upper part of the city. No
lounge, but the apartments are comfortable and well appointed.

Nacional without rest 　　　　　🛒 🎙️ 🚗 🆚🅰️ 🆚🅰️ 🆎 🅾️

Rua Castilho 34 ⊠ 1250-070 – Ⓜ *Marquês de Pombal –* ✆ *213 55 44 33*
– hotelnacional@mail.telepac.pt – Fax 213 56 11 22 – www.hotel-nacional.com
61 rm ⚏ **–** ♦75/150 € ♦♦87/170 € 　　　　　　　　　　　G3
◆ Urban ◆ Classical ◆
Very professionally run with attentive service and a setting that is both functional
and contemporary.

Itália without rest 　　　　　　🛒 🆚🅰️ 🆚🅰️ 🆎 🅾️

Av. Visconde de Valmor 67 ⊠ 1050-239 – Ⓜ *Saldanha –* ✆ *217 97 77 36*
– reservas@residencial-italia.com – Fax 217 61 14 99
– www.residencial-italia.com 　　　　　　　　　　　　　　G-H2
44 rm ⚏ **–** ♦42/80 € ♦♦50/100 €
◆ Family ◆ Urban ◆ Functional ◆
The attractive patio with its tables, lawn and orange trees comes as a pleasant surprise in the centre of the city. The guestrooms are modern, simple and functional.

Eleven (Joachim Koerper) ⇐Totally no smoking ⇔ 🄿

Rua Marquês de Fronteira ✉ *1070 –* 🄜 *São Sebastião* VISA ⓞⓞ AE ①
– ☎ 213 86 22 11 – 11@restauranteleven.com – Fax 213 86 22 14
– www.restauranteleven.com – closed Sunday **G2**
Rest – Menu 69 € – Carte 64/76 € ⌘

Spec. Tártaro de santola confitada e vinagrete de caril de Madrás (January-June). Carré de cordeiro biológico em crosta. Soufflé de maracujá com gelado de banana (December-June).

 ♦ Inventive ♦ Modern ♦

Attractive restaurant with a private bar/hall. The modern dining room has wonderful views of the park, the river and the city. Well-presented, creative cuisine.

Saraiva's VISA ⓞⓞ AE ①

Rua Engenheiro Canto Resende 3 ✉ *1050-104 –* 🄜 *São Sebastião – ☎ 213 54 06 09*
– Fax 213 53 19 87 – closed Friday dinner, Saturday and Bank Holidays
Rest – Carte 20/32 € **G2**

 ♦ Traditional ♦ Contemporary ♦

Excellent, well-run restaurant decorated in a modern style reminiscent of the 1980s. Good choice of dishes on the menu, which features both traditional and international cuisine.

Clube do Peixe VISA ⓞⓞ AE ①

Av. 5 de Outubro 180 ✉ *1050-063 –* 🄜 *Campo Pequeno – ☎ 217 97 34 34*
– Fax 217 97 34 33 – www.clube-do-peixe.com – closed Sunday **H1**
Rest – Carte 25/39 €

 ♦ Fish and shellfish ♦ Formal ♦

A popular local restaurant with an attractive display of fish and seafood at the entrance. The dining room is classic-contemporary in style with the occasional maritime detail in the decor.

Adega Tia Matilde ⇔ VISA ⓞⓞ AE ①

Rua da Beneficência 77 ✉ *1600-017 –* 🄜 *Praça de Espanha – ☎ 217 97 21 72*
– adegatiamatilde@netcabo.pt – Fax 217 97 21 72 – www.adegatiamatilde.com
– closed Saturday dinner and Sunday **Rest** – Carte 25/40 € **G1**

 ♦ Traditional ♦ Formal ♦

Family-run restaurant with a good local reputation. Spacious dining rooms and traditional cuisine. The large underground car park makes up for the poor location.

Varanda da União ⇐ VISA ⓞⓞ AE ①

Rua Castilho 14 C-7° ✉ *1250-069 –* 🄜 *Marquês de Pombal – ☎ 213 14 10 45*
– varandauniao@sapo.pt – Fax 213 14 10 46 – www.varandauniao.restaunet.pt
– closed Saturday lunch, Sunday and Bank Holidays lunch *Plan II* **E1**
Rest – Carte 32/40 €

 ♦ Traditional ♦ Formal ♦

This successful restaurant on the seventh floor of an apartment building enjoys splendid views of the rooftops of Lisbon. High quality cuisine served by a plethora of waiters.

O Polícia ⇔ VISA ⓞⓞ AE

Rua Marquês Sá da Bandeira 112 ✉ *1050-150 –* 🄜 *São Sebastião – ☎ 217 96 35 05*
– Fax 217 96 97 91 – closed Saturday dinner, Sunday and Bank Holidays
Rest – Carte 25/37 € **G2**

 ♦ Traditional ♦ Family ♦

This busy family-run restaurant is renowned for its fish. Display counter, attractive table settings and two entrances. Dining area divided into four rooms. Reservations recommended.

Mezzaluna VISA ⓞⓞ AE ①

Rua Artilharia Um 16 ✉ *1250-039 – ☎ 213 87 99 44 – mg@chefguerrieri.com*
– Fax 213 85 16 61 – www.mezzalunalisboa.com
– closed Saturday lunch, Sunday and Bank Holidays **G3**
Rest – Carte approx. 30 €

 ♦ Italian ♦ Formal ♦

A classic-style restaurant run by its owner-chef. Attractive layout, although the tables are set somewhat close together. High quality Italian cuisine.

✗   **Mãe d'Água**   _VISA_ ⦿ _AE_ ⓘ
Travessa das Amoreiras 10 ✉ *1250-025* – Ⓜ *Rato* – ℰ *213 88 28 20*
– Fax 213 87 12 66
– closed 17 July-28 August, Saturday and Sunday   **G3**
Rest – Carte 28/36 €
♦ Traditional ♦ Family ♦

The limited space in this restaurant adds to its cosy ambience. The dining room
beyond the bar is decorated with bullfighting pictures and photos. Excellent service.

PARQUE DAS NAÇÕES   *Plan I*

🏨   **Tivoli Tejo**   ℔ 🖥 ⅋ rm ▦ ℣ ⅍ 🀫 _VISA_ ⦿ _AE_ ⓘ
Av. D. João II (Parque das Nações) ✉ *1990-083* – Ⓜ *Oriente* – ℰ *218 91 51 00*
– httejo@tivolihotels.com – Fax 218 91 53 45 – www.tivolitejo.com
262 rm – ♥♥420 €, ☑ 10 € – 17 suites   **D1**
Rest *VIII Colina* – – Carte 31/55 €
♦ Chain hotel ♦ Classical ♦

Attractive building next to the Oriente railway station. It offers contemporary
guestrooms with small bathrooms. Pleasant public areas, albeit lacking in space.
The VIII Colina restaurant enjoys superb panoramic views.

🏨   **Olissippo Oriente**   ▦ ℣ ⅍ 🀫 _VISA_ ⦿ _AE_ ⓘ
Av. D. João II (Parque das Nações) ✉ *1990-083* – Ⓜ *Oriente* – ℰ *218 92 91 00*
– reservas@olissippohotels.com – Fax 218 92 91 19 – www.olissippohotels.com
182 rm ☑ – ♥160/200 € ♥♥180/220 €   **Rest** – Menu 21 €   **D1**
♦ Chain hotel ♦ Modern ♦

Situated on the Expo site, this hotel boasts modern facilities. It includes extensive
public areas and lounges, meeting rooms and comfortable guestrooms. A refined
dining room where guests can enjoy a full buffet or a menu featuring traditional
cuisine.

🏨   **Tryp Oriente**   ⅋ ▦ ℣ ⅍ 🀫 _VISA_ ⦿ _AE_ ⓘ
Av. D. João II (Parque das Nações) ✉ *1990-083* – Ⓜ *Oriente* – ℰ *218 93 00 00*
– tryp.oriente@solmeliaportugal.com – Fax 218 93 00 99 – www.solmelia.com
206 rm ☑ – ♥120/153 € ♥♥135/175 €   **Rest** – Menu 14 €   **D1**
♦ Chain hotel ♦ Classical ♦

Situated on the Expo site, this functional hotel has a pleasant lounge-bar and spacious guestrooms - those on the upper floors enjoy lovely views. A bright restaurant with a limited menu. Separate entrance from the hotel.

AT WEST   *Plan I*

🏨🏨   **Lapa Palace** ⤴   ≤ ⚎ ⚏ ℔ ⅀ 🖥 ⅋ rm ▦ ℣ ⅍ 🄿 🀫
Rua do Pau de Bandeira 4 ✉ *1249-021* – Ⓜ *Rato*   _VISA_ ⦿ _AE_ ⓘ
– ℰ 213 94 94 94 – info@lapa-palace.com – Fax 213 95 06 65
– www.lapa-palace.com   **B3**
102 rm ☑ – ♥♥340/775 € – 7 suites   **Rest *Hotel Cipriani*** – Carte 52/65 €
♦ Grand Luxury ♦ Classical ♦

On a hill, with the Tagus river in the distance, this 19C palace is a luxurious hidea-
way in a quiet and elegant part of the city. Intimate lounges, and delightful tree-
lined gardens with a waterfall add to the overall charm. The restaurant serves fine
cuisine with a focus on Italian and Portuguese specialities.

🏨🏨   **Pestana Palace** ⤴   ⚎ ℔ ⅀ 🖥 ⅋ rm ▦ ℣ ⅍ 🀫 _VISA_ ⦿ _AE_ ⓘ
Rua Jau 54 ✉ *1300-314* – ℰ *213 61 56 00* – *sales.cph@pestana.com*
– Fax 213 61 56 01 – www.pestana.com   **B3**
177 rm ☑ – ♥370 € ♥♥390 € – 17 suites   **Rest *Valle Flor*** – Carte 57/73 €
♦ Luxury ♦ Palace ♦ Stylish ♦

Beautifully restored 19C palace with period decor, luxurious lounges and guestrooms filled with decorative detail. Well-maintained grounds with an abundance
of flora. Magnificent restaurant both in terms of its cuisine and the beautiful and
luxurious dining rooms.

As Janelas Verdes *without rest* 🔲 🍴 VISA ✪ AE ①

Rua das Janelas Verdes 47 ✉ 1200-690 – ℰ 213 96 81 43
– jverdes@heritage.pt – Fax 213 96 81 44 – www.heritage.pt **B3**
29 rm – ♦210/280 € ♦♦225/298 €, ☲ 14 €
♦ Mansion ♦ Classical ♦

Partially housed in an 18C mansion, this welcoming hotel has a delightful lounge-library and beautiful views. A romantic feel and classic style.

York House 🏠 🔲 🍴 ⅍ VISA ✪ AE ①

Rua das Janelas Verdes 32 ✉ 1200-691 – Ⓜ Cais do Sodré
– ℰ 213 96 24 35 – reservations@yorkhouselisboa.com
– Fax 213 97 27 93 – www.yorkhouselisboa.com **B3**
32 rm – ♦135/225 € ♦♦155/270 €, ☲ 15 € **Rest** – Carte 30/45 €
♦ Convent ♦ Contemporary ♦

Housed in a 17C convent, this hotel has a comfortable, contemporary interior. Its modern decor is furnished with period pieces. Classic-style restaurant adorned with an attractive frieze of old azulejo tiles.

A Travessa 🏠 VISA ✪ AE

Travessa do Convento das Bernardas 12 ✉ 1200-638 – Ⓜ Cais do Sodré
– ℰ 213 90 20 34 – info@atravessa.com – Fax 213 94 08 39 – www.atravessa.com
– closed Saturday lunch, Sunday and Monday lunch **B3**
Rest – Carte 30/42 €
♦ French ♦ Cosy ♦

This restaurant occupies a 17C monastery. The dining room has a lovely vaulted ceiling, rustic-style flooring and an attractive terrace in the cloister.

Solar dos Nunes ✿ VISA ✪ AE ①

Rua dos Lusíadas 68-72 ✉ 1300-372 – ℰ 213 64 73 59 – Fax 213 63 16 31
– www.solardosnunes.pt
– closed 5-25 August and Sunday **B3**
Rest – Carte approx. 30 €
♦ Traditional ♦ Typical ♦

This restaurant has a friendly atmosphere, traditional-style dining rooms and a lovely paved floor. Wide choice of traditional Portuguese dishes and a good wine list.

Tromba Rija Totally no smoking VISA ✪ AE ①

Rua Cintura do Porto de Lisboa - edif 254 ✉ 1200-109 – Ⓜ Cais do Sodré
– ℰ 213 97 15 07 – reservaslisboa@trombarija.com – Fax 213 97 12 03
– www.trombarija.com – closed Sunday dinner and Monday lunch
Rest – Menu 36 € **B3**
♦ Traditional ♦ Neo-rustic ♦

Located in a former warehouse at the port. This restaurant offers a full buffet of traditional Portuguese cuisine featuring over 50 different dishes.

BELÉM *Plan I*

Jerónimos 8 *without rest* 🔲 🍴 ⅍ VISA ✪ AE ①

Rua dos Jerónimos 8 ✉ 1400-211 – ℰ 213 60 09 00 – jeronimos8@
almeidahotels.com – Fax 213 60 09 08 – www.jeronimos8.com **A3**
65 rm ☲ – ♦160/220 € ♦♦180/240 €
♦ Business ♦ Modern ♦

This comfortable hotel is located next to the Monasterio de Los Jerónimos. It occupies an old building that has been completely renovated with a minimalist feel.

Vela Latina 🏠 ✿ VISA ✪ AE ①

Doca do Bom Sucesso ✉ 1400-038 – ℰ 213 01 71 18 – reservas@velalatina.pt
– Fax 213 01 93 11 – www.velalatina.pt – closed Sunday and Bank Holidays
Rest – Carte 34/50 € **A3**
♦ Traditional ♦ Formal ♦

Located near the Torre de Belém with an elegant private bar, splendid private dining room and a main lounge with typical maritime decor. Pleasant, glass-fronted terrace.

SPAIN
ESPAÑA

PROFILE

→ **AREA:**
504 645 km².

→ **POPULATION:**
46 063 511
inhabitants (est.
2008), density = 91.2
per km².

→ **CAPITAL:**
Madrid (conurbation
6 112 078
inhabitants).

→ **CURRENCY:**
Euro (€); rate of
exchange: € 1 =
US$ 1.32 (Jan 2009).

→ **GOVERNMENT:**
Constitutional
parliamentary
monarchy (since
1978). Member of
European Union since
1986.

→ **LANGUAGES:**
Spanish (Castilian)
but also Catalan in
Catalonia, Gallego
in Galicia, Euskera in
the Basque Country,
Valencian in the
Valencian Region
and Mallorquin in the
Balearic Isles.

→ **SPECIFIC PUBLIC
HOLIDAYS:**
Epiphany (6 January);
San Jose (19 March);
Maundy Thursday
(the day before
Good Friday); Good
Friday (Friday before

Easter); National
Day (12 October);
Constitution Day
(6 December);
Immaculate
Conception
(8 December). Some
public holidays
may be replaced by
the autonomous
communities with
another date.

→ **LOCAL TIME:**
GMT + 1 hour in
winter and GMT
+ 2 hours in summer.

→ **CLIMATE:**
Temperate
Mediterranean with
mild winters (colder
in interior) and sunny,
hot summers (Madrid:
January: 6°C, July:
25°C).

→ **IINTERNATIONAL
DIALLING CODE:**
00 34 followed
by full 9-digit
number. Directory
enquiries: ℰ **11822**.
International
directory enquiries:
ℰ **11825**. On-line
telephone directory:
www.blancas.
paginasamarillas.es

→ **EMERGENCY:**
Dial ℰ **112**;
National Police:
ℰ **091**.

→ **ELECTRICITY:**
220 or 225 volts AC
(previously 110 V),
50 Hz; 2-pin round-
shaped continental
plugs.

→ **FORMALITIES**
Travellers from the
European Union
(EU), Switzerland,
Iceland and
the main countries
of North and South
America need a
national identity
card or passport
(America: passport
required) to visit
Spain for less than
three months
(tourism or business
purpose). For visitors
from other countries
a visa may be
required, in addition
to a passport,
especially for those
wishing to stay for
longer than three
months. We advise
you to check with
your embassy before
travelling.

MADRID

MADRID

Population (est. 2008): 3 238 208 (conurbation 6 245 883) – Altitude: 655m

Y. Travert/PHOTONONSTOP

Madrid is a city on the rise. The nightlife in Spain's proud capital is now second to none and the superb museums of art which make up the city's 'golden triangle' have all undergone thrilling reinvention in recent years.

The next big plan for Madrid is to have a square kilometre park near the river Manzanares, which runs just west of the city. In a big bid to give *madrileños* more clean air, the new park will be free of cars, and will boast bike lanes intermingled with eight thousand trees – and there'll be an artificial beach, too. The renaissance of Madrid has seen it develop as a big player on the world cultural stage, attracting more international music, theatre and dance than it would have dreamed of a decade ago. The new Royal Spanish Ballet will be based here, a testament to its rising cachet in the arts. This is a city that might think it has some catching up to do: it was only made the capital in 1561 on the whim of ruler, Felipe II. But its position was crucial: slap bang in the middle of the Iberian Peninsula. Ruled by Habsburgs and Bourbons, it soon made a mark in Europe.

The contemporary big wigs of Madrid are out to have the same effect with a 21C twist.

LIVING THE CITY

The central heart of Madrid is compact, defined by the teeming Habsburg hubs of **Puerta del Sol** and **Plaza Mayor**, and the mighty **Palacio Real**. East of here are the grand squares, fountains and fine museums of the Bourbon district with its easterly boundary, the **Retiro** park. West of the historical centre are the capacious green acres of **Casa de Campo**, while the affluent, regimented grid streets of **Salamanca** are to the east. Modern Madrid is just to the north, embodied in the grand north-south boulevard **Paseo de la Castellana**.

PRACTICAL INFORMATION

ARRIVAL-DEPARTURE

Madrid-Barajas Airport is approximately 13km east of the city. A taxi should cost around €25. Metro Line 8 runs every 4-7min, with a journey time of 50min. Chamartin Station is the railway station for services to the north of Spain and France ; Atocha Station for those to the south.

TRANSPORT

Madrid is covered by a bus and metro public transport system. You can buy single journey tickets, but a better bet for longer visits is a ten-trip Metrobus ticket, valid on both bus and metro networks, and better value than tickets bought individually. Get them from underground stations, bus ticket offices, newsstands and tobacconists.

Consider also the Tourist Travel Card, which is valid from one to seven days for unlimited travel on all public transport in Zone A or Zone T in the Madrid region. As well as usual outlets, it's also on sale at the city's two long-distance train stations, Chamartín and Atocha.

It's well worth forking out for a Madrid Card. You can get them for one, two, or three-day periods from a wide range of outlets. They entitle you to travel on all forms of public transport, and grant admission to more than forty museums. They're also valid for discounts in some nightclubs, shops and restaurants.

EXPLORING MADRID

All roads in Spain lead to the Puerta del Sol. This is not as fanciful as it

sounds: the square - where it seems every tourist in Madrid has congregated for orientation guidelines - also bears a symbol on the ground marking Kilometre Zero, considered the centre of Spain's road network. This was once the eastern entrance to Madrid, with a castle and gatehouse. You'd never guess it now. With its iconic 'Tio Pepe' sherry sign leering overhead, the cafés and shops here are a non-stop buzz of activity as visitors plan their itineraries in the surrounding knot of narrow streets. The crescent shaped Puerta del Sol has its charms, but the area's finest square is a little way to the west.

Plaza Mayor is a beautifully arcaded rectangle which has been the focal point over the centuries of everything from bullfights to the trials of the Inquisition. It's still the ceremonial heart of the city, so one day you can expect a fiesta, the next a political rally. Despite all this, it can be surprisingly peaceful here during weekdays, and makes the perfect setting for a coffee or a meal at one of the many cafés whose tables spill out from the arcades. It boasts a distinctly Castilian character, and its theatrical face is best shown above the arcades of the Casa de la Panadería, which is decorated with eye-catching allegorical paintings. Just two hundred metres further west is the third of the old quarter's great squares, **Plaza de la Villa**, an atmospheric space surrounded by many historic buildings, such as the early fifteenth-century **Torre de los Lujanes**, which mixes Gothic embellishments with arches in a dramatic horse-shoe style.

→ REAL HEAD-TURNER

Head even further west, up a steep slope towards the river, and you come to Madrid's ultimate showpiece building: the **Palacio Real**. This is the biggest official royal residence in the world with a bewildering three thousand rooms. It took two 18C Bourbon monarchs twenty eight years to build themselves this cosy little number. You come to it across the huge semi-circular **Plaza de Oriente**, a theatrical concoction in itself. Inside, the show continues, with highlights left, right and centre. These include the superb Throne Room with its sculptures by Velázquez, the main staircase sculpted from Toledo marble, the lavishly decorated Garparini Rooms (all silk, stucco and chinoiserie), the magnificent State Dining Room, and the Royal Armoury, which includes the armour of El Cid and his horse.

Don't get the impression Madrid is all plaza and palaccio. You can come up for air at a number of imposing green spaces. Close to the Palaccio Real is the gracefully sloping **Campo del Moro**, while the western boundary of the city is the massive Casa de Campo, almost seven square miles of tennis courts, swimming pools, funfair, pines and scrubland. Madrid's favourite park, though, is on the eastern side of town. Retiro Park was once a three hundred acre royal palace garden. When it opened to the public in 1869 *madrileños* came in their thousands, and it's still the city's number one destination for chilling out. There's a large boating lake in the middle, and two elegant glasshouses useful for delving around as they house interesting free art exhibitions.

If you're at the Retiro, you're in the city's Bourbon quarter, named after the dynasty which developed it in the eighteenth century. Strolling around the park, there's every chance you've been to, or are heading towards, one of the three fabulous museums in the area: art lovers in this neck of the woods aren't just spoilt for choice, they can positively wallow in it. Top spot goes to the **Prado**, one of the world's great museums and the capital's top cultural attraction. It contains the world's richest assembly of Spanish painting, covering the 12 to 19C, with a magnificent range of works by Velázquez, Goya and El Greco. There's also a wealth of Italian Renaissance masterpieces and Flemish works. Ground floor highlights include Hieronymus Bosch's *The Garden of Earthly Delights*, and *The Annunciation* by Fra Angelico.

→ SEVEN CENTURIES OF ART

Cross the street and you're at another superb artistic offering. The **Museo Thyssen-Bornemisza** was bequeathed to Spain as recently as 1993, and is one of the most important private collections in the world. Installed in an 18C palace, its three floors cover seven centuries of Western art, from Van Eyck, Holbein, Titian, Durer and Rubens (top floor) to the Dutch Golden Age, German Expressionism and French Impressionism (first floor), and ending up with Picasso, Hopper and Freud at ground level. If you have the energy, saunter down the Paseo del Prado for less than half a mile and you'll reach the third of the triumvirate, the **Centro de Arte Reina Sofía**, the city's museum of modern art. Most people come here primarily to take in Picasso's haunting *Guernica*, but when they arrive they're knocked out by the whole place. It's an 18C former hospital, and its exhibition space is vast. The focus is on Spanish work (the 20C was a monumental century for Spanish art), and there are rooms devoted to Miró, Dalí and the surrealist film-maker Luis Buñuel.

→ GRAN TOUR

It's useful to have eyes not only in the back of your head but on top of it too when you're passing along the **Gran Vía**. This is Madrid's bustling main thoroughfare, whose construction started exactly one hundred years ago (1908) and was completed twenty years later. Sure, you have to watch out for the traffic streaming along it, but don't miss the fine 20C buildings towering above you, either. They represent a vivid panorama of modern architecture, from neo-classical to art deco. Gran Vía even has a structure straight out of a Jimmy Cagney movie: the 1920s **Telefónica** building is a slightly squashed version of a Manhattan skyscraper. A different style of street, and a different style of window gazing, can be found further east in the Salamanca district. Here you'll come across wide, sophisticated boulevards on a grid system where the shops and boutiques are of the smartly expensive variety.

Madrid is a hip and happening place wherever you turn at whatever time of day, and tourists from, say, northern Europe may have to adjust their body clocks to the city's late hour culture. However, even in this city, there are two areas just north of Gran Vía that are instantly recognisable for their extra cool vibe. **Chueca** and **Malasaña** have an arty, bohemian feel, defined by hip bars and sassy little shops. Chueca is the gay/lesbian quarter of the city; Malasaña's grungy ambience is, if anything, heightened by its charming cobbled streets, fountains and trees. Whichever quarter you hit on, you won't forget the nightlife in a hurry.

CALENDAR HIGHLIGHTS

The highlight of the year comes in May: the Fiesta de San Isidro, the feast of the region's patron saint. For a week either side of the fifteenth, the city pulsates with fiestas, music and dance; focal points are the Plaza Mayor and Jardines de las Vistillas. Just before this, on 2 May, Dos de Mayo

MADRID IN...

→ ONE DAY
Puerta del Sol, Plaza Mayor, Palacio Real, Prado

→ TWO DAYS
Museo Thyssen-Bornemisza, Retiro, Gran Vía, tapas at a traditional taberna

→ THREE DAYS
Chueca, Malasaña, Centro de Arte Reina Sofía

festivities in Malasaña commemorate a rebellion against French occupying forces. A more sedate air surrounds the Madrid Book Fair in Retiro Park at the end of the month. The summer's main festival is Los Veranos de la Villa, a series of concerts featuring international musicians in various city venues: for two months, Madrid is ablaze with opera, tango, flamenco, jazz, Spanish musicals, exhibitions and films. September sees Festival de Otoño, when drama, ballet and opera descend upon they city's concert venues. One of the most colourful sights of the Madrid winter is the Twelfth Night procession (5 January) which goes from Retiro to Plaza Mayor and is full of floats and accompanying animals. Art lovers don their coats and scarves and head for ARCO in February: this is the city's internationally renowned contemporary art fair, held in Parque Ferial Juan Carlos I. And then there's Carnaval, with fancy dress parties and a parade from Plaza de Colón to Plaza de Cibeles. Día de Cervantes (23 April) celebrates the great author's death with a book fair in Alcalá de Henares.

EATING OUT

Madrileños know how to pace themselves. Breakfast is around 8am, lunch 2pm or 3pm, 5pm is the beginning of the afternoon and dinner won't be until 10pm or 11pm. A late night? Until dawn the next day or later. Madrid is the European capital which has best managed to absorb the regional cuisine of the country, largely due to massive internal migration to the city. Spain has the highest bar-restaurant per inhabitant ratio in Europe, and Madrid clocks in with one bar-restaurant per 171 inhabitants. Strange as it may seem given its geography, the quality and range of fish available in Madrid is exceptional: it's the second largest central fish market in the world, after Tokyo. Two reasons: it's established a land port in the nearby town of Coslada, and ocean fresh seafood is transported to the capital on a daily basis from the Galician coast. If you want to tuck into local specialities, you'll find them everywhere around the city. But what to try? *Callos a la madrileña* is Madrid-style tripe, dating back to 1559, while *sopas de Ajo* (garlic soup) is a favourite on cold winter days. Another popular soup (also a main course) is *cocido madrileño*, hearty and aromatic and comprised of chick peas, meat, tocino belly pork, potatoes and vegetables, slowly cooked in a rich broth. Two top fish dishes are *besugo a la madrileña* (baked sea bream with white wine, parsley and potatoes), and *bacalao a la madrileña* (Madrid-style cod, with potatoes, onions, tomatoes, garlic and olive oil). Or, of course, there's always the ubiquitous *tortilla de patata* (potato omelette) found in any bar, taberna or cafetería. To experience the real Madrid dining ambience, get to a traditional taberna in the heart of the old neighbourhood: there are about one hundred remaining in the area, distinguished by large clock, carved wooden bar with zinc counter and wine flasks, marble table tops and ceramic tiles. At the end of a meal, the bill will include service, but tips in cash are commonplace: around five per cent of the total.

→ THE OLDEST

A taberna to make for when in the old town is Botín. The roast suckling pig on offer is renowned throughout Spain, and Ernest Hemingway was known to tuck in here. The establishment's real claim to fame, though, is its appearance in the Guinness Book of Records: it dates back to 1725, making it the oldest restaurant in the world.

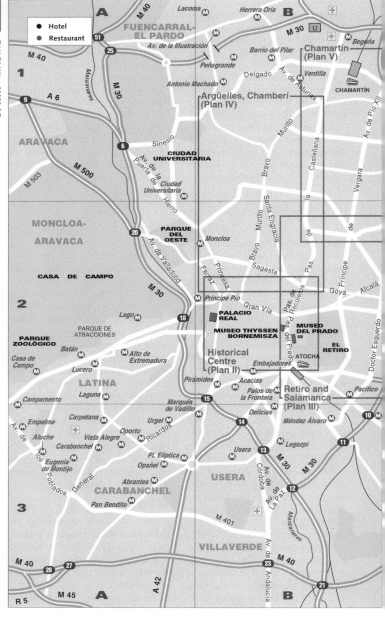

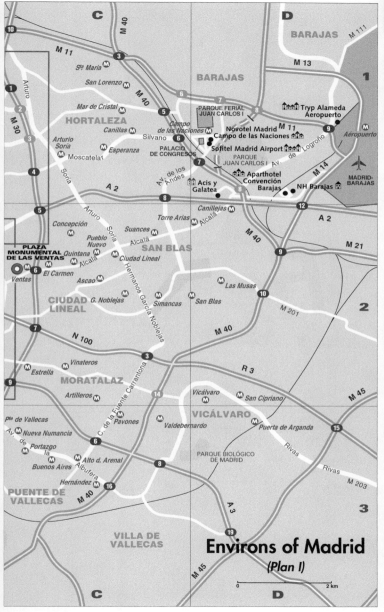

Environs of Madrid
(Plan I)

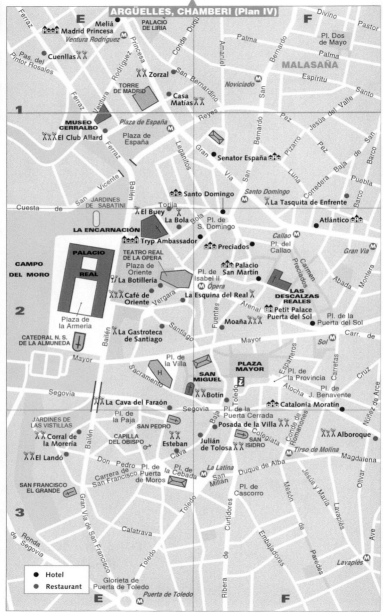

ARGÜELLES, CHAMBERI (Plan IV)

E
F

SPAIN - MADRID

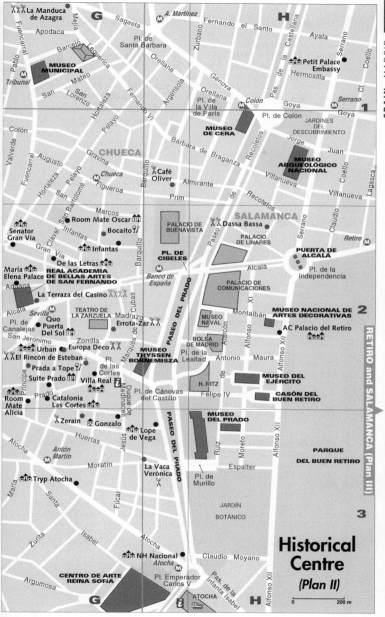

Historical
Centre
(Plan II)

0   200 m

Villa Real 🏨🏨🏨

pl. de las Cortes 10 ✉ *28014 –* Ⓜ *Sevilla –* ✆ *914 20 37 67*
– villareal@derbyhotels.com – Fax 914 20 25 47 – www.derbyhotels.com
96 rm – †175/384 €, ††160/425 €, ⌑ 21 € – 19 suites **MY**
Rest *East 47* – Carte approx. 55 €

♦ Urban ♦ Personalised ♦

This hotel displays a valuable collection of Greek and Roman art in many of its public areas. The comfortable guestrooms are attractively decorated with mahogany furniture. Charming restaurant decorated with contemporary lithography.

Urban 🏨🏨🏨

Carrera de San Jerónimo 34 ✉ *28014 –* Ⓜ *Sevilla –* ✆ *917 87 77 70*
– urban@derbyhotels.com – Fax 917 87 77 99 – www.derbyhotels.com
87 rm – †215/426 €, ††200/475 €, ⌑ 21 € – 9 suites **G2**
Rest Europa Decó – see below

♦ Urban ♦ Design ♦

An avant-garde hotel with high quality furnishings, attractive lighting effects and numerous works of art on display. Well-equipped guestrooms with real attention to detail.

Husa Princesa 🏨🏨🏨 Smokers rest.

Princesa 40 ✉ *28008 –* Ⓜ *Argüelles –* ✆ *915 42 21 00 – husaprincesa@husa.es*
– Fax 915 42 73 28 – www.hotelhusaprincesa.com *Plan IV* **K3**
263 rm – †140/300 €, ††165/375 €, ⌑ 25 € – 12 suites
Rest *– (Closed August, Sunday and Monday dinner)* Carte 52/69 €

♦ Chain hotel ♦ Classical ♦

Magnificent hotel located on one of the city's main avenues. It has large public rooms and spacious, extremely well-equipped guestrooms. Modern dining room with an intimate feel and a menu featuring classic international cuisine.

Meliá Madrid Princesa 🏨🏨🏨

Princesa 27 ✉ *28008 –* Ⓜ *Ventura Rodríguez –* ✆ *915 41 82 00*
– melia.madrid.princesa@solmelia.com – Fax 915 41 19 88
– www.meliamadridprincesa.com **E1**
237 rm – ††140/290 €, ⌑ 25 € – 37 suites
Rest *– (closed August)* Carte 41/67 €

♦ Chain hotel ♦ Classical ♦

This hotel boasts a charming location and a wide range of facilities. Elegant lobby with designer furniture and reasonably modern, well-equipped guestrooms. The hotel restaurant offers its guests a carefully prepared menu of Mediterranean cuisine.

Tryp Ambassador 🏨🏨🏨 Smokers rest.

Cuesta de Santo Domingo 5 ✉ *28013 –* Ⓜ *Santo Domingo –* ✆ *915 41 67 00*
– tryp.ambassador@solmelia.com – Fax 915 59 10 40 – www.solmelia.com
159 rm – ††85/210 €, ⌑ 18 € – 24 suites
Rest – Carte 35/53 € **E-F2**

♦ Chain hotel ♦ Classical ♦

The Tryp Ambassador has a stately atmosphere with an attractive patio typical of this exclusive district of the city. Comfortable guestrooms with elegant, high quality furniture. Restaurant with a glass ceiling, in the style of a winter garden.

De las Letras 🏨🏨

Gran Vía 11 ✉ *28013 –* Ⓜ *Sevilla –* ✆ *915 23 79 80*
– info@hoteldelasletras.com – Fax 915 23 79 81 – www.hoteldelasletras.com
103 rm – ††120/300 €, ⌑ 15.50 € **Rest** – Carte 38/48 € **G2**

♦ Urban ♦ Design ♦

The restored exterior contrasts with a contemporary, colourful interior. The guestrooms are described as having a 'New York' style with intimate lighting and poems on the walls. A unique, modern restaurant where guests can prepare their own dishes.

María Elena Palace

Aduana 19 ✉ *28013* – 🚇 *Sol* – 𝒞 *913 60 49 30* – *mariaelenapalace@chh.es* – *Fax 913 60 47 89* – *www.chh.es* **G2**
87 rm ☲ – 🛏100/250 € 🛏🛏125/350 €   **Rest** – Menu 23 €
♦ Traditional ♦ Classical ♦
This hotel has an open lobby and a magnificent patio crowned by a glass dome. Classical-style bedrooms with quality furnishings, carpets and marble baths.

NH Nacional

paseo del Prado 48 ✉ *28014* – 🚇 *Atocha* – 𝒞 *914 29 66 29* – *nhnacional@nh-hotels.com* – *Fax 913 69 15 64* – *www.nh-hotels.com*
213 rm – 🛏91/209 € 🛏🛏101/232 €, ☲ 19 € **G3**
Rest – *(closed 15 July-August)* Menu 33 €
♦ Urban ♦ Contemporary ♦
An attractive façade and excellent location. Spacious lobby-reception area, and cosy, well-appointed guestrooms decorated in a bright, contemporary-style.

Catalonia Las Cortes No smokers rest.

Prado 6 ✉ *28014* – 🚇 *Antón Martín* – 𝒞 *913 89 60 51* – *lascortes@ hoteles-catalonia.es* – *Fax 913 89 60 52* – *www.hoteles-catalonia.com*
65 rm – 🛏155/250 € 🛏🛏195/290 €, ☲ 15 € **G2**
Rest – *(dinner only)* Menu 26 €
♦ Traditional ♦ Classical ♦
This 18C building once belonged to the Dukes of Noblejas. Fully-equipped guestrooms and a bright interior that combines the traditional and modern.

Senator España No smokers rest.

Gran Vía 70 ✉ *28013* – 🚇 *Plaza de España* – 𝒞 *915 22 82 65* – *senator.espana@playasenator.com* – *Fax 915 22 82 64* – *www.playasenator.com* **F1**
171 rm – 🛏100/300 € 🛏🛏100/500 €, ☲ 15 €   **Rest** – Menu 21 €
♦ Chain hotel ♦ Functional ♦
This hotel boasts excellent leisure facilities, including a beauty centre and hydromassage pools. The well-appointed guestrooms are fitted with excellent soundproofing. The Senator España's restaurant offers guests a choice between the salad buffet and a creative à la carte menu.

Infantas Smokers rest.

Infantas 29 ✉ *28004* – 🚇 *Chueca* – 𝒞 *915 21 28 28* – *hotelinfantas@ lussohoteles.com* – *Fax 915 21 66 88* – *www.lussohoteles.com* **G2**
40 rm – 🛏🛏75/275 €, ☲ 14 €   **Rest *Ex Libris*** – Carte 31/44 €
♦ Urban ♦ Modern ♦
The Infantas occupies an old building that has been completely renovated in contemporary-style. Well-appointed guestrooms and bathrooms. A minimalist-style restaurant serving creative cuisine.

Palacio San Martín No smokers rest.

pl. San Martín 5 ✉ *28013* – 🚇 *Callao* – 𝒞 *917 01 50 00* – *sanmartin@intur.com* – *Fax 917 01 50 10* – *www.intur.com* **F2**
93 rm – 🛏120/187 € 🛏🛏120/232 €, ☲ 16 €
Rest – *(closed August, Sunday and Bank Holidays)* Menu 35 €
♦ Urban ♦ Stylish ♦
This hotel occupies an old building that served as the American embassy in the 1950s. The lounge is situated in a patio crowned by a glass roof. Traditional-style bedrooms. A top floor restaurant with lovely views.

Room Mate Alicia without rest

Prado 2 ✉ *28014* – 🚇 *Sevilla* – 𝒞 *913 89 60 95* – *alicia@ room-matehoteles.com* – *Fax 913 69 47 95* – *www.room-matehotels.com*
34 rm ☲ – 🛏90/140 € 🛏🛏100/170 € **G2**
♦ Urban ♦ Contemporary ♦
The façade of this restored old building contrasts with the contemporary interior. Spacious, well-appointed bedrooms with designer furniture.

Senator Gran Vía
No smokers rest. 📶 ⁾⁾ 👍 VISA ⁍⁍ AE ⓞ

Gran Vía 21 ✉ *28013* – Ⓜ *Gran Vía* – 𝒞 *915 31 41 51* – *senator.granvia@*
playasenator.com – *Fax 915 24 07 99* – *www.playasenator.com* **G2**
136 rm – 🛏79/299 € 🛏🛏89/329 €, ⌷ 12 €   **Rest** – Carte 26/46 €
◆ Chain hotel ◆ Functional ◆
The emblematic classic façade of this hotel contrasts with its contemporary creature comforts. Up-to-date guestrooms, and a café that is the hotel's only lounge
area. Simple, functional restaurant offering à la carte and buffet options.

Santo Domingo
No smokers rest. 📶 ⁾⁾ 👍 VISA ⁍⁍ AE ⓞ

pl. de Santo Domingo 13 ✉ *28013* – Ⓜ *Santo Domingo* – 𝒞 *915 47 98 00*
– *reserva@hotelsantodomingo.com* – *Fax 915 47 59 95*
– *www.hotelsantodomingo.com* **F2**
120 rm – 🛏127/170 € 🛏🛏140/220 €, ⌷ 12.40 €   **Rest** – Menu 33 €
◆ Traditional ◆ Personalised ◆
Pleasantly comfortable guestrooms in varied tones with modern bathrooms, some
of which have hydromassage baths. Outstanding display of art on the walls.

Preciados
📶 ⁾⁾ 👍 🚗 VISA ⁍⁍ AE ⓞ

Preciados 37 ✉ *28013* – Ⓜ *Callao* – 𝒞 *914 54 44 00* – *preciadoshotel@*
preciadoshotel.com – *Fax 914 54 44 01* – *www.preciadoshotel.com*
68 rm – 🛏95/160 € 🛏🛏105/250 €, ⌷ 15 € – 5 suites **F2**
Rest – Carte 34/41 €
◆ Urban ◆ Modern ◆
The plain classic architectural style of this building, dating back to the 19C, contrasts with the modern, fully equipped interior. Smallish, cosy lounge area.

Tryp Atocha without rest
📶 ⁾⁾ 👍 VISA ⁍⁍ AE ⓞ

Atocha 83 ✉ *28012* – Ⓜ *Antón Martín* – 𝒞 *913 30 05 00* – *tryp.atocha@*
solmelia.com – *Fax 914 20 15 60* – *www.solmelia.com* **G3**
150 rm – 🛏95/225 € 🛏🛏95/245 €, ⌷ 16 €
◆ Chain hotel ◆ Functional ◆
Palace-like building from 1913 with modern, functional facilities. Spacious public
areas, such as the ballroom with its large windows, and magnificent staircase.

Catalonia Moratín without rest
📶 ⁾⁾ 👍 VISA ⁍⁍ AE ⓞ

Atocha 23 ✉ *28012* – Ⓜ *Sol* – 𝒞 *913 69 71 71* – *moratin@hoteles-catalonia.es*
– *Fax 913 60 12 31* – *www.hoteles-catalonia.es* **F2-3**
59 rm – 🛏150/240 € 🛏🛏190/280 €, ⌷ 15 € – 4 suites
◆ Chain hotel ◆ Functional ◆
Housed in an 18C building, this hotel has retained some of its original features,
such as the staircase, and combined them with a more practical design. Inner
patio with a glass ceiling and modern guestrooms.

Lope de Vega without rest
📶 ⁾⁾ 👍 🚗 VISA ⁍⁍ AE ⓞ

Lope de Vega 49 ✉ *28014* – Ⓜ *Banco de España* – 𝒞 *913 60 00 11*
– *lopedevega@hotellopedevega.com* – *Fax 914 29 23 91*
– *www.hotellopedevega.com* **G3**
59 rm – 🛏89/199 € 🛏🛏99/255 €, ⌷ 15 €
◆ Urban ◆ Contemporary ◆
Modern hotel with a marble reception area and an adjoining convention centre.
Modern guestrooms decorated with references to Lope de Vega and 17C Madrid.

Atlántico without rest
📶 ⁾⁾ 👍 VISA ⁍⁍ AE ⓞ

Gran Vía 38 ✉ *28013* – Ⓜ *Callao* – 𝒞 *915 22 64 80* – *informacion@*
hotelatlantico.es – *Fax 915 31 02 10* – *www.hotelatlantico.es* **F2**
116 rm – 🛏100/140 € 🛏🛏120/200 €, ⌷ 10 €
◆ Family ◆ Classical ◆
A majestic hotel that has upgraded its facilities and comfort since being renovated.
Spacious guestrooms, the older of which are decorated in white tones; the newer
rooms are more contemporary in style.

SPAIN - MADRID

Husa Moncloa   ‡ℰ 🖭 (ʳ)ᵖ P̲ 🚗 VISA 🐼 AE ①

Serrano Jover 1 ⊠ *28015 –* Ⓜ *Argüelles –* ℰ *915 42 45 85 – husamoncloa@husa.es – Fax 915 42 71 69 – www.hotelhusamoncloa.com*   *Plan IV* **K3**
116 rm – †100/200 € ††115/250 €, ⊑ 19 € – 12 suites
Rest *– (at Hotel Husa Princesa)*
♦ Chain hotel ♦ Classical ♦
This bed and breakfast is an annex to the Husa Princesa hotel, which provides the majority of its services. Spacious, well-equipped rooms.

Petit Palace Puerta del Sol without rest   🖭 (ʳ)ᵖ VISA 🐼 AE ①

Arenal 4 ⊠ *28013 –* Ⓜ *Sol –* ℰ *915 21 05 42 – sol@hthoteles.com – Fax 915 21 05 61 – www.hthoteles.com*   **F2**
64 rm – ††100/320 €, ⊑ 12 €
♦ Chain hotel ♦ Functional ♦
Contemporary hotel with a spacious lobby, a lounge area, and free Internet access. Functional bedrooms with hydromassage showers.

Suite Prado without rest   🖭 (ʳ)ᵖ VISA 🐼 AE ①

Manuel Fernández y González 10 ⊠ *28014 –* Ⓜ *Antón Martín – ℰ 914 20 23 18 – hotel@suiteprado.com – Fax 914 20 05 59 – www.suiteprado.com*   **G2**
9 rm – †90/126 € ††90/158 €, ⊑ 13 € – 9 suites
♦ Urban ♦ Family ♦
This hotel has a classic contemporary façade and a delightful old staircase. Family atmosphere and apartment-style bedrooms, each with their own lounge and kitchen.

Quo Puerta del Sol without rest   🖭 (ʳ)ᵖ VISA 🐼 AE ①

Sevilla 4 ⊠ *28014 –* Ⓜ *Sevilla –* ℰ *915 32 90 49 – puertadelsol@hotelesquo.com – Fax 915 31 28 34 – www.hotelesquo.com*   **G2**
61 rm – †125/245 € ††125/305 €, ⊑ 17 €
♦ Urban ♦ Design ♦
This hotel has small but well-appointed guestrooms decorated in attractive minimalist style. Limited lounge area.

Room Mate Oscar without rest   (ℰ)ᵖ VISA 🐼 AE ①

pl. Vázquez de Mella 12 – Ⓜ *Gran Vía –* ℰ *91 701 11 73 – oscar@room-matehotels.com – Fax 91 521 62 96 – www.room-matehotels.com*
75 rm ⊑ *–* ††90/170 €   **G2**
♦ Chain hotel ♦ Design ♦
This delightful hotel has excellent facilities including numerous designer details. Lounge bar at the entrance with background music and separate access.

Gonzalo without rest   VISA 🐼

Cervantes 34-3° ⊠ *28014 –* Ⓜ *Antón Martín –* ℰ *914 29 27 14 – hostal@hostalgonzalo.com – Fax 914 20 20 07 – www.hostalgonzalo.com*
15 rm – †45 € ††55 €   **G3**
♦ Urban ♦ Family ♦
Excellent guesthouse in a residential building in the Las Letras district. Spacious guestrooms with good soundproofing and attractive Provençal-style furniture.

🕸🕸🕸 La Terraza del Casino (Paco Roncero)   🕸 VISA 🐼 AE ①
🕸

Alcalá 15-3° ⊠ *28014 –* Ⓜ *Sevilla –* ℰ *91 532 12 75 – terraza.casino@nh-hotels.com – Fax 91 523 44 36 – www.casinodemadrid.es – closed August, Saturday lunch, Sunday and Bank Holidays*   **G2**
Rest – Menu 120 € – Carte 69/85 € 🍸
Spec. Judión con almejas en salsa verde. Sopa de aceite de oliva virgen extra, variedad arbequina, con langostinos. Pichón con gelé-cru manzana al cassis.
♦ Inventive ♦ Formal ♦
Housed in an attractive 19C building, this restaurant has a palatial atmosphere, contemporary decor and one of the most elegant terraces in the city. Innovative cuisine.

XXX ✿

El Club Allard (Diego Guerrero) Smokers rest. ✿ *VISA* ⓪ *AE* ①

Ferraz 2 ✉ *28008 – Ⓜ Plaza España – ✆ 915 59 09 39*
– mpellicer@elcluballard.com – Fax 915 59 12 29 – www.elcluballard.com
– closed August, Saturday lunch, Sunday and Monday dinner **E1**
Rest – Menu 61 € – Carte 43/59 €

Spec. Huevos con pan y panceta sobre crema ligera de patatas. Bombón de bacalao y pil pil, lecho esponjoso de brandada y churros de pan de ajo. La ternera en terrina con natillas ligeras de foie.
♦ Inventive ♦ Formal ♦

This restaurant occupying the ground floor of a Modernist, early 20C building serves carefully prepared, innovative dishes using fresh market produce. Classical, dining room with high ceiling.

XXX

Café de Oriente ✿ *VISA* ⓪ *AE* ①

pl. de Oriente 2 ✉ *28013 – Ⓜ Ópera – ✆ 915 47 15 64 – cafeoriente@ grupolezama.com – Fax 915 47 77 07 – www.grupolezama.es*
Rest – Carte 47/55 € ⅋ **E2**
♦ International ♦ Formal ♦

Conveniently located opposite the Royal Palace, this restaurant has a luxurious cafeteria, attractive wine bar-cum-dining room, and several private rooms. Innovative international cuisine.

XXX

La Manduca de Azagra *VISA* ⓪ *AE* ①

Sagasta 14 ✉ *28004 – Ⓜ Alonso Martínez – ✆ 915 91 01 12*
– Fax 915 91 01 13
– closed August, Sunday and Bank Holidays **G1**
Rest – Carte 42/52 €
♦ Traditional ♦ Minimalist ♦

This spacious, well-located restaurant is decorated in minimalist style with particular attention paid to the design and lighting. The menu focuses on high quality produce.

XXX

Moaña ✿ *VISA* ⓪ *AE* ①

Hileras 4 ✉ *28013 – Ⓜ Ópera – ✆ 915 48 29 14 – Fax 915 41 65 98*
– closed Sunday dinner and Monday
Rest – Carte 43/65 € **F2**
♦ Galician ♦ Formal ♦

Comfortable and elegant restaurant in a central, historic district. Bar, several private rooms and a fresh seafood tank.

XXX ✿

Alboroque (Andrés Madrigal) *VISA* ⓪ *AE* ①

Atocha 34 – Ⓜ Antón Martín – ✆ 91 389 65 70 – alboroque@alboroque.es
– www.alboroque.es
– closed Holy Week, Sunday and Bank Holidays **F3**
Rest – Menu 55/75 € – Carte 54/67 € ⅋

Spec. Ajoverde de pistachos, helado de almendras amargas, huevo de codorniz, langostinos y olivas. Cous-cous de pichón con láminas de trufa de verano. Tatin de piña con helado de pistachos.
♦ Inventive ♦ Contemporary ♦

Access to this restaurant is via the old courtyard of a classical-style building once used by horse drawn carriages. Two attractive contemporary-style dining rooms. Inventive à la carte options, three menus, and an extensive wine list.

XX

Errota-Zar ✿ *VISA* ⓪ *AE* ①

Jovellanos 3-1° ✉ *28014 – Ⓜ Sevilla – ✆ 915 31 97 90*
– errota@errota-zar.com – Fax 915 31 25 64 – www.errota-zar.com
– closed 25 July-25 August, Sunday and Bank Holidays **G2**
Rest – Carte 47/53 €
♦ Basque cuisine ♦ Family ♦

Situated opposite the Zarzuela theatre, this restaurant has a plain but elegant dining room, as well as a private room. Basque specialities accompanied by a good selection of wines and cigars.

SPAIN - MADRID

XX Casa Matías
San Leonardo 12 ⊠ 28015 – ⓜ Plaza España – ℰ 915 41 76 83
– casamatias@casamatias.es – Fax 915 41 93 70 – www.casamatias.es
– closed Sunday dinner **E1**
Rest – Carte 44/51 €
♦ Grills ♦ Rustic ♦

Decorated in the style of a Basque cider bar with large barrels from which customers can pour cider. Two spacious dining rooms in a rustic, modern style and a grill visible to diners.

XX Julián de Tolosa
Smokers rest.
Cava Baja 18 ⊠ 28005 – ⓜ La Latina – ℰ 913 65 82 10 – Fax 913 66 33 08
– www.casajuliandetolosa.com
– closed Sunday dinner **F3**
Rest – Carte 35/58 €
♦ Grills ♦ Rustic ♦

Excellent carvery offering some of the best T-bone steaks in the city. The lack of choice on the menu is compensated by the high quality cuisine.

XX Posada de la Villa
Cava Baja 9 ⊠ 28005 – ⓜ La Latina – ℰ 913 66 18 60 – reservas@
posadadelavilla.com – Fax 913 66 70 90 – www.posadadelavilla.com
– closed August and Sunday dinner, except May **F3**
Rest – Carte 38/59 €
♦ Spanish ♦ Rustic ♦

A popular, lively old inn with a charming atmosphere and Castilian decor. The menu features regional cuisine and traditional dishes prepared in a wood oven.

XX Europa Decó – Hotel Urban
Carrera de San Jerónimo 34 ⊠ 28014 – ⓜ Sevilla – ℰ 917 87 77 80
– europadeco@derbyhotels.com – Fax 917 87 77 70 – www.derbyhotels.com
– closed August, Saturday lunch and Sunday **G2**
Rest – Carte approx. 65 €
♦ Inventive ♦ Fashionable ♦

Increasingly popular for its innovative design and excellent service. Mediterranean and ethnic cuisine prepared using fresh and exotic produce.

XX El Landó
Smokers rest.
pl. Gabriel Miró 8 ⊠ 28005 – ⓜ La Latina – ℰ 913 66 76 81
– ellando@telefonica.net – Fax 913 66 25 56
– closed Holy Week, August and Sunday **E3**
Rest – Carte 46/60 €
♦ Spanish ♦ Formal ♦

Situated close to the San Francisco el Grande basilica. This restaurant has a bar, a dining room in the cellar and a small private room, all decorated in classic style with a profusion of wood.

XX Cuenllas
Ferraz 5 ⊠ 28008 – ⓜ Ventura Rodríguez – ℰ 915 42 56 21
– f.cuenllas@cuenllas.com – Fax 915 59 79 01 – www.cuenllas.com
– closed 1–10 January, 10-31 August, Saturday lunch and Sunday
Rest – Carte 52/65 € ⅊ **E1**
♦ Inventive ♦ Formal ♦

Restaurant along modern lines, split over two floors with two compact dining rooms, several private rooms and a wine-bar at the entrance. Creative cuisine and an excellent wine cellar.

XX Corral de la Morería
Totally no smoking
Morería 17 ⊠ 28005 – ⓜ Ópera – ℰ 913 65 84 46
– info@corraldelamorería.com – Fax 913 64 12 19 – www.corraldelamoreria.com
Rest – (dinner only) Carte 57/79 € **E3**
♦ Spanish ♦ Musical ♦

Restaurant with a high quality flamenco show. The closely packed tables are grouped around the stage. À la carte options, as well as various gastronomic menus.

719

SPAIN - MADRID

XX Botín
Totally no smoking VISA ◑◉ AE ①

Cuchilleros 17 ✉ *28005 –* ◍ *Sol –* ☏ *913 66 42 17 – Fax 913 66 84 94*
– www.botin.es **F2**
Rest – Carte 33/53 €

◆ Spanish ◆ Rustic ◆

Founded in 1725, this restaurant is said to be the oldest in the world. The decor and wood fire oven add to its authentic old-world ambience.

XX El Rincón de Esteban
VISA ◑◉ AE ①

Santa Catalina 3 ✉ *28014 –* ◍ *Sevilla –* ☏ *914 29 92 89 – Fax 913 65 87 70*
– www.elrincondeesteban.com
– closed August and Sunday **G2**
Rest – Carte 40/58 €

◆ Spanish ◆ Family ◆

Well-known politicians are often spotted in this restaurant, which is situated close to the Palacio del Congreso. An intimate atmosphere with an elegant clientele and traditional cuisine.

XX Esteban
⇕ VISA ◑◉

Cava Baja 36 ✉ *28005 –* ◍ *La Latina –* ☏ *913 65 90 91*
– info@rte-esteban.com – Fax 913 66 93 91 – www.rte-esteban.com
– closed 15 July-15 August, Sunday and Monday dinner **E3**
Rest – Carte 38/52 €

◆ De Terroir ◆ Castilian ◆

A welcoming hotel decorated in typical Castilian style with photos of famous characters on the walls. The restaurant serves traditional cuisine.

XX Zorzal
VISA ◑◉ AE ①

🏠

San Bernardino 13 ✉ *28015 –* ◍ *Plaza España –* ☏ *91 541 20 26*
– closed Holy Week, August, Sunday dinner, Monday and Tuesday dinner
Rest – Carte approx. 35 € **E1**

◆ Traditional ◆ Contemporary ◆

This restaurant extends over two floors. The upper floor dining area with its designer feel is particularly impressive. Young staff, traditional cuisine and elegantly presented cuisine.

XX La Cava del Faraón
VISA ◑◉ AE ①

Segovia 8 ✉ *28005 –* ◍ *Tirso de Molina –* ☏ *915 42 52 54 – f@defuny.com*
– Fax 914 57 45 30 – www.buenpaladar.com
– closed Monday **E2**
Rest – *(dinner only)* Carte 31/45 €

◆ Egyptian ◆ Exotic ◆

Egypt is the theme of this restaurant, which has a tea room and dining rooms with arched ceilings. Sample typical Egyptian cuisine, smoke a traditional shisha pipe or enjoy the belly dancing show.

X La Tasquita de Enfrente
VISA ◑◉ AE

Ballesta 6 ✉ *28004 –* ◍ *Callao –* ☏ *91 532 54 49*
– latasquitadeenfrente@hotmail.com
– closed Holy Week, August, Sunday, Monday dinner and Tuesday dinner
Rest – *(booking essential)* Carte 41/63 € **F1**

◆ Market ◆ Family ◆

A family-run restaurant that has always had to struggle with the poor reputation brought on by its location. However, it has maintained a loyal following and continues to serve good, seasonal cuisine.

X La Esquina del Real
Smokers rest. VISA ◑◉ AE ①

Amnistía 4 ✉ *28013 –* ◍ *Ópera –* ☏ *915 59 43 09 – Fax 915 59 43 09*
– www.laesquinadelreal.com
– closed 15 August-15 September, Saturday lunch and Sunday **E-F2**
Rest – Carte 43/50 €

◆ International ◆ Friendly ◆

A charming and intimate restaurant decorated in rustic style with stone and brick walls. Good service and an attractive menu with an emphasis on French cuisine.

X **Zerain** ⟡ VISA ⓪ⓞ AE ①

Quevedo 3 ⊠ 28014 – Ⓜ Antón Martín – ℰ 914 29 79 09 – Fax 914 29 17 20
– closed Holy Week, August and Sunday **G3**
Rest – Carte 30/43 €
♦ Basque cuisine ♦ Rustic ♦
Typical Basque cider bar decorated with large barrels. Friendly atmosphere and
cheerful decor with photographs of typical towns and villages. Affordable menu
with an emphasis on roasted meats.

X **Café Oliver** VISA ⓪ⓞ AE

Almirante 12 ⊠ 28004 – Ⓜ Colón – ℰ 915 21 73 79 – info@cafeoliver.com
– www.cafeoliver.com **G1**
Rest – Carte 38/45 €
♦ International ♦ Bistro ♦
Spacious, yet intimate restaurant with stone walls and individual table lighting. The
menu features an interesting fusion of international and traditional Arabic cuisine.

X **El Buey** VISA ⓪ⓞ

*pl. de la Marina Española 1 ⊠ 28013 – Ⓜ Ópera – ℰ 915 41 30 41 – info@
restauranteelbuey.com – Fax 915 59 27 21 – www.restauranteelbuey.com*
– closed Sunday dinner **E1-2**
Rest – Carte approx. 33 €
♦ Meat ♦ Formal ♦
This classic-style restaurant with a bar is conveniently located opposite the Senate.
The menu focuses on meat dishes; the delicious lomo de buey (ox loin) is the
house speciality.

X **La Gastroteca de Santiago** Smokers rest. VISA ⓪ⓞ AE ①

pl. Santiago 1 ⊠ 28013 – Ⓜ Ópera – ℰ 915 48 07 07
– lagastrotecadesantiago@yahoo.es
– Closed 15-31 August, Monday and Sunday dinner **E2**
Rest – Carte 45/56 €
♦ A la mode ♦ Cosy ♦
A small, cosy restaurant with two large French windows and a modern decor.
Friendly staff, contemporary cuisine and a kitchen that is partially visible to diners.

X **La Bola** Totally no smoking VISA ⓪ⓞ AE ①
☺
Bola 5 ⊠ 28013 – Ⓜ Santo Domingo – ℰ 915 47 69 30
– labola1870@hotmail.com – Fax 915 41 71 64 – www.labola.es
*– closed Saturday dinner and Sunday in the summer, Sunday dinner the rest of
the year* **E2**
Rest – Carte 30/35 €
♦ Spanish ♦ Regional ♦
An old, typical Madrid-style tavern, which cooks many of its dishes in traditional
clay pots. The cocido madrileño, a local stew, is particulary recommended.

X **La Vaca Verónica** Smokers rest. VISA ⓪ⓞ AE ①

Moratín 38 ⊠ 28014 – Ⓜ Antón Martín – ℰ 914 29 78 27
– www.lavacaveronica.es
– closed Saturday lunch and Sunday dinner **G3**
Rest – Carte 26/34 €
♦ International ♦ Cosy ♦
Cosy and intimate with friendly staff. Original decor with colourful paintings, chandeliers, mirrors on the ceilings and candlelit tables at dinner.

ⴿ/ **La Botillería del Café de Oriente** VISA ⓪ⓞ AE ①

*pl. de Oriente 4 ⊠ 28013 – Ⓜ Ópera – ℰ 915 48 46 20 – botilleria@
grupolezama.es – Fax 915 47 77 07 – www.grupolezama.es* **E2**
Tapa 4 € **Ración** approx. 9 €
♦ Spanish ♦ Tapas bar ♦
Situated in a lively area of bars and restaurants. This Viennese-style café serves a
wide variety of snacks and canapés, as well as excellent wines by the glass.

Prada a Tope

Smokers rest. 📶 🔵🔵 🔘

Príncipe 11 ✉ *28012 –* Ⓜ *Sevilla –* ☎ *914 29 59 21 – Fax 914 29 59 21*
– closed August, Sunday dinner and Monday **G2**
Tapa 6 € **Ración** approx. 11 €
◆ Spanish ◆ Tapas bar ◆

This restaurant is typical of the El Bierzo region with a bar at the entrance and rustic-style tables. The decor features wood, photographs and various products that can be purchased by customers.

Bocaito

Smokers rest. 📶 🔵🔵 🔲 🔘

Libertad 6 ✉ *28004 –* Ⓜ *Chueca –* ☎ *915 32 12 19 – bocaito@bocaito.com*
– Fax 915 22 56 29 – www.bocaito.com
– closed August, Saturday lunch and Sunday **G2**
Tapa 2.60 € **Ración** approx. 11.30 €
◆ Spanish ◆ Tapas bar ◆

The atmosphere and decor in this restaurant reflect the world of bullfighting. Enjoy tapas at the splendid bar or at your table, where you can choose from a variety of scrambled egg (revueltos) or fried dishes.

Taberna de San Bernardo

Smokers rest. 📶 🔵🔵

San Bernardo 85 ✉ *28015 –* Ⓜ *San Bernardo –* ☎ *914 45 41 70* *Plan IV* **K3**
Tapa 2 € **Ración** approx. 7 €
◆ Spanish ◆ Tapas bar ◆

This traditional, informal restaurant is divided into three areas. Good choice of dishes, including the popular papas con huevo (potatoes and eggs) and fritura de verduras (fried vegetables).

RETIRO and SALAMANCA

Plan III

Ritz

No smokers rest. 🔲 Ⓖ 🔲 📶 🔲 📶 🔵🔵 🔲 🔘

pl. de la Lealtad 5 ✉ *28014 –* Ⓜ *Banco de España –* ☎ *917 01 67 67*
– reservations@ritz.es – Fax 917 01 67 76 – www.ritzmadrid.com
137 rm – 🛏405 € 🛏🛏645 €, ⊑ 33 € – 30 suites **Rest** – Carte 75/95 € **I2**
◆ Grand Luxury ◆ Traditional ◆ Classical ◆

This elegant, internationally renowned hotel occupies an early 20C mansion, which has historical associations with the diplomatic world. Lavish decor in the guestrooms and beautiful lounges. The Ritz's restaurant is endowed with an elegant dining room and pleasant summer terrace.

Gran Meliá Fénix

Ⓖ 🔲 📶 🔲 📶 📶 🔵🔵 🔲 🔘

Hermosilla 2 ✉ *28001 –* Ⓜ *Serrano –* ☎ *914 31 67 00 – gran.melia.fenix*
@solmelia.com – Fax 915 76 06 61 – www.granmeliafenix.com
199 rm – 🛏170/345 € 🛏🛏205/410 €, ⊑ 27.80 € – 16 suites **I2**
Rest – Menu 27 €
◆ Luxury ◆ Chain hotel ◆ Classical ◆

This smart, distinctive hotel has bedrooms in an elegant, classical style equipped to a very high standard. Spacious public areas, including an impressive lounge crowned by a domed ceiling. A small, yet elegant restaurant serving modern, imaginative cuisine.

Wellington

🔲 📶 📶 📶 📶 🔵🔵 🔲 🔘

Velázquez 8 ✉ *28001 –* Ⓜ *Retiro –* ☎ *915 75 44 00 – wellington@*
hotel-wellington.com – Fax 915 76 41 64 – www.hotel-wellington.com
233 rm – 🛏140/325 € 🛏🛏140/410 €, ⊑ 25 € – 28 suites **I2**
Rest Goizeko Wellington y Kabuki Wellington – see below
◆ Luxury ◆ Classical ◆

In an elegant district near the Retiro Park. Classic in style with recently modernised lounges and guestrooms. A popular haunt for bullfighting aficionados.

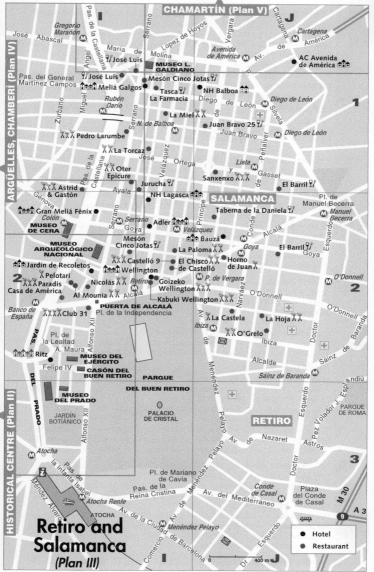

Retiro and Salamanca
(Plan III)

ARGÜELLES, CHAMBERÍ (Plan IV)

HISTORICAL CENTRE (Plan II)

José Abascal

Gregorio Marañón

Pas. de la Castellana

Serrano

López de Hoyos

Vergara

Cartagena

Cartagena

América

José

Angel

Maria de Molina

Avenida de América

Av.

de

AC Avenida de América

José Luis

MUSEO L. GALDIANO

Mesón Cinco Jotas

NH Balboa

Pas. del General Martínez Campos

Miguel

José Luis

Meliá Galgos

Tasca
La Farmacia

Diego de León

Diego de León

1

Zurbano

Rubén Darío

N. de Balboa

La Miel

Juan Bravo 25

Silvela

Peñalver

Diego de León

Pedro Larumbe

La Torcaz

José

Velázquez

Ortega

Lista

y

Gasset

Sanxenxo

El Barril

Génova

Oter Epicure

Jurucha

Ayala

SALAMANCA

Pl. de Manuel Becerra

Astrid & Gastón

NH Lagasca

Taberna de la Daniela

Manuel Becerra

Gran Meliá Fénix

Colón

MUSEO DE CERA

Serrano

Goya

Adler

Príncipe

Conde

Alcalá

Velázquez

Esguerra

El Barril

MUSEO ARQUEOLÓGICO NACIONAL

Mesón Cinco Jotas

Castelló 9

La Paloma

Goya

Bauzá

Horno de Juan

Jardin de Recoletos

Wellington

El Chisco de Castelló

O'Donnell

2

Pelotari

Nicolás

Retiro

Goizeko Wellington

P. de Vergara

Paradis

Casa de América

Al Mounia

Alcalá

Kabuki Wellington

Narváez

O'Donnell

O'Donnell

Banco de España

Club 31

PUERTA DE ALCALÁ
Pl. de la Independencia

Ibiza

La Castela

La Hoja

O'Donnell

Pl. de la Lealtad
A. Maura

O'Grelo

Doctor

Sáinz de Baranda

Baranda

Ritz

Felipe IV

MUSEO DEL EJÉRCITO

CASÓN DEL BUEN RETIRO

Menéndez

Ibiza

Alcalde

Sáinz de Baranda

PARQUE

MUSEO DEL PRADO

JARDÍN BOTÁNICO

DEL BUEN RETIRO

PALACIO DE CRISTAL

RETIRO

Alfonso XII

Pelayo

Av.

de

Nazaret

Astros

Esguerra

PARQUE DE ROMA

Atocha

Pl. de Mariano de Cavia

Menéndez

Pelayo

Conde de Casal

Doctor

Plaza del Conde de Casal

3

Méndez Álvaro

la Infanta Isabel

Atocha Renfe

ATOCHA

Pas. de la Reina Cristina

Av. de la Ciudad de Barcelona

Menéndez Pelayo

Av. del Mediterráneo

Esguerra

M 30

A 3

9

Comercio

Dr.

PAS. DEL PRADO

● Hotel

● Restaurant

0   400 m

Meliá Galgos

Claudio Coello 139 ✉ *28006* – Ⓜ *Gregorio Marañón* – ✆ *915 62 66 00*
– melia.galgos@solmelia.com – Fax 915 61 76 62 – www.solmelia.com
350 rm – †70/160 € ††85/270 €, ⧠ 19 € – 6 suites
Rest *Diábolo* – Carte 36/59 €
I1

♦ Chain hotel ♦ Business ♦ Classical ♦

Aimed at business travellers, this hotel has comfortable bedrooms, attractive lounge areas, a gym on the top floor and a rooftop sun terrace. Restaurant with a refined classical-style decor and excellent service.

Adler   Smokers rest.

Velázquez 33 ✉ *28001* – Ⓜ *Velázquez* – ✆ *914 26 32 20*
– hoteladler@iova-sa.com – Fax 914 26 32 21 – www.hoteladler.es
45 rm – †250/400 € ††300/495 €, ⧠ 27 €   **Rest** – Menu 70 €
I2

♦ Luxury ♦ Personalised ♦

This exclusive, select hotel has an elegant interior decorated with high quality furnishings. Comfortable guestrooms equipped to the highest standard. Restaurant with a charming atmosphere and impressive attention to detail in its decor.

AC Palacio del Retiro

Alfonso XII-14 ✉ *28014* – Ⓜ *Retiro* – ✆ *915 23 74 60 – pretiro@ac-hotels.com*
– Fax 915 23 74 61 – www.ac-hotels.com   *Plan II* **H2**
49 rm – †236 € ††338 €, ⧠ 29 € – 1 suite   **Rest** – Menu 55 €

♦ Luxury ♦ Personalised ♦

Early-20C mansion with a reception area situated in what was once a passageway for horse-drawn carriages. Elegant public area and superb guestrooms. Modern-style restaurant with designer details in dark tones.

Vincci Soma

Goya 79 ✉ *28001* – Ⓜ *Goya* – ✆ *914 35 75 45 – info@hotelbauza.com*
– Fax 914 31 09 43 – www.vinccihoteles.com
169 rm – †96/385 € ††120/481 €, ⧠ 17 €   **Rest** – Carte 36/48 €
J2

♦ Business ♦ Modern ♦

A designer hotel with an attractive lounge-library with a fireplace. Fully equipped guestrooms, some of which have their own terrace. This bright, modern restaurant decorated in varying shades of white serves innovative, creative cuisine.

Petit Palace Embassy   No smokers rest.

Serrano 46 ✉ *28001* – Ⓜ *Serrano* – ✆ *914 31 30 60 – emb@hthoteles.com*
– Fax 914 31 30 62 – www.hthoteles.com
75 rm – †120/400 € ††150/400 €, ⧠ 16 €
H1
Rest – *(closed August, Saturday, Sunday and Bank Holidays)* Carte 36/46 €

♦ Chain hotel ♦ Design ♦

A combination of a beautiful 19C building with a designer interior, resulting in a bold but cosy atmosphere. Fully equipped bedrooms, each with a computer. This restaurant has a modern decor with a predominance of grey and metallic shades.

AC Avenida de América without rest

Cartagena 83 ✉ *28028* – Ⓜ *Av. de América*
– ✆ 917 24 42 40 – acamerica@ac-hotels.com – Fax 917 24 42 41
– www.ac-hotels.com
145 rm – ††82/170 €, ⧠ 16 €
J1

♦ Business ♦ Chain hotel ♦ Functional ♦

This modern and well-designed hotel offers good transport connections aimed at the business traveller. It has a multipurpose lounge, which also serves as a bar and café depending on the time of day.

Jardín de Recoletos

Gil de Santivañes 4 ✉ *28001* – Ⓜ *Serrano* – ✆ *917 81 16 40 – rc@*
vphoteles.com – Fax 917 81 16 41 – www.vphoteles.com
43 rm – †152/228 € ††160/238 €, ⧠ 23 €   **Rest** – Carte 66/87 €
I2

♦ Urban ♦ Classical ♦

Attractive façade with balustraded balconies. The hotel has an elegant reception hall with a glass ceiling, large studio-style guestrooms and an attractive patio-terrace. Small dining room with landscapes painted on the walls.

SPAIN - MADRID

NH Lagasca

No smokers rest. 📺 📶 ✦ VISA ✦ AE ✦

Lagasca 64 ✉ *28001 –* Ⓜ *Serrano –* ☎ *915 75 46 06 – nhlagasca@*
nh-hotels.com – Fax 915 75 16 94 – www.nh-hotels.com   **I2**
100 rm – ♦95/260 € ♦♦100/265 €, ⌂ 17 €
Rest – *(closed August, Saturday, Sunday and Bank Holidays)* Menu 30 €
♦ Chain hotel ♦ Functional ♦
Functional hotel with well-appointed, functional guestrooms. A well-run hotel with
pleasing attention to guest comfort and detail.

NH Balboa without rest

📺 📶 ✦ VISA ✦ AE ✦

Núñez de Balboa 112 ✉ *28006 –* Ⓜ *Príncipe de Vergara –* ☎ *915 63 03 24*
– nhbalboa@nh-hotels.com – Fax 915 62 69 80 – www.nh-hotels.com
120 rm – ♦200 € ♦♦245 €, ⌂ 16 €   **J1**
♦ Urban ♦ Classical ♦
Functional, well-located hotel. It has a multi-purpose area that acts as a breakfast
room, lounge, bar and café (with a snack menu). Well-appointed guestrooms.

Club 31

Smokers rest. ⇔ VISA ✦ AE ✦

Alcalá 58 ✉ *28014 –* Ⓜ *Retiro –* ☎ *915 31 00 92 – club31@club31.net*
– Fax 915 31 00 92 – www.club31.net
– closed August   **I2**
Rest – Carte 50/62 €
♦ International ♦ Formal ♦
The decor in this typical restaurant is a fusion of the traditional and modern. Inter-
national cuisine and an excellent wine list.

Sanxenxo

⇔ VISA ✦ AE ✦

José Ortega y Gasset 40 ✉ *28006 –* Ⓜ *Núñez de Balboa –* ☎ *915 77 82 72*
– combarro@combarro.com – Fax 914 35 95 12 – www.sanxenxo.com.es
– closed Holy Week, August and Sunday dinner   **J1**
Rest – Carte approx. 71 €
♦ Galician ♦ Formal ♦
This restaurant serves traditional Galician cuisine based on quality fish and seafood. Covering two floors, the superb dining rooms are decorated with a profusion
of granite and wood.

Pedro Larumbe

VISA ✦ AE ✦

Serrano 61 (2nd floor) ✉ *28006 –* Ⓜ *Rubén Darío –* ☎ *915 75 11 12*
– info@larumbe.com – Fax 915 76 60 19 – www.larumbe.com
– closed August, Sunday, Monday dinner and Bank Holidays   **I1**
Rest – Carte 48/66 €
♦ International ♦ Retro ♦
Housed on the top floor of a mansion, this restaurant has three elegant dining
rooms with a unique and tasteful decor. International menu with a creative touch.

Goizeko Wellington – Hotel Wellington

VISA ✦ AE ✦

Villanueva 34 ✉ *28001 –* Ⓜ *Retiro –* ☎ *915 77 01 38 – goizeko@*
goizekowellington.com – Fax 915 57 60 26 – www.goizekogaztelupe.com
– closed 7 days in August and Sunday   **I2**
Rest – Carte 60/80 € ⽊
♦ Spanish ♦ Minimalist ♦
This elegant restaurant decorated in classic-modern style serves traditional, international cuisine with creative touches. Comprehensive wine list.

Kabuki Wellington – Hotel Wellington

VISA ✦ AE ✦

Velazquez 6 ✉ *28001 –* Ⓜ *Retiro –* ☎ *915 77 78 77 – wellington@*
resturantekabuki.com – www.restaurantekabuki.com
– closed 7 days in August, Saturday lunch and Sunday   **I2**
Rest – Carte 50/75 €
♦ Japanese ♦ Design ♦
Part of the Wellington hotel, this restaurant offers a large dining room on two
levels and attentive service. Restrained, elegant decor with numerous designer
details. Sushi bar.

XXX **Paradis Casa de América**   🍴 ⇔ VISA ⚭ AE ⓪

paseo de Recoletos 2 ⊠ 28001 – ⓜ Banco de España – ℰ 915 75 45 40
– Fax 915 76 02 15 – www.paradis.es
– closed Saturday lunch, Sunday and Bank Holidays   **I2**
Rest – Carte 40/49 €
♦ Inventive ♦ Minimalist ♦
Attractive, elegantly decorated restaurant in the Palacio de Linares. The modern, mini-malist dining room provides the backdrop for an interesting and innovative menu.

XXX **Castelló 9**   ⇔ VISA ⚭ AE ⓪

Castelló 9 ⊠ 28001 – ⓜ Príncipe de Vergara – ℰ 914 35 00 67
– castello9@castello9.es – Fax 914 35 91 34 – www.castello9.es
– closed Holy Week, August, Sunday and Bank Holidays   **I2**
Rest – Carte approx. 50 €
♦ International ♦ Formal ♦
An elegant, traditional restaurant in the Salamanca district. It has several intimate dining rooms, a classic international menu and a varied tasting menu.

XXX **Astrid & Gastón**   VISA ⚭ AE ⓪

paseo de la Castellana 13 – ⓜ Serrano – ℰ 91 702 62 62 – Fax 91 702 59 75
– www.astridygastonmadrid.com   **I1-2**
Rest – Carte 47/58 €
♦ International ♦ Contemporary ♦
Extending over two floors, this restaurant has spacious dining areas decorated in contemporary-style. Bar for pre-dinner cocktails, and a menu specialising in Peru-vian cuisine.

XX **La Paloma**   Smokers rest. ⇔ VISA ⚭ AE ⓪

Jorge Juan 39 ⊠ 28001 – ⓜ Príncipe de Vergara – ℰ 915 76 86 92
– Fax 915 75 51 41 – www.rtelapaloma.com
– closed Holy Week, August, Sunday and Bank Holidays   **I2**
Rest – Carte 54/64 €
♦ International ♦ Fashionable ♦
A professionally run restaurant catering to a sophisticated clientele. Dining room on two levels, where the focus is on international and traditional cuisine. Excellent service.

XX **O'Grelo**   ⇔ VISA ⚭ AE ⓪

Menorca 39 ⊠ 28009 – ⓜ Ibiza – ℰ 914 09 72 04 – Fax 914 09 72 04
– www.restauranteogrelo.com
– closed August and Sunday dinner   **J2**
Rest – Carte approx. 55 €
♦ Galician ♦ Neo-rustic ♦
Enjoy excellent traditional Galician cuisine in this restaurant decorated in a neo-rustic style. Wide selection of fish and seafood and a tapas bar at the entrance.

XX **La Torcaz**   Smokers rest. ⇔ VISA ⚭ AE ⓪

Lagasca 81 ⊠ 28006 – ⓜ Núñez de Balboa – ℰ 915 75 41 30
– info@latorcaz.com – Fax 914 31 83 88 – www.latorcaz.com
– closed Holy Week, August and Sunday   **I1**
Rest – Carte 45/56 €
♦ International ♦ Formal ♦
Friendly restaurant with an attractive wine display. The dining room, decorated in classical-contemporary style, is divided into three different ambiences. Excellent service and an extensive wine list.

XX **Dassa Bassa**   VISA ⚭ AE ⓪

Villalar 7 ⊠ 28001 – ⓜ Retiro – ℰ 915 76 73 97
– dassabassa@dassabassa.com – www.dassabassa.com
– closed Holy Week and 15 days in August   *Plan II* **H2**
Rest – Carte 58/65 €
♦ Inventive ♦ Design ♦
This restaurant occupying what was once a coal cellar has an attractive foyer, and four modern dining rooms with designer detail. Creative cuisine with a particular focus on interesting flavours.

XX **Oter Epicure** ⟳ VISA ⓪⊙ AE ①
Claudio Coello 71 ⊠ 28001 – Ⓜ Serrano – ℰ 914 31 67 70
– Fax 914 31 67 71 – www.oterepicure.com
– closed Sunday I1
Rest – Carte 45/55 €
♦ De Terroir ♦ Contemporary actual ♦
The dining room of this restaurant is decorated in a classical-contemporary
style in grey tones. There are also three private rooms in the basement. Find
Basque-Navarran specialities, a well-stocked cellar and a wide selection of
cigars.

XX **La Miel** Smokers rest. VISA ⓪⊙ AE ①
Maldonado 14 ⊠ 28006 – Ⓜ Núñez de Balboa – ℰ 914 35 50 45
– manuelcoto@restaurantelamiel.com – www.restaurantelamiel.com
– closed August and Sunday I1
Rest – Carte 38/51 €
♦ International ♦ Family ♦
Classic style restaurant with a husband and wife team in the kitchen and dining
room. Comfortable dining room, attentive service and international cuisine. Good
wine list.

XX **Al Mounia** VISA ⓪⊙ AE ①
Recoletos 5 ⊠ 28001 – Ⓜ Banco de España – ℰ 914 35 08 28
– info@almounia.es – Fax 915 75 01 73 – www.almounia.es
– closed Holy Week, August and Sunday I2
Rest – Carte 27/53 €
♦ International ♦ Exotic ♦
Exotically decorated restaurant near the National Archaeological Museum. Moroccan decoration with carved woodwork, stucco and typical low tables on carpeted
floors. Traditional North African dishes.

XX **Nicolás** Smokers rest. ⟳ VISA ⓪⊙ AE ①
Villalar 4 ⊠ 28001 – Ⓜ Retiro – ℰ 914 31 77 37 – resnicolas@hotmail.com
– Fax 915 77 86 65
– closed Holy Week, August, Sunday and Monday I2
Rest – Carte 33/46 €
♦ Spanish ♦ Minimalist ♦
Although the traditional menu is somewhat limited, it features a number of excel-
lent homemade dishes. Select wine list. Modern, minimalist decor.

XX **El Chiscón de Castelló** Smokers rest. ⟳ VISA ⓪⊙ AE ①
Castelló 3 ⊠ 28001 – Ⓜ Príncipe de Vergara – ℰ 915 75 56 62
– Fax 915 75 56 62 – www.elchiscon.com
– closed August, Sunday, Monday dinner and Bank Holidays I2
Rest – Carte 36/49 €
♦ Spanish ♦ Friendly ♦
Behind the typical façade is a warmly decorated interior similar in style to a pri-
vate home, especially in the first floor dining rooms. Reasonably priced traditional
cuisine.

XX **La Hoja** VISA ⓪⊙ AE
Doctor Castelo 48 ⊠ 28009 – Ⓜ O'Donnell – ℰ 914 09 25 22
– info@lahoja.es – Fax 915 74 14 78 – www.lahoja.es
– closed Sunday and Monday dinner J2
Rest – Carte 40/55 €
♦ Asturian ♦ Formal ♦
This restaurant has two classic style dining rooms furnished with wood. Generous
portions of traditional Asturian cooking, including bean dishes and chicken raised
on the owner's farm.

SPAIN - MADRID

✗ Pelotari   ⇕ 💳 VISA ⊛⊛ AE ⓪

Recoletos 3 ✉ 28001 – �Ⓜ *Colón –* ✆ *915 78 24 97 – informacion@
asador-pelotari.com – Fax 914 31 60 04 – www.asador-pelotari.com
– closed 10-16 August and Sunday*   **I2**
Rest – Carte 37/50 €
  ◆ Basque cuisine ◆ Rustic ◆
This typical Basque eatery specialising in roasted meats is run by its owners, with
one in the kitchen and the other front of house. Four regional style dining rooms,
two of which can be used as private rooms.

✗ Horno de Juan   VISA ⊛⊛ AE ⓪

Lope de Rueda 4 ✉ 28009 – Ⓜ *Goya –* ✆ *915 75 69 16 – ldr@hornodejuan.net
– Fax 915 76 01 88 – www.hornodejuan.net*   **J2**
Rest – Carte 32/40 €
  ◆ Roasts ◆ Castilian ◆
Small but welcoming restaurant decorated in Castilian style with a wood oven at
the entrance and a simply furnished dining room. Traditional à la carte menu.

✗ La Castela   Smokers rest. VISA ⊛⊛ AE ⓪

Doctor Castelo 22 ✉ 28009 – Ⓜ *Ibiza –* ✆ *915 74 00 15 – info@lacastela.com
– www.lacastela.com
– closed Holy Week, August and Sunday*   **J2**
Rest – Carte 35/42 €
  ◆ Traditional ◆ Formal ◆
A traditional Madrid style tavern with a tapas bar at the entrance. The menu in the
traditional dining room is centred on international cuisine.

℉ Juan Bravo 25   Smokers rest. 🍴 VISA ⊛⊛ AE ⓪

Juan Bravo 25 ✉ 28006 – Ⓜ *Núñez de Balboa –* ✆ *914 11 60 25
– jmb@juanbravo25.com – Fax 914 11 82 31 – www.juanbravo25.com
– closed Holy Week, 15 days in August and Sunday*   **J1**
Tapa 3.25 € **Ración** approx. 14.50 €
  ◆ Spanish ◆ Tapas bar ◆
Large restaurant located on the mezzanine level with a central bar serving Basque
style tapas and hors d'oeuvres. The adjoining dining room offers a traditional
menu.

℉ José Luis   Smokers rest. 🍴 VISA ⊛⊛ AE ⓪

General Oráa 5 ✉ 28006 – Ⓜ *Rubén Darío –* ✆ *915 61 64 13
– joseluis@joseluis.es – www.joseluis.es*   **I1**
Tapa 2 € **Ración** approx. 10 €
  ◆ Spanish ◆ Tapas bar ◆
This famous restaurant is located in a smart part of town. It serves a large choice of
appetisers and tapas in an elegant setting with a classic decor.

℉ Mesón Cinco Jotas   🍴 VISA ⊛⊛ AE ⓪

Puigcerdá ✉ 28001 – Ⓜ *Serrano –* ✆ *915 75 41 25 – m5jjorgejuan@osborne.es
– Fax 915 75 56 35 – www.mesoncincojotas.com*   **I2**
Tapa 3 € **Ración** approx. 15 €
  ◆ Spanish ◆ Tapas bar ◆
This mesón is renowned for its excellent hams and tapas. The restaurant has a
splendid terrace, and three cosy dining rooms spread across three floors.

℉ Tasca La Farmacia   Totally no smoking VISA ⊛⊛ AE ⓪

Diego de León 9 ✉ 28006 – Ⓜ *Núñez de Balboa –* ✆ *915 64 86 52
– Fax 915 56 62 02 – www.asadordearanda.com
– closed 15-31 July, 1-15 August and Sunday*   **I1**
Tapa 4 € **Ración** approx. 12 €
  ◆ Codfish specialities ◆ Tapas bar ◆
Traditional style tasca, with a beautifully tiled bar adorned with elegant motifs.
House specialities include cod and 'zancarrón' (meat on the bone) tapas and
snacks.

SPAIN - **MADRID**

Ψ/ **Mesón Cinco Jotas**   VISA ◉◎ AE ◉

Serrano 118 ✉ *28006 –* Ⓜ *Núñez de Balboa –* ℰ *915 63 27 10*
– m5jserrano@osborne.es – Fax 915 61 32 84 – www.mesoncincojotas.com
Tapa *3.50 €* **Ración** *approx. 16 €*   **I1**
♦ Spanish ♦ Tapas bar ♦
Contemporary-style mesón serving a varied array of tapas, snacks and sandwiches
with an emphasis on Spanish hams and pork. Attractive dining room.

Ψ/ **El Barril**   VISA ◉◎ AE ◉

Goya 86 ✉ *28009 –* Ⓜ *Goya –* ℰ *915 78 39 98 – www.elbarrildegoya.com*
– closed Sunday dinner   **J2**
Ración *approx. 18 €*
♦ Seafood ♦ Tapas bar ♦
Good seafood restaurant with an air-conditioned bar displaying an impressive
range of high quality products. Dining room with a reasonable menu to the rear
of the building.

Ψ/ **José Luis**   Smokers rest. 🌣 VISA ◉◎ AE ◉

Serrano 89 ✉ *28006 –* Ⓜ *Gregorio Marañón –* ℰ *915 63 09 58*
– joseluis@joseluis.es – Fax 915 63 31 02 – www.joseluis.es   **I1**
Tapa *2.50 €* **Ración** *approx. 15 €*
♦ Spanish ♦ Tapas bar ♦
This restaurant is really two restaurants in one, with two entrances, two bars and
two dining rooms. Pleasant terrace for summer dining. Basque style tapas, snacks
and a concise à la carte menu.

Ψ/ **Taberna de la Daniela**   Smokers rest. VISA ◉◎ AE ◉

General Pardiñas 21 ✉ *28001 –* Ⓜ *Goya –* ℰ *915 75 23 29 – Fax 914 35 24 22*
Tapa *3.50 €* **Ración** *approx. 10 €*   **J2**
♦ Spanish ♦ Tapas bar ♦
Typical tavern in the Salamanca district, with a glass façade and several dining
rooms. A good place to sample tapas, more substantial snacks, or to try the restau-
rant's famous stew, the cocido madrileño.

Ψ/ **El Barril**   VISA ◉◎ AE ◉

Don Ramón de la Cruz 91 ✉ *28006 –* Ⓜ *Manuel Becerra –* ℰ *914 01 33 05*
– www.elbarrilalcantara.com   **J1**
Tapa *6 €* **Ración** *approx. 23 €*
♦ Seafood ♦ Tapas bar ♦
Renowned seafood restaurant with an excellent reputation for its cuisine and service. Enjoy seafood specialities and snacks either in the pub or in one of the two
dining rooms.

Ψ/ **Jurucha**   Smokers rest.

Ayala 19 ✉ *28001 –* Ⓜ *Serrano –* ℰ *915 75 00 98 – jurucha@telefonica.net*
– closed August, Sunday and Bank Holidays   **I1**
Tapa *1.80 €*
♦ Spanish ♦ Tapas bar ♦
One of Madrid's most popular tapas bars. Delicious Basque style pinchos, tapas,
tortillas and croquettes.

ARGÜELLES   *Plan IV*

🏨 **Sofitel Madrid Plaza de España** *without rest*   SAT 📶

Tutor 1 ✉ *28008 –* Ⓜ *Ventura Rodríguez*   VISA ◉◎ AE ◉
– ℰ 915 41 98 80 – h1320@accor.com – Fax 915 42 57 36 – www.sofitel.com
96 rm – 🛏113/321 € 🛏🛏130/343 €, ⌑ 25.15 €   **K3**
♦ Chain hotel ♦ Cosy ♦
Elegance, comfort and attention to detail are the hallmarks of this recently remo-
delled hotel. Guestrooms with high quality furniture and marble bathrooms.

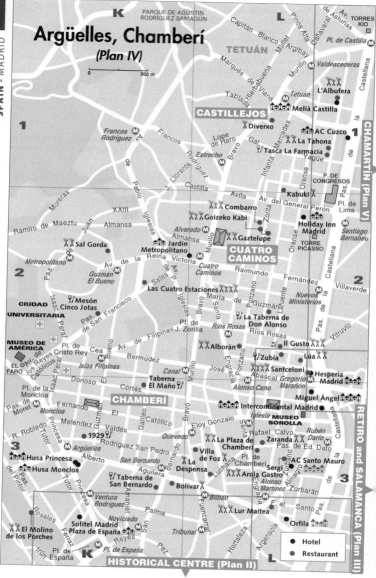

Argüelles, Chamberí
(Plan IV)

0 _____ 500 m

PARQUE DE AGUSTÍN
RODRÍGUEZ SAMAGUN

TETUÁN

TORRES
KIO
Pl. de Castilla

Capitán Blanco Argibay

Valdeacederas

XXX L'Albufera

Meliá Castilla

CASTILLEJOS

Diverxo

AC Cuzco

La Tahona

Tasca La Farmacia

CHAMARTÍN (Plan VI)

Kabuki

P. DE CONGRESOS

Pl. de Lima

Combarro

Goizeko Kabi

Holiday Inn Madrid

Santiago Bernabeu

Gaztelupe

CUATRO CAMINOS

TORRE PICASSO

Sal Gorda

Jardín Metropolitano

Guzmán El Bueno

Mesón Cinco Jotas

CIUDAD UNIVERSITARIA

Las Cuatro Estaciones XXXX

Nuevos Ministerios

Villaverde

La Taberna de Don Alonso

MUSEO DE AMÉRICA

Alborán

Il Gusto XXX

EL FARO

Zubia

Lúa

Santceloni

Hesperia Madrid

Taberna El Maño

Gregorio Marañón

Miguel Ángel

CHAMBERÍ

Intercontinental Madrid

Iglesia **MUSEO SOROLLA**

1929

Husa Princesa

Husa Moncloa

La Plaza de Chamberí

Zaranda

Rubén Darío

AC Santo Mauro

Villa de Foz

La Despensa

Pl. de Chamberí

Arola Gastro

Taberna de San Bernardo

Bolívar

RETIRO and SALAMANCA (Plan III)

Lur Maitea

Sofitel Madrid Plaza de España

El Molino de los Porches

Orfila

● Hotel
● Restaurant

HISTORICAL CENTRE (Plan II)

XX **El Molino de los Porches**   m̂ *VISA* ⭕⭕ AE ⑪

paseo Pintor Rosales 1 ⊠ *28008 –* ⓜ *Plaza España –* ℰ *915 48 13 36*
– Fax 915 47 97 61 – www.asadorelmolino.com
– closed Sunday dinner in winter   **K3**
Rest – Carte 40/48 €
♦ Grills ♦ Rustic ♦
Located in Parque del Oeste, this restaurant has several lounges and a charming
glass enclosed terrace. The roasts from the wood-burning oven and the delicious
grilled dishes are the house specialities.

CHAMBERÍ   *Plan IV*

🏨🏨🏨 **AC Santo Mauro**   No smokers rest. m̂ *Ĺᵨ* 🖥 🖵 ⑪ 🖖 🚗

Zurbano 36 ⊠ *28010 –* ⓜ *Alonso Martínez*   *VISA* ⭕⭕ AE ⑪
– ℰ *913 19 69 00 – hotelacsantomauro@ac-hotels.com – Fax 913 08 54 77*
– www.ac-hotels.com   **L3**
43 rm – ♦295 € ♦♦355 €, � 30 € – 8 suites
Rest Santo Mauro *– (closed August)* Carte 95/120 €
♦ Palace ♦ Grand Luxury ♦ Classical ♦
Delightful French style mansion located in the city's former aristocratic district,
which is now home to a number of foreign embassies. Elegant setting with an
attractive garden, and luxurious features in every guestroom. The restaurant occupies a beautiful library-lounge, providing a distinctive backdrop to lunch.

🏨🏨🏨 **Intercontinental Madrid**   m̂ *Ĺᵨ* 🖥 ⑪ 🖖 🚗 *VISA* ⭕⭕ AE ⑪

paseo de la Castellana 49 ⊠ *28046 –* ⓜ *Gregorio Marañón*
– ℰ *917 00 73 00 – icmadrid@ihg.com – Fax 913 19 58 53*
– www.madrid.intercontinental.com   **L3**
279 rm – ♦♦199/550 €, ⊆ 32 € – 28 suites   **Rest** – Menu 45 €
♦ Luxury ♦ Classical ♦
This hotel has an elegant marble adorned lobby crowned with a cupola. Attractive
inner terrace-patio and extremely comfortable guestrooms. The restaurant, located next to the bar, serves fine international cuisine.

🏨🏨🏨 **Miguel Ángel**   m̂ *Ĺᵨ* 🖥 ⑪ 📞 🖖 🚗 *VISA* ⭕⭕ AE ⑪

Miguel Ángel 31 ⊠ *28010 –* ⓜ *Gregorio Marañón*
– ℰ *914 42 00 22 – comercial.hma@oh-es.com – Fax 914 42 53 20*
– www.miguelangelhotel.com   **L3**
243 rm – ♦♦160/350 €, ⊆ 25 € – 20 suites   **Rest Arco** – Carte 40/59 €
♦ Luxury ♦ Classical ♦
Situated in the middle section of the Castellana avenue, this prestigious hotel
offers guest the very the latest in technology. Large, elegant lounges and guestrooms decorated with real attention to detail. Elegant restaurant with an outdoor
terrace for summer dining.

🏨🏨🏨 **Hesperia Madrid**   *Ĺᵨ* 🖥 ⑪ 🖖 *VISA* ⭕⭕ AE ⑪

paseo de la Castellana 57 ⊠ *28046 –* ⓜ *Gregorio Marañón*
– ℰ *912 10 88 00 – hotel@hesperia-madrid.com – Fax 912 10 88 99*
– www.hesperia-madrid.com   **FU**
139 rm – ♦160/403 € ♦♦165/463 €, ⊆ 27 € – 32 suites
Rest Santceloni – see below
Rest – Menu 35 €
♦ Urban ♦ Modern ♦
Conveniently located in a central business district, this hotel has a small lobby and
a number of different lounge areas. Elegant, guestrooms that are in traditional in
style. Hotel with modern decoration and attractive interior design. It has a spacious
lounge area, with well-lit foyer-reception and a bright, central courtyard. Classical
rooms.

SPAIN - MADRID

Orfila 🏠 🗃 ((•)) 🛁 🚗 VISA ⚫⚫ AE ①

Orfila 6 ✉ *28010 –* ⓜ *Alonso Martínez –* ☎ *917 02 77 70*
– inforeservas@hotelorfila.com – Fax 917 02 77 72 – www.hotelorfila.com
– closed 21 days in August **L3**
28 rm – ♦230/345 € ♦♦230/415 €, ⛱ 30 € – 4 suites **Rest** – Menu 65 €
♦ Palace ♦ Luxury ♦ Classical ♦
A 19C mansion located in an exclusive residential area. A stately atmosphere pervades every room with furnishings that are classically elegant. À la carte dining in the Orfila's welcoming dining room or the indoor garden.

Santceloni (Óscar Velasco) – Hotel Hesperia Madrid ⇔

paseo de la Castellana 57 ✉ *28046* VISA ⚫⚫ AE ①
– ⓜ *Gregorio Marañón –* ☎ *912 10 88 40 – santceloni@hesperia-madrid.com*
– Fax 912 10 88 92 – www.restaurantesantceloni.com
– closed Holy Week, August, Saturday lunch, Sunday and Bank Holidays
Rest – Menu 132 € – Carte 90/120 € **L2**
Spec. Navajas con el aceite de tomate seco y membrillo. Jarrete de ternera blanca con puré de patatas. Galleta de almendra con crema de azafrán y el sorbete de naranja sanguina.
♦ Inventive ♦ Minimalist ♦
A wonderful culinary experience enhanced by superb service. Traditional cuisine with a creative twist served in an elegant dining room extending over two levels.

Las Cuatro Estaciones VISA ⚫⚫ AE ①

General Ibáñez de Íbero 5 ✉ *28003 –* ⓜ *Guzmán El Bueno –* ☎ *915 53 63 05*
– lascuatroestaciones@flanigansa.com – Fax 915 35 05 23
– www.lascuatroestaciones.info
– closed August, Saturday lunch and Sunday **K2**
Rest – Carte approx. 60 €
♦ International ♦ Formal ♦
An original restaurant with 1980s decor and a carpeted dining room that extends across several levels. Private bar and a comprehensive wine list.

Il Gusto VISA ⚫⚫ AE ①

Espronceda 27 ✉ *28003 –* ⓜ *Canal –* ☎ *915 35 39 02 – Fax 915 35 08 61*
– www.restauranteilgusto.com
– closed Sunday dinner **L2**
Rest – Carte 31/47 €
♦ Italian ♦ Design ♦
Italian cuisine takes pride of place in this modern restaurant. It has an elegant dining room decorated with a profusion of marble and wood.

Sergi Arola Gastro Totally no smoking VISA ⚫⚫ AE ①

Zurbano 31 ✉ *28010 –* ⓜ *Rubén Darío –* ☎ *91 310 21 69 – info@sergiarola.es*
– Fax 91 310 04 51 – www.sergiarola.es
– closed Christmas, Holy Week, 21 days in August, Saturday lunch and Sunday
Rest *– (set menu only)* Menu 85/140 € **L3**
Spec. Ravioli de cigala y foie-gras con parmentier. Arroz basmati guisado con fruta escarchada y pichón navarro. Esfera de chocolate rellena de mousse de azafrán y sopa caliente de chocolate.
♦ Inventive ♦ Contemporary ♦
A restaurant full of surprises with a cocktail bar on the mezzanine level, a glass-fronted wine cellar, a simply lit dining room and an unusual private dining area in the kitchen itself. Creative cuisine.

Lur Maitea VISA ⚫⚫ AE ①

Fernando el Santo 4 ✉ *28010 –* ⓜ *Alonso Martínez –* ☎ *913 08 03 50*
– alex@restaurantelurmaitea.com – Fax 913 91 38 21
– www.restaurantelurmaitea.com
– closed Holy Week, August and Sunday **L3**
Rest – Carte 57/77 €
♦ Basque cuisine ♦ Formal ♦
Lur Maitea has become one of the city's best-known restaurants. It serves contemporary Basque cuisine in an elegant dining room with blue-inspired decor and wood flooring.

SPAIN - MADRID

XX **Alborán** ⌒ VISA ⟲ AE ①

Ponzano 39-41 ⌧ *28003 –* ⓜ *Alonso Cano –* ℰ *913 99 21 50*
– alboran@alboran-rest.com – Fax 913 99 21 50 – www.alboran-rest.com
– closed Sunday dinner **L2**
Rest – Carte 50/63 €
♦ Traditional ♦ Rustic ♦
Tapas are served in the cafeteria by the entrance with more extensive choices in the two well-furnished dining rooms. The decor here is nautical in theme with wood floors and panelling.

XX **Zaranda** (Fernando Arellano)   Smokers rest. VISA ⟲ AE ①
❀
paseo de Eduardo Dato 5 ⌧ *28010 –* ⓜ *Iglesia –* ℰ *914 46 45 48*
– zaranda@zaranda.es – www.zaranda.es
– closed August, Sunday and Monday **L3**
Rest – Menu 56/78 € – Carte 53/87 €
Spec. Espardeñas a la brasa sobre estofado de lentejas y papada de ibérico ahumada. Cochinillo en choucroute oriental (Winter-Spring). Cremoso de queso de cabra con sorbete de fresa al Rioja y albahaca.
♦ Inventive ♦ Cosy ♦
An efficiently managed restaurant in which the owners run the dining room and kitchen. Two modern dining rooms with a focus on creative cuisine, including two tasting menus.

XX **La Plaza de Chamberí** VISA ⟲ AE ①

pl. de Chamberí 10 ⌧ *28010 –* ⓜ *Iglesia –* ℰ *914 46 06 97 – Fax 915 94 21 20*
– www.restaurantelaplazadechamberi.com
– closed Sunday **L3**
Rest – Carte 35/44 €
♦ Traditional ♦ Formal ♦
A well-established and popular restaurant with an old-style dining room extending over two floors. The culinary focus here is on traditional cuisine.

XX **Lúa** Smokers rest. VISA ⟲ AE ①

Zurbano 85 ⌧ *28003 –* ⓜ *Gregorio Marañón –* ℰ *913 95 28 53*
– www.restaurantelua.com
– closed 10-20 August and Sunday **L2**
Rest – *(set menu only)* Menu 42 €
♦ Inventive ♦ Cosy ♦
This small, trendy restaurant has a lively atmosphere with the dining room separated into three sections. Creative, contemporary cuisine, including a tasting menu.

X **Bolívar** VISA ⟲ AE ①

Manuela Malasaña 28 ⌧ *28004 –* ⓜ *San Bernardo –* ℰ *914 45 12 74*
– angellosadalopez@yahoo.com – www.restaurantebolivar.com
– closed Holy Week, August and Sunday **K3**
Rest – Carte 31/46 €
♦ Traditional ♦ Family ♦
This family-run restaurant in the traditional Malasaña district has excellent service and a reasonably priced, varied menu. Welcoming dining room with a modern feel.

X **Villa de Foz** Smokers rest. ⌒ VISA ⟲ AE ①

Gonzálo de Córdoba 10 ⌧ *28010 –* ⓜ *Bilbao –* ℰ *914 46 89 93*
– www.villadefoz.com
– closed August and Sunday **L3**
Rest – Carte 36/49 €
♦ Galician ♦ Fashionable ♦
Traditional Galician cuisine served in an attractive, contemporary-style dining room. A somewhat limited menu but with a high standard across the board.

Mesón Cinco Jotas

🚭 Totally no smoking VISA ◎◎ AE ①

paseo de San Francisco de Sales 27 ✉ *28003 –* Ⓜ *Guzmán El Bueno*
– ℰ 915 44 01 89 – m5jsfsales@osborne.es – Fax 915 49 06 51
– www.mesoncincojotas.com

K2

Tapa 3.50 € **Ración** approx. 16 €
♦ Traditional ♦ Tapas bar ♦

Decorated in the chain's usual contemporary-style, this restaurant has two dining rooms where customers can enjoy snacks or à la carte dishes. Good selection of tapas at the bar, including superb Spanish hams.

Zubia

Smokers rest. VISA ◎◎ AE ①

Espronceda 28 ✉ *28003 –* Ⓜ *Ríos Rosas – ℰ 914 41 04 32*
– info@restaurantezubia.com – Fax 914 41 10 43 – www.restaurantezubia.com
– closed August, Saturday lunch and Sunday

L2

Tapa 2 € **Ración** approx. 10 €
♦ Traditional ♦ Tapas bar ♦

Extensive menu of tapas and snacks at the bar, as well as a few tables for informal dining. The restaurant has a small dining room.

La Taberna de Don Alonso

Smokers rest.

Alonso Cano 64 ✉ *28003 –* Ⓜ *Ríos Rosas – ℰ 915 33 52 49*
– closed Holy Week, 20 July-20 August, Sunday dinner and Monday

Tapa 2 € **Ración** approx. 12 €

L2

♦ Traditional ♦ Tapas bar ♦

This tavern has a small choice of tapas on display at the bar, and a blackboard highlighting the dishes available direct from the kitchen. Selection of wines by the glass.

Taberna El Maño

Smokers rest. 🚭 VISA ◎◎

Vallehermoso 59 ✉ *28015 –* Ⓜ *Canal – ℰ 914 48 40 35*
– closed Sunday dinner and Monday

Tapa 5 € **Ración** approx. 12 €

K3

♦ Traditional ♦ Tapas bar ♦

Old, traditional restaurant decorated with a bullfighting theme. Tapas and snacks of a high quality.

1929

Smokers rest. VISA ◎◎

Rodríguez San Pedro 66 ✉ *28015 –* Ⓜ *Argüelles – ℰ 915 49 91 16*
– www.taberna1929.com
– closed August and Sunday

K3

Tapa 3 € **Ración** approx. 14.60 €
♦ Traditional ♦ Tapas bar ♦

Rustic restaurant run by its owner. Well- stocked bar, barrels used as tables, and two dining rooms.

CASTILLEJOS and CUATRO CAMINOS

Plan IV

Meliá Castilla

🍴 🖥 ☎ 🛎 🚗 VISA ◎◎ AE ①

Capitán Haya 43 ✉ *28020 –* Ⓜ *Cuzco – ℰ 915 67 50 00*
– melia.castilla@solmelia.com – Fax 915 67 50 51 – www.meliacastilla.com
904 rm – 👫110/395 €, 🍽 25 € – 12 suites
Rest L'Albufera – see below

L1

♦ Chain hotel ♦ Modern ♦

This hotel is renowned for its public areas, including a large auditorium and numerous banqueting and conference rooms. Elegant bedrooms.

AC Cuzco

No smokers rest. 🛗 🖥 ☎ 🛎 🅿 🚗 VISA ◎◎ AE ①

paseo de la Castellana 133 ✉ *28046 –* Ⓜ *Cuzco – ℰ 915 56 00 00*
– reservas.accuzco@ac-hotels.com – Fax 915 56 03 72 – www.ac-hotels.com
315 rm – 👫100/255 €, 🍽 21 € – 4 suites
Rest – Carte approx. 50 €

L1

♦ Chain hotel ♦ Business ♦ Modern ♦

This completely renovated hotel offers guests a choice of modern, comfortable and well-designed rooms typical of the AC chain.

Holiday Inn Madrid

pl. Carlos Trías Beltrán 4 (access by Orense 22-24) ✉ *28020*
– Ⓜ *Santiago Bernabeu* – ℰ *914 56 80 00* – *tojsp.reservations@*
ichotelsgroup.com – *Fax 914 56 80 01* – *www.holidayinnmadrid.net*
280 rm – ♦130/250 € ♦♦150/270 €, ⌷ 23 € – 33 suites **L2**
Rest *Big Blue* – Carte 30/45 €
♦ Chain hotel ♦ Functional ♦

Convenient location next to the Azca complex, a financial centre with a plethora of offices, shops and restaurants. Contemporary-style guestrooms, and an extensive range of additional services. The Big Blue restaurant is decorated in a cheerful, Modernist style.

Jardín Metropolitano

av. Reina Victoria 12 ✉ *28003* – Ⓜ *Cuatro Caminos* – ℰ *911 83 18 10*
– *metropolitano@vphoteles.com* – *Fax 911 83 18 11* – *www.vphoteles.com*
96 rm – ♦118/187 € ♦♦121/234 €, ⌷ 19.80 € – 6 suites **K-L2**
Rest – Menu 25 €
♦ Urban ♦ Classical ♦

This contemporary-style hotel occupies a building surrounding a central patio crowned by a skylight. Spacious, classical, and well-equipped bedrooms.

L'Albufera – Hotel Meliá Castilla

Capitán Haya 45 ✉ *28020* – Ⓜ *Cuzco* – ℰ *915 67 51 97* – *Fax 915 67 50 51*
Rest – Carte 40/54 € **L1**
♦ Rice ♦ Formal ♦

This restaurant has three classically elegant dining rooms, as well as an enclosed winter garden-style patio with a profusion of greenery.

Combarro

Reina Mercedes 12 ✉ *28020* – Ⓜ *Nuevos Ministerios* – ℰ *915 54 77 84*
– *combarro@combarro.com* – *Fax 915 34 25 01* – *www.combarro.com*
– *closed Holy Week, August and Sunday dinner* **L2**
Rest – Carte approx. 60 €
♦ Galician ♦ Formal ♦

Galician cuisine with an emphasis on fresh quality produce, including live fish tanks. Public bar, dining on the first floor and a number of rooms in the basement. Classic and elegant in style.

Goizeko Kabi

Smokers rest.
Comandante Zorita 37 ✉ *28020* – Ⓜ *Alvarado* – ℰ *915 33 01 85*
– *Fax 915 33 02 14* – *www.goizekogaztelupe.com*
– *closed Sunday* **L2**
Rest – Carte 55/77 €
♦ Basque cuisine ♦ Formal ♦

Prestigious address serving modern Basque cuisine. Although the tables are somewhat close together, the overall feel is one of refined elegance.

La Tahona

Capitán Haya 21 (side) ✉ *28020* – Ⓜ *Cuzco* – ℰ *915 55 04 41*
– *Fax 915 56 62 02* – *www.asadordearanda.com*
– *closed August and Sunday dinner* **L1**
Rest – Carte 36/43 €
♦ Roast lamb ♦ Rustic ♦

Bar in the entrance with a wood oven and wood panelling, followed by various dining rooms decorated in medieval Castilian style. Enjoy traditional roast dishes accompanied by the restaurant's own house red.

Gaztelupe

Comandante Zorita 32 ✉ *28020* – Ⓜ *Alvarado* – ℰ *915 34 90 28*
– *Fax 915 54 65 66* – *www.goizekogaztelupe.com*
– *closed Sunday in July-August and Sunday dinner the rest of the year*
Rest – Carte 52/62 € **L2**
♦ Basque cuisine ♦ Cosy ♦

Bar at the entrance, dining rooms renovated in cosy, neo-rustic style, and two private rooms in the basement. The extensive menu focuses on traditional Basque cuisine.

Sal Gorda
Smokers rest. 〜〜

Beatriz de Bobadilla 9 ✉ *28040 –* Ⓜ *Guzmán El Bueno –* ☏ *915 53 95 06*
– closed August and Sunday   **K2**
Rest – Carte 31/35 €
♦ Traditional ♦ Formal ♦
A small restaurant run by renowned professionals with a loyal and regular clientele.
Reasonably priced menu featuring classic, traditional cuisine.

Diverxo
〜〜

Francisco Medrano 5 ✉ *28020 –* Ⓜ *Tetuán –* ☏ *91570 07 66*
– kocifree@hotmail.com – www.diverxo.com
– closed Sunday and Monday   **L1**
Rest – *(booking essential)* Menu 60 €
♦ Inventive ♦ Contemporary ♦
Basic decor centred on varying shades of grey, allied with contemporary table settings. Creative cuisine combining a variety of influences.

Kabuki
〜〜

av. Presidente Carmona 2 ✉ *28020 –* Ⓜ *Santiago Bernabeu*
– ☏ *914 17 64 15 – kabuki@ya.com – Fax 915 56 02 32*
– closed Holy Week, 21 days in August, Saturday lunch, Sunday and Bank
Holidays   **L1-2**
Rest – Carte approx. 60 €
♦ Japanese ♦ Minimalist ♦
Intimate Japanese restaurant with tasteful, minimalist decor. Modern terrace and a
kitchen counter where all the dishes, including the popular sushi, are prepared.

Tasca La Farmacia
Totally no smoking 〜〜

Capitán Haya 19 ✉ *28020 –* Ⓜ *Cuzco –* ☏ *915 55 81 46 – Fax 915 56 62 02*
– www.asadorodearanda.com
– closed 10 August-10 September and Sunday   **L1**
Tapa 3 € **Ración** approx. 10 €
♦ Codfish specialities ♦ Tapas bar ♦
Delightful restaurant decorated with azulejo tiles, stone arches, exposed brickwork,
wrought iron lattice windows and an impressive glass ceiling. La Farmacia is
famous for its cod dishes.

CHAMARTÍN
Plan V

Puerta América
〜〜

av. de América 41 ✉ *28002 –* Ⓜ *Cartagena –* ☏ *917 44 54 00*
– hotel.puertamerica@hoteles-silken.com – Fax 917 44 54 01
– www.hotelpuertamerica.com   **N3**
330 rm – ♥♥159/450 €, ⊏ 27 € – 12 suites
Rest *Lágrimas Negras* – *(closed August, Saturday lunch and Sunday)*
Carte 62/88 € 🍴
♦ Business ♦ Design ♦
Colourfully decorated and with numerous designer features, each of the floors of
this hotel reflects the creativity of a renowned artist. The guestrooms are very original in style. This modern restaurant has a certain New York feel, with its bar area
and high ceilings.

AC Aitana
No smokers rest. 〜〜

paseo de la Castellana 152 ✉ *28046 –* Ⓜ *Cuzco –* ☏ *914 58 49 70*
– aitana@ac-hotels.com – Fax 914 58 49 71 – www.ac-hotels.com
109 rm – ♥♥107/289 €, ⊏ 21 € – 2 suites   **M2**
Rest – *(closed August)* Carte 35/41 €
♦ Chain hotel ♦ Functional ♦
An avant-garde style both in the interior design and in the furniture, with an abundant use of wood. Contemporary-style guestrooms with parquet flooring. A multi-
purpose restaurant used for breakfast, lunch and dinner.

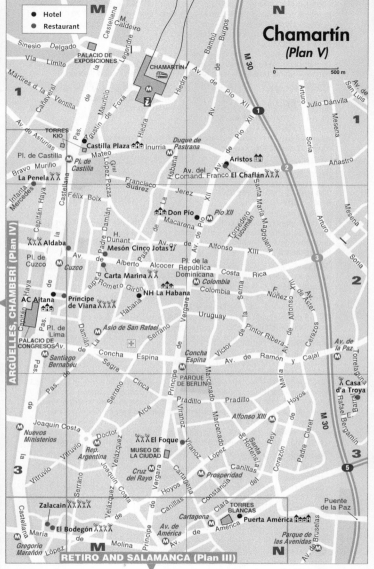

Chamartín
(Plan V)

0   500 m

- Hotel
- Restaurant

PALACIO DE EXPOSICIONES

CHAMARTÍN

TORRES KIO

Castilla Plaza · Inurria

Pl. de Castilla

La Penela

Duque de Pastrana

Aristos

Av. del Comand. Franco El Chaflán

Don Pío

Aldaba

Mesón Cinco Jotas

Pl. de Cuzco

Carta Marina

NH La Habana

AC Aitana

Príncipe de Viana

Asio de San Rafael

PALACIO DE CONGRESOS

Santiago Bernabéu

PARQUE DE BERLÍN

Casa d'a Troya

Nuevos Ministerios

El Foque

MUSEO DE LA CIUDAD

Cruz del Rayo

Prosperidad

Zalacaín

El Bodegón

Gregorio Marañón

TORRES BLANCAS

Puerta América

Puente de la Paz

Parque de las Avenidas

SPAIN - MADRID

NH La Habana
No smokers rest. 🗺️ 📶 🏃 🚗 VISA ◎ AE ①
paseo de La Habana 73 ⊠ *28036 –* Ⓜ *Colombia –* ☎ *914 43 07 20*
– nhhabana@nh-hotels.com – Fax 914 57 75 79 – www.nh-hotels.com
155 rm – †85/210 € ††110/250 €, � 16.50 €
Rest – Menu 30 €   M2

♦ Chain hotel ♦ Functional ♦

Contemporary-style hotel aimed at a business clientele. The somewhat compact but comfortable bedrooms have modern furnishings and wood flooring.

Don Pío
without rest 👜 🗺️ 📶 🏃 🅿 VISA ◎ AE ①
av. Pío XII-25 ⊠ *28016 –* Ⓜ *Pío XII –* ☎ *913 53 07 80 – hoteldonpio@*
hoteldonpio.com – Fax 913 53 07 81 – www.hoteldonpio.com
41 rm – †80/160 € ††80/175 €, ⊇ 13 €   N2

♦ Traditional ♦ Cosy ♦

Attractive patio-lobby crowned by a modern skylight overlooked by all the guest-rooms. These are spacious and include features such as hydromassage bathtubs.

Castilla Plaza
👜 🗺️ 📶 🏃 🚗 VISA ◎ AE ①
paseo de la Castellana 220 ⊠ *28046 –* Ⓜ *Plaza Castilla –* ☎ *915 67 43 00*
– castilla-plaza@abbahoteles.com – Fax 913 15 54 06 – www.abbahoteles.com
228 rm – †70/281 € ††70/294 €, ⊇ 18 €
Rest – Carte 40/46 €   M1

♦ Business ♦ Classical ♦

Beautiful glass fronted building, which along with the Kio Towers, is part of the Puerta de Europa complex. Comfortable, contemporary-style with a wealth of decorative detail. Attention to detail and traditional cuisine are the hallmarks of this restaurant.

Aristos
🗺️ 📶 VISA ◎ AE ①
av. Pío XII-34 ⊠ *28016 –* Ⓜ *Pío XII –* ☎ *913 45 04 50 – hotelaristos@gmail.com*
– Fax 913 45 10 23 – www.hotelaristos.com   N1
22 rm – †110 € ††150 €, ⊇ 10 €   **Rest** El Chaflán – see below

♦ Traditional ♦ Functional ♦

Behind the red brick exterior is a functional hotel. It offers fully equipped guest-rooms with wood floors and contemporary furnishings.

Zalacaín (Juan Antonio Medina)
↔ VISA ◎ AE ①
🍃
Álvarez de Baena 4 ⊠ *28006 –* Ⓜ *Gregorio Marañón –* ☎ *915 61 48 40*
– Fax 915 61 47 32 – www.restaurantezalacain.com
– closed Holy Week, August, Saturday lunch, Sunday and Bank Holidays
Rest – Menu 96 € – Carte 60/83 €   M3
Spec. Pequeño búcaro Don Pío con huevos de codorniz, salmón ahumado y caviar. Filetes de lenguado en caracolas con vinagreta de marisco y espa-guetti de patata. Costillar de cordero lechal asado con su riñón y pisto.

♦ International ♦ Formal ♦

A stylish restaurant with classical, cosy lounges that combine an elegant atmo-sphere with delicate decorative details. Traditional and international menu.

Príncipe de Viana
VISA ◎ AE ①
Manuel de Falla 5 ⊠ *28036 –* Ⓜ *Santiago Bernabeu –* ☎ *914 57 15 49*
– restaurante@principeviana.com – Fax 914 57 52 83
– closed Holy Week, August, Saturday lunch, Sunday and Bank Holidays
Rest – Carte 68/79 € 🌿   M2

♦ Basque cuisine ♦ Formal ♦

This restaurant has a long-standing reputation for its excellent cuisine, which takes its inspiration from the Basque country and Navarra. Attractive decor and table set-tings.

El Bodegón
↔ VISA ◎ AE ①
Pinar 15 ⊠ *28006 –* Ⓜ *Gregorio Marañón –* ☎ *915 62 88 44*
– Fax 915 62 97 25 – www.grupovips.com
– closed August, Saturday lunch, Sunday and Bank Holidays
Rest – Carte 69/86 €   M3

♦ Traditional ♦ Formal ♦

Elegant restaurant in classical style with a private bar and dining rooms on various levels. The menu here focuses on traditional cuisine.

XXX ❄

El Chaflán (Juan Pablo Felipe) – Hotel Aristos   🏠 VISA ⬤⬤ AE ⓞ
av. Pío XII-34 ✉ *28016 –* Ⓜ *Pío XII – 𝒞 913 50 61 93*
– restaurante@elchaflan.com – Fax 913 45 10 23 – www.elchaflan.com
– closed 10 days in August, Saturday lunch and Sunday   **N1**
Rest – Menu 91/115 € – Carte 80/110 € ❀
Spec. Alcachofas y vieiras en ensalada, con vinagreta emulsionada. Costillas de buey Wagyu, lentamente guisadas, manzana y puré de apio. Tarta al whisky, la de siempre, pero diferente.
◆ Inventive ◆ Minimalist ◆
Attractive minimalist-style restaurant with the kitchen in view of diners. The à la carte menu here is both interesting and innovative.

XXX

Aldaba   ⇔ VISA ⬤⬤ AE ⓞ
av. de Alberto Alcocer 5 ✉ *28036 –* Ⓜ *Cuzco – 𝒞 913 59 73 86*
– Fax 913 45 21 93
– closed Holy Week, August, Saturday lunch, Sunday and Bank Holidays
Rest – Carte 64/74 € ❀   **M2**
◆ Traditional ◆ Cosy ◆
This restaurant has a bar at the entrance, followed by an attractive dining room in classic-modern style and several small rooms for private dining. Excellent wine list.

XXX

El Foque   Smokers rest. VISA ⬤⬤ AE ⓞ
Suero de Quiñones 22 ✉ *28002 –* Ⓜ *Cruz del Rayo – 𝒞 915 19 25 72*
– restaurante@elfoque.com – Fax 915 19 25 73 – www.elfoque.com
– closed Sunday   **M3**
Rest – Carte 41/56 €
◆ Codfish specialities ◆ Cosy ◆
Conveniently located close to the Auditorio Nacional de Música, this restaurant on two levels has an attractive nautical decor with a mast and sails adorning the dining room. The house speciality is cod.

XX

Carta Marina   No smokers rest. ⇔ VISA ⬤⬤ AE ⓞ
Padre Damián 40 ✉ *28036 –* Ⓜ *Cuzco – 𝒞 914 58 68 26 – Fax 914 57 08 21*
– www.restaurantecartamarina.com
– closed Holy Week, August and Sunday   **M2**
Rest – Carte 41/56 €
◆ Galician ◆ Formal ◆
This restaurant has an attractive wood decor, private bar, and cosy dining rooms with a summer and winter terrace. Traditional Galician menu.

XX

La Penela   ⇔ VISA ⬤⬤
Infanta Mercedes 98 ✉ *28020 –* Ⓜ *Valdeacederas – 𝒞 915 79 91 78*
– www.lapenela.com
– closed Sunday dinner   **M1-2**
Rest – Carte 33/50 €
◆ Galician ◆ Formal ◆
A Galician restaurant with a bar and a modern dining room split over two floors. The focus here is on fresh produce, much of which is brought in daily from Galicia.

X

Casa d'a Troya   ⇔ VISA ⬤⬤ AE ⓞ
Emiliano Barral 14 ✉ *28043 –* Ⓜ *Avenida de la Paz – 𝒞 914 16 44 55*
– Fax 914 16 42 80
– closed 24 December-2 January, Holy Week, 15 July-August, nights from Monday to Thursday, Sunday and Bank Holidays   **N3**
Rest – Carte 45/57 €
◆ Galician ◆ Family ◆
A family-run business offering simply prepared, traditional Galician cuisine. Lobby-bar and two comfortable dining rooms.

Ɏ/

Mesón Cinco Jotas   🏠 VISA ⬤⬤ AE ⓞ
Padre Damián 42 ✉ *28036 –* Ⓜ *Cuzco – 𝒞 913 50 31 73 – m5jpdamian@ osborne.es – Fax 913 45 79 51 – www.mesoncincojotas.com*   **M2**
Tapa 3 € **Ración** approx. 12 €
◆ Traditional ◆ Tapas bar ◆
This chain restaurant specialises in top quality Iberian ham and chorizos. Varied tapas and à la carte menus served in two pleasant dining rooms.

Sofitel Madrid Campo de las Naciones ⛄ 📺 📶 🛗 🚗 💳 ⓿ 🅰 🆔

av. de la Capital de España Madrid 10 ✉ *28042*
– ⓜ *Campo de las Naciones* – ☎ *917 21 00 70 – h1606@accor.com*
– *Fax 917 21 05 15 – www.sofitel.com* **D1**
176 rm – 🛏🛏85/375 €, ⊑ 24.50 € – 3 suites
Rest *Mare Nostrum* – *(closed August, Saturday and Sunday)* Carte 59/76 €
♦ Business ♦ Chain hotel ♦ Classical ♦
Situated near the Recinto Ferial de Madrid convention centre, this hotel has an attractive foyer and a pleasant dining room that is reminiscent of an Andalusian patio. Comfortable, fully equipped guestrooms. The Mare Nostrum restaurant has an elegant atmosphere and interesting menu.

Novotel Madrid Campo de las Naciones No smokers rest.

Amsterdam 3 ✉ *28042* 🛋 ⛄ 📺 📶 🛗 🚗 💳 ⓿ 🅰 🆔
– ⓜ *Campo de las Naciones* – ☎ *917 21 18 18 – h1636@accor.com*
– *Fax 917 21 11 22 – www.novotel.com* **D1**
240 rm – 🛏🛏260 €, ⊑ 17 € – 6 suites **Rest** *Claravía* – Carte 33/49 €
♦ Business ♦ Chain hotel ♦ Functional ♦
Classic, modern building complex next to the Parque Ferial. Reasonably spacious lounges, and comfortable guestrooms with functional furnishings. Bright dining room with a terrace for the summer months.

Acis y Galatea without rest ⚓ 📺 📶 🅿 💳 ⓿

Galatea 6 ✉ *28042* – ⓜ *Canillejas* – ☎ *917 43 49 01 – res.acisgalatea@hotelesglobales.com – Fax 917 41 76 97 – www.acisygalatea.com*
20 rm – 🛏71/181 € 🛏🛏76/186 €, ⊑ 12 € **D1**
♦ Family ♦ Modern ♦
A friendly, family-run hotel with a certain charm. Modern decor with a contrasting light and dark colour scheme. Well-appointed guestrooms.

Tryp Alameda Aeropuerto 📺 📞 🛗 🅿 💳 ⓿ 🅰 🆔

av. de Logroño 100 - A 2 and turn off to Barajas village : 15 km ✉ *28042*
– ⓜ *Barajas* – ☎ *917 47 48 00 – tryp.alameda.aeropuerto@solmelia.com*
– *Fax 917 47 89 28 – www.trypalamedaaeropuerto.solmelia.com* **D1**
145 rm – 🛏60/200 € 🛏🛏65/220 €, ⊑ 15 € – 3 suites **Rest** – Menu 26 €
♦ Business ♦ Chain hotel ♦ Modern ♦
The public areas in this hotel are in the process of being modernised. The bright guestrooms offer modern comforts with cherry coloured furniture and well-equipped bathrooms.

Aparthotel Convención Barajas without rest 📺 📶 🛗 🚗

Noray 10 - A 2 and turn off to Barajas village and 💳 ⓿ 🅰 🆔
Industrial Area : 10 km ✉ *28042* – ⓜ *El Capricho* – ☎ *913 71 74 10*
– *aparthotel@hotel-convencion.com – Fax 913 71 79 01*
– *www.hotel-convencion.com* **D1**
95 suites – 🛏🛏80/220 €, ⊑ 14 €
♦ Business ♦ Functional ♦
Two twin blocks with limited public areas but with spacious apartment-style guestrooms, each with a small living room and kitchen.

NH Barajas without rest 📺 📶 🚗 💳 ⓿ 🅰 🆔

Catamarán 1 - A 2 and turn off to Barajas village and Industrial Area: 10 km
✉ *28042* – ⓜ *El Capricho* – ☎ *917 42 02 00 – exbarajas@nh-hoteles.es*
– *Fax 917 41 11 00 – www.nh-hotels.com* **D1**
173 rm – 🛏🛏65/157 €, ⊑ 9 €
♦ Business ♦ Chain hotel ♦ Functional ♦
This airport hotel offers the usual comforts associated with the NH chain. Somewhat limited public areas but a good choice in its price range.

Population (est 2008): 1 595 110 (conurbation 5 346 715) – Altitude: sea level

B. Brillion/MICHELIN

It can't be overestimated how important Catalonia is to the locals of Barcelona. Pride in their autonomous region of Spain runs deep in the blood. Barcelona loves to mix the traditional with the avant-garde, and this exuberant opening of arms has seen it grow over the years into a pulsating city for visitors. Its rash of theatres, museums and concert halls is unmatched by most other European cities, and many artists and architects have chosen to live here. Testament to the creative zest of Barcelona lies in the fact that Picasso, Miró and Dalí, along with Gaudí and Subirachs, chose to make it their home.

The nineteenth century was a golden period in the city's artistic development, with the growth of the great Catalan Modernism movement. It was knocked back on its heels after the Spanish Civil War and the rise to power of the dictator Franco, who destroyed the hopes for an independent Catalonia. After his death, democracy came to Spain and in the last 30 years Barcelona has relished its position as capital of a restored autonomous region. Whether it's via fun-loving locals, record numbers of tourists thronging its streets, or the beloved Barça football team that reached the pinnacle of success with victory in the 2006 European Champions League, this is a city that lives by the headlines it creates.

LIVING THE CITY

If you're up on **Montjuïc**, you get a great overview of the city below. Barcelona's atmospheric old town is near the harbour and reaches into the teeming streets of the **Gothic Quarter**, while the newer area is north of this, the elegant avenues in grid formation that make up Eixample. The coastal quarter of **Barça** has been transformed in recent times with the development of Barceloneta and its trendy informality. For many, though, the epicentre of this bubbling city is **The Ramblas**, scything through the centre of town.

PRACTICAL INFORMATION

ARRIVAL-DEPARTURE

Barcelona airport is located 13km southwest of the city. A taxi will cost around €25. Alternatively take the train (marked C beside Terminal A) every 30min or Aerobýs which runs approximately every 10min.

TRANSPORT

Barcelona Card – two to five days of unlimited travel, starting at 24 euros, on metro and buses; discounts on airport bus and cable cars; reduced entry to museums and attractions; discounts in several restaurants, bars and shops. It's sold at airport, tourist offices and various participating venues.

Articket – 20 euros: gives free entry to seven museums and galleries over six months and is available from tourist offices.

Look out for two tourist buses – orange Barcelona Tours and white Bus Turistic; both offer comprehensive tours of the city.

Walking tours include Modernisme, Picasso, Gothic and Gourmet – the latter includes stops in best cafés, food shops and markets.

EXPLORING BARCELONA

Has the vibrant and visceral Catalonian capital grown too popular for its own good? Some might say so but it's not hard to make the opposite case: Barcelona has always been a city that wears its heart on its sleeve, eager to show the world a love of eccentricity and affection for life after dark. No wonder the modernist master **Gaudí** flourished here: his ideals of creativity and vivacity fitted perfectly with those of the locals.

Following the 'grey years' of Franco, Barcelona really took off. It was awarded the 1992 Olympics, and the city fathers granted free reign to acclaimed architects and designers for a face-lifting blitz. From a virtual 'green-free' city, 19 new parks were created and nearly 30,000 new trees took root. Neglected squares were transformed with paved surfaces, shimmering mosaics and innovative sculptures, not to mention new seats from which to appreciate them. And the run-down seafront was spruced up, so that swathes of shiny new beach and bustling marina were created from wasteland. It's now possible to walk along five kilometres of waterfront or laze on a beach, though you might wish to avert your gaze from the senors of a certain vintage who have taken this late opportunity in life to stand naked at the water's edge.

➜ RAMBLING ON

Polls indicate that Barcelona is the European city best loved by visitors. Its beating heart, The **Ramblas**, runs straight up from the port, inexorably sucking in the world's tourists. Plane trees fan the way, and you can buy all manner of bird-life and flowers, or watch locals chatting at the newsstands. Along its three-quarter mile stretch, the Ramblas boasts numerous places to linger, from the exhibitions of the Centre d'Art Santa Mónica and waxwork likenesses at the Museu de Cera at one end, to the splendid 19C **Palau Moja** and famous Canaletes drinking fountain at the other. In between it's possible to get a feel for Gaudí's curves at the Palau Güell with its magnificently ornate chimneys, indulge in a treasure trove of musical paraphernalia at Casa Beethoven, or submerge into a feast of colourful fruit, fish and veg at the mighty Boquería market with its sturdy cast iron exterior and stained glass decorations.

You can retreat from the clamour of the Ramblas onto two of the city's most charming squares: **Plaça del Pi**, where buskers make the most of wonderful acoustics, or **Plaça Reial**, a harmonious spot with palm trees, fountains, classical buildings and lanterns designed by Gaudí.

In a city of churches, two stand out. The **Catedral de Santa Eulalia**, an imposing medieval giant that actually wasn't finished until 1913, is the star attraction of the Gothic quarter adjacent to the Ramblas. Its longevity of construction is being mirrored further across the city, where Gaudí's **Sagrada Familia**, Barcelona's most famously photographed landmark, remains unfinished, over 80 years after its creator was run down and killed by a trolley bus. Its circular towers, stretching conically to the heavens, look down eerily on a hollow interior, the project's completion date vaguely set for some time in the future. Gaudí spent the last 16 years of his life working on La Sagrada Familia. His name is entrenched in the city's recent history, his monuments to Modernism consigning design rulebooks to the scrap heap. No visitor should miss his work. La Pedrera ('The Stone Quarry' to natives) is an imposing apartment house with a fantastical, rippling façade and roof, while Casa Batlló's wonderfully sinister face depicts Sant Jordi and the Dragon: the cross on the top of the building is the knight's lance, the roof is the back of the beast, and the skeletal balconies are the skulls and bones of its wretched victims.

UNESCO has been busy in Barça. **Casa Batlló** is now one of its sites, as is the 100 year-old Palau de la Música Catalana, a richly ornate concert hall in the modernist style. Quirkiness pops up in all corners of the city with a wealth of offbeat museums dedicated to the likes of sewers, funeral carriages and shoes. The one most people head for, though, is the **Museu Picasso**, housed in five beautiful palaces, and containing over 3,600 of the great man's works, mostly from his early years and Blue Period. Picasso would have approved of the La Ribera district in which the museum is found: it's a bohemian, cutting edge area, and teems with boutiques, trendy cafés and snazzy restaurants.

➜ HEAD FOR THE HILL

For a different view of the city, then **Montjuïc** is the place to head for. The 700ft. hill, home of most events at the

'92 Olympics, provides Barça's lungs. You can reach the summit in style by cable car, and take in the views via new gardens and walkways. Don't miss out on a swim in the Olympic pool while you're there. Then soak up the glories of the world-renowned **Museu Nacional d'Art de Catalunya**, in the massive Palau Nacional. This contains a unique collection of Romanesque frescoes peeled carefully from the walls of churches in remote Pyrenean valleys.

Barcelona has changed much since George Orwell stayed in the city in the mid-thirties during the time of the Civil War. He wrote in Homage to Catalonia: "The working-class was in the saddle. Practically every building of any size had been seized by the workers." You could argue that artists and architects have now seized those very buildings. A former bullring in the city (bullfighting no longer exists now in Barcelona) is being transformed into an avant-garde shopping centre by Lord Rogers: an old infatuation being replaced by a very modern one.

CALENDAR HIGHLIGHTS

Think Barcelona and you think celebration. Unsurprisingly, the city enjoys a rich musical calendar. Maldades, in May, is a fiery flamenco festival which has strong similarities with the popular Rumba Catalana, while in the same month, the Barcelona Guitar Festival highlights international talent and emerging performers in locations around the city. From October through to July, the Gran Teatre del Liceu presents a wide-ranging programme of classical performances in luxurious surroundings. Also in October, the International Jazz Festival is one of Europe's longest-running and most well respected events, and the range of styles on offer is all-encompassing.

Away from the music hall, you can get out and about on two wheels in the much-hyped Bicycle Week every June, and keep the midnight fires burning during the dramatic Fiesta de la Merce in September, when a spectacular late night train of dragons, eagles and devils haunt the streets to a sizzling backdrop of fireworks. There's another great knees-up in June in celebration of Saint John's Day when concerts, dances and bonfires come together in a dazzling explosion. For those in a quieter frame of mind, the Barcelona Book Market, every September, is a fine place to find a second hand book and appreciate charming Passeig de Gràcia in Eixample.

BARCELONA IN...

→ ONE DAY
Catedral de Santa Eulalia, the Ramblas, La Pedrera, Museu Picasso, Sagrada Familia, chocolate shop

→ TWO DAYS
Montjuïc, Parc Güell, Nou Camp stadium, Barceloneta waterfront, Tibidabo (hill with 19C amusement park)

→ THREE DAYS
Barri Gotic and Palau de la Musica Catalana, Via Laietana (street with elegant façades and buzzy cafés), a trip to the resort of Sitges along the coast

EATING OUT

Barcelona has long had a good gastronomic tradition, not least because geographically it's been more influenced by France and Italy than other Spanish regions. But these days the sensual enjoyment of food has become something of a mainstream religion here. Not surprising, when you remember that Ferran Adriá's shrine-like El Bulli restaurant is along the Catalan coast, his reputation leading to an explosion of creative kitchens in the area. But if you want to stick with more traditional fare, the city has hundreds of tapas bars, and these are very refreshing knocked back with a draught beer. The city's location brings together produce from the land and the sea, with a firm emphasis on seasonality and quality produce. This explains why there are 39 markets in the city, all in great locations. Specialities to look out for include Pantumaca: slices of toasted bread with tomato and olive oil; Escalibada which is made with roasted vegetables; Esqueixada, a typically Catalan salad and Crema Catalana, a light custard. One little known facet of Barcelona life is its exquisite chocolate and sweet shops. Two stand out: Fargas, in the Barri Gothic, is the city's most famous chocolate shop, its 19C air giving it the status of a shrine, while Cacao Sampaka is the most elegant chocolate store you could ever wish to find and its creative concoctions, made with authentic cocoa, would make even Willie Wonka drool.

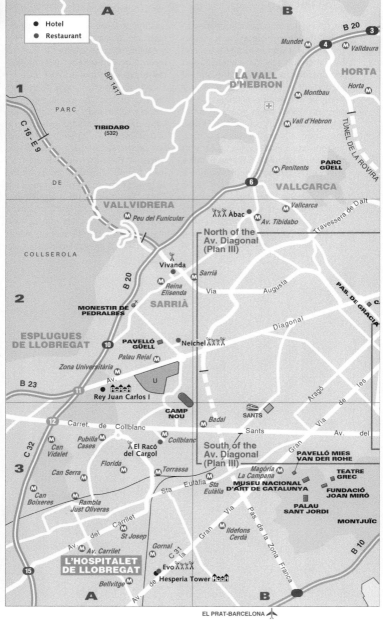

- ● Hotel
- ● Restaurant

A

BP 1417

PARC

C 16 - E 9

TIBIDABO
(532)

DE

VALLVIDRERA

Peu del Funicular

COLLSEROLA

B 20

Vivanda

Reina
Elisenda

MONESTIR DE
PEDRALBES

SARRIÀ

ESPLUGUES
DE LLOBREGAT

PAVELLÓ
GÜELL

Palau Reial

Zona Universitària

Av.

Rey Juan Carlos I

CAMP
NOU

Carret. de Collblanc

Pubilla
Cases

Can
Vidalet

El Racó
del Cargol

Collblanc

Florida

Can Serra

Torrassa

Can
Boixeres

Rambla
Just Oliveras

Sta Eulàlia

Carrilet

St Josep

Av. del

Av. Carrilet

Gornal

L'HOSPITALET
DE LLOBREGAT

Evo

Hesperia Tower

Bellvitge

Av.

A

B

B 20

Mundet

Valldaura

LA VALL
D'HEBRON

Montbau

Horta

HORTA

Vall d'Hebron

TÚNEL DE LA ROVIRA

Penitents

PARC
GÜELL

VALLCARCA

Vallcarca

Àbac

Av. Tibidabo

Travessera de Dalt

North of the
Av. Diagonal
(Plan III)

Sarrià

Via

Augusta

PAS DE GRACIA

Diagonal

C.

Neichel

U

Badal

SANTS

Sants

Aragó

de

les

Via

Av. del

South of the
Av. Diagonal
(Plan III)

PAVELLÓ MIES
VAN DER ROHE

Magòria
La Campana

Gran

TEATRE
GREC

MUSEU NACIONAL
D'ART DE CATALUNYA

FUNDACIÓ
JOAN MIRÓ

PALAU
SANT JORDI

MONTJUÏC

Ildefons
Cerdà

Gran

Via

Pas de la Zona Franca

B 10

B

EL PRAT-BARCELONA ✈

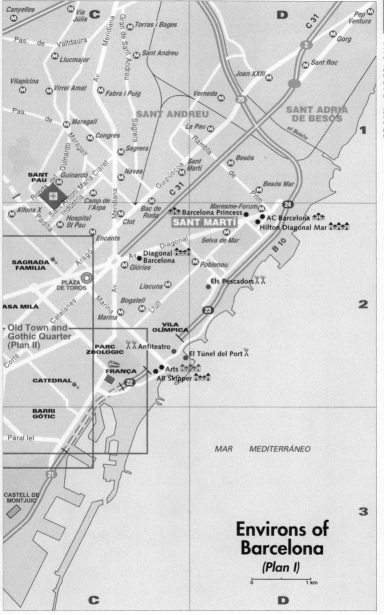

Environs of Barcelona
(Plan I)

0   1 km

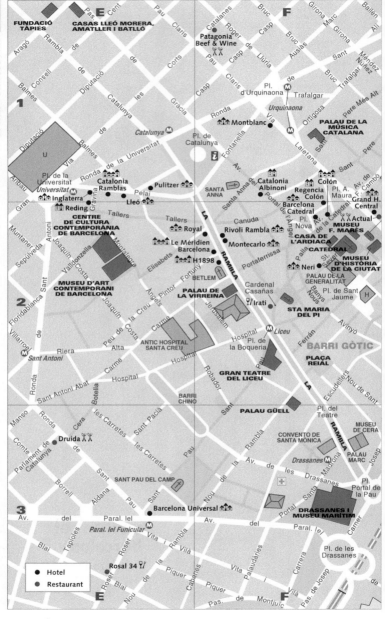

E

FUNDACIÓ TÀPIES

CASAS LLEÓ MORERA, AMATLLER I BATLLÓ

F

Patagonia Beef & Wine

Pl. d'Urquinaona

Trafalgar

Urquinaona

PALAU DE LA MÚSICA CATALANA

Montblanc

1

U

Pl. de Catalunya

Pl. de la Universitat

Catalonia Ramblas

Pulitzer

Catalonia Albinoni

Colón

Pl. A. Maura

Grand H. Central

Inglaterra

Lleó

SANTA ANNA

Regencia Colón

Barcelona Catedral

Reding

CENTRE DE CULTURA CONTEMPORÀNIA DE BARCELONA

Tallers

Royal

Rivoli Rambla

Pl. Nova

MUSEU F. MARÈS

Actual

Le Méridien Barcelona

Montecarlo

CASA DE L'ARDIACA

H1898

CATEDRAL

MUSEU D'HISTÒRIA DE LA CIUTAT

MUSEU D'ART CONTEMPORANI DE BARCELONA

BETLEM

Neri

PALAU DE LA GENERALITAT

PALAU DE LA VIRREINA

Cardenal Casañas

Irati

Pl. de Sant Jaume

H

2

Sant Antoni

STA MARIA DEL PI

ANTIC HOSPITAL SANTA CREU

Liceu

Pl. de la Boqueria

BARRI GÒTIC

GRAN TEATRE DEL LICEU

PLAÇA REIAL

BARRI CHINO

PALAU GÜELL

Pl. del Teatre

MUSEU DE CERA

Druida

CONVENTO DE SANTA MONICA

Drassanes

PALAU MARC

SANT PAU DEL CAMP

Pl. Portal de la Pau

3

Barcelona Universal

DRASSANES I MUSEU MARÍTIM

Paral·lel Funicular

Rosal 34

Pl. de les Drassanes

E

F

- ● Hotel
- ● Restaurant

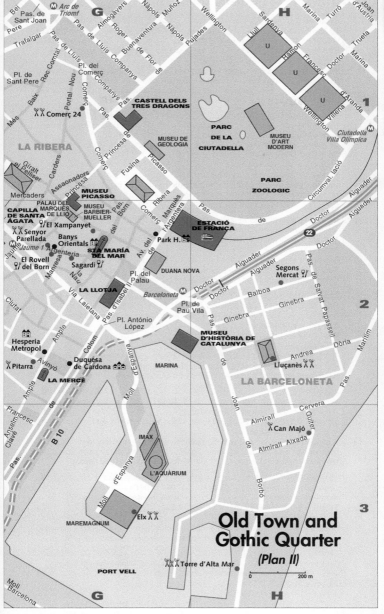

Bel
Pas. de
Sant Joan

M Arc de
Triomf

G

Almogàvers

Nàpols

Muñoz

Wellington

Sardenya

Marina

Turró

Joan
d'Àustria

H

Pere

Trafalgar

Roger

Pas. de Lluís Companys

Buenaventura

Nàpols

Pujades

Flor
de

Lluïl

Ramón

Francesc

Doctor

Marina

Pl. de
Sant Pere

Rec Comtal

Baix

Portal Nou

Comerç

Comerç

Pl. del
Comerç

Companys

Pas.

Pas.

CASTELL DELS
TRES DRAGONS

U

U

U

1

d'Aranda

Vilena

Wellington

Ciutadella
Villa Olímpica

Més

✕✕ Comerç 24

Comerç

Princesa

Carders

MUSEU DE
GEOLOGIA

PARC
DE LA
CIUTADELLA

MUSEU
D'ART
MODERN

LA RIBERA

Girait
el Tellisser

Assaonadors

Princesa

Fusina

Picasso

Ribera

PARC
ZOOLOGIC

Mercaders

MUSEU
PICASSO

Pas.

Comerç

Marquès

Circumval.lació

Aiguader

Aiguader

CAPILLA
DE SANTA
ÀGATA

PALAU DEL
MARQUÈS
DE LLIÓ

MUSEU
BARBIER-
MUELLER

Pas. de l'Argentera

ESTACIÓ
DE FRANÇA

de

Doctor

Aiguader

22

Doctor

Aiguader

✕✕ El Senyor
Parellada

♊ El Xampanyet

Banys
Orientals

Argenteria

Av. del Marquès

Comerç

Park H. 🏨

Jaume 1 M

Jaume 1

STA. MARÍA
DEL MAR

Aiguader

Pas. de Salvat Papasseit

El Rovell
♊ del Born

Manresa

Sagardi ♊

la
Nau

DUANA
NOVA

Alguader

Aiguader

Balboa

Segons
Mercat ♊

LA LLOTJA

Via Laietana

Pas. d'Isabel II

Pl. del
Palau

Barceloneta M

Doctor

Ginebra

Ginebra

Dòria

2

Ciutat

Pl. António
López

Pl. de
Pau Vila

Martím

🏛 Hesperia
Metropol

Ample

Colom

MUSEU
D'HISTÒRIA DE
CATALUNYA

Pas.

Andrea

✕ Pitarra

Avinyo

Duquesa
de Cardona 🏨

MARINA

de

Lluçanès ✕✕

LA MERCÈ

Ample

Moll d'Espanya

LA BARCELONETA

Francesc

Anselm

Clavé

B 10

Pas.

IMAX

Joan

Almirall

Cervera

Guiter

de

✕ Can Majó

L'AQUARIUM

Almirall Aixada

Moll d'Espanya

Borbó

3

Elx ✕✕

MAREMAGNUM

Old Town and
Gothic Quarter
(Plan II)

0   200 m

PORT VELL

✕✕♊ Torre d'Alta Mar

Moll
Barcelona

G

H

H1898
No smokers rest. ♿ 🏊 ⬚ 🖥 📶 🛎 🚗 VISA ⑳ AE ①

La Rambla 109 ✉ *08002 –* Ⓜ *Catalunya –* 🖉 *935 52 95 52 – 1898@nnhotels.es*
– Fax 935 52 95 50 – www.hotel1898.com **F2**
166 rm – 🛉199 € 🛉🛉450 €, ⬚ 20 € – 3 suites **Rest –** Carte approx. 45 €

♦ Chain hotel ♦ Colonial ♦

This hotel occupies the former Tabacos de Filipinas headquarters, which explains its modern, colonial style. Well-appointed guestrooms, spa centre, and a rooftop solarium-terrace with views of the city. The restaurant's menu features a full range of international dishes.

Le Méridien Barcelona
No smokers rest. 🖥 📶 🛎 VISA ⑳ AE ①

La Rambla 111 ✉ *08002 –* Ⓜ *Catalunya –* 🖉 *933 18 62 00 – info.barcelona@
lemeridien.com – Fax 933 01 77 76 – www.lemeridiem.com* **F2**
217 rm – 🛉🛉179/450 €, ⬚ 25 € – 16 suites **Rest –** Menu 25 €
Rest *Cent Onze* – Carte 31/46 €

♦ Urban ♦ Contemporary ♦

An elegant, emblematic hotel combining local flavour and contemporary, cosmopolitan style. Excellent location alongside the Ramblas. A bright, informal restaurant offering an imaginative à la carte menu.

Colón
No smokers rest. 🖥 📶 🛎 VISA ⑳ AE ①

av. de la Catedral 7 ✉ *08002 –* Ⓜ *Jaume I –* 🖉 *933 01 14 04
– info@hotelcolon.es – Fax 933 17 29 15 – www.hotelcolon.es* **F2**
142 rm – 🛉90/160 € 🛉🛉100/230 €, ⬚ 16.75 € – 5 suites **Rest –** Menu 21 €

♦ Urban ♦ Classical ♦

Boasting a magnificent location opposite the cathedral with a pleasant terrace in front of the hotel. Classical in style with functional, comfortable guestrooms. The Colón's dining room has a cosy, intimate atmosphere.

Catalonia Ramblas
Smokers rest. ♿ 🏊 🖥 📶 🛎 VISA ⑳ AE ①

Pelai 28 ✉ *08001 –* Ⓜ *Catalunya –* 🖉 *933 16 84 00 – ramblas@
hoteles-catalonia.es – Fax 933 16 84 01 – www.hoteler-catalonia.com*
219 rm – 🛉173/304 € 🛉🛉206/347 €, ⬚ 15 € – 2 suites **E1**
Rest *Pelai* – Carte 35/47 €

♦ Urban ♦ Design ♦

This hotel has an attractive façade linking two early 20C Modernist buildings. Well-appointed guestrooms and a swimming pool and sun terrace. The Pelai restaurant has its own entrance. Traditional cuisine with a modern twist.

Pulitzer
🖥 📶 🚗 VISA ⑳ AE ①

Bergara 8 ✉ *08002 –* Ⓜ *Catalunya –* 🖉 *934 81 67 67 – info@hotelpulitzer.es
– Fax 934 81 64 64 – www.hotelpulitzer.es* **E1**
92 rm – 🛉109/215 € 🛉🛉120/230 €, ⬚ 15 € **Rest –** Menu 20 €

♦ Urban ♦ Design ♦

A modern hotel decorated with design features and high quality furnishings. Elegant lounge area and well-appointed guestrooms, albeit on the small side. Contemporary décor in the restaurant, with views of a courtyard and terrace.

Montecarlo
without rest 🖥 📶 🚗 VISA ⑳ AE ①

La Rambla 124 ✉ *08002 –* Ⓜ *Liceu –* 🖉 *934 12 04 04 – hotel@
montecarlobcn.com – Fax 933 18 73 23 – www.montecarlobcn.com*
50 rm – 🛉108/154 € 🛉🛉165/413 €, ⬚ 12 € **F2**

♦ Mansion ♦ Classical ♦

Housed in a 19C mansion, this splendid hotel is a harmonious blend of old-world classicism and modern design. Spacious, extremely well-appointed guestrooms.

Neri
🖥 📶 VISA ⑳ AE ①

Sant Sever 5 ✉ *08002 –* Ⓜ *Liceu –* 🖉 *933 04 06 55 – info@hotelneri.com
– Fax 933 04 03 37 – www.hotelneri.com* **F2**
21 rm – 🛉🛉265/525 €, ⬚ 21 € **Rest –** Menu 25 €

♦ Mansion ♦ Design ♦

This 18C mansion, just a few metres from the cathedral, has a unique avant-garde appearance. The hotel has a small lounge-library and magnificent guestrooms. An intimate restaurant dominated by two stone arches. It offers an inventive and innovative menu.

SPAIN - BARCELONA

Grand H. Central 🛋 🔽 📶 📞 🏊 💳 ⚫ 🅰🅴 ⓪

Via Laietana 30 ⊠ *08003 –* Ⓜ *Jaume I –* ☎ *932 95 79 00*
– info@grandhotelcentral.com – Fax 932 68 12 15
– www.grandhotelcentral.com   **F2**
141 rm – 🛏190/300 € 🛏🛏210/700 €, � 20 € – 6 suites
Rest Actual – see below
♦ Urban ♦ Design ♦
This contemporary hotel emphasises modern design and functionality. Guestrooms feature great attention to detail. Terrace with a swimming pool and panoramic views.

Duquesa de Cardona   No smokers rest. 📶 📞 🏊 💳 ⚫ 🅰🅴 ⓪

passeig de Colom 12 ⊠ *08002 –* Ⓜ *Drassanes –* ☎ *932 68 90 90*
– info@hduquesadecardona.com – Fax 932 68 29 31
– www.hduquesadecardona.com   **G2**
40 rm – 🛏🛏160/265 €, ⊇ 14 €
Rest *– (closed Sunday) (lunch only except Thursday , Friday and Saturday)*
Menu 16 €
♦ Mansion ♦ Cosy ♦
This hotel occupies a charming 19C mansion that has retained many of its original features. Excellent guestrooms and an attractive terrace-solarium on the roof. A restaurant that is impressively classical in style with large arches and vaults.

Rivoli Rambla   🍴 📶 📞 🏊 💳 ⚫ 🅰🅴 ⓪

La Rambla 128 ⊠ *08002 –* Ⓜ *Catalunya –* ☎ *934 81 76 76*
– reservas@rivolihotels.com – Fax 933 17 50 53 – www.rivolihotels.com
119 rm – 🛏150/277 € 🛏🛏180/303 €, ⊇ 19 € – 6 suites   **F2**
Rest – Menu 30 €
♦ Urban ♦ Classical ♦
This historical building has an attractive façade and a classic-contemporary décor with Art Deco features. Comfortable guestrooms and a pleasant interior terrace. A restaurant with a menu resolutely focused on international cuisine.

Royal   No smokers rest. 📶 📞 🍴 💳 ⚫ 🅰🅴 ⓪

La Rambla 117 ⊠ *08002 –* Ⓜ *Catalunya –* ☎ *933 01 94 00*
– info@royalramblashotel.com – Fax 933 17 31 79
– www.royalramblashotel.com   **F2**
119 rm – 🛏🛏105/280 €, ⊇ 10 €   **Rest La Poma** – Carte approx. 40 €
♦ Urban ♦ Classical ♦
Located in one of the most atmospheric districts of the city. The Royal's traditional style is gradually being replaced by a more modern, contemporary look. This spacious restaurant, specialising in grilled meats, has a separate entrance.

Barcelona Catedral   🍴 🛋 🔽 📶 📞 🏊 ⚫ 🅰🅴 ⓪

Dels Capellans 4 ⊠ *08002 –* Ⓜ *Catalunya –* ☎ *933 04 22 55*
– hotel@barcelonacatedral.com – Fax 933 04 23 66
– www.barcelonacatedral.com   **F2**
80 rm – 🛏🛏139/289 €, ⊇ 18 €
Rest *– (closed August, Saturday and Sunday) (lunch only)* Menu 18 €
♦ Urban ♦ Modern ♦
A contemporary-style hotel with designer furnishings and tasteful decor. Fully equipped guestrooms and an attractive interior patio. A restaurant with an informal atmosphere, located next to the bar.

Montblanc   No smokers rest. 📶 📞 🏊 🍴 💳 ⚫ 🅰🅴 ⓪

Via Laietana 61 ⊠ *08003 –* Ⓜ *Urquinaona –* ☎ *933 43 55 55*
– montblanc@hcchotels.es – Fax 933 43 55 58 – www.hcchotels.es
157 rm – 🛏129/202 € 🛏🛏149/247 €, ⊇ 18.19 €   **F1**
Rest – Menu 22 €
♦ Chain hotel ♦ Urban ♦ Functional ♦
The Montblanc has a spacious lounge area and a piano-bar with live music. Functional but comfortable guestrooms, as well as a small swimming pool, terrace and solarium. Dining room with a circular design, offering a limited choice of international dishes.

SPAIN - BARCELONA

Barcelona Universal
No smokers rest. 🏃 ☃ 📺 🛜 🛁

av. del Paral.lel 80 ✉ *08001 –* Ⓜ *Paral.lel*   🆅🇮🇸🇦 ⚈ 🅰🇪 ⓪
– 📞 935 67 74 47 – bcnuniversal@nnhotels.com – Fax 935 67 74 40
– www.nnhotels.com   **E3**
164 rm – ♥♥90/400 €, � 14 € – 3 suites   **Rest** – *(dinner only)* Menu 24 €
♦ Chain hotel ♦ Urban ♦ Contemporary ♦
This modern hotel offers spacious, well-appointed guestrooms and a lounge area
with bar. Panoramic swimming pool with a solarium on the top floor. A simply furnished restaurant serving a buffet of grilled meats.

Inglaterra
No smokers rest. 📺 🛜 🛁 🆅🇮🇸🇦 ⚈ 🅰🇪 ⓪

Pelai 14 ✉ *08001 –* Ⓜ *Universitat – 📞 935 05 11 00 – recepcion@*
hotel-inglaterra.com – Fax 935 05 11 09 – www.hotel-inglaterra.com
60 rm – ♥♥119/240 €, ⊊ 14 €   **Rest** – Menu 20 €   **E1**
♦ Urban ♦ Cosy ♦
A modern but charming hotel with a beautiful classical façade. Multipurpose
lounge, and rooms dominated by large wooden headboards. Pleasant terrace-
solarium. Simple, contemporary-style restaurant with a predominantly red colour
scheme.

Lleó *without rest*
📺 🛜 🛁 🆅🇮🇸🇦 ⚈ 🅰🇪

Pelai 22 ✉ *08001 –* Ⓜ *Universitat – 📞 933 18 13 12 – reservas@hotel-lleo.es*
– Fax 934 12 26 57 – www.hotel-lleo.es   **E1**
89 rm – ♥135/160 € ♥♥165/190 €, ⊊ 12 €
♦ Urban ♦ Functional ♦
Hotel with an elegant façade and functional style. Comfortable, contemporary-
style guestrooms, spacious lounge area and professional, family management.

Catalonia Albinoni
📺 🆅🇮🇸🇦 ⚈ 🅰🇪 ⓪

av. Portal de l'Àngel 17 ✉ *08002 –* Ⓜ *Catalunya – 📞 933 18 41 41 – albinoni@*
hoteles-catalonia.es – Fax 933 01 26 31 – www.hoteles-catalonia.com
83 rm – ♥138/200 € ♥♥171/214 €, ⊊ 15 €   **Rest** – Menu 20 €   **F1**
♦ Chain hotel ♦ Urban ♦ Functional ♦
Conveniently situated near the Gothic quarter, this hotel occupies the former Roca-
mora palace. Original decorative details in the lounge area and contemporary-style
guestrooms.

Park H. *without rest*
📺 🛜 🆅🇮🇸🇦 ⚈ 🅰🇪 ⓪

av. Marqués de l'Argentera 11 ✉ *08003 –* Ⓜ *Barceloneta – 📞 933 19 60 00*
– parkhotel@parkhotelbarcelona.com – Fax 933 19 45 19
– www.parkhotelbarcelona.com   **G2**
91 rm – ♥93/171 € ♥♥116/218 €, ⊊ 12 €
♦ Urban ♦ Modern ♦
Contemporary in style, this welcoming hotel is well furnished with modern, well-
equipped and comfortable guestrooms. Attractive lobby-reception area with a
bar on one side.

Reding
📺 🛜 🆅🇮🇸🇦 ⚈ 🅰🇪 ⓪

Gravina 5-7 ✉ *08001 –* Ⓜ *Universitat – 📞 934 12 10 97 – reding@oh-es.com*
– Fax 932 68 34 82 – www.hotelreding.com   **E1-2**
44 rm – ♥99/365 € ♥♥109/375 €, ⊊ 14 €
Rest – *(closed Sunday and Bank Holidays)* Menu 12 €
♦ Urban ♦ Functional ♦
Situated close to the Plaça de Catalunya. This hotel has a small lounge area and
adequate facilities, including comfortable, well-appointed guestrooms. The simply
designed dining room offers a menu featuring traditional and Catalan dishes.

Banys Orientals
📺 📞 🆅🇮🇸🇦 ⚈ 🅰🇪 ⓪

L'Argenteria 37 ✉ *08003 –* Ⓜ *Jaume I – 📞 932 68 84 60 – reservas@*
hotelbanysorientals.com – Fax 932 68 84 61 – www.hotelbanysorientals.com
56 rm – ♥83 € ♥♥99.50 €, ⊊ 10 €   **G2**
Rest Senyor Parellada – *see below*
♦ Urban ♦ Design ♦
This hotel has comfortable, minimalist-style rooms. They feature plenty of design
features, wooden floors and canopies above the beds. No lounge.

Regencia Colón without rest `SAT VISA ∞ AE ①`

Sagristans 13 ⊠ 08002 – ⓜ Jaume I – ℰ 933 18 98 58 – info@
hotelregenciacolon.com – Fax 933 17 28 22 – www.hotelregenciacolon.com
50 rm – ♦65/140 € ♦♦65/183 €, � 12 €   **F1-2**
♦ Urban ♦ Functional ♦

A good location in one of the most typical districts of the city. Functional rooms
with wood floors and fully equipped bathrooms.

Hesperia Metropol without rest `SAT ((●)) VISA ∞ AE ①`

Ample 31 ⊠ 08002 – ⓜ Drassanes – ℰ 933 10 51 00 – hotel@
hesperia-metropol.com – Fax 933 19 12 76 – www.hesperia-metropol.com
71 rm – ♦60/180 € ♦♦70/195 €, ⊑ 11.50 €   **G2**
♦ Chain hotel ♦ Functional ♦

Located in the historic quarter of the city, this hotel has comfortable, well-decorated guestrooms. Warm atmosphere and friendly staff.

Torre d'Alta Mar   No smokers rest. ≼ VISA ∞ AE ①

passeig Joan de Borbó 88 ⊠ 08039 – ⓜ Barceloneta – ℰ 932 21 00 07
– reserves@torredealtamar.com – Fax 932 21 00 90 – www.torredealtamar.com
– closed Christmas, Sunday lunch and Monday lunch   **H3**
Rest – Carte 70/95 €
♦ Traditional ♦ Fashionable ♦

A striking location at the top of a 75m metal tower. Modern circular dining room
with large glass windows and spectacular views.

Actual – Hotel Grand H. Central   Totally no smoking VISA ∞ AE ①

Pare Gallifa 3 ⊠ 08003 – ⓜ Jaume I – ℰ 932 95 79 05 – actual@
grandhotelcentral.com – Fax 932 68 12 15 – www.grandhotelcentral.com
Rest – Carte 31/35 €   **F2**
♦ Inventive ♦ Modern ♦

A restaurant with its own distinctive personality and a young and friendly staff.
Modern, designer-style decor and a creative set price menu.

Lluçanès (Angel Pascual)   Totally no smoking ⇔ VISA ∞ AE

pl. de la Font 1 ⊠ 08003 – ⓜ Barceloneta – ℰ 932 24 25 25 – cuina@
restaurantllucanes.com – www.restaurantllucanes.com
– closed Sunday dinner and Monday   **H2**
Rest – Menu 68/95 € – Carte 58/69 €
Spec. Ventresca de atún con risotto crujiente, crema de jengibre y wasabi
(November-June). Solomillo de ternera Kobe, tatin de calabaza, espárragos
verdes y rúcula. Tocinillo con trufa negra del Lluçanès, su helado y pan crujiente tostado (January-April).
♦ Inventive ♦ Family ♦

Located in the working class Barceloneta district, Lluçanès remains loyal to its
roots. Attractively urban in style with an open kitchen serving innovative cuisine.

Druída   Smokers rest. ⇔ VISA ∞ AE ①

Parlament 54 ⊠ 08015 – ⓜ Sant Antoni – ℰ 934 41 10 45 – druida@
restaurantedruida.com – Fax 933 24 84 67 – www.restaurantedruida.com
– closed 15-31 August, Sunday dinner, Monday and Bank Holidays dinner
Rest – Carte 45/55 €   **E3**
♦ Innovative ♦ Cosy ♦

Cosy restaurant decorated with Louis XV furnishings and with tableware that matches the period design. Creative menu, and an open kitchen in view of diners.

Comerç 24 (Carles Abellán)   Totally no smoking VISA ∞ AE ①

Comerç 24 ⊠ 08003 – ⓜ Arc de Triomf – ℰ 933 19 21 02 – info@
comerc24.com – Fax 933 19 10 74 – www.carlesabellan.com
– closed Sunday and Monday   **G1**
Rest – Menu 62/78 € – Carte 46/62 €
Spec. Infusión fría de vegetales, flores y frutos del mar. Arroz de cigala y
pollo de corral. Canelones de setas con salsa reducida de carne (Autumn).
♦ Inventive ♦ Design ♦

Modern restaurant with a cutting-edge feel. Creative cuisine, including a tapas tasting menu and limited à la carte choices.

XX **Patagonia Beef & Wine** *VISA* **CO** *AE* **(1)**

Gran Via de les Corts Catalanes 660 ⊠ *08010 –* **Ⓜ** *Passeig de Gràcia*
– ℰ 933 04 37 35 – info.bcn@patagoniabw.com – Fax 933 04 37 34
– www.patagoniabw.com
– closed Sunday   **F1**
Rest – Carte 38/56 €
♦ Argentinian ♦ Minimalist ♦
An attractive restaurant decorated in minimalist style. A comprehensive menu, with an emphasis on Argentinean red meat dishes.

XX **Senyor Parellada** – Hotel Banys Orientals   *VISA* **CO** *AE* **(1)**

L'Argenteria 37 ⊠ *08003 –* **Ⓜ** *Jaume I – ℰ 933 10 50 94*
– diana@senyorparellada.com – Fax 932 68 31 57 – www.senyorparellada.com
Rest – Carte 26/35 €   **G2**
♦ Catalan cuisine ♦ Cosy ♦
Charming restaurant in a traditional-modern style. It features a bar, various dining rooms and an attractive small patio with a glass roof. Reasonably priced regional cuisine.

XX **Elx**   No smokers rest. ⇐ 🕼 *VISA* **CO** *AE*

Moll d'Espanya-Maremagnum, Local 9 ⊠ *08039 –* **Ⓜ** *Drassanes*
– ℰ 932 25 81 17 – elx@restaurantelx.com – Fax 932 25 81 20
– www.restaurantelx.com   **G3**
Rest – Carte 30/43 €
♦ Rice ♦ Formal ♦
This restaurant has a rustic-modern dining room and an attractive terrace with views of the marina. Fish, seafood and a good selection of rice dishes on the menu.

X **Pitarra**   Totally no smoking ⇔ *VISA* **CO** *AE* **(1)**

Avinyó 56 ⊠ *08002 –* **Ⓜ** *Liceu – ℰ 933 01 16 47 – info@restaurantpitarra.cat*
– Fax 933 01 85 62 – www.restaurantpitarra.cat
– closed August, Sunday and Bank Holidays dinner   **G2**
Rest – Carte 27/46 €
♦ Traditional ♦ Cosy ♦
This restaurant creates a warm and friendly atmosphere with its interior decor of numerous mementoes, antique clocks and reminders of the poet Pitarra. Traditional, reasonably priced menu.

X **Can Majó**   🕼 *VISA* **CO** *AE* **(1)**

Almirall Aixada 23 ⊠ *08003 –* **Ⓜ** *Barceloneta – ℰ 932 21 54 55*
– majocan@terra.es – Fax 932 21 54 55 – www.canmajo.es
– closed Sunday dinner and Monday   **H3**
Rest – Carte 35/53 €
♦ Fish and shellfish ♦ Family ♦
Renowned, family-run restaurant serving an excellent menu focusing on seafood and rice dishes, hence the impressive seafood counter. Terrace.

℟∤ **El Rovell del Born**   Smokers rest. *VISA* **CO**

L'Argenteria 6 ⊠ *08003 –* **Ⓜ** *Jaume I – ℰ 932 69 04 58*
– info@elrovelldelborn.com – www.elrovelldelborn.com
– closed Monday except Bank Holidays   **G2**
Tapa 2.50 € **Ración** approx. 8 €
♦ Traditional ♦ Tapas bar ♦
Contemporary-style bar with high tables and an impressive selection of excellent tapas. The à la carte menu features traditional dishes with a modern twist.

℟∤ **Sagardi**   🕼 *VISA* **CO** *AE* **(1)**

L'Argenteria 62 ⊠ *08003 –* **Ⓜ** *Jaume I – ℰ 933 19 99 93*
– reservas@sagardi.com – Fax 932 68 48 86 – www.sagardi.com   **G2**
Tapa 1.80 € **Ración** approx. 14 €
♦ Basque cuisine ♦ Tapas bar ♦
This Basque cider bar close to the historic Santa Maria del Mar church serves a fine selection of tapas. The dining room is decorated with cider barrels and has a charcoal barbecue in view of diners.

SPAIN - BARCELONA

Ψ✗ **Irati**   VISA ◑◐ AE ⓪

Cardenal Casanyes 17 ✉ *08002* – ◍ *Liceu* – ☎ *933 02 30 84*
– irati@sagardi.com – Fax 934 12 73 76 – www.sagardi.com   **F2**
Tapa 2 €
◆ Basque cuisine ◆ Tapas bar ◆
A typical Basque tavern close to the Gran Teatre del Liceu. Traditional carvery-style dining room where the menu focuses on innovative Basque cuisine. Good selection of tapas at the bar.

Ψ✗ **El Xampanyet**   Totally no smoking VISA ◑◐

Montcada 22 ✉ *08003* – ◍ *Jaume I* – ☎ *933 19 70 03*
– xampanyet@telefonica.net
– closed Holy Week, August, Sunday dinner and Monday   **G2**
Tapa 3 € **Ración** approx. 6 €
◆ Traditional ◆ Tapas bar ◆
This old tavern with a long-standing family tradition is decorated with typical azulejo tiles. Good selection of tapas with an emphasis on cured meats and high quality canned products.

Ψ✗ **Segons Mercat**   🏠 VISA ◑◐

Balboa 16 ✉ *08003* – ◍ *Barceloneta* – ☎ *933 10 78 80*
– sm@segonsmercat.com – www.segonsmercat.com   **H2**
Tapa 5 € **Ración** approx. 12 €
◆ Traditional ◆ Tapas bar ◆
This restaurant has a bar with an impressive display of fresh produce, in particular fish and seafood. A separate room is available for tapas, snacks and daily specials.

Ψ✗ **Rosal 34**   Smokers rest. VISA ◑◐ AE

Roser 34 ✉ *08004* – ◍ *Paral.lel* – ☎ *933 24 90 46* – *info@rosal34.com*
– Fax 933 24 90 46 – www.rosal34.com
– closed 1-15 January, 15-30 August, Sunday and Monday lunch
Ración approx. 15 €   **E3**
◆ Traditional ◆ Rustic ◆
Rosal 34 is located in an old family wine cellar, where the rustic stonework blends in with the contemporary decor. Extensive seasonal menu.

SOUTH of AV. DIAGONAL   *Plan III*

🏨 **Rey Juan Carlos I** ❧   No smokers rest. ≼ 🚗 🏠 🖪 🏊 🏞 🆒 ¶¶

av. Diagonal 661 ✉ *08028*   🅰 🅿 🏠 VISA ◑◐ AE
– ◍ Zona Universitaria – ☎ 933 64 40 40 – hotel@hrjuancarlos.com
– Fax 933 64 42 64 – www.hrjuancarlos.com   *Plan I* **A2**
395 rm – ¶¶187/481 €, ⌑ 25.15 € – 38 suites   **Rest** – Menu 41 €
◆ Grand Luxury ◆ Classical ◆
Impressively modern in style, the hotel is surrounded by a park with a lake and swimming pool. An exclusive atmosphere pervades all the tastefully decorated guestrooms. A variety of culinary options, including à la carte and buffet choices.

🏨 **Majestic**   🖪 🏊 🆒 ¶¶ 🅰 🏠 VISA ◑◐ AE ⓪

passeig de Gràcia 68 ✉ *08007* – ◍ *Passeig de Gràcia*
– ☎ 934 88 17 17 – recepcion@hotelmajestic.es – Fax 934 88 18 80
– www.hotelmajestic.es   **K2**
271 rm – ¶¶199/430 €, ⌑ 23 € – 32 suites
Rest Drolma – see below
Rest – Menu 37 €
◆ Traditional ◆ Classical ◆
A renovated classic hotel on the Paseo de Gràcia. Superbly appointed guestrooms, although some are not particularly spacious. Impeccable service.

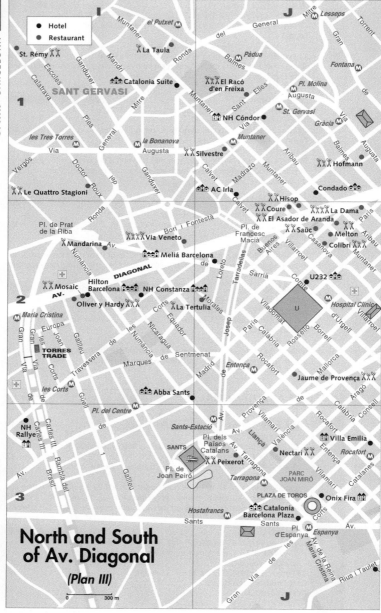

**North and South
of Av. Diagonal**

(Plan III)

0   300 m

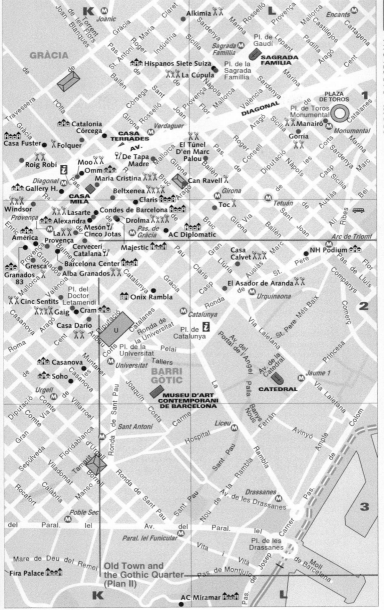

SPAIN - BARCELONA

Condes de Barcelona – (Monument i Centre) 🖼 📶 🛄 🚗

passeig de Gràcia 73-75 ✉ *08008* – 🚇 *Diagonal*   🆅🆂🅰 ⓒⓢ 🆀🅴
– ☎ *934 45 00 00* – *reservas@condesdebarcelona.com* – *Fax 934 45 32 32*
– *www.condesdebarcelona.com*   **K2**
228 rm – 🛏135/315 €, ☑ 17 € – 7 suites
Rest Lasarte – see below
Rest *Loidi* – *(closed on Sunday dinner) (set menu only)* Menu 36/44 €
◆ Monumental ◆ Contemporary classic ◆
This hotel occupies two of the city's most emblematic buildings, Casa Batlló and Casa Durella. A combination of modern comfort and period decor. Attractive sun terrace. The informal Loidi bistro offers a set menu that changes on a weekly basis.

NH Constanza   No smokers rest. 🆂 🖼 📶 🛄 🚗 🆅🆂🅰 ⓒⓢ 🆀🅴

Deu i Mata 69-99 ✉ *08029* – 🚇 *Les Corts* – ☎ *932 81 15 00*
– *nhconstanza@nh-hotels.com* – *Fax 934 10 03 35* – *www.nh-hotels.com*
300 rm – 🛏105/325 €, ☑ 19.50 € – 8 suites   **I2**
Rest – Carte 30/42 €
◆ Avant-garde ◆ Contemporary ◆
Designed by Rafael Moneo, the building makes full use of natural light and clean lines. Large lobby, modular meeting rooms and luxurious, functional bedrooms. The restaurant occupies a room decorated in varying tones of white. Traditional cuisine.

Meliá Barcelona   No smokers rest. ≤ 🖪 🖼 📶 🛄 🚗

av. de Sarrià 50 ✉ *08029* – 🚇 *Hospital Clínic*   🆅🆂🅰 ⓒⓢ 🆀🅴
– ☎ *934 10 60 60* – *melia.barcelona@solmelia.com* – *Fax 934 10 77 44*
– *www.solmelia.com*   **J2**
333 rm – 🛏100/390 €, ☑ 20 € – 21 suites   **Rest** – Menu 50 €
◆ Business ◆ Contemporary ◆
A recently renovated hotel. It has guestrooms and public areas that combine contemporary design with high quality furnishings and excellent facilities.

Hilton Barcelona   🖪 🖼 📶 🛄 🚗 🆅🆂🅰 ⓒⓢ 🆀🅴

av. Diagonal 589 ✉ *08014* – 🚇 *María Cristina* – ☎ *934 95 77 77*
– *barcelona@hilton.com* – *Fax 934 95 77 00* – *www.barcelona.hilton.com*
275 rm – 🛏175/355 € 🛏197/377 €, ☑ 24 € – 11 suites   **I2**
Rest *Mosaic* – see below
◆ Urban ◆ Contemporary ◆
This hotel is situated in one of the city's main thoroughfares. It has a spacious foyer and well-equipped lounges. The contemporary-style guestrooms feature cutting-edge design.

AC Miramar   ≤ 🍽 🖪 🛀 🗔 🖼 📶 🛄 🚗 🆅🆂🅰 ⓒⓢ 🆀🅴

pl. Carlos Ibáñez 3 ✉ *08038* – 🚇 *Paral.lel* – ☎ *932 81 16 00* – *acmiramar@*
ac-hotels.com – *Fax 932 81 16 01* – *www.hotelacmiramar.com*   **K3**
73 rm – 🛏210/1210 €, ☑ 25 € – 2 suites   **Rest** – Carte 52/73 €
◆ Chain hotel ◆ Contemporary ◆
Renovated by Oscar Tusquets, who has retained the monumental façade. Spacious rooms, cutting-edge design, excellent facilities and good views. A pleasant restaurant with a terrace that provides the perfect setting for a relaxing meal.

Claris ⌂   No smokers rest. 🍽 🖪 🛀 🖼 📶 🛄 🚗 🆅🆂🅰 ⓒⓢ 🆀🅴

Pau Claris 150 ✉ *08009* – 🚇 *Passeig de Gràcia* – ☎ *934 87 62 62*
– *claris@derbyhotels.es* – *Fax 932 15 79 70* – *www.derbyhotels.com*
80 rm – 🛏175/426 € 🛏199/475 €, ☑ 21 € – 40 suites   **K2**
Rest *East 47* – Menu 22 €
◆ Traditional ◆ Modern ◆
This elegant, stately hotel occupies the former Vedruna palace. It offers a perfect fusion of tradition, cutting-edge design and technology. Impressive archaeological collection. This attractively presented restaurant is decorated in a style that recalls the work of Andy Warhol.

Barcelona Center without rest   Ⅰ₆ ⓢⓐⓣ ⓦ ⅁ ⓥⒾⓢⓐ ⓪ ⒜Ⓔ ⓪

*Balmes 103 ⊠ 08008 – Ⓜ Passeig de Gràcia – 𝒞 932 73 00 00 – barcelona@
hotelescenter.com – Fax 932 73 00 02 – www.hotelescenter.com*   **K2**
129 rm – ♟♟110/490 €, ⫶ 17 € – 3 suites

♦ Chain hotel ♦ Cosy ♦

Sheltered behind a striking, well-maintained façade, this hotel boasts superbly
equipped modern guestrooms, impressive public areas and a huge solarium on
the roof terrace.

Fira Palace   No smokers rest. Ⅰ₆ ⎚ ⓢⓐⓣ ⓦ ⅁ ⌂ ⓥⒾⓢⓐ ⓪ ⒜Ⓔ ⓪

*av. Rius i Taulet 1 ⊠ 08004 – Ⓜ Espanya – 𝒞 934 26 22 23 – reservations@
fira-palace.com – Fax 934 25 50 47 – www.fira-palace.com*   **J-K3**
258 rm – ♟314 € ♟♟330 €, ⫶ 17 € – 18 suites   **Rest** *El Mall* – Carte 45/57 €

♦ Conventions ♦ Classical ♦

Traditional in style, the Fira Palace prides itself on its excellent service and high
quality furnishings. Well-appointed lounges and spacious guestrooms. A rustic-
style restaurant with exposed brick walls.

AC Diplomatic   No smokers rest. Ⅰ₆ ⓢⓐⓣ ⓦ ⅁ ⌂ ⓥⒾⓢⓐ ⓪ ⒜Ⓔ ⓪

*Pau Claris 122 ⊠ 08009 – Ⓜ Passeig de Gràcia – 𝒞 932 72 38 10
– diplomatic@ac-hotels.com – Fax 932 72 38 11 – www.ac-hotels.com*
209 rm – ♟♟130/295 €, ⫶ 21 € – 2 suites   **K2**
Rest – Carte 36/55 €

♦ Urban ♦ Contemporary ♦

Redecorated in line with the AC chain's typical look, the Diplomatic combines
designer features, comfort, and excellent facilities for guests. Modernised
bedrooms and a choice of meeting rooms.

Catalonia Barcelona Plaza   Ⅰ₆ ⎗ ⎚ ⓢⓐⓣ ⓦ ⅁ ⌂ ⓥⒾⓢⓐ ⓪ ⒜Ⓔ ⓪

*pl. d'Espanya 6 ⊠ 08014 – Ⓜ Espanya – 𝒞 934 26 26 00 – plaza@
hoteles-catalonia.es – Fax 934 26 04 00 – www.hoteles-catalonia.es*
338 rm – ♟89/262 € ♟♟104/299 €, ⫶ 15 € – 9 suites   **J3**
Rest *Gourmet Plaza* – Carte 32/50 €

♦ Business ♦ Functional ♦

Located opposite the city's exhibition centre this establishment has functional furnishings, good facilities and meeting rooms for business travellers. There is a swimming pool with retractable roof on the top floor. A functional restaurant with restrained decor.

Omm   Ⅰ₆ ⎗ ⓢⓐⓣ ⓦ ⅁ ⌂ ⓥⒾⓢⓐ ⓪ ⒜Ⓔ ⓪

*Rosselló 265 ⊠ 08008 – Ⓜ Diagonal – 𝒞 934 45 40 00 – reservas@
hotelomm.es – Fax 934 45 40 04 – www.hotelomm.es*   **K1**
87 rm – ♟♟250/445 €, ⫶ 24 € – 4 suites   **Rest** *Moo* – see below

♦ Urban ♦ Design ♦

Hidden behind the original façade is a highly contemporary hotel with spacious
public areas divided into three sections. Extremely well-appointed guestrooms,
and an attractive spa.

Cram   ⓢⓐⓣ ⓦ ⌂ ⓥⒾⓢⓐ ⓪ ⒜Ⓔ ⓪

*Aribau 54 ⊠ 08011 – Ⓜ Universitat – 𝒞 932 16 77 00 – info@hotelcram.com
– Fax 932 16 77 07 – www.hotelcram.com*   **K2**
67 rm – ♟♟130/253 €, ⫶ 21 €   **Rest** *Gaig* – see below

♦ Urban ♦ Avant-garde ♦

Although the guestrooms are on the small side, this is counter balanced by cutting-edge technology and the superb contemporary interior – the work of several
famous designers.

Granados 83   No smokers rest. ⌂ ⓢⓐⓣ ⓦ ⅁ ⌂ ⓥⒾⓢⓐ ⓪ ⒜Ⓔ ⓪

*Enric Granados 83 ⊠ 08008 – Ⓜ Provença – 𝒞 934 92 96 70 – granados83@
derbyhotels.com – Fax 934 92 96 90 – www.derbyhotels.com*   **K2**
77 rm – ♟130/243 € ♟♟160/408 €, ⫶ 17 €
Rest – *(closed Sunday and Monday dinner)* Carte 36/45 €

♦ Chain hotel ♦ Design ♦

Unusual cutting-edge hotel built with a predominance of glass, steel and brick.
Superbly appointed bedrooms decorated with 10C Asian works of art. A restaurant
with a pleasant terrace.

SPAIN - BARCELONA

Abba Sants
No smokers rest. 🛏 🛜 🔊 🚗 VISA ⓒ AE ⓞ

Numància 32 ✉ *08029 –* Ⓜ *Sants-Estació –* 𝒞 *936 00 31 00 – abba-sants@abbahoteles.com – Fax 936 00 31 01 – www.abbahoteles.com* **I2**
140 rm ⚏ – ♦96/321 € ♦♦107/332 €   **Rest** *Amalur* – Menu 28 €
♦ Urban ♦ Functional ♦

This comfortable, modern and well-run hotel is popular with business travellers. Functional guestrooms and several multi-purpose meeting rooms. The Amalur offers attractive à la carte choices, although the daily set menu continues to be the restaurant's best seller.

Alexandra
🛏 🔊 🚗 VISA ⓒ AE ⓞ

Mallorca 251 ✉ *08008 –* Ⓜ *Passeig de Gràcia –* 𝒞 *934 67 71 66 – informacion@hotel-alexandra.com – Fax 934 88 02 58 – www.hotel-alexandra.com* **K2**
106 rm – ♦110/330 € ♦♦110/350 €, ⚏ 18 € – 3 suites   **Rest** – Menu 22 €
♦ Urban ♦ Contemporary ♦

A cosy, modern hotel with spacious, well-appointed guestrooms. They are furnished in contemporary-style, with wall-to-wall carpeting and glass partitioned bathrooms. The menu in this simply furnished restaurant focuses on traditional and international cuisine.

U 232 without rest
🛏 🔊 🚗 VISA ⓒ AE ⓞ

Comte d'Urgell 232 ✉ *08036 –* Ⓜ *Hospital Clinic –* 𝒞 *933 22 41 53 – reservas-u232@nnhotels.com – Fax 934 19 01 06 – www.nnhotels.com*
102 rm – ♦100/190 € ♦♦110/210 €, ⚏ 13 € **J2**
♦ Business ♦ Contemporary classic ♦

Recently renovated, this classic, contemporary-style hotel has comfortable guestrooms with open wardrobes and marble bathrooms.

Soho without rest
🔲 🛏 📞 🚗 VISA ⓒ AE ⓞ

Gran Via de les Corts Catalanes 543-545 ✉ *08011 –* Ⓜ *Urgell – 𝒞 935 52 96 10 – soho@nnhotels.com – Fax 935 52 96 11 – www.hotelsohobarcelona.com* **K2**
51 rm – ♦107/257 € ♦♦117.70/315.65 €, ⚏ 14 €
♦ Urban ♦ Design ♦

The Soho combines cutting-edge style with designer detail, the decorative use of light and the interplay of space. An interesting fusion of modern comfort and technology.

América without rest
🛗 🔲 🛏 🔊 🚗 VISA ⓒ AE ⓞ

Provença 195 ✉ *08008 –* Ⓜ *Provença –* 𝒞 *934 87 62 92 – america@hotelamericabarcelona.com – Fax 934 87 25 18 – www.hotelamericabarcelona.com* **K2**
60 rm – ♦100/196 € ♦♦100/230 €, ⚏ 15 €
♦ Urban ♦ Contemporary ♦

Bright, contemporary hotel decorated in an attractive combination of red and white tones. Interior patio and functional, comfortable guestrooms.

Gallery H.
No smokers rest. 🍴 🛗 🛏 🔊 🚗 VISA ⓒ AE ⓞ

Rosselló 249 ✉ *08008 –* Ⓜ *Diagonal –* 𝒞 *934 15 99 11 – galleryhotel@galleryhoteles.com – Fax 934 15 91 84 – www.galleryhotel.com* **K1**
110 rm – ♦95/220 € ♦♦120/305 €, ⚏ 19 € – 5 suites   **Rest** – Menu 24 €
♦ Urban ♦ Functional ♦

Renovated, contemporary-style hotel with several meeting rooms and comfortable guestrooms. Fully equipped bathrooms showing careful attention to detail. The restaurant has large windows and a pleasant terrace in an interior courtyard.

Casanova
📞 🔊 🚗 VISA ⓒ AE ⓞ

Gran Vía de les Corts 559 ✉ *08011 –* 𝒞 *933 96 48 00 – reservas@casanovabcnhotel.com – Fax 933 96 48 10 – www.casanovabcnhotel.com*
118 rm – ♦♦185 €, ⚏ 20 € – 6 suites   **Rest** – Menu 20 € **K2**
♦ Chain hotel ♦ Urban ♦ Contemporary ♦

The classical façade of this hotel contrasts with its contemporary-style interior. Attractive lobby, modern guestrooms and a small spa. This restaurant features a fusion of Mexican and Mediterranean cuisine.

NH Podium

No smokers rest. ⅁ ☒ 🖳 ℡ ⅍ 🚗 𝘝𝘐𝘚𝘈 ⓪ ᴀᴇ ⓪

Bailén 4 ⊠ *08010* – Ⓜ *Arc de Triomf* – 𝒞 *932 65 02 02*
– nhpodium@nh-hotels.com – Fax 932 65 05 06 – www.nh-hotels.com
140 rm – ⸙108/221 € ⸙⸙120/279 €, ⚏ 18 € – 5 suites **L2**
Rest *Corella* – Carte 31/37 €

♦ Urban ♦ Functional ♦

Located in the Modernist Ensanche district, the Podium has a classical façade with a contemporary interior and cosy guestrooms. Swimming pool and a fitness room with sauna on the top floor. Restaurant with an intimate and personal atmosphere, warm decor and contemporary paintings on the walls.

Villa Emilia without rest

🖵 ℡ ⅍ 𝘝𝘐𝘚𝘈 ⓪ ᴀᴇ ⓪

Calábria 115-117 ⊠ *08015* – Ⓜ *Rocafort* – 𝒞 *932 52 52 85*
– comercial@hotelvillaemilia.com – Fax 932 52 52 86
– www.hotelvillaemilia.com **J3**
53 rm – ⸙110/275 € ⸙⸙120/350 €, ⚏ 14 €

♦ Urban ♦ Contemporary ♦

This urban hotel combines contemporary and traditional design. Extremely comfortable guestrooms and a delightful roof terrace.

NH Rallye

No smokers rest. ⅁ ☒ 🖳 ℡ ⅍ 🚗 𝘝𝘐𝘚𝘈 ⓪ ᴀᴇ ⓪

Travessera de les Corts 150 ⊠ *08028* – Ⓜ *Les Corts* – 𝒞 *933 39 90 50*
– nhrallye@nh-hotels.com – Fax 934 11 07 90 – www.nh-hotels.com
105 rm – ⸙68/165 € ⸙⸙93/240 €, ⚏ 15 € **I3**
Rest – *(closed August)* Carte 35/46 €

♦ Chain hotel ♦ Functional ♦

Modern and functional in the characteristic style of the NH chain. A comfortable hotel with excellent facilities, an attractive swimming pool and fitness centre on the top floor. A simple, contemporary-style restaurant offering à la carte and buffet choices.

Onix Fira without rest

☒ 🖳 🖵 ℡ ⅍ 🚗 𝘝𝘐𝘚𝘈 ⓪ ᴀᴇ ⓪

Llançà 30 ⊠ *08015* – Ⓜ *Espanya* – 𝒞 *934 26 00 87*
– reservas.hotelsonix@icyesa.es – Fax 934 26 19 81 – www.hotelsonix.com
80 rm – ⸙70/139 € ⸙⸙80/171 €, ⚏ 10 € **J3**

♦ Urban ♦ Functional ♦

This simple, comfortable hotel is a good option for delegates attending the nearby 'Fira de Barcelona' complex. Spacious cafeteria and functional guest rooms.

Onix Rambla without rest

⅁ ☒ 🖳 ℡ ℡ ⅍ 🚗 𝘝𝘐𝘚𝘈 ⓪ ᴀᴇ ⓪

Rambla de Catalunya 24 ⊠ *08007* – Ⓜ *Catalunya*
– 𝒞 933 42 79 80 – reservas.hotelsonix@icyesa.es – Fax 933 42 51 52
– www.hotelsonix.com **K2**
40 rm – ⸙124/216 € ⸙⸙136/228 €, ⚏ 11.77 €

♦ Urban ♦ Functional ♦

Simple, understated contemporary design with an emphasis on wood, white tones and concrete. The functional guestrooms are adorned with wooden laminate flooring.

XXXX £3 Drolma (Fermí Puig) – Hotel Majestic

⇔ 𝘝𝘐𝘚𝘈 ⓪ ᴀᴇ ⓪

passeig de Gràcia 68 ⊠ *08007* – Ⓜ *Passeig de Gràcia* – 𝒞 *934 96 77 10*
– drolma@hotelmajestic.es – Fax 934 45 38 93 – www.drolma.cat
– closed Sunday **K2**
Rest – Menu 90/135 € – Carte 94/137 € ⅋

Spec. Cabrito embarrado a la cuchara. Canelones de faisana con trufas (15 December-15 March). Tarta fina de gambas y espardenyes.

♦ International ♦ Formal ♦

The impeccable table settings and meticulous, classical style decoration create an elegant and distinguished atmosphere, with wood taking centre-stage. Select cuisine.

XXXX
ॐ **Gaig** (Carles Gaig) – Hotel Cram ⇔ VISA ◑◐ AE ⑩

Aragó 214 ⊠ 08011 – **Ⓜ** Universitat – 𝒞 934 29 10 17
– info@restaurantgaig.com – Fax 934 29 70 02 – www.restaurantgaig.com
– closed Holy Week, 3 weeks in August, Sunday and Monday **K2**
Rest – Menu 85 € – Carte 64/81 € 🕸
Spec. Crujiente de manita de cerdo y vieiras. Fricassé de bogavante del país.
Chocolate negro sobre arena y sorbete.
♦ Inventive ♦ Avant-garde ♦
This contemporary-style restaurant is elegant in tone with great attention to detail.
High quality cuisine and excellent service. Splendid wine cellar.

XXXX **La Dama** VISA ◑◐ AE ⑩

av. Diagonal 423 ⊠ 08036 – **Ⓜ** Diagonal – 𝒞 932 02 06 86 – reservas@
ladama-restaurant.com – Fax 932 00 72 99 – www.ladama-restaurant.com
– closed 3 weeks in August **J2**
Rest – Carte 55/72 €
♦ International ♦ Retro ♦
La Dama has a classically elegant atmosphere with splendid Modernist detail both
on the façade and within its walls. Excellent service.

XXXX **Beltxenea** VISA ◑◐ AE ⑩

Mallorca 275 ⊠ 08008 – **Ⓜ** Diagonal – 𝒞 932 15 30 24 – info@beltxenea.com
– Fax 934 87 00 81
– closed Christmas, Holy Week, August, Saturday lunch and Sunday
Rest – Carte 41/55 € **K1**
♦ Traditional ♦ Formal ♦
Located in an elegant mansion with a certain old world charm. Refined, classical
cuisine with two dining rooms overlooking a small garden.

XXX
ॐ **Lasarte** (Alex Gares) – Hotel Condes de Barcelona Smokers rest.

Mallorca 259 ⊠ 08008 – **Ⓜ** Diagonal – 𝒞 934 45 32 42 VISA ◑◐ AE
– info@restaurantlasarte.com – Fax 934 45 32 32 – www.restaurantlasarte.com
– closed Holy Week, August, Saturday and Sunday
Rest – Menu 62/105 € – Carte 87/104 € **K2**
Spec. Gazpacho de melocotón de viña, escamas heladas de berberechos,
hierbas, txacolí y gamba roja. Bocadillo de ventresca de atún, chutney de
tomate y cilantro con berenjenas a la brasa. Rodaballo con manzana ácida,
tubérculos asados y cremosos y pequeña ensalada de tallos.
♦ Inventive ♦ Contemporary ♦
This restaurant bears the hallmark of Martín Berasategui and his group, with two
attractive rooms decorated in contemporary-style. Creative menu which includes
some traditional Basque dishes.

XXX **Casa Calvet** Totally no smoking ⇔ VISA ◑◐ AE ⑩

Casp 48 ⊠ 08010 – **Ⓜ** Urquinaona – 𝒞 934 12 40 12
– restaurant@casacalvet.es – Fax 934 12 43 36 – www.casacalvet.es
– closed August, Sunday and Bank Holidays **L2**
Rest – Carte 54/71 €
♦ Inventive ♦ Formal ♦
Housed in an attractive Modernist building designed by Gaudí. Well-presented tra-
ditional cuisine with a contemporary flavour, centred around the very best ingre-
dients.

XXX **Windsor** VISA ◑◐ AE ⑩

Còrsega 286 ⊠ 08008 – **Ⓜ** Diagonal – 𝒞 934 15 84 83 – info@
restaurantwindsor.com – Fax 932 38 66 08 – www.restaurantwindsor.com
– closed 1-7 January, Holy Week, August, Saturday lunch and Sunday
Rest – Carte 43/61 € 🕸 **K2**
♦ Catalan cuisine ♦ Formal ♦
Elegant, classical style restaurant with several private rooms and a main dining
room that overlooks a garden. Good selection of contemporary Catalan dishes, as
well as an excellent wine list.

SPAIN - BARCELONA

XXX   **Colibrí**   No smokers rest. *VISA* ⓪ⓈⒶⒺ ①
Casanova 212 ✉ *08036 –* Ⓜ *Hospital Clinic –* ℰ *934 43 23 06*
– info@restaurantcolibri.com – Fax 934 42 61 27 – www.restaurantcolibri.com
– closed Monday and Bank Holidays   **J2**
Rest – Carte 44/69 €
   ♦ Inventive ♦ Formal ♦
Large restaurant with an elegant decor and excellent service. Enjoy innovative cuisine created from seasonal ingredients in the light, bright dining room.

XXX   **Maria Cristina**   *VISA* ⓪ⓈⒶⒺ ①
Provença 271 ✉ *08008 –* Ⓜ *Passeig de Gràcia –* ℰ *932 15 32 37*
– margaret_marga@hotmail.com – Fax 932 15 83 23
– www.restaurante-mariacristina.com   **K1**
Rest – Carte 45/61 €
   ♦ Traditional ♦ Formal ♦
Behind the beautiful exterior of this restaurant, with its large opaque windows, is a small foyer and several dining rooms decorated in classical-contemporary style. Traditional cuisine prepared with quality produce.

XXX   **Oliver y Hardy**   🍴 *VISA* ⓪ⓈⒶⒺ ①
av. Diagonal 593 ✉ *08014 –* Ⓜ *María Cristina –* ℰ *934 19 31 81*
– oliveryhardy@husa.es – Fax 934 19 18 99 – www.husarestauracion.com
– closed Saturday lunch and Sunday   **I2**
Rest – Carte 43/54 €
   ♦ International ♦ Formal ♦
A real classic of Barcelona nightlife, this restaurant has two sections: a night club on one side and an attractively laid-out dining room on the other. The terrace is used for private events.

XXX   **Jaume de Provença**   *VISA* ⓪ⓈⒶⒺ ①
Provença 88 ✉ *08029 –* Ⓜ *Entença –* ℰ *934 30 00 29 – restaurant@
jaumeprovenza.com – Fax 934 29 29 50 – www.jaumeprovenza.com*
– closed Holy Week, August, Sunday dinner and Monday   **J2**
Rest – Carte 44/71 €
   ♦ International ♦ Formal ♦
Run by its owner, this classical style restaurant has a bar, various wine cellars and a pleasant dining room with wood panelled walls.

XX   **Melton**   Smokers rest. *VISA* ⓪ⓈⒶⒺ ①
Muntaner 189 ✉ *08036 –* Ⓜ *Hospital Clinic –* ℰ *933 63 27 76*
– meltonrestaurante@hotmail.com – Fax 933 63 27 76
– www.restaurante-melton.com
– closed Holy Week, 21 days in August, Sunday dinner and Monday
Rest – Carte approx. 39 €   **J2**
   ♦ Italian ♦ Fashionable ♦
A small, contemporary-style restaurant specialising in innovative Italian cuisine. Real attention to detail in the decor and lighting. Good service.

XX   **Cinc Sentits** (Jordi Artal)   Totally no smoking *VISA* ⓪ⓈⒶⒺ ①
🕸   *Aribau 58* ✉ *08011 –* Ⓜ *Universitat –* ℰ *933 23 94 90 – info@cincsentits.com*
– Fax 933 23 94 91 – www.cincsentits.com
– closed Holy Week, 15 days in August, Sunday and Monday   **K2**
Rest – Menu 49/69 € – Carte 64/69 €
Spec. Colas de cigalas, estofado de garbanzos, rovellons y aceite de picada. Lubina salvaje, fideua de mariscos y all i oli espumoso.Chocolate con pan, sal y aceite.
   ♦ Inventive ♦ Minimalist ♦
A sparsely decorated yet attractive restaurant that is minimalist in feel. Inventive dishes made from quality Catalan produce.

763

XX
ε3
Moo (Felip Llufriu) – Hotel Omm   Totally no smoking 𝘝𝘐𝘚𝘈 ⓪ 🅰🄴 ⓪
Rosselló 265 ⊠ 08008 – ◍ Diagonal – ℰ 934 45 40 00
– restaurante.moo@hotelomm.es – Fax 934 45 40 04
– www.hotelomm.es
– closed 21 days in August and Sunday   **K1**
Rest – Menu 45/81 € – Carte 45/51 € 🕸
Spec. Gamba con pies de cerdo crujientes. Grano de café. Maridaje entre plato y vino.
♦ Inventive ♦ Avant-garde ♦
Coffee bar and a modern, open dining room with stunning skylights and designer detail. Signature cuisine and an original wine list. Cosmopolitan atmosphere.

XX
ε3
Saüc (Xavier Franco)   Totally no smoking 𝘝𝘐𝘚𝘈 ⓪ 🅰🄴
passatge Lluís Pellicer 12 ⊠ 08036 – ◍ Hospital Clínic – ℰ 933 21 01 89
– sauc@saucrestaurant.com – www.saucrestaurant.com
– closed 5-11 January, 21 days in August, Sunday and Monday   **J2**
Rest – Menu 52/72 € – Carte 49/63 €
Spec. Garbanzos con cap-i-pota, huevo de payés y caviar. Bacalao con salsifis, bourguignone de caracoles y vino tinto. Jarrete de ternera lechal, trinxat de patata y perona.
♦ Inventive ♦ Family ♦
Functional restaurant with contemporary decorative touches. Personalised cuisine, including several signature dishes, all based around quality ingredients.

XX
😊
La Provença   𝘝𝘐𝘚𝘈 ⓪ 🅰🄴 ⓪
Provença 242 ⊠ 08008 – ◍ Diagonal – ℰ 933 23 23 67
– restofi@laprovenza.com – Fax 934 51 23 89 – www.laprovenza.com
Rest – Carte 29/35 €   **K2**
♦ De Terroir ♦ Formal ♦
A cosy restaurant along classic-modern lines with numerous private dining areas. Popular with business clientele, the menu here is varied with a good choice of daily specials.

XX
El Túnel D'en Marc Palou   Smokers rest. 𝘝𝘐𝘚𝘈 ⓪ 🅰🄴 ⓪
Bailén 91 ⊠ 08009 – ◍ Girona – ℰ 932 65 86 58 – info@eltuneldenmarc.com
– Fax 932 46 01 14 – www.eltuneldenmarc.com
– Closed August, Sunday and Monday dinner   **L1**
Rest – Carte 38/47 €
♦ Inventive ♦ Contemporary ♦
This corner restaurant has three small, contemporary-style dining rooms on several levels. The chef here is known for his interesting, inventive food.

XX
Peixerot   Totally no smoking 𝘝𝘐𝘚𝘈 🅰🄴 ⓪
av. Tarragona 177 ⊠ 08014 – ◍ Sants Estació – ℰ 934 24 69 69
– central@peixerot.net – Fax 934 26 10 63 – www.peixerot.com
– closed 9-23 August and Sunday dinner   **J3**
Rest – Carte 41/59 €
♦ Fish and shellfish ♦ Sea style ♦
Classical style restaurant with rooms on different floors. Good service and a wideranging menu that varies daily, depending on the fish available in the market.

XX
Alba Granados   𝘝𝘐𝘚𝘈 ⓪ 🅰🄴 ⓪
Enric Granados 34 ⊠ 08036 – ◍ Passeig de Gràcia – ℰ 934 54 61 16
– info@albagranados.com – Fax 934 54 83 74 – www.albagranados.com
– closed Sunday dinner   **K2**
Rest – Carte 27/42 €
♦ Mediterranean ♦ Rustic ♦
Unusual decor, entirely centred around the world of wine. Dining rooms on two floors, where the traditional menu offers a good choice of grilled meats.

SPAIN - BARCELONA

XX **El Asador de Aranda** [VISA] [CO] [AE] [O]

Londres 94 ✉ *08036 –* ⓜ *Hospital Clinic –* ☎ *934 14 67 90*
– barcelona@asadordearanda.com – Fax 934 14 67 90
– www.asadordearanda.com
– closed Sunday dinner **L2**
Rest *– Carte 35/44 €*
♦ Roast lamb ♦ Rustic ♦
Situated in a side street off the Avenida Diagonal, this spacious restaurant is decorated in Castilian style. The wood oven, in full view of diners, is where the restaurant's traditional lamb dishes are cooked. Bar.

XX **Gorría** [VISA] [CO] [AE] [O]

Diputació 421 ✉ *08013 –* ⓜ *Sagrada Familia –* ☎ *932 45 11 64*
– info@restaurantegorria.com – Fax 932 32 78 57
– www.restaurantegorria.com
– closed Holy Week, August, Sunday, Monday dinner and Bank Holidays dinner
Rest *– Carte 38/52 €* ⅗ **L1**
♦ Traditional ♦ Navarian ♦
A well-established Basque restaurant with rustic style decor. The excellent menu is complemented by an extensive wine list. Attentive service.

XX **Mosaic** – Hotel Hilton Barcelona   No smokers rest. ⌂ [VISA] [CO] [AE] [O]

av. Diagonal 589 ✉ *08014 –* ⓜ *María Cristina –* ☎ *934 95 77 60*
– Fax 934 95 77 00 – www.barcelona.hilton.com **I2**
Rest *– Carte 40/60 €*
♦ International ♦ Contemporary ♦
Contemporary-style interior combining high ceilings, straight lines and dark wood. International and Mediterranean cuisine.

XX **Nectari** ⇔ [VISA] [CO] [AE] [O]

València 28 – ⓜ *Tarragona –* ☎ *93 226 87 18 – nectari@nectari.es*
– Fax 93 226 68 24 – www.nectari.es **J3**
Rest *– (closed 17-30 August) Carte 34/52 €*
♦ A la mode ♦ Contemporary ♦
Occupying the lower floors of a residential building, this restaurant has two contemporary-style dining areas and one private dining room. Inventive Mediterranean cuisine from the owner-chef.

XX **El Asador de Aranda** [VISA] [CO] [AE] [O]

Pau Clarís 70 ✉ *08010 –* ⓜ *Urquinaona –* ☎ *933 42 55 77*
– barcelona@asadordearanda.com – Fax 933 42 55 78
– www.asadordearanda.com
– closed Sunday dinner **J2**
Rest *– Carte 35/45 €*
♦ Roast lamb ♦ Rustic ♦
Typical of this chain of carveries, this restaurant has a bar at the entrance, a rotisserie in full view of diners, as well as attractive dining rooms with elegant Castilian decor.

XX **Casa Darío** ⇔ [VISA] [CO] [AE] [O]

Consell de Cent 256 ✉ *08011 –* ⓜ *Universitat –* ☎ *934 53 31 35*
– casadario@casadario.com – Fax 934 51 33 95
– www.casadario.com
– closed August and Sunday **K2**
Rest *– Carte 47/68 €*
♦ Galician ♦ Formal ♦
A well-established restaurant with a good reputation for the quality of its ingredients. The restaurant has a private bar, three dining rooms and three private rooms. Galician dishes and seafood are the house specialities.

XX **Manairó** (Jordi Herrera)　　　　Totally no smoking 𝗩𝗜𝗦𝗔 ⑩ 𝗔𝗘 ⑩
🏵 *Diputació 424 ⊠ 08013 – Ⓜ Monumental – ℰ 932 31 00 57*
– info@manairo.com – Fax 932 65 23 81 – www.manairo.com
– closed 1-7 January, Sunday and Bank Holidays　　　　　**L1**
Rest – Menu 55/72 € – Carte 50/60 €
Spec. Raviolis con foie-gras y colmenillas. Bacalao con patatas de azafrán y picada de frutos secos. Sopa de fruta de la pasión con naranja y sorbete de albahaca.
♦ Inventive ♦ Contemporary ♦
Popular with locals, this restaurant has a small dining room decorated with works by various artists. Creative cuisine offering an innovative approach to traditional recipes.

X **Gresca**　　　　　　　　　𝗩𝗜𝗦𝗔 ⑩ ⑩
Provença 230 ⊠ 08036 Barcelona – Ⓜ Diagonal – ℰ 93 451 61 93
– www.gresca.net
– closed Christmas, Holy Week, 15-31 August, Saturday lunch and Sunday
Rest – Carte 31/45 €　　　　　　　**K2**
♦ A la mode ♦ Contemporary ♦
The discreet façade leads to a spacious, minimalist-style dining room, decorated in contrasting shades of black and white. Contemporary cuisine from the conscientious chef.

X **Toc**　　　　　　　　　　𝗩𝗜𝗦𝗔 ⑩ 𝗔𝗘 ⑩
Girona 59 ⊠ 08009 – Ⓜ Girona – ℰ 934 88 11 48 – toc@tocbcn.com
– www.tocbcn.com – closed 10-30 August, Saturday lunch and Sunday
Rest – Carte 38/53 €　　　　　　　**L2**
♦ Catalan cuisine ♦ Contemporary ♦
This restaurant extending over two floors has modern, 1970s inspired decor. Contemporary Catalan cuisine.

X **La Tertulia**　　　　　Smokers rest. 🏠 𝗩𝗜𝗦𝗔 ⑩ 𝗔𝗘 ⑩
😊 *Morales 15 ⊠ 08029 – Ⓜ Entença – ℰ 934 19 58 97 – tertulia@*
arrosseriaxativa.com – Fax 933 63 21 58 – www.arrosseriaxativa.com
– closed Sunday dinner　　　　　　　**J2**
Rest – Carte 25/41 €
♦ Traditional ♦ Rustic ♦
This cosy restaurant with a rustic atmosphere has large windows and a pleasant terrace. Traditional cuisine offering good value for money.

X **Can Ravell**　　　　　　　𝗩𝗜𝗦𝗔 ⑩ 𝗔𝗘 ⑩
Aragó 313 ⊠ 08009 – Ⓜ Girona – ℰ 934 57 51 14 – direccio@ravell.com
– Fax 934 59 39 56 – www.ravell.com – closed Sunday　　　**K1**
Rest – (lunch only except Thursday and Friday) Carte 44/66 €
♦ Traditional ♦ Family ♦
This unusual restaurant with one dining room and two private rooms is situated on the second floor of an old grocery store. Catalan cuisine and a good selection of wines.

𝕐/ **Mesón Cinco Jotas**　　　　　🏠 𝗩𝗜𝗦𝗔 ⑩ 𝗔𝗘 ⑩
Rambla de Catalunya 91-93 ⊠ 08008 – Ⓜ Diagonal – ℰ 934 87 89 42
– m5jrambla@osborne.es – Fax 934 87 91 21 – www.mesoncincojotas.com
Tapa 4 € **Ración** approx. 14 €　　　　　　**K2**
♦ Traditional ♦ Tapas bar ♦
Spacious and rustic bar decorated with a profusion of wood. Enjoy the mouthwatering array of hams at a table by the entrance or in the rear dining room. Extensive tapas menu.

𝕐/ **Cervecería Catalana**　　　🏠Totally no smoking 𝗩𝗜𝗦𝗔 ⑩ 𝗔𝗘 ⑩
Mallorca 236 ⊠ 08008 – Ⓜ Diagonal – ℰ 932 16 03 68
– jordiahumada@gmail.com – Fax 934 88 17 97　　　**K2**
Tapa 5 € **Ración** approx. 10 €
♦ Traditional ♦ Tapas bar ♦
This popular local pub, decorated with racks full of bottles, serves a comprehensive choice of top quality tapas.

SPAIN - BARCELONA

Ψ/ **De Tapa Madre** 🛋 VISA ◎◎ AE

Mallorca 301 ⊠ *08037 –* **Ⓜ** *Verdaguer –* 𝒞 *934 59 31 34 – detapamadre@
hotmail.com – Fax 934 57 28 61 – www.detapamadre.com* **K1**
Tapa 4 € **Ración** approx. 14 €
◆ Traditional ◆ Rustic ◆
Rustic tapas bar with a small terrace, dining room and a private room on the upper
floor. The tapas here are all produced from high quality ingredients.

SANT MARTÍ

Plan I

🏨🏨🏨🏨 **Arts** 🏖 No smokers rest. ⩤ 🛋 Ⅰ৯ ⌱ ⊡ ⌁ 🄼 🏊 VISA ◎◎ AE ⓘ

Marina 19 ⊠ *08005 –* **Ⓜ** *Ciutadella-Villa Olímpica –* 𝒞 *932 21 10 00 – rc.barcelona
reservations@ritzcarlton.com – Fax 932 21 10 70 – www.hotelartsbarcelona.com*
397 rm – ♦♦295/525 €, ⇆ 32 € **C2**
Rest Arola – *(closed Monday and Tuesday)* Carte 44/63 €
Rest Enoteca – *(closed Sunday) (dinner only except Monday and Tuesday)*
Carte 32/86 €
◆ Grand Luxury ◆ Contemporary ◆
Splendid hotel occupying a glass tower overlooking the Olympic port. It has
magnificent views of the city and rooms that combine luxury and ultramodern
design. The Arts is home to several restaurants. The most outstanding of which is
Arola, renowned for the creativity of its cuisine.

🏨🏨🏨🏨 **Hilton Diagonal Mar** No smokers rest. ⩤ 🛋 Ⅰ৯ ⌱ ⊡ ⌁ 🄼 🏊

passeig del Taulat 262-264 ⊠ *08019* VISA ◎◎ AE ⓘ
– **Ⓜ** *El Maresme/Forum –* 𝒞 *935 07 07 07 – diagonalmarbarcelona@hilton.com
– Fax 935 07 07 00 – www.hilton.com* **D2**
413 rm – ♦215/410 € ♦♦237/432 €, ⇆ 24 € – 20 suites **Rest** – Carte 40/60 €
◆ Conventions ◆ Contemporary ◆
Located near the Fórum, the Hilton is heavily orientated towards conference delegates. The guestrooms have a clean, modern design with high quality contemporary furnishings. Enjoy views of the large entrance hall and the sea from the hotel's
first floor restaurant.

🏨🏨🏨 **Diagonal Barcelona** ⌱ ⊡ ⌂ 🄼 🏊 VISA ◎◎ AE ⓘ

av. Diagonal 205 ⊠ *08018 –* **Ⓜ** *Glòries –* 𝒞 *934 89 53 00 – reservas.diagonal@
hoteles-silken.com – Fax 934 89 53 09 – www.hoteldiagonalbarcelona.com*
228 rm – ♦110/350 € ♦♦125/380 €, ⇆ 17 € – 12 suites **C2**
Rest – *(closed August and Sunday)* Carte 38/60 €
◆ Urban ◆ Design ◆
Several well-known artists have given vent to their creativity in this designer hotel.
Highly modern guestrooms with open bathrooms and a sun terrace on the top
floor. Restaurant simply laid out along modern lines.

🏨🏨🏨 **AB Skipper** 🛋 Ⅰ৯ ⌱ ⊡ ⌁ 🄼 🏊 VISA ◎◎ AE ⓘ

av. del Litoral 10 ⊠ *08005 –* **Ⓜ** *Ciutadella-Vila Olímpica –* 𝒞 *932 21 65 65
– skipper@hotelabskipper.com – Fax 932 21 36 00 – www.hotelabskipper.com*
236 rm – ♦♦225/350 €, ⇆ 25 € – 5 suites **Rest** – Menu 45 € **C2**
Rest Syrah – *(closed Sunday, Monday and Bank Holidays)* Carte 45/59 €
◆ Traditional ◆ Contemporary ◆
This hotel combines designer detail and technology with a warm, welcoming environment. Varied lounge areas, comfortable guestrooms and a swimming pool on
the attractive roof terrace. The focus in the Syrah gastronomic restaurant is on
creative, contemporary cuisine.

🏨🏨🏨 **Barcelona Princess** ⩤ Ⅰ৯ ⌱ ⊡ ⌂ 🄼 🏊 VISA ◎◎ AE ⓘ

av. Diagonal 1 ⊠ *08019 –* **Ⓜ** *El Maresme/Forum –* 𝒞 *93 356 10 00
– bcn.reservas@princess-hotels.com – Fax 93 356 10 22 – www.princess-hotels.com*
364 rm – ♦106/270 € ♦♦114/325 €, ⇆ 17 € **D2**
Rest – Menu 23 €
◆ Business ◆ Contemporary ◆
The Princess occupies two modern tower blocks in the Fórum district of the city.
Colourful lobby and contemporary-style guestrooms with good views and glass-
enclosed bathrooms. A bright, functional restaurant serving a traditional menu.

AC Barcelona

passeig del Taulat 278 ✉ *08019 Barcelona* – ⓜ *El Maresme/Forum* – ℰ *93 489 82 00*
– acbarcelona@ac-hotels.com – Fax 93 489 82 01 – www.ac-hotels.com
368 rm – ♥♥113/234 €, ⌷ 20 €   **Rest** – Carte approx. 37 €   **D2**
♦ Business ♦ Contemporary ♦
Situated in the Fórum district of the city with direct access to the International Conference Centre. Comfortable, contemporary-style guestrooms with suites in the corners of the building. A modern restaurant unusual in that its kitchen remains open 24-hours a day.

Anfiteatro

av. Litoral (Parc del Port Olímpic) ✉ *08005* – ⓜ *Ciutadella-Vila Olímpica*
– ℰ 659 69 53 45 – anfiteatrobcn@telefonica.net – Fax 934 57 14 19
– www.anfiteatro-restaurante.com – closed August, Sunday dinner and Monday
Rest – *(set menu only)* Menu 45 €   **C2**
♦ Inventive ♦ Contemporary ♦
Contemporary-style restaurant on a large avenue overlooking a small lake. An abundance of natural light in the dining room, where the main culinary focus is the popular tasting menu.

Els Pescadors

pl. Prim 1 ✉ *08005* – ⓜ *Poblenou* – ℰ *932 25 20 18 – contacte@elspescadors.com*
– Fax 932 24 00 04 – www.elspescadors.com – closed Holy Week   **D2**
Rest – Carte 38/57 €
♦ De Terroir ♦ Modern ♦
This restaurant has three dining rooms, one in early-20C café style and two with a more modern decor. A generous menu based on fish and seafood with rice dishes and cod to the fore.

El Túnel del Port

Moll de Gregal 12 (Port Olímpic) ✉ *08005* – ⓜ *Ciutadella-Vila Olímpica*
– ℰ 932 21 03 21 – eltunel@eltuneldelport.com – Fax 932 21 35 86
– www.eltuneldelport.com – closed Sunday dinner and Monday   **C2**
Rest – Carte 34/48 €
♦ De Terroir ♦ Formal ♦
A spacious, attractively laid out restaurant with two dining rooms on different levels, one of which has glass windows and attractive views. Canopied terrace.

NORTH of AV. DIAGONAL   *Plan III*

Casa Fuster

passeig de Gràcia 132 ✉ *08008* – ⓜ *Diagonal* – ℰ *932 55 30 00 – casafuster@*
hotelescenter.com – Fax 932 55 30 02 – www.hotelcasafuster.com
66 rm – ♥♥189/665 €, ⌷ 25 € – 39 suites   **Rest** *Galaxó* – Carte 54/73 €   **K1**
♦ Luxury ♦ Historic building ♦ Contemporary ♦
This magnificent hotel occupies a beautiful Modernist building dating back to 1908. Attractive lounge-bar and high quality, comfortable guestrooms with fully equipped bathrooms. This elegant restaurant serves innovative, creative cuisine.

Hispanos Siete Suiza

Sicilia 255 ✉ *08025* – ⓜ *Sagrada Familia* – ℰ *932 08 20 51*
– comercial@hispanos7suiza.com – Fax 932 08 20 52 – www.h7s.es
19 suites ⌷ – ♥♥170/230 €   **Rest** *La Cúpula* – see below   **L1**
♦ Traditional ♦ Classical ♦
This comfortable, traditional property has apartments with two bedrooms, two bathrooms, a lounge and fully equipped kitchen. Most of the apartments have a terrace.

AC Irla *without rest*

Calvet 40-42 ✉ *08021* – ⓜ *Muntaner* – ℰ *932 41 62 10*
– acirla@ac-hotels.com – Fax 932 41 62 11 – www.ac-hotels.com   **J1**
36 rm – ♥♥98/275 €, ⌷ 17 €
♦ Chain hotel ♦ Traditional ♦ Contemporary ♦
An attractive hotel combining quality materials with functionality and design. All the guestrooms are equipped with modern bathrooms and impressive showers.

SPAIN - BARCELONA

Condado without rest   [symbols] ✆ 📠 VISA ⓪ AE ①

Aribau 201 ✉ *08021* – Ⓜ *Diagonal* – 𝒞 *932 00 23 11* – *administracion@*
condadohotel.com – *Fax 932 00 25 86* – *www.condadohotel.com*
75 rm – ♟♟95/225 €, ⨅ 12 € – 1 suite   **J1**
♦ Urban ♦ Classical ♦
Following a complete overhaul, the hotel now has a traditional yet contemporary
look which combines high quality materials and light colours. Spacious and bright
bedrooms with wood flooring.

Catalonia Suite   No smokers rest. 📶 ⁽¹⁾ 🛁 🛏 VISA ⓪ AE ①

Muntaner 505 ✉ *08022* – Ⓜ *El Putxet* – 𝒞 *932 12 80 12*
– *suite@hoteles-catalonia.es* – *Fax 932 11 23 17* – *www.hoteles-catalonia.com*
117 rm – ♟119/200 €, ♟♟152/214 €, ⨅ 15 €   **I1**
Rest – *(set menu only)* Menu 18 €
♦ Chain hotel ♦ Traditional ♦ Contemporary ♦
Located in a residential and business area. Functional, contemporary-style rooms
with large bathrooms, most of which have separate showers and hydromassage
baths.

Catalonia Córcega   📶 ⁽¹⁾ VISA ⓪ AE ①

Còrsega 368 ✉ *08037* – Ⓜ *Verdaguer* – 𝒞 *932 08 19 19* – *corcega@*
hoteles-catalonia.es – *Fax 932 08 08 57* – *www.hoteles-catalonia.com*
77 rm – ♟134/167 €, ♟♟200/214 €, ⨅ 15 € – 2 suites   **K1**
Rest – Menu 18 €
♦ Chain hotel ♦ Traditional ♦ Contemporary classic ♦
This contemporary-style hotel has well-maintained guestrooms with classical-contemporary furniture and wood flooring. Compact public areas. The focus here is
on set menus, although the restaurant also offers limited à la carte choices.

NH Cóndor   No smokers rest. 📶 ⁽¹⁾ 🛁 VISA ⓪ AE ①

Via Augusta 127 ✉ *08006* – Ⓜ *Muntaner* – 𝒞 *932 09 45 11*
– *nhcondor@nh-hotels.com* – *Fax 932 02 27 13* – *www.nh-hotels.com*
66 rm – ♟90/150 €, ♟♟95/230 €, ⨅ 15 € – 12 suites   **J1**
Rest – *(closed August and weekends)* Menu 30 €
♦ Chain hotel ♦ Traditional ♦ Functional ♦
A well-designed, comfortable hotel in keeping with the usual decor of the NH
chain. Small lounge area and well-appointed guestrooms with modern furnishings.

Neichel (Jean Louis Neichel)   🔄 VISA ⓪ AE ①
🕄

Beltran i Rózpide 1 ✉ *08034* – Ⓜ *María Cristina* – 𝒞 *932 03 84 08*
– *neichel@relaischateaux.com* – *Fax 932 05 63 69* – *www.neichel.es*
– *closed 1 week in January, August, Sunday, Monday and Bank Holidays*
Rest – Menu 75/95 € – Carte 70/85 € ⅜   *Plan I* **A2**
Spec. Tartar de atún del Mediterráneo, erizos de mar y Wakame al jengibre,
cebiche de atún. Becada del país en dos cocciones, muslo en civet y sup-
rema sangrante, canapé al foie trufado (Winter). Tartar de fresones y
mango relleno de Mascarpone, helado de flor de lavanda, gelé de rosas.
♦ Innovative ♦ Formal ♦
Neichel's talented chef has created a varied menu of traditional and contemporary
dishes for a highly discerning clientele. Elegant and bright setting next to a beautiful garden.

Via Veneto (Carles Tejedor)   VISA ⓪ AE ①
🕄

Ganduxer 10 ✉ *08021* – Ⓜ *Hospital Clinic* – 𝒞 *932 00 72 44*
– *pmonje@adam.es* – *Fax 932 01 60 95* – *www.viavenetorestaurant.com*
– *closed 1-20 August, Saturday lunch and Sunday*   **I2**
Rest – Menu 95 € – Carte 69/89 € ⅜
Spec. Trilogía de gambas en tartar, con crujiente de aceitunas negras, a la
parrilla y en canelón relleno. Salmonetes de roca dorados, con arroz meloso
al azafrán y flor de naranjo. Costillar de cordero lechal asado con costra de
finas hierbas y milhojas de butifarra de perol.
♦ International ♦ Retro ♦
Elegant Belle Époque décor, impeccable service and an interesting, classical menu.
This well-established restaurant also boasts a magnificent wine cellar.

XXX
🕊🕊
Àbac (Xavier Pellicer) with rm 🛏 Totally no smoking ✿ 🚙
av. del Tibidabo 1 ⊠ 08022 – ⓜ Tibidabo
– 𝒞 93 319 66 00 – info@abacbarcelona.com – Fax 93 319 66 01
– www.abacbarcelona.com – closed August, Sunday and Monday
15 rm – ⭐⭐220/875 €, ⌂ € *Plan I* **B2**
Rest – Menu 117 € – Carte 80/110 €
Spec. Tendones de ternera, almejas, brócoli y caviar. Lenguado, espinacas, perrechicos y pan de ajo. Pichón a la brasa y muslos en ensalada.
♦ Inventive ♦ Modern ♦
This restaurant is housed in an unusual villa in the upper part of the city. It has a terrace, designer bar, and modern dining room serving creative cuisine. This restaurant is housed in an unusual villa in the upper part of the city. It has a terrace, designer bar, and modern dining room serving creative cuisine.

XXX
🕊
El Racó d'en Freixa (Ramón Freixa) Smokers rest. 𝗩𝗜𝗦𝗔 ⓸⦵ 𝗔𝗘 ⓞ
Sant Elíes 22 ⊠ 08006 – ⓜ Plaça Molina – 𝒞 932 09 75 59
– info@elracodenfreixa.com – Fax 932 09 79 18 – www.elracodenfreixa.com
– closed Holy Week, 21 days in August, Sunday and Monday **J1**
Rest – Carte 75/89 € 🎋
Spec. Sopa-ensalada de huevo frito, espárragos y seta de primavera (Spring). Cigala real. Chocolate 2009.
♦ Innovative ♦ Contemporary ♦
A modern restaurant with clean, minimalist lines, designer touches and excellent service. High quality, creative cuisine.

XXX
🕊
Hofmann (Mey Hofmann) ✿ 𝗩𝗜𝗦𝗔 ⓸⦵ 𝗔𝗘 ⓞ
La Granada del Penedès 14-16 ⊠ 08006 – ⓜ Diagonal – 𝒞 93 218 71 65
– restaurante@hofmann-bcn.com – Fax 93 218 98 67 – www.hofmann-bcn.com
– closed Holy Week, August, Saturday and Sunday **J1**
Rest – Menu 80 € – Carte 67/79 €
Spec. Cigalas envueltas con láminas de ceps sobre Parmentier y su jugo. Arroz bomba con setas, foie salteado y reducción de Oporto. Bacalao glaseado con all i oli sobre lecho de espinacas a la catalana.
♦ Inventive ♦ Elegant ♦
Contemporary in style, this restaurant has several semi-private dining areas and a main dining room separated from the kitchen via a large window. Innovative menu.

XXX
La Cúpula – Hotel Hispanos Siete Suiza 𝗩𝗜𝗦𝗔 ⓸⦵ 𝗔𝗘 ⓞ
Sicilia 255 ⊠ 08025 – ⓜ Sagrada Familia – 𝒞 932 08 20 61 – info@
lacupularestaurant.com – Fax 932 08 20 52 – www.lacupularestaurant.com
– closed August, Sunday and Monday **L1**
Rest – Carte 40/60 €
♦ Traditional ♦ Formal ♦
This restaurant displays a wonderful collection of Hispano-Suiza cars from the beginning of the 20C. The restaurant has two dining rooms on two floors, both exquisitely decorated in classical style with high quality furniture.

XX
Roig Robí 🛏 𝗩𝗜𝗦𝗔 ⓸⦵ 𝗔𝗘 ⓞ
Sèneca 20 ⊠ 08006 – ⓜ Diagonal – 𝒞 932 18 92 22 – roigrobi@roigrobi.com
– Fax 934 15 78 42 – www.roigrobi.com
– closed 7 days in January, 21 days in August, Saturday lunch and Sunday
Rest – Carte 61/79 € **K1**
♦ De Terroir ♦ Formal ♦
Contemporary-style restaurant with a cosy atmosphere in a splendid location. Varied menu with individual touches. Pleasant garden-terrace.

XX
🕊
Alkimia (Jordi Vilà) Totally no smoking 𝗩𝗜𝗦𝗔 ⓸⦵ ⓞ
Indústria 79 ⊠ 08025 – ⓜ Sagrada Familia – 𝒞 932 07 61 15 – alkimia@
telefonica.net – closed Holy Week, 21 days in August, Saturday and Sunday
Rest – Menu 54/68 € – Carte 58/62 € **K1**
Spec. Bombón de huevo frito con patata, sobrasada y membrillo. Arroz de ñoras y azafrán con cigalas. Steak tartar a la soja con patatas soufflé y mantequilla especiada.
♦ Inventive ♦ Minimalist ♦
Understated, minimalist decor illuminated by individual lighting. Modern, Catalan inspired cuisine, including several signature dishes. Attentive service.

XX **Coure**   *VISA* **©©** AE

passatge de Marimon 20 ⊠ 08021 – Ⓜ Hospital Clinic – 𝒞 932 00 75 32
– restaurantcoure@hotmail.com – closed 21 days in August, Sunday and Monday
Rest – Carte 46/54 €   **J2**
♦ A la mode ♦ Contemporary ♦
A modern restaurant with bright colours and a minimalist inspired decoration.
Interesting and innovative cuisine from the owner-chef.

XX **Hisop**   Smokers rest. *VISA* **©©** AE ①

passatge de Marimon 9 ⊠ 08021 – Ⓜ Hospital Clinic – 𝒞 932 41 32 33
– hisop@hisop.com – www.hisop.com – closed 7 days in January, 21 days in
August, Saturday lunch, Sunday and Bank Holidays   **J2**
Rest – Carte 48/63 €
♦ Inventive ♦ Minimalist ♦
This restaurant is minimalist in style with floral motifs on the walls. Good local repu-
tation and excellent service. Creative, innovative cuisine.

XX ☺ **St. Rémy**   *VISA* **©©** AE ①

Iradier 12 ⊠ 08017 – 𝒞 934 18 75 04 – Fax 934 34 04 34
– www.stremyrestaurant.com – closed Sunday dinner   **I1**
Rest – Carte 28/35 €
♦ De Terroir ♦ Contemporary ♦
The St Rémy occupies a small mansion with spacious dining rooms, modern furni-
ture and elegant lighting. Catalan inspired cuisine.

XX **Le Quattro Stagioni**   🛋 ✿ *VISA* **©©** AE ①

Dr. Roux 37 ⊠ 08017 – Ⓜ Les Tres Torres – 𝒞 932 05 22 79
– restaurant@4stagioni.com – Fax 932 05 78 65 – www.4stagioni.com
– closed Holy Week, Sunday and Monday lunch (July-August), Sunday dinner
and Monday for rest of the year   **Rest** – Carte 30/39 € 🈺   **I1**
♦ Italian ♦ Contemporary ♦
Dining rooms on two floors with a glass-fronted terrace and outdoor patio. Mediterranean ambience, Italian cuisine and a wide selection of Italian wines.

XX ☺ **Silvestre**   *VISA* **©©** AE

Santaló 101 ⊠ 08021 – Ⓜ Muntaner – 𝒞 932 41 40 31 – Fax 932 41 40 31
– www.restaurantesilvestre.com – closed Holy Week, 21 days in
August, Saturday lunch, Sunday and Bank Holidays   **J1**
Rest – Carte 30/35 €
♦ Traditional ♦ Formal ♦
The couple who own this restaurant have created a classical ambience with a num-
ber of separate dining areas providing a certain intimacy. Reasonably priced menu
based around fresh market produce.

X ☺ **Mandarina**   🛋 *VISA* **©©** AE ①

Caravel.la "La Niña" ⊠ 08017 – Ⓜ María Cristina – 𝒞 932 05 60 04
– info@mandarinarestaurant.com – Fax 932 80 19 72
– www.mandarinarestaurant.com – closed 6-26 August and Sunday
Rest – Carte 24/35 €   **I2**
♦ Inventive ♦ Contemporary ♦
A bright and youthful atmosphere, which adds to the sensation of eating light,
healthy cuisine. Split over two floors with the kitchen partially in view and a pleasant terrace.

X ☺ **La Taula**   Totally no smoking *VISA* **©©** AE ①

Sant Màrius 8-12 ⊠ 08022 – Ⓜ El Putxet – 𝒞 934 17 28 48 – Fax 934 34 01 27
– www.lataula.com – closed August, Saturday lunch, Sunday and Bank Holidays
Rest – Carte 30/35 €   **I1**
♦ International ♦ Formal ♦
A small and welcoming restaurant with interesting decorative detail. Two types of
menu and a choice of daily specials are on offer in this busy and popular eatery.

Vivanda
🕭 VISA ⏍ AE

Major de Sarrià 134 ⊠ 08017 – ℰ 932 03 19 18 – asisted@asisted.com
– Fax 932 12 48 85 – closed Sunday and Monday lunch Plan I **A2**
Rest – Carte 33/35 €
♦ Market ♦ Contemporary ♦
Located in the residential suburb of Sarria, Vivanda has a modern dining room with wicker furniture. Interesting, reasonably priced menu. Attentive service.

Folquer
Smokers rest. 🕭 ⇩ VISA ⏍ AE ⏀

Torrent de l'Olla 3 ⊠ 08012 – Ⓜ Diagonal – ℰ 932 17 43 95
– carrillojuanjo@yahoo.es – closed Christmas, Holy Week, 21 days in August,
Saturday lunch, Sunday and Bank Holidays **K1**
Rest – Carte 27/35 €
♦ A la mode ♦ Bistro ♦
Typical bistro decoration with 1920s style cafeteria chairs and tables. Modern menu, focusing on three set menus at lunchtime.

AT L'HOSPITALET de LLOBREGAT
Plan I

Hesperia Tower
⇐ Ⅰ£ 🖾 ᵗᵖ 🖙 🖘 VISA ⏍ AE ⏀

Gran Via 144 ⊠ 08907 – Ⓜ Bellvitge – ℰ 934 13 50 00 – hotel@
hesperia-tower.com – Fax 934 13 50 10 – www.hesperia-tower.com
258 rm – ⍦125/350 € ⍦⍦145/370 €, � 24 € – 22 suites **BT**
Rest *Evo* – see below
Rest *Bouquet* – Carte 48/53 €
♦ Chain hotel ♦ Business ♦ Modern ♦
An innovatively designed hotel with a 'hi-tech' architectural style. Spacious public areas, convention centre and well-equipped bedrooms. The emphasis in this contemporary restaurant on the second floor is on creative cuisine.

Evo (Ismael Alegría) – Hotel Hesperia Tower
Smokers rest. ⇐

Gran Via 144 ⊠ 08907 – Ⓜ Bellvitge – ℰ 934 13 50 30 VISA ⏍ AE ⏀
– evo@hesperia-tower.com – Fax 934 13 50 17 – www.evorestaurante.com
– closed August, Sunday and Bank Holidays
Rest – Menu 135 € **A3**
Spec. Langosta plancha con guisantes, colmenillas y aceite de rostit. Costilla de ternera lacada al horno con manzana asada a la canela y judías violeta. Tarta de caramelo con sorbete de pera y crocanti de piñones.
♦ Innovative ♦ Design ♦
This restaurant has an original layout: under a glass dome is a panoramic dining area providing splendid views. Signature cuisine with a focus on quality produce.

El Racó del Cargol
Smokers rest. VISA ⏍

Dr. Martí Julià 54 ⊠ 08903 L'Hospitalet de Llobregat – Ⓜ Collblanc
– ℰ 934 49 77 18 – restaurantecargol@hotmail.com – Fax 934 49 08 16
– www.rocxi.es – closed Christmas, Sunday and Monday dinner **A3**
Rest – Carte 25/38 €
♦ Traditional ♦ Formal ♦
An efficiently run restaurant serving reasonably priced traditional cuisine. Dining room with classical style decor and two smaller, more modern rooms on the upper floor.

AT EL PRAT AIRPORT

Tryp Barcelona Aeropuerto
No smokers rest. Ⅰ£ 🕽 🖙 🖘

pl. del Pla de L'Estany 1-2 ⊠ 08820 – ℰ 933 78 10 00 VISA ⏍ AE ⏀
– tryp.barcelona.aeropuerto@solmelia.com – Fax 933 78 10 01
– www.trypbarcelonaaeropuerto.solmelia.com
205 rm – ⍦⍦80/210 €, ⊠ 15 € **Rest** – Menu 30 €
♦ Business ♦ Contemporary ♦
Functional hotel located in a business park near the airport. The lobby has an original layout with corridors leading off from it to the comfortable guestrooms.

VALENCIA
VALÈNCIA

Population (2008): 800 666 (Conurbation 1 500 000) - Altitude: 15m

Turismo Valencia/www.turisvalencia.es

Spain's third largest city remained to all intents and purposes a tourist no-go destination for too many years, hidden beneath its sunny shell. Not any more. In 2007 the prestigious America's Cup set sail from its shores in the shadow of the most eye-catching leisure complex in Europe, a stunning twenty-first century addition to the city's skyline. Valencia has announced itself in a big way.

Why it was ever relegated in the visitor stakes is a mystery to all Valencians. Friendly and unpretentious, they're only too willing to tell you of the city's undeniable character and charm, its unspoilt beaches, museums, amazing nightlife and rip-roaring fiestas. And they have a point. The buildings of the city's beautiful old town are testament to its rich history: medieval churches, Renaissance halls of trade and baroque mansions are layered on top of an earlier Roman city. This is the home of paella, and a thriving café scene gives you ample opportunity to tuck into it. The sun shines most of the time here, but if you want shelter there are more than thirty museums on hand offering a cool escape.

LIVING THE CITY

Valencia sits in an enviable position on the Mediterranean coast; the city's port and its long golden beach are to the east. A mile or so inland is the heart of the city, its old town, a labyrinth of ancient cobbled streets. It's bounded to the north by the Turia River Park, created when the actual river was diverted after floods a half a century ago, and to the south by a semicircle of wide boulevards, which follow the line of the ancient city walls. The renowned nightlife district of Carmen is the northwest area of the old town.

PRACTICAL INFORMATION

ARRIVAL-DEPARTURE

Valencia-Manises Airport is 8km west of the city and a taxi to the centre will cost about €20. Alternatively take the Metro train (lines 3 and 5) or the Airport bus which runs every 20min and takes around 15min.

TRANSPORT

Valencia has an integrated transport system, with metro, buses and trams. Single tickets for the modern metro, which has four lines, are cheap and can be purchased from station machines or ticket offices. You can buy a one-day pass for the metro, trams and buses or, alternatively, a 10-trip pass for about twice the price.

Another useful investment is the Valencia Tourist Card, available from tourism offices, hotels, tobacconists and kiosks. It offers free travel on all forms of public transport, as well as discounts in museums, shops, restaurants and various leisure activities. The cards last for one, two, or three days.

EXPLORING VALENCIA

This is a city whose centre resembles a Gothic-Renaissance theme park. Valencia can trace two thousand years of history, and at times you might well believe there's a mazy little street or alleyway for each of those years. Certainly newcomers will get lost in the compact centre, but that's part of the charm of the place. Anyway, you'll always come to a hefty landmark before too long. The reason for all the cobbled warrens and hidden plazas, the grand mixture of architectural styles is simple: over time Valencia has seen many invaders come and go, from the Romans to the Visigoths, from the Aragonese to the Moors. Each has left behind a mark of its presence.

The city's focal point is the **Plaza de la Virgen**. This is at the hub of the old town, a square constructed of marble with central fountain and array of buzzy street cafés. What mark it out as special are the two mighty churches that dominate it. The **Cathedral** is the most important religious building in the city, a beguiling mishmash of Moorish, gothic and Baroque styles built between 1262 and 1426. Alabaster windows bathe the interior in a warm Mediterranean light, suitably mellow to appreciate two paintings by Goya in a private chapel instigated by the renowned Borgia family. Climb the octagonal bell tower, 165ft above the ground, for some spectacular vertiginous views across the old rooftops. Once you've stepped out from the Cathedral, you can step straight into the neighbouring **Basílica** and admire its seventeenth century baroque geography and gaze up at the dome for a beautiful fresco restored to its original glory. But don't look for candles to light: none are allowed in order to save the fresco from the effects of blackening.

→ SILKY SMOOTH

A hop, skip and jump to the south west – so close you're unlikely even to get lost – stands the jewel in Valencia's gothic crown: **La Lonja**. This fabulous one-time Silk Exchange was constructed in the 15C in the days when Valencia was the Spanish capital of prosperity. These days it's a UNESCO World Heritage Site. The façade is impressive enough, but it's the interior that catches your breath with its elegant columns of white stone carved to resemble twisted bolts of silk. There are high vaulted ceilings, wrought-iron chandeliers, a hall with splendid carved figures and impish gargoyles, and a prison tower where disreputable silk merchants would be sent. There's also a hidden garden with orange trees where you can sit and contemplate all you've seen. La Lonja is still in use today – for stamp fairs…

→ MARKET SHARES

Stamp lover or not, you'll come out of the Silk Exchange and face one of Valencia's most popular landmarks, the art nouveau **Central Market**, which has been a colourful centrepiece of local life for eighty years. It's a vast vaulted scrum of activity, one of the largest markets in Europe. The stalls, laden with gleaming tomatoes, hams, peppers and, above all, fish and shellfish, are an experience in themselves, set off by the wonderfully worn tiled and domed surroundings. If you counted the stalls here, you'd eventually reach an astronomical 959, so make sure you don't arrange to meet someone by the one that sells vegetables. They say that Valencians don't do things by halves, which is why there's a second great market to be found in the city: the **Mercado Colón**. This is a beautifully restored place with an ornate façade to the east of town. What it lacks in the fruit and veg stakes, it makes up for in cool cafés and boutiques which now populate most of the interior.

→ FUTURISTIC CITY

Culturally, the city has been propelled into the major league in the last decade. What's taken it there is the exciting **City of Arts and Sciences** complex, which draws over four million visitors each year. Valencian authorities had the inspired notion to build it in the confines of the Turia River Park, the fabulous nine-mile green space created when the river was diverted after flooding in 1957. This futuristic 'city' is made up of four stunning buildings made of white concrete and glass; these are home to a science museum, an opera house, an aquarium and an Imax cinema with a planetarium and laserium. Whether you're planning to go in any of them, or come face-to-face with them on a stroll through the parkland, there's no way you can ignore these weirdly compelling, other-worldly domes and pods.

For the more conventionally-minded, there are two great art galleries in Valencia. Both are on the northern edge of the old town, one just to the south of the river park, the other just to its north. The first, the Valencian Institute of Modern Art (IVAM), is only twenty years old (as of 2009) but surprisingly it's Spain's oldest contemporary art museum. It boasts a brilliant display of sculpture by local artist Julio González, whose expressive iron masks and figures make him a true icon of modern sculpture. His work is backed up by a strong collection of international pop art and photography. Cross the Turia river bed and you'll soon arrive at the city's Museum of Fine Arts, one of the most important in Spain and generally regarded as a 'must see' by visitors. It's an easily identifiable place, with its blue-tiled dome jutting above the park; inside, it's a treasure trove of great works. There's much religious art from the 13C to 15C, mixed in with Bosch's breath-taking Triptych of the Passion. You'll also find works by most of Spain's greats such as Goya, El Greco and Velázquez, as well as plenty of modern art depicting the life of Valencia.

→ CLASSIC CARMEN

This part of town – between the hip and happening Calle Caballeros and the Turia River Park – is also the main area to hit for nightlife and bars. It's

the district known as **Carmen**, and fittingly boasts its very own operatic style. Even for a late-night country like Spain, Valencia has a revered position in the good-time stakes, and Carmen is where it happens. At the weekends the smart clubs and bars are overflowing with locals and tourists alike: there's not much point in arriving before 11pm, while it's a sure-fire bet that the sunshine will be accompanying you on your way back to your hotel. If you're more interested in a quiet stroll than the bright lights, then a good walk in the old town is to the **Serranos Tower** on Plaza Fueros by the side of the park. It's a heavily fortified survivor from the city's medieval walls, and as it doesn't close till 8.30 in the evening, climb up to its battlements as the sun goes down. From here, take in the sparkling views as you look across the lights of the old town and down the length of the Turia River Park, where the spookily illuminated City of Arts and Sciences looks like a multi-pronged night-travelling space voyager.

CALENDAR HIGHLIGHTS

Valencia is a religious city, and nowhere is this more evident than in its festivals, which fill the streets throughout the year. These are not sombre affairs, and fireworks play a significant – and noisy – role on practically every occasion. It all gets underway on 5 January when the Three Wise Men are

VALENCIA IN...

→ ONE DAY

Plaza de la Virgen, La Lonja, central market, City of Arts and Sciences, a trip to the beach

→ TWO DAYS

IVAM (or Valencian Institute of Modern Art), another visit to City of Arts and Sciences, Carmen district nightlife

→ THREE DAYS

Long, slow stroll along the Turia River Park, followed by equally long, relaxing meal of paella at café on Plaza de la Virgen or along the beach promenade lifted onto the City Hall balcony. Later that month the city's patron saint, St Vincent, is honoured in a procession from outside the cathedral. Easter sees Sailors' Holy Week and more rip-roaring processions, while kite-flying at the Turia River Park marks Easter Sunday and Monday. On the second Sunday of May all sorts of festivities coincide with the feast day of Our Lady of the Forsaken. Two months after Easter comes the feast of Corpus Christi (celebrated here for over 650 years), which sees a giant procession take to the streets led fittingly by eye-catching giant figures. As we say, a city of religion…Two festivals with a more secular tone are the Bienal de Valencia, an art-themed event from September to November (every second year, the next is in 2009) and the city's greatest extravaganza, Las Fallas. This is quite simply one of the greatest and craziest festivals in Europe; it always runs from 12-19 March and incorporates eardrum-shattering fireworks, brilliant parades, full-on parties and the ritual burning (on the last day) of satirical figures made from papier-mâché, some as tall as 25m. All this to celebrate the arrival of spring. And to add to its bizarre element, one of the giant figures is saved every year from conflagration, and stored in a special museum – the Guild of Fallas Artists Museum – way to the north of the city.

EATING OUT

Valencia is the city of paella. It was invented here, and this is the place to try it in infinite varieties. For a gargantuan helping, head off to the Las Arenas beach promenade, which is lined with a whole legion of seafood restaurants, anxious to send great platefuls your way. On a hot day (which is most days) the traditional liquid accompaniment is *agua de Valencia*, a potentially lethal combination of orange juice, Cava and vodka. Alternatively, if you're in town for Las Fallas, join a nomadic Fallas community group and eat it on the pavement amidst the firecrackers and parties. Generally speaking, food in Valencia is of the no-nonsense variety. Most restaurants remain very Spanish in character, and if you're not eating paella, then you'll probably be enjoying tapas, with an emphasis on the excellent local cured hams and cheeses. Slightly more 'off the wall' is the local delicacy of *all i pebre*, a mouth-watering meal of stewed eels from the local wetlands served in a garlic and red pepper sauce. The drink to cool down with is *horchata*. It's tigernut milk (a mixture of nuts, cinnamon, sugar and water) and is best enjoyed with a doughy cake. Meal times can throw the unwary visitor. Lunch is often not served until two in the afternoon, and dinner, in general, is never taken before nine at night. Adjust your eating habits accordingly. One thing that will be easy to get used to: service charge is always included in your bill, though if you wish to tip then five to ten per cent is ample.

→ ON THE TILES

One of the best buildings in the city is home to the Ceramics Museum. It's the 15C Palacio del Marqués de Dos Aguas, just south of Plaza de la Virgen, and it's a baroque beauty (it was revamped in 1740). The over-the-top alabaster front door surround is something to behold, as is the sumptuous interior. Oh yes, and it has a superlative range of tiles, too.

VALENCIA-MANISES

A GODELLA **B** Palmaret

Burjassot-Godella

BORBÒTO

Ctra del Pla del Pou

CV 31

TVV

Fíra

V. Andrés E.

Campus

U

St. Joan

BURJASSOT

Burjassot

La Granja

Moncada

Benimàmet

Les Carolines

Canterería

Empalme

Juan

XXIII

Av. de los

PATERNA

Campament

CV 31

CV 31

PALACIO DE CONGRESOS

Av.

Palau de Congresos

Florista

Av. de

Juan XXIII

Sorolla Palace

Novotel Valencia

Palacio de Congresos

Hilton Valencia

Camp

del Turia

Garbí

Benicalap

Tránsits

Benifierri

de

Av. Dr. Peset Aleixandre

Marxalenes

Av.

Reus

Sagunt

Safor

Cortes

Valencianes

Avilés

Burjassot

Reus

Av.

de Sagunto

Maestro

Gil

Campanar

MISLATA

Mislata-Almassil

Antonio

Av.

9 de Octubre

Rodrigo

CAMPANAR

Valencia Centre (Plan II)

San

Nuevo

Ronda

Ronda

Cauce

Míslata

Av. M. de Falla

Paseo

Pechina

Av. de Pérez Galdós

Gran Via de Fernando el Católico

Gran Via de Ramón y Cajal

CATEDRAL

ESTACIÓN DEL NORTE

338

Nou d'Octubre

Av. del Cid

XIRIVELLA

Av. del Cid

Av. Tres

Forques

Río

Marginal

Turia

de

Nuevo

Tres

Picaña

Cruces

Archiduque Carlos

Av. de G. Aguilar

Hospital

Patraix

Jesús

Av. de Peris

Av. de

Giorgeta

Martir

Sant Vicente

Sant Isidre

Av. del Pianista M. Carrasco

CV 36

Camino

València-Sud

V 30

V 30

Ronda

Ronda

Barranc

Picanya

PICANYA

Paiporta

Xiva

Av. del Sur

V 400

Av. Réal de Madrid

BENETÚSSER

Av. del País Valenciano

V 31

PAIPORTA

SEDAVÍ

● Hotel
● Restaurant

A **B**

778

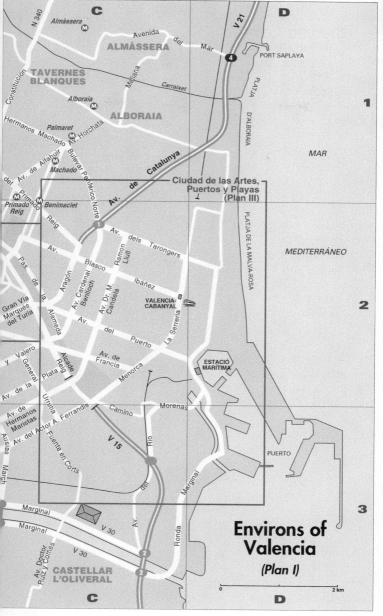

Environs of Valencia

(Plan I)

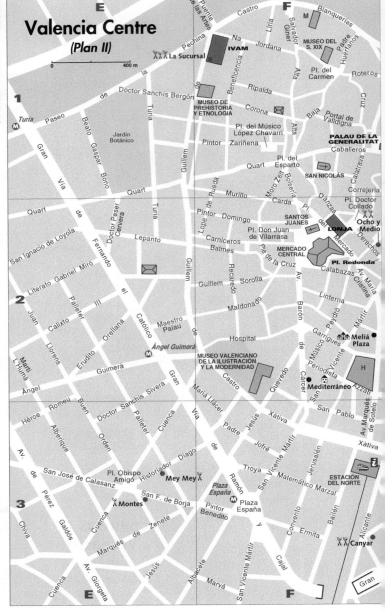

Valencia Centre
(Plan II)

0   400 m

SPAIN - VALENCIA

Puente de las Artes

Castro

Pechina

Na Jordana

Liria

Salvador Giner

Blanquerías

M

MUSEO DEL S. XIX

Padre Huérfanos

La Sucursal

IVAM

Beneficencia

Ripalda

Alta

Pl. del Carmen

Roteros

Doctor Sanchis Bergón

Turia

Corona

Baja

Cruz

Portal de Valldigna

Turia

M

Paseo

Gran Vía

Beato Gaspar Bono

Jardín Botánico

Guillem

Pl. del Músico López Chavarri

Pintor Zariñena

Corona

PALAU DE LA GENERALITAT

Caballeros

Quart

Pl. del Esparto

Calatrava

Correjería

Murillo

Moro Zeit

Boisería

SAN NICOLÁS

Danzas

Pl. Doctor Collado

Quart

Quart

Doctor Peset Cervera

Fernando

Turia

López de Rueda

Pintor Domingo

Carda

Pl. de Carmen

SANTOS JUANES

Ocho y Medio

San Ignacio de Loyola

Lepanto

Carniceros

Pl. Don Juan de Vilarrasa

LONJA

Derechos

Literato Gabriel Miró

Católico

Balmes

Pie de la Cruz

MERCADO CENTRAL

Pl. Redonda

Juan

Calixto III

Palleter

Orellana

Guillem

Recaredo

Sorolla

Av. María Cristina

Calabazas

Llorens

Erudito

Maestro Palau

Maldonado

Barón

Linterna

Pedro

Martir

Meliá Plaza

Martí L'Huma

Angel

Guimerá

Ángel Guimerá

Hospital

Garrigues

Músico Periodista

H

Héroe

Romeu

Buen

Doctor Sanchis Sivera

Palleter

Gran Vía

Castro

María Llácer

MUSEO VALENCIANO DE LA ILUSTRACIÓN Y LA MODERNIDAD

Quevedo

Cárcer

Mediterráneo

San Pablo

Azzati

Av. Marqués de Sotelo

Alberique

Orden

Cuenca

Padre

Jesús

Xàtiva

Jofré

San Vicente Martir

Jerusalén

Xàtiva

Av.

de

San José de Calasanz

Pl. Obispo Amigó

Historiador Diago

Mey Mey

Plaza España

Ramón

Troya

Matemático Marzal

ESTACIÓN DEL NORTE

Chiva

Pérez Galdós

Cuenca

San F. de Borja

Montes

Zenete

Pintor Benedito

M

Plaza España

Convento

Bailén

Alicante

Cuenca

Av. Giorgeta

Marqués de

Jesús

Albacete

Marvá

San Vicente Martir

Calaf

Ermita

Canyar

Gran

E   F

780

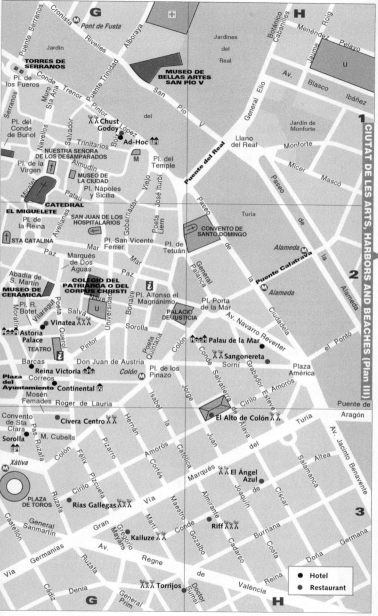

SPAIN - VALENCIA

Ayre Astoria Palace
pl. Rodrigo Botet 5 ⊠ *46002* – ⓜ *Colón* – ℰ *963 98 10 00* – *astoriapalace@ayrehoteles.com* – *Fax 963 98 10 10* – *www.ayrehoteles.com* **G2**
197 rm – ♦105/295 € ♦♦105/375 €, ⌇ 14 € – 7 suites
Rest Vinatea – see below
♦ Urban ♦ Classical ♦
An elegant, classical style and central location are the main selling points of the Ayre Astoria. The executive rooms on the third floor are particularly comfortable. Fitness room with large Jacuzzi.

Palau de la Mar
Smokers rest.
Navarro Reverter 14 ⊠ *46004* – ⓜ *Colón* – ℰ *963 16 28 84* – *hospes.palaudelamar@hospes.es* – *Fax 963 16 28 85* – *www.hospes.es*
65 rm – ♦175/325 € ♦♦175/375 €, ⌇ 19 € **H2**
Rest – Menu 20 €
Rest *Senzone* – Carte 43/46 €
♦ Mansion ♦ Modern ♦
The 'Sea Palace' partially occupies two 19C mansions. These house the hotel's public areas and most of its fully equipped, minimalist-style rooms. Spa centre. The bright, minimalist-style restaurant specialises in creative, Mediterranean cuisine, as well as rice dishes with a contemporary twist.

Meliá Plaza
Smokers rest.
pl. del Ayuntamiento 4 ⊠ *46002* – ⓜ *Xàtiva* – ℰ *963 52 06 12* – *reservas@plazavalencia.com* – *Fax 963 52 04 26* – *www.solmelia.com*
100 rm – ♦♦100/190 €, ⌇ 15 € **Rest** – Menu 26 € **F2**
♦ Chain hotel ♦ Urban ♦ Classical ♦
Following gradual renovation over the years, this comfortable hotel is known for its elegant decor and carefully chosen furnishings. Well-equipped guestrooms. The restaurant serves Mediterranean and international cuisine, alongside a good selection of savoury rice dishes.

Reina Victoria
No smokers rest.
Barcas 4 ⊠ *46002* – ⓜ *Xàtiva* – ℰ *963 52 04 87* – *hreinavictoriavalencia@husa.es* – *Fax 963 52 27 21* – *www.husa.es* **G2**
95 rm – ♦70/160 € ♦♦70/222 €, ⌇ 13 € **Rest** – *(closed August)* Menu 29 €
♦ Chain hotel ♦ Urban ♦ Classical ♦
Beautiful façade and an excellent location just a stone's throw from the city's main museums. Elegant facilities with an appealing lounge area and attractive contemporary-style guestrooms. Simple dining room on the first floor, next to the English style bar.

Ad-Hoc
Smokers rest.
Boix 4 ⊠ *46003* – ℰ *963 91 91 40* – *adhoc@adhochoteles.com* – *Fax 963 91 36 67* – *www.adhochoteles.com* **G1**
28 rm – ♦89/174 € ♦♦89/207 €, ⌇ 12 € **Rest** – *(closed Sunday)* Menu 25 €
♦ Urban ♦ Cosy ♦
This hotel occupies an attractive 19C building. It has a small lounge area and rooms decorated in neo-rustic style with exposed brickwork, wooden beams and clay tiles. The restaurant has a pleasant and relaxing atmosphere, making it the perfect place for an after dinner cocktail.

Sorolla without rest
Convento Santa Clara 5 ⊠ *46002* – ⓜ *Xàtiva* – ℰ *963 52 33 92* – *reservas@hotelsorollacentro.com* – *Fax 963 52 14 65* – *www.hotelsorollacentro.com*
58 rm – ♦88/165 € ♦♦88/230 €, ⌇ 9.50 € **G3**
♦ Urban ♦ Functional ♦
The Sorolla boasts a glazed façade and fully refurbished reception area. A contemporary-style hotel with functional, comfortable guestrooms and modern bathrooms.

Mediterráneo without rest [SAT] [📶] [VISA] [OO] [AE] [O]

Barón de Cárcer 45 ✉ *46001 –* ⓜ *Xàtiva –* ℰ *963 51 01 42 – reservas@*
hotel-mediterraneo.es – Fax 963 51 01 42 – www.hotel-mediterraneo.es
34 rm – ♦65/110 € ♦♦65/160 €, ⚌ 8 €   **F2**
♦ Urban ♦ Functional ♦

This centrally located hotel has a breakfast room on the first floor and classic
bedrooms. Each of which has a fitted carpet and the full range of facilities you
would expect of a hotel of this standard.

Continental without rest [SAT] [VISA] [OO] [AE] [O]

Correos 8 ✉ *46002 –* ⓜ *Colón –* ℰ *963 53 52 82 – continental@contitel.es*
– Fax 963 53 11 13 – www.contitel.es   **G2**
46 rm ⚌ – ♦60/70 € ♦♦69/113 €
♦ Family ♦ Urban ♦ Functional ♦

A central hotel with a contemporary design and functional furniture. The lounge
area is fairly small, but the bedrooms, half of which overlook an interior courtyard,
are comfortable.

Rías Gallegas   Smokers rest. ⇔ [P.] [VISA] [OO] [AE] [O]

Cirilo Amorós 4 ✉ *46004 –* ⓜ *Xàtiva –* ℰ *963 52 51 11*
– riasgallegas@riasgallegas.es – Fax 963 51 99 10 – www.riasgallegas.es
– closed Sunday and Monday dinner   **G3**
Rest – Carte 48/75 €
♦ Inventive ♦ Contemporary ♦

This restaurant has undergone radical changes, both in terms of its decor and cuisine. The menu is now highly creative, featuring seafood specialities and a tasting
menu.

Torrijos (Josep Quintana)   ⇔ [VISA] [OO] [AE] [O]
£3

Dr. Sumsi 4 ✉ *46005 –* ⓜ *Colón –* ℰ *963 73 29 49 – info@*
restaurantetorrijos.com – Fax 963 73 29 49 – www.restaurantetorrijos.com
– closed 10 days in January, 10 days in April, 10 days in September, Sunday
and Monday   **G-H3**
Rest – Menu 80 € – Carte 59/71 € ⅏
Spec. Milhojas de foie-gras con mojama y manzana. Kokotxas de merluza al
pil pil con puré de limón. Pichón con moras, violetas y eucaliptos.
♦ Inventive ♦ Modern ♦

A stylish, modern restaurant with excellent service and an interesting menu based
around the chef's own creations. A beautiful glass-enclosed wine cellar, and two
private rooms, one with views of the kitchen.

La Sucursal (Jorge Bretón)   [VISA] [OO] [AE] [O]
£3

Guillém de Castro 118 ✉ *46003 –* ⓜ *Túria –* ℰ *963 74 66 65 – info@*
restaurantelasucursal.com – Fax 963 92 41 54 – www.restaurantelasucursal.com
– closed 9-29 August, Saturday lunch and Sunday   **F1**
Rest – Carte 55/56 € ⅏
Spec. Arroz meloso de pulpitos y navajas con cubo de all i oli. Salmonete de
roca con emulsión de all i pebre. Sorbete de panacota con hoja de cacao y
torrefactos.
♦ Creative ♦ Modern ♦

This restaurant housed in the Valencian Institute of Modern Art has a public café
on the ground floor and a minimalist dining room on the first floor. A combination
of innovative and traditional cuisine.

Vinatea – Hotel Ayre Astoria Palace   Smokers rest. ⇔ [VISA] [OO] [AE] [O]

Vilaragut 4 ✉ *46002 –* ⓜ *Colón –* ℰ *963 98 10 00 – astoriapalace@*
ayrehoteles.com – Fax 963 98 10 10 – www.ayrehoteles.com
– closed Sunday   **G2**
Rest – Carte 34/54 €
♦ International ♦ Formal ♦

Restaurant with its own separate entrance. The cuisine here is of a high standard
with a particular emphasis on rice dishes. Elegant, classic decor.

XXX
☼

Riff (Bernd Knoller) Smokers rest. 𝘝𝘐𝘚𝘈 ⓒⓞ AE ⓘ

Conde de Altea 18 ✉ *46005 –* Ⓜ *Colón –* 𝒞 *963 33 53 53 – restaurante@restaurante-riff.com – Fax 963 35 31 78 – www.restaurante-riff.com – closed 1-15 September, Sunday and Monday* **H3**

Rest – Menu 69 € – Carte 45/63 € ⅋

Spec. Arroz negro con tocino y bonito marinado. Colita de rape, jugo de trufa negra de Carrión, apio y Oporto. Sopita de chocolate con naranjas caramelizadas, helado de yogur y cardamomo.

◆ Creative ◆ Modern ◆

In keeping with the latest restaurant trends, the Riff produces creative cuisine in a minimalist, designer setting. The restaurant has a delicatessen shop next door.

XX

El Alto de Colón 𝘝𝘐𝘚𝘈 ⓒⓞ AE ⓘ

Jorge Juan 19 ✉ *46004 –* Ⓜ *Colón –* 𝒞 *963 53 09 00 – elaltodecolon@grupoelalto.com – Fax 963 10 68 90 – www.grupoelalto.com – closed Holy Week, 1-24 August, Saturday lunch and Sunday* **H3**

Rest – Carte 44/54 €

◆ Mediterranean ◆ Modernist ◆

This remarkable restaurant located in one of the towers of the Colón market is resolutely modern in style. Attractive tiled ceilings and contemporary Mediterranean cuisine.

XX

Kailuze Smokers rest. ⇔ 𝘝𝘐𝘚𝘈 ⓒⓞ AE

Gregorio Mayáns 5 ✉ *46005 –* Ⓜ *Xàtiva –* 𝒞 *963 35 45 39 – kailuze@menjariviure.com – Fax 963 35 48 93 – www.kailuze.com – closed Holy Week, August, Saturday lunch, Sunday and Bank Holidays*

Rest – Carte 49/57 € **G3**

◆ Traditional ◆ Cosy ◆

Restaurant with an entrance hall and a classical-style dining room. Good traditional cuisine with a contemporary flavour. Excellent service.

XX

El Ángel Azul Smokers rest. ⇔ 𝘝𝘐𝘚𝘈 ⓒⓞ AE ⓘ

Conde de Altea 33 ✉ *46005 –* Ⓜ *Colón –* 𝒞 *963 74 56 56 – www.restauranteelangelazul.com – closed 15 August-15 September, Sunday and Monday* **H3**

Rest – Carte 44/52 €

◆ Inventive ◆ Contemporary actual ◆

A centrally located restaurant with a main dining room designed in an elegant, classical style. Two private lounges also available. Creative à la carte choices plus several tasting menus.

XX

Ocho y Medio ☺ 𝘝𝘐𝘚𝘈 ⓒⓞ AE ⓘ

pl. Lope de Vega 5 ✉ *46001 –* Ⓜ *Xàtiva –* 𝒞 *963 92 20 22 – info@elochoymedio.com – Fax 963 92 21 79 – www.elochoymedio.com – closed Holy Week, Saturday lunch and Sunday* **F2**

Rest – Carte 42/50 €

◆ Creative ◆ Cosy ◆

This welcoming restaurant in a central location has a private bar, neo-rustic style decor, and two dining rooms on the first floor. Innovative, international menu.

XX

Civera Centro ☺ ⇔ 𝘝𝘐𝘚𝘈 ⓒⓞ AE ⓘ

Mosén Femades 10 ✉ *46002 –* Ⓜ *Colón –* 𝒞 *963 52 97 64 – civeracentro@marisqueriascivera.com – Fax 963 46 50 50 – www.marisqueriascivera.com – closed 15-31 July* **G3**

Rest – Carte 38/54 €

◆ Seafood ◆ Sea style ◆

This restaurant specialising in fish, seafood and rice dishes has a tapas bar, maritime inspired dining room and several private rooms. The seafood platter here is particularly memorable.

SPAIN - VALENCIA

XX **Canyar** _VISA_ _OO_ _AE_ _O_

Segorbe 5 ⊠ *46004 –* 𝒞 *963 41 80 82 – Fax 963 41 66 37*
– closed August, Saturday lunch and Sunday **F3**
Rest *– (set menu only)* Menu 75 €
♦ Traditional ♦ Formal ♦

A family-run restaurant decorated in Art Deco style with contemporary touches.
The menu focuses uniquely on fish and seafood, with particular emphasis on
local red prawns from Denia.

XX **Chust Godoy** Smokers rest. ⇧ _VISA_ _OO_ _AE_

Boix 6 ⊠ *46003 –* 🅜 *Colón –* 𝒞 *963 91 38 15 – chustgodoy@chustgodoy.com*
– Fax 963 92 22 39 – www.chustgodoy.com
– closed Holy Week, August, Saturday lunch and Sunday **G1**
Rest *–* Carte 51/58 €
♦ Traditional ♦ Cosy ♦

Run by the chef and his wife, this reputable restaurant has a neo-rustic style dining
room and two private rooms, one with a wine cellar atmosphere. Seasonal menu
with a good selection of rice dishes.

XX **Sangonereta** Smokers rest. _VISA_ _OO_ _AE_

Sorni 31 ⊠ *46004 –* 🅜 *Colón –* 𝒞 *963 73 81 70 – info@sangonereta.com*
– Fax 96 373 81 70 – www.sangonereta.com
– closed Holy Week, Saturday lunch and Sunday **H2**
Rest *–* Carte 37/56 €
♦ Inventive ♦ Contemporary ♦

This restaurant has a contemporary feel, with four small rooms that can also be
used as private dining areas. Creative cuisine, and a tasting menu.

X **Montes** Smokers rest. _VISA_ _OO_ _AE_ _O_

pl. Obispo Amigó 5 ⊠ *46007 –* 🅜 *Pl. Espanya –* 𝒞 *963 85 50 25*
– closed Holy Week, August, Sunday dinner, Monday and Tuesday dinner
Rest *–* Carte 28/34 € **E3**
♦ Traditional ♦ Formal ♦

This restaurant serves traditional cuisine at reasonable prices. It has a small entrance hall, a long dining room, and at the back of the building, the main restaurant
is decorated in classical style with regionally inspired decor.

X **Mey Mey** Smokers rest. _VISA_ _OO_ _AE_ _O_

Historiador Diago 19 ⊠ *46007 –* 🅜 *Pl. Espanya –* 𝒞 *963 84 07 47*
– Fax 961 85 71 76 – www.mey-mey.com
– closed Holy Week and the last 3 weeks in August **E3**
Rest *–* Carte 18/32 €
♦ Chinese ♦ Exotic ♦

Decorated in typical Chinese style, this well-run restaurant has an attractive circular
fountain with colourful fish. Cantonese cuisine with an emphasis on steamed
dishes.

CIUDAD DE LAS ARTES, HARBOURS AND BEACHES *Plan III*

The Westin València No smokers rest. 🛱 🏋 🖻 🖭 💈 🚗

Amadeo de Saboya 16 ⊠ *46010 –* 🅜 *Alameda* _VISA_ _OO_ _AE_ _O_
– 𝒞 *963 62 59 00 – hotel.westinvalencia@westin.com – Fax 963 62 59 09*
– www.westin.com **J1**
130 rm *–* ♟♟135/475 €, ⊑ 24 € – 5 suites
Rest *Oscar Torrijos – (closed Sunday)* Carte approx. 60 €
♦ Luxury ♦ Classical ♦

Located in an attractive historic building with a large interior patio adorned with
pergolas. The Westin offers very spacious, well-appointed rooms decorated in an
elegant, classical style. The gastronomic restaurant is run by a chef with an excellent reputation in the city.

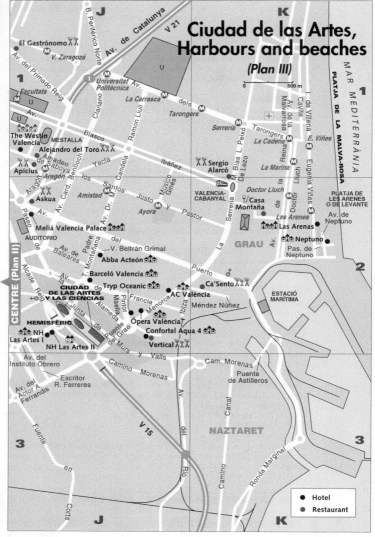

Ciudad de las Artes,
Harbours and beaches
(Plan III)

CENTRE (Plan II)

Hotel
Restaurant

Meliá València Palace ⮕ 🏊 🖥 📶 📞 🧖 VISA ⊗ AE ①

paseo de la Alameda 32 ⊠ *46023* – **Ⓜ** *Aragón* – 𝒞 *963 37 50 37*
– *melia.valencia.palace@solmelia.com* – *Fax 963 37 55 32* – *www.solmelia.com*
233 rm – ♦♦93/385 €, ⌑ 18 € – 5 suites **Rest** – Menu 35 €   **J2**
♦ Chain hotel ♦ Business ♦ Contemporary ♦
A very comfortable hotel with a large lobby, spacious lounge areas and well-appointed guestrooms, most of which have been modernised. A contemporary-style restaurant serving traditional cuisine, including a varied selection of rice dishes.

 Las Arenas ⮕ 🚗 🏠 📶 🏊 🖥 📶 📞 🧖 🚘 VISA ⊗ AE ①

Eugenia Viñes 22 ⊠ *46011* – **Ⓜ** *Neptú* – 𝒞 *963 12 06 00*
– *reservas@hotel-lasarenas.com* – *Fax 963 12 06 16* – *www.h-santos.es*
243 rm – ♦170/535 € ♦♦195/535 €, ⌑ 22 € – 10 suites   **K2**
Rest – Carte approx. 50 €
Rest *Sorolla* – Carte 50/66 €
♦ Luxury ♦ Business ♦ Classical ♦
A luxurious hotel located opposite the beach. Split between three buildings, the hotel boasts comfortable lounge areas, superb meeting rooms, and extremely well-equipped bedrooms.

 Opera València 🏠 📶 📶 📞 🧖 🚘 VISA ⊗ AE ①

Menorca 22 ⊠ *46023* – 𝒞 *902 16 16 20* – *info@hoteloperavalencia.com*
– *Fax 963 31 21 29* – *www.hoteloperavalencia.com*   **J2**
253 rm – ♦♦70/320 €, ⌑ 14 € – 9 suites
Rest – *(closed Sunday dinner and Monday)* Carte 43/54 €
♦ Business ♦ Urban ♦ Modern ♦
This modern hotel boasts several interesting design features, and an attractive garden area with trees and terraces. Well-appointed guestrooms. This glass adorned restaurant is modern in style with a distinctive and imaginative menu.

 NH Las Artes I No smokers rest. 📶 🖥 📶 📞 🧖 🚘 VISA ⊗ AE ①

av. Instituto Obrero 28 ⊠ *46013* – 𝒞 *963 35 13 10* – *nhlasartes@nh-hotels.com*
– *Fax 963 74 86 22* – *www.nh-hotels.com*   **J2**
172 rm – ♦65/200 € ♦♦80/350 €, ⌑ 15 € – 2 suites **Rest** – Menu 25 €
♦ Chain hotel ♦ Urban ♦ Contemporary ♦
Excellent facilities and elegant comfort in this modern hotel. It offers meticulous guestrooms and an extensive range of additional services for guests. A multi-purpose hotel restaurant.

 Neptuno ⮕ 📶 📶 📞 VISA ⊗ AE ①

paseo de Neptuno 2 ⊠ *46011* – **Ⓜ** *Neptú* – 𝒞 *963 56 77 77*
– *reservas@hotelneptunovalencia.com* – *Fax 963 56 04 30*
– *www.hotelneptunovalencia.com*   **K2**
48 rm ⌑ – ♦110/235 € ♦♦125/290 €
Rest *Tridente* – *(closed Monday)* Carte 49/60 €
♦ Beach ♦ Urban ♦ Modern ♦
A contemporary-style hotel situated on the seafront. Well-equipped guestrooms designed in a minimalist style with quality materials and hydromassage bathtubs. The restaurant serves interesting, inventive cuisine, as well as savoury rice dishes.

Barceló València No smokers rest. ⮕ 📶 📶 📞 🧖 🚘
av. de Francia 11 ⊠ *46023* – **Ⓜ** *Amistat*   VISA ⊗ AE ①
– 𝒞 *963 30 63 44* – *valencia@barcelovalencia.com* – *Fax 963 30 68 31*
– *www.barcelovalencia.com*   **J2**
175 rm – ♦♦82/415 €, ⌑ 17 € – 12 suites **Rest** – Menu 25 €
♦ Chain hotel ♦ Modern ♦
A superb location with beautiful views of the City of Arts and Sciences. Spacious, modern guestrooms, as well as a spa on the roof terrace. A contemporary-style restaurant serving traditional and international cuisine.

SPAIN - VALENCIA

Confortel Aqua 4
No smokers rest. 🍴 🛗 🚗 VISA ⓪ AE ⓪

Luis Garcia Berlanga 19-21 ✉ *46023* – ✆ *963 18 71 00*
– *reservasagua4@confortel.com* – *Fax 963 18 71 67*
– *www.confortelhoteles.com*   **J2**
176 rm – 🛏79/105 €, ⌷ 16 € – 8 suites   **Rest** – Menu 20 €
♦ Chain hotel ♦ Modern ♦
A combination of two hotels that share their facilities and lounges. Located above
a shopping centre, the hotel is striking for its interesting combination of design
and functionality.

Abba Acteón
🛗 🕭 🍴 🛗 🚗 VISA ⓪ AE ⓪

Vicente Beltrán Grimal 2 ✉ *46023* – Ⓜ *Ayora* – ✆ *963 31 07 07*
– *reservas-acteon@abbahoteles.com* – *Fax 963 30 22 30*
– *www.abbahotels.com*   **J2**
182 rm – 🛏70/300 € 🛏🛏70/320 €, ⌷ 14.45 € – 5 suites
Rest *Amalur* – *(closed Sunday dinner)* Carte 32/43 €
♦ Chain hotel ♦ Contemporary ♦
A high quality, designer focused hotel. It offers spacious, carefully furnished guestrooms with excellent facilities and marble bathrooms. The bright, modern restaurant is meticulously arranged.

AC València
No smokers rest. 🛗 🕭 🍴 🛗 🚗 VISA ⓪ AE ⓪

av. de Francia 67 ✉ *46023* – Ⓜ *Serrería* – ✆ *963 31 70 00*
– *acvalencia@ac-hotels.com* – *Fax 963 31 70 01*
– *www.ac-hotels.com*   **J2**
172 rm – 🛏🛏75/215 €, ⌷ 15 € – 2 suites   **Rest** – Menu 23 €
♦ Chain hotel ♦ Modern ♦
Modern, functional and geared towards business travellers, this hotel has a spacious lounge and a café divided into different sections. Comfortable guestrooms.
The menu at the hotel's first-floor restaurant is a blend of the traditional and
modern.

Tryp Oceanic
No smokers rest. 🛗 🏊 🕭 📞 🛗 🚗 VISA ⓪ AE ⓪

Pintor Maella 35 ✉ *46023* – Ⓜ *Serrería* – ✆ *963 35 03 00*
– *tryp.oceanic@solmelia.com* – *Fax 963 35 03 11*
– *www.solmelia.com*   **J2**
195 rm – 🛏🛏70/500 €, ⌷ 15 € – 2 suites   **Rest** – Menu 30 €
♦ Chain hotel ♦ Contemporary ♦
This hotel is located next to the City of Arts & Sciences. Pleasant lounge area, well-
appointed rooms and a swimming pool surrounded by a garden. Modern, functional restaurant serving traditional cuisine.

NH Las Artes II *without rest*
🕭 🍴 🛗 🚗 VISA ⓪ AE ⓪

av. Instituto Obrero 26 ✉ *46013* – ✆ *963 35 60 62*
– *exlasartes@nh-hotels.com* – *Fax 963 33 46 83*
– *www.nh-hotels.com*   **J2**
121 rm – 🛏57/150 € 🛏🛏65/240 €, ⌷ 12 €
♦ Chain hotel ♦ Urban ♦ Functional ♦
A new, functional-style hotel with good facilities. Limited lounge area and simple
yet cheerfully decorated bedrooms.

Ca'Sento *(Raúl Aleixandre)*
Smokers rest. VISA ⓪ AE ⓪

Méndez Núñez 17 ✉ *46024* – Ⓜ *Ayora* – ✆ *963 30 17 75*
– *casento@sento.e.telefonica.net*
– *closed 15-31 March, Sunday and Monday*   **K2**
Rest – Menu 110 € – Carte 75/95 €
Spec. Bogavante asado. Cigalas en costra de sal. Canelón de piña con sorbete de piña colada e hinojo.
♦ Inventive ♦ Modern ♦
This long-standing, family-run restaurant has a surprisingly modern layout. Unpretentious dishes based on fish and seafood with a hint of nouvelle cuisine.

XXX 🕄

Alejandro del Toro   Smokers rest. ⬧ VISA AE

Amadeo de Saboya 15 ⊠ 46010 – ⓜ Aragón – ☎ 963 93 40 46
– info@restaurantealejandrodeltoro.com – Fax 96 369 84 86
– www.restaurantealejandrodeltoro.com
– closed Saturday lunch and Sunday   **J1**
Rest – Menu 75/90 € – Carte 53/72 €
Spec. Esponja de huevo de corral con angulas salteadas al ajo y guindilla. Chuleta de vaca con falso tartar de patata. Bizcocho de pasas y gelatina de anís estrellado.
◆ Inventive ◆ Modern ◆

The owner-chef here serves creative cuisine in a spacious dining room with a minimalist aesthetic. Glazed wine cellar that leaves the kitchen visible to diners.

XXX 🕄

Vertical (Jorge Andrés)   ⬧ VISA ⓒ AE ⓞ

Luis Garcia Berlanga 19 ⊠ 46013 – ☎ 963 30 38 00 – info@restaurantevertical.com – Fax 963 30 38 00 – www.resturantevertical.com
– closed Sunday   **J2**
Rest – *(tasting menu only)* Menu 48/58 €
Spec. Crema de foie con calabaza. Arroz de pulpitos y gambas. Bizcocho de dátiles con helado de maracuyá.
◆ Creative ◆ Modern ◆

This unusual restaurant is situated on the roof terrace of the Confortel Aqua 4 hotel. The modern design dining room boasts a beautiful panoramic view. Tasting menu.

XX

Sergio Alarcó   ⬧ VISA ⓒ AE

Marino Blas de Lezo 23 ⊠ 46022 – ⓜ Serrería – ☎ 963 55 22 80
– rest.sergioalarco@hotmail.com – Fax 963 55 22 80
– closed Sunday dinner and Monday   **K1-2**
Rest – Carte 38/47 €
◆ Traditional ◆ Contemporary ◆

Run by the owner-chef, this restaurant has a minimalist style dining room that is striking with its glass-enclosed wine cellar. Menu based on traditional and international cuisine. Excellent service.

XX

Askua   VISA ⓒ AE

Felip María Garín 4 ⊠ 46021 – ⓜ Aragón – ☎ 963 37 55 36
– ricardo@askuarestaurante.com – www.restauranteaskua.com
– closed Christmas, Holy Week, 15 days in August, Saturday lunch, Sunday and Bank Holidays   **J2**
Rest – Carte 45/70 € 🍴
◆ Traditional ◆ Modern ◆

A restaurant with a solid reputation and popular with a well-heeled clientele. The dining room is modern in design, while the restricted menu specialises in grilled meat.

XX

El Gastrónomo   Smokers rest. VISA ⓒ AE

av. Primado Reig 149 ⊠ 46020 – ⓜ Benimaclet – ☎ 963 69 70 36
– elgastronomo@gmail.com – www.elgastronomorestaurante.com
– closed Holy Week, August, Sunday, Monday and Tuesday dinner
Rest – Carte 30/40 €   **J1**
◆ International ◆ Formal ◆

An old-fashioned, highly professional restaurant with traditional decor. Good choice of dishes, including the house speciality, steak tartare.

XX

Apicius   VISA ⓒ AE

Finlandia 7 ⊠ 46010 – ⓜ Aragón – ☎ 963 93 63 01
– info@restaurante-apicius.com – www.restaurante-apicius.com
– closed 20 July-10 August, Sunday and Monday dinner   **J1**
Rest – Carte 42/53 €
◆ Inventive ◆ Functional ◆

This restaurant has an informal dining room, in addition to a functional and contemporary main dining room towards the back of the building. Restricted yet imaginative à la carte choices plus a tasting menu.

Casa Montaña   *VISA* ●● AE

José Benlliure 69 ✉ *46011 –* ⓜ *Serrería –* 𝄐 *963 67 23 14*
– catas@emilianobodega.com – www.emilianobodega.com
– closed Sunday dinner   **K2**
Tapa 2.50 € **Ración** approx. 12 €
◆ Traditional ◆ Tavern ◆

This delightful old restaurant is decorated with traditional features and large wine barrels. It also has a number of dining rooms that can be used for private functions, a good tapas menu and an impressive wine cellar.

AT PALACIO DE CONGRESOS   *Plan I*

Hilton València   ⅃ゟ 🗌 🗌 SAT ⁙♍ ⅏ 🚗 *VISA* ●● AE ⓞ

av. Cortes Valencianas 52 ✉ *46015 –* ⓜ *Beniferri –* 𝄐 *963 03 00 00*
– info.valencia@hilton.com – Fax 963 03 00 01 – www.valencia.hilton.com
269 rm – 🛉🛉100/600 €, ☕ 19.50 € **– 35 suites**   **B1**
Rest *Azahar* – Carte 44/62 €
Rest *Bice* – Carte 40/54 €
◆ Business ◆ Contemporary ◆

Located opposite the Palacio de Congresos, this hotel is particularly geared towards business travellers. It has spacious public areas, meeting rooms and extremely comfortable bedrooms.

Sorolla Palace   ⅃ゟ ⌥ 🗌 SAT ⁙♍ ⅏ 🚗 *VISA* ●● AE ⓞ

av. Cortes Valencianas 58 ✉ *46015 –* ⓜ *Burjassot –* 𝄐 *961 86 87 00*
– reservas@hotelsorollapalace.com – Fax 961 86 87 05
– www.hotelsorollapalace.com   **B1**
246 rm – 🛉79/250 € 🛉🛉79/300 €, ☕ 15 € **– 25 suites   Rest** – Carte 34/52 €
◆ Business ◆ Functional ◆

A hotel popular with business clientele due to its contemporary facilities and proximity to the Palacio de Congresos. Modern, functional guestrooms. An attractive restaurant with several private dining rooms.

Novotel València Palacio de Congresos   No smokers rest.

Valle de Ayora 1 ✉ *46015*   ⅃ゟ ⌥ SAT ⁙♍ ⅏ 🚗 *VISA* ●● AE ⓞ
– ⓜ *Beniferri –* 𝄐 *963 99 74 00 – H3315@accor.com – Fax 963 40 12 94*
– www.novotel.com   **B1**
148 rm – 🛉🛉72/210 €, ☕ 16 € **– 3 suites   Rest** – Menu 25 €
◆ Chain hotel ◆ Business ◆ Functional ◆

This hotel has a decent sized lobby, a variety of lounge areas and pleasantly equipped guestrooms, all with desks and fully equipped bathrooms. The kitchen in this contemporary-style restaurant is in full view of the dining room.

SWEDEN
SVERIGE

PROFILE

→ **AREA:**
449 964 km²
(173 731 sq mi).

→ **POPULATION:**
9 003 000 inhabitants
(est. 2006), density
= 20 per km².

→ **CAPITAL:**
Stockholm 781 000
(conurbation
1 912 000
inhabitants).

→ **CURRENCY:**
Swedish Kronor
(Skr or SEK); rate
of exchange:
SEK 1 = € 0.09
= US$ 0.12
(Dec 2008).

→ **GOVERNMENT:**
Constitutional
parliamentary
monarchy (since
1950). Member of
European Union since
1995.

→ **LANGUAGE:**
Swedish; many
Swedes also speak
good English.

→ **SPECIFIC PUBLIC
HOLIDAYS:**
Epiphany (6 January),
Good Friday (Friday
before Easter),
National Day, 6
June, Midsummer's
Day (Saturday

between June 20-26),
Halloween
(Saturday between
Oct 31-Nov 6),
Christmas Day
(25 December),
Boxing Day
(26 December).

→ **LOCAL TIME:**
GMT + 1 hour in
winter and GMT
+ 2 hours in summer.

→ **CLIMATE:**
Temperate
continental with cold
winters and mild
summers (Stockholm:
January: -3°C, July:
16°C).

→ **INTERNATIONAL
DIALLING CODE:**
00 46 followed by
area code without
the initial **0** and then
the local number.
International
Directory Enquiries:
☏ **079 77.**

→ **EMERGENCY:**
Dial ☏ **112** for
Police, Fire Brigade,
Ambulance, Poison
hot-line, on-call
doctors and 24hr
Roadside breakdown
service.

→ **ELECTRICITY:**
220 volts AC, 50 Hz;

STOCKHOLM
Gothenburg

2-pin round-shaped
continental plugs.

→ **FORMALITIES**
Travellers from the
European Union
(EU), Switzerland,
Iceland and the main
countries of North
and South America
need a national
identity card or
passport (America:
passport required)
to visit Sweden
for less than three
months (tourism or
business purpose).
For visitors from
other countries
a visa may be
required, in addition
to a passport,
especially for those
wishing to stay for
longer than three
months. We advise
you to check with
your embassy before
travelling.

Population: 782 000 (conurbation 1 912 000) – Altitude: sea level

R. Ryan/Stockholm Visitors Board/www.imagebank.swe

Stockholm is the place to go for clean air, big skies and handsome architecture. And water. One of the great beauties of the city, possibly *the* great beauty, is the amount of water that runs through and around it. It's built on fourteen islands, and looks out on twenty four thousand of them. Ferries glide out to the larger ones, and some, such as Vaxholm and Grinda, are great for swimming, others for picnicking, cycling and walking. An astounding two-thirds of the area within the city limits is made up of water, parks and woodland, and there are dozens of little bridges to cross to get from one part of town to another. No wonder Swedes appear so calm and relaxed.

It's in Stockholm that the salty waters of the Baltic meet head-on the fresh waters of Lake Mälaren, reflecting the broad boulevards and elegant buildings that shimmer along their edge. Truly, this is 'The City That Floats On Water'. Chain stores that seem so unavoidable in other European cities seem to have given Stockholm a wide berth, while domes, spires and turrets dot a skyline that in the summertime never truly darkens. It wasn't too long ago that this was a city with practically no nightlife, but now it rivals other European capitals for its after dark attractions. Admirers call Stockholm the most beautiful city in the world – day or night, you can see their point.

LIVING THE CITY

The city of Stockholm is enough to give you double vision. Alongside the important looking buildings is an almost rural quality of open space and water. The heart of the city is the Old Town, **Gamla Stan**, full of alleyways and lanes little changed from their medieval origins. Just to the north is the modern centre, **Norrmalm**, the part of the city with the least pastoral appeal: a buzzing quarter of shopping malls, restaurants and bars. East of Gamla Stan you reach the small island of **Skeppsholmen**, which boasts fine views of the waterfront. Directly north from here is **Östermalm**, an area full of grand residences, while south-east is the lovely park island of Djurgården, where you can find two of the city's most popular attractions. South and west of Gamla Stan are the two areas where Stockholmers like to hang out, the trendy (and hilly) Södermalm, and Kungsholmen.

PRACTICAL INFORMATION

ARRIVAL-DEPARTURE

Stockholm Arlanda Airport is 40km northwest of the city. The Arlanda Expresso train takes 20min to Centralstation and departs every 15min. The airport bus (Flygbuss) to Cityterminalen takes 40min. A taxi will cost around SEK 375.

TRANSPORT

Invest in a Stockholm Card, available from tourist offices. It is valid for one, two or three days and offers free travel on public transport, including sightseeing boats, and free entry to over 70 attractions (museums, galleries and castles).

If you're using public transport, it's best to go by metro, as it offers a more direct route than the buses. The No 7 tram, which runs throughout the summer, takes in quite a few of the main attractions.

You can buy single tickets for the bus, tram and metro, but if you're planning to do lots of travelling about the city, you can also get passes which cover a whole day or three whole days.

EXPLORING STOCKHOLM

Stockholm's old town, Gamla Stan, is the focal point of any visit, and that's as true now as it was in the thirteenth

century, when its naturally fortuitous position between two channels of water made it the ideal setting for a fortress and the foundations of the city. It's a wonderfully enticing tangle of cobbled streets, small squares and gabled roofs. Remarkably, over eight hundred years it's been untouched by war or even the merest rumblings of local dissent. Its most imposing building is the Royal Palace, which has 600 rooms and good accessibility for the public. What it doesn't have is any royalty: they upped sticks and moved away to Drottningholm further along Lake Mälaren. What it retains is a museum dedicated to the Nobel Prize, art shops, galleries, antique shops, and the joyous feeling that although you might get lost in its maze of medieval stone streets, you'll reach water before too long. Near the opulent German Church (Tyska Kyrkan) try and find Marten Trotzigs Grand, the narrowest street in Stockholm. It's little more than a yard wide and has a beguiling lamp-lit atmosphere (it's also pretty steep).

➜ QUAY MOMENTS

To escape any feelings of claustrophobia, head to the adjacent island of **Riddarholmen**, stand on its quay, breathe in its blasts of fresh air, and take in awesome views of **Lake Mälaren**, as well as the green heights of Southern Stockholm, and the vertical red-brick surprise of the City Hall, which seems to thrust straight out of the water. This is a graceful and imposing building, made up of eight million bricks, black granite reliefs, topped by three golden crowns; its first floor Golden Hall is decorated with nearly 20lb of gold leaf and eighteen million pieces of mosaic. If you're here in the summer, a great way of appreciating the visual splendour of the City Hall is to get to Riddarholmen at 3am (yes, three in the morning) and marvel at the changing hues of the early-hour light, from pastel blue to misty salmon, taking in the subtly changing shades of the brickwork. Catch up on your sleep later.

➜ GET SKEPPTICAL

With all this light, shade and water, the last thing you might feel like doing is submerging yourself indoors, but if you miss the museums of Stockholm, you miss an essential part of the city's character. Actually, most of them are conveniently located on the city's 'museum island', **Skeppsholmen**. As you approach it, you see its most striking edifice, the **National Museum of Fine Arts**, over 200 years old, with a superb old masters collection, including works by Rembrandt, El Greco and Canaletto, and more recent paintings by Gauguin, Cézanne and Renoir. Further along the island are three more intriguing museums: the Museum of Modern Art, with works by Matisse, Klee and Modigliani; the Architecture Museum, which showcases one thousand years of Scandinavian design; and the Museum of Far Eastern Antiquities, a former stable with an enormous collection of Asian art. The two most popular attractions, though, are just to the east in the 'National City Park' of **Djurgården**. This unspoiled island of natural beauty contains miles of trails, grand oaks, handy restaurants and coffee shops, and two world-famous museums. The first of these, the **Vasa Museum**, is commonly considered the very best Stockholm has to offer, even though it only features one exhibit! The *Vasa* warship sank on its maiden voyage in Stockholm harbour in 1628, and was preserved for 300 years beneath the Baltic. Raised in 1961, it now stands magnificently complete in its vast 'hangar' by the water. See it, and prepare to gasp…

Inland from here is the world's most famous open-air museum, **Skansen**, located perfectly atop a hill and covering seventy-four wondrous acres. Skansen's over a hundred years old, and contains over a hundred and fifty reconstructed buildings depicting the lives of Swedes over different eras. You can see everything from windmills and farms to an entire township. It's beautifully put together, with not an ounce of tackiness, and even serves you delicious traditional food. In winter, warm up with a big bowl of soup.

➜ DANCING QUEEN TO DRAMA QUEENS

Culture lovers can get a double hit in the smartly affluent area of **Östermalm**, 'over the water' northwest of Skansen. The Music Museum not only charts the history of music in Sweden but also allows visitors to experiment with the different instruments they find there. And yes, there's a section given over to ABBA. Leave here, and just in front of you is the suitably dramatic looking Royal Theatre of Drama, the place where Garbo, both Bergmans and Von Sydow cut their teeth. It's a great place to get your own canines into a bit of Swedish angst, though obviously, if you haven't mastered the language, then actions may speak louder than words.

One part of the Swedish capital not so easy to negotiate for the cycling fraternity is the southern island of **Södermalm**, which has steeply craggy cliffs plunging down into the sea and the lake. Buildings look a bit perilous as they perch on the edge, but venture into their midst and come across a green and pleasant land. As in other European cities, this is a working class area that's been 'gentrified' to the extent that it contains some strikingly trendy bars, fashion boutiques and cafés, along with a number of charming small parks. And, of course, some of the views from these dizzy heights looking towards the city centre are spectacular.

➜ WEST END IS NIGH

The western island of Stockholm, **Kungsholmen**, is where you'll find the previously mentioned City Hall; apart from that it has a rather sedate, neighbourhood feel, but one that's gradually acquiring a real buzz as swish little restaurants, bars and bistros start to pop up all over it. There was a bit of a 'big bang' around here a few years ago with the opening of a particularly smart boutique mall, and since then it's been rivalling Södermalm as the hippest place in town. It also boasts a promenade much loved by Stockholmers. The landscaped Norr Mälarstrand runs for a mile or so all the way along the water's edge from the City Hall, giving lovely lake views to the south, and proving once again that in this city the urban is always likely to play second fiddle to the pastoral.

CALENDAR HIGHLIGHTS

The Swedes may be modern in outlook, but culturally speaking they like to look to their past. Celebrations can tend towards the traditional, and they don't come much more traditional than the January Viking Run, a skiing race, starting in the town of Uppsala and finishing in Stockholm. Viking influence is to the fore again on Walpurgis Night, at the end of April, when bonfires light up the night sky in celebration of the arrival of Spring: various city venues reflect the night's activities. In June, the Stockholm Marathon begins and ends at the Olympic Stadium, while Gamla Stan provides a fitting

STOCKHOLM IN...

➜ ONE DAY
Gamla Stan, City Hall, Vasa or Skansen museums, meal on Södermalm

➜ TWO DAYS
Coffee in Kungsholmen, museums in Skeppsholmen, Djurgården stroll, another evening in Södermalm

➜ THREE DAYS
Shopping in Norrmalm, boat trip round the archipelago

backdrop for the Early Music Festival, featuring music of pre-1750. Everyone heads over to Skansen Museum on Midsummer Eve to dance and drink the night (which looks like day, of course) away…there's no guarantee that the drinks are any cheaper than usual, though. July's Jazz Festival also includes blues, soul and reggae, while in the run-up to Christmas there's the world-famous Nobel Prize Day, around 10th December, and St Lucia Day (13th) when candles burn in coffee shops and restaurants, and young girls are crowned with wreaths of lighted candles: it's all to signify the light that will eventually break through winter's gloom.

EATING OUT

Everyone thinks that eating out in Stockholm is invariably expensive, but with a little forward planning it doesn't have to be. In the middle of the day, most restaurants and cafés offer very good value set menus. Keep in mind that, unlike in Southern Europe, the Swedes like to get their eating done early. Lunch is considered fair game from 11am (until 2pm), while dinner is on the go from 6pm, and they might want to start putting chairs on the tables sometime after 9pm. Don't nip out for breakfast: there are few places open in the early morning. Picking wild food is a birthright of Swedes, and there's no law to stop you going into forest or field to pick blueberries, cloudberries, cranberries, strawberries, mushrooms and the like. This love of outdoor, natural fare means that Stockholmers have a special bond with menus which relate to the seasons: keep your eyes open for restaurants that feature *husmanskost,* or traditional Swedish dishes. Try and find somewhere with a good **smörgåsbord**: if you're lucky, this should include soup, herring, warm potatoes and gravlax, followed by salads, cold meats, meatballs, beef and chicken, washed down with beer. As for tipping, well, the service charge is included in the bill, but charming service (common in Stockholm) might make you add on a bit more for the waiting staff.

→ FULL STEAM AHEAD

More memorable than a trip on a motorised launch - why not head out from Stockholm's waterfront on a full-blown steamship? There are about ten plying the archipelago and Lake Mälaren. There used to be hundreds, but the introduction of car travel put paid to most of them. One blast from the funnel and you'll be smitten.

Apart from Södermalm, Stockholm's a pretty flat city that is ideal for cycling around. Alternatively, see its natural wonders from above – this is a rare example of a world capital that allows hot-air balloons to fly over.

Catching the metro (or tunnelbana, to be precise) in Stockholm is less of a chore than in other cities. That's because it's the world's longest art gallery! It displays artwork by the city's most creative talents along its underground system – so watch out for paintings, mosaics, sculptures and murals where you wouldn't normally expect to find them.

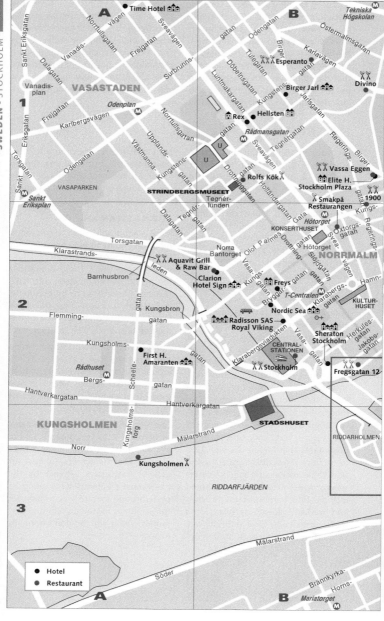

Time Hotel

A

B

Tekniska
Högskolan

Norrtullsgatan
vägen

Sveavägen

Freigatan

Surbrunns-

gatan

Odengatan

Östermalmsgatan

Sankt Eriksgatan

Vanadis-

Dalagatan

Tulegatan

Döbelnsgatan

Birger

Karlavägen

Esperanto

gatan

Divino

Vanadis-
plan

VASASTADEN

Luntmakargatan

Kungstens-

Jarlsgatan

Birger Jarl

Frejgatan

Odenplan

Norrtullsgatan

gatan

Hellsten

1

Karlbergsvägen

Uplands-

Rex

Rådmansgatan

Sveavägen

Tegnérgatan

Regeringsgatan

Sankt Eriksgatan

Odengatan

Västmanna-

gatan

Kungstens-

gatan

Drottninggatan

Rolfs Kök

Vassa Eggen

Elite H.
Stockholm Plaza

Birger

Torsgatan

VASAPARKEN

STRINDBERGSMUSEET

Tegnér-
lunden

Tegnér-
gatan

Hollandargatan

Smak på
Restaurangen

1900

Sankt
Eriksplan

Dalagatan

gatan

Gata

Kungs-

Torsgatan

Klarastrands-

Torsgatan

Norra
Bantorget

Olof Palmes

Drottning

KONSERTHUSET

Hötorget

Oxtorgs-
gatan

Sveavägen

Regerings-

Hötorget

NORRMALM

Barnhusbron

leden

gatan

Aquavit Grill
& Raw Bar

Vasa-

Kungs-

gatan

Sturegatan

2

Flemming-

gatan

Kungsbron

Clarion
Hotel Sign

Freys

Bryggar

T-Centralen

gatan

Klarabergs-

Hamn-

KULTUR-
HUSET

Kungsholms-

gatan

Nordic Sea

Radisson SAS
Royal Viking

Klarabergsviadukten

Sheraton
Stockholm

Herkules-
gatan

Jakobs-
gatan

Rådhuset

First H.
Amaranten

Scheele-

gatan

Bergs-

gatan

CENTRAL-
STATIONEN

Vasa-

gatan

Stockholm

Fregsgatan 12

Hantverkargatan

Hantverkargatan

KUNGSHOLMEN

Kungsholms-
torg

Mälarstrand

STADSHUSET

RIDDARHOLMEN

Norr

Kungsholmen

RIDDARFJÄRDEN

3

Mälarstrand

● Hotel
● Restaurant

Söder

A

Brännkyrka-

Horns-

B

Mariatorget

798

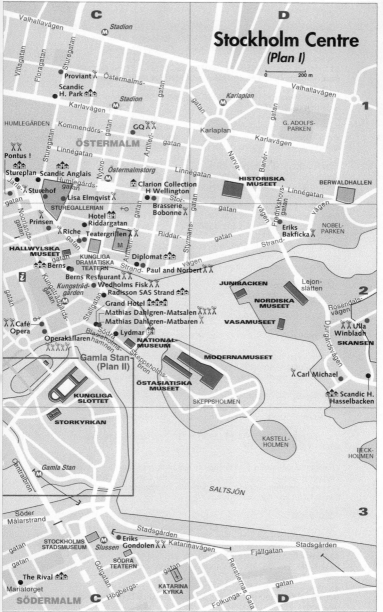

Stockholm Centre
(Plan I)

0   200 m

Valhallavägen

Stadion

Sturegatan

Floragatan

Villagatan

Proviant ✕

Scandic
H. Park 🏠🏠

Karlavägen

Stadion

M

Karlaplan

M

Valhallavägen

G. ADOLFS-
PARKEN

HUMLEGÅRDEN

Kommendörs-

Karlaplan

Karlavägen

GQ ✕✕

gatan

Linnégatan

ÖSTERMALM

Artilleri-

gatan

Banér-

Narva-

Fredrikshovs-

HISTORISKA
MUSEET

Linnégatan

BERWALDHALLEN

Pontus !

Stureplan Scandic Anglais

Stureplan

Humlegårds-

🏠🏠

🏠🏠

Nybro-

Östermalmstorg

Linnégatan

M

gatan

Norrlands-

Jarls-

gatan

Sturehof

Lisa Elmqvist ✕

STUREGALLERIAN

Clarion Collection
H Wellington

Stor-

gatan

NOBEL-
PARKEN

Eriks
Bakficka ✕

Prinsen

Hotel 🏨
Riddargatan

Riche

Teatergriffen ✕✕

M

Brasserie
Bobonne ✕

Riddar-

Strand-

HALLWYLSKA
MUSEET

🏠🏠 Berns

KUNGLIGA
DRAMATISKA
TEATERN

Diplomat 🏠🏠

Paul and Norbert ✕✕

Stymans-

vägen

JUNIBACKEN

Lejons-
slätten

Kungsträd-
gården

Berns Restaurant ✕✕

Wedholms Fisk ✕✕

Radisson SAS Strand 🏠🏠

Stallgatan

Kungsträdgårds-

gatan

NORDISKA
MUSEET

Rosendals-
vägen

✕✕ Café
Opera

Grand Hotel 🏠🏠🏠

Mathias Dahlgren-Matsalen ✕✕✕✕

Mathias Dahlgren-Matbaren ✕

Lydmar 🏨

VASAMUSEET

Ulla
Winbladh ✕✕

Djurgårdsvägen

SKANSEN

Operakällaren ✕✕✕✕

Blasieholms-

hamnen

Södra

Blasieholmshamnen

NATIONAL-
MUSEUM

Skeppsholms-

bron

MODERNAMUSEET

Carl Michael ✕

Gamla Stan
(Plan II)

KUNGLIGA
SLOTTET

ÖSTASIATISKA
MUSEET

SKEPPSHOLMEN

🏠🏠 Scandic H.
Hasselbacken

STORKYRKAN

Centralbron

Gamla Stan

M

KASTELL-
HOLMEN

BECK-
HOLMEN

SALTSJÖN

Söder
Mälarstrand

Stadsgården

Eriks
Gondolen ✕✕

Katarinavägen

Stadsgården

Renstiernas Gata

STOCKHOLMS
STADSMUSEUM

Slussen

Götgatan

SÖDRA
TEATERN

Högbergs-

The Rival 🏠🏠

Mariatorget

SÖDERMALM

KATARINA
KYRKAN

Folkunga-

gatan

Grand Hôtel ≤ ᠘ ⅏ ㊧ ↳ 🖾 ℉ ﹩ 🚗 VISA ⓪ ᴁ ①

Södra Blasieholmshamnen 8 ⊠ *S-103 27* – Ⓜ *Kungsträdgården*
– ℰ *(08) 679 35 00* – *info@grandhotel.se* – *Fax (08) 611 86 86*
– *www.grandhotel.se*   **C2**
331 rm – 🛉3600/6600 SEK 🛉🛉6900 SEK, ⌖ 255 SEK – 37 suites
Rest *Mathias Dahlgren-Matsalen and Mathias Dahlgren-Matbaren*
– see below
Rest *The Veranda* – ℰ *(08) 679 35 86* – Menu 580 SEK (dinner)
– Carte 430/705 SEK
◆ Grand Luxury ◆ Classic ◆
Sweden's top hotel occupies a late 19C mansion on the waterfront overlooking the
Royal Palace and Old Town. Existing rooms refurbished; elegant new rooms boast
latest facilities. The Veranda boasts famous smörgåsbord.

Radisson SAS Royal Viking ᠘ ⅏ 🖾 ↳ 🖾 ⓦ ﹩ 🚗

Vasagatan 1 ⊠ *S-101 24* – Ⓜ *T-Centralen* – ℰ *(08)*   VISA ⓪ ᴁ ①
506 540 00 – *sales.royal.stockholm@radissonsas.com* – *Fax (08) 506 540 01*
– *www.royalviking.stockholm.radissonsas.com*   **B2**
456 rm – 🛉1095/2995 SEK 🛉🛉1295/2995 SEK, ⌖ 125 SEK – 3 suites
Rest *Stockholm Fisk* – ℰ *(08) 506 541 02 (Closed lunch Saturday and Sunday)*
Menu 385 SEK (dinner) – Carte 356/585 SEK
◆ Business ◆ Modern ◆
Large hotel in central location, with spacious, busy lobby. Panoramic Sky Bar with
impressive views over Stockholm and 9 floors of comfortable bedrooms. Stylish
contemporary restaurant offers an array of seafood dishes.

Sheraton Stockholm ≤ ㊰ ᠘ ⅏ ㊧ 🖾 ↳ 🖾 ℉ ﹩ 🚗

Tegelbacken 6 ⊠ *S-101 23* – Ⓜ *T-Centralen* – ℰ *(08)*   VISA ⓪ ᴁ ①
412 34 00 – *sheraton.stockholm.@sheraton.com* – *Fax (08) 412 34 09*
– *www.sheratonstockholm.com*   **B2**
459 rm – 🛉3345 SEK 🛉🛉3545 SEK, ⌖ 245 SEK – 6 suites
Rest *360°* – ℰ *(08) 412 34 72 (buffet lunch)* Menu 245 SEK – Carte 385/585 SEK
◆ Business ◆ Modern ◆
Contemporary international hotel overlooking Gamla Stan, with ample lobby and
offering comprehensive business facilities. Spacious bedrooms, refurbished in a
modern style. Open-plan all day restaurant serving international dishes.

Radisson SAS Strand ⅏ ㊧ 🖾 ↳ 🖾 ℉ ﹩ VISA ⓪ ᴁ ①

Nybrokajen 9 ⊠ *S-103 27* – Ⓜ *Kungsträdgården* – ℰ *(08) 506 640 00*
– *sales.strand.stockholm@radissonsas.com* – *Fax (08) 506 640 02*
– *www.strand.stockholm.radissonsas.com*   **C2**
133 rm – 🛉1995/2995 SEK 🛉🛉2295/3295 SEK, ⌖ 180 SEK – 19 suites
Rest – Carte 290/535 SEK
◆ Business ◆ Classic ◆
Characterful old world architecture in red brick overlooking the harbour. Most
bedrooms feature elegant décor and traditional furniture although the newest
are more contemporary in style. Open-plan lobby restaurant with accomplished
Swedish and international cooking.

Diplomat ㊰ ⅏ ↳ 🖾 ℉ ﹩ VISA ⓪ ᴁ ①

Strandvägen 7c ⊠ *S-104 40* – Ⓜ *Kungsträdgården* – ℰ *(08) 459 68 00*
– *info@diplomathotel.com* – *Fax (08) 459 68 20* – *www.diplomathotel.com*
– *Closed 21-28 December*   **C2**
126 rm – 🛉1725/2595 SEK 🛉🛉2475/3295 SEK, ⌖ 180 SEK – 4 suites
Rest *T Bar* – ℰ *(08) 459 68 02 (brunch Saturday and Sunday)*
Carte 315/578 SEK
◆ Traditional ◆ Classic ◆
Elegant 1911 Art Nouveau building converted into hotel from diplomatic lodgings
pleasantly located overlooking the harbour. Traditional and contemporary
bedrooms. A popular terrace adjoins contemporary-style hotel restaurant offering
traditional Swedish cooking.

SWEDEN - STOCKHOLM

Berns
⤶ 🖭 ℐ 🛁 VISA ⚏ AE ⓘ

Näckströmsgatan 8, Berzelii Park ⊠ S-111 47 – Ⓜ Kungsträdgården
– 𝒞 (08) 566 322 00 – sales@berns.se – Fax (08) 566 322 30 – www.berns.se
61 rm ⊇ – ⫟2650/2950 SEK ⫟⫟4200 SEK – 4 suites **C2**
Rest *Berns Restaurant* – see below
♦ Business ♦ Stylish ♦

Boutique hotel with a modern minimalist interior décor verging on trendy; details in cherry wood and marble. Modern facilities in bedrooms, some have balconies.

Nordic Light
🖪 ℐ ⅙ 🅰🅲 ⤶ 🖭 ℐ 🛁 🚗 VISA ⚏ AE ⓘ

Vasaplan ⊠ S-101 37 – Ⓜ T-Centralen – 𝒞 (08) 505 630 00
– info@nordichotels.se – Fax (08) 505 630 90 – www.nordiclighthotel.com
175 rm – ⫟1530/1730 SEK ⫟⫟1730/3170 SEK, ⊇ 180 SEK **B2**
Rest – Carte 255/450 SEK ⅋⅋
♦ Business ♦ Design ♦

Stylish, modern hotel, whose harmonious black and white designer décor features a symphony of lights on the Nordic Lights theme. Cool bar and lounge. Comfortable bedrooms. Modern restaurant in the main hall: modish international cooking.

First H. Amaranten
🖪 ℐ ⅙ 🅰🅲 rest ⤶ 🖭 ℐ 🛁 🚗

Kungsholmsgatan 31 ⊠ S-104 20 – Ⓜ Rådhuset VISA ⚏ AE ⓘ
– 𝒞 (08) 692 52 00 – amaranten@firsthotels.se – Fax (08) 652 62 48
– www.firsthotels.com/amaranten **A2**
423 rm ⊇ – ⫟1000/2050 SEK ⫟⫟1300/2450 SEK
Rest *Amaranten* – *(Closed Saturday lunch and Sunday)* Menu 265/337 SEK
– Carte 271/585 SEK
♦ Business ♦ Modern ♦

Modernised, commercial hotel conveniently located with easy access to subway. Stylish, quiet public areas with American Bar; compact but up-to-date bedrooms. Stylish modern eating area with a large menu of modern Swedish cooking.

Scandic H. Park
🚗 ℐ ⅙ ⤶ 🖭 ℐ 🛁 🚗 VISA ⚏ AE ⓘ

Karlavägen 43 ⊠ S-102 46 – Ⓜ Stadion – 𝒞 (08) 517 348 00
– park@scandichotels.com – Fax (08) 517 348 11 – www.scandichotels.com/park
193 rm ⊇ – ⫟990/2690 SEK ⫟⫟1090/2790 SEK – 8 suites **C1**
Rest *Park Village* – Carte 245/515 SEK
♦ Business ♦ Functional ♦

Convenient location by one of the city's prettiest parks (view from suites). All rooms a good size, modern and comfortable with good range of facilities. Contemporary lounge. Modern restaurant with small summer terrace; traditional Swedish and international fare.

Birger Jarl
🖪 ℐ ⅙ ⤶ 🖭 ℐ 🛁 🚗 VISA ⚏ AE ⓘ

Tulegatan 8 ⊠ S-104 32 – Ⓜ Rådmansgatan – 𝒞 (08) 674 18 00
– info@birgerjarl.se – Fax (08) 673 73 66 – www.birgerjarl.se **B1**
230 rm ⊇ – ⫟890/2170 SEK ⫟⫟2900 SEK – 5 suites
Rest – *(Closed lunch Saturday and Sunday)* Carte 327/608 SEK
♦ Business ♦ Modern ♦

Modern hotel in quieter part of city. Lobby features art and sculpture displays. Individually styled bedrooms; 17 of them decorated by Swedish artists of international repute. Simple and stylish restaurant with unfussy Swedish cooking.

Time Hotel *without rest*
ℐ ⅙ ⤶ 🖭 ℐ 🛁 🚗 VISA ⚏ AE ⓘ

Vanadisvägen 12 ⊠ 113 46 – Ⓜ Odenplan – 𝒞 (08) 545 47 300
– info@timehotel.se – Fax (08) 545 47 3 01 – www.timehotel.se **A1**
144 rm ⊇ – ⫟1195/1645 SEK ⫟⫟1395/3995 SEK
♦ Business ♦ Modern ♦

Brand new business hotel in residential area, featuring spacious, functional rooms in warm colours. Contemporary breakfast room with buffet. Popular lounge bar.

Scandic Anglais

Humlegardsgatan 23 ✉ *102 44* – **Ⓜ** *Östermalmstorg* – 𝒞 *(08) 517 340 00*
– *anglais@scandichotels.com* – *Fax (08) 517 340 11* – *www.scandichotels.com*
217 rm ⌷ – †1190/3290 SEK ††1290/3390 SEK – 13 suites **C1**
Rest – *(buffet lunch)* Menu 145 SEK – Carte dinner 260/608 SEK

♦ Chain hotel ♦ Modern ♦

Recently refurbished hotel featuring large, stylishly-furnished lobby, popular
ground floor bar and contemporary bedrooms, ideal for the business traveller.
Modern open plan restaurant serves international cuisine.

Clarion H. Sign

Östra Järnvägsgatan 35 ✉ *S-101 26* – **Ⓜ** *T-Centralen* – 𝒞 *(08) 676 98 00*
– *cl.sign@choice.se* – *Fax (08) 676 98 99* – *www.clarionsign.com* **B2**
558 rm ⌷ – †1095/2995 SEK ††1095/3195 SEK
Rest *Aquavit Grill & Raw Bar* – see below

♦ Business ♦ Chain hotel ♦ Modern ♦

This large, purpose-built hotel opened in early 2008, overlooks a square and
boasts comprehensive conference facilities. Each floor of rooms boast a different
design. Rooftop pool heated to 35 degrees!

Stureplan

Birger Jarlsgatan 24 ✉ *S-11434* – **Ⓜ** *Östermalmstorg* – 𝒞 *(08) 440 66 00*
– *reservation@hotelstureplan.se* – *Fax (08) 440 66 11* – *www.hotelstureplan.se*
– *Closed July and 23-27 December* **C1**
101 rm ⌷ – †1350/4350 SEK ††1350/4350 SEK
Rest *Per Lei* – *(Closed July, Christmas, Saturday lunch, Sunday and Monday)*
Menu 320/445 SEK – Carte 505/520 SEK

♦ Traditional ♦ Classic ♦

Converted 19C building with classic Gustavian interiors juxtaposed with modern
amenities. Individually styled bedrooms; Loft rooms the more contemporary,
Cabin rooms more compact. Flavoursome, Italian influenced cooking.

Lydmar

Södra Blasieholmshamnen 2 ✉ *S-103 24* – **Ⓜ** *Kungsträdgården*
– 𝒞 *(08) 223 160* – *info@lydmar.com* – *Fax (08) 223 1 70* – *www.lydamar.com*
46 rm ⌷ – †2500 SEK ††3500/5500 SEK **C2**
Rest – Carte 445/555 SEK

♦ Townhouse ♦ Stylish ♦

Enviable location for this stylish townhouse, opened in late 2008. Its striking art,
modern facilities and easy-going atmosphere appeal to a creative clientele.
Relaxed dining room doubles as the bar, with a flexible menu.

Elite H. Stockholm Plaza

Birger Jarlsgatan 29 ✉ *S-103 95* – **Ⓜ** *Östermalmstorg*
– 𝒞 *(08) 566 220 00* – *info.stoplaza@elite.se* – *Fax (08) 566 220 20*
– *www.elite.se* **B1**
139 rm ⌷ – †1250/2300 SEK ††1650/2500 SEK – 4 suites
Rest *Vassa Eggen* – see below

♦ Business ♦ Functional ♦

Well preserved 1884 building with up-to-date comforts. Compact, well-run commercial hotel with conference rooms and basement sauna. Some rooms
refurbished in a modish style.

Freys

Bryggargatan 12 ✉ *S-101 31* – **Ⓜ** *T-Centralen* – 𝒞 *(08) 506 213 00*
– *freys@freyshotels.com* – *Fax (08) 506 213 13* – *www.freyshotels.com*
– *Closed 22-28 December* **B2**
123 rm ⌷ – †890/2390 SEK ††1090/2590 SEK – 1 suite
Rest *Belgobaren* – *(Closed Sunday lunch)* Menu 295 SEK (dinner)
– Carte 348/460 SEK

♦ Business ♦ Functional ♦

Located near Central station with good conference facilities and first-floor terrace.
Fairly compact rooms with informal furnishings; superior rooms with balconies.
Belgian specialities, including more than 100 different beers, on exclusive menu.

SWEDEN - STOCKHOLM

Hotel Riddargatan without rest 　　🎉 ⁽ᵗ⁾ 𝒱𝒾𝒮𝒜 ⓪ 🄰🄴 ①

Riddargatan 14 ☒ S-114 35 – **Ⓜ** *Östermalmstorg –* 𝒞 *(08) 555 730 00*
– hotelriddargatan@profilhotels.se – Fax (08) 555 730 11
– www.profilhotels.se
– Closed Christmas　　　　　　　　　　　　　　　　　**C2**
75 rm ⌂ – ⛬1225/2150 SEK ⛬⛬1425/2550 SEK – 3 suites
♦ Business ♦ Modern ♦

Modern, boutique-style hotel in quiet location behind the Royal Dramatik Theatre, near shops and restaurants. Functional, modern bedrooms; 20 new rooms boast designer styling.

Hellsten without rest 　　🎉 ᵻ 🎉 🄲🄼 ⁽ᵗ⁾ ⚁ 𝒱𝒾𝒮𝒜 ⓪ 🄰🄴 ①

Luntmakargatan 68 ☒ 113 51 – **Ⓜ** *Rådmannsgatan*
– 𝒞 (08) 661 86 00 – hotel@hellsten.se – Fax (08) 661 86 01
– www.hellsten.se
– Closed 20 December-4 January　　　　　　　　　　　**B1**
78 rm ⌂ – ⛬990/2190 SEK ⛬⛬1490/3090 SEK
♦ Townhouse ♦ Personalised ♦

Unique hotel in residential area, with warm atmosphere, filled with trinkets and antiques picked up by its globetrotting owner. Individually-styled rooms with modern bathrooms.

Clarion Collection H. Wellington without rest 　🎉 ᵻ 🎉 🄲🄼 ⁽ᵗ⁾

Storgatan 6 ☒ S-114 51 – **Ⓜ** *Östermalmstorg*　　🚗 𝒱𝒾𝒮𝒜 ⓪ 🄰🄴 ①
– 𝒞 (08) 667 09 10 – cc.wellington@choice.se – Fax (08) 667 12 54
– www.wellington.se
– Closed 23 December-2January
60 rm ⌂ – ⛬1195/2895 SEK ⛬⛬1895/3195 SEK – 1 suite　　**C1**
♦ Business ♦ Functional ♦

Apartment block converted to hotel in 1960s, well placed for shopping. Compact, well-equipped rooms; good city views from upper floor balconies. Complimentary dinner buffet.

Rex without rest 　　　　　　　　🄲🄼 ⁽ᵗ⁾ 𝒱𝒾𝒮𝒜 ⓪ 🄰🄴 ①

Luntmakargatan 73 ☒ 113 51 – **Ⓜ** *Rådmannsgatan*
– 𝒞 (08) 16 00 40 – reception@rexhotel.se – Fax (08) 6 61 86 01
– www.rexhotel.se
– Closed 20 December-4 January　　　　　　　　　　　**B1**
32 rm ⌂ – ⛬790/2090 SEK ⛬⛬1190/2290 SEK
♦ Townhouse ♦ Modern ♦

Building dating from 1866, set in a residential area not far from metro station. Functional, modern bedrooms; grey slate bathrooms. Owner's black and white photos decorate.

XXXXX　**Operakällaren** (Stefano Catenacci)　　🎉 ⇕ 𝒱𝒾𝒮𝒜 ⓪ 🄰🄴 ①
❀❀

Operahuset, Karl XII's Torg ☒ S-111 86 – **Ⓜ** *Kungsträdgården*
– 𝒞 (08) 676 58 01 – matsal@operakallaren.se
– Fax (08) 676 58 72 – www.operakallaren.se
– Closed July-August, 25 December-7 January, Sunday and Monday
Rest – *(dinner only)* Carte 675/953 SEK 🍴　　　　　**C2**
Spec. Langoustine with lobster salad and citrus fruit. Venison with horn of plenty mushrooms and blackcurrant sauce. Banana mousse, chocolate jelly and vanilla ice cream.
♦ Classic ♦ Formal ♦

Grand and elegant dining room with striking 19C carved wood décor and fresco paintings, situated in the historic Opera House. Skilled and artistic cooking blends the classic with the modern.

Mathias Dahlgren - Matsalen – at Grand Hotel

Södra Blasieholmshamnen 6 ⊠ 103 27
– **M** Kungsträdgården – ℰ (08) 679 35 84 – reservations@mdghs.com
– Fax (08) 679 36 27 – www.mdghs.com
– Closed 20 July-9 August, Christmas, 13 April, Sunday and Monday
Rest – (booking essential) (dinner only) Menu 850 SEK – Carte   **C2**
880/1005 SEK
Spec. Tartare of beef and oysters with watercress and tallow. Fusion of langoustine and cauliflower with lemon and crown dill. Baked wild chocolate with sour cream, malt and beetroot sorbet.
◆ Modern ◆ Elegant ◆
Fine dining in classically comfortable Matsalen, where the charming and helpful service ensures the atmosphere remains relaxed. Tasty and inventive modern Swedish cooking makes vibrant use of high quality ingredients.

Esperanto (Sayan Isaksson)

Kungstensgatan 2 ⊠ 114 25 – **M** Tekniska Högskolan – ℰ (08) 696 2323
– esperanto@sollevi.se – www.esperantorestaurant.se
– Closed 2 weeks Christmas, Sunday dinner and Monday dinner   **B1**
Rest – (dinner only) (set menu only) Menu 855/1075 SEK
Spec. Langoustine and monkfish liver with ocean tea and rice flour. Pigeon with 'pastella classique' and blackcurrant jus. Jasmine rice in vanilla milk with frozen peach.
◆ Innovative ◆ Formal ◆
On the first floor of a converted theatre, where candlelight adds warmth to the understated décor. Structured and detailed service; innovative cooking with the emphasis on originality.

Fredsgatan 12 (Danyel Couet)

Fredsgatan 12 ⊠ S-111 52 – **M** T-Centralen – ℰ (08) 24 80 52
– info@fredsgatan12.com – Fax (08) 23 76 05 – www.f12.se
– Closed 4 weeks July, 25 December, Saturday lunch and Sunday
Rest – (booking essential) Menu 350 SEK (lunch) – Carte 620/   **B2**
920 SEK
Spec. Jerusalem artichoke with Swedish blue lobster and pomegranate. Duck with carrots and whipped hazelnut milk. Pear with cured lemon and browned butter.
◆ Innovative ◆ Fashionable ◆
Sophisticated and stylish restaurant in a wing of the Academy of Arts, with warm yet contemporary feel. Choice of menus but cooking is largely creative and original. Service is attentive and intelligent.

Pontus!

Brunnsgatan 1 ⊠ 111 38 – **M** Östermalmstorg – ℰ (08) 54 52 73 00
– bokningenbg1@pontusfrithiof.com – Fax (08) 7 96 60 69
– www.pontusfrithiof.com
– Closed July, 24-26 December, Saturday lunch and Sunday   **C1**
Rest – (booking essential) Menu 390/650 SEK – Carte 540/925 SEK
◆ Inventive ◆ Fashionable ◆
Appealing atmosphere at this stylish venue, divided into three: oysters by the entrance; Asian-influenced food around the bar and contemporary cuisine in the lower 'Library' restaurant.

GQ

Kommendörsgatan 23 ⊠ S-114 48 – **M** Stadion – ℰ (08) 545 674 30
– upplev@gqrestaurang.se – Fax (08) 662 25 06 – www.gqrestaurang.se
– Closed 21 December- 7 January, Sunday and Monday   **C1**
Rest – (dinner only) Carte 605/655 SEK
◆ Modern ◆ Friendly ◆
The owner is as passionate about his restaurant as he is about wines; wine evenings and cookery classes are common. Cooking has a traditional base while the room is bright and modern.

XX
Divino
↳ ⇆ 🆚 ⚫ 🅰 ⓪

Karlavägen 28 ⊠ *114 31 –* Ⓜ *Tekniska Högskolan –* ℰ *(08) 611 02 69*
– info@divino.se – Fax (08) 611 12 04 – www.divino.se
– Closed Sunday **B1**
Rest *– (dinner only)* Menu 565 SEK – Carte 555/660 SEK 🏵
♦ Italian ♦ Elegant ♦
19C townhouse with elegant, intimate dining room. Seasonal menus offer flavourful, Italian cooking. Wine cellar and deli. Attentive, friendly service and warm atmosphere.

XX
Paul and Norbert
↳ 🆚 ⚫ 🅰 ⓪

Strandvägen 9 ⊠ *S-114 56 –* Ⓜ *Kungsträdgården –* ℰ *(08) 663 81 83*
– restaurang.paul.norbert@telia.com – Fax (08) 661 72 36
– www.paulochnorbert.se
– Closed Christmas-New Year, lunch July-August, Monday lunch and Sunday
Rest *– (booking essential)* Menu 350 SEK (lunch) – Carte 535/ **C2**
690 SEK
♦ Classic ♦ Formal ♦
Small, sophisticated, well-run restaurant on harbour, with stylish, modern décor and artwork. Some tables in booths. Numerous menus feature classic dishes made with seasonal produce.

XX
Stockholm
🛋 ↳ 🆚 ⚫ 🅰 ⓪

Centralplan/Ingång från Vasagatan ⊠ *101 35 –* Ⓜ *T-Centralen*
– ℰ *(08) 20 20 49 – info@restaurangstockholm.se – Fax (08) 613 62 98*
– www.restaurangstockholm.se
– Closed Saturday lunch, Sunday and Bank Holidays **B 2**
Rest – Menu 290/525 SEK – Carte 450/590 SEK
♦ Swedish ♦ Fashionable ♦
Restaurant within a glass cube in front of the central station. Stylish and retro-style decoration, with lounge bar. Friendly and organised service; modern Swedish cuisine with some classic touches.

XX
Berns Restaurant – at Berns Hotel
↳ ⇆ 🆚 ⚫ 🅰 ⓪

Näckströmsgatan 8, Berzelii Park ⊠ *S-111 47 –* Ⓜ *Kungsträdgården*
– ℰ *(08) 566 322 22 – info@berns.se – Fax (08) 566 323 23 – www.berns.se*
Rest – Menu 435 SEK (dinner) – Carte 425/625 SEK **C2**
♦ Asian influences ♦ Fashionable ♦
A stunningly-restored 19C rococo ballroom with galleries overlooking the dining room. Modern cuisine with strong Asian influences. Live music. The place to be seen.

XX
Teatergrillen
↳ 🆚 ⚫ 🅰 ⓪

Nybrogatan 3 ⊠ *S-111 48 –* Ⓜ *Östermalmstorg –* ℰ *(08) 545 035 62*
– info@riche.se – Fax (08) 545 035 69 – www.teatergrillen.se
– Closed Saturday lunch and Sunday
Rest – Menu 445/550 SEK – Carte 410/895 SEK **C2**
♦ Traditional ♦ Intimate ♦
Intimate, traditional city institution, most pleasant in the evening. Menus are more expensive than its sister Riche. Expect traditional cooking of Scandinavian classics.

XX
Wedholms Fisk
🛋 🅺 ↳ 🆚 ⚫ 🅰 ⓪

Nybrokajen 17 ⊠ *S-111 48 –* Ⓜ *Kungsträdgården –* ℰ *(08) 611 78 74*
– info@wedholmsfisk.se – Fax (08) 678 60 11 – www.wedholmsfisk.se
– Closed 24 December-2 January, Saturday lunch, Sunday and Bank Holidays
Rest *– (booking essential)* Carte 420/920 SEK **C2**
♦ Seafood ♦ Formal ♦
Classic 19-20C building near harbour. Busy, elegant restaurant serving a good choice of fish and shellfish, simply but accurately prepared; similar dishes in the bar.

Café Opera 🕏 AK ⅊ VISA ⊕ AE ⓘ

Operahuset, Karl XII's Torg ⊠ *S-111 86 –* Ⓜ *Kungsträdgården*
– 𝒞 (08) 676 58 07 – info@cafeopera.se – Fax (08) 676 58 71
– www.cafeopera.se
– Closed Monday in Winter **C2**
Rest *– (booking essential) (dinner only - music and dancing after 12am)*
Carte 354/677 SEK
♦ International ♦ Brasserie ♦
Characterful rotunda-style historic restaurant with ceiling painted in 1895, Corinthian pillars, fine mouldings and covered terrace. Swedish-influenced, international menu.

Vassa Eggen – at Elite Hotel Stockholm Plaza AK ⅊ VISA ⊕ AE ⓘ

Birger Jarlsgatan 29 ⊠ *S-103 25 –* Ⓜ *Östermalmstorg – 𝒞 (08) 21 61 69*
– info@vassaeggen.com – Fax (08) 20 34 46 – www.vassaeggen.com
Rest *–* Menu 465/865 SEK (lunch) – Carte 585/775 SEK **B1**
♦ Inventive ♦ Fashionable ♦
Refined, well run restaurant popular with those in the know. Modern, fashionable styling and friendly service. Ambitious, innovative cooking.

1900 VISA ⊕ AE

Regeringsgatan 66 ⊠ *S- 111 39 –* Ⓜ *Hötorget – 𝒞 (08) 20 60 10*
– info@r1900.se – www.r1900.se
– Closed 2 weeks Christmas and Sunday **B2**
Rest *–* Carte 390/545 SEK
♦ Traditional ♦ Cosy ♦
Niklas Ekstëdt's paean to traditional Swedish cooking and flavours, using the best seasonal produce, attracts a loyal following. Comfortable booths and warm lighting create a cosy feel.

Aquavit Grill & Raw Bar – at Clarion Hotel Sign

Östra Järnvägsgatan 35 ⊠ *S-101 26 –* Ⓜ *T-Centralen – 𝒞 (08) 676 98 50*
– aquavit.sign@choice.se – Fax (08) 676 98 99 – www.aquaavitgrillrawbar.se
Rest *–* Carte 460/555 SEK **B2**
♦ International ♦ Minimalist ♦
Scandinavia meets the Big Apple at this bright spot at the front of the Clarion hotel. Raw bar for oysters and the catch of the day; Grill for strip steak and rib-eye.

Mathias Dahlgren - Matbaren – at Grand Hotel ≤ ⅊

Södra Blasieholmshamnen 6 ⊠ *103 27* VISA ⊕ AE ⓘ
– Ⓜ *Kungsträdgården – 𝒞 (08) 679 35 84 – reservations@mdghs.com*
– Fax (08) 679 36 27 – www.mdghs.com
– Closed 13 April, 20 July-9 August, 24-27 December, Sunday and
lunch 10-12 April, 19 June and 28-31 December **C2**
Rest *–* Carte 445/665 SEK
Spec. Brill with scallop, bok choy and soy beurre blanc. Porter-braised beef cheek, onions, potatoes and pickled cucumber. Fried apples with cinnamon, sugar and vanilla ice cream.
♦ Modern ♦ Trendy ♦
Matbaren means 'the food bar,' a relaxed but stylish spot with an informal atmosphere and great service. Order one dish at a time - they come in medium-sized portions and are full of flavour and expertly crafted, using top quality produce.

Smak På Restaurangen 🕏 ⅊ VISA ⊕ AE ⓘ

Oxtorgsgatan 14 ⊠ *S-111 57 –* Ⓜ *Hötorget – 𝒞 (08) 22 09 52 – reservation@*
restaurangtm.com – Fax (08) 22 09 54 – www.restaurangentm.com
– Closed 22 July-30 December, Saturday lunch and Sunday **B2**
Rest *– (booking essential)* Menu 350/550 SEK
♦ Innovative ♦ Trendy ♦
Contemporary interior with clean-cut minimalist décor and stylish furnishings. Unusual, modern menu concept based on a tasting of several small dishes. Lively atmosphere.

✗ **Kungsholmen** ⊲ 🛱 🔝 ↳ 𝓥𝓘𝓢𝓐 ⊕ 🖭 ⓪

Norr Mälarstrand, Kajplats 464 ⊠ *112 20* – ⓜ *Rådhuset* – 𝒞 *(08) 50 52 44 50*
– info@kungsholmen.se – Fax (08) 50 52 44 55 – www.kungsholmen.com
Rest – *(dinner only)* Carte 390/720 SEK   **A3**
♦ International ♦ Trendy ♦

Trendy restaurant on the waterfront. Comfy furnishings; lounge feel. 7 open kitchens separately themed: sushi, bistro, grill, soup, bread, salad and ice cream. Friendly service.

✗ **Brasserie Bobonne** ↳ 𝓥𝓘𝓢𝓐 ⊕ 🖭

Storegatan 12 ⊠ *114 44* – ⓜ *Östermalmstorg* – 𝒞 *(08) 660 03 18*
– bobonne@telia.com – www.brasseriebobonne.se
– Closed 6 weeks in Summer and Sunday   **C1**
Rest – *(booking essential) (dinner only)* Menu 498 SEK – Carte 405/595 SEK
♦ Bistro ♦ Cosy ♦

Small, busy French-style brasserie located in a residential area, serving flavourful French and Swedish dishes. Relaxing, welcoming atmosphere.

✗ **Proviant** ↳ 𝓥𝓘𝓢𝓐 ⊕ 🖭
㊧
Sturegatan 19 ⊠ *114 36* – ⓜ *Stadion* – 𝒞 *(08) 22 60 50* – *info@proviant.se*
– Fax (08) 20 39 17 – www.proviant.se
– Closed 3 weeks mid July-August, 22 December, Saturday and Bank Holidays
Rest – Menu 395 SEK (dinner)/525 SEK – Carte 375/570 SEK   **C1**
♦ Swedish ♦ Bistro ♦

Simply furnished, professionally run restaurant near Humlegärden Park. Accomplished Swedish cooking. Friendly, efficient service.

✗ **Rolfs Kök** 🛱 ↳ 𝓥𝓘𝓢𝓐 ⊕ 🖭 ⓪
㊧
Tegnérgatan 41 ⊠ *S-111 61* – ⓜ *Rådmansgatan* – 𝒞 *(08) 10 16 96*
– info@rolfskok.se – Fax (08) 789 88 80 – www.rolfskok.se
– Closed July, Midsummer, Christmas-New Year, and lunch Saturday, Sunday and Bank Holidays   **B1**
Rest – *(booking essential) (light lunch)* Carte 425/600 SEK 🏵
♦ Modern ♦ Bistro ♦

Compact, trendy bar-restaurant; buzzy atmosphere guaranteed. Mix of modern and traditional international cooking. Home made bread and ice cream and up to 750 wines by the glass! Efficient service.

✗ **Lisa Elmqvist** ↳ 𝓥𝓘𝓢𝓐 ⊕ 🖭 ⓪

Östermalms Saluhall ⊠ *114 39* – ⓜ *Östermalmstorg* – 𝒞 *(08) 553 40410*
– info@lisaelmqvist.se – Fax (08) 553 4 04 05 – www.lisaelmqvist.se
– Closed Easter, Christmas-New Year, Sunday and Bank Holidays
Rest – *(booking essential (bookings not accepted on Saturday))*   **C 1**
(lunch only) (communal dining) Carte 500/750 SEK
♦ Seafood ♦ Friendly ♦

A fourth generation family affair where shared tables and fresh seafood combine to create a contented and lively atmosphere. Open kitchen with seasonal fish display and deli.

BRASSERIES AND BISTRO

✗ **Prinsen** 🛱 ↳ ✿ 𝓥𝓘𝓢𝓐 ⊕ 🖭 ⓪

Mäster Samuelsgatan 4 ⊠ *S-111 44* – ⓜ *Östermalmstorg* – 𝒞 *(08) 611 13 31*
– kontoret@restaurangprinsen.se – Fax (08) 611 70 79
– www.restaurangprinsen.se
– Closed Christmas, New Year, 19-20 June and Sunday lunch   **C2**
Rest – *(booking essential)* Carte 407/689 SEK
♦ Traditional ♦ Brasserie ♦

Long-standing, busy and well-run brasserie with literary associations. Spread over ground and lower floor with traditional décor and well-priced Swedish and French classics.

X **Eriks Bakficka** 🏠 ⇐ 𝘝𝘐𝘚𝘈 ⓞ𝘰 𝘼𝘌 ⓪

Fredrikshovsgatan 4 ⊠ S-115 23 – ℰ (08) 660 15 99 – info.bakfickan@eriks.se
– Fax (08) 663 25 67 – www.eriks.se
– Closed Easter, July-mid August, Saturday lunch and Sunday **D2**
Rest – Menu 475 SEK (dinner) – Carte 325/560 SEK
♦ Modern ♦ Bistro ♦

Quiet residential setting and well-run bistro and bar-counter with small terrace.
Cosy dining rooms in the basement. Traditional Swedish dishes with modern global twists.

X **Sturehof** 🏠 ⇐ 𝘝𝘐𝘚𝘈 ⓞ𝘰 𝘼𝘌 ⓪

Stureplan 2-4 ⊠ S-114 46 – Ⓜ Östermalmstorg – ℰ (08) 440 57 30
– info@sturehof.com – Fax (08) 678 11 01 – www.sturehof.com **C1**
Rest – Carte 445/690 SEK
♦ Traditional ♦ Brasserie ♦

Very popular classic café-brasserie with closely packed tables and a busy atmosphere due to the steady stream of local business clientele. Good choice of seafood dishes.

X **Riche** ⇐ 𝘝𝘐𝘚𝘈 ⓞ𝘰 𝘼𝘌 ⓪

Birger Jarlsgatan 4 ⊠ S-114 53 – Ⓜ Östermalmstorg – ℰ (08) 545 035 60
– info@riche.se – Fax (08) 545 035 69 – www.riche.se
– closed Sunday **C2**
Rest – (brunch saturday) Carte 280/620 SEK
♦ Traditional ♦ Brasserie ♦

Lively bar and friendly, bustling brasserie; very different from, but with same menu
as, its sister Teatergrillen. Serves classic Scandinavian as well as international
dishes.

at Gamla Stan (Old Stockholm) *Plan II*

🏠 **First H. Reisen** ⇐ 🅰️🅲 rest ⇐ 📧 ᵗ⁰ 🛁 𝘝𝘐𝘚𝘈 ⓞ𝘰 𝘼𝘌 ⓪

Skeppsbron 12 ⊠ S-111 30 – Ⓜ Gamla Stan – ℰ (08) 22 32 60
– reisen@firsthotels.se – Fax (08) 20 15 59 – www.firsthotels.com/reisen
137 rm ⊇ – � 1390/3240 SEK ♦♦1590/3440 SEK – 7 suites **F1**
Rest *Reisen Bar and Dining Room* – Carte 335/530 SEK
♦ Business ♦ Classic ♦

19C hotel on waterfront with original maritime décor. Popular piano bar. Sauna in
17C vault. Classically-styled rooms; de luxe and superior offer quayside view and
small balconies. Modern, airy brasserie-style restaurant with a welcoming atmosphere. Traditional Swedish and international menu.

🏠 **Victory** ᵗ⁰ 🅰️🅲 ⇐ 📧 ᵗ⁰ 🛁 𝘝𝘐𝘚𝘈 ⓞ𝘰 𝘼𝘌 ⓪

Lilla Nygatan 5 ⊠ S-111 28 – Ⓜ Gamla Stan – ℰ (08) 506 400 00
– info@victoryhotel.se – Fax (08) 506 400 10 – www.victoryhotel.se
– Closed 20 December-10 January **E1**
42 rm ⊇ – ♦1450/3850 SEK ♦♦2450/3850 SEK – 3 suites
Rest *Leijontornet* – see below
♦ Historic ♦ Classic ♦

Pleasant 17C hotel with Swedish rural furnishings and maritime antiques. Rooms
named after sea captains with individually-styled fittings, mixing modern and
antique.

🏠 **Rica H. Gamla Stan** without rest ⇐ 📧 ᵗ⁰ 🛁 𝘝𝘐𝘚𝘈 ⓞ𝘰 𝘼𝘌 ⓪

Lilla Nygatan 25 ⊠ S-111 28 – Ⓜ Gamla Stan – ℰ (08) 723 72 50
– info.gamlastan@rica.se – Fax (08) 723 72 59 – www.rica.se
50 rm ⊇ – ♦1195/2645 SEK ♦♦2745 SEK – 1 suite **F1**
♦ Business ♦ Classic ♦

Conveniently located 17C house with welcoming style. Well-furnished rooms with
traditional décor and antique-style furniture. Pleasant top-floor terrace with rooftop outlook.

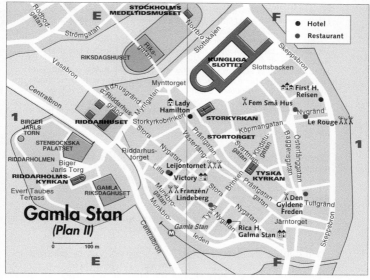

STOCKHOLMS MEDELTIDSMUSEET

Strömgatan

Rödbodgatan

Riks gatan

RIKSDAGSHUSET

Vasabron

Norrbro

Slottskajen

Skeppsbron

KUNGLIGA SLOTTET Slottsbacken

● Hotel
● Restaurant

Centralbron

Rådhusgränd

Riddarhusgränd

Myntgatan

Mynttorget

First H. Reisen

Fem Små Hus

1

BIRGER JARLS TORN

RIDDARHUSET

Storkyrkobrinken

Lady Hamilton

STORKYRKAN

Nygränd

Le Rouge

STENBOCKSKA PALATSET

Stora Nygatan

Prästgatan

Köpmangatan

Österlånggatan

Baggensgatan

RIDDARHOLMEN

Biger Jarls Torg

Riddarhus-torget

Västerlång

STORTORGET

Skärmarbrink Kindsgatan

1

RIDDARHOLMS-KYRKAN

GAMLA RIKSDAGSHUSET

Lilla Nygatan

Leijontornet

Victory

TYSKA KYRKAN

Prästgatan

Evert Taubes Terrass

Munkbron

Franzén/ Lindeberg

Stora Nygatan

Brinken

Den Gyldene Freden Tullgränd

Gamla Stan
(Plan II)

Munkbro-

Tysk Nygatan

Gamla Stan leden

Nygatan

Rica H. Galma Stan

Järntorget

Skeppsbron

0   100 m

E   **F**

🏠 **Lady Hamilton** without rest   🕭 ↳ 🖭 ⁽ᵗ⁾ 📶 **VISA** 🚭 **AE** ①

Storkyrkobrinken 5 ⊠ S-111 28 – ⓜ Gamla Stan – ℰ (08) 506 401 00
– info@ladyhamiltonhotel.se – Fax (08) 506 401 10
– www.ladyhamiltonhotel.se   **E-F1**
34 rm � – †1250/3290 SEK ††2050/3290 SEK
   ♦ Historic ♦ Cosy ♦
15C houses of character full of fine Swedish rural furnishings. Rooms boast antique
pieces and modern facilities. Sauna and 14C well plunge pool in basement.

XXX **Leijontornet** – at Victory Hotel   🅰️ ↳ 📶 **VISA** 🚭 **AE** ①
✿
Lilla Nygatan 5 ⊠ S-111 28 – ⓜ Gamla Stan – ℰ (08) 506 400 80
– info@leijontornet.se – Fax (08) 506 400 85 – www.leijontornet.se
– Closed 18 June-2 August, 20 December-6 January, Sunday and Bank Holidays
Rest – *(booking essential)* Menu 695/1050 SEK ꙮ   **E1**
Spec. Langoustine and pig's cheek in pork consommé. Duck breast with liver
terrine, rosehips and juniper. Cloudberry pudding, jelly and cream.
   ♦ Innovative ♦ Elegant ♦
Smart cellar restaurant built around the ruins of a 14C fortified tower. Accomplis-
hed and inventive cooking, with Nordic flavours to the fore. Excellent wine list
and knowledgeable service.

XXX **Le Rouge**   📶 **VISA** 🚭 **AE** ①

Brunnsgränd 2-4 ⊠ 111 30 – ⓜ Gamla Stan – ℰ (08) 505 244 30
– info@lerouge.se – Fax (08) 505 244 35
– www.lerouge.se
– Closed Saturday lunch and Sunday   **F1**
Rest – Menu 750 SEK (dinner) – Carte 550/845 SEK
Rest *Le Bar Rouge* – Menu 650 SEK – Carte 245/415 SEK
   ♦ French traditional ♦ Musical ♦
Richly decorated, contagiously exuberant in atmosphere and influenced by the
Moulin Rouge. But the French-influenced cooking is still undertaken with care.
Separate, busy and bustling Le Bar Rouge is aimed at younger crowd.

Frantzén/Lindeberg (Bjorn Frantzén/Daniel Lindeberg)

Lilla Nygatan 21 ✉ *S-111 28* – **Ⓜ** *Gamla Stan*   VISA ⬤⑨ AE ⓪
– 𝒞 *(08) 20 85 80* – *info@frantzen-lindeberg.com*
– *www.frantzen-lindeberg.com*
– *Closed mid July- mid August, 20 December-9 January, Sunday and Monday*
Rest – *(booking essential) (dinner only)* Menu 995/1295 SEK   **F1**
Spec. Carpaccio of scallops with truffle vinaigrette. Salt-baked celeriac, 'tarte
fine' with melting bone marrow. Salted caramel ice cream with roasted rape-
seed oil and bitter chocolate cream.
   ♦ Innovative ♦ Romantic ♦
Two highly skilled chefs bring their impressive international experience to bear at
this compact but expertly run restaurant. The cooking may be innovative but it
also boasts depth and personality.

Fem Små Hus   AC ↳ VISA ⬤⑨ AE ⓪

Nygränd 10 ✉ *S-111 30* – **Ⓜ** *Gamla Stan* – 𝒞 *(08) 10 87 75*
– *info@femsmahus.se* – *Fax (08) 14 96 95* – *www.femsmahus.se*
– *Closed 23-26 December, 1 January and 1 May*   **F1**
Rest – *(dinner only)* Menu 415 SEK – Carte 420/710 SEK 🏵
   ♦ Traditional ♦ Rustic ♦
Lively, characterful restaurant set in 9 rooms located in the 17C cellars of 'five small
houses.' Popular with tourists. Several menus available offering traditional cuisine.

Den Gyldene Freden   ↳ 🏛 VISA ⬤⑨ AE ⓪

Österlånggatan 51 ✉ *S-103 17* – **Ⓜ** *Gamla Stan* – 𝒞 *(08) 24 97 60*
– *info@gyldenefreden.se* – *Fax (08) 21 38 70* – *www.gyldenefreden.se*
– *Closed Sunday and Bank Holidays*   **F1**
Rest – *(booking essential)* Menu 345/595 SEK – Carte 475/725 SEK
   ♦ Traditional ♦ Rustic ♦
Popular restaurant in attractive early 18C inn, divided into assorted rooms inclu-
ding vaulted cellar. Friendly service and robust cooking incorporating plenty of fla-
vours.

---

at Djurgården   *Plan I*

Scandic H. Hasselbacken   �│ 🏠 👥 🔌 AC ↳ 📺 📶 ⚓ P 🌳

Hazeliusbacken 20 ✉ *S-100 55* – 𝒞 *(08) 517 343 00*   VISA ⬤⑨ AE ⓪
– *hasselbacken@scandichotels.com* – *Fax (08) 517 343 11*
– *www.scandichotels.com/hasselbacken*   **D2**
111 rm ☕ – 💂990/2790 SEK 💂💂1090/2890 SEK – 1 suite
Rest *Restaurang Hasselbacken* – *(buffet lunch Monday-Saturday)*
Menu 155/470 SEK – Carte dinner 315/385 SEK
   ♦ Business ♦ Modern ♦
Modern hotel situated on island in former Royal park, close to the Vasa Museum.
Comfortable, contemporary bedrooms; some refurbished, some with views. Regular musical events. Restaurant with ornate mirrored ceilings, attractive terrace and
pleasant outlook; traditional Swedish cooking.

Ulla Winbladh   🏛 ↳ VISA ⬤⑨ AE ⓪

Rosendalsvägen 8 ✉ *S-115 21* – 𝒞 *(08) 534 897 01* – *info@ullawinbladh.se*
– *Fax (08) 534 89 7 00* – *www.ullawinbladh.se*
– *Closed 25-26 December*   **D2**
Rest – *(booking essential)* Menu 183 SEK (dinner)/665 SEK – Carte 233/635 SEK
   ♦ Traditional Swedish ♦ Formal ♦
Late 19C pavilion in former Royal hunting ground houses several welcoming
dining rooms with terraces. Mix of traditional and modern Swedish cuisine, with
international influences.

SWEDEN - STOCKHOLM

✕ **Carl Michael**   🛣 🗳 VISA ⦾⦾ AE ⓞ
Allmänna Gränd 6 ✉ *115 21* – 𝒞 *(08) 667 45 96* – *info@carlmichael.se*
– *Fax (08) 662 43 61* – *www.carlmichael.se*
– *Closed 24-26 December, 1-10 January and Monday dinner*   **D2**
Rest – Menu 375/540 SEK – Carte 259/670 SEK
♦ Swedish ♦ Cosy ♦
Father and son owners took over in late 2008. Charming bistro-style restaurant in
18C house with warm and welcoming feel. Focus is on traditional Swedish flavours
and dishes.

at Södermalm   *Plan I*

🏠🏠 **The Rival**   🛣 🕭 🗳 ⦾ ⁍⁍ 🐾 ⮐ VISA ⦾⦾ AE ⓞ
Mariatorget 3 ✉ *S-118 91* – ⓜ *Mariatorget* – 𝒞 *(08) 545 789 00*
– *rival@rival.se* – *Fax (08) 545 789 24* – *www.rival.se*   **C3**
97 rm – 🛏1190/2890 SEK 🛏🛏1590/3090 SEK, ⌸ 175 SEK – 2 suites
Rest *The Bistro* – Carte 329/496 SEK
♦ Business ♦ Stylish ♦
Modern boutique hotel and Art Deco cinema in 1930s building, owned by ex-
ABBA singer Benny Andersson. Cosy, stylish bedroooms with cinema theme
décor and high-tech facilities. First floor restaurant serves modern international
dishes.

🏠🏠 **Clarion H. Stockholm**   🛗 🕭 🕭 🏧 🗳 ⦾ ⁍⁍ 🐾 🚗 VISA ⦾⦾ AE ⓞ
Ring Vägen 98 ✉ *104 60* – ⓜ *Skanstull* – 𝒞 *(08) 462 1000*
– *cl.stockholm@choice.se* – *Fax (08) 462 10 99*
– *www.clarionstockholm.se*
531 rm ⌸ – 🛏895/2695 SEK 🛏🛏1095/2895 SEK – 1 suite
Rest *Greta's Kok* – Carte approx. 580 SEK
♦ Business ♦ Modern ♦
Displaying more character than most modern, purpose built hotels, with impressive collection of Nordic art. Comfortable lounge, functional bedrooms and good
conference facilities. Restaurant named after Greta Garbo who was born locally;
international menu.

✕✕ **Eriks Gondolen**   ⬋ 🛣 🗳 VISA ⦾⦾ AE ⓞ
Stadsgården 6 (11th floor) ✉ *S-104 56* – ⓜ *Slussen* – 𝒞 *(08) 641 70 90*
– *info@eriks.se* – *Fax (08) 641 11 40* – *www.eriks.se*
– *Closed Sunday*   **C3**
Rest – Menu 495 SEK – Carte 380/615 SEK
♦ Traditional ♦ Brasserie ♦
Glass-enclosed suspended passageway, renowned for stunning panoramic view of
city and water. Open-air dining and barbecue terraces on 12th floor. Traditional
Swedish fare.

at Arlanda Airport

🏠🏠 **Radisson SAS Sky City**   🛗 🕭 🕭 🏧 🗳 ⦾ ⁍⁍ 🐾 VISA ⦾⦾ AE ⓞ
at Terminals 4-5, 2nd floor above street level (Stockholm-Arlanda, Sky City)
✉ *190 45* – 𝒞 *(08) 506 740 00*
– *reservations.skycity.stockholm@radissonsas.com* – *Fax (08) 506 740 01*
– *www.skycity.arlanda.stockholm.radissonsas.com*
229 rm – 🛏1350/2195 SEK 🛏🛏1350/2195 SEK, ⌸ 135 SEK – 1 suite
Rest *Stockholm Fish* – Carte 360/500 SEK
♦ Business ♦ Modern ♦
The perfect place not to miss your plane: modern, corporate airport hotel. Refurbished bedrooms in Scandinavian style or with maritime décor. Balcony restaurant
overlooking airport terminal offering fish-based menu.

ENVIRONS OF STOCKHOLM

to the North 2 km by Sveavägen (at beginning of E 4)

Stallmästaregården 　🏠 🖑 📧 📞 🖾 🅿 VISA ⊙⊙ AE ⓪

Nortull (North : 2 km by Sveavägen (at beginning of E 4)) ⊠ *S-113 47*
– ℰ *(08) 610 13 00* – *info@stallmastaregarden.se* – *Fax (08) 610 13 40*
– *www.stallmastaregarden.se*
46 rm ⌁ – ♦1395/2695 SEK ♦♦2295/3695 SEK – 3 suites
Rest – Menu 495 SEK – Carte 510/635 SEK
◆ Inn ◆ Cosy ◆

Attractive 17C inn with central courtyard and modern bedroom wing. Quieter rooms overlook waterside and park. 18C-style rustic Swedish décor with modern comforts. Restaurant serves modern Swedish cuisine.

at Ladugårdsgärdet

Villa Källhagen 　≼ 🖍 🕅 🖑 📧 🍴 🖾 🅿 VISA ⊙⊙ AE ⓪

Djurgårdsbrunnsvägen 10 (East: 3 km by Strandvägen) ⊠ *S-115 27*
– ℰ *(08) 665 03 00* – *villa@kallhagen.se* – *Fax (08) 665 03 99*
– *www.kallhagen.se*
– *Closed 22-27 December*
36 rm ⌁ – ♦1230/2300 SEK ♦♦1630/2500 SEK – 2 suites
Rest Villa Källhagen – *see below*
Rest Bistro – *(lunch only and dinner Sunday)* Carte 145/418 SEK
◆ Inn ◆ Modern ◆

A relaxing hotel in a lovely waterside setting with extensive open-air terraces among the trees. Contemporary bedrooms, some brand new; some with views. Simple bistro with international menu.

🗙🗙 Villa Källhagen – at Villa Källhagen 　≼ 🖍 🕅 🖑 🅿 VISA ⊙⊙ AE ⓪

Djurgårdsbrunnsvägen 10 (East: 3 km by Strandvägen) ⊠ *S-115 27*
– ℰ *(08) 665 03 00* – *villa@kallhagen.se* – *Fax (08) 665 03 99*
– *www.kallhagen.se*
– *Closed Sunday dinner*
Rest – Carte 301/560 SEK
◆ Traditional ◆ Brasserie ◆

Busy restaurant with terrace in great spot overlooking lake. Popular lunch with mostly traditional fare; more international influences at dinner. Raised area the best place to sit.

at Fjäderholmarna Island

🗙🗙 Fjäderholmarnas Krog 　≼ 🍴 VISA ⊙⊙ AE ⓪

Stora Fjäderholmen ⊠ *S-100 05* – ℰ *(08) 718 33 55* – *fjaderholmarna@atv.se*
– *Fax (08) 716 39 89* – *www.fjaderholmarnaskrog.se*
– *Closed 7 September-30 April except 26-31 December*
Rest – *(booking essential)* Menu 345 SEK (lunch) – Carte 330/775 SEK
◆ Seafood ◆ Friendly ◆

Delightful waterside setting on archipelago island with fine view. Fresh produce, mainly fish, delivered daily by boat. Wide selection of traditional Swedish dishes.

at Nacka Strand Southeast : 10 km by Stadsgården or 20 mins by boat from Nybrokajen

Hotel J 🌢 　≼ 🖍 🕹 🖾 🖑 📧 📞 🅿 VISA ⊙⊙ AE ⓪

Ellensviksvägen 1 ⊠ *S-131 28* – ℰ *(08) 601 30 00* – *nackastrand@hotelj.com*
– *Fax (08) 601 30 09* – *www.hotelj.com*
40 rm ⌁ – ♦1245/1995 SEK ♦♦1845/2595 SEK – 5 suites
Rest Restaurant J – *see below*
◆ Historic ◆ Design ◆

Former politician's early 20C summer residence in quiet waterside setting. 'Boutique'- style hotel with maritime theme. Stylish spacious rooms, some with sea view.

╳ **Restaurant J** ⌉ ⌂ ⇩ VISA ⊕ AE ⓪

Augustendalsvägen 52 ⊠ *S-131 28 –* ℃ *(08) 601 30 25 – info@restaurantj.com*
– Fax (08) 601 30 09 – www.restaurantj.com
Rest *– (closed 23-31 December)* Carte 474/652 SEK
◆ Traditional ◆ Brasserie ◆

Bright, informal restaurant with sleek maritime décor and attractive terrace beside marina. Selective menu of Swedish and international dishes.

at Lilla Essingen West : 5.5 km by Norr Mälarstrand

╳╳ **Lux Stockholm** (Henrik Norström) ⌉ ⌂ AC ⇩ VISA ⊕ AE ⓪
☆

Primusgatan 116 ⊠ *S-112 67 –* ℃ *(08) 619 01 90 – info@luxstockholm.com*
– Fax (08) 619 04 47 – www.luxstockholm.com
– Closed 21 July-17 August, 20 December-12 January, Saturday lunch, Sunday and Monday
Rest *– (booking essential) (light lunch)* Carte 775/840 SEK
Spec. Pike perch with smoked salted egg and herring caviar. Braised venison with fried ceps and parsley roots. Nougatine-sugared raspberries with chilled fresh milk.
◆ Innovative ◆ Fashionable ◆

Bright and stylish former Electrolux factory with delightful terrace. Innovative Swedish cooking makes good use of regional products. Restaurant has its own bakery and shop around the corner.

at Bromma West : 5.5 km by Norr Mälarstrand and Drottningholmsvägen

╳ **Sjöpaviljongen** ⌉ ⌂ AC ⇩ VISA ⊕ AE ⓪

Traneberg Strand 4, Alvik (East : 1.5 km) ⊠ *167 40 –* Ⓜ *Alvik*
– ℃ *(08) 704 04 24 – info@sjopaviljongen.se – Fax (08) 704 82 40*
– www.sjopaviljongen.se
– Closed 23 December-6 January and Sunday dinner
Rest *– (booking essential)* Carte 280/515 SEK
◆ Traditional ◆ Friendly ◆

Modern pavilion in attractive lakeside setting, with pleasant waterfront terrace. Swedish-style décor with busy, friendly atmosphere. Good value classic Swedish cuisine.

at Bockholmen Island Northwest : 7 km by Sveavägen and E18

╳ **Bockholmen** ⌉ ⌂ ⇅ P VISA ⊕ AE ⓪

Bockholmsvägen ⊠ *170 78 Solna –* ℃ *(08) 624 22 00 – info@bockholmen.com*
– www.bockholmen.com
– May-September, dinner late November-21 December and March-April and weekend brunch.
Rest *– (booking essential)* Menu 380 SEK bi/495 SEK – Carte 368/610 SEK
◆ Traditional ◆ Friendly ◆

Former merchant's villa in an enchanting island setting, overlooking the lake, with large terrace. Traditional roots underpin the young kitchen's classic repertoire. Friendly, relaxed feel.

to the Northwest 8 km by Sveavägen and E 18 towards Norrtälje

╳╳ **Ulriksdals Wärdshus** ⌉ 🚌 ⌂ ⇩ P VISA ⊕ AE ⓪

(take first junction for Ulriksdals Slott) ⊠ *170 79 Solna –* ℃ *(08) 85 08 15*
– info@ulriksdalswardshus.se – Fax (08) 85 08 58 – www.ulriksdalswardshus.se
– Closed 2 weeks July, 1 week Febuary, 26-30 December, Tuesday dinner and Monday in low season and Bank Holidays
Rest *– (booking essential)* Menu 385 SEK – Carte 415/645 SEK ♻
◆ Traditional ◆ Inn ◆

19C former inn in Royal Park with classic winter garden-style décor, delightful summer terrace and wine cellar. Traditional Swedish cooking; extensive smörgåsbord at weekends.

at Sollentuna Northwest : 15 km by Sveavägen and E 4, (exit Sollentuna c)

Edsbacka Krog

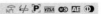

Sollentunavägen 220 ✉ 191 35 – ℰ (08) 96 33 00
– info@edsbackakrog.se – Fax (08) 96 40 19
– www.edsbackakrog.se
– Closed Midsummer weekend, 5 July-6 August, 23 December-8
January, Sunday and Bank Holidays
Rest – *(dinner only and Saturday lunch)* Menu 875 SEK – Carte 810/940 SEK
Spec. Cured bleak with king crab, crisp bread and bleak roe. Variation of red deer and bacon with pear and mushrooms.Candied pastry of apples with almonds and brown sugar ice cream.
♦ Classic ♦ Elegant ♦
Delightful 17C inn in small park with elegantly understated décor, divided into 5 rooms. Long-standing chef now at the helm; his cooking is intricate yet balanced. Thoughtful and well-paced service.

Edsbacka Bistro

Sollentunavägen 223 ✉ 191 35 – ℰ (08) 631 00 34
– bistro@edsbackakrog.se – Fax (08) 96 40 19
– www.edsbackakrog.se
– Closed Midsummer weekend, 12 July-2 August, 24-28 December and
31 December-1 January
Rest – *(booking essential)* Menu 385 SEK – Carte 320/475 SEK
♦ Traditional ♦ Bistro ♦
Simple modern bistro with black and white décor. Smart rear terrace shielded from traffic. Good value menu of tasty classic Swedish dishes. Friendly, informal service.

GOTHENBURG
GÖTEBORG

Population: 489 500 (conurbation 872 200) - Altitude: sea level

Kjell Holmner/Göteborg & Co/www.imagebank.sweden.se

It's not everywhere you find a cook's face on a postage stamp, but Gothenburg's Leif Mannerström has achieved this curious honour, as good an indication as any that in this attractive west coast city, cuisine is a major priority, and seafood its *cause célèbre*. Gothenburg is universally considered to be Sweden's friendliest town, a throwback to its days as a leading trading centre and seaport, a cosmopolitan place where you're as likely to strike up a conversation with a local as come face-to-face with a restaurant – and there are over 650 of those.

This is a compact, pretty city whose roots go back four hundred years. It has trams, broad avenues and canals – the Dutch designed it all. Its centre is boisterous but never feels tourist heavy and overcrowded; Gothenburgers take life at a more leisurely pace than their Stockholm cousins over on the east coast. The mighty shipyards that once dominated the shoreline are now quiet. Go to the centre, though, and you find the good-time ambience of Avenyn, a vivacious thoroughfare full of places to eat and drink. But for those still itching for a feel of the heavy industry that once defined the place, there's a Volvo museum sparkling with chrome and shiny steel. Truly, a city for all comers.

LIVING THE CITY

Unless you really do fancy the visit to the Volvo museum (which is north of the Göta river) there's not much point in crossing from the southern side of Gothenburg. The Old Town is the historic heart: its tight grid of streets has grand façades and a fascinating waterfront. Southeast of here is the commercial and retail hub of **Avenyn**, where the pretty people like to be seen. Just west is the **Vasastan** quarter, full of fine National Romantic buildings. Further west again is **Haga**, an old working-class district which – you've guessed it – has been gentrified, its cobbled streets sprawling with cafes and boutiques. Adjacent to Haga is the district of **Linné**, a racy and vibrant area that has catapulted itself into the same league as Avenyn – its elegantly tall nineteenth-century Dutch-inspired buildings perhaps giving it the edge.

PRACTICAL INFORMATION

ARRIVAL-DEPARTURE

Landvetter Airport is 25km east of the city although City Airport in the northwest is increasingly popular. A taxi from either airport will cost approximately SEK350, although there are also bus connections. There are regular ferry services from Kiel.

TRANSPORT

The Gothenburg Pass gives you unlimited bus, tram and boat travel within the city. It will also guarantee you a sightseeing tour, admission to the Liseberg amusement park, entry to all museums, and discounts in certain shops and restaurants.

They are valid for either one or two days, and are available from Tourist Information offices, the amusement park, newspaper kiosks, hotels and campsites.

Doing a fair amount of bus and tram travel? Then get a 10-trip carnet of tickets from the driver, or from Travel Information Centres. Single tickets are also available.

Punts – flat Paddan boats - are a pleasant way to explore this maritime city, gliding past stately canalside buildings. They pass under 20 bridges; you're advised to duck on numerous occasions, as a lot of them were built for the vertically challenged.

EXPLORING GOTHENBURG

If you've been to San Francisco and liked what you saw, then you'll probably be partial to Gothenburg. It's often compared to the hip US city: it occupies a breezy west coast location, has plenty of bridges, hills, water and trams and, as with Fisherman's Wharf, it boasts an abundance of seafood restaurants. Like San Francisco, there's a welcoming spirit about the place, and a true cosmopolitan air. Canals, silently ringing the city, bring the emphasis back to Europe, as does the grand Neoclassical architecture, a product of Gothenburg's spirited history of trading, as merchants from around the continent stayed on and built grand houses in which to live.

→ CRANE SUPREME

As this is a maritime town, down along the quayside is as good a place to get your bearings as any. There is much character here, as the grandly decaying shipyards sadly eye your progress along the waterfront. Here, at Lilla Bommen harbour, the sombre glory of the rusting, arching cranes are juxtaposed against temples of modernism, such as the iconic **Utkiken Tower** from the late 1980s, better known as 'The Lipstick Tower' because of its lusty scarlet tip, offering a great viewing platform over Gothenburg. And just along the blustery waterfront, competing with it in the iconic stakes, is another relatively recent arrival, 1994's strikingly modern **Opera House,** designed with its location uppermost, to resemble a fine ship. It puts on not just opera, but ballet and musicals, too. The salty location meets its match two minutes' stroll further along at the **Maritiman**, a truly floating maritime museum which can rightly label itself the 'largest ship museum in the world'. It's a retirement home for twenty boats – a cross-section of Sweden's naval heritage. These include a lightship, a fire-fighting vessel, a vast destroyer and a submarine that should be avoided by claustrophobia sufferers at all costs.

→ MAKING HIS POINT

It won't take you long to turn inland and reach the heart of the Old Town. You'll know when you're there, because you'll see a big copper statue of Gustav II Adolf pointing down to the spot where he allegedly declared he would build his city. This is **Gustav Adolf's Torg**, the stately main square, and close by are two buildings worth

visiting. The **Kronhuset** was built by the Dutch over 350 years ago and is the city's oldest secular building, while the **Stadsmuseum** is a cultural powerhouse, boasting exhibits of Gothenburg's rich history all the way back to the days of the Vikings and including a very impressive long-boat. All around this area are 17C streets, canals and buildings; and the Stadsmuseum itself is housed inside the former auction house of the Swedish East India Company, richly endowed with stone pillars, frescoes and stained glass.

Both these buildings are dwarfed by a monstrous interloper, one which owes its origins to twenty first century consumerism. The gigantic **Nordstan** is Sweden's biggest shopping centre and it has some eye-catching modern Nordic design amongst its sparkly boutiques and chain stores. It should satisfy any shopping itch you were waiting to scratch, but if not then head due south to the main thoroughfare of Kungsportsavenyn, more elegantly known as **Avenyn**, which, to be more accurate, is actually a place to be seen rather than to shop. It's adorned with grand nineteenth century houses, and their ground floors have been transformed into swish cafés, bars or restaurants, for this is the avenue with the highest density of places to eat in Sweden. In the summer, tables spill out, a chrome carnival shimmering along Avenyn's spacious, cobbled length, the young and the wish-they-were-still-young adding their own lustre. One of the city's abiding delights is that the centre, though lively, never feels over-crowded or in a rush: the sense of harmony and space is never strained.

→ NORTHERN LIGHT

At the southern end of Avenyn stands one of the city's best attractions, the **Art Museum**, housed in a massive building, which, rather impressively, claims the finest collection of Nordic art in Scandinavia. Head for the sixth floor where the Furstenberg Galleries are full of work by revered early 20C century artists which brings to life the landscapes, shades and nuances of the Nordic countries. On other floors there are also works by the French Impressionists, Munch, Van Gogh and Gauguin. Half-way down Avenyn, just over in the adjoining area of Vasastan, can be found the Röhsska Museum of Design and Applied Art, which takes you on an excellent trip through the centuries and continents, looking at aesthetic glories from ancient Asian ceramics to 21C mod cons.

Gothenburg boasts another 'biggest in Scandinavia' if you meander southeast from Avenyn. It's **Liseberg** - a magical name to those in the know, conjuring up roller coaster rides, shocking pink paintwork, fairy lights and sweet-scented waffles. Opened in 1923, it's Scandinavia's biggest amusement park, bigger even than Copenhagen's Tivoli, and reaches the parts of adults other amusement parks fail to reach, as it boasts trees, fountains and flowers to give it the authentic feel of a 'proper' park. There's another reason to go to Liseberg now: it's right next door to a museum, opened only in 2004, that's won a host of plaudits including Sweden's most prestigious architecture award, plus worldwide praise for its refreshing exhibitions. This is the **Museum of World Culture**, which apart from its startling four-storey glass atrium, also offers a clear-sighted angle on the diverse variety of world cultures through a series of changing exhibitions. The café/restaurant here is pretty good, too.

→ HAGA SAGA

Gothenburg's most remarkably transformed quarter is **Haga**, its south-western suburb. Not so long ago it was so run-down that it was on the verge of demolition, but the nineteenth-century artisan houses were replenished in the 1980s and now some of the coolest of the city's cool hang out here. During the daytime it can be a delightful place to visit with its village-like ambience – sip a coffee at an outside table on a cobbled street, or wander round the stylish boutiques. Carry on a bit further west and you're in **Linné**, the smart area named after famed Swedish scientist Carl von Linné (whose 300th birthday was celebrated in style in the country in 2007). Linné has a rash of trendy places to eat and drink, and is now considered a second Avenyn, but without the tourist gloss. There are nineteen century buildings in the Dutch style, atmospheric antique shops and sex stores, all melding together to create a quarter very much with its own style and patina.

→ STOCK COMMENT

If you hear a Gothenburger making a dismissive remark about an 08-er, it's not some kind of Swedish rhyming slang. 08 is the telephone code for Stockholm, and saying something not

GOTHENBURG IN…

→ **ONE DAY**
The old town, the harbour, a meal in Haga, a stroll around Linné

→ **TWO DAYS**
Liseburg, The Museum of World Culture, Art Museum

→ **THREE DAYS**
A trip on a Pattan boat, a night at the Opera House (or a boat trip around the archipelago)

so nice about Stockholm is par for the course in Gothenburg.

→ STATUESQUE

At the southern end of Avenyn, in Götaplatsen square, stands the unmissable bronze statue of the nude Poseidon. In 1931, when he first appeared, the outlandish size of his male member caused outrage amongst the citizenry, so it was chopped painfully short, leaving modern onlookers to wonder at the somewhat out of proportion 7m high statue staring at them.

CALENDAR HIGHLIGHTS

Gothenburg is a serious party city, and the stress is on the serious side of things in May when the International Science Festival hits town. This is closely followed by the party element when, the same month, the Gothenburg Jazz Festival explodes into life. A sporting and musical dimension is much to the fore in June and July: June's Nokia Oops Cup is a well-established yachting event, with spectators close to the action as the trimarans race near to shore; blues fans should head to Slottsparken zoo the same month for the Gothenburg Blues Party. Then in July, the Gothia Cup at the Ullevi Stadium is a massively important youth cup for footballers from around the world, established for over thirty years with representations from over a hundred countries, and, yes, boasting more wins for Swedish teams than any other. August's Gothenburg Party is the biggest city festival in Sweden, taking up every inch the town has to offer, with more than six hundred concerts, cultural events and fireworks. Culture vultures can gorge themselves on the Art Biennial from September to November – a contemporary art smorgasbord with seminars and workshops at various city locations. As the nights get darker in October, Kulturnatta brings much light relief with events ranging from poetry readings to theatrical productions.

EATING OUT

No wonder Gothenburg's oldest food market is called Feskekörka or 'Fish Church'. Locals will always give thanks for the humble herring and the Fish Church does indeed look like a place of worship, but its pews are stalls of oysters, prawns and salmon, and where you might expect to find an organ loft, you'll find a restaurant instead. There are more than 650 of them in the city, a bewildering total for a population of around half a million. Food – and in particular the piscine variety - is a big reason for visiting Gothenburg. Its restaurants have earned a plethora of Michelin stars which are dotted all over the compact city. As is often the case in Scandinavia, best practice is to eat your main meal at lunchtime, when fixed price specials are such good value. Restaurants with a European base are worth trying out: there are a lot of them here and often they use a Swedish fishy staple as a starting point. If you're in town in the summer, don't miss out on the delicious local fruits for dessert: soft and juicy, they're a must. Gothenburgers also love coffee and cake, a combination they twin under the umbrella term 'fika', and ideal after a glass of traditional brannvin (vodka) and marinated herring. You're not expected to tip in Gothenburg's eateries, though it is customary to round the bill up to the nearest 10-20kr.

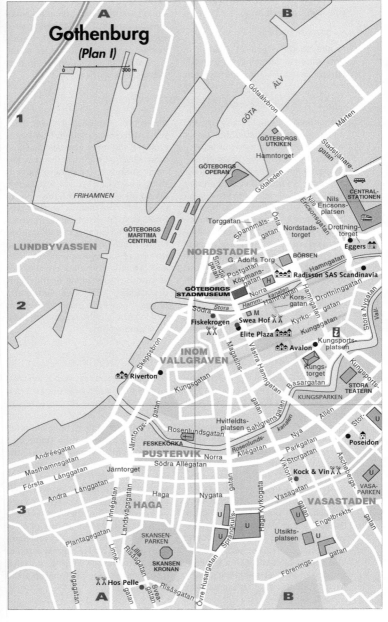

Gothenburg
(Plan I)

0   300 m

A

B

1

2

3

GÖTA ÄLV

GÖTAÄLVBRON

GÖTA

Mårten

Stadstjänare-gatan

GÖTEBORGS UTKIKEN

Hamntorget

GÖTEBORGS OPERAN

Götaleden

CENTRAL-STATIONEN

FRIHAMNEN

Nils Ericsons-platsen

Nils Ericsonsgatan

Torggatan

Spannmåls-gatan

Östra Nordstadstorget

Drottning-torget

LUNDBYVASSEN

GÖTEBORGS MARITIMA CENTRUM

NORDSTADEN

G. Adolfs Torg

BÖRSEN

Eggers

Snedje-gatan

Postgatan

Köpmans-gatan

Hamngatan

Radisson SAS Scandinavia

GÖTEBORGS STADMUSEUM

Norra Hamn-kanalen

Hamngatan

Drottninggatan

Stora Nygatan

Södra Stora

Hamngatan

Kors-gatan

Kyrko-gatan

Valli

Fiskekrogen

Swea Hof

Elite Plaza

Kungsgatan

Skeppsbron

INOM VALLGRAVEN

Magasins-gatan

Vastra Hamngatan

Avalon

Kungsports-platsen

Riverton

Kungsgatan

Kungs-torget

Basargatan

Kungsportsavenyn

STORA TEATERN

KUNGSPARKEN

Hvitfeldts-platsen

Sahlgrensgatan

Alléen

Stor

Järntorgs-gatan

Rosenlundsgatan

kanalen

U

FESKEKÖRKA

Rosenlunds-Allégatan

Nya

Parkgatan

Poseidon

Andréegatan

PUSTERVIK

Norra

Södra Allégatan

Storgatan

Viktoria

Kock & Vin

Aschebergs

Masthamnsgatan

Järngatan

Nygata

Vasagatan

VASA-PARKEN

Första Långgatan

Andra Långgatan

Haga

U

Hagal Kyrkogata

VASASTADEN

HAGA

Linnégatan

Landsvägsgatan

Nygata

Sprängkulls-gatan

U

Engelbrekts-

Plantagegatan

SKANSEN-PARKEN

U

Utsiktsplatsen

U

Linné

Lilla Risåsgatan

SKANSEN KRONAN

Övre Husargatan

Föreningsgatan

Vegagatan

Hos Pelle

Swea-gatan

Risåsgatan

A

B

C
D

E 20
E 6

Tidbloms

Krakowgatan

Redbergsvägen

Gubberogatan

GULLBERGSVASS

Kruthusgatan

1

Lagorströms-
platsen

Friggagatan

Notra

Perssonsgatan

Odinsplatsen

Stampgatan

STAMPEN

E 6-E 20

Willinsbron

Valåsgatan

Clarion Collection
H. Odin

Odinsgatan

Folkunga-
gatan

Anders

Scandic Crown

Dämme-
vägen

Polhems-
platsen

Stampgatan

Ulevi-
gatan

Skånegatan

ULLEVI

GÅRDA

E 6-E 20

TRÄDGÅRDS-
PALMHUSET

Levgrens-
vägen

Gårda-
vägen

FÖRENINGENS

Bohusgatan

Fabriks-

ÖVERÅS-
PARKER

2

PARK

Sten Sturegatan

HEDEN

BURGÅRDS
PARKEN

gatan

Nya Allén

Parkgatan

Södra
gatan

Mornington

Scandic H. Opalen

Skåne-
gatan

ETNOGRAFISKA
MUSEET

Kungsbackaleden

Vasagatan

Vägen

Engelbrektsgatan

Valhallagatan

RÖHSSKA
KONSTLÖJSDMUSEET

U

Scandic H. Rubinen

Berzeliigatan

SVENSKA
MÄSSAN

Tvåkanten

LORENSBERG

Sankt
Sigfrids
Plan

Basement

avenyn

Elite Park Avenue

STADS-
TEATERN

La Cucina
Italiana

Örgrytevägen

Gothia Towers

28+

Götabergs-
gatan

GÖTAPLATSEN

KONSERTHUSET

Korsvägen

3

Fond

LISEBERGS

Mölndalsån

E 6-E 20

GÖTEBORGS
KONSTMUSEET

Olof Wijksgatan

U

NÖJESPARK

Viktor

Rydberggatan

Södra
Vägen

Eklanda-
gatan

Thörnströms Kök

U

C
D

● Hotel
● Restaurant

821

SWEDEN - GOTHENBURG

Elite Park Avenue
⪡ 🛋 ╚ 🛁 ⑱ 🀄 ⅙ rest 🗚 ⅙ 🖴 ⑨ 🛰 🚗

Kungsportsavenyn 36-38 ⊠ S-400 15 – ℰ (031) **VISA 🌑 AE ⑩**
727 1000 – info.parkavenue@elite.se – Fax (031) 727 10 10 – www.elite.se
269 rm ⊡ – 🛇1000/2700 SEK 🛇🛇1200/2900 SEK – 48 suites   **C3**
Rest *Park Aveny Cafe* – Menu 325 SEK – Carte 235/585 SEK
◆ Business ◆ Modern ◆

Fully refurbished 1950s hotel with new spa, set on a busy main street. Decorated in shades of cream and chocolate, well-proportioned bedrooms offer high levels of comfort. Informal restaurant with pavement terrace offers classical French and international cooking.

Radisson SAS Scandinavia
╚ 🀄 ▢ ╚ 🗚 ⅙ 🖴 🛰 🚗 🚗 VISA 🌑 AE ⑩

Södra Hamngatan 59 ⊠ S-401 24 – ℰ (031) 758 50 00 **VISA 🌑 AE ⑩**
– reservations.gothenburg@radissonsas.com – Fax (031) 758 50 01
– www.gothenburg.radissonsas.com   **B2**
349 rm ⊡ – 🛇890/2345 SEK 🛇🛇990/2445 SEK – 18 suites
Rest *Atrium Bar & Restaurant* – *(Closed lunch Saturday, Sunday and in summer)* Menu 215/530 SEK – Carte 355/575 SEK
◆ Business ◆ Modern ◆

Grand commercial hotel with impressive atrium courtyard complete with water features and glass elevators. Refurbished, modern rooms boast choice of décor and impressive mod cons. A range of international dishes offered in restaurant housed within the atrium.

Gothia Towers
⪡ 🀄 ╚ 🗚 ⅙ 🖴 🛰 🚗 🚗 VISA 🌑 AE ⑩

Mässans Gata 24 ⊠ S-402 26 – ℰ (031) 750 88 00 – infomasters@
gothiatowers.com – Fax (031) 750 88 85 – www.gothiatowers.com
697 rm ⊡ – 🛇995/2595 SEK 🛇🛇1145/2595 SEK – 7 suites   **D3**
Rest *Heaven 23* – Menu 255/515 SEK – Carte 475/605 SEK
Rest *Incontro* – ℰ (031) 750 88 05 *(Closed Sunday dinner)* Menu 125/425 SEK
– Carte 395/677 SEK
◆ Business ◆ Modern ◆

Set by the largest amusement park in Sweden, this spacious twin-towered hotel boasts elegant modern Scandinavian décor and is popular with businesspeople. Top floor Heaven 23 offers spectacular city views and contemporary cuisine, while Incontro serves modern Italian and international dishes.

Elite Plaza
╚ 🀄 🗚 ⅙ 🖴 🛰 🚗 🚗 VISA 🌑 AE ⑩

Västra Hamngatan 3 ⊠ S-402 22 – ℰ (031) 720 40 40 – info.gbgplaza@elite.se
– Fax (031) 720 40 10 – www.elite.se – Closed 3 days Christmas   **B2**
140 rm ⊡ – 🛇1200/1500 SEK 🛇🛇2500 SEK – 6 suites
Rest *Swea Hof* – see below
◆ Luxury ◆ ◆ Modern ◆

Discreet and stylishly converted late 19C building. Rooms embody understated luxury with those overlooking the atrium sharing its lively atmosphere. Smart cocktail bar.

Avalon
🛋 🀄 ▢ ╚ 🗚 ⅙ 🖴 🛰 🚗 🚗 VISA 🌑 AE ⑩

Kungstorget 9 ⊠ S-411 17 – ℰ (031) 751 02 00 – info@avalonhotel.se
– Fax (031) 751 02 08 – www.avalonhotel.se   **B2**
101 rm ⊡ – 🛇1190/2990 SEK 🛇🛇1490/2990 SEK – 3 suites
Rest – *(Closed Sunday January-March)* Menu 275/650 SEK – Carte 489/665 SEK
◆ Business ◆ Modern ◆

Modern hotel near tourist office in the city centre. Spacious, contemporary bedrooms boast all mod cons; some have open baths; others, mini-spa or mini-gym. Rooftop swimming pool. International dishes offered in ground floor restaurant.

Clarion Collection H. Odin *without rest*
╚ 🀄 ⅙ 🖴 🛰 🚗 P

Odinsgatan 6 ⊠ S-411 03 – ℰ (031) 745 22 00 **VISA 🌑 AE ⑩**
– reservation.cc.odin@choice.se – Fax (031) 711 24 60 – www.hotelodin.se
156 rm ⊡ – 🛇1045/2145 SEK 🛇🛇1245/2395 SEK – 24 suites   **C2**
◆ Business ◆ Modern ◆

Central location near railway station. Smart, Scandic-style, well-equipped, serviced apartments with mini-kitchen; also spacious and appealing suites.

Scandic H. Rubinen 🛜 & 📶 rest ↔ 🖵 ☎ 🛐 💶 VISA 🆎 ⓞ

Kungsportsavenyn 24 ✉ *S-400 14* – ℰ *(031) 751 54 00* – *rubinen@
scandichotels.com* – *Fax (031) 751 54 11* – *www.scandichotels.com/rubinen*
191 rm ⌲ – 📱950/2150 SEK 📱📱1250/2250 SEK – 1 suite **C3**
Rest – *(Closed Sunday)* Menu 98 SEK (lunch) – Carte 150/300 SEK
✦ Business ✦ Modern ✦

Well-located central hotel with smart, modern style and international atmosphere.
Comfy, modern bedrooms in warm shades. Top-floor suites boast delightful roof
terraces. Modish restaurant with dominant bar; trendy "New Latino" style cuisine.

Riverton ≼ 🕥 & 📶 rest ↔ 🖵 🛐 🅿 VISA 🆎 ⓞ

Stora Badhusgatan 26 ✉ *S-411 21* – ℰ *(031) 750 10 00* – *riverton@riverton.se*
– *Fax (031) 750 10 01* – *www.riverton.se* **A2**
186 rm ⌲ – 📱995/1995 SEK 📱📱1295/2295 SEK – 8 suites
Rest – *(Closed Sunday)* Carte 350/510 SEK
✦ Business ✦ Modern ✦

Modern hotel offering fine view of city and docks from upper floors. Some rooms
redecorated in a contemporary style; others have sleek Swedish décor. Good business facilities. 12th floor restaurant, overlooking Göta Älv river and docks. Local
and international cuisine.

Scandic Crown 🛵 🕥 & 📶 ↔ 🖵 🛐 🅿 🚗 VISA 🆎 ⓞ

Polhemsplatsen 3 ✉ *S-411 11* – ℰ *(031) 751 51 00* – *crown@scandichotels.com*
– *Fax (031) 751 51 11* – *www.scandichotels.com* **C2**
338 rm ⌲ – 📱1250/2150 SEK 📱📱1350/2250 SEK – 4 suites
Rest – *(Closed Sunday)* *(buffet lunch)* Menu 139 SEK – Carte approx. 448 SEK
✦ Business ✦ Modern ✦

Modern group hotel in good location for transport connections. Fresh, bright, functional rooms with wood floors and colourful fabrics. Executive rooms with balconies. Top floor gym and sauna. Pleasant atrium restaurant with a wide range of
Swedish and international cuisine.

Scandic H. Opalen 🛵 🕥 & 📶 ↔ 🖵 🛐 🛐 🚗 VISA 🆎 ⓞ

Engelbrektsgatan 73 ✉ *S-412 52* – ℰ *(031) 751 53 00* – *opalen@
scandichotels.com* – *Fax (031) 751 53 11* – *www.scandichotels.com*
239 rm – 📱650/2300 SEK 📱📱950/2400 SEK, ⌲ 130 SEK – 4 suites **C2**
Rest – *(Closed Sunday)* Menu 199 SEK – Carte 350/389 SEK
✦ Business ✦ Modern ✦

Corporate hotel with pleasant relaxation zone, set close to the business centre and
stadium. Classical bedrooms vary in size but all offer good facilities. Restaurant
offers wide ranging Swedish and international fare.

Eggers 🛜 ↔ 🖵 🛐 🛐 VISA 🆎 ⓞ

Drottningtorget ✉ *S-404 24* – ℰ *(031) 333 44 40* – *hotel.eggers@telia.com*
– *Fax (031) 333 44 49* – *www.hoteleggers.se* – *Closed 23-27 December*
69 rm ⌲ – 📱835/1945 SEK 📱📱1290/2260 SEK **B2**
Rest – *(Closed July, 23-27 December and Bank Holidays)* Menu 190/500 SEK
– Carte 360/525 SEK
✦ Traditional ✦ Classic ✦

Charming 1850s hotel, one of Sweden's oldest: wrought iron and stained glass on
staircase, Gothenburg's oldest lift. Rooms feature period furniture and fittings.
Ornate restaurant busy during day, more elegant in evening. Traditional Swedish
and international cuisine.

Novotel Göteborg ≼ 🕥 & ↔ 🖵 🛐 🛐 🅿 VISA 🆎 ⓞ

*Klippan 1 (Southwest : 3.5 km by Andréeg taking Kiel-Klippan Ö exit,
or boat from Rosenlund)* ✉ *S-414 51* – ℰ *(031) 720 22 00* – *info@novotel.se*
– *Fax (031) 720 22 99* – *www.novotel.se*
151 rm ⌲ – 📱1540/1640 SEK 📱📱1690/1790 SEK – 4 suites
Rest *Carnegie Kaj* – *(buffet lunch)* Carte 253/500 SEK
✦ Chain hotel ✦ Business ✦ Functional ✦

Converted brewery set on the waterfront, with attractive atrium style lobby, views
of the Göta Älv river and spacious bedrooms displaying international styling and
décor. Serving international dishes, Carnegie Kaj offers views over the harbour. Sjo-
magasinet restaurant is close by.

Mornington 🛋 ⅏ 🅰🅲 rest ⅏ 🖭 ¶ 🕍 ⇆ 🆅🅸🆂🅰 ⓐ 🅰🅴 ⓞ

Kungsportsavenyn 6 ⊠ S-411 36 – ℰ (031) 767 34 00
– goteborg@mornington.se – Fax (031) 711 34 39 – www.mornington.se
98 rm ⌂ – ♦636/2950 SEK ♦♦1076/2950 SEK   **C2**
Rest *Brasserie Lipp* – Menu 479 SEK (dinner) – Carte 350/500 SEK
◆ Business ◆ Classic ◆

Set on a famous shopping street, a modern 'office block' façade conceals this hotel.
Compact, wood-furnished bedrooms range in size and comfort, with some overlooking the Avenue. Pleasant brasserie-style restaurant offers hearty home cooking.

Tidbloms ⅏ ⅏ ¶ 🕍 🅿 🆅🅸🆂🅰 ⓐ 🅰🅴 ⓞ

Olskroksgatan 23 ⊠ S-416 66 – ℰ (031) 707 50 00 – info@tidbloms.se – Fax (031)
707 50 99 – www.tidbloms.se – Closed 10-13 April and 20 December-8 January
42 rm ⌂ – ♦750/1275 SEK ♦♦895/1575 SEK   **D1**
Rest – *(closed Sunday)* Menu 155 SEK
◆ Business ◆ Traditional ◆ Functional ◆

Old red-brick hotel set in a quiet residential area, a short tram ride from the town.
The new owners plan to refurbish the classical bedrooms throughout 2009. Peaceful library. Casual dining in the relaxed, friendly restaurant.

Poseidon without rest 🅰🅲 ⅏ 🖭 ¶ 🆅🅸🆂🅰 ⓐ 🅰🅴 ⓞ

Storgatan 33 ⊠ S-411 38 – ℰ (031) 10 05 50 – info@hotelposeidon.com
– Fax (031) 13 83 91 – www.hotelposeidon.com   **B3**
49 rm ⌂ – ♦745/1550 SEK ♦♦995/1550 SEK
◆ Family ◆ Functional ◆

Informal hotel in residential area not far from main shopping street. Comfortable neutral décor and functional furnishings in rooms. Accommodation for families available.

Sjömagasinet (Leif Mannerström) ⇐ 🛋 ⇔ 🅿 🆅🅸🆂🅰 ⓐ 🅰🅴 ⓞ

Klippans Kulturreservat 5 (Southwest : 3.5 km by Andréeg
taking Kiel-Klippan Ö exit, or boat from Rosenlund.
Also evenings and weekends in summer from Lilla Bommens Hamn) ⊠ S-414
– ℰ (031) 775 59 20 – info@sjomagasinet.se – Fax (031) 24 55 39
– www.sjomagasinet.se – Closed Midsummer, 24-25 & 31 December, 1 January,
lunch Saturday, Sunday & Bank Holidays and Sunday January-April
Rest – *(booking essential)* Menu 425/545 SEK (lunch) – Carte 690/910 SEK 🕸
Spec. Kalix bleak roe with red onions, chives, sour cream and fried toast.
Anglerfish with mushroom consommé, Svecia cheese and spinach. Crème
brûlée with plums and plum sorbet.
◆ Seafood ◆ Cosy ◆

Delightful 18C former warehouse on the waterfront. Busy restaurant on two floors
with ship's mast and charming terrace. Accomplished, flavourful seafood cooking
uses quality ingredients.

Thörnströms Kök 🅰🅲 ⅏ ⇔ 🆅🅸🆂🅰 ⓐ 🅰🅴 ⓞ

Teknologgatan 3 ⊠ S-41132 – ℰ (031) 16 20 66 – info@thornstromskok.com
– Fax (031) 16 40 17 – www.thornstromskok.com – Closed 13 July-11 August,
Christmas, Sunday, Monday and Bank Holidays   **C3**
Rest – *(booking essential) (dinner only)* Menu 495 SEK – Carte 545/645 SEK 🕸
◆ Seasonal cuisine ◆ Neighbourhood ◆

Well-established, elegant restaurant in a quiet neighbourhood area. Blending
modern French and Swedish techniques, the ambitious kitchen produce carefully
conceived dishes. Professional service.

28+ 🅰🅲 ⅏ ⇔ 🆅🅸🆂🅰 ⓐ 🅰🅴 ⓞ

Götabergsgatan 28 ⊠ S-411 34 – ℰ (031) 20 21 61 – info@28plus.se
– Fax (031) 81 97 57 – www.28plus.se – Closed 10-13 April, 28 June-26 August,
23-27 & 31 December, 1-2 & 6-10 January and Sunday   **C3**
Rest – *(dinner only)* Carte 585/620 SEK 🕸
Spec. Scallops with Baeri caviar, beetroot and cep bouillon. Venison with
Brussels sprouts, chanterelles and a parsnip and gin sauce. Apple and vanilla
mousse with caramel ice cream.
◆ Modern ◆ Formal ◆

Well-established, enthusiastically run restaurant in an enchanting candlelit cellar.
Well-crafted cooking is intricate, and detailed. Set menus offer wine pairings;
cheese course taken seriously.

XX   **Kock & Vin**   AC ↵ VISA ⚫ AE ①
※

Viktoriagatan 12 ⊠ *S-411 25 – ℰ (031) 701 79 79 – info@kockvin.se*
– www.kockvin.se – Closed 5 July-5 August, Christmas and New Year
Rest *– (dinner only)* Menu 595/795 SEK – Carte 555/625 SEK ఄ   **B3**
Spec. Scallops and oysters with a parsley and cauliflower snow. Ling poached in ham bouillon with beetroot and hazelnut vinaigrette. Cloudberries
baked with sour cream, almonds and crumbs of toffee.
♦ Innovative ♦ Friendly ♦

Agenda-setting, candlelit restaurant with ornate 19C ceiling and modern basement bar. Confidently blending textures and colours, the original, artistic cooking
displays strength and ambition.

XX   **Basement** (Ulf Wagner)   AC ↵ VISA ⚫ AE ①
※

Götabergsgatan 28 ⊠ *S-411 – ℰ (031) 28 27 29 – bokning@restbasement.com*
– Fax (031) 28 27 37 – www.restbasement.com
– Closed 15 July-15 August, Christmas-New Year and Sunday   **C3**
Rest *– (dinner only) (set menu only)* Menu 550/650 SEK ఄ
Spec. Shellfish 'in mist'. Lamb with truffle polenta and goat cheese nouga-
tine. Chocolate ganache with yoghurt ice cream.
♦ Innovative ♦ Fashionable ♦

Modern basement restaurant with relaxed atmosphere and friendly service. Passionate, highly imaginative cooking produces artistic, flavoursome dishes that explore
unusual combinations.

XX   **Fiskekrogen**   AC ↵ VISA ⚫ AE ①

Lilla Torget 1 ⊠ *S-411 18 – ℰ (031) 10 10 05 – info@fiskekrogen.com*
– Fax (031) 10 10 06 – www.fiskekrogen.com
– Closed 4 weeks Summer, Christmas-New Year and Sunday   **B2**
Rest *–* Menu 295/645 SEK – Carte 590/690 SEK ఄ
♦ Seafood ♦ Brasserie ♦

Striking 1920s restaurant with wood panelling and smart columns. Extensive buffet
lunch upholds the restaurant's reputation for quality seafood. Wine list boasts over
500 bins.

XX   **Hos Pelle**   ↵ VISA ⚫ AE ①

Djupedalsgatan 2 ⊠ *S-413 07 – ℰ (031) 12 10 31 – info@hospelle.com*
– Fax (031) 775 38 32 – www.hospelle.com
– Closed 6 weeks Summer, Sunday, lunch Saturday and Bank Holidays
Rest *–* Menu 250/375 SEK – Carte lunch 375 SEK   **A3**
♦ Traditional ♦ Neighbourhood ♦

Popular local restaurant with comfortable atmosphere, displaying Swedish art. Serves
classic and modern Swedish cuisine prepared to high standard. Ground floor bistro.

XX   **Swea Hof** *– at Elite Plaza Hotel*   AC VISA ⚫ AE ①

Västra Hamngatan 3 ⊠ *S-404 22 – ℰ (031) 720 40 40 – sweahof@elite.se*
– Fax (031) 720 40 10 – www.elite.se/sweahof – Closed 3 days Christmas
Rest *– (Closed lunch Saturday and Sunday)* Menu 425/625 SEK   **B2**
Carte 515/665 SEK
♦ Modern ♦ Formal ♦

Striking atrium-style restaurant in heart of hotel with glass roof on metal framework and open-plan kitchen. Dinner menu offers elaborate and accomplished
modern cuisine.

X   **Fond**   AC ↵ VISA ⚫ AE ①
※

Götaplatsen ⊠ *S 412 56 – ℰ (031) 81 25 80 – fond@fondrestaurang.com*
– Fax (031) 18 37 90 – www.fondrestaurang.com – closed 4 weeks Summer,
2 weeks Christmas, Sunday, Saturday lunch and Bank Holidays   **C3**
Rest *–* Carte 505/740 SEK ఄ
Spec. Langoustines with black pepper carrots and orange sauce. Rack of
lamb with smoked leg and a sweet and sour gravy. Pear with toffee sauce
and a lingonberry sorbet.
♦ Modern ♦ Trendy ♦

Well-established restaurant with bright, stylish interior and relaxed atmosphere.
Simple, well-informed Swedish cooking has a classical base and unique, contemporary touches.

La Cucina Italiana
�̂ 🌿 VISA 🆗 AE ①

Skånegatan 33 ✉ *S-412 52 – 𝒞 (031) 16 63 07 – pietro@swipnet.ie*
– Fax (031) 81 12 19 – www.lacucinaitaliana.nu
– Restricted opening Christmas, closed 31 December, 1 January and Sunday
Rest *– (booking essential) (dinner only)* Menu 620 SEK   **C3**
– Carte approx. 580 SEK
♦ Italian ♦ Friendly ♦

Intimate, keenly run restaurant by the convention centre. Enthusiastic kitchen borrows inspiration from all over Italy. 6 course 'Creative' and 'Italiano' menus or an à la carte.

Tvåkanten
🛂 🌿 ⇄ VISA 🆗 AE ①

Kungsportsavenyn 27 ✉ *S-411 36 – 𝒞 (031) 18 21 15 – info@tvakanten.se*
– Fax (031) 81 11 98 – www.tvakanten.se
– Closed 25 December, 1 January and Sunday lunch   **C3**
Rest *–* Carte 395/710 SEK 🍷
♦ Traditional ♦ Brasserie ♦

Busy characterful restaurant with simpler lunch and more extensive dinner menus. Dining rooms with brick walls, plus elegant first-floor private dining room. Rustic fare.

at Eriksberg **West : 6 km by Götaälvbron and Lundbyleden, or boat from Rosenlund**

Quality Hotel 11
≼ 👘 ⅃ 🔟 🌿 🖭 ¶° 🖪 🅿 VISA 🆗 AE ①

Maskingatan 11 ✉ *S-417 64 – 𝒞 (031) 779 11 11 – q.hotel11@choice.se*
– Fax (031) 779 11 10 – www.hotel11.se
260 rm ⌧ *–* †790/2199 SEK ††990/2399 SEK
Rest *Kök & Bar 67 – (dinner only)* Carte 350/400 SEK
♦ Business ♦ Functional ♦

Striking former shipbuilding warehouse, part see-through; there is so much glass! Rooms feature stylish modern Scandinavian interior design with pale wood and bright fabrics. Gym and sauna with a view. Upper floor restaurant with bar area, waterway views and international cooking.

Villan *without rest*
≼ 🖭 ¶° 🅿 VISA 🆗 AE ①

Sjöportsgatan 2 ✉ *S-417 64 – 𝒞 (31) 725 77 77 – info@hotelvillan.com*
– Fax (31) 725 77 70 – www.hotelvillan.com
26 rm ⌧ *–* †1000/1300 SEK ††1100/1700 SEK
♦ Modern ♦

Modern, intimate hotel set in a developing area; easily reached by boat. Simple, contemporary bedrooms display subtle hues and good mod cons – one boasts a private sauna and great views. Breakfast is served at the River Café restaurant on the pier.

River Café
≼ 🛂 🔟 🌿 VISA 🆗 AE ①

Dockepiren ✉ *S-417 64 – 𝒞 (031) 51 00 00 – info@rivercafe.se*
– Fax (31) 51 00 01 – www.rivercafe.se – Closed Sunday
Rest *–* Menu 295/549 SEK
♦ Seasonal cuisine ♦ Friendly ♦

Delightfully set on the pier in Eriksburg with fine view to harbour. Agreeable bar; elegant first-floor restaurant with panoramic glass frontage. Seasonal, international cooking.

at Landvetter Airport **East : 30 km by Rd 40**

Landvetter Airport Hotel
🛂 🛗 👘 ⅃ 🔟 🌿 🖭 ¶° 🖪 🅿

Flygets Hotellväg ✉ *S-438 13 – 𝒞 (031) 97 75 50*   VISA 🆗 AE ①
– info@landvetterairporthotel.se – Fax (031) 94 64 70
– www.landvetterairporthotel.se
134 rm ⌧ *–* †1445/1595 SEK ††1595 SEK – 1 suite
Rest *– (buffet lunch)* Menu 198 SEK – Carte 225/508 SEK
♦ Business ♦ Modern ♦

Adjacent to airport. Welcoming bedrooms; 'old' style rooms are bright and feature Swedish décor in bright colours; 'new' rooms are more contemporary. Modern and business facilities. Relaxed restaurant and terrace off the main lobby. Offers Swedish and global fare.

SWITZERLAND
SUISSE, SCHWEIZ, SVIZZERA

PROFILE

→ **AREA:**
41 284 km² (15 940 sq mi).

→ **POPULATION:**
7 460 000 (est. 2006), density = 181 per km².

→ **CAPITAL:**
Bern (Berne) (conurbation 349 100 inhabitants).

→ **CURRENCY:**
Swiss Franc (CHF); rate of exchange CHF 1 = € 0.65 = US$ 0.83 (Dec 2008).

→ **GOVERNMENT:**
Federation of 26 cantons with 2 assemblies (National Council and Council of State) forming the Federal Assembly.

→ **LANGUAGES:**
German (64% of population), French (20%), Italian (7%) are spoken in all administrative departments, shops, hotels and restaurants. Romansh (1%) in the Grisons canton.

→ **SEPCIFIC PUBLIC HOLIDAYS:**
Berchtold's Day (2 January); Good Friday (Friday before Easter);
Swiss National Holiday (1 August); St. Stephen's Day (26 December). Thanksgiving (Jeûne Fédéral in French; Bettag in German) is observed in all cantons, except Geneva, on the third Sunday in September; the Geneva canton holds Thanksgiving on the second Thursday in September.

→ **LOCAL TIME:**
GMT + 1 hour in winter, GMT+ 2 hours in summer.

→ **CLIMATE**
Temperate continental, varies with altitude – most of the country has cold winters and warm summers (Bern: January: 0°C, July: 19°C).

→ **INTERNATIONAL DIALLING CODE**
00 41 followed by the area or city code (Geneva: **22**, Bern: **31**, Zurich: **44** or **43**) and then the local number.

→ **EMERGENCY**
Police: ☎ **117**; Medical emergencies: ☎ **144**; Fire Brigade: ☎ **118**.

Anglo-Phone (24 hr information and helpline in English): ☎ **0900 576 444**.

→ **ELECTRICITY:**
220 volts AC, 50 Hz; 2-pin round-shaped continental plugs.

→ **FORMALITIES**
Travellers from the European Union (EU), Iceland and the main countries of North and South America need a national identity card or passport (America: passport required) to visit Switzerland for less than three months (tourism or business purpose). For visitors from other countries a visa may be required, in addition to a passport, especially for those wishing to stay for longer than three months. We advise you to check with your embassy before travelling.

BERN
BERNE

Population: 122 300 (conurbation 349 100) – Altitude: 548m

Bern Tourisme

To look at Bern, you'd never believe it a capital city. Small and beautifully proportioned, its old town sits sedately on a spur overlooking the river Aare, at a point where the river bends back on itself, giving a graceful curve to the landscape. UNESCO was so impressed it gave Bern World Heritage status.

In fact, the little city is the best preserved medieval centre north of the Alps, and the layout of the streets has barely changed since the Duke of Zahringen chose the superbly defended site to found a city over eight hundred years ago. Most of the buildings date from the period between the 14 and 16C when Bern was at the height of its power – one good reason why it feels much more human than many other European cities. The cluster of cobbled lanes, surrounded by ornate sandstone arcaded buildings and numerous fountains and wells, give it the feel of a delightfully overgrown village. Albert Einstein felt so secure here that while ostensibly employed as a clerk in the Bern patent office he managed to find the time to work out his Theory of Relativity.

LIVING THE CITY

Bern is a wonderfully compact city. Its **Old Town** stretches eastwards over a narrow peninsula, and is surrounded by the curving **River Aare**. The eastern limit of the Old Town is the **Nydeggbrücke** (bridge); the western end is the **Käfigturm** tower, once a city gate and prison. On the southern side of the Aare lies the small **Kirchenfeld** quarter which houses some impressive museums. The capital's famous brown bears are over the river via the Nydeggbrücke.

PRACTICAL INFORMATION

ARRIVAL-DEPARTURE

Bern-Belp International Airport is 9km southeast of the city. There's a shuttle bus every 30 minutes which takes 20 minutes to the city centre. A taxi will cost around 50CHF.

TRANSPORT

The Bern Card is well worth investing in. It gives unlimited travel, free admission to museums and gardens, and various reductions around the city. It's available from the Tourist Office, museums and hotels, and is valid for 24hr, 48hr or 72hr.

As Bern is small enough to walk around, it requires no more than a super-efficient bus and tram network. A short cable-railway links the Marzili quarter to the Bundeshaus. You can buy your ticket at the bus or tram stop.

EXPLORING BERN

It might sound like a cliché, but Bern is the secret jewel of the Alps. Its spectacular setting takes newcomers aback. Perched aloft on its precipice, surrounded by steep, wooded hills and mountains, who could resist a visit to one of the city's fifty-foot high bridges to watch the gushing grey-green foaming glacier waters of the Aare below? It's not hard to see why UNESCO bestowed its seal of approval upon Bern in 1983. Its perfectly preserved ancient centre comprises superb five-storey red-roofed houses, many of which date back to the 15C, separated by broad, cobbled streets enlivened by equally ancient, brightly coloured fountains. From springtime onwards, the rich sandstone of the buildings is shocked into life by dazzlingly-hued hanging baskets and the heraldic pennants of the Swiss cantons. It's an easy place to explore on foot, and even easier to get your bearings. With dominant landmarks all around your eyes would have to be closed to miss either the river, the Prison Tower, the **Clock Tower**, or the spiralling splendour of the Gothic **Cathedral.**

➜ TOWERING ACHIEVEMENT

Bern's dramatic Cathedral is the tallest church in Switzerland. It was a long time in creation: over four hundred and fifty years, from 1421 until 1893, when the spire was finally added. The least you can do is pay it a visit, and when you do, don't miss the dramatic 15C stained glass windows in the choir. The tower is unusual in that it still has tower-keepers to look after it. If you're feeling energetic, you can climb to the top yourself, and take in a fine view of the city's curves. There's barely a straight line to be seen as cobbled streets wind every which way, forming fascinating parabolas. Back down at *gasse* level, a little way west from the Cathedral, is the central landmark of Bern, the Clock Tower. Its beautiful astronomical clockface has been keeping time here since 1530 and its elaborate chimes start at four minutes before the hour, when mechanical bears and a crowing cock start their regular procession in front of captivated visitors.

→ SHOPPING? IT'S COVERED

Appearances can deceive. On first acquaintance, the Swiss capital may hardly seem like a retail hot-spot. But rather surprisingly, this is a city beloved for its shopping opportunities. Not for Bern the antiseptic malls or cloned high streets of less fortunate towns. Instead, it boasts the longest covered shopping promenade in Europe. Sheltering underneath arcades with medieval vaulted roofs covering the pavement below, these dainty shops take the form of small boutiques selling a bewildering assortment of things. And they're entwined with charming cafés and restaurants, many within atmospheric vaulted cellars. Most of these arcades are along an east-west axis running from the Nydeggbrücke ; at its western end a sprinkling of colourful markets brings you back out into the open air.

→ FEAT OF KLEE

The world of art has a picture-perfect setting here. Until 2005, the main attraction was based at the **Museum of Fine Arts** (on the old town's north side), and with good reason: its globally renowned collection spans the 14C to 20C and includes everything from early Renaissance to Old Master to French Impressionist, not forgetting a broad representation of Switzerland's finest, including Albert Anker and Ferdinand Hodler. Since 2005, many visitors to Bern have been beating a path to the easterly **Schöngrün** quarter, to an audacious and extraordinary wave-shaped museum which emerges from a hillside: The **Zentrum Paul Klee**. This holds a mind-boggling amount of paintings (shown in rotation) by Bern's most famous artist, including four thousand works donated by a couple of collectors alone. The building was designed by Renzo Piano, creator of Paris's Pompidou Centre, and also includes a chamber concert hall.

Cross the **Kirchenfeldbrücke** to the southern side of the Aare, and you're in a museum wonderland. There's the **Bern Museum of History** in a building like a grand medieval castle; the **Art Gallery** with its rolling programme of modern art exhibitions; the **Swiss Alpine Museum**, which offers an engrossing look at environmental issues as well as the history, flora and fauna of the Alps; and three other museums with an eclectic focus ranging from human communications, to Swiss rifles to natural history.

Being out of doors is the real clue to getting the most out of Bern. A top walk is beside the Aare through the former artisans' quarter of **Matte**, or, in the eastern section of the main axis through the old town, the streets of **Postgasse** and **Gerechtigkeitsgasse**. Some of the oldest and most appealing of Bern's arcaded buildings are here: many were built as guild houses, and sport decorative motifs proudly pointing out the relevant trade.

→ A FINE TOWN, RELATIVELY SPEAKING

Albert Einstein was a man who loved the outdoors: he would famously shuffle around the streets of Bern, often in green slippers, carrying a net bag for his shopping. He lived on **Kramgasse** for two years from 1903, and it was while here that he began to develop his Theory of Relativity. His small apartment is now a little museum, hung with documents and photos, and containing his writing desk. There's not much doubt the great man would have related strongly to the street in which he lived: in an earlier decade, the poet Goethe called Kramgasse "the most beautiful street in the world".

→ FRINGE BENEFITS

Adding to the beauty and beguilement of Bern's streets are a warren of fringe theatres, many of them tucked comfortably away in the cellars of houses along the thoroughfares of the old town. More conventionally, performance lovers can head for the very visible Stadttheater on centrally located Kornhausplatz, to get a more mainstream dramatic fix. This is Bern's most beautiful theatre, the primary venue for the city's resident opera company and contemporary dance troupe. Another fine show is offered at the Bundesplatz, home of the Swiss Federal Parliament. The fountain in the square has twenty-six jets, each one representing a canton. In the summer months, these shoot skywards every thirty minutes, stopping passers-by in their tracks, and enhancing the centuries-old feeling that in its modest way Bern is just a delightful place to be.

CALENDAR HIGHLIGHTS

It's not often that deepest November plays host to a city's biggest annual bash; even less so when onions are involved. But Bern's November Onion Market takes pride of place in the events calendar. Taking over the old town between the railway station and the Bundesplatz, over fifty tons of onions from all over Switzerland guarantee a tear-jerking celebration. Incongruously, jazz is the other big-hitter in the city. There are four annual festivals, two of which take place in January and February (the Jazz Weekend and the Be-Jazz Winterfestival). The biggest is the week-long International Jazz Festival in May, which features top stars from the worlds of jazz, blues, gospel and Latin. Costumed parades light up the streets at the Fasnacht Carnival in February, while the summer's two top events are the Gurtenfestival (July), a high-powered rock music event in Gurtenpark, over the river to the south of the old town, and Altstadtsommer,

BERN IN...

→ ONE DAY
River walk, Old Town (Cathedral, Clock Tower, arcades), Museum of Fine Arts, cellar fringe theatre

→ TWO DAYS
Zentrum Paul Klee, Einstein's house, Stadttheater

→ THREE DAYS
Repeat some of the delights of the first two days...but more slowly!

a series of concerts in the magical setting of the old town itself. There's also an absorbing Bern Dance Festival in June, in which people arrive from all over the world to give displays of their country's dance styles. You can check it out in bars, restaurants, concert halls and theatres.

EATING OUT

Bern is a great place to sit and enjoy a meal. Pride of place must go to the good range of al fresco venues in the squares of the old town, invariably popular spots to enjoy coffee and cake. Hiding away in the arcades are many delightful dining choices; some of the best for location alone are in vaulted cellars that breathe historic ambience. There's no shortage of international restaurants, either, but if you want to feel what a real Swiss restaurant is like, head for a traditional old-style rustic eatery complete with cow-bells, and sample local dishes like the Berner Platte - a heaving plate of hot and cold meats, served with beans and sauerkraut – or treberwurst, a sausage poached with fermented grape skins. Along with German restaurants, French and Italian Switzerland each has its own distinctive cuisine well represented here, so it's not difficult to go from rösti to risotto and gnocchi, raclette and fondue. And, of course, there's always cheese and chocolate waiting in the wings. A fifteen percent service charge is always added, but it's customary to round the bill up.

→ **BEAR NECESSITIES**

For good or bad, there are bears in Bern, in the bear pits, just across from the Nydeggbrücke. The city is named after bears, and they've been kept in the city since the early sixteenth century. Despite constant protests from animal rights activists, the bears are a very popular tourist attraction.

→ **MOUNTAIN CLIMB**

If you fancy a memorable day trip from Bern, the city is handily placed for excursions to the dramatic mountain ranges of the Bernese Oberland. It's only twenty minutes by train to Thun, where lake cruise boats leave from outside the station. You can easily get to Interlaken, but best of all, perhaps, is the unforgettable journey to Europe's highest railway station at Jungfraujoch, an easy day trip.

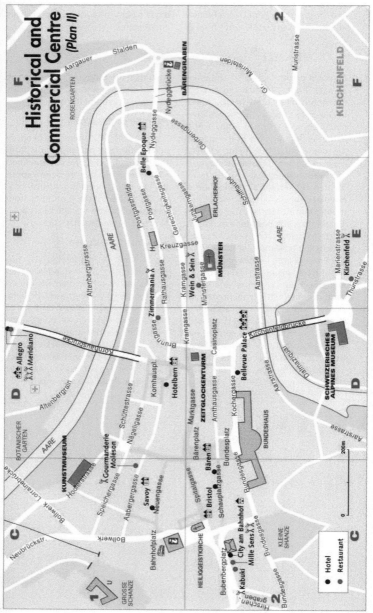

Historical and Commercial Centre *(Plan II)*

Hotel ●

Restaurant ●

Bellevue Palace ⟨⟩ 🏠 ⟨⟩ 🅰🅒 rm 🖂 ⟨⟩ ⟨⟩ 🅟 🅰🅔 🅥🅢🅐 ⟨⟩ 🅐🅔 ⟨⟩
Kochergasse 3 ⊠ *3000 –* ⟨⟩ *031 320 45 45 – info@bellevue-palace.ch*
– Fax 031 320 46 46 – www.bellevue-palace.ch   **D2**
115 rm – 🛏380/475 CHF 🛏🛏495/590 CHF, ⥿ 36 CHF – 15 suites
Rest *Bellevue Terrasse* – Menu 72 CHF (lunch)/135 CHF
– Carte 83/152 CHF 🍃
♦ Palace ♦ Classic ♦
Situated next door to the parliament building, the Grand Hotel breathes exclusiveness. Note its luxurious setting, very comfortable classical rooms and elegant suites. Enjoy a beautiful view of the Aare from the terrace of the restaurant.

Allegro ⟨⟩ 🏠 🎰 🎰 ⟨⟩ 🅰🅒 ⟨⟩ 🖂 ⟨⟩ 🅟 🅿 ⟨⟩ 🅥🅢🅐 ⟨⟩ 🅐🅔 ⟨⟩
Kornhausstr. 3 ⊠ *3013 –* ⟨⟩ *031 339 55 00 – info@kursaal-bern.ch*
– Fax 031 339 55 10 – www.kursaal-bern.ch   **D1**
171 rm – 🛏250/660 CHF 🛏🛏310/660 CHF, ⥿ 30 CHF
Rest *Meridiano* – see below
Rest *Yù* – *(closed 1 - 6 January, 6 - 21 April, 27 July - 19 August and Saturday lunch, Monday – Tuesday)* Menu 28 CHF (lunch)/78 CHF – Carte 53/92 CHF
Rest *Giardino* – Carte 46/84 CHF
♦ Business ♦ Modern ♦
This trendy hotel is a highly modern, functionally equipped business venue, which even has its own casino. The two penthouse suites are particularly fine. Chinese specialities are served in Yù. The Giardino offers Italian cuisine.

Hotelbern 🏠 ⟨⟩ ⟨⟩ 🖂 ⟨⟩ 🅿 🅥🅢🅐 ⟨⟩ 🅐🅔 ⟨⟩
Zeughausgasse 9 ⊠ *3011 –* ⟨⟩ *031 329 22 22 – hotelbern@hotelbern.ch*
– Fax 031 329 22 99 – www.hotelbern.ch   **D1**
95 rm ⥿ – 🛏190/295 CHF 🛏🛏250/330 CHF
Rest *Kurierstube* – *(closed 6 July - 23 August and Sunday)* Menu 38 CHF (lunch)/82 CHF – Carte 54/98 CHF
Rest *7-Stube* – Carte 39/82 CHF
♦ Business ♦ Modern ♦
This centrally located hotel named after the town and canton, is in an old townhouse offering modern, colourful rooms and seminar facilities. The Kurierstube is classic and elegant. The 7-Stube : a rustic restaurant.

Savoy *without rest* 🅰🅒 ⟨⟩ 🖂 ⟨⟩ 🅥🅢🅐 ⟨⟩ 🅐🅔 ⟨⟩
Neuengasse 26 ⊠ *3011 –* ⟨⟩ *031 311 44 05 – reservation-sav@zghotels.ch*
– Fax 031 312 19 78 – www.zghotels.ch   **C1**
56 rm ⥿ – 🛏255/285 CHF 🛏🛏340/360 CHF
♦ Business ♦ Classic ♦
This hotel in an old townhouse has a central location in a pedestrian area not far from the station. Its rooms are in a classical style with contemporary fittings.

Belle Epoque 🏠 ⟨⟩ 🖂 ⟨⟩ 🅿 🅥🅢🅐 ⟨⟩ 🅐🅔 ⟨⟩
Gerechtigkeitsgasse 18 ⊠ *3011 –* ⟨⟩ *031 311 43 36 – info@belle-epoque.ch*
– Fax 031 311 39 36 – www.belle-epoque.ch   **E1**
17 rm – 🛏250 CHF 🛏🛏350 CHF, ⥿ 21 CHF **Rest** – Carte 41/78 CHF
♦ Business ♦ Cosy ♦
This small hotel in the town centre has been beautifully fitted with Belle Epoque and Art Nouveau features – you will find pictures and antiques all over the building. The restaurant serves classical cuisine – steak tartare is a speciality.

Bristol *without rest* 🎰 ⟨⟩ 🖂 ⟨⟩ 🅥🅢🅐 ⟨⟩ 🅐🅔 ⟨⟩
Schauplatzgasse 10 ⊠ *3011 –* ⟨⟩ *031 311 01 01 – reception@bristolbern.ch*
– Fax 031 311 94 79 – www.bristolbern.ch   **C2**
92 rm ⥿ – 🛏200/295 CHF 🛏🛏270/330 CHF
♦ Business ♦ Modern ♦
The old, renovated townhouse has modern rooms with light-coloured solid wood furniture. The small sauna is shared with the Hotel Bern.

Bären without rest 》》 AC ⫞ SAT 🎙 VISA ∞ AE ①

Schauplatzgasse 4 ⊠ 3011 – 𝒞 031 311 33 67 – reception@baerenbern.ch
– Fax 031 311 69 83 – www.baerenbern.ch   **C2**
57 rm ⊿ – 🛏180/240 CHF 🛏🛏200/330 CHF
♦ Business ♦ Modern ♦

Just a stone's throw from the Bundesplatz, this hotel offers modern-styled rooms,
well equipped with everything for the business traveller.

City am Bahnhof without rest ⫞ SAT 🎙 VISA ∞ AE ①

Bubenbergplatz 7 ⊠ 3011 – 𝒞 031 311 53 77 – cityab@fhotels.ch
– Fax 031 311 06 36 – www.fhotels.ch   **C2**
58 rm – 🛏145/230 CHF 🛏🛏185/260 CHF, ⊿ 18 CHF
♦ Business ♦ Functional ♦

Centrally located town hotel opposite the station square. It offers contemporary
and functionally equipped rooms.

Meridiano – Hotel Allegro ⪕ 🛖 AC ⟺ P VISA ∞ AE ①

Kornhausstr. 3 ⊠ 3013 – 𝒞 031 339 52 45 – info@kursaal-bern.ch
– Fax 031 339 55 10 – www.kursaal-bern.ch
– closed 1 – 13 January, 5 - 27 July and Saturday lunch, Sunday - Monday
Rest – Menu 59 CHF (lunch)/160 CHF – Carte 108/156 CHF   **D1**
♦ Modern ♦ Trendy ♦

Seasonal, contemporary cuisine is served in a modern, elegant atmosphere on the
sixth floor of the Hotel Allegro. The restaurant affords a fantastic view, especially
from the terrace.

Mille Sens ⫞ VISA ∞ AE ①

Bubenbergplatz 9 (in the market hall) ⊠ 3011 – 𝒞 031 329 29 29
– info@millesens.ch – Fax 031 329 29 29 – www.millesens.ch
– closed July 3 weeks, Sunday and bank holidays   **C2**
Rest – Menu 64 CHF (lunch)/98 CHF – Carte 81/109 CHF 🍴
Rest *Marktplatz* – Menu 86 CHF (dinner) – Carte 51/87 CHF 🍴
♦ Modern ♦ Fashionable ♦

The market hall with its numerous shops, taverns and bars is the site of this
modern styled restaurant. It offers contemporary cuisine and a business lunch at
midday. Good value modest menu in the bistro Marktplatz. Tapas bar next door.

Kirchenfeld 🛖 ⫞ ⟺ VISA ∞ AE ①

Thunstr. 5 ⊠ 3005 – 𝒞 031 351 02 78 – restaurant@kirchenfeld.ch
– Fax 031 351 84 16 – www.kirchenfeld.ch – closed Sunday and Monday
Rest – Menu 62 CHF – Carte 49/80 CHF   **E2**
♦ Modern ♦ Brasserie ♦

Contemporary dining in this historic townhouse. It has an unassuming lounge and
a brasserie-style, prettily decorated restaurant. Economically priced two-course
lunch menu. Easily reached by tram from the city.

Wein & Sein (Beat Blum) 🛖 ⫞ VISA ∞

Münstergasse 50 ⊠ 3011 – 𝒞 031 311 98 44 – blum@weinundsein.ch
– www.weinundsein.ch – closed 19 July - 10 August, Sunday and Monday
Rest – *(dinner only) (booking essential) (menu only)* Menu 92   **E2**
CHF 🍴
Spec. Sommerwild (June - August). Schokoladen-Nusssoufflé.
♦ Modern ♦ Trendy ♦

A pleasant informal atmosphere reigns in the lovely vaulted dining room. Patrons
can select the wine to suit the four-course evening menu themselves, or ask the
friendly staff for advice. The wine is chosen from a well-stocked, air-conditioned
wine rack.

Zimmermania VISA ∞

Brunngasse 19 ⊠ 3011 – 𝒞 031 311 15 42 – info@zimmermania.ch – Fax 031 312 28 22
– www.zimmermania.net – closed 5 July - 3 August and Sunday-Monday
Rest – Menu 78 CHF – Carte 47/86 CHF   **D1**
♦ Traditional ♦ Bistro ♦

Sit in cosy comfort in this traditional establishment in a narrow alley in the old
town. The pleasant bistro serves traditional and seasonal cuisine.

✂ ### Gourmanderie Moléson 🛖 ⅔ 🔄 VISA ⓪ ①

*Aarbergergasse 24 ⊠ 3011 – ℰ 031 311 44 63 – info@moleson-bern.ch
– Fax 031 312 01 45 – www.moleson-bern.ch – closed 1-9 January and Saturday
lunch, Sunday* **Rest** – Menu 69/79 CHF – Carte 58/88 CHF **C1**
♦ Traditional ♦ Brasserie ♦

The Moléson, established in 1865, is a snug old-town restaurant. It serves everything from Alsace Flammkuchen to a multi-course menu.

✂ ### Kabuki AC ⅔ VISA ⓪ AE

*Bubenbergplatz 9 (in the market hall) ⊠ 3011 – ℰ 031 329 29 19
– kabuki@kabuki.ch – Fax 031 329 29 17 – www.kabuki.ch – closed 26 July -
2 August and Sunday* **Rest** – Menu 92 CHF (dinner) – Carte 41/88 CHF
♦ Japanese ♦ Exotic ♦ **C2**

An unostentatiously modern restaurant offering Japanese cuisine and sushi in the
basement of the market hall. Interesting glimpses into the kitchen from the immediately adjoining bar.

ENVIRONS OF BERN *Plan I*

🏠 ### Innere Enge ॐ 🛖 ⅘ 🖼 ⟨⟩ ⅔ 🅿 VISA ⓪ AE ①

*Engestr. 54 ⊠ 3012 – ℰ 031 309 61 11 – reservation-ieb@zghotels.ch
– Fax 031 309 61 12 – www.zghotels.ch* **A1**
26 rm ⌂ – †325 CHF ††380 CHF **Rest** – (closed Sunday dinner from October
- May) Menu 50 CHF (lunch)/79 CHF – Carte 48/88 CHF
♦ Business ♦ Classic ♦

This quiet house, almost out in the country, offers elegant rooms in Provençal
colour schemes. You can breakfast in the historic pavilion. The Jazz cellar is well-
known in the town. Inviting café and restaurant in bistro-brasserie style.

🏠 ### Sternen 🛖 ⅘ 🖼 ⟨⟩ ⅔ 🅿 🚗 VISA ⓪ AE

Thunstr. 80 – ℰ 031 950 71 11 – info@sternenmuri.ch – Fax 031 950 71 00 – www.sternenmuri.ch
44 rm ⌂ – †170/320 CHF ††230/350 CHF **Rest** – (closed **B2**
19 December - 3 January and 25 July - 9 August) Menu 45 CHF – Carte 49/110 CHF
♦ Traditional ♦ Functional ♦

This traditional Bern guesthouse offers modern, functional rooms in both the main
building and the extension. Läubli and restaurant offer contemporary cuisine.

🏠 ### Astoria 🛖 ⅘ 🖼 ⟨⟩ ⅔ 🅿 VISA ⓪ AE ①

*Zieglerstr. 66 ⊠ 3007 – ℰ 031 378 66 66 – info@astoria-bern.ch – Fax 031 378 66 00
– www.astoria-bern.ch* **63 rm** ⌂ – †150/170 CHF ††180/200 CHF
Rest – (closed 18 December - 6 January, 17 July - 3 August, Saturday - Sunday
and bank holidays) Menu 30 CHF (lunch) – Carte 32/59 CHF **A2**
♦ Townhouse ♦ Business ♦ Contemporary ♦

This contemporary hotel near the town centre is tailor-made for business guests.
Agreeable breakfast room with comfortable basket chairs and a small terrace.
Bistro-style restaurant offering traditional and Greek dishes.

🏠 ### Ador without rest ⅔ ⅘ 🖼 ⟨⟩ ⅔ VISA ⓪ AE ①

*Laupenstr. 15 ⊠ 3001 – ℰ 031 388 01 11 – info@hotelador.ch
– Fax 031 388 01 10 – www.hotelador.ch – closed 18 December - 3 January*
57 rm ⌂ – †125/219 CHF ††150/308 CHF **A2**
♦ Business ♦ Modern ♦

The hotel is situated near the station and is ideal for business people. The rooms
are technically well-equipped and have a simple and modern design.

✂✂ ### Landhaus Liebefeld with rm 🛖 ⅔ ⅘ 🖼 ⟨⟩ ⅔ 🅿 VISA ⓪ AE ①

*Schwarzenburgstr. 134 – ℰ 031 971 07 58 – info@landhaus-liebefeld.ch – Fax 031 972 02 49
– www.landhaus-liebefeld.ch* **6 rm** ⌂ – †175 CHF ††240 CHF **A2**
Rest – (closed Sunday) (booking advisable) Menu 59/135 CHF – Carte 56/105 CHF ॐ
Rest Gaststube – (closed Sunday) Carte 53/78 CHF
♦ Seasonal cuisine ♦ Cosy ♦

The pastorally elegant grillroom is in a charming former bailiff's residence. It offers
contemporary cuisine and friendly service under the chef's direction The secluded
garden terrace is also agreeable. Good value classics and seasonal dishes in the bar
parlour. Tasteful, richly appointed guestrooms.

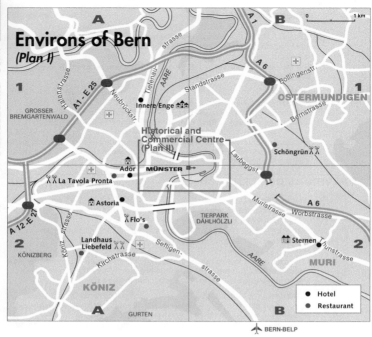

Environs of Bern
(Plan I)

GROSSER
BREMGARTENWALD

OSTERMUNDIGEN

Innere/Enge

Historical and
Commercial Centre
(Plan II)

Ador
MÜNSTER

Schöngrün

La Tavola Pronta

Astoria

Flo's

TIERPARK
DAHLHÖLZLI

A 6

Landhaus
Liebefeld

KÖNIZBERG

Sternen

KÖNIZ

MURI

GURTEN

● Hotel
● Restaurant

BERN-BELP

✗✗ **La Tavola Pronta**   🖼 ⇔ VISA ⓶ AE ⓵

*Laupenstr. 57 ✉ 3008 – ✆ 031 382 66 33 – Fax 031 381 56 93 – www.latavolapronta.ch
– closed 6 July - 4 August, Saturday lunch, Sunday - Monday*   **A2**
Rest – *(booking advisable)* Menu 45 CHF (lunch)/108 CHF – Carte 68/99 CHF
♦ Italian ♦ Cosy ♦

This pleasant little basement restaurant in the inner city is a cosy venue offering its
guests Piedmontese cuisine.

✗✗ **Schöngrün**   🖼 AC ⇔ ✧ VISA ⓶ AE ⓵

*Monument im Fruchtland 1 ✉ 3006 – ✆ 031 359 02 90
– info@restaurants-schoengruen.ch – Fax 031 359 02 91
– www.restaurants-schoengruen.ch
– closed Monday - Tuesday*   **B1**
Rest – *(booking advisable)* Menu 59 CHF (lunch)/140 CHF – Carte 80/118 CHF
♦ International ♦ Fashionable ♦

Near the famous Paul Klee Centre, find this trendy glass structure adjoining a historic building. Beautifully presented contemporary food is served.

✗ **Flo's**   ⇔ VISA ⓶
😊

*Weissenbühlweg 40 ✉ 3007 – ✆ 031 372 05 55 – info@flos-restaurant.ch
– Fax 031 372 05 54 – www.flos-restaurant.ch
– closed 24 December – 18 January, 6 - 13 April, 21 June - 15 August,
20 September - 4 October, Sunday, Monday and Tuesday*   **A2**
Rest – *(dinner only) (booking advisable)* Carte 55/76 CHF
♦ Modern ♦ Fashionable ♦

The two Manz siblings manage this modern restaurant enthusiastically with
relaxed but friendly service. The integral display kitchen prepares market fresh produce. Cooking courses available in the afternoon.

Population (est. 2005): 198 500 (conurbation 698 000) - Altitude: 375m

P. Wysocki/HEMIS.fr

In just about every detail except efficiency, Geneva exudes a distinctly Latin feel. It boasts a proud cosmopolitanism, with about one in three of its residents being non-Swiss, drawn here by the presence of the largest UN office outside New York, as well as a whole swathe of international organisations dealing with every human concern under the – frequently dazzling - sun. Its renowned *savoir-vivre* challenges that of equally swishy Zurich, while it also enjoys cultural ties with Paris, and is often called 'the twenty first arrondissement'.

It could hardly have a better setting. It's strung around the sparkling shores of Europe's largest alpine lake. Enter the city on that lake and you have mountains to either side – take your pick from Jura or Alps. There are manicured city parks and the world's tallest fountain, the bisecting River Rhone and the world's longest bench on which to sit and take it all in. Geneva is renowned for its orderliness: the Reformation was born here under the austere preachings of Calvin, and the city has been a place of refuge to Europeans for at least five centuries, providing sanctuary for religious dissidents, revolutionaries and elopers. Hell-raising poets, too, in the shape of Byron and Shelley. Nowadays, new arrivals tend to be of a more conservative persuasion, as they go their elegant way balancing international affairs alongside *la belle vie*.

LIVING THE CITY

Geneva may be in Switzerland, but it's almost totally surrounded by France. The **River Rhône** snakes through the centre, dividing the city into **the right bank** (north side, the **'international quarter'**), and the **left bank** (south side, the **old town**). To the east of Geneva is **Lake Léman** (Lake Geneva in English), while the **Jura** mountains dominate the right bank, and the **Alps** form a backdrop to the left bank. Geneva's **international airport** is to the north-west of the city, while the popular suburb of **Carouge** is to the south.

PRACTICAL INFORMATION

ARRIVAL-DEPARTURE

Geneva International Airport is just 4km from the city centre and a taxi will cost around 35CHF. Trains depart every 15min and take just 6min. Bus 10 runs every 10min.

TRANSPORT

Geneva is served by an efficient public transport network which, true to the cliché, runs like clockwork. There are various timed cards depending on how much travelling you intend to do: for one hour, one day, or 9am-midnight.

A useful alternative: if you're making several trips, pick up a 48- or 72-hour Geneva Transport Card from the tourist office for unlimited use of the city's trams, trains, buses and boats. It also offers free admission to many top museums and attractions, plus reductions in some restaurants and shops.

There's nothing better than a cycle ride along the long quaysides by the lake. The city encourages pedal power, and from May to October bikes can be borrowed for free. More information from Geneva Tourism on Rue du Mont-Blanc.

EXPLORING GENEVA

It may be one of the most famous cities in the world, in one of the world's most beautiful locations, but Geneva is actually pretty small, not much bigger than a medium-sized town. The fame that goes before it stems mostly from all those organisations

based here whose tentacles embrace the world. And, of course, everyone knows about the Lake. This is what makes Geneva extra special, giving it that sense of a bygone seaside resort. The huge expanse of water is a perfect foil for the majesty of the surrounding mountains. Its mirror-like surface is as flat as a pancake, save for an iconic landmark that has first-time visitors drawing breath before the search for superlatives. The **Jet d'Eau** is a stirring sight from the aeroplane window coming in to land. The world's tallest fountain, it shoots water with incredible force 140m into the air, and when the sun shines creates a shimmering rainbow. Watch out, though: spectators on the adjacent pier get a regular spraying.

Its forceful presence is at odds with the quiet and measured calm of the medieval old town, which lies nearby along the left bank. Here, the cobbled streets invariably lead to the dominant **St Peter's Cathedral**, sitting proudly atop its hill. This medieval monolith has Romanesque and Gothic origins hidden behind a neoclassical façade; its huge rose window is a glowing gem in the sunlight. You can go from the highs (via steep spiral steps for a look at the bell tower and awesome views of the lake and mountains) to the subterranean lows (an underground archaeological site that traces the cathedral's early foundations).

→ SEEDS OF TIME

Back up at lake level, and standing in an enviable position close to the water's edge, is a permanent tribute to 'Swiss timing' - the **Floral Clock**. This is a favourite spot for clicking cameras. It's certainly colourful: over six thousand dazzling flowers and plants are arranged in new displays each spring and autumn in celebration of local watch-making. You won't need to check your timepiece to get to one of the old town's most fascinating attractions – **Maison Tavel** is just a short stroll south. This is the place to visit to get an idea of what Geneva looked like in the Middle Ages. Set in the city's oldest house, dating back to the fourteenth century, there are displays of antique furniture, silverware and tapestries spanning six hundred years. Highlight is a seven-metre-long model of Geneva pre-1850. It took the very patient Auguste Magnin eighteen years to make it out of zinc and copper.

→ WALL OF DEFIANCE

Magnin's honest endeavours would have met with the approval of Jean Calvin, the father of the 16C Protestant movement who lived and lectured in Geneva, and set in stone the city's 'work ethic'

image that lives on to this day. There are two lasting memorials to him: one is the recently opened **International Museum of the Reformation,** near the Cathedral, which is chock-full of objects, books and paintings about the religious upheavals of the time; and then there's the breathtaking, hundred-yard long **Reformation Wall** in the **Parc des Bastions**, a dazzlingly white construction, a century old, with a fifteen-foot high statue of Calvin at its heart. If all this earnestness has left you feeling the need to chill out a bit, then the park itself is an ideal place. Its wide, tree-lined avenues are tailor-made for strolling, stopping off to watch chess being played on giant boards, while locals jog along trying to decide which of the thousand restaurants in town will play host to their expense account tonight.

For the ultimate Genevan chill-out, the coolest place in town in the summer months is **Bains des Paquis** on the Right Bank – just look for the soaring white lighthouse. Some forty years ago, this area had a bad boy reputation forged by its proximity to the dodgy Paquis district. Today, not only is Paquis the multicultural buzzword for boho chic, but the Bains itself is now a fun-filled pier and beach zone that entices a veritable league of nations to sample its charms. This is where, whether Rastafarian or restaurateur, the world comes to hang around, to graze on a lazy lunchtime picnic, read a paperback, swim in the lake, or just enjoy the sun. Beaches, boardwalk or rocks – take your pick of where you want to flop down. When it gets chilly, a big draw is the state-of-the-art spa complex on the pier, where you can steam in the hammams, sauna or solarium.

→ DRAWN AWAY

There comes a time when everyone has to forego the delights of the Lake, and Geneva has a sprinkling of top museums to investigate.

Modernists should head for **MAMCO – the Museum of Contemporary Art** – which, suitably enough, is housed in a refitted industrial factory from the 1950s. It puts on a whole raft of fresh, cutting edge exhibitions that cover a range of mediums. Across town is the more conservative but equally riveting **Art & History Museum**, a cavernous place that makes the most of its space with paintings, sculpture, arty room interiors and medieval weaponry. Roman pottery and Egyptian antiquities are popular attractions, as are masterpieces from the likes of Van Gogh, Rembrandt and Monet, but the highlight is a fifteenth century altarpiece by Konrad Witz. Meanwhile, right in the centre of the old town, on **Place Neuve**, the **Rath Museum** is dedicated to fine arts and is well known for putting on excellent temporary exhibitions. For something completely different, the **International Red Cross Museum**, way up north on the right bank near the massive HQ of the United Nations, is a thought-provoking museum with multimedia displays that highlights the work through the decades of the world's largest humanitarian network,

started by Genevan philanthropist Henri Dunant in 1864. The soundtracks, photos and films that accompany this sometimes-harrowing exhibition enhance the Red Cross's compelling story. That other Swiss speciality, timekeeping, is celebrated in a treasure trove of ticks and tocks at **Patek Philippe Museum**, next to the Museum of Contemporary Art. On show is everything from exquisite seventeenth century pocket watches to stylish art nouveau creations.

→ THE GENEVA UNCONVENTION

When Genevans seek a musical fix, their natural port of call is the **Grand Theatre**, in the heart of Place Neuve, which is internationally famous for its world-class theatre, ballet, dance and opera. Those looking for more edgy material have a pretty impressive choice: **Salle Centrale** puts on everything from art-house movies to improvised plays; **Theatre du Grütli** takes the term 'experimental' to new levels in its theatre and comedy productions; and **L'Usine** – an old gold-roughing factory – contributes art happenings, dance nights and weird cabaret to Geneva's cultural map.

CALENDAR HIGHLIGHTS

One event stands head and shoulders above any other here: the Escalade. This atmospheric procession through the old town over the weekend closest to 12 December commemorates the

battle to defend the Protestant city against the Catholic House of Savoy. The attack, in 1602, was repulsed, and Geneva's celebratory costumed procession takes place by the light of

GENEVA IN...

→ ONE DAY
St Peter's Cathedral, Maison Tavel, Jet d'Eau. Reformation Wall

→ TWO DAYS
MAMCO (or Art & History Museum), a stroll along the edge of the lake, a trip to Carouge

→ THREE DAYS
A day in Paquis, with a lazy time at the Bains des Paquis

torches to the sound of drums, fifes, trumpets and musketeers opening fire on horseback. It can get quite noisy. The volume's pretty high in August, too, when another big event, The Geneva Fête, kicks off. Days of music, shows, dancing and gastronomy are concluded with a firework display that lights up the lakeside. Other summer highlights include June's Bol d'Or Race, when the peace of Lake Geneva succumbs to over six hundred boats and yachts contesting the Golden Cup; the Fête de la Musique, also in June, which sees open-air stages in many streets and squares for a riot of concerts featuring every kind of musical form; and August's Fêtes de Geneve, when the streets are again awash with colour for fireworks, parties and parades (and it's all free!). There's more of a 'Protestant friendly' air about the Antiques and Bric-A-Brac Fair (October) in the Plaine de Plainpalais, an immense showcase of dealers' stalls by the Rhône. But the temperature rises again in October for the Flamenco Festival, a week-long celebration that brings the spirit of Seville to the Swiss Alps.

EATING OUT

One thing's for sure: you won't be hard pressed to find an eating establishment in Geneva. All those big international organisations take a bit of feeding, and so you'll find over a thousand dining establishments in the city and its surrounds. If you're looking for elegance, then head to a restaurant overlooking the lake; if your tastes are more for the 'nonna' style of home-cooked Sardinian fare, make tracks for the charming Italianate suburb of Carouge just to the south, where little cafés serve up delicious antipasti, risotto and fresh fish. If you haven't an expense account to blow, but fancy something with an international accent, then Paquis has it all, and at a fair price. This trendy part of Geneva offers flavours on a truly global scale from Moroccan to Mexican, from Jordanian to Japanese. The old town is the place for Swiss staples, packed as it is with delightful brasseries and alpine-style chalets: you can't go wrong here if your fancy is for fondue, or a heartily rustic papet vaudois (cream-leek casserole). Longeole (pork sausage enlivened with cumin and fennel) is a popular choice for meat eaters. Rösti, of course, is ubiquitous. For a bit of extra atmosphere, head downstairs to dine in a vaulted cellar with flickering candles. Though restaurants include a service charge of fifteen per cent, it's customary to leave a tip if you were happy with the service – round up the bill or give the waiter a tip between five and ten per cent.

→ CAROUSE IN CAROUGE

For Geneva with a true Latin heart, take a tram to Carouge. From 1754 till 1816, this now hip suburb was part of the kingdom of Sardinia. Designed by Piedmontese architects, its chessboard pattern of blocks enclosing courtyard gardens provides a wonderfully understated charm, enhanced by funky bars, boutiques, Italian cafés and artists' workshops.

→ CHILLON OUT

Byron and Shelley visited Geneva in 1816, and the Lord wrote a poem afterwards about the four-year imprisonment of Prior Bonivard in the fabulous castle of Chillon overlooking Lake Geneva. You can see the castle, and others, on an idyllic lake cruise. Vessels – some of them paddlesteamers – serve forty-two piers, and are a delightfully relaxing way of getting to see many of the places around the lake.

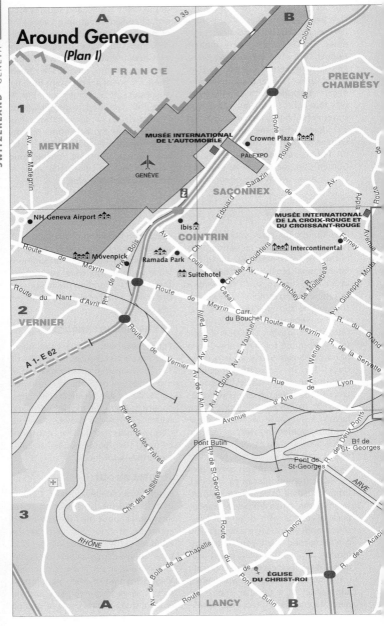

Around Geneva
(Plan I)

FRANCE

A

B

D 35

Colovrex

PREGNY-CHAMBÉSY

MEYRIN

Av. de Mategnin

MUSÉE INTERNATIONAL
DE L'AUTOMOBILE

Crowne Plaza

Route de

Route

Sarazin

Édouard

Appia

Avenue

Ferney

Route

PALEXPO

GENÈVE

SACONNEX

NH Geneva Airport

Route de Meyrin

Prés Bois

de

Ibis

COINTRIN

Ch. Louis

Av.

Mövenpick

Ramada Park

Casaï

Suitehotel

MUSÉE INTERNATIONAL
DE LA CROIX-ROUGE ET
DU CROISSANT-ROUGE

Intercontinental

Ch. des Coudriers

Av. J. Trembley de Molliebeau

R. du Grand

Av. Giuseppe Motta

Route du Nant d'Avril

VERNIER

Route de Meyrin

Pailly

Carr.
du Bouchet Route de Meyrin

Av. E. Vaucher

R. de la Servette

A 1 - E 62

Route de Vernier

Av. H. Golay

Av. de l'Ain

Av. du

Av. Wendt

Rue de Lyon

d'Aire

Avenue

Rte du Bois des Frères

Pont Butin

Rte de St-Georges

Route du St-Georges

Pont de
St-Georges

R. des Deux Ponts

Bd de
St-Georges

ARVE

RHÔNE

Chin des Sellières

Chancy

R. des Acaci

Av. du Bois de la Chapelle

Route du

de
Pont

ÉGLISE
DU CHRIST-ROI

A

LANCY

Pont Butin

B

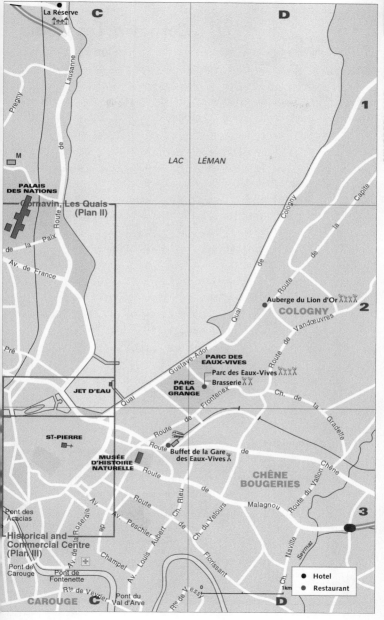

La Réserve C

D

1

PRÉGNY

Lausanne

de

M

PALAIS
DES NATIONS

Cornavin, Les Quais
(Plan II)

Route

de la Paix

de la

Av. de France

Pré

LAC LÉMAN

Cologny

de

la

Capite

Route

de

Auberge du Lion d'Or XXXX

COLOGNY

2

Quai

Vandœuvres

Route de

Gustave-Ador

PARC DES
EAUX-VIVES

Parc des Eaux-Vives XXXX
Brasserie XX

JET D'EAU

Quai

PARC
DE LA
GRANGE

Route de Frontenex

Ch. de la Gradelle

ST-PIERRE

Route de

Route

Buffet de la Gare
des Eaux-Vives X

de

Chêne

MUSÉE
D'HISTOIRE
NATURELLE

Route

CHÊNE
BOUGERIES

Route du Vallon

Pont des
Acacias

Av. de

Route

de

Ch. Rieu

Malagnou

Naville

3

Historical and
Commercial Centre
(Plan III)

Av. de la Roseraie

Av. Peschier

Av. Louis-Aubert

Ch. du Velours

Florissant

Sézenaz

Pont de
Carouge

Pont de
Fontenette

Champel

de

Ch. de

Vessy

CAROUGE C

Rte de Veyrier

Pont du
Val d'Arve

Rte de Vessy

0   1km

● Hotel
● Restaurant

D

845

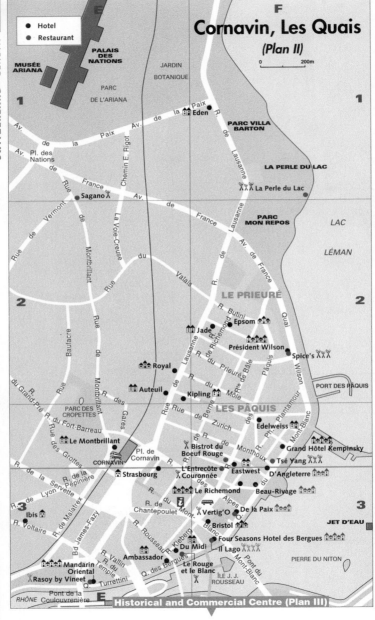

Cornavin, Les Quais
(Plan II)

- ● Hotel
- ● Restaurant

0   200m

MUSÉE ARIANA

PALAIS DES NATIONS

JARDIN BOTANIQUE

PARC DE L'ARIANA

Eden

PARC VILLA BARTON

LA PERLE DU LAC

La Perle du Lac

Av. de la Paix

Av. de la Paix

Pl. des Nations

Av. de la France

Sagano

Chemin E. Rigot

Av. de France

PARC MON REPOS

LAC LÉMAN

Rue de Vermont

La Voie-Creuse

Rue de Montbrillant

R. du Valais

Av. de Lausanne

Av. de France

LE PRIEURÉ

R. Butini

Epsom

Jade

R. de Richemond

Président Wilson

Spice's

Royal

R. de Lausanne

R. du Prieuré

R. du Môle

Quai Wilson

PORT DES PÂQUIS

Auteuil

Kipling

Baulacre

Rue de Montbrillant

Rue des Gares

R. de Berne

R. de Zurich

R. des Pâquis

Ph. Plantamour

LES PÂQUIS

Edelweiss

Mont-Blanc

R. du Grand-Pré

R. du Fort-Barreau

PARC DES CROPETTES

Rue des Grottes

Le Montbrillant

Pl. de Cornavin

CORNAVIN

Bistrot du Boeuf Rouge

R. de Monthoux

Grand Hôtel Kempinsky

Tsé Yang

L'Entrecôte Couronnée

Eastwest

D'Angleterre

Beau-Rivage

Strasbourg

R. des Alpes

Le Richemond

R. de la Servette

R. de la Pépinière

Ibis

R. de Lyon

R. de Malatrex

R. Voltaire

R. de Chantepoulet

R. du Mont-Blanc

Vertig'O

De la Paix

JET D'EAU

Bristol

Bd James-Fazy

R. Rousseau

R. Kléber

Four Seasons Hotel des Bergues

PIERRE DU NITON

R. du Temple

R. Vallin

Du Midi

Lago

Ambassador

Q. des Bergues

Le Rouge et le Blanc

Pont du Mont-Blanc

Mandarin Oriental

Rasoy by Vineet

Q. Turrettini

ÎLE J. J. ROUSSEAU

RHÔNE

Pont de la Coulouvrenière

Historical and Commercial Centre (Plan III)

846

SWITZERLAND - GENEVA

Four Seasons Hôtel des Bergues   ← ƒふ &゙ Ẩ ⅔ ⁇ ⅙ ⌂

33 quai des Bergues ⊠ *1201* – ℰ *022 908 70 00*
– *info.gen@fourseasons.com* – *Fax 022 908 74 00*
– *www.fourseasons.com/geneva*   **F3**
83 rm – †760/950 CHF ††810/1000 CHF, � 55 CHF – 20 suites
Rest *Il Lago* – see below
♦ Palace ♦ Stylish ♦

Recently renovated, the oldest and most luxurious hotel in Geneva (1834) offers lounges adorned with gleaming marble, an elegant bar, guestrooms and suites decorated in Empire style. Excellent service.

Mandarin Oriental   ← 🍽 ƒふ ⅗ &゙ Ẩ ⅔ rm 📺 ⁇ ⅙ ⌂

1 quai Turrettini ⊠ *1201* – ℰ *022 909 00 00*
– *mogva-enquiry@mohg.com* – *Fax 022 909 00 10*
– *www.mandarinoriental.com/geneva*   **E3**
166 rm – †840/1200 CHF ††900/1260 CHF, ⊠ 47 CHF – 31 suites
Rest *Rasoi by Vineet* – see below
Rest *Le Sud* – ℰ *022 909 00 05* – Carte 63/110 CHF
♦ Grand Luxury ♦ Art Deco ♦

Choice of sumptuous, Art Deco furnished, Rhone-side or courtyard rooms and suites. Le Sud offers both a Mediterranean atmosphere and menu.

Le Richemond   🍽 ƒふ ⅗ &゙ Ẩ ⅔ ⁀ ⅙ ⌂ 🆅🅸🆂🅰 ◑ 🅰🅴

8 r. Adhémar- Fabri ⊠ *1201* – ℰ *022 715 70 00* – *reservations.lerichemond@*
roccofortecollection.com – *Fax 022 715 70 01* – *www.roccofortecollection.com*
99 rm – †735/910 CHF ††735/910 CHF, ⊠ 45 CHF – 10 suites   **F3**
Rest *Sapori* – Menu 68 CHF (lunch)/85 CHF – Carte 96/136 CHF
♦ Grand Luxury ♦ Modern ♦

Opened in 1863 and completely renovated in 2007, this hotel offers a choice of standard rooms, junior suites and suites decorated in chic, contemporary style. Those on the upper floors have a view of the lake and the Jet d'Eau. Italian specialities, a smart, modern decor and an attractive terrace overlooking the Brunswick Garden are the highlights of the Sapori.

Président Wilson   ← 🍽 ƒふ ⅗ 🏊 &゙ Ẩ 📺 ⁇ ⅙ ⌂

47 quai Wilson ⊠ *1201* – ℰ *022 906 66 66* – *sales@*
hotelpwilson.com – *Fax 022 906 66 67* – *www.hotelpwilson.com*   **F2**
219 rm – †730/890 CHF ††820/980 CHF, ⊠ 43 CHF – 11 suites
Rest *Spice's* – see below
Rest *L'Arabesque* – Menu 56 CHF (lunch)/105 CHF – Carte 62/88 CHF
Rest *Pool Garden* – (closed mid-September – May) Menu 58 CHF (lunch)/80 CHF
– Carte 86/144 CHF
♦ Grand Luxury ♦ Stylish ♦

Overlooking the lake, this hotel is adorned with marble decor, fine wood furnishings and attractive flower arrangements. Enjoy the subtle flavours of Lebanese cuisine amid the enchanting decor (goldleaf mosaics) of L'Arabesque. The Pool Garden is ideal for summer dining, with tables set around the swimming pool.

Grand Hôtel Kempinski   ← 🍽 ƒふ 🈺 🔲 &゙ Ẩ ⅔ rm 📺 ⁇ ⅙

19 quai du Mont-Blanc ⊠ *1201* – ℰ *022 908 90 81*
– *reservations.grandhotelgeneva@kempinski.com* – *Fax 022 908 90 90*
– *www.kempinski-geneva.com*   **F3**
409 rm – †600/1000 CHF ††700/1100 CHF, ⊠ 47 CHF – 14 suites
Rest *Le Floor Two* – Carte 73/124 CHF
Rest *Le Grill* – (closed Sunday and Monday) Carte 87/206 CHF
♦ Grand Luxury ♦ Classic ♦

A fully renovated lakeside hotel. Modern public areas, rooms and suites. Convention centre, fully equipped fitness room and spa. The Floor Two offers a lounge bar, fashionable decor and terrace facing the fountain. The Grill offers a warm, modern setting with an open kitchen and a fine lake view.

Beau-Rivage ≤ 🛜 ⅃ⅆ AC ↳ rm 🖭 ¶¹ 🕍 🚗 VISA ⓒⓓ AE ⓘ

13 quai du Mont-Blanc ⊠ *1201 –* ℰ *022 716 66 66*
– info@beau-rivage.ch – Fax 022 716 60 60
– www.beau-rivage.ch   **F3**
80 rm – ⅆ800/1200 CHF ⅆⅆ900/1400 CHF, � 45 CHF – 11 suites
Rest *Le Chat Botté* – Menu 70 CHF (lunch)/180 CHF – Carte 127/208 CHF 🌿
Rest *Patara* – ℰ *022 731 55 66 (closed 21 December - 4 January, Saturday
lunch and Sunday lunch)* Menu 43 CHF (lunch)/145 CHF – Carte 56/107 CHF
◆ Grand Luxury ◆ Stylish ◆
The same family has run this hotel facing the lake since 1865. The stylish guest-rooms have an elegant atmosphere and the hotel has a fine atrium adorned with colonnades and a fountain. Modern cuisine in a cosy atmosphere in Le Chat Botté. The Patara specialises in Thai cuisine.

D'Angleterre ≤ ⅃ⅆ 🐾 AC ↳ rm 🖭 ¶¹ 🕍 🚗 VISA ⓒⓓ AE ⓘ

17 quai du Mont-Blanc ⊠ *1201 –* ℰ *022 906 55 55*
– angleterre@rchmail.com – Fax 022 906 55 56
– www.hoteldangleterre.ch   **F3**
45 rm – ⅆ680/990 CHF ⅆⅆ680/1020 CHF, ⊑ 48 CHF
Rest *Windows* – Menu 55 CHF (lunch)/199 CHF – Carte 100/148 CHF
◆ Luxury ◆ Classic ◆
Dating from 1872, this elegant neo-Classical building overlooks Lake Geneva. Excellent service, tastefully decorated rooms with individual touches, and a cosy colonial decor in the Leopard Lounge. This exclusive restaurant-veranda overloo-king the lake serves traditional French cuisine.

De la Paix ≤ AC ↳ 🖭 ¶¹ 🕍 VISA ⓒⓓ AE ⓘ

11 quai du Mont-Blanc ⊠ *1201 –* ℰ *022 909 60 00*
– info-hdlp@concorde-hotels.com – Fax 022 909 60 01
– www.hoteldelapaix.ch   **F3**
84 rm – ⅆ750/1100 CHF ⅆⅆ750/1100 CHF, ⊑ 40 CHF
Rest *Vertig'O* – see below
◆ Luxury ◆ Classic ◆
A palatial hotel built in 1865 and renovated in 2005. Luxurious public areas, inclu-ding a vertiginous, gold-adorned patio. Personalised guestrooms decorated accor-ding to two themes: "water drops" and "rose petals".

InterContinental ≤ 🛜 ⅃ⅆ 🕥 🐾 🏊 AC ↳ 🤙 🕍 P P 🚗

7 ch. du Petit-Saconnex ⊠ *1209 –* ℰ *022 919 39 39*   VISA ⓒⓓ AE ⓘ
– inter-geneva@intercontinental-geneva.ch – Fax 022 919 38 38
– www.intercontinental.com/geneva   *Plan I* **B2**
266 rm – ⅆ395/670 CHF ⅆⅆ445/720 CHF, ⊑ 44 CHF – 62 suites
Rest *Woods* – Menu 59 CHF (lunch)/98 CHF – Carte 78/131 CHF
◆ Chain hotel ◆ Classic ◆
This hotel is located in a 1960s building near the Palais des Nations. Renovated public areas, excellent conference facilities and rooms awaiting renovation. A spa-cious and comfortable restaurant serving modern cuisine in a contemporary set-ting.

Bristol ⅃ⅆ 🐾 AC ↳ rm 🖭 ¶¹ 🕍 VISA ⓒⓓ AE ⓘ

10 r. du Mont-Blanc ⊠ *1201 –* ℰ *022 716 57 00 – reservations@bristol.ch*
– Fax 022 738 90 39 – www.bristol.ch   **F3**
95 rm – ⅆ355/630 CHF ⅆⅆ485/670 CHF, ⊑ 36 CHF – 5 suites
Rest *Relais Bristol* – ℰ *022 716 57 58* – Menu 52 CHF (lunch)/87 CHF
– Carte 68/106 CHF
◆ Business ◆ Classic ◆
Situated near the lakeside, the Bristol has a luxurious lobby, vertiginous winding staircase and spacious guestrooms (ask for one overlooking the square). Fitness room, sauna and hammam. Up-to-date cuisine in an impeccable classical dining room. Piano bar.

SWITZERLAND - GENEVA

Epsom
⟨symbols⟩ rm ⟨symbols⟩ VISA ⟨symbols⟩ AE ⟨symbols⟩

18 r. Richemont ⊠ *1202 –* ⟨phone⟩ *022 544 66 66 – epsom@manotel.com*
– Fax 022 544 66 99 – www.manotel.com **F2**
153 rm – †300/595 CHF ††300/595 CHF, ⊊ 30 CHF
Rest *Portobello* – Menu 40 CHF (lunch)/61 CHF – Carte 54/88 CHF
♦ Business ♦ Classic ♦

Contemporary-style hotel situated in a quiet road in the city centre. Relaxing atmosphere and pleasant guestrooms. Conference rooms also available. Contemporary cuisine and wines from around the world feature in this restaurant, with its conservatory-style dining room. The parquet floor, rattan chairs and potted plants add an exotic touch.

Royal
⟨symbols⟩ rm ⟨symbols⟩ VISA ⟨symbols⟩ AE ⟨symbols⟩

41 r. de Lausanne ⊠ *1201 –* ⟨phone⟩ *022 906 14 14 – royal@manotel.com*
– Fax 022 906 14 99 – www.manotel.com **E2**
197 rm – †350/595 CHF ††350/595 CHF, ⊊ 30 CHF – 5 suites
Rest *Rive Droite* – Carte 50/89 CHF
♦ Business ♦ Classic ♦

Busy roadside and modern business hotel, set between the railway station and the lake. Some rooms have been renovated in warm shades (stone and wood). Conference centre. The Rive Droite offers modern cuisine in a stylish brasserie setting. Terrace under arches.

Eastwest
⟨symbols⟩ VISA ⟨symbols⟩ AE ⟨symbols⟩

6 r. des Pâquis ⊠ *1201 –* ⟨phone⟩ *022 708 17 17 – info@eastwesthotel.ch*
– Fax 022 708 17 18 – www.eastwesthotel.ch **F3**
37 rm – †395/715 CHF ††470/715 CHF, ⊊ 35 CHF
Rest *Sens* – *(closed Sunday)* Menu 89 CHF – Carte 64/107 CHF
♦ Townhouse ♦ Modern ♦

This centrally located hotel offers a modern Japanese-style setting. Warm, modern rooms, fitness area and sauna. Restaurant with a modern Mediterranean menu. The Pourcel brothers have advised the chef. Tapas bar.

Le Montbrillant
⟨symbols⟩ P. VISA ⟨symbols⟩ AE ⟨symbols⟩

2 r. de Montbrillant ⊠ *1201 –* ⟨phone⟩ *022 733 77 84 – contact@montbrillant.ch*
– Fax 022 733 25 11 – www.montbrillant.ch **E3**
82 rm – †225/295 CHF ††355/385 CHF **Rest** – Carte 48/86 CHF
♦ Family ♦ Personalised ♦

A reliable hotel in the vicinity of the station. Public areas with a mountain chalet-style decor, bedrooms of varying size and studios with small kitchenettes. Massages upon request. Parisian brasserie with a welcoming restaurant combining French traditional and Italian cuisine (wood oven cooked pizzas).

Jade without rest
⟨symbols⟩ VISA ⟨symbols⟩ AE ⟨symbols⟩

55 r. Rothschild ⊠ *1202 –* ⟨phone⟩ *022 544 38 38 – jade@manotel.com*
– Fax 022 544 38 99 – www.manotel.com **F2**
47 rm – †210/420 CHF ††210/520 CHF, ⊊ 18 CHF
♦ Business ♦ Modern ♦

This hotel has been redecorated in ultra modern style according to the principles of Feng Shui. Harmony and serenity in a refined, modern environment.

Kipling without rest
⟨symbols⟩ P. ⟨symbols⟩ VISA ⟨symbols⟩ AE ⟨symbols⟩

27 r. de la Navigation ⊠ *1201 –* ⟨phone⟩ *022 544 40 40 – kipling@manotel.com*
– Fax 022 544 40 99 – www.manotel.com **E-F2**
62 rm – †260/420 CHF ††260/420 CHF, ⊊ 18 CHF
♦ Business ♦ Modern ♦

This pleasant hotel with a colonial-style decor pays tribute to the famous author of the "Jungle Book". Aroma of incense in the entrance hall.

Auteuil without rest
⟨symbols⟩ VISA ⟨symbols⟩ AE ⟨symbols⟩

33 r. de Lausanne ⊠ *1201 –* ⟨phone⟩ *022 544 22 22 – auteuil@manotel.com*
– Fax 022 544 22 99 – www.manotel.com **E2**
104 rm – †320/520 CHF ††320/520 CHF, ⊊ 28 CHF
♦ Business ♦ Classic ♦

A modern lobby adorned with portraits of film stars, guestrooms with dark wooden furniture brightened with velvet fabrics, and a trendy breakfast area.

849

Edelweiss
🔳 ↪ rm 📺 🛜 VISA ⊛ AE ①

2 pl. de la Navigation ✉ *1201* – ☏ *022 544 51 51* – *edelweiss@manotel.com*
– Fax 022 544 51 99 – *www.manotel.com*   **F3**
42 rm – ♦290/520 CHF ♦♦290/520 CHF, � 18 CHF
Rest *– (closed 1 - 19 January) (dinner only)* Menu 55 CHF – Carte 48/82 CHF
♦ Business ♦ Cosy ♦

Decorated inside and out in the style of a typical Swiss chalet, this hotel offers cosy, comfortable guestrooms. Welcoming dining room with a mezzanine level. Traditional regional dishes, including fondue and raclette, are served in this typical Swiss setting.

Du Midi
🔳 ₺ 🔳 🛜 🛜 🆔 VISA ⊛ AE ①

4 pl. Chevelu ✉ *1201* – ☏ *022 544 15 00* – *info@hotel-du-midi.ch*
– Fax 022 544 15 20 – *www.hotel-du-midi.ch*   **E-F3**
78 rm – ♦300/400 CHF ♦♦350/500 CHF, ⊵ 26 CHF
Rest *– (closed Saturday and Sunday)* Menu 40 CHF (lunch)/80 CHF
– Carte 58/71 CHF
♦ Business ♦ Functional ♦

This family-run hotel stands on a small square overlooking the Rhône. Features include an elegant lobby adorned with colonnades, a cosy lounge, a modern art collection and renovated rooms with contemporary decor. Modern, cosy restaurant and an outdoor terrace for summer dining.

Ambassador
🔳 🔳 ↪ rm 📺 🛜 🆔 VISA ⊛ AE ①

21 quai des Bergues ✉ *1201* – ☏ *022 908 05 30* – *info@hotel-ambassador.ch*
– Fax 022 738 90 80 – *www.hotel-ambassador.ch*   **E3**
66 rm – ♦250/450 CHF ♦♦400/650 CHF, ⊵ 25 CHF
Rest *– (closed Saturday, Sunday lunch and bank holidays)* Menu 41 CHF
(lunch)/66 CHF – Carte 57/80 CHF
♦ Business ♦ Classic ♦

Hotel on a busy road overlooking the Rhône. Ask for one of the recently refurbished rooms which have been decorated in a modern style. Traditional dishes served in a wood-panelled dining room or on the summer terrace.

Eden
🔳 📺 🛜 VISA ⊛ AE ①

135 r. de Lausanne ✉ *1202* – ☏ *022 716 37 00* – *eden@eden.ch*
– Fax 022 731 52 60 – *www.eden.ch*   **F1**
54 rm ⊵ – ♦180/280 CHF ♦♦235/330 CHF
Rest *– (closed 20 December - 4 January, 18 July – 9 August, Saturday and Sunday)* Menu 36/52 CHF – Carte 44/61 CHF
♦ Business ♦ Classic ♦

Regularly refurbished hotel opposite the Palais des Nations. The classic rooms are bright and functional. A traditional restaurant which is popular with locals and visitors alike.

Strasbourg without rest
↪ 📺 🛜 VISA ⊛ AE ①

10 r. Pradier ✉ *1201* – ☏ *022 906 58 00* – *info@hotelstrasbourg.ch*
– Fax 022 906 58 14 – *www.hotelstrasbourg.ch*   **E3**
51 rm ⊵ – ♦170/220 CHF ♦♦220/270 CHF
♦ Business ♦ Functional ♦

A traditional hotel with rather small, but functional rooms, just a stone's throw from the station and Cornavin car park. Welcoming wood-panelled reception area.

Ibis without rest
₺ 🔳 ↪ 📺 VISA ⊛ AE ①

10 r. Voltaire ✉ *1201* – ☏ *022 338 20 20* – *h2154@accor.com*
– Fax 022 338 20 30 – *www.ibishotel.com*   **E3**
64 rm – ♦147/200 CHF ♦♦147/200 CHF, ⊵ 15 CHF
♦ Chain hotel ♦ Minimalist ♦

This non-smoking chain hotel is situated in a rather dull part of Geneva. Functional guestrooms, some of which are family rooms.

XXXX **Il Lago** – Four Seasons Hôtel des Bergues   🛜 AC ⟷ VISA ⦿ AE ⓞ
33 quai des Bergues ✉ *1201* – ✆ *022 908 70 00* – *info.gen@fourseasons.com*
– *Fax 022 908 74 00* – *www.fourseasons.com/geneva*   **F3**
Rest – *(booking essential)* Menu 79 CHF (lunch)/135 CHF – Carte 111/179 CHF 🍴
♦ Italian ♦ Classic ♦

Enjoy well-prepared Italian dishes in a rich classical setting. Precious hand-painted wallpaper (lake scenes). Good wine list and efficient service.

XXX **La Perle du Lac**   ⟨ 🌙 🛜 AC ⟷ P VISA ⦿ AE ⓞ
126 r. de Lausanne ✉ *1202* – ✆ *022 909 10 20* – *info@laperledulac.ch*
– *Fax 022 909 10 30* – *www.laperledulac.ch*
– *closed 24 December - 15 January and Monday*   **F1**
Rest – Menu 62 CHF (lunch)/120 CHF – Carte 83/134 CHF
♦ Traditional ♦ Classic ♦

This hundred-year-old chalet, surrounded by a large outdoor dining area, enjoys an attractive location in the middle of a park facing the lake. Bright tones in the more modern of the two dining rooms.

XXX **Spice's** – Hôtel Président Wilson   ⟨ 🛜 ⴳ ⳧ AC VISA ⦿ AE ⓞ
47 quai Wilson ✉ *1201* – ✆ *022 906 66 66* – *sales@hotelpwilson.com*
– *Fax 022 906 66 67* – *www.hotelpwilson.com*
– *closed 2 - 12 January, 5 July – 16 August, Saturday lunch and Sunday*
Rest – Menu 59 CHF (lunch)/140 CHF – Carte 105/163 CHF   **F2**
♦ Euro-asiatic ♦ Fashionable ♦

A cosmopolitan menu, fashionable decor and trendy atmosphere are the order of the day in this restaurant, which also has a boutique selling a range of products from around the world.

XX **Tsé Yang**   ⟨ AC ⟷ VISA ⦿ AE ⓞ
19 quai du Mont-Blanc (1st floor) ✉ *1201* – ✆ *022 732 50 81*
– *Fax 022 731 05 82*   **F3**
Rest – Menu 46 CHF (lunch)/145 CHF – Carte 65/158 CHF
♦ Chinese ♦ Exotic ♦

Elegant dining room with a Far Eastern decor, separated into alcoves by carved wood partitions. Savour Chinese specialities while enjoying the view of Lake Geneva.

X **Rasoi by Vineet** – Hôtel Mandarin Oriental   🛜 AC VISA ⦿ AE ⓞ
1 quai Turrettini ✉ *1201* – ✆ *022 909 00 06* – *mogva-enquiry@mohg.com*
– *Fax 022 909 00 10* – *www.mandarinoriental.com/geneva*   **E3**
Rest – *(booking advisable)* Menu 75 CHF (lunch)/160 CHF – Carte 95/166 CHF
♦ Indian ♦ Design ♦

Sample the Indian cuisine with delicious personal touches. It is served in a fashionable setting with a modern-style tandoori oven in which the naans (bread) are baked. Simple comfort, good service and cosmopolitan atmosphere.

X **Vertig'O** – Hôtel de la Paix   ⟨ VISA ⦿ AE ⓞ
11 quai du Mont-Blanc ✉ *1201* – ✆ *022 909 60 66*
– *info-hdlp@concorde-hotels.com* – *Fax 022 909 60 01* – *www.hoteldelapaix.ch*
– *closed 22 December - 6 January, 13 July – 17 August, Saturday and Sunday*
Rest – Menu 55 CHF (lunch)/125 CHF – Carte 92/124 CHF   **F3**
♦ Traditional ♦ Fashionable ♦

Hotel restaurant serving modernised traditional cuisine in a very fashionable modern setting, combining shades of orange, grey and blue. Bistro-style comfort.

X **Bistrot du Boeuf Rouge**   VISA ⦿ AE
(😊)
17 r. Alfred-Vincent ✉ *1201* – ✆ *022 732 75 37* – *Fax 022 731 46 84*
– *www.boeufrouge.ch*
– *closed 24 December - 4 January, 18 July – 16 August, Saturday and Sunday*
Rest – Menu 38 CHF (lunch)/54 CHF – Carte 52/81 CHF   **F3**
♦ Bistro ♦ Brasserie ♦

A French-style bistro with a bar, benches, old advertisements and mirrors on the walls. Specialities from Lyon, local dishes and gourmet specials.

Sagano

86 r. de Montbrillant ⊠ *1202 –* ℰ *022 733 11 50 – Fax 022 733 27 50*
– closed Saturday lunch and Sunday   **E1**
Rest – Menu 40 CHF (lunch)/90 CHF – Carte 38/102 CHF

♦ Japanese ♦ Exotic ♦

This restaurant offers a good introduction to Japanese cuisine, with decor typical of Japan, including tatamis (Japanese floor cushions) and low tables.

L'Entrecôte Couronnée

5 r. des Paquis ⊠ *1201 –* ℰ *022 732 84 45 – Fax 022 732 84 46*
– closed Saturday lunch and Sunday   **F3**
Rest – Menu 60 CHF – Carte 57/84 CHF

♦ Modern ♦ Bistro ♦

Attractive residence housing a small bistro with a typical local atmosphere. Retro decor and specialities made with regional produce and served by the chefs themselves.

Le Rouge et le Blanc

27 quai des Bergues ⊠ *1201 –* ℰ *022 731 15 50*
– closed 22 December - 6 January and Sunday   **E3**
Rest – Carte 59/65 CHF

♦ Modern ♦ Wine bar ♦

This friendly wine-bar-cum-restaurant serves contemporary dishes at lunchtime (the waiter will tell you what's available) and a more traditional menu in the evening. Home-made charcuterie and excellent wines.

LEFT BANK   *Plan III*

Swissôtel Métropole

34 quai Général-Guisan ⊠ *1204 –* ℰ *022 318 32 00 – geneva@swissotel.com*
– Fax 022 318 33 00 – www.swissotel.com/geneva   **H1**
118 rm – ♦440/890 CHF ♦♦500/890 CHF, ⊊ 41 CHF – 9 suites
Rest *Le Grand Quai* – Carte 87/122 CHF

♦ Luxury ♦ Classic ♦

This hotel facing the famous Jet d'Eau dates from 1854. Traditional rooms (those overlooking the lake are the most spacious), pleasant piano bar, panoramic terrace and fitness room. The Grand Quai offers seasonal up-to-date cuisine in a brown, modern setting.

Les Armures

1 r. du Puits-Saint-Pierre ⊠ *1204 –* ℰ *022 310 91 72 – armures@span.ch*
– Fax 022 310 98 46 – www.hotel-les-armures.ch   **H2**
32 rm ⊊ – ♦415/505 CHF ♦♦635/660 CHF
Rest – *(closed Christmas and New Year)* Carte 52/90 CHF

♦ Traditional ♦ Historic ♦

This 17C building, nestling at the heart of old Geneva, has a welcoming interior that tastefully combines old and new. Choice of modern or more rustic rooms. Restaurant with a pleasant terrace and a popular 'carnotzet' - a wine cellar for tastings. Fondues and raclettes or up-to-date dishes are served.

De la Cigogne

17 pl. Longemalle ⊠ *1204 –* ℰ *022 818 40 40 – cigogne@relaischateaux.com*
– Fax 022 818 40 50 – www.cigogne.ch   **H1-2**
46 rm ⊊ – ♦390/495 CHF ♦♦495/605 CHF – 6 suites
Rest – *(closed Saturday from July to August and Sunday lunch)*
Menu 65/120 CHF – Carte 84/106 CHF

♦ Traditional ♦ Historic ♦

Early-20C façade overlooking a busy square. Elegant fittings, public areas embellished with objets d'art, guestrooms and suites furnished with attractive antiques. Traditional cuisine is served in this restaurant with a glass ceiling and Art Deco design.

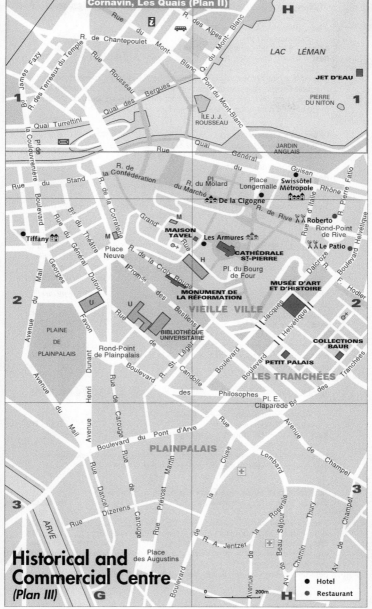

Cornavin, Les Quais (Plan II)

H

Rue du Mont-Blanc

R. de Chantepoulet

R. des Alpes

Q. du Mont-Blanc

Pont du Mont-Blanc

LAC LÉMAN

JET D'EAU

PIERRE
DU NITON

1

R. de la Couluvrenière

Bd James Fazy

R. des Terreaux du Temple

Rue Rousseau

Quai des Bergues

ÎLE J. J.
ROUSSEAU

Quai Turrettini

Quai

Quai Général

JARDIN
ANGLAIS

Rue

Rue du Stand

R. de la Confédération

R. du Marché

Pl du Molard

Place
Longemalle

Guisan

Swissôtel
Métropole

Rhône

R. Pierre Fatio

Boulevard

Rue du Théâtre

Bd du Général Dufour

R. de la Corraterie

Grand

De la Cigogne

Roberto

R. de Rive

Rue d'Italie

Rond-Point
de Rive

Boulevard Helvétique

Tiffany

M

M

MAISON
TAVEL

Place
Neuve

R. de la Croix-Rouge

Les Armures

H

Le Patio

CATHÉDRALE
ST-PIERRE

Pl. du Bourg
de Four

Dalcroze

R. Hodler

2

Georges

Favon

U

U

Prom de des Bastions

MONUMENT DE
LA RÉFORMATION

VIEILLE VILLE

MUSÉE D'ART
ET D'HISTOIRE

R. Jacques

Helvétique

2

PLAINE
DE
PLAINPALAIS

Avenue du Mail

Henri Dunant

Rue de

BIBLIOTHÈQUE
UNIVERSITAIRE

Rond-Point
de Plainpalais

R. St- Léger

R. de Candolle

Boulevard

Boulevard

COLLECTIONS
BAUR

PETIT PALAIS

LES TRANCHÉES

des Tranchées

Boulevard

des

Philosophes

Pl. E.
Claparède Bd

Avenue du Mail

Rue de Carouge

Boulevard du Pont d'Arve

Rue Martin

Rue Prévost

Cluse

Rue

Avenue de Champel

PLAINPALAIS

ARVE

Rue Dizerens

Rue Dancet

de Carouge

R. A. Jentzet

de la Roseraie

Séjour

Beau

Avenue de Beau Séjour

Thury

Chemin

de

Champel

3

Historical and
Commercial Centre
(Plan III)

G

Place
des Augustins

Boulevard

0   200m

● Hotel
● Restaurant

H

Tiffany
🏠 🕭 📶 rm 🖵 📶 VISA ⓒⓞ AE ①

20 r. de l'Arabesque ✉ *1204 –* ☎ *022 708 16 16*
– info@tiffanyhotel.ch – Fax 022 708 16 17
– www.tiffanyhotel.ch   **G2**
46 rm – 🛏270/385 CHF 🛏🛏380/465 CHF, ⌷ 28 CHF
Rest – *(closed Christmas, New Year and Easter)* Carte 54/106 CHF
♦ Traditional ♦ Classic ♦

Housed in a late-19C residence, this elegant hotel has public rooms decorated in chic Belle Époque style, guestrooms with individual touches and excellent quality bedding. Retro decor, an outdoor terrace for summer dining, and a contemporary menu offering gourmet cuisine and low-calorie dishes.

Parc des Eaux-Vives
≤ 🕭 🖘 & ⇔ 🅿 VISA ⓒⓞ AE ①

82 quai Gustave-Ador (1st floor) ✉ *1207 –* ☎ *022 849 75 75*
– info@parcdeseauxvives.ch – Fax 022 849 75 70
– www.parcdeseauxvives.ch   *Plan I* **D2**
Rest Brasserie – see below
Rest – *(closed 1 - 18 January, Sunday and Monday)* Menu 79 CHF (lunch)/ 260 CHF – Carte 170/236 CHF 🍴
Spec. Tourteau de casier et caviar Osciètre. Homard bleu des côtes Bretonnes rôti entier dans sa coque. Lièvre à la royale avec truffes et foie gras (autumn).
♦ Modern ♦ Design ♦

Sumptuous 18C house set in a park. The chef, Olivier Samson, offers a menu of dishes from his native Brittany. Good wines from around the world. Low-key lounge and dining room near the kitchen. Terrace with a panoramic view.

Roberto
📶 ⇔ VISA ⓒⓞ AE

10 r. Pierre-Fatio ✉ *1204 –* ☎ *022 311 80 33 – Fax 022 311 84 66*
– closed Saturday dinner, Sunday and bank holidays   **H2**
Rest – Carte 68/133 CHF
♦ Italian ♦ Cosy ♦

Renowned for its cosy decor, authentic Italian cuisine and excellent service, this restaurant is perfect for an intimate candlelit meal. Ask for a table in the main dining room.

Brasserie – Parc des Eaux-Vives
≤ 🕭 & 🅿 VISA ⓒⓞ AE ①

82 quai Gustave-Ador ✉ *1207 –* ☎ *022 849 75 75*
– info@parcdeseauxvives.ch – Fax 022 849 75 70
– www.parcdeseauxvives.ch   *Plan I* **D2**
Rest – Menu 49 CHF (lunch) – Carte 69/91 CHF
♦ Modern ♦ Trendy ♦

Elegant modern brasserie on the ground floor of the Eaux-Vives Park lodge. Up-to-date cuisine, fine view of the lake and inviting teak terrace.

Buffet de la Gare des Eaux-Vives (Serge Labrosse)
🕭

7 av. de la Gare des Eaux-Vives ✉ *1207 –* ☎ *022 840 44 30*   VISA ⓒⓞ AE
– Fax 022 840 44 31
– closed 20 December - 5 January, 18 July – 10 August, Saturday and Sunday
Rest – Menu 59 CHF (lunch)/175 CHF – Carte 105/135 CHF 🍴   *Plan I* **D3**
Spec. Gambas et poulpe en croustilles, compote de tomates et piquillos, emulsion d'une crème de chorizo piquant. Filet de rouget et pignon de pin, jus de courgette et geranium odorant. Le veau cuit en basse temperature, cannelloni de jarret confit, condiment de capres et citron de menton.
♦ Inventive ♦ Classic ♦

A "station buffet" that stands out from the crowd, with its very modern interior, summer terrace next to the platforms, up-to-date cuisine and good selection of wines from Switzerland and the Rhone Valley.

✖ **Le Patio**   VISA ⓪ AE ⓪

19 bd Helvétique ✉ *1207 – ☏ 022 736 66 75 – lepatio.ch@bluewin.ch*
– Fax 022 786 40 74
– closed 24 December - 4 January, Saturday and Sunday   **H2**
Rest – Menu 48 CHF (lunch) – Carte 68/94 CHF
◆ Traditional ◆ Neighbourhood ◆

Run by an art enthusiast, this neighbourhood restaurant features large paintings by a Cuban artist in the dining room. Traditional menu and daily seasonal specials.

ENVIRONS AND COINTRIN AIRPORT   *Plan I*

🏨 **La Réserve** ᨰ   ≼ 🕭 🖰 ᵭ🌣 ⌖ 🕃 ⍟ ▣ ✖ ᵭ 𝔸𝕮 ⤴ rm 🖭 ᵞ 🅿

301 rte de Lausanne – ☏ 022 959 59 59   🚗 VISA ⓪ AE ⓪
– info@lareserve.ch – Fax 022 959 59 60 – www.lareserve.ch   **C1**
87 rm – ♦600 CHF ♦♦750/1000 CHF, ⛌ 45 CHF – 15 suites
Rest *Le Loti* – Menu 115/145 CHF – Carte 82/161 CHF
Rest *Tsé-Fung* – Menu 75/150 CHF – Carte 69/170 CHF
◆ Grand Luxury ◆ Design ◆

This luxury hotel boasts modern rooms and suites with terraces, most of which overlook the park and swimming pool. Magnificent decor designed by Garcia, plus a superb spa. Italian-influenced menu and stylish exotic decor at Le Loti. Enjoy inventive Chinese cuisine in elegant surroundings at the Tsé-Fung.

🏨 **Crowne Plaza**   ⍟ ᵭ🌣 ᵭ ▣ ᵭ 𝔸𝕮 ⤴ rm 🖭 ᵞ ᵴᵭ 🚗

34 r. François-Peyrot – ☏ 022 747 02 02 – reservations@   VISA ⓪ AE ⓪
cpgeneva.ch – Fax 022 747 03 03 – www.crowneplazageneva.ch   **B1**
496 rm – ♦315/550 CHF ♦♦315/550 CHF, ⛌ 39 CHF
Rest *Carlights* – Menu 55 CHF (lunch)/69 CHF – Carte 60/85 CHF
Rest *L'Olivo* – (closed 20 December - 5 January, Saturday and Sunday)
Carte 82/104 CHF
◆ Business ◆ Contemporary ◆

Business hotel near the airport specialising in conferences and congresses. Modern bedrooms, trendy public areas and a fitness club. The Carlights serves fusion cuisine in a modern and functional setting. Contemporary cuisine and a Mediterranean ambience at L'Olivo.

🏨 **Mövenpick**   ⍟ ᵭ🌣 ᵭ 𝔸𝕮 ⤴ rm 🖭 ᵞ ᵴᵭ 🚗 VISA ⓪ AE ⓪

20 rte de Pré-Bois – ☏ 022 717 11 11 – hotel.geneva.airport@moevenpick.com
– Fax 022 717 11 22 – www.moevenpick-geneva-airport.com   **A2**
344 rm – ♦220/590 CHF ♦♦250/630 CHF, ⛌ 36 CHF – 6 suites
Rest *Latitude* – Menu 57/59 CHF – Carte 52/94 CHF
Rest *Kamomé* – (closed 26 July – 16 August, Monday lunch, Saturday lunch and Sunday) Menu 45 CHF (lunch)/110 CHF – Carte 52/109 CHF
◆ Chain hotel ◆ Modern ◆

Business hotel with lounge, bars, casino and various types of guestrooms, the newest of which are the executive rooms. Trendy decor and fusion cuisine at the Latitude. The Kamomé offers Japanese dishes at the sushi bar or around hot plate tables (teppanyaki).

🏨 **Ramada Park**   ᵭ🌣 ᵭ 𝔸𝕮 ⤴ rm 🖭 ᵞ ᵴᵭ 🚗 VISA ⓪ AE ⓪

75 av. Louis-Casaï – ☏ 022 710 30 00 – info@ramadaparkhotel.ch
– Fax 022 710 31 00 – www.ramadaparkhotel.ch   **A2**
302 rm – ♦270/500 CHF ♦♦320/500 CHF, ⛌ 37 CHF – 6 suites
Rest *La Récolte* – Carte 50/97 CHF
◆ Chain hotel ◆ Modern ◆

Hotel near the airport offering a wide range of amenities, including a news-stand, hairdresser's, sauna, fitness centre and meeting rooms. Modern guestrooms. This contemporary-style restaurant organises weekly events based on different culinary themes.

NH Geneva Airport

21 av. de Mategnin – *022 989 90 00 – nhgenevaairport@nh-hotels.ch*
– *Fax 022 989 99 99 – www.nh-hotels.com*   **A2**
190 rm – †155/450 CHF ††155/450 CHF, ⌑ 27 CHF
Rest *Le Pavillon* – *(closed Saturday lunch and Sunday lunch)* Menu 65 CHF
– Carte 50/96 CHF
♦ Chain hotel ♦ Design ♦

This hotel has a distinctive circular shape built in red brick, in keeping with its
modern style interiors. Designer lobby, with an attractive bar and well-kept
rooms. Enjoy up-to-date cuisine in a modern setting under the Pavillon's dome.

Suitehotel

28 av. Louis-Casaï – *022 710 46 46 – h5654@accor.com – Fax 022 710 46 00*
– *www.suite-hotel.com*   **B2**
86 rm – †187/270 CHF ††187/270 CHF, ⌑ 11 CHF
Rest *Swiss Bistro* – *(closed Saturday, Sunday lunch and bank holidays)*
Carte 37/67 CHF
♦ Chain hotel ♦ Modern ♦

Located between the airport and the town centre, this hotel offers contemporary-
style rooms with an office separated by a sliding door. Modern and light public
areas. Brasserie with a modern setting. Its bistro-type menu has Swiss touches.

Ibis

10 ch. de la Violette – *022 710 95 00 – h3535@accor.com – Fax 022 710 95 95*
– *www.ibishotel.com*   **A2**
109 rm – †147/220 CHF ††147/220 CHF, ⌑ 15 CHF
Rest – *(closed 23 December - 5 January) (dinner only)* Carte 49/58 CHF
♦ Chain hotel ♦ Minimalist ♦

Situated near the motorway and Geneva airport, this hotel has all the facilities you
would expect of the Ibis chain. Functional rooms with bathrooms. This restaurant
has a tavern-style decor and a menu featuring contemporary cuisine.

Auberge du Lion d'Or (Thomas Byrne et Gilles Dupont)

5 pl. Pierre-Gautier – *022 736 44 32*
– *liondorcologny@bluewin.ch – Fax 022 786 74 62 – www.liondor.ch*
– *closed 19 December - 8 January, Saturday and Sunday*
Rest – Menu 145 CHF (lunch)/220 CHF – Carte 156/189 CHF   **D2**
Rest *Le Bistro de Cologny* – Menu 70/90 CHF – Carte 67/90 CHF
Spec. Ravioli de crabe royal et langoustine aux élans de citronelle et gingembre. Parilla de poissons et crustacés de l'Atlantique. Millefeuille de selle
d'agneau et aubergine, persil plat et fèvettes.
♦ Modern ♦ Elegant ♦

Magnificent view from the stylish dining room, modern bar and terrace shaded by
a great plane tree. Two chefs offer delicious up-to-date dishes. A modern bistro
and an outdoor restaurant with a flower-filled garden for summer dining.

Domaine de Châteauvieux (Philippe Chevrier) with rm

16 ch. de Châteauvieux
*(West: 10 km) – *022 753 15 11 – info@chateauvieux.ch – Fax 022 753 19 24*
– *www.chateauvieux.ch*
– *closed 21 December - 5 January, 12 - 20 April and 26 July – 10 August*
13 rm ⌑ – †265/405 CHF ††315/455 CHF
Rest – *(closed Sunday and Monday)* Menu 92 CHF (lunch)/270 CHF
– Carte 196/249 CHF
Spec. Les jambonnettes de grenouilles sautées et tempura d'escargots petit-
gris, mousseline de pommes de terre. Bar de ligne cuit dans le gros sel par-
fumé au lemon grass. Côte de bison poelée aux zestes de citrons confits et
au poivre vert.
♦ Innovative ♦ Formal ♦

This former farmhouse is now a hostelry at the heart of the vineyard. Exquisite,
creative cuisine, prestigious wine list, fine terrace and all the amenities you would
expect from such a renowned restaurant. Stylish rooms with excellent bedding
and modern bathrooms. Carefully prepared breakfast.

XXX
£3
La Chaumière (Richard Cressac) 　　　　　　 ⌂ & ♧ P̲ *VISA* ◎◎ ᴬᴱ ◉

16 ch. de la Fondelle (South: 5 km by Carouge C3) – ℰ 022 784 30 66
– info@lachaumiere.ch – Fax 022 784 60 48 – www.lachaumiere.ch
– closed 21 December - 6 January, 10 - 13 April, 10 - 14 September, Sunday and
Monday
Rest – Menu 70 CHF (lunch)/175 CHF – Carte 97/136 CHF ⅏
Rest *Brasserie* – Menu 45 CHF (lunch) – Carte 57/88 CHF
Spec. L'omble chevalier du lac à la meunière. Entrecôte du Simmental, jus au
poivre de Szechuan. Millefeuille aux fraises, glace à la double crème de la
Gruyère.
　◆ Modern ◆ Elegant ◆
Former inn converted into a comfortable restaurant, surrounded by greenery.
Modern cuisine accompanied by the best local wines. Summer terrace. Brasserie-
type restaurant in a rotunda. Terrace with a grill.

XX
£3
Le Cigalon (Jean-Marc Bessire) 　　　　　　 ⌂ ⅟⅟ P̲ *VISA* ◎◎ ᴬᴱ

39 rte d'Ambilly (South-East: 5 km by Route de Chêne D3)
– ℰ 022 349 97 33 – jmbessire@le-cigalon.ch – Fax 022 349 97 39
– www.le-cigalon.ch
– closed 21 December - 6 January, 10 - 20 April, 26 July – 18 August, Sunday
and Monday
Rest – Menu 52 CHF (lunch)/135 CHF – Carte 83/131 CHF
Spec. Menu Tapas (only for the whole table). Poissons de Sète selon arri-
vage. Agneau de lait des Pyrénées.
　◆ Fish ◆ Family ◆
Tasty fish dishes served in an ocean atmosphere or near the kitchen, at the chef's
table. Also enjoy the fine seaside cuisine on the summer terrace.

Population (est.2005): 345 300 (conurbation 1 081 700) – Altitude: 409m

M. Bauer/Zürich Tourismus

Zurich has a lot of things going for it. A lot of history (two thousand years' worth), a lot of water (two rivers and a huge lake), a lot of beauty (its old town is a visual feast), and, let's face it, a lot of wealth (it's Switzerland's richest city). It's an important financial and commercial centre, and has a well-earned reputation for good living with a rich cultural life, reflected in an abundance of smart restaurants and outdoor cafés.

The place strikes a nice balance – it's large enough to boast some world-class facilities but small enough to hold on to its charm and old-world ambience. The window-shopping here sets it apart from many other European cities – from tiny boutiques and specialist emporiums to a shopping boulevard that's famed across the globe. Although it's not Switzerland's political capital, it's the spiritual one because of its pulsing arts scene: for those who might think the Swiss a bit staid, think again – this is where the nihilistic, anti-art Dada movement began.

LIVING THE CITY

The attractive **Lake Zurich** flows northwards into the city, which forms a pleasingly symmetrical arc around it. From the lake, the river **Limmat** bisects Zurich, flowing north until it reaches another river, the narrower **Sihl.** On the Limmat's west bank lies the **Old Town**, the medieval hub, overlooked by two dominant churches. The stylishly vibrant **Bahnhofstrasse**, the smartest shopping street in town, follows the line of the former city walls. Across the Limmat on the east side, the unmissable landmark is the magnificent twin-towered **Grossmünster**, while just beyond is the charmingly historic district of **Niederdorf**. Way down south is the city's largest green space, the **Zürichhorn Park.**

PRACTICAL INFORMATION

ARRIVAL-DEPARTURE

Zurich International Airport (Kloten) is located 10km north of the city. Trains run every 10-15min and take 10min. A taxi will be about 50CHF. Zürich Hauptbahnhof is the main railway station for international and inter-city trains.

TRANSPORT

As this is Switzerland, you can guarantee that the public transport system runs like clockwork. The city operates an efficient system on bus, tram, metro, train and boat. You can buy a single ticket, day ticket, or 9 o'clock Pass. Tickets are available from ticket machines and tourist offices. Remember to validate your ticket at the ticket machine or special orange-coloured machine before boarding.

The Zurichcard grants unlimited travel on all public transport (including river and lake boats). It also gives you admission to more than forty museums and art collections. The card can be purchased for twenty-four or seventy-two hours.

Cycle riding is encouraged here. Hire bikes for free for the day from beside the main railway station. All you have to do is leave ID and a local currency deposit.

EXPLORING ZURICH

Mention Zurich and your first thoughts may turn to bankers and precision timing. But Zurich is a beautiful, medieval city that has been a respected base of European culture for centuries. To wander round and about the alleyways of its Old Town (the **Altstadt**) is to explore a fascinating labyrinth of cobbled streets, flower-filled squares and ancient pastel-shaded houses. Momentous events have happened here. In the cobbled **Münsterhof Square**, in the Old Town's heart, Winston Churchill delivered a famous speech after World War II, declaring "Europe Arise!" in praise of a postwar European union. These words are on a plaque set into the cobbles,

a reminder that this city has played a recognisable part in the continent's history. Further proof is just over the water at the imposing Grossmünster, where the zealous preaching of radical cleric Huldrych Zwingli set in motion the wheels of the sixteenth-century Reformation.

→ BAHN-STORMER

The plaque to Churchill is no more than a cuckoo's call from the Bahnhofstrasse, a mile-long, tram-packed avenue stretching south to the edge of Lake Zurich. The city's commercial centre, Bahnhoffstrasse is lined with upmarket shops and chic restaurants, its gravitas enhanced by the headquarters of several major Swiss banks. Between it and the river lies a warren of medieval lanes full of small, individual shops selling a range of quirky things. Act like a smart local, and get some respite from the bustle by ducking into the lanes that head up to the **Lindenhof.** This tree-covered hill is where Zurich began: the Romans founded a customs post here as early as the first century BC. It's a delightful spot to take a rest; an observation platform gives you views of the surrounding rooftops and the Limmat gliding along below. There's a giant chessboard on the hill-top where old boys wreathed in concentration search for checkmate underneath the lime trees.

On this west side of the Limmat there are two distinctive churches, less than two hundred metres apart. The **Church of St Peter**, whose main body is exactly three hundred years old, seems to be an ideal landmark for the punctual Swiss: its clockface, at twenty-eight feet in diameter, is the largest in Europe, so you'll know if you have the time to nip south a little way and pay a visit to **Fraumünster**. This is a graceful building whose history stretches back over a thousand years, but its main claim to fame is more recent. The

breathtaking stained glass windows were added in 1970, and were the inspiration of Marc Chagall. They're a delicious fusion of ethereal light and colour.

→ SWISS ROLE

At the top end of Bahnhofstrasse, past the grand railway station, is the equally imposing **Swiss National Museum**. Ideal for a rainy day, this vast collection covers everything you'll need to know about Switzerland from prehistoric times to the 21C. Its main highlight is a beautifully preserved 18C Benedictine pharmacy. Head across the river, though, for the top cultural attraction of the city: if you go on past the Grossmünster, you'll reach the **Kunsthaus**, Switzerland's premier art gallery. It's easy to get round, and its permanent art collection is outstanding. You can admire thrilling paintings by Swiss artists such as Giacometti and Fussli, plus a broad range of work that takes in medieval religious paintings, Dutch Old Masters, Impressionists and Surrealists. Dadaists are there too, of course, but it might be fun to see their actual birthplace before encountering them at the Kunsthaus. For this, stroll up through the pretty eastern section of the Altstadt – Niederdorf – till you come to the near-mystical **Cabaret Voltaire** on the corner of **Niederdorfstrasse** and **Spiegelgasse**. This updated café-bar and arts centre is where artist Tristan Tzara and like-minded refugees from World War I founded an avant-garde artistic movement in 1916 as an anarchic reaction against all the horrifying carnage – Dada.

→ LOOK WHO'S AT THE ODEON

At the same time as Tzara and his pals were in the process of revolutionising art, guess who was down the road killing time before the armistice ? None other than James Joyce and Vladimir Ilyich Lenin. They'd both become devotees of another legendary Zurich watering hole, the **Café Odeon** (although, unfortunately, there's no record of them ever having met). What would have captivated the great writer and the great revolutionary was the wonderful atmosphere of this Viennese-style coffee house. Looking out over bustling **Bellevueplatz**, the Café Odeon had, and still has, all the grand trimmings, including plate-glass windows, polished red marble and deep leather armchairs.

→ GO WEST

The shock of the new has slammed into Zurich. Go north of the main station and you'll come to Zurich West. But this is no railway terminus; it's the evolutionary outcome of the city's vibrant cultural scene and its cutting-edge reputation in the worlds of fashion and design. Zurich West is set in a former industrial and red light area that's taken on a new life. It's now an arty warehouse zone with a funky, chic, up-and-coming feel. Full of clubs, cinemas and restaurants, it's centred round **Langstrasse**, a road crisscrossed by flyovers and railway bridges, and is the complete antithesis to the idea of Zurich as an icy financial centre.

→ LAKE ARRIVAL

Search out a more peaceful, relaxing vibe at the other end of the city. If you head south from Grossmünster, there's a delightful narrow strip of parkland running parallel to the lake's eastern shore alongside the arrow-straight **Utoquai**. It's full of trees and flowerbeds and ends up at the idyllically set Zürichhorn Park, which rubs verdant shoulders with the wide expanses of Lake Zurich. From here, watch the boats in and out of the Limmat: catch one yourself from the city's landing stage at **Bürkliplatz**. A trip on the water is a must here. The lovely forty-kilometre lake stretches in an arc from Zurich to the foot of the Alps. There's a good choice of trips, from short sorties to cruises of half a day, taking in a range of lakeshore towns and villages. The water is crystal clear and unpolluted, so if you fancy, you can take a dip, too.

On your walk down Utoquai, you might like to take a little detour at **Falkenstrasse** and check out the glorious **Opera House**. Better still, try and get some tickets for a performance. This is one of Europe's leading opera and ballet theatres, a neo-Baroque beauty, designed by nineteenth century Viennese architects who knew a thing or two about this kind of opulence.

CALENDAR HIGHLIGHTS

Zurich's renown as a cultural leader reaches its annual highpoint at the Zurich Festival, every June and July, during which much of the city resounds to

ZURICH IN...

→ ONE DAY
Old Town, Bahnhofstrasse, Zurich West, Grossmünster

→ TWO DAYS
Watch the chessplayers on Lindenhof, see Chagall's glorious windows at Fraumünster, Kunsthaus, Cabaret Voltaire, Café Odeon

→ THREE DAYS
Utoquai, Zürichhorn Park, a night at the Opera House

international music, opera, theatre and dance, and thousands pour in to visit the performances. Theatre lovers can indulge their habit for longer at August's Theatre Spectacle, where innovative productions take centre stage, while in September athletics fans flock to the Letzigrund Stadium – the 'magic track' – for the legendary Weltklasse, which in 2008 celebrates eighty years of the event. The Zurich International Art Fair at Kongresshaus in October features everything from painting to sculpture and photography to video, but by then many will be outdoors in training for December's Silvesterlauf, a festively decorated race through the Old Town in which ten thousand competitors select various distances to run. February's Art On Ice at Hallenstadium is a 'feelgood' mix of musical stars, ice skaters and dynamic lightshow, while the same month's Carnival Procession transforms the city centre into a garish float-fest, highlighted by guggen music, when groups of musicians and non-musicians bang out an impromptu blast of rhythms, culminating in the Guggen Monster Concert in Münsterhof Square.

EATING OUT

Zurich stands out in Switzerland (along with Geneva) for its top-class restaurants serving international cuisine. Zurich, though, takes the prize when it comes to trendy, cutting-edge places to dine, whether restaurant or bar, whether along the lakeside or in the converted loft of an old factory. In the middle of the day, most locals go for the cheaper daily lunchtime menus, saving themselves for the glories of the evening. The city is host to many traditional, longstanding Italian restaurants, but if you want to try something 'totally Zurcher', you can't do any better than tackle geschnetzeltes with rösti: sliced veal fried in butter, simmered with onions and mushrooms, with a dash of white wine and cream, served with hashed brown potatoes. A good place for simple restaurants and bars is Niederdorf, while Zurich West is coming on strong with its twenty first century zeitgeist diners. When you're happy with the service you usually round up a small bill or leave up to ten percent on a larger one.

➔ PANORAMA

Take a 15-minute train journey from the main station for quite simply the very best view of Zurich. Known to Zurchers as the 'top of Zurich', Uetliberg is an 871m mountain with a forested mountain ridge, lush green meadows, tinkling cowbells and, best of all, fantastic 360-degree views of the city, the lake and the Alps. The train will take you to the summit, or you can walk up yourself: it should take a fit person about one and a half hours.

➔ AN ARTY BREW

An old brewery is now the home of two of Zurich's very best contemporary art museums. The former home of Löwenbräu in Limmatstrasse has been converted into bright, white rooms which house the Migros Museum, with its huge permanent collection, and the Kunsthalle Zurich, which puts on temporary exhibitions for up-and-coming stars of the art world.

➔ AND FINALLY...

In case anyone still thinks of Zurich as a staid place for intrepid clockwatchers: it has the highest density of pavement cafés in the world; its opera house has staged more premieres than any other; and its river and lake are home to no less than eighteen sandy beaches.

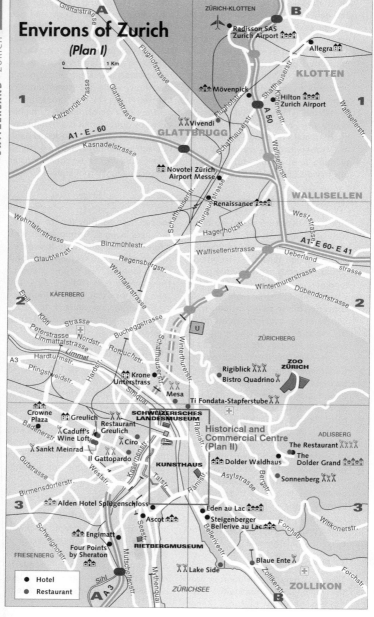

Environs of Zurich
(Plan I)

0   1 Km

ZÜRICH-KLOTTEN

Radisson SAS
Zurich Airport

Allegra

KLOTTEN

Mövenpick

Hilton
Zurich Airport

A 50

Vivendi

GLATTBRUGG

A1 - E - 60

Kasnadelstrasse

WALLISELLEN

Novotel Zürich
Airport Messe

Renaissance

A1 - E 60 - E 41

Wehntalerstrasse

Binzmühlestr.

Glaubtenstr.

Regensbergstr.

Wallisellenstrasse

Ueberland strasse

Winterthurerstrasse

Dübendorfstrasse

KÄFERBERG

ZÜRICHBERG

U

Bucheggstrasse

Nordstr.

Limmattalstrasse

Hardturmstr.

Limmat

Pfingstweidstr.

A3

Krone
Unterstrass

Mesa

Rigiblick

Bistro Quadrino

ZOO
ZÜRICH

Ti Fondata-Stapferstube

Crowne
Plaza

Greulich

Restaurant
Greulich

SCHWEIZERISCHES
LANDESMUSEUM

Historical and
Commercial Centre
(Plan II)

ADLISBERG

The Restaurant

Caduff's
Wine Loft

Ciro

Sankt Meinrad

Il Gattopardo

KUNSTHAUS

Dolder Waldhaus

The
Dolder Grand

Sonnenberg

Asylstrasse

Birmensdorferstr.

Alden Hotel Splügenschloss

Eden au Lac

Ascot

Steigenberger
Bellerive au Lac

Wittikonerstr.

Engimatt

Four Points
by Sheraton

RIETBERGMUSEUM

Blaue Ente

FRIESENBERG

Lake Side

ZÜRICHSEE

ZOLLIKON

● Hotel
● Restaurant

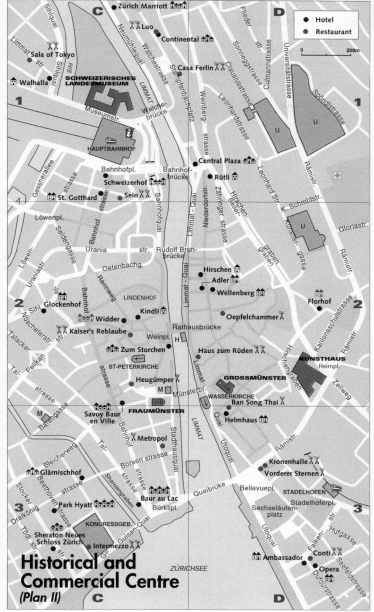

SWITZERLAND - ZURICH

● Hotel
● Restaurant

0   200m

Zürich Marriott
Luo
Continental
Casa Ferlin
Sala of Tokyo
Walhalla
SCHWEIZERISCHES
LANDESMUSEUM
HAUPTBAHNHOF
Central Plaza
Bahnhofpl.
Bahnhof-
brücke
Schweizerhof
Rütli
St. Gotthard
Sein
Löwenpl.
Urania
Rudolf Brun-
brücke
Hirschen
Adler
Glockenhof
Wellenberg
Florhof
LINDENHOF
Kindli
Widder
Oepfelchammer
Kaiser's Reblaube
Weinpl.
Zum Storchen
Rathausbrücke
Haus zum Rüden
KUNSTHAUS
ST-PETERKIRCHE
GROSSMÜNSTER
Heimpl.
Heugümper
WASSERKIRCHE
Ban Song Thai
FRAUMÜNSTER
Savoy Baur
en Ville
Helmhaus
Metropol
Glärnischhof
Kronenhalle
Vorderer Sternen
STADELHOFEN
Park Hyatt
Baur au Lac
Bürklipl.
Quaibrüke
Bellevuepl.
Stadelhoferpl.
Sechseläuten-
platz
Sheraton Neues
Schloss Zürich
Intermezzo
KONGRESSGEB.
Ambassador
Conti
Opera
ZÜRICHSEE

Historical and
Commercial Centre
(Plan II)

SWITZERLAND - ZURICH

Zürich Marriott ≤ ⅃ ㏗ ☒ ☖ ㎞ ⅔ ⊡ ♈ ⅍ ⇔ 𝖵𝖨𝖲𝖠 ☒

Neumühlequai 42 ☒ 8001 – ℰ 044 360 70 70 – marriott.zurich@
marriotthotels.com – Fax 044 360 77 77 – www.zurichmarriott.com
255 rm – ♟355/635 CHF ♟♟355/685 CHF, ☷ 37 CHF – 9 suites **C1**
Rest *White Elephant* – *(closed Saturday lunch and Sunday lunch)* Menu
65 CHF (dinner buffet) – Carte 64/77 CHF
Rest *Echo* – *(dinner only)* Carte 64/97 CHF
♦ Chain hotel ♦ Classic ♦
Beside the river, this multi-storey building has its own underground parking. The
rooms differ in size and layout but are all comfortable and contemporary. Modern
and with clean lines, the White Elephant is known for its Thai specialities.

Continental ☖ ☖ ㎞ ⅔ rm ⊡ ♈ ⅍ ⇔ 𝖵𝖨𝖲𝖠 ☒ ☒ ☒

Stampfenbachstr. 60 ☒ 8006 – ℰ 044 360 60 60 – h1196@accor.com
– Fax 044 360 60 61 – www.continentalzuerich.com **C1**
134 rm – ♟220/450 CHF ♟♟270/545 CHF, ☷ 32 CHF – 4 suites
Rest *Luo* – see below
Rest *Bel Etage* – *(closed Saturday – Sunday lunch)* Carte 54/110 CHF
♦ Chain hotel ♦ Functional ♦
From the reception area, which is decorated in the style of an elegant Swiss chalet
to the sound-insulated rooms, wood and warm colours characterise the interior of
this hotel. The Bel Etage is rustic yet refined; the cuisine is contemporary.

Central Plaza ☖ ⅃ ☖ ㎞ rm ⅔ rm ⊡ ♈ ⅍ ⇔ 𝖵𝖨𝖲𝖠 ☒ ☒ ☒

Central 1 ☒ 8001 – ℰ 044 256 56 56 – info@central.ch – Fax 044 256 56 57
– www.central.ch **D1**
101 rm – ♟390/415 CHF ♟♟390/415 CHF, ☷ 18 CHF – 4 suites
Rest *King's Cave* – ℰ 044 256 55 55 – Carte 60/87 CHF
♦ Business ♦ Modern ♦
This hotel is opposite the railway station, beside the Limmat. The comfortable
guest rooms are all furnished with modern style and design. The King's Cave grill
restaurant has beautiful atmosphere: the basement vaults previously served as the
safe for the UBS bank.

Florhof ☖ ⅔ rm ⊡ ☏ 𝖵𝖨𝖲𝖠 ☒ ☒ ☒

Florhofgasse 4 ☒ 8001 – ℰ 044 250 26 26 – info@florhof.ch
– Fax 044 250 26 27 – www.florhof.ch **D2**
35 rm ☷ – ♟265/305 CHF ♟♟380/400 CHF
Rest – *(closed 24 December – 5 January, 18 April - 4 May and Saturday lunch,
Sunday – Monday)* Menu 47 CHF (lunch)/110 CHF – Carte 82/107 CHF ⅊
♦ Traditional ♦ Personalised ♦
Dating from 1576, this fine, thin patrician townhouse is a very individual venue.
The rooms are tastefully equipped in a highly liveable style, and the two junior sui-
tes in the attics are sumptuously appointed. A comfortable and elegant restaurant.

Ambassador ㎞ ⅔ rm ⊡ ♈ 𝖵𝖨𝖲𝖠 ☒ ☒ ☒

Falkenstr. 6 ☒ 8008 – ℰ 044 258 98 98 – welcome@ambassadorhotel.ch
– Fax 044 258 98 00 – www.ambassadorhotel.ch **D3**
45 rm – ♟260/480 CHF ♟♟395/540 CHF, ☷ 28 CHF
Rest *A l'Opera* – Menu 36 CHF (lunch)/76 CHF – Carte 44/95 CHF
♦ Business ♦ Modern ♦
This former patrician house is located on the edge of the city centre, very close to
the opera house. It features modern, well equipped guest rooms. Wall paintings
and scenes from the opera adorn the A l'Opera restaurant.

Opera without rest ㎞ ⅔ ⊡ ♈ 𝖵𝖨𝖲𝖠 ☒ ☒ ☒

Dufourstr. 5 ☒ 8008 – ℰ 044 258 99 99 – welcome@operahotel.ch
– Fax 044 258 99 00 – www.operahotel.ch **D3**
58 rm – ♟245/440 CHF ♟♟360/490 CHF, ☷ 26 CHF
♦ Business ♦ Modern ♦
This business hotel faces the opera house which has given it its name. The rooms
are modern and homey, decorated in warm colours.

Wellenberg without rest   ⇖ 🖭 ⁽ᵗ⁾ 💳 ◉ 🅰🅴 ⓪

Niederdorfstr. 10 ⊠ *8001 –* 𝒞 *043 888 44 44 – reservation@hotel-wellenberg.ch*
– Fax 043 888 44 45 – www.hotel-wellenberg.ch   **D2**
45 rm ⊡ – ♥325/410 CHF ♥♥420/470 CHF
◆ Business ◆ Functional ◆
This house deep in the old town offers modern rooms, some of them in Art Deco
style. Elegant breakfast room with a leafy shaded terrace.

Adler   🍴 ⇖ rm 🖭 ⁽ᵗ⁾ 💳 ◉ 🅰🅴 ⓪

Rosengasse 10 (at Hirschenplatz) ⊠ *8001 –* 𝒞 *044 266 96 96*
– info@hotel-adler.ch – Fax 044 266 96 69 – www.hotel-adler.ch   **D2**
52 rm ⊡ – ♥150/290 CHF ♥♥230/350 CHF
Rest *Swiss Chuchi –* 𝒞 *044 266 96 66 (closed Christmas)* Carte 42/77 CHF
◆ Business ◆ Functional ◆
The rooms have light-coloured, functional wood furnishings and modern technology and also feature artwork depicting views of Zurich's old town by the painter
Heinz Blum. Enjoy the rustic atmosphere in the Swiss Chuchi, located on the
street.

Helmhaus without rest   🅰🅲 ⇖ 🖭 ⁽ᵗ⁾ 💳 ◉ 🅰🅴 ⓪

Schifflände 30 ⊠ *8001 –* 𝒞 *044 266 95 95 – info@helmhaus.ch*
– Fax 044 266 95 66 – www.helmhaus.ch   **D3**
24 rm ⊡ – ♥220/300 CHF ♥♥300/430 CHF
◆ Traditional ◆ Functional ◆
A house in the heart of the city with functionally appointed guestrooms – some
with particularly modern furnishings. Pleasant breakfast room on the first floor.

Hirschen without rest   ⇖ 🖭 ⁽ᵗ⁾ 💳 ◉

Niederdorfstr. 13 ⊠ *8001 –* 𝒞 *043 268 33 33 – info@hirschen-zuerich.ch*
– Fax 043 268 33 34 – www.hirschen-zuerich.ch   **D2**
27 rm ⊡ – ♥150/170 CHF ♥♥190/220 CHF
◆ Family ◆ Functional ◆
A 300-year-old inn with functional and modern rooms and a wine tavern in the his-
toric 16th century vaulted cellar. A beautiful roof terrace opens in the summer.

Rütli without rest   ⇖ 🖭 ⁽ᵗ⁾ 💳 ◉ 🅰🅴 ⓪

Zähringerstr. 43 ⊠ *8001 –* 𝒞 *044 254 58 00 – info@rutli.ch*
– Fax 044 254 58 01 – www.rutli.ch
– closed 20 December – 4 January   **D1**
62 rm ⊡ – ♥185/250 CHF ♥♥260/340 CHF
◆ Business ◆ Functional ◆
This hotel near the train station has a pleasant reception area and simple modern
guest rooms. Of special interest are the graffiti rooms.

Conti   🍴 💳 ◉ 🅰🅴 ⓪

Dufourstr. 1 ⊠ *8008 –* 𝒞 *044 251 06 66 – ristorante.conti@bindella.ch*
– Fax 044 251 06 86 – www.bindella.ch   **D3**
Rest – Carte 70/120 CHF
◆ Italian ◆ Formal ◆
This restaurant is immediately next to the opera. Find an interior of classical dignity
with a lovely high stucco ceiling, an exhibition of paintings, and Italian cuisine.

Kronenhalle   🅰🅲 ⇔ 💳 ◉ 🅰🅴 ⓪

Rämistr. 4 ⊠ *8001 –* 𝒞 *044 262 99 00 – info@kronenhalle.com*
– Fax 044 262 99 19 – www.kronenhalle.com   **D3**
Rest *– (booking advisable)* Carte 75/122 CHF
◆ Traditional ◆ Formal ◆
This elegant, well-established Zurich institution has a long tradition and offers
attentive service. Noteworthy art collection.

XX **Haus zum Rüden**   🗚 ⇔ 𝘝𝘐𝘚𝘈 ⓒ AE ⓞ

Limmatquai 42 (1st floor) ✉ *8001* – ☎ *044 261 95 66*
– *info@hauszumrueden.ch* – *Fax 044 261 18 04* – *www.hauszumrueden.ch*
– *closed Christmas and Saturday - Sunday*   **D2**
Rest – Menu 63 CHF (lunch)/138 CHF – Carte 74/126 CHF
◆ Classic ◆ Formal ◆
The Gothic ceiling of the restaurant in this lovely 13th century Guildhall is surprisingly made of wooden barrels. Refined historical ambience and a classic menu.

XX **Ti-Fondata-Stapferstube**   🍴 ⇔ 𝘝𝘐𝘚𝘈 ⓒ AE

Culmannstr. 45 ✉ *8006* – ☎ *044 350 11 00* – *info@restauranti.ch*
– *Fax 044 350 11 01* – *www.restauranti.ch*
– *closed 19 July - 10 August, Saturday lunch, Sunday – Monday and bank holidays*   *Plan I* **A3**
Rest – Menu 39 CHF (lunch) – Carte 65/105 CHF
◆ Italian ◆ Friendly ◆
This traditional restaurant specialises in products from the Ticino region: fresh, typical cuisine as well as a large selection of Ticino wines and grappa.

XX **Luo** – Hotel Continental   🗚 𝘝𝘐𝘚𝘈 ⓒ AE

Stampfenbachstr. 60 ✉ *8006* – ☎ *043 810 00 65* – *Fax 043 322 58 18*
– *closed 23 December – 3 January, 27 July - 22 August and Saturday lunch, Sunday*   **C1**
Rest – Menu 65/95 CHF – Carte 46/93 CHF
◆ Chinese ◆ Friendly ◆
Brick walls and a beautiful wood ceiling give this restaurant its refined, rustic character. Delicious Chinese cuisine is served.

XX **Casa Ferlin**   🗚 𝘝𝘐𝘚𝘈 ⓒ AE ⓞ

Stampfenbachstr. 38 ✉ *8006* – ☎ *044 362 35 09* – *casaferlin@bluewin.ch*
– *Fax 044 362 35 34* – *www.casaferlin.ch*
– *closed mid July – mid August and Saturday - Sunday*   **C-D1**
Rest – (booking advisable) Menu 56 CHF (lunch)/130 CHF – Carte 78/114 CHF
◆ Italian ◆ Family ◆
A traditional, family-run establishment with a classic, countrified atmosphere. The restaurant was first opened in 1907 and offers Italian cooking.

X **Oepfelchammer**   🍴 ⇔ 𝘝𝘐𝘚𝘈 ⓒ AE ⓞ

Rindermarkt 12 (1st floor) ✉ *8001* – ☎ *044 251 23 36* – *Fax 044 262 75 33*
– *www.oepfelchammer.ch*
– *closed 22 December – 5 January, 13 July - 10 August, Sunday – Monday and bank holidays*   **D2**
Rest – Carte 62/80 CHF
◆ Modern ◆ Rustic ◆
The poet Gottfried Keller was a regular guest at the original wine tavern. Contemporary as well as traditional cuisine is served in this 19th century inn.

X **Vorderer Sternen**   🍴 ⇼ 𝘝𝘐𝘚𝘈 ⓒ AE ⓞ

Theaterstr. 22 ✉ *8001* – ☎ *044 251 49 49* – *info@vorderer-sternen.ch*
– *Fax 044 252 90 63* – *www.vorderer-sternen.ch*   **D3**
Rest – Carte 51/77 CHF
◆ Traditional ◆ Brasserie ◆
On the ground floor is a simple café, while upstairs there is a cosy restaurant decorated in dark wood, offering a traditional menu.

X **Ban Song Thai**   ⇼ 𝘝𝘐𝘚𝘈 ⓒ AE

Kirchgasse 6 ✉ *8001* – ☎ *044 252 33 31* – *bansong@bluewin.ch*
– *Fax 044 252 33 15* – *www.bansongthai.com*
– *closed 1 – 4 January, 20 July - 9 August, Saturday lunch and Sunday*
Rest – (booking advisable) Carte 44/82 CHF   **D2**
◆ Asian ◆ Exotic ◆
This restaurant is located near the Kunsthaus and the Grossmünster cathedral. The name says it all: the cuisine invites you on a trip to Thailand.

Baur au Lac

Talstr. 1 ✉ *8001* – ℰ *044 220 50 20* – *info@bauraulac.ch*
– *Fax 044 220 50 44* – *www.bauraulac.ch* **C3**
110 rm – †520 CHF ††820 CHF, ⊑ 42 CHF – 14 suites
Rest *Le Pavillon / Le Français* – Menu 98 CHF – Carte 74/160 CHF
Rest *Rive Gauche* – *(closed 14 July - 3 August and Sunday)* Carte 63/132 CHF
♦ Grand Luxury ♦ Stylish ♦
This traditional, stately 19th century hotel includes a spacious lobby, luxurious rooms and a beautiful garden. Mediterranean cuisine is served in the summer in Le Pavillon and in winter in Le Français. A stylish favourite: the Rive Gauche.

Park Hyatt

Beethovenstr. 21 ✉ *8002* – ℰ *043 883 12 34* – *zurich.park@hyatt.com*
– *Fax 043 883 12 35* – *www.zurich.park.hyatt.ch* **C3**
138 rm – †480/1030 CHF ††630/1180 CHF, ⊑ 45 CHF – 4 suites
Rest *Parkhuus* – ℰ *043 883 10 75 (closed Saturday lunch, Sunday)*
Menu 59 CHF (lunch)/92 CHF – Carte 71/119 CHF
♦ Grand Luxury ♦ Stylish ♦
Behind a modern glass façade are tasteful, luxurious rooms outfitted with the latest technology, as well as professional service. Snacks available in the lounge. Onyx bar. The elegant Parkhuus has floor-to-ceiling windows and a fine, glazed wine cellar on two floors.

Savoy Baur en Ville

Poststr. 12 (at Paradeplatz) ✉ *8001* – ℰ *044 215 25 25*
– *welcome@savoy-zuerich.ch* – *Fax 044 215 25 00*
– *www.savoy-zuerich.ch* **C3**
104 rm ⊑ – †520/800 CHF ††800/840 CHF – 8 suites
Rest *Baur* – *(closed Saturday, Sunday and bank holidays)* Menu 75 CHF (lunch)
– Carte 98/148 CHF
Rest *Orsini* – ℰ *044 215 27 27 (booking advisable)* Menu 75 CHF (lunch)
– Carte 97/144 CHF
♦ Grand Luxury ♦ Classic ♦
This hotel in the heart of town creates a stylish setting with its grand 19th century architecture. It is distinguished by its service and modern, elegant interior. Classic and elegant: the Baur on the first floor. The Italian alternative: the Orsini.

Widder

Rennweg 7 ✉ *8001* – ℰ *044 224 25 26* – *home@widderhotel.ch*
– *Fax 044 224 24 24* – *www.widderhotel.ch* **C2**
42 rm – †590/615 CHF ††770/1000 CHF, ⊑ 48 CHF – 7 suites
Rest – *(closed Sunday lunch)* Menu 125/140 CHF – Carte 91/102 CHF ❀
♦ Luxury ♦ Design ♦
The hotel is a neat group of eight historic houses in the old town, with contemporary architectural features artfully incorporated. The noble interior is in excellent taste. Two beautiful restaurants, each with its own charm and character.

Schweizerhof

Bahnhofplatz 7 ✉ *8021* – ℰ *044 218 88 88*
– *info@hotelschweizerhof.com* – *Fax 044 218 81 81*
– *www.hotelschweizerhof.com* **C1**
115 rm – †470/580 CHF ††580/770 CHF
Rest *La Soupière* – ℰ *044 218 88 20 (closed Saturday lunch, July - August Saturday - Sunday)* Menu 77 CHF (lunch) – Carte 88/123 CHF
♦ Luxury ♦ Classic ♦
In the centre of town, directly opposite the main railway station, you will find this hotel which is steeped in tradition. Behind its imposing façade lie modern elegance and comfort. The La Soupière restaurant is classic and refined.

Four Points by Sheraton

Kalandergasse 1 (Sihlcity) ✉ *8045* – ☏ *044 554 00 00*
– *sihlcity@fourpoints.com* – *Fax 044 554 00 01* – *www.fourpoints.com/zurich*
128 rm – ☷230/490 CHF ☷☷230/490 CHF, ☵ 30 CHF – 4 suites   *Plan I* **A3**
Rest *Rampe Süd* – *(closed Sunday and bank holidays)* Menu 84 CHF (dinner)
– Carte 59/88 CHF
  ◆ Chain hotel ◆ Design ◆
In the Sihlcity, with a large shopping centre, is this large, comfortable hotel with well equipped rooms and modern design. This stylish restaurant serves international cuisine.

Zum Storchen

Am Weinplatz 2 ✉ *8001* – ☏ *044 227 27 27* – *info@storchen.ch*
– *Fax 044 227 27 00* – *www.storchen.ch*   **C2**
65 rm ☵ – ☷415/475 CHF ☷☷580/790 CHF
Rest *Rôtisserie* – ☏ *044 227 21 13* – Menu 95 CHF – Carte 71/117 CHF
  ◆ Traditional ◆ Classic ◆
This traditional hotel, one of the oldest in town, is located directly on the Limmat. Tasteful Jouy fabrics adorn the elegant and comfortable rooms. A beautiful terrace by the river complements the restaurants and offers views over the old part of town.

Sheraton Neues Schloss Zürich

Stockerstr. 17 ✉ *8002* – ☏ *044 286 94 00*
– *sheraton.neuesschloss.zuerich@arabellastarwood.com* – *Fax 044 286 94 45*
– *www.sheraton.com/zuerich* – *closed 29 June - 30 August*   **C3**
60 rm – ☷280/620 CHF ☷☷280/620 CHF, ☵ 39 CHF
Rest *Le Jardin* – *(closed Saturday – Sunday)* Carte 53/97 CHF
  ◆ Business ◆ Classic ◆
This hotel is not far from the lake and is an excellent starting point for your activities. The guest rooms are furnished in an elegant, modern style. Ground-floor restaurant with contemporary cuisine.

Glärnischhof

Claridenstr. 30 ✉ *8002* – ☏ *044 286 22 22* – *info@hotelglaernischhof.ch*
– *Fax 044 286 22 86* – *www.hotelglaernischhof.ch*   **C3**
62 rm ☵ – ☷240/440 CHF ☷☷290/500 CHF
Rest *Le Poisson* – *(closed Saturday - Sunday and bank holidays)* Menu 59 CHF (lunch)/79 CHF – Carte 71/102 CHF
Rest *Vivace* – Carte 45/86 CHF
  ◆ Business ◆ Classic ◆
This townhouse is on the edge of the city centre and offers large guest rooms with high ceilings and beautiful walnut furniture. Le Poisson features delicious fish specialities.

St. Gotthard

Bahnhofstr. 87 ✉ *8023* – ☏ *044 227 77 00* – *reservation@hotelstgotthard.ch*
– *Fax 044 227 77 50* – *www.hotelstgotthard.ch*   **C1**
143 rm – ☷320/485 CHF ☷☷500/500 CHF, ☵ 29 CHF
Rest *Hummerrestaurant & Austernbar* – ☏ *044 211 55 00 (closed 21 July -
17 August and Sunday - Monday)* Menu 130/150 CHF – Carte 92/151 CHF
Rest *Lobbybar-Bistro* – ☏ *044 211 55 00* – Carte 67/102 CHF
  ◆ Traditional ◆ Classic ◆
A hotel rich in tradition, dating from 1889, just a stone's throw from the main station. A classical setting with guestrooms equipped in a predominantly modern style. In the dignified elegance of the restaurant's Lobster and Oyster Bar, crustaceans and French cuisine are available.

Glockenhof

Sihlstr. 31 ✉ *8022* – ☏ *044 225 91 91* – *info@glockenhof.ch*
– *Fax 044 225 92 92* – *www.glockenhof.ch*   **C2**
91 rm ☵ – ☷290/420 CHF ☷☷400/560 CHF
Rest – Menu 46 CHF (lunch) – Carte 41/92 CHF
  ◆ Business ◆ Modern ◆
The central location is just one of the advantages of this well-run hotel. In addition to traditional rooms there are tastefully modern designer rooms. Glogge-Stube restaurant with a lovely, quiet terrace. Glogge-Egge Bistro.

🏠 **Kindli** 🍴 ⚙ (º) VISA ⊚ AE ①
Pfalzgasse 1 ⊠ 8001 – ℰ 043 888 76 76 – hotel@kindli.ch – Fax 043 888 76 77
– www.kindli.ch **C2**
19 rm ⌑ – 🛏260/380 CHF 🛏🛏400/440 CHF
Rest Zum Kindli – *(closed Sunday and bank holidays)* Carte 64/103 CHF
♦ Traditional ♦ Cosy ♦
This very traditional Zurich townhouse offers you a homey atmosphere and comfortable, individual rooms, most of which are in a classic Laura Ashley style and some of which are modern. A refined, elegant restaurant with contemporary cuisine.

🏠 **Walhalla** without rest ↳ ⚙ (º) 🏋 VISA ⊚ AE ①
Limmatstr. 5 ⊠ 8005 – ℰ 044 446 54 00 – walhalla-hotel@bluewin.ch
– Fax 044 446 54 54 – www.walhalla-hotel.ch **C1**
48 rm – 🛏140/170 CHF 🛏🛏180/220 CHF, ⌑ 18 CHF
♦ Business ♦ Functional ♦
Convenient to transportation, located at a tram station behind the train station. Beautiful painted scenes of the gods adorn the rooms, which are furnished in dark wood.

✕✕ **Sein** 🍴 VISA ⊚ AE ①
Schützengasse 5 ⊠ 8001 – ℰ 044 221 10 65 – info@zuerichsein.ch
– Fax 044 212 65 80 – www.zuerichsein.ch
– closed 24 December – 4 January, 6 - 19 April, 20 July - 9 August
Rest – *(closed Saturday - Sunday, mid-November – mid-December:* **C1**
open Saturday dinner) Menu 72 CHF (lunch)/150 CHF – Carte 65/131 CHF
Rest Tapas Bar – *(closed Saturday - Sunday)* Carte 42/71 CHF
♦ Modern ♦ Fashionable ♦
Located in a pedestrian area, contemporary cooking is offered by this modern restaurant with a touch of elegance. Gourmet cuisine is served in the evening with a simpler menu at midday. Little delicious bites in the Tapas Bar.

✕✕ **Kaiser's Reblaube** 🍴 VISA ⊚
Glockengasse 7 ⊠ 8001 – ℰ 044 221 21 20 – info@kaisers-reblaube.ch
– Fax 044 221 21 55 – www.kaisers-reblaube.ch
– closed 2 weeks July, 1 week August and Saturday lunch, Sunday
Rest – *(booking advisable)* Menu 58 CHF (lunch)/165 CHF **C2**
– Carte 73/128 CHF
♦ Modern ♦ Rustic ♦
In a historic old townhouse in the midst of old alleyways is the Goethe-Stübli. Located on the first floor and boasting a lively wine tavern with a garden. Contemporary cuisine.

✕✕ **Intermezzo** AK ⇔ VISA ⊚ AE
Beethovenstr. 2 (in the Kongresshaus) ⊠ 8002 – ℰ 044 206 36 42
– intermezzo@kongresshaus.ch – Fax 044 206 36 59 – www.kongresshaus.ch
– closed 13 July - 9 August, Saturdays, Sundays and bank holidays
Rest – Menu 58 CHF (lunch) – Carte 81/122 CHF **C3**
♦ Modern ♦ Formal ♦
Up-to-date dining in a bright, elegant restaurant in the conference building. Friendly, attentive service at well-presented tables.

✕✕ **Sala of Tokyo** 🍴 VISA ⊚ AE ①
Limmatstr. 29 ⊠ 8005 – ℰ 044 271 52 90 – sala@active.ch – Fax 044 271 78 07
– www.sala-of-tokyo.ch – closed 22 December – 5 January, 19 July - 10 August
and Saturday lunch, Sunday - Monday **C1**
Rest – Menu 125 CHF – Carte 51/96 CHF
♦ Japanese ♦ Fashionable ♦
Along with the sushi bar and restaurant, authentic dishes are served here, prepared on special Sankaiyaki grill tables, in an atmosphere featuring clean lines and modern design.

✕ **Metropol** 🍴 ⅙ ↳ ⇔ VISA ⊚ AE ①
Fraumünsterstr. 12 ⊠ 8001 – ℰ 044 200 59 00 – welcome@metropol-restaurant.ch
– Fax 044 200 59 01 – www.metropol-restaurant.ch – closed Sunday and bank holidays
Rest – Menu 85/122 CHF – Carte 71/125 CHF **C3**
♦ International ♦ Fashionable ♦
This beautiful, neo-Baroque house in the banking quarter houses the cleanly-styled modern restaurant with café, bar and lounge. International cuisine includes sushi and sashimi.

☒ **Heugümper** 🍴 ⅃ ⅃ AC ⇪ VISA ⬤⬤ AE ⓪

*Waaggasse 4 ✉ 8001 – ☎ 044 211 16 60 – info@restaurantheuguemper.ch
– Fax 044 211 16 61 – www.restaurantheuguemper.ch
– closed 22 December – 4 January, 13 July - 9 August and Saturday - Sunday,
October – December: Saturday lunch, Sunday* **C2**
Rest – Menu 143 CHF – Carte 61/110 CHF
♦ Euro-asiatic ♦ Fashionable ♦
In a house near the Fraumünster in the old town, this smart-casual, modern bistro
has been created that serves tasty international cuisine.

NEAR THE AIRPORT
Plan I

🏨 **Radisson SAS Zurich Airport** ⩻ ⅃ 𝄆 ⅃ AC ⤧ 📠 📶 ⅃
✉ 8058 – ☎ 044 800 40 40 – info.zurich@ VISA ⬤⬤ AE ⓪
radissonsas.com – Fax 044 800 40 50 – www.zurich.radissonsas.com
330 rm – ♦225/495 CHF ♦♦225/495 CHF, ☲ 39 CHF **B1**
Rest *filini* – Carte 48/83 CHF
Rest *Angels' Wine Tower Grill* – (closed Sunday) (dinner only)
Carte 45/115 CHF
♦ Business ♦ Conference hotel ♦ Modern ♦
A business hotel designed by star architect Matteo Thun. It has an impressive
atrium hall and modern rooms in the styles of 'At Home', 'Chic', 'Fresh' and
'Charm'. Find retro style and Italian cuisine in Filini. The Angels' Wine Tower Grill
offers grilled dishes.

🏨 **Renaissance** ⅃ 𝄆 ▢ ⅃ AC ⤧ 📠 📶 ⅃ 🚗 VISA ⬤⬤ AE ⓪
*Thurgauerstr. 101 (Glattpark) – ☎ 044 874 50 00 – renaissance.zurich@
renaissancehotels.com – Fax 044 874 50 01 – www.renaissancezurich.com*
196 rm – ♦215/495 CHF ♦♦215/495 CHF, ☲ 37 CHF – 8 suites **B2**
Rest *Asian Place* – (closed 13 July - 22 August) Carte 47/117 CHF
Rest *Brasserie* – Menu 40 CHF (lunch) – Carte 43/94 CHF
♦ Business ♦ Functional ♦
The hotel boasts large, public leisure facilities in the basement and spacious rooms
with dark-coloured, solid wood furnishings. In the Asian Place, the cuisine ranges
from Chinese and Thai through to Japanese and Indonesian. Traditional: the Brasserie.

🏨 **Hilton Zurich Airport** ⅃ 𝄆 ⅃ AC ⤧ rm 📠 📶 ⅃ 🅿
Hohenbühlstr. 10 – ☎ 044 828 50 50 VISA ⬤⬤ AE ⓪
– zurich@hilton.com – Fax 044 828 51 51 – www.hilton.ch **B1**
310 rm – ♦265/625 CHF ♦♦265/625 CHF, ☲ 39 CHF – 13 suites
Rest *Market Place* – Menu 59 CHF (buffet) – Carte 48/117 CHF
♦ Chain hotel ♦ Functional ♦
This hotel provides pleasantly appointed rooms in a location near the airport.
Accommodation available on two floors in 'Executive Rooms'. The Market Place
offers guests a view of the open kitchen.

🏨 **Mövenpick** 🍴 ⅃ ⅃ AC ⤧ rm 📠 📶 ⅃ 🅿 VISA ⬤⬤ AE ⓪
*Walter Mittelholzerstr. 8 – ☎ 044 808 88 88
– hotel.zurich.airport@moevenpick.com – Fax 044 808 88 77
– www.moevenpick-zurich.com* **B1**
333 rm – ♦215/525 CHF ♦♦215/525 CHF, ☲ 33 CHF
Rest – Carte 41/85 CHF
Rest *Appenzeller Stube* – ☎ 044 808 85 55 (closed 2 weeks August and Satur-
day lunch) Carte 64/109 CHF
Rest *Dim Sum* – ☎ 044 808 84 44 (closed 3 weeks July - August and Saturday
lunch, Sunday) Carte 47/75 CHF
♦ Chain hotel ♦ Modern ♦
The hotel is situated right next to the motorway. It offers modern rooms comfortably
and functionally appointed to a high standard, with plenty of space. The Appenzeller
Stube has a traditional Swiss style. The Dim Sum serves Chinese cuisine.

Novotel Zürich Airport Messe 🛏 ⚿ 🎿 ♿ 🅰️🅲 rm 🚭 📠 📶 🏋️

Lindbergh - Platz 1 (Glattpark) – 𝒞 *044 829 90 00* 🅿️ 🚗 💳 ⓿ 🄰🄴 ⓿
– *h0884@accor.com* – *Fax 044 829 99 99* – *www.novotel-zurich-airport-messe.com*
255 rm – 🛏185/400 CHF 🛏🛏185/400 CHF, ⥮ 26 CHF **A-B1**
Rest – Carte 55/76 CHF
♦ Chain hotel ♦ Modern ♦

Tailor-made for business guests, this hotel in the Office and Trade Centre offers contemporary-style rooms and good transport connections. The restaurant offers international cuisine.

Allegra 🛏 ⚿ ♿ 🚭 rm 📶 🏋️ 🅿️ 💳 🄾🄾 🄰🄴 ⓿

Hamelirainstr. 3 – 𝒞 *044 804 44 44* – *reservation@hotel-allegra.ch*
– *Fax 044 804 41 41* – *www.hotel-allegra.ch* **B1**
132 rm – 🛏135/195 CHF 🛏🛏160/230 CHF, ⥮ 18 CHF
Rest – Carte 40/87 CHF
♦ Business ♦ Modern ♦

This modern business hotel offers generous rooms with functional, cheerfully coloured furnishings. Free shuttle service to and from the airport.

Vivendi 🛏 🅰️🅲 🅿️ 💳 🄾🄾 🄰🄴 ⓿

Europastr. 2 – 𝒞 *043 211 32 42* – *info@restaurant-vivendi.ch*
– *Fax 043 211 32 41* – *www.restaurant-vivendi.ch*
– *closed 24 December – 5 January, Saturday - Sunday and bank holidays*
Rest – Carte 61/78 CHF **B1**
♦ Traditional ♦ Friendly ♦

A modern, refined restaurant, characterised by bold lines and subtle colours, serving traditional cuisine with contemporary touches.

ENVIRONS OF ZURICH *Plan I*

The Dolder Grand 🞄 ← 🚗 🛏 ⚿ 🆙 🎿 🗨 🏊 ♿ 🅰️🅲 🚭 📶 🏋️

Kurhausstr. 65 ✉ *8032* – 𝒞 *044 456 60 00* 🏋️ 🚗 💳 🄾🄾 🄰🄴 ⓿
– *info@thedoldergrand.com* – *Fax 044 456 60 01* – *www.thedoldergrand.com*
162 rm – 🛏540/950 CHF 🛏🛏850/950 CHF, ⥮ 24 CHF – 11 suites **B3**
Rest The Restaurant – *see below*
Rest Garden Restaurant – Carte 83/113 CHF
♦ Grand Luxury ♦ Modern ♦

The former spa building of 1899 has been renovated to the highest standards and enlarged with two modern extensions. It is now an elegant, luxury hotel magnificently situated with a panoramic view over the town. The 4,000sqm spa park is as tasteful and sumptuous as the whole house. Garden Restaurant with large terrace and a fine view.

Eden au Lac ← 🚭 🅰️🅲 🚭 📶 🏋️ 🅿️ 💳 🄾🄾 🄰🄴 ⓿

Utoquai 45 ✉ *8008* – 𝒞 *044 266 25 25* – *info@edenaulac.ch*
– *Fax 044 266 25 00* – *www.edenaulac.ch* **B3**
46 rm – *(closed Saturday lunch)* 🛏450/590 CHF 🛏🛏690/765 CHF, ⥮ 40 CHF – 4 suites
Rest – *(closed Saturday lunch)* Menu 48 CHF (lunch)/145 CHF – Carte 84/133 CHF
♦ Luxury ♦ Classic ♦

This neo-Baroque hotel is something of a cultural monument, which has decisively imprinted its character on the lakefront since 1909. Inside, find everything you would expect of a luxury hotel. A classic gourmet Restaurant with seasonal, contemporary cuisine.

Steigenberger Bellerive au Lac ← 🛏 🚭 ♿ 🚭 📶 🏋️ 🅿️

Utoquai 47 ✉ *8008* – 𝒞 *044 254 40 00* – *bellerive@* 💳 🄾🄾 🄰🄴 ⓿
steigenberger.ch – *Fax 044 254 40 01* – *www.zuerich.steigenberger.ch*
51 rm – 🛏370/450 CHF 🛏🛏480/540 CHF, ⥮ 30 CHF **B3**
Rest – *(closed Saturday lunch)* Menu 55 CHF – Carte 64/110 CHF
♦ Business ♦ Modern ♦

The hotel, modern yet elegantly decorated in the style of the 1920s, is located on the lakeside. The rooms are contemporary in design, technology and comfort. This restaurant offers perfectly executed 5-element cuisine made from regional products.

Alden Hotel Splügenschloss 🛋 🕭 🗚 ↔ rm 🖭 ⁽ᵗ⁾ 🔏 🅿

Splügenstr. 2 ✉ *8002* – ☎ *044 289 99 99* 🚺 🐧 🖭 🕥
– *welcome@alden.ch* – *Fax 044 289 99 98* – *www.alden.ch* **A3**
10 rm – 🛉700/1500 CHF 🛉🛉700/1500 CHF – **12 suites** ⌿

Rest *Gourmet* – Carte 66/117 CHF

♦ Luxury ♦ Stylish ♦

Behind the grand façade of this building that dates from 1895 are very modern suites with elegant designer furnishings. Contemporary cuisine is served in the tasteful and refined Gourmet.

Crowne Plaza 🛋 🕭 🕭 🖾 🕭 🗚 ↔ 🖭 ⁽ᵗ⁾ 🔏 🚗 🚺 🐧 🖭 🕥

Badenerstr. 420 ✉ *8040* – ☎ *044 404 44 44* – *info@cpzurich.ch*
– *Fax 044 404 44 40* – *www.crowneplaza.com/zurich* **A3**
364 rm – 🛉280/550 CHF 🛉🛉280/550 CHF, ⌿ 33 CHF

Rest *Relais des Arts* – Menu 45 CHF (lunch) – Carte 58/95 CHF

♦ Business ♦ Retro ♦

Among the amenities of this hotel are comfortable, modern rooms, functionally equipped, as well as good transport connections. Fitness room. The Relais des Arts' decor has a touch of elegance.

Ascot 🛋 🗚 rm ↔ rm ⁽ᵗ⁾ 🔏 🚗 🚺 🐧 🖭 🕥

Tessinerplatz 9 ✉ *8002* – ☎ *044 208 14 14* – *info@ascot.ch*
– *Fax 044 208 14 20* – *www.ascot.ch* **A3**
74 rm ⌿ – 🛉460/600 CHF 🛉🛉580/680 CHF

Rest *Lawrence* – *(closed Saturday and Sunday)* Menu 65 CHF
– Carte 72/130 CHF

♦ Traditional ♦ Classic ♦

This stylishly appointed building offers comfortable rooms with fittings in dark mahogany or pale bleached oak. The Lawrence features a beautiful Tudor style.

Dolder Waldhaus ⌇ ≼ 🚗 🛋 🕭 🖾 ✕ 🗚 rest ↔ 🖭 ⁽ᵗ⁾ 🔏 🅿

Kurhausstr. 20 ✉ *8032* – ☎ *044 269 10 00* 🚗 🚺 🐧 🖭 🕥
– *info@dolderwaldhaus.ch* – *Fax 044 269 10 01*
– *www.dolderwaldhaus.ch* **B3**
70 rm – 🛉265/345 CHF 🛉🛉380/480 CHF, ⌿ 22 CHF – 30 suites

Rest – Carte 49/94 CHF

♦ Business ♦ Functional ♦

The building is located in a quiet area and offers up-to-date rooms with balcony and views over the town and lake. The modern apartments are recommended for families or longer stays. Restaurant with a classic, refined ambience and a beautiful terrace.

Engimatt 🛋 ✕ 🗚 rm 🖭 ⁽ᵗ⁾ 🔏 🅿 🚗 🚺 🐧 🖭 🕥

Engimattstr. 14 ✉ *8002* – ☎ *044 284 16 16*
– *info@engimatt.ch* – *Fax 044 201 25 16*
– *www.engimatt.ch* **A3**
73 rm ⌿ – 🛉190/295 CHF 🛉🛉250/340 CHF

Rest – Menu 45 CHF (lunch)/80 CHF – Carte 47/81 CHF

♦ Business ♦ Modern ♦

The hotel is located near the centre of town and yet has a country-like setting. The rooms - each with its own balcony - are individually designed and feature solid, modern furnishings. The Orangerie has modern winter garden-style glass and steel construction and a pleasant garden terrace.

Greulich 🕭 ↔ 🖭 ⁽ᵗ⁾ 🔏 🅿 🚺 🐧 🖭 🕥

Herman-Greulich-Str. 56 ✉ *8004* – ☎ *043 243 42 43*
– *mail@greulich.ch* – *Fax 043 243 42 00*
– *www.greulich.ch* **A3**
18 rm – 🛉225 CHF 🛉🛉305 CHF, ⌿ 28 CHF

Rest *Greulich* – see below

♦ Business ♦ Modern ♦

In an inner courtyard lined with birch trees are garden rooms and junior suites furnished in a clean, pure, modern design.

SWITZERLAND - ZURICH

Krone Unterstrass   AC rm ⅍ rm [img] ⁽ᵖ⁾ 𝑆𝐴̀ VISA ⁰⁰ AE ⓪

Schaffhauserstr. 1 ✉ *8006 –* ℰ *044 360 56 56 – info@hotel-krone.ch*
– Fax 044 360 56 00 – www.hotel-krone.ch   **A2**
57 rm – †185/280 CHF ††260/280 CHF, ⌣ 19 CHF
Rest – Menu 77 CHF – Carte 52/75 CHF
   ◆ Business ◆ Modern ◆

The rooms in this hotel, which is a short distance from the city centre, are tastefully decorated in a contemporary style and offer modern comfort. An elegant a-la-carte restaurant and a simpler daytime restaurant facing the street.

XXXX
❀

The Restaurant – Hotel The Dolder Grand   ⪕ 斉 & AC

Kurhausstr. 65 ✉ *8032 –* ℰ *044 456 60 00 – info@*   VISA ⁰⁰ AE ⓪
thedoldergrand.com – Fax 044 456 60 01
– www.thedoldergrand.com   **B3**
Rest – *(closed Saturday lunch, Sunday dinner and Monday) (booking advisable)*
Menu 98 CHF (lunch)/198 CHF – Carte 114/178 CHF
Spec. Meeresschnecken mit Ochsenbrust, Kohl und Paprikafond. Seeteufel mit Mark, Bohnen und Anis. Fencheltarte mit Orange und Milcheis.
   ◆ Inventive ◆ Fashionable ◆

Sit in a modern setting beneath the carefully preserved, high coffered ceiling to enjoy Heiko Nieder's outstanding creative cuisine. Small terrace with a very fine view over Zurich.

XXX
❀

Rigiblick - Spice (Felix Eppisser) with rm ⌇   ⪕ 斉 ⁽ᵖ⁾ 🛥

Germaniastr. 99 ✉ *8044 –* ℰ *043 255 15 70*   VISA ⁰⁰ AE ⓪
– eppisser@restaurantrigiblick.ch – Fax 043 255 15 80
– www.restaurantrigiblick.ch   **B2**
7 rm ⌣ – †490/800 CHF ††490/800 CHF
Rest *Bistro Quadrino* – see below
Rest – *(closed Sunday and Monday) (booking advisable)*
Menu 62 CHF (lunch)/152 CHF – Carte 112/116 CHF
Spec. Gebackener Carabiniero auf Pak-Choi mit Lotuswurzel-Chips. Sashimi, Tatar und Panna Cotta vom Schottischen Wildlachs mit Wasabi-Espuma. Bengalisch gewürztes Lammfilet.
   ◆ Euro-asiatic ◆ Formal ◆

The atmosphere in the Restaurant Spice is bright, cleanly styled and elegant. Patrons enjoy Euro-Asian cuisine and an amazing view over Zurich. The junior suites are furnished in the most modern style.

XXX
❀

Sonnenberg   ⪕ 斉 & AC P. VISA ⁰⁰ AE ⓪

Hitzigweg 15 ✉ *8032 –* ℰ *044 266 97 97 – restaurant@sonnenberg-zh.ch*
– Fax 044 266 97 98 – www.sonnenberg-zh.ch   **B3**
Rest – *(booking essential)* Carte 69/145 CHF ✿
   ◆ Classic ◆ Formal ◆

Located high up in the FIFA building with a splendid view of the town, lake and mountains. The panoramic restaurant specialises in veal and beef dishes.

XX
❀

Mesa   斉 AC VISA ⁰⁰ AE

Weinbergstr. 75 ✉ *8006 –* ℰ *043 321 75 75 – info@mesa-restaurant.ch*
– Fax 043 321 75 77 – www.mesa-restaurant.ch
– closed 23 December – 15 January, 21 July - 13 August, Saturday lunch,
Sunday and Monday   **A2**
Rest – *(booking advisable)* Menu 55 CHF (lunch)/165 CHF – Carte 104/152 CHF
Spec. Jakobsmuschel mit Weideschwein, Gurke, Passionsfrucht und Senf-crème. Mariniertes Lammkotelett mit Chermoula und Safran-Minz-Kichererb-sen. Joghurtmousse mit Erdbeer-Basilikum-Eis.
   ◆ Modern ◆ Minimalist ◆

A restaurant with a simple, contemporary decor (its Spanish name means 'table'), which carries conviction by its good, modern cuisine and very attentive service. Lower priced lunch menu.

Il Gattopardo ⚌ XX

Rotwandstr. 48 ✉ 8004 – ☎ 043 443 48 48 – Fax 043 243 85 51
– www.ilgattopardo.ch
– closed 27 July - 24 August, May – September: Saturday lunch, Sunday and
Monday lunch   **Rest** – Menu 90 CHF – Carte 68/110 CHF   **A3**
◆ Italian ◆ Trendy ◆

This restaurant offers attentive service and top-notch Italian cuisine. The setting is a successful mixture of classical and modern. Walk-in wine cellar (for groups).

Greulich – Hotel Greulich XX

Herman-Greulich-Str. 56 ✉ 8004 – ☎ 043 243 42 43 – mail@greulich.ch
– Fax 043 243 42 00 – www.greulich.ch – closed Saturday lunch, Sunday
Rest – Menu 84/144 CHF – Carte 77/96 CHF   **A3**
◆ Inventive ◆ Trendy ◆

Guests are greeted with a modern ambience, clean lines and creative, Spanish-inspired cuisine in this restaurant, which also features a beautiful inner courtyard terrace.

Lake Side XX

Bellerivestr. 170 ✉ 8008 – ☎ 044 385 86 00 – info@lake-side.ch
– Fax 044 385 86 01 – www.lake-side.ch   **Rest** – Carte 66/106 CHF
◆ Modern ◆ Trendy ◆   **B3**

Located in the Seepark Zürichhorn, this modern restaurant features contemporary cuisine and a sushi bar. A summer attraction is the large deck on the shore of the lake.

Sankt Meinrad X

Stauffacherstr. 163 ✉ 8004 – ☎ 043 534 82 77 – restaurant@sanktmeinrad.ch
– www.sanktmeinrad.ch – closed 21 December - 6 January, 19 July - 11 August,
Saturday lunch, Sunday and Monday   **A3**
Rest – (booking advisable) Menu 120 CHF – Carte 79/109 CHF
◆ Inventive ◆ Fashionable ◆

In the modern restaurant not far from the bakery, creative cuisine awaits you. It is served by very friendly staff in a pleasantly relaxed atmosphere.

Caduff's Wine Loft X

Kanzleistr. 126 ✉ 8004 – ☎ 044 240 22 55 – caduff@wineloft.ch
– Fax 044 240 22 56 – www.wineloft.ch
– closed 24 December - 4 January, Saturday lunch and Sunday   **A3**
Rest – (booking advisable) Menu 52 CHF (lunch)/115 CHF – Carte 60/117 CHF
◆ Modern ◆ Trendy ◆

Once a flower wholesaler's, today this is a modern restaurant offering delicious, contemporary cuisine using selected fresh produce. Remarkable range of wines.

Bistro Quadrino – Restaurant Rigiblick X

Germaniastr. 99 ✉ 8044 – ☎ 043 255 15 70 – eppisser@restaurantrigiblick.ch
– Fax 043 255 15 80 – www.restaurantrigiblick.ch – closed Sunday and Monday
Rest – Carte 55/77 CHF   **B2**
◆ Modern ◆ Trendy ◆

A bistro in contemporary-style, offering a happy combination of food bar, lounge and walk-in wine cellar. Dishes are prepared predominantly from organic produce.

Blaue Ente X

Seefeldstr. 223 (Tiefenbrunnen mill) ✉ 8008 – ☎ 044 388 68 40 – info@
blaue-ente.ch – Fax 044 422 77 41 – www.blaue-ente.ch
– closed 2 weeks February, 2 weeks July   **B3**
Rest – (booking advisable) Carte 71/121 CHF
◆ Modern ◆ Trendy ◆

A trendy restaurant in the historic former mill building – the impressive machinery is an eye-catcher. Innovative, modern dishes from the partly visible kitchen.

Ciro X

Militärstr. 16 ✉ 8004 – ☎ 044 241 78 41 – ciro@swissonline.ch
– Fax 044 291 14 24 – closed 30 July - 10 August and Sunday   **A3**
Rest – Carte 50/85 CHF
◆ Italian ◆ Friendly ◆

This small restaurant near the train station serves typical Italian dishes and wines.

PROFILE

→ **AREA:**
244 157 km²
(94 269 sq mi).

→ **POPULATION:**
60 776 000
inhabitants
(est. 2007), density
= 248 per km².

→ **CAPITAL:**
London (conurbation
9 332 000
inhabitants).

→ **CURRENCY:**
Pound sterling (£);
rate of exchange:
£ 1 = € 1.07 =
US$ 1.32
(Jan 2009).

→ **GOVERNMENT:**
Constitutional
parliamentary
monarchy
(since 1707). Member
of European Union
since 1973.

→ **LANGUAGE:**
English.

→ **SPECIFIC PUBLIC
HOLIDAYS:**
Good Friday (Friday
before Easter), first
and last Monday in
May, last Monday in
August, Boxing Day
(26 December).

→ **LOCAL TIME:**
GMT in winter and
GMT + 1 hour in
summer.

→ **CLIMATE:**
Temperate
maritime with cool
winters and mild
summers (London:
January:
3°C, July: 17°C);
rainfall evenly
distributed
throughout the year.

→ **INTERNATIONAL
DIALLING CODE:**
00 44 followed by
area or city code
(London: **20**,
Glasgow: **141**, etc.)
and then the local
number.

→ **EMERGENCY:**
Police, Fire Brigade,
Ambulance: ☎ **999**.

→ **ELECTRICITY:**
240 volts AC, 50 Hz.
3 flat pin plugs.

→ **FORMALITIES**
Travellers from the
European Union (EU),
Switzerland, Iceland,
the main countries
of North and South

America and some
Commonwealth
countries need a
national identity
card or passport
(except for Irish
nationals; America:
passport required)
to visit the United
Kingdom for
less than three
months (tourism
or business purpose).
For visitors from
other countries
a visa may be
required, in addition
to a passport,
especially for those
wishing to stay for
longer than three
months. We advise
you to check with
your embassy
before travelling.

LONDON

LONDON

Population: 2 914 000 (conurbation 9 332 000) – Altitude: sea level

R. Mattès/HEMIS.fr

The term 'world city' could have been invented for London. Time zones radiate from Greenwich, and global finances zap round the Square Mile, while a phalanx of international restaurants is the equal of anywhere on earth. A stunning diversity of population is testament to the city's famed tolerance; different lifestyles and languages are as much a part of the London scene as cockneys and black cabs. This mesmerising blur of life lures long-term visitors from abroad; recently, for example, many thousands of French and Polish workers have laid down roots within the M25.

Whereas Paris evolved through a grand design of formal planning, London grew over time in a pretty haphazard way, swallowing up surrounding villages, but retaining an enviable acreage of green 'lungs': a comforting 30 per cent of London's area is made up of open space. The drama of the city is reflected in its history. From Roman settlement to banking centre to capital of a 19C empire, the city's pulse has never missed a beat; it's no surprise that a dazzling array of theatres, restaurants, museums, markets and art galleries populate its streets. Plus, of course, over 3,500 pubs, the like of which you won't find anywhere else in the world.

LIVING THE CITY

London's piecemeal character has endowed it with distinctly different areas, often breathing down each other's necks. North of Piccadilly lie the playgrounds of Soho and Mayfair, while south is the classier gentleman's clubland of St James's. On the other side of town are Clerkenwell and Southwark, historically artisan areas that have been scrubbed down, freshened up and populated with hip offices and trendy places to eat and drink. The cool sophistication of Kensington and Knightsbridge is to the west, while a more touristy aesthetic is found in the heaving piazza zone of Covent Garden further east along the river.

PRACTICAL INFORMATION

ARRIVAL-DEPARTURE

Heathrow Express to Paddington is the quickest way of getting into the city from Heathrow Airport which is 20 miles west of London. A black cab will cost about £55. There are also bus and underground connections. From Gatwick Airport, take the Gatwick Express to Victoria station. Stansted Airport is 34 miles northeast of London and Luton 35 miles north and both are served by rail links.

TRANSPORT

If you're in London for a short period, get a Travelcard, which will take you all over the city's transport system. If you're around for the longer haul, invest in an Oyster Card, much beloved by locals: these are smartcards with electronically stored pre-pay credit, and they offer good savings on fares.

Just when everyone had got used to calling Waterloo the home of their Eurostar journey to the likes of Paris and Brussels, lo and behold the London terminus changed, and these days you should head for St Pancras.

EXPLORING LONDON

In a city that grew organically without planning committee, is there anywhere you'd call the centre? Instinctively, most locals would probably say

Piccadilly Circus if only because all that neon advertising gives it the feel of a focal point. It can certainly make a claim as gateway to the West End: when you see the statue of Eros, you know you've 'arrived'. Along Piccadilly itself, the main attractions are a top end version of what draws people to London: culture (at the Royal Academy of Arts), retail (at Fortnum & Mason) and tradition (at The Ritz). From here, London sprawls out in all directions. To the south and west are the wide-open expanses of **Green Park** and **Hyde Park**. In the latter, riders trot their horses along Rotten Row and swimmers chill out in the cool waters of the snaking Serpentine. To the north, the habitués of **Mayfair** tend towards the monied, their dark suits flitting round the environs of Bond Street (with its Premier League shops), Grosvenor Square and the swanky Dorchester hotel. Go east, meanwhile, and you're in **Soho**, home to a lively gay culture and a dazzling array of little eateries and hip lounge bars in an equally bewildering maze of narrow streets.

→ THE GHERKIN CLASSES

The engine-room of London is the **City**, where the bonus levels paid to bankers are almost as high as the vertiginous buildings in which they work. The skyline here is a blur of steel and glass, in recent years dominated by the highly distinctive Swiss Re building, affectionately known as The Gherkin. The City, and its upstream location, has been London's centre of commerce for nearly a thousand years. In the 11C, Edward The Confessor separated it from Westminster, where he concentrated royal power. But these days the area is not all about corporate finance. Flanking the City are Shoreditch, Hoxton, Finsbury and Clerkenwell, former run-down areas that have undergone a resurgence powered by a young(ish) and creatively-minded crowd.

→ MARKET FRESH

For those who prefer their retail establishments of a more traditional kind, smart **Knightsbridge** is a perennial choice. Harrods and Harvey Nichols have stood proudly along the road from each other for many decades, the epitome of SW1 sophistication, but one of the great things about London is that street markets hold (nearly) as much cachet as the consumerist shrines. There are a great many of them, and they're dotted around all over the place. Food lovers should head for **Borough market**, under the railway arches at London Bridge. It's a gourmet's paradise, offering top quality produce from all over Britain. A grander setting is **Leadenhall market** in the City, which boasts cobbled walkways, glass roof and rare meats. **Portobello Road** in Notting Hill is world famous for its bric-à-brac, fruit and veg, and East End favourites **Brick Lane** and Ridley Road markets will keep you well stocked with everything from cheap perfume to blackened smoked fish heads! A top destination for plant lovers is **Columbia Road** market in the East End, while Old Spitalfields in the City is a great place to go for stylish handicrafts from the area's young artists.

Your Oyster card will take you far and wide sussing out the markets, but if a musical's your thing after a day battling for bargains, then you probably won't even need to take the Tube since the Leicester Square/Piccadilly area in the heart of town crams in enough board-treading venues to overwhelm even the most voracious addict of stage extravaganzas. Fringe theatre tends to play on the, well, fringes of town, so if you're looking for something a bit more thought-provoking than Abba, Queen or Andrew Lloyd Webber, then you might be better served looking to the likes of the Royal Court in Chelsea, the Old Vic at Waterloo or Islington's Kings Head or Almeida.

→ POWER MAD

London's a great place to look at pictures. Who would have believed even a decade ago that the capital's leading tourist venue would be a disused old power station on the 'wrong' side of the Thames, but the **Tate Modern**, scrubbed up and, cocking a snook at St Paul's over the river, has proved itself a record-breaker and continues to draw the crowds. As ever, London's art galleries of an older vintage also attract visitors like bees to the honeypot, so prepare to stand a few tourists deep as you admire the world's greatest artists at the likes of The **National Gallery**, The **National Portrait**

Gallery and The **Royal Academy of Arts**. Museums – there are over 200 of them in London – are an institution here, and the Imperial War Museum in Lambeth is one of the best: first-rate exhibits on the First and Second World Wars offer fascinating and sobering perspectives on the realities of conflict.

→ CAPITAL ACTION

Despite all its other claims to fame, you'd lay short odds that most of London's headlines around the world revolve around sport. On the football front, Chelsea FC's recent successes have doused the Royal Borough in even more glamorous gold-dust (getting a ticket for a home game, though, can be challenging); the brand new, behind-schedule, wow-factor **Wembley** opened its doors in 2007 and looks set for an illustrious future; the London Marathon, run every April since 1981, was the first big-city 26 miler, and competitor numbers increase each year; there's the perennial newsworthiness of **Wimbledon** fortnight and the University boat race; and, of course, the city will remain in the sporting spotlight as the 2012 Olympics edges closer by the day.

It's not hard to see London as a melding together of its constituent parts, its 'villages': Kensington and Chelsea, Hampstead and Highgate, Bayswater and Maida Vale, Richmond and Twickenham. Each of these boasts its own community feel and its own areas of treasured green space. Don't be afraid to jump on a bus or dive onto a tube and find out for yourself what each has to offer. There are nearly 4,000 pubs around the city and each one offers a clue to the character of the area you're in. If you want to join the dots and link up lots of areas in one go, take a walk along the **Thames Path**, which covers the whole length of the river from source to sea – it's a stress-free way to take in some cracking views of a pulsating city.

CALENDAR HIGHLIGHTS

Some things never change. You can set your watch by some of London's calendar highlights: from the Boat Race in April to the Chelsea Flower Show in May, from Wimbledon Fortnight in June to the Great British Beer Festival in August, from the Notting Hill Carnival, also in August, to the London Film Festival in October. Other annual highlights are of more recent vintage. The New Year's Day Parade of extravagant floats starting from Parliament Square is settling in nicely, as is the St Patrick's Day Parade through Whitehall in March. The South Bank Beach, 'laid' in July to August, would have been considered a joke even 10 years ago, while ice rinks at the Natural History Museum, Hampton Court Palace, Tower of London, Somerset House and Kew Gardens now give an extra glow to Christmas revellers.

LONDON IN...

→ ONE DAY
British Museum, Tower of London, St Paul's Cathedral, Tate Modern

→ TWO DAYS
National Gallery, London Eye, Natural History Museum

→ THREE DAYS
Science Museum, Victoria and Albert Museum, National Portrait Gallery

EATING OUT

Some years ago you could dine out in London on anything from a bacon and egg sandwich to its cucumber variant. Or so popular memory has it. These days it's one of the food capitals of the world, and you really can eat Malay to Mediterranean, Latin American to Lebanese right across zones one to five. But those wishing to sample classic British dishes also have more choice these days as more and more chefs are rediscovering home-grown ingredients, regional classics and traditional recipes. Eating in the capital can be pricey, so check out good value pre- and post-theatre menus, or tuck into lunch at one of the many eateries that drop their prices, but not their standards, in the middle of the day.

With over 6,000 restaurants in London (to say nothing of its cafés), it's possible to eat at any time. But central London restaurants can get very busy from about 7.30pm; if you haven't booked well in advance you might have more luck trying somewhere a bit further out.

"Would I were in an alehouse in London! I would give all my fame for a pot of ale and safety," says Shakespeare's Henry V. Samuel Johnson tended to agree, waxing lyrical upon the happiness produced by a good tavern or inn. Two examples of the dewy-eyed love the Londoner (albeit one a monarch) has for beer. Pubs are often open these days from 11am to 11pm (and beyond) so this particular love now knows no bounds, and any tourist is welcome to come along and enjoy the romance. It is not just the cooking that has improved in pubs - wine, too, has gained in popularity in recent years: woe betide any establishment in this city that can't distinguish its Chardonnay from its Pinot Grigio. And with more Champagne being quaffed in London than any city outside France, it's fair to say the taste for a tipple offers up a wide range of opportunities to anyone within the M25.

→ THERE'S NO RHYME OR REASON...

...when it comes to a formal tipping procedure. Some restaurants leave the amount open, while others add on anything up to 15%. Leaving a cash tip on the table guarantees the tip goes to the people it's meant for, the waiters. If you're not sure whether it's heading for their pockets then just ask them.

RESTAURANTS - ALPHABETICAL LIST

OPEN ON SATURDAY AND SUNDAY

A

Aaya	XX	904
Amaya	XXX⁂	915
Angelus	XX	936
Arbutus	X⁂	905
Arturo	X	938
L'Atelier de Joël Robuchon N	X⁂	913
L'Autre Pied N	XX⁂	926
Awana	XXX	954

B

Barrafina	X	906
Bedford & Strand	X	914
Benares	XXX⁂	899
Bengal Clipper	XX	944
Bentley's (Oyster Bar)	X	903
Bibendum	XXX	953
Bluebird	XX	956
Bombay Brasserie	XXX	960
The Botanist	XX	957
Brasserie Roux	XX	909
Bumpkin	X	966
Butlers Wharf Chop House	X	945

C

Le Café Anglais N	XX	935
Cafe Boheme	X	906
Le Café du Jardin	X	914
Cantina Del Ponte	X	945
The Capital Restaurant	XXX⁂⁂	953
Le Caprice	XX	908
Chelsea Brasserie	XX	955
China Tang	XXXX	897
Chutney Mary	XXX	954
Cigala	X	931
Clarke's	XX	963

D à O

Daphne's	XX	955
Le Deuxième	XX	913
E&O	XX	965
L'Etranger	XX	960
Foliage	XXX⁂	932
The Forge	XX	913
Foxtrot Oscar N	X⊕	957
Galvin at Windows	XXXX	897
Galvin	XX⊕	926
Gordon Ramsay at Claridge's	XXXX⁂	897
Hakkasan	XX⁂	930
Haozhan	XX	904
Hereford Road N	X⊕	938
Imli	X	906

Inn the Park	X	910
Island	XX	937
The Ivy	XXX	912
Jamuna	XX	936
J. Sheekey	XX	912
Kai N	XXX⁂	900
Kensington Place	X	964
Kiasu	X	938
Launceston Place	XXX	963
The Ledbury	XXX⁂	965
Locanda Locatelli	XXX⁂	925
L Restaurant & Bar	XX	964
Malabar	X⊕	964
Mr Chow	XX	933
The Narrow	ĐⒶ	948
Noura Central	XX	909
Nozomi	XX	955
One-O-One	XXX	954
The Only Running Footman	Đ	903
Oscar	XX	926
Ozer	XX	927

P à Z

Papillon	XX	955
Pasha	XX	960
Phoenix Palace	XX	927
La Porte des Indes	XX	926
Portrait	X	910
La Poule au Pot	X	921
The Providores	XX	926
Quaglino's	XX	909
Quilon	XXX⁂	920
Racine	XX	955
Rhodes W1 Brasserie	XX	926
The Ritz Restaurant	XXXXX	908
Roka	XX	927
Rules	XX	913
St Alban	XXX	908
Sake No Hana	XXX	908
Scott's	XXX	897
Skylon	XXX	914
Snazz Sichuan	XX	931
Tamarind	XXX	899
Tom's Kitchen	X	957
Urban Turban	X	938
Veeraswamy	XX	902
Village East	X	945
Wild Honey	XX⁂	900
The Wolseley	XXX	908
Yauatcha	XX⁂	905
Zafferano	XXX⁂	918
Zuma	XX	933

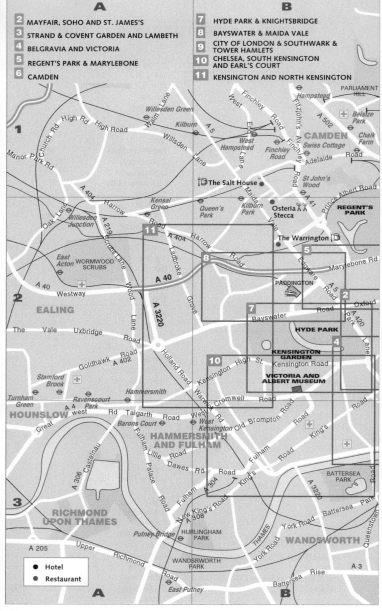

A

2	MAYFAIR, SOHO AND ST. JAMES'S
3	STRAND & COVENT GARDEN AND LAMBETH
4	BELGRAVIA AND VICTORIA
5	REGENT'S PARK & MARYLEBONE
6	CAMDEN

B

7	HYDE PARK & KNIGHTSBRIDGE
8	BAYSWATER & MAIDA VALE
9	CITY OF LONDON & SOUTHWARK & TOWER HAMLETS
10	CHELSEA, SOUTH KENSINGTON AND EARL'S COURT
11	KENSINGTON AND NORTH KENSINGTON

- ● Hotel
- ● Restaurant

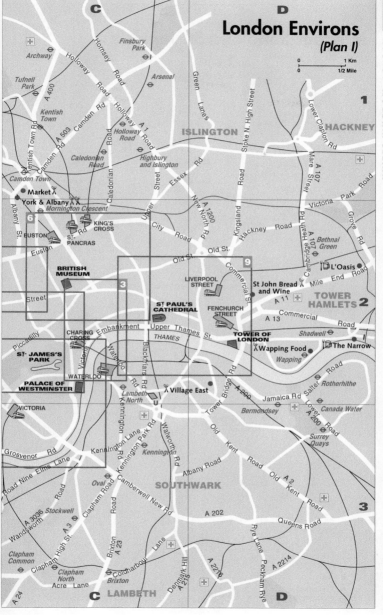

London Environs
(Plan I)

0   1 Km
0   1/2 Mile

C   **D**

Archway

Finsbury Park

Tufnell Park

Arsenal

Hornsey Road

Holloway Road

Green Lanes

Lower Clapton Rd

1

HACKNEY

Kentish Town

A 400

A 503

Camden Rd

Camden Rd

Holloway Road

A 1

Stoke N. High Street

Mare Street

A 107

ISLINGTON

Highbury and Islington

Victoria Park Road

Grove Rd

Caledonian Road

Camden Town

Kentish Town Rd

Camden Town Rd

Mornington Crescent

Caledonian Rd

Upper Street

Essex Rd

New North Rd

Kingsland Road

Hackney Road

A 107

Cambridge Heath Rd

Bethnal Green

L'Oasis

● Market ╳
● York & Albany ╳╳

Albany St.

6

EUSTON

St PANCRAS

Euston

KING'S CROSS

A 1200

City Road

Old St.

Old St.

9

LIVERPOOL STREET

Commercial St.

St John Bread and Wine ╳

A 11

Mile End Road

TOWER HAMLETS

2

BRITISH MUSEUM

3

Street

St PAUL'S CATHEDRAL

FENCHURCH STREET

Commercial

A 13

Road

CHARING CROSS

Embankment

Upper Thames St.

TOWER OF LONDON

Shadwell

Piccadilly

Victoria

Waterloo

THAMES

Blackfriars Rd

╳ Wapping Food ●

Wapping

The Narrow

St JAMES'S PARK

WATERLOO

PALACE OF WESTMINSTER

Waterloo Rd

Lambeth North

╳ Village East ●

Tower Bridge Rd

A 200

Jamaica Rd

Saltier Road

Rotherhithe

Lower Road

Canada Water

VICTORIA

Kennington Lane

Bermondsey

A 200

Grosvenor Rd

Kennington Rd

Kennington Park Rd

Walworth Rd

Old Kent Road

Surrey Quays

Nine Elms Lane

Road

Oval

Clapham Road

Camberwell New Rd

Kennington

Albany Road

A 2

Kent Road

3

SOUTHWARK

Wandsworth

A 3036

Stockwell

A 3

Clapham High St.

Brixton Rd

A 23

Coldharbour Lane

Denmark Hill

A 202

A 215

Queens Road

Rye Lane

Peckham Rye

A 2214

Clapham Common

A 24

Clapham North

Acre Lane

Brixton

C   **LAMBETH**   **D**

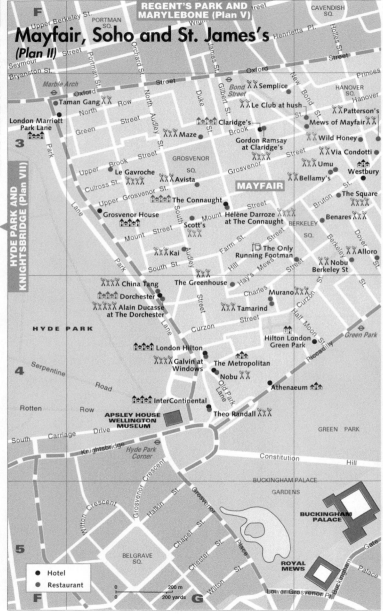

Mayfair, Soho and St. James's
(Plan II)

REGENT'S PARK AND MARYLEBONE (Plan V)

MAYFAR

HYDE PARK AND KNIGHTSBRIDGE (Plan VII)

HYDE PARK

UNITED KINGDOM - LONDON

- Hotel
- Restaurant

0   200 m
0   200 yards

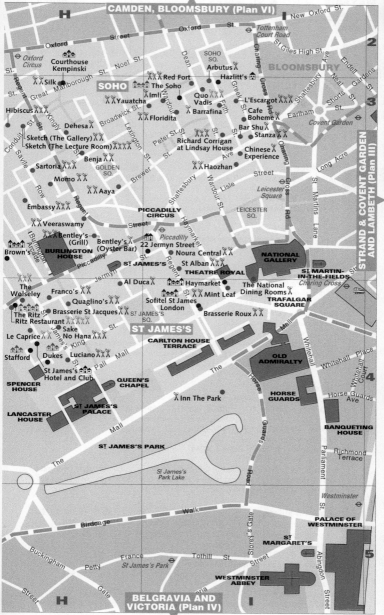

CAMDEN, BLOOMSBURY (Plan VI)

New Oxford St.

Oxford St.

Tottenham Court Road

St Giles High St.

Oxford Street

Oxford Circus

Courthouse Kempinski

Silk

Noel St.

Dean St.

SOHO SQ.

BLOOMSBURY

Endell St.

Great Marlborough St.

SOHO

Red Fort

The Soho

Arbutus

Hazlitt's

Shaftesbury Ave.

Hibiscus

Yauatcha

Imli

Quo Vadis

L'Escargot

Neal St.

Shorts Gardens

Dehesa

Kingly St.

Broadwick St.

Floridita

Barrafina

Cafe Boheme

Bar Shu

Stanza

Earlham St.

Covent Garden

Sketch (The Gallery)

Sketch (The Lecture Room)

Lexington St.

Peter St.

Wardour St.

Richard Corrigan at Lindsay House

Chinese Experience

Long Acre

Sartoria

Benja

GOLDEN SQ.

Haozhan

Momo

Brewer St.

Shaftesbury Ave.

Lisle St.

Leicester Square

St Martin's Lane

Aaya

Regent St.

LEICESTER SQ.

Cross Rd.

Embassy

PICCADILLY CIRCUS

Veeraswamy

Street

Haymarket

Piccadilly

Bentley's (Grill)

Bentley's (Oyster Bar)

22 Jermyn Street

Noura Central

NATIONAL GALLERY

Brown's

BURLINGTON HOUSE

Piccadilly

St Alban

St. James's

ST JAMES'S

St Martin's Place

THEATRE ROYAL

ST MARTIN-IN-THE-FIELDS

Charing Cross

The Wolseley

Franco's

Al Duca

Jermyn St.

Haymarket

Mint Leaf

The National Dining Rooms

TRAFALGAR SQUARE

Quaglino's

Sofitel St James London

Brasserie Roux

Whitehall

The Ritz

Ritz Restaurant

Brasserie St Jacques

ST JAMES'S ST.

Le Caprice

Sake No Hana

King St.

ST JAMES'S

Stafford

Dukes

Luciano

St James's Hotel and Club

CARLTON HOUSE TERRACE

OLD ADMIRALTY

Whitehall Place

Whitehall Court

SPENCER HOUSE

ST JAMES'S PALACE

QUEEN'S CHAPEL

The Mall

HORSE GUARDS

Horse Guards Ave.

LANCASTER HOUSE

Inn The Park

Horse Guards Rd.

BANQUETING HOUSE

The Mall

Richmond Terrace

ST JAMES'S PARK

St James's Park Lake

Westminster Bridge St.

Birdcage Walk

Storey's Gate

PALACE OF WESTMINSTER

Buckingham Gate

Petty France

St James's Park

Tothill St.

ST MARGARET'S

Abingdon St.

WESTMINSTER ABBEY

BELGRAVIA AND VICTORIA (Plan IV)

STRAND & COVENT GARDEN AND LAMBETH (Plan III)

893

UNITED KINGDOM - LONDON

Mayfair

Dorchester
Park Lane ⌂ *W1K 1QA* – Ⓜ *Hyde Park Corner* – ℰ *(020) 7629 8888*
– info@thedorchester.com – Fax (020) 7629 80 80 – www.thedorchester.com
200 rm – ♦£ 335/699 ♦♦£ 652/828 – 49 suites   **G4**
Rest Alain Ducasse at The Dorchester and **China Tang** *– see below*
Rest Grill Room *– ℰ (020) 7317 6336 –* Menu £ 28 – Carte £ 40/69
♦ Grand Luxury ♦ Classic ♦
A sumptuously decorated, luxury hotel offering every possible facility. Impressive
marbled and pillared promenade. Rooms quintessentially English in style. Faultless
service. Bold Scottish-themed decoration in the Grill Room.

Claridge's
Brook St ⌂ *W1K 4HR* – Ⓜ *Bond Street* – ℰ *(020) 7629 8860*
– guest@claridges.co.uk – Fax (020) 7499 22 10 – www.claridges.co.uk
143 rm – ♦£ 576/658 ♦♦£ 776, ⛌ £ 28 – 60 suites   **G3**
Rest Gordon Ramsay at Claridge's *– see below*
♦ Grand Luxury ♦ Stylish ♦
The epitome of English grandeur, celebrated for its Art Deco. Exceptionally well-
appointed and sumptuous bedrooms, all with butler service. Magnificently restored foyer.

The Connaught
Carlos Place ⌂ *W1K 2AL* – Ⓜ *Bond St* – ℰ *(020) 7499 7070*
– info@theconnaught.co.uk – Fax (020) 7495 32 62 – www.the-connaught.co.uk
95 rm – ♦£ 387/717 ♦♦£ 434/717, ⛌ £ 28 – 27 suites   **G3**
Rest Hélène Darroze at The Connaught *– see below*
Rest Espelette *–* Carte £ 44/63
♦ Grand Luxury ♦ Classic ♦
This famous hotel reopened in 2008 after a major renovation. Luxury bedrooms
updated in style and mod cons while retaining that elegant British feel. Choice of
two stylish bars. Espelette for all-day, informal dining.

InterContinental
1 Hamilton Place, Park Lane ⌂ *W1J 7QY*
– Ⓜ *Hyde Park Corner* – ℰ *(020) 7409 3131 – london@ihg.com*
– Fax (020) 7493 34 76 – www.london.intercontinental.com   **G4**
399 rm – ♦£ 282/388 ♦♦£ 282/388, ⛌ £ 27 – 48 suites
Rest Theo Randall *– see below*
Rest Cookbook Café *–* Carte £ 30/44
♦ Business ♦ Modern ♦
International hotel relaunched in 2007 after major refit. English style bedrooms
with high tech equipment and large, open plan lobby. Cookbook Café invites visi-
ting chefs to showcase their talents.

London Hilton
22 Park Lane ⌂ *W1K 1BE* – Ⓜ *Hyde Park Corner* – ℰ *(020) 7493 8000*
– reservations.parklane@hilton.com – Fax (020) 7208 41 42
– www.hilton.co.uk/londonparklane   **G4**
395 rm – ♦£ 234/516 ♦♦£ 328/563, ⛌ £ 27 – 56 suites
Rest Galvin at Windows *– see below*
Rest Trader Vics *– (closed lunch Saturday and Sunday)* Carte £ 32/47
Rest Podium *–* Menu £ 22/30 – Carte £ 29/40
♦ Business ♦ Classic ♦
This 28 storey tower is one of the city's tallest hotels, providing impressive views
from the upper floors. Club floor bedrooms are particularly comfortable. Exotic
Trader Vics with bamboo and plants. Modern European food in Podium.

Grosvenor House without rest

Park Lane ✉ W1K 7TN – Ⓜ Marble Arch – ✆ (020) 7499 6363 – grosvenor.house@marriotthotels.com – Fax (020) 7493 33 41 – www.grosvenorhouse.co.uk **G3**

378 rm – †£ 299/399 ††£ 299/399, ☕ £ 21.50 – 55 suites

◆ Business ◆ Classic ◆

Refurbished hotel in commanding position by Hyde Park. Uniform, comfortable bedrooms in classic Marriott styling. Boasts the largest ballroom in Europe.

Brown's

Albemarle St ✉ W1S 4BP – Ⓜ Green Park – ✆ (020) 7493 6020 – reservations.browns@roccofortecollection.com – Fax (020) 7493 93 81 – www.roccofortecollection.com **H3**

105 rm – †£ 415/575 ††£ 540/725, ☕ £ 27 – 12 suites

Rest *The Albermarle* – ✆ *(020) 7518 4004* – Carte £ 28/52

◆ Luxury ◆ Stylish ◆

After a major refit, this urbane hotel offers a swish bar featuring Terence Donovan prints, up-to-the minute rooms and a quintessentially English sitting room for tea. Cavernous room decorated by Olga Polizzi to reflect hotel's heritage: dark wood panelling, lime green banquettes. Well executed and unashamedly traditional English cooking.

London Marriott H. Park Lane

140 Park Lane ✉ W1K 7AA – Ⓜ Marble Arch – ✆ (020) 7493 7000 – Fax (020) 7493 83 33 – www.marriott.com/lonpl **F3**

148 rm – ††£ 347/370, ☕ £ 18.95 – 9 suites

Rest *140 Park Lane* – Menu £ 19 – Carte £ 23/39

◆ Luxury ◆ Design ◆

Superbly located 'boutique' style hotel at intersection of Park Lane and Oxford Street. Attractive basement health club. Spacious, well-equipped rooms with luxurious elements. Attractive restaurant overlooking Marble Arch.

Westbury without rest

Bond St ✉ W1S 2YF – Ⓜ Bond Street – ✆ (020) 7629 7755 – sales@westburymayfair.com – Fax (020) 7495 11 63 – www.westburymayfair.com **H3**

232 rm – †£ 504/539 ††£ 539, ☕ £ 22.50 – 17 suites

◆ Business ◆ Modern ◆

Surrounded by London's most fashionable shops; the renowned Polo bar and lounge provide soothing sanctuary. Some suites have their own terrace.

The Metropolitan

Old Park Lane ✉ W1K 1LB – Ⓜ Hyde Park Corner – ✆ (020) 7447 1000 – res.lon@metropolitan.como.bz – Fax (020) 7447 11 00 – www.metropolitan.como.bz **G4**

147 rm – †£ 763 ††£ 763, ☕ £ 26 – 3 suites **Rest *Nobu*** – see below

◆ Modern ◆

Minimalist interior and a voguish reputation make this the favoured hotel of pop stars and celebrities. Sleek design and fashionably attired staff set it apart.

Athenaeum

116 Piccadilly ✉ W1J 7BJ – Ⓜ Hyde Park Corner – ✆ (020) 7499 3464 – info@athenaeumhotel.com – Fax (020) 7493 18 60 – www.athenaeumhotel.com **G4**

145 rm – ††£ 176/411, ☕ £ 27 – 12 suites

Rest *Damask* – Menu £ 21/26 – Carte £ 36/46

◆ Luxury ◆ Classic ◆

Built in 1925 as a luxury apartment block. Comfortable bedrooms with video and CD players. Individually designed suites are in an adjacent Edwardian townhouse. Conservatory roofed dining room renowned for its mosaics and malt whiskies.

Hilton London Green Park   ⚿ rm 🅰🄲 rest 📶 📞 ⚒

Half Moon St ⊠ *W1J 7BN* – ⓜ *Green Park* – ✆ *(020)*   🆅🅸🆂🅰 ⓦ🄾 🄰🄴 ⓞ
7629 7522 – reservations.greenpark@hilton.com – Fax (020) 7491 89 71
– www.hilton.co.uk/greenpark   **H4**
162 rm – ♥£ 140/311 ♥♥£ 152/311, ☒ £ 19.50
Rest – *(bar lunch)* Carte £ 31/37
♦ Business ♦ Functional ♦
A row of sympathetically adjoined townhouses, dating from the 1730s. Well maintained bedrooms share the same décor but vary in size and shape. Monet prints decorate light, airy dining room.

Alain Ducasse at The Dorchester   ⇔ 🆅🅸🆂🅰 ⓦ🄾 🄰🄴 ⓞ
XXXXX
❀ ❀

Park Lane ⊠ *W1K 1QA* – ⓜ *Hyde Park Corner* – ✆ *(020) 7629 8866*
– alainducasse@thedorchester.com – Fax (020) 7629 86 86
– www.alainducasse-dorchester.com
– closed 3 weeks summer, 5 days early January, Saturday lunch, Sunday and Monday   **G4**
Rest – Menu £ 45/75 🍸
Spec. Soft-boiled egg, crayfish, wild mushrooms and Nantua sauce. Fillet of beef and seared foie gras Rossini, sacristain potatoes and Périgueux sauce. 'Baba like in Monte-Carlo'.
♦ French ♦ Fashionable ♦
Luxury and extravagance are the hallmarks of this Alain Ducasse outpost. Dining room is elegant without being staid; food is modern and refined yet satisfying and balanced. Service is formal and well organised.

Hélène Darroze at The Connaught   🆅🅸🆂🅰 ⓦ🄾 🄰🄴 ⓞ
XXXX
❀

Carlos Place ⊠ *W1K 2AL* – ⓜ *Bond St* – ✆ *(020) 3147 7200*
– info@theconnaught.co.uk – www.the-connaught.co.uk   **G3**
Rest – *(closed Saturday and Sunday) (booking essential)* Menu £ 39/75 🍸
Spec. Lobster ravioli with spices, citrus and carrot mousseline. Wild Irish salmon, puy lentils, carrots and spring onions. Peach with pistachio ice cream and sponge.
♦ French ♦ Luxury ♦
With influences from Landes and SW of France; the accomplished cooking is creative and flavours are bold and confident. Formal and elegant room; original mahogany panelling.

Le Gavroche (Michel Roux)   🅰🄲 🆅🅸🆂🅰 ⓦ🄾 🄰🄴 ⓞ
XXXX
❀ ❀

43 Upper Brook St ⊠ *W1K 7QR* – ⓜ *Marble Arch* – ✆ *(020) 7408 0881*
– bookings@le-gavroche.com – Fax (020) 7491 43 87 – www.le-gavroche.co.uk
– closed Christmas-New Year, Sunday, Saturday lunch and Bank Holidays
Rest – *(booking essential)* Menu £ 48 (lunch) – Carte £ 58/137 🍸   **G3**
Spec. Hot duck foie gras, grapes, and crispy duck pancake flavoured with cinnamon. Roast saddle of rabbit with crispy potatoes and parmesan. Bitter chocolate and praline 'indulgence'.
♦ French ♦ Formal ♦
Long-standing, renowned restaurant with a clubby, formal atmosphere. Accomplished classical French cuisine, served by smartly attired and well-drilled staff.

The Square (Philip Howard)   🅰🄲 ⇔ 🆅🅸🆂🅰 ⓦ🄾 🄰🄴 ⓞ
XXXX
❀ ❀

6-10 Bruton St ⊠ *W1J 6PU* – ⓜ *Green Park* – ✆ *(020) 7495 7100 – reception@*
squarerestaurant.com – Fax (020) 7495 71 50 – www.squarerestaurant.com
– closed 25 December, 1 January and Saturday lunch, Sunday and Bank Holidays   **H3**
Rest – Menu £ 35/75 🍸
Spec. Crab lasagne, cappuccino of shellfish, champagne foam. Herb crusted saddle of lamb, rosemary and shallot purée. Assiette of chocolate.
♦ French ♦ Formal ♦
Smart, busy restaurant; comfortable and never overformal. Cooking is thoughtful and honest, with a dextrous balance of flavours and textures. Prompt, efficient service.

Sketch (The Lecture Room & Library)   AC VISA ©© AE ①
❀❀

First Floor, 9 Conduit St ⊠ *W1S 2XG* – Ⓜ *Oxford Street*
– ℰ *(020) 76594500 – info@sketch.uk.com – Fax (020) 76 29 16 83*
– *www.sketch.uk.com*
– *closed 25-30 December, 2 weeks summer, Saturday lunch, Sunday,*
Monday and Bank Holidays   **H3**
Rest – *(booking essential)* Menu £ 35/65 – Carte £ 65/94 ❀❀
Spec. Langoustines 'addressed in five ways'. Fillet of Simmental beef, pan-
cake and truffle. Caraïbe chocolate and ground nuts.
  ◆ French ◆ Luxury ◆
A work of animated art, full of energy, vitality and colour; an experience of true
sensory stimulation. Ambitious, highly elaborate and skilled cooking; try the tasting
menu.

China Tang – at Dorchester Hotel   AC ⇔ VISA ©© AE ①

Park Lane ⊠ *W1A 2HJ* – Ⓜ *Hyde Park Corner* – ℰ *(020) 7629 9988*
– *chinatang@dorchesterhotel.com – Fax (020) 7629 95 95*
– *www.thedorchester.com*
– *closed 25 December*   **G4**
Rest – Menu £ 15 (lunch) – Carte £ 40/100
  ◆ Chinese ◆ Fashionable ◆
A striking mix of Art Deco, Oriental motifs, hand-painted fabrics, mirrors and marbled table tops. Carefully prepared, traditional Cantonese dishes using quality ingredients.

Galvin at Windows – at London Hilton Hotel   ≤ AC

22 Park Lane ⊠ *W1K 1BE* – Ⓜ *Hyde Park Corner*   VISA ©© AE ①
– ℰ *(020) 7208 4021 – reservations@galvinatwindows.com*
– *Fax (020) 7208 41 44 – www.galvinatwindows.com*
– *Closed Saturday lunch and Bank Holidays*
Rest – Menu £ 29/58 – Carte £ 60/75   **G4**
  ◆ French ◆ Formal ◆
On the 28th floor, so the views are spectacular. Contemporary styling includes silk
curtains and opulent gold leaf effect sculpture on ceiling. Detailed and elaborate
cooking.

Gordon Ramsay at Claridge's   AC VISA ©© AE ①
❀

Brook St ⊠ *W1K 4HR* – Ⓜ *Bond St* – ℰ *(020) 7499 0099*
– *reservations@gordonramsay.com – Fax (020) 7499 30 99*
– *www.gordonramsay.com*   **G3**
Rest – *(booking essential)* Menu £ 30/70 ❀❀
Spec. Salad of crab with carrot à la grecque, ginger and carrot dressing.
Roast rib of beef with cep relish and smoked potato purée. Valrhona choco-
late and honeycomb fondant with orange yoghurt sorbet.
  ◆ Modern European ◆ Pub ◆
A thoroughly comfortable dining room with a charming and gracious atmosphere.
Serves classically-inspired food executed with a high degree of finesse.

Scott's   AC ⇔ VISA ©© AE ①

20 Mount St ⊠ *W1K 2HE* – Ⓜ *Bond St*
– ℰ *(020) 7495 7309 – Fax (020) 7647 63 27*
– *www.scotts-restaurant.com*
– *Closed 25-26 December, 1 January and August Bank holiday*   **G3**
Rest – Carte £ 38/87
  ◆ Seafood ◆ Fashionable ◆
A landmark London institution reborn. Stylish yet traditional; oak panelling juxta-
posed with vibrant artwork from young British artists. Top quality seafood, kept
simple.

XXX ✫

The Greenhouse   🏧 ⇄ 💳 ⊙⊙ 🅰🅴 ⓪

27a Hay's Mews ⊠ W1J 5NY – ⓜ Hyde Park Corner
– 𝒞 *(020) 7499 3331*
– *reservations@greenhouserestaurant.co.uk*
– *Fax (020) 7499 53 68*
– *www.greenhouserestaurant.co.uk*
– *Closed 24 December - 6 January, Saturday lunch, Sunday and Bank Holidays*
Rest – Menu £ 29/65 🕸   **G4**
Spec. Foie gras glazed with lemon, honey, apricot and begonia flowers. Veal rump with asparagus and tamarind reduction. "Snix" - chocolate, salted caramel and peanuts.
♦ Innovative ♦ Fashionable ♦
Smart, elegant restaurant broken up into sections by glass screens. Innovative selection of elaborately presented dishes, underpinned with sound French culinary techniques.

XXX ✫✫

Hibiscus (Claude Bosi)   🏧 ⇄ 💳 ⊙⊙ 🅰🅴

29 Maddox St ⊠ W1S 2PA – ⓜ Oxford Circus
– 𝒞 *(020) 7629 2999*
– *enquiries@hibiscusrestaurant.co.uk*
– *Fax (020) 7514 95 52*
– *www.hibiscusrestaurant.co.uk*
– *closed 2 weeks summer, 2 weeks Christmas, Saturday except dinner*
1 November - 20 December and Sunday   **H3**
Rest – Menu £ 25 (lunch)/60
Spec. Sweetbeads, oak smoked goat's cheese, onion fondue. Chicken stuffed with crayfish, girolles and green mango. Tart of sweet peas, mint and sheep's whey with coconut ice cream.
♦ Innovative ♦ Elegant ♦
French oak wood panelling and Welsh slate walls reminiscent of its previous incarnation in Ludlow. Shropshire ingredients feature; cooking is accomplished and bold.

XXX ✫

Murano   💳 ⊙⊙ 🅰🅴 ⓪

20 Queen St ⊠ W1J 5PR – ⓜ Green Park
– 𝒞 *(020) 7592 1222 – murano@gordonramsay.com*
– *Fax (020) 7592 12 13*
– *www.angelahartnett.com*
– *closed Sunday*   **G4**
Rest – Menu £ 25/55
Spec. Scallop, watermelon and Joselito ham salad. Duck breast and confit of leg with mustard fruits and potato cakes. Apricot soufflé with Amaretto di Saronno ice cream.
♦ Italian influences ♦
Angela Hartnett's bright and stylish restaurant, in collaboration with Gordon Ramsay, provides a luminous setting for her refined and balanced cooking, with its strong Italian influences.

XXX ✫

Maze   🏧 ⇄ 💳 ⊙⊙ 🅰🅴

10-13 Grosvenor Sq ⊠ W1K 6JP – ⓜ Bond Street
– 𝒞 *(020) 7107 0000 – maze@gordonramsay.com – Fax (020) 7107 00 01*
– *www.gordonramsay.com*   **G3**
Rest – Carte approx. £ 57 🕸
Spec. Crab salad with mooli and apple jelly. Red mullet and sardine with saffron rice and pimento purée. Pineapple carpaccio with seaweed croquette and Malibu lime jelly.
♦ Innovative ♦ Fashionable ♦
Choose between a variety of small dishes at this sleek, contemporary restaurant. Innovative, balanced and precise, cooking has a French base and the occasional Asian influence.

XXX
❀

Benares (Atul Kochhar)   AC ⇄ VISA ◑◐ AE ⓪

12a Berkeley Square House ⊠ W1J 6BS – ⓜ *Green Park –* ☎ *(020) 7629 8886*
– reservations@benaresrestaurant.com – Fax (020) 7499 24 30
– www.benaresrestaurant.com
– closed 25-26 December, 1 January, and Bank Holidays   **H3**
Rest – Menu £ 30 (lunch) – Carte £ 39/61
Spec. Tandoori roasted quails' with red chilli and yoghurt marinade. Tiger prawns with curry leaf, onion and tomato sauce. Saffron and mango jelly with coconut.
♦ Indian ♦ Formal ♦
A smart and stylish, first floor Indian restaurant. Many of the regional dishes are given innovative twists but flavours remain authentic. Convivial atmosphere and pleasant service.

XXX
❀

Umu   AC VISA ◑◐ AE ⓪

14-16 Bruton Pl ⊠ W1J 6LX – ⓜ *Bond Street –* ☎ *(020) 7499 8881*
– reception@umurestaurant.com – Fax (020) 7016 51 20
– www.umurestaurant.com
– Closed 24 December - 7 January, Saturday lunch, Sunday and Bank Holidays
Rest – Menu £ 21 (lunch) – Carte £ 34/73 ♪   **H3**
Spec. Sweet shrimp with sake jelly and caviar. Grilled skill fish teriyaki, yuzu and citrus flavoured grated radish. Black bean ice cream.
♦ Japanese ♦ Fashionable ♦
Stylish, discreet interior using natural materials, with central sushi bar. Japanese dishes, specialising in Kyoto cuisine; choose one of the Kaiseki menus. Over 160 different labels of sake.

XXX

Theo Randall – at InterContinental Hotel   AC ⇄ VISA ◑◐ AE ⓪

1 Hamilton Place, Park Lane ⊠ W1J 7QY – ⓜ *Hyde Park Corner*
– ☎ *(020) 7318 8747 – www.theorandall.com*
– closed 25-26 December, Saturday lunch, Sunday and Bank Holidays
Rest – Menu £ 25 (weekday lunch) – Carte £ 43/50   **G4**
♦ Italian ♦ Fashionable ♦
Stylish and spacious ground floor restaurant; helpful and chatty service. Rustic, seasonal Italian dishes focus on the best ingredients; wood oven the speciality.

XXX

Embassy   🌂 AC VISA ◑◐ AE

29 Old Burlington St ⊠ W1S 3AN – ⓜ *Green Park –* ☎ *(020) 7851 0956*
– embassy@embassylondon.com – Fax (020) 7434 30 74
– www.embassylondon.com
– closed Saturday lunch, Sunday, Monday and Bank Holidays   **H3**
Rest – Menu £ 25 (lunch) – Carte £ 24/45
♦ Modern European ♦ Trendy ♦
Marble floors, ornate cornicing and a long bar create a characterful, moody dining room. Tables are smartly laid and menus offer accomplished, classic dishes.

XXX

Tamarind   AC VISA ◑◐ AE ⓪

20 Queen St ⊠ W1J 5PR – ⓜ *Green Park –* ☎ *(020) 7629 3561 – manager@ tamarindrestaurant.com – Fax (020) 7499 50 34*
– www.tamarindrestaurant.com
– closed 25-26 December, 1 January and lunch Saturday and Bank Holidays
Rest – Menu £ 22/52 – Carte £ 39/61   **G4**
♦ Indian ♦ Formal ♦
The starting point is the Moghul cooking of the North West and the use of the tandoor oven – kebabs are a speciality. The spacious and stylish basement restaurant is popular with the smart set.

XXX

Bentley's (Grill)   AC ⇄ VISA ◑◐ AE

11-15 Swallow St ⊠ W1B 4DG – ⓜ *Piccadilly Circus –* ☎ *(020) 7734 4756*
– reservations@bentleys.org – www.bentleysoysterbarandgrill.co.uk
– closed 25-26 December, 1 January, Saturday lunch and Sunday
Rest – Menu £ 22 (lunch) – Carte £ 36/62   **H3**
♦ British ♦ Elegant ♦
Entrance into striking bar; panelled staircase to richly decorated restaurant. Carefully sourced seafood or meat dishes enhanced by clean, crisp cooking. Unruffled service.

XXX **Sartoria** 〔AC〕⇔ ☜ VISA ◑◐ AE

20 Savile Row ⊠ *W1S 3PR* – **Ⓜ** *Green Park* – *℘ (020) 7534 7000*
– sartoriareservations@danddlondon.com – Fax (020) 7534 70 70
– www.danddlondon.com
– closed 25-26 December, 1 January, Sunday and Bank Holidays
Rest – Menu £ 25 – Carte £ 35/46   **H3**
◆ Italian ◆ Formal ◆
In the street renowned for English tailoring, a coolly sophisticated restaurant to suit those looking for classic Italian cooking with modern touches.

XXX **Avista** 〔AC〕⇔ VISA ◑◐ AE ◑

Millennium Mayfair H, 39 Grosvenor Sq ⊠ *W1K 2HP* – **Ⓜ** *Bond Street*
– ℘ (020) 7596 3444 – reservations@avistarestaurant.com
– Fax (020) 7596 34 43 – www.avistarestaurant.com
– Closed 25 December and 1 January   **G3**
Rest – Menu £ 24 (lunch) – Carte £ 26/46
◆ Italian ◆ Luxury ◆
A large room, softened by neutral shades, within the Millennium Hotel. The menu traverses Italy and the cooking marries the rustic with the more refined. Pasta dishes are a highlight.

XXX **Kai** 〔AC〕⇔ VISA ◑◐ AE ◑
ॐ
65 South Audley St ⊠ *W1K 2QU* – **Ⓜ** *Hyde Park Corner* – *℘ (020) 7493 8988*
– kai@kaimayfair.com – Fax (020) 7493 14 56 – www.kaimayfair.com
– Closed 25-26 December and 1 January   **G3**
Rest – *(booking essential)* Menu £ 24 (lunch) – Carte £ 34/84
Spec. Pan-fried prawns with mustard greens and buttered lettuce. Lamb with Sichuan peppercorns, flower mushroom and bamboo shoot. 'Pumpkin Cream' with purple rice, coconut ice cream.
◆ Chinese ◆ Intimate ◆
Stylish and slick surroundings spread over two floors, with unobtrusive and sweet natured service. Highly skilled cooking blends the traditional with the modern to good effect on extensive menu.

XX **Wild Honey** 〔AC〕☜ VISA ◑◐ AE
ॐ
12 St George St ⊠ *W1S 2FB* – **Ⓜ** *Oxford Circus* – *℘ (020) 7758 9160*
– info@wildhoneyrestaurant.co.uk – Fax (020) 7493 45 49
– www.wildhoneyrestaurant.co.uk
– Closed 25-26 December and 1 January   **H3**
Rest – Menu £ 17 (lunch) – Carte £ 23/37
Spec. Dorset crab, salad of peas and young shoots. Saddle and shoulder of rabbit, gnocchi, olives and tomatoes. Rum 'Baba' , raspberries, Chantilly cream.
◆ Modern European ◆ Design ◆
High-ceilinged, oak-panelled restaurant, with banquette and booth seating; sister to Arbutus in Soho. Easy to eat, gimmick-free food with flavoursome and seasonal ingredients.

XX **Semplice** *(Marco Torri)* 〔AC〕VISA ◑◐ AE
ॐ
9-10 Blenheim St ⊠ *W1S 1LJ* – **Ⓜ** *Bond Street* – *℘ (020) 7495 1509*
– info@ristorantesemplice.com – Fax (020) 7493 70 74
– www.ristorantesemplice.com
– Closed Christmas, Easter, Saturday lunch, Sunday and Bank Holidays
Rest – *(booking essential at dinner)* Menu £ 19 (lunch) – Carte   **G3**
£ 31/47 ♨
Spec. Pan-fried goat's cheese with beetroot and balsamic vinegar. Fassone beef with spiced French beans and salad. Domori chocolate fondant and pistachio ice cream.
◆ Italian ◆ Fashionable ◆
Comfortable and stylish with custom laquered ebony, wavy gold walls and leather seating. Owners' passion about produce evident on the plate; northern Italy influences.

XX **Bellamy's** AC VISA ⓞ AE

18 Bruton Pl ⊠ W1J 6LY – ⓜ Bond Street – ℰ (020) 7491 2727
– info@bellamysrestaurant.co.uk – Fax (020) 7491 99 90
– www.bellamysrestaurant.co.uk
– closed Saturday lunch, Sunday, Christmas, Easter and Bank Holidays
Rest – Menu £ 29 – Carte £ 36/54   **H3**
♦ Traditional ♦ Brasserie ♦

French deli/brasserie tucked down a smart mews. Go past the caviar and cheeses into the restaurant proper for a very traditional, but well-executed, range of Gallic classics.

XX **Patterson's** AC ⇔ VISA ⓞ AE

4 Mill St ⊠ W1S 2AX – ⓜ Oxford Street – ℰ (020) 7499 1308
– info@pattersonsrestaurant.co.uk – Fax (020) 7491 21 22
– www.pattersonsrestaurant.com
– Closed Saturday lunch, Sunday and Bank Holidays
Rest – Menu £ 25 (lunch) – Carte £ 20/45   **H3**
♦ Modern European ♦ Intimate ♦

Stylish modern interior in black and white. Elegant tables and attentive service. Modern British cooking with concise wine list and sensible prices.

XX **Alloro** AC ⇔ VISA ⓞ AE ⓞ

19-20 Dover St ⊠ W1S 4LU – ⓜ Green Park – ℰ (020) 7495 4768
– alloro@finedininggroup.com – Fax (020) 7629 53 48
– www.londonfinedininggroup.com
– Closed Easter, 25 December, 1 January, Saturday lunch and Sunday
Rest – Menu £ 32/35 – Carte £ 40/60   **H3**
♦ Italian ♦ Fashionable ♦

One of the new breed of stylish Italian restaurants with contemporary art and leather seating. A separate, bustling bar. Smoothly run with modern cooking.

XX **Hush** ☆ AC ⇔ VISA ⓞ AE

8 Lancashire Court, Brook St ⊠ W1S 1EY – ⓜ Bond Street
– ℰ (020) 7659 1500 – info@hush.co.uk – Fax (020) 7659 15 01
– www.hush.co.uk   **H3**
Rest – (Closed 25 December, 31 December, 1 January and Sunday except lunch April-September) (booking essential) Carte £ 23/49
♦ Modern European ♦ Fashionable ♦

Tucked away down a delightful mews courtyard, this brasserie - with sunny courtyard terrace - is an informal and lively little place to eat rustic Mediterranean fare.

XX **Nobu** – at The Metropolitan Hotel ≤ AC ⇔ VISA ⓞ AE
ⓢ

19 Old Park Lane ⊠ W1Y 1LB – ⓜ Hyde Park Corner – ℰ (020) 7447 4747
– london@noburestaurants.com – Fax (020) 7447 47 49
– www.noburestaurants.com
– Closed 25-26 December and 1 January   **G4**
Rest – (booking essential) Menu £ 50/90 – Carte £ 32/50
Spec. Tuna sashimi salad with matsuhiza dressing. Black cod with miso. Suntory whisky cappuccino.
♦ Japanese ♦ Fashionable ♦

Its celebrity clientele has made this one of the most glamorous spots. Staff are fully conversant in the unique menu that adds South American influences to Japanese cooking.

XX **Via Condotti** AC ⇔ ⅋ VISA ⓞ AE
ⓢ

23 Conduit St ⊠ W1S 2XS – ⓜ Oxford Circus – ℰ (020) 7493 7050
– info@viacondotti.co.uk – Fax (020) 7409 79 85 – www.viacondotti.co.uk
– Closed Christmas, New Year, Sunday and Bank Holidays   **H3**
Rest – Menu £ 19/28
♦ Italian ♦ Fashionable ♦

Reliable and keenly run Italian, as warm and welcoming as the pretty façade suggests. Balanced and appetising cooking, using influences from the north of Italy, and all fairly priced.

XX **Taman Gang**   AC VISA ⓸ AE

141 Park Lane ⊠ *W1K 7AA* – Ⓜ *Marble Arch* – 𝒞 *(020) 7518 3160*
– info@tamangang.com – Fax (020) 7518 31 61 – www.tamangang.com
– closed Sunday and Bank Holidays   **F3**
Rest – *(dinner only)* Carte £ 28/73
♦ Asian ♦ Exotic ♦
Basement restaurant with largish bar and lounge area. Stylish but intimate décor.
Informal and intelligent service. Pan-Asian dishes presented in exciting modern
manner.

XX **Mews of Mayfair**   VISA ⓸ AE ⓪

10-11 Lancashire Court, Brook St (first floor) ⊠ *W1S 1EY* – Ⓜ *Bond Street*
– 𝒞 (020) 7518 9388 – info@mewsofmayfair.com – Fax (020) 7518 93 89
– www.mewsofmayfair.com
– closed 25-26 December and Sunday   **H3**
Rest – Menu £ 23/40 – Carte £ 36/48
♦ International ♦ Friendly ♦
Converted mews houses once used as storage rooms for Savile Row. Ground floor
bar with French windows. Pretty first floor restaurant where eclectic modern
menus are served.

XX **Sketch (The Gallery)**   AC VISA ⓸ AE ⓪

9 Conduit St ⊠ *W1S 2XG* – Ⓜ *Oxford Street* – 𝒞 *(020) 7659 4500*
– info@sketch.uk.com – Fax (020) 7629 16 83 – www.sketch.uk.com
– closed 25-26 December Sunday and Bank Holidays   **H3**
Rest – *(dinner only) (booking essential)* Carte £ 32/52
♦ International ♦ Trendy ♦
On the ground floor of the Sketch building: daytime video art gallery metamor-
phoses into evening brasserie with ambient wall projections and light menus
with eclectic range.

XX **Nobu Berkeley St**   AC VISA ⓸ AE
ⓒ
15 Berkeley St ⊠ *W1J 8DY* – Ⓜ *Green Park* – 𝒞 *(020) 7290 9222*
– nobuberkeleyst@noburestaurants.com – Fax (020) 7290 92 23
– www.noburestaurants.com
– Closed 25-26 December, Saturday lunch, Sunday lunch and Bank Holidays
Rest – Menu £ 28/85 – Carte £ 33/49   **H3**
Spec. Octopus carpaccio with botarga. Duck breast with wasabi salsa. Chocolate santandagi with pistachios.
♦ Japanese ♦ Fashionable ♦
In a prime position off Berkeley Square: downstairs 'destination' bar and above, a
top quality, soft-hued restaurant. Innovative Japanese dishes with original combi-
nations.

XX **Momo**   ⛱ AC VISA ⓸ AE ⓪

25 Heddon St ⊠ *W1B 4BH* – Ⓜ *Oxford Circus* – 𝒞 *(020) 7434 4040*
– info@momoresto.com – Fax (020) 7287 04 04 – www.momoresto.com
– closed Sunday lunch   **H3**
Rest – Menu £ 24/40 – Carte £ 30/43
♦ Moroccan ♦ Exotic ♦
Elaborate adornment of rugs, drapes and ornaments mixed with Arabic music lend
an authentic feel to this busy Moroccan restaurant. Helpful service. Popular basement bar.

XX **Veeraswamy**   AC ⇔ 🕸 VISA ⓸ AE ⓪

Victory House, 99 Regent St (entrance on Swallow St) ⊠ *W1B 4RS*
– Ⓜ Piccadilly Circus – 𝒞 (020) 7734 1401 – veeraswamy@realindianfood.com
– Fax (020) 7439 84 34 – www.realindianfood.com
– Closed dinner 25 December   **H3**
Rest – Menu £ 20 (lunch) – Carte £ 36/44
♦ Indian ♦ Design ♦
The country's oldest Indian restaurant enlivened by vivid coloured walls and glass
screens. The menu also combines the familiar with some modern twists.

XX **Silk** – at Courthouse Kempinksi Hotel `AC` `VISA` `OO` `AE`

19-21 Great Marlborough St ✉ W1F 7HL – Ⓜ Oxford Circus
– ℰ (020) 7297 5567 – info@courthouse-hotel.com – Fax (020) 7297 55 99
– www.courthouse-hotel.com
– Closed 22 December-1 January, Sunday and Monday   **H3**
Rest – (dinner only) Menu £ 25 – Carte £ 23/38
♦ International ♦ Formal ♦

Former magistrate's court with original panelling. Menu follows the journey of the
Silk Route: this translates as mostly Indian flavours with some Thai; desserts more
European.

XX **Stanza** `AC` `↳` `☕` `VISA` `OO` `AE` `①`

97-107 Shaftesbury Ave ✉ W1D 5DY – Ⓜ Leicester Square
– ℰ (020) 7494 3020 – reception@stanzalondon.com – Fax (020) 7494 30 50
– www.stanzalondon.com
– Closed Saturday lunch and Sunday   **I3**
Rest – Menu £ 14 (lunch) – Carte £ 28/64
♦ Modern European ♦

On the first floor in the heart of theatre-land, with a large and glitzy bar attached.
Good value pre-theatre menu; à la carte name-checks key suppliers and kitchen
displays a degree of originality.

XX **Benja** `AC` `VISA` `OO` `AE`
☺

17 Beak St ✉ W1F 9RW – Ⓜ Oxford Circus – ℰ (020) 7287 0555
– info@krua.co.uk – Fax (020) 7287 00 56 – www.benjarestaurant.com
– Closed 24-25 December and Sunday   **H3**
Rest – Carte approx. £ 34
♦ Thai ♦ Intimate ♦

Soho townhouse, seductively and colourfully styled; first floor is the most appealing. Go for the interesting and unusual specialities in among the more familiar
classics.

XX **Yauatcha** `AC` `VISA` `OO` `AE`
❀

15 Broadwick St ✉ W1F 0DL – Ⓜ Tottenham Court Road – ℰ (020) 7494 8888
– mail@yauatcha.com – Fax (020) 7494 88 89
– Closed 24-25 December   **I3**
Rest – Carte £ 20/78
Spec. Chilean sea bass mooli roll. Crispy aromatic duck with Thai spring
onion and cucumber. Coconut soufflé with lime sorbet.
♦ Chinese ♦ Design ♦

Choose between darker, more atmospheric basement or lighter, brighter ground
floor. Refined and delicate modern Chinese dim sum served on both levels; ideal
for sharing.

X **Arbutus** (Anthony Demetre) `AC` `☕` `VISA` `OO` `AE`
❀

63-64 Frith St ✉ W1D 3JW – Ⓜ Tottenham Court Road – ℰ (020) 7734 4545
– info@arbutusrestaurant.co.uk – Fax (020) 7287 86 24
– www.arbutusrestaurant.co.uk
– Closed 25-26 December and 1 January   **I3**
Rest – Menu £ 16 (lunch) – Carte £ 31/36
Spec. Smoked eel, beetroot and horseradish cream. Saddle of rabbit, cottage
pie and peas. Doughnuts, pistachio, honey and lemon thyme ice cream.
♦ Modern European ♦ Bistro ♦

Dining room and bar that's bright and stylish without trying too hard. Bistro classics
turned on their head: poised, carefully crafted cooking - but dishes still pack a punch.

X **Dehesa** `📻` `AC` `↔` `VISA` `OO` `AE`
☺

25 Ganton St ✉ W1F 9BP – Ⓜ Oxford Circus – ℰ (020) 7494 4170
– info@dehesa.co.uk – Fax (020) 7494 41 75 – www.dehesa.co.uk
– closed 1 week Christmas and Sunday dinner   **H3**
Rest – Carte £ 20/40 ⅛
♦ Mediterranean ♦ Tapas bar ♦

Repeats the success of its sister restaurant, Salt Yard, by offering tasty, good value
Spanish and Italian tapas. Unhurried atmosphere in appealing corner location. Terrific drinks list too.

Barrafina   _VISA_ ◎◎ _AE_

54 Frith St ⊠ W1D 3SL – Ⓜ Tottenham Court Rd – ℰ (020) 7813 8016
– info@barrafina.co.uk – Fax (020) 7734 75 93 – www.barrafina.co.uk
– Closed Christmas, Easter and Bank Holidays   **I3**
Rest *– (bookings not accepted)* Carte £ 18/37
♦ Spanish ♦ Tapas bar ♦
Centred around a counter with seating for 20, come here if you want authentic
Spanish tapas served in a buzzy atmosphere. Seafood is a speciality and the Jabugo
ham a must.

Imli   _AC_ _VISA_ ◎◎ _AE_ ⓪

167-169 Wardour St ⊠ W1F 8WR – Ⓜ Tottenham Court Road
– ℰ (020) 7287 4243 – info@imli.co.uk – Fax (020) 7287 42 45 – www.imli.co.uk
– Closed 25-28 December, 1 January and lunch Bank Holidays   **I3**
Rest *– Menu £ 18 (lunch) – Carte £ 15/23*
♦ Indian ♦ Bistro ♦
Long, spacious interior is a busy, buzzy place. Good value, fresh and tasty Indian
tapas style dishes prove a popular currency. Same owners as Tamarind.

Bar Shu   _AC_ ⇔ _VISA_ ◎◎ _AE_

28 Frith St ⊠ W1D 5LF – Ⓜ Leicester Square – ℰ (020) 7287 8822
– Fax (020) 7287 88 58
– Closed 25-26 December   **I3**
Rest *– (booking advisable)* Carte £ 20/25
♦ Chinese ♦ Exotic ♦
The fiery flavours of authentic Sichuan cooking are the draw here; dishes have
some unusual names but help is at hand as menu has pictures. Best atmosphere
is on the ground floor.

Chinese Experience   _AC_ _VISA_ ◎◎

118 Shaftesbury Ave ⊠ W1D 5EP – Ⓜ Leicester Square – ℰ (020) 7437 0377
– info@chineseexperience.com – www.chineseexperience.com
– Closed 25 December   **I3**
Rest *– Menu £ 15 – Carte approx. £ 19*
♦ Chinese ♦ Fashionable ♦
Bright, buzzy restaurant: sit at long bench or chunky wood tables. Large, sensibly
priced menus with a wide range of Chinese dishes; good dim sum. Knowledgable
service.

Cafe Boheme   ☞ 🗐 _VISA_ ◎◎ _AE_

13 Old Compton St ⊠ W1D 5GQ – Ⓜ Leicester Square – ℰ (020) 77340623
– info@cafeboheme.co.uk – Fax (020) 74 34 37 75 – www.cafeboheme.co.uk
– Closed 25 December   **I3**
Rest *– Carte £ 24/36*
♦ French ♦ Brasserie ♦
Expect classic Gallic comfort-food and a zinc-topped bar surrounded by wine drin-
kers. Remade as a Parisian brasserie in 2008, ideal for pre/post theatre meals. Open
from dawn to the wee small hours.

St James's

The Ritz   🖧 _AC_ 🖳 🕻 🛠 _VISA_ ◎◎ _AE_ ⓪

150 Piccadilly ⊠ W1J 9BR – Ⓜ Green Park – ℰ (020) 7493 8181
– enquire@theritzlondon.com – Fax (020) 7493 26 87
– www.theritzlondon.com   **H4**
116 rm – ♥£ 294/552 ♥♥£ 458/552, � £ 30 – 17 suites
Rest *The Ritz Restaurant* – see below
♦ Grand Luxury ♦ Stylish ♦
Opened 1906, a fine example of Louis XVI architecture and decoration. Elegant
Palm Court famed for afternoon tea. Many of the lavishly appointed rooms overlook the park.

Sofitel St James London

6 Waterloo Pl ⊠ SW1Y 4AN – **Ⓜ** *Piccadilly Circus* – *ℰ (020) 7747 2200*
– *H3144@accor.com* – *Fax (020) 7747 22 10* – *www.sofitelstjames.com*
179 rm – ♥£ 382/441 ♥♥£ 441, ⊡ £ 21 – 6 suites   I4
Rest *Brasserie Roux* – see below
◆ Luxury ◆ Classic ◆

Grade II listed building in smart Pall Mall location. Classically English interiors include floral Rose Lounge and club-style St. James bar. Comfortable, well-fitted
bedrooms.

Haymarket

1 Suffolk Place ⊠ SW1Y 4BP – **Ⓜ** *Piccadilly Circus* – *ℰ (020) 7470 4000*
– *haymarket@firmdale.com* – *Fax (020) 7470 40 04* – *www.haymarkethotel.com*
47 rm – ♥£ 294 ♥♥£ 382, ⊡ £ 18.50 – 3 suites   I4
Rest *Brumus* – *ℰ (020) 7451 1012* – Carte £ 25/45
◆ Luxury ◆ Stylish ◆

Smart, spacious hotel in John Nash Regency building, with stylish blend of modern
and antique furnishings. Large, comfortable bedrooms in soothing colours. Impressive pool. Brumus bar and restaurant puts focus on Italian cooking.

Stafford ⌂
16-18 St James's Pl ⊠ SW1A 1NJ – **Ⓜ** *Green Park* – *ℰ (020) 7493 0111*
– *information@thestaffordhotel.co.uk* – *Fax (020) 7493 71 21*
– *www.thestaffordhotel.co.uk*   H4
73 rm – ♥£ 353/494 ♥♥£ 623/682, ⊡ £ 24 – 32 suites
Rest – *(Closed Saturday lunch)* Menu £ 30 (lunch) – Carte dinner £ 28/62
◆ Townhouse ◆ Stylish ◆

A genteel atmosphere prevails in this discreet country house in the city. Bedrooms
divided between main house, converted 18C stables and newer Mews. Refined,
elegant, intimate dining room.

Dukes ⌂

35 St James's Pl ⊠ SW1A 1NY – **Ⓜ** *Green Park* – *ℰ (020) 7491 4840*
– *bookings@dukeshotel.com* – *Fax (020) 7493 12 64* – *www.dukeshotel.com*
83 rm – ♥£ 282/376 ♥♥£ 323/417, ⊡ £ 22 – 7 suites   H4
Rest – Menu £ 18/28 – Carte £ 29/41
◆ Traditional ◆ Luxury ◆ Classic ◆

Refurbished fully in 2008 but still retaining that discreet, traditionally British quality. Central but quiet location. Dukes bar famous for its martinis. Elegant bedrooms
with country house feel. Discreet dining room.

St James's Hotel and Club ⌂
7-8 Park Place ⊠ SW1A 1LP – **Ⓜ** *Green Park* – *ℰ (020) 7725 0274*
– *reservation@stjameshotelandclub.com* – *Fax (020) 7725 03 01*
– *www.stjameshotelandclub.com*   H4
50 rm – ♥£ 288/405 ♥♥£ 347/441, ⊡ £ 26 – 10 suites
Rest *Andaman by Dieter Müller* – *(booking essential)* Menu £ 55
– Carte £ 41/60
◆ Business ◆ Modern ◆

1890s house in cul-de-sac, formerly a private club, reopened as a hotel in 2008.
Modern, boutique–style interior with over 400 paintings. Fine finish to compact,
but well-equipped bedrooms. Small restaurant blends with bar; original and ambitious tasting plates.

22 Jermyn Street without rest

22 Jermyn St ⊠ SW1Y 6HL – **Ⓜ** *Piccadilly Circus* – *ℰ (020) 7734 2353*
– *office@22jermyn.com* – *Fax (020) 7734 07 50* – *www.22jermyn.com*
5 rm – ♥£ 259 ♥♥£ 259 – **14 suites**   I3
◆ Townhouse ◆

Exclusive boutique hotel with entrance amid famous shirt-makers' shops. Stylishly
decorated bedrooms more than compensate for the lack of lounge space. Room
service available.

XXXXX **The Ritz Restaurant** – at The Ritz Hotel 🕏 🗚 ᵛⁱˢᵃ ⚬⚬ 🗚 ⓞ
150 Piccadilly ⊠ W1J 9BR – Ⓜ *Green Park –* ℰ *(020) 7493 8181*
– enquire@theritzlondon.com – Fax (020) 7493 26 87 – www.theritzlondon.com
Rest – Menu £ 36/45 – Carte £ 46/88 **H4**
♦ Traditional ♦ Formal ♦
The height of opulence: magnificent Louis XVI décor with trompe l'oeil and ornate
gilding. Delightful terrace over Green Park. Refined service, classic and modern
menu.

XXX **The Wolseley** 🗚 ᵛⁱˢᵃ ⚬⚬ 🗚 ⓞ
160 Piccadilly ⊠ W1J 9EB – Ⓜ *Green Park –* ℰ *(020) 7499 6996*
– Fax (020) 7499 68 88 – www.thewolseley.com
– Closed 25 December, 1 January, August Bank Holiday and dinner 24 and 31
December **H4**
Rest – *(booking essential)* Carte £ 26/53
♦ Modern European ♦ Fashionable ♦
Has the feel of a grand European coffee house: pillars, high vaulted ceiling, mezza-
nine tables. Menus range from caviar to a hot dog. Also open for breakfast and tea.

XXX **Sake No Hana** 🗚 ⇔ ᵛⁱˢᵃ ⚬⚬ 🗚
23 St James's St ⊠ SW1A 1HA – Ⓜ *Green Park –* ℰ *(020) 7925 8988*
– reservations@sakenohana.com – Fax (020) 7925 89 99
– www.sakenohana.com
– closed 24-25 December **H4**
Rest – Carte £ 20/85
♦ Japanese ♦ Design ♦
Reached via elevator, a stylish room with striking cedar wood décor. 8 page menu
mixes new-style Japanese with more traditional kaiseki, with sharing the best
option. Large sake list and separate sushi bar.

XXX **St Alban** 🗚 🕏 ᵛⁱˢᵃ ⚬⚬ 🗚 ⓞ
4-12 Regent St ⊠ SW1Y 4PE – Ⓜ *Piccadilly Circus –* ℰ *(020) 7499 8558*
– info@stalban.net – Fax (020) 7499 68 88 – www.stalban.net
– Closed 25-26 December and 1 January **I3**
Rest – Menu £ 20 – Carte £ 22/39
♦ Mediterranean ♦
Light, airy restaurant with colourful booth seating and feeling of space. Weekly-
changing southern European menu; specialities from the wood-fired oven and
charcoal grill.

XXX **Luciano** 🗚 ⇔ ᵛⁱˢᵃ ⚬⚬ 🗚
72-73 St James's St ⊠ SW1A 1PH – Ⓜ *Green Park –* ℰ *(020) 7408 1440*
– info@lucianorestaurant.co.uk – Fax (020) 7493 66 70
– www.lucianorestaurant.co.uk
– Closed 25-26 December and Sunday **H4**
Rest – Menu £ 22 (lunch) – Carte £ 30/46
♦ Italian ♦ Brasserie ♦
Art Deco, David Collins styled bar leads to restaurant sympathetic to its early 19C
heritage. Mix of Italian and English dishes cooked in rustic, wholesome and earthy
manner.

XX **Le Caprice** 🗚 ᵛⁱˢᵃ ⚬⚬ 🗚 ⓞ
Arlington House, Arlington St ⊠ SW1A 1RJ – Ⓜ *Green Park*
– ℰ *(020) 7629 2239 – reservation@le-caprice.co.uk – Fax (020) 7493 90 40*
– www.le-caprice.co.uk
– Closed 24-26 December, 1 January and 31 August **H4**
Rest – *(Sunday brunch)* Carte £ 37/50
♦ Modern European ♦ Fashionable ♦
Still attracting a fashionable clientele and as busy as ever. Dine at the bar or in the
smoothly run restaurant. Food combines timeless classics with modern dishes.

XX **Quaglino's**   AC ⟷ ⚏ VISA ⓪ AE ⓪

16 Bury St ⊠ *SW1Y 6AL –* Ⓜ *Green Park –* ℰ *(020) 7930 6767*
– quags-res@danddlondon.com – Fax (020) 7930 27 32
– www.quaglinos.co.uk
– Closed 25-26 December   **H4**
Rest *– (booking essential) Menu £ 20 (lunch) – Carte £ 25/46*
  ♦ Modern European ♦ Design ♦

Descend the sweeping staircase into the capacious room where a busy and buzzy atmosphere prevails. Watch the chefs prepare everything from osso bucco to fish and chips.

XX **Mint Leaf**   AC ⚏ VISA ⓪ AE ⓪

Suffolk Pl ⊠ *SW1Y 4HX –* Ⓜ *Piccadilly Circus –* ℰ *(020) 7930 9020*
– reservations@mintleafrestaurant.com – Fax (020) 7930 62 05
– www.mintleafrestaurant.com
– Closed Saturday lunch and Sunday   **I4**
Rest *– Carte £ 27/37*
  ♦ Indian ♦ Design ♦

Basement restaurant in theatreland. Cavernous dining room incorporating busy, trendy bar with unique cocktail list and loud music. Helpful service. Contemporary Indian dishes.

XX **Brasserie Roux**   AC ⚏ VISA ⓪ AE ⓪

8 Pall Mall ⊠ *SW1Y 5NG –* Ⓜ *Piccadilly Circus –* ℰ *(020) 7968 2900*
– h3144@accor.com – Fax (020) 7747 22 51 – www.sofitelstjames.com
Rest *– Menu £ 20 – Carte £ 32/55*   **I4**
  ♦ French ♦ Brasserie ♦

Informal, smart, classic brasserie style with large windows making the most of the location. Large menu of French classics with many daily specials; comprehensive wine list.

XX **Franco's**   AC ⚏ VISA ⓪ AE

61 Jermyn St ⊠ *SW1Y 6LX –* Ⓜ *Green Park –* ℰ *(020) 7499 2211*
– reserve@francoslondon.com – Fax (020) 7495 13 75
– www.francoslondon.com
– Closed Christmas- New Year and Sunday   **H4**
Rest *– (booking essential) Menu £ 30 (lunch) – Carte £ 34/49*
  ♦ Italian ♦

Great all-day menu at 'the café'. Further in, regulars have taken to smart refurbishment. Classic/modern Italian cooking allows bold but refined flavours to shine through.

XX **Noura Central**   AC VISA ⓪ AE ⓪

22 Lower Regent St ⊠ *SW1Y 4UJ –* Ⓜ *Piccadilly Circus –* ℰ *(020) 7839 2020*
– nouracentral@noura.co.uk – Fax (020) 7839 77 00 – www.noura.co.uk
Rest *– Menu £ 18/40 – Carte £ 20/39*   **I3**
  ♦ Lebanese ♦ Exotic ♦

Eye-catching Lebanese façade, matched by sleek interior design. Buzzy atmosphere enhanced by amplified background music. Large menus cover all aspects of Lebanese cuisine.

XX **Brasserie St Jacques**   AC ⟷ VISA ⓪ AE ⓪

33 St James's Street ⊠ *SW1A 1HD –* Ⓜ *Green Park –* ℰ *(020) 7839 1007*
– info@brasseriestjacques.co.uk – Fax (020) 7839 32 04
– www.brasseriestjacques.co.uk
– closed Christmas and New Year   **H4**
Rest *– Carte £ 26/38*
  ♦ French ♦ Brasserie ♦

With its high ceiling and narrow layout, it may lack the buzz one finds in a typical French brasserie, but is nearer the mark with a menu that features all the classic brasserie favourites.

Al Duca
AC · VISA · ◎ · AE · ①

4-5 Duke of York St ⊠ SW1Y 6LA – Ⓜ *Piccadilly Circus*
– ℰ *(020) 7839 3090 – info@alduca-restaurants.co.uk*
– *Fax (020) 7839 40 50 – www.alduca-restaurant.co.uk*
– *Closed Christmas, New Year, Sunday and Bank Holidays*   **H4**
Rest – Menu £ 27/28
♦ Italian ♦ Friendly ♦
Relaxed, modern, stylish restaurant. Friendly and approachable service of robust
and rustic Italian dishes. Set priced menu is good value.

Inn the Park
⟨ · 🕮 · VISA · ◎ · AE

St James's Park ⊠ SW1A 2BJ – Ⓜ *Charing Cross* – ℰ *(020) 7451 9999*
– *info@innthepark.com – Fax (020) 7451 99 98*
– *www.innthepark.com*
– *Closed 25 December and dinner January-February and October-November*
Rest – Carte £ 28/32   **I4**
♦ British ♦ Design ♦
Eco-friendly restaurant with grass covered roof; pleasant views across park and
lakes. Super-heated dining terrace. Modern British menus of tasty, wholesome
dishes.

Portrait
⟨ · AC · VISA · ◎ · AE

3rd Floor, National Portrait Gallery, St Martin's Pl ⊠ WC2H 0HE
– Ⓜ *Charing Cross* – ℰ *(020) 7312 2490 – portrait.restaurant@searcys.co.uk*
– *Fax (020) 7925 02 44 – www.searcys.co.uk*
– *Closed 25-26 December*   *Plan III* **I3**
Rest – *(lunch only and dinner Thursday and Friday) (booking essential)*
Carte £ 23/32
♦ Modern European ♦
On the top floor of National Portrait Gallery with rooftop local landmark views: a
charming spot for lunch. Modern British/European dishes; weekend brunch.

The National Dining Rooms
AC · VISA · ◎ · AE

Sainsbury Wing, The National Gallery, Trafalgar Sq ⊠ WC2N 5DN
– Ⓜ *Charing Cross* – ℰ *(020) 7747 2525 – enquiries@*
thenationaldiningrooms.co.uk – www.thenationaldiningrooms.co.uk
– *Closed Christmas*   **I3-4**
Rest – *(lunch only and dinner Wednesday)* Carte £ 28/45
♦ British ♦ Design ♦
Set on the East Wing's first floor, you can tuck into cakes in the bakery or grab a
prime corner table in the restaurant for great views and proudly seasonal British
menus.

STRAND, COVENT GARDEN & LAMBETH   *Plan III*

Strand and Covent Garden

One Aldwych
ℐ₆ · 🛁 · ⬚ · ⅙ · rm · AC · 🖾 · 🕆 · ⅙ · P · VISA · ◎ · AE · ①

1 Aldwych ⊠ WC2B 4RH – Ⓜ *Temple* – ℰ *(020) 7300 1000*
– *sales@onealdwych.com – Fax (020) 7300 10 01*
– *www.onealdwych.com*   **J3**
96 rm – ❰£ 223/447 ❰❰£ 223/447, � £ 24.75 – 9 suites
Rest *Axis* – see below
Rest *Indigo* – Carte £ 34/43
♦ Grand Luxury ♦ Stylish ♦
Decorative Edwardian building, former home to the Morning Post newspaper.
Now a stylish and contemporary address with modern artwork, a screening
room and hi-tech bedrooms. All-day restaurant looks down on fashionable
bar.

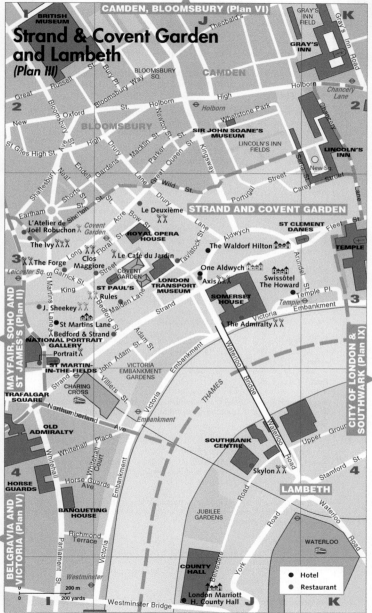

CAMDEN, BLOOMSBURY (Plan VI)

GRAY'S INN FIELD

Strand & Covent Garden and Lambeth
(Plan III)

BRITISH MUSEUM

GRAY'S INN

Theobald's

CAMDEN

BLOOMSBURY SQ.

Holborn

Bury St.

Bloomsbury Way

High

Holborn

Whetstone Park

Chancery Lane

BLOOMSBURY

Oxford St.

High

Newton St.

Macklin St.

Parker St.

SIR JOHN SOANE'S MUSEUM

LINCOLN'S INN FIELDS

LINCOLN'S INN

New Sq.

St Giles High St.

Drury Lane

Great Queen St.

Kingsway

Shaftesbury Ave.

Earlham

Shorts Gardens

Endell St.

Wild St.

Drury Lane

Portugal Street

Carey St.

Serle St.

STRAND AND COVENT GARDEN

Neal St.

Shelton St.

Covent Garden

Acre

Bow St.

Le Deuxième

ST CLEMENT DANES

Fleet St.

L'Atelier de Joël Robuchon

ROYAL OPERA HOUSE

Floral St.

Aldwych

The Waldorf Hilton

TEMPLE

The Ivy

Long

Le Café du Jardin

Tavistock St.

One Aldwych

Arundel St.

The Forge

Clos Maggiore

COVENT GARDEN

LONDON TRANSPORT MUSEUM

Axis

Swissôtel The Howard

Leicester Sq.

Garrick St.

Street

ST PAUL'S

SOMERSET HOUSE

Temple Pl.

Temple

St Martin's Lane

King St.

Rules

Maiden Lane

Strand

Victoria Embankment

J. Sheekey

Bedford St.

Adam St.

The Admiralty

St Martins Lane

Bedford & Strand

NATIONAL PORTRAIT GALLERY

Portrait

John Adam St.

ST MARTIN-IN-THE-FIELDS

Villiers St.

VICTORIA EMBANKMENT GARDENS

Embankment

Strand

TRAFALGAR SQUARE

CHARING CROSS

THAMES

Northumberland Ave.

Victoria

Embankment

Waterloo Bridge

CITY OF LONDON & SOUTHWARK (Plan IX)

OLD ADMIRALTY

Whitehall Place

SOUTHBANK CENTRE

Waterloo Road

Upper Groun

Whitehall

Whitehall Court

Horse Guards Ave.

Embankment

Stamford St.

HORSE GUARDS

Skylon

LAMBETH

MAYFAIR, SOHO AND ST JAMES'S (Plan II)

BANQUETING HOUSE

Richmond Terrace

JUBILEE GARDENS

Road

Waterloo

BELGRAVIA AND VICTORIA (Plan IV)

Parliament St.

Victoria

Westminster

WATERLOO

COUNTY HALL

York Road

Belvedere Road

London Marriott H. County Hall

● Hotel
● Restaurant

200 m

200 yards

Westminster Bridge

Swissôtel The Howard

Temple Pl ✉ *WC2R 2PR* – Ⓜ *Temple* – ☎ *(020) 7836 3555*
– *reservations.london@swissotel.com* – *Fax (020) 7379 45 47*
– *www.london.swissotel.com*   **J3**
177 rm – ♦£ 557 ♦♦£ 557, ⊆ £ 23.50 – 12 suites
Rest *12 Temple Place* – Menu £ 24 (lunch) – Carte approx. £ 37
♦ Luxury ♦ Modern ♦

Discreet elegance is the order of the day at this handsomely appointed hotel.
Many of the comfortable rooms enjoy balcony views of the Thames. Attentive service. Large terrace to restaurant serving modern European dishes.

The Waldorf Hilton

Aldwych ✉ *WC2B 4DD* – Ⓜ *Covent Garden* – ☎ *(020) 7836 2400*
– *enquiry.waldorflondon@hilton.com* – *Fax (020) 7836 46 48*
– *www.hilton.co.uk/waldorf*   **J3**
293 rm – ♦£ 199/469 ♦♦£ 199/469, ⊆ £ 22 – 6 suites
Rest *Homage* – *(Closed lunch Saturday and Sunday)* Menu £ 20
– Carte £ 28/58
♦ Luxury ♦ Modern ♦

Impressive curved and columned façade: an Edwardian landmark. Basement leisure club. Ornate meeting rooms. Two bedroom styles: one contemporary, one more traditional. Large, modish brasserie with extensive range of modern menus.

St Martins Lane

45 St Martin's Lane ✉ *WC2N 4HX* – Ⓜ *Charing Cross* – ☎ *(020) 7300 5500*
– *stmartinslane@morganshotelgroup.com* – *Fax (020) 7300 55 01*
– *www.morganshotelgroup.com*   **I3**
202 rm – ♦£ 253/370 ♦♦£ 253/370, ⊆ £ 25 – 2 suites
Rest *Asia de Cuba* – Carte £ 50/115
♦ Luxury ♦ Design ♦

The unmistakable hand of Philippe Starck evident at this most contemporary of hotels. Unique and stylish, from the starkly modern lobby to the state-of-the-art rooms. 350 varieties of rum and tasty Asian dishes at fashionable Asia de Cuba.

The Ivy

1-5 West St ✉ *WC2H 9NQ* – Ⓜ *Leicester Square* – ☎ *(020) 7836 4751*
– *Fax (020) 7240 93 33* – *www.the-ivy.co.uk*
– *Closed 24-26 December, 1 January and August Bank Holiday*   **I3**
Rest – Carte £ 26/50
♦ International ♦ Fashionable ♦

Wood panelling and stained glass combine with an unpretentious menu to create a veritable institution. A favourite of 'celebrities', so securing a table can be challenging.

Axis

1 Aldwych ✉ *WC2B 4RH* – Ⓜ *Temple* – ☎ *(020) 7300 0300*
– *axis@onealdwych.com* – *Fax (020) 7300 03 01* – *www.onealdwych.com*
– *closed Saturday lunch, Sunday and Bank Holidays*   **J3**
Rest – Menu £ 18 (lunch) – Carte £ 28/37
♦ Modern European ♦ Fashionable ♦

Spiral staircase down to this modern restaurant with very high ceiling; new fabrics and bamboo-effect façade in front of futuristic mural. British ingredients to the fore in carefully crafted dishes.

J. Sheekey

28-32 St Martin's Court ✉ *WC2 4AL* – Ⓜ *Leicester Square* – ☎ *(020) 7240 2565*
– *reservations@j-sheekey.co.uk* – *Fax (020) 7497 08 91* – *www.j-sheeky.co.uk*
– *Closed 25-26 December, 1 January and August Bank Holiday*   **I3**
Rest – *(booking essential)* Carte £ 31/51
♦ Seafood ♦ Fashionable ♦

Festooned with photographs of actors and linked to the theatrical world since opening in 1890. Wood panels and alcove tables add famed intimacy. Accomplished seafood cooking.

XX **Rules** AC ⊕ VISA ◑◉ AE

35 Maiden Lane ⊠ *WC2E 7LB –* ◍ *Leicester Square –* ℰ *(020) 7836 5314*
– info@rules.co.uk – Fax (020) 7497 10 81 – www.rules.co.uk
– closed 4 days Christmas   J3
Rest *– (booking essential) Carte £ 33/47*
◆ British ◆ Formal ◆
London's oldest restaurant boasts a fine collection of antique cartoons, drawings
and paintings. Tradition continues in the menu, specialising in game from its own
estate.

XX **Clos Maggiore** AC ⊕ ⊕ VISA ◑◉ AE ◑

33 King St ⊠ *WC2E 8JD –* ◍ *Leicester Square –* ℰ *(020) 7379 9696*
– enquiries@closmaggiore.com – Fax (020) 7379 67 67
– www.closmaggiore.com
– Closed lunch Saturday and Sunday   IJ3
Rest *– Menu £ 20 (lunch) – Carte £ 35/47* 🍃
◆ French ◆ Formal ◆
Walls covered with flowering branches create delightful woodland feel to rear
dining area with retractable glass roof. French cooking shows flair, creativity and
ambition.

XX **Admiralty** VISA ◑◉ AE ◑

Somerset House, The Strand ⊠ *WC2R 1LA –* ◍ *Temple –* ℰ *(020) 7845 4646*
– info@theadmiraltyrestaurant.com – Fax (020) 7845 46 58
– www.theadmiraltyrestaurant.com
– Closed 25-26 December and Sunday   J3
Rest *– Menu £ 22/25 – Carte £ 27/38*
◆ French ◆ Brasserie ◆
Within the magnificent surroundings of 18C Somerset House. Pretty dining room
divided into two rooms, both with plenty of light; the cooking ranges from regional French to international.

XX **The Forge** AC ⊕ VISA ◑◉ AE

14 Garrick Street ⊠ *WC2E 9BJ –* ◍ *Leicester Square –* ℰ *(020) 73791432*
– info@theforgerestaurant.co.uk – Fax (020) 73 79 15 30
– www.theforgerestaurant.co.uk
– Closed 24 and 25 December   I3
Rest *– Menu £ 17 (lunch) – Carte £ 31/35*
◆ Modern European ◆
Long and appealing menu, from eggs Benedict to Dover sole; good value theatre
menus and last orders at midnight. Most influences from within Europe. Large
room with downstairs bar.

XX **Le Deuxième** AC ⊕ VISA ◑◉ AE

65a Long Acre ⊠ *WC2E 9JH –* ◍ *Covent Garden –* ℰ *(020) 7379 0033*
– info@ledeuxieme.com – Fax (020) 7379 00 66 – www.ledeuxieme.com
– Closed 24-25 December   J3
Rest *– Menu £ 17 (lunch) – Carte £ 28/33*
◆ Modern European ◆ Brasserie ◆
Caters well for theatregoers: opens early, closes late. Buzzy eatery, quietly decora-
ted in white with subtle lighting. Varied international menu: Japanese to Mediter-
ranean.

X **L'Atelier de Joël Robuchon** AC ⊕ VISA ◑◉ AE

🍃🍃 *13-15 West St* ⊠ *WC2H 9NE –* ◍ *Leicester Square –* ℰ *(020) 7010 8600*
– info@joelrobuchon.co.uk – Fax (020) 7010 86 01 – www.joel-robuchon.com
Rest *– Menu £ 25 (lunch) – Carte £ 33/85*   I3
Rest *La Cuisine – (dinner only) Carte £ 45/105*
Spec. *Pig's trotter on parmesan toast with black truffle. Langoustine with
mango and basil relish. La Boule surprise.*
◆ French ◆ Fashionable ◆
Entrance into trendy atelier with counter seating; upstairs the more structured La
Cuisine; wonderfully delicate, precise modern French cooking. Cool top floor
lounge bar.

✗ Le Café du Jardin   AC 🦮 VISA ⓪ AE ⓪

28 Wellington St ✉ *WC2E 7BD* – Ⓜ *Covent Garden* – ✆ *(020) 7836 8769*
– *info@lecafedujardin.com* – *Fax (020) 7836 41 23*
– *www.lecafedujardin.com*
– *Closed 24-25 December*   **J3**
Rest – Menu £ 17 (lunch) – Carte £ 25/32 🕭

♦ Mediterranean ♦

Spread over two floors, with the bustle on the ground floor. Sunny, mostly Mediterranean cooking. Very busy early and late evening thanks to the good value theatre menus which change weekly.

✗ Bedford & Strand   VISA ⓪ AE

1a Bedford St ✉ *WC2E 9HH* – Ⓜ *Charing Cross* – ✆ *(020) 7836 3033*
– *hello@bedford-strand.com* – *www.bedford-strand.com*
– *Closed 25-26 and 31 December, 1 January, Saturday lunch, Sunday and Bank Holidays*   **J3**
Rest – *(booking essential)* Carte £ 22/35

♦ British ♦ Wine bar ♦

Basement bistro/wine bar with simple décor and easy-going atmosphere; kitchen sources well and has a light touch with Italian, French and British dishes.

Lambeth

🏨 London Marriott H. County Hall   ⇐ 𝄃 ⑳ 🕸 ▤ ᴕ rm AC ⚑

Westminster Bridge Rd ✉ *SE1 7PB*   𝄃 VISA ⓪ AE ⓪
– Ⓜ *Westminster* – ✆ *(020) 7928 5200* – *mhrs.lonch.salesadmin*
@marriotthotels.com – *Fax (020) 7928 53 00*
– *www.marriott.countyhall.com*   **J5**
195 rm – ♟£ 328 ♟♟£ 363, ⌸ £ 21.95 – 5 suites
Rest *County Hall* – Menu £ 26 – Carte £ 33/45

♦ Luxury ♦ Classic ♦

Occupying the historic County Hall building. Many of the spacious and comfortable bedrooms enjoy river and Parliament outlook. Impressive leisure facilities. World famous views from restaurant.

✗✗✗ Skylon   ⇐ AC VISA ⓪ AE ⓪

1 Southbank Centre, Belvedere Rd ✉ *SE1 8XX* – Ⓜ *Waterloo* – ✆ *(020) 7654 7800* – *skylon@danddlondon.com* – *Fax (020) 7654 78 01*
– *www.skylonrestaurant.co.uk*   **J4**
Rest – Menu £ 27 (lunch) – Carte £ 29/40 🕭

♦ Modern European ♦ Design ♦

1950s style dining flagship in Royal Festival Hall. Grill with bar, river views and easy-to-eat menu. Restaurant offers more ambitious dishes, which means higher prices.

BELGRAVIA & VICTORIA   *Plan IV*

Belgravia

🏨 The Berkeley   𝄃 ⑳ 🕸 ▤ AC ⚑ 𝄃 ☕ VISA ⓪ AE ⓪

Wilton Pl ✉ *SW1X 7RL* – Ⓜ *Knightsbridge* – ✆ *(020) 7235 6000*
– *info@the-berkeley.co.uk* – *Fax (020) 7235 43 30*
– *www.the-berkeley.co.uk*   **G4**
189 rm – ♟£ 552/658 ♟♟£ 658, ⌸ £ 26 – 25 suites
Rest *Marcus Wareing at The Berkeley* – see below
Rest *Boxwood Café* – Carte £ 28/35.50

♦ Grand Luxury ♦ Stylish ♦

Discreet and rejuvenated hotel with roof-top pool and opulently decorated bedrooms. Relax in the gilded and panelled Caramel Room or have a drink in the cool Blue Bar. Split-level basement restaurant, divided by bar with modern stylish décor; New York-style dining.

UNITED KINGDOM - LONDON

The Lanesborough

Hyde Park Corner ⊠ *SW1X 7TA –* Ⓜ *Hyde Park Corner*
– 𝒞 *(020) 7259 5599 – info@lanesborough.com*
– *Fax (020) 7259 56 06 – www.lanesborough.com* **G4**
86 rm – ♥£ 441/582 ♥♥£ 582, ⊊ £ 30 – 9 suites
Rest *Apsleys* – Carte £ 41/61
♦ Grand Luxury ♦ Classic ♦

Converted in the 1990s from 18C St George's Hospital. Butler service offered. Regency-era decorated, lavishly appointed rooms with impressive technological extras. Opulent, glass-roofed Italian restaurant with rustic food.

The Halkin

5 Halkin St ⊠ *SW1X 7DJ –* Ⓜ *Hyde Park Corner*
– 𝒞 *(020) 7333 1000 – res@halkin.como.bz*
– *Fax (020) 7333 11 00*
– *www.halkin.como.bz* **G5**
35 rm – ♥£ 458 ♥♥£ 458, ⊊ £ 26 – 6 suites
Rest *Nahm* – see below
♦ Luxury ♦ Stylish ♦

One of London's first minimalist hotels. The cool, marbled reception and bar have an understated charm. Spacious rooms have every conceivable facility.

Diplomat without rest

2 Chesham St ⊠ *SW1X 8DT –* Ⓜ *Sloane Square –* 𝒞 *(020) 7235 1544*
– *diplomat.hotel@btinternet.com – Fax (020) 7259 61 53*
– *www.btinternet.com/diplomat.hotel* **G5**
26 rm ⊊ – ♥£ 95/115 ♥♥£ 175
♦ Traditional ♦ Classic ♦

Imposing Victorian corner house built in 1882 by Thomas Cubitt. Attractive glass-domed stairwell and sweeping staircase. Spacious and well-appointed bedrooms.

Marcus Wareing at The Berkeley

Wilton Pl ⊠ *SW1X 7RL –* Ⓜ *Knightsbridge –* 𝒞 *(020) 7235 1200*
– *marcuswareing@the-berkeley.co.uk – Fax (020) 7235 12 66*
– *www.marcuswareing.com*
– *Closed 25-26 December, Saturday lunch and Sunday* **G4**
Rest – Menu £ 35/75
Spec. Poached lobster with braised trotters, vanilla butter and roasted salsify. Roasted veal, fricassee of snails, wild garlic and bacon. Lemon crème, salted caramel popcorn and milk ice cream.
♦ French ♦ Formal ♦

Intimate, richly-appointed restaurant serving exceptionally well-crafted, classically-inspired cuisine. Watch the kitchen at work from the chef's table. Polished, graceful service.

Amaya

Halkin Arcade, 19 Motcomb St ⊠ *SW1X 8JT –* Ⓜ *Knightsbridge*
– 𝒞 *(020) 7823 1166 – amaya@realindianfood.com*
– *Fax (020) 7259 64 64 – www.realindianfood.com*
– *closed 25 December* **F5**
Rest – Menu £ 22/40 – Carte approx. £ 34
Spec. Tandoori ocean wild prawns, tomato and ginger. Grilled lamb chops with lime and coriander. Whipped chocolate and yoghurt.
♦ Indian ♦ Fashionable ♦

Light, piquant and aromatic Indian cooking specialising in kebabs from a tawa skillet, sigri grill or tandoor oven. Chic comfortable surroundings, modern and subtly exotic.

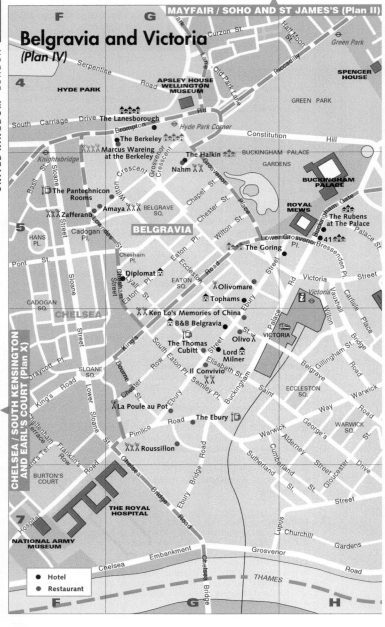

UNITED KINGDOM - LONDON

Belgravia and Victoria
(Plan IV)

CHELSEA / SOUTH KENSINGTON AND EARL'S COURT (Plan X)

HYDE PARK

APSLEY HOUSE
WELLINGTON
MUSEUM

SPENCER HOUSE

Green Park

GREEN PARK

The Lanesborough

The Berkeley

Marcus Wareing
at the Berkeley

The Halkin

Nahm

Knightsbridge

The Pantechnicon
Rooms

Zafferano

Amaya

BELGRAVE
SQ.

BELGRAVIA

BUCKINGHAM PALACE

GARDENS

BUCKINGHAM
PALACE

ROYAL
MEWS

The Rubens
at The Palace

41

HANS
PL.

Diplomat

EATON
SQ.

Olivomare

Tophams

The Goring

Lower Grosvenor
Pl.

CADOGAN
SQ.

CHELSEA

Ken Lo's Memories of China

B&B Belgravia

The Thomas
Cubitt

Il Convivio

Olivo

Lord
Milner

VICTORIA

SLOANE
SQ.

La Poule au Pot

The Ebury

ECCLESTON
SQ.

WARWICK
SQ.

Roussillon

BURTON'S
COURT

THE ROYAL
HOSPITAL

NATIONAL ARMY
MUSEUM

THAMES

● Hotel
● Restaurant

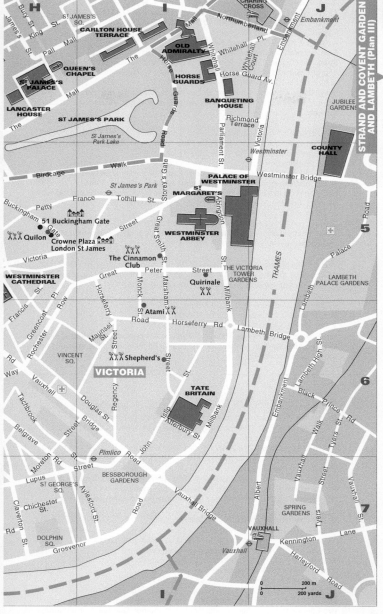

CHARING CROSS

Embankment

Northumberland

St James's Park

CARLTON HOUSE TERRACE

Bury St

King St

James's St

St JAMES'S SQ.

Pall Mall

The Mall

OLD ADMIRALTY

Whitehall

Whitehall Pl.

Whitehall Court

JUBILEE GARDENS

QUEEN'S CHAPEL

HORSE GUARDS

Horse Guard Av.

St JAMES'S PALACE

Horse Guards Road

BANQUETING HOUSE

LANCASTER HOUSE

The Mall

ST JAMES'S PARK

Richmond Terrace

Victoria

COUNTY HALL

St James's Park Lake

Westminster

Birdcage

Walk

St James's Park

Westminster Bridge

THAMES

Buckingham

Petty

France

Tothill St.

Storey's Gate

Great George's

PALACE OF WESTMINSTER

Abingdon

St MARGARET'S

51 Buckingham Gate

Gate

Street

Great Smith St.

WESTMINSTER ABBEY

Palace Road

Quilon

Crowne Plaza London St James

The Cinnamon Club

Peter

Street

THE VICTORIA TOWER GARDENS

LAMBETH PALACE GARDENS

Victoria

Great

Monck

Quirinale

St

Marsham

Millbank

WESTMINSTER CATHEDRAL

Street

St

Francis

St

Horseferry

Atami

Horseferry Rd.

Lambeth Bridge

Greencoat Pl.

Row

Rochester

Road

Maunsel Street

Embankment

Lambeth High St.

VINCENT SQ.

Shepherd's

Street

Black

Prince

Rd

Way

Vauxhall

Regency St.

VICTORIA

TATE BRITAIN

Walk

Tyers St.

Vauxhall St.

Tachbrook

Douglas St.

Street

Bridge

Islip St.

Atterbury St.

Millbank

Belgrave

Moreton

Rd.

St.

Pimlico

John

Road

Lupus

St GEORGE'S SQ.

Street

BESSBOROUGH GARDENS

Aylesford St.

Vauxhall Bridge

Chichester St.

Albert

SPRING GARDENS

Tyers Street

Vauxhall St.

Claverton St.

Rd

DOLPHIN SQ.

Grosvenor

VAUXHALL

Kennington

Lane

Harleyford Road

Vauxhall

0   200 m
0   200 yards

917

XXX ✿ Zafferano   AC ⇔ VISA ⚭ AE ⓪

15 Lowndes St ⊠ SW1X 9EY – Ⓜ Knightsbridge – ℰ (020) 7235 5800
– info@zafferanorestaurant.com – Fax (020) 7235 19 71
– www.zafferanorestaurant.com
– closed 2 weeks Christmas-New Year   **F5**
Rest *– (booking essential)* Menu £ 35/45 ⅋
Spec. Sliced cured beef, rocket and goat's cheese. Grilled monkfish with courgettes and sweet chilli. Chocolate fondant with gianduia ice cream.
♦ Italian ♦ Fashionable ♦
Busy, three–roomed restaurant decorated in Mediterranean colours. Classic, unfussy, flavoursome Italian cooking, where the quality of the ingredients shines through.

XX ✿ Nahm – at The Halkin Hotel   AC ⇔ VISA ⚭ AE ⓪

5 Halkin St ⊠ SW1X 7DJ – Ⓜ Hyde Park Corner – ℰ (020) 7333 1234
– res@nahm.como.bz – Fax (020) 7333 11 00
– www.halkin.como.bz   **G5**
Rest *– (closed 25 December, 1 January, Easter, Saturday-Sunday lunch and Bank Holidays) (booking advisable)* Menu £ 26/55 – Carte £ 40/46
Spec. Salted chicken wafers, longans and Thai basil. Pork belly braised with peanuts. Coconut cake with rambutans and perfumed syrup.
♦ Thai ♦ Design ♦
Discreet, comfortable dining room; sleek understated décor. Sophisticated cooking showcases the harmony of Thai cooking achieved through careful combinations of textures and flavours.

🛏 The Pantechnicon Rooms   VISA ⚭ AE ⓪

10 Motcomb St ⊠ SW1X 8LA – Ⓜ Knightsbridge – ℰ (020) 77306074
– reservations@thepantechnicon.com – Fax (020) 77 30 60 55
– www.thepantechnicon.com
– Closed 25 December and Good Friday   **G5**
Rest – Menu £ 25 (lunch) – Carte £ 25/50
♦ Modern European ♦ Pub ♦
Same owners as the nearby Thomas Cubitt; a smart pub with more formal dining room upstairs. Shellfish and seafood a speciality. Bright, comfortable surroundings with enthusiastic service.

Victoria

🏨 The Goring   🚗 AC 🖥 📞 🛁 VISA ⚭ AE ⓪

15 Beeston Pl, Grosvenor Gdns ⊠ SW1W 0JW – Ⓜ Victoria
– ℰ (020) 7396 9000 – reception@goringhotel.co.uk – Fax (020) 7834 43 93
– www.goringhotel.co.uk   **H5**
65 rm – ♦£ 234/388 ♦♦£ 246/717, ⌑ £ 24 – 6 suites
Rest *– (Closed Saturday lunch)* Menu £ 37/49 ⅋
♦ Traditional ♦ Luxury ♦ Classic ♦
Opened in 1910 as a quintessentially English hotel. The fourth generation of Goring is now at the helm. Many of the attractive rooms overlook a peaceful garden. Elegantly appointed restaurant provides memorable dining experience.

🏨 Crowne Plaza London - St James   🖿 🕅 ⅃ rm AC 🖥 📞 🛁

45 Buckingham Gate ⊠ SW1E 6AF   VISA ⚭ AE ⓪
– Ⓜ St James's Park – ℰ (020) 7834 6655 – sales@cplonsj.co.uk
– Fax (020) 7630 75 87 – www.london.crowneplaza.com   **H5**
323 rm – ♦£ 323 ♦♦£ 388, ⌑ £ 14.25 – 19 suites
Rest *Quilon* and **Bank** – see below
Rest *Bistro 51* – Menu £ 18/22 – Carte £ 32/43
♦ Luxury ♦ Classic ♦
Built in 1897 as serviced accommodation for visiting aristocrats. Behind the impressive Edwardian façade lies an equally elegant interior. Quietest rooms overlook courtyard. Bright and informal café-style restaurant.

51 Buckingham Gate without rest

51 Buckingham Gate ⌧ *SW1E 6AF* – Ⓜ *St James's Park*
– ℰ *(020) 7769 7766* – info@51-buckinghamgate.co.uk
– *Fax (020) 7828 59 09* – www.51-buckinghamgate.com　　　**H5**
86 suites – ♥♥£ 452/670, ⌸ £ 22
Rest Quilon and **Bank** – see below
♦ Luxury ♦ Classic ♦

Canopied entrance leads to luxurious suites: every detail considered, every mod con provided. Colour schemes echoed in plants and paintings. Butler and nanny service.

41 without rest

41 Buckingham Palace Rd ⌧ *SW1W 0PS* – Ⓜ *Victoria*
– ℰ *(020) 7300 0041* – book41@rchmail.com – *Fax (020) 7300 01 41*
– www.41hotel.com　　　**H5**
28 rm – ♥£ 264/382 ♥♥£ 288/415, ⌸ £ 25 – 1 suite
♦ Luxury ♦ Classic ♦

Discreet appearance; exudes exclusive air. Leather armchairs; bookcases line the walls. Intimate service. State-of-the-art rooms where hi-tec and fireplace merge appealingly.

The Rubens at The Palace

39 Buckingham Palace Rd ⌧ *SW1W 0PS* – Ⓜ *Victoria*
– ℰ *(020) 7834 6600* – bookrb@rchmail.com – *Fax (020) 7828 54 01*
– www.rubenshotel.com　　　**H5**
159 rm – ♥£ 292/304 ♥♥£ 304/320, ⌸ £ 18.50 – 2 suites
Rest – *(closed lunch Saturday and Sunday)* Menu £ 28 – Carte dinner £ 28/45
♦ Traditional ♦ Classic ♦

Traditional hotel with an air of understated elegance. Tastefully furnished rooms: the Royal Wing, themed after Kings and Queens, features TVs in bathrooms. Smart carvery restaurant.

Tophams without rest

24-32 Ebury Street ⌧ *SW1W 0LU* – Ⓜ *Victoria*
– ℰ *(020) 7730 3313* – tophams.reservations@zolahotels.com
– *Fax (020) 7730 00 08* – www.zolahotels.com/tophams　　　**G5**
47 rm – ♥£ 160/195 ♥♥£ 175/195, ⌸ £ 11 – 1 suite
♦ Townhouse ♦ Personalised ♦

Reopened in 2008, after a major refit. A row of five terraced houses, in a good spot for tourists. Neat bedrooms with large bathrooms and good mod cons. Comfortable breakfast room.

B + B Belgravia without rest

64-66 Ebury St ⌧ *SW1W 9QD* – Ⓜ *Victoria* – ℰ *(020) 7259 8570*
– info@bb-belgravia.com – *Fax (020) 7259 85 91* – www.bb-belgravia.com
17 rm ⌸ – ♥£ 99 ♥♥£ 125/130　　　**G6**
♦ Townhouse ♦ Personalised ♦

Two houses, three floors, and, considering the location, some of the best value accommodation in town. Sleek, clean-lined rooms. Breakfast overlooking little garden terrace.

Lord Milner without rest

111 Ebury Street ⌧ *SW1W 9QU* – Ⓜ *Victoria* – ℰ *(020) 7881 9880*
– info@lordmilner.com – *Fax (020) 7730 80 27*
– www.lordmilner.com　　　**G6**
11 rm – ♥£ 115 ♥♥£ 145/255, ⌸ £ 11.50
♦ Townhouse ♦ Classic ♦

A four storey terrace house, with individually decorated bedrooms, three with four-poster beds and all with marble bathrooms. Garden Suite the best room, with its own patio. No public areas.

XXX ⊗

Roussillon (Alex Gauthier)　　　　　　　AC VISA ⊚ AE

16 St Barnabas St ⊠ SW1W 8PE – Ⓜ Sloane Square – ℰ (020) 7730 5550
– alexis@roussillon.co.uk – Fax (020) 7824 86 17 – www.roussillon.co.uk
– Closed 25-26 December, Easter, Saturday lunch and Sunday　　　　**G6**
Rest – Menu £ 35/55 ఞ
Spec. Sesame seed crusted langoustines with basil and tomato broth. Red deer with celeriac and truffle purée, poached pear. Louis XV crunchy praline and chocolate.

◆ French ◆ Neighbourhood ◆

Tucked away in a smart residential area. Cooking clearly focuses on the quality of the ingredients. Seasonal menu with inventive elements and a French base.

XXX ⊗

Quilon – at Crowne Plaza London - St James Hotel　　AC VISA ⊚ AE

41 Buckingham Gate ⊠ SW1 6AF – Ⓜ St James's Park – ℰ (020) 7821 1899
– info@quilonrestaurant.co.uk – Fax (020) 7233 95 97 – www.quilon.co.uk
– Closed Saturday lunch　　　　**H5**
Rest – Menu £ 20/35 – Carte £ 35/46
Spec. Marinated scallops grilled and served with spiced coconut cream. Lobster with mango, ginger, kokum and curry leaves. Almond delight with praline, yoghurt and almond ice cream.

◆ Indian ◆

Original, vibrant and well balanced Indian dishes, many of which originate from the South West coast. Excellent use of spices, appealing seafood specialities and graceful service.

XXX

The Cinnamon Club　　AC ⇔ P. ⊟ VISA ⊚ AE ⓪

30-32 Great Smith St ⊠ SW1P 3BU – Ⓜ St James's Park – ℰ (020) 7222 2555
– info@cinnamonclub.com – Fax (020) 7222 13 33 – www.cinnamonclub.com
– Closed 26 December, 1 January, Sunday and Bank Holiday Mondays
Rest – Menu £ 22 (lunch) – Carte £ 34/54　　　　**I5**
◆ Indian ◆

Housed in former Westminster Library: exterior has ornate detail, interior is stylish and modern. Walls are lined with books. New Wave Indian cooking with plenty of choice.

XXX

Shepherd's　　AC ⇔ VISA ⊚ AE ⓪

Marsham Court, Marsham St ⊠ SW1P 4LA – Ⓜ Pimlico – ℰ (020) 7834 9552
– admin@langansrestaurants.co.uk – Fax (020) 7233 60 47
– www.langansrestaurants.co.uk – Closed Saturday, Sunday and Bank Holidays
Rest – (booking essential) Menu £ 34　　　　**I6**
◆ British ◆ Formal ◆

A truly English restaurant where game and traditional puddings are a highlight. Popular with those from Westminster - the booths offer a degree of privacy.

XX

Atami　　AC VISA ⊚ AE

37 Monck St (entrance on Great Peter St) ⊠ SW1P 2BL – Ⓜ Pimlico
– ℰ (020) 7222 2218 – mail@atami-restaurant.com – Fax (020) 7222 27 88
– www.atami-restaurant.com – Closed Saturday lunch　　　　**I6**
Rest – Menu £ 23/45 – Carte approx. £ 35
◆ Japanese ◆ Design ◆

Clean, modern lines illuminated by vast ceiling orbs induce a sense of calm. Menus true to Japanese roots feature sushi and sashimi turning down interesting modern highways.

XX

Il Convivio　　AC ⇔ VISA ⊚ AE

143 Ebury St ⊠ SW1W 9QN – Ⓜ Sloane Square – ℰ (020) 7730 4099
– comments@etruscarestaurants.com – Fax (020) 7730 41 03
– www.etruscarestaurants.com
– closed 25-26 December, Sunday and Bank Holidays　　　　**G6**
Rest – Menu £ 22 (lunch) – Carte £ 33/41
◆ Italian ◆ Design ◆

A retractable roof provides alfresco dining to part of this comfortable and modern restaurant. Contemporary and traditional Italian menu with home-made pasta specialities.

UNITED KINGDOM - LONDON

XX **Ken Lo's Memories of China**   AC ⇄ VISA ⬤ AE ①
65-69 Ebury St ⊠ SW1W 0NZ – ⓜ *Victoria –* ℰ *(020) 7730 7734*
– Fax (020) 7730 29 92 – www.memories-of-china.co.uk
– Closed 25-26 December, Sunday lunch and Bank Holidays   **G6**
Rest – Menu £ 20/32 – Carte £ 31/51
♦ Chinese ♦ Neighbourhood ♦
An air of tranquillity pervades this traditionally furnished room. Lattice screens
add extra privacy. Extensive Chinese menu: bold flavours with a clean, fresh
style.

XX **Quirinale**   VISA ⬤ AE ①
North Court, 1 Great Peter St ⊠ SW1P 3LL – ⓜ *Westminster*
– ℰ (020) 7222 7080 – info@quirinale.co.uk – www.quirinale.co.uk
– Closed August, 1 week Christmas - New Year, Saturday, Sunday and Bank
Holidays   **I5**
Rest – Carte £ 34/40
♦ Italian ♦ Neighbourhood ♦
Light and bright Italian restaurant with contemporary, minimalist feel typified
by cream leather banquettes. Seasonally-changing menu encompasses all things
Italian.

X **Olivo**   AC VISA ⬤ AE ①
21 Eccleston St ⊠ SW1W 9LX – ⓜ *Victoria –* ℰ *(020) 7730 2505*
– maurosanna@oliveto.fsnet.co.uk – Fax (020) 7823 53 77
– www.olivorestaurant.com
– Closed Bank Holidays, lunch Saturday and Sunday   **G6**
Rest – Menu £ 23 (lunch) – Carte £ 25/33
♦ Italian ♦ Neighbourhood ♦
Rustic, informal Italian restaurant. Relaxed atmosphere provided by the friendly
staff. Simple, non-fussy cuisine with emphasis on best available fresh produce.

X **La Poule au Pot**   ⌂ AC VISA ⬤ AE ①
231 Ebury St ⊠ SW1W 8UT – ⓜ *Sloane Square –* ℰ *(020) 7730 7763*
– Fax (020) 7259 96 51
– Closed 25-26 December and 1 January   **G6**
Rest – Menu £ 18 (lunch) – Carte £ 29/42
♦ French ♦ Bistro ♦
The subdued lighting and friendly informality make this one of London's more
romantic restaurants. Classic French menu with extensive plats du jour.

X **Olivomare**   ⌂ AC VISA ⬤ AE ①
10 Lower Belgrave St ⊠ SW1W 0LJ – ⓜ *Victoria –* ℰ *(020) 7730 9022*
– maurosanna@oliveto.fsnet.co.uk – Fax (020) 7823 53 77
– www.olivorestaurants.com
– Closed Sunday and Bank Holidays   **G5**
Rest – Carte £ 28/33
♦ Seafood ♦ Design ♦
Chic minimalist décor with magic-eye mural of intertwined fish. The food is robust
and full-flavoured; seafood is the theme, with a subtle Sardinian subtext. Assured
service.

⌂ **The Ebury**   AC VISA ⬤ AE
11 Pimlico Rd ⊠ SW1W 8NA – ⓜ *Sloane Square –* ℰ *(020) 7730 6784*
– info@theebury.co.uk – Fax (020) 7730 61 49
– www.theebury.co.uk
– Closed 25 December   **G6**
Rest – Menu £ 20 (lunch) – Carte £ 30/45
♦ Pub ♦
Victorian corner pub restaurant with walnut bar, simple tables and large seafood
bar. Friendly service. Wide-ranging menu from snacks to full meals.

🏠 **The Thomas Cubitt** VISA ⓌⓈ AE Ⓞ

44 Elizabeth Street ✉ SW1W 9PA – Ⓜ *Sloane Square*. – ℰ *(020) 7730 6060*
– *reservations@thethomascubitt.co.uk – Fax (020) 7730 60 55*
– *www.thethomascubitt.co.uk*
– *Closed 25 December, Good Friday* **G6**
Rest – *(booking essential)* Carte £ 30/60
♦ Pub ♦

Georgian pub refurbished and renamed after master builder. He'd approve of elegant, formal dining room. Carefully supplied ingredients underpin tasty, seasonal English dishes.

REGENT'S PARK & MARYLEBONE *Plan V*

🏨 **Landmark London** without rest 🛗 🕙 🐾 ☒ ⅙ 🅰 📠 📞 🛄 🏌 🏌

222 Marylebone Rd ✉ NW1 6JQ – Ⓜ *Edgware Rd* VISA ⓌⓈ AE Ⓞ
– ℰ *(020) 7631 8000 – reservations@thelandmark.co.uk – Fax (020) 7631 80 80*
– *www.landmarklondon.co.uk* **F1**
290 rm – 🛏£ 329/535 🛏£ 364/535, ☐ £ 28 – 9 suites
♦ Grand Luxury ♦ Classic ♦

Imposing Victorian Gothic building with a vast glass enclosed atrium, overlooked by many of the modern, well-equipped bedrooms.

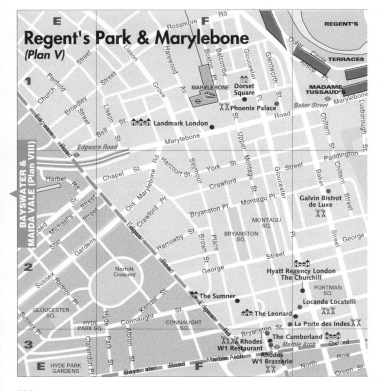

Langham *Lb* 🕸 🖾 ⅍ rm AC SAT 🕿 🔏 VISA 🗯 AE ①

1c Portland Pl, Regent St ⊠ *W1B 1JA –* Ⓜ *Oxford Circus –* ℰ *(020) 7636 1000*
– loninfo@langhamhotels.com – Fax (020) 7323 23 40
– www.langhamhotels.com   **H2**
365 rm – 🛉£ 476 🛉🛉£ 476, ⊈ £ 27.50 – 17 suites
Rest – Menu £ 37.50/45 – Carte £ 39/47
♦ Luxury ♦ Classic ♦
A classic Victorian hotel with a long history, opposite the BBC. Currently undergoing a major refurbishment to be completed by early 2009.

The Cumberland *Lb* ₺ AC ⅝¹ 🔏 VISA 🗯 AE ①

Great Cumberland Place ⊠ *W1H 4DL –* Ⓜ *Marble Arch –* ℰ *(0870) 3339280*
– enquiries@thecumberland.co.uk – Fax (0870) 3 33 92 81 – www.guoman.com
1010 rm ⊈ – 🛉£ 358 🛉🛉£ 366   **FG3**
Rest Rhodes W1 Restaurant and **Rhodes W1 Brasserie** – *see below*
♦ Business ♦ Design ♦
Fully refurbished, conference oriented hotel whose vast lobby boasts modern art,
sculpture and running water panels. Distinctive bedrooms with a host of impressive extras.

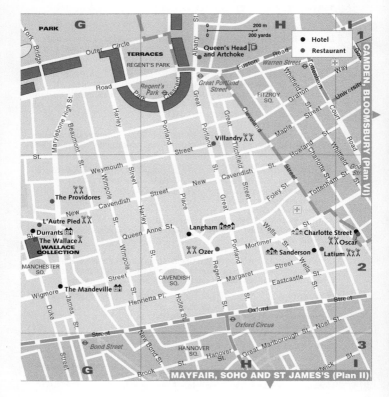

Hyatt Regency London-The Churchill

30 Portman Sq ✉ *W1H 7BH*
– Ⓜ *Marble Arch* – ℰ *(020) 7486 5800 – london.churchill@hyatt.com*
– *Fax (020) 7486 12 55 – www.london.churchill.hyatt.com*
404 rm – †£ 194/447 ††£ 217/470, ⊿ £ 25 – 40 suites

G2

Rest *The Montagu* – Menu £ 22/25 – Carte £ 35/47
♦ Luxury ♦ Classic ♦
Smart property overlooking attractive square. Elegant marbled lobby. Well-appointed and recently refurbished rooms have the international traveller in mind. Restaurant provides popular Sunday brunch entertainment.

Charlotte Street

15 Charlotte St ✉ *W1T 1RJ* – Ⓜ *Goodge Street* – ℰ *(020) 7806 2000*
– *charlotte@firmdale.com – Fax (020) 7806 20 02*
– *www.charlottestreethotel.co.uk*

I2

48 rm – †£ 259/294 ††£ 364, ⊿ £ 19 – 4 suites   **Rest *Oscar*** – see below
♦ Luxury ♦ Stylish ♦
Interior designed with a charming and understated English feel. Welcoming lobby laden with floral displays. Individually decorated rooms with CDs and mobile phones.

Sanderson

50 Berners St ✉ *W1T 3NG* – ⓂOxford Circus* – ℰ *(020) 7300 1400*
– *sanderson@morganshotelgroup.com – Fax (020) 7300 14 01*
– *www.morganshotelgroup.com*

H2

150 rm – †£ 282/423 ††£ 282/423, ⊿ £ 25
Rest *Suka* – Menu £ 24 – Carte £ 27/55
♦ Luxury ♦ Minimalist ♦
Designed by Philipe Starck: the height of contemporary design. Bar is the place to see and be seen. Bedrooms with minimalistic white décor have DVDs and striking bathrooms. Malaysian dishes designed for sharing in Suka.

The Leonard

15 Seymour St ✉ *W1H 7JW* – ⓂMarble Arch* – ℰ *(020) 7935 2010*
– *reservations@theleonard.com – Fax (020) 7935 67 00 – www.theleonard.com*
32 rm – †£ 153 ††£ 293, ⊿ £ 19.50 – 16 suites

G2

Rest – *(Closed Sunday dinner)* Carte £ 21/27
♦ Townhouse ♦ Classic ♦
Around the corner from Selfridges, an attractive Georgian townhouse: antiques and oil paintings abound. Well-appointed rooms in classic country house style. Intimate front dining room.

Dorset Square

39-40 Dorset Sq ✉ *NW1 6QN* – ⓂMarylebone* – ℰ *(020) 7723 7874*
– *reservations@dorsetsquare.co.uk – Fax (020) 7724 33 28*
– *www.dorsetsquare.co.uk*
– *Closed 1 week Christmas*

F1

37 rm – †£ 165/282 ††£ 206/329, ⊿ £ 14.50
Rest *The Potting Shed* – *(Closed Saturday lunch and Sunday dinner) (booking essential)* Menu £ 23
♦ Townhouse ♦ Classic ♦
Converted Regency townhouses in a charming square and the site of the original Lord's cricket ground. A relaxed country house in the city. Individually decorated rooms. The Potting Shed features modern cuisine and a set business menu.

Durrants

26-32 George St ✉ *W1H 5BJ* – ⓂBond Street* – ℰ *(020) 7935 8131*
– *enquiries@durrantshotel.co.uk – Fax (020) 7487 35 10*
– *www.durrantshotel.co.uk*

G2

89 rm – †£ 125 ††£ 175, ⊿ £ 14.50 – 3 suites
Rest – Menu £ 22 – Carte £ 30/43
♦ Traditional ♦ Classic ♦
Traditional, privately owned hotel with friendly, long-standing staff. Newly refurbished bedrooms are brighter in style but still English in character. Clubby dining room for mix of British classics and lighter, European dishes.

UNITED KINGDOM - LONDON

The Mandeville ⅍ 🏧 ⅍ 📺 ⸾⸾ 🐾 🆅🆂🅰 ⊚ 🅰🅴 ⊙

Mandeville Pl ⊠ W1V 2BE – Ⓜ Bond Street
– 𝒞 (020) 79355599 – info@mandeville.co.uk
– Fax (020) 79 35 95 88   **G2**
135 rm – ♥£ 250/275 ♥♥£ 275/450, � £ – 7 suites
Rest *de Ville* – *(Closed Sunday)* Menu £ 25 – Carte £ 37/44
♦ Chain hotel ♦ Design ♦

Fashionably located hotel, refurbished in 2005 with marbled reception and strikingly colourful bar. Stylish rooms have flatscreen TVs and make good use of the space available. Informal restaurant serving modern British cuisine.

The Sumner *without rest* ⅍ 🏧 ⸾⸾ 🆅🆂🅰 ⊚ 🅰🅴 ⊙

54 Upper Berkeley St ⊠ W1H 7QR – Ⓜ Marble Arch – 𝒞 (020) 7723 2244
– hotel@thesumner.com – Fax (0870) 705 87 67 – www.thesumner.com
20 rm ⊟ – ♥£ 165 ♥♥£ 188   **F2**
♦ Townhouse ♦ Personalised ♦

Two Georgian terrace houses in developing area of town. Comfy, stylish sitting room; basement breakfast room. Largest bedrooms, 101 and 201, have sunny, full-length windows.

Rhodes W1 (Restaurant) – *at The Cumberland Hotel* 🆅🆂🅰 ⊚ 🅰🅴
𝟪𝟯

Great Cumberland Place ⊠ W1H 7DL – Ⓜ Marble Arch – 𝒞 (020) 7616 5930
– restaurant@rhodesw1.com – Fax (020) 7479 38 88
– www.rhodesw1.com
– Closed Christmas - New Year, 1 week August, Saturday lunch, Sunday and Monday   **F3**
Rest – *(booking advisable)* Menu £ 32/65 – Carte £ 65/83 🍴
Spec. Crispy pork belly, langoustine, caramelised apple and vanilla. Roast pigeon, pig's trotter, navet and chutney sauce. Hot chocolate moelleux, salted chocolate mousse, crème fraîche sorbet.
♦ French ♦

Just 12 tables in a warm and textured room designed by Kelly Hoppen. Influences are more European than usual for a Gary Rhodes restaurant but with the same emphasis on clear, uncluttered flavours.

Locanda Locatelli 🏧 🆅🆂🅰 ⊚ 🅰🅴
𝟪𝟯

8 Seymour St ⊠ W1H 7JZ – Ⓜ Marble Arch – 𝒞 (020) 7935 9088
– info@locandalocatelli.com – Fax (020) 7935 11 49
– www.locandalocatelli.com
– Closed 25 December   **G2**
Rest – Carte £ 41/58 🍴
Spec. Deep fried calf's foot salad and mustard fruit. Veal with Parma ham, sage and aubergine. Tasting of Amedei chocolate.
♦ Italian ♦ Fashionable ♦

Forever popular restaurant serving authentic, seasonal Italian cooking of outstanding quality, complemented by a comprehensive wine list. Best tables are the corner booths.

Latium 🏧 🆅🆂🅰 ⊚ 🅰🅴 ⊙

21 Berners St, Fitzrovia ⊠ W1T 3LP – Ⓜ Oxford Circus
– 𝒞 (020) 7323 9123 – info@latiumrestaurant.com
– Fax (020) 7323 32 05
– www.latiumrestaurant.com
– Closed Christmas, New Year, Saturday lunch, Sunday and Bank Holidays
Rest – Menu £ 20/30   **H2**
♦ Italian ♦ Neighbourhood ♦

Welcoming restaurant owned by affable chef. Smart feel with well-spaced linen-clad tables, tiled floors and rural pictures. Italian country cooking in the heart of town.

XX **L'Autre Pied** (Marcus Eaves)   AC VISA ©© AE
£3
5-7 Blandford Street ⊠ W1U 3DB – ⓜ Bond Street – ℰ (020) 74869696
– info@lautrepied.co.uk – Fax (020) 74 86 50 67 – www.lautrepied.co.uk
– closed 23-29 December   **G2**
Rest – Menu £ 20 (lunch) – Carte £ 35/46 ⅋
Spec. Seared foie gras, artichokes and pineapple sorbet. Saddle of rabbit,
courgette, polenta with chorizo and black olive jus. Black Forest millefeuille.
♦ Modern European ♦
A more informal sibling to Pied à Terre, with red leather seating, closely set tables
and relaxed atmosphere. But cooking is just as ambitious: it is original, creative and
technically adroit.

XX **Rhodes W1 Brasserie** – at The Cumberland H.   AC ⅋ VISA ©© AE
Great Cumberland Pl ⊠ W1A 4RF – ⓜ Marble Arch – ℰ (020) 7616 5930
– brasserie@rhodesw1.com – Fax (020) 7479 38 88 – www.garyrhodes.com
Rest – Carte £ 25/42   **F3**
♦ British ♦ Brasserie ♦
In the heart of the Cumberland Hotel, a very stylish dining experience with impres-
sively high ceiling and classical Gary Rhodes dishes bringing out the best of the
seasons.

XX **Galvin Bistrot de Luxe**   AC ⅋ VISA ©© AE
☺
66 Baker St ⊠ W1U 7DJ – ⓜ Baker Street – ℰ (020) 7935 4007
– info@galvinuk.com – Fax (020) 7486 17 35 – www.galvinuk.com
– Closed 25-26 December and 1 January   **G2**
Rest – Menu £ 16 (lunch) – Carte £ 24/35
♦ French ♦ Bistro ♦
A modern take on the classic Gallic bistro with ceiling fans, globe lights, rich wood
panelled walls and French influenced dishes where precision and good value are
paramount.

XX **Oscar** – at Charlotte Street Hotel   AC VISA ©© AE ⓪
15 Charlotte St ⊠ W1T 1RJ – ⓜ Goodge Street – ℰ (020) 7907 4005
– charlotte@firmdale.com – Fax (020) 7806 20 02
– www.charlottestreethotel.co.uk
– Closed Sunday lunch   **I2**
Rest – (booking essential) Carte £ 31/46
♦ Modern European ♦ Trendy ♦
Bright room with busy bar at the front and dominated by a large, vivid
mural. Sunny Mediterranean-influenced dishes, served by attentive staff.

XX **The Providores**   AC VISA ©© AE
109 Marylebone High St ⊠ W1U 4RX – ⓜ Bond Street – ℰ (020) 7935 6175
– anyone@theprovidores.co.uk – Fax (020) 7935 68 77
– www.theprovidores.co.uk
– Closed 25-26 December and 1-2 January   **G2**
Rest – Menu £ 44 (dinner) – Carte £ 19/61
♦ Innovative ♦ Trendy ♦
Packed ground floor for tapas; upstairs for innovative fusion cooking, with spices
and ingredients from around the world, including Australasia. Starter-size dishes
at dinner allow for greater choice.

XX **La Porte des Indes**   AC ⇔ VISA ©© AE ⓪
32 Bryanston St ⊠ W1H 7EG – ⓜ Marble Arch – ℰ (020) 7224 0055
– london.reservation@laportedesindes.com – Fax (020) 7224 11 44
– www.laportedesindes.com
– Closed 25-26 December, 1 January and Saturday   **F2**
Rest – Menu £ 15/28 – Carte £ 27/42
♦ Indian ♦ Exotic ♦
Don't be fooled by the discreet entrance: inside there is a spectacularly unrestrained display of palm trees, murals and waterfalls. French influenced Indian
cuisine.

XX **Ozer**   `AC` `VISA` `MO` `AE` `O`

4-5 Langham Pl, Regent St ✉ *W1B 3DG* – Ⓜ *Oxford Circus*
– ☎ *(020) 7323 0505 – info@sofra.co.uk – Fax (020) 7323 01 11*
– www.sofra.co.uk   **H2**
Rest – Menu £ 21 – Carte £ 17/25
♦ Turkish ♦ Design ♦
Behind the busy and vibrantly decorated bar you'll find a smart modern restaurant.
Lively atmosphere and efficient service of modern, light and aromatic Turkish cooking.

XX **Roka**   `AC` `VISA` `MO` `AE` `O`

37 Charlotte St ✉ *W1T 1RR* – Ⓜ *Tottenham Court Road* – ☎ *(020) 7580 6464*
– info@rokarestaurant.com – Fax (020) 7580 02 20 – www.rokarestaurant.com
– Closed 25 December and 1 January   *Plan VI* **I2**
Rest – Carte approx. £ 29
♦ Japanese ♦ Fashionable ♦
Striking glass and steel frontage. Airy, atmospheric interior of teak, oak and paper
wall screens. Authentic, flavoursome Japanese cuisine with variety of grill dishes.

XX **Phoenix Palace**   `AC` `⇔` `VISA` `MO` `AE`

3-5 Glentworth St ✉ *NW1 5PG* – Ⓜ *Baker Street* – ☎ *(020) 7486 3515*
– info@phoenixpalace.uk.com – Fax (020) 7486 34 01
– www.phoenixpalace.uk.com   **F1**
Rest – Menu £ 25 (dinner) – Carte approx. £ 20
♦ Chinese ♦ Friendly ♦
Tucked away near Baker Street; lots of photos of celebrities who've eaten here.
Huge room for 200 diners where authentic, fresh, well prepared Chinese dishes
are served.

XX **Villandry**   `AC` `VISA` `MO` `AE` `O`

170 Great Portland St ✉ *W1W 5QB* – Ⓜ *Regent's Park* – ☎ *(020) 7631 3131*
– contactus@villandry.com – Fax (020) 7631 30 30 – www.villandry.com
– Closed 25-26 and 31 December, 1 January and Sunday dinner   **H1**
Rest – Menu £ 30/35 – Carte £ 27/43
♦ French ♦
The senses are heightened by passing through the well-stocked deli to the dining
room behind. Bare walls, wooden tables and a menu offering simple, tasty dishes.

XX **Osteria Stecca**   `🌭` `AC` `VISA` `MO` `AE` `O`

1 Blenheim Terrace ✉ *NW8 0EH* – Ⓜ *St John's Wood* – ☎ *(020) 7328 5014*
– info@osteriastecca.com – www.osteriastecca.com
– Closed Monday lunch   *Plan I* **B2**
Rest – Menu £ 16 (lunch) – Carte dinner approx. £ 40
♦ Italian ♦
Terrace, conservatory and brilliant white walls ensure a bright atmosphere. Reope-
ned in 2008, with a former chef back as owner. Undemanding menu of fully gar-
nished dishes covers all parts of Italy.

X **The Wallace**   `↳` `VISA` `MO` `AE`

Hertford House, Manchester Sq ✉ *W1U 3BN* – Ⓜ *Bond St* – ☎ *(020) 7563 9505*
– reservations@thewallacerestaurant.com – www.thewallacerestaurant.com
– Closed 25 December   **G2**
Rest – *(lunch only and dinner Friday-Saturday)* Menu £ 25 – Carte £ 30/41
♦ French ♦ Friendly ♦
Situated in the Wallace Collection's delightful glass-roofed courtyard, divided by
Japanese maple trees. Comprehensive selection of classic French fare; terrines a
speciality.

🍴 **The Salt House**   `🌭` `VISA` `MO` `AE`

63 Abbey Road, St John's Wood ✉ *NW8 0AE* – Ⓜ *St John's Wood.*
– ☎ *(020) 7328 6626 – salthousemail@majol.co.uk – www.thesalthouse.co.uk*
Rest – Carte £ 20/36   *Plan I* **B1**
♦ Pub ♦
Grand Victorian pub appearance in bottle green. Busy bar at the front; main dining
room, in calm duck egg blue, to the rear. Modern menus boast a distinct Mediterranean style.

🛏️ **Queen's Head & Artichoke** 　　AC VISA ⓞⓞ AE

30-32 Albany St ⊠ *NW1 4EA –* Ⓜ *Great Portland Street.*
– ℰ (020) 7916 6206 – info@theartichoke.net
– www.theartichoke.net　　　　　　　　　　　　　　　　**H1**
Rest – Carte £ 19/25
♦ Pub ♦

Busy, wood-panelled bar and eccentrically-styled upstairs restaurant. Modern,
European influenced food mixed with a large selection of all-day international
'tapas.'

CAMDEN　　　　　　　　　　　　　　　　　　　　　　　*Plan VI*

Bloomsbury

🏨 **Covent Garden** 　　L♿ AC 🖥 📶 ♨ VISA ⓞⓞ AE ⓞ

10 Monmouth St ⊠ *WC2H 9HB –* Ⓜ *Covent Garden*
– ℰ (020) 7806 1000 – covent@firmdale.com – Fax (020) 7806 11 00
– www.coventgardenhotel.co.uk　　　　　　　　　　　　　　**I3**
56 rm – �person£ 264/323 ♥♥£ 376, ⊑ £ 19.50 – 2 suites
Rest *Brasserie Max* – *(closed Sunday lunch) (booking essential)*
Carte £ 30/46
♦ Luxury ♦ Stylish ♦

Individually designed and stylish bedrooms, with CDs and VCRs discreetly conceal-
ed. Boasts a very relaxing first floor oak-panelled drawing room with its own
honesty bar. Informal restaurant.

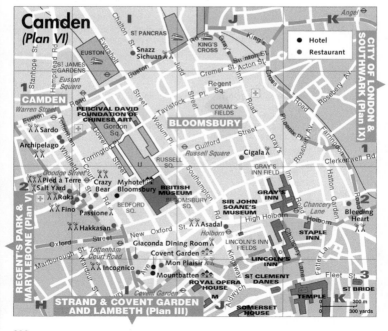

Mountbatten   🏨   🖥 🔲 📶 🔺 🅅🅄🅂🅐 🆖 🄰🄴 ⓘ

20 Monmouth St ⊠ *WC2H 9HD* – Ⓜ *Covent Garden*
– ℰ *(020) 7836 4300 – dial@radisson.com – Fax (020) 7240 35 40*
– *www.radissonedwardian.com*   **I3**
149 rm ⊿ – ♥£ 90/227 ♥♥£ 140/249 – 3 suites
Rest *Dial* – *(Closed Saturday lunch, Sunday and Bank Holidays)* Menu £ 25
– Carte £ 28/34

♦ Business ♦ Functional ♦

Photographs and memorabilia of the eponymous Lord Louis adorn the walls and corridors. Ideally located in the heart of Covent Garden. Compact but comfortable bedrooms. Bright, stylish restaurant.

Myhotel Bloomsbury   🏨   🖥 🔲 📶 🔺 🅅🅄🅂🅐 🆖 🄰🄴 ⓘ

11-13 Bayley St, Bedford Sq ⊠ *WC1B 3HD* – Ⓜ *Tottenham Court Road*
– ℰ *(020) 3004 6000 – bloomsbury@myhotels.com*
– *Fax (020) 3004 60 44 – www.myhotels.com*   **I2**
78 rm – ♥£ 128/240 ♥♥£ 151/276, ⊿ £ 18
Rest *Yo! Sushi* – ℰ *(020) 7667 6000* – Menu £ 16 (lunch)
– Carte £ 22/33

♦ Business ♦ Minimalist ♦

The minimalist interior is designed on the principles of feng shui; even the smaller bedrooms are stylish and uncluttered. Mybar is a fashionable meeting point. Diners can enjoy Japanese food from conveyor belt.

Pied à Terre (Shane Osborn)   🔲 ⇄ 🅅🅄🅂🅐 🆖 🄰🄴

34 Charlotte St ⊠ *W1T 2NH* – Ⓜ *Goodge Street*
– ℰ *(020) 7636 1178 – reservations@pied-a-terre.co.uk*
– *Fax (020) 7916 11 71 – www.pied-a-terre.co.uk*
– *closed first week January, Saturday lunch and Sunday*   **I2**
Rest – Menu £ 32/69 ⅋

Spec. Crayfish and garlic gnocchi, broccoli, Lardo di Colonnata and grapefruit. Suckling pig with beetroot, girolles and apple cider sauce. Bitter sweet chocolate tart, stout ice cream and macadamia nut cream.

♦ Innovative ♦ Fashionable ♦

Smart, low-key exterior; stylish but compact interior with intimately-set tables and well-structured service. Elaborate, expertly-crafted classical dishes, artfully presented.

Mon Plaisir   🍽 🅅🅄🅂🅐 🆖 🄰🄴 ⓘ

21 Monmouth St ⊠ *WC2H 9DD* – Ⓜ *Covent Garden*
– ℰ *(020) 7836 7243 – monplaisirrestaurant@googlemail.com*
– *Fax (020) 7240 47 74 – www.monplaisir.co.uk*
– *closed 25 December-2 January, Saturday lunch and Bank Holidays*
Rest – Menu £ 17 (lunch) – Carte £ 28/41   **I3**

♦ French ♦ Family ♦

London's oldest French restaurant and family-run for over fifty years. Divided into four rooms, all with a different feel but all proudly Gallic in their decoration.

Incognico   🔲 ⇄ 🅅🅄🅂🅐 🆖 🄰🄴 ⓘ

117 Shaftesbury Ave ⊠ *WC2H 8AD* – Ⓜ *Tottenham Court Road*
– ℰ *(020) 7836 8866 – incognicorestaurant@gmail.com*
– *Fax (020) 7240 95 25 – www.incognico.com*
– *Closed 1 week Christmas, Sunday and Bank Holidays*   **I3**
Rest – Menu £ 33 (lunch) – Carte £ 30/35

♦ French ♦ Brasserie ♦

Firmly established with robust décor of wood panelling and brown leather chairs. Downstairs bar has a window into the kitchen, from where French and English classics derive.

XX **Hakkasan** AC VISA ◑◉ AE
£3

8 Hanway Place ✉ W1T 1HD – ⓜ *Tottenham Court Road*
– ℰ (020) 7927 7000 – reservations@hakkasan.com – Fax (020) 7907 18 89
– www.hakkasan.com
– closed 24-25 December **I2**
Rest – Menu £ 40/55 – Carte £ 37/110
Spec. Roasted mango duck with lemon sauce. Stir-fried ostrich in yellow
bean sauce. Rum and caramel banana cookie crumble.
♦ Chinese ♦
Contemporary basement restaurant, with sexy, sophisticated styling and bustling
atmosphere. Well-organised staff serve expertly crafted and innovative Chinese
cooking. Dim sum at lunch.

XX **Sardo** AC VISA ◑◉ AE ◑

45 Grafton Way ✉ W1T 5DQ – ⓜ *Warren Street – ℰ (020) 7387 2521*
– info@sardo-restaurant.com – Fax (020) 7387 25 59
– www.sardo-restaurant.com
– Closed 24-29 December, 1 January, Saturday lunch and Sunday
Rest – Carte £ 23/32 **H1**
♦ Italian ♦ Family ♦
Simple, stylish interior run in a very warm and welcoming manner with very effici-
ent service. Rustic Italian cooking with a Sardinian character and a modern tone.

XX **Fino** VISA ◑◉ AE

33 Charlotte St (entrance on Rathbone St) ✉ W1T 1RR – ⓜ *Goodge Street*
– ℰ (020) 7813 8010 – reception@finorestaurant.com – Fax (020) 7813 80 11
– www.finorestaurant.com
– closed 25 December, Saturday lunch, Sunday and Bank Holidays
Rest – Carte approx. £ 30 **I2**
♦ Spanish ♦ Fashionable ♦
Spanish-run basement bar with modern style décor and banquette seating. Wide-
ranging menu of authentic dishes; 2 set-price selections offering an introduction to
tapas.

XX **Crazy Bear** AC VISA ◑◉ AE

26-28 Whitfield St ✉ W1T 2RG – ⓜ *Goodge Street – ℰ (020) 7631 0088*
– enquiries@crazybear-london.co.uk – Fax (020) 7631 11 88
– www.crazybeargroup.co.uk
– Closed Saturday lunch, Sunday and Bank Holidays **I2**
Rest – Carte £ 29/41
♦ Asian ♦ Trendy ♦
Exotic destination: downstairs bar geared to fashionable set; ground floor dining
room is art deco inspired. Asian flavoured menus, with predominance towards
Thai dishes.

XX **Archipelago** VISA ◑◉ AE ◑

110 Whitfield St ✉ W1T 5ED – ⓜ *Goodge Street – ℰ (020) 7383 3346*
– info@archipelago-restaurant.co.uk – Fax (020) 7383 71 81
– www.archipelago-restaurant.co.uk
– closed Christmas -New Year, Saturday lunch and Sunday **H1**
Rest – Carte £ 27/37
♦ Innovative ♦ Exotic ♦
Eccentric in both menu and décor and not for the faint hearted. Crammed with
knick-knacks from cages to Buddhas. Menu an eclectic mix of influences from
around the world.

X **Passione** VISA ◑◉ AE ◑

10 Charlotte St ✉ W1T 2LT – ⓜ *Tottenham Court Road – ℰ (020) 7636 2833*
– liz@passione.co.uk – Fax (020) 7636 28 89 – www.passione.co.uk
– Closed Christmas-New Year, Bank Holidays, Saturday lunch and Sunday
Rest – (booking essential) Carte £ 40/47 **I2**
♦ Italian ♦ Friendly ♦
Compact but light and airy. Modern Italian cooking served in informal surroun-
dings, with friendly and affable service. Particularly busy at lunchtime.

Cigala
⚔️✂   AC VISA ◉◉ AE ◎

54 Lamb's Conduit St ✉ *WC1N 3LW –* **Ⓜ** *Russell Square –* ℰ *(020) 7405 1717*
– tasty@cigala.co.uk – Fax (020) 7242 99 49 – www.cigala.co.uk
– Closed 24-26 December, 1 January and Easter **J1**
Rest – *(booking essential)* Menu £ 18 (lunch) – Carte £ 24/35
♦ Spanish ♦ Neighbourhood ♦

Spanish restaurant on corner of attractive street. Simply furnished; open-plan kitchen. Robust Iberian cooking, with some dishes designed for sharing; interesting drinks list.

Giaconda Dining Room
AC VISA ◉◉ AE

9 Denmark Street ✉ *WC2H 8LS London –* **Ⓜ** *Tottenham Court Road*
– ℰ *(020) 72403334 – paulmerrony@gmail.com – www.giacondadining.com*
– closed Saturday, Sunday, August and 1 week between Christmas and New Year **I2**
Rest – *(booking essential)* Carte £ 22/27
♦ Modern European ♦

Aussie owners run a small, fun and very busy place in an unpromising location. The very well priced menu offers an appealing mix of gutsy, confident, no-nonsense food, with French and Italian influences.

Salt Yard
AC VISA ◉◉ AE

54 Goodge St ✉ *W1T 4NA –* **Ⓜ** *Goodge Street –* ℰ *(020) 7637 0657*
– info@saltyard.co.uk – Fax (020) 7580 74 35 – www.saltyard.co.uk
– closed 24 December -3 January, Sunday, Saturday lunch and Bank Holidays
Rest – Carte £ 20/37 ♨ **H2**
♦ Mediterranean ♦ Tapas bar ♦

Vogue destination with buzzy downstairs restaurant specialising in inexpensive sharing plates of tasty Italian and Spanish dishes: try the freshly cut hams. Super wine list.

Camden Town

York & Albany *with rm*
⚔️♿ ∻ 🛋 VISA ◉◉ AE ◎

127-129 Parkway ✉ *NW1 7PS –* **Ⓜ** *Camden Town –* ℰ *(020) 7388 3344*
– y&a@gordonramsay.com – www.gordonramsay.com *Plan I* **C1**
10 rm ⛶ – ♦£ 155 ♦♦£ 205 **Rest** – *(booking essential)* Carte £ 26/33
♦ Modern European ♦

Gordon Ramsay's first hotel, with the restaurant as focal point. Dishes are comforting, straightforward but still deftly prepared. Lower level for views of the kitchen. Cosy bedrooms combine antiques with mod cons.

Market
AC VISA ◉◉ AE ◎

43 Parkway ✉ *NW1 7PN –* **Ⓜ** *Camden Town –* ℰ *(020) 72679700*
– primrose.gourmet@btconnect.com – www.marketrestaurant.co.uk
– closed Christmas-New Year, Sunday dinner and Bank Holidays *Plan I* **C1**
Rest – *(booking essential)* Menu £ 15 (lunch) – Carte £ 20/30
♦ British ♦

The highlights of the well-priced, daily menu are the classic British dishes, using market fresh ingredients. Simple comforts of exposed brick walls, zinc-topped tables and school chairs work well.

Euston

Snazz Sichuan
🛋 VISA ◉◉ ◎

37 Chalton St ✉ *NW1 1JD –* **Ⓜ** *Euston –* ℰ *(020) 7388 0808*
– www.newchinaclub.co.uk **I0**
Rest – Menu £ 19/39 – Carte £ 10/50
♦ Chinese ♦ Fashionable ♦

Authentic Sichuan atmosphere and cooking, with gallery and traditional tea room. Menu split into hot and cold dishes; the fiery Sichuan pepper helps heat you from inside out.

UNITED KINGDOM - LONDON

Hatton Garden

XX **Bleeding Heart** 🚗 ⇔ 💳 ⦿ AE ⦿

Bleeding Heart Yard (off Greville St) ⊠ *EC1N 8SJ* – ⓜ *Farringdon*
– ℰ (020) 7242 8238 – bookings@bleedingheart.co.uk – Fax (020) 7831 14 02
– www.bleedingheart.co.uk
– closed Christmas-New Year, Sunday and Bank Holidays **K2**
Rest *– (booking essential)* Carte £ 25/39 🏶
 ◆ French ◆ Romantic ◆
Busy downstairs restaurant, popular with City suits. Fast-paced service, terrific wine list and well-practised cooking. Seasonally-changing French menu with traditional core.

Holborn

XX **Asadal** AC 💳 ⦿ AE

227 High Holborn ⊠ *WC1V 7DA* – ⓜ *Holborn* – ℰ *(020) 7430 9006*
– info@asadal.co.uk – www.asadal.co.uk
– closed 25-26 December, 1 January and Sunday lunch **J2**
Rest – Menu £ 10 (lunch) – Carte £ 10/18
 ◆ Korean ◆ Friendly ◆
A hectic, unprepossessing location, but delivers the authenticity of a modest Korean café with the comfort and service of a proper restaurant. Good quality Korean cooking.

HYDE PARK & KNIGHTSBRIDGE *Plan VII*

🏨🏨🏨 **Mandarin Oriental Hyde Park** ≤ 🕼 ⑳ 🐎 ⅙ rm AC 🖂 📞 🕸

66 Knightsbridge ⊠ *SW1X 7LA* – ⓜ *Knightsbridge* 💳 ⦿ AE ⦿
– ℰ (020) 7235 2000 – molon-dine@mohg.com – Fax (020) 7235 20 01
– www.mandarinoriental.com/london **F4**
173 rm – ♦£ 452/652 ♦♦£ 593/652, ⊑ £ 29 – 25 suites
Rest *Foliage* – see below
Rest *The Park* – Menu £ 33 – Carte £ 35/57
 ◆ Grand Luxury ◆ Classic ◆
Built in 1889 this classic hotel, with striking façade, remains one of London's grandest. Many of the luxurious bedrooms enjoy Park views. Immaculate and detailed service. Smart ambience in The Park.

🏨 **Knightsbridge Green** without rest AC 🕸 💳 ⦿ AE ⦿

159 Knightsbridge ⊠ *SW1X 7PD* – ⓜ *Knightsbridge* – ℰ *(020) 7584 6274*
– reservations@thekghotel.com – Fax (020) 7225 16 35 – www.thekghotel.com
– Closed 25-26 December **F4**
16 rm – ♦£ 150/180 ♦♦£ 200/250 – 12 suites
 ◆ Traditional ◆ Classic ◆
Just yards from Hyde Park and all the smartest shops. Small lounge; breakfast served in the well-proportioned bedrooms spread over six floors. Privately owned.

XXX **Foliage** – at Mandarin Oriental Hyde Park Hotel AC ✂
🅰 *66 Knightsbridge* ⊠ *SW1X 7LA* – ⓜ *Knightsbridge* 💳 ⦿ AE ⦿
– ℰ (020) 7201 3723 – molon-dine@mohg.com – Fax (020) 7235 45 52
– www.mandarinoriental.com/london
– closed 26 December and 1 January
Rest – Menu £ 35/40 **F4**
Spec. Sweetbreads, glazed leeks and morels. Pigeon, red cabbage, endive tart tatin. Calvados soufflé, iced apple parfait, sea salt caramel.
 ◆ Innovative ◆
Sophisticated, modern cooking features experimental combinations and unexpected flavours. View of the park through the windows reflected by earthy colours and foliage motif.

XX **Zuma** 　AK VISA ⓒⓄ AE

5 Raphael St ⊠ SW7 1DL – Ⓜ Knightsbridge – ℰ (020) 7584 1010
– info@zumarestaurant.com – Fax (020) 7584 50 05
– www.zumarestaurant.com
– Closed 25 December and 1 January **F5**
Rest – Carte approx. £ 26
♦ Japanese ♦ Fashionable ♦
Eye-catching design that blends east with west. Bustling atmosphere; fashionable clientele; popular sushi bar. Varied and interesting contemporary Japanese food.

XX **Mr Chow** 　AK VISA ⓒⓄ AE ⓞ

151 Knightsbridge ⊠ SW1X 7PA – Ⓜ Knightsbridge – ℰ (020) 7589 7347
– mrchowuk@aol.com – Fax (020) 7584 57 80 – www.mrchow.com
– closed 24-26 December and 1 January **F4**
Rest – Menu £ 27/38 – Carte dinner £ 39/48
♦ Chinese ♦ Friendly ♦
Long-standing Chinese restaurant, opened in 1968. Smart clientele, stylish and comfortable surroundings and prompt service from Italian waiters. Carefully prepared and satisfying food.

BAYSWATER & MAIDA VALE 　　　　　*Plan VIII*

🏨 **Hilton London Paddington** 　Lб 𝔫 ₺ rm AK SAT ⁽ᵗ⁾ ₅А

146 Praed St ⊠ W2 1EE – Ⓜ Paddington – ℰ (020) 　VISA ⓒⓄ AE ⓞ
7850 0500 – sales.paddington@hilton.com – Fax (020) 7850 06 00
– www.hilton.co.uk/paddington **E2**
344 rm – ♦£ 328 ♦♦£ 328, ☑ £ 19.95 – 20 suites
Rest *The Brasserie* – Carte £ 29/46
♦ Business ♦ Chain hotel ♦ Modern ♦
Early Victorian railway hotel, sympathetically restored in contemporary style with Art Deco details. Co-ordinated bedrooms with high tech facilities continue the modern style. Contemporarily styled brasserie offering a modern menu.

🏨 **Royal Lancaster** 　≤ ₺ AK ⁽ᵗ⁾ ₅А P VISA ⓒⓄ AE ⓞ

Lancaster Terrace ⊠ W2 2TY – Ⓜ Lancaster Gate – ℰ (020) 7262 6737
– sales@royallancaster.com – Fax (020) 7724 31 91 – www.royallancaster.com
394 rm – ♦£ 304 ♦♦£ 304, ☑ £ 19 – 22 suites **E3**
Rest *Island* and **Nipa** – see below
♦ Business ♦ Classic ♦
Imposing 1960s purpose-built hotel overlooking Hyde Park. Some of London's most extensive conference facilities. Well-equipped bedrooms are decorated in traditional style.

🏛 **The Hempel** 🍃 　🏊 Lб ₺ rm AK ⁽ᵗ⁾ VISA ⓒⓄ AE ⓞ

31-35 Craven Hill Gdns ⊠ W2 3EA – Ⓜ Queensway – ℰ (020) 7298 9000
– hotel@the-hempel.co.uk – Fax (020) 7402 46 66 – www.the-hempel.co.uk
– closed 24-28 December **D3**
46 rm – ♦£ 210/304 ♦♦£ 210/304, ☑ £ 21.50 – 4 suites
Rest *The Hempel* – (closed Sunday and Bank Holidays) (dinner only)
Carte £ 33/54
♦ Luxury ♦ Minimalist ♦
A striking example of minimalist design. Individually appointed bedrooms are understated yet very comfortable. Relaxed ambience. Modern basement restaurant.

🏠 **Colonnade Town House** without rest 　AK ⁽ᵗ⁾ VISA ⓒⓄ AE ⓞ

2 Warrington Crescent ⊠ W9 1ER – Ⓜ Warwick Avenue – ℰ (020) 7286 1052
– rescolonnade@theetoncollection.com – Fax (020) 7286 10 57
– www.theetoncollection.com 　*Plan XI* **D1**
43 rm – ♦£ 116/182 ♦♦£ 135/264, ☑ £ 15
♦ Townhouse ♦ Classic ♦
Two Victorian townhouses with comfortable well-furnished communal rooms decorated with fresh flowers. Stylish and comfortable bedrooms with many extra touches.

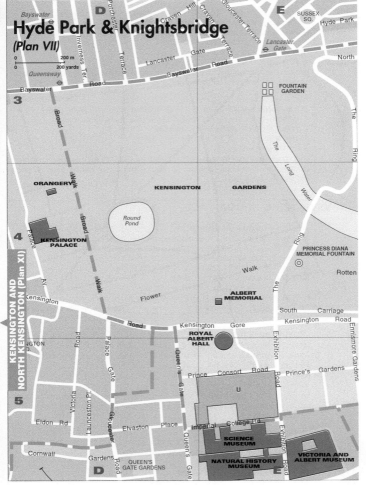

Hyde Park & Knightsbridge
(Plan VII)

0 — 200 m
0 — 200 yards

New Linden without rest ℡ VISA ⑩ AE

58-60 Leinster Sq ⊠ W2 4PS – Ⓜ Bayswater
– 𝒞 (020) 7221 4321 – newlindenhotel@mayflower-group.co.uk
– Fax (020) 7727 31 56 – www.newlinden.co.uk

50 rm – ♥£ 79/109 ♥♥£ 115/145 **C2**

♦ Family ♦ Functional ♦

Smart four storey white stucco façade. Basement breakfast room with sunny aspect. Bedrooms are its strength: flat screen TVs and wooden floors; two split level family rooms.

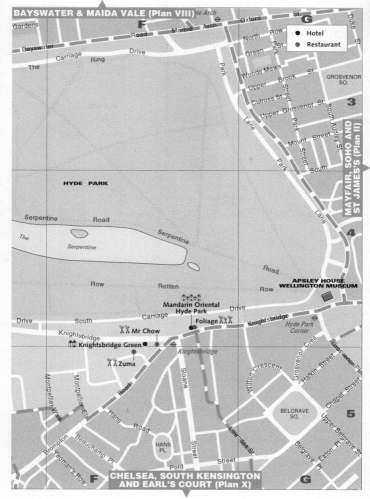

BAYSWATER & MAIDA VALE (Plan VIII)

● Hotel
● Restaurant

HYDE PARK

MAYFAIR, SOHO AND ST JAMES'S (Plan II)

APSLEY HOUSE WELLINGTON MUSEUM

Mandarin Oriental Hyde Park

Foliage ※※※

Mr Chow ※※

Knightsbridge Green

Zuma ※※

BELGRAVE SQ.

CHELSEA, SOUTH KENSINGTON AND EARL'S COURT (Plan X)

※※ **Le Café Anglais**　　　　　　　　　AC VISA ① AE

8 Porchester Gardens ⊠ W2 4BD – Ⓜ *Bayswater –* ℰ *(020) 72211415*
– info@lecafeanglais.co.uk – www.lecafeanglais.co.uk
– closed 26 December　　　　　　　　　　　　　　　　　　　**D2**
Rest *– Menu £ 20 – Carte £ 23/47*
♦ Modern European ♦
Opened in late 2007, a large, modern brasserie with art deco styling within White-ley's shopping centre. Large and very appealing selection of classic brasserie food; the rotisserie is the centrepiece.

935

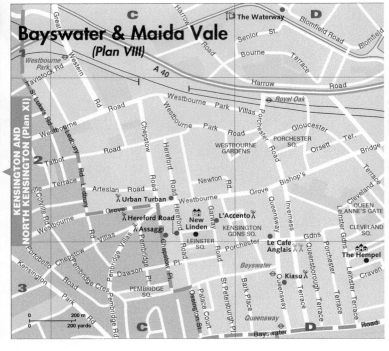

Bayswater & Maida Vale
(Plan VIII)

XX **Angelus**   AC ⟺ VISA ⦿ AE

*4 Bathurst St ⊠ W2 2SD – Ⓜ Lancaster Gate – ℰ (020) 7402 0083 – info@
angelusrestaurant.co.uk – Fax (020) 7402 53 83 – www.angelusrestaurant.co.uk
– Closed Christmas-New Year and Monday*   **E3**

Rest – Menu £ 36 (lunch) – Carte £ 39/55

♦ French ♦ Brasserie ♦

In the style of a French brasserie, with studded leather banquettes, huge art nouveau mirror, Murano chandeliers and lounge bar. Unfussy, French dishes; clean,
precise cooking.

XX **Trenta**   AC VISA ⦿ AE

*30 Connaught St ⊠ W2 2AF – Ⓜ Marble Arch – ℰ (020) 7262 9623 – trenta@
btconnect.com – Fax (020) 7262 96 36
– closed Christmas-New Year, Sunday and Bank Holidays*   **F2**

Rest – (dinner only and lunch Thursday and Friday) Carte £ 23/31

♦ Italian ♦ Neighbourhood ♦

Only 7 tables on ground floor and 5 more downstairs; red and cream with comfy
leather seats. Uncomplicated Italian cooking on constantly changing menu.

XX **Jamuna**   AC VISA ⦿ AE

*38A Southwick St ⊠ W2 1JQ – Ⓜ Edgware Road – ℰ (020) 7723 5056 – info@
jamuna.co.uk – Fax (020) 7706 18 70 – www.jamuna.co.uk
– Closed 25-26 December*   **E2**

Rest – (dinner only) Menu £ 30 – Carte £ 37/60

♦ Indian ♦ Neighbourhood ♦

Don't be put off by the unprepossessing nature of the area: this is a modern out of
the ordinary Indian restaurant with cooking that's well presented, refined and flavoursome.

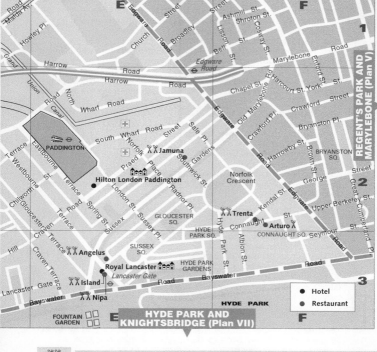

Edgware Road, Church Street, Broadley Street, Ashmill St., Shroton St., Cosway St., Lisson St., Marylebone Road, Enford St., Howley Pl., Maida Av., Road, Harrow Road, Wharf Road, South Wharf Road, Praed Street, Chapel St., Old Marylebone Rd., Harcourt St., York St., Crawford Street, Crawford Pl., Bryanston Pl., BRYANSTON SQ., Harrowby St., Brown St., George St., Great Cumberland Pl., Upper Berkeley St., CONNAUGHT SQ., Seymour St., Kendal St., Connaught St., Albion St., Norfolk Crescent, HYDE PARK SQ., SUSSEX SQ., HYDE PARK GARDENS, Bayswater Road, Sale Pl., Norfolk Place, Southwick St., Gloucester Sq., Sussex Pl., Sussex Gardens, Radnor Pl., Hyde Park St., Grand Union Canal, Eastbourne Terrace, Westbourne Terrace, Chilworth St., Gloucester Terrace, Craven Terrace, Lancaster Gate, Lancaster Terrace, Bayswater, Craven Hill, FOUNTAIN GARDEN

PADDINGTON

🏥 Jamuna

Hilton London Paddington

Trenta, Arturo

Angelus

Royal Lancaster

Island

Nipa

HYDE PARK

● Hotel
● Restaurant

XX **Island** – at Royal Lancaster Hotel   AC VISA ⦵ AE ⦵

Lancaster Terrace ⊠ W2 2TY
– Ⓜ Lancaster Gate
– ℰ (020) 7551 6070
– eat@islandrestaurant.co.uk
– Fax (020) 7551 60 71
– www.islandrestaurant.co.uk   **E3**
Rest – Carte £ 28/43

♦ Modern European ♦ Brasserie ♦

Modern, stylish restaurant with buzzy open kitchen. Full length windows allow good views of adjacent Hyde Park. Seasonally based, modern menus with wide range of dishes.

XX **Nipa** – at Royal Lancaster Hotel   AC P VISA ⦵ AE ⦵

Lancaster Terrace ⊠ W2 2TY
– Ⓜ Lancaster Gate
– ℰ (020) 7551 6039
– Fax (020) 7724 31 91
– www.niparestaurant.co.uk
– Closed 24-30 December, 1-4 January, Saturday lunch,
Sunday and Bank Holidays   **E3**
Rest – Menu £ 27 – Carte £ 23/32

♦ Thai ♦ Exotic ♦

On the 1st floor and overlooking Hyde Park. Authentic and ornately decorated restaurant offers subtly spiced Thai cuisine. Keen to please staff in traditional silk costumes.

937

Assaggi (Nino Sassu) $\boxed{AC}$ $\boxed{VISA}$ ◉◎ ◐

39 Chepstow Pl, (above Chepstow pub) ⊠ *W2 4TS –* Ⓜ *Bayswater*
– ℰ (020) 7792 5501 – nipi@assaggi.demon.co.uk – www.assaggi.com
– closed 2 weeks Christmas and Sunday **C2**
Rest *– (booking essential)* Carte £ 31/46

Spec. Pecorino con San Daniele e Rucola. Pan-fried calf's liver with balsamic vinegar. Bitter chocolate tart with pastry cream.
♦ Italian ♦ Rustic ♦

Tall windows add to the brightness of this room above a pub. High quality ingredients are used to create appetisingly rustic dishes with more than a hint of Sardinia.

Hereford Road $\boxed{AC}$ $\boxed{VISA}$ ◉◎ $\boxed{AE}$

3 Hereford Road ⊠ *W2 4AB –* Ⓜ *Bayswater – ℰ (020) 7727 1144*
– info@herefordroad.org – www.herefordroad.org
– Closed 25-30 December **C2**
Rest *– (booking essential)* Carte £ 24/32
♦ British ♦

Converted butcher's shop now specialises in classic British dishes and recipes, with first rate, seasonal ingredients. Booths for six people are the prize seats. Friendly and relaxed feel.

L'Accento $\boxed{VISA}$ ◉◎ $\boxed{AE}$

16 Garway Rd ⊠ *W2 4NH –* Ⓜ *Bayswater – ℰ (020) 7243 2201*
– laccentorest@aol.com – Fax (020) 7243 22 01
– www.laccentorestaurant.co.uk
– Closed Sunday and Bank Holidays **C2**
Rest *– Menu £ 24 –* Carte £ 27/33
♦ Italian ♦ Rustic ♦

Rustic surroundings and provincial, well priced, Italian cooking. Menu specialises in tasty pasta, made on the premises, and shellfish. Rear conservatory for the summer.

Arturo $\boxed{AC}$ $\boxed{VISA}$ ◉◎ $\boxed{AE}$

23 Connaught St ⊠ *W2 2AY –* Ⓜ *Marble Arch – ℰ (020) 7706 3388*
– enquiries@arturorestaurant.co.uk – Fax (020) 7402 91 95
– www.arturorestaurant.co.uk
– Closed 25-26 December, 1 January, Good Friday and Easter Sunday
Rest *– Menu £ 17 (lunch) –* Carte £ 22/30 **F2**
♦ Italian ♦

On a smart street near Hyde Park: sleek, modish feel imbues interior with intimate, elegant informality. Tuscan and Sicilian dishes cooked with confidence and originality.

Kiasu $\boxed{AC}$ $\boxed{VISA}$ ◉◎

48 Queensway ⊠ *W2 3RY –* Ⓜ *Bayswater – ℰ (020) 7727 8810*
– info@kiasu.co.uk – Fax (020) 7727 72 20 – www.kiasu.co.uk **D3**
Rest *–* Carte £ 12/26
♦ Asian ♦ Friendly ♦

Its name means 'afraid to be second best.' Malaysian owner; some dishes are hot and spicy, others light and fragrant; all designed for sharing. Brightly decorated; good fun.

Urban Turban $\boxed{AC}$ ⇔ $\boxed{VISA}$ ◉◎ $\boxed{AE}$

98 Westbourne Grove ⊠ *W2 5RU –* Ⓜ *Bayswater – ℰ (020) 7243 4200*
– info@urbanturban.uk.com – Fax (020) 72 43 40 80
– www.urbanturban.uk.com **C2**
Rest *–* Carte £ 24/26
♦ Indian ♦ Exotic ♦

Mumbai street food is the inspiration behind this venture from Vineet Bhatia. Order a number of dishes to share. Ground floor for the bustle and bar; the downstairs area is calmer.

The Waterway ⟨ 🍴 AC P VISA ⊙ AE

54 Formosa St ⊠ W9 2JU – **Ⓜ** *Warwick Avenue –* 𝒞 *(020) 7266 3557*
– info@thewaterway.co.uk – Fax (020) 7266 35 47 – www.thewaterway.co.uk
Rest *– Carte £ 30/40*   **D1**
♦ Pub ♦
Pub with a thoroughly modern, metropolitan ambience. Spacious bar and large
decked terrace overlooking canal. Concise, well-balanced menu served in open
plan dining room.

The Warrington AC ⇔ VISA ⊙ AE

93 Warrington Crescent ⊠ W9 1EH – **Ⓜ** *Maida Vale. –* 𝒞 *(020) 7592 7960*
– thewarrington@gordonramsay.com – Fax (020) 7592 16 03
– www.gordonramsay.com   *Plan I* **B2**
Rest *– Carte £ 25/35*
♦ Modern European ♦ Pub ♦
Imposing Victorian pub, now owned by Gordon Ramsay, with traditional feel to the
ground floor bar. Upstairs is the smarter dining room with appealing menu of
French and British classics.

CITY OF LONDON, SOUTHWARK & TOWER HAMLETS *Plan IX*

City of London

Andaz Liverpool Street 𝄢 & rm AC 🖥 📶 ☆ VISA ⊙ ⓞ

Liverpool St ⊠ EC2M 7QN – **Ⓜ** *Liverpool Street –* 𝒞 *(020) 7961 1234*
– info.londonliv@andaz.com – Fax (020) 7961 12 35
– www.london.liverpoolstreet.andaz.com   **M2**
264 rm ⚏ *–* **♥**£ 428 **♥♥**£ 605 *– 3 suites*
Rest *1901 –* 𝒞 *(020) 7618 7000 (closed Saturday lunch and Sunday)*
Carte approx. £ 44 ⅋
♦ Grand Luxury ♦ Design ♦
A contemporary and stylish interior hides behind the classic Victorian façade. Part
of Hyatt group. Bright and spacious bedrooms with state-of-the-art facilities. European cooking on offer in Grade II listed 1901.

Crowne Plaza London - The City 𝄢 ⋒ & rm AC 📶 ☆

19 New Bridge St ⊠ EC4V 6DB – **Ⓜ** *Blackfriars*   VISA ⊙ AE ⓞ
– 𝒞 *(0870) 4009190 – loncy.info@ihg.com – Fax (020) 7438 80 80*
– www.crowneplaza.com   **K3**
201 rm *–* **♥**£ 347/423 **♥♥**£ 347/423, ⚏ £ 19.50 *– 2 suites*
Rest *Refettorio –* 𝒞 *(020) 7438 8052 (Closed Saturday lunch, Sunday and Bank
Holidays) Menu £ 23 (dinner) – Carte £ 31/39*
Rest *Spicers –* 𝒞 *(020) 7438 8051 (lunch only Monday - Saturday) Menu £ 15
– Carte £ 25/30*
♦ Business ♦ Chain hotel ♦ Modern ♦
Art deco façade by the river; interior enhanced by funky chocolate, cream and
brown palette. Compact meeting room; well equipped fitness centre. Sizable, sty-
lish rooms. Modish Refettorio for Italian cuisine. British dishes with a modern twist
at Spicers.

Threadneedles & AC 🖥 📶 ☆ VISA ⊙ AE ⓞ

5 Threadneedle St ⊠ EC2R 8AY – **Ⓜ** *Bank –* 𝒞 *(020) 7657 8080*
– resthreadneedles@theetoncollection.com – Fax (020) 7657 81 00
– www.theetoncollection.com   **M3**
68 rm *–* **♥**£ 264/394 **♥♥**£ 264/394, ⚏ £ 19 *– 1 suite*
Rest *Bonds – see below*
♦ Business ♦ Modern ♦
A converted bank, dating from 1856, with a stunning stained-glass cupola in the
lounge. Rooms are very stylish and individual featuring CD players and Egyptian
cotton sheets.

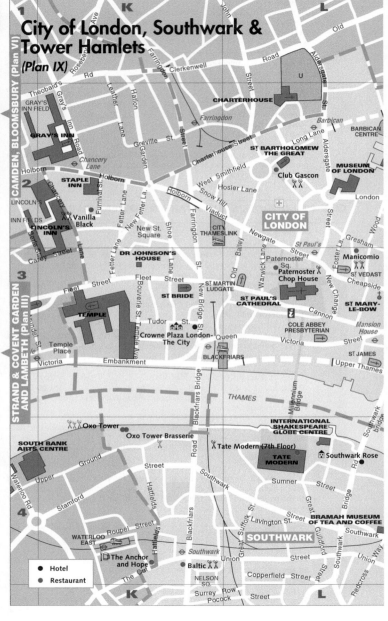

City of London, Southwark & Tower Hamlets
(Plan IX)

CHARTERHOUSE

ST BARTHOLOMEW THE GREAT

Club Gascon

BARBICAN CENTRE

MUSEUM OF LONDON

GRAY'S INN FIELD

GRAY'S INN

STAPLE INN

LINCOLN'S INN FIELDS

LINCOLN'S INN

Vanilla Black

CITY OF LONDON

CITY THAMESLINK

DR JOHNSON'S HOUSE

Manicomio

ST VEDAST

ST MARTIN LUDGATE

Paternoster Sq.
Paternoster Chop House

ST BRIDE

ST PAUL'S CATHEDRAL

ST MARY-LE-BOW

TEMPLE

Crowne Plaza London-The City

COLE ABBEY PRESBYTERIAN

Mansion House

ST JAMES

BLACKFRIARS

Embankment

THAMES

Oxo Tower

Oxo Tower Brasserie

Tate Modern (7th Floor)

INTERNATIONAL SHAKESPEARE GLOBE CENTRE

Southwark Rose

SOUTH BANK ARTS CENTRE

TATE MODERN

BRAMAH MUSEUM OF TEA AND COFFEE

WATERLOO EAST

The Anchor and Hope

Baltic

SOUTHWARK

NELSON SQ.

- Hotel
- Restaurant

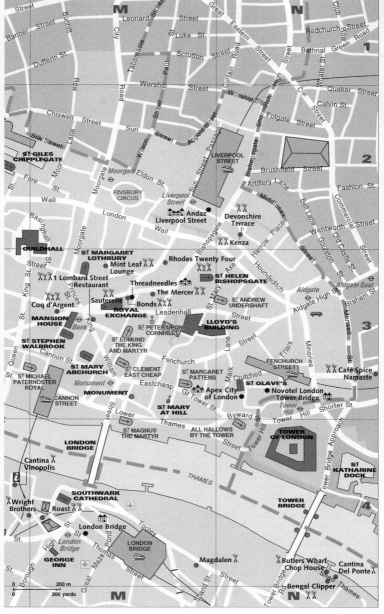

941

Apex City of London

No 1, Seething Lane ✉ *EC3N 4AX* – Ⓜ *Fenchurch Street* – ☎ *(020) 7702 2020*
– *london.guestrelations@apexhotels.co.uk* – *Fax (020) 7702 22 17*
– *www.apexhotels.co.uk*   **N3**
129 rm – ♦£ 311 ♦♦£ 311, ⊑ £ 10 – 1 suite
Rest *Addendum Bar* – Carte £ 17/27
♦ Business ♦ Modern ♦

Tucked away behind Tower of London, overlooking leafy square. Smart meeting facilities, well-equipped gym and treatment rooms. Bedrooms are super sleek with bespoke extras.

Novotel London Tower Bridge

10 Pepys St ✉ *EC3N 2NR* – Ⓜ *Tower Hill* – ☎ *(020)*
7265 6000 – *h3107@accor.com* – *Fax (020) 7265 60 60* – *www.accorhotels.com*
199 rm – ♦£ 280 ♦♦£ 300/235, ⊑ £ 13.95 – 4 suites   **N3**
Rest *The Garden Brasserie* – *(buffet lunch, bar lunch Saturday-Sunday)*
Menu £ 20 (buffet lunch)/25 – Carte £ 23/36
♦ Business ♦ Chain hotel ♦ Functional ♦

Modern, purpose-built hotel with carefully planned, comfortable bedrooms. Useful City location and close to Tower of London which is visible from some of the higher rooms. Informally styled brasserie.

Rhodes Twenty Four

24th floor, Tower 42, 25 Old Broad St ✉ *EC2N 1HQ* – Ⓜ *Liverpool Street*
– ☎ *(020) 7877 7703* – *reservations@rhodes24.co.uk* – *Fax (020) 7877 77 88*
– *www.rhodes24.co.uk*
– *closed Christmas-New Year, Saturday, Sunday and Bank Holidays*
Rest – Carte £ 37/55   **M3**
Spec. Seared scallops, mashed potato and shallot mustard sauce. Steamed mutton and onion suet pudding with buttered carrots. Bread and butter pudding.
♦ British ♦ Formal ♦

Panoramic views are afforded from this contemporary restaurant, set on the 24th floor of Tower 42; the former Natwest building. Well balanced British dishes, appetisingly presented.

Coq d'Argent

✉ *EC2R 8EJ* – Ⓜ *Bank* – ☎ *(020) 7395 5000* – *coqd-argent@*
danddlondon.com – *Fax (020) 7395 50 50* – *www.danddlondon.com*
– *closed Christmas, Easter, Saturday lunch and Bank Holidays*
Rest – *(booking essential)* Menu £ 29 – Carte £ 34/50   **M3**
♦ French ♦ Design ♦

Take the dedicated lift to the top of this modern office block. Tables on the rooftop terrace have city views; busy bar. Gallic menus highlighted by popular shellfish dishes.

1 Lombard Street

1 Lombard St ✉ *EC3V 9AA* – Ⓜ *Bank* – ☎ *(020) 7929 6611*
– *hb@1lombardstreet.com* – *Fax (020) 7929 66 22* – *www.1lombardstreet.com*
– *closed 25 December- 6 January, Saturday, Sunday and Bank Holidays*
Rest – *(booking essential at lunch)* Menu £ 44/45 – Carte £ 52/62   **M3**
♦ French ♦ Formal ♦

Grade II listed banking hall; rear room for elaborately presented, classical cooking using luxury ingredients. Bustling front brasserie and bar.

Bonds – at Threadneedles H.

5 Threadneedle St ✉ *EC2R 8AY* – Ⓜ *Bank* – ☎ *(020) 7657 8088* – *bonds@*
theetongroup.com – *Fax (020) 7657 80 89* – *www.theetoncollection.com*
– *closed Saturday, Sunday and Bank Holidays*   **M3**
Rest – Menu £ 18 (lunch) – Carte £ 28/46
♦ Modern European ♦ Retro ♦

Modern interior juxtaposed with the grandeur of a listed city building. Vast dining room with high ceiling and tall pillars. Attentive service of hearty, contemporary food.

XX · ⌘

Club Gascon (Pascal Aussignac)   `AC` `VISA` `OO` `AE`

57 West Smithfield ✉ *EC1A 9DS –* Ⓜ *Barbican – ℰ (020) 7796 0600*
– info@clubgascon.com – Fax (020) 7796 06 01 – www.clubgascon.com
– closed January, Saturday lunch, Sunday and Bank Holidays   **L2**
Rest *– (booking essential)* Menu £ 28/42 *–* Carte £ 34/48 ⅋

Spec. Abalone and razor clams à la plancha, parsnip and seaweed tartare. Cappuccino of black pudding and lobster. Rhubarb and champagne sorbet, rose Chantilly.

♦ French ♦

Former bank; its marble walls now softened by big floral displays and mirrors. Elegantly crafted 'petits plats' are a paean to Gascony and the gastronomy of South West France.

XX

Mint Leaf Lounge   `AC` `VISA` `OO` `AE` `①`

12 Angel Court, Lothbury ✉ *EC2R 7HB –* Ⓜ *Bank – ℰ (020) 76000992*
– reservations@mintleaflounge.com – Fax (020) 76 00 66 28
– www.mintleaflounge.com
– closed 22 December-3 January, Saturday lunch and Sunday   **M3**
Rest *–* Menu £ 23 (lunch) *–* Carte £ 28/44

♦ Indian ♦ Design ♦

Sister branch to the original in St James's. Slick and stylish, with busy bar. Well paced service of carefully prepared contemporary Indian food, with many of the influences from the south.

XX

Vanilla Black   `AC` `VISA` `OO` `AE`

17-18 Tooks Court ✉ *EC4A 1LB –* Ⓜ *Chancery Lane – ℰ (020) 72422622*
– www.vanillablack.co.uk
– Closed Saturday, Sunday and 2 weeks Christmas   **K2**
Rest *–* Menu £ 23/30

♦ Vegetarian ♦ Minimalist ♦

Proving that vegetarian food can be flavoursome and satisfying, with a menu that is varied and imaginative. This is a well run, friendly restaurant with understated décor, run by a husband and wife team.

XX

Kenza   `AC` `⇆` `VISA` `OO` `AE` `①`

10 Devonshire Square ✉ *EC2M 4YP –* Ⓜ *Liverpool Street – ℰ (020) 79295533*
– info@kenza-restaurant.com – Fax (020) 79 29 03 03
– www.kenza-restaurant.com
– closed Saturday lunch and Sunday   **N2**
Rest *–* Carte approx. £ 35

♦ Lebanese ♦ Exotic ♦

Exotic basement restaurant, with lamps, carvings, pumping music and nightly belly dancing. Lebanese and Moroccan cooking are the menu influences and the cooking is authentic and accurate.

XX

Devonshire Terrace   `⌖` `AC` `⇆` `VISA` `OO` `AE`

Devonshire Sq ✉ *EC2M 4YY –* Ⓜ *Liverpool Street – ℰ (020) 72563233*
– info@devonshireterrace.co.uk – Fax (020) 72 56 32 44
– www.devonshireterrace.co.uk
– Closed Christmas-New Year, Saturday and Sunday   **N2**
Rest *–* Carte £ 22/34

♦ Modern European ♦ Brasserie ♦

Brasserie-style cooking, where you choose the sauce and side dish to accompany your main course. Bright and busy restaurant with open kitchen and choice of two terraces, one within large atrium.

XX

The Mercer   `AC` `VISA` `OO` `AE`

34 Threadneedle St ✉ *EC2R 8AY –* Ⓜ *Bank – ℰ (020) 7628 0001*
– info@themercer.co.uk – Fax (020) 7588 28 22 – www.themercer.co.uk
– Closed 25 December - 1 January, Saturday, Sunday and Bank Holidays
Rest *–* Carte £ 29/50 ⅋   **M2**

♦ Modern European ♦ Brasserie ♦

Converted bank, with airy feel thanks to high ceilings and large windows. Brasserie style menu with appealing mix of classics and comfort food. Huge choice of wines available by glass or carafe.

XX **Sauterelle**   AC ✦ VISA ⓪ AE ①

The Royal Exchange ⊠ *EC3V 3LR –* Ⓜ *Bank*
– 𝒞 (020) 7618 2483
– www.restaurantsauterelle.com
– Closed Saturday and Sunday   **M3**
Rest – Menu £ 21 (dinner) – Carte £ 33/56
♦ French ♦ Design ♦

Located on mezzanine level of Royal Exchange, a stunning 16C property with ornate columns and pillars. Appealing and rustic French menus attract plenty of lunchtime diners.

XX **Manicomio**   AC VISA ⓪ AE

6 Gutter Lane ⊠ *EC2V 7AD –* Ⓜ *St Paul's*
– 𝒞 (020) 7265010 – gutterlane@manicomio.co.uk
– Fax (020) 7 26 50 11 – www.manicomio.co.uk
– Closed Christmas-New Year, Saturday and Sunday   **L3**
Rest – Carte £ 22/35
♦ Italian ♦ Brasserie ♦

Second branch to follow the first in Chelsea. Regional Italian fare, with top-notch ingredients. Bright and fresh first floor restaurant, with deli-café on the ground floor and bar on top floor.

X **Paternoster Chop House**   ⌕ AC VISA ⓪ AE ①

Warwick Court, Paternoster Square ⊠ *EC4N 7DX –* Ⓜ *St Paul's*
– 𝒞 (020) 7029 9400
– paternosterr@conran-restaurants.co.uk
– Fax (020) 7029 94 09
– www.paternosterchophouse.com
– closed 10 days Christmas, dinner Sunday, Saturday and Bank Holidays
Rest – Carte £ 31/41   **L3**
♦ British ♦ Brasserie ♦

On ground floor of office block, with large terrace. Classic and robust British cooking; menu a mix of traditional favourites, shellfish and comfort food. Busy and noisy.

Southwark

Bermondsey

🏠 **London Bridge**   ⨎ ᕓ rm AC ⁋⁰ ⟐ VISA ⓪ AE ①

8-18 London Bridge St ⊠ *SE1 9SG –* Ⓜ *London Bridge*
– 𝒞 (020) 7855 2200
– sales@londonbridgehotel.com
– Fax (020) 7855 22 33 – www.londonbridgehotel.com   **M4**
135 rm – ♦£ 229 ♦♦£ 229, ⊃ £ 14.95 – 3 suites
Rest *Georgetown* – *(dinner only)* Carte £ 26/33
♦ Business ♦ Classic ♦

In one of the oldest parts of London, independently owned with an ornate façade dating from 1915. Modern interior with classically decorated bedrooms and an impressive gym. Restaurant echoing the colonial style serving Malaysian dishes.

XX **Bengal Clipper**   AC VISA ⓪ AE

Cardamom Building, Shad Thames, Butlers Wharf ⊠ *SE1 2YR*
– Ⓜ *London Bridge – 𝒞 (020) 7357 9001*
– mail@bengalclipper.co.uk – Fax (020) 7357 90 02
– www.bengalclipper.co.uk   **N4**
Rest – Carte £ 14/20
♦ Indian ♦ Friendly ♦

Housed in a Thames-side converted warehouse, a smart Indian restaurant with original brickwork and steel supports. Menu features Bengali and Goan dishes. Evening pianist.

✗ Magdalen

AK **VISA** **✆✆** **AE**

*152 Tooley St ⊠ SE1 2TU – **Ⓜ** London Bridge – 𝒞 (020) 7403 1342*
– info@magdalenrestaurant.co.uk – Fax (020) 7403 99 50
– www.magdalenrestaurant.co.uk
– closed last 2 weeks August, 1 week Christmas, Saturday lunch and Sunday
Rest – Menu £ 19 (lunch) – Carte £ 28/45 **M4**
♦ British ♦ Bistro ♦

Appealing bistro style restaurant set over two floors, with aubergine-coloured walls and chandeliers. Seasonal menus offer precise, well-executed and simply presented cooking.

✗ Village East

AK **⟷** **VISA** **✆✆** **AE**

*171 Bermondsey St ⊠ SE1 3UW – **Ⓜ** London Bridge – 𝒞 (020) 7357 6082*
– info@villageeast.co.uk – Fax (020) 7403 33 60 – www.villageeast.co.uk
– closed 25-26 December *Plan I* **D2**
Rest – Carte £ 23/34
♦ Modern European ♦ Trendy ♦

In a glass fronted block sandwiched by Georgian townhouses, this trendy restaurant has two loud, buzzy bars and dining areas serving ample portions of modern British fare.

✗ Cantina Del Ponte

≼ **⌂** **VISA** **✆✆** **AE** **Ⓞ**

*36c Shad Thames, Butlers Wharf ⊠ SE1 2YE – **Ⓜ** London Bridge*
– 𝒞 (020) 7403 5403 – cantina@danddlondon.com – Fax (020) 7940 18 45
– www.conran.com
– closed 24-26 December **N4**
Rest – Menu £ 18 (lunch) – Carte £ 22/36
♦ Italian ♦

An Italian stalwart, refurbished late in 2007. Simple menu offers an appealing mix of classic dishes, with a good value set menu until 7pm. Riverside setting with pleasant terrace.

✗ Butlers Wharf Chop House

≼ **⌂** **VISA** **✆✆** **AE** **Ⓞ**

*36e Shad Thames, Butlers Wharf ⊠ SE1 2YE – **Ⓜ** London Bridge*
– 𝒞 (020) 7403 3403 – bwchophouse@dandddlondon.com
– Fax (020) 7940 18 55 – www.danddlondon.com – closed 1-2 January
Rest – Menu £ 26 – Carte £ 26/38 **N4**
♦ British ♦ Rustic ♦

Book the terrace in summer and dine in the shadow of Tower Bridge. Rustic feel to the interior, with obliging service. Menu focuses on traditional English dishes.

Southwark

🏠 Southwark Rose

₺ rm **AK** **▦** **⟨⟩** **🛦** **P** **VISA** **✆✆** **AE**

*43-47 Southwark Bridge Rd ⊠ SE1 9HH – **Ⓜ** London Bridge*
– 𝒞 (020) 7015 1480 – info@southwarkrosehotel.co.uk
– Fax (020) 7015 14 81 – www.southwarkrosehotel.co.uk **L4**
78 rm – ♥£ 105/190 ♥♥£ 105/190, � £ 12.95 – 6 suites
Rest – *(dinner only)* Carte £ 14/22
♦ Business ♦ Functional ♦

Purpose built budget hotel south of the City, near the Globe Theatre. Top floor dining room with bar. Uniform style, reasonably spacious bedrooms with writing desks.

✗✗✗ Oxo Tower

≼ **⌂** **AK** **VISA** **✆✆** **AE** **Ⓞ**

*(8th Floor) Oxo Tower Wharf, Barge House St ⊠ SE1 9PH – **Ⓜ** Southwark*
– 𝒞 (020) 7803 3888 – oxo.reservations@harveynichols.co.uk
– Fax (020) 7803 38 38 – www.harveynichols.com
– closed 25-26 December **K4**
Rest *Oxo Tower Brasserie* – see below
Rest – Menu £ 30 – Carte dinner £ 42/57
♦ Modern ♦ Formal ♦

Top of a converted factory, providing stunning views of the Thames and beyond. Stylish, minimalist interior with huge windows. Smooth service of modern cuisine.

UNITED KINGDOM - LONDON

XX **Roast**   AC 🕼 VISA ⦾ AE

The Floral Hall, Borough Market ⊠ *SE1 1TL –* Ⓜ *London Bridge*
– 𝒞 (020) 7940 1300 – info@roast-restaurant.com – Fax (020) 7655 20 79
– www.roast-restaurant.com
– closed 25 December and Sunday dinner   **M4**
Rest *– (booking essential)* Carte £ 33/48
♦ British ♦ Fashionable ♦

Set into the roof of Borough Market's Floral Hall. Extensive cocktail list in bar; split-level restaurant has views to St. Paul's. Robust English cooking using market produce.

XX **Baltic**   VISA ⦾ AE ⓪

74 Blackfriars Rd ⊠ *SE1 8HA –* Ⓜ *Southwark – 𝒞 (020) 7928 1111 – info@*
balticrestaurant.co.uk – Fax (020) 7928 84 87 – www.balticrestaurant.co.uk
Rest *– Menu £ 14 –* Carte £ 23/28   **K4**
♦ Eastern European ♦ Brasserie ♦

Set in a Grade II listed 18C former coach house. Enjoy authentic and hearty east European and Baltic influenced food. Interesting vodka selection and live jazz on Sundays.

X **Oxo Tower Brasserie**   ⩽ 🛋 AC VISA ⦾ AE ⓪

(8th Floor) Oxo Tower Wharf,Barge House St ⊠ *SE1 9PH –* Ⓜ *Southwark*
– 𝒞 (020) 7803 3888 – oxo.reservations@harveynichols.co.uk
– Fax (020) 7803 38 38 – www.harveynichols.com
– closed 25-26 December   **K4**
Rest *– Menu £ 22 –* Carte £ 30/41
♦ Modern ♦ Brasserie ♦

Same views but less formal than the restaurant. Open-plan kitchen, relaxed service, the modern menu is slightly lighter. In summer, try to secure a table on the terrace.

X **Cantina Vinopolis**   AC VISA ⦾ AE ⓪

No 1 Bank End ⊠ *SE1 9BU –* Ⓜ *London Bridge – 𝒞 (020) 7940 8333*
– cantina@vinopolis.co.uk – Fax (020) 7940 83 34
– www.cantinavinopolis.com
– closed Christmas, New Year and Sunday dinner   **L4**
Rest *– Menu £ 18 –* Carte £ 20/28 ⅜
♦ Modern ♦ Bistro ♦

Large, solid brick vaulted room under Victorian railway arches, with an adjacent wine museum. Modern menu with a huge selection of wines by the glass.

X **Tate Modern**   ⩽ ⅍ VISA ⦾ AE ⓪

Tate Modern, Bankside ⊠ *SE1 9TG –* Ⓜ *Southwark – 𝒞 (020) 7401 5020*
– Fax (020) 7401 51 71 – www.tate.org.uk
– closed 24-26 December   **L4**
Rest *–* Carte £ 20/32
♦ Innovative ♦ Design ♦

Modernity to match the museum, with vast murals and huge windows affording stunning views. Canteen-style menu at a sensible price with obliging service.

X **Wright Brothers**   VISA ⦾ AE

11 Stoney St, Borough Market ⊠ *SE1 9AD –* Ⓜ *London Bridge*
– 𝒞 (020) 7403 9554 – reservations@wrightbros.eu.com
– Fax (020) 7403 95 58 – www.wrightbros.eu.com
– closed Sunday, Christmas and Bank Holidays   **L4**
Rest *–* Carte £ 22/35
♦ Seafood ♦ Wine bar ♦

Classic style oyster and porter house - a large number of porter ales on offer. Simple settings afford a welcoming ambience to enjoy huge range of oysters and prime shellfish.

Anchor and Hope   *VISA* **◎**

*36 The Cut ⌧ SE1 8LP – **Ⓜ** Southwark – 𝒞 (020) 7928 9898*
– Fax (020) 7928 45 95
– closed Christmas-New Year, 2 weeks August, Sunday, Monday lunch and Bank
Holidays   **K4**
Rest – Carte £ 20/30
◆ Modern ◆ Pub ◆

Close to Waterloo, the distinctive dark green exterior lures visitors in droves. Bare floorboards, simple wooden furniture. Seriously original cooking with rustic French base.

Tower Hamlets

Bow

The Morgan Arms   ⌂ **ⒶⓀ** *VISA* **◎** **ⒶⒺ**

*43 Morgan St ⌧ E3 5AA – **Ⓜ** Bow Road. – 𝒞 (020) 8980 6389*
– themorgan@geronimo-inns.co.uk – www.geronimo-inns.co.uk
– Closed 24-26 December, 1 January
Rest – (Closed Sunday dinner) (bookings not accepted) Carte £ 20/31
◆ Pub ◆

Characterful pub with mismatch of furniture and shabby chic appeal. Constantly evolving menu offers robust cooking, using some unusual and sometimes unfamiliar ingredients.

Canary Wharf

Four Seasons   ⇐ **Ⅰ₅** ⌾ ⌧ & **ⒶⓀ** 〒 ⁽ᵖ⁾ **⁂** ⌁ *VISA* **◎** **ⒶⒺ** **⓪**

*Westferry Circus ⌧ E14 8RS – **Ⓜ** Canary Wharf – 𝒞 (020) 7510 1999*
– sales.caw@fourseasons.com – Fax (020) 7510 19 98
– www.fourseasons.com/canarywharf
128 rm – **♦**£ 252/434 **♦♦**£ 270/494, ⌕ £ 25 – 14 suites
Rest *Quadrato* – see below
◆ Grand Luxury ◆ Classic ◆

Sleek and stylish with striking river and city views. Atrium lobby leading to modern bedrooms boasting every conceivable extra. Detailed service.

XX   **Quadrato** – at Four Seasons H.   ⌂ **ⒶⓀ** **Ⓟ** *VISA* **◎** **ⒶⒺ** **⓪**

*Westferry Circus ⌧ E14 8RS – **Ⓜ** Canary Wharf (DLR) – 𝒞 (020) 7510 1999*
– Fax (020) 7510 19 98 – www.fourseasons.com/canarywharf
Rest – Menu £ 27/33 – Carte £ 27/41
◆ Italian ◆ Design ◆

Striking, modern restaurant with terrace overlooking river. Sleek, stylish dining room with glass-fronted open-plan kitchen. Menu of northern Italian dishes; swift service.

XX   **Plateau**   **ⒶⓀ** *VISA* **◎** **ⒶⒺ** **⓪**

*Canada Place, Canada Square ⌧ E14 5ER – **Ⓜ** Canary Wharf (DLR)*
– 𝒞 (020) 7715 7100 – Fax (020) 7715 71 10 – www.conran.com
Rest – Menu £ 20/35 – Carte £ 24/35
◆ Modern ◆ Design ◆

Situated on fourth floor of 21C building; adjacent to Plateau Restaurant, with simpler table settings. Classical dishes, with seasonal base, employing grill specialities.

The Gun   ⌂ *VISA* **◎** **ⒶⒺ**

*27 Coldharbour ⌧ E14 9NS – **Ⓜ** Blackwall (DLR) – 𝒞 (020) 7515 5222*
– info@thegundocklands.com – www.thegundocklands.com
Rest – Carte £ 20/33
◆ Modern ◆ Pub ◆

Restored historic pub with a terrace facing the Dome: tasty dishes, including Billingsgate market fish, balance bold simplicity and a bit of French finesse. Efficient service.

Limehouse

The Narrow 🛋 AC ↵ ⇔ P VISA ◎ AE

Narrow Street ⊠ E14 8DP – Ⓜ Limehouse (DLR) – ✆ (020) 7592 7950
– thenarrow@gordonramsay.com – Fax (020) 7265 95 03
– www.gordonramsay.com *Plan I* **D2**
Rest – *(booking essential)* Carte £ 35/45
♦ British ♦ Pub ♦

Gordon Ramsay's Grade II listed former dockmaster's house on the edge of the Thames, restyled and serving good value old school British favourites. Spacious terrace.

Mile End

L'Oasis AC VISA ◎ AE

237 Mile End Rd ⊠ E1 4AA – Ⓜ Stepney Green. – ✆ (020) 7702 7051
– info@loasisstepney.co.uk – Fax (020) 7265 98 50
– www.loasisstepney.co.uk
– Closed Monday and Bank Holidays *Plan I* **D2**
Rest – Carte £ 20/33
♦ Pub ♦

Narrow, cavernous and bright, its original features include ornamental Victorian ceiling. Concise menus offer hearty, rustic cooking with influences from all over the world.

Spitalfields

St John Bread and Wine AC VISA ◎ AE

94-96 Commercial St ⊠ E1 6LZ – Ⓜ Shoreditch – ✆ (020) 7247 8724
– Fax (020) 7247 89 24 – www.stjohnbreadandwine.com *Plan I* **D2**
Rest – Carte £ 25/29
♦ Innovative ♦ Bistro ♦

Very popular neighbourhood bakery providing wide variety of home-made breads. Appealing, intimate dining section: all day menus that offer continually changing dishes.

Wapping

Wapping Food 🛋 P VISA ◎ AE

Wapping Wall ⊠ E1W 3ST – Ⓜ Wapping – ✆ (020) 7680 2080
– info@wapping-wpt.com – www.thewappingproject.com *Plan I* **D2**
Rest – Carte £ 26/42
♦ Modern ♦ Design ♦

Something a little unusual; a combination of restaurant and gallery in a converted hydraulic power station. Enjoy the modern menu surrounded by turbines and TV screens.

Whitechapel

Cafe Spice Namaste AC VISA ◎ AE ⓪

16 Prescot St ⊠ E1 8AZ – Ⓜ Tower Hill – ✆ (020) 7488 9242
– info@cafespice.co.uk – Fax (020) 7481 05 08 – www.cafespice.co.uk
Rest – Menu £ 30 – Carte £ 17/29 **N3**
♦ Indian ♦ Neighbourhood ♦

A riot of colour from the brightly painted walls to the flowing drapes. Sweet-natured service adds to the engaging feel. Fragrant and competitively priced Indian cooking.

Chelsea

Jumeirah Carlton Tower

Cadogan Pl ✉ *SW1X 9PY* – Ⓜ *Knightsbridge*
– ✆ *(020) 7235 1234* – *jctinfo@jumeirah.com* – *Fax (020) 7235 91 29*
– *www.jumeirah.com* **F5**

190 rm – †£ 288/550 ††£ 288/550, ☕ £ 30 – 30 suites
Rest *Rib Room* – Carte £ 40/68

◆ Grand Luxury ◆ Classic ◆

Imposing international hotel overlooking a leafy square. Well-equipped roof-top health club has funky views. Generously proportioned rooms boast every conceivable facility. Rib Room restaurant has a clubby atmosphere.

Wyndham Grand

Chelsea Harbour ✉ *SW10 0XG* – Ⓜ *Fulham Broadway*
– ✆ *(020) 7823 3000*
– *wyndhamlondon@wyndham.com*
– *Fax (020) 7352 81 74*
– *www.wyndhamgrandlondon.co.uk* **D8**

160 suites – ††£ 558, ☕ £ 20
Rest *Aquasia* – see below
Rest *Aquasia* – Carte £ 25/45

◆ Luxury ◆ Modern ◆

Modern, all-suite hotel within an exclusive marina and retail development. Many of the spacious and well-appointed rooms have balconies and views across the Thames.

Sheraton Park Tower

101 Knightsbridge ✉ *SW1X 7RN* – Ⓜ *Knightsbridge*
– ✆ *(020) 7235 8050*
– *central.london.reservations@sheraton.com*
– *Fax (020) 7235 82 31*
– *www.luxurycollection.com/parktowerlondon* **F4**

275 rm – †£ 505 ††£ 705, ☕ £ 25 – 5 suites **Rest *One-O-One*** – see below

◆ Luxury ◆ Business ◆

Built in the 1970s in a unique cylindrical shape. Well-equipped bedrooms are all identical in size. Top floor executive rooms have commanding views of Hyde Park and City.

Capital

22-24 Basil St ✉ *SW3 1AT* – Ⓜ *Knightsbridge* – ✆ *(020) 7589 5171*
– *reservations@capitalhotel.co.uk* – *Fax (020) 7225 00 11*
– *www.capitalhotel.co.uk* **F5**

49 rm – †£ 253 ††£ 345/523, ☕ £ 18.50
Rest *The Capital Restaurant* – see below

◆ Luxury ◆ Traditional ◆ Classic ◆

Discreet and privately owned town house with distinct English charm. Individually decorated rooms with plenty of thoughtful touches.

Draycott

26 Cadogan Gdns ✉ *SW3 2RP* – Ⓜ *Sloane Square*
– ✆ *(020) 7730 6466* – *reservations@draycotthotel.com*
– *Fax (020) 7730 02 36* – *www.draycotthotel.com* **F6**

31 rm – †£ 158/183 ††£ 233/370, ☕ £ 21.95 – 4 suites
Rest – *(room service only)*

◆ Townhouse ◆ Stylish ◆

Charmingly discreet 19C house with elegant sitting room overlooking tranquil garden, for afternoon tea. Individual rooms in a country house style, named after writers or actors.

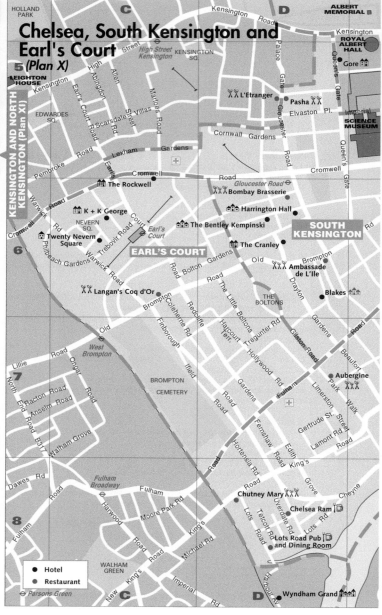

Chelsea, South Kensington and Earl's Court
(Plan X)

HOLLAND PARK

ALBERT MEMORIAL

Kensington Road

LEIGHTON HOUSE

High Street Kensington

KENSINGTON SQ.

Kensington ROYAL ALBERT HALL

Gore

L'Etranger

Pasha

Elvaston Pl.

EDWARDES SQ.

Earl's Court Road

Scarsdale Villas

Marloes Road

Cornwall Gardens

SCIENCE MUSEUM

Pembroke Road

Lexham Gardens

Cromwell Road

Cromwell Road

The Rockwell

Gloucester Road

Bombay Brasserie

K + K George

NEVERN SQ.

Trebovir Road

Earl's Court

EARL'S COURT

Harrington Hall

The Bentley Kempinski

SOUTH KENSINGTON

Twenty Nevern Square

Philbeach Gardens

Warwick Road

Old Brompton Road

The Cranley

Brompton

Ambassade de L'Ile

Blakes

Langan's Coq d'Or

Bolton Gardens

The Little Boltons

THE BOLTONS

Brompton

Coleherne Rd

Redcliffe

Finborough Road

Ifield

West Brompton

BROMPTON CEMETERY

Harcourt Terr.

Tregunter Rd

Hollywood Rd

Gardens

Gunter Grove

Aubergine

Lillie Road

North End Road

Racton Road

Anselm Road

Walham Grove

Fernshaw Road

Edith Grove

Gertrude St.

Lamont Road

Dawes Rd

Fulham Broadway

Moore Park Rd

King's Road

Hortensia Rd

Chutney Mary

Chelsea Ram

Uverdale Rd

WALHAM GREEN

Parsons Green

Harwood Road

Michael Rd

King's Road

Imperial Rd

New King's Rd

Telcott Rd

Lots Road

Lots Road Pub and Dining Room

Cheyne

Harbour Av.

Wyndham Grand

● Hotel

● Restaurant

950

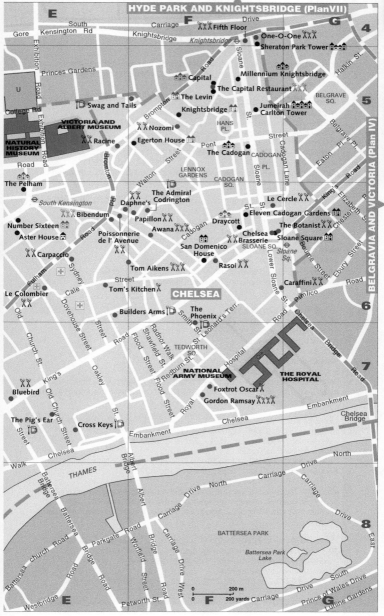

HYDE PARK AND KNIGHTSBRIDGE (Plan VII)

Gore
South Kensington Rd
Carriage
Drive
Fifth Floor
Knightsbridge
Knightsbridge
One-O-One
Sheraton Park Tower
Halkin St.
BELGRAVE SQ.

Princes Gardens

Exhibition Road

College Rd

U

Capital
Millennium Knightsbridge
The Capital Restaurant
Swag and Tails
The Levin
Brompton
Knightsbridge
Jumeirah
Carlton Tower

VICTORIA AND ALBERT MUSEUM

NATURAL HISTORY MUSEUM

Nozomi
Racine
Egerton House
HANS PL.
Street
Cadogan Lane
Pont
The Cadogan
CADOGAN

The Pelham

South Kensington

LENNOX GARDENS
CADOGAN SQ.
CADOGAN PL.

Walton
Street

Le Cercle
Eleven Cadogan Gardens
Draycott
The Botanist
Chelsea
Brasserie
Sloane Square
Eaton Pl.
Belgrave Pl.
King's
Elizabeth
Street

The Admiral Codrington
Daphne's
Bibendum
Papillon
Awana
Poissonnerie de l'Avenue
San Domenico House
SLOANE SQ.
Sloane Sq.
Rasoi

Number Sixteen
Aster House
Carpaccio
Bourne Street
Ebury Street

Tom Aikens
Caraffini
Pimlico
Fulham
Tom's Kitchen
Street
CHELSEA

Le Colombier
Cale
Street
Dovehouse Street
Sydney
Builders Arms
The Phoenix
St. Leonard's Terr.
Chelsea
Bridge
Road

Church St.
Oakley
TEDWORTH SQ.
Radnor Walk
Shawfield St.
Flood Street
Royal Hospital

NATIONAL ARMY MUSEUM
THE ROYAL HOSPITAL

Bluebird
King's
Old Church Street
Foxtrot Oscar
Gordon Ramsay
Embankment
Chelsea Bridge
Chelsea Bridge Road

The Pig's Ear
Cross Keys
Chelsea
Embankment
North

Walk
Chelsea
THAMES
Albert Bridge
Carriage
Drive
North
Carriage
Drive East

Battersea Bridge
Battersea church Road
Albert Bridge
Parkgate Road
Woodfield Street
Carriage Drive West
Petworth St.

BATTERSEA PARK

Battersea Park Lake

Westbridge Road
0   200 m
0   200 yards
Prince of Wales Drive
Lurline Gardens

951

UNITED KINGDOM - LONDON

The Cadogan � ᴌ㕭 ℀ AC sat ℣ �2A VISA ⓪③ AE ⓪

75 Sloane St ⊠ *SW1X 9SG* – Ⓜ *Knightsbridge* – ℰ *(020) 7235 7141*
– *info@thesteingroup.com* – *Fax (020) 7245 09 94* – *www.cadogan.com*
63 rm – ♥£ 300/347 ♥♥£ 347, ⊊ £ 24 – 2 suites   **F5**
Rest – Menu £ 23 – Carte £ 38/50
♦ Luxury ♦ Cosy ♦

An Edwardian town house, where Oscar Wilde was arrested; modernised and
refurbished with a French accent. Contemporary drawing room. Stylish bedrooms;
latest facilities.

Millennium Knightsbridge ᒻ rm AC sat ℣ �2A VISA ⓪③ AE ⓪

17-25 Sloane St ⊠ *SW1X 9NU* – Ⓜ *Knightsbridge* – ℰ *(020) 7235 4377*
– *reservations.knightsbridge@mill-cop.com* – *Fax (020) 7235 37 05*
– *www.millenniumhotels.co.uk/knightsbridge*   **F5**
218 rm – ♥£ 176/323 ♥♥£ 265/393, ⊊ £ 25.75 – 4 suites
Rest *Mju* – ℰ *(020) 7201 6330* – Menu £ 24/36
♦ Business ♦ Modern ♦

Modern, corporate hotel in the heart of London's most fashionable shopping district. Club bedrooms are well-appointed and equipped with the latest technology.

Knightsbridge ᒻ rm AC sat ℣ VISA ⓪③ AE ⓪

10 Beaufort Gdns ⊠ *SW3 1PT* – Ⓜ *Knightsbridge* – ℰ *(020) 7584 6300*
– *knightsbridge@firmdale.com* – *Fax (020) 7584 63 55*
– *www.knightsbridgehotel.com*   **F5**
44 rm – ♥£ 200/247 ♥♥£ 345/405, ⊊ £ 17.50
Rest – *(room service only)* *(room service only)*
♦ Luxury ♦ Townhouse ♦ Stylish ♦

Attractively furnished town house with a very stylish, discreet feel. Every bedroom
is immaculately appointed and has an individuality of its own; fine detailing
throughout.

The Sloane Square H. ᒻ AC ℣ VISA ⓪③ AE

Sloane Sq ⊠ *SW1W 8EG* – Ⓜ *Sloane Square* – ℰ *(020) 7896 9988*
– *reservations@sloanesquarehotel.co.uk* – *Fax (020) 7751 42 11*
– *www.sloanesquarehotel.co.uk*   **F6**
102 rm – ♥£ 125/168 ♥♥£ 175/245, ⊊ £ 10.75
Rest Chelsea Brasserie – see below
♦ Business ♦ Modern ♦

Redbrick hotel opened in 2007, boasts bright, contemporary décor. Stylish, coordi-
nated bedrooms, with laptops; library of DVDs and games available. Rooms at back
slightly quieter.

The Levin AC ℣ VISA ⓪③ AE ⓪

28 Basil St ⊠ *SW3 1AS* – Ⓜ *Knightsbridge* – ℰ *(020) 7589 6286*
– *reservations@thelevinhotel.co.uk* – *Fax (020) 7823 78 26*
– *www.thelevinhotel.co.uk*   **F5**
12 rm – ♥♥£ 300/535, ⊊ £ 16.50
Rest Le Metro – *(Closed Sunday dinner)* Carte £ 27/37
♦ Townhouse ♦ Classic ♦

Impressive façade, contemporary interior and comfortable bedrooms in subtle art
deco style, boasting marvellous champagne mini bars. Sister to The Capital hotel.
Informal brasserie offers classic bistro fare; includes blackboard menu and pies of
the week.

San Domenico House ጛ AC ℣ VISA ⓪③ AE ⓪

29-31 Draycott Pl ⊠ *SW3 2SH* – Ⓜ *Sloane Square* – ℰ *(020) 7581 5757*
– *info@sandomenicohouse.com* – *Fax (020) 7584 13 48*
– *www.sandomenicohouse.com*   **F6**
15 rm – ♥£ 210/246 ♥♥£ 255/299, ⊊ £ 22   **Rest** – *(room service only)*
♦ Townhouse ♦ Classic ♦

Intimate and discreet Victorian town house with an attractive rooftop terrace. Individually styled and generally spacious rooms with antique furniture and rich
fabrics.

Egerton House
17-19 Egerton Terrace ⊠ *SW3 2BX –* Ⓜ *South Kensington*
– 𝒞 (020) 7589 2412 – bookeg@rchmail.com
– Fax (020) 7584 65 40
– www.egertonhousehotel.com **F5**
27 rm – ♦£ 300 ♦♦£ 370, ⌷ £ 24.50 – 1 suite
Rest *– (room service only)*
♦ Townhouse ♦ Classic ♦

Discreet, compact but comfortable townhouse in a good location, recently refurbished throughout and owned by Red Carnation group. High levels of personal service make the hotel stand out.

Eleven Cadogan Gardens
11 Cadogan Gardens ⊠ *SW3 2RJ –* Ⓜ *Sloane Square*
– 𝒞 (020) 7730 7000 – info@no11london.com – Fax (020) 7730 52 17
– www.no11london.com **I6**
60 rm – ♦£ 194/553 ♦♦£ 294/617, ⌷ £ 20
Rest *– Carte £ 31/45*
♦ Townhouse ♦ Classic ♦

Made up of four Victorian houses; decorated in a flamboyant style, particularly the richly furnished lounge. Bedrooms currently more traditional in style. Concise menu in basement dining room.

Gordon Ramsay
✿✿✿
68-69 Royal Hospital Rd ⊠ *SW3 4HP –* Ⓜ *Sloane Square*
– 𝒞 (020) 7352 4441 – Fax (020) 7352 33 34
– www.gordonramsay.com
– Closed 1 week Christmas - New Year, Saturday and Sunday **F7**
Rest *– (booking essential)* Menu £ 45/90 ⅋
Spec. Roasted Scottish lobster tail, bouillabaisse sauce, cabbage and ratatouille. Best end of lamb and confit shoulder, provençale vegetables, spinach, thyme jus. Prune and armagnac soufflé with chocolate sorbet.
♦ French ♦ Formal ♦

Discreetly located, with meticulous service; its best tables by the windows. Luxury ingredients employed in perfectly balanced classical dishes. Book 2 months in advance.

The Capital Restaurant – at Capital Hotel
✿✿
22-24 Basil St – Ⓜ *Knightsbridge – 𝒞 (020) 7589 5171*
– reservations@capitalhotel.co.uk – Fax (020) 7225 00 11
– www.capitalhotel.co.uk **F5**
Rest *– (booking essential)* Menu £ 38/58 ⅋
Spec. Crab lasagne with langoustine cappuccino. Saddle of rabbit provençale with seared calamari. Iced coffee parfait with chocolate fondant.
♦ French ♦ Formal ♦

Hotel restaurant imbued with an understated elegance. Confident, precise cooking; classical dishes come with impishly ingenious touches. Enthusiastic and knowledgeable staff.

Bibendum
Michelin House, 81 Fulham Rd ⊠ *SW3 6RD –* Ⓜ *South Kensington*
– 𝒞 (020) 7581 5817 – reservations@bibendum.co.uk
– Fax (020) 7823 79 25 – www.bibendum.co.uk
– Closed 25-26 December and 1 January **E6**
Rest *– Menu £ 30 – Carte £ 41/60* ⅋
♦ French ♦ Design ♦

A fine example of Art Nouveau architecture; a London landmark. 1st floor restaurant with striking stained glass 'Michelin Man'. Attentive service of modern British cooking.

XXX �

Tom Aikens   🆔 VISA ⊙⊙ AE

43 Elystan St ⊠ SW3 3NT – ⓜ *South Kensington –* ℰ *(020) 7584 2003*
– info@tomaikens.co.uk – Fax (020) 7584 20 01 – www.tomaikens.co.uk
– closed last two weeks August, 10 days Christmas-New Year, Saturday,
Sunday and Bank Holidays   **E6**
Rest – Menu £ 29/65 ⅏

Spec. Lobster and rabbit roasted in vanilla butter with cannelloni. Cutlet and belly of pork with squid. Truffle and vanilla panna cotta with truffle mousse.
◆ Innovative ◆ Fashionable ◆

Minimalist in style, with a warm feel. Classically based French cooking features original touches, with the focus firmly on seasonal, traceable ingredients. Attentive service.

XXX ⊙

Aubergine (William Drabble)   🆔 VISA ⊙⊙ AE ⊙

11 Park Walk ⊠ SW10 0AJ – ⓜ *South Kensington –* ℰ *(020) 7352 3449*
– info@auberginerestaurant.co.uk – Fax (020) 7351 17 70
– www.auberginerestaurant.co.uk
– closed 2 weeks Christmas, Easter, Saturday lunch, Sunday and Bank Holidays
Rest – *(booking essential)* Menu £ 34/64   **D7**
Spec. Assiette of foie gras. Baked fillets of sole, apple, mussels and chives. Iced clementine mousse with rhubarb.
◆ French ◆ Formal ◆

Longstanding restaurant in heart of Chelsea, serving classic French cooking which shows off the kitchen's considerable skill. Elegant, intimate feel; immaculately laid tables.

XXX

One-O-One – at Sheraton Park Tower H.   🆔 VISA ⊙⊙ AE ⊙

101 Knightsbridge ⊠ SW1X 7RN – ⓜ *Knightsbridge –* ℰ *(020) 7290 7101*
– Fax (020) 7235 61 96 – www.onetoonerestaurant.com   **F4**
Rest – *(closed 25-26 December and 1 January)* Menu £ 19 – Carte £ 19/69
◆ Seafood ◆ Design ◆

Brittany-born chef focuses primarily on seafood, especially Norwegian, served either in standard sizes or 'petits plats' for a more flexible eating experience.

XXX

Fifth Floor – at Harvey Nichols   🆔 🕾 VISA ⊙⊙ AE ⊙

Knightsbridge ⊠ SW1X 7RJ – ⓜ *Knightsbridge –* ℰ *(020) 7235 5250*
– reception@harveynicols.com – Fax (0870) 1 91 60 19
– www.harveynichols.com
– closed Christmas and Sunday dinner   **F4**
Rest – Menu £ 20 – Carte £ 29/47 ⅏
◆ Modern European ◆ Fashionable ◆

Stylish, colour-changing surroundings on Harvey Nichols' fifth floor, reached via its own lift. Modern cooking with some originality and the emphasis on France. Good wine list.

XXX

Awana   🆔 VISA ⊙⊙ AE ⊙

85 Sloane Ave ⊠ SW3 3DX – ⓜ *South Kensington –* ℰ *(020) 7584 8880*
– info@awana.co.uk – Fax (020) 7584 61 88 – www.awana.co.uk
– Closed 25-26 December and 1 January   **F6**
Rest – *(booking essential)* Menu £ 15 (lunch) – Carte £ 26/43
◆ Malaysian ◆ Exotic ◆

Enter into stylish cocktail bar. Traditional Malay elements adorn restaurant. Satay chef cooks to order. Malaysian dishes authentically prepared and smartly presented.

XXX

Chutney Mary   🆔 ✧ VISA ⊙⊙ AE ⊙

535 King's Rd ⊠ SW10 0SZ – ⓜ *Fulham Broadway –* ℰ *(020) 7351 3113*
– chutneymary@realindianfood.com – Fax (020) 7351 76 94 – www.
realindianfood   **D8**
Rest – *(dinner only and lunch Saturday and Sunday)* Carte £ 34/45
◆ Indian ◆ Exotic ◆

Soft lighting and sepia etchings hold sway at this forever popular restaurant. Extensive menu of specialities from all corners of India. Complementary wine list.

XX **Daphne's** `AC` `⇆` `VISA` `OO` `AE` `O`

112 Draycott Ave ✉ *SW3 3AE* – Ⓜ *South Kensington* – ℰ *(020) 7589 4257*
– reservations@daphnes-restaurant.co.uk – Fax (020) 7225 27 66
– www.daphnes-restaurant.co.uk
– closed 25-26 December   **E6**
Rest *– (booking essential)* Menu £ 17 (lunch) – Carte £ 33/49
 ◆ Italian ◆ Fashionable ◆
Positively buzzes in the evening, the Chelsea set gelling smoothly and seamlessly with the welcoming Tuscan interior ambience. A modern twist updates classic Italian dishes.

XX **Rasoi** (Vineet Bhatia) `AC` `⇆` `VISA` `OO` `AE` `O`
ಜ
10 Lincoln St ✉ *SW3 2TS* – Ⓜ *Sloane Square* – ℰ *(020) 7225 1881*
– info@rasoirestaurant.co.uk – Fax (020) 7581 02 20
– www.rasoirestaurant.co.uk
– closed 25 -26 December, Saturday lunch, and Sunday   **F6**
Rest – Menu £ 26 (lunch) – Carte £ 55/80
Spec. Mustard infused chicken tikka with milk fritter and chilli chutney. Lamb shank and morels with saffron mash, rosemary naan. Rose petal sandwich with saffron yoghurt and fruit jelly.
 ◆ Indian ◆ Intimate ◆
L-shaped dining room and conservatory decorated with Indian trinkets; intimate upstairs rooms. Contemporary Indian cooking with subtle spicing and innovative flavour combinations.

XX **Racine** `AC` `🖘` `VISA` `OO` `AE`

239 Brompton Rd ✉ *SW3 2EP* – Ⓜ *South Kensington* – ℰ *(020) 7584 4477*
– Fax (020) 7584 49 00
– closed 25 December   **E5**
Rest – Menu £ 20 – Carte £ 31/47
 ◆ French ◆ Brasserie ◆
Dark leather banquettes, large mirrors and wood floors create the atmosphere of a genuine Parisienne brasserie. Tasty, well crafted, regional French fare.

XX **Chelsea Brasserie** – at The Sloane Square Hotel   `AC` `🖘`

7-12 Sloane Sq. ✉ *SW1W 8EG* – Ⓜ *Sloane Square*   `VISA` `OO` `AE` `O`
– ℰ (020) 7881 5999 – robert@chelsea-brasserie.co.uk
– www.sloanesquarehotel.co.uk
– closed 25 December
Rest *– (closed Sunday dinner)* Carte £ 24/42   **F6**
 ◆ French ◆ Brasserie ◆
Glass doors open into roomy brasserie-style restaurant, with smoky green lamps and brick walls inlaid with mirror tiles. A European menu includes some classic French dishes.

XX **Papillon** `AC` `⇆` `VISA` `OO` `AE`

96 Draycott Ave ✉ *SW3 3AD* – Ⓜ *South Kensington* – ℰ *(020) 7225 2555*
– info@papillonchelsea.co.uk – Fax (020) 7225 25 54
– www.papillonchelsea.co.uk
– closed 24-26 December and 1January   **F6**
Rest *– (closed Sunday dinner)* Menu £ 17 (lunch) – Carte £ 33/51
 ◆ French ◆ Brasserie ◆
Classic French regional fare, from fish soup to Chateaubriand, all feature at this well run brasserie. French windows, lamps and a fleur-de-lys motif add to the authenticity.

XX **Nozomi** `AC` `⇆` `VISA` `OO` `AE`

15 Beauchamp Pl ✉ *SW3 1NQ* – Ⓜ *Knightsbridge* – ℰ *(020) 7838 1500*
– marios@nozomi.co.uk – Fax (020) 7838 10 01 – www.nozomi.co.uk
– Closed Sunday   **F5**
Rest – Carte £ 50/80
 ◆ Japanese ◆ Minimalist ◆
DJ mixes lounge music at the front bar; up the stairs in the restaurant the feeling is minimal with soft lighting. Innovative Japanese menus provide an interesting choice.

XX **Bluebird**   AC ⇔ ☜ VISA ☜ AE ☜

350 King's Rd ⊠ *SW3 5UU –* Ⓜ *Sloane Square –* ℰ *(020) 7559 1000*
– enquiries@bluebird-restaurant.co.uk – Fax (020) 7559 11 15
– www.bluebird-restaurant.com   **E7**
Rest – Menu £ 19 – Carte £ 32/52
♦ British ♦ Design ♦
A foodstore, café and homeware shop also feature at this impressive skylit restaurant. Much of the modern British food is cooked in wood-fired ovens. Lively atmosphere.

XX **Poissonnerie de l'Avenue**   AC ⇔ VISA ☜ AE ☜

82 Sloane Ave ⊠ *SW3 3DZ –* Ⓜ *South Kensington –* ℰ *(020) 7589 2457*
– peterr@poissoneire.co.uk – Fax (020) 7581 33 60
– www.poissonneriedelavenue.co.uk
– closed 24-26 December and Sunday   **E6**
Rest – Menu £ 24 (lunch) – Carte £ 29/45
♦ French ♦ Formal ♦
A Chelsea institution with a loyal following. Classically decorated and comfortable. Emphasis on well-sourced and very fresh seafood, in dishes with a Mediterranean accent.

XX **Le Cercle**   AC VISA ☜ AE

1 Wilbraham Pl ⊠ *SW1X 9AE –* Ⓜ *Sloane Square –* ℰ *(020) 7901 9999*
– info@lecercle.co.uk – Fax (020) 7901 91 11 – www.lecercle.co.uk
– closed Christmas - New Year, Sunday, Monday and Bank Holidays
Rest – Menu £ 15 (lunch) – Carte £ 18/31   **F6**
♦ French ♦ Fashionable ♦
Discreetly signed basement restaurant down residential side street. High, spacious room with chocolate banquettes. Tapas style French menus; accomplished cooking.

XX **Le Colombier**   ⇔ ☜ VISA ☜ AE

145 Dovehouse St ⊠ *SW3 6LB –* Ⓜ *South Kensington –* ℰ *(020) 7351 1155*
– lecolombier1998@aol.com – Fax (020) 7351 51 24
– www.lecolombier-sw3.co.uk   **E6**
Rest – Menu £ 16/19 – Carte £ 30/40
♦ French ♦ Neighbourhood ♦
Proudly Gallic corner restaurant in an affluent residential area. Attractive enclosed terrace. Bright and cheerful surroundings and service of traditional French cooking.

XX **Caraffini**   ☜ AC VISA ☜ AE

61-63 Lower Sloane St ⊠ *SW1W 8DH –* Ⓜ *Sloane Square –* ℰ *(020) 7259 0235*
– info@caraffini.co.uk – Fax (020) 7259 02 36 – www.caraffini.co.uk
– closed 25 December, Easter, Sunday and Bank Holidays   **F6**
Rest – *(booking essential)* Carte £ 27/38
♦ Italian ♦ Friendly ♦
The omnipresent and ebullient owner oversees the friendly service in this attractive neighbourhood restaurant. Authentic and robust Italian cooking; informal atmosphere.

XX **Carpaccio**   AC ⇔ VISA ☜ AE

4 Sydney St ⊠ *SW3 6PP –* Ⓜ *South Kensington –* ℰ *(020) 7352 3435*
– carpacciorest@aol.com – Fax (020) 7622 83 04
– www.carpacciorestaurant.co.uk
– closed 25 December, Easter, last 2 weeks August, Sunday and Bank Holidays
Rest – Carte £ 23/35   **E6**
♦ Italian ♦ Neighbourhood ♦
Fine Georgian exterior housing James Bond stills, 1920s silent Italian comedies, Ayrton Senna's Honda cockpit, witty waiters, and enjoyable, classical Trattoria style cooking.

XX **The Botanist** AC VISA ©© AE

7 Sloane Square ✉ SW1W 8EE – Ⓜ Sloane Square – ℰ (020) 7730 0077
– info@thebotanistonsloanesquare.com – Fax (020) 7730 71 77
– www.thebotanistonsloanesquare.com **F6**
Rest – Carte £ 26/43
♦ Modern European ♦ Wine bar ♦

Busy bar, popular with after-work crowd; the swish and stylish restaurant occupies the other half of this corner site. Crisp and clean cooking, with influences kept within Europe.

X **Foxtrot Oscar** AC VISA ©© AE ①

79 Royal Hospital Rd ✉ SW3 4HN – Ⓜ Sloane Square – ℰ (020) 7349 9595
– foxtrotoscar@gordonramsay.com – Fax (020) 7592 16 03
– www.gordonramsay.com **F7**
Rest – (booking essential) Carte £ 20/30
♦ Traditional ♦ Cosy ♦

A real Chelsea institution, now under the ownership of the Gordon Ramsay group. Expect authentic comfort food from cassoulet and coq au vin to burgers and eggs Benedict and all at sensible prices.

X **Tom's Kitchen** VISA ©© AE

27 Cale St ✉ SW3 3QP – Ⓜ South Kensington – ℰ (020) 7349 0202
– info@tomskitchen.co.uk – Fax (020) 7823 36 52 – www.tomskitchen.co.uk
– Closed 25 Decmeber and 1 January **E6**
Rest – Carte £ 29/51
♦ French ♦ Neighbourhood ♦

A converted pub, whose white tiles and mirrors help to give it an industrial feel. Appealing and wholesome dishes come in man-sized portions. The eponymous Tom is Tom Aikens.

🍴🍴 **The Admiral Codrington** 🛎 AC ⇄ VISA ©© AE ①

17 Mossop St ✉ SW3 2LY – Ⓜ South Kensington – ℰ (020) 7581 0005
– admiral-codrington@333holdingsltd.com – Fax (020) 7589 24 52
– www.theadmiralcodrington.com
– Closed 24-27 December **F6**
Rest – Carte £ 25/32
♦ Pub ♦

Local landmark pub, with separate dining room complete with retractable roof. Menu is an appealing mix of satisfying British and European classics. The bar gets busy in the evenings.

🍴🍴 **Chelsea Ram** AC VISA ©©

32 Burnaby St ✉ SW10 0PL – Ⓜ Fulham Broadway – ℰ (020) 7351 4008
– bookings@chelsearam.co.uk **D8**
Rest – Carte £ 20/27
♦ Pub ♦

A stalwart of the London pub scene. Full table service of honest home-cooking and comforting classics, from lamb chops to cottage pies and heart-warming puddings. Over 20 wines by the glass.

🍴🍴 **Swag and Tails** VISA ©© AE

10-11 Fairholt St, Knightsbridge ✉ SW7 1EG – Ⓜ Knightsbridge
– ℰ (020) 7584 6926 – theswag@swagandtails.com – Fax (020) 7581 99 35
– www.swagandtails.com
– Closed Christmas-New Year, Saturday, Sunday and Bank Holidays
Rest – Carte £ 22/32 **EF5**
♦ Pub ♦

Attractive Victorian pub close to Harrods and the fashionable Knightsbridge shops. Polite and approachable service of a blackboard menu of light snacks and seasonal dishes.

Builders Arms
AK VISA ©© AE

13 Britten St ⊠ SW3 3TY – Ⓜ *South Kensington –* ℰ *(020) 7349 9040*
– buildersarms@geronimo-inns.co.uk – www.geronimo-inns.co.uk
– Closed 25-26 December **E6**
Rest *– (bookings not accepted)* Carte £ 20/35
◆ Pub ◆
Extremely busy modern 'gastropub' favoured by the locals. Eclectic menu of contemporary dishes with blackboard specials. Polite service from a young and eager team.

The Pig's Ear
VISA ©© AE

35 Old Church St ⊠ SW3 5BS – Ⓜ *Sloane Square –* ℰ *(020) 7352 2908*
– thepigsear@hotmail.co.uk – Fax (020) 7352 93 21 – www.thepigsear.co.uk
– Closed 10 days Christmas to New Year **E7**
Rest *–* Carte £ 30/50
◆ Pub ◆
Busy bar, romantic panelled dining room and cosy, curtained-off Blue Room with fire. Modern British meets Mediterranean menu; dishes like beef marrow or lamb stew and dumplings.

The Phoenix
⏚ AK VISA ©© AE

23 Smith St ⊠ SW3 4EE – Ⓜ *Sloane Square –* ℰ *(020) 7730 9182*
– thephoenix@geronimo-inns.co.uk – www.geronimo-inns.co.uk
– Closed 25-26 December **F6-7**
Rest *–* Carte £ 15/25
◆ Pub ◆
The main bar is popular with locals but go through to the dining room at the back which was redecorated in 2008. Expect proper pub food with interesting and seasonal daily specials.

The Cross Keys
AK VISA ©© AE

1 Lawrence St ⊠ SW3 5NB – Ⓜ *South Kensington –* ℰ *(020) 7349 9111*
– xkeys.nicole@hotmail.co.uk – Fax (020) 7349 93 33 – www.thexkeys.net
– Closed 24-25 December, 1 January, Bank Holidays **E7**
Rest *–* Carte £ 25/30
◆ Pub ◆
Hidden away near the Embankment, this 18C pub has period furniture and impressive carved stone fireplaces. Interesting, modern menus include blackboard of daily specials.

Lots Road Pub & Dining Room
AK VISA ©© AE

114 Lots Rd ⊠ SW10 0RJ – Ⓜ *Fulham Broadway –* ℰ *(020) 7352 6645*
– lotsroad@foodandfuel.co.uk – Fax (020) 7376 49 75 – www.lotsroadpub.com
Rest *– (Closed Sunday)* Carte £ 20/26 **D8**
◆ Pub ◆
Traditional corner pub with an open-plan kitchen, flowers at each table and large modern pictures on the walls. Contemporary menus change daily.

South Kensington

The Pelham
Ⅰ₄ AK ☐ ᵠ VISA ©© AE ⓪

15 Cromwell Pl ⊠ SW7 2LA – Ⓜ *South Kensington –* ℰ *(020) 7589 8288*
– reservations@pelhamhotel.co.uk – Fax (020) 7584 84 44
– www.pelhamhotel.co.uk **E6**
51 rm *–* ♦£ 212/235 ♦♦£ 341, ⊇ £ 17.50 – 1 suite
Rest *Kemps –* Menu £ 18 – Carte £ 29/41
◆ Luxury ◆ Stylish ◆
Attractive Victorian town house with a discreet and comfortable feel. Wood panelled drawing room and individually decorated bedrooms with marble bathrooms. Detailed service. Warm basement dining room.

UNITED KINGDOM - LONDON

Blakes *$\downarrow$ AC rest "1" VISA ∞ AE $\oplus$*

33 Roland Gdns ⊠ SW7 3PF – **⊕** Gloucester Road – $\mathcal{C}$ (020) 7370 6701
– blakes@blakeshotels.com – Fax (020) 7373 04 42 – www.blakeshotels.com
40 rm – **†**£ 176/311 **††**£ 382/441, ⊆ £ 25 – 8 suites
Rest – Carte £ 60/90   **D6**

♦ Luxury ♦ Design ♦

Behind the Victorian façade lies one of London's first 'boutique' hotels. Dramatic,
bold and eclectic décor, with oriental influences and antiques from around the
globe. Fashionable restaurant with bamboo and black walls.

The Bentley *$\downarrow$ $\gg$ AC $\boxdot$ $\langle$"$\rangle$ $\acute{A}$ VISA ∞ AE $\oplus$*

27-33 Harrington Gdns ⊠ SW7 4JX – **⊕** Gloucester Road – $\mathcal{C}$ (020) 7244 5555
– info@thebentley-hotel.com – Fax (020) 7244 55 66
– www.thebentley-hotel.com   **D6**
52 rm – **†**£ 353 **††**£ 470, ⊆ £ 22.50 – 12 suites
Rest 1880 – (closed Sunday-Monday) (dinner only) Menu £ 26/32 – Carte £ 34/
53

♦ Grand Luxury ♦ Classic ♦

A number of stucco-fronted 19C houses were joined to create this opulent, lavish
hotel decorated with marble, mosaics and ornate gold leaf. Bedrooms with gorgeous silk fabrics. 1880 for formal dining and ambitious cooking.

NH Harrington Hall *$\downarrow$ $\gg$ AC $\boxdot$ "1" $\acute{A}$ VISA ∞ AE $\oplus$*

5-25 Harrington Gdns ⊠ SW7 4JB – **⊕** Gloucester Road – $\mathcal{C}$ (020) 7396 9696
– nhharringtonhall@nh-hotels.com – Fax (020) 7396 17 19
– www.nh-hotels.com   **D6**
200 rm – **†**£ 210 **††**£ 270, ⊆ £ 18
Rest Wetherby's – Menu £ 16 – Carte £ 26/35

♦ Business ♦ Functional ♦

A series of adjoined terraced houses, with an attractive period façade that belies
the size. Tastefully furnished bedrooms, with an extensive array of facilities. Classically decorated dining room.

Number Sixteen without rest *$\rightleftharpoons$ AC $\langle$"$\rangle$ VISA ∞ AE*

16 Sumner Pl ⊠ SW7 3EG – **⊕** South Kensington – $\mathcal{C}$ (020) 7589 5232
– sixteen@firmdale.com – Fax (020) 7584 86 15
– www.numbersixteenhotel.co.uk   **E6**
42 rm – **†**£ 141/235 **††**£ 317, ⊆ £ 17.50

♦ Townhouse ♦ Stylish ♦

Enticingly refurbished 19C town houses in smart area. Discreet entrance, comfy sitting room and charming breakfast terrace. Bedrooms in English country house
style.

The Cranley *AC $\langle$"$\rangle$ VISA ∞ AE $\oplus$*

10 Bina Gardens ⊠ SW5 0LA – **⊕** Gloucester Road – $\mathcal{C}$ (020) 7373 0123
– info@thecranley.com – Fax (020) 7373 94 97 – www.thecranley.com
38 rm – **†**£ 264/294 **††**£ 294, ⊆ £ 19.50 – 1 suite
Rest – (room service only)   **D6**

♦ Townhouse ♦ Stylish ♦

Delightful Regency town house combines charm and period details with modern
comforts and technology. Individually styled bedrooms; some with four-posters.
Room service available.

The Gore *AC $\langle$"$\rangle$ $\acute{A}$ VISA ∞ AE $\oplus$*

190 Queen's Gate ⊠ SW7 5EX – **⊕** Gloucester Road – $\mathcal{C}$ (020) 7584 6601
– reservations@gorehotel.com – Fax (020) 7589 81 27 – www.gorehotel.com
50 rm – **†**£ 212/269 **††**£ 269, ⊆ £ 16.95   **D5**
Rest 190 Queensgate – (booking essential) Carte £ 27/39

♦ Townhouse ♦ Personalised ♦

Idiosyncratic Victorian house, with lobby covered with pictures and prints. Individually styled bedrooms have discreet mod cons and charming bathrooms. Informal bistro with European menu.

UNITED KINGDOM - LONDON

The Rockwell

181-183 Cromwell Rd ⊠ SW5 0SF – Ⓜ Earl's Court – ℘ (020) 7244 2000
– enquiries@therockwell.com – Fax (020) 7244 20 01 – www.therockwell.com
40 rm – ♦£ 120/180 ♦♦£ 180/200, ☑ £ 12.50   **C5**
Rest – Carte £ 23/34
♦ Townhouse ♦ Design ♦

Two Victorian houses with open, modern lobby and secluded, south-facing garden terrace. Bedrooms come in bold warm colours; 'Garden rooms' come with their own patios. Small dining room offers easy menu of modern European staples.

Aster House without rest

3 Sumner Pl ⊠ SW7 3EE – Ⓜ South Kensington – ℘ (020) 7581 5888
– asterhouse@btinternet.com – Fax (020) 7584 49 25 – www.asterhouse.com
13 rm ☑ – ♦£ 80/135 ♦♦£ 120/180   **E6**
♦ Townhouse ♦ Cosy ♦

End of terrace Victorian house with a pretty little rear garden and first floor conservatory. Ground floor rooms available. A wholly non-smoking establishment.

Ambassade de L'Ile (Jean-Christophe Ansanay-Alex)

117-119 Old Brompton Rd ⊠ SW7 3RN London
– Ⓜ Gloucester Road – ℘ (020) 73737774 – direction@ambassadedelile.com
– Fax (020) 73 73 44 72 – www.ambassadedelile.com
– closed Sunday
Rest – Menu £ 65 – Carte £ 63/88   **D6**
Spec. Watermelon gazpacho, avocado and langoustines. Rib of milk fed veal with girolles, spinach and potato gnocchi. White peach soufflé.
♦ French ♦ Design ♦

Eccentric 1970s retro décor of shag-pile carpet and white leather. This is the London outpost of the Lyonnais restaurant L'Auberge de L'Ile. The French cooking is original, detailed and ambitious.

Bombay Brasserie

Courtfield Rd ⊠ SW7 4QH – Ⓜ Gloucester Road – ℘ (020) 7370 4040
– bombay1brasserie@aol.com – Fax (020) 7835 16 69
– www.bombaybrasserielondon.com
– closed 25-26 December   **D6**
Rest – Menu £ 19 (weekday lunch) – Carte £ 42/52
♦ Indian ♦ Exotic ♦

Something of a London institution: an ever busy Indian restaurant with Raj-style décor. Ask to sit in the brighter plant-filled conservatory. Popular lunchtime buffet.

L'Etranger

36 Gloucester Rd ⊠ SW7 4QT – Ⓜ Gloucester Road – ℘ (020) 7584 1118
– etranger@etranger.co.uk – Fax (020) 7584 88 86 – www.circagroupltd.co.uk
– closed 25-26 December and Saturday lunch   **D5**
Rest – (booking essential) Menu £ 20 (lunch) – Carte £ 31/86
♦ Innovative ♦ Neighbourhood ♦

Corner restaurant with mosaic entrance floor and bay window. Modern décor. Tables extend into adjoining wine shop. French based cooking with Asian influences.

Pasha

1 Gloucester Rd ⊠ SW7 4PP – Ⓜ Gloucester Road – ℘ (020) 7589 7969
– info@pasha-restaurant.co.uk – Fax (020) 7581 99 96
– www.pasha-restaurant.co.uk
– closed 24-25 December and 1 January   **D5**
Rest – Menu £ 15/37 – Carte £ 24/42
♦ Moroccan ♦ Exotic ♦

Relax over ground floor cocktails, then descend to mosaic floored restaurant where the rose-petal strewn tables are the ideal accompaniment to tasty Moroccan home cooking.

Earl's Court

K + K George

1-15 Templeton Pl ⊠ *SW5 9NB –* Ⓜ *Earl's Court*
– ℰ (020) 7598 8700 – hotelgeorge@kkhotels.co.uk – Fax (020) 7370 22 85
– www.kkhotels.com **C6**
154 rm ⌑ *–* **♦**£ 259 **♦♦**£ 294 **Rest** *–* Carte £ 20/32
♦ Business ♦ Modern ♦

Five converted 19C houses overlooking large rear garden. Scandinavian style to rooms with low beds, white walls and light wood furniture. Breakfast room has the garden view. Informal dining in the bar.

Twenty Nevern Square without rest

20 Nevern Sq ⊠ *SW5 9PD –* Ⓜ *Earl's Court*
– ℰ (020) 7565 9555 – hotel@twentynevernsquare.co.uk
– Fax (020) 7565 94 44 – www.twentynevernsquare.co.uk **C6**
20 rm *–* **♦**£ 85/115 **♦♦**£ 110/150, ⌑ £ 9
♦ Townhouse ♦ Functional ♦

In an attractive Victorian garden square, an individually designed, privately owned town house. Original pieces of furniture and some rooms with their own terrace.

✕✕ Langan's Coq d'Or

254-260 Old Brompton Rd ⊠ *SW5 9HR –* Ⓜ *Earl's Court*
– ℰ (020) 7259 2599 – admin@langansrestaurant.co.uk
– Fax (020) 7370 77 35 – www.langansrestaurants.co.uk
– closed 25-26 December **C6**
Rest *–* Menu £ 24 *–* Carte approx. £ 28
♦ Traditional ♦ Brasserie ♦

Classic, buzzy brasserie and excellent-value menu to match. Walls adorned with pictures of celebrities: look out for more from the enclosed pavement terrace. Smooth service.

KENSINGTON, NORTH KENSINGTON & NOTTING HILL *Plan XI*

Kensington

Royal Garden

2-24 Kensington High St ⊠ *W8 4PT –* Ⓜ *High Street Kensington*
– ℰ (020) 7937 8000 – sales@royalgardenhotel.co.uk
– Fax (020) 7361 19 91 – www.royalgardenhotel.co.uk **D4**
376 rm *–* **♦**£ 175/388 **♦♦**£ 175/388, ⌑ £ 19 *–* 20 suites
Rest *Min Jiang –* see below
Rest *Park Terrace –* Menu £ 18/30
Rest *The Tenth – ℰ (020) 7361 1910 –* Menu £ 23/65 *–* Carte £ 36/45
♦ Business ♦ Functional ♦

A tall, modern hotel with many of its rooms enjoying enviable views over the adjacent Kensington Gardens. All the modern amenities and services, with well-drilled staff. Bright, spacious Park Terrace offers British, Asian and modern European cuisine. Modern menu and commanding views from the top floor Tenth restaurant.

The Milestone

1-2 Kensington Court ⊠ *W8 5DL –* Ⓜ *High Street Kensington*
– ℰ (020) 7917 1000 – bookms@rchmail.com
– Fax (020) 7917 10 10 – www.milestonehotel.com **D4**
57 rm *–* **♦**£ 276/311 **♦♦**£ 370/405, ⌑ £ 25 *–* 6 suites
Rest *– (booking essential for non-residents)* Menu £ 27 (lunch) *–* Carte £ 42/67
♦ Luxury ♦ Stylish ♦

Elegant hotel with decorative Victorian façade and English feel. Charming oak panelled lounge and snug bar. Meticulously decorated bedrooms with period detail. Panelled dining room with charming little oratory for privacy seekers.

UNITED KINGDOM - **LONDON**

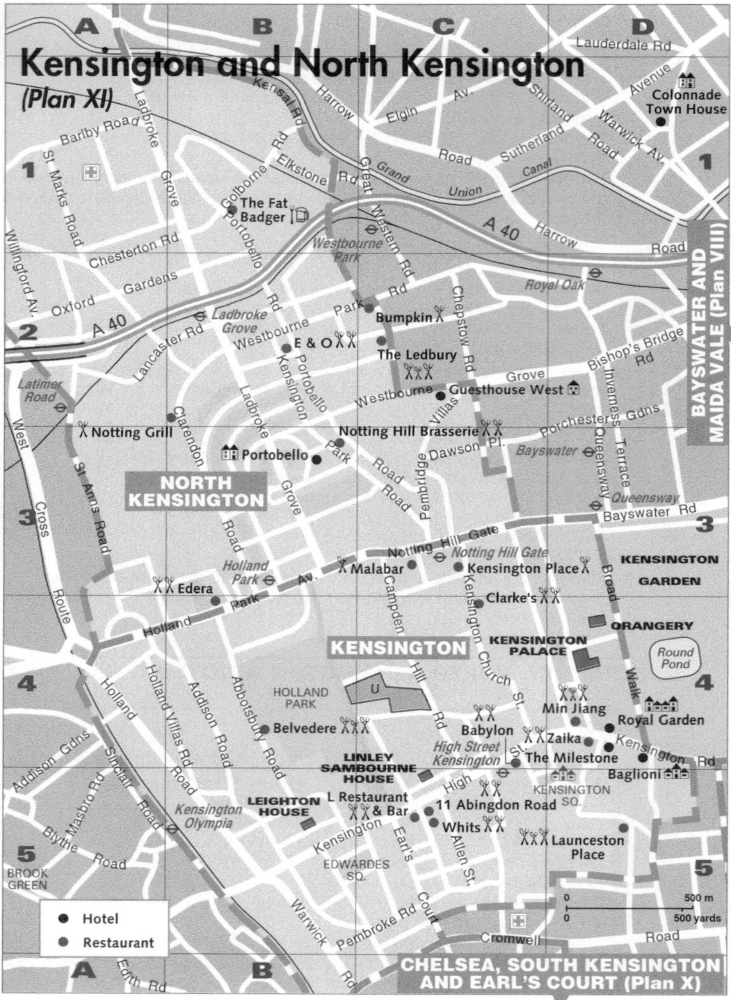
Kensington and North Kensington
(Plan XI)
A
B
C
D
1
2
3
4
5
Lauderdale Rd
Colonnade Town House
Barlby Road
Ladbroke Grove
St Marks Road
Kensal Rd
Harrow Road
Elgin Av.
Shirland
Avenue
Warwick Road
Warwick Av.
Sutherland
Canal
Grand Union
Golborne Rd
Elkstone Rd
Great Western Rd
The Fat Badger
Westbourne Park
A 40
Harrow Road
Chesterton Rd
Willingford Av.
Oxford Gardens
Royal Oak
BAYSWATER AND MAIDA VALE (Plan VIII)
Ladbroke Grove
Lancaster Rd
Westbourne Park Rd
Bumpkin
E & O
The Ledbury
Chepstow Rd
Bishop's Bridge Rd
Latimer Road
Westbourne Grove
Guesthouse West
Notting Grill
Clarendon
Kensington
Portobello
Ladbroke
Villas
Inverness Terrace
Notting Hill Brasserie
Porchester Gdns
West Cross Route
St Anns Road
Portobello
Park
Pembridge
Dawson Pl.
Bayswater
Queensway
NORTH KENSINGTON
Grove
Road
Queensway
Bayswater Rd
Notting Hill Gate
Notting Hill Gate
Kensington Place
Holland Park
Malabar
KENSINGTON GARDEN
Edera
Holland Park Av.
Campden Hill
Clarke's
Broad Walk
ORANGERY
KENSINGTON
KENSINGTON PALACE
Kensington Church St.
Round Pond
Holland Road
Holland Villas Rd
Addison Road
Abbotsbury Road
HOLLAND PARK
Min Jiang
Royal Garden
Belvedere
Babylon
Zaika
Addison Gdns
Sinclair Road
High Street Kensington
The Milestone
Kensington Rd
LINLEY SAMBOURNE HOUSE
Baglioni
KENSINGTON SQ.
Masbro Rd
LEIGHTON HOUSE
L Restaurant & Bar
11 Abingdon Road
Kensington Olympia
Kensington High St.
Whits
Launceston Place
Blythe Road
Earl's Court
Allen St.
BROOK GREEN
EDWARDES SQ.
0
500 m
0
500 yards
Hotel
Restaurant
Warwick Rd
Pembroke Rd
Cromwell Road
Edith Rd
CHELSEA, SOUTH KENSINGTON AND EARL'S COURT (Plan X)

Baglioni

60 Hyde Park Gate ✉ SW7 5BB – Ⓜ High Street Kensington
– ✆ (020) 7368 5700 – info@baglionihotellondon.com
– Fax (020) 7368 57 01 – www.baglionihotels.com **D4**
52 rm – †£ 423 ††£ 423, ☕ £ 25 – 15 suites
Rest *Brunello* – *✆ (020) 7368 5900* – Menu £ 24 (lunch) – Carte £ 37/51
◆ Luxury ◆ Stylish ◆
Opposite Kensington Palace: ornate interior, trendy basement bar. Impressively high levels of service. Small gym/sauna. Superb rooms in cool shades boast striking facilities. Restaurant specialises in rustic Italian cooking.

Belvedere

Holland House, off Abbotsbury Rd ✉ *W8 6LU –* Ⓜ *Holland Park*
– ℰ (020) 7602 1238 – info@belvedererestaurant.co.uk
– Fax (020) 7610 43 82 – www.belvedererestaurant.co.uk
– closed 26 December, 1 January and Sunday dinner **B4**
Rest – Menu £ 18/25 (lunch) – Carte £ 28/53
◆ French ◆ Romantic ◆

Former 19C orangery in a delightful position in the middle of the Park. On two floors with a bar and balcony terrace. Huge vases of flowers. Modern take on classic dishes.

Min Jiang – at Royal Garden Hotel

10th Floor, 2-24 Kensington High St ✉ *W8 4PT –* Ⓜ *High Street Kensington*
– ℰ (020) 7361 1988 – reservations@minjiang.co.uk – Fax (020) 7361 19 87
– www.minjiang.co.uk **D4**
Rest – Carte £ 30/50
◆ Chinese ◆

Stylish and comfortable Chinese restaurant on the 10th floor of the hotel, with terrific views. Lunchtime dim sum a strength; the Beijing duck is a speciality and comes roasted in a wood-fired oven.

Launceston Place

1a Launceston Pl ✉ *W8 5RL –* Ⓜ *Gloucester Road – ℰ (020) 7937 6912*
– lpr-res@danddlondon.com – Fax (020) 7938 24 12
– www.launcestonplace-restaurant.co.uk
– Closed Christmas and New Year and Monday lunch **D5**
Rest – Menu £ 24/38 – Carte £ 35/48
◆ Modern European ◆ Neighbourhood ◆

Re-launched and reinvigorated, with dark walls and moody lighting, but still with that local feel. Cooking is original and deftly executed and uses ingredients largely from the British Isles.

Clarke's

124 Kensington Church St ✉ *W8 4BH –* Ⓜ *Notting Hill Gate*
– ℰ (020) 7221 9225 – restaurant@sallyclarke.com
– Fax (020) 7229 45 64 – www.sallyclarke.com
– closed 2 weeks Christmas - New Year and Bank Holidays **C4**
Rest – Menu £ 47 (dinner) – Carte lunch £ 29/32
◆ Modern European ◆ Neighbourhood ◆

Forever popular restaurant, now serving a choice of dishes boasting trademark fresh, seasonal ingredients and famed lightness of touch. Loyal following for over 20 years.

Zaika

1 Kensington High St ✉ *W8 5NP –* Ⓜ *High Street Kensington*
– ℰ (020) 7795 6533 – info@zaika-restaurant.co.uk – Fax (020) 7937 88 54
– www.zaika-restaurant.co.uk
– closed Saturday lunch, Christmas, New Year and Bank Holidays
Rest – Menu £ 20 (lunch) – Carte £ 29/43 **D4**
◆ Indian ◆ Exotic ◆

A converted bank, sympathetically restored, with original features and Indian artefacts. Well organised service of modern Indian dishes.

Whits

21 Abingdon Rd ✉ *W8 6AH –* Ⓜ *High Street Kensington – ℰ (020) 7938 1122*
– eva@whits.co.uk – Fax (020) 7937 61 21 – www.whits.co.uk
– closed Christmas - New Year, Easter, Saturday lunch, Sunday dinner and Monday **C5**
Rest – (dinner only and Sunday lunch) Menu £ 19/24 – Carte £ 29/37
◆ Modern European ◆ Neighbourhood ◆

Run by friendly owner. Bar runs length of lower level. Most diners migrate upstairs with its modish art work and intimate tables. Modern cooking with generous portions.

XX **11 Abingdon Road**   AC VISA OO AE

11 Abingdon Rd ⊠ W8 6AH – ⓂHigh Street Kensington – ℰ (020) 7937 0120
– eleven@abingdonroad.co.uk – www.abingdonroad.co.uk
– Closed Bank Holidays   **C5**
Rest – Carte £ 26/33
♦ Mediterranean ♦ Brasserie ♦
Part of a little 'eating oasis' off Ken High Street. Stylish frosted glass façade with a
clean, white interior. Cooking's from the modern British stable with Euro accents.

XX **L Restaurant & Bar**   AC ⇔ VISA OO AE

2 Abingdon Rd ⊠ W8 6AF – ⓂHigh Street Kensington – ℰ (020) 7795 6969
– info@l-restaurant.co.uk – Fax (020) 7795 66 99 – www.l-restaurant.co.uk
– closed 25 December and Monday lunch   **C5**
Rest – Carte £ 26/36
♦ Spanish ♦ Design ♦
Wonderfully airy glass-roofed dining room with tastefully designed wood work
and mirrors. Authentic Iberian menus with an emphasis on tapas matched by
good-value wine list.

XX **Babylon** – at The Roof Gardens   ≲ ⌂ AC ⇔ VISA OO AE

99 Kensington High St (entrance on Derry St) ⊠ W8 5SA
– ⓂHigh Street Kensington – ℰ (020) 7368 3993 – babylon@
roofgardens.virgin.co.uk – Fax (020) 7368 39 95 – www.roofgardens.com
– closed Christmas-New Year and Sunday dinner   **C4**
Rest – Menu £ 20 (lunch) – Carte £ 39/55
♦ Modern European ♦ Fashionable ♦
Situated on the roof of this pleasant London building affording attractive views of
the London skyline. Stylish modern décor in keeping with the contemporary, British cooking.

X **Kensington Place**   AC VISA OO AE OD

201 Kensington Church St ⊠ W8 7LX – ⓂNotting Hill Gate
– ℰ (020) 7727 3184 – kprreservations@danddlondon.com
– Fax (020) 7792 93 88 – www.kensingtonplace-restaurant.co.uk   **C3**
Rest – (booking essential) Menu £ 20/25 – Carte £ 22/46
♦ Modern European ♦ Fashionable ♦
A cosmopolitan crowd still head for this establishment that set the trend for large,
bustling and informal restaurants. Professionally run with skilled modern cooking.

X **Malabar**   AC VISA OO AE

27 Uxbridge St ⊠ W8 7TQ – ⓂNotting Hill Gate – ℰ (020) 7727 8800
– feedback@malabar-restaurant.co.uk – www.malabar-restaurant.co.uk
– closed 23-27 December   **C3**
Rest – (buffet lunch Sunday) Menu £ 23 – Carte £ 21/28
♦ Indian ♦ Neighbourhood ♦
Indian restaurant in a residential street. Three rooms with individual personalities
and informal service. Extensive range of good value dishes, particularly vegetarian.

North Kensington

🏠 **The Portobello** without rest   ▨ ᵗᵗ VISA OO AE

22 Stanley Gdns ⊠ W11 2NG – ⓂNotting Hill Gate – ℰ (020) 7727 2777
– info@portobello-hotel.co.uk – Fax (020) 7792 96 41
– www.portobello-hotel.co.uk
– closed 23-29 December   **B3**
21 rm – ♦£ 150/180 ♦♦£ 355, ⊑ £ 17
♦ Townhouse ♦ Personalised ♦
An attractive Victorian town house in an elegant terrace. Original and theatrical
décor. Circular beds, half-testers, Victorian baths: no two bedrooms are the same.

Guesthouse West
🛏 AC ⚙ 📶 VISA ⓪ AE

163-165 Westbourne Grove ✉ *W11 2RS –* Ⓜ *Notting Hill Gate*
– ℰ (020) 7792 9800 – reception@guesthousewest.com
– Fax (020) 7792 97 97 – www.guesthousewest.com **C2**
20 rm – †£ 194 ††£ 229, ⌥ £ 15 **Rest** – Carte £ 27/37
♦ Townhouse ♦ Stylish ♦

Attractive Edwardian house in the heart of Notting Hill, close to its shops and restaurants. Contemporary bedrooms boast the latest in audio visual gadgetry. Chic Parlour Bar for all-day light dishes in a tapas style.

The Ledbury
🛏 AC VISA ⓪ AE
🌸

127 Ledbury Rd ✉ *W11 2AQ –* Ⓜ *Notting Hill Gate – ℰ (020) 7792 9090*
– info@theledbury.com – Fax (020) 7792 91 91 – www.theledbury.com
– closed 24-26 December and August Bank Holiday **C2**
Rest – Menu £ 60 (dinner) – Carte lunch £ 38/50 ☕
Spec. Flame-grilled mackerel with a mackerel tartare, avocado and shiso. Breast and confit of pigeon, sweetcorn, almond and girolles. Date and vanilla tart with cardamom and orange ice cream.
♦ French ♦ Neighbourhood ♦

Former pub with elegant, minimalist décor. Seasonal menu with innovative edge; flavours are pronounced and well judged; ingredients are superbly sourced.

Notting Hill Brasserie
AC ⇄ VISA ⓪ AE

92 Kensington Park Rd ✉ *W11 2PN –* Ⓜ *Notting Hill Gate*
– ℰ (020) 7229 4481 – enquiries@nottinghillbrasserie.com
– Fax (020) 7221 12 46 – www.nottinghillbrasserie.com
– closed Bank Holidays and lunch Monday and Tuesday **B3**
Rest – Menu £ 23/30 – Carte £ 40/48
♦ French ♦ Neighbourhood ♦

Modern, comfortable restaurant with quiet, formal atmosphere set over four small rooms. Authentic African artwork on walls. Contemporary dishes with European influence.

Edera
AC ⇄ VISA ⓪ AE

148 Holland Park Ave ✉ *W11 4UE –* Ⓜ *Holland Park – ℰ (020) 7221 6090*
– Fax (020) 7313 97 00
– Closed Bank Holidays **B4**
Rest – Carte £ 32/49
♦ Italian ♦ Neighbourhood ♦

Split level restaurant with outdoor tables. Modern Italian cooking with some unusual ingredients and combinations. Sardinian specialities include Bottarga and homemade pastas.

E&O
AC ⇄ VISA ⓪ AE ⓪

14 Blenheim Crescent ✉ *W11 1NN –* Ⓜ *Ladbroke Grove – ℰ (020) 7229 5454*
– eando@rickerrestaurants.com – Fax (020) 7229 55 22
– www.rickerrestaurants.com
– closed Christmas, New Year and August Bank Holiday **B2**
Rest – Carte £ 31/42
♦ Asian ♦ Minimalist ♦

Mean, dark and moody: never mind the exterior, we're talking about the A-list diners. Minimalist chic meets high sound levels. Menus scour Far East: cutlery/ chopstick choice.

Notting Grill
🛏 VISA ⓪ AE ⓪

123A Clarendon Rd ✉ *W11 4JG –* Ⓜ *Holland Park – ℰ (020) 7229 1500*
– nottinggrill@awtrestaurants.com – Fax (020) 7229 88 89 – www.awt.com
– closed 25-26 December and Monday-Friday lunch except December
Rest – Carte £ 32/35 **B2**
♦ Beef specialities ♦ Neighbourhood ♦

Converted pub that retains a rustic feel, with bare brick walls and wooden tables. Specialises in well sourced, quality meats.

Bumpkin

209 Westbourne Park Rd ✉ W11 1EA – Ⓜ Westbourne Park – ☎ (020) 7243 9818 – Fax (020) 7229 18 26 – www.bumpkinuk.com – Closed 25-26 December and 1 January **C2**

Rest – *(closed Sunday dinner and Monday) (dinner only and Sunday lunch)* Carte £ 27/40

Rest *Brasserie* – Carte £ 27/40

◆ Modern European ◆ Family ◆

Converted pea-green pub with casual, clubby feel and wholesome philosophy of cooking seasonal, carefully-sourced and organic food. Whisky tasting and private dining on top floors. First floor restaurant offers modern Mediterranean menu.

The Fat Badger

310 Portobello Road ✉ W10 5TA – Ⓜ Ladbroke Grove. – ☎ (020) 8969 4500 – rupert@thefatbadger.com – Fax (020) 8969 67 14 – www.thefatbadger.com – Closed 25-26 December **B1**

Rest – Menu £ 15 – Carte £ 30/50

◆ British ◆ Pub ◆

Large rustic pub with old sofas, chandeliers, upstairs dining room and some intriguing wallpaper. Seasonal and earthy British food, with whole beasts delivered to the kitchen.

LONDON AIRPORTS

Heathrow Airport West : 17 m. by A 4 and M 4

London Heathrow Marriott

Bath Rd, Hayes ✉ UB3 5AN – ☎ (020) 8990 1100 – salesadmin.heathrow@marriotthotels.com – Fax (020) 8990 11 10 – www.londonheathrowmarriott.co.uk

391 rm – †£ 182 ††£ 182, ☕ £ 16.95 – 2 suites

Rest *Tuscany* – *☎ (0870) 400 7250 (Closed Sunday) (dinner only)* Menu £ 39 – Carte £ 33/46

Rest *Allie's grille* – *☎ (0870) 400 7250* – Carte £ 21/38

◆ Chain hotel ◆ Business ◆ Functional ◆

Built at the end of 20C, this modern, comfortable hotel is centred around a large atrium, with comprehensive business facilities: there is an exclusive Executive floor. Italian cuisine at bright and convivial Tuscany. Grill favourites at Allie's.

Sheraton Skyline

Bath Rd, Hayes ✉ UB3 5BP – ☎ (020) 8759 2535 – res268-skyline@sheraton.com – Fax (020) 8750 91 51 – www.sheraton.com/skyline

348 rm – †£ 69/245 ††£ 349, ☕ £ 17 **Rest *Al Dente*** – Carte £ 21/30

◆ Chain hotel ◆ Business ◆ Functional ◆

Well known for its unique indoor swimming pool surrounded by a tropical garden which is overlooked by many of the bedrooms. Business centre available. Italian dining in Al Dente.

Hilton London Heathrow Airport

Terminal 4 ✉ TW6 3AF – ☎ (020) 8759 7755 – gm-heathrow@hilton.com – Fax (020) 8759 75 79 – www.hilton.co.uk/heathrow

390 rm – †£ 292 ††£ 292, ☕ £ 20.50 – 5 suites

Rest *Brasserie* – *(closed lunch Saturday and Sunday) (buffet lunch)* Menu £ 28/35 – Carte dinner £ 33/50

Rest *Zen Oriental* – *(closed Bank Holidays)* Carte £ 23/24

◆ Chain hotel ◆ Business ◆ Functional ◆

Group hotel with a striking modern exterior and linked to Terminal 4 by a covered walkway. Good sized bedrooms, with contemporary styled suites. Spacious Brasserie in vast atrium. Zen Oriental offers formal Chinese experience.

Gatwick Airport South : 28 m. by A 23 and M 23

Hilton London Gatwick Airport   ⅃₅ ♿ rm 🅰🅲 ℡ 🔊 🅿

South Terminal ✉ RH6 0LL – ℰ *(01293) 518080*   *VISA* ⓒⓓ 🄰🄴 ⓘ
– londongatwick@hilton.com – Fax (01293) 52 89 80
– www.hilton.co.uk/gatwick
823 rm – 🛉£ 195/239 🛉🛉£ 195/239, ⊑ £ 18.50
Rest – Menu £ 18 – Carte £ 35/40
♦ Chain hotel ♦ Business ♦ Functional ♦

Large, well-established hotel, popular with business travellers. Two ground floor bars. Older rooms co-ordinated, newer ones more minimalist in style. Restaurant enlivened by floral profusions.

Stansted Airport North : 37 m. by M 11 and A 120

Radisson SAS H. London Stansted Airport   ⅃₅ ⊛ 〰 🍸

Waltham Close ✉ CM24 1PP   ♿ rm 🅰🅲 🛜 🔊 🅿 *VISA* ⓒⓓ 🄰🄴 ⓘ
– ℰ (01279) 661012 – info.stansted@radissonsas.com – Fax (01279) 66 10 13
– www.stansted.radissonsas.com
484 rm – 🛉£ 135 🛉🛉£ 135, ⊑ £ 14.95 – 16 suites
Rest *New York Grill Bar* – *(Closed lunch Saturday and Sunday)* Carte £ 33/58
Rest *Wine Tower* – Carte £ 22/30
Rest *Filini* – Carte (dinner only) £ 22/35
♦ Business ♦ Functional ♦

Impressive hotel just two minutes from main terminal; vast open atrium housing 40 foot wine cellar. Extensive meeting facilities. Very stylish bedrooms in three themes. Small, formal New York Grill Bar. Impressive Wine Tower. Filini for Italian dishes.

Hilton London Stansted Airport   ⅃₅ 〰 🍽 ♿ rm 🅰🅲 rest 🔊

Round Coppice Rd ✉ CM24 1SF – ℰ *(01279)*   🅿 *VISA* ⓒⓓ 🄰🄴 ⓘ
680800 – reservations.stansted@hilton.com – Fax (01279) 68 08 90
– www.hilton.co.uk
237 rm – 🛉£ 79/115 🛉🛉£ 79/115, ⊑ £ 17.95 – 2 suites
Rest – *(closed lunch Saturday and Bank Holidays)* Menu £ 27
♦ Business ♦ Functional ♦

Bustling hotel whose facilities include leisure club, hairdressers and beauty salon. Modern rooms, with two of executive style. Transport can be arranged to and from terminal. Restaurant/bar has popular menu; sometimes carvery lunch as well.

BIRMINGHAM
BIRMINGHAM

Population: 889 000 (conurbation 2 371 000) – Altitude: 98m

Duclerc/COLORISE

I t takes a pretty big backwards leap of the imagination to visualise Birmingham as an insignificant market town, but England's second city was just such a place through much of its history. Then came the boom times of the Industrial Revolution, the town fattening up on the back of the local iron and coal trades. In many people's minds that legacy lives on, the city seen as a rather dour place with shoddy Victorian housing, but 21C Brum has swept away much of its factory grime and polished up its civic face.

I ts first 'makeover' was nearly a century ago when Neville Chamberlain's dad Joseph, the then mayor, enlarged the city's boundaries to make it the second largest in the country. Today it's feeling the benefits of a second modernist surge - a multi-million pound regeneration, typified by a fusion of appealing squares and modern shopping arcades: the 'armadillo' shaped Selfridges store became a fashion icon and city symbol when it opened a few years ago. Being pretty much in the centre of England, Birmingham is easily accessible from all areas and is within a curtain call of Shakespeare's Stratford while the charming Cotswolds are practically in its southern suburbs (if you stretch the imagination a bit more). To add to its impressive credentials, it can boast more canal miles than Venice and more trees than it has inhabitants.

LIVING THE CITY

Birmingham is surrounded by towns of all shapes and sizes, from the glories of Stratford-on-Avon in the south and Bridgnorth and Ironbridge in the west, to the more 'subtle' attractions of Wolverhampton and Coventry in its hinterland. Birmingham's landscape inspired a certain resident, JRR Tolkien, to write 'Lord of the Rings', but he'd be lost nowadays, what with the undulating contours of the flyovers, the self-important muscle of the adjoining National Indoor Arena and International Convention Centre, and the nearby trendy makeover of the Gas Street Basin. To say nothing with what they've done to the Bullring …he wouldn't know where he was in the Balti Triangle (south of the centre) but perhaps would feel more at home in the elegant Jewellery Quarter further north.

PRACTICAL INFORMATION

ARRIVAL-DEPARTURE

Birmingham International Airport is 8 miles east of the city. There's free Air-Rail connection to Birmingham International Station every 2mins. From there, frequent trains to New St Station take 20min.

TRANSPORT

Three miles an hour might seem like a slow way to get round the city, but canal travel by narrowboat is stress-free and relaxing. Alternatively, take a cycle ride or walk along the towpaths. Stop off at Brindleyplace's floating café, or take a short summer trip from there.

Birmingham has eight local rail lines for travel to anywhere in the country. A recent addition, Midland Metro, is a light railway linking Snow Hill station with Wolverhampton.

Centro provides a regular service around the city. Give the exact fare to your driver as you board or purchase day or off-peak weekly Centrocards.

EXPLORING BIRMINGHAM

A sassy blend of refined arcades, stylish malls, well-stocked markets and the world-famous Jewellery Quarter just up the road, not to mention miles of canal

pathways and impressive galleries… strolling round Brum has a lot going for it. In the past, you'd have thought 'coal' or 'cars', even 'great key locks' when you thought of this city, but now a more likely reaction would be "Oh, let's go there for our shopping." Historically, there's no reason why this shouldn't be the case. Many world famous British brands were created here, ranging from Bakelite to Cadbury's, HP Sauce and Typhoo Tea to Brylcreem.

→ RAG TO A BULL (RING)

Much of the action takes place in the **Bullring** mega-complex, overseen by the shimmering ego of the Selfridges building, less a department store, more a self-assured statement of intent from Future Systems, who designed it. Slightly more down-to-earth, and a mere stone's throw from the Bullring, is the flea market in Saint Martin's Market, known affectionately for 50 years as The Rag. Its 350 stalls complement the Bullring's grandeur rather well, and the antiques' and collectors' fairs it puts on are renowned amongst in-the-know locals. One less salubrious claim to fame...it also has a bit of a risqué reputation for early morning 'business transactions' before the stallholders arrive.

On the other side of the city, in the northern area of Hockley, is the **Jewellery Quarter**, the place to head for if you're after a quality piece of body adornment or silverware. Also known as 'The Golden Triangle', it's an area of smart Victorian buildings between Warstone Lane and Vyse Street, and it's steeped in 19C folklore: it democratized writing by supplying the world with cheap pen nibs for 130 years; it was where Joseph Hudson invented the police whistle, borrowing £20 from the Metropolitan Police so that he could get his hands on enough brass for 21,000 of them to be produced; and it's where the same man made the doomed whistles for the Titanic lifeboats (Kate Winslet used a 'rescued' one in the movie!). There are fascinating museums in the area too, such as the Jewellery Quarter Discovery Centre, which does pretty much what it says on the label.

→ A POSTING TO THE MAILBOX

You feel like you've moved forward a century or two when you step into the **Mailbox** area, not a half-mile from the main New Street railway station. It has a distinct noughties feel to it, proudly referring to itself as the UK's 'largest mixed use building'. What that actually means is that it incorporates penthou-

se style apartments, health clubs, office space, hotels, restaurants and shops... not a bad refit for a former mail sorting office. It's the West Midlands' answer to Bond Street, and it's where you'll find Britain's biggest Malmaison Hotel. But it's not the only area laying claim to being Brum's coolest. Just a waterbus ride away along the quaintly named Gas Street Basin sits **Brindleyplace**, an impressive and vibrant canalside destination, boasting tree-lined streets, eye-catching water features, striking architecture and a good few clear open spaces. It's got the Sea Life Centre, too, complete with a fully transparent underwater tube letting you walk, suspended in mid-'ocean', completely surrounded by sharks, skate, rays and all manner of marine life. One final conversion that's of interest: about 700 paces from the Bullring, southeast in the area of Digbeth, stands another icon of Birmingham's branded past: the Bird's custard factory. They don't make yellow gooey stuff there anymore though: The **Custard Factory** is now an arts and media quarter with a trendy pub, The Medicine Bar, and a host of urban style shops, green spaces, fountains and sculpture. It's in a smart square too.

→ ART ATTACK

Not everything in England's second city is rebranded, spruced up or brand new. There's still a reverence for old-fashioned style and taste embodied in a variety of esteemed establishments around the city. Take the **Barber Institute of Fine Art,** on the University of Birmingham campus in Edgbaston. This impressive art deco building, opened by Queen Mary in 1939, contains one of the finest small collections of European art in the UK, including Botticelli, Holbein, Rembrandt, Rubens, Van Gogh, Turner and Monet. Go up to the central Chamberlain Square to be equally impressed by the **Museum & Art Gallery**, which boasts a renowned collection of Pre-Raphaelite paintings, as well as works by Degas, Renoir and Canaletto. It also houses popular natural and local history sections, and the archaeology department is highly acclaimed. The Edwardian tearoom's not a bad place to relax for a spot of cultural reflection. Further north is Aston Hall, a fine Jacobean mansion built between 1618 and 1635 with friezes and plaster ceilings, a 40m long panelled gallery, gables and turrets, and with a collection that features textiles, furniture and paintings from the Birmingham Museum.

The world of science comes to life at **Millennium Point**, 10 minutes walk from the centre, its public areas dominated by an awesome central Hub with soaring atrium. This is where you'll find two visitor attractions, Thinktank, the city's science museum, and IMAX cinema. If you're more at home outdoors, then The Birmingham Botanical Gardens and Glasshouses is probably more your style. Based in Edgbaston, they opened in 1832, and today their 15 acres are an ideal place to wind down and find tranquility.

Of course, the city is only some 20 miles from the birthplace of William Shakespeare, **Stratford-upon-Avon**, and it's not unknown for visitors to forego even the delights of Birmingham in order to breathe in a bit of the Bard's magic. If you're lucky enough to be around on a summer Sunday (between July and September) there's really only one way to do the trip, and that's on the Shakespeare Express, a wonderful steam locomotive which starts from Snow Hill station, picks up passengers at Moor Street, and chugs its way through leafy Warwickshire countryside to Stratford. There's Pullman class dining if you're feeling extravagant: you can take breakfast on the way out, and high tea on the return journey.

CALENDAR HIGHLIGHTS

They like a party in Birmingham. There's a St George's Day Celebration every April, while in Handsworth the Caribbean-style Birmingham International Carnival takes place in August every second year, and winds its way to Perry Barr Park. Birmingham Pride attracts 100,000 visitors each year to the Hurst Street 'gay village' location. The largest single-day event, though, is the St. Patrick's Day Parade, which can claim to be the second biggest in Europe, after the one held in Dublin.

BIRMINGHAM IN...

→ **ONE DAY**
The Rag, The Bullring, a museum

→ **TWO DAYS**
Brindleyplace, a trip on the waterbus to The Mailbox, and a cycle ride round the canals.

→ **THREE DAYS**
If you're around on a summer Sunday, take the Shakespeare Express to Stratford. Or visit Bridgnorth and Ironbridge, cradle of the Industrial Revolution. Venture south to the idyllic Cotswolds.

EATING OUT

Temptation isn't far away from students at the city's main centre of learning, the University of Birmingham, to the south-west of the city, and not a million miles away from Cadbury World, the UK's only purpose-built visitor centre devoted entirely to chocolate. Located in the evocative sounding Bourneville area, staff are on hand to tell visitors the history of chocolate and how it's made, but, let's face it, most people go along to get a face full of the stuff in fresh liquid form straight from the vat.

More conventionally, many people who come to Birmingham make for the now legendary area of Sparkbrook, Balsall Heath and Moseley. In itself that may not sound too funky, but over the last 30 years it's become the area known as the Balti Triangle. The balti was 'officially' discovered in Birmingham in 1976, a full-on dish of aromatic spices, fresh herbs and rich curries, and The Triangle now boasts over 50 establishments dedicated to the dish.

For those after something a little more subtle, the city offers a growing number of lively and fashionable restaurants, offering assured and contemporary cuisine.

UNITED KINGDOM - BIRMINGHAM

Radisson SAS

⪜ & rm 🅰🅲 🆂🅰 📶 ⚐ 🆅🅸🆂🅰 ⓿ 🅰🅴 ⓘ

12 Holloway Circus ⊠ *B1 1BT* – ℰ *(0121) 654 6000* – *info.birmingham@radissonsas.com* – *Fax (0161) 654 60 01* – *www.birmingham.radissonsas.com*
204 rm – †£ 99/205, ††£ 99/205, ⊊ £ 14.95 – 7 suites
Rest *Filini* – *(Closed Saturday lunch and Sunday)* Carte £ 20/48
♦ Business ♦ Modern ♦

Occupies 18 uber-modern floors of a city centre skyscraper. Well-equipped business facilities; ultra stylish bedrooms in three distinctly slinky themes. Modern bar leads to airy, easy-going Italian restaurant, Filini.

Hyatt Regency

⪜ 🅵🅰 🌐 📶 🖥 & rm 🅰🅲 🆂🅰 📶 ⚐ 🆅🅸🆂🅰 ⓿ 🅰🅴 ⓘ

2 Bridge St ⊠ *B1 2JZ* – ℰ *(0121) 643 1234* – *birmingham@hyattintl.com* – *Fax (0121) 616 23 23* – *www.birmingham.hyatt.com* **D2**
315 rm – †£ 199, ††£ 199, ⊊ £ 15.25 – 4 suites
Rest *Aria* – Menu £ 14/17 – Carte £ 25/41
♦ Luxury ♦ Modern ♦

Striking mirrored exterior. Glass enclosed lifts offer panoramic views. Sizeable rooms with floor to ceiling windows. Covered link with International Convention Centre. Contemporary style restaurant in central atrium; modish cooking.

Malmaison

🅵🅰 📶 & rm 🅰🅲 🆂🅰 📶 ⚐ 🆅🅸🆂🅰 ⓿ 🅰🅴

Mailbox, 1 Wharfside St ⊠ *B1 1RD* – ℰ *(0121) 246 5000* – *birmingham@malmaison.com* – *Fax (0121) 246 50 02* – *www.malmaison.com* **E2**
184 rm – †£ 170, ††£ 495, ⊊ £ 13.95 – 5 suites
Rest *Brasserie* – Menu £ 16 (dinner) – Carte £ 26/33
♦ Luxury ♦ Stylish ♦

Stylish, modern boutique hotel, forms centrepiece of Mailbox development. Stylish bar. Spacious contemporary bedrooms with every modern facility; superb petit spa. Brasserie serving contemporary French influenced cooking at reasonable prices.

Hotel Du Vin

🏠 🅵🅰 📶 & rm 🅰🅲 rm 📶 ⚐ 🆅🅸🆂🅰 ⓿ 🅰🅴

25 Church St ⊠ *B3 2NR* – ℰ *(0121) 200 0600* – *info.birmingham@hotelduvin.com* – *Fax (0121) 236 08 89* – *www.hotelduvin.com* **E2**
66 rm – †£ 150/185, ††£ 150/185, ⊊ £ 13.50
Rest *Bistro* – Carte £ 25/35 ⅌
♦ Business ♦ Design ♦

Former 19C eye hospital in heart of shopping centre; has relaxed, individual, boutique style. Low lighting in rooms of muted tones: Egyptian cotton and superb bathrooms. Champagne in "bubble lounge"; Parisian style brasserie.

The Burlington

🅵🅰 📶 & rm 🅰🅲 ☎ ⚐ 🆅🅸🆂🅰 ⓿ 🅰🅴 ⓘ

Burlington Arcade, 126 New St ⊠ *B2 4JQ* – ℰ *(0844) 879 9019* – *general.burlington@macdonald-hotels.co.uk* – *Fax (0121) 628 50 05* – *www.macdonaldhotels.co.uk* – *Closed 25-26 December* **E2**
110 rm – †£ 175, ††£ 195, ⊊ £ 17.50 – 2 suites
Rest *Berlioz* – ℰ *(0121) 643 9191 (dinner only)* Carte £ 20/35
♦ Traditional ♦ Classic ♦

Approached by a period arcade. Restored Victorian former railway hotel retains much of its original charm. Period décor to bedrooms yet with fax, modem and voice mail. Elegant dining room: ornate ceiling, chandeliers and vast mirrors.

City Inn

🏠 🅵🅰 & rm 🅰🅲 🆂🅰 ⚐ 🆅🅸🆂🅰 ⓿ 🅰🅴 ⓘ

1 Brunswick Sq, Brindley Pl ⊠ *B1 2HW* – ℰ *(0121) 643 1003* – *birmingham.reservations@cityinn.com* – *Fax (0121) 643 10 05* – *www.cityinn.com* **D2**
238 rm – †£ 89/225, ††£ 89/225, ⊊ £ 12.50
Rest *City Café* – Menu £ 15/17 – Carte £ 19/48
♦ Chain hotel ♦ Business ♦ Functional ♦

In heart of vibrant Brindley Place; the spacious atrium with bright rugs and blond wood sets the tone for equally stylish rooms. Corporate friendly with many meeting rooms. Eat in restaurant, terrace or bar.

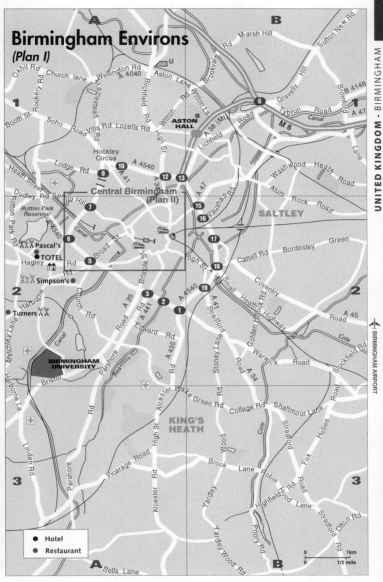

Birmingham Environs
(Plan I)

O'hill Rd
Church lane
Church Rd
Rookery Rd
Wellington Rd
A 4040
Aston Lane
Wit
Rd
Brookvale
Rd
Marsh Hill

B

Sutton New Rd
Gravelly Hill
A 4148
A 47
Bromford

1

Booth St
Soho Road
Hamstead Rd
Villa Rd
Lozells Rd
Birchfield Rd
Witton Rd
High St.
Witton Rd
Lichfield Road
Tyburn Road
Canal
M 6
Lane

6

ASTON HALL

Heath Street
Lodge Rd
Hockley Circus
A 4540
A 41
A 38 (M)
Washwood Heath Road

Dudley Rd
Spring Hill
Central Birmingham (Plan II)
A 47
Vauxhall Rd
Alum Rock Road
SALTLEY

10
9
12
13
7
15
16

Rotton Park Reservoir
Canal
Broad
St.
Bristol St.
High St.
Cattell Rd
Bordesley Green

Pascal's
TOTEL
Hagley Rd
Simpson's

6
5
17
18

2

Harborne
Turners
Metchley Lane
Church Rd
A 38
A 441
Edward Rd
A 4540
Stratford
A 41
Small Heath
Coventry Road
Hobmoor Highway
Warwick Road
A 45
Cole
Road
Stockfield Rd

3
2
1
19

2

Harborne La.
Linder Rd
Bristol Rd
Pershore Rd
Rea
A 435
Stoney Lane
Golden Hillock Road
A 34
Reddings
BIRMINGHAM UNIVERSITY

Alcester Rd
Wake Green Rd
Collage Rd
Shaftmoor Lane
Stratford Rd
Fox Hollies Road

KING'S HEATH

3

Pershore Rd
Vicarage Road
High St.
Alcester Rd
Cole
Wood
Brook
Lane
Robin Hood Lane
Highfield Rd
Stratford Rd
Olton Rd
Priory Rd
Yardley Wood Rd

| Hotel |
| Restaurant |

0   1km
0   1/2 mile

Bells Lane
A
B

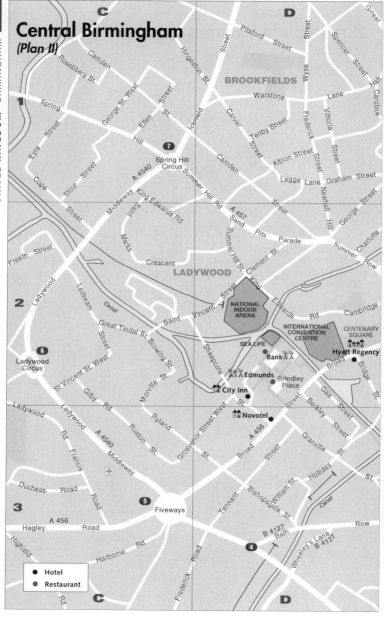

Central Birmingham
(Plan II)

BROOKFIELDS

LADYWOOD

NATIONAL INDOOR ARENA

INTERNATIONAL CONVENTION CENTRE

CENTENARY SQUARE

SEA LIFE

Bank

Hyatt Regency

Edmunds

Brindley Place

City Inn

Novotel

Ladywood Circus

Fiveways

- ● Hotel
- ● Restaurant

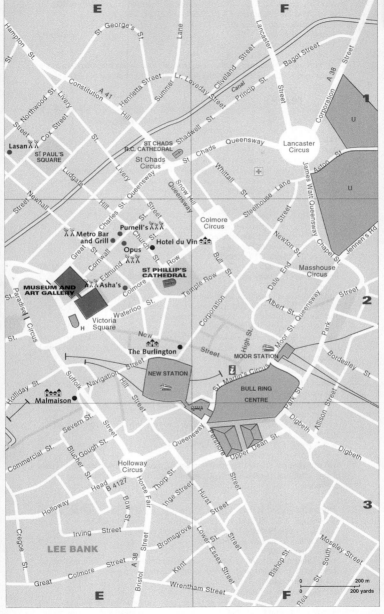

E

F

St. George's St.

Lane

Lancaster Street

Bagot Street

Corporation

A 38 Street

1

U

Hampton St.

St. George's St.

Constitution A 41 Hill

Henrietta Street

Summer Lr. Loveday Street

Cliveland Street

Canal Princip St.

Lancaster Circus

James Watt Queensway

Aston St.

U

Jennen's Rd.

Northwood St.

Cox Street

Livery Street

Shadwell St.

Queensway

St. Chads

●**Lasan** ✕✕
ST PAUL'S SQUARE

ST CHADS R.C. CATHEDRAL

St Chads Circus

St. Chads

Whittall St.

Steelhouse Lane

✚

Ludgate Hill

Livery Street

Snow Hill Queensway

Colmore Circus

Newton St.

Newhall Street

Charles St. Queensway

Church Street

Masshouse Circus

Paradise Circus

Great Charles St.

Cornwall St.

Purnell's ✕✕✕

Hotel du Vin ⊞⊞

Bull St.

Dale End

Albert St. Queensway

Moor St. Queensway

Park St.

Bordesley

2

✕✕ **Metro Bar and Grill**
Opus ●
✕✕✕

●

ST PHILLIP'S CATHEDRAL

Temple Row

Corporation Street

High St.

MUSEUM AND ART GALLERY

St. Edmund

✕✕ **Asha's**

Colmore St.

Waterloo St.

Temple Row

Moor St.

MOOR STATION 🚉

Allison Street

Digbeth

St.

Victoria Square

H

New Street

The Burlington ⊞⊞

Corporation Street

St. Martin's Circus

BULL RING CENTRE

Park St.

Digbeth

Holliday St.

Suffolk

Navigation Hill Street

New Street

NEW STATION 🚉

𝒊

Park St.

▣ **Malmaison**

Queensway

Smallbrook

Upper Dean St.

Commercial St.

Severn St.

Blucher St.

Gough St.

Queensway

Smallbrook

Holloway Circus

B 4127

Horse Fair

Thorp Street

Inge Street

Hurst Street

Bromsgrove Street

Kent St.

Lower Essex St.

Bishop St.

Moseley Street

3

Cregoe St.

Holloway Head

Bow St.

Irving Street

LEE BANK

Great Colmore Street

A 38 Bristol St.

Bromsgrove Street

Wrentham Street

Rea St.

0   200 m

0   200 yards

E

F

TOTEL without rest   P VISA ⚫⚫ AE

19 Portland Rd, Edgbaston ⊠ B16 9HN – ℰ (0121) 454 5282
– info@toteluk.com – Fax (0121) 456 46 68
– www.toteluk.com   *Plan I* **A2**
1 rm – 10 suites – ♦♦ £ 75/105
♦ Business ♦ Design ♦

19C house converted into comfortable, spacious fully-serviced apartments, individually styled with modern facilities. Friendly service. Continental breakfast served in room.

Novotel   🐾 🕭 ⅙ rm 🖭 🎙 🛗 🚗 VISA ⚫⚫ AE ⓞ

70 Broad St ⊠ B1 2HT – ℰ (0121) 643 2000 – h1077@accor.com
– Fax (0121) 643 97 86 – www.novotel.com   **D3**
148 rm – ♦ £ 152 **♦♦** £ 152, ⊑ £ 12.50
Rest – *(meals in bar)* Menu £ 20 – Carte £ 21/28
♦ Chain hotel ♦ Business ♦ Functional ♦

Well located for the increasingly popular Brindleyplace development. Underground parking. Modern, well-kept, branded bedrooms suitable for families. Modern, open-plan restaurant.

✗✗✗   Simpsons (Andreas Antona) with rm   🚄 🛏 AC rest ⇆ P
☸️

20 Highfield Rd, Edgbaston ⊠ B15 3DU – ℰ (0121)   VISA ⚫⚫ AE ⓞ
454 3434 – info@simpsonsrestaurant.co.uk – Fax (0121) 454 33 99
– www.simpsonsrestaurant.co.uk
– closed 24-27 and 31 December-1 January
4 rm – ♦♦ £ 160/225   *Plan I* **A2**
Rest – *(closed Sunday dinner and Bank Holidays)* Menu £ 28/33
– Carte £ 45/53 ⅏
Spec. Ravioli of scallops with baby vegetables, ginger and lemon grass sauce. Confit of rabbit with pancetta and sweet and sour sauce. Chocolate and passion fruit délice with coconut ice cream.
♦ Innovative ♦ Fashionable ♦

Impressive Georgian mansion with blend of contemporary furnishings and period touches. L-shaped dining room set around terrace. Classically based menus with a personal twist. Large, individually themed bedrooms.

✗✗✗   Pascal's   VISA ⚫⚫
☺️

1 Montague Rd ⊠ B16 9HN – ℰ (0121) 455 0999
– info@pascalsrestaurant.co.uk – Fax (0121) 455 09 99
– www.pascalsrestaurant.co.uk
– closed 1 week Easter, last 2 weeks July, 1 week Christmas, Saturday lunch,
Sunday and Monday   *Plan I* **A2**
Rest – Menu £ 20/29 – Carte £ 20/29
♦ French ♦ Formal ♦

Two main rooms; a darker inner hall and lighter, more airy conservatory with views of the small rear garden. Classical, carefully priced cooking with strong French overtones.

✗✗✗   Purnell's (Glynn Purnell)   ↳ VISA ⚫⚫ AE
☸️

55 Cornwall St ⊠ B3 2DH – ℰ (0121) 212 9799 – www.purnellsrestaurant.com
– closed 1 week Easter, last week July, 1st week August, 1 week Christmas,
Saturday lunch, Sunday and Monday   **E2**
Rest – Menu £ 20/40
Spec. Salad of crab with smoked paprika and honeycomb. Slow cooked ox cheek with monkfish and spiced lentils. Raspberry pavlova with lavender and raspberry sorbet.
♦ Innovative ♦ Design ♦

Red brick Victorian building in heart of city, boasting large arched floor to ceiling windows and central bar. Well-priced, modern and innovative food uses quality ingredients.

XXX **Opus**   [AC] ⇔ [VISA] [OO] [AE]

54 Cornwall St ⊠ *B3 2DE –* ℰ *(0121) 200 2323 – restaurant@*
opusrestaurant.co.uk – Fax (0121) 200 20 90 – www.opusrestaurant.co.uk
– closed 25 December-4 January, Saturday lunch, Sunday and Bank Holidays
Rest – Menu £ 20 – Carte £ 30/38   **E2**
♦ Modern ♦ Design ♦
Restaurant of floor-to-ceiling glass in evolving area of city. Seafood and shellfish
bar for diners on the move. Assured cooking underpins modern menus with traditional base.

XXX **Asha's**   [VISA] [OO] [AE]

12-22 Newhall St ⊠ *B3 3LX –* ℰ *(0121) 2002767 – info@ashasrestaurants.co.uk*
– www.ashasrestaurants.co.uk
– Closed 25 December, 1 January and lunch Saturday, Sunday and Bank
Holidays   **E2**
Rest – Carte £ 20/28
♦ Indian ♦
Smart restaurant with delightful décor and vivid artwork. Owned by renowned
artiste/gourmet Asha Bhosle. Authentic North West Indian cuisine cooked by
chefs originally from that region.

XXX **Edmunds**   [VISA] [OO] [AE]

6 Brindley Place ⊠ *B1 2JB –* ℰ *(0121) 633 4944*
– info@edmundsbirmingham.com – Fax (0121) 4 97 49 74
– www.edmundsbirmingham.com
– Closed 1 week per season, Saturday lunch, Sunday and Bank Holidays
Rest – Menu £ 20/40   **D2**
♦ Modern European ♦ Friendly ♦
Formal restaurant in heart of city. Smart interior with neutral décor and modern
lighting. Immaculately laid tables boast fine china and glassware. Smart, attentive
staff.

XX **Turners** (Richard Turner)   [VISA] [OO]
ఔ
69 High Street, Harborne ⊠ *B17 9NS –* ℰ *(0121) 426 4440*
– closed Saturday lunch, Sunday dinner and Monday   Plan I **A2**
Rest – *(booking advisable)* Menu £ 18 (lunch) – Carte £ 35/50
Spec. Roast and confit quail with soft boiled egg, and walnut vinaigrette.
Assiette of lamb, shallot purée and thyme sauce. Raspberry sablé Breton
with basil ice cream.
♦ Modern European ♦ Friendly ♦
Unlikely venue in a parade of shops; simple, crisp interior. The cooking reflects the
experienced chef's classical background; flavours are clean and dishes well balan-
ced.

XX **Lasan**   [VISA] [OO] [AE]

3-4 Dakota Buildings, James St ⊠ *B3 1SD –* ℰ *(0121) 212 3664*
– info@lasan.co.uk – Fax (0121) 212 36 65 – www.lasan.co.uk
– closed 25-26 December and Saturday lunch   **E1**
Rest – Carte £ 26/40
♦ Indian ♦ Design ♦
Jewellery quarter restaurant of sophistication and style; good quality ingredients
allow the clarity of the spices to shine through in this well-run Indian establishment.

XX **Bank**   ⌂ [AC] ⇔ [Eऀ] [VISA] [OO] [AE] [O]

4 Brindleyplace ⊠ *B1 2JB –* ℰ *(0121) 633 4466*
– birmres@bankrestaurants.com – Fax (0121) 633 44 65
– www.bankrestaurants.com   **D2**
Rest – Menu £ 15 – Carte approx. £ 29
♦ Modern ♦ Brasserie ♦
Capacious, modern and busy bar-restaurant where chefs can be watched through
a glass wall preparing the tasty modern dishes. Pleasant terrace area.

XX **Metro Bar and Grill** Ⓐ𝐂 𝘝𝘐𝘚𝘈 ⓒⓞ 𝔸𝔼

73 Cornwall St ⊠ B3 2DF – ℰ (0121) 200 1911
– birmingham@metrobarandgrill.co.uk – Fax (0121) 200 16 11
– www.metrobarandgrill.co.uk
– closed 25 December-2 January, Sunday and Bank Holidays **E2**
Rest *– (booking essential)* Menu £ 18 (dinner) – Carte £ 22/32
♦ Modern ♦ Brasserie ♦

Gleaming chrome and mirrors in a bright, contemporary basement restaurant. Modern cooking with rotisserie specialities. Spacious, ever-lively bar serves lighter meals.

at Birmingham Airport

 Novotel Birmingham Airport & rm 🖭 ¶" 🔏 𝘝𝘐𝘚𝘈 ⓒⓞ 𝔸𝔼 ⓞ

Terminal 1 ⊠ B26 3QL – ℰ (0121) 782 7000 – h1058@accor.com
– Fax (0121) 782 04 45 – www.novotel.com
195 rm – ♦£ 139 ♦♦£ 139, � £ 14.50
Rest *– (bar lunch Saturday, Sunday and Bank Holidays)* Menu £ 17 (lunch)
– Carte £ 23/35
♦ Chain hotel ♦ Business ♦ Functional ♦

Opposite main terminal building: modern hotel benefits from sound proofed doors and double glazing. Mini bars and power showers provided in spacious rooms with sofa beds. Open-plan garden brasserie.

at National Exhibition Centre

 Crowne Plaza 🛪 🕉 & rm Ⓐ𝐂 🖭 ¶" 🔏 ℙ 𝘝𝘐𝘚𝘈 ⓒⓞ 𝔸𝔼 ⓞ

Pendigo Way ⊠ B40 1PS – ℰ (0870) 400 9160 – necroomsales@ihg.com
– Fax (0121) 781 43 21 – www.crowneplaza.co.uk
– closed 21 December-4 January
242 rm � – ♦£ 89/269 ♦♦£ 89/269
Rest *– (bar lunch Saturday)* Carte £ 29/32
♦ Business ♦ Modern ♦

Modern hotel adjacent to NEC. Small terrace area overlooks lake. Extensive conference facilities. State-of-the-art bedrooms with a host of extras.

EDINBURGH

Population: 430 082 (conurbation 452 194 – Altitude: 50m

T. Bognar/PHOTONONSTOP

Edinburgh is often called 'the Athens of the North', but the beautiful Scottish capital can also bear comparison with Rome: like the Italian capital, it's laid out on seven hills. These were once of a volcanic nature, in contrast to the modern city, which is elegant, cool and sophisticated. It's essentially two cities in one, the medieval Old Town, huddled around and beneath the crags and battlements of the castle, and the smart Georgian terraces of the New Town, overseen by the eighteenth century architect Robert Adam. You could say there's a third element to the equation: the port of Leith, two miles from the centre, which has undergone a revamp over the last decade to take its place as Edinburgh's proud little relative.

This is a city that's been attracting tourists since the nineteenth century. You could even make a claim for Edinburgh being one of the places where the tourist industry came of age. That's why it sits so easily with the annual August invasion of the Edinburgh Festival. Since 1999 it's also been the home of the Scottish Parliament, adding a new dimension to its worldwide reputation. It accepts its plaudits with the same ease that it accepts an extra half million visitors at the height of summer. Its status as a UNESCO World Heritage site confirms it as a city that knows how to be both ancient and modern.

981

LIVING THE CITY

In the middle is the **castle**; to the south is the **old town;** to the north is the **new town**. There, in a nutshell, you have Edinburgh. But within that briefest of outlines lies so much life and colour you could find a new facet to interest you each day for a week. There's a natural boundary to the north at the Firth of Forth, while to the south lie the rolling Pentland Hills. Unless you've had a few too many drams, it's just about impossible to get lost here, as prominent landmarks like the Castle, Arthur's Seat and Calton Hill access all areas. Filleting the centre of town is the main artery of Princes Street, one side of which invites you to shop, the other to sit and relax in your own space.

PRACTICAL INFORMATION

ARRIVAL-DEPARTURE

8 miles to the west of the city is Edinburgh International Airport. There is an Airlink Bus Service to Waveley Bridge every 10min. A taxi to the city centre will cost around £17.

TRANSPORT

A great way of gaining access to many of Edinburgh's top sights is by getting an Edinburgh Pass. It gives you free entry to over 30 of the city's attractions and includes loads of great offers.

There's no underground or tram system in the city, so it might be wise to invest in a Daysaver ticket for the buses. For £2.50 you'll have the freedom of Edinburgh for 24 hours.

There are plenty of guided options for showing you around. Choose from an open-top bus, a walking or cycling tour, or, slightly more off the wall, a ghost tour of the old town. All city bus tours leave from Waverley Bridge and the hop-on, hop-off nature of the ticket will last you 24 hours.

EXPLORING EDINBURGH

The Castle Rock, epicentre of the Scottish capital, has been an elevated and indomitable refuge for over a thousand years, and it's from here that the city grew, abetted by Stuart kings who favoured Edinburgh as their royal residence. Breathe in its air and pick up its scent. Wherever you are, its ancient geography seeps into your pores. Whether it's from the extinct volcanic mound of Arthur's Seat in Holyrood Park, or the pivotal lump of rock upon which the castle hovers; whether you're atop the craggy splendour of Calton Hill or down in the mysterious dank of a medieval wynd, this is a city scraped from the work of primeval forces.

The old town is hued from stone, with tightly packed, granite grey houses, each having their own story to tell. **The Royal Mile** is the main spine of the area, running downhill from the castle through Lawnmarket past St Giles' Cathedral, through Canongate to Holyroodhouse and the Scottish Parliament building. The bottom section is far quieter than the tourist-oriented upper part, but all the way down, every narrow wynd (stone staircase) and (nearly) every building withholds ancient secrets, bound up in wondrous gables, turrets and towering chimneys. Two places to seek out in this vicinity: one is the **Writers' Museum** in Lady Stair's Close off Lawnmarket. This is full of the paraphernalia of three of Scotland's most famous writers – Robert Burns, Sir Walter Scott and Robert Louis Stevenson. The latter got his inspiration for Dr. Jekyll and Mr. Hyde from a notorious local schizophrenic who was a respectable councillor and cabinet-maker by day, burglar and thief by night. The man was eventually caught and hanged, but his name lives on at Deacon Brodie's Tavern further along Lawnmarket.

Try and avoid the crowds for a while by wandering off into a charming little close, or exploring the tunnels and wynds that connect streets on different levels - these can be the most fascinating elements of the Royal Mile. Gladstone's Land in Lawnmarket will enhance this feel for the sixteenth century: it's a six-storey former merchant's home and shop, and it's been restored to its former glory. You can actually partake in this yourself, as four of the apartments are available to rent. Any stroll down the Royal Mile wouldn't be complete without coming under the lowering glare of **St Giles Cathedral**, or to give it its proper Scottish name, The High Kirk. It's a magnificently sombre place dating from 1120, but don't expect the interior to be too ornate: Calvinist zealots during the Reformation saw to

that. This deep, dark landmark acts as a kind of focal point for Festival revellers, but of more relevance it's where ghost-tour companies pitch up and lead you off to spooky cellars and shabby arches.

→ SO WHAT'S NEW?

A different feel pervades the New Town, which you reach via a pleasant walk over the Waverley railway bridge and across Princes Street. 'New' in this case is a relative term. This part of town was pastureland known as The Long Dikes and architect Robert Adam transformed it in the latter part of the 18C, when union with England was bringing the city new prosperity. It's an area with wide, spacious streets, open grassy squares and classical lines: essentially it's the diametric opposite of the Old Town. Its rectangle of streets and terraces is one of the first and finest examples of town planning in Europe. The elegant Georgian architecture you find here now acts as the backdrop to a yummy collection of equally stylish shops, restaurants and bars; rather out of the ordinary in a stylistic sense is the distinctive neo-Gothic **Scottish National Portrait Gallery**, a great place to spend a wet afternoon, taking in the visual history of the country's rebels, philosophers, heroes and villains. Contemporary portraits include the likes of novelist Irvine Welsh, actor Sean Connery and ex-footballer Danny McGrain, possibly a surprise inclusion since he made his name playing for a Glasgow club...

Edinburgh never really takes on an 'industrial' aspect; with the likes of **Princes Street Gardens** right there in the heart of things, it's easy to feel green here. Nevertheless, there's a wonderful place to go if you want to take things to a more rural plane. It's The Water of Leith, a short bus ride out of the centre; it starts close to the entrance to Murrayfield Rugby Stadium and meanders along a walkway for all of 21 miles, taking in the delightful Dean Village, a former grain-milling centre dating from the twelfth century, plunged down a valley 30 metres deep. The village's old buildings have been restored and converted into apartments and houses: there's a famous view here looking downstream beneath the thrusting arches of Thomas Telford's Dean Bridge (close by you can get a cultural hit at the Scottish National Gallery of Modern Art, which includes works by Vuillard, Matisse, Lichtenstein and Giacometti, as well as Scottish painters of the vibrant Colourist school).

The Water of Leith Walkway is one of the city's most tranquil strolls, with a pleasant mix of village and woodland along the way. An ideal end point for many is the **Royal Botanic Garden**, which boasts the world's largest collection of rhododendrons, plus rock gardens with a waterfall and redwoods in a mini-forest.

→ KEEPING YOU PAGED

Per capita head, Edinburgh boasts more booksellers than any other city in Britain. In 2004 it became the first city in the world to be named City of Literature by UNESCO.

→ TAKE IT OR LEITH IT

At the end of the engaging Walkway, **Leith** is a very agreeable place to pitch up. The former dockland area staring out onto the Firth of Forth was a typical run-down port of aching infrastructure and rough-and-ready seamen's bars until the late 80s, when it experienced a renaissance. Nineteenth century warehouses were converted into loft apartments and a coterie of stylish bars and restaurants opened their doors. Proof of their impact came when two eating establishments in the area earned Michelin stars: Martin Wishart and The Kitchin. Both are located in old dockside conversions. There's also the smart Ocean Terminal shopping complex adding a retail landmark to the serene waterfront ambience.

Edinburgh is a superb city to explore. Its topography and its architecture give it varied nuance and colour. It can also be a pretty cool city, and not just in the cultural sense. Summer temperatures are unlikely to climb much above 18 Celsius, but in a place as fascinating as this, wrap up warm and you'll hardly notice.

→ REEL LIFE

Edinburgh's a popular place with filmmakers. Movies shot in and around the city include Trainspotting, The Prime of Miss Jean Brodie, The Da Vinci Code, The 39 Steps, and Mary Reilly.

EDINBURGH IN...

→ ONE DAY
Calton Hill, Royal Mile, Edinburgh Castle, New Town café, Old town pub

→ TWO DAYS
Water of Leith, Scottish National Gallery of Modern Art, Leith and one of its smart restaurants, Forth Rail Bridge

→ THREE DAYS
Arthur's Seat, National Museum of Scotland, Holyrood Park, a trip to the Pentland Hills

CALENDAR HIGHLIGHTS

Festivals are a part and parcel of Edinburgh life, and not just the famous jamboree every August. In the spring, the Ceilidh Culture Festival highlights local performers as well as others from around the world, and takes place over three weeks in 30 different venues. Mary King's Ghost Fest is a 10-day bonanza for anyone interested in the city's haunted sites, and includes overnight vigils and experiments. December is a special time of year here. There are all kinds of markets and fun fairs at Christmas, while Hogmanay is a four day spor-rans-up with a torchlight procession on the 29th, a carnival on George Street on the 30th, a street party (to end all street parties) on New Year's Eve, plus a host of events to detox and energise on the first day of the year. The Summer Festival, the one that the world not only knows about but appears to attend en masse, is in fact an umbrella term for many distinct cultural events taking place, including an international festival and others for film, fringe, art, books, jazz and blues.

EATING OUT

Food and drink in Edinburgh takes on many forms. It can range from the 'tartan menus' fodder for tourists to the very best, via the smart conversions of Leith or the exquisite central hotels, as in the case of the landmark Balmoral, at the head of Princes Street with its immaculate basement restaurant, Number One. Edinburgh is said to have more restaurants per head of population than anywhere else in the UK, and you can admire the city from a rooftop table, or dine with ghosts in a basement eatery. There are some good pubs in the old town, such as the tiny but hip Black Bo's in Blackfriars Street, or the authentically atmospheric Ensign Ewart on Lawnmarket. Drinking dens also abound in Cowgate and Grassmarket. Further away, in West End, you'll find enticing late-night bars, while the stylish variety, serving cocktails, are more in order in the George Street area of new town. What to drink in Scotland's capital? Any beer by Deuchar's gets the thumbs-up, or a pint of Dark Island from Orkney. Peaty flavoured Laphroaig is a highly recommended dram of whisky. For those who might want to buy their grub and take it away to eat, then a visit to Valvona & Crolla is a must. It's in Elm Row near Calton Hill, and is a great Italian deli: a weekly van from Italy brings wonderful cheeses, olive oils, wine and salamis, and if the temptation's too strong, you can try them at once in the café at the back. The nineteenth century Cadenhead's on the Royal Mile is the place to go for whiskies: it sells a mind-boggling range of rare distillations.

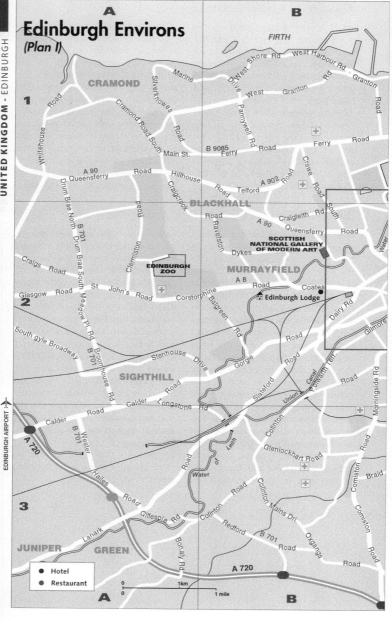

Edinburgh Environs
(Plan I)

CRAMOND

BLACKHALL

SCOTTISH NATIONAL GALLERY OF MODERN ART

MURRAYFIELD

EDINBURGH ZOO

Edinburgh Lodge

SIGHTHILL

JUNIPER GREEN

FIRTH

EDINBURGH AIRPORT

- ● Hotel
- ● Restaurant

0 ___ 1km
0 ___ 1 mile

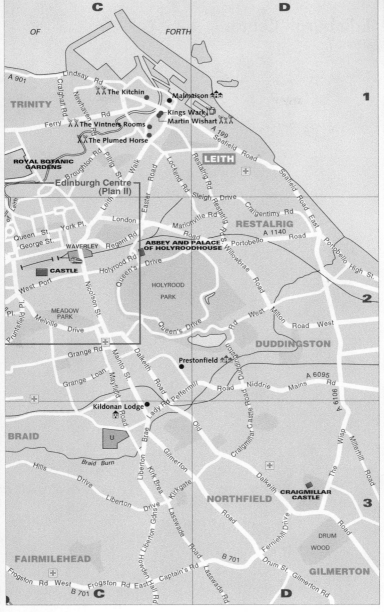

OF

FORTH

A 901

Lindsay Rd

TRINITY

Craighall Rd

Newhaven Rd

X X The Kitchin

Malmaison

Ferry

Rd

X X The Vintners Rooms

Kings Wark

Martin Wishart X X X

A 199

Seafield Road

X The Plumed Horse

ROYAL BOTANIC
GARDENS

Broughton Rd

Pilrig St

Walk

LEITH

Leith

Lochend Rd

Restalrig Rd

Seafield Road East

Portobello High St.

Edinburgh Centre
(Plan II)

Leith

Easter

Road

Sleigh

Drive

Craigentiny Rd

London

Marionville Rd

Restalrig Rd

RESTALRIG

A 1140

Portobello

Road

Queen St.

York Pl.

George St.

WAVERLEY

Regent Rd

ABBEY AND PALACE
OF HOLYROODHOUSE

Willowbrae

Road

CASTLE

Holyrood Rd

Queen's

Drive

West Port

Nicolson St.

HOLYROOD
PARK

West

Milton

Road

West

Pl.

MEADOW
PARK

Melville

Drive

Queen's Drive

Rd

DUDDINGSTON

Prunstield Pl.

Grange Rd

Mayfield

Dalkeith

Road

Duddingston

Grange Loan

Prestonfield

Niddrie

Mains

A 6095

Rd

Braid

Road

Kildonan Lodge

Lady Rd

Peffermill

Road

BRAID

U

Craigmillar Castle Road

Old

Dalkeith

Road

The

Wisp

Millerhill

Road

Braid Burn

Gilmerton

Dalkeith

CRAIGMILLAR
CASTLE

Hills

Drive

Liberton

Kirk Brae

Road

Ferniehill Drive

B 6095

Liberton

Drive

Kirkgate

Lasswade

NORTHFIELD

Road

3

DRUM
WOOD

FAIRMILEHEAD

Frogston Rd West

B 701

Frogston Rd

Howden Hall Rd

Captain's Rd

Lasswade Road

B 701

Drum St.

Gilmerton Rd

GILMERTON

C

D

987

Edinburgh Centre
(Plan II)

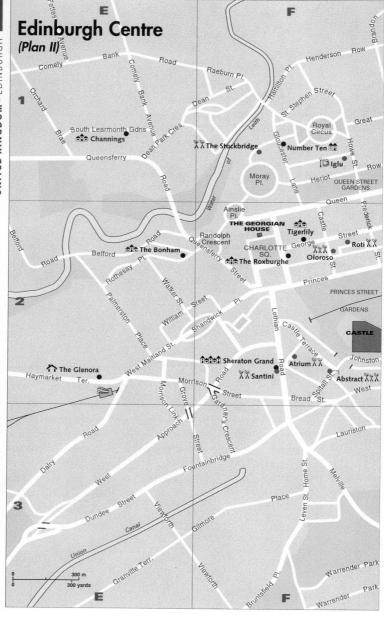

E

F

1

Fettes Avenue
Comely Bank
Orchard Brae
Comely Bank Avenue
Bank Road
Queensferry
Dean Park Cres.
Raeburn Pl.
Dean St.
Water of Leith
Hamilton Pl.
Henderson Row
Brandon
St. Stephen Street
Glenfinlas Lane
Gloucester Lane
Royal Circus
Great
Howe St.
Heriot
Row
QUEEN STREET GARDENS

South Learmonth Gdns
🏠 Channings
❌ ❌ The Stockbridge
Moray Pl.
Number Ten 🏠
🏠 Iglu

2

Belford
Road
Belford
Rothesay Pl.
Palmerston Place
Walker St.
William Street
Queensferry Road
Randolph Crescent
Ainslie Pl.
THE GEORGIAN HOUSE
CHARLOTTE SQ.
🏠 The Roxburghe
🏠 The Bonham
Queen Street
Tigerlily 🏠
Castle Street
George Street
Oloroso ❌❌❌
Roti ❌❌
Frederick St.
Princes
PRINCES STREET GARDENS

The Glenora 🏠
Haymarket Ter.
West Maitland St.
Shandwick Pl.
Morrison Link
Grove Street
Gardner's Crescent
Morrison Street
Lothian Road
Castle Terrace
Sheraton Grand 🏠
❌❌ Santini
Atrium ❌❌
Bread St.
Spittal St.
CASTLE
Johnston
Abstract ❌❌❌
West

3

Dalry Road
West
Dundee Street
Viewforth
Canal
Union
Fountainbridge
Gilmore Place
Granville Terr.
Viewforth
Leven St. Home St.
Melville Place
Lauriston
Brunsfield Pl.
Warrender Park
Warrender Park

0 ——— 300 m
0 ——— 300 yards

E

F

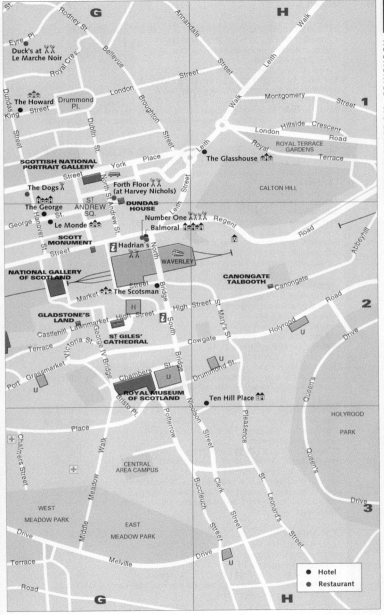

G

Eyre Pl.
Duck's at
Le Marche Noir
Rodney St.
Annandale
Walk
H

Royal Cres.
Bellevue
Street
Leith

Dundas St.
Drummond Pl.
The Howard
London
Montgomery
Street
1

King
Street
Dublin St.
Broughton Street
Hillside Crescent
London
Road
ROYAL TERRACE
GARDENS
Leith Walk
York
Place
Royal Terrace
SCOTTISH NATIONAL
PORTRAIT GALLERY
Street
The Glasshouse
CALTON HILL

The Dogs
North St Andrew St.
Forth Floor
(at Harvey Nichols)
The George
ST
ANDREW
SQ.
DUNDAS
HOUSE
George St.
Hanover St.
Le Monde
Number One
Balmoral
Leith Street
Regent
Road
Abbeyhill
SCOTT
MONUMENT
Hadrian's
North
WAVERLEY
St.
NATIONAL GALLERY
OF SCOTLAND
Street
Market
The Scotsman
Bridge
CANONGATE
TALBOOTH
Canongate
Road
2

GLADSTONE'S
LAND
High Street
High Street
St. Mary's St.
Holyrood
U
Castlehill
Lawnmarket
George IV Bridge
South Bridge
Cowgate
Drive
Terrace
Victoria St.
ST GILES'
CATHEDRAL
Port
Grassmarket
Chambers
U
Drummond St.
U
U
ROYAL MUSEUM
OF SCOTLAND
St. Bridge
Ten Hill Place
HOLYROOD

Chalmers Street
Place
Bristo Pl.
Potterrow
Nicolson Street
Pleasance
PARK
Queen's

Meadow Walk
CENTRAL
AREA CAMPUS
Drive
3

WEST
MEADOW PARK
Middle Meadow
EAST
MEADOW PARK
Buccleuch Street
St. Leonard's Street
Clerk Street
Queen's
Drive
Terrace
Drive
Melville
Drive
U
Road
G
H

Hotel ●
Restaurant ●

989

The Balmoral

1 Princes St ⊠ EH2 2EQ – ℰ (0131) 556 2414
– reservations.balmoral@roccofortecollection.com
– Fax (0131) 557 87 40
– www.roccofortecollection.com **G2**
167 rm – ♥£ 305/320 ♥♥£ 535/555, ⊇ £ 18.50 – 21 suites
Rest Number One and **Hadrian's** – see below
◆ Grand Luxury ◆ Classic ◆
Richly furnished rooms in grand baronial style complemented by contemporary furnishings in the Palm Court exemplify this de luxe Edwardian railway hotel and city landmark.

Sheraton Grand H. & Spa

1 Festival Sq ⊠ EH3 9SR – ℰ (0131) 229 9131
– grandedinburgh.sheraton@sheraton.com
– Fax (0131) 221 62 54
– www.sheraton.com/grandedinburgh **F2**
244 rm – ♥£ 293/334 ♥♥£ 323/364, ⊇ £ 19 – 16 suites
Rest Santini – see below
Rest Terrace – (buffet) Menu £ 21/22 – Carte £ 23/33
◆ Grand Luxury ◆ Business ◆ Modern ◆
A modern, centrally located and smartly run hotel. A popular choice for the working traveller, as it boasts Europe's most advanced urban spa. Comfy, well-kept rooms. Glass expanse of Terrace restaurant overlooks Festival Square.

The George

19-21 George St ⊠ EH2 2PB – ℰ (0131) 225 1251
– george.reservations@principal-hayley.com
– Fax (0131) 226 56 44
– www.principal-hayley.com **G2**
247 rm – ♥£ 99/299 ♥♥£ 99/299, ⊇ £ 16.50 – 1 suite
Rest The Tempus – Carte £ 25/40
◆ Luxury ◆ Classic ◆
Grade II listed Georgian classic in the heart of the city's most chic street; makes the most of Robert Adam's listed design. Modern decor allied to smartly refurbished rooms. Interesting modern menus at The Tempus.

Prestonfield

Priestfield Rd ⊠ EH16 5UT – ℰ (0131) 225 7800
– mail@prestonfield.com – Fax (0131) 220 43 92
– www.prestonfield.com *Plan I* **C2**
20 rm ⊇ – ♥£ 225/275 ♥♥£ 225/275 – 2 suites
Rest Rhubarb – Menu £ 17/25 – Carte £ 39/51
◆ Townhouse ◆ Stylish ◆
Superbly preserved interior, tapestries and paintings in the main part of this elegant country house, built in 1687 with modern additions. Set in parkland below Arthur's Seat. Two-roomed, period-furnished 18C dining room with fine views of the grounds.

The Howard

34 Great King St ⊠ EH3 6QH – ℰ (0131) 274 7402
– reserve@thehoward.com – Fax (0131) 274 74 05
– www.thehoward.com **G1**
14 rm ⊇ – ♥£ 100/275 ♥♥£ 190/275 – 4 suites
Rest The Atholl – (booking essential for non-residents) Carte £ 33/43
◆ Townhouse ◆ Stylish ◆
Crystal chandeliers, antiques, richly furnished rooms and the relaxing opulence of the drawing room set off a fine Georgian interior. An inviting "boutique" hotel. Elegant, linen-clad tables for sumptuous dining.

The Scotsman　　ほ ⑩ 🏊 🖥 & rm 🖭 ⁽ᵀ⁾ 🍴 🅿 ⅦⅣ ⓦ Æ ⓪

20 North Bridge ⊠ EH1 1YT – ℰ (0131) 556 5565 – reservations@tshg.com
– Fax (0131) 652 36 52 – www.theetoncollection.com　　**G2**
69 rm – ♦£ 350/500 ♦♦£ 350/500, ⊊ £ 18.50 – 2 suites
Rest Vermilion – (closed Monday-Tuesday) (dinner only) Carte £ 32/47
Rest North Bridge Brasserie – Carte £ 24/35
♦ Luxury ♦ Classic ♦

Imposing former offices of "The Scotsman" newspaper, with marble reception hall and historic prints. Notably impressive leisure facilities. Well-equipped modern bedrooms. Vibrant, richly red Vermilion. North Bridge Brasserie serves seasonal, modern Scottish dishes.

Channings　　🚗 🛋 ⁽ᵛ⁾ 🍴 ⅦⅣ ⓦ Æ

15 South Learmonth Gdns ⊠ EH4 1EZ – ℰ (0131) 274 7401
– reserve@channings.co.uk – Fax (0131) 274 74 05 – www.channings.co.uk
38 rm – ♦£ 100/200 ♦♦£ 140/200, ⊊ £ 11.50 – 3 suites　　**E1**
Rest – Menu £ 17 (lunch) – Carte £ 28/36
♦ Townhouse ♦ Stylish ♦

Sensitively refurbished rooms and fire-lit lounges blend an easy country house elegance with original Edwardian character. Individually appointed bedrooms. A warm, contemporary design doesn't detract from the formal ambience pervading this basement restaurant in which classic Gallic flavours hold sway.

The Bonham　　& rm ⁽ᵛ⁾ 🍴 🅿 ⅦⅣ ⓦ Æ

35 Drumsheugh Gdns ⊠ EH3 7RN – ℰ (0131) 274 7400
– reserve@thebonham.com – Fax (0131) 274 74 05 – www.thebonham.com
46 rm – ♦£ 110/185 ♦♦£ 175/215, ⊊ £ 11.50 – 2 suites　　**E2**
Rest – Menu £ 16 – Carte £ 27/44
♦ Townhouse ♦ Stylish ♦

A striking synthesis of Victorian architecture, eclectic fittings and bold, rich colours of a contemporary décor. Numerous pictures by "up-and-coming" local artists. Chic dining room with massive mirrors and "catwalk" in spotlights.

The Glasshouse without rest　　≤ 🚗 & AC ⁽ᵛ⁾ 🍴 ⅦⅣ ⓦ Æ ⓪

2 Greenside Pl ⊠ EH1 3AA – ℰ (0131) 525 8200
– resglasshouse@theetoncollection.com – Fax (0131) 525 82 05
– www.theetoncollection.com
– closed Christmas　　**H1**
65 rm – ♦£ 160/355 ♦♦£ 200/510, ⊊ £ 16.50
♦ Business ♦ Modern ♦

Glass themes dominate the discreet style. Modern bedrooms, with floor to ceiling windows, have views of spacious roof garden or the city below. Breakfast room to the rear.

The Roxburghe　　ほ 🏊 🖥 & rm AC rest ⁽ᵛ⁾ 🍴 ⅦⅣ ⓦ Æ ⓪

38 Charlotte Sq ⊠ EH2 4HQ – ℰ (0844) 879 9063
– roxburghe@macdonald-hotels.co.uk – Fax (0131) 240 55 55
– www.macdonaldhotels.co.uk/roxburghe　　**F2**
196 rm ⊊ – ♦£ 95/200 ♦♦£ 95/255 – 1 suite
Rest The Melrose – Carte £ 17/43
♦ Business ♦ Classic ♦

Attentive service, understated period-inspired charm and individuality in the British style. Part modern, part Georgian but roomy throughout; welcoming bar. Restaurant reflects the grandeur of architect Robert Adam's exterior.

Tigerlily　　& rm AC 🖭 ⁽ᵀ⁾ ⅦⅣ ⓦ Æ

125 George St ⊠ EH2 4JN – ℰ (0131) 225 5005 – info@tigerlilyedinburgh.co.uk
– Fax (0131) 225 70 46 – www.tigerlilyedinburgh.co.uk
– closed 25 December　　**F2**
33 rm – ♦£ 195 ♦♦£ 195　　**Rest** – Carte £ 25/34
♦ Townhouse ♦ Design ♦

Coverted Georgian townhouse boasting hip interior, including pink furnished bar, buzzy basement nightclub and glamourous, well-appointed bedrooms. Busy dining room offers wide choice of dishes, with Asian tendencies.

Le Monde   &. rm AC 🖥 🛜 VISA ⚫⚫ AE ⓪

16 George St ⊠ *EH2 2PF – ℰ (0131) 270 3900*
– info@lemondehotel.co.uk – Fax (0131) 270 39 01
– www.lemondehotel.co.uk
– Closed 24-26 December   **G2**
18 rm ⌲ – ♦£ 125/195 ♦♦£ 145/295   **Rest** *Paris* – Carte £ 18/32
♦ Business ♦ Modern ♦
Smartly appointed hotel in city centre, with two trendy bars and a nightclub. Contemporary bedrooms are themed on cities from around the world, even down to the DVDs. First floor restaurant offers simple menu.

Number Ten without rest   🛜 VISA ⚫⚫ AE ⓪

10 Gloucester Place ⊠ *EH3 6EF – ℰ (0131) 225 2720*
– reservations@hotelnumberten.co.uk – Fax (0131) 220 47 06
– www.hotelnumberten.co.uk   **F1**
28 rm ⌲ – ♦£ 98/158 ♦♦£ 118/248
♦ Townhouse ♦ Classic ♦
Georgian house on cobbled street in quiet residential area; a chintzy feel overlays the contemporary interior. Eclectically styled bedrooms feature homely extra touches.

Ten Hill Place without rest   &. AC 📞 VISA ⚫⚫ AE

10 Hill Place ⊠ *EH8 9DS – ℰ (0131) 662 2080*
– reservations@tenhillplace.com – Fax (0131) 662 20 82
– www.tenhillplacehotel.com
– Closed Christmas   **H2**
78 rm ⌲ – ♦£ 110/150 ♦♦£ 110/150
♦ Business ♦ Modern ♦
Brand new hotel owned by Royal College of Surgeons and next to main college. Contemporary bedrooms boast state-of-the-art facilities; views from Skyline rooms worth extra cost.

Edinburgh Lodge without rest   🚗 📞 P VISA ⚫⚫ AE

6 Hampton Terrace, West Coates ⊠ *EH12 5JD – ℰ (0131) 337 3682*
– info@thelodgehotel.co.uk – Fax (0131) 313 17 00
– www.thelodgehotel.co.uk   *Plan I* **B2**
12 rm ⌲ – ♦£ 50/70 ♦♦£ 80/135
♦ Family ♦ Classic ♦
A converted Georgian manse, family owned and immaculately kept. Individually designed bedrooms and lounge decorated with taste and care; close to Murrayfield rugby stadium.

Kildonan Lodge without rest   🛜 P VISA ⚫⚫ AE ⓪

27 Craigmillar Park ⊠ *EH16 5PE – ℰ (0131) 667 2793*
– info@kildonanlodgehotel.co.uk – Fax (0131) 667 97 77
– www.kildonanlodgehotel.co.uk
– closed week Christmas   *Plan I* **C3**
12 rm ⌲ – ♦£ 65/98 ♦♦£ 78/149
♦ Family ♦ Cosy ♦
Privately managed, with a cosy, firelit drawing room which feels true to the Lodge's origins as a 19C family house. One room has a four-poster bed and a fine bay window.

The Glenora without rest   🖥 🛜 VISA ⚫⚫ ⓪

14 Rosebery Crescent ⊠ *EH12 5JY – ℰ (0131) 337 1186*
– enquiries@glenorahotel.co.uk – Fax (0131) 337 11 19
– www.theglenorahotel.co.uk   **E2**
11 rm ⌲ – ♦£ 58/75 ♦♦£ 90/140
♦ Family ♦ Modern ♦
Capacious Georgian house split over three floors with modern, stylish décor and generously sized bedrooms. Exclusively organic produce served at breakfast.

XXXX
ঃঃ

Number One – at The Balmoral Hotel · AC VISA ⬤ AE ⓞ

1 Princes St ⊠ *EH2 2EQ* – ✆ *(0131) 622 8831*
– *numberone@roccofortecollection.com* – *Fax (0131) 557 87 40*
– *www.roccofortecollection.com*
– *Closed first 2 weeks January* · **G2**
Rest – *(dinner only)* Menu £ 55 🏵

Spec. Citrus scallops with braised artichokes and lentils. Lamb with lettuce and niçoise garnish. Prune soufflé and armagnac ice cream.
♦ Modern ♦ Formal ♦
Opulently-appointed basement restaurant offering fine dining in grand railway
hotel. Luxurious feel. Complex and elaborate cooking showcases Scottish produce.

XXX

Oloroso · ≼ 🏠 AC ⇧ VISA ⬤ AE

33 Castle St ⊠ *EH2 3DN* – ✆ *(0131) 226 7614* – *info@oloroso.co.uk*
– *Fax (0131) 226 76 08* – *www.oloroso.co.uk*
– *closed first 3 weeks January and 25-26 December* · **F2**
Rest – Carte £ 33/52

♦ Innovative ♦ Design ♦
Modish third floor restaurant in heart of city. Busy, atmospheric bar. Lovely terrace
with good castle views to the west. Stylish, modern cooking with Asian influence.

XXX

Abstract · VISA ⬤ AE ⓞ

33-35 Castle Terrace ⊠ *EH1 2EL* – ✆ *(0131) 229 1222*
– *reservations@abstractrestaurant.com* – *Fax (0131) 228 23 98*
– *www.abstractrestaurant.com*
– *Closed Sunday and Monday* · **F2**
Rest – Menu £ 17 (weekday lunch) – Carte £ 32/45

♦ French ♦ Formal ♦
Tucked away behind the castle, all mock snakeskin furniture and vibrant wallpaper.
Seasonal French cooking is balanced and thoughtful; formal service by a well-ver-
sed team.

XX

Santini – at Sheraton Grand H. & Spa. · AC P VISA ⬤ AE ⓞ

8 Conference Sq ⊠ *EH3 8AN* – ✆ *(0131) 221 7788*
– *grandeedinburgh.sheraton@sheraton.com* – *Fax (0131) 221 77 89*
– *www.sheraton.com/grandeedinburgh* · **F2**
Rest – Menu £ 10/19 – Carte £ 16/44

♦ Italian ♦ Formal ♦
The personal touch is predominant in this stylish restaurant appealingly situated
under a superb spa. Charming service heightens the enjoyment of tasty, modern
Italian food.

XX
😊

Atrium · AC VISA ⬤ AE ⓞ

10 Cambridge St ⊠ *EH1 2ED* – ✆ *(0131) 228 8882*
– *eat@atriumrestaurant.co.uk* – *Fax (0131) 228 88 08*
– *www.atriumrestaurant.co.uk*
– *closed 24-26 December, 1 January, Sunday and Saturday lunch except during*
Edinburgh Festival and Rugby matches · **F2**
Rest – Menu £ 20/27 – Carte £ 35/46 🏵
♦ Modern ♦ Design ♦
Located inside the Traverse Theatre, an adventurous repertoire enjoyed on tables
made of wooden railway sleepers. Twisted copper lamps subtly light the ultra-
modern interior.

XX

Hadrian's – at The Balmoral Hotel · AC 🍴 VISA ⬤ AE ⓞ

2 North Bridge ⊠ *EH1 1TR* – ✆ *(0131) 557 5000*
– *hadrians@roccofortecollection.com* – *Fax (0131) 557 37 47* · **G2**
Rest – Menu £ 22 (lunch) – Carte £ 25/41
♦ Modern ♦ Brasserie ♦
Drawing on light, clean-lined styling, reminiscent of Art Deco, and a "British new
wave" approach; an extensive range of contemporary brasserie classics and smart
service.

XX **Forth Floor - Restaurant (at Harvey Nichols)** ← 🏠 AK 🗓

30-34 St Andrew Sq ⊠ EH2 2AD – 🕿 *(0131) 524 8350* VISA ◑◐ AE ⓞ
– forthfloorreservations@harveynichols.com – Fax (0131) 524 83 51
– www.harveynichols.com **G1**
Rest *– (closed Sunday dinner and Monday)* Menu £ 24 (lunch) – Carte £ 31/40
♦ Modern ♦ Brasserie ♦
Stylish restaurant with delightful outside terrace affording views over the city. Half the room in informal brasserie-style and the other more formal. Modern, Scottish menus.

XX **The Stockbridge** VISA ◑◐ AE

54 St Stephens St ⊠ EH3 5AL – 🕿 *(0131) 226 6766*
– www.thestockbridgerestaurant.com
– closed first 2 weeks January, 25, 31 December, Monday and lunch Tuesday
Rest – Menu £ 22 – Carte (dinner) £ 28/41 **F1**
♦ Modern ♦ Intimate ♦
Intimate neighbourhood restaurant, its black walls hung with colourful Scottish art. Professional staff serve a mix of classical and more modern dishes, precisely prepared.

XX **Duck's at Le Marche Noir** ⇆ VISA ◑◐ AE ⓞ
😊
14 Eyre Pl ⊠ EH3 5EP – 🕿 *(0131) 558 1608 – enquiries@ducks.co.uk*
– Fax (0131) 556 07 98 – www.ducks.co.uk
– Closed 25-26 December, Sunday and Monday **G1**
Rest – Menu £ 16 – Carte £ 24/39
♦ Innovative ♦ Bistro ♦
Confident, inventive cuisine with a modern, discreetly French character, served with friendly efficiency in bistro-style surroundings - intimate and very personally run.

XX **Roti** VISA ◑◐ AE

73 Morrison St ⊠ EH3 8BU – 🕿 *(0131) 221 9998 – info@roti.uk.com*
– Fax (0131) 225 53 74 – www.roti.uk.com
– Closed Sunday **F2**
Rest – Carte £ 23/27
♦ Indian ♦ Friendly ♦
Modern Indian restaurant in central location; traditional carved wood meets funky new fittings. Accomplished kitchen serves authentic dishes; tasting menus a highlight.

X **The Dogs** VISA ◑◐
😊
110 Hanover St. ⊠ EH2 1DR – 🕿 *(0131) 220 1208 – info@thedogsonline.co.uk*
– www.thedogsonline.co.uk
– Closed 25 December-1 January **G1**
Rest – Carte £ 16/20
♦ Minimalist ♦
Set on the first floor of a classic Georgian mid-terrace; impressive staircase, simple décor, high-ceilings. Robust, good value comfort food crafted from local, seasonal produce.

🛏 **Iglu** VISA ◑◐ AE

2B Jamaica Street ⊠ EH3 6HH – 🕿 *(0131) 476 5333 – mail@theiglu.com*
– www.theiglu.com
– Closed 25 December dinner, 26 December, 1-2 January **F1**
Rest *– (booking essential)* Menu £ 12 (lunch) – Carte £ 22/32
♦ Modern ♦ Pub ♦
Vivid blue façade. Plasma screens, low tub chairs and funky music; fish tanks and potted plants upstairs. Their ethos is ethical eating; their motto 'wild, organic and local.'

UNITED KINGDOM - EDINBURGH

Malmaison 🏠 ⌂ 🖻 rm 🕽 🔊 🅿 VISA ⬤ AE ⓪

1 Tower Pl ⊠ *EH6 7DB* – 🕾 *(0131) 468 5000*
– *edinburgh@malmaison.com* – *Fax (0131) 468 50 02*
– *www.malmaison.com*   **C1**
95 rm – ♦£ 150 ♦♦£ 150, ☞ £ 13.95 – 5 suites
Rest *Brasserie* – Menu £ 14/15 – Carte £ 26/41
♦ Business ♦ Stylish ♦
Imposing quayside sailors' mission converted in strikingly elegant style. Good-sized rooms, thoughtfully appointed, combine more traditional comfort with up-to-date overtones. Sophisticated brasserie with finely wrought iron.

𝕏𝕏𝕏 Martin Wishart VISA ⬤ AE
🕸

54 The Shore ⊠ *EH6 6RA* – 🕾 *(0131) 553 3557*
– *info@martin-wishart.co.uk* – *Fax (0131) 467 70 91*
– *www.martin-wishart.co.uk*
– *closed first 2 weeks January, last week July, 25 December, Sunday and Monday*
Rest – *(booking essential)* Menu £ 25/55 – Carte approx. £ 55   **C1**
Spec. Ceviche of halibut with mango, passion fruit and coriander. Shin of beef with pumpkin purée and wild mushroom risotto. St. Felicien and apple cannelloni, blueberry brûlée and apple sorbet.
♦ Innovative ♦ Formal ♦
Simply decorated dockside conversion with a fully formed reputation. Modern French-accented menus characterised by clear, intelligently combined flavours. Formal service.

𝕏𝕏 The Kitchin (Tom Kitchin) 🏠 VISA ⬤ AE
🕸

78 Commercial Quay ⊠ *EH6 6LX* – 🕾 *(0131) 555 1755*
– *info@thekitchin.com* – *Fax (0131) 553 06 08* – *www.thekitchin.com*
– *closed Christmas - 7 January, Sunday and Monday*   **C1**
Rest – Menu £ 25 (lunch) – Carte £ 44/59
Spec. Roast langoustine with pig's head and crispy ear salad. Roast duck with endive, roasted fig and orange sauce. Orange tuille with lemon mousse, citrus marmalade and Earl Grey sorbet.
♦ Contemporary ♦ Design ♦
Former dockside warehouse, the industrial feel enhanced by original metal supp-orts and battleship grey décor. Well-priced menus offering skilful, accomplished, modern cooking.

𝕏𝕏 Plumed Horse (Tony Borthwick) ⇌ VISA ⬤ AE
🕸

50-54 Henderson St ⊠ *EH6 6DE* – 🕾 *(0131) 554 5556* – *plumedhorse@aol.com*
– *www.plumedhorse.co.uk*
– *closed 2 weeks July, 2 weeks November, 25-26 December, 1 January,*
Sunday and Monday   **C1**
Rest – Menu £ 21/39
Spec. Foie gras terrine withwater melon, Sauternes and golden raisin vinaig-rette. Scallop and langoustine lasagne, sea bass and champagne sauce. Fudge and ginger parfait, vanilla, lime and 'Sailor Jerry' granita.
♦ Modern ♦ Neighbourhood ♦
Stylish, personally run restaurant with ornate ceiling, vivid paintings, an intimate feel and formal service. Precise, well-crafted cooking makes good use of Scottish ingredients.

𝕏𝕏 The Vintners Rooms VISA ⬤ AE

The Vaults, 87 Giles St ⊠ *EH6 6BZ* – 🕾 *(0131) 554 6767*
– *enquiries@thevintnersrooms.com* – *Fax (0131) 555 56 53*
– *www.thevintersrooms.com*
– *closed 23 December-9 January, Sunday and Monday*   **C1**
Rest – Carte £ 37/48
♦ Mediterranean ♦ Rustic ♦
Atmospheric 18C bonded spirits warehouse with high ceilings, stone floor, rug-covered walls and candlelit side-room with ornate plasterwork. French/Mediterra-nean cooking.

The Kings Wark

36 The Shore ⊠ *EH6 6QU –* 𝒞 *(0131) 554 9260*
– Closed 25-26 December and 1 January

C1

Rest – Carte £ 13/29

♦ Modern ♦ Pub ♦

Distinctive blue façade and cosy, characterful interior with exposed stone and beams. Hearty, unpretentious Scottish cooking. Well known for its all day weekend breakfasts.

Population: 616 000 (conurbation 1 228 000) – Altitude: 8m

M. Fife/Zefa/CORBIS

R ising like the proverbial phoenix from the ashes, Glasgow can claim to be one of the great urban success stories of the past 20 years. Like a punch-drunk boxer, Scotland's second city was slumped against the ropes throughout much of the post-World War II era, its shipbuilding industry in tatters, its troubled, drink-fuelled reputation a byword for the poverty endemic to its inner areas. But the place that Daniel Defoe once called "the cleanest and beautifullest and best built city in Britain, London excepted" had an ace up its sleeve: the 1990 City of Culture award that turned its PR image upside down. From that time on, Glasgow has grown immensely as an arts, business and retail centre, and tourists have discovered for themselves its grand Victorian façade and eye-catching riverside milieu.

T he Clyde played a pivotal role in the original growth of Glasgow: in the 18C as a source of trade with the Americas, and in the 19th as the centre for one of the world's major shipbuilding industries. During this period many of the imposing buildings on show today were constructed, a testament to the wealth of the city. Enlightened patrons held sway, and the world of art benefited handsomely from their endowments. Now Glasgow reaps a rich cultural harvest, a dynamic image hard to imagine in the debris of a generation ago.

LIVING THE CITY

Look at a map of Glasgow and see just how the centre is laid out, Manhattan style, in a neat grid system that makes getting around town a piece of cake. Cocooned within the curving arm of the M8 motorway, the area is home to most of Glasgow's main cultural venues. "Old Glasgow", just to the east, was the original medieval centre, but is now a thriving arts quarter, and also incorporates a large part of the city's gay scene. The West End, in a kind of hinterland away from the grid system, has practically invented itself as a town in its own right. It's a bohemian district filled with cafés, bars and restaurants, a million miles from the old image of a rough, tough city, and it's where you'll also find the main art gallery and museum at Kelvingrove. Go across the Clyde, to the south, and amongst the sprawling suburbs you come across gems like The Burrell Collection and Charles Rennie Mackintosh's Scotland Street School Museum and House for an Art Lover.

PRACTICAL INFORMATION

ARRIVAL-DEPARTURE

Glasgow International Airport is 8 miles west. A taxi costs approximately £20 or there are buses that stop close to Central Station.

TRANSPORT

Glasgow has a circular underground system covering the centre and west of the city – to go right round it only takes 24 minutes! Adult single fares are £1, returns £2. 10 and 20 multi-journey tickets are available, as are seven-day passes and day passes (the Discovery ticket).

Black cabs are easy to hail all over the city: expect your driver to have a smile on his face as Glasgow cabbies are some of the friendliest in the world.

A good idea on the buses is to buy a FirstDay ticket from your driver; this will let you hop on or off buses all day until midnight.

EXPLORING GLASGOW

If you'd been bold enough to take a walk around Glasgow in its days of great industrial output, you'd have been forgiven for thinking the buil-

dings had been constructed of black slate, such was the soot and pollutant grime that attached itself to them. Actually, many of those buildings were things of beauty constructed with red or blond sandstone, and in more recent times they've been restored to their striking original appearance. **George Square** - the heart of the city - typifies all this. It's an inspiring place to stand, its splendidly ornate nineteenth century buildings confidently reflecting the era in which they were built; in the City Chambers to this day sits the City Council. But Glasgow wouldn't be Glasgow if there weren't a temple of culture nearby, and round the corner in Queen Street stands the **Gallery of Modern Art**, housed in a stunning neo-classical building. Outside London, it's the UK's second most visited contemporary art gallery; this is a city that knows how to put on a show.

→ BIG MACK

In the relentless days of heavy industry around the Clyde, one man's aesthetic vision helped raise people's sights above the back-breaking level of the shipyard and steel furnace. Charles Rennie Mackintosh kept alive the idea of architectural creativity with his stunning Art Nouveau 'Glasgow Style' designs. Go to Renfrew Street at the northern end of the central grid to find his elegant and unmistakable masterpiece, the **Glasgow School of Art**, started in 1899 and finished a decade later. Its stunning façade has been compared in scale and majesty to Michelangelo. On a slightly lesser scale, Mackintosh's distinctive lines are also evident at The Willow Tea Rooms in Sauchiehall Street and Buchanan Street (they're a great place to admire his work over a cuppa). Across the river, House For an Art Lover pretty much sums up its appeal. The legacy of CRM lives on: in 1999 Glasgow was the UK's City of Architecture and Design, and one of Mackintosh's buildings, the Glasgow Herald newspaper office, began a new life as **The Lighthouse**, Scotland's national centre for architecture and design. Since it opened its doors, The Lighthouse has attracted over three quarters of a million visitors making the most of attractions such as the Mackintosh Centre and The Mackintosh Tower with its spectacular views of the city.

→ WE NEED TO TALK ABOUT KELVIN

It's quite handy that it rains so much in Glasgow. It's a very good excuse for visiting any of the thirteen museums and galleries that scatter themselves around the city, which, through its teeming industrial and cultural heritage, owns one of the richest collections in Europe. There's the **People's Palace** on Glasgow Green, for instance, which lives up to its name by telling the social history of the city from 1750 to the present day, including the rise of the tobacco lords, the poverty of the 'single end' tenement house families of the 1930s…and the eye-catching banana boots Billy Connolly wore on stage in the 1970s. A trip down to the Clyde brings you to the Science Centre and IMAX theatre, a state-of-the-art attraction setting a benchmark for scientific discovery, and most definitely not the place for visitors with a creationist slant on life. Carry on down into the depths of the southern suburbs for **The Burrell Collection**, quite simply a magnificent display of works of art from all periods and all continents, or head eastwards to the eerie shadow of the Necropolis (where Glasgow's industrial barons keep silent watch over their one-time nest-egg) where you'll find Provand's Lordship, the medieval city's only surviving house, now extensively restored to give a real fifteenth century feel. It's in the West End of the city, though, that arguably Glasgow's favourite landmark can be found: **The Kelvingrove** Art Gallery and Museum was reopened two years ago after renovations, and it houses one of the finest civic collections in Europe, including fine art, archaeology and exhibits from the natural world. And if that's not enough to sate your appetite, the impressive Hunterian Museum and Art Gallery is just across Kelvingrove Park.

→ TOPS FOR SHOPS

You might not be surprised to find that the shopping's rather good in Glasgow; in fact it's second only to London for retail power in the UK. In the central grid are no fewer than three precincts, in Argyle, Sauchiehall and Buchanan Streets. There are shopping malls (Buchanan Galleries and St. Enoch Centre), and boutique designer malls (Princes Square and the Italian Centre). Out in the slightly more rarefied air of the West End, you'll find a treasure trove of antiques and rare books, while back in the heart of town, the art galleries of West Regent Street highlight the contemporary works of both up-and-coming and established artists.

→ CLYDE VIBES

If you want to have a good time in this city it's almost impossible to fail in your quest. There's a vibrant music scene: in fact, Time Magazine not so long ago likened Glasgow to Detroit during its 1960s Motown heyday. Certainly the city has a happy knack of throwing up talented bands – of recent vintage are, for example, Franz Ferdinand, Belle & Sebastian and The Fratellis. And it was at the now legendary venue King Tut's Wah Wah Hut that Oasis were discovered by Glasgow's most famous record mogul Alan McGee. There are lots of venues to watch live music, from small pubs to landmark spaces such as the Glasgow Royal Concert Hall, the Scottish Exhibition Centre (impressively modernistic next to the Clyde), and the Barrowlands, a byword for musical excellence in the east end of the city.

Glasgow's legendary drinking culture does still live on, albeit in a noticeably more laidback 'European' style than of old, and nowhere more so than the cobbled Ashton Lane off trendy Byres Road in the West End. Jinty McGinty's bar is a favourite here, along with the locally renowned Chip. Beware strolling here on weekend evenings, as the cobbles disappear beneath the ever-burgeoning wave of humanity. Another establishment that will impress is Babbity Bowster, set in a carefully renovated townhouse in Blackfriars Street in the city centre, where the ale is invariably top-notch and the surroundings impressively informal.

If you should tire of this endlessly inspiring city, you'd be amazed at how close you are to the rugged Scottish countryside. Grab a seat on a West Highland line train out of Queen Street and you're staring at the wondrous hills within minutes…

CALENDAR HIGHLIGHTS

Glasgow's never short of a festival or two, and Glaswegians flock to them in their thousands. Celtic Connections, in January, is a widely acclaimed celebration of international roots music, while the Comedy Festival, each March, is the biggest in Europe, with the likes of Russell Brand and Joan Rivers doing a turn. Each June, The West End Festival, around Byres Road, is the

GLASGOW IN…

→ ONE DAY
Kelvingrove Art Gallery, the West End, Glasgow School of Art

→ TWO DAYS
Sauchiehall Street (including Willow Tea Rooms), Provand's Lordship and Necropolis, Glasgow Green, a trip on the Clyde, Science Centre

→ THREE DAYS
A train journey to the rolling hills of the Clyde Valley, a concert at one of Glasgow's top ranking venues

city's biggest, featuring a wide range of street bands and costume groups. The same month, the International Jazz Festival does exactly what it says on the label. There's a Merchant City Festival in September, in which that part of Glasgow plays host to a wide variety of cultural shows, but it's the event in chilly November that many locals keep a weather eye open for. Whisky Live, at the Exhibition Centre, is, quite simply, the world's greatest celebration of Scotland's (arguably) finest export.

EATING OUT

The dreaded legend of the deep-fried Mars bar did no favours for the reputation of the Scottish diet. Don't mention it in Glasgow, though. In the last decade, the place has undergone a gourmet revolution, and these days you can enjoy good food in restaurants from all areas of the world. There are now many establishments specializing in modern Scottish cooking and fish menus have come of age. Go to the trendy West End or Merchant City quarters to find bistros and brasseries that wouldn't be out of place in France or Italy. Glasgow has made the most of the glorious natural larder on its doorstep: spring lamb from the Borders, Perthshire venison, fresh fish and shellfish from the Western Highlands and Aberdeen Angus beef. It's always had a lot of respect for its liquid refreshment: if you want beer, you can't go far wrong with a pint of Deuchar's, the award-winning Bitter & Twisted, or an 'imported' Dark Island from the Orkneys: locals have taken to real ale from the Scottish regions in a big way.

UNITED KINGDOM - GLASGOW

Hotel du Vin at One Devonshire Gardens

1 Devonshire Gardens ✉ G12 OUX – ✆ (0141) 339 2001 – Fax (0141) 337 16 63 – www.onedevonshiregardens.com
45 rm – †£ 145 ††£ 145/395, ☕ £ 17 – 4 suites Plan I **A1**
Rest *Bistro* – *(Closed Saturday lunch)* Menu £ 18/21 – Carte £ 33/56
◆ Townhouse ◆ Stylish ◆
Collection of adjoining 19C houses in terrace, refurbished with attention to detail. Warm, intimate and comfortable bedrooms are named after wines. High levels of service. Smart Bistro offers classic grill menu as well as more innovative carte.

Radisson SAS

301 Argyle St ✉ G2 8DL – ✆ (0141) 204 3333 – reservations.glasgow@radissonsas.com – Fax (0141) 204 33 44 – www.glasgow.radissonsas.com
246 rm – †£ 220 ††£ 220, ☕ £ 15.50 – 1 suite **D2**
Rest *Collage* – Carte £ 15/55
Rest *TaPaell'Ya* – *(Closed Sunday-Monday)* Carte £ 15/35
◆ Business ◆ Modern ◆
A stunning, angular, modish exterior greets visitors to this consummate, modern commercial hotel. Large, stylish, eclectically furnished bedrooms. Collage is a bright modern restaurant. Ta Paell'Ya serves tapas.

Hilton Glasgow

1 William St ✉ G3 8HT – ✆ (0141) 204 5555 – reservations.glasgow@hilton.com – Fax (0141) 204 50 04 – www.hilton.com/glasgow **C2**
317 rm – †£ 90/250 ††£ 90/250, ☕ £ 17.95 – 2 suites
Rest *Camerons* – *(Closed Saturday lunch and Sunday)* Carte approx. £ 40
Rest *Minsky's* – Menu £ 15/25
◆ Luxury ◆ Business ◆ Modern ◆
A city centre tower with impressive views on every side. Comfortable, comprehensively fitted rooms. Extensive leisure and conference facilities. Spacious, modern Minsky's has the style of a New York deli. Contemporary cuisine served in formal Camerons.

Malmaison

278 West George St ✉ G2 4LL – ✆ (0141) 572 1000 – glasgow@malmaison.com – Fax (0141) 572 10 02 – www.malmaison.com **C2**
68 rm – †£ 170/220 ††£ 170/220, ☕ £ 13.95 – 4 suites
Rest *The Brasserie* – Menu £ 16 – Carte £ 26/41
◆ Business ◆ Stylish ◆
Visually arresting former Masonic chapel. Comfortable, well-proportioned rooms seem effortlessly stylish with bold patterns and colours and thoughtful extra attentions. Informal Brasserie with French themed menu and Champagne bar.

Abode Glasgow

129 Bath St ✉ G2 2SZ – ✆ (0141) 221 6789 – reservationsglasgow@abodehotels.co.uk – Fax (0141) 221 67 77 – www.abodehotels.co.uk
60 rm ☕ – †£ 99/245 ††£ 99/245 **D2**
Rest *Michael Caines* – see below
◆ Business ◆ Stylish ◆
Near Mackintosh's School of Art, an early 20C building decorated with a daring modern palette: striking colour schemes and lighting in the spacious, elegantly fitted rooms.

Carlton George

44 West George St ✉ G2 1DH – ✆ (0141) 353 6373 – resgeorge@carltonhotels.co.uk – Fax (0141) 353 62 63 – www.carltonhotels.co.uk – Closed 24-26 December and 1-2 January **D2**
64 rm – ††£ 130/220, ☕ £ 14
Rest *Windows* – Menu £ 19 (lunch) – Carte £ 27/35
◆ Business ◆ Classic ◆
A quiet oasis away from the city bustle. Attractive tartan decorated bedrooms bestow warm tidings. Comfortable 7th floor business lounge. An overall traditional ambience. Ask for restaurant table with excellent view across city's rooftops.

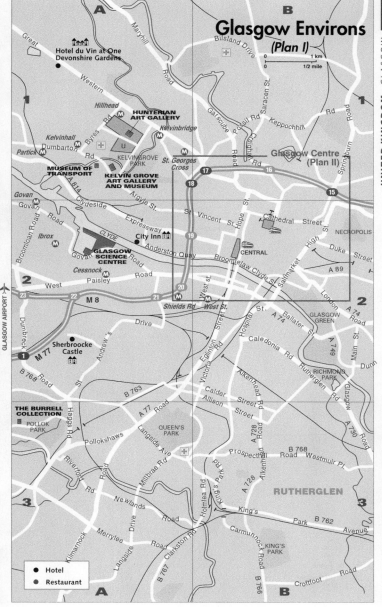

Glasgow Environs
(Plan I)

Great

Maryhill

Bilsland Drive

Hotel du Vin at One
Devonshire Gardens

Western

Road

0   1 km
0   1/2 mile

Hillhead

Byres

HUNTERIAN
ART GALLERY

Kelvinbridge

Saracen St.

Keppochhill

Rd

Road

1

Kelvinhall

Bd

Garscube

Basil Rd

Springburn

Partick

Dumbarton

Rd

KELVINGROVE
PARK

St. Georges
Cross

Glasgow Centre
(Plan II)

MUSEUM OF
TRANSPORT

KELVIN GROVE
ART GALLERY
AND MUSEUM

Argyle St.

17

16

15

Govan

M

Clydeside

Expressway

St Vincent

St.

Hope St.

Cathedral

Street

NECROPOLIS

Govan

Road

CLYDE

18

Ibrox

M

City Inn

Anderston Quay

19

CENTRAL

High

Duke

Street

GLASGOW
SCIENCE
CENTRE

Govan

Road

Broomielaw Clyde St.

Saltmarket

London

A 89

Cessnock

M

Paisley

Road

West St.

20

A 74

2

West

Road

23

22

M 8

21

Shields Rd

West St.

Drive

Eglinton

Street

Hospital

St.

Ballater

St.

GLASGOW
GREEN

A 74

Road

Main   St.

Dumbreck

M 77

Sherbroocke
Castle

Andrew's

St.

Victoria

Rd

Aitkenhead

Rd

Caledonia

Road

Rutherglen

A 749

RICHMOND
PARK

Glasgow

A 730

Dunn

B 768

Road

B 763

A 77

Road

Calder

Allison

Street

A 728

Road

Road

B 768

Road Westmuir Pl.

RUTHERGLEN

THE BURRELL
COLLECTION

POLLOK
PARK

Haggs Rd

Pollokshaws

Riverford

Rd

Road

Langside Ave

Milnbrae Rd

QUEEN'S
PARK

King's Park Rd

Holmlea Rd

A 728

Aitkenhead

Prospecthill

Road

B 768

A 730

Road

Newlands

Road

King's

Park

B 762

Avenue

3

Kilmarnock

Merrylee

Drive

Langside

Road

Clarkston Rd

B 767

King's

Carmunnock Road

B 766

KING'S
PARK

Crotfoot

Road

● Hotel
● Restaurant

GLASGOW AIRPORT

1

A

B

1003

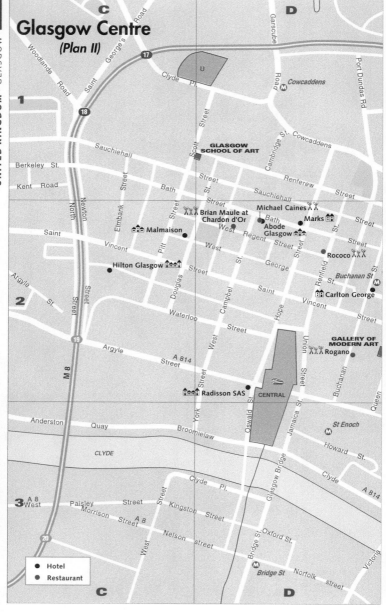

Glasgow Centre
(Plan II)

- **Hotel** ●
- **Restaurant** ●

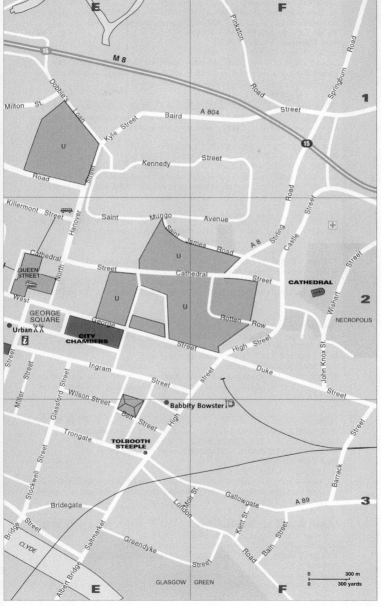

E

F

M 8

16

15

Milton St.

Dobbie's Loan

Kyle Street

Baird

A 804

Pinkston

Road

Street

Springburn

Road

1

U

Road

Kennedy

Street

Street

Killermont Street

Hanover

Saint

Mungo

Avenue

Road

Stirling

Castle

Street

Street

Cathedral

North

Street

Saint James Road

U

A 8

QUEEN
STREET

Street

Cathedral

U

Street

CATHEDRAL

West

GEORGE
SQUARE

Urban

George

U

U

Rotten

Row

2

NECROPOLIS

Wishart

Street

CITY
CHAMBERS

Street

High

Street

John Knox St.

Street

Ingram

Street

Duke

Street

Miller

Street

Glassford Street

Wilson Street

Street

street

Babbity Bowster

Barrack

Street

Trongate

Bell

Street

High

TOLBOOTH
STEEPLE

Stockwell

Street

Bridgate

Saltmarket

Moir St.

London

Gallowgate

Kent St.

A 89

Bain Street

3

Bridge

Street

Greendyke

Road

Albert Bridge

CLYDE

Street

GLASGOW GREEN

E

F

| 0 | | 300 m |
| 0 | | 300 yards |

Sherbrooke Castle

🚗 &. rm 🅰🅲 rest ⁇¶ 🔌 🅿 VISA ☺ 🅰🅴 ⓘ

11 Sherbrooke Ave, Pollokshields ✉ *G41 4PG –* ℰ *(0141) 427 4227 – mail@sherbrooke.co.uk – Fax (0141) 427 56 85 – www.sherbrooke.co.uk*

16 rm ⊆ – ♥£ 105 ♥♥£ 155 – 2 suites   *Plan I* **A2**

Rest *Morrisons* – Carte £ 18/32

◆ Castle ◆ Classic ◆

Late 19C baronial Romanticism given free rein inside and out. The hall is richly furnished and imposing; rooms in the old castle have a comfortable country house refinement. Panelled Victorian dining room with open fire.

City Inn

≤ 🏠 &. rm 🅰🅲 🖭 ⁇¶ 🔌 🅿 VISA ☺ 🅰🅴 ⓘ

Finnieston Quay ✉ *G3 8HN –* ℰ *(0141) 240 1002 – glasgow.reservations@cityinn.com – Fax (0141) 248 27 54 – www.cityinn.com*
– closed 24-25 December   *Plan I* **A2**

164 rm – ♥£ 79/179 ♥♥£ 89/189, ⊆ £ 12.50

Rest *City Cafe* – Menu £ 15/16.50 – Carte £ 19/34

◆ Chain hotel ◆ Business ◆ Functional ◆

Quayside location and views of the Clyde. Well priced hotel with a "business-friendly" ethos; neatly maintained modern rooms with sofas and en suite power showers.

Marks

&. rm 🅰🅲 rest ⁇¶ VISA ☺ 🅰🅴 ⓘ

110 Bath St ✉ *G2 2EN –* ℰ *(0141) 353 0800 – info@markshotels.com*
– Fax (0141) 353 09 00 – www.markshotels.com
– Closed 25 December   **D2**

102 rm – ♥£ 149 ♥♥£ 149, ⊆ £ 12.50 – 1 suite   **Rest *Loop*** – Carte £ 18/22

◆ Business ◆ Functional ◆

In the middle of Glasgow's shopping streets, with fashionable front bar. Modern bedrooms have bold fushia print wallpaper; mezzanine suites are worth the upgrade.

Rococo

🅰🅲 🍽 VISA ☺ 🅰🅴 ⓘ

48 West Regent St ✉ *G2 1LP –* ℰ *(0141) 221 5004 – info@rococoglasgow.co.uk*
– Fax (0141) 221 50 06 – www.rococoglasgow.co.uk   **D2**

Rest – Menu £ 20/42 – Carte lunch approx. £ 42

◆ Contemporary ◆ Design ◆

In style, more like studied avant-garde: stark, white-walled cellar with vibrant modern art and high-backed leather chairs. Accomplished, fully flavoured contemporary menu.

Lux

🅰🅲 🅿 VISA ☺ 🅰🅴

1051 Great Western Rd ✉ *G12 0XP –* ℰ *(0141) 576 7576 – enquiries@luxstazione.co.uk – Fax (0141) 576 01 62 – www.luxstazione.co.uk*
– Closed 25-26 December, 1-2 January, Sunday and Monday

Rest – *(dinner only)* Menu £ 34

◆ Modern ◆ Design ◆

19C railway station converted with clean-lined elegance: dark wood, subtle lighting and vivid blue banquettes. Fine service and flavourful, well-prepared modern menus.

Brian Maule at Chardon d'Or

🍽 VISA ☺ 🅰🅴

176 West Regent St ✉ *G2 4RL –* ℰ *(0141) 248 3801 – info@brianmaule.com*
– Fax (0141) 248 39 01 – www.brianmaule.com
– Closed 2 weeks January, 25-26 December, Saturday lunch, Sunday and Bank Holidays   **D2**

Rest – Menu £ 20 (lunch) – Carte £ 36/54

◆ Modern ◆ Brasserie ◆

Large pillared Georgian building. Airy refurbished interior with ornate carved ceiling. Classical French cooking made with fine Scottish produce. Function rooms in basement.

XXX **Rogano**   🛍 AC 📷 VISA ⊙⊙ AE

11 Exchange Place ⊠ *G1 3AN –* ✆ *(0141) 248 4055 – rogano@btconnect.com*
– www.roganoglasgow.com
– Closed 25 December and 1 January   **D2**
Rest – Menu £ 15 (lunch) – Carte £ 31/56
♦ Seafood ♦ Retro ♦

Long-standing Glasgow institution; art deco, with original panelling, stained glass
windows and etched mirrors. Classic menus lean towards local seafood. Table 16
most popular.

XX **Michael Caines** – at Abode Glasgow Hotel   AC VISA ⊙⊙ AE ⊙

129 Bath St ⊠ *G2 2SZ –* ✆ *(0141) 572 6011*   **D2**
Rest – *(closed Sunday and Monday)* Menu £ 10 (lunch) – Carte £ 30/45
♦ Modern ♦ Fashionable ♦

Smart, stylish restaurant in boutique hotel, a mirrored wall creating impression of
size. Quality décor matched by clean, unfussy cooking prepared with finesse and
skill.

XX **Urban**   AC ⇔ VISA ⊙⊙ AE

23-25 St Vincent Place ⊠ *G1 2DT –* ✆ *(0141) 248 5720*
– info@urbanbrasserie.co.uk – www.urbanbrasserie.co.uk
– Closed 1-2 January and 25-26 December   **E2**
Rest – Menu £ 18 (lunch) – Carte £ 24/36
♦ Modern ♦ Brasserie ♦

Imposing 19C building in heart of city centre. Stylish, modern interior with individual booths and illuminated glass ceiling. Modern English cooking. Live piano at
weekends.

🍺 **Babbity Bowster**   🛍 VISA ⊙⊙ AE

16-18 Blackfriars St ⊠ *G1 1PE –* ✆ *(0141) 552 5055 – Fax (0141) 552 77 74*
– Closed 25 December   **E3**
Rest – Carte £ 16/26
♦ Traditional ♦ Pub ♦

Well regarded pub of Georgian origins with columned façade. Paradoxically simple
ambience: gingham-clothed tables, hearty Scottish dishes, slightly more formal in
evenings.

Eurozone : €

  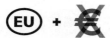

   EU states

Schengen Countries

Area of free movement between member states

    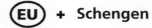 EU + Schengen

     EU + Schengen

    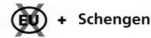 EU + Schengen

Driving in Europe

The information panels which follow give the principal motoring regulations in force when this guide was prepared for press; an explanation of the symbols is given below, together with some additional notes.

Speed restrictions in kilometres per hour applying to:

 motorways

 dual carriageways

 single carriageways

 urban areas

 Maximum permitted level of alcohol in the bloodstream. This should not be taken as an acceptable level - it is NEVER sensible to drink and drive.

 Whether tolls are payable on motorways and/or other parts of the road network.

 Whether seatbelts are compulsory for the driver and all passengers in both front and back seats.

 Whether seatbelts must be worn by the driver and front seat passenger.

 Whether headlights must be on at all time.

Driving in Europe

		🛣	🛣	🛣	🏙	🍷	🛣	🦺	🔦
AUSTRIA	**A**	130		100	50	0,05	●	●	
BELGIUM	**B**	120	120	90	50	0,05		●	
CZECH REPUBLIC	**CZ**	130		90	50	**0,00**	●	●	31/10 -31/3
DENMARK	**DK**	130		80	50	0,05		●	●
FINLAND	**FIN**	120		80	50	0,05		●	●
FRANCE	**F**	130	110	90	50	0,05	●	●	
GERMANY	**D**			100	50	0,05		●	
GREECE	**GR**	120		90	50	0,05	●	●	
HUNGARY	**H**	130	110	90	50	**0,00**	●	●	●
IRELAND	**IRL**	120		80	50	0,08		●	
ITALY	**I**	130		90	50	0,05	●	●	●
LUXEMBOURG	**L**	130		90	50	0,08		●	
NETHERLANDS	**NL**	120	100	80	50	0,05		●	
NORWAY	**N**	90		80	50	0,02	●	●	●
POLAND	**PL**	130	120	90	50	0,02	●	●	1/10 -28/2
PORTUGAL	**P**	120	100	90	50	0,05	●	●	
SPAIN	**E**	120		90	50	0,05	●	●	
SWEDEN	**S**	110		70	50	0,02		●	●
SWITZERLAND	**CH**	120	100	80	50	0,05	●	●	
UNITED KINGDOM	**GB**	112		96	48	0,08		●	

●   Compulsory

1/11-30/4   Period of regulation enforcement

Distances

(A) AUSTRIA
(AL) ALBANIE
(B) BELGIUM
(BG) BULGARIA
(BIH) BOSNIA-HERZEGOVINA
(BY) BELORUSSIA
(CZ) CZECH REPUBLIC
(CH) SWITZERLAND
(D) GERMANY
(DK) DENMARK
(E) SPAIN
(EST) ESTONIA
(F) FRANCE
(FIN) FINLAND
(GB) UNITED KINGDOM
(GR) GREECE
(H) HUNGARY
(HR) CROATIA
(I) ITALY
(IRL) IRELAND
(L) LUXEMBOURG
(LT) LITHUANIA
(LV) LATVIA
(M) MALTA
(MD) MOLDAVIA
(MK) MACEDONIA (F.Y.R.O.M.)
(N) NORWAY
(NL) NETHERLANDS
(P) PORTUGAL
(PL) POLAND
(S) SWEDEN
(RO) ROMANIA
(RUS) RUSSIA
(SCG) SERBIA
      AND MONTENEGRO
(SK) SLOVAK REPUBLIC
(SLO) SLOVENIA
(TR) TURKEY
(UA) UKRAINE

123 : distances by road in kilometers

Glasgow 76 Edinburgh

(IRL)

DUBLIN

673

Birmingham 462 (GB)

202 Rotterdam

LONDON 150

114

226

223

401

PARIS

127

Orléans

307

(F)

Gene

154

554

648 620

Toulouse 242

293 Montpellier

390

513

619

Barcelona

305

LISBON 627 **MADRID**

(P)

(E)

Time zones

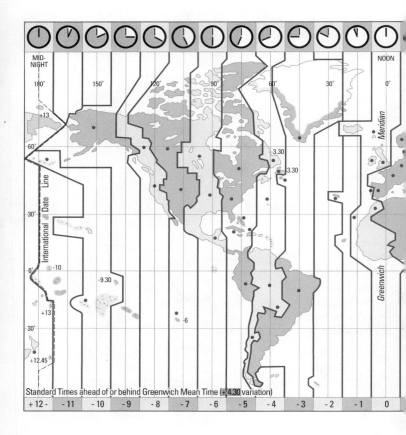

Standard Times ahead of or behind Greenwich Mean Time (+ 4.30 variation)

| + 12 - | - 11 | - 10 | - 9 | - 8 | - 7 | - 6 | - 5 | - 4 | - 3 | - 2 | - 1 | 0 |

MID-
NIGHT

NOON

180°   150°   120°   90°   60°   30°   0°

+13

60°

-3.30

3.30

International Date Line

30°

0°

-10

-9.30

Greenwich

+13

-6

30°

+12.45

Meridian

Time zones

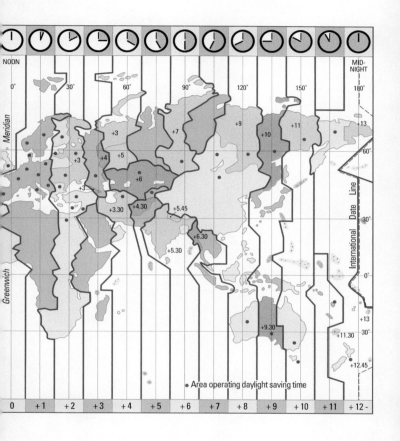

Town plans

● Hotels   ● Restaurants

Sights

▬ Place of interest

🚪 Interesting place of worship

Roads

═ Motorway

═ Dual carriageway

▬ Pedestrian street

① Junctions: complete

① Junctions: limited

🚉 Station and railway

Various Signs

🛈 Tourist Information Centre

◼◻ Mosque

◼▨ Synagogue

♣♣ Ruins

▨ Garden, Park, Wood

🚌 Coach station

✈ Airport

Ⓜ Metro station

✚ Hospital

✉ Covered market

▬ Public buildings:

H Town Hall

R Town Hall (Germany)

M Museum

U University

Manufacture française des pneumatiques Michelin

Société en commandite par actions au capital de 304 000 000 EUR
Place des Carmes-Déchaux – 63 Clermont-Ferrand (France)
R.C.S. Clermond-Fd B 855 200 507

Michelin et Cie, Propriétaires-éditeurs, 2009

Dépôt légal : mars 2009

No part of this publication may be reproduced in any form
without the prior permission of the publisher.

"Based on Ordnance Survey Ireland by permission of the Government
Permit No 8509 © Government of Ireland"

Town plans of Bern, Basle, Geneva and Zürich :
with the permission of Federal directorate for cadastral surveys

"Based on Ordnance Survey of Great Britain with the permission
of the Controller of Her Majest'ys Stationery Office, © Crown Copyright 100000247"

Printed in Belgium : 02-2009/6-1

Compogravure : MCP Jouve, Saran

Impression : CASTERMAN, Tournai (Belgium)

Reliure : S.I.R.C., Marigny-le-Châtel

Cover photograph : MAISANT Ludovic/hemis.fr

Our editorial team has taken the greatest care in writing this and checking
the information in it. However, pratical information (administrative formalities, prices,
addresses, telephone numbers, Internet addresses, etc) is subject to frequent change
and such information should therefore be used for guidance only.
it is possible that some of the information in this guide may not be a accurate
or exhaustive as of the date of publication. Before taking action (in particular
in regard to administrative and customs regulations and procedures),
you should contact the appropriate official administration.
We hereby accept no liability in regard to such information